Features for Students

MyStatLab provides students with a personalized, interactive environment where they can learn at their own pace and measure their progress.

Interactive tutorial exercises

MyStatLab's homework and practice exercises, correlated to the exercises in the textbook, are generated algorithmically, giving students unlimited opportunity for practice and mastery. Exercises include guided solutions, sample problems, and learning aids for extra help at point-of-use, and they offer helpful feedback when students enter incorrect answers.

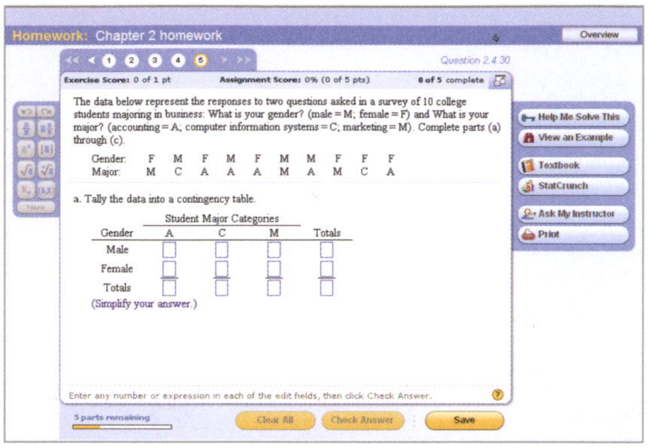

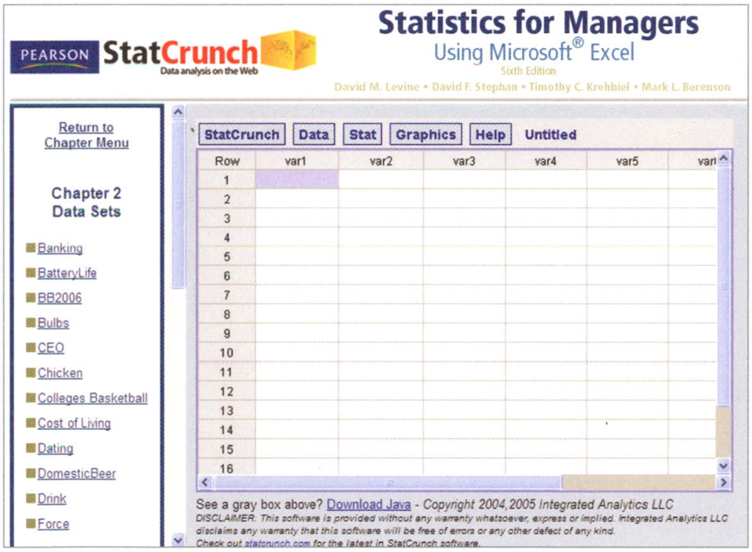

StatCrunch

StatCrunch offers both numerical and data analysis and uses interactive graphics to illustrate the connection between objects selected in a graph and the underlying data. In most MyStatLab courses, all data sets from the textbook are pre-loaded in StatCrunch, and StatCrunch is also available as a tool from all online homework and practice exercises.

Student Purchasing Options

There are many ways for students to sign up for MyStatLab:

- Use the access kit bundled with a new textbook
- Purchase a stand-alone access kit from the bookstore
- Register online through www.coursecompass.com

PEARSON

www.pearsonhighered.com

A ROADMAP FOR SELECTING A STATISTICAL METHOD

Type of Analysis	TYPE OF DATA: Numerical	TYPE OF DATA: Categorical
Describing a group or several groups	Ordered array, stem-and-leaf display, frequency distribution, relative frequency distribution, percentage distribution, cumulative percentage distribution, histogram, polygon, cumulative percentage polygon **(Sections 2.3, 2.5)** Mean, median, mode, quartiles, geometric mean, range, interquartile range, standard deviation, variance, coefficient of variation, boxplot **(Sections 3.1, 3.2, 3.3)** Index numbers **(Online Topic 16.8)**	Summary table, bar chart, pie chart, Pareto chart **(Sections 2.2, 2.4)**
Inference about one group	Confidence interval estimate of the mean **(Sections 8.1 and 8.2)** *t* test for the mean **(Section 9.2)** Chi-square test for a variance **(Section 12.5)**	Confidence interval estimate of the proportion **(Section 8.3)** *Z* test for the proportion **(Section 9.4)**
Comparing two groups	Tests for the difference in the means of two independent populations **(Section 10.1)** Paired *t* test **(Section 10.2)** *F* test for the difference between two variances **(Section 10.4)** Wilcoxon rank sum test **(Section 12.6)** Wilcoxon signed ranks test **(Online Topic 12.8)**	*Z* test for the difference between two proportions **(Section 10.3)** Chi-square test for the difference between two proportions **(Section 12.1)** McNemar test for the difference between two proportions in related samples **(Section 12.4)**
Comparing more than two groups	One-way analysis of variance **(Section 11.1)** Randomized block design **(Section 11.2)** Two-way analysis of variance **(Section 11.3)** Kruskal-Wallis test **(Section 12.7)** Friedman rank test **(Online Topic 12.9)**	Chi-square test for differences among more than two proportions **(Section 12.2)**
Analyzing the relationship between two variables	Scatter plot, time series plot **(Section 2.6)** Covariance, coefficient of correlation **(Section 3.5)** Simple linear regression **(Chapter 13)** *t* test of correlation **(Section 13.7)** Time series forecasting **(Chapter 16)**	Contingency table, side-by-side bar chart, **(Sections 2.2, 2.4)** Chi-square test of independence **(Section 12.3)**
Analyzing the relationship between two or more variables	Multiple regression **(Chapters 14 and 15)**	Multidimensional contingency tables **(Section 2.7)** Logistic regression **(Section 14.7)**

Basic Business Statistics: Concepts and Applications

TWELFTH EDITION

Basic Business Statistics: Concepts and Applications

TWELFTH EDITION

Mark L. Berenson

Department of Management and Information Systems

School of Business, Montclair State University

David M. Levine

Department of Statistics and Computer Information Systems

Zicklin School of Business, Baruch College, City University of New York

Timothy C. Krehbiel

Department of Management

Richard T. Farmer School of Business, Miami University

Prentice Hall

Boston Columbus Indianapolis New York San Francisco Upper Saddle River
Amsterdam Cape Town Dubai London Madrid Milan Munich Paris Montreal Toronto
Delhi Mexico City Sao Paulo Sydney Hong Kong Seoul Singapore Taipei Tokyo

Editorial Director: Sally Yagan
Editor in Chief: Eric Svendsen
Senior Acquisitions Editor: Chuck Synovec
Editorial Project Manager: Mary Kate Murray
Editorial Assistant: Jason Calcano
Director of Marketing: Patrice Lumumba Jones
Senior Marketing Manager: Anne Fahlgren
Marketing Assistant: Melinda Jensen
Senior Managing Editor: Judy Leale
Project Manager: Kerri Tomasso
Senior Operations Supervisor: Arnold Vila
Senior Art Director: Kenny Beck
Text Designers: Dina Curro/Suzanne Behnke
Cover Designer and Art: LCI Design
Media Editor: Allison Longley
Media Project Manager: John Cassar
Full-Service Project Manager: Jen Carley
Composition: PreMediaGlobal
Printer/Binder: Courier/Kendallville
Cover Printer: Lehigh-Phoenix Color/Hagerstown
Text Font: TimesNewRomanPS
Technical Editor: David Stephan

Photo Credits: front, page viii, courtesy of Rudy Krehbiel; pp. 2–3: Photos.com; pp. 3, 7: Maga, Shutterstock; pp. 14–15: Don Farrall, PhotoDisc/Getty Images; pp. 15, 59:Steve Coleccs, iStockphoto; pp. 84–85: Don Farrall, PhotoDisc/Getty Images; pp. 85, 121: Steve Coleccs, iStockphoto; pp. 132–133: Ljupco Smokovski, Shutterstock; pp. 133, 154: © Alan Levenson/Corbis, all rights reserved; pp. 160–161: Sebastian Kaulitzki, Shutterstock; pp. 161, 183: Monkey Business Images, Shutterstock; pp. 192–193: Alexander Kalina, Shutterstock; pp. 193, 215: Lee Morris, Shutterstock; pp. 222–223: R. Mackay Photography, Shutterstock; pp. 223, 243: © Corbis, all rights reserved; pp. 250–251: Kristy Pargeter, Shutterstock; pp. 251, 283: Marcin Balcerzak, Shutterstock; pp. 296–297: Peter Close, Shutterstock; pp. 297, 326: Maja Schon, Shutterstock; pp. 334–335: Travis Manley, Shutterstock; pp. 335, 366: Michael Bradley, Getty Images; p. 381: Joggie Botma, Shutterstock; pp. 381, 408: Alexey U, Shutterstock; p. 423: KzlKurt, Shutterstock; pp. 423, 458: Zastolískiyí victor Leonidovich, Shutterstock; p. 471: crystalfoto, Shutterstock; pp. 471, 511: Dmitriy Shironosov, Shutterstock; p. 527: Courtesy of Sharon Rosenberg; pp. 527, 558: George Bailey, Shutterstock; pp. 570–571: Giedrius Dagys, iStockphoto.com; pp. 571, 596: Rob Crandall, Stock Boston; p. 604: Rudyanto Wijaya, iStockphoto.com; pp. 604, 643: Cathy Melloan/PhotoEdit Inc.; pp. 654–655: Ian Logan/Taxi/Getty Images; pp. 655, 684: Kim Steele/Image Bank/Getty; pp. 701, 706: Stepan Popov, iStockphoto.com; Ch. 19 Photos: Thinkstock.

Credits and acknowledgments borrowed from other sources and reproduced, with permission, in this textbook appear on appropriate page within text.

CIP data for this title is available on file at the Library of Congress

Prentice Hall
is an imprint of

PEARSON

www.pearsonhighered.com

10 9 8 7 6 5 4 3 2 1
ISBN 10: 0-13-216838-3
ISBN 13: 978-0-13-216838-0

To our wives,
Rhoda B., Marilyn L., and, Patti K.,

and to our children,
Kathy, Lori, Sharyn, Ed, Rudy, and Rhonda

About the Authors

The textbook authors meet to discuss statistics at a Mets baseball game. Shown left to right: David Levine, Mark Berenson, and Tim Krehbiel.

Mark L. Berenson is Professor of Management and Information Systems at Montclair State University (Montclair, New Jersey) and also Professor Emeritus of Statistics and Computer Information Systems at Bernard M. Baruch College (City University of New York). He currently teaches graduate and undergraduate courses in statistics and in operations management in the School of Business and an undergraduate course in international justice and human rights that he co-developed in the College of Humanities and Social Sciences.

Berenson received a B.A. in economic statistics and an M.B.A. in business statistics from City College of New York and a Ph.D. in business from the City University of New York.

Berenson's research has been published in *Decision Sciences Journal of Innovative Education*, *Review of Business Research*, *The American Statistician*, *Communications in Statistics*, *Psychometrika*, *Educational and Psychological Measurement*, *Journal of Management Sciences and Applied Cybernetics*, *Research Quarterly*, *Stats Magazine*, *The New York Statistician*, *Journal of Health Administration Education*, *Journal of Behavioral Medicine*, and *Journal of Surgical Oncology*. His invited articles have appeared in *The Encyclopedia of Measurement & Statistics* and *Encyclopedia of Statistical Sciences*. He is co-author of 11 statistics texts published by Prentice Hall, including *Statistics for Managers Using Microsoft Excel*, *Basic Business Statistics: Concepts and Applications*, and *Business Statistics: A First Course*.

Over the years, Berenson has received several awards for teaching and for innovative contributions to statistics education. In 2005, he was the first recipient of The Catherine A. Becker Service for Educational Excellence Award at Montclair State University.

David M. Levine is Professor Emeritus of Statistics and Computer Information Systems at Baruch College (City University of New York). He received B.B.A. and M.B.A. degrees in Statistics from City College of New York and a Ph.D. from New York

University in Industrial Engineering and Operations Research. He is nationally recognized as a leading innovator in statistics education and is the co-author of 14 books, including such best-selling statistics textbooks as *Statistics for Managers Using Microsoft Excel*, *Basic Business Statistics: Concepts and Applications*, *Business Statistics: A First Course*, and *Applied Statistics for Engineers and Scientists Using Microsoft Excel and Minitab*.

He also is the co-author of *Even You Can Learn Statistics: A Guide for Everyone Who Has Ever Been Afraid of Statistics*, currently in its 2nd edition, *Six Sigma for Green Belts and Champions* and *Design for Six Sigma for Green Belts and Champions*, and the author of *Statistics for Six Sigma Green Belts*, all published by FT Press, a Pearson imprint, and *Quality Management*, 3rd edition, McGraw-Hill/Irwin. He is also the author of *Video Review of Statistics* and *Video Review of Probability*, both published by Video Aided Instruction, and the statistics module of the MBA primer published by Cengage Learning. He has published articles in various journals, including *Psychometrika*, *The American Statistician*, *Communications in Statistics*, *Decision Sciences Journal of Innovative Education*, *Multivariate Behavioral Research*, *Journal of Systems Management*, *Quality Progress*, and *The American Anthropologist*, and given numerous talks at the Decision Sciences Institute (DSI), American Statistical Association (ASA), and Making Statistics More Effective in Schools and Business (MSMESB) conferences. Levine has also received several awards for outstanding teaching and curriculum development from Baruch College.

Timothy C. Krehbiel is Professor of Management and Senior Associate Dean of the Farmer School of Business at Miami University in Oxford, Ohio. He teaches undergraduate and graduate courses in business statistics. In 1996, he received the prestigious Instructional Innovation Award from the Decision Sciences Institute. He has also received the Farmer School of Business Effective Educator Award and has twice been named MBA professor of the year.

Krehbiel's research interests span many areas of business and applied statistics. His work has appeared in numerous journals, including *Quality Management Journal*, *Ecological Economics*, *International Journal of Production Research*, *Journal of Purchasing and Supply Management*, *Journal of Applied Business Research*, *Journal of Marketing Management*, *Communications in Statistics*, *Decision Sciences Journal of Innovative Education*, *Journal of Education for Business*, *Marketing Education Review*, *Journal of Accounting Education*, and *Teaching Statistics*. He is a co-author of three statistics textbooks published by Prentice Hall: *Business Statistics: A First Course*, *Basic Business Statistics*, and *Statistics for Managers Using Microsoft Excel*. Krehbiel is also a co-author of the book *Sustainability Perspectives in Business and Resources*.

Krehbiel graduated *summa cum laude* with a B.A. in history from McPherson College and earned an M.S. and a Ph.D. in statistics from the University of Wyoming.

Brief Contents

Contents

Online Chapter: 19 Decision Making

Preface

Educational Philosophy

Seeking ways to continuously improve the teaching of business statistics is the core value that guides our works. We actively participate in Decision Sciences Institute (DSI), American Statistical Association (ASA), and Making Statistics More Effective in Schools and Business (MSMESB) conferences. We use the Guidelines for Assessment and Instruction (GAISE) reports as well as our reflections on teaching business statistics to a diverse student body at several large universities. These experiences have helped us identify the following key principles:

1. **Show students the relevance of statistics** Students need a frame of reference when learning statistics, especially when statistics is not their major. That frame of reference for business students should be the functional areas of business, such as accounting, finance, information systems, management, and marketing. Each statistics topic needs to be presented in an applied context related to at least one of these functional areas. The focus in teaching each topic should be on its application in business, the interpretation of results, the evaluation of the assumptions, and the discussion of what should be done if the assumptions are violated.
2. **Familiarize students with the statistical applications used in the business world** Integrating these programs into all aspects of an introductory statistics course allows the course to focus on interpretation of results instead of computations. Introductory business statistics courses should recognize that programs with statistical functions are commonly found on a business decision maker's desktop computer, therefore making the *interpretation* of results more important than the tedious hand calculations required to produce them.
3. **Provide clear instructions to students for using statistical applications** Books should explain clearly how to use programs such as Excel and Minitab with the study of statistics, without having those instructions dominate the book or distract from the learning of statistical concepts.
4. **Give students ample practice in understanding how to apply statistics to business** Both classroom examples and homework exercises should involve actual or realistic data as much as possible. Students should work with data sets, both small and large, and be encouraged to look beyond the statistical analysis of data to the interpretation of results in a managerial context.

New to This Edition: MyStatLab

MyStatLab

Custom MyStatLab course materials designed for specific use with this book are available. MyStatLab is Pearson Education's online learning, homework, and assessment tool that provides a rich and flexible set of course materials, including free-response exercises that are algorithmically generated for unlimited practice and mastery. MyStatLab provides students with a personalized, interactive learning environment that helps them to independently improve their understanding and performance in a course. MyStatLab allows instructors to deliver portions of a course online, to perform course management functions, and to create a supportive online community. In addition, instructors can use the MyStatLab homework and test manager to select and assign their own online exercises as well as import TestGen tests.

The MyStatLab for *Basic Business Statistics* features several improvements over earlier versions including a more intuitive user design that presents a simpler interface with fewer pop-up windows. This MyStatLab also provides mobile device access through free apps that can be downloaded for iPhones, iPads, and Andriod phones. (iPad users can even download a free app to access all of their Pearson eTexts, seeing their instructors annotations and gaining links to Do Homework, Take a Test, and Study Plan functions.)

New to This Edition: Enhanced Statistical Coverage

This 12th edition of *Basic Business Statistics* builds on previous editions with these new and enhanced features:

- New chapter-ending "Using Statistics ... Revisited" sections that reinforce the statistical methods and applications discussed in each chapter.
- The use of the DCOVA (**D**efine, **C**ollect, **O**rganize, **V**isualize, and **A**nalyze) framework as an integrated approach for applying statistics to help solve business problems.
- Many new applied examples and exercises, with data from *The Wall Street Journal*, *USA Today*, and other sources.
- "Managing Ashland MultiComm Services," a new integrated case that appears at the ends of chapters throughout the book (replacing the *Springville Herald* case).
- "Digital Cases," interactive PDF files that create a new series of cases that appear at the ends of chapters throughout the book (replacing the Web Cases).
- An expanded discussion of using Excel and Minitab to summarize and explore multidimensional data.
- Revised and updated "Think About This" essays (formerly entitled "From the Author's Desktop") that provide greater insight into what has just been learned and raise important issues about the application of statistical knowledge.
- Additional in-chapter Excel and Minitab results.
- A new online section that discusses analytics and data mining.

New to This Edition: Expanded Excel and Minitab Guides

In this 12th edition of *Basic Business Statistics*, the instructions for using Excel and Minitab have been revised, reorganized, and enhanced in new end-of-chapter guides and back-of-the book appendices. These sections support students by:

- Providing a readiness checklist and orientation that guide students through the process of getting ready to use Excel or Minitab (see Chapter 1 and the Chapter 1 Excel and Minitab Guides).
- Incorporating Excel Guide workbooks that serve as models and templates for using Excel for statistical problem solving. These free and reusable workbooks, annotated examples of which appear throughout the chapters of this book, can be used by students in their other courses or in their jobs.
- Allowing students to use Excel with or without PHStat2 and with or without the Analysis ToolPak (an Excel component that is not available in Mac Excel 2008).
- Expanding the scope of Minitab Guide instructions.
- Reviewing common operations, such as opening, saving, and printing results (see Chapter 1 Excel and Minitab Guides).
- Explaining the different types of files available online that support this book and how to download those free files from this book's companion website (Appendix C).
- Providing a separate appendix that discusses software configuration issues, including how to check for Excel and Minitab updates and how to configure Excel for use with PHStat2 or the Analysis ToolPak (Appendix D).
- An appendix that discusses formatting and other intermediate-level Excel operations (Appendix F).
- Answering frequently asked questions about Excel, PHStat2, the Pearson statistical add-in for Microsoft Windows–based Excel versions, and Minitab (the new Appendix G).
- In Appendix Section C.4, offering a complete list of all downloadable files and programs for this book. (See "Student Resources" on page xxvi for more details about the files and programs that can be downloaded.)

Chapter-by-Chapter Changes in the 12th Edition

Chapters begin with a redesigned opening page that displays the chapter sections and subsections and conclude with the new Excel and Minitab Guides that discuss how to apply Excel and Minitab to the statistical methods discussed in a chapter. Minitab Guides have been expanded to better match the scope of the Excel Guides. End-of-chapter Digital Cases that use interactive documents, in lieu of simulated web pages, update the former Web Cases. There is a new integrated case, "Managing Ashland MultiComm Services," that replaces the "Managing the *Springville Herald*" case (see Chapters 2, 3, 5 through 7, 9 through 14, 16, and 17). Appendices B through D and F and G have been revised, reorganized, and updated.

Highlights of changes to individual chapters follow.

Chapter 1 The 11th edition's Section 1.4 has been moved to Chapter 2. Section 1.6 has been rewritten and retitled "How to Use This Book" and now includes the "Checklist for Getting Started" (with Excel or Minitab). There are new undergraduate and graduate surveys.

Chapter 2 This chapter has been completely reorganized. Sections 1.4 of the previous edition, concerning data collection, has been moved to this chapter. The Define, Collect, Organize, Visualize, and Analyze approach to solving business problems has been incorporated. The material on tables and charts has been reorganized so that the sections on organizing data into tables is presented first, in Sections 2.2 and 2.3, followed by sections on visualizing data in graphs in Sections 2.4–2.7. There is a new section on organizing multidimensional data (Section 2.7). There are new Excel and Minitab Guide sections that discuss multidimensional data. The Minitab Guide that replaces the Minitab Appendix has been greatly expanded. In addition, there are new examples throughout the chapter, and a new data set on bond funds has been created.

Chapter 3 A new data set on bond funds has been created. The section "Numerical Measures for a Population" has been moved after the section on quartiles and boxplots. "Numerical Descriptive Measures from a Population" has been deleted.

Chapter 4 The chapter example has been updated. There are new problems throughout the chapter. The "Think About This" essay about Bayes' theorem has been condensed and updated. In combinations and permutations, x is used instead of X to be consistent with binomial notation in Chapter 5.

Chapter 5 This chapter has revised notation for the binomial, Poisson, and hypergeometric distributions. It uses lower-case x and includes the parameter after an | sign in the equation. To reduce the size of the book, the tables of the binomial and Poisson distributions (Tables E.6 and E.7) have been placed online. There are new problems throughout the chapter.

Chapter 6 This chapter has an updated Using Statistics scenario. The "Think About This" essay on the importance of the normal distribution has been revised. The discussion of the exponential distribution has been revised.

Chapter 7 A new "Think About This" essay replaces and expands on the pros and cons of web-based surveys, using a famous historical example. "Sampling from Finite Populations" is now an online topic.

Chapter 8 This chapter includes problems on sigma known in Section 8.1.

Chapter 9 This chapter includes problems on sigma known in Section 9.1. "Power of a Test" is now an online topic.

Chapter 10 This chapter has a new example on the paired t-test on textbook prices.

Chapter 11 This chapter has an "Online Topic" subsection titled "The Analysis of Means (ANOM)."

Chapter 12 This chapter has an "Online Topic" subsection titled "The Analysis of Proportions (ANOP)." The Wilcoxon signed ranks test and the Friedman test are now online topicss.

Chapter 13 The "Think About This" essay has been revised. There are new problems throughout the chapter.

Chapter 14 This chapter has various new problems.

Chapter 15 This chapter has a new "Online Topic" section titled "Analytics and Data Mining." There are new problems throughout the chapter.

Chapter 16 This chapter has updated examples throughout the chapter. "Index Numbers" is now an online topic.

Chapter 17 This chapter has been edited for conciseness without any loss of concepts or clarity.

Chapter 18 This chapter now includes an interactive roadmap for analyzing data as part of a new Digital Case. There are many new problems in the chapter.

Chapter 19 This chapter (formerly Chapter 17) has become an online chapter and is available for download through this book's companion website.

Hallmark Features

We have continued many of the traditions of past editions and have highlighted some of these features below.

Using Statistics Business Scenarios—Each chapter begins with a Using Statistics example that shows how statistics is used in the functional areas of business—accounting, finance, information systems, management, and marketing. Each scenario is used throughout the chapter to provide an applied context for the concepts.

Emphasis on Data Analysis and Interpretation of Software Results—We believe that the use of computer software is an integral part of learning statistics. Our focus emphasizes analyzing data by interpreting results while reducing emphasis on doing computations. For example, in the coverage of tables and charts in Chapter 2, the focus is on the interpretation of various charts and on when to use each chart. In our coverage of hypothesis testing in Chapters 9 through 12, and regression and time series forecasting in Chapters 13–16, extensive computer results have been included so that the p-value approach can be emphasized.

Pedagogical Aids—An active writing style is used, with boxed numbered equations, set-off examples to provide reinforcement for learning concepts, problems divided into "Learning the Basics" and "Applying the Concepts," key equations, and key terms.

Answers—Many answers to the even-numbered exercises are included at the end of the book.

Flexibility Using Excel—For almost every statistical method discussed, this book presents more than one way of using Excel. Students can use *In-Depth Excel* instructions to directly work with the worksheet cell-level details *or* they can use the *PHStat2* instructions *or* use the *Analysis ToolPak* instructions to automate the creation of those same details.

Digital Cases—An end-of-chapter Digital Case is included for each of the first 16 chapters. Most Digital Cases extend a Using Statistics business scenario by posing additional questions and raising issues about the scenario. Students examine interactive documents to sift through claims and assorted information in order to discover the data most relevant to a scenario. Students then determine whether the conclusions and claims are supported by the data. In doing so, students discover and learn how to identify common misuses of statistical information. (Instructional tips for using the Digital Cases and solutions to the Digital Cases are included in the Instructor's Solutions Manual.)

Case Studies and Team Projects—Detailed case studies are included in numerous chapters. A "Managing Ashland MultiComm Services" continuing case, a team project related to bond funds, and undergraduate and graduate student surveys are included at the end of most chapters, and these serve to integrate learning across the chapters.

Visual Explorations—The Excel add-in workbook allows students to interactively explore important statistical concepts in descriptive statistics, the normal distribution, sampling distributions, and regression analysis. For example, in descriptive statistics, students observe the effect of changes in the data on the mean, median, quartiles, and standard deviation. With the normal distribution, students see the effect of changes in the mean and standard deviation on the areas under the normal curve. In sampling distributions, students use simulation to explore the effect of sample size on a sampling distribution. In regression analysis, students have the opportunity to fit a line and observe how changes in the slope and intercept affect the goodness of fit.

Student Resources

Student Solutions Manual—Created by Professor Pin Tian Ng of Northern Arizona University, this manual provides detailed solutions to virtually all the even-numbered exercises and worked-out solutions to the self-test problems.

Companion website—This book comes with a companion website from which the following resources can be downloaded for free (see Appendix C that starts on page 784 for more details about these resources, including how to visit the companion website):

- **Data files** Excel and Minitab data files used by in-chapter examples and problems (in **.xls** and **.mtw** formats).
- **Online Chapter** The electronic-only Chapter 19: Decision Making in PDF format.
- **Online Topics** Online topics are PDF files that discuss additional topics for Chapters 5, 6, 7, 8, 9, 11, 12, 15, and 16.
- **Excel Guide workbooks** Self-documenting Excel Guide workbooks illustrate solutions for more than 60 statistical topics that serve as freely reusable templates for future problem solving.
- **Case files** Supporting files are provided for the Digital Cases and the Managing Ashland MultiComm Services Case.
- **Visual Explorations** The files needed to use the Visual Explorations Excel add-in workbook.
- **Using Excel 2003 Guide** This guide presents, where necessary, alternate Excel Guide instructions for users of this older version of Excel.
- **PHStat2** The latest version of PHStat2, the Pearson statistical add-in for Windows-based Excel, version 2003 and later. This version eliminates the use of the Excel Analysis ToolPak add-ins, thereby simplifying installation and setup.

MyStatLab™

MyStatLab—MyStatLab provides students with direct access to the companion website resources as well as the following exclusive online features and tools:

- **Interactive tutorial exercises** A comprehensive set of exercises have been written especially for use with this book that are algorithmically generated for unlimited practice and mastery. Most exercises are free-response exercises and provide guided solutions, sample problems, and learning aids for extra help at point of use.
- **Personalized study plan** A plan indicates which topics have been mastered and creates direct links to tutorial exercises for topics that have not been mastered. MyStatLab manages the study plan, updating its content based on the results of future online assessments.
- **Pearson Tutor Center (www.pearsontutorservices.com)** The MyStatlab student access code grants access to this online resource, staffed by qualified instructors who provide book-specific tutoring via phone, fax, e-mail, and interactive web sessions.
- **Integration with Pearson eTexts** iPad users can download a free app at www.apple.com/ipad/apps-for-ipad/ and then sign in using their MyStatLab account to access a bookshelf of all their Pearson eTexts. The iPad app also allows access to the Do Homework, Take a Test, and Study Plan pages of their MyStatLab course.
- **Mobile Dashboard** Allows students to use their mobile devices to log in and review information from the dashboard of their courses: announcements, assignments, results, and progress bars for completed work. This app is available for iPhones, iPads, and Android phones, and is designed to promote effective study habits rather than to allow students to complete assignments on their mobile devices.

@RISK trial Palisade Corporation, the maker of the market-leading risk and decision analysis Excel add-ins, @RISK and the DecisionTools® Suite, provides special academic versions of its software to students (and faculty). Its flagship product, @RISK, debuted in 1987 and performs risk analysis using Monte Carlo simulation.

@RISK and the DecisionTools Suite are used widely in undergraduate and graduate business programs worldwide. Thanks to the company's generous academic sales program, more than 40,000 students learn to make better decisions using @RISK and the DecisionTools Suite each year.

To download a trial version of @RISK software, visit **www.palisadecom/academic/**.

Instructor Resources

Instructor's Resource Center—Reached through a link at **www.pearsonhighered.com/levine**, the Instructor's Resource Center contains the electronic files for the complete Instructor's Solutions Manual, the Test Item File, and PowerPoint lecture presentations.

- **Register, redeem, log in** At **www.pearsonhighered.com/irc**, instructors can access a variety of print, media, and presentation resources that are available with this book in downloadable digital format. Resources are also available for course management platforms such as Blackboard, WebCT, and CourseCompass.

- **Need help?** Pearson Education's dedicated technical support team is ready to assist instructors with questions about the media supplements that accompany this text. Visit **http://247.prenhall.com** for answers to frequently asked questions and toll-free user support phone numbers. The supplements are available to adopting instructors. Detailed descriptions are provided at the Instructor's Resource Center.

Instructor's Solutions Manual—Created by Professor Pin Tian Ng of Northern Arizona University, this manual includes solutions for end-of-section and end-of-chapter problems, answers to case questions, where applicable, and teaching tips for each chapter. Electronic solutions are provided in PDF and Word formats.

Lecture PowerPoint Presentations—A PowerPoint presentation, created by Professor Patrick Schur of Miami University, is available for each chapter. The PowerPoint slides provide an instructor with individual lecture outlines to accompany the text. The slides include many of the figures and tables from the text. Instructors can use these lecture notes as is or can easily modify the notes to reflect specific presentation needs.

Test Item File—Created by Professor Pin Tian Ng of Northern Arizona University, the Test Item File contains true/false, multiple-choice, fill-in, and problem-solving questions based on the definitions, concepts, and ideas developed in each chapter of the text.

TestGen—The computerized TestGen package allows instructors to customize, save, and generate classroom tests. The test program permits instructors to edit, add, and delete questions from the test bank; edit existing graphics and create new graphics; analyze test results; and organize a database of test and student results. This software provides ease of use and extensive flexibility, and it provides many options for organizing and displaying tests, along with search and sort features. The software and the test banks can be downloaded from the Instructor's Resource Center.

MathXL for Statistics—MathXL for Statistics is a powerful online homework, tutorial, and assessment system that accompanies Pearson Education statistics textbooks. With MathXL for Statistics, instructors can create, edit, and assign online homework and tests using algorithmically generated exercises correlated at the objective level to the textbook. They can also create and assign their own online exercises and import TestGen tests for added flexibility. All student work is tracked in MathXL's online grade book. Students can take chapter tests in MathXL and receive personalized study plans based on their test results. Each study plan diagnoses weaknesses and links the student directly to tutorial exercises for the objectives he or she needs to study and retest. Students can also access supplemental animations and video clips directly from selected exercises. MathXL for Statistics is available to qualified adopters. For more information, visit **www.mathxl.com** or contact your sales representative.

MyStatLab™

MyStatLab—Part of the MyMathLab and MathXL product family, MyStatLab is a text-specific, easily customizable online course that integrates interactive multimedia instruction with textbook content. MyStatLab gives you the tools you need to deliver all or a portion of your course online, whether your students are in a lab setting or working from home. The latest version of MyStatLab offers a new, intuitive design that features more direct access to MathXL for Statistics pages (Gradebook, Homework & Test Manager, Home Page Manager, etc.) and provides enhanced functionality for communicating with students and customizing courses. Other key features include:

- **Assessment manager** An easy-to-use assessment manager lets instructors create online homework, quizzes, and tests that are automatically graded and correlated directly to your textbook. Assignments can be created using a mix of questions from the MyStatLab exercise bank, instructor-created custom exercises, and/or TestGen test items.
- **Grade book** Designed specifically for mathematics and statistics, the MyStatLab grade book automatically tracks students' results and gives you control over how to calculate final grades. You can also add offline (paper-and-pencil) grades to the grade book.
- **MathXL Exercise Builder** You can use the MathXL Exercise Builder to create static and algorithmic exercises for your online assignments. A library of sample exercises provides an easy starting point for creating questions, and you can also create questions from scratch.
- **eText-MathXL for Statistics Full Integration** Students using appropriate mobile devices can use your eText annotations and highlights for each course, and iPAd users can download

a free app that allows them access to the Do Homework, Take a Test, and Study Plan pages of their course.

- **"Ask the Publisher" Link in "Ask My Instructor" Email** You can easily notify the content team of any irregularities with specific questions by using the "Ask the Publisher" functionality in the "Ask My Instructor" emails you receive from students.
- **Tracking Time Spent on Media** Because the latest version of MyStatLab requires students to explicitly click a "Submit" button after viewing the media for their assignments, you will be able to track how long students are spending on each media file.

Palisade Corporation software—Palisade Corporation, the maker of the market-leading risk and decision analysis Excel add-ins, @RISK and the DecisionTools® Suite, provides special academic versions of its software. Its flagship product, @RISK, debuted in 1987 and performs risk analysis using Monte Carlo simulation. With an estimated 150,000 users, Palisade software can be found in more than 100 countries and has been translated into five languages.

@RISK and the DecisionTools Suite are used widely in undergraduate and graduate business programs worldwide and can be bundled with this textbook. To download a trial version of @RISK software, visit **www.palisade.com/academic/**.

Acknowledgments

We are extremely grateful to the Biometrika Trustees, American Cyanamid Company, the RAND Corporation, and the American Society for Testing and Materials for their kind permission to publish various tables in Appendix E, and the American Statistical Association for its permission to publish diagrams from the *American Statistician*. Also, we are grateful to Professors George A. Johnson and Joanne Tokle of Idaho State University and Ed Conn, Mountain States Potato Company, for their kind permission to incorporate parts of their work as our Mountain States Potato Company case in Chapter 15.

A Note of Thanks

We would like to thank Kevin Caskey, SUNY–New Paltz; Zhi Min Huang, Adelphi University; David Huff, Wayne State University; Eugene Jones, Ohio State University; Glen Miller, Piedmont College; Angela Mitchell, Wilmington College; Daniel Montgomery, Delta State University; Patricia Mullins, University of Wisconsin–Madison; Robert Pred, Temple University; Gary Smith, Florida State University; and Robert Wharton, Fordham University for their comments, which have made this a better book.

We would especially like to thank Chuck Synovec, Mary Kate Murray, Jason Calcano, Judy Leale, Anne Fahlgren, Melinda Jensen, and Kerri Tomasso of the editorial, marketing, and production teams at Prentice Hall. We would like to thank our statistical reader and accuracy checker Annie Puciloski for her diligence in checking our work; Susan Pariseau, Merrimack College, for assisting in the reading of the page proofs; Kitty Wilson for her copyediting; Lori Cavanaugh for her proofreading; and Jen Carley of PreMediaGlobal for her work in the production of this text.

Finally, we would like to thank our families for their patience, understanding, love, and assistance in making this book a reality. It is to them that we dedicate this book.

Concluding Remarks

We have gone to great lengths to make this text both pedagogically sound and error free. If you have any suggestions or require clarification about any of the material, or if you find any errors, please contact us at **davidlevine@davidlevinestatistics.com**. Include the phrase "BBS edition 12" in the subject line of your e-mail. For technical support for PHStat2 beyond what is presented in the appendices and in the PHStat2 readme file that accompanies PHStat2, visit the PHStat2 website, **www.pearsonhighered.com/phstat** and click on the **Contact Pearson Technical Support** link.

Mark L. Berenson

David M. Levine

Timothy C. Krehbiel

Basic Business Statistics: Concepts and Applications

TWELFTH EDITION

1 Introduction

Learning Objectives

In this chapter, you learn:

- How businesses use statistics
- The basic vocabulary of statistics
- The types of data used in business
- How to use Microsoft Excel and/or Minitab with this book

USING STATISTICS

@ Good Tunes & More

Managers at Good Tunes & More, a consumer electronics retailer, are looking to expand their chain to take advantage of recent store closings by their competitors. These managers have decided to approach local banks for the funding needed to underwrite the expansion. The managers know that they will have to present information about Good Tunes & More that will convince the bankers that the retailer is a good candidate for expansion.

The managers ask you to help prepare the supporting documents to be submitted to the bankers. To this end, they give you access to the retailer's sales transactions for the past five years. What should you do with the data? To help find a starting point for the task, you decide to learn more about statistics.

1.1 Why Learn Statistics

Statistics is the branch of mathematics that transforms numbers into useful information for decision makers. Statistics lets you know about the risks associated with making a business decision and allows you to understand and reduce the variation in the decision-making process.

Statistics provides you with methods for making better sense of the numbers used every day to describe or analyze the world we live in. For example, consider these news stories:

- **"More Clicks to Escape an Email List" (*The New York Times*, March 29, 2010, p. B2)** A study of 100 large online retailers reported that 39% required three or more clicks to opt out of an email list in 2009, compared to 7% in 2008.
- **"Green Power Purchases Targeted to Wind, Solar" (P. Davidson, *USA Today*, April 1, 2009, p. 3B)** Approximately 55% of green power sales was for wind energy.
- **"Follow the Tweets" (H. Rui, A. Whinston, and E. Winkler, *The Wall Street Journal*, November 30, 2009, p. R4)** In this study, the authors used the number of tweets that mention specific products to make accurate predictions of sales trends.

Do these numbers represent useful information? How can you decide? Statistical methods help you understand the information contained in "the numbers" and determine whether differences in "the numbers" are meaningful or are just due to chance.

Why learn statistics? First and foremost, statistics helps you make better sense of the world. Second, statistics helps you make better business decisions.

1.2 Statistics in Business

In the business world, statistics has these important specific uses:

- To summarize business data
- To draw conclusions from those data
- To make reliable forecasts about business activities
- To improve business processes

The statistical methods you use for these tasks come from one of the two branches of statistics: descriptive statistics and inferential statistics.

DESCRIPTIVE STATISTICS

Descriptive statistics are the methods that help collect, summarize, present, and analyze a set of data.

INFERENTIAL STATISTICS

Inferential statistics are the methods that use the data collected from a small group to draw conclusions about a larger group.

Many of the tables and charts found in a typical presentation are the products of descriptive methods, as are statistics such as the mean or median of a group, which you may have encountered previously. (The mean and median are among the concepts discussed in Chapter 3.) When you use statistical methods to help choose which investment from a set of investments might lead to a higher return or which marketing strategy might lead to increased sales, you are using inferential methods.

There are four important uses of statistics in business:

- To visualize and summarize your data (an example of using descriptive methods)
- To reach conclusions about a large group based on data collected from a small group (an example of using inferential methods)

- To make reliable forecasts that are based on statistical models for prediction (inferential methods)
- To improve business processes using managerial approaches such as Six Sigma that focus on quality improvement

To use descriptive and inferential methods correctly, you must also learn the conditions and assumptions required for using those methods. And since many of the statistical methods used in business must be computerized in order to be of practical benefit, you also need to know how computers can help you apply statistics in the business world.

To help you develop and integrate these skills, which will give you a basis for making better decisions, every chapter of *Basic Business Statistics* begins with a Using Statistics scenario. Each scenario describes a realistic business situation in which you are asked to make decisions that can be enhanced by applying statistical methods. For example, in one chapter you must decide the location in a supermarket that best enhances sales of a cola drink, while in another chapter you need to forecast sales for a clothing store.

In the scenario on page 3, you need to answer the following questions: What data should you include to convince bankers to extend the credit that Good Tunes & More needs? How should you present those data?

Because Good Tunes & More is a retailer, collecting data about the company's sales would be a reasonable starting point. You could present the details of every sales transaction for the past few years as a way of demonstrating that the business is thriving. However, presenting the bankers with the thousands of transactions would overwhelm them and not be very useful. You need to summarize the details of each transaction in some useful way that will give the bankers the information to (perhaps) uncover a favorable pattern about the sales over time.

One piece of information that the bankers would presumably want to see is the yearly dollar sales totals. Tallying and totaling sales is a common summary task. When you tally sales—or any other relevant data about Good Tunes & More that you choose to use—you follow standard business practice and tally by a business period, such as by month, quarter, or year. When you do so, you end up with multiple values: sales for this year, sales for last year, sales for the year before that, and so on.

Knowing more about statistics will definitely help you prepare a better presentation for the bankers! And the best way to begin knowing more about statistics is to learn the basic vocabulary of statistics.

1.3 Basic Vocabulary of Statistics

Seven terms—*variable*, *data*, *operational definition*, *population*, *sample*, *parameter*, and *statistic* (singular)—identify the fundamental concepts of the subject of statistics. Learning about and making sense of the statistical methods discussed in later chapters is nearly impossible if you do not first understand the meaning of these words.

Variables are characteristics of items or individuals. They are what you analyze when you use a statistical method. For the Good Tunes & More scenario, sales, expenses by year, and net profit by year are variables that the bankers would want to analyze. When used in everyday speech, *variable* suggests that something changes or varies, and you would expect sales, expenses, and net profit to have different values from year to year. These different values are the *data* associated with a variable or, more simply, the "data to be analyzed."

VARIABLE

A **variable** is a characteristic of an item or individual.

DATA

Data are the different values associated with a variable.

Variables can differ for reasons other than time. For example, if you conducted an analysis of the composition of a large lecture class, you would probably want to include the variables class standing, gender, and major field of study. These variables would also vary because each student in the class is different. One student might be a sophomore, a male, and an accounting major, while another might be a junior, a female, and a finance major.

Variable values are meaningless unless their corresponding variables have **operational definitions**. These definitions are universally accepted meanings that are clear to all associated with an analysis. Even though the operational definition for sales per year might seem clear, miscommunication could occur if one person were to refer to sales per year for the entire chain of stores and another to sales per year per store. Even individual values for variables sometimes need to be defined. For the class standing variable, for example, what *exactly* is meant by the words *sophomore* and *junior*? (Perhaps the most famous examples of vague definitions have been election disputes, such as the one that occurred in Florida during the 2000 U.S. presidential election that involved the definitions for "valid" and "invalid" ballots.)

The subject of statistics creates useful information from either populations or samples.

POPULATION

A **population** consists of all the items or individuals about which you want to reach conclusions.

SAMPLE

A **sample** is the portion of a population selected for analysis.

A *population* consists of all the items or individuals about which you want to reach conclusions. All the Good Tunes & More sales transactions for a specific year, all the customers who shopped at Good Tunes & More this weekend, all the full-time students enrolled in a college, and all the registered voters in Ohio are examples of populations.

A *sample* is the portion of a population selected for analysis. From the four examples of populations just given, you could select a sample of 200 Good Tunes & More sales transactions randomly selected by an auditor for study, a sample of 30 Good Tunes & More customers asked to complete a customer satisfaction survey, a sample of 50 full-time students selected for a marketing study, and a sample of 500 registered voters in Ohio contacted by telephone for a political poll. In each of these examples, the transactions or people in the sample represent a portion of the items or individuals that make up the population.

Parameter and *statistic* complete the basic vocabulary of statistics.

PARAMETER

A **parameter** is a measure that describes a characteristic of a population.

STATISTIC

A **statistic** is a measure that describes a characteristic of a sample.

The average amount spent by all customers who shopped at Good Tunes & More this weekend is an example of a parameter because this amount refers to the amount spent in the entire population. In contrast, the average amount spent by the 30 customers completing the customer satisfaction survey is an example of a statistic because it refers only to the amount spent by the sample of 30 customers.

1.4 Identifying Types of Variables

Identifying the characteristic of an item or individual to study and assigning an operational definition to that characteristic is only part of the variable definition process. For each variable, you must also establish the type of values it will have.

Categorical variables (also known as **qualitative variables**) have values that can only be placed into categories such as yes and no. "Do you currently own bonds?" (yes or no) and the level of risk of a bond fund (below average, average, or above average) are examples of categorical variables.

Numerical variables (also known as **quantitative variables**) have values that represent quantities. Numerical variables are further identified as being either discrete or continuous variables.

Discrete variables have numerical values that arise from a counting process. "The number of premium cable channels subscribed to" is an example of a discrete numerical variable because the response is one of a finite number of integers. You subscribe to zero, one, two, or more channels. "The number of items purchased" is also a discrete numerical variable because you are counting the number of items purchased.

Continuous variables produce numerical responses that arise from a measuring process. The time you wait for teller service at a bank is an example of a continuous numerical variable because the response takes on any value within a *continuum*, or an interval, depending on the precision of the measuring instrument. For example, your waiting time could be 1 minute, 1.1 minutes, 1.11 minutes, or 1.113 minutes, depending on the precision of the measuring device used. (Theoretically, no two continuous values would ever be identical. However, because no measuring device is perfectly precise, identical continuous values for two or more items or individuals can occur.)

At first glance, identifying the variable type may seem easy, but some variables that you might want to study could be either categorical or numerical, depending on how you define them. For example, "age" would seem to be an obvious numerical variable, but what if you are interested in comparing the buying habits of children, young adults, middle-aged persons, and retirement-age people? In that case, defining "age" as a categorical variable would make better sense. Again, this illustrates the earlier point that without operational definitions, variables are meaningless.

Asking questions about the variables you have identified for study can often be a great help in determining the variable type you want. Table 1.1 illustrates the process. Note that the "answers" to the questions are labeled *responses*. The word *responses* is sometimes used in statistics to refer to the values of a variable.

TABLE 1.1

Types of Variables

Question	Responses		Data Type
Do you currently have a profile on Facebook?	❑ Yes ❑ No	→	Categorical
How many text messages have you sent in the past week?	____	→	Numerical (discrete)
How long did it take to download a video game?	____ seconds	→	Numerical (continuous)

Measurement Scales

The values for variables can themselves be classified by the level of measurement, or measurement scale. Statisticians use the terms *nominal scale* and *ordinal scale* to describe the values for a categorical variable and use the terms *interval scale* and *ratio scale* to describe numerical values.

Nominal and Ordinal Scales Values for a categorical variable are measured on a nominal scale or on an ordinal scale. A **nominal scale** (see Table 1.2) classifies data into distinct categories in which no ranking is implied. Examples of a nominal scaled variable are your favorite soft drink, your political party affiliation, and your gender. Nominal scaling is the weakest form of measurement because you cannot specify any ranking across the various categories.

TABLE 1.2

Examples of Nominal Scales

Categorical Variable	Categories
Do you currently have a Facebook profile?	❑ Yes ❑ No
Types of investments	❑ Stocks ❑ Bonds ❑ Other ❑ None
Internet email provider	❑ Gmail ❑ Windows Live ❑ Yahoo ❑ Other

An **ordinal scale** classifies values into distinct categories in which ranking is implied. For example, suppose that Good Tunes & More conducted a survey of customers who made a purchase and asked the question "How do you rate the overall service provided by Good Tunes & More during your most recent purchase?" to which the responses were "excellent," "very good," "fair," and "poor." The answers to this question would constitute an ordinal scaled variable because the responses "excellent," "very good," "fair," and "poor" are ranked in order of satisfaction. Table 1.3 lists other examples of ordinal scaled variables.

TABLE 1.3

Examples of Ordinal Scales

Categorical Variable		Ordered Categories
Student class designation	→	Freshman Sophomore Junior Senior
Product satisfaction	→	Very unsatisfied Fairly unsatisfied Neutral Fairly satisfied Very satisfied
Faculty rank	→	Professor Associate Professor Assistant Professor Instructor
Standard & Poor's bond ratings	→	AAA AA A BBB BB B CCC CC C DDD DD D
Student grades	→	A B C D F

Ordinal scaling is a stronger form of measurement than nominal scaling because an observed value classified into one category possesses more of a property than does an observed value classified into another category. However, ordinal scaling is still a relatively weak form of measurement because the scale does not account for the amount of the differences *between* the categories. The ordering implies only *which* category is "greater," "better," or "more preferred"—not by *how much*.

Interval and Ratio Scales Values for a numerical variable are measured on an interval scale or a ratio scale. An **interval scale** (see Table 1.4) is an ordered scale in which the difference between measurements is a meaningful quantity but does not involve a true zero point. For example, a noontime temperature reading of 67 degrees Fahrenheit is 2 degrees warmer than a noontime reading of 65 degrees. In addition, the 2 degrees Fahrenheit difference in the noontime temperature readings is the same as if the two noontime temperature readings were 74 and 76 degrees Fahrenheit because the difference has the same meaning anywhere on the scale.

TABLE 1.4

Examples of Interval and Ratio Scales

Numerical Variable		Level of Measurement
Temperature (in degrees Celsius or Fahrenheit)	→	Interval
Standardized exam score (e.g., ACT or SAT)	→	Interval
Time to download a file (in seconds)	→	Ratio
Age (in years or days)	→	Ratio
Cost of a personal computer system (in U.S. dollars)	→	Ratio

A **ratio scale** is an ordered scale in which the difference between the measurements involves a true zero point, as in height, weight, age, or salary measurements. If Good Tunes & More conducted a survey and asked the amount of money that you expected to spend on audio equipment in the next year, the responses to such a question would be an example of a ratio scaled variable. As another example, a person who weighs 240 pounds is twice as heavy as someone who weighs 120 pounds. Temperature is a trickier case: Fahrenheit and Celsius (centigrade) scales are interval but not ratio scales; the "zero" value is arbitrary, not real. You cannot say that a noontime temperature reading of 4 degrees Fahrenheit is twice as hot as 2 degrees Fahrenheit. But a Kelvin temperature reading, in which 0 degrees means no molecular motion, is ratio scaled. In contrast, the Fahrenheit and Celsius scales use arbitrarily selected 0-degree beginning points.

Data measured on an interval scale or on a ratio scale constitute the highest levels of measurement. They are stronger forms of measurement than an ordinal scale because you can determine not only which observed value is the largest but also by how much.

Problems for Section 1.4

LEARNING THE BASICS

1.1 Four different beverages are sold at a fast-food restaurant: soft drinks, tea, coffee, and bottled water.

a. Explain why the type of beverage sold is an example of a categorical variable.

b. Explain why the type of beverage sold is an example of a nominal scaled variable.

1.2 Coffee is sold in three sizes at a fast-food restaurant: small, medium, and large. Explain why the beverage size of coffee is an example of an ordinal scaled variable.

1.3 Suppose that you measure the time it takes to download a video from the Internet.

a. Explain why the download time is a continuous numerical variable.

b. Explain why the download time is a ratio scaled variable.

APPLYING THE CONCEPTS

SELF Test **1.4** For each of the following variables, determine whether the variable is categorical or numerical. If the variable is numerical, determine whether the variable is discrete or continuous. In addition, determine the measurement scale.

a. Number of telephones per household

b. Length (in minutes) of the longest telephone call made in a month

c. Whether someone in the household owns a Wi-Fi-capable cell phone

d. Whether there is a high-speed Internet connection in the household

1.5 The following information is collected from students upon exiting the campus bookstore during the first week of classes.

a. Amount of time spent shopping in the bookstore

b. Number of textbooks purchased

c. Academic major

d. Gender

Classify each of these variables as categorical or numerical. If the variable is numerical, determine whether the variable is discrete or continuous. In addition, determine the measurement scale for each of these variables.

1.6 For each of the following variables, determine whether the variable is categorical or numerical. If the variable is numerical, determine whether the variable is discrete or continuous. In addition, determine the measurement scale for each variable.

a. Name of Internet service provider
b. Time in hours spent surfing the Internet per week
c. Number of emails received in a week
d. Number of online purchases made in a month

1.7 For each of the following variables, determine whether the variable is categorical or numerical. If the variable is numerical, determine whether the variable is discrete or continuous. In addition, determine the measurement scale for each variable.

a. Amount of money spent on clothing in the past month
b. Favorite department store
c. Most likely time period during which shopping for clothing takes place (weekday, weeknight, or weekend)
d. Number of pairs of shoes owned

1.8 Suppose the following information is collected from Robert Keeler on his application for a home mortgage loan at the Metro County Savings and Loan Association.

a. Monthly payments: $1,927
b. Number of jobs in past 10 years: 1
c. Annual family income: $76,000
d. Marital status: Married

Classify each of the responses by type of data and measurement scale.

1.9 One of the variables most often included in surveys is income. Sometimes the question is phrased "What is your income (in thousands of dollars)?" In other surveys, the respondent is asked to "Select the circle corresponding to your income level" and is given a number of income ranges to choose from.

a. In the first format, explain why income might be considered either discrete or continuous.
b. Which of these two formats would you prefer to use if you were conducting a survey? Why?

1.10 If two students score a 90 on the same examination, what arguments could be used to show that the underlying variable—test score—is continuous?

1.11 The director of market research at a large department store chain wanted to conduct a survey throughout a metropolitan area to determine the amount of time working women spend shopping for clothing in a typical month.

a. Describe both the population and the sample of interest. Indicate the type of data the director might want to collect.
b. Develop a first draft of the questionnaire needed in (a) by writing three categorical questions and three numerical questions that you feel would be appropriate for this survey.

1.5 Statistical Applications for Desktop Computing

Advances in computing during the past 40 years have brought statistical applications to the business desktop. Statistical functionality is so commonplace today that many simple statistical tasks once done exclusively with pencil and paper or hand calculators are now done electronically, with the assistance of statistical applications.

Excel and Minitab are examples of desktop applications that people use for statistics. Excel is the Microsoft Office data analysis application that evolved from earlier electronic spreadsheets used in accounting and financial applications. Minitab, a dedicated statistical application, or **statistical package**, was developed from the ground up to perform statistical analysis as accurately as possible. Versions of Minitab run on larger computer systems and can perform heavy-duty corporate analyses involving very large data sets. Excel and Minitab are two very different programs, and their differences have led to an ongoing debate as to which program is more appropriate for use in an introductory business statistics course. Proponents of each program point to their program's strengths: Minitab as a complete statistical solution; Excel as a common desktop tool found in many business functional areas (and in many different business school courses).

Although you are probably more familiar with Excel than with Minitab, both programs share many similarities, starting with their shared use of **worksheets** (or spreadsheets) to store data for analysis. Worksheets are tabular arrangements of data, in which the intersections of rows and columns form **cells**, boxes into which you make entries. In Minitab, the data for each variable are placed in separate columns, and this is also the standard practice when using Excel. Generally, to perform a statistical analysis in either program, you select one or more columns of data and then apply the appropriate command.

Both Excel and Minitab allow you to save worksheets, programming information, and results as one file, called a **workbook** in Excel and a **project** in Minitab. In Excel, workbooks are collections of worksheets and chart sheets. You save a workbook when you save "an Excel file" (as either an **.xls** or **.xlsx** file). In Minitab, a project includes data worksheets, all the results shown in a **session window**, and all graphs created for the data. Unlike in Excel, in Minitab you can save individual worksheets (as **.mtw** worksheet files) as well as save the entire project (as an **.mpj** project file).

You can use either Excel or Minitab to learn and practice the statistical methods learned in this book. The end of each chapter, except for the last chapter, presents guides that contain detailed instructions for applying Microsoft Excel and Minitab to the statistical methods taught in the chapter. These Excel and Minitab Guides use some of the downloadable files discussed in Appendix C to illustrate the step-by-step process by which you apply a method. The Excel Guides additionally offer a choice of techniques—all leading to the same results—that allow you to use Excel either in a semi-automated way to get quick results or as a "sandbox" in which you construct results from scratch or from model templates. This is further explained in Section EG1.1 of the Chapter 1 Excel Guide.

1.6 How to Use This Book

This book organizes its material around the four important uses of statistics in business (see Section 1.2). Chapters 2 and 3 present methods that summarize business data to address the first use listed. Chapters 4 through 12 discuss methods that use sample data to draw conclusions about populations (the second use). Chapters 13 though 16 review methods to make reliable forecasts (the third use). Chapter 17 introduces methods that you can use to improve business processes (the fourth use). In addition, Chapter 2 introduces a problem-solving approach that will help you learn individual methods and help you apply your knowledge beyond the statistics course. Chapter 18 further illustrates this approach and also summarizes the methods discussed in earlier chapters.

As explained in Section 1.2, each chapter begins with a scenario that establishes a business situation to which you can apply the methods of the chapter. At the end of each chapter, you revisit the scenario to learn how the methods of the chapter could be applied in the scenario. Following the revisited scenario, you will find such sections as Summary, Key Terms, Key Equations, and Chapter Review Problems that help you review what you have learned.

Following this review material in most chapters, you will find a continuing case study that allows you to apply statistics to problems faced by the management of Ashland MultiComm Services, a residential telecommunications provider. Most chapters continue with a Digital Case, in which you examine information in a variety of media forms and apply your statistical knowledge to resolve problems or address issues and concerns of the case. Many of these cases will help you think about what constitutes the proper or ethical use of statistics. ("Learning with the Digital Cases" on page 15 introduces you to this unique set of business cases.) Finally, at the very end of each chapter, except for the last chapter, are the Excel Guides and Minitab Guides discussed in Section 1.5.

Don't worry if your instructor does not cover every section of every chapter. Introductory business statistics courses vary in their scope, length, and number of college credits. Your chosen functional area of specialization (accounting, management, finance, marketing, etc.) may also affect what you learn in class or what you are assigned or choose to read in this book.

Checklist for Getting Started

To make the best use of this book, you need to work with Excel or Minitab and download and use files and other electronic resources that are available from the companion website (discussed fully in Appendix C). To minimize problems you may face later when using these resources, review and complete the Table 1.5 checklist. When you have checked off all the tasks necessary for your own work, you will be ready to begin reading the Chapter 1 Excel or Minitab Guide and using the supplemental material in Appendices B, C, D, F and G, as necessary.

When you have completed the checklist, you are ready to begin using the Excel Guides and Minitab Guides that appear at the end of chapters. These guides discuss how to apply

TABLE 1.5

Checklist for Getting Started with *Basic Business Statistics*

- ❑ Select which program, Excel or Minitab, you will use with this book. (Your instructor may have made this decision for you.)
- ❑ Read Appendix A if you need to learn or review basic math concepts and notation.
- ❑ Read Appendix B if you need to learn or review basic computing concepts and skills.
- ❑ Download the files and other electronic resources needed to work with this book. Read Appendix C to learn more about the things you can download from the companion website for this book. (This process requires Internet access.)
- ❑ Successfully install the chosen program and apply all available updates to the program. Read Appendix Section D.1 to learn how to find and apply updates. (This process requires Internet access.)
- ❑ If you plan to use PHStat2 with Excel, complete the special checklist in Appendix Section D.2. If you plan to use the Analysis ToolPak with Excel, read and follow the instructions in Appendix Section D.5.
- ❑ Skim Appendices F and G to be aware of how these appendices can help you as you use this book with Excel or Minitab.

Excel and Minitab to the statistical methods discussed in the chapter. The Excel Guides and Minitab Guides for this chapter (which begin on pages 17 and 22, respectively) review the basic operations of these programs and explain how Excel and Minitab handle the concept of type of variable discussed in Section 1.4.

Instructions in the Excel Guides and Minitab Guides and related appendices use the conventions for computer operations presented in Table 1.6. Read and review Appendix B if some of the vocabulary used in the table is new to you.

TABLE 1.6

Conventions for Computing Operations

Operation	Examples	Interpretation
Keyboard keys	**Enter** **Ctrl** **Shift**	Names of keys are always the object of the verb *press*, as in "press **Enter**."
Keystroke combination	**Crtl+C** **Crtl+Shift+Enter**	Some keyboarding actions require you to press more than one key at the same time. **Crtl+C** means press the **C** key while holding down the **Ctrl** key. **Crtl+Shift+Enter** means press the **Enter** key while holding down the **Ctrl** and **Shift** keys.
Click object	Click **OK**. Click **All** in the **Page Range** section.	A *click object* is a target of a mouse click. When click objects are part of a window that contains more than one part, the part name is also given, e.g., "in the **Page Range** section." Review Appendix Section B.2 to learn the verbs this book uses with click objects.
Menu or ribbon selection	**File → New** **Layout → Trendline → Linear Trendline**	A sequence of menu or ribbon selections is represented by a list of choices separated by the **→** symbol. **File → New** means first select **File** and then, from the list of choices that appears, select **New**.
Placeholder object	Select ***variablename***	An italicized object means that the actual object varies, depending on the context of the instruction. "Select ***variablename***" might, for one problem, mean "select the **Yearly Sales** variable" and might mean "select the **Monthly Sales** variable" for another.

USING STATISTICS @ Good Tunes & More Revisited

In the Using Statistics scenario at the beginning of this chapter, you were asked to help prepare documents to support the Good Tunes & More expansion. The managers had decided to approach local banks for funding the expansion of their company, and you needed to determine what type of data to present and how to present those data. As a first step, you decided to summarize the details of thousands of transactions into useful information in the form of yearly dollar sales totals.

SUMMARY

Learning about statistics begins with learning the seven terms that are the basic vocabulary of statistics. With this vocabulary, you can begin to understand how statistics helps you make better sense of the world. Businesses use statistics to summarize and reach conclusions from data, to make reliable forecasts, and to improve business processes. You learned some of the basic vocabulary used in statistics and the various types of data used in business. In the next two chapters, you will study data collection and a variety of tables and charts and descriptive measures that are used to present and analyze data.

KEY TERMS

CHAPTER REVIEW PROBLEMS

CHECKING YOUR UNDERSTANDING

1.12 What is the difference between a sample and a population?

1.13 What is the difference between a statistic and a parameter?

1.14 What is the difference between descriptive statistics and inferential statistics?

1.15 What is the difference between a categorical variable and a numerical variable?

1.16 What is the difference between a discrete numerical variable and a continuous numerical variable?

1.17 What is an operational definition, and why are operational definitions so important?

1.18 What are the four measurement scales?

APPLYING THE CONCEPTS

1.19 Visit the official website for either Excel or Minitab, **www.office.microsoft.com/excel** or **www.minitab.com/products/minitab**. Read about the program you chose and then think about the ways the program could be useful in statistical analysis.

1.20 In 2008, a university in the midwestern United States surveyed its full-time first-year students after they completed their first semester. Surveys were electronically distributed to all 3,727 students, and responses were obtained from 2,821 students. Of the students surveyed, 90.1% indicated that they had studied with other students, and 57.1% indicated that they had tutored another student. The report also noted that 61.3% of the students surveyed came to class late at least once, and 45.8% admitted to being bored in class at least once.

a. Describe the population of interest.

b. Describe the sample that was collected.

c. Describe a parameter of interest.
d. Describe the statistic used to estimate the parameter in (c).

1.21 The Gallup organization releases the results of recent polls at its website, **www.gallup.com**. Visit this site and read an article of interest.
a. Describe the population of interest.
b. Describe the sample that was collected.
c. Describe a parameter of interest.
d. Describe the statistic used to describe the parameter in (c).

1.22 A Gallup poll indicated that 20% of Americans had confidence in U.S. banks. Interestingly, 58% also said that they had confidence in their main or primary bank. (data extracted from D. Jacobs, "Americans' Confidence in Banks Is at Historical Low," **www.gallup.com**, April 7, 2010). The results are based on telephone interviews conducted March 24, 2010, with 1,006 adults living in the United States, aged 18 and older.
a. Describe the population of interest.
b. Describe the sample that was collected.
c. Is 20% a parameter or a statistic? Explain.
d. Is 58% a parameter or a statistic?

1.23 According to its home page, "Swivel is a website where people share reports of charts and numbers. Businesses use swivel to dashboard their metrics. Students use Swivel to find and share research data." Visit **www.swivel.com** and explore a data set of interest to you.
a. Describe a variable in the data set you selected.
b. Is the variable categorical or numerical?
c. If the variable is numerical, is it discrete or continuous?

1.24 Download and examine the U.S. Census Bureau's "2007 Survey of Business Owners and Self-Employed Persons," directly available at **bhs.econ.census.gov/BHS/SBO/sbo1_07.pdf** or through the **Get Help with Your Form** link at **www.census.gov/econ/sbo**.
a. Give an example of a categorical variable included in the survey.
b. Give an example of a numerical variable included in the survey.

1.25 Three professors at Northern Kentucky University compared two different approaches to teaching courses in the school of business (M. W. Ford, D. W. Kent, and S. Devoto, "Learning from the Pros: Influence of Web-Based Expert Commentary on Vicarious Learning About Financial Markets," *Decision Sciences Journal of Innovative Education*, January 2007, 5(1), 43–63). At the time of the study, there were 2,100 students in the business school, and 96 students were involved in the study. Demographic data collected on these 96 students included class (freshman, sophomore, junior, senior), age, gender, and major.
a. Describe the population of interest.
b. Describe the sample that was collected.
c. Indicate whether each of the four demographic variables mentioned is categorical or numerical.
d. For each of the four demographic variables mentioned, indicate the measurement scale.

1.26 A manufacturer of cat food was planning to survey households in the United States to determine purchasing habits of cat owners. Among the variables to be collected are the following:
i. The primary place of purchase for cat food
ii. Whether dry or moist cat food is purchased
iii. The number of cats living in the household
iv. Whether any cat living in the household is pedigreed
a. For each of the four items listed, indicate whether the variable is categorical or numerical. If it is numerical, is it discrete or continuous?
b. Develop five categorical questions for the survey.
c. Develop five numerical questions for the survey.

1.27 A sample of 62 undergraduate students answered the following survey:
1. What is your gender? Female ______ Male ______
2. What is your age (*as of last birthday*)? ______
3. What is your current registered class designation?
Freshman ______ Sophomore ______ Junior ______
Senior ______
4. What is your major area of study?
Accounting ______
Computer Information Systems ______ Economics/Finance ______
International Business ______ Management ______
Retailing/Marketing ______
Other ______ Undecided ______
5. At the present time, do you plan to attend graduate school?
Yes ______ No ______ Not sure ______
6. What is your current cumulative grade point average?
______
7. What is your current employment status?
Full time ______ Part time ______ Unemployed ______
8. What would you expect your starting annual salary (*in $000*) to be if you were to seek full-time employment immediately after obtaining your bachelor's degree? ______
9. For how many social networking sites are you registered? ______
10. How satisfied are you with the food and dining services on campus? ______

1	2	3	4	5	6	7
Extremely unsatisfied			Neutral			Extremely satisfied

11. About how much money did you spend this semester for textbooks and supplies? ______
12. What type of computer do you prefer to use for your studies?
Desktop ______ Laptop ______
Tablet/notebook/netbook ______
13. How many text messages do you send in a typical week? ______
14. How much wealth (income, savings, investment, real estate, and other assets) would you have to accumulate

(in millions of dollars) before you would say you are rich? ______

a. Which variables in the survey are categorical?
b. Which variables in the survey are numerical?
c. Which variables are discrete numerical variables?

The results of the survey are stored in **UndergradSurvey**

1.28 A sample of 44 graduate students answered the following survey:

1. What is your gender? Female ______ Male ______
2. What is your age (*as of last birthday*)? ______
3. What is your current major area of study?
   Accounting ______
   Economics/Finance ______
   Management ______
   Retailing/Marketing ______
   Other ______ Undecided ______
4. What is your current graduate cumulative grade point average? ______
5. What was your undergraduate major?
   Biological Sciences ______ Business ______
   Computers ______
   Engineering ______
   Other ______
6. What was your undergraduate cumulative grade point average? ______
7. What is your current employment status?
   Full time ______ Part time ______ Unemployed ______
8. How many different full-time jobs have you held in the past 10 years? ______
9. What do you expect your annual salary (*in $000*) to be immediately after completion of your graduate studies if you are employed full time? ______
10. About how much money did you spend this semester for textbooks and supplies? ______
11. How satisfied are you with the MBA program advisory services on campus?
    1 2 3 4 5 6 7
    Extremely unsatisfied — Neutral — Extremely satisfied
12. What type of computer do you prefer to use for your studies?
    Desktop ______ Laptop ______ Tablet/notebook/netbook ______
13. How many text messages do you send in a typical week? ______
14. How much wealth (income, savings, investment, real estate, and other assets) would you have to accumulate (in millions of dollars) before you would say you are rich? ______

a. Which variables in the survey are categorical?
b. Which variables in the survey are numerical?
c. Which variables are discrete numerical variables?

The results of the survey are stored in **GradSurvey**

END-OF-CHAPTER CASES

At the end of most chapters, you will find a continuing case study that allows you to apply statistics to problems faced by the management of the Ashland MultiComm Services, a residential telecommunications provider. You will also find a series of Digital Cases that extend many of the Using Statistics scenarios that begin each chapter.

LEARNING WITH THE DIGITAL CASES

People use statistical techniques to help communicate and present important information to others both inside and outside their businesses. Every day, as in these examples, people misuse these techniques. Identifying and preventing misuses of statistics, whether intentional or not, is an important responsibility for all managers. The Digital Cases help you develop the skills necessary for this important task.

A Digital Case asks you to review electronic documents related to a company or statistical issue discussed in the chapter's Using Statistics scenario. You review the contents of these documents, which may contain internal confidential as well as publicly stated facts and claims, seeking to identify and correct misuses of statistics. Unlike a traditional case study, but like many business situations, not all of the information you encounter will be relevant to your task, and you may occasionally discover conflicting information that you have to resolve in order to complete the case.

To assist your learning, each Digital Case begins with a learning objective and a summary of the problem or issue at hand. Each case directs you to the information necessary to reach your own conclusions and to answer the case questions. You can work with the documents for the Digital Cases offline, after downloading them from the companion website (see Appendix C). Or you can work with the Digital Cases online, chapter-by-chapter, at the companion website.

DIGITAL CASE EXAMPLE

This section illustrates learning with a Digital Case. To begin, open the Digital Case file **GTM.pdf**, which contains contents from the Good Tunes & More website. Recall that the privately held Good Tunes & More, the subject of the

Using Statistics scenario in this chapter, is seeking financing to expand its business by opening retail locations. Because the managers are eager to show that Good Tunes & More is a thriving business, it is not surprising to discover the "our best sales year ever" claim in the "Good Times at Good Tunes & More" section on the first page.

Click the **our best sales year ever** link to display the page that supports this claim. How would you support such a claim? With a table of numbers? A chart? Remarks attributed to a knowledgeable source? Good Tunes & More has used a chart to present "two years ago" and "latest twelve months" sales data by category. Are there any problems with the choices made on this web page? *Absolutely*!

First, note that there are no scales for the symbols used, so it is impossible to know what the actual sales volumes are. In fact, as you will learn in Section 2.8, charts that incorporate symbols in this way are considered examples of *chartjunk* and would never be used by people seeking to properly use graphs.

This important point aside, another question that arises is whether the sales data represent the number of units sold or something else. The use of the symbols creates the impression that unit sales data are being presented. If the data are unit sales, does such data best support the claim being made, or would something else, such as dollar volumes, be a better indicator of sales at the retailer?

Then there are those curious chart labels. "Latest twelve months" is ambiguous; it could include months from the current year as well as months from one year ago and therefore may not be an equivalent time period to "two years ago." But the business was established in 1997, and the claim being made is "best sales year ever," so why hasn't management included sales figures for *every* year?

Are Good Tunes & More managers hiding something, or are they just unaware of the proper use of statistics? Either way, they have failed to properly communicate a vital aspect of their story.

In subsequent Digital Cases, you will be asked to provide this type of analysis, using the open-ended questions in the case as your guide. Not all the cases are as straightforward as this example, and some cases include perfectly appropriate applications of statistics.

REFERENCES

1. McCullough, B. D., and D. Heiser, "On the Accuracy of Statistical Procedures in Microsoft Excel 2007," *Computational Statistics and Data Analysis*, 52 (2008), 4568–4606.
2. McCullough, B. D., and B. Wilson, "On the Accuracy of Statistical Procedures in Microsoft Excel 97," *Computational Statistics and Data Analysis*, 31 (1999), 27–37.
3. McCullough, B. D., and B. Wilson, "On the Accuracy of Statistical Procedures in Microsoft Excel 2003," *Computational Statistics and Data Analysis*, 49 (2005), 1244–1252.
4. *Microsoft Excel 2010* (Redmond, WA: Microsoft Corporation, 2010).
5. Minitab *Release 16* (State College, PA: Minitab, Inc., 2010).
6. Nash, J. C., "Spreadsheets in Statistical Practice—Another Look," *The American Statistician*, 60 (2006), 287–289.

CHAPTER 1 EXCEL GUIDE

EG1.1 GETTING STARTED with EXCEL

You are almost ready to use Excel if you have completed the Table 1.5 checklist and reviewed the Table 1.6 conventions for computing on page 12. Before going further, decide how you plan to use Excel with this book. The Excel Guides include *In-Depth Excel* instructions that require no additional software and *PHStat2* instructions that use PHStat2, an add-in that simplifies using Excel while creating results identical to those you would get using the Excel instructions. Table EG1.1 lists the advantages and disadvantages of each type of instruction. Because of the equivalency of these two types, you can switch between them at any time while using this book.

TABLE EG1.1

Types of Excel Guide Instructions

***In-Depth Excel* Instructions**
Provides step-by-step instructions for applying Excel to the statistical methods of the chapter. **Advantages** Applicable to all Excel versions. Creates "live" worksheets and chart sheets that automatically update when the underlying data change. **Disadvantages** Can be time-consuming, frustrating, and error prone, especially for novices. May force you to focus on low-level Excel details, thereby distracting you from learning statistics.
***PHStat2* Instructions**
Provides step-by-step instructions for using the PHStat2 add-in with Excel. (To learn more about PHStat2, see Appendix G.) **Advantages** Creates live worksheets and chart sheets that are the same as or similar to the ones created in the *In-Depth Excel* instructions. Frees you from having to focus on low-level Excel details. Can be used to quickly double-check results created by the *In-Depth Excel* instructions. **Disadvantages** Must be installed separately and therefore requires an awareness about installing software on your system. (See Appendix D for the technical details.) Not compatible with OpenOffice.org Calc 3.

If you want to develop a mastery of Excel and gain practice building solutions from the bottom up, you will want to use the *In-Depth Excel* instructions. If you are more of a top-down person, who first wants quick results and then, later, looks at the details of a solution, you will want to maximize your use of the *PHStat2* instructions. At any time, you can switch between these methods without any loss of comprehension. Both methods lead to identical, or nearly identical, results. These results are mostly in the form of reusable workbooks. These workbooks, as well as the workbooks you can download (see Appendix C) are yours to keep and reuse for other problems, in other courses, or in your workplace.

When relevant, the Excel Guides also include instructions for the Analysis ToolPak, an optional component of Excel that Microsoft distributes with many versions of Excel, although not with the current version of Mac Excel.

The rest of this Excel Guide reviews the basic concepts and common operations encountered when using Excel with this book.

The Excel Guide instructions feature Windows Excel versions 2010 and 2007 and note their differences, when those differences are significant. The instructions have been written for maximum compatibility with current versions of Mac Excel and OpenOffice.org Calc, an Excel work-alike. If you use either Mac Excel or OpenOffice.org Calc, you will be able to use almost all the workbooks discussed in the *In-Depth Excel* instructions. If you use the older Windows-based Excel 2003, you can use the *PHStat2* instructions as is and can download from this book's companion website the *Using Excel 2003 with Basic Business Statistics* document that adapts the *In-Depth Excel* instructions for use with Excel 2003.

EG1.2 ENTERING DATA and VARIABLE TYPE

As first discussed in Section 1.5, you enter the data for each variable in a separate column. By convention, you start with column A and enter the name of each variable into the cells of the first row, and then you enter the data for the variable in the subsequent rows, as shown in Figure EG1.1.

FIGURE EG1.1
An example of a data worksheet

	A	B	C	D	E	F	G	H	I
1	Fund Number	Type	Assets	Fees	Expense Ratio	Return 2009	3-Year Return	5-Year Return	Risk
2	FN-1	Intermediate Government	7268.1	No	0.45	6.9	6.9	5.5	Below average
3	FN-2	Intermediate Government	475.1	No	0.50	9.8	7.5	6.1	Below average
4	FN-3	Intermediate Government	193.0	No	0.71	6.3	7.0	5.6	Average

Excel infers the variable type from the data you enter into a column. If Excel discovers a column containing numbers, for example, it treats the column as a numerical variable. If Excel discovers a column containing words or alphanumeric entries, it treats the column as a non-numerical (categorical) variable. This imperfect method works most of the time in Excel, especially if you make sure that the categories for your categorical variables are words or phrases such as "yes" and "no" and are not coded values that could be mistaken for numerical values, such as "1," "2," and "3." However, because you cannot explicitly define the variable type, Excel occasionally makes "mistakes" by either offering or allowing you to do nonsensical things such as using a statistical method that is designed for numerical variables on categorical variables.

When you enter data, never skip any rows in a column, and as a general rule, also avoid skipping any columns. Pay attention to any special instructions that occur throughout the book for the order of the entry of your data. For some statistical methods, entering your data in an order that Excel does not expect will lead to incorrect results.

Most of the Excel workbooks that you can download from this book's companion website (Appendix C) and use with the Excel Guides contain a DATA worksheet that follows the rules of this section. Any of those worksheets can be used as additional models for the method you use to enter variable data in Excel.

EG1.3 OPENING and SAVING WORKBOOKS

You open and save workbooks by first selecting the folder that stores the workbook and then specifying the file name of the workbook. In Excel 2010, you select **File → Open** to open a workbook file or **File → Save As** to save a workbook. In Excel 2007, you select **Office Button → Open** to open a workbook file or **Office Button → Save As** to save a workbook. **Open** and **Save As** display nearly identical dialog boxes that vary only slightly among the different Excel versions. Figure EG1.2 shows the Excel 2010 Open and Save As dialog boxes.

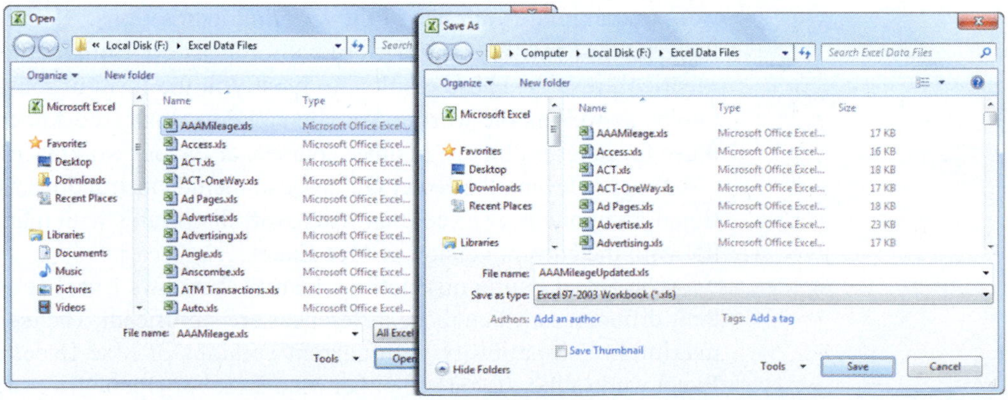

FIGURE EG1.2
Excel 2010 Open and Save As dialog boxes

You select the storage folder by using the drop-down list at the top of either of these dialog boxes. You enter, or select from the list box, a file name for the workbook in the **File name** box. You click **Open** or **Save** to complete the task. Sometimes when saving files, you may want to change the file type before you click **Save**. If you want to save your workbook in the format used by Excel 2003 and earlier versions, select **Excel 97-2003 Workbook (*.xls)** from the **Save as type** drop-down list (shown in Figure EG1.2) before you click **Save**. If you want to save data in a form that can be opened by programs that cannot open Excel workbooks, you might select either **Text (Tab delimited) (*.txt)** or **CSV (Comma delimited) (*.csv)** as the save type.

When you want to open a file and cannot find its name in the list box, double-check that the current **Look in** folder is the folder you intend. If it is, change the file type to **All Files (*.*)** to see all files in the current folder. This technique can help you discover inadvertent misspellings or missing file extensions that otherwise prevent the file from being displayed.

Although all versions of Microsoft Excel include a **Save** command, you should avoid this choice until you gain experience. Using Save makes it too easy to inadvertently overwrite your work. Also, you cannot use the Save command for any open workbook that Excel has marked as read-only. (Use Save As to save such workbooks.)

EG1.4 CREATING and COPYING WORKSHEETS

You create new worksheets by either creating a new workbook or by inserting a new worksheet in an open workbook. To create a new workbook, select **File → New** (Excel 2010) or **Office Button → New** (Excel 2007) and in the pane that appears, double-click the **Blank workbook** icon.

New workbooks are created with a fixed number of worksheets. To delete extra worksheets or insert more sheets, right-click a sheet tab and click either **Delete** or **Insert** (see Figure EG1.3). By default, Excel names a worksheet serially in the form Sheet1, Sheet2, and so on. You should change these names to better reflect the content of your worksheets. To rename a worksheet, double-click the sheet tab of the worksheet, type the new name, and press **Enter**.

FIGURE EG1.3
Sheet tab shortcut menu and the Move or Copy dialog box

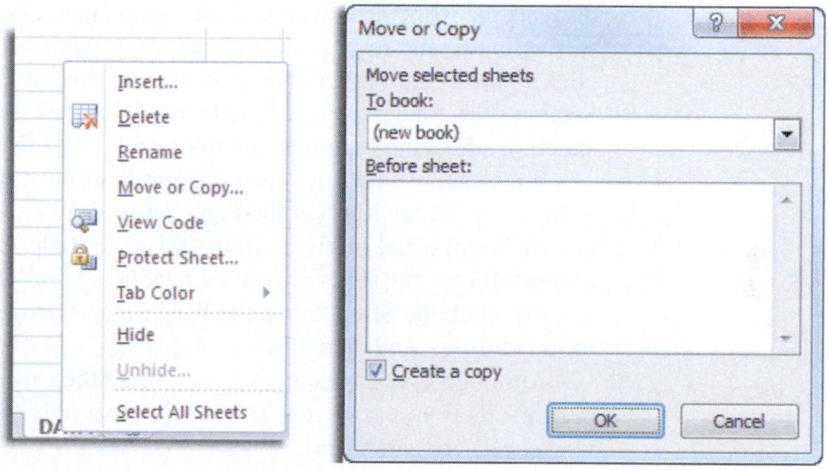

You can also make a copy of a worksheet or move a worksheet to another position in the same workbook or to a second workbook. Right-click the sheet tab and select **Move or Copy** from the shortcut menu that appears. In the **To book** drop-down list of the Move or Copy dialog box (see Figure EG1.3), first select **(new book)** (or the name of the pre-existing target workbook), check **Create a copy**, and then click **OK**.

EG1.5 PRINTING WORKSHEETS

To print a worksheet (or a chart sheet), first open to the worksheet by clicking its sheet tab. Then, in Excel 2010, select **File → Print**. If the print preview displayed (see Figure EG1.4) contains errors or displays the worksheet in an undesirable manner, click **File**, make the necessary corrections or adjustments, and repeat **File → Print**. When you are satisfied with the preview, click the large **Print** button.

FIGURE EG1.4

Excel 2010 and Excel 2007 (inset) Print Preview (left) and Page Setup dialog box (right)

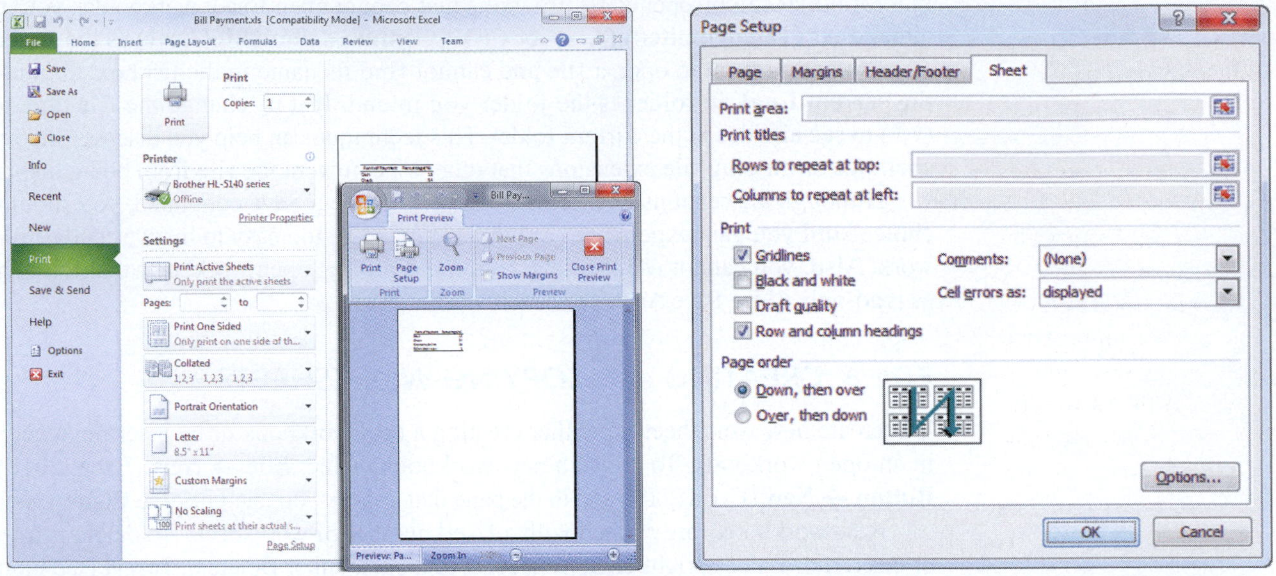

In Excel 2007, the same process requires more mouse clicks. First click **Office Button** and then move the mouse pointer over (but do not click) **Print**. In the Preview and Print gallery, click **Print Preview**. If the preview displayed (see Figure EG1.4) contains errors or displays the worksheet in an undesirable manner, click **Close Print Preview**, make the necessary changes, and reselect the print preview. After completing all corrections and adjustments, click **Print** in the Print Preview window to display the Print dialog box (shown in Appendix Section B.3). Select the printer to be used from the **Name** drop-down list, click **All** and **Active sheet(s)**, adjust the **Number of copies**, and click **OK**.

If necessary, you can adjust print formatting while in print preview by clicking the **Page Setup** icon (Excel 2007) or the **Page Setup** link (Excel 2010) to display the Page Setup dialog box (the right panel of Figure EG1.4). For example, to print your worksheet with gridlines and numbered row and lettered column headings (similar to the appearance of the worksheet on-screen), click the **Sheet** tab in the Page Setup dialog box, check **Gridlines** and **Row and column headings**, and click **OK**.

Although every version of Excel offers the (print) **Entire workbook** choice, you get the best results if you print each worksheet separately when you need to print out more than one worksheet (or chart sheet).

EG1.6 WORKSHEET ENTRIES and REFERENCES

When you open to a specific worksheet in a workbook, you use the cursor keys or your pointing device to move a **cell pointer** through the worksheet to select a specific cell for entry. As you type an entry, it appears in the formula bar, and you place that entry in the cell by either pressing the **Tab** key or **Enter** key or clicking the checkmark button in the formula bar.

In worksheets that you use for intermediate calculations or results, you might enter **formulas**, instructions to perform a calculation or some other task, in addition to the numeric and text entries you otherwise make in cells. Formulas typically use values found in other cells to compute a result that is displayed in the cell that stores the formula. With formulas, the displayed result automatically changes as the dependent values in the other cells change. This process, called **recalculation**, was the original novel feature of spreadsheet programs and led to these programs being widely used in accounting. (Worksheets that contain formulas are sometimes called "live" worksheets to distinguish them from "dead" worksheets—worksheets without any formulas and therefore not capable of recalculation.)

To refer to a cell in a formula, you use a **cell address** in the form ***SheetName*!*ColumnRow***. For example, **Data!A2** refers to the cell in the Data worksheet that is in column A and row 2. You can also use just the *ColumnRow* portion of a full address, for example, **A2**, if you are referring to a cell on the same worksheet as the one into which you are entering a formula. If the sheet name contains spaces or special characters, for example, **CITY DATA** or **Figure_1.2**, you must enclose the sheet name in a pair of single quotes, as in **'CITY DATA'!A2** or **'Figure_1.2'!A2**.

When you want to refer to a group of cells, such as the cells of a column that store the data for a particular variable, you use a **cell range**. A cell range names the upper-leftmost cell and the lower-rightmost cell of the group using the form ***SheetName*! *UpperLeftCell*:*LowerRightCell***. For example, the cell range **DATA!A1:A11** identifies the first 11 cells in the first column of the **DATA worksheet**. Cell ranges can extend over multiple columns; the cell range **DATA!A1:D11** would refer to the first 11 cells in the first 4 columns of the worksheet.

As with a single cell reference, you can skip the *SheetName*! part of the reference if you are referring to a cell range on the current worksheet and you must use a pair of single quotes if a sheet name contains spaces or special characters. However, in some dialog boxes, you must include the sheet name in a cell reference in order to get the proper results. (In such cases, the instructions in this book include the sheet name; otherwise, they do not.)

Although not used in this book, cell references can include a workbook name in the form **'[*WorkbookName*] *SheetName*'! *ColumnRow*** or **'[*WorkbookName*] *SheetName*'! *UpperLeft Cell*: *LowerRightCell***. You might discover such references if you inadvertently copy certain types of worksheets or chart sheets from one workbook to another.

EG1.7 ABSOLUTE and RELATIVE CELL REFERENCES

Many worksheets contain columns (or rows) of similar-looking formulas. For example, column C in a worksheet might contain formulas that sum the contents of the column A and column B rows. The formula for cell C2 would be **=A2 + B2**, the formula for cell C3 would be **=A3 + B3**, for cell C4, **=A4 + B4**, and so on down column C. To avoid the drudgery of typing many similar formulas, you can copy a formula and paste it into all the cells in a selected cell range. For example, to copy a formula that has been entered in cell C2 down the column through row 12:

1. Right-click cell **C2** and click **Copy** from the shortcut menu. A movie marquee–like highlight appears around cell C2.
2. Select the cell range **C3:C12**. (See Appendix B if you need help selecting a cell range.)
3. With the cell range highlighted, right-click over the cell range and click **Paste** from the shortcut menu.

When you perform this copy-and-paste operation, Excel adjusts the cell references in formulas so that copying the formula **=A2 + B2** from cell C2 to cell C3 results in the formula **=A3 + B3** being pasted into cell C3, the formula **=A4 + B4** being pasted into cell C4, and so on.

There are circumstances in which you do not want Excel to adjust all or part of a formula. For example, if you were copying the cell C2 formula **=(A2 + B2)/B15**, and cell B15 contained the divisor to be used in all formulas, you would not want to see pasted into cell C3 the formula **=(A3 + B3)/B16**. To prevent Excel from adjusting a cell reference, you use an **absolute cell reference** by inserting dollar signs ($) before the column and row references. For example, the absolute cell reference **$B$15** in the copied cell C2 formula **=(A2 + B2)/$B$15** would cause Excel to paste **=(A3 + B3)/$B$15** into cell C3. (For ease of reading, formulas shown in the worksheet illustrations in this book generally do not include absolute cell references.)

Do not confuse the use of the U.S. dollar symbol in an absolute reference with the formatting operation that displays numbers as U.S. currency values.

EG1.8 ENTERING FORMULAS into WORKSHEETS

You enter formulas by typing the equal sign (=) followed by a combination of mathematical and data-processing operations. For simple formulas, you use the symbols +, –, *, /, and ^ for the operations addition, subtraction, multiplication, division, and exponentiation (a number raised to a power), respectively. For example, the formula **=DATA!B2 + DATA!B3 + DATA!B4** adds the contents of cells B2, B3, and B4 of the DATA worksheet and displays the sum as the value in the cell containing the formula.

You can also use **worksheet functions** in formulas to simplify formulas. To use a worksheet function in a formula, either type the function as shown in the instructions in this book or use the Excel Function Wizard feature to insert the function. To use this feature, select **Formulas → Insert Function** and then make the necessary entries and selections in one or more dialog boxes that follow.

If you enter formulas in your worksheets, you should review and verify those formulas before you use their results. To view the formulas in a worksheet, press **Ctrl+`** (grave accent). To restore the original view, the re´sults of the formulas, press **Ctrl+`** a second time. (A "formulas view" accompanies most of the worksheet illustrations in this book.)

EG1.9 USING APPENDICES D and F

Appendices D and F contain additional Excel-related material that you may need to know, depending on how you use this book. If you plan to use PHStat2, make sure you have read Sections D.1 through D.3 in Appendix D. If you would like to learn formatting worksheet details such as how to make the contents of cells appear boldfaced or how to control the number of decimal places displayed, read Sections F.1 and F.2 in Appendix F.

CHAPTER 1 MINITAB GUIDE

MG1.1 GETTING STARTED with MINITAB

You are almost ready to use Minitab if you have completed the Table 1.5 checklist and reviewed the Table 1.6 computing conventions on page 12. Before using Minitab for a specific analysis, you should practice using the Minitab user interface.

Minitab project components appear in separate windows *inside* the Minitab window. In Figure MG1.1 these separate windows have been overlapped, but you can arrange or hide these windows in any way you like. When you start Minitab, you typically see a new project that contains only the session area and one worksheet window. (You can view other components by selecting them in the Minitab **Window** menu.) You can open and save an entire project or, as is done in this book, open and save individual worksheets.

FIGURE MG1.1
Minitab main worksheet with overlapping session, worksheet, chart, and Project Manager windows

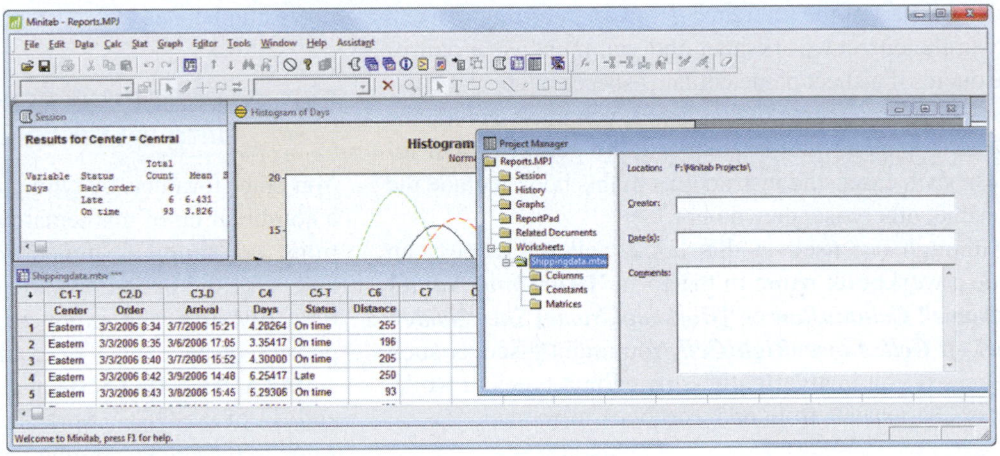

MG1.2 ENTERING DATA and VARIABLE TYPE

As first discussed in Section 1.5, you enter the data for each variable in a separate column. By convention, you start with the first column, initially labeled **C1** by Minitab, and enter the name of each variable into the cells of the unnumbered, shaded first row and then the data for the variable into the numbered rows, as shown in Figure MG1.1.

Minitab infers the variable type from the data you enter in a column. If Minitab discovers a column containing numbers, it treats the column as a numerical variable. If Minitab discovers a column containing words or alphanumeric entries, it treats the column as "text" variable (appropriate for use as a categorical variable). If Minitab discovers a column containing entries that can be interpreted as dates or times, it treats the column as a date/time variable, a special type of numerical variable. This imperfect method works most of the time in Minitab, especially if you make sure that the categories for your categorical variables are words or phrases such as "yes" and "no."

When Minitab identifies a text or date/time variable, it appends a "-T" or "-D" to its column heading for the variable. For example, in Figure MG1.1 above:

- C1-T and C5-T mean that the first and fifth columns contain text variables.
- C2-D and C3-D mean that the second and third columns contain date/time variables.
- C4 and C6 mean that the fourth and sixth columns contain numerical variables.

Because Minitab explicitly defines the variable type, unlike in Excel, your ability to do nonsensical things (such as use a statistical method that is designed for numerical variables on categorical data) is limited. If Minitab misinterprets your data, you can attempt to change the variable type by selecting **Data → Change Data Type** and then selecting the appropriate change from the submenu.

When you enter data, never skip any rows in a column. Minitab interprets skipped rows as missing values. You can use the Minitab workbooks that you can download from this book's companion website (see Appendix C) as models for the method you use to enter variable data in Minitab.

MG1.3 OPENING and SAVING WORKSHEETS and PROJECTS

You open and save Minitab worksheet or project files by first selecting the folder that stores a workbook and then specifying the file name of the workbook. To open a worksheet, you select **File → Open Worksheet**. To open a project, you select **File → Open Project**. To save a worksheet, you select **File → Save Current Worksheet As**. To save a project, you select **File → Save Project As**.

Both pairs of open and save commands display nearly identical dialog boxes. Figure MG1.2 shows the Minitab 16 Open Worksheet and Save Current Worksheet As dialog boxes.

FIGURE MG1.2
Minitab 16 Open Worksheet and Save Current Worksheet As dialog boxes

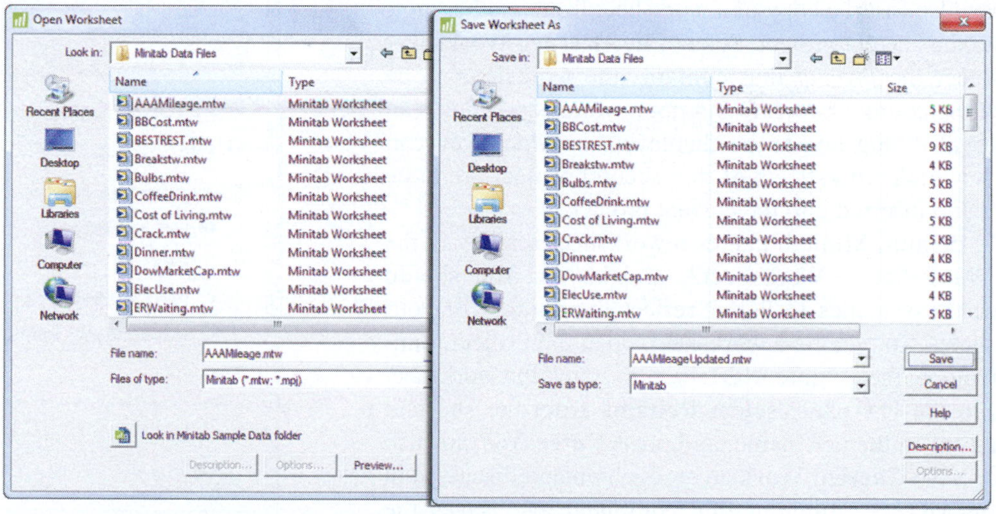

Inside the open or save dialog boxes, you select the storage folder by using the drop-down list at the top of either dialog box. You enter or select from the list box a file name for the workbook in the **File name** box. You click **Open** or **Save** to complete the task. Sometimes when saving files, you might want to change the file type before you click **Save**. If you want to save your data as an Excel worksheet, select **Excel 97-2003** from the **Save as type** drop-down list before you click **Save**. If you want to save data in a form that can be opened by programs that cannot open Excel workbooks, you might select one of the **Text** or **CSV** choices as the **Save as type** type.

When you want to open a file and cannot find its name in the list box, double-check that the current **Look in** folder is the folder you intend. If it is, change the file type to **All (*.*)** to see all files in the current folder. This technique can help you discover inadvertent misspellings or missing file extensions that otherwise prevent the file from being displayed.

When you save a project, you can click **Options** in the Save Project As dialog box and then specify which parts of the project you want to save in a Save Project - Options dialog box (not shown).

Although Minitab includes **Save Current Worksheet** and a **Save Project** commands (commands without the "**As**"), you should avoid this choice until you gain experience. Using Save makes it too easy to inadvertently overwrite your work. Also, you cannot use the Save command for any open workbook that Minitab has marked as read-only. (Use Save As to save such workbooks.)

Individual graphs and a project's session window can also be opened and saved separately in Minitab, although these operations are never used in this book.

MG1.4 CREATING and COPYING WORKSHEETS

You create new worksheets by either creating a new project or by inserting a new worksheet in an open project. To create a new project, select **File → New** and in the New dialog box, click **Minitab Project** and then click **OK**. To insert a new worksheet, also select **File → New** but in the New dialog box click **Minitab Worksheet** and then click **OK**.

A new project is created with one new worksheet. To insert another worksheet, select **File → New** and in the New dialog box click **Minitab Worksheet** and then click **OK**. You can also insert a copy of a worksheet from another project into the current project. Select **File → Open Worksheet** and select the *project* that contains the worksheet to be copied. Selecting a project (and not a worksheet) causes an additional dialog box to be displayed, in which you can specify which worksheets of that second project are to be copied and inserted into the current project.

By default, Minitab names a worksheet serially in the form Worksheet1, Worksheet2, and so on. You should change these names to better reflect the content of your worksheets. To rename a worksheet, open the Project Manager window (see Figure MG1.1), right-click the worksheet name in the left pane, select **Rename** from the shortcut menu, type in the new name, and press **Enter**. You can also use the **Save Current Worksheet As** command discussed in Section MG1.3, although this command also saves the worksheet as a separate file.

MG1.5 PRINTING PARTS of a PROJECT

To print a worksheet, a graph, or the contents of a session, first select the window that corresponds to the object you want to print. Then select **File → Print *object***, where ***object*** is either **Worksheet**, **Graph**, or **Session Window**, depending on which object you first selected.

If you are printing a graph or a session window, selecting the **Print** command displays the Print dialog box. The Print dialog box contains settings to select the printer to be used, what pages to print, and the number of copies to produce. If you need to change these settings, change them before clicking **OK** to create your printout.

If you are printing a worksheet, selecting **Print Worksheet** displays the Data Window Print Options dialog box (see Figure MG1.3). In this dialog box, you specify the formatting options for your printout (the default selections should be fine), enter a **Title**, and click **OK**. Minitab then presents the Print dialog box discussed in the previous paragraph.

FIGURE MG1.3
Data Window Print Options dialog box

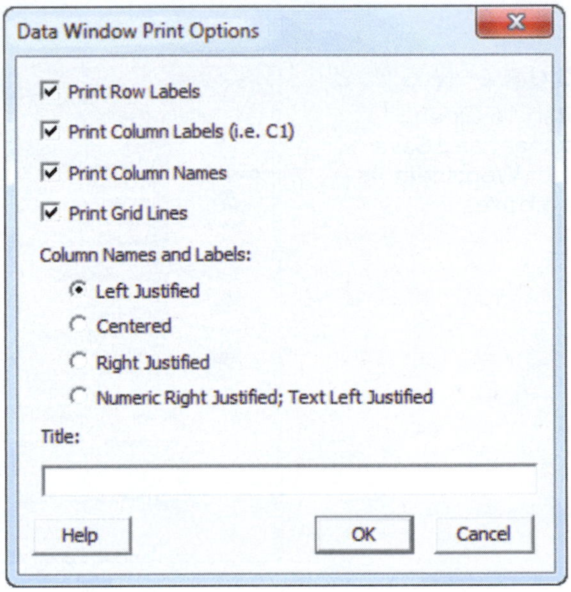

If you need to change the paper size or paper orientation of your printout, select **File → Print Setup** before you select the Print command, make the appropriate selections in the dialog box that appears, and click **OK**.

MG1.6 WORKSHEET ENTRIES and REFERENCES

You refer to individual variables in one of two ways. You can use their column number, such as C1 in Figure MG1.1 on page 22, that appears at the top of a worksheet. Or you can use the variable name that you entered into the cells of the unnumbered, shaded second row, such as Center or Order (in Figure MG1.1). For most statistical analyses, Minitab presents a list of column numbers and their corresponding variable names (if any) from which you make selections. For a variable name such as **Return 2009**, that contain spaces or other special characters, Minitab displays the name using a pair of single quotation marks—for example, **'Return 2009'**—an'd you need to include those quotation marks any time you type such a variable name in a Minitab dialog box.

For clarity and to minimize errors, this book generally refers to columns by their variable names. In later chapters, you will see that Minitab allows you to refer to several consecutive columns by using a hyphen. For example, either **C1-C6** or **Center-Distance** would refer to all six columns of the Shipping data worksheet shown in Figure MG1.1.

MG1.7 USING APPENDICES D and F

Appendices D and F contain additional Minitab-related material of a general nature. Consult these appendices if you have a question about using Minitab that is not answered in the Minitab Guides of this book.

2 Organizing and Visualizing Data

Learning Objectives

In this chapter, you learn:

- The sources of data used in business
- To construct tables and charts for numerical data
- To construct tables and charts for categorical data
- The principles of properly presenting graphs

USING STATISTICS

@ Choice Is Yours, Part I

The Choice Is Yours investment service helps clients with their investment choices. Choice Is Yours evaluates investments as diverse as real estate, direct private equity investments, derivatives, and various specialized types of mutual funds. You've been hired to assist clients who seek to invest in mutual funds, which pool the money of many individual clients and invest the money in a mix of securities and other investments. (To learn more about mutual funds, visit **investopedia.com/university/mutualfunds**.)

Because mutual funds that are highly invested in common stocks have had mixed returns recently, Choice Is Yours wants to examine mutual funds that focus on investing in certain types of bonds. Company analysts have selected a sample of 184 such funds that they believe might interest clients. You have been asked to present data about these funds in a way that will help customers make good investment choices. What facts about each bond mutual fund would you collect to help customers compare and contrast the many funds?

A good starting point would be to collect data that would help customers classify mutual funds into various categories. You could research such things as the amount of risk involved in a fund's investment strategy and the type of bonds in which the mutual fund primarily invests. Of course, you would want to learn how well the fund performed in the past, and you would want to supply the customer with several measures of each fund's past performance. (Although past performance is no assurance of future performance, past data could give customers insight into how well each mutual fund has been managed.)

As you further think about your task, you realize that the data for all 184 mutual funds would be a lot for anyone to review. You have been asked to present data about these funds in a way that will help customers make good investment choices. How can you review and explore such data in a comprehensible manner? What facts about each fund would you collect to help customers compare and contrast the many funds?

The challenge you face in Part I of the Choice Is Yours scenario is to examine a large amount of data and reach conclusions based on those data. You can make this business task more manageable by breaking it into these five steps:

- **Define** the variables that you want to study in order to solve a business problem or meet a business objective
- **Collect** the data from appropriate sources
- **Organize** the data collected by developing tables
- **Visualize** the data by developing charts
- **Analyze** the data by examining the appropriate tables and charts (and in later chapters by using other statistical methods) to reach conclusions.

These five steps, known by the acronym **DCOVA** (for **D**efine, **C**ollect, **O**rganize, **V**isualize, and **A**nalyze), are used throughout this book as the basis for statistical problem solving (see Reference 2). In Chapter 1, you already learned that defining a variable includes developing an operational definition and identifying the type of variable. In this chapter, you will learn more about the steps involved in collecting, organizing, visualizing, and analyzing the data.

To help illustrate the DCOVA approach, this chapter frequently uses for its examples the sample of 184 mutual funds that specialize in bond investments mentioned in Part I of the Choice Is Yours scenario. (To examine this sample, open **Bond Funds**, one of the data files you can download for use with this book as explained in Appendix C.) By the end of the chapter, you will be able to answer the questions posed in the scenario. For example, you will be able to answer questions that compare two categories of bond funds, such as "Is there a difference in the returns of intermediate government bond funds and short-term corporate bond funds?" or "Do intermediate government bond funds tend to be less risky investments than short-term corporate bond funds?"

2.1 Data Collection

Once you have defined your variables, you may need to collect the data for those variables. Examples of **data collection** include the following:

- A marketing analyst who needs to assess the effectiveness of a new television advertisement
- A pharmaceutical manufacturer that needs to determine whether a new drug is more effective than those currently in use
- An operations manager who wants to improve a manufacturing or service process
- An auditor who wants to review the financial transactions of a company in order to determine whether the company is in compliance with generally accepted accounting principles

When you collect data, you use either a **primary data source** or a **secondary data source.** You are using a primary data source when you collect your own data for analysis, and you are using a secondary source if the data for your analysis have been collected by someone else. Data collection almost always involves collecting data from a sample because collecting data from every item or individual in a population is typically too difficult or too time-consuming. (See Chapter 7 to learn more about sample selection methods.)

Organizations and individuals that collect and publish data often use their data as a primary source and may let others use those data as a secondary source. For example, the U.S. federal government collects and distributes data in this way for both public and private purposes. The Bureau of Labor Statistics collects data on employment and also distributes the monthly consumer price index. The Census Bureau oversees a variety of ongoing surveys regarding population, housing, and manufacturing and undertakes special studies on topics such as crime, travel, and health care.

Data sources are created in one of four ways:

- As data distributed by an organization or individual
- As outcomes of a designed experiment

- As responses from a survey
- As a result of conducting an observational study

Market research companies and trade associations distribute data pertaining to specific industries or markets. Investment services such as Mergent (**www.mergent.com**) provide financial data on a company-by-company basis. Syndicated services such as Nielsen provide clients with data that enables client products to be compared with those of their competitors. On the other hand, daily newspapers are secondary sources that are filled with numerical information regarding stock prices, weather conditions, and sports statistics obtained from primary sources.

Conducting a designed experiment is another source of data. For example, one such experiment might test several laundry detergents to compare how well each detergent removes a certain type of stain. Developing proper experimental designs is a subject mostly beyond the scope of this book because such designs often involve sophisticated statistical procedures. However, some of the fundamental experimental design concepts are discussed in Chapters 10 and 11.

Conducting a survey is a third type of data source. People being surveyed are asked questions about their beliefs, attitudes, behaviors, and other characteristics. For example, people could be asked their opinion about which laundry detergent best removes a certain type of stain. (This could lead to a result different from a designed experiment seeking the same answer.) One good way to avoid data-collection flaws when using such a survey is to distribute the questionnaire to a random sample of respondents. (Chapter 7 explains how to collect a random sample.) A bad way would be to rely on a business-rating website that allows online visitors to rate a merchant. Such websites cannot provide assurance that those who do the ratings are representative of the population of customers—or that they even *are* customers.

Conducting an observational study is the fourth data source. A researcher collects data by directly observing a behavior, usually in a natural or neutral setting. Observational studies are a common tool for data collection in business. For example, market researchers use focus groups to elicit unstructured responses to open-ended questions posed by a moderator to a target audience. You can also use observational study techniques to enhance teamwork or improve the quality of products and services.

Problems for Section 2.1

APPLYING THE CONCEPTS

2.1. According to its home page, "Swivel is a website where people share reports of charts and numbers. Businesses use Swivel to dashboard their metrics. Students use Swivel to find and share research data." Visit **www.swivel.com** and explore a data set of interest to you. Which of the four sources of data best describes the sources of the data set you selected?

2.2. Visit the website of the Gallup organization, at **www.gallup.com**. Read today's top story. What type of data source is the top story based on?

2.3. A supermarket chain wants to determine the best placement for the supermarket brand of soft drink. What type of data collection source do you think that the supermarket chain should use?

2.4. Visit the "Longitudinal Employer-Household Dynamics" page of the U.S. Census Bureau website, **lehd.did.census.gov/led/**. Examine the "Did You Know" panel on the page. What type of data source is the information presented here based on?

ORGANIZING DATA

After you define your variables and collect your data, you organize your data to help prepare for the later steps of visualizing and analyzing your data. The techniques you use to organize your data depend on the type of variable (categorical or numerical) associated with your data.

2.2 Organizing Categorical Data

You organize categorical data by tallying responses by categories and placing the results in tables. Typically, you construct a summary table to organize the data for a single categorical variable and you construct a contingency table to organize the data from two or more categorical variables.

Starting with this section, the sections of the Excel and Minitab Guides duplicate the sections in the main chapter. For example, to learn how to use Excel or Minitab to organize categorical data, see either Section EG2.2 or MG2.2.

The Summary Table

A **summary table** presents tallied responses as frequencies or percentages for each category. A summary table helps you see the differences among the categories by displaying the frequency, amount, or percentage of items in a set of categories in a separate column. Table 2.1 shows a summary table (stored in **Bill Payment**) that tallies the responses to a recent survey that asked adults how they pay their monthly bills.

TABLE 2.1

Types of Bill Payment

Form of Payment	Percentage (%)
Cash	15
Check	54
Electronic/online	28
Other/don't know	3

Source: *Data extracted from "How Adults Pay Monthly Bills,"* USA Today, *October 4, 2007, p. 1.*

From Table 2.1, you can conclude that more than half the people pay by check and 82% pay by either check or by electronic/online forms of payment.

EXAMPLE 2.1

Summary Table of Levels of Risk of Bond Funds

The 184 bond funds involved in Part I of the Choice Is Yours scenario (see page 27) are classified according to their risk level, categorized as below average, average, and above average. Construct a summary table of the bond funds, categorized by risk.

SOLUTION From Table 2.2, you can see that about the same number of funds are below average, average, and above average in risk. This means that 69.57% of the bond funds are classified as having an average or above average level of risk.

TABLE 2.2

Frequency and Percentage Summary Table Pertaining to Risk Level for 184 Bond Funds

Fund Risk Level	Number of Funds	Percentage of Funds (%)
Below average	56	30.43%
Average	69	37.50%
Above average	59	32.07%
Total	184	100.00%

The Contingency Table

A **contingency table** allows you to study patterns that may exist between the responses of two or more categorical variables. This type of table cross-tabulates, or tallies jointly, the responses of the categorical variables. In the simplest case of two categorical variables, the joint responses appear in a table such that the category tallies of one variable are located in the rows and the category tallies of the other variable are located in the columns. Intersections of the rows and columns are called **cells**, and each cell contains a value associated with a unique pair of responses for the two variables (e.g., Fee: Yes and Type: Intermediate Government in Table 2.3). Cells can contain the frequency, the percentage of the overall total, the percentage of the row total, or the percentage of the column total, depending on the type of contingency table being used.

In Part I of the Choice Is Yours scenario, you could create a contingency table to examine whether there is any pattern between the type of bond fund (intermediate government or short-term corporate) and whether the fund charges a fee (yes or no). You would begin by tallying the joint responses for each of the mutual funds in the sample of 184 bond mutual funds (stored in Bond Funds). You tally a response into one of the four possible cells in the table, depending on the type of bond fund and whether the fund charges a fee. For example, the first fund listed in the sample is classified as an intermediate government fund that does not charge a fee. Therefore, you tally this joint response into the cell that is the intersection of the Intermediate Government row and the No column. Table 2.3 shows the completed contingency table after all 184 bond funds have been tallied.

TABLE 2.3

Contingency Table Displaying Type of Fund and Whether a Fee Is Charged

	FEE		
TYPE	**Yes**	**No**	**Total**
Intermediate government	34	53	87
Short-term corporate	20	77	97
Total	54	130	184

To look for other patterns between the type of bond fund and whether the fund charges a fee, you can construct contingency tables that show cell values as a percentage of the overall total (the 184 mutual funds), the row totals (the 87 intermediate government funds and the 97 short-term corporate bond funds), and the column totals (the 54 funds that charge a fee and the 130 funds that do not charge a fee). Tables 2.4, 2.5, and 2.6 present these contingency tables.

Table 2.4 shows that 47.28% of the bond funds sampled are intermediate government funds, 52.72% are short-term corporate bond funds, and 18.48% are intermediate government funds that charge a fee. Table 2.5 shows that 39.08% of the intermediate government funds charge a fee, while 20.62% of the short-term corporate bond funds charge

TABLE 2.4

Contingency Table Displaying Type of Fund and Whether a Fee Is Charged, Based on Percentage of Overall Total

	FEE		
TYPE	**Yes**	**No**	**Total**
Intermediate government	18.48	28.80	47.28
Short-term corporate	10.87	41.85	52.72
Total	29.35	70.65	100.00

TABLE 2.5

Contingency Table Displaying Type of Fund and Whether a Fee Is Charged, Based on Percentage of Row Total

	FEE		
TYPE	**Yes**	**No**	**Total**
Intermediate government	39.08	60.92	100.00
Short-term corporate	20.62	79.38	100.00
Total	29.35	70.65	100.00

a fee. Table 2.6 shows that of the funds that charge a fee, 62.96% are intermediate government funds. From the tables, you see that intermediate government funds are much more likely to charge a fee.

TABLE 2.6
Contingency Table Displaying Type of Fund and Whether a Fee Is Charged, Based on Percentage of Column Total

	FEE		
TYPE	**Yes**	**No**	**Total**
Intermediate government	62.96	40.77	47.28
Short-term corporate	37.04	59.23	52.72
Total	100.00	100.00	100.00

Problems for Section 2.2

LEARNING THE BASICS

2.5 A categorical variable has three categories, with the following frequencies of occurrence:

Category	Frequency
A	13
B	28
C	9

a. Compute the percentage of values in each category.
b. What conclusions can you reach concerning the categories?

2.6 The following data represent the responses to two questions asked in a survey of 40 college students majoring in business: What is your gender? (M = male; F = female) and What is your major? (A = Accounting; C = Computer Information Systems; M = Marketing):
a. Tally the data into a contingency table where the two rows represent the gender categories and the three columns represent the academic major categories.
b. Construct contingency tables based on percentages of all 40 student responses, based on row percentages and based on column percentages.

Gender:	M	M	M	F	M	F	F	M	F	M	F	M	M	M	M	F	F	M	F	F
Major:	A	C	C	M	A	C	A	A	C	C	A	A	A	M	C	M	A	A	A	C
Gender:	M	M	M	M	F	M	F	F	M	M	F	M	M	M	M	F	M	F	M	M
Major:	C	C	A	A	M	M	C	A	A	A	C	C	A	A	A	A	C	C	A	C

APPLYING THE CONCEPTS

2.7 The Transportation Security Administration reported that from January 1, 2008, to February 18, 2009, more than 14,000 banned items were collected at Palm Beach International Airport. The categories were as follows:

Category	Frequency
Flammables/irritants	8,350
Knives and blades	4,134
Prohibited tools	753
Sharp objects	497
Other	357

a. Compute the percentage of values in each category.
b. What conclusions can you reach concerning the banned items?

SELF Test **2.8** The Energy Information Administration reported the following sources of electricity in the United States in 2008:

Source of Electricity	Net Electricity Generation (millions of megawatt-hours)
Coal	1,994.4
Hydroelectric	248.1
Natural gas	876.9
Nuclear	806.2
Other	184.7

Source: Energy Information Administration, 2008.

a. Compute the percentage of values in each category.
b. What conclusions can you reach concerning the sources of electricity in the United States in 2008?

2.9 Federal obligations for benefit programs and the national debt were $63.8 trillion in 2008. The cost per household ($) for various categories was as follows:

Category	Cost per Household ($)
Civil servant retirement	15,851
Federal debt	54,537
Medicare	284,288
Military retirement	29,694
Social Security	160,216
Other	2,172

Source: Data extracted from "What We Owe," *USA Today*, May 29, 2009, p. 1A.

a. Compute the percentage of values in each category.
b. What conclusions can you reach concerning the benefit programs?

2.10 A sample of 500 shoppers was selected in a large metropolitan area to determine various information concerning consumer behavior. Among the questions asked was "Do you enjoy shopping for clothing?" The results are summarized in the following table:

ENJOY SHOPPING FOR CLOTHING	GENDER		
	Male	**Female**	**Total**
Yes	136	224	360
No	104	36	140
Total	240	260	500

a. Construct contingency tables based on total percentages, row percentages, and column percentages.
b. What conclusions do you reach from these analyses?

2.11 Each day at a large hospital, several hundred laboratory tests are performed. The rate at which these tests are done improperly (and therefore need to be redone) seems steady, at about 4%. In an effort to get to the root cause of these nonconformances, tests that need to be redone, the director of the lab decided to keep records over a period of one week. The laboratory tests were subdivided by the shift of workers who performed the lab tests. The results are as follows:

LAB TESTS PERFORMED	SHIFT		
	Day	**Evening**	**Total**
Nonconforming	16	24	40
Conforming	654	306	960
Total	670	330	1,000

a. Construct contingency tables based on total percentages, row percentages, and column percentages.
b. Which type of percentage—row, column, or total—do you think is most informative for these data? Explain.
c. What conclusions concerning the pattern of nonconforming laboratory tests can the laboratory director reach?

2.12 Does it take more time to get yourself removed from an email list than it used to? A study of 100 large online retailers revealed the following:

	NEED THREE OR MORE CLICKS TO BE REMOVED	
YEAR	**Yes**	**No**
2009	39	61
2008	7	93

Source: Data extracted from "Drill Down," *The New York Times*, March 29, 2010, p. B2.

What do these results tell you about whether more online retailers were requiring three or more clicks in 2009 than in 2008?

2.3 Organizing Numerical Data

You organize numerical data by creating ordered arrays or distributions. The amount of data you have and what you seek to discover about your variables influences which methods you choose, as does the arrangement of data in your worksheet.

Stacked and Unstacked Data

In Section 1.5, you learned to enter variable data into worksheets by columns. When organizing numerical data, you must additionally consider if you will need to analyze a numerical variable by subgroups that are defined by the values of a categorical variable.

For example, in **Bond Funds** you might want to analyze the numerical variable **Return 2009**, the year 2009 percentage return of a bond fund, by the two subgroups that are defined by the categorical variable **Type**, intermediate government and short-term corporate. To perform this type of subgroup analysis, you arrange your worksheet data either in stacked format or unstacked format, depending on the requirements of the statistical application you plan to use.

In **Bond Funds**, the data has been entered in **stacked** format, in which the all of the values for a numerical variable appear in one column and a second, separate column contains the categorical values that identify which subgroup the numerical values belong to. For example, all values for the **Return 2009** variable are in one column (the sixth column) and the values in the second column (for the **Type** variable) would be used to determine which of the two **Type** subgroups an individual **Return 2009** value belongs to.

None of the data sets used in the examples found in the Excel and Minitab Guides require that you stack (or unstack) data. However, you may need to stack (or unstack) data to solve some of the problems in this book.

In **unstacked** format, the values for each subgroup of a numerical variable are segregated and placed in separate columns. For example, **Return 2009 Unstacked** contains the **IG_Return_2009** and **STC_Return 2009** variable columns that contain the data of **Return 2009** in unstacked format by the two subgroups defined by **Type,** intermediate government (IG) and short-term corporate (STC).

While you can always manually stack or unstack your data, Minitab and PHStat2 both provide you with commands that automate these operations. If you use Excel without PHStat2, you *must* use a manual procedure.

The Ordered Array

An **ordered array** arranges the values of a numerical variable in rank order, from the smallest value to the largest value. An ordered array helps you get a better sense of the range of values in your data and is particularly useful when you have more than a few values. For example, Table 2.7A shows the data collected for a study of the cost of meals at 50 restaurants located in a major city and at 50 restaurants located in that city's suburbs (stored in **Restaurants**). The unordered data in Table 2.7A prevent you from reaching any quick conclusions about the cost of meals.

TABLE 2.7A

Cost per Person at 50 City Restaurants and 50 Suburban Restaurants

City Restaurant Meal Cost

62	67	23	79	32	38	46	43	39	43
44	29	59	56	32	56	23	40	45	44
40	33	57	43	49	28	35	79	42	21
40	49	45	54	64	48	41	34	53	27
44	58	68	59	61	59	48	78	65	42

Suburban Restaurant Meal Cost

53	45	39	43	44	29	37	34	33	37
54	30	49	44	34	55	48	36	29	40
38	38	55	43	33	44	41	45	41	42
37	56	60	46	31	35	68	40	51	32
28	44	26	42	37	63	37	22	53	62

In contrast, Table 2.7B, the ordered array version of the same data, enables you to quickly see that the cost of a meal at the city restaurants is between \$21 and \$79 and that the cost of a meal at the suburban restaurants is between \$22 and \$68.

When you have a data set that contains a large number of values, reaching conclusions from an ordered array can be difficult. For such data sets, creating a frequency or percentage distribution and a cumulative percentage distribution (see following sections) would be a better choice.

TABLE 2.7B

Ordered Arrays of Cost per Person at 50 City Restaurants and 50 Suburban Restaurants

City Restaurant Meal Cost

21	23	23	27	28	29	32	32	33	34
35	38	39	40	40	40	41	42	42	43
43	43	44	44	44	45	45	46	48	48
49	49	53	54	56	56	57	58	59	59
59	61	62	64	65	67	68	78	79	79

Suburban Restaurant Meal Cost

22	26	28	29	29	30	31	32	33	33
34	34	35	36	37	37	37	37	37	38
38	39	40	40	41	41	42	42	43	43
44	44	44	44	45	45	46	48	49	51
53	53	54	55	55	56	60	62	63	68

The Frequency Distribution

A **frequency distribution** summarizes numerical values by tallying them into a set of numerically ordered **classes**. Classes are groups that represent a range of values, called a **class interval**. Each value can be in only one class and every value must be contained in one of the classes.

To create a useful frequency distribution, you must think about how many classes are appropriate for your data and also determine a suitable *width* for each class interval. In general, a frequency distribution should have at least 5 classes but no more than 15 classes because having too few or too many classes provides little new information. To determine the **class interval width** (see Equation 2.1), you subtract the lowest value from the highest value and divide that result by the number of classes you want your frequency distribution to have.

DETERMINING THE CLASS INTERVAL WIDTH

$$\text{Interval width} = \frac{\text{highest value} - \text{lowest value}}{\text{number of classes}} \qquad \textbf{(2.1)}$$

Because the city restaurant data consist of a sample of only 50 restaurants, between 5 and 10 classes are acceptable. From the ordered city cost array in Table 2.7B, the difference between the highest value of \$79 and the lowest value of \$21 is \$58. Using Equation (2.1), you approximate the class interval width as follows:

$$\text{Interval width} = \frac{58}{10} = 5.8$$

This result suggests that you should choose an interval width of \$5.80. However, your width should always be an amount that simplifies the reading and interpretation of the frequency distribution. In this example, an interval width of \$10 would be much better than an interval width of \$5.80.

Because each value can appear in only one class, you must establish proper and clearly defined **class boundaries** for each class. For example, if you chose \$10 as the class interval for the restaurant data, you would need to establish boundaries that would include all the values and simplify the reading and interpretation of the frequency distribution. Because the cost of a city restaurant meal varies from \$21 to \$79, establishing the first class interval as from \$20 to less than \$30, the second from \$30 to less than \$40, and so on, until the last class interval is from \$70 to less than \$80, would meet the requirements. Table 2.8 is a frequency distribution of the cost per meal for the 50 city restaurants and the 50 suburban restaurants that uses these class intervals.

TABLE 2.8

Frequency Distributions of the Cost per Meal for 50 City Restaurants and 50 Suburban Restaurants

Cost per Meal ($)	City Frequency	Suburban Frequency
20 but less than 30	6	5
30 but less than 40	7	17
40 but less than 50	19	17
50 but less than 60	9	7
60 but less than 70	6	4
70 but less than 80	3	0
Total	50	50

The frequency distribution allows you to reach conclusions about the major characteristics of the data. For example, Table 2.8 shows that the cost of meals at city restaurants is concentrated between $40 and $50, while for suburban restaurants the cost of meals is concentrated between $30 and $50.

For some charts discussed later in this chapter, class intervals are identified by their **class midpoints**, the values that are halfway between the lower and upper boundaries of each class. For the frequency distributions shown in Table 2.8, the class midpoints are $25, $35, $45, $55, $65, and $75 (amounts that are simple to read and interpret).

If a data set does not contain a large number of values, different sets of class intervals can create different impressions of the data. Such perceived changes will diminish as you collect more data. Likewise, choosing different lower and upper class boundaries can also affect impressions.

EXAMPLE 2.2

Frequency Distributions of the 2009 Return for Intermediate Government and Short-Term Corporate Bond Mutual Funds

In the Using Statistics scenario, you are interested in comparing the 2009 return of intermediate government and short-term corporate bond mutual funds. Construct frequency distributions for the intermediate government funds and the short-term corporate bond funds.

SOLUTION The 2009 returns of the intermediate government bond funds are highly concentrated between 0 and 10, whereas the 2009 returns of the short-term corporate bond funds are highly concentrated between 5 and 15 (see Table 2.9).

For the bond fund data, the number of *values* is different in the two groups. When the number of *values* in the two groups is not the same, you need to use proportions or relative frequencies and percentages in order to compare the groups.

TABLE 2.9

Frequency Distributions of the 2009 Return for Intermediate Government and Short-Term Corporate Bond Funds

2009 Return	Intermediate Government Frequency	Short-Term Corporate Frequency
−10 but less than −5	0	1
−5 but less than 0	13	0
0 but less than 5	35	15
5 but less than 10	30	38
10 but less than 15	6	31
15 but less than 20	1	9
20 but less than 25	1	1
25 but less than 30	1	1
30 but less than 35	0	1
Total	87	97

The Relative Frequency Distribution and the Percentage Distribution

When you are comparing two or more groups, as is done in Table 2.10, knowing the proportion or percentage of the total that is in each group is more useful than knowing the frequency count of each group. For such situations, you create a relative frequency distribution or a percentage distribution instead of a frequency distribution. (If your two or more groups have different sample sizes, you *must* use either a relative frequency distribution or a percentage distribution.)

TABLE 2.10

Relative Frequency Distributions and Percentage Distributions of the Cost of Meals at City and Suburban Restaurants

	CITY		SUBURBAN	
COST PER MEAL ($)	Relative Frequency	Percentage (%)	Relative Frequency	Percentage (%)
20 but less than 30	0.12	12.0	0.10	10.0
30 but less than 40	0.14	14.0	0.34	34.0
40 but less than 50	0.38	38.0	0.34	34.0
50 but less than 60	0.18	18.0	0.14	14.0
60 but less than 70	0.12	12.0	0.08	8.0
70 but less than 80	0.06	6.0	0.00	0.0
Total	1.00	100.0	1.00	100.0

The **proportion**, or **relative frequency**, in each group is equal to the number of *values* in each class divided by the total number of values. The percentage in each group is its proportion multiplied by 100%.

COMPUTING THE PROPORTION OR RELATIVE FREQUENCY

The proportion, or relative frequency, is the number of *values* in each class divided by the total number of values:

$$\text{Proportion} = \text{relative frequency} = \frac{\text{number of values in each class}}{\text{total number of values}} \quad \textbf{(2.2)}$$

If there are 80 values and the frequency in a certain class is 20, the proportion of values in that class is

$$\frac{20}{80} = 0.25$$

and the percentage is

$$0.25 \times 100\% = 25\%$$

You form the **relative frequency distribution** by first determining the relative frequency in each class. For example, in Table 2.8 on page 36, there are 50 city restaurants, and the cost per meal at 9 of these restaurants is between \$50 and \$60. Therefore, as shown in Table 2.10, the proportion (or relative frequency) of meals that cost between \$50 and \$60 at city restaurants is

$$\frac{9}{50} = 0.18$$

You form the **percentage distribution** by multiplying each proportion (or relative frequency) by 100%. Thus, the proportion of meals at city restaurants that cost between \$50 and $60 is 9 divided by 50, or 0.18, and the percentage is 18%. Table 2.10 presents the relative frequency distribution and percentage distribution of the cost of meals at city and suburban restaurants.

From Table 2.10, you conclude that meals cost slightly more at city restaurants than at suburban restaurants. Also, 12% of the meals cost between $60 and $70 at city restaurants as compared to 8% of the meals at suburban restaurants; and 14% of the meals cost between $30 and $40 at city restaurants as compared to 34% of the meals at suburban restaurants.

EXAMPLE 2.3

Relative Frequency Distributions and Percentage Distributions of the 2009 Return for Intermediate Government and Short-Term Corporate Bond Mutual Funds

In the Using Statistics scenario, you are interested in comparing the 2009 return of intermediate government and short-term corporate bond mutual funds. Construct relative frequency distributions and percentage distributions for these funds.

SOLUTION You conclude (see Table 2.11) that the 2009 return for the corporate bond funds is much higher than for the intermediate government funds. For example, 31.96% of the corporate bond funds have returns between 10 and 15, while 6.90% of the intermediate government funds have returns between 10 and 15. Of the corporate bond funds, only 15.46% have returns between 0 and 5 as compared to 40.23% of the intermediate government funds.

TABLE 2.11
Relative Frequency Distributions and Percentage Distributions of the 2009 Return for Intermediate Government and Short-Term Corporate Bond Mutual Funds

	INTERMEDIATE GOVERNMENT		SHORT-TERM CORPORATE	
2009 RETURN	Proportion	Percentage	Proportion	Percentage
−10 but less than −5	0.0000	0.00	0.0103	1.03
−5 but less than 0	0.1494	14.94	0.0000	0.00
0 but less than 5	0.4023	40.23	0.1546	15.46
5 but less than 10	0.3448	34.48	0.3918	39.18
10 but less than 15	0.0690	6.90	0.3196	31.96
15 but less than 20	0.0115	1.15	0.0928	9.28
20 but less than 25	0.0115	1.15	0.0103	1.03
25 but less than 30	0.0115	1.15	0.0103	1.03
30 but less than 35	0.0000	0.00	0.0103	1.03
Total	1.0000	100.00	1.0000	100.00

The Cumulative Distribution

The **cumulative percentage distribution** provides a way of presenting information about the percentage of values that are less than a specific amount. For example, you might want to know what percentage of the city restaurant meals cost less than $40 or what percentage cost less than $50. You use the percentage distribution to form the cumulative percentage distribution. Table 2.12 shows how percentages of individual class intervals are combined to form the cumulative percentage distribution for the cost of meals at city restaurants. From this table, you see that none (0%) of the meals cost less than $20, 12% of meals cost less than $30, 26% of meals cost less than $40 (because 14% of the meals cost between $30 and $40), and so on, until all 100% of the meals cost less than $80.

Table 2.13 summarizes the cumulative percentages of the cost of city and suburban restaurant meals. The cumulative distribution shows that the cost of meals is slightly lower in suburban restaurants than in city restaurants. Table 2.13 shows that 44% of the meals at suburban restaurants cost less than $40 as compared to 26% of the meals at city restaurants; 78% of the

TABLE 2.12

Developing the Cumulative Percentage Distribution for the Cost of Meals at City Restaurants

Cost per Meal ($)	Percentage (%)	Percentage of Meals Less Than Lower Boundary of Class Interval (%)
20 but less than 30	12	0
30 but less than 40	14	12
40 but less than 50	38	26 = 12 + 14
50 but less than 60	18	64 = 12 + 14 + 38
60 but less than 70	12	82 = 12 + 14 + 38 + 18
70 but less than 80	6	94 = 12 + 14 + 38 + 18 + 12
80 but less than 90	0	100 = 12 + 14 + 38 + 18 + 12 + 6

meals at suburban restaurants cost less than $50 as compared to 64% of the meals at city restaurants; and 92% of the meals at suburban restaurants cost less than $60 as compared to 82% of the meals at city restaurants.

TABLE 2.13

Cumulative Percentage Distributions of the Cost of City and Suburban Restaurant Meals

Cost ($)	Percentage of City Restaurants With Meals Less Than Indicated Amount	Percentage of Suburban Restaurants With Meals Less Than Indicated Amount
20	0	0
30	12	10
40	26	44
50	64	78
60	82	92
70	94	100
80	100	100

EXAMPLE 2.4

Cumulative Percentage Distributions of the 2009 Return for Intermediate Government and Short-Term Corporate Bond Mutual Funds

In the Using Statistics scenario, you are interested in comparing the 2009 return for intermediate government and short-term corporate bond mutual funds. Construct cumulative percentage distributions for the intermediate government and short-term corporate bond mutual funds.

SOLUTION The cumulative distribution in Table 2.14 indicates that returns are much lower for the intermediate government bond funds than for the short-term corporate funds. The table shows that 14.94% of the intermediate government funds have negative returns as compared to 1.03% of the short-term corporate bond funds; 55.17% of the intermediate government funds have returns below 5 as compared to 16.49% of the short-term corporate bond funds; and 89.65% of the intermediate government funds have returns below 10 as compared to 55.67% of the short-term corporate bond funds.

TABLE 2.14

Cumulative Percentage Distributions of the 2009 Return for Intermediate Government and Short-Term Corporate Bond Funds

2009 Return	Intermediate Government Percentage Less Than Indicated Value	Short-Term Corporate Percentage Less Than Indicated Value
−10	0.00	0.00
−5	0.00	1.03
0	14.94	1.03
5	55.17	16.49
10	89.65	55.67
15	96.55	87.63
20	97.70	96.91
25	98.85	97.94
30	100.00	98.97
35	100.00	100.00

Problems for Section 2.3

LEARNING THE BASICS

2.13 Construct an ordered array, given the following data from a sample of $n = 7$ midterm exam scores in accounting:

68 94 63 75 71 88 64

2.14 Construct an ordered array, given the following data from a sample of midterm exam scores in marketing:

88 78 78 73 91 78 85

2.15 The GMAT scores from a sample of 50 applicants to an MBA program indicate that none of the applicants scored below 450. A frequency distribution was formed by choosing class intervals 450 to 499, 500 to 549, and so on, with the last class having an interval from 700 to 749. Two applicants scored in the interval 450 to 499, and 16 applicants scored in the interval 500 to 549.

a. What percentage of applicants scored below 500?
b. What percentage of applicants scored between 500 and 549?
c. What percentage of applicants scored below 550?
d. What percentage of applicants scored below 750?

2.16 A set of data has values that vary from 11.6 to 97.8.

a. If these values are grouped into nine classes, indicate the class boundaries.
b. What class interval width did you choose?
c. What are the nine class midpoints?

APPLYING THE CONCEPTS

2.17 The file **BBCost** contains the total cost ($) for four tickets, two beers, four soft drinks, four hot dogs, two game programs, two baseball caps, and parking for one vehicle at each of the 30 Major League Baseball parks during the 2009 season. These costs were

164,326,224,180,205,162,141,170,411,187,185,165,151,166,114
158,305,145,161,170,210,222,146,259,220,135,215,172,223,216

Source: Data extracted from **teammarketing.com**, April 1, 2009.

a. Organize these costs as an ordered array.
b. Construct a frequency distribution and a percentage distribution for these costs.
c. Around which class grouping, if any, are the costs of attending a baseball game concentrated? Explain.

SELF Test **2.18** The file **Utility** contains the data in the next column about the cost of electricity during July 2010 for a random sample of 50 one-bedroom apartments in a large city.

a. Construct a frequency distribution and a percentage distribution that have class intervals with the upper class boundaries \$99, \$119, and so on.
b. Construct a cumulative percentage distribution.
c. Around what amount does the monthly electricity cost seem to be concentrated?

Raw Data on Utility Charges ($)

96	171	202	178	147	102	153	197	127	82
157	185	90	116	172	111	148	213	130	165
141	149	206	175	123	128	144	168	109	167
95	163	150	154	130	143	187	166	139	149
108	119	183	151	114	135	191	137	129	158

2.19 One operation of a mill is to cut pieces of steel into parts that will later be used as the frame for front seats in an automobile. The steel is cut with a diamond saw and requires the resulting parts to be within $\pm$ 0.005 inch of the length specified by the automobile company. Data are collected from a sample of 100 steel parts and stored in **Steel**. The measurement reported is the difference in inches between the actual length of the steel part, as measured by a laser measurement device, and the specified length of the steel part. For example, the first value, -0.002, represents a steel part that is 0.002 inch shorter than the specified length.

a. Construct a frequency distribution and a percentage distribution.
b. Construct a cumulative percentage distribution.
c. Is the steel mill doing a good job meeting the requirements set by the automobile company? Explain.

2.20 A manufacturing company produces steel housings for electrical equipment. The main component part of the housing is a steel trough that is made out of a 14-gauge steel coil. It is produced using a 250-ton progressive punch press with a wipe-down operation that puts two 90-degree forms in the flat steel to make the trough. The distance from one side of the form to the other is critical because of weatherproofing in outdoor applications. The company requires that the width of the trough be between 8.31 inches and 8.61 inches. The widths of the troughs, in inches, are collected from a sample of 49 troughs and stored in **Trough** and shown here:

8.312	8.343	8.317	8.383	8.348	8.410	8.351	8.373
8.481	8.422	8.476	8.382	8.484	8.403	8.414	8.419
8.385	8.465	8.498	8.447	8.436	8.413	8.489	8.414
8.481	8.415	8.479	8.429	8.458	8.462	8.460	8.444
8.429	8.460	8.412	8.420	8.410	8.405	8.323	8.420
8.396	8.447	8.405	8.439	8.411	8.427	8.420	8.498
8.409							

a. Construct a frequency distribution and a percentage distribution.
b. Construct a cumulative percentage distribution.
c. What can you conclude about the number of troughs that will meet the company's requirements of troughs being between 8.31 and 8.61 inches wide?

2.21 The manufacturing company in Problem 2.20 also produces electric insulators. If the insulators break when in use, a short circuit is likely to occur. To test the strength of the insulators, destructive testing in high-powered labs is carried out to determine how much *force* is required to break the insulators. Force is measured by observing how many pounds must be applied to the insulator before it breaks. Force measurements are collected from a sample of 30 insulators and stored in **Force** and shown here:

1,870	1,728	1,656	1,610	1,634	1,784	1,522	1,696
1,592	1,662	1,866	1,764	1,734	1,662	1,734	1,774
1,550	1,756	1,762	1,866	1,820	1,744	1,788	1,688
1,810	1,752	1,680	1,810	1,652	1,736		

a. Construct a frequency distribution and a percentage distribution.
b. Construct a cumulative percentage distribution.
c. What can you conclude about the strength of the insulators if the company requires a force measurement of at least 1,500 pounds before the insulator breaks?

2.22 The file **Bulbs** contains the life (in hours) of a sample of 40 100-watt light bulbs produced by Manufacturer A and a sample of 40 100-watt light bulbs produced by Manufacturer B. The following table shows these data as a pair of ordered arrays:

Manufacturer A					Manufacturer B				
684	697	720	773	821	819	836	888	897	903
831	835	848	852	852	907	912	918	942	943
859	860	868	870	876	952	959	962	986	992
893	899	905	909	911	994	1,004	1,005	1,007	1,015
922	924	926	926	938	1,016	1,018	1,020	1,022	1,034
939	943	946	954	971	1,038	1,072	1,077	1,077	1,082
972	977	984	1,005	1,014	1,096	1,100	1,113	1,113	1,116
1,016	1,041	1,052	1,080	1,093	1,153	1,154	1,174	1,188	1,230

a. Construct a frequency distribution and a percentage distribution for each manufacturer, using the following class interval widths for each distribution:

Manufacturer A: 650 but less than 750, 750 but less than 850, and so on.
Manufacturer B: 750 but less than 850, 850 but less than 950, and so on.

b. Construct cumulative percentage distributions.
c. Which bulbs have a longer life—those from Manufacturer A or Manufacturer B? Explain.

2.23 The following data (stored in **Drink**) represent the amount of soft drink in a sample of 50 2-liter bottles:

2.109	2.086	2.066	2.075	2.065	2.057	2.052	2.044	2.036	2.038
2.031	2.029	2.025	2.029	2.023	2.020	2.015	2.014	2.013	2.014
2.012	2.012	2.012	2.010	2.005	2.003	1.999	1.996	1.997	1.992
1.994	1.986	1.984	1.981	1.973	1.975	1.971	1.969	1.966	1.967
1.963	1.957	1.951	1.951	1.947	1.941	1.941	1.938	1.908	1.894

a. Construct a cumulative percentage distribution.
b. On the basis of the results of (a), does the amount of soft drink filled in the bottles concentrate around specific values?

VISUALIZING DATA

When you organize your data, you sometimes begin to discover patterns or relationships in your data, as examples in Sections 2.2 and 2.3 illustrate. To better explore and discover patterns and relationships, you can visualize your data by creating various charts and special "displays." As is the case when organizing data, the techniques you use to visualize your data depend on the *type of* variable (categorical or numerical) of your data.

2.4 Visualizing Categorical Data

The chart you choose to visualize the data for a single categorical variable depends on whether you seek to emphasize how categories directly compare to each other (bar chart) or how categories form parts of a whole (pie chart), or whether you have data that are concentrated in only a few of your categories (Pareto chart). To visualize the data for two categorical variables, you use a side-by-side bar chart.

The Bar Chart

A **bar chart** compares different categories by using individual bars to represent the tallies for each category. The length of a bar represents the amount, frequency, or percentage of values falling into a category. Unlike with a histogram, discussed in Section 2.5, a bar chart separates the bars between the categories. Figure 2.1 displays the bar chart for the data of Table 2.1 on page 30, which is based on a recent survey that asked adults how they pay their monthly bills ("How Adults Pay Monthly Bills," *USA Today*, October 4, 2007, p. 1).

FIGURE 2.1

Bar chart for how adults pay their monthly bills

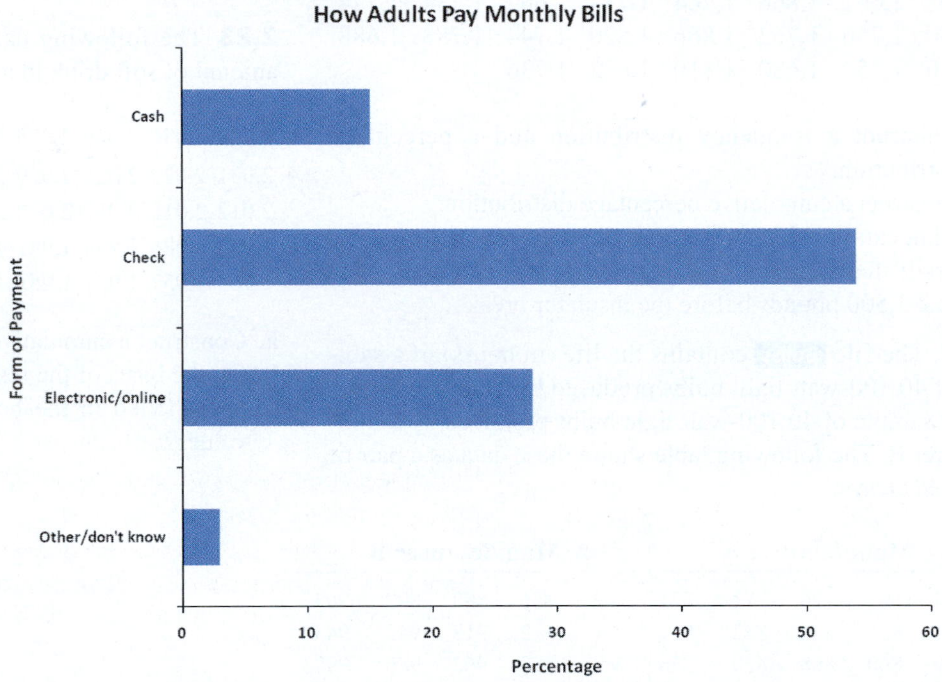

Reviewing Figure 2.1, you see that respondents are most likely to pay by check or electronically/online, followed by paying by cash. Very few respondents mentioned other or did not know.

EXAMPLE 2.5

Bar Chart of Levels of Risk of Bond Mutual Funds

In Part I of the Choice Is Yours scenario, you are interested in examining the risk of the bond funds. You have already defined the variables and collected the data from a sample of 184 bond funds. Now, you need to construct a bar chart of the risk of the bond funds (based on Table 2.2 on page 30) and interpret the results.

SOLUTION Reviewing Figure 2.2, you see that average is the largest category, closely followed by above average, and below average.

FIGURE 2.2
Bar chart of the levels of risk of bond mutual funds

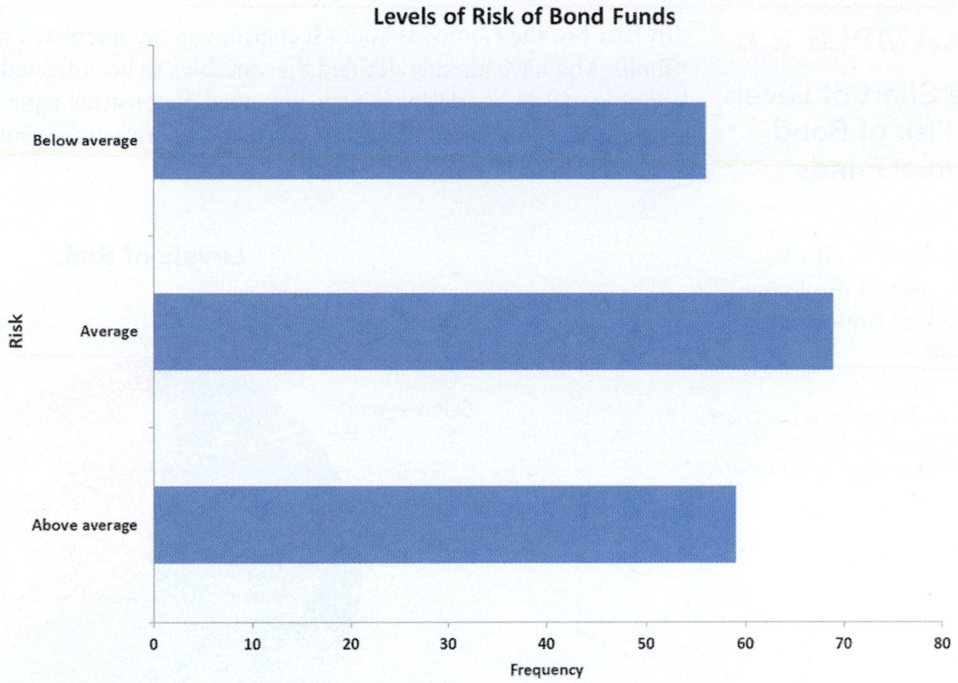

The Pie Chart

A **pie chart** uses parts of a circle to represent the tallies of each category. The size of each part, or pie slice, varies according to the percentage in each category. For example, in Table 2.1 on page 30, 54% of the respondents stated that they paid bills by check. To represent this category as a pie slice, you multiply 54% by the 360 degrees that makes up a circle to get a pie slice that takes up 194.4 degrees of the 360 degrees of the circle. From Figure 2.3, you can see that the pie chart lets you visualize the portion of the entire pie that is in each category. In this figure, paying bills by check is the largest slice, containing 54% of the pie. The second largest slice is paying bills electronically/online, which contains 28% of the pie.

FIGURE 2.3
Pie chart for how people pay their bills

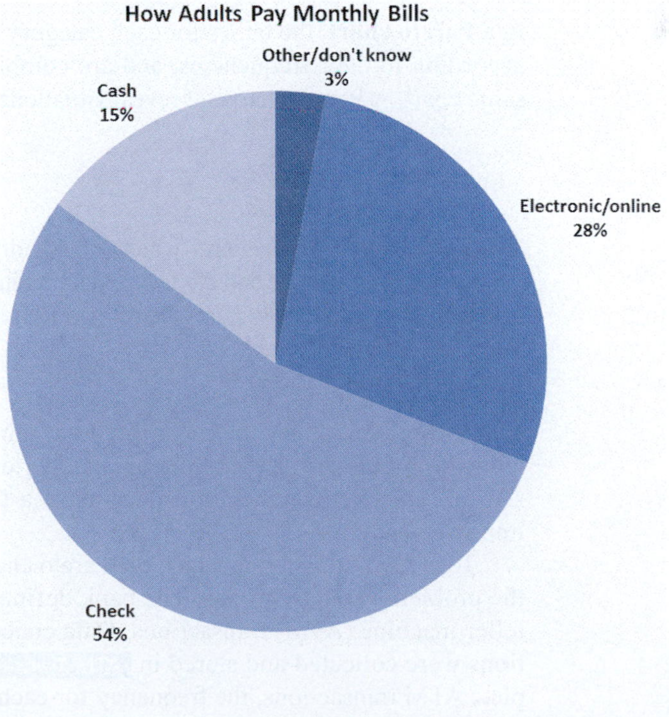

EXAMPLE 2.6

Pie Chart of Levels of Risk of Bond Mutual Funds

In Part I of the Choice Is Yours scenario, you are interested in examining the risk of the bond funds. You have already defined the variables to be collected and collected the data from a sample of 184 bond funds. Now, you need to construct a pie chart of the risk of the bond funds (based on Table 2.2 on page 30) and interpret the results.

FIGURE 2.4

Pie chart of the levels of risk of bond mutual funds

Figure 2.4 shows a pie chart created using Minitab; Figure 2.3 shows a pie chart created using Excel.

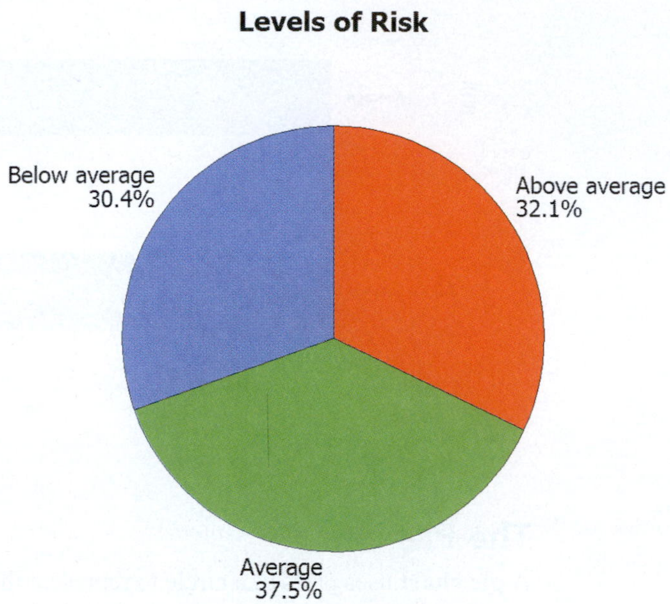

SOLUTION Reviewing Figure 2.4, you see that approximately a little more than one-third of the funds are average risk, about one-third are above average risk, and fewer than one-third are below-average risk.

The Pareto Chart

In a **Pareto chart**, the tallies for each category are plotted as vertical bars in descending order, according to their frequencies, and are combined with a cumulative percentage line on the same chart. A Pareto chart can reveal situations in which the Pareto principle occurs.

> PARETO PRINCIPLE
>
> The **Pareto principle** exists when the majority of items in a set of data occur in a small number of categories and the few remaining items are spread out over a large number of categories. These two groups are often referred to as the "vital few" and the "trivial many."

A Pareto chart has the capability to separate the "vital few" from the "trivial many," enabling you to focus on the important categories. In situations in which the data involved consist of defective or nonconforming items, a Pareto chart is a powerful tool for prioritizing improvement efforts.

To study a situation in which the Pareto chart proved to be especially appropriate, consider the problem faced by a bank. The bank defined the problem to be the incomplete automated teller machine (ATM) transactions. Data concerning the causes of incomplete ATM transactions were collected and stored in **ATM Transactions**. Table 2.15 shows the causes of incomplete ATM transactions, the frequency for each cause, and the percentage of incomplete ATM transactions due to each cause.

TABLE 2.15

Summary Table of Causes of Incomplete ATM Transactions

Cause	Frequency	Percentage (%)
ATM malfunctions	32	4.42
ATM out of cash	28	3.87
Invalid amount requested	23	3.18
Lack of funds in account	19	2.62
Magnetic strip unreadable	234	32.32
Warped card jammed	365	50.41
Wrong key stroke	23	3.18
Total	724	100.00

Source: Data extracted from A. Bhalla, "Don't Misuse the Pareto Principle," *Six Sigma Forum Magazine*, May 2009, pp. 15–18.

Table 2.16 presents a summary table for the incomplete ATM transactions data in which the categories are ordered based on the frequency of incomplete ATM transactions present (rather than arranged alphabetically). The percentages and cumulative percentages for the ordered categories are also included as part of the table.

TABLE 2.16

Ordered Summary Table of Causes of Incomplete ATM Transactions

Cause	Frequency	Percentage (%)	Cumulative Percentage (%)
Warped card jammed	365	50.41%	50.41%
Magnetic strip unreadable	234	32.32%	82.73%
ATM malfunctions	32	4.42%	87.15%
ATM out of cash	28	3.87%	91.02%
Invalid amount requested	23	3.18%	94.20%
Wrong key stroke	23	3.18%	97.38%
Lack of funds in account	19	2.62%	100.00%
Total	724	100.00%	

Figure 2.5 shows a Pareto chart based on the results displayed in Table 2.16.

FIGURE 2.5

Pareto chart for the incomplete ATM transactions data

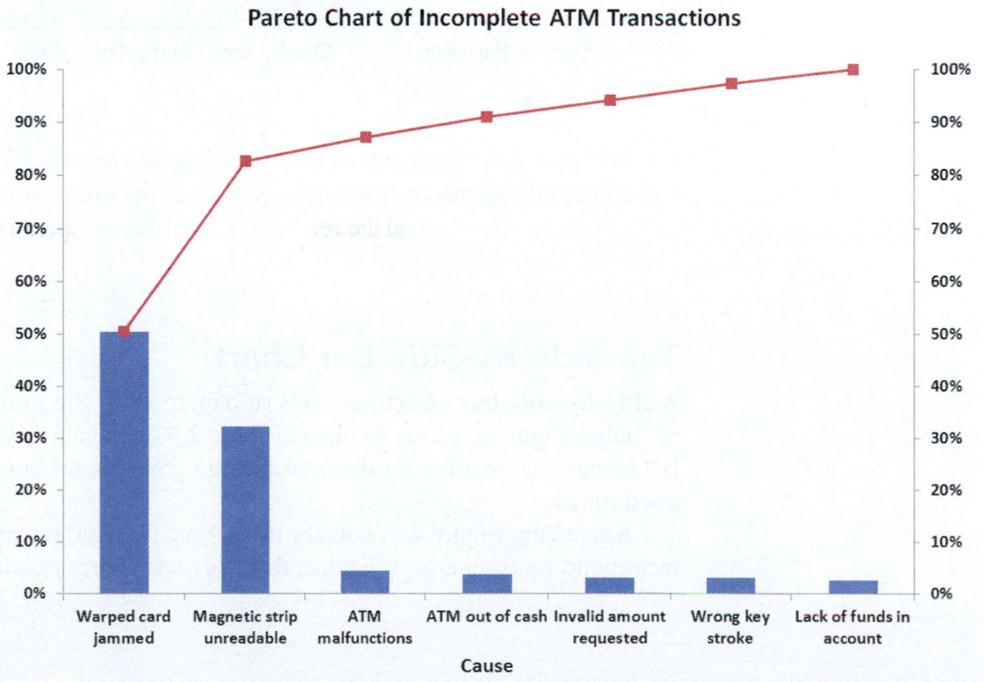

A Pareto chart presents the bars vertically, along with a cumulative percentage line. The cumulative line is plotted at the midpoint of each category, at a height equal to the cumulative percentage. In order for a Pareto chart to include all categories, even those with few defects, in some situations, you need to include a category labeled *Other* or *Miscellaneous*. In these situations, the bar representing these categories should be placed to the right of the other bars.

Because the categories in a Pareto chart are ordered by the frequency of occurrence, you can see where to concentrate efforts to improve the process. Analyzing the Pareto chart in Figure 2.5, if you follow the line, you see that these first two categories account for 82.73% of the incomplete ATM transactions. The first category listed is warped card jammed (with 50.41% of the defects), followed by magnetic strip unreadable (with 32.32%). Attempts to reduce incomplete ATM transactions due to warped card jammed and magnetic strip unreadable should produce the greatest payoff. The team should focus on finding why these errors occurred.

EXAMPLE 2.7

Pareto Chart of Types of Bill Payment

Construct a Pareto chart of the types of bill payment (see Table 2.1 on page 30)

FIGURE 2.6

Pareto chart of bill payment

Figure 2.6 shows a Pareto chart created using Minitab; Figure 2.5 shows a Pareto chart created using Excel.

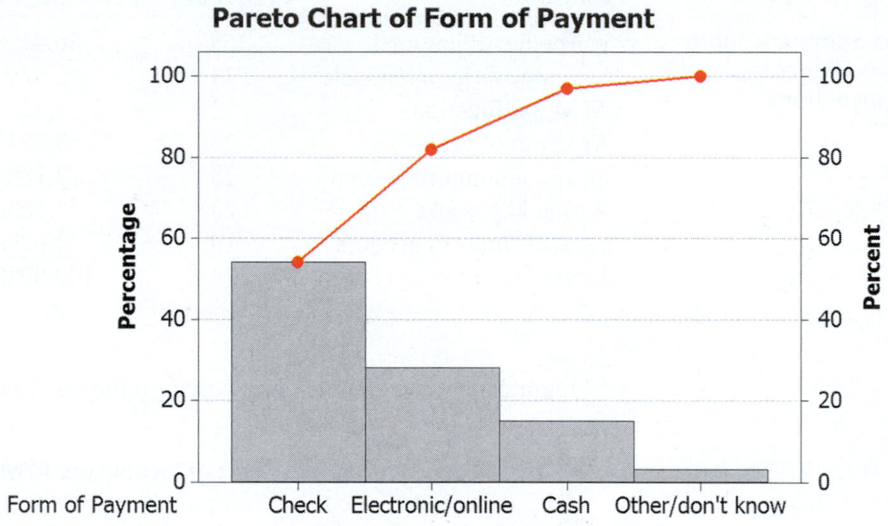

In Figure 2.6, check and electronic/online account for 82% of the bill payments and check, electronic/online, and cash account for 97% of the bill payments.

The Side-by-Side Bar Chart

A **side-by-side bar chart** uses sets of bars to show the joint responses from two categorical variables. Figure 2.7 uses the data of Table 2.3 on page 31, which shows the frequency of bond funds that charge a fee for the intermediate government bond funds and short-term corporate bond funds.

Reviewing Figure 2.7, you see that a much higher percentage of the intermediate government bond funds charge a fee than the short-term corporate bond funds.

FIGURE 2.7
Side-by-side bar chart of fund type and whether a fee is charged

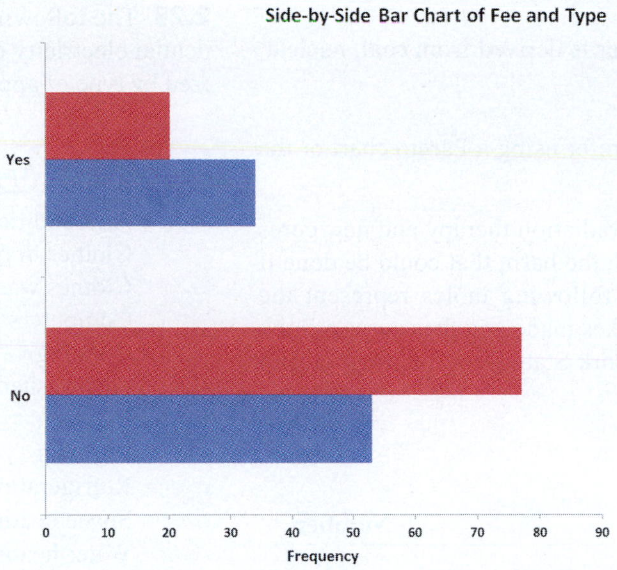

Problems for Section 2.4

APPLYING THE CONCEPTS

SELF Test **2.24** A survey asked 1,264 women who were their most trusted shopping advisers. The survey results were as follows:

Shopping Advisers	Percentage (%)
Advertising	7
Friends/family	45
Manufacturer websites	5
News media	11
Online user reviews	13
Retail websites	4
Salespeople	1
Other	14

Source: Data extracted from "Snapshots," *USA Today,* October 19, 2006, p. 1B.

a. Construct a bar chart, a pie chart, and a Pareto chart.
b. Which graphical method do you think is best for portraying these data?
c. What conclusions can you reach concerning women's most trusted shopping advisers?

2.25 What would you do if you won $1 million? A survey was taken of 1,078 adults who were asked what they would spend money on first if they won $1 million in a March Madness NCAA pool. The results are shown at the top of the next column:

a. Construct a bar chart, a pie chart, and a Pareto chart.
b. Which graphical method do you think is best for portraying these data?
c. What conclusions can you reach concerning what adults would do with $1 million?

Spending Choice	Percentage (%)
Buy Final Four tickets	4
Charity	4
Pay off debt	59
Save it	16
Take a cruise	8
Take money, never enter pool again	4
Take luck to Las Vegas	5

Source: Data extracted from "If I Win $1 Million," *USA Today,* March 19, 2009, p. 1A.

2.26 The Energy Information Administration reported the following sources of electricity in the United States in 2010:

Source of Electricity	Percentage (%)
Coal	44
Hydroelectric	7
Natural gas	24
Nuclear	20
Other	5

Source: Energy Information Administration, 2010.

a. Construct a Pareto chart.
b. What percentage of power is derived from coal, nuclear, or natural gas?
c. Construct a pie chart.
d. For these data, do you prefer using a Pareto chart or the pie chart? Why?

2.27 An article discussed radiation therapy and new cures from the therapy, along with the harm that could be done if mistakes were made. The following tables represent the results of the types of mistakes made and the causes of mistakes reported to the New York State Department of Health from 2001 to 2009:

Radiation Mistakes	Number
Missed all or part of intended target	284
Wrong dose given	255
Wrong patient treated	50
Other	32

a. Construct a bar chart and a pie chart for the types of radiation mistakes.
b. Which graphical method do you think is best for portraying these data?

Causes of Mistakes	Number
Quality assurance flawed	355
Data entry or calculation errors by personnel	252
Misidentification of patient or treatment location	174
Blocks, wedges, or collimators misused	133
Patient's physical setup wrong	96
Treatment plan flawed	77
Hardware malfunction	60
Staffing	52
Computer software or digital information transfer malfunction	24
Override of computer data by personnel	19
Miscommunication	14
Unclear/other	8

Source: Data extracted from W. Bogdanich, "A Lifesaving Tool Turned Deadly," *The New York Times,* January 24, 2010, pp. 1, 15, 16.

c. Construct a Pareto chart for the causes of mistakes.
d. Discuss the "vital few" and "trivial many" reasons for the causes of mistakes.

2.28 The following table indicates the percentage of residential electricity consumption in the United States, organized by type of appliance in a recent year:

Type of Appliance	Percentage (%)
Air conditioning	18
Clothes dryers	5
Clothes washers/other	24
Computers	1
Cooking	2
Dishwashers	2
Freezers	2
Lighting	16
Refrigeration	9
Space heating	7
Water heating	8
TVs and set top boxes	6

Source: Data extracted from J. Mouawad, and K. Galbraith, "Plugged-in Age Feeds a Hunger for Electricity," *The New York Times,* September 20, 2009, pp. 1, 28.

a. Construct a bar chart, a pie chart, and a Pareto chart.
b. Which graphical method do you think is best for portraying these data?
c. What conclusions can you reach concerning residential electricity consumption in the United States?

2.29 A study of 1,000 people asked what respondents wanted to grill during barbecue season. The results were as follows:

Type of Food	Percentage (%)
Beef	38
Chicken	23
Fruit	1
Hot dogs	6
Pork	8
Seafood	19
Vegetables	5

Source: Data extracted from "What Folks Want Sizzling on the Grill During Barbecue Season," *USA Today,* March 29, 2009, p. 1A.

a. Construct a bar chart, a pie chart, and a Pareto chart.
b. Which graphical method do you think is best for portraying these data?
c. What conclusions can you reach concerning what folks want sizzling on the grill during barbecue season?

2.30 A sample of 500 shoppers was selected in a large metropolitan area to learn more about consumer behavior.

Among the questions asked was "Do you enjoy shopping for clothing?" The results are summarized in the following table:

ENJOY SHOPPING FOR CLOTHING	GENDER		
	Male	Female	Total
Yes	136	224	360
No	104	36	140
Total	240	260	500

a. Construct a side-by-side bar chart of enjoying shopping and gender.
b. What conclusions do you reach from this chart?

2.31 Each day at a large hospital, several hundred laboratory tests are performed. The rate at which these tests are done improperly (and therefore need to be redone) seems steady, at about 4%. In an effort to get to the root cause of these nonconformances, tests that need to be redone, the director of the lab decided to keep records over a period of one week. The laboratory tests were subdivided by the shift of workers who performed the lab tests. The results are as follows:

LAB TESTS PERFORMED	SHIFT		
	Day	Evening	Total
Nonconforming	16	24	40
Conforming	654	306	960
Total	670	330	1,000

a. Construct a side-by-side bar chart of nonconformances and shift.
b. What conclusions concerning the pattern of nonconforming laboratory tests can the laboratory director reach?

2.32 Does it take more time to get yourself removed from an email list than it used to? A study of 100 large online retailers revealed the following:

YEAR	NEED THREE OR MORE CLICKS TO BE REMOVED	
	Yes	No
2009	39	61
2008	7	93

Source: Data extracted from "Drill Down," *The New York Times,* March 29, 2010, p. B2.

a. Construct a side-by-side bar chart of year and whether you need to click three or more times to be removed from an email list.
b. What do these results tell you about whether more online retailers were requiring three or more clicks in 2009 than in 2008?

2.5 Visualizing Numerical Data

Among the charts you use to visualize numerical data are the stem-and-leaf display, the histogram, the percentage polygon, and the cumulative percentage polygon (ogive).

The Stem-and-Leaf Display

A **stem-and-leaf display** allows you to see how the data are distributed and where concentrations of data exist. The display organizes data into groups (the stems) row-wise, so that the values within each group (the leaves) branch out to the right of their stem. For stems with more than one leaf, the leaves are presented in ascending order. On each leaf, the values are presented in ascending order. For example, suppose you collect the following lunch costs ($) for 15 classmates who had lunch at a fast-food restaurant:

5.40 4.30 4.80 5.50 7.30 8.50 6.10 4.80 4.90 4.90 5.50 3.50 5.90 6.30 6.60

To construct the stem-and-leaf display, you use whole dollar amounts as the stems and round the cents, the leaves, to one decimal place. For the first value, 5.40, the stem would be 5 and its leaf would be 4. For the second value, 4.30, the stem would be 4 and its leaf 3. The completed stem-and-leaf display for these data is

3	5
4	38899
5	4559
6	136
7	3
8	5

EXAMPLE 2.8

Stem-and-Leaf Display of the 2009 Return of the Short-Term Corporate Bond Funds

In Part I of the Choice Is Yours scenario, you are interested in studying the past performance of the short-term corporate bond funds. One measure of past performance is the return in 2009. You have already defined the variables to be collected and collected the data from a sample of 97 short-term corporate bond funds. Now, you need to construct a stem-and-leaf display of the return in 2009.

SOLUTION Figure 2.8 illustrates the stem-and-leaf display of the return in 2009 for short-term corporate bond funds.

FIGURE 2.8

Stem-and-leaf display of the return in 2009 of short-term corporate bond funds

Figure 2.8 shows a stem-and-leaf display created using Minitab and modified so that each stem occupies only one row. The leaves using PHStat2 will differ from Figure 2.8 slightly because PHStat2 and Minitab use different methods.

Stem-and-Leaf Display: Return 2009_Short Term Corporat

```
Stem-and-leaf of Return 2009_Short Term Corporat  N  = 97
Leaf Unit = 1.0

 1    -0  8
(53)   0   11222223334444455555555556666666666777777888888999999
 43    1   0000001111122222222333333333444555566679
 3     2   4
 2     2   9
 1     3   2
```

Analyzing Figure 2.8, you conclude the following:

- The lowest return in 2009 was –8.
- The highest return in 2009 was 32.
- The returns in 2009 were concentrated between 0 and 20.
- Only one fund had a negative 2009 return, and three funds had 2009 returns 20 and above.

The Histogram

A **histogram** is a bar chart for grouped numerical data in which you use vertical bars to represent the frequencies or percentages in each group. In a histogram, there are no gaps between adjacent bars. You display the variable of interest along the horizontal (X) axis. The vertical (Y) axis represents either the frequency or the percentage of values per class interval.

Figure 2.9 displays frequency histograms for the cost of meals at city restaurants and suburban restaurants. The histogram for city restaurants shows that the cost of meals is concentrated between approximately \$40 and \$50. Very few meals at city restaurants cost more than

FIGURE 2.9

Histograms for the cost of restaurant meals at city and suburban restaurants

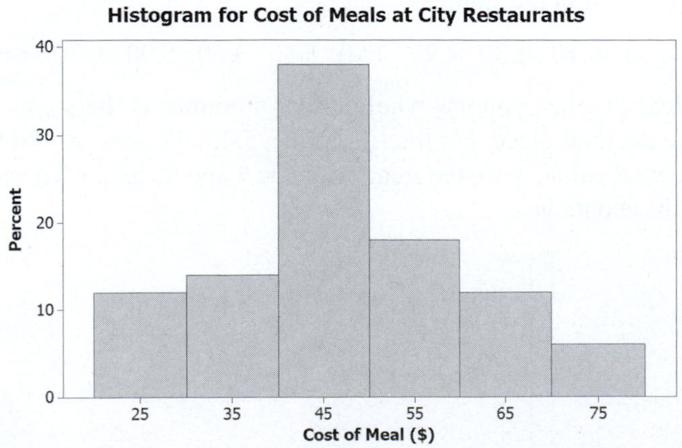

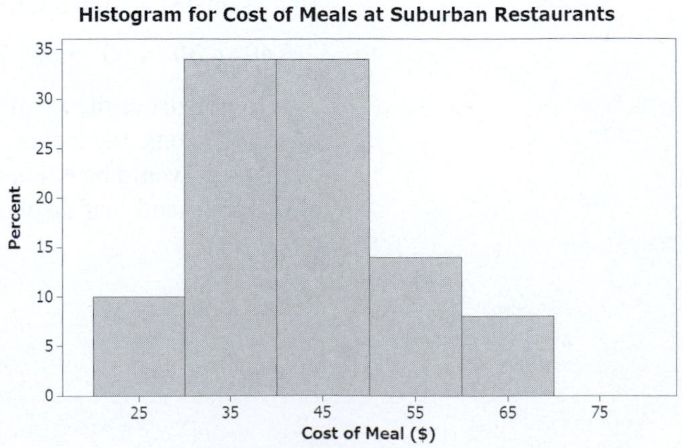

$70. The histogram for suburban restaurants shows that the cost of meals is concentrated between $30 and $50. Very few meals at suburban restaurants cost more than $60.

EXAMPLE 2.9

Histograms of the 2009 Return for the Intermediate Government and Short-Term Corporate Bond Funds

In Part I of the Choice Is Yours scenario, you are interested in comparing the past performance of the intermediate government bond funds and the short-term corporate bond funds. One measure of past performance is the return in 2009. You have already defined the variables to be collected and collected the data from a sample of 184 bond funds. Now, you need to construct histograms for the intermediate government and the short-term corporate bond funds.

SOLUTION Figure 2.10 displays frequency histograms for the 2009 return for the intermediate government and short-term corporate bond funds.

FIGURE 2.10

Frequency histograms of the 2009 return for the intermediate government and short-term corporate bond funds

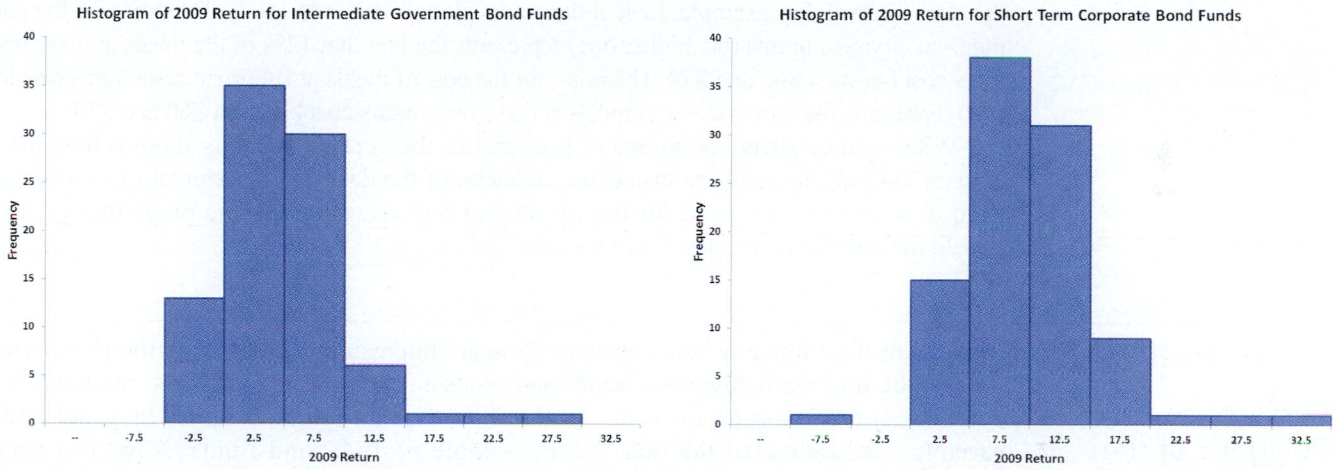

Figure 2.10 shows histograms created using Excel and PHStat2; Figure 2.9 shows histograms created using Minitab.

Reviewing the histograms in Figure 2.10 leads you to conclude that the returns were much higher for the short-term corporate bond funds than for the intermediate government bond funds. The return for intermediate government bond funds is concentrated between 0 and 10, and the return for the short-term corporate bond funds is concentrated between 5 and 15.

The Percentage Polygon

If you tried to construct two or more histograms on the same graph, you would not be able to easily interpret each histogram because the bars would overlap. When there are two or more groups, you should use a percentage polygon. A **percentage polygon** uses the midpoints of each class interval to represent the data of each class and then plots the midpoints, at their respective class percentages, as points on a line.

Figure 2.11 displays percentage polygons for the cost of meals at city and suburban restaurants.

Reviewing the two polygons in Figure 2.11 leads you to conclude that the highest concentration of the cost of meals at city restaurants is between $40 and $50, while the cost of meals at suburban restaurants is evenly concentrated between $30 and $50. Also, city restaurants have a higher percentage of meals that cost $60 or more than suburban restaurants.

FIGURE 2.11
Percentage polygons of the cost of restaurant meals for city and suburban restaurants

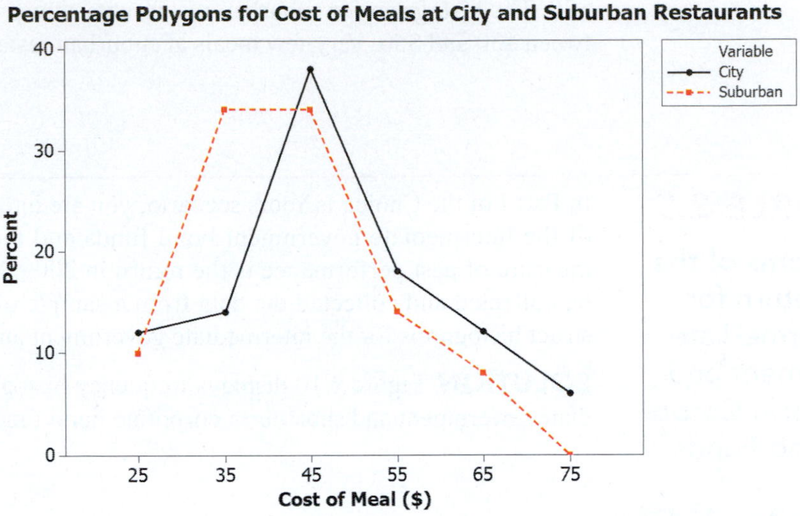

The polygons in Figure 2.11 have points whose values on the X axis represent the midpoint of the class interval. For example, look at the points plotted at $X = 65$ ($65). The point for the cost of meals at city restaurants (the higher one) represents the fact that 12% of the meals at these restaurants cost between $60 and $70. The point for the cost of meals at suburban restaurants (the lower one) represents the fact that 8% of meals at these restaurants cost between $60 and $70.

When you construct polygons or histograms, the vertical (Y) axis should show the true zero, or "origin," so as not to distort the character of the data. The horizontal (X) axis does not need to show the zero point for the variable of interest, although the range of the variable should include the major portion of the axis.

EXAMPLE 2.10

Percentage Polygons of the 2009 Return for the Intermediate Government and Short-Term Corporate Bond Funds

In Part I of the Choice Is Yours scenario, you are interested in comparing the past performance of the intermediate government bond funds and the short-term corporate bond funds. One measure of past performance is the return in 2009. You have already defined the variables and collected the data from a sample of 184 bond funds. Now, you need to construct percentage polygons for the intermediate government bond and short-term corporate bond funds.

SOLUTION Figure 2.12 displays percentage polygons of the 2009 returns for the intermediate government bond and short-term corporate bond funds.

FIGURE 2.12
Percentage polygons of the 2009 return for the intermediate government bond and short-term corporate bond funds

Figure 2.12 shows percentage polygons created using Excel; Figure 2.11 shows percentage polygons created using Minitab.

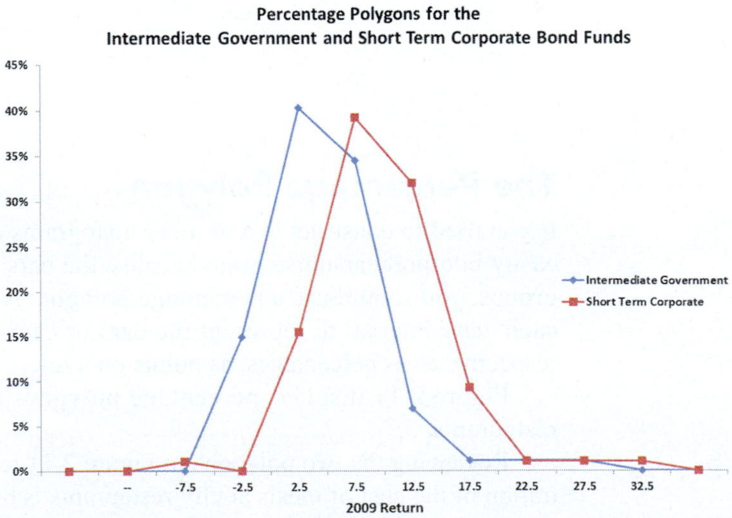

Analyzing Figure 2.12 leads you to conclude that the 2009 return of short-term corporate funds is much higher than for intermediate government bond funds. The polygon for the short-term corporate funds is to the right (the returns are higher) of the polygon for the intermediate government bond funds. The return for intermediate government funds is concentrated between 0 and 10, whereas the return for the short-term corporate bond funds is concentrated between 5 and 15.

The Cumulative Percentage Polygon (Ogive)

The **cumulative percentage polygon**, or **ogive**, uses the cumulative percentage distribution discussed in Section 2.3 to display the variable of interest along the *X* axis and the cumulative percentages along the *Y* axis.

Figure 2.13 shows cumulative percentage polygons for the cost of meals at city and suburban restaurants.

FIGURE 2.13
Cumulative percentage polygons of the cost of restaurant meals at city and suburban restaurants

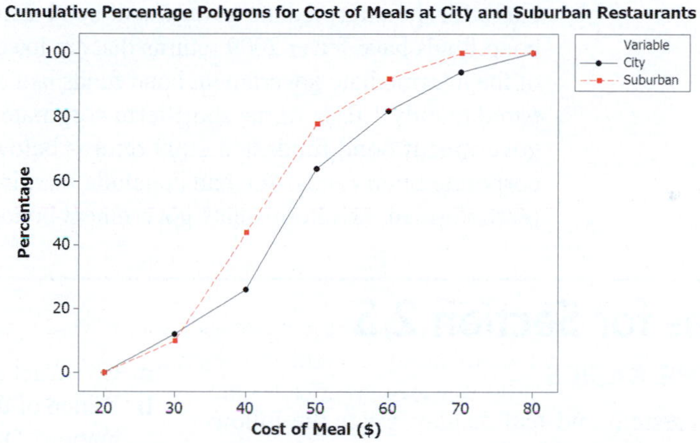

Reviewing the curves leads you to conclude that the curve of the cost of meals at the city restaurants is located to the right of the curve for the suburban restaurants. This indicates that the city restaurants have fewer meals that cost less than a particular value. For example, 64% of the meals at city restaurants cost less than $50, as compared to 78% of the meals at suburban restaurants.

EXAMPLE 2.11
Cumulative Percentage Polygons of the 2009 Return for the Intermediate Government and Short-Term Corporate Bond Funds

In Part I of the Choice Is Yours scenario, you are interested in comparing the past performance of the intermediate government bond funds and the short-term corporate bond funds. One measure of past performance is the return in 2009. You have already defined the variables and collected the data from a sample of 184 bond funds. Now, you need to construct cumulative percentage polygons for the intermediate government bond and the short-term corporate bond funds.

SOLUTION Figure 2.14 on page 54 displays cumulative percentage polygons for the 2009 return for the intermediate government bond and short-term corporate bond funds.

FIGURE 2.14

Cumulative percentage polygons of the 2009 return of intermediate government bonds and short-term corporate bond funds

Figure 2.14 shows cumulative percentage polygons created using Excel; Figure 2.13 shows cumulative percentage polygons created using Minitab.

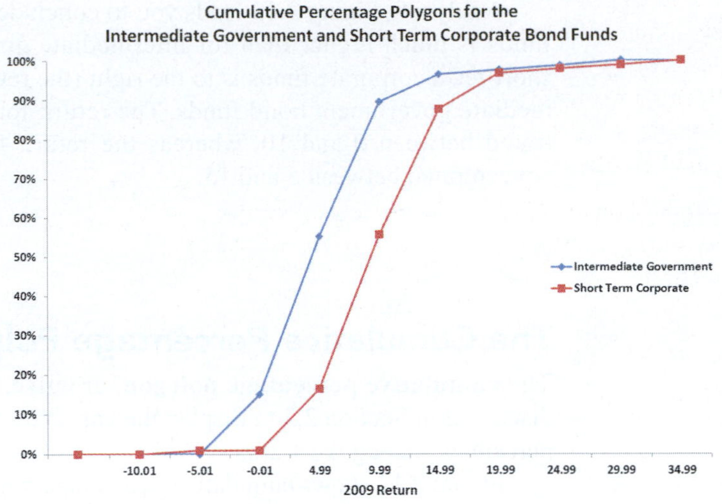

Reviewing the cumulative percentage polygons in Figure 2.14 leads you to conclude that the curve for the 2009 return of short-term corporate bond funds is located to the right of the curve for the intermediate government bond funds. This indicates that the short-term corporate bond funds have fewer 2009 returns that are lower than a particular value. For example, 14.94% of the intermediate government bond funds had negative (returns below 0) 2009 returns as compared to only 1.03% of the short-term corporate bond funds. Also, 55.17% of the intermediate government bond funds had 2009 returns below 5, as compared to 16.49% of the short-term corporate bond funds. You can conclude that, in general, the short-term corporate bond funds outperformed the intermediate government bond funds in 2009.

Problems for Section 2.5

LEARNING THE BASICS

2.33 Construct a stem-and-leaf display, given the following data from a sample of midterm exam scores in finance:

54 69 98 93 53 74

2.34 Construct an ordered array, given the following stem-and-leaf display from a sample of $n = 7$ midterm exam scores in information systems:

5	0
6	
7	446
8	19
9	2

APPLYING THE CONCEPTS

2.35 The following is a stem-and-leaf display representing the amount of gasoline purchased, in gallons (with leaves in tenths of gallons), for a sample of 25 cars that use a particular service station on the New Jersey Turnpike:

9	147
10	02238
11	125566777
12	223489
13	02

a. Construct an ordered array.
b. Which of these two displays seems to provide more information? Discuss.
c. What amount of gasoline (in gallons) is most likely to be purchased?
d. Is there a concentration of the purchase amounts in the center of the distribution?

SELF Test **2.36** The file **BBCost** contains the total cost ($) for four tickets, two beers, four soft drinks, four hot dogs, two game programs, two baseball caps, and parking for one vehicle at each of the 30 Major League Baseball parks during the 2009 season.

Source: Data extracted from **teammarketing.com,** April 1, 2009.

a. Construct a stem-and-leaf display for these data.
b. Around what value, if any, are the costs of attending a baseball game concentrated? Explain.

2.37 The file **DarkChocolate** contains the cost per ounce ($) for a sample of 14 dark chocolate bars:

0.68	0.72	0.92	1.14	1.42	0.94	0.77
0.57	1.51	0.57	0.55	0.86	1.41	0.90

Source: Data extracted from "Dark Chocolate: Which Bars Are Best?" *Consumer Reports,* September 2007, p. 8.

a. Construct an ordered array.
b. Construct a stem-and-leaf display.
c. Does the ordered array or the stem-and-leaf display provide more information? Discuss.
d. Around what value, if any, is the cost of dark chocolate bars concentrated? Explain.

2.38 The file **Utility** contains the following data about the cost of electricity during July 2010 for a random sample of 50 one-bedroom apartments in a large city:

96	171	202	178	147	102	153	197	127	82
157	185	90	116	172	111	148	213	130	165
141	149	206	175	123	128	144	168	109	167
95	163	150	154	130	143	187	166	139	149
108	119	183	151	114	135	191	137	129	158

a. Construct a histogram and a percentage polygon.
b. Construct a cumulative percentage polygon.
c. Around what amount does the monthly electricity cost seem to be concentrated?

2.39 As player salaries have increased, the cost of attending baseball games has increased dramatically. The following histogram visualizes the total cost ($) for four tickets, two beers, four soft drinks, four hot dogs, two game programs, two baseball caps, and parking for one vehicle at each of the 30 Major League Baseball parks during the 2009 season that is stored in **BBCost**.

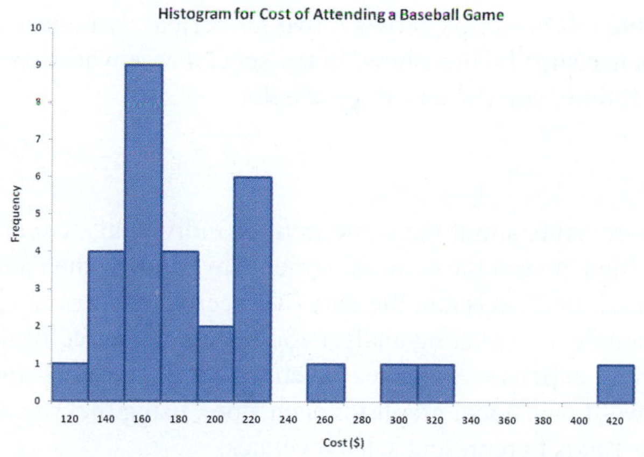

What conclusions can you reach concerning the cost of attending a baseball game at different ballparks?

2.40 The following histogram visualizes the data about the property taxes per capita for the 50 states and the District of Columbia, stored in **PropertyTaxes**.

What conclusions can you reach concerning the property taxes per capita?

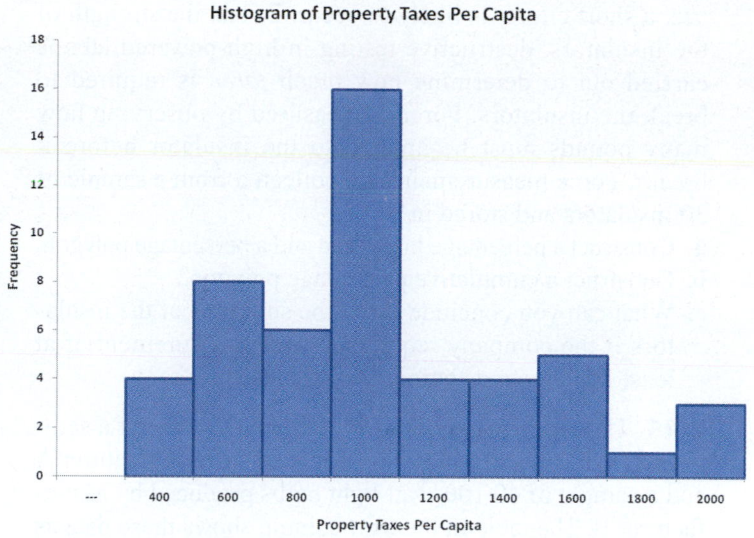

2.41 One operation of a mill is to cut pieces of steel into parts that will later be used as the frame for front seats in an automobile. The steel is cut with a diamond saw and requires the resulting parts to be within ±0.005 inch of the length specified by the automobile company. The data are collected from a sample of 100 steel parts and stored in **Steel**. The measurement reported is the difference in inches between the actual length of the steel part, as measured by a laser measurement device, and the specified length of the steel part. For example, the first value, −0.002, represents a steel part that is 0.002 inch shorter than the specified length.
a. Construct a percentage histogram.
b. Is the steel mill doing a good job meeting the requirements set by the automobile company? Explain.

2.42 A manufacturing company produces steel housings for electrical equipment. The main component part of the housing is a steel trough that is made out of a 14-gauge steel coil. It is produced using a 250-ton progressive punch press with a wipe-down operation that puts two 90-degree forms in the flat steel to make the trough. The distance from one side of the form to the other is critical because of weatherproofing in outdoor applications. The company requires that the width of the trough be between 8.31 inches and 8.61 inches. The widths of the troughs, in inches, are collected from a sample of 49 troughs and stored in **Trough**.
a. Construct a percentage histogram and a percentage polygon.
b. Plot a cumulative percentage polygon.
c. What can you conclude about the number of troughs that will meet the company's requirements of troughs being between 8.31 and 8.61 inches wide?

2.43 The manufacturing company in Problem 2.42 also produces electric insulators. If the insulators break when in use, a short circuit is likely to occur. To test the strength of the insulators, destructive testing in high-powered labs is carried out to determine how much *force* is required to break the insulators. Force is measured by observing how many pounds must be applied to the insulator before it breaks. Force measurements are collected from a sample of 30 insulators and stored in **Force**.

a. Construct a percentage histogram and a percentage polygon.
b. Construct a cumulative percentage polygon.
c. What can you conclude about the strengths of the insulators if the company requires a force measurement of at least 1,500 pounds before the insulator breaks?

2.44 The file **Bulbs** contains the life (in hours) of a sample of 40 100-watt light bulbs produced by Manufacturer A and a sample of 40 100-watt light bulbs produced by Manufacturer B. The table in the next column shows these data as a pair of ordered arrays:

Manufacturer A					Manufacturer B				
684	697	720	773	821	819	836	888	897	903
831	835	848	852	852	907	912	918	942	943
859	860	868	870	876	952	959	962	986	992
893	899	905	909	911	994	1,004	1,005	1,007	1,015
922	924	926	926	938	1,016	1,018	1,020	1,022	1,034
939	943	946	954	971	1,038	1,072	1,077	1,077	1,082
972	977	984	1,005	1,014	1,096	1,100	1,113	1,113	1,116
1,016	1,041	1,052	1,080	1,093	1,153	1,154	1,174	1,188	1,230

Use the following class interval widths for each distribution:

Manufacturer A: 650 but less than 750, 750 but less than 850, and so on.
Manufacturer B: 750 but less than 850, 850 but less than 950, and so on.

a. Construct percentage histograms on separate graphs and plot the percentage polygons on one graph.
b. Plot cumulative percentage polygons on one graph.
c. Which manufacturer has bulbs with a longer life—Manufacturer A or Manufacturer B? Explain.

2.45 The data stored in **Drink** represents the amount of soft drink in a sample of 50 2-liter bottles:

a. Construct a histogram and a percentage polygon.
b. Construct a cumulative percentage polygon.
c. On the basis of the results in (a) and (b), does the amount of soft drink filled in the bottles concentrate around specific values?

2.6 Visualizing Two Numerical Variables

Often you will want to explore possible relationships between two numerical variables. You use a scatter plot as a first step to visualize such relationships. In the special case where one of your variables represents the passage of time, you use a time-series plot.

The Scatter Plot

Often, you have two numerical measurements about the same item or individual. A **scatter plot** can explore the possible relationship between those measurements by plotting the data of one numerical variable on the horizontal, or X, axis and the data of a second numerical variable on the vertical, or Y, axis. For example, a marketing analyst could study the effectiveness of advertising by comparing advertising expenses and sales revenues of 50 stores. Using a scatter plot, a point is plotted on the two-dimensional graph for each store, using the X axis to represent advertising expenses and the Y axis to represent sales revenues.

Table 2.17 presents the revenues and value (both in millions of dollars) for all 30 NBA professional basketball teams that is stored in **NBAValues**. To explore the possible relationship between the revenues generated by a team and the value of a team, you can create a scatter plot.

TABLE 2.17
Values and Revenues for NBA Teams

Team	Value	Revenues	Team	Value	Revenues
Atlanta	306	103	Milwaukee	254	91
Boston	433	144	Minnesota	268	96
Charlotte	278	96	New Jersey	269	92
Chicago	511	168	New Orleans	267	95
Cleveland	476	159	New York	586	202
Dallas	446	154	Oklahoma City	310	111
Denver	321	115	Orlando	361	107
Detroit	479	171	Philadelphia	344	115
Golden State	315	113	Phoenix	429	148
Houston	470	160	Portland	338	121
Indiana	281	97	Sacramento	305	109
Los Angeles Clippers	295	102	San Antonio	398	133
Los Angeles Lakers	607	209	Toronto	386	133
Memphis	257	88	Utah	343	118
Miami	364	126	Washington	313	110

Source: Data extracted from **www.forbes.com/lists/2009/32/basketball-values-09_NBA-Team-Valuations_Rank.html**.

For each team, you plot the revenues on the *X* axis and the values on the *Y* axis. Figure 2.15 presents a scatter plot for these two variables.

FIGURE 2.15
Scatter plot of revenue and value

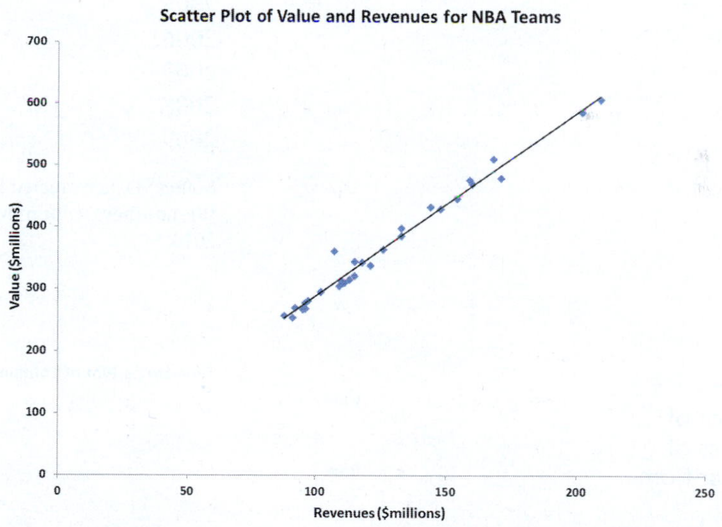

Reviewing Figure 2.15, you see that there appears to be a very strong increasing (positive) relationship between revenues and the value of a team. In other words, teams that generate a smaller amount of revenues have a lower value, while teams that generate higher revenues have a higher value. Notice the straight line that has been superimposed on the plotted data in Figure 2.15. For these data, this line is very close to the points in the scatter plot. This line is a linear regression prediction line that will be discussed in Chapter 13. (In Section 3.5, you will return to this example when you learn about the covariance and the coefficient of correlation.)

Other pairs of variables may have a decreasing (negative) relationship in which one variable decreases as the other increases. In other situations, there may be a weak or no relationship between the variables.

The Time-Series Plot

A **time-series plot** plots the values of a numerical variable on the *Y* axis and plots the time period associated with each numerical value on the *X* axis. A time-series plot can help explore trends in data that occur over time. For example, Table 2.18 presents the combined gross (in millions of dollars) of movies released from 1996 to 2009 that is stored in MovieGross. To better visualize this data, you create the time-series plot shown in Figure 2.16.

From Figure 2.16, you see that there was a steady increase in the combined gross of movies between 1996 and 2009. During that time, the combined gross increased from under $6 billion in 1996 to more than $10 billion in 2009.

TABLE 2.18

Combined Gross of Movies

Year	Combined Gross
1996	5,669.20
1997	6,393.90
1998	6,523.00
1999	7,317.50
2000	7,659.50
2001	8,077.80
2002	9,146.10
2003	9,043.20
2004	9,359.40
2005	8,817.10
2006	9,231.80
2007	9,685.70
2008	9,707.40
2009	10,675.60

Source: Data extracted from **www.the-numbers. com/movies**, February 16, 2010.

FIGURE 2.16

Time-series plot of combined gross of movies per year from 1996 to 2009

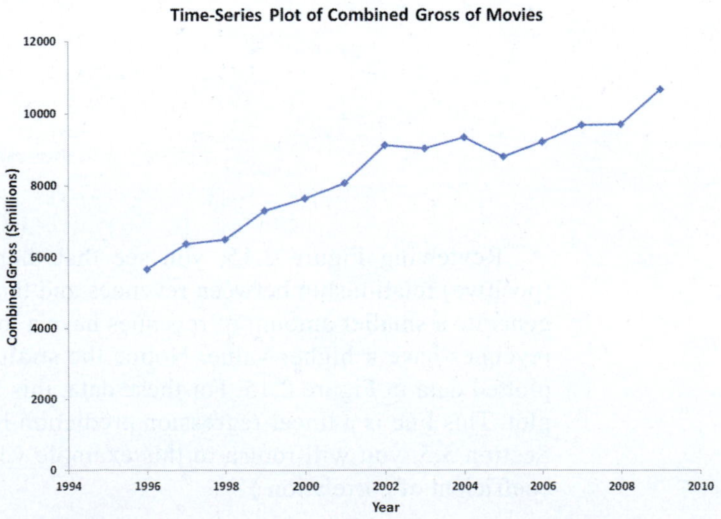

Problems for Section 2.6

LEARNING THE BASICS

2.46 The following is a set of data from a sample of $n = 11$ items:

X:	7	5	8	3	6	0	2	4	9	5	8
Y:	1	5	4	9	8	0	6	2	7	5	4

a. Construct a scatter plot.
b. Is there a relationship between *X* and *Y*? Explain.

2.47 The following is a series of annual sales (in millions of dollars) over an 11-year period (2000 to 2010):

Year:	2000	2001	2002	2003	2004	2005	2006	2007	2008	2009	2010
Sales:	13.0	17.0	19.0	20.0	20.5	20.5	20.5	20.0	19.0	17.0	13.0

a. Construct a time-series plot.
b. Does there appear to be any change in annual sales over time? Explain.

APPLYING THE CONCEPTS

SELF Test **2.48** Movie companies need to predict the gross receipts of individual movies once the movie has debuted. The following results, stored in PotterMovies, are the first weekend gross, the U.S. gross, and the worldwide gross (in millions of dollars) of the six Harry Potter movies that debuted from 2001 to 2009.

Title	First Weekend	U.S. Gross	Worldwide Gross
Sorcerer's Stone	90.295	317.558	976.458
Chamber of Secrets	88.357	261.988	878.988
Prisoner of Azkaban	93.687	249.539	795.539
Goblet of Fire	102.335	290.013	896.013
Order of the Phoenix	77.108	292.005	938.469
Half-Blood Prince	77.836	301.460	934.601

Source: Data extracted from **www.the-numbers.com/interactive/comp-Harry-Potter.php**.

a. Construct a scatter plot with first weekend gross on the *X* axis and U.S. gross on the *Y* axis.
b. Construct a scatter plot with first weekend gross on the *X* axis and worldwide gross on the *Y* axis.
c. What can you say about the relationship between first weekend gross and U.S. gross and first weekend gross and worldwide gross?

2.49 The file VeggieBurger contains data on the calories and total fat (in grams per serving) for a sample of 12 veggie burgers.

Source: *Data extracted from "Healthful Burgers That Taste Good,"* Consumer Reports, *June 2008, p 8.*

a. Construct a scatter plot with calories on the *X* axis and total fat on the *Y* axis.
b. What conclusions can you reach about the relationship between the calories and total fat in veggie burgers?

2.50 College basketball is big business, with coaches' salaries, revenues, and expenses in millions of dollars. The file College Basketball contains the coaches' salary and revenue for college basketball at 60 of the 65 schools that played in the 2009 NCAA men's basketball tournament (data extracted from "Compensation for Division 1 Men's Basketball Coaches," *USA Today*, April 2, 2010, p. 8C; and C. Isadore, "Nothing but Net: Basketball Dollars by School," **money.cnn.com/2010/03/18/news/companies/basketball_profits/**).

a. Do you think schools with higher revenues also have higher coaches' salaries?
b. Construct a scatter plot with revenue on the *X* axis and coaches' salaries on the *Y* axis.
c. Does the scatter plot confirm or contradict your answer to (a)?

2.51 College football players trying out for the NFL are given the Wonderlic standardized intelligence test. The file Wonderlic contains the average Wonderlic scores of football players trying out for the NFL and the graduation rate for football players at selected schools (data extracted from S. Walker, "The NFL's Smartest Team," *The Wall Street Journal*, September 30, 2005, pp. W1, W10).

a. Construct a scatter plot with average Wonderlic score on the *X* axis and graduation rate on the *Y* axis.
b. What conclusions can you reach about the relationship between the average Wonderlic score and graduation rate?

2.52 How have stocks performed in the past? The following table presents the data stored in Stock Performance that shows the performance of a broad measure of stocks (by percentage) for each decade from the 1830s through the 2000s:

Decade	Performance (%)
1830s	2.8
1840s	12.8
1850s	6.6
1860s	12.5
1870s	7.5
1880s	6.0
1890s	5.5
1900s	10.9
1910s	2.2
1920s	13.3
1930s	–2.2
1940s	9.6
1950s	18.2
1960s	8.3
1970s	6.6
1980s	16.6
1990s	17.6
2000s*	–0.5

* Through December 15, 2009.

Source: Data extracted from T. Lauricella, "Investors Hope the '10s" Beat the '00s," *The Wall Street Journal,* December 21, 2009, pp. C1, C2.

a. Construct a time-series plot of the stock performance from the 1830s to the 2000s.
b. Does there appear to be any pattern in the data?

2.53 According to the U.S. Census Bureau, the average price of a new home declined in 2008 and 2009. The file **New Home Prices** contains the average price paid for a new home from 1990 to 2009 (extracted from **www.census.gov**, March 15, 2010).
a. Construct a time-series plot of new home prices.
b. What pattern, if any, is present in the data?

2.54 The following table uses the data in **Solar Power** to show the yearly amount of solar power installed (in megawatts) in the United States from 2000 through 2008:

Year	Amount of Solar Power Installed
2000	18
2001	27
2002	44
2003	68
2004	83
2005	100
2006	140
2007	210
2008	250

Source: Data extracted from P. Davidson, "Glut of Rooftop Solar Systems Sinks Price," *USA Today,* January 13, 2009, p. 1B.

a. Construct a time-series plot for the yearly amount of solar power installed (in megawatts) in the United States.
b. What pattern, if any, is present in the data?

2.55 The file **Audits** contains the number of audits of corporations with assets of more than $250 million conducted by the Internal Revenue Service (data extracted from K. McCoy, "IRS Audits Big Firms Less Often," *USA Today*, April 15, 2010, p. 1B).
a. Construct a time-series plot.
b. What pattern, if any, is present in the data?

2.7 Organizing Multidimensional Data

In this chapter, you have learned methods for organizing and visualizing a single variable and methods for jointly organizing and visualizing two variables. More and more, businesses need to organize and visualize more than two variables to mine data to discover possible patterns and relationships that simpler explorations might miss. While any number of variables can be used, subject to limits of computation and storage, examples of more than three or four variables can be hard to interpret when simple tables are used to present results. Both Excel and Minitab can organize multidimensional data but the two applications have different strengths: Excel contains **PivotTables**, a type of interactive table that facilitates exploring multidimensional data, while Minitab has specialized statistical and graphing procedures (that are beyond the scope of this book to fully discuss).

Multidimensional Contingency Tables

A **multidimensional contingency table** tallies the responses of three or more categorical variables. In the simplest case of three categorical variables, each cell in the table contains the tallies of the third variable organized by the subgroups represented by the row and column variables.

Consider the Table 2.3 contingency table, which displays the type of fund and whether a fee is charged for the sample of 184 mutual funds. Figure 2.17 presents this table as an Excel PivotTable. Adding a third categorical variable, Risk, to the PivotTable, forms the new multidimensional PivotTable shown in Figure 2.18. The new table reveals that following patterns that cannot be seen in the original Table 2.3 contingency table:

- Although the ratio of fee–yes to fee–no bond funds for the intermediate government category seems to be about 2 to 3 (34 to 53), the ratio for above-average-risk intermediate government bond funds is about 1 to 1 (15 to 14) while the ratio for below average-risk funds is less than 1 to 3 (6 to 20).
- While the group "short-term corporate funds that charge a fee" has nearly equal numbers of above-average-risk, average-risk, and below-average-risk funds (7, 7, and 6), the group "intermediate government bond funds that charge a fee" contains many fewer below-average-risk funds (6) than average risk (13) or above-average (15) ones.
- The pattern of risk tallies differs between the fee–yes and fee–no funds in each of the bond fund categories.

Using methods presented in later chapters, you can confirm whether these first impressions are statistically significant.

FIGURE 2.17

Excel PivotTable version of the Table 2.3 contingency table

	A	B	C	D
1	PivotTable of Type and Fees			
2				
3	Count of Fees	Fees		
4	Type	Yes	No	Grand Total
5	Intermediate Government	34	53	87
6	Short Term Corporate	20	77	97
7	Grand Total	54	130	184

FIGURE 2.18

Excel and Minitab multidimensional contingency table of type, risk, and fees

	A	B	C	D	E
1	Multidimensional Contingency Table of Type, Risk, and Fees				
2					
3	Count of Fees		Fees		
4	Type	Risk	Yes	No	Grand Total
5	⊟ Intermediate Government	Above average	15	14	29
6		Average	13	19	32
7		Below average	6	20	26
8	Intermediate Government Total		34	53	87
9	⊟ Short Term Corporate	Above average	7	23	30
10		Average	7	30	37
11		Below average	6	24	30
12	Short Term Corporate Total		20	77	97
13	Grand Total		54	130	184

Tabulated statistics: Type, Risk, Fees

```
Rows: Type / Risk   Columns: Fees

                                                  No  Yes  All
Intermediate Government
                          Above average           14   15   29
                          Average                 19   13   32
                          Below average           20    6   26
Short Term Corporate
                          Above average           23    7   30
                          Average                 30    7   37
                          Below average           24    6   30
All
                          All                    130   54  184

Cell Contents:      Count
```

Adding Numerical Variables

Multidimensional contingency tables can contain numerical variables. When you add a numerical variable to a multidimensional analysis, you use categorical variables or variables that represent units of time for the rows and columns that will form the subgroups by which the numerical variable will be analyzed.

For example, Figure 2.19 on page 62 shows a table that cross classifies fees and type in which the cell amounts are the sums of the asset variable for each subgroup, and Figure 2.20 on page 62 shows the same table formatted to show percentages of assets. Comparing Figure 2.21—the table shown in Figure 2.17 but formatted for percentage of the overall total—to Figure 2.20 shows that the percentage of assets for the intermediate government funds by fee category does not mimic the fees category percentages.

FIGURE 2.19

Excel and Minitab multidimensional contingency table of type, fees, and sums of assets

	A	B	C	D
1	Contingency Table of Type, and Fees, and Sums of Assets			
2				
3	Sum of Assets	Fees		
4	Type	Yes	No	Grand Total
5	Intermediate Government	26252.7	56692.2	82944.9
6	Short Term Corporate	16842.1	67772.3	84614.4
7	Grand Total	43094.8	124464.5	167559.3

Tabulated statistics: Type, Fees

Rows: Type Columns: Fees

	No	Yes	All
Intermediate Government	56692	26253	82945
Short Term Corporate	67772	16842	84614
All	124465	43095	167559

Cell Contents: Assets : Sum

FIGURE 2.20

Multidimensional contingency table of type of fund, fee category, and percentages of assets

	A	B	C	D
1	Contingency Table of Type, and Fees, and Percentages of Assets			
2				
3	Sum of Assets	Fees		
4	Type	Yes	No	Grand Total
5	Intermediate Government	15.67%	33.83%	49.50%
6	Short Term Corporate	10.05%	40.45%	50.50%
7	Grand Total	25.72%	74.28%	100.00%

FIGURE 2.21

Contingency table of type and percentages of fees

	A	B	C	D
1	Contingency Table of Type and Percentages of Fees			
2				
3	Count of Fees	Fees		
4	Type	Yes	No	Grand Total
5	Intermediate Government	18.48%	28.80%	47.28%
6	Short Term Corporate	10.87%	41.85%	52.72%
7	Grand Total	29.35%	70.65%	100.00%

When you include a numerical variable, you typically compute one of the numerical descriptive statistics discussed in Sections 3.1 and 3.2. For example, Figure 2.22 shows a multidimensional contingency table in which the mean, or average 2009 rate of return for each of the subgroups, is computed.[1] This table reveals, among other things, that although there was virtually no difference in the 2009 return depending on whether a fee was charged, for funds with above-average risk, the return was much higher (4.89) for intermediate government funds that charged a fee than for funds that did not charge a fee (1.41).

[1] See Section 3.1 to learn more about the mean.

FIGURE 2.22

Excel and Minitab multidimensional contingency table of type, risk, fees, and the mean 2009 rates of return

	A	B	C	D	E
1	Contingency Table of Type, Risk, Fees and Means of 2009 Return				
2					
3	Average of Return 2009		Fees		
4	Type	Risk	Yes	No	Grand Total
5	⊟Intermediate Government	Above average	4.89	1.41	3.21
6		Average	3.39	3.74	3.60
7		Below average	5.98	7.17	6.90
8	Intermediate Government Total		4.51	4.42	4.45
9	⊟Short Term Corporate	Above average	15.99	12.42	13.25
10		Average	9.87	9.66	9.70
11		Below average	6.53	5.63	5.81
12	Short Term Corporate Total		11.01	9.23	9.60
13	Grand Total		6.92	7.27	7.16

Tabulated statistics: Type, Risk, Fees

Rows: Type / Risk Columns: Fees

		No	Yes	All
Intermediate Government				
	Above average	1.407	4.887	3.207
	Average	3.737	3.392	3.597
	Below average	7.170	5.983	6.896
Short Term Corporate				
	Above average	12.417	15.986	13.250
	Average	9.663	9.871	9.703
	Below average	5.629	6.533	5.810
All				
	All	7.267	6.917	7.164

Cell Contents: Return 2009 : Mean

Problems for Section 2.7

APPLYING THE CONCEPTS

SELF Test **2.56** For this problem, use the data in **BondFunds2008**.

a. Construct a table that tabulates type, fees, and risk.

b. What conclusions can you reach concerning differences among the types of mutual funds (intermediate government and short-term corporate), based on fees (yes or no) and the risk factor (low, average, and high)?

c. Compare the results of (b) with those shown in Figure 2.18.

2.57 For this problem, use the data in **Mutual Funds**.

a. Construct a table that tabulates category, objective, and fees.

b. What conclusions can you reach concerning differences among the categories of mutual funds (large cap, medium cap, and small cap), based on objective (growth and value) and fees (yes and no)?

2.58 For this problem, use the data in **Mutual Funds**.

a. Construct a table that tabulates category, fees, and risk.

b. What conclusions can you reach concerning differences among the categories of mutual funds (large cap, medium cap, and small cap), based on fees (yes and no) and the risk factor (low, average, and high)?

2.59 For this problem, use the data in **Mutual Funds**.

a. Construct a table that tabulates category, objective, fees, and risk.

b. What conclusions can you reach concerning differences among the categories of mutual funds (large cap, medium cap, and small cap), based on objective (growth and value), the risk factor (low, average, and high), and fees (yes and no)?

c. Which table do you think is easier to interpret, the one in this problem or the ones in Problems 2.56 and 2.57? Explain.

2.8 Misuses and Common Errors in Visualizing Data

Good graphical displays clearly and unambiguously reveal what the data convey. Unfortunately, many graphs presented in the media (broadcast, print, and online) are incorrect, misleading, or so unnecessarily complicated that they should never be used. To illustrate the misuse of graphs, the chart presented in Figure 2.23 is similar to one that was printed in *Time* magazine as part of an article on increasing exports of wine from Australia to the United States.

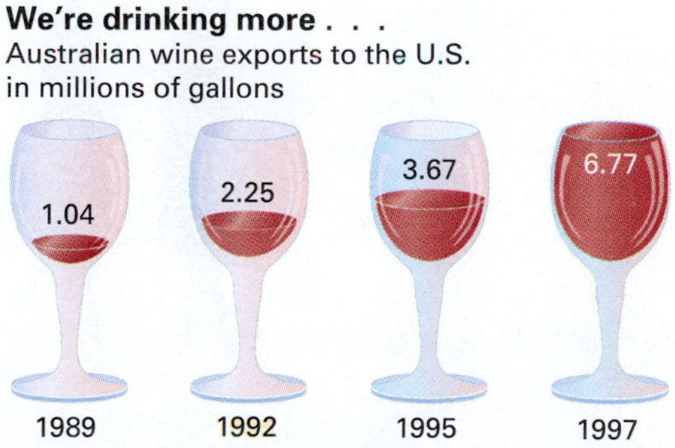

FIGURE 2.23
"Improper" display of Australian wine exports to the United States, in millions of gallons

Source: *Based on S. Watterson, "Liquid Gold—Australians Are Changing the World of Wine. Even the French Seem Grateful,"* Time, *November 22, 1999, p. 68.*

In Figure 2.23, the wineglass icon representing the 6.77 million gallons for 1997 does not appear to be almost twice the size of the wineglass icon representing the 3.67 million gallons for 1995, nor does the wineglass icon representing the 2.25 million gallons for 1992 appear to be twice the size of the wineglass icon representing the 1.04 million gallons for 1989. Part of the reason for this is that the three-dimensional wineglass icon is used to represent the two dimensions of exports and time. Although the wineglass presentation may catch the eye, the data should instead be presented in a summary table or a time-series plot.

In addition to the type of distortion created by the wineglass icons in the *Time* magazine graph displayed in Figure 2.23, improper use of the vertical and horizontal axes leads to distortions. Figure 2.24 presents another graph used in the same *Time* magazine article.

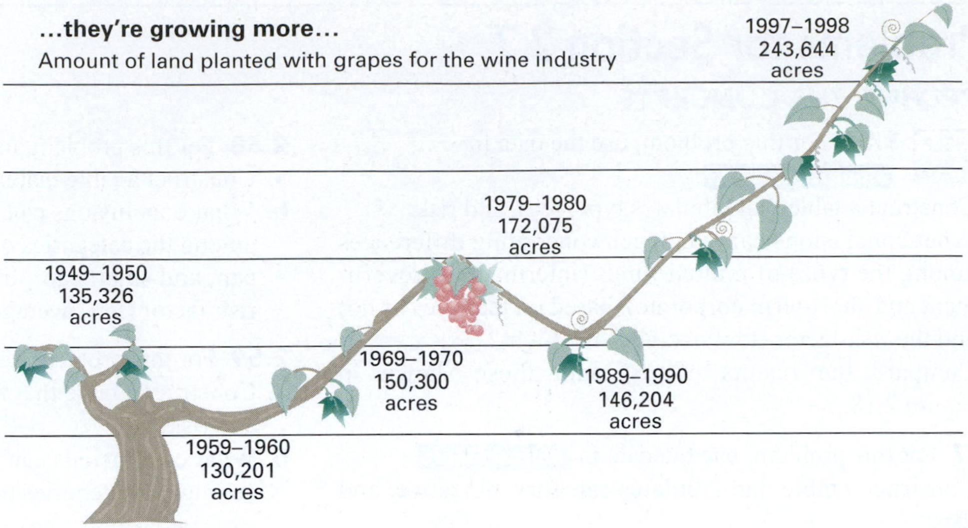

FIGURE 2.24
"Improper" display of amount of land planted with grapes for the wine industry

Source: *Based on S. Watterson, "Liquid Gold—Australians Are Changing the World of Wine. Even the French Seem Grateful,"* Time, *November 22, 1999, pp. 68–69.*

There are several problems in this graph. First, there is no zero point on the vertical axis. Second, the acreage of 135,326 for 1949–1950 is plotted above the acreage of 150,300 for 1969–1970. Third, it is not obvious that the difference between 1979–1980 and 1997–1998 (71,569 acres) is approximately 3.5 times the difference between 1979–1980 and 1969–1970 (21,775 acres). Fourth, there are no scale values on the horizontal axis. Years are plotted next to the acreage totals, not on the horizontal axis. Fifth, the values for the time dimension are not properly spaced along the horizontal axis. For example, the value for 1979–1980 is much closer to 1989–1990 than it is to 1969–1970. Other types of eye-catching displays that you typically see in magazines and newspapers often include information that is not necessary and just adds excessive clutter. Figure 2.25 represents one such display.

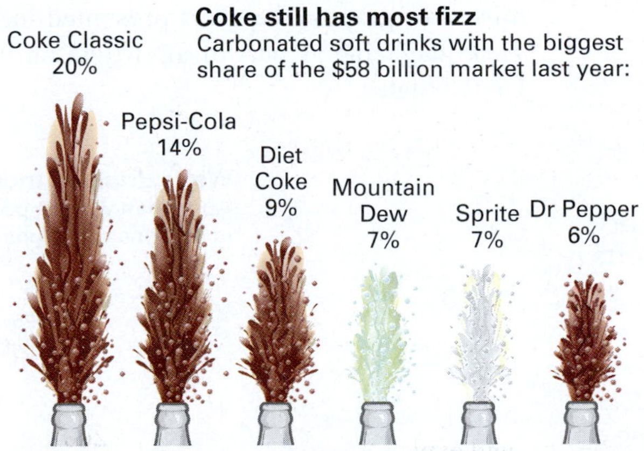

FIGURE 2.25
"Improper" plot of market share of soft drinks

Source: *Based on Anne B. Carey and Sam Ward, "Coke Still Has Most Fizz,"* USA Today, *May 10, 2000, p. 1B.*

The graph in Figure 2.25 shows the products with the largest market share for soft drinks. The graph suffers from too much clutter, although it is designed to show the differences in market share among the soft drinks. The display of the fizz for each soft drink takes up too much of the graph relative to the data. The same information could be better conveyed with a bar chart or pie chart.

The following are some guidelines for developing good graphs:

- A graph should not distort the data.
- A graph should not contain **chartjunk**, unnecessary adornments that convey no useful information.
- Any two-dimensional graph should contain a scale for each axis.
- The scale on the vertical axis should begin at zero.

- All axes should be properly labeled.
- The graph should contain a title.
- The simplest possible graph should be used for a given set of data.

Often individuals unaware of how to construct appropriate graphs violate these guidelines. Some applications, including Excel, tempt you to create "pretty" charts that may be fancy in their designs but that represent unwise choices. For example, making a simple pie chart fancier by adding exploded 3D slices is unwise as this can complicate a viewer's interpretation of the data. Uncommon chart choices such as doughnut, radar, surface, bubble, cone, and pyramid charts may look visually striking, but in most cases they obscure the data.

Problems for Section 2.8

APPLYING THE CONCEPTS

2.60 **(Student Project)** Bring to class a chart from either a website, newspaper, or magazine published this month that you believe to be a poorly drawn representation of a numerical variable. Be prepared to submit the chart to the instructor with comments about why you believe it is inappropriate. Do you believe that the intent of the chart is to purposely mislead the reader? Also, be prepared to present and comment on this in class.

2.61 **(Student Project)** Bring to class a chart from either a website, newspaper, or magazine published this month that you believe to be a poorly drawn representation of a categorical variable. Be prepared to submit the chart to the instructor with comments about why you consider it inappropriate. Do you believe that the intent of the chart is to purposely mislead the reader? Also, be prepared to present and comment on this in class.

2.62 **(Student Project)** According to its home page, Swivel is "Swivel is a website where people share reports of charts and numbers. Businesses use Swivel to dashboard their metrics. Students use Swivel to find and share research data." Go to **www.swivel.com** and explore some of the various graphical displays.

a. Select a graphical display that you think does a good job revealing what the data convey. Discuss why you think it is a good graphical display.

b. Select a graphical display that you think needs a lot of improvement. Discuss why you think that it is a poorly constructed graphical display.

2.63 The following visual display contains an overembellished chart similar to one that appeared in *USA Today*, dealing with the average consumer's Valentine's Day spending ("USA Today Snapshots: The Price of Romance," *USA Today*, February 14, 2007, p. 1B).

a. Describe at least one good feature of this visual display.

b. Describe at least one bad feature of this visual display.

c. Redraw the graph, using the guidelines given on page 64 and above.

2.64 The following visual display contains an overembellished chart similar to one that appeared in *USA Today*, dealing with the estimated number of hours the typical American spends using various media ("USA Today Snapshots: Minding Their Media," *USA Today*, March 2, 2007, p. 1B).

a. Describe at least one good feature of this visual display.
b. Describe at least one bad feature of this visual display.
c. Redraw the graph, using the guidelines given on pages 64–65.

2.65 The following visual display contains an overembellished chart similar to one that appeared in *USA Today*, dealing with which card is safer to use ("USA Today Snapshots: Credit Card vs. Debit Card," *USA Today*, March 14, 2007, p. 1B).

a. Describe at least one good feature of this visual display.
b. Describe at least one bad feature of this visual display.
c. Redraw the graph, using the guidelines given on pages 64–65.

2.66 Professor Deanna Oxender Burgess of Florida Gulf Coast University conducted research on annual reports of corporations (see D. Rosato, "Worried About the Numbers? How About the Charts?" *The New York Times*, September 15, 2002, p. B7) and found that even slight distortions in a chart changed readers' perception of the information. Using Internet or library sources, select a corporation and study the most recent annual report. Find at least one chart in the report that you think needs improvement and develop an improved version of the chart. Explain why you believe the improved chart is better than the one included in the annual report.

2.67 Figures 2.1 and 2.3 show a bar chart and a pie chart for how adults pay their monthly bills (see pages 42 and 43).
a. Create an exploded pie chart, a doughnut chart, a cone chart, or a pyramid chart that shows how adults pay their monthly bills.
b. Which graphs do you prefer—the bar chart or pie chart or the exploded pie chart, doughnut chart, cone chart, and pyramid chart? Explain.

2.68 Figures 2.2 and 2.4 show a bar chart and a pie chart for the risk level for the bond fund data (see pages 43 and 44).
a. Create an exploded pie chart, a doughnut chart, a cone chart, and a pyramid chart that shows the risk level of bond funds.
b. Which graphs do you prefer—the bar chart or pie chart or the exploded pie chart, doughnut chart, cone chart, and pyramid chart? Explain.

USING STATISTICS @ Choice Is Yours, Part I Revisited

In the Using Statistics scenario, you were hired by the Choice Is Yours investment company to assist clients who seek to invest in mutual funds. A sample of 184 bond mutual funds was selected, and information on the funds and past performance history was recorded. For each of the 184 funds, data were collected on eight variables. With so much information, visualizing all these numbers required the use of properly selected graphical displays.

From bar charts and pie charts, you were able to illustrate that about one-third of the funds were classified as having below-average risk, about one-third had average risk, and about one-third had above-average risk. Cross tabulations of the funds by whether the fund charged a fee and whether the fund invested in intermediate government bonds or short-term corporate bonds revealed that intermediate government bond funds are more likely to charge fees. After constructing histograms on the 2009 return, you were able to conclude that the returns were much higher for the short-term corporate bond funds than for the intermediate government bonds. The return for intermediate government bond funds is concentrated between 0 and 10, whereas the return for the short-term corporate bond funds is concentrated between 5 and 15.

With these insights, you can inform your clients about how the different funds performed. Of course, past performance history does not guarantee future performance. In fact, if you look at returns in 2008, stored in **BondFunds2008**, you will discover that the returns were much *lower* for the short-term corporate bond funds than for the intermediate government bonds!

Using graphical methods such as these is an important first step in summarizing and interpreting data. Although the proper display of data (as discussed in Section 2.8) helps to avoid ambiguity, graphical methods always contain a certain degree of subjectivity. Next, you will need descriptive statistics to further analyze the past performance of the mutual funds. Chapter 3 presents descriptive statistics (e.g., mean, median, and mode).

SUMMARY

Organizing and visualizing data involves using various tables and charts to help draw conclusions about data. In several different chapter examples, tables and charts helped you reach conclusions about how people prefer to pay their bills and about the cost of restaurant meals in a city and its suburbs; they also provided some insights about the sample of bond mutual funds in the Using Statistics scenario.

The tables and charts you use depend on the type of data you have. Table 2.19 summarizes the proper choices for the type of data and the tables and charts discussed in this chapter. In Chapter 3 you will learn about a variety of descriptive statistics useful for data analysis and interpretation.

TABLE 2.19

Selecting Tables and Charts

	Type of Data	
Type of Analysis	**Numerical**	**Categorical**
Organizing data	Ordered array, frequency distribution, relative frequency distribution, percentage distribution, cumulative percentage distribution (Section 2.3)	Summary table, contingency table (Section 2.2)
Visualizing one variable	Stem-and-leaf display, histogram, percentage polygon, cumulative percentage polygon (ogive) (Section 2.5)	Bar chart, pie chart, Pareto chart (Section 2.4)
Visualizing two variables	Scatter plot, time-series plot (Section 2.6)	Side-by-side bar chart (Section 2.4)
Organizing multidimensional data	Multidimensional tables (Section 2.7)	Multidimensional tables (Section 2.7)

KEY EQUATIONS

Determining the Class Interval Width

$$\text{Interval width} = \frac{\text{highest value} - \text{lowest value}}{\text{number of classes}} \tag{2.1}$$

Computing the Proportion or Relative Frequency

$$\text{Proportion} = \text{relative frequency} = \frac{\text{number of values in each class}}{\text{total number of values}} \tag{2.2}$$

KEY TERMS

CHAPTER REVIEW PROBLEMS

CHECKING YOUR UNDERSTANDING

2.69 How do histograms and polygons differ in their construction and use?

2.70 Why would you construct a summary table?

2.71 What are the advantages and disadvantages of using a bar chart, a pie chart, and a Pareto chart?

2.72 Compare and contrast the bar chart for categorical data with the histogram for numerical data.

2.73 What is the difference between a time-series plot and a scatter plot?

2.74 Why is it said that the main feature of a Pareto chart is its ability to separate the "vital few" from the "trivial many"?

2.75 What are the three different ways to break down the percentages in a contingency table?

2.76 How can a multidimensional table differ from a two variable contingency table?

2.77 What type of insights can you gain from a three-way table that are not available in a two-way table?

APPLYING THE CONCEPTS

2.78 The following summary table presents the breakdown of the price of a new college textbook:

Revenue Category	**Percentage (%)**	
Publisher	64.8	
Manufacturing costs		32.3
Marketing and promotion		15.4
Administrative costs and taxes		10.0
After-tax profit		7.1
Bookstore	22.4	
Employee salaries and benefits		11.3
Operations		6.6
Pretax profit		4.5
Author	11.6	
Freight	1.2	

Source: Data extracted from T. Lewin, "When Books Break the Bank," *The New York Times,* September 16, 2003, pp. B1, B4.

a. Using the four categories publisher, bookstore, author, and freight, construct a bar chart, a pie chart, and a Pareto chart.

b. Using the four subcategories of publisher and three subcategories of bookstore, along with the author and freight categories, construct a Pareto chart.

c. Based on the results of (a) and (b), what conclusions can you reach concerning who gets the revenue from the sales of new college textbooks? Do any of these results surprise you? Explain.

2.79 The following table represents the market share (in number of movies, gross in millions of dollars, and in number of tickets sold in millions) of each type of movie in 2009:

Type	Number	Gross ($ millions)	Tickets (millions)
Based on book/short story	66	2042.9	272.4
Based on comic/graphic novel	6	376.2	50.2
Based on factual book/article	5	280.7	37.4
Based on game	3	9.2	1.2
Based on musical/opera	1	13.7	1.8
Based on play	8	172.0	22.9
Based on real life events	95	334.9	44.7
Based on toy	1	150.2	20.0
Based on TV	7	267.5	35.7
Compilation	1	0.6	0.1
Original screenplay	203	4,335.7	578.1
Remake	18	422.6	56.3
Sequel	20	2,064.2	275.2
Spin-off	1	179.9	24.0

Source: Data extracted from **www.the-numbers.com/market/Sources2009.php**.

a. Construct a bar chart, a pie chart, and a Pareto chart for the number of movies, gross (in millions of dollars), and number of tickets sold (in millions).

b. What conclusions can you reach about the market share of the different types of movies in 2009?

2.80 A survey was conducted from 665 consumer magazines on the practices of their websites. The results are summarized in a copyediting table and a fact-checking table:

Copyediting as Compared to Print Content	Percentage
As rigorous	41
Less rigorous	48
Not copyedited	11

a. For copyediting, construct a bar chart, a pie chart, and a Pareto chart.

b. Which graphical method do you think is best for portraying these data?

Fact Checking as Compared to Print Content	Percentage
Same	57
Less rigorous	27
Online not fact checked	8
Neither online nor print is fact-checked	8

Source: Data extracted from S. Clifford, "Columbia Survey Finds a Slack Editing Process of Magazine Web Sites," *The New York Times*, March 1, 2010, p. B6.

c. For fact checking, construct a bar chart, a pie chart, and a Pareto chart.

d. Which graphical method do you think is best for portraying these data?

e. What conclusions can you reach concerning copy editing and fact checking of print and online consumer magazines?

2.81 The owner of a restaurant that serves Continental-style entrées has the business objective of learning more about the patterns of patron demand during the Friday-to-Sunday weekend time period. Data were collected from 630 customers on the type of entrée ordered and organized in the following table:

Type of Entrée	Number Served
Beef	187
Chicken	103
Mixed	30
Duck	25
Fish	122
Pasta	63
Shellfish	74
Veal	26
Total	630

a. Construct a percentage summary table for the types of entrées ordered.

b. Construct a bar chart, a pie chart, and a Pareto chart for the types of entrées ordered.

c. Do you prefer using a Pareto chart or a pie chart for these data? Why?

d. What conclusions can the restaurant owner reach concerning demand for different types of entrées?

2.82 Suppose that the owner of the restaurant in Problem 2.81 also wanted to study the demand for dessert during the same time period. She decided that in addition to studying whether a dessert was ordered, she would also study the gender of the individual and whether a beef entrée was ordered. Data were collected from 600 customers and organized in the following contingency tables:

DESSERT ORDERED	GENDER		
	Male	Female	Total
Yes	40	96	136
No	240	224	464
Total	280	320	600

DESSERT ORDERED	BEEF ENTRÉE		
	Yes	No	Total
Yes	71	65	136
No	116	348	464
Total	187	413	600

a. For each of the two contingency tables, construct contingency tables of row percentages, column percentages, and total percentages.

b. Which type of percentage (row, column, or total) do you think is most informative for each gender? For beef entrée? Explain.

c. What conclusions concerning the pattern of dessert ordering can the restaurant owner reach?

2.83 The following data represent the pounds per capita of fresh food and packaged food consumed in the United States, Japan, and Russia in 2009:

FRESH FOOD	COUNTRY		
	United States	Japan	Russia
Eggs, nuts, and beans	88	94	88
Fruit	124	126	88
Meat and seafood	197	146	125
Vegetables	194	278	335

PACKAGED FOOD	COUNTRY		
	United States	Japan	Russia
Bakery goods	108	53	144
Dairy products	298	147	127
Pasta	12	32	16
Processed, frozen, dried and chilled food, and ready-to-eat meals	183	251	70
Sauces, dressings, and condiments	63	75	49
Snacks and candy	47	19	24
Soup and canned food	77	17	25

Source: Data extracted from H. Fairfield, "Factory Food," *The New York Times,* April 4, 2010, p. BU5.

a. For the United States, Japan, and Russia, construct a bar chart, a pie chart, and a Pareto chart for different types of fresh foods consumed.

b. For the United States, Japan, and Russia, construct a bar chart, a pie chart, and a Pareto chart for different types of packaged foods consumed.

c. What conclusions can you reach concerning differences between the United States, Japan, and Russia in the fresh foods and packaged foods consumed?

2.84 In 2000, a growing number of warranty claims on Firestone tires sold on Ford SUVs prompted Firestone and Ford to issue a major recall. An analysis of warranty claims data helped identify which models to recall. A breakdown of 2,504 warranty claims based on tire size is given in the following table:

Tire Size	Number of Warranty Claims
23575R15	2,030
311050R15	137
30950R15	82
23570R16	81
331250R15	58
25570R16	54
Others	62

Source: Data extracted from Robert L. Simison, "Ford Steps Up Recall Without Firestone," *The Wall Street Journal,* August 14, 2000, p. A3.

The 2,030 warranty claims for the 23575R15 tires can be categorized into ATX models and Wilderness models. The type of incident leading to a warranty claim, by model type, is summarized in the following table:

Incident Type	ATX Model Warranty Claims	Wilderness Warranty Claims
Tread separation	1,365	59
Blowout	77	41
Other/ unknown	422	66
Total	1,864	166

Source: Data extracted from Robert L. Simison, "Ford Steps Up Recall Without Firestone," *The Wall Street Journal,* August 14, 2000, p. A3.

a. Construct a Pareto chart for the number of warranty claims by tire size. What tire size accounts for most of the claims?

b. Construct a pie chart to display the percentage of the total number of warranty claims for the 23575R15 tires that come from the ATX model and Wilderness model. Interpret the chart.

c. Construct a Pareto chart for the type of incident causing the warranty claim for the ATX model. Does a certain type of incident account for most of the claims?

d. Construct a Pareto chart for the type of incident causing the warranty claim for the Wilderness model. Does a certain type of incident account for most of the claims?

2.85 One of the major measures of the quality of service provided by an organization is the speed with which the organization responds to customer complaints. A large family-held department store selling furniture and flooring, including carpet, had undergone a major expansion in the past several years. In particular, the flooring department had expanded from 2 installation crews to an installation supervisor, a measurer, and 15 installation crews. A business objective of the company was to reduce the time between when the complaint is received and when it is resolved. During a recent year, the company received 50 complaints concerning carpet installation. The data from the 50 complaints, stored in **Furniture**, represent the number of days between the receipt of the complaint and the resolution of the complaint:

54	5	35	137	31	27	152	2	123	81	74	27
11	19	126	110	110	29	61	35	94	31	26	5
12	4	165	32	29	28	29	26	25	1	14	13
13	10	5	27	4	52	30	22	36	26	20	23
33	68										

a. Construct a frequency distribution and a percentage distribution.

b. Construct a histogram and a percentage polygon.

c. Construct a cumulative percentage distribution and plot a cumulative percentage polygon (ogive).

d. On the basis of the results of (a) through (c), if you had to tell the president of the company how long a customer should expect to wait to have a complaint resolved, what would you say? Explain.

2.86 The file **DomesticBeer** contains the percentage alcohol, number of calories per 12 ounces, and number of carbohydrates (in grams) per 12 ounces for 139 of the best-selling domestic beers in the United States.

Source: Data extracted from **www.Beer100.com,** March 18, 2010.

a. Construct a percentage histogram for each of the three variables.

b. Construct three scatter plots: percentage alcohol versus calories, percentage alcohol versus carbohydrates, and calories versus carbohydrates.

c. Discuss what you learn from studying the graphs in (a) and (b).

2.87 The file **CigaretteTax** contains the state cigarette tax ($) for each state as of December 31, 2009.

a. Construct an ordered array.

b. Plot a percentage histogram.

c. What conclusions can you reach about the differences in the state cigarette tax between the states?

2.88 The file **SavingsRate-MMCD** contains the yields for a money market account and a five-year certificate of deposit (CD) for 25 banks in the United States, as of March 29, 2010.

Source: Data extracted from **www.Bankrate.com**, March 29, 2010.

a. Construct a stem-and-leaf display for each variable.

b. Construct a scatter plot of money market account versus five-year CD.

c. What is the relationship between the money market rate and the five-year CD rate?

2.89 The file **CEO-Compensation** includes the total compensation (in millions of $) of CEOs of 197 large public companies and the investment return in 2009.

Source: Data extracted from D. Leonard, "Bargains in the Boardroom," *The New York Times,* April 4, 2010, pp. BU1, BU7, BU10, BU11.

a. Construct a frequency distribution and a percentage distribution.

b. Construct a histogram and a percentage polygon.

c. Construct a cumulative percentage distribution and plot a cumulative percentage polygon (ogive).

d. Based on (a) through (c), what conclusions can you reach concerning CEO compensation in 2009?

e. Construct a scatter plot of total compensation and investment return in 2009.

f. What is the relationship between the total compensation and investment return in 2009?

2.90 Studies conducted by a manufacturer of Boston and Vermont asphalt shingles have shown product weight to be a major factor in customers' perception of quality. Moreover, the weight represents the amount of raw materials being used and is therefore very important to the company from a cost standpoint. The last stage of the assembly line packages the shingles before the packages are placed on wooden pallets. The variable of interest is the weight in pounds of the pallet which for most brands holds 16 squares of shingles. The company expects pallets of its Boston brand-name shingles to weigh at least 3,050 pounds but less than 3,260 pounds. For the company's Vermont brand-name shingles, pallets should weigh at least 3,600 pounds but less than 3,800. Data are collected from a sample of 368 pallets of Boston shingles and 330 pallets of Vermont shingles and stored in **Pallet**.

a. For the Boston shingles, construct a frequency distribution and a percentage distribution having eight class intervals, using 3,015, 3,050, 3,085, 3,120, 3,155, 3,190, 3,225, 3,260, and 3,295 as the class boundaries.
b. For the Vermont shingles, construct a frequency distribution and a percentage distribution having seven class intervals, using 3,550, 3,600, 3,650, 3,700, 3,750, 3,800, 3,850, and 3,900 as the class boundaries.
c. Construct percentage histograms for the Boston shingles and for the Vermont shingles.
d. Comment on the distribution of pallet weights for the Boston and Vermont shingles. Be sure to identify the percentage of pallets that are underweight and overweight.

2.91 What was the average price of a room at two-star, three-star, and four-star hotels in cities around the world in 2009? The file **HotelPrices** contains the prices in English pounds (about US $1.57 as of October 2010). Complete the following for two-star, three-star, and four-star hotels.

Source: Data extracted from **www.hotels.com/press/hotel-price-index-2009-h2.html.**

a. Construct a frequency distribution and a percentage distribution.
b. Construct a histogram and a percentage polygon.
c. Construct a cumulative percentage distribution and plot a cumulative percentage polygon (ogive).
d. What conclusions can you reach about the cost of two-star, three-star, and four-star hotels?
e. Construct separate scatter plots of the cost of two-star hotels versus three-star hotels, two-star hotels versus four-star hotels, and three-star hotels versus four-star hotels.
f. What conclusions can you reach about the relationship of the price of two-star, three-star, and four-star hotels?

2.92 The file **Protein** contains calorie and cholesterol information concerning popular protein foods (fresh red meats, poultry, and fish).

Source: U.S. Department of Agriculture.

a. Construct a percentage histogram for the number of calories.
b. Construct a percentage histogram for the amount of cholesterol.
c. What conclusions can you reach from your analyses in (a) and (b)?

2.93 The file **Gas Prices** contains the monthly average price of gasoline in the United States from January 1, 2006, to March 1, 2010. Prices are in dollars per gallon.

Source: "Energy Information Administration," **www.eia.doe.gov**, March 26, 2010.

a. Construct a time-series plot.
b. What pattern, if any, is present in the data?

2.94 The following data (stored in **Drink**) represent the amount of soft drink in a sample of 50 consecutively filled 2-liter bottles. The results are listed horizontally in the order of being filled:

2.109	2.086	2.066	2.075	2.065	2.057	2.052	2.044	2.036	2.038
2.031	2.029	2.025	2.029	2.023	2.020	2.015	2.014	2.013	2.014
2.012	2.012	2.012	2.010	2.005	2.003	1.999	1.996	1.997	1.992
1.994	1.986	1.984	1.981	1.973	1.975	1.971	1.969	1.966	1.967
1.963	1.957	1.951	1.951	1.947	1.941	1.941	1.938	1.908	1.894

a. Construct a time-series plot for the amount of soft drink on the *Y* axis and the bottle number (going consecutively from 1 to 50) on the *X* axis.
b. What pattern, if any, is present in these data?
c. If you had to make a prediction about the amount of soft drink filled in the next bottle, what would you predict?
d. Based on the results of (a) through (c), explain why it is important to construct a time-series plot and not just a histogram, as was done in Problem 2.45 on page 56.

2.95 The S&P 500 Index tracks the overall movement of the stock market by considering the stock prices of 500 large corporations. The file **Stock Prices** contains weekly data for this index as well as the daily closing stock prices for three companies from January 2, 2009, to December 28, 2009. The following variables are included:

WEEK—Week ending on date given
S&P—Weekly closing value for the S&P 500 Index
GE—Weekly closing stock price for General Electric
DISC—Weekly closing stock price for Discovery Communications
AAPL—Weekly closing stock price for Apple

Source: Data extracted from **finance.yahoo.com,** March 26, 2010.

a. Construct time-series plots for the weekly closing values of the S&P 500 Index, General Electric, Discovery, and Apple.
b. Explain any patterns present in the plots.
c. Write a short summary of your findings.

2.96 (Class Project) Have each student in the class respond to the question "Which carbonated soft drink do you most prefer?" so that the instructor can tally the results into a summary table.

a. Convert the data to percentages and construct a Pareto chart.
b. Analyze the findings.

2.97 (Class Project) Let each student in the class be cross-classified on the basis of gender (male, female) and current employment status (yes, no) so that the instructor can tally the results.

a. Construct a table with either row or column percentages, depending on which you think is more informative.
b. What would you conclude from this study?
c. What other variables would you want to know regarding employment in order to enhance your findings?

REPORT WRITING EXERCISES

2.98 Referring to the results from Problem 2.90 on page 72 concerning the weight of Boston and Vermont shingles, write a report that evaluates whether the weight of the pallets of the two types of shingles are what the company expects. Be sure to incorporate tables and charts into the report.

2.99 Referring to the results from Problem 2.84 on page 70 concerning the warranty claims on Firestone tires, write a report that evaluates warranty claims on Firestone tires sold on Ford SUVs. Be sure to incorporate tables and charts into the report.

TEAM PROJECT

The file **Bond Funds** contains information regarding nine variables from a sample of 184 mutual funds:

Fund number—Identification number for each bond fund
Type—Bond fund type (intermediate government or short-term corporate)
Assets—In millions of dollars
Fees—Sales charges (no or yes)
Expense ratio—Ratio of expenses to net assets in percentage
Return 2009—Twelve-month return in 2009
Three-year return—Annualized return, 2007–2009
Five-year return—Annualized return, 2005–2009
Risk—Risk-of-loss factor of the mutual fund (below average, average, or above average)

2.100 For this problem, consider the expense ratio.

a. Construct a percentage histogram.
b. Using a single graph, plot percentage polygons of the expense ratio for bond funds that have fees and bond funds that do not have fees.
c. What conclusions about the expense ratio can you reach, based on the results of (a) and (b)?

2.101 For this problem, consider the three-year annualized return from 2007 to 2009.

a. Construct a percentage histogram.
b. Using a single graph, plot percentage polygons of the three-year annualized return from 2007 to 2009 for intermediate government funds and short-term corporate funds.
c. What conclusions about the three-year annualized return from 2007 to 2009 can you reach, based on the results of (a) and (b)?

2.102 For this problem, consider the five-year annualized return from 2005 to 2009.

a. Construct a percentage histogram.
b. Using a single graph, plot percentage polygons of the five-year annualized return from 2005 to 2009 for intermediate government funds and short-term corporate funds.
c. What conclusions about the five-year annualized return from 2005 to 2009 can you reach, based on the results of (a) and (b)?

STUDENT SURVEY DATABASE

2.103 Problem 1.27 on the page 14 describes a survey of 62 undergraduate students (stored in **UndergradSurvey**). For these data, construct all the appropriate tables and charts and write a report summarizing your conclusions.

2.104 Problem 2.103 describes a survey of 62 undergraduate students (stored in **UndergradSurvey**).

a. Select a sample of undergraduate students at your school and conduct a similar survey for those students.
b. For the data collected in (a), construct all the appropriate tables and charts and write a report summarizing your conclusions.
c. Compare the results of (b) to those of Problem 2.103.

2.105 Problem 1.28 on the page 15 describes a survey of 44 graduate students (see the file **GradSurvey**). For these data, construct all appropriate tables and charts and write a report summarizing your conclusions.

2.106 Problem 2.105 describes a survey of 44 MBA students (stored in **GradSurvey**).

a. Select a sample of MBA students in your MBA program and conduct a similar survey for those students.
b. For the data collected in (a), construct all the appropriate tables and charts and write a report summarizing your conclusions.
c. Compare the results of (b) to those of Problem 2.105.

MANAGING ASHLAND MULTICOMM SERVICES

Recently, Ashland MultiComm Services has been criticized for its inadequate customer service in responding to questions and problems about its telephone, cable television, and Internet services. Senior management has established a task force charged with the business objective of improving customer service. In response to this charge, the task force collected data about the types of customer service errors, the cost of customer service errors, and the cost of wrong billing errors. It found the following data:

Types of Customer Service Errors

Type of Errors	Frequency
Incorrect accessory	27
Incorrect address	42
Incorrect contact phone	31
Invalid wiring	9
On-demand programming error	14
Subscription not ordered	8
Suspension error	15
Termination error	22
Website access error	30
Wrong billing	137
Wrong end date	17
Wrong number of connections	19
Wrong price quoted	20
Wrong start date	24
Wrong subscription type	33
Total	448

Cost of Customer Service Errors in the Past Year

Type of Errors	Cost ($ thousands)
Incorrect accessory	17.3
Incorrect address	62.4
Incorrect contact phone	21.3
Invalid wiring	40.8
On-demand programming errors	38.8
Subscription not ordered	20.3
Suspension error	46.8
Termination error	50.9
Website access errors	60.7
Wrong billing	121.7
Wrong end date	40.9
Wrong number of connections	28.1
Wrong price quoted	50.3
Wrong start date	40.8
Wrong subscription type	60.1
Total	701.2

Type and Cost of Wrong Billing Errors

Type of Wrong Billing Errors	Cost ($ thousands)
Declined or held transactions	7.6
Incorrect account number	104.3
Invalid verification	9.8
Total	121.7

1. Review these data (stored in AMS2-1). Identify the variables that are important in describing the customer service problems. For each variable you identify, construct the graphical representation you think is most appropriate and explain your choice. Also, suggest what other information concerning the different types of errors would be useful to examine. Offer possible courses of action for either the task force or management to take that would support the goal of improving customer service.
2. As a follow-up activity, the task force decides to collect data to study the pattern of calls to the help desk (stored in AMS2-2). Analyze these data and present your conclusions in a report.

DIGITAL CASE

In the Using Statistics scenario, you were asked to gather information to help make wise investment choices. Sources for such information include brokerage firms, investment counselors, and other financial services firms. Apply your knowledge about the proper use of tables and charts in this Digital Case about the claims of foresight and excellence by an Ashland-area financial services firm.

Open **EndRunGuide.pdf,** which contains the EndRun Financial Services "Guide to Investing." Review the guide, paying close attention to the company's investment claims and supporting data and then answer the following.

1. How does the presentation of the general information about EndRun in this guide affect your perception of the business?

2. Is EndRun's claim about having more winners than losers a fair and accurate reflection of the quality of its investment service? If you do not think that the claim is a fair and accurate one, provide an alternate presentation that you think is fair and accurate.

3. Review the discussion about EndRun's "Big Eight Difference" and then open and examine **Mutual Funds**, a sample of mutual funds. Are there any other relevant data from that file that could have been included in the Big Eight table? How would the new data alter your perception of EndRun's claims?

4. EndRun is proud that all Big Eight funds have gained in value over the past five years. Do you agree that EndRun should be proud of its selections? Why or why not?

REFERENCES

1. Huff, D., *How to Lie with Statistics* (New York: Norton, 1954).
2. Levine, D. and D. Stephan, "Teaching Introductory Business Statistics Using the DCOVA Framework," *Decision Science Journal of Innovative Education*, January 2011.
3. *Microsoft Excel 2010* (Redmond, WA: Microsoft Corporation, 2010).
4. *Minitab Release 16* (State College, PA: Minitab, Inc., 2010).
5. Tufte, E. R., *Beautiful Evidence* (Cheshire, CT: Graphics Press, 2006).
6. Tufte, E. R., *Envisioning Information* (Cheshire, CT: Graphics Press, 1990).
7. Tufte, E. R., *The Visual Display of Quantitative Information*, 2nd ed. (Cheshire, CT: Graphics Press, 2002).
8. Tufte, E. R., *Visual Explanations* (Cheshire, CT: Graphics Press, 1997).
9. Wainer, H., *Visual Revelations: Graphical Tales of Fate and Deception from Napoleon Bonaparte to Ross Perot* (New York: Copernicus/Springer-Verlag, 1997).

EG2.2 ORGANIZING CATEGORICAL DATA

The Summary Table

PHStat2 Use **One-Way Tables & Charts** to create a summary table. For example, to create a summary table similar to Table 2.2 on page 30, open to the **DATA worksheet** of the **Bond Funds workbook**. Select **PHStat → Descriptive Statistics → One-Way Tables & Charts**. In the procedure's dialog box (shown below):

1. Click **Raw Categorical Data**.
2. Enter **I1:I185** as the **Raw Data Cell Range** and check **First cell contains label**.
3. Enter a **Title**, check **Percentage Column**, and click **OK**.

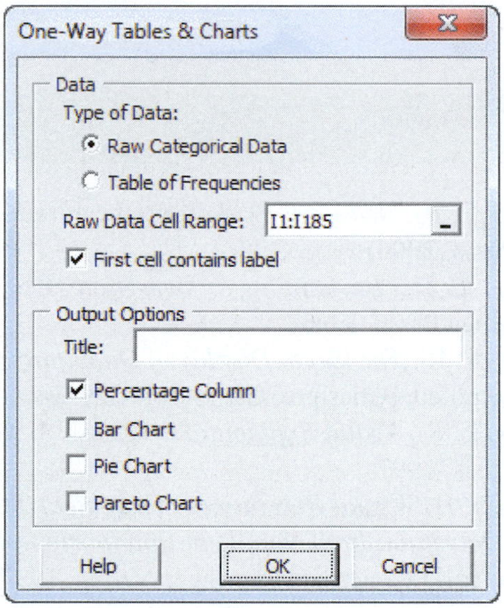

The DATA worksheet contains unsummarized data. For data that have already been tallied into categories, click **Table of Frequencies**.

In-Depth Excel For data that need to be tallied, use the PivotTable feature to create a summary table. (For the case in which data have already been tallied, use the **SUMMARY _SIMPLE worksheet** of the **Chapter 2 workbook** as a model for creating a summary table.)

For example, to create a summary table similar to Table 2.2 on page 30, open to the **DATA worksheet** of the **Bond Funds workbook** and select **Insert → PivotTable**. In the Create PivotTable dialog box (shown at the top of the next column):

1. Click **Select a table or range** and enter **I1:I185** as the **Table/Range** cell range.
2. Click **New Worksheet** and then click **OK**.

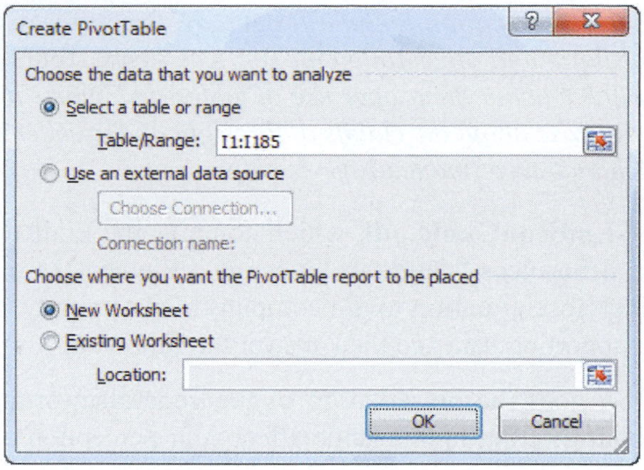

In the PivotTable Field List task pane (shown below):

3. Check **Risk** in the **Choose fields to add to report** box.
4. Drag the checked **Risk** label and drop it in the **Row Labels** box. Drag a second copy of this checked **Risk** label and drop it in the Σ **Values** box. This second label changes to **Count of Risk** to indicate that a count, or tally, of the occurrences of each risk category will be displayed in the PivotTable.

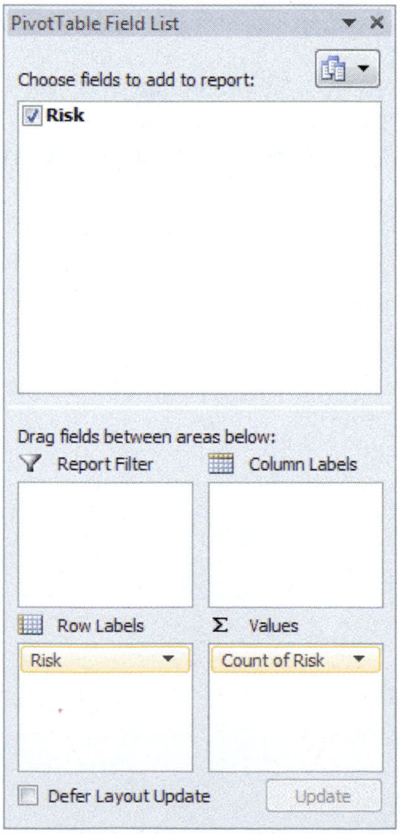

In the PivotTable being created:

5. Right-click and then click **PivotTable Options** in the shortcut menu that appears.

In the PivotTable Options dialog box (shown below):

6. Click the **Layout & Format** tab.
7. Check **For empty cells show** and enter **0** as its value. Leave all other settings unchanged.
8. Click **OK** to complete the PivotTable.

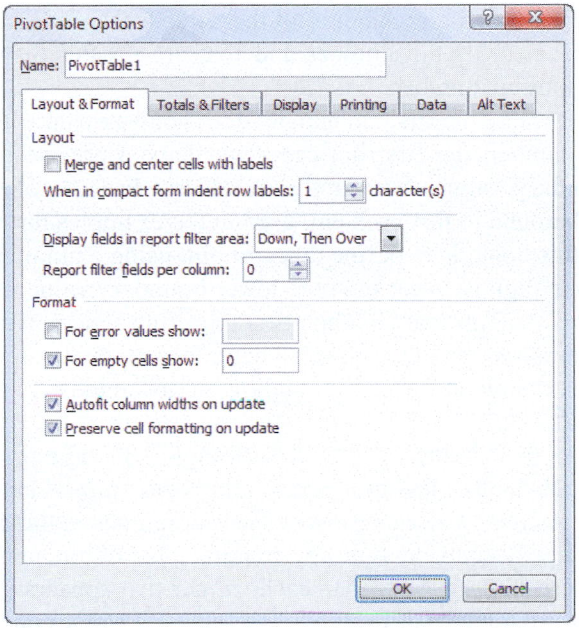

To add a column for the percentage frequency:

9. Enter **Percentage** in cell C4. Enter the formula **=B5/B$8** in cell **C5** and copy it down through row 7.
10. Select cell range **C5:E5**, right-click, and select **Format Cells** in the shortcut menu.
11. In the **Number** tab of the Format Cells dialog box, select **Percentage** as the **Category** and click **OK**.
12. Adjust cell borders, if desired (see Appendix F).

The Contingency Table

PHStat2 Use **Two-Way Tables & Charts** to create a contingency table for data that need to be tallied. For example, to create the Table 2.3 contingency table on page 31, open to the **DATA worksheet** of the **Bond Funds workbook**. Select **PHStat → Descriptive Statistics → Two-Way Tables & Charts**. In the procedure's dialog box (shown below):

1. Enter **B1:B185** as the **Row Variable Cell Range**.
2. Enter **D1:D185** as the **Column Variable Cell Range**.
3. Check **First cell in each range contains label**.
4. Enter a **Title** and click **OK**.

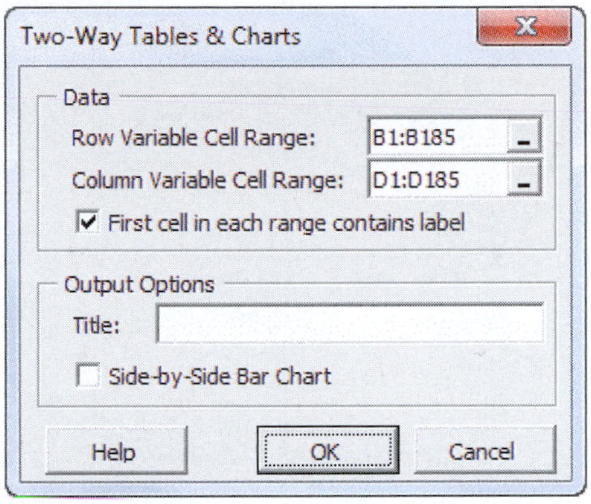

After the procedure creates the PivotTable, rearrange the order of the "No" and "Yes" columns:

5. Click the **Fees** drop-down list in cell B3 and select **Sort Z to A**.

In-Depth Excel For data that need to be tallied, use the PivotTable feature to create a contingency table. (For the case in which data have already been tallied, use the **CONTINGENCY_SIMPLE worksheet** of the **Chapter 2 workbook** as a model for creating a contingency table.) For example, to create the Table 2.3 contingency table on page 31, open to the **DATA worksheet** of the **Bond Funds workbook**. Select **Insert → PivotTable**. In the Create PivotTable dialog box:

1. Click **Select a table or range** and enter **B1:D185** as the **Table/Range** cell range. (Although **Type** is in column B and **Fees** is in column D, Excel does not allow you to enter a range comprised of nonadjacent columns.)
2. Click **New Worksheet** and then click **OK**.

In the PivotTable Field List task pane (shown at the top of page 78):

3. Check **Type** and **Fees** in the **Choose fields to add to report** box.
4. Drag the checked **Type** label and drop it in the **Row Labels** box.
5. Drag a second copy of the check **Type** label and drop it in the **Σ Values** box. (This label changes to **Count of Type**.) Then drag the checked **Fees** label and drop it in the **Column Labels** area.

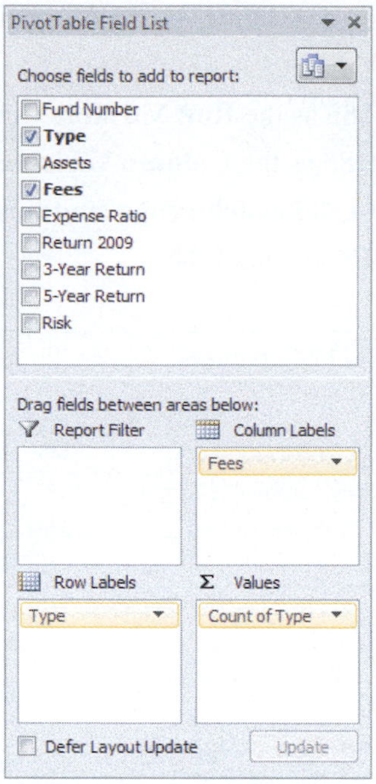

In the PivotTable being created:

6. Click the **Fees** drop-down list in cell B3 and select **Sort Z to A** to rearrange the order of the "No" and "Yes" columns.
7. Right-click and then click **PivotTable Options** in the shortcut menu that appears.

In the PivotTable Options dialog box:

8. Click the **Layout & Format** tab.
9. Check **For empty cells show** and enter **0** as its value. Leave all other settings unchanged.
10. Click the **Total & Filters** tab.
11. Check **Show grand totals for columns** and **Show grand totals for rows**.
12. Click **OK** to complete the table.

EG2.3 ORGANIZING NUMERICAL DATA

Stacked and Unstacked Data

PHStat2 Use **Stack Data** or **Unstack Data** to rearrange data. For example, to unstack the **Return 2009** variable in column F of the **DATA worksheet** of the **Bond Funds workbook**, open to that worksheet. Select **Data Preparation → Unstack Data**. In that procedure's dialog box, enter **B1:B185** (the Type variable cell range) as the **Grouping Variable Cell Range** and enter **F1:F185** as the **Stacked Data Cell Range**. Check **First cells in both ranges contain label** and click **OK**. The unstacked data appears on a new worksheet.

The Ordered Array

In-Depth Excel To create an ordered array, first select the data to be sorted. Then select **Home → Sort & Filter** (in the **Editing group**) **→ Sort Smallest to Largest**.

The Frequency Distribution, Part I

To create a frequency distribution, you must first translate your classes into what Excel calls *bins*. Bins approximate the classes of a frequency distribution. Unlike classes, bins do not have precise lower and upper boundary values. You establish bins by entering, in ascending order, a list of "bin numbers" into a column cell range. Each bin number, in turn, defines a bin: A bin is all the values that are less than or equal to its bin number and that are greater than the previous bin number.

Because the first bin number does not have a "previous" bin number, the first bin can never have a precise lower boundary value, as a first class always has. A common workaround to this problem, used in the examples throughout this book, is to define an extra bin, using a bin number that is slightly lower than the lower boundary value of the first class. This extra bin number, appearing first, will allow the now-second bin number to better approximate the first class, though at the cost of adding an unwanted bin to the results.

In this chapter, Tables 2.8 through 2.11 on pages 36 through 38 use class groupings in the form "*valueA* but less than *valueB*." You can translate class groupings in this form into nearly equivalent bins by creating a list of bin numbers that are slightly lower than each *valueB* that appears in the class groupings. For example, the Table 2.9 classes on page 36 could be translated into nearly equivalent bins by using this bin number list: –10.01 (the extra bin number), –5.01 ("slightly less" than –5), –0.01, –0.01, 4.99 (slightly less than 5), 9.99, 14.99, 19.99, 24.99, 29.99, and 34.99.

For class groupings in the form "all values from *valueA* to *valueB*," such as the set 0.0 through 4.9, 5.0 through 9.9, 10.0 through 14.9, and 15.0 through 19.9, you can approximate each class grouping by choosing a bin number slightly more than each *valueB*, as in this list of bin numbers: (the extra bin number), 4.99 (slightly more than 4.9), 9.99, 14.99, and 19.99.

Use an empty column in the worksheet that contains your untallied data to enter your bin numbers (in ascending order). Enter **Bins** in the row 1 cell of that column as the column heading. Enter your bin numbers before you use the Part II instructions to create frequency distributions.

When you create your own frequency distributions, you can include frequency, percentage, and/or cumulative percentages as columns of one distribution, unlike what is shown in Tables 2.8 through 2.11. Also, when you use Excel, you create frequency distributions for individual categories separately (e.g., a frequency distribution for intermediate government bond funds, followed by one for short-term corporate bond funds). To form worksheets that look like two-category Tables 2.8 through 2.11, you cut and paste parts of separately created frequency distributions. (Examine the **FD_IG** and **FD_STC worksheets** of the **Chapter 2 workbook** and then examine the **FD_COMBINED worksheet** to see how frequency distributions for an individual category can be cut and pasted to form one table.)

The Frequency Distribution, Part II

PHStat2 Use **Frequency Distribution** to create a frequency distribution. For example, to create the Table 2.9 frequency distribution on page 36, open to the **DATA worksheet** of the **Bond Funds workbook**. Select **PHStat → Descriptive Statistics → Frequency Distribution**. In the procedure's dialog box (shown below):

1. Enter **F1:F185** as the **Variable Cell Range**, enter **J1:J11** as the **Bins Cell Range**, and check **First cell in each range contains label**.
2. Click **Multiple Groups - Stacked** and enter **B1:B185** as the **Grouping Variable Cell Range**. (In the DATA worksheet, the 2009 returns for both types of bond funds are stacked, or placed in a single column. The column B values allow PHStat2 to unstack the returns for intermediate government funds from the returns for the short-term corporate funds.)
3. Enter a **Title** and click **OK**.

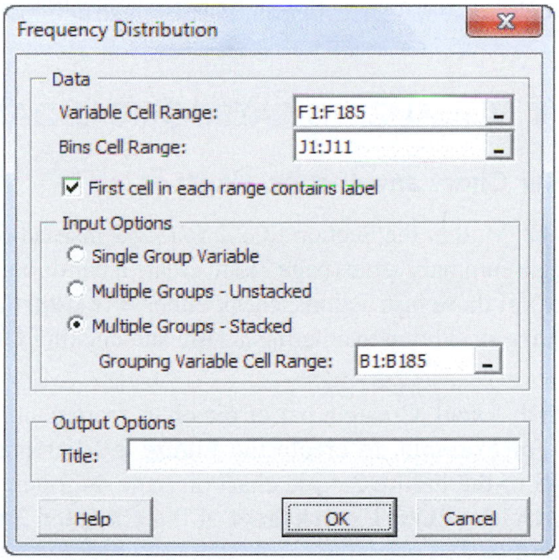

When creating other frequency distributions, if you use a worksheet that contains data for a single group, such as the **IGDATA** or **STCDATA worksheets**, click **Single Group Variable** in step 2. Note that the **Histogram & Polygons** procedure, discussed in Section EG2.5, also creates frequency distributions.

In-Depth Excel Use the **FREQUENCY** worksheet function and a bin number list (see "The Frequency Distribution, Part I" on page 78) to create a frequency distribution. For example, to create the Table 2.9 frequency distribution on page 36, open to and review the **IGDATA** and **STCDATA worksheets** of the **Bond Funds workbook**. Note that the worksheets divide the bond funds sample by fund type and that the two worksheets contain identical bin number lists in column J. With the workbook open to the IGDATA worksheet:

1. Right-click the **IGDATA sheet tab** and then click **Insert** in the shortcut menu. In the Insert dialog box, click the **Worksheet** icon and click **OK** to insert a new worksheet.
2. In the new worksheet, enter a worksheet title in cell **A1**, **Bins** in cell **A3**, and **Frequency** in cell **B3**.
3. Copy the **bin number list** that is in the cell range **J2:J11** of the IGDATA worksheet and paste this list into column A of the new worksheet, starting with cell **A4**.
4. Select the cell range **B4:B13** that will contain the frequency function.
5. Type, but do not press the **Enter** or **Tab** key, the formula **=FREQUENCY(IGDATA!$F$1:$F$88, $A$4:$A$13)**. Then, while holding down the **Ctrl** and **Shift** keys (or the **Apple** key on a Mac), press the **Enter** key. (This combination keystroke enters an "array formula," explained in Appendix F, in the cell range **B4:B13**.)

To create the frequency distribution for short-term corporate bonds, repeat steps 1 through 5 but enter the formula **=FREQUENCY(STCDATA!$F$1:$F$98, $A$4:$A$13)** in step 5. Then cut and paste the results from the two frequency distributions to create a table similar to Table 2.9.

Note that in step 5, you entered the cell range as **IGDATA!$F$1:$F$88** (or **STCDATA!$F$1:$F$98**) and not as **F1:F88** (or **F1:F98**) because the data to be summarized are located on another worksheet, and you wanted to use absolute cell references to facilitate the copying of the frequency column to create a table similar to Table 2.9.

Analysis ToolPak Use **Histogram** with a bin number list (see "The Frequency Distribution, Part I" on page 78) to create a frequency distribution. For example, to create the Table 2.9 frequency distribution on page 36, open to the **IGDATA worksheet** of the **Bond Funds workbook** and select **Data → Data Analysis**. In the Data Analysis dialog box, select **Histogram** from the **Analysis Tools** list and then click **OK**. In the Histogram dialog box (see the top of page 80):

1. Enter **F1:F88** as the **Input Range** and enter **J1:J11** as the **Bin Range**. (If you leave **Bin Range** blank, the procedure creates a set of bins that will not be as well-formed as the ones you can specify.)
2. Check **Labels** and click **New Worksheet Ply**.
3. Click **OK** to create the frequency distribution on a new worksheet.

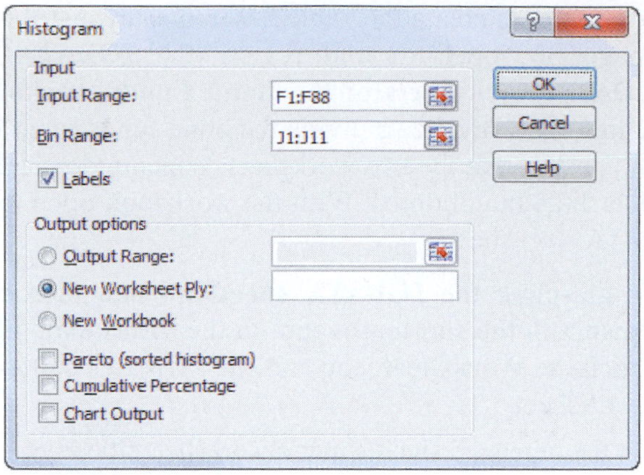

In the new worksheet:

4. Select row 1. Right-click row 1 and click the **Insert** shortcut menu. Repeat. (This creates two blank rows at the top of the worksheet.)
5. Enter a title for the frequency distribution in cell A1.

The ToolPak creates a frequency distribution that contains an improper bin labeled **More**. Correct this error as follows:

6. Manually add the frequency count of the **More** row to the count of the preceding bin. (This is unnecessary if the **More** count is 0, as it is in this Table 2.9 example.)
7. Click the worksheet row number for the **More** row (to select the entire worksheet row), right-click on the row, and click **Delete** in the shortcut menu that appears.

Open to the **STCDATA worksheet** and repeat steps 1 through 7 with rows 1 through 98. Then cut and paste the results from the two frequency distributions to create a table similar to Table 2.9.

The Relative Frequency, Percentage, or Cumulative Percentage Distribution

PHStat2 To create these other distributions, first use the *PHStat2* instructions in "The Frequency Distribution, Part II" to create a frequency distribution that contains a column of percentages and cumulative percentages. To create a column of relative frequencies, reformat the percentage column. Select the cells containing the percentages, right-click, and then select **Format Cells** from the shortcut menu. In the **Number** tab of the Format Cells dialog box, select **Number** as the **Category** and click **OK**.

In-Depth Excel To create these other distributions, modify a frequency distribution created using the *In-Depth Excel* instructions in "The Frequency Distribution, Part II" by adding a column for percentages (or relative frequencies) and a column for cumulative percentages. For example, open to the **FD_IG worksheet** of the **Chapter 2 workbook**. This worksheet contains the frequency distribution for the intermediate government bond funds. To modify this worksheet to include percentage and cumulative percentage distributions:

1. Enter **Total** in cell **A14** and enter **=SUM(B4:B13)** in cell **B14**.
2. Enter **Percentage** in cell **C3** and **Cumulative Pctage** in cell **D3**.
3. Enter **=B4/$B$14** in cell **C4** and copy this formula down through all the rows of the frequency distribution.
4. Enter **= C4** in cell **D4**. Enter **=D4 + C5** in cell **D5** and copy this formula down through all the rows of the frequency distribution.
5. Select the cell range **C4:D13**, right-click, and click **Format Cells** in the shortcut menu.
6. In the **Number** tab of the Format Cells dialog box, select **Percentage** as the **Category** and click **OK**.

If you want a column of relative frequencies instead of percentages, change the cell **C4** column heading to **Rel. Frequencies**. Then select the cell range **C4:C13**, right-click, and click **Format Cells** in the shortcut menu. In the **Number** tab of the Format Cells dialog box, select **Number** as the **Category** and click **OK**.

Analysis ToolPak Use the preceding *In-Depth Excel* instructions to modify a frequency distribution created using the "The Frequency Distribution, Part II" instructions.

EG2.4 VISUALIZING CATEGORICAL DATA

The Bar Chart and the Pie Chart

PHStat2 Modify the Section EG2.2 *PHStat2* instructions for creating a summary table (page 76) to create a bar or pie chart. In step 3 of those instructions, check either **Bar Chart** and/or **Pie Chart** in addition to entering a **Title** and clicking **OK**.

In-Depth Excel Create a bar or pie chart from a summary table. For example, to create the Figure 2.2 bar chart on page 43 or the Figure 2.4 pie chart on page 44, open to the **SUMMARY_PIVOT worksheet** of the **Chapter 2 workbook** and:

1. Select cell range **A4:B7** (Begin your selection at cell B7 and not at cell A4, as you would normally do).
2. Click **Insert**. For a bar chart, click **Bar** in the **Charts group** and then select the first **2-D Bar** gallery choice (**Clustered Bar**). For a pie chart, click **Pie** in the **Charts group** and then select the first **2-D Pie** gallery choice (**Pie**).
3. Relocate the chart to a chart sheet and adjust chart formatting by using the instructions in Appendix Section F.4 on page 815.

For a pie chart, select **Layout ➔Data Labels ➔ More Data Label Options**. In the Format Data Labels dialog box, click **Label Options** in the left pane. In the Label Options right pane, check **Category Name** and **Percentage** and clear the other check boxes. Click **Outside End** and then click **Close**.

For a bar chart, if the horizontal axis scale does not begin with 0, right-click the horizontal (value) axis and click **Format Axis** in the shortcut menu. In the Format Axis dialog box, click **Axis Options** in the left pane. In the Axis Options right pane, click the first **Fixed** option button (for Minimum) and enter **0** in its box. Click **Close**.

The Pareto Chart

PHStat2 Modify the Section EG2.2 *PHStat2* instructions for creating a summary table on page 76 to create a Pareto chart. In step 3 of those instructions, check **Pareto Chart** in addition to entering a **Title** and clicking **OK**.

In-Depth Excel To create a Pareto chart, modify the summary table that was originally created using the instructions in Section EG2.3. In the original table, first sort the table in order of decreasing frequencies and then add a column for cumulative percentage. Use the sorted, modified table to create the Pareto chart.

For example, to create the Figure 2.5 Pareto chart, open to the **ATMTable worksheet** of the **ATM Transactions workbook**. Begin by sorting the modified table by decreasing order of frequency:

1. Select row **11** (the Total row), right-click, and click **Hide** in the shortcut menu. (This prevents the total row from getting sorted.)
2. Select cell **B4** (the first frequency), right-click, and select **Sort ➔ Sort Largest to Smallest**.
3. Select rows **10** and **12** (there is no row 11), right-click, and click **Unhide** in the shortcut menu.

Next, add a column for cumulative percentage:

4. Enter **Cumulative Pctage** in cell **D3**. Enter **=C4** in cell **D4**. Enter **=D4 + C5** in cell **D5** and copy this formula down through row 10.
5. Select the cell range **C4:D10**, right-click, and click **Format Cells** in the shortcut menu.
6. In the **Number** tab of the Format Cells dialog box, select **Percentage** as the **Category** and click **OK**.

Next, create the Pareto chart:

7. Select the cell range **A3:A10** and while holding down the **Ctrl** key also select the cell range **C3:D10**.
8. Select **Insert ➔ Column** (in the Charts group) and select the first **2-D Column** gallery choice (**Clustered Column**).
9. Select **Format** (under **Chart Tools**). In the Current Selection group, select the entry for the cumulative percentage series from the drop-down list and then click **Format Selection**.
10. In the Format Data Series dialog box, click **Series Options** in the left pane and in the **Series Options** right pane, click **Secondary Axis**. Click **Close**.
11. With the cumulative percentage series still selected in the Current Selection group, select **Design ➔ Change Chart Type**, and in the **Change Chart Type** gallery, select the fourth **Line** gallery choice (**Line with Markers**). Click **OK**.

Next, set the maximum value of the primary and secondary (left and right) *Y* axes scales to 100%. For each *Y* axis:

12. Right-click on the axis and click **Format Axis** in the shortcut menu.
13. In the Format Axis dialog box, click **Axis Options** in the left pane and in the **Axis Options** right pane, click the second **Fixed** option button (for Maximum) and enter **1** in its box. Click **Close**.

Relocate the chart to a chart sheet and adjust chart formatting by using the instructions in Appendix Section F.4 on page.

When using a PivotTable as a summary table, table sorting is simpler: Right-click the cell that contains the first frequency (cell B5 in the sample worksheet) and select **Sort ➔ Sort Largest to Smallest**. However, creating a Pareto chart from a PivotTable with additional columns for percentage and cumulative percentage is much more difficult than creating a chart from a simple summary table. The best workaround is to convert the PivotTable to a simple summary table by copying the category names and frequencies in the PivotTable, along with the additional columns, to an empty worksheet area.

The Side-by-Side Chart

PHStat2 Modify the Section EG2.2 *PHStat2* instructions for creating a contingency table on page 77 to create a side-by-side chart. In step 4 of those instructions, check **Side-by-Side Bar Chart** in addition to entering a **Title** and clicking **OK**.

In-Depth Excel Create a chart based on a contingency table to create a side-by-side chart. For example, to create the Figure 2.7 side-by-side bar chart on page 47, open to the **CONTINGENCY_PIVOT worksheet** of the **Chapter 2 workbook** and:

1. Select cell **A4** (or any other cell inside the PivotTable).
2. Select **Insert ➔ Bar** and select the first **2-D Bar** gallery choice (**Clustered Bar**). Relocate the chart to a chart sheet and adjust the chart formatting by using the instructions in Appendix Section F.4 on page, but with this exception: When you click **Legend**, select **Show Legend at Right**.

When creating a chart from a contingency table that is not a PivotTable, select the cell range of the contingency table, including row and column headings, but excluding the total row and total column, before selecting **Insert → Bar**.

Occasionally when you create a side-by-side chart, the row and column variables need to be swapped. If a PivotTable is the source for the chart, rearrange the PivotTable by making the row variable the column variable and vice versa. If the chart is not based on a PivotTable, right-click the chart and then click **Select Data** in the shortcut menu. In the Select Data Source dialog box, click **Switch Row/Column** and then click **OK**. (In Excel 2010, you can also use this second method for PivotTable-based charts.)

You may also need to rearrange the order of categories shown on the chart. To flip their positions for a chart based on a PivotTable, click the pull-down list for the categorical variable that needs to be rearranged and select **Sort A to Z**. In this example, after step 2, click the **Fees** pull-down list for the categorical variable that needs to be rearranged and select **Sort A to Z**. To rearrange the order of categories for a chart not based on a PivotTable, physically rearrange the worksheet columns that contain the data for the chart.

EG2.5 VISUALIZING NUMERICAL DATA

The Stem-and-Leaf Display

PHStat2 Use the **Stem-and-Leaf Display** procedure to create a stem-and-leaf display. For example, to create a stem-and-leaf display similar to Figure 2.8 on page 50, open to the **STCDATA worksheet** of the **Chapter 2 workbook**. Select **PHStat → Descriptive Statistics → Stem-and-Leaf Display**. In the procedure's dialog box (shown below):

1. Enter **F1:F98** as the **Variable Cell Range** and check **First cell contains label**.
2. Leave **Autocalculate stem unit** selected.
3. Enter a **Title** and click **OK**.

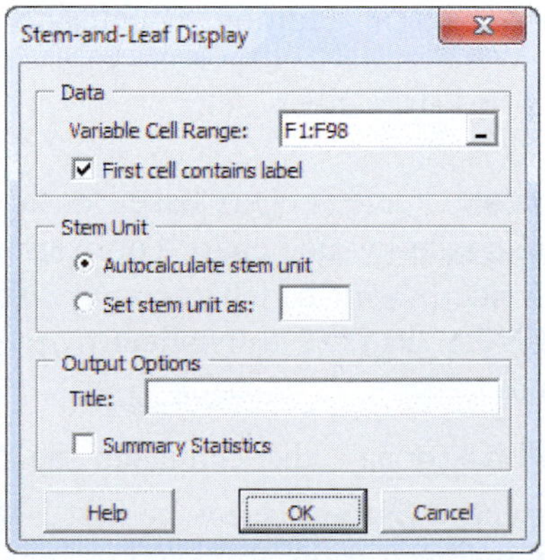

Because Minitab uses a truncation method and PHStat2 uses a rounding method, the leaves of the PHStat2 display differ slightly from Figure 2.8 (created using Minitab).

When creating other displays, use the **Set stem unit as** option sparingly and only if **Autocalculate stem unit** creates a display that has too few or too many stems. (Any stem unit you specify must be a power of 10.)

In-Depth Excel Manually construct the stems and leaves on a new worksheet to create a stem-and-leaf display. Use the **STEM_LEAF worksheet** of the **Chapter 2 workbook** as a guide to formatting your display.

The Histogram

PHStat2 Use the **Histogram & Polygons** procedure to create a histogram from unsummarized data. For example, to create the pair of histograms shown in Figure 2.10 on page 51, open to the **DATA worksheet** of the **Bond Funds workbook**. Select **PHStat → Descriptive Statistics → Histogram & Polygons**. In the procedure's dialog box (shown below):

1. Enter **F1:F185** as the **Variable Cell Range**, **J1:J11** as the **Bins Cell Range**, **K1:K10** as the **Midpoints Cell Range**, and check **First cell in each range contains label**.
2. Click **Multiple Groups - Stacked** and enter **B1:B185** as the **Grouping Variable Cell Range**. (In the DATA worksheet, the 2009 returns for both types of bond funds are stacked, or placed in a single column. The column B values allow PHStat2 to separate the returns for intermediate government funds from the returns for the short-term corporate funds.)
3. Enter a **Title**, check **Histogram**, and click **OK**.

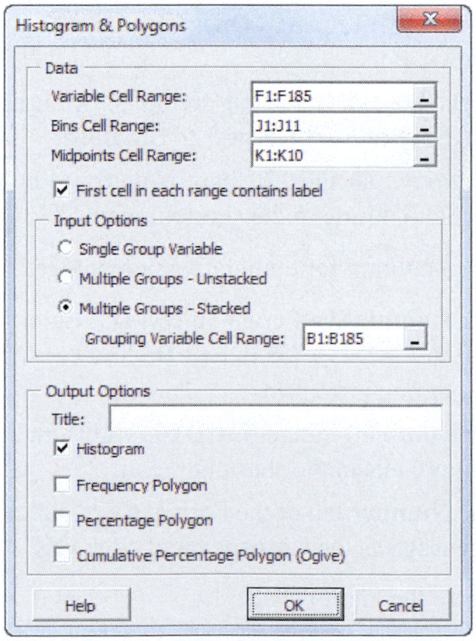

The **Bins Cell Range** and the **Midpoints Cell Range** should appear in the same worksheet as the unsummarized data, as the DATA worksheet of the Bond Funds workbook illustrates. Because a first bin can never have a midpoint (because that bin does not have a lower boundary value defined), the procedure assigns the first midpoint to the second bin and uses "---" as the label for the first bin. Therefore, the **Midpoints Cell Range** you enter must be one cell smaller in size than the **Bins Cell Range**. Read "The Histogram: Follow-up" in the next column for an additional adjustment that you can apply to the histograms created.

In-Depth Excel Create a chart from a frequency distribution. For example, to create the Figure 2.10 pair of histograms on page 51, first use the Section EG2.4 "The Frequency Distribution, Part II" *In-Depth Excel* instructions on page 79.

Follow those instructions to create a pair of frequency distributions, one for the intermediate government bond funds, and the other for the short-term corporate bond funds, on separate worksheets. In each worksheet, add a column of midpoints by entering the column heading **Midpoints** in cell **C3**, **'---** in cell **C4**, and starting in cell **C5**, the midpoints **-7.5, -2.5, 2.5, 7.5, 12.5, 17.5, 22.5, 27.5, and 32.5.** In each worksheet:

1. Select the cell range **B3:B13** (the cell range of the frequencies).
2. Select **Insert → Column** and select the first **2-D Column** gallery choice (**Clustered Column**).
3. Right-click the chart background and click **Select Data**.

In the Select Data Source dialog box:

4. Click **Edit** under the **Horizontal (Categories) Axis Labels** heading.
5. In the Axis Labels dialog box, enter the cell range *formula* in the form =***SheetName*!C4:C13** (where ***SheetName*** is the name of the current worksheet) and then click **OK** to return to the Select Data Source dialog box.
6. Click **OK**.

In the chart:

7. Right-click inside a bar and click **Format Data Series** in the shortcut menu.

In the Format Data Series dialog box:

8. Click **Series Options** in the left pane. In the Series Options right pane, change the **Gap Width** slider to **No Gap**. Click **Close**.

Relocate the chart to a chart sheet and adjust the chart formatting by using the instructions in Appendix Section F.4 on page. Read "The Histogram: Follow-up" on page for an additional adjustment that you can apply to the histograms created.

Analysis ToolPak Modify the Section EG2.3 Analysis ToolPak instructions for "The Frequency Distribution, Part II" on page 79 to create a histogram. In step 5 of those instructions, check **Chart Output** before clicking **OK**.

For example, to create the pair of histograms in Figure 2.10 on page 51, use the modified step 5 with both the **IGDATA** and **STCDATA** worksheets of the **Chapter 2 workbook** (as discussed on page 79) to create a pair of worksheets that contain a frequency distribution and a histogram. Each histogram will have (the same) two formatting errors that you can correct:

To eliminate the gaps between bars:

1. Right-click inside one of the histogram bars and click **Format Data Series** in the shortcut menu that appears.
2. In the **Series Options pane** of the Format Data Series dialog box, move the **Gap Width** slider to **No Gap** and click **Close**.

To change the histogram bin labels:

1. Enter the column heading **Midpoints** in cell **C3** and enter **'---** in cell **C4** (the first bin has no midpoint). Starting in cell **C5**, enter the midpoints −7.5, −2.5, 2.5, 7.5, 12.5, 17.5, 22.5, 27.5, and 32.5, in column C. (The midpoints will serve as the new bin labels in step 3.)
2. Right-click the chart background and click **Select Data**.
3. In the Select Data Source dialog box, click **Edit** under the **Horizontal (Categories) Axis Labels** heading. In the Axis Labels dialog box, enter the cell range *formula* in the form =***SheetName*!C4:C13** as the **Axis label range** and click **OK**. Back in the Select Data Source dialog box, click **OK** to complete the task.

In step 3, substitute the name of the worksheet that contains the frequency distribution and histogram for ***SheetName*** and note that the cell range **C4:C13** does not include the column heading cell. Read the next section for an additional adjustment that you can apply to the histograms created.

The Histogram: Follow-up

Because the example used throughout "The Histogram" uses a technique that uses an extra bin (see "The Frequency Distribution, Part I" in Section EG2.4), the histogram created will have the extra, meaningless bin. If you would like to remove this extra bin, as was done for the histograms shown in Figure 2.10, right-click the histogram background and click **Select Data**. In the Select Data Source Data dialog box, first click **Edit** under the **Legend Entries (Series)** heading. In the Edit Series dialog box, edit the **Series values** cell range formula. Then click **Edit** under the **Horizontal (Categories) Axis Labels** heading. In the Axis Labels dialog box, edit the **Axis label range**. For the example used in the previous section, change the starting cell for the **Series values** cell range formula from B4 to B5 and change the starting cell for the **Axis label range** cell range formula from C4 to C5.

The Percentage Polygon

PHStat2 Modify the *PHStat2* instructions for creating a histogram on page 82 to create a percentage polygon. In step 3 of those instructions, click **Percentage Polygon** before clicking **OK**.

In-Depth Excel Create a chart based on a modified percentage distribution to create a percentage polygon. For example, to create the Figure 2.12 percentage polygons on page 52, open to the **CPD_IG worksheet** of the **Bond Funds workbook**. (This worksheet contains a frequency distribution for the intermediate government bond funds and includes columns for the percentages and cumulative percentages in column C and D.) Begin by modifying the distribution:

1. Enter the column heading **Midpoints** in cell **E3** and enter **'---** in cell **E4** (the first bin has no midpoint). Starting in cell **E5**, enter **-7.5, -2.5, 2.5, 7.5, 12.5, 17.5, 22.5, 27.5, and 32.5,** in column E.
2. Select row 4 (the first bins row), right-click, and select **Insert** in the shortcut menu.
3. Select row 15 (the total row), right-click, and select **Insert** in the shortcut menu.
4. Enter **0** in cells **C4**, **D4** and **C15**.
5. Select the cell range **C3:C15**.

Next, create the chart:

6. Select **Insert → Line** and select the fourth **2-D Line** gallery choice (**Line with Markers**).
7. Right-click the chart and click **Select Data** in the shortcut menu.

In the Select Data Source dialog box:

8. Click **Edit** under the **Legend Entries (Series)** heading. In the Edit Series dialog box, enter the formula **="Intermediate Government"** for the Series name and click **OK**.
9. Click **Edit** under the **Horizontal (Categories) Axis Labels** heading. In the Axis Labels dialog box, enter the cell range formula **=CPD_IG!E4:E15** for the **Axis label range** and click **OK**.
10. Back in the Select Data Source dialog box, click **OK**.

Back in the chart sheet:

11. Right-click the vertical axis and click **Format Axis** in the shortcut menu.
12. In the Format Axis dialog box, click **Number** in left pane and then select **Percentage** from the **Category** list in the Number right pane. Enter **0** as the **Decimal places** and click **OK**.

Relocate the chart to a chart sheet and adjust chart formatting by using the instructions in Appendix Section F.4 on page.

Figure 2.12 on page 52 also contains the percentage polygon for the short-term corporate bond funds. To add this polygon to the chart just created, open to the **CPD_STC worksheet**. Repeat steps 1 through 5 to modify this distribution. Then open to the chart sheet that contains the intermediate government polygon. Select **Layout → Legend → Show Legend at Right**. Right-click the chart and click **Select Data** in the shortcut menu. In the Select Data Source dialog box, click **Add**. In the Edit Series dialog box, enter the formula **="Short Term Corporate"** as the **Series name** and enter the cell range formula **=CPD_STC!C4:C15** as the **Series values**. Click **OK**. Back in the Select Data Source dialog box, click **OK**.

The Cumulative Percentage Polygon (Ogive)

PHStat2 Modify the *PHStat2* instructions for creating a histogram on page 82 to create a cumulative percentage polygon, In step 3 of those instructions, click **Cumulative Percentage Polygon (Ogive)** before clicking **OK**.

In-Depth Excel Create a cumulative percentage polygon by modifying the *In-Depth Excel* instructions for creating a percentage polygon. For example, to create the Figure 2.14 cumulative percentage polygons on page 54, use the instructions for creating percentage polygons, replacing steps 4 and 8 with the following:

4. Select the cell range **D3:D14.**
8. Click **Edit** under the **Horizontal (Categories) Axis Labels** heading. In the Axis Labels dialog box, enter the cell range formula **=CPD_IG!A4:A14** for the **Axis label range** and click **OK**.

Later, when adding the second polygon for the short-term corporate bond funds, enter the cell range formula **=CPD_STC!D4:D14** as the **Series values** in the Edit Series dialog box.

EG2.6 VISUALIZING TWO NUMERICAL VARIABLES

The Scatter Plot

PHStat2 Use the **Scatter Plot** procedure to create a scatter plot. For example, to create a scatter plot similar to the one shown in Figure 2.15 on page 57, open to the **DATA worksheet** of the **NBAValues workbook**. Select **PHStat2 → Descriptive Statistics → Scatter Plot**. In the procedure's dialog box (shown below):

1. Enter **C1:C31** as the **Y Variable Cell Range**.
2. Enter **B1:B31** as the **X Variable Cell Range**.
3. Check **First cells in each range contains label**.
4. Enter a **Title** and click **OK**.

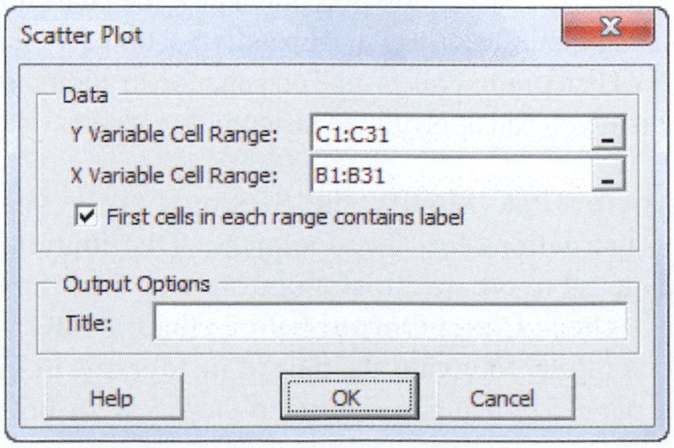

You can also use the **Scatter Plot** output option of the **Simple Linear Regression** procedure to create a scatter plot. Scatter plots created using this alternative will contain a superimposed line like the one seen in Figure 2.15. (See the Excel Guide for Chapter 13 for the instructions for using the Simple Linear Regression procedure.)

In-Depth Excel Use a worksheet in which the column for the *X* variable data is to the left of the column for the *Y* variable data to create a scatter plot. (If the worksheet is arranged *Y* then *X*, cut and paste the *Y* variable column to the right of the *X* variable column.)

For example, to create a scatter plot similar to the one shown in Figure 2.15 on page 57, open to the **DATA worksheet** of the **NBAValues workbook** and:

1. Select the cell range **B1:C31.**
2. Select **Insert ➔ Scatter** and select the first **Scatter** gallery choice (**Scatter with only Markers**).
3. Select **Layout ➔ Trendline ➔ Linear Trendline**.

Relocate the chart to a chart sheet and adjust the chart formatting by using the instructions in Appendix Section F.4 on page.

The Time-Series Plot

In-Depth Excel Create a chart from a worksheet in which the column for the time variable data appears to the immediate left of the column for the numerical variable data. (Use cut and paste to rearrange columns, if necessary.)

For example, to create the Figure 2.16 time-series plot on page 58, open to the **DATA worksheet** of the **MovieGross workbook** and:

1. Select the cell range **A1:B15**.
2. Select **Insert ➔ Scatter** and select the fourth **Scatter** gallery choice (**Scatter with Straight Lines and Markers**).

Relocate the chart to a chart sheet and adjust chart formatting by using the instructions in Appendix Section F.4 on page.

EG2.7 ORGANIZING MULTIDIMENSIONAL DATA

Multidimensional Contingency Tables

In-Depth Excel Use PivotTables to create multidimensional contingency tables. For example, to create the Figure 2.18 fund type, risk, and fees table on page 61, open to the **DATA worksheet** of the **Bond Funds workbook** and select **Insert ➔ PivotTable**. In the Create PivotTable dialog box:

1. Click **Select a table or range** and enter **A1:I185** as the **Table/Range**.
2. Click **New Worksheet** and then click **OK**.

In the PivotTable Field List task pane (shown below):

3. Drag **Type** in the **Choose fields to add to report** box and drop it in the **Row Labels** box.
4. Drag **Risk** in the **Choose fields to add to report** box and drop it in the **Row Labels** box.
5. Drag **Fees** in the **Choose fields to add to report** box and drop it in the **Column Labels** box.
6. Drag **Fees** in the **Choose fields to add to report** box a second time and drop it in the **Σ Values** box. (This label changes to **Count of Fees**.)

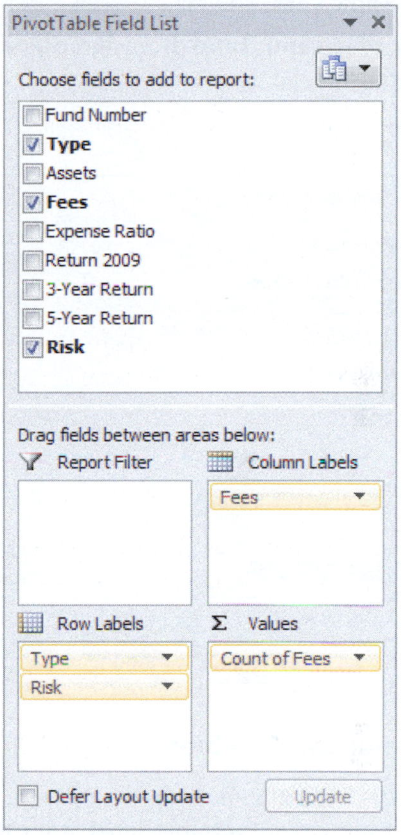

In the PivotTable being created:

7. Click the **Fees** drop-down list in cell B3 and select **Sort Z to A** to rearrange the order of the "No" and "Yes" columns.
8. Right-click and then click **PivotTable Options** in the shortcut menu that appears.

In the PivotTable Options dialog box:

9. Click the **Layout & Format** tab.
10. Check **For empty cells, show** and enter **0** as its value. Leave all other settings unchanged.
11. Click the **Total & Filters** tab.
12. Check **Show grand totals for columns** and **Show grand totals for rows.**
13. Click **OK** to complete the table.

If you create a PivotTable from an **.xlsx** file in Excel 2007 or later, the default formatting of the PivotTable will differ from the formatting of the PivotTables shown in Section 2.7. Also, in step 7 you will always see **Column Labels** as the name of drop-down list and that drop-down list will appear in cell B3.

To display the cell values as percentages, as was done in Figures 2.20 and 2.21 on page 62, click **Count of Fees** in the PivotTable Field List task pane and then click **Value Field Settings** from the shortcut menu. In the Value Field Settings dialog box (shown below):

1. Click the **Show Values As** tab.
2. Select **% of Grand Total** from the **Show values as** drop-down list.
3. Click **OK**.

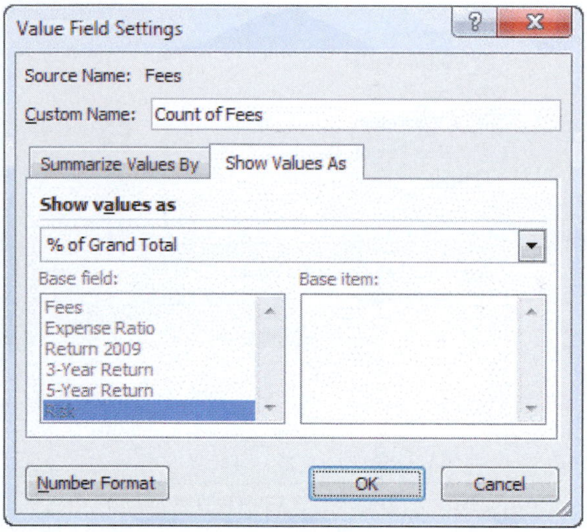

Adding Numerical Variables

In-Depth Excel Add a numerical variable to a PivotTable by dragging a numerical variable label from the **Choose fields to add to report** box to the Σ **Values** box and deleting the **Count of *categorical variable*** label (by dragging the label and dropping it anywhere outside the Σ **Values** box). To display something other than the sum of the numerical variable, click the **Sum of *numerical variable*** and then click **Value Field Settings** and make the appropriate entries in the Value Field Settings dialog box.

For example, to create the Figure 2.22 PivotTable of fund type, risk, and fees, showing averages of the 2009 return (see page 62) from the Figure 2.18 PivotTable, first create the Figure 2.18 PivotTable using steps 1 through 12 of the preceding section. Then continue with these steps:

13. Drag **Return 2009** in the **Choose fields to add to report** box and drop it in the Σ Values box. (This label changes to **Sum of Return 2009**.)
14. Drag **Count of Fees** in the Σ **Values** box and drop it anywhere outside that box.
15. Click **Sum of Return 2009** and click **Value Field Settings** from the shortcut menu.

In the Value Field Settings dialog box (shown below):

16. Click the **Summarize Values By** tab and select **Average** from the list. The label **Sum of Return 2009** changes to **Average of Return 2009**.
17. Click **OK**.

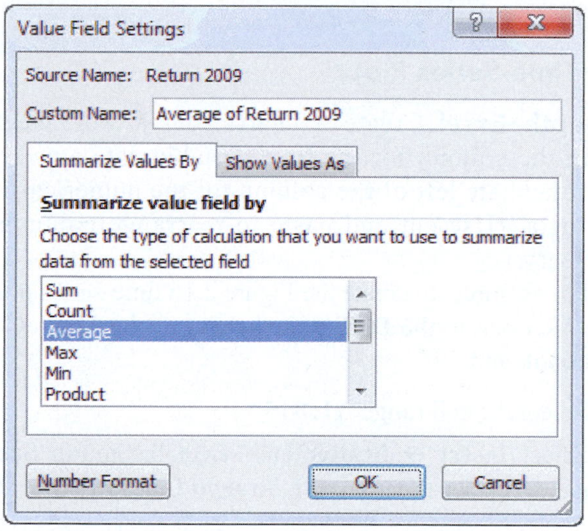

Adjust cell formatting and decimal place display as required (see Appendix F).

CHAPTER 2 MINITAB GUIDE

MG2.2 ORGANIZING CATEGORICAL DATA

The Summary Table

Use **Tally Individual Variables** to create a summary table. For example, to create a summary table similar to Table 2.2 on page 30, open to the **Bond Funds worksheet**. Select **Stat → Tables → Tally Individual Variables**. In the procedure's dialog box (shown below):

1. Double-click **C9 Risk** in the variables list to add **Risk** to the **Variables** box.
2. Check **Counts** and **Percents**.
3. Click **OK**.

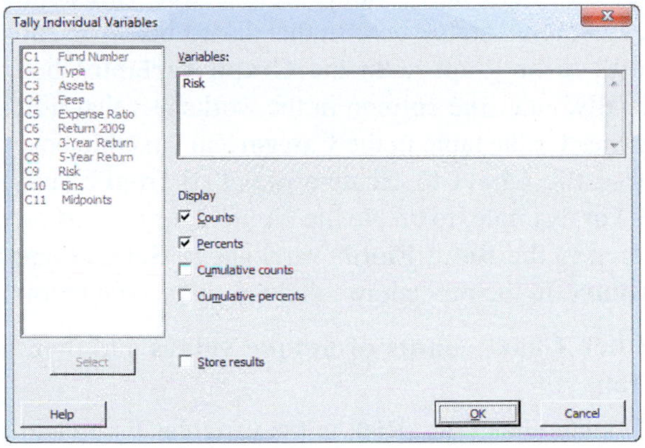

The Contingency Table

Use **Cross Tabulation and Chi-Square** to create a contingency table. For example, to create a contingency table similar to Table 2.3 on page 31, open to the **Bond Funds worksheet**. Select **Stat → Tables → Cross Tabulation and Chi-Square**. In the procedure's dialog box (shown below):

1. Enter **Type** in the **For rows** box.
2. Enter **Fees** in the **For columns** box
3. Check **Counts**.
4. Click **OK**.

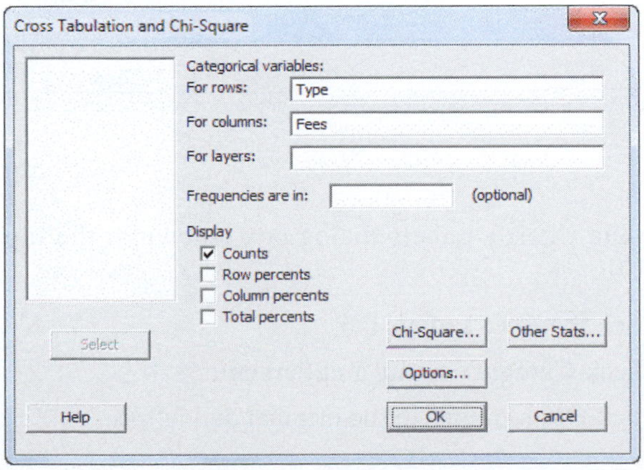

To create the other types of contingency tables shown in Tables 2.4 through 2.6, change step 3 by checking other additional **Display** items.

MG2.3 ORGANIZING NUMERICAL DATA

Stacked and Unstacked Data

Use **Stack** or **Unstack Columns** to rearrange data. For example, to unstack the **Return 2009** variable in column C6 of the **Bond Funds worksheet**, open to that worksheet. Select **Data → Unstack Columns**. In the procedure's dialog box (shown below):

1. Double-click **C6 Return 2009** in the variables list to add **'Return 2009'** to the **Unstack the data in** box and press **Tab**.
2. Double-click **C2 Type** in the variables list to add **Type** to the **Using subscripts in** box.
3. Click **After last column in use**.
4. Check **Name the columns containing the unstacked data**.
5. Check **OK**.

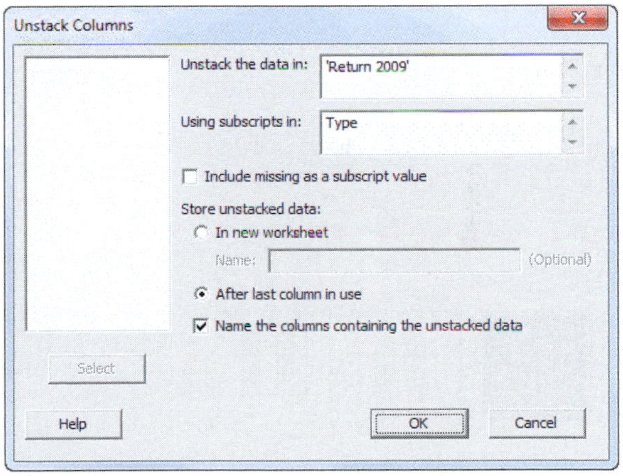

Minitab inserts two new columns, **Return 2009_Intermediate Government** and **Return 2009_Short Term Corporate**, the names of which you can edit.

To stack columns, select **Data → Stack → Columns**. In the Stack Columns dialog box, add the names of columns that contain the data to be stacked to the **Stack the following columns** box and then click either **New worksheet** or **Column of current worksheet** as the place to store the stacked data.

The Ordered Array

Use **Sort** to create an ordered array. Select **Data → Sort** and in the Sort dialog box (not shown), double-click a column name in the variables list to add it to the **Sort column(s)** box and then press **Tab.** Double-click the same column name in the variables list to add it to the first **By column** box. Click either **New worksheet**, **Original column(s)**, or **Column(s) of current worksheet**. (If you choose the third option, also enter the name of the column in which to place the ordered data in the box). Click **OK**.

The Frequency Distribution

There are no Minitab commands that use classes that you specify to create frequency distributions of the type seen in Tables 2.8 through 2.11. (See also "The Histogram" in Section MG2.5.)

MG2.4 VISUALIZING CATEGORICAL DATA

The Bar Chart and the Pie Chart

Use **Bar Chart** to create a bar chart from a summary table and use **Pie Chart** to create a pie chart from a summary table. For example, to create the Figure 2.2 bar chart on page 43, open to the **Bond Funds worksheet**. Select **Graph ➔ Bar Chart**. In the procedure's dialog box (shown below):

1. Select **Counts of unique values** from the **Bars represent** drop-down list.
2. In the gallery of choices, click **Simple**.
3. Click **OK**.

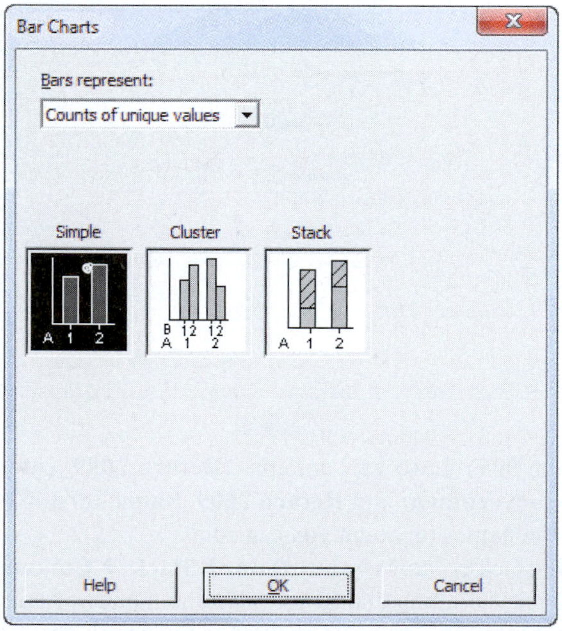

In the Bar Chart - Counts of unique values, Simple dialog box (see the top of the next column):

4. Double-click **C9 Risk** in the variables list to add **Risk** to **Categorical variables**.
5. Click **OK**.

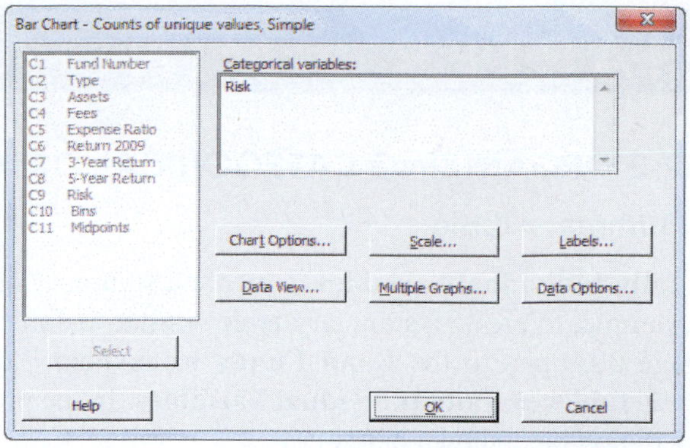

If your data are in the form of a table of frequencies, select **Values from a table** from the **Bars represent** drop-down list in step 1. With this selection, clicking **OK** in step 3 will display the "Bar Chart - Values from a table, One column of values, Simple" dialog box. In this dialog box, you enter the columns to be graphed in the **Graph variables** box and, optionally, enter the column in the worksheet that holds the categories for the table in the **Categorical variable** box.

Use **Pie Chart** to create a pie chart from a summary table. For example, to create the Figure 2.4 pie chart on page 44, open to the **Bond Funds worksheet**. Select **Graph ➔ Pie Chart**. In the procedure's dialog box (shown below):

1. Click **Chart counts of unique values** and then press **Tab**.
2. Double-click **C9 Risk** in the variables list to add **Risk** to **Categorical variables**.
3. Click **Labels**.

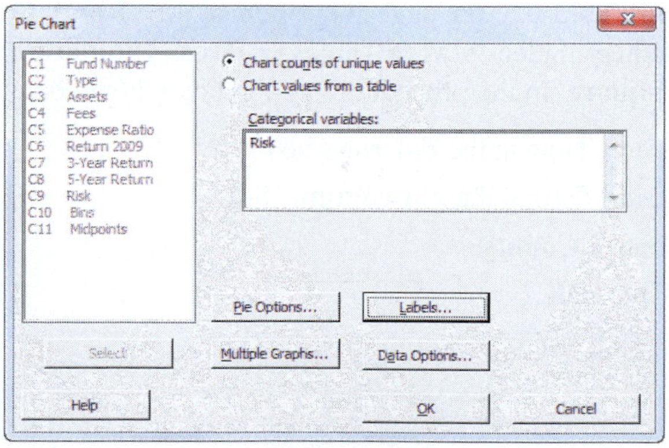

In the Pie Chart - Labels dialog box (shown at the top of page 89):

4. Click the **Slice Labels** tab.
5. Check **Category name** and **Percent**.
6. Click **OK** to return to the original dialog box.

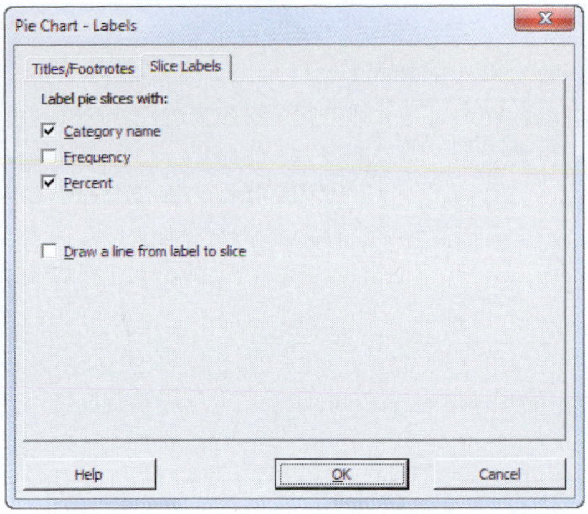

Back in the original Pie Chart dialog box:

7. Click **OK**.

The Pareto Chart

Use **Pareto Chart** to create a Pareto chart. For example, to create the Figure 2.5 Pareto chart on page 45, open to the **ATM Transactions worksheet**. Select **Stat → Quality Tools → Pareto Chart**. In the procedure's dialog box (shown below):

1. Double-click **C1 Cause** in the variables list to add **Cause** to the **Defects or attribute data in** box.
2. Double-click **C2 Frequency** in the variables list to add **Frequency** to the **Frequencies in** box.
3. Click **Do not combine**.
4. Click **OK**.

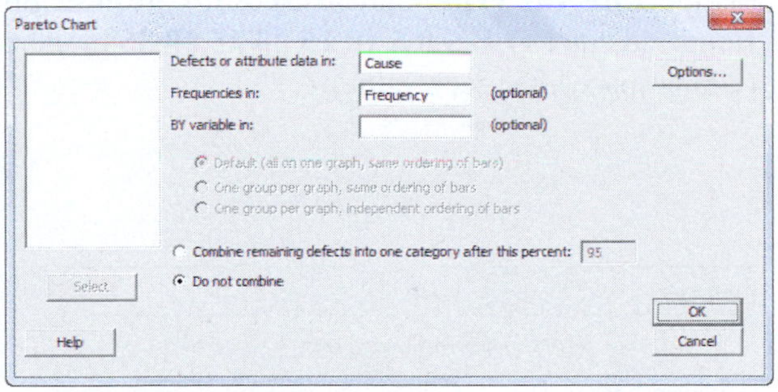

The Side-by-Side Chart

Use **Bar Chart** to create a side-by-side chart. For example, to create the Figure 2.7 side-by-side chart on page 47, open to the **Bond Funds worksheet**. Select **Graph → Bar Chart**. In the procedure's dialog box:

1. Select **Counts of unique values** from the **Bars represent** drop-down list.
2. In the gallery of choices, click **Cluster**.
3. Click **OK**.

In the "Bar Chart - Counts of unique values, Cluster" dialog box (shown below):

4. Double-click **C2 Type** and **C4 Fees** in the variables list to add **Type** and **Fees** to the **Categorical variables (2–4, outermost first)** box.
5. Click **OK**.

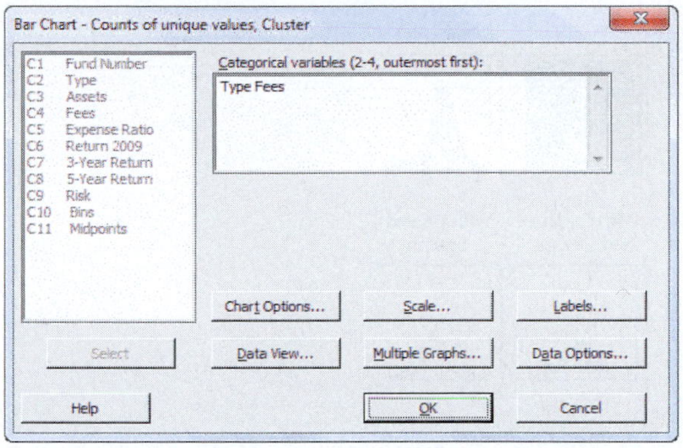

MG2.5 VISUALIZING NUMERICAL DATA

The Stem-and-Leaf Display

Use **Stem-and-Leaf** to create a stem-and-leaf display. For example, to create the Figure 2.8 stem-and-leaf display on page 50, open to the **Bond Funds worksheet**. Select **Graph → Stem-and-Leaf**. In the procedure's dialog box (shown below):

1. Double-click **C6 Return 2009** in the variables list to add **'Return 2009'** in the **Graph variables** box.
2. Click **OK.**

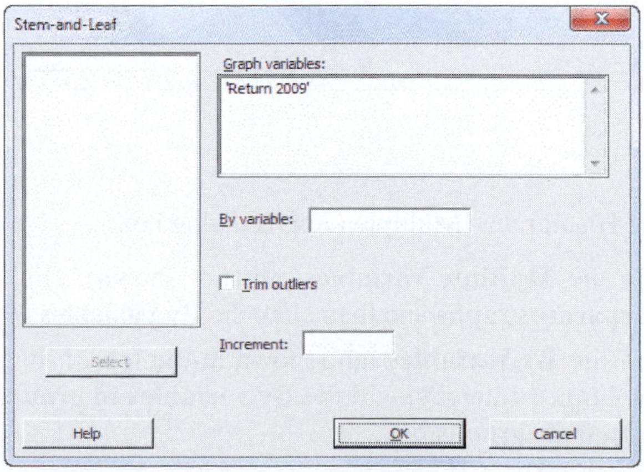

The Histogram

Use **Histogram** to create a histogram. For example, to create the pair of histograms shown in Figure 2.10 on page 51, open to the **Bond Funds worksheet**. Select **Graph → Histogram**. In the Histograms dialog box (shown below):

1. Click **Simple** and then click **OK**.

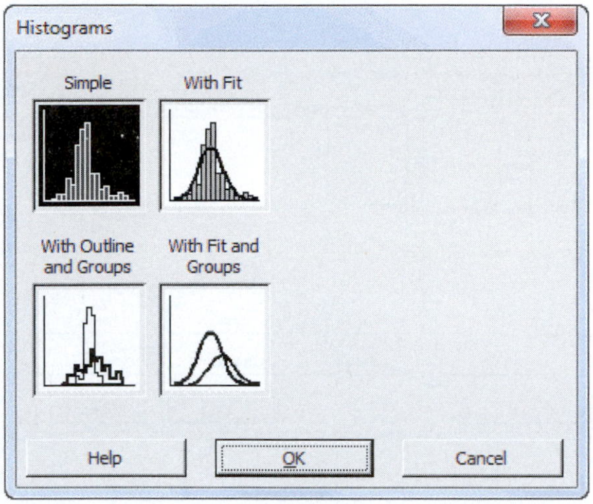

In the Histogram - Simple dialog box (shown below):

2. Double-click **C6 Return 2009** in the variables list to add **'Return 2009'** in the **Graph variables** box.
3. Click **Multiple Graphs**.

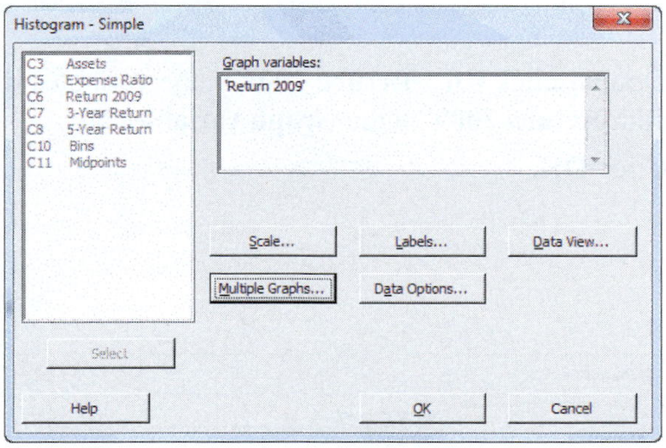

In the Histogram - Multiple Graphs dialog box:

4. In the **Multiple Variables** tab (not shown), click **On separate graphs** and then click the **By Variables** tab.
5. In the **By Variables** tab (shown at the top of the next column), enter **Type** in the **By variables in groups on separate graphs** box.
6. Click **OK**.

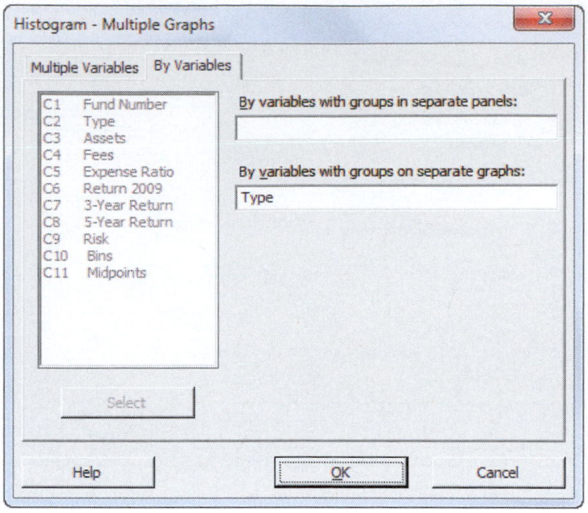

Back in the Histogram - Simple dialog box:

7. Click **OK**.

The histograms created use classes that differ from the classes used in Figure 2.10 (and in Table 2.9 on page 36) and do not use the midpoints shown in Figure 2.10. To better match the histograms shown in Figure 2.10, for each histogram:

8. Right-click the *X* axis and then click **Edit X Scale** from the shortcut menu.

In the Edit Scale dialog box (shown below):

9. Click the **Binning** tab (shown below). Click **Cutpoint** (as the **Interval Type**) and **Midpoint/Cutpoint positions** and enter **-10 -5 0 5 10 15 20 25 30 35** in the box (with a space after each value).

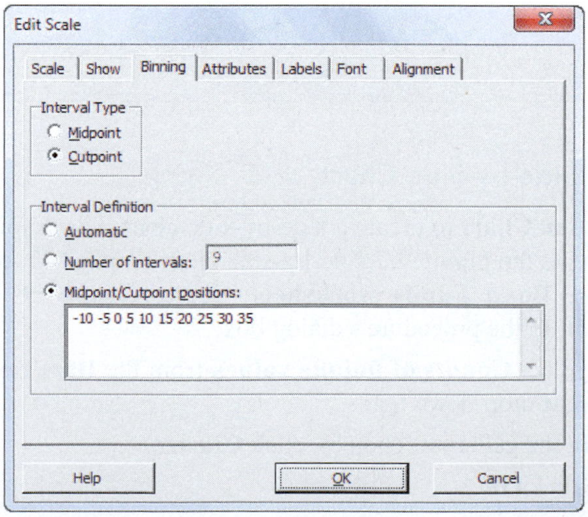

10. Click the **Scale** tab (shown below). Click **Position of ticks** and enter **-7.5 -2.5 2.5 7.5 12.5 17.5 22.5 27.5 32.5** in the box (with a space after each value).
11. Click **OK**.

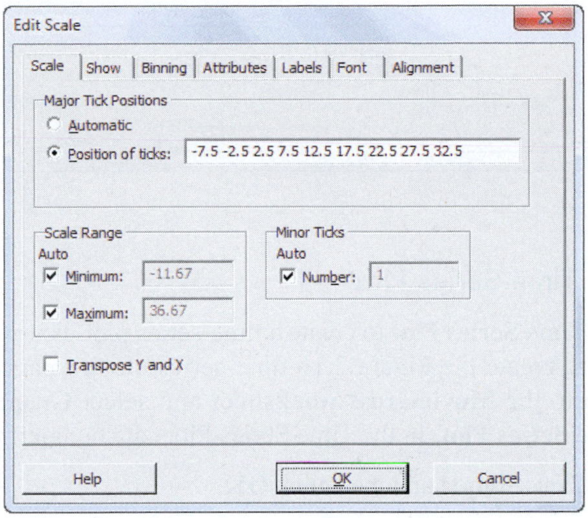

To create the histogram of the 2009 returns for all the bond funds, repeat steps 1 through 11, but in step 5 delete **Type** from the **By variables in groups on separate graphs** box. In the general case, if you have not just created histograms by subgroups (as was done in the example), then follow steps 1 through 4, changing step 4 to "Click **OK**" to create a single histogram that contains all the values of a variable.

To modify the histogram bars, double-click over the histogram bars and make the appropriate entries and selections in the Edit Bars dialog box. To modify an axis, double-click the axis and make the appropriate entries and selections in the Edit Scale dialog box.

The Percentage Polygon

Use **Histogram** to create a percentage polygon. For example, to create the pair of percentage polygons shown in Figure 2.12 on page 52, open to the **Return 2009 Unstacked worksheet**. Select **Graph ➔ Histogram**. In the Histograms dialog box:

1. Click **Simple** and then click **OK**.

In the Histogram - Simple dialog box:

2. Double-click **C1 Intermediate Government** in the variables list to add **'Intermediate Government'** in the **Graph variables** box.
3. Double-click **C2 Short-Term Corporate** in the variables list to add **'Short-Term Corporate'** in the **Graph variables** box.
4. Click **Scale.**

In the Histogram - Scale dialog box:

5. Click the **Y-Scale Type** tab. Click **Percent**, clear **Accumulate values across bins**, and then click **OK.**

Back again in the Histogram - Simple dialog box:

6. Click **Data View**.

In the Histogram - Data View dialog box:

7. Click the **Data Display** tab and then check **Symbols**.
8. Click the **Smoother** tab and then click **Lowness** and enter **0** as the **Degree of smoothing** and **1** as the **Number of steps**.
9. Click **OK**.

Back again in the Histogram - Simple dialog box:

10. Click **OK** to create the polygons.

The percentage polygons created use classes that differ from the classes used in Figure 2.12 (and in Table 2.9 on page 36) and do not use the midpoints shown in Figure 2.12. To better match the polygons shown in Figure 2.12:

11. Right-click the X axis and then click Edit X Scale from the shortcut menu.

In the Edit Scale dialog box:

12. Click the **Binning** tab. Click **Cutpoint** as the **Interval Type** and **Midpoint/Cutpoint positions** and enter **-10 -5 0 5 10 15 20 25 30 35** in the box (with a space after each value).
13. Click the **Scale** tab. Click **Position of ticks** and enter **-7.5 -2.5 2.5 7.5 12.5 17.5 22.5 27.5 32.5** in the box (with a space after each value).
14. Click **OK**.

The Cumulative Percentage Polygon (Ogive)

If you have access to image or photo editing software, use the instructions in the section "The Percentage Polygon" to create a cumulative percentage polygon. In step 5, click **Percent** *and* check **Accumulate values across bins** before clicking **OK**. At this point, the data points will be plotted (incorrectly) to the midpoints and not the ends of the classes (the cutpoints). With the graph open, select **File ➔ Save Graph As** and save the graph using a **Save as type** format compatible with your image or photo-editing software. Open the software and replace the *X* axis labels (the midpoints) with the proper cutpoint values.

Otherwise, use **Scatterplot** with columns of data that represent a cumulative percentage distribution to create a cumulative percentage polygon. For example, to create the Figure 2.13 cumulative percentage polygons of the cost of restaurant meals at city and suburban restaurants, open to the **Restaurant Cumulative Percentages worksheet.** Select **Graph → Scatterplot**. In the Scatterplots dialog box:

1. Click **With Connect Line** and then click **OK**.

In the Scatterplot - With Connect Line dialog box (shown below):

2. Double-click **C2 City Restaurants** in the variables list to enter **'City Restaurants'** in the **Y variables row 1** cell.
3. Double-click **C1 Cost of Meal** in the variables list to enter **'Cost of Meal'** in the **X variables row 1** cell.
4. Double-click **C3 Suburban Restaurants** in the variables list to enter **'Suburban Restaurants'** in the **Y variables row 1** cell.
5. Double-click **C1 Cost of Meal** in the variables list to enter **'Cost of Meal'** in the **X variables row 2** cell.
6. Click **OK.**

In the chart, right-click the *Y* axis label and then click **Edit Y Axis Label** from the shortcut menu. In the Edit Axis Label dialog box, enter **Percentage** in the **Text box** and then click **OK**.

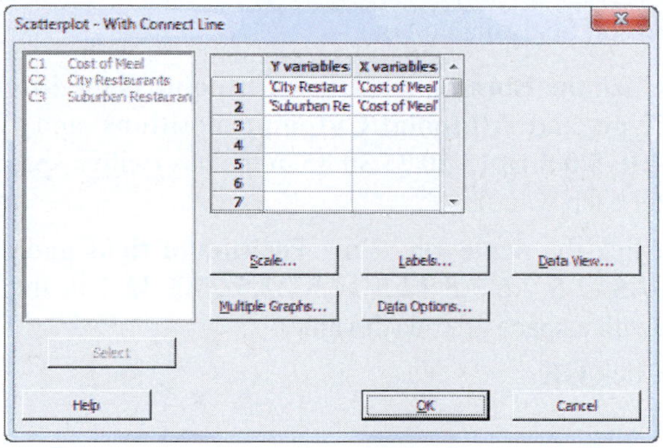

MG2.6 VISUALIZING TWO NUMERICAL VARIABLES

The Scatter Plot

Use **Scatterplot** to create a scatter plot. For example, to create a scatter plot similar to the one shown in Figure 2.15 on page 57, open to the **NBAValues worksheet**. Select **Graph → Scatterplot**. In the Scatterplots dialog box:

1. Click **With Regression** and then click **OK**.

In the Scatterplot - With Regression dialog box (shown at the top of the next column):

2. Enter **Value** in the **row 1 Y variables** cell.
3. Enter **Revenue** in the **row 1 X variables** cell.
4. Click **OK**.

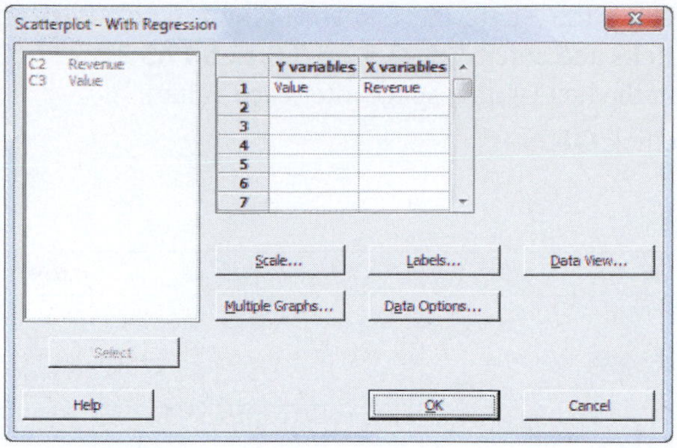

The Time-Series Plot

Use **Time Series Plot** to create a time-series plot. For example, to create the Figure 2.16 time-series plot on page 58, open to the **MovieGross worksheet** and select **Graph → Time Series Plot**. In the Time Series Plots dialog box:

1. Click **Simple** and then click **OK**.

In the Time Series Plot - Simple dialog box (shown below):

2. Double-click **C2 Combined Gross** in the variables list to add **'Combined Gross'** in the **Series** box.
3. Click **Time/Scale**.

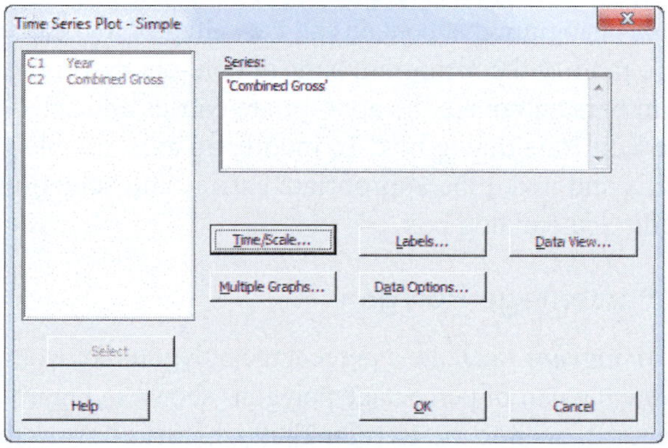

In the Time Series Plot - Time/Scale dialog box (shown at the top of page 93):

4. Click **Stamp** and then press **Tab**.
5. Double-click **C1 Year** in the variables list to add **Year** in the **Stamp columns (1-3, innermost first)** box.
6. Click **OK**.

Back in the Time Series Plot - Simple dialog box:

7. Click **OK**.

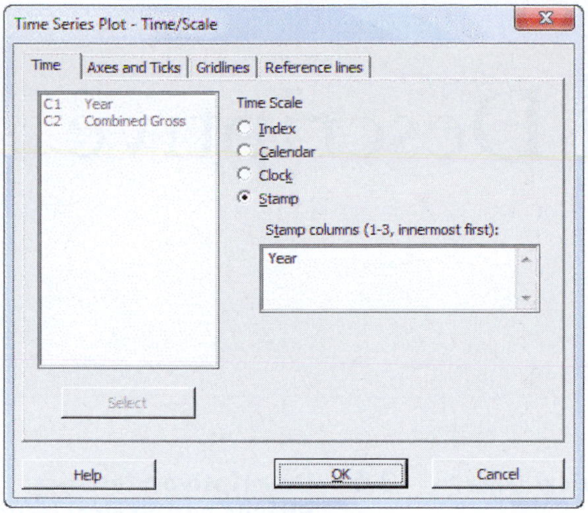

MG2.7 ORGANIZING MULTIDIMENSIONAL DATA

Multidimensional Contingency Tables

Use **Cross Tabulation and Chi-Square** to create a multidimensional contingency table. For example, to create a table similar to the Figure 2.18 fund type, risk, and fees table on page 61, open to the **Bond Funds worksheet**. Select **Stat ➔ Tables ➔ Cross Tabulation and Chi-Square**. In the procedure's dialog box:

1. Double-click **C2 Type** in the variables list to add **Type** to the **For rows** box.
2. Double-click **C9 Risk** in the variables list to add **Risk** to the **For rows** box and then press **Tab.**
3. Double-click **C4 Fees** in the variables list to add **Fees** to the **For columns** box.
4. Check **Counts**.
5. Click **OK**.

To display the cell values as percentages, as was done in Figures 2.20 and 2.21 on page 62, check **Total percents** instead of **Counts** in step 4.

Adding Numerical Variables

Use **Descriptive Statistics** to create a multidimensional contingency table that contains a numerical variable. For example, to create the Figure 2.22 table of fund type, risk, and fees on page 62, showing averages of the 2009 return, open to the **Bond Funds worksheet**. Select **Stat ➔ Tables ➔ Descriptive Statistics**. In the Table of Descriptive Statistics dialog box (shown below):

1. Double-click **C2 Type** in the variables list to add **Type** to the **For rows** box.
2. Double-click **C9 Risk** in the variables list to add **Risk** to the **For rows** box and then press **Tab.**
3. Double-click **C4 Fees** in the variables list to add **Fees** to the **For columns** box.
4. Click **Associated Variables**.

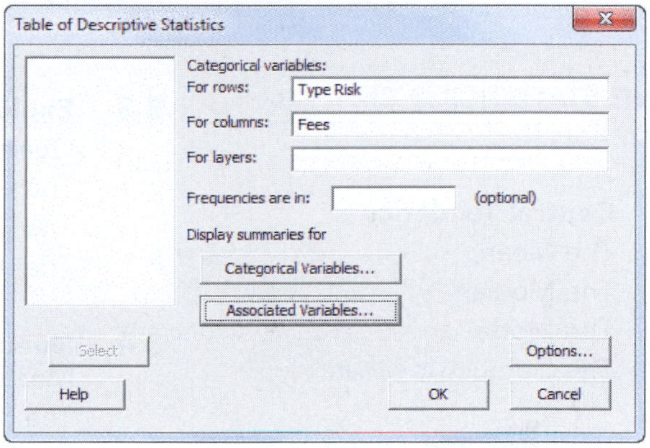

In the Descriptive Statistics - Summaries for Associated Variables dialog box (shown below):

5. Double-click **C6 Return 2009** in the variables list to add **'Return 2009'** to the **Associated variables** box.
6. Check **Means**.
7. Click **OK**.

Back in Table of Descriptive Statistics dialog box:

8. Click **OK**.

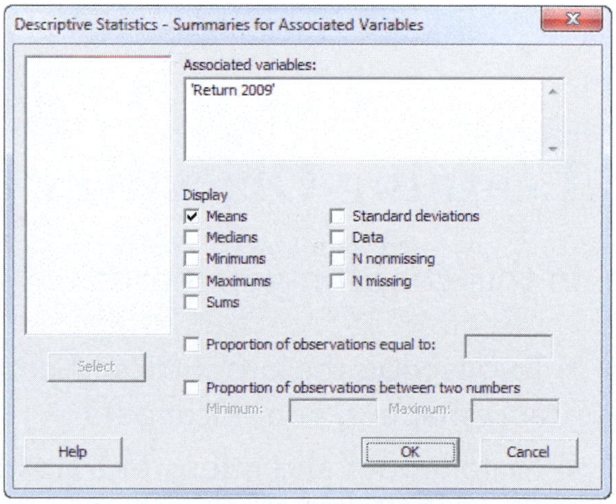

3 Numerical Descriptive Measures

Learning Objectives

In this chapter, you learn:

- To describe the properties of central tendency, variation, and shape in numerical data
- To construct and interpret a boxplot
- To compute descriptive summary measures for a population
- To compute the covariance and the coefficient of correlation

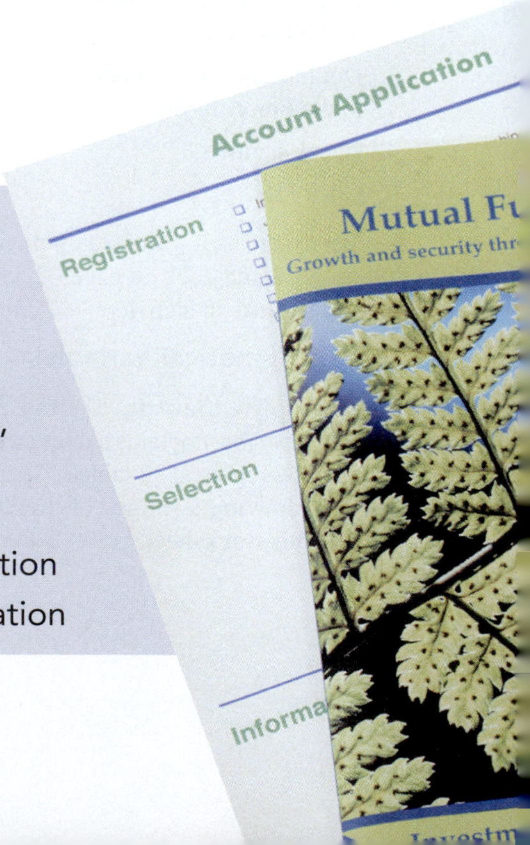

USING STATISTICS

@ Choice Is Yours, Part II

The tables and charts you prepared for the sample of 184 bond mutual funds has been useful to the customers of the Choice Is Yours service. However, customers have become frustrated trying to evaluate bond fund performance. Although they know how the 2009 returns are distributed, they have no idea what a typical 2009 rate of return is for a particular category of bond funds, such as intermediate government and short-term corporate bond funds. They also have no idea of the extent of the variability in the 2009 rate of return. Are all the values relatively similar, or do they include very small and very large values? Are there a lot of small values and a few large ones, or vice versa, or are there a similar number of small and large values?

How could you help the customers get answers to these questions so that they could better evaluate the bond funds?

The customers in Part II of the Choice Is Yours scenario are asking questions about numerical variables. When summarizing and describing numerical variables, you need to do more than just prepare the tables and charts discussed in Chapter 2. You also need to consider the central tendency, variation, and shape of each numerical variable.

CENTRAL TENDENCY

The **central tendency** is the extent to which the data values group around a typical or central value.

VARIATION

The **variation** is the amount of dispersion, or scattering, of values away from a central value.

SHAPE

The **shape** is the pattern of the distribution of values from the lowest value to the highest value.

This chapter discusses ways you can measure the central tendency, variation, and shape of a variable. You will also learn about the covariance and the coefficient of correlation, which help measure the strength of the association between two numerical variables. Using these measures would give the customers of the Choice Is Yours service the answers they seek.

3.1 Central Tendency

Most sets of data show a distinct tendency to group around a central value. When people talk about an "average value" or the "middle value" or the "most frequent value," they are talking informally about the mean, median, and mode—three measures of central tendency.

The Mean

The **arithmetic mean** (typically referred to as the **mean**) is the most common measure of central tendency. The mean is the only common measure in which all the values play an equal role. The mean serves as a "balance point" in a set of data (like the fulcrum on a seesaw). You compute the mean by adding together all the values in a data set and then dividing that sum by the number of values in the data set.

The symbol $\bar{X}$, called *X-bar*, is used to represent the mean of a sample. For a sample containing n values, the equation for the mean of a sample is written as

$$\bar{X} = \frac{\text{sum of the values}}{\text{number of values}}$$

Using the series $X_1, X_2, \ldots, X_n$ to represent the set of n values and n to represent the number of values in the sample, the equation becomes

$$\bar{X} = \frac{X_1 + X_2 + \cdots + X_n}{n}$$

By using summation notation (discussed fully in Appendix A), you replace the numerator $X_1 + X_2 + \cdots + X_n$ with the term $\sum_{i=1}^{n} X_i$, which means sum all the X_i values from the first X

value, X_1, to the last X value, X_n, to form Equation (3.1), a formal definition of the sample mean.

SAMPLE MEAN

The **sample mean** is the sum of the values in a sample divided by the number of values in the sample.

$$\bar{X} = \frac{\sum_{i=1}^{n} X_i}{n} \tag{3.1}$$

where

$\bar{X}$ = sample mean
n = number of values or sample size
X_i = ith value of the variable X
$\sum_{i=1}^{n} X_i$ = summation of all X_i values in the sample

Because all the values play an equal role, a mean is greatly affected by any value that is greatly different from the others. When you have such extreme values, you should avoid using the mean as a measure of central tendency.

The mean can suggest a typical or central value for a data set. For example, if you knew the typical time it takes you to get ready in the morning, you might be able to better plan your morning and minimize any excessive lateness (or earliness) going to your destination. Following the Define, Collect, Organize, Visualize, and Analyze approach, you first define the time to get ready as the time (rounded to the nearest minute) from when you get out of bed to when you leave your home. Then, you collect the times shown below for 10 consecutive workdays (stored in **Times**):

Day:	1	2	3	4	5	6	7	8	9	10
Time (minutes):	39	29	43	52	39	44	40	31	44	35

The first statistic that you compute to analyze these data is the mean. For these data, the mean time is 39.6 minutes, computed as follows:

$$\bar{X} = \frac{\text{sum of the values}}{\text{number of values}}$$

$$\bar{X} = \frac{\sum_{i=1}^{n} X_i}{n}$$

$$\bar{X} = \frac{39 + 29 + 43 + 52 + 39 + 44 + 40 + 31 + 44 + 35}{10}$$

$$= \frac{396}{10} = 39.6$$

Even though no individual day in the sample actually had the value 39.6 minutes, allotting about 40 minutes to get ready would be a good rule for planning your mornings. The mean is a good measure of central tendency here because the data set does not contain any exceptionally small or large values.

Consider a case in which the value on Day 4 is 102 minutes instead of 52 minutes. This extreme value causes the mean to rise to 44.6 minutes, as follows:

$$\bar{X} = \frac{\text{sum of the values}}{\text{number of values}}$$

$$\bar{X} = \frac{\sum_{i=1}^{n} X_i}{n}$$

$$\bar{X} = \frac{446}{10} = 44.6$$

The one extreme value has increased the mean from 39.6 to 44.6 minutes. In contrast to the original mean that was in the "middle" (i.e., was greater than 5 of the getting-ready times and less than the 5 other times), the new mean is greater than 9 of the 10 getting-ready times. Because of the extreme value, now the mean is not a good measure of central tendency.

EXAMPLE 3.1

The Mean Calories for Cereals

Nutritional data about a sample of seven breakfast cereals (stored in **Cereals**) includes the number of calories per serving:

Cereal	Calories
Kellogg's All Bran	80
Kellogg Corn Flakes	100
Wheaties	100
Nature's Path Organic Multigrain Flakes	110
Kellogg Rice Krispies	130
Post Shredded Wheat Vanilla Almond	190
Kellogg Mini Wheats	200

Compute the mean number of calories in these breakfast cereals.

SOLUTION The mean number of calories is 130, computed as follows:

$$\bar{X} = \frac{\text{sum of the values}}{\text{number of values}}$$

$$\bar{X} = \frac{\sum_{i=1}^{n} X_i}{n}$$

$$= \frac{910}{7} = 130$$

The Median

The **median** is the middle value in an ordered array of data that has been ranked from smallest to largest. Half the values are smaller than or equal to the median, and half the values are larger than or equal to the median. The median is not affected by extreme values, so you can use the median when extreme values are present.

To compute the median for a set of data, you first rank the values from smallest to largest and then use Equation (3.2) to compute the rank of the value that is the median.

MEDIAN

$$\text{Median} = \frac{n + 1}{2} \text{ ranked value} \qquad \textbf{(3.2)}$$

You compute the median by following one of two rules:

- **Rule 1** If the data set contains an *odd* number of values, the median is the measurement associated with the middle-ranked value.
- **Rule 2** If the data set contains an *even* number of values, the median is the measurement associated with the *average* of the two middle-ranked values.

To further analyze the sample of 10 times to get ready in the morning, you can compute the median. To do so, you rank the daily times as follows:

Ranked values:	29	31	35	39	39	40	43	44	44	52
Ranks:	1	2	3	4	5	6	7	8	9	10

↑

Median = 39.5

Because the result of dividing $n + 1$ by 2 is $(10 + 1)/2 = 5.5$ for this sample of 10, you must use Rule 2 and average the measurements associated with the fifth and sixth ranked values, 39 and 40. Therefore, the median is 39.5. The median of 39.5 means that for half the days, the time to get ready is less than or equal to 39.5 minutes, and for half the days, the time to get ready is greater than or equal to 39.5 minutes. In this case, the median time to get ready of 39.5 minutes is very close to the mean time to get ready of 39.6 minutes.

EXAMPLE 3.2

Computing the Median From an Odd-Sized Sample

Nutritional data about a sample of seven breakfast cereals (stored in Cereals) includes the number of calories per serving (see Example 3.1 on page 98). Compute the median number of calories in breakfast cereals.

SOLUTION Because the result of dividing $n + 1$ by 2 is $(7 + 1)/2 = 4$ for this sample of seven, using Rule 1, the median is the measurement associated with fourth ranked value. The number of calories per serving data are ranked from the smallest to the largest:

Ranked values:	80	100	100	110	130	190	200
Ranks:	1	2	3	4	5	6	7

↑

Median = 110

The median number of calories is 110. Half the breakfast cereals have equal to or less than 110 calories per serving, and half the breakfast cereals have equal to or more than 110 calories.

The Mode

The **mode** is the value in a set of data that appears most frequently. Like the median and unlike the mean, extreme values do not affect the mode. Often, there is no mode or there are several modes in a set of data. For example, consider the following time-to-get-ready data:

29 31 35 39 39 40 43 44 44 52

There are two modes, 39 minutes and 44 minutes, because each of these values occurs twice.

EXAMPLE 3.3

Determining the Mode

A systems manager in charge of a company's network keeps track of the number of server failures that occur in a day. Determine the mode for the following data, which represents the number of server failures in a day for the past two weeks:

1 3 0 3 26 2 7 4 0 2 3 3 6 3

SOLUTION The ordered array for these data is

0 0 1 2 2 3 3 3 3 3 4 6 7 26

Because 3 occurs five times, more times than any other value, the mode is 3. Thus, the systems manager can say that the most common occurrence is having three server failures in a day. For this data set, the median is also equal to 3, and the mean is equal to 4.5. The value 26 is an extreme value. For these data, the median and the mode are better measures of central tendency than the mean.

A set of data has no mode if none of the values is "most typical." Example 3.4 presents a data set that has no mode.

EXAMPLE 3.4

Data with No Mode

The bounced check fees ($) for a sample of 10 banks is

26 28 20 21 22 25 18 23 15 30

Compute the mode.

SOLUTION These data have no mode. None of the values is most typical because each value appears once.

The Geometric Mean

When you want to measure the rate of change of a variable over time, you need to use the geometric mean instead of the arithmetic mean. Equation (3.3) defines the geometric mean.

GEOMETRIC MEAN

The **geometric mean** is the nth root of the product of n values.

$$\bar{X}_G = (X_1 \times X_2 \times \cdots \times X_n)^{1/n} \qquad \textbf{(3.3)}$$

The **geometric mean rate of return** measures the average percentage return of an investment per time period. Equation (3.4) defines the geometric mean rate of return.

GEOMETRIC MEAN RATE OF RETURN

$$\bar{R}_G = [(1 + R_1) \times (1 + R_2) \times \cdots \times (1 + R_n)]^{1/n} - 1 \qquad \textbf{(3.4)}$$

where

$R_i =$ rate of return in time period i

To illustrate these measures, consider an investment of $100,000 that declined to a value of $50,000 at the end of Year 1 and then rebounded back to its original $100,000 value at the end of Year 2. The rate of return for this investment per year for the two-year period is 0 because the starting and ending value of the investment is unchanged. However, the arithmetic mean of the yearly rates of return of this investment is

$$\bar{X} = \frac{(-0.50) + (1.00)}{2} = 0.25 \text{ or } 25\%$$

because the rate of return for Year 1 is

$$R_1 = \left(\frac{50{,}000 - 100{,}000}{100{,}000}\right) = -0.50 \text{ or } -50\%$$

and the rate of return for Year 2 is

$$R_2 = \left(\frac{100{,}000 - 50{,}000}{50{,}000}\right) = 1.00 \text{ or } 100\%$$

Using Equation (3.4), the geometric mean rate of return per year for the two years is

$$\begin{aligned} \bar{R}_G &= [(1 + R_1) \times (1 + R_2)]^{1/n} - 1 \\ &= [(1 + (-0.50)) \times (1 + (1.0))]^{1/2} - 1 \\ &= [(0.50) \times (2.0)]^{1/2} - 1 \\ &= [1.0]^{1/2} - 1 \\ &= 1 - 1 = 0 \end{aligned}$$

Thus, the geometric mean rate of return more accurately reflects the (zero) change in the value of the investment per year for the two-year period than does the arithmetic mean.

EXAMPLE 3.5

Computing the Geometric Mean Rate of Return

The percentage change in the Russell 2000 Index of the stock prices of 2,000 small companies was −33.79% in 2008 and 27.17% in 2009. Compute the geometric mean rate of return per year.

SOLUTION Using Equation (3.4), the geometric mean rate of return per year in the Russell 2000 Index for the two years is

$$\begin{aligned} \bar{R}_G &= [(1 + R_1) \times (1 + R_2)]^{1/n} - 1 \\ &= [(1 + (-0.3379)) \times (1 + (0.2717))]^{1/2} - 1 \\ &= [(0.6621) \times (1.2717)]^{1/2} - 1 \\ &= [0.8419925]^{1/2} - 1 \\ &= 0.9176 - 1 = -0.0824 \end{aligned}$$

The geometric mean rate of return in the Russell 2000 Index for the two years is −8.24% per year.

3.2 Variation and Shape

In addition to central tendency, every data set can be characterized by its variation and shape. Variation measures the **spread**, or **dispersion**, of values in a data set. One simple measure of variation is the range, the difference between the largest and smallest values. More commonly used in statistics are the standard deviation and variance, two measures explained later in this section. The shape of a data set represents a pattern of all the values, from the lowest to highest value. As you will learn later in this section, many data sets have a pattern that looks approximately like a bell, with a peak of values somewhere in the middle.

The Range

The range is the simplest numerical descriptive measure of variation in a set of data.

RANGE

The **range** is equal to the largest value minus the smallest value.

$$\text{Range} = X_{\text{largest}} - X_{\text{smallest}} \quad \textbf{(3.5)}$$

To further analyze the sample of 10 times to get ready in the morning, you can compute the range. To do so, you rank the data from smallest to largest:

29 31 35 39 39 40 43 44 44 52

Using Equation (3.5), the range is $52 - 29 = 23$ minutes. The range of 23 minutes indicates that the largest difference between any two days in the time to get ready in the morning is 23 minutes.

EXAMPLE 3.6

Computing the Range in the Calories in Cereals

Nutritional data about a sample of seven breakfast cereals (stored in **Cereals**) includes the number of calories per serving (see Example 3.1 on page 98). Compute the range of the number of calories for the cereals.

SOLUTION Ranked from smallest to largest, the calories for the seven cereals are

80 100 100 110 130 190 200

Therefore, using Equation (3.5), the range $= 200 - 80 = 120$. The largest difference in the number of calories between any cereals is 120.

The range measures the *total spread* in the set of data. Although the range is a simple measure of the total variation in the data, it does not take into account *how* the data are distributed between the smallest and largest values. In other words, the range does not indicate whether the values are evenly distributed throughout the data set, clustered near the middle, or clustered near one or both extremes. Thus, using the range as a measure of variation when at least one value is an extreme value is misleading.

The Variance and the Standard Deviation

Being a simple measure of variation, the range does not consider how the values distribute or cluster between the extremes. Two commonly used measures of variation that take into account how all the data values are distributed are the **variance** and the **standard deviation**. These statistics measure the "average" scatter around the mean—how larger values fluctuate above it and how smaller values fluctuate below it.

A simple measure of variation around the mean might take the difference between each value and the mean and then sum these differences. However, if you did that, you would find that because the mean is the balance point in a set of data, for *every* set of data, these differences sum to zero. One measure of variation that differs from data set to data set *squares* the difference between each value and the mean and then sums these squared differences. In statistics, this quantity is called a **sum of squares (*SS*)**. This sum is then divided by the number of values minus 1 (for sample data), to get the sample variance (S^2). The square root of the sample variance is the sample standard deviation (S).

Because this sum of squares will always be nonnegative according to the rules of algebra, *neither the variance nor the standard deviation can ever be negative*. For virtually all sets of data, the variance and standard deviation will be a positive value. Both of these statistics will be zero only if there is no variation in a set of data which happens only when each value in the sample is the same.

For a sample containing n values, $X_1, X_2, X_3, \ldots, X_n$, the sample variance (given by the symbol S^2) is

$$S^2 = \frac{(X_1 - \bar{X})^2 + (X_2 - \bar{X})^2 + \cdots + (X_n - \bar{X})^2}{n - 1}$$

Equation (3.6) expresses the sample variance using summation notation, and Equation (3.7) expresses the sample standard deviation.

SAMPLE VARIANCE

The **sample variance** is the sum of the squared differences around the mean divided by the sample size minus 1.

$$S^2 = \frac{\sum_{i=1}^{n}(X_i - \bar{X})^2}{n - 1} \quad \textbf{(3.6)}$$

where

$\bar{X}$ = sample mean
n = sample size
X_i = ith value of the variable X
$\sum_{i=1}^{n}(X_i - \bar{X})^2$ = summation of all the squared differences between the X_i values and $\bar{X}$

SAMPLE STANDARD DEVIATION

The **sample standard deviation** is the square root of the sum of the squared differences around the mean divided by the sample size minus 1.

$$S = \sqrt{S^2} = \sqrt{\frac{\sum_{i=1}^{n}(X_i - \bar{X})^2}{n - 1}} \quad \textbf{(3.7)}$$

If the denominator were n instead of $n - 1$, Equation (3.6) [and the inner term in Equation (3.7)] would compute the average of the squared differences around the mean. However, $n - 1$ is used because the statistic S^2 has certain mathematical properties that make it desirable for statistical inference (see Section 7.4 on page 258). As the sample size increases, the difference between dividing by n and by $n - 1$ becomes smaller and smaller.

In practice, you will most likely use the sample standard deviation as the measure of variation [defined in Equation (3.7)]. Unlike the sample variance, which is a squared quantity, the standard deviation is always a number that is in the same units as the original sample data. The standard deviation helps you see how a set of data clusters or distributes around its mean. For almost all sets of data, the majority of the observed values lie within an interval of plus and minus one standard deviation above and below the mean. Therefore, knowledge of the mean and the standard deviation usually helps define where at least the majority of the data values are clustering.

To hand-compute the sample variance, S^2, and the sample standard deviation, S, do the following:

1. Compute the difference between each value and the mean.
2. Square each difference.
3. Add the squared differences.
4. Divide this total by $n - 1$ to get the sample variance.
5. Take the square root of the sample variance to get the sample standard deviation.

To further analyze the sample of 10 times to get ready in the morning, Table 3.1 shows the first four steps for calculating the variance and standard deviation with a mean ($\bar{X}$) equal to 39.6. (See page 97 for the calculation of the mean.) The second column of Table 3.1 shows step 1. The third column of Table 3.1 shows step 2. The sum of the squared differences (step 3) is shown at the bottom of Table 3.1. This total is then divided by $10 - 1 = 9$ to compute the variance (step 4).

TABLE 3.1

Computing the Variance of the Getting-Ready Times

$\bar{X} = 39.6$

Time (X)	*Step 1:* $(X_i - \bar{X})$	*Step 2:* $(X_i - \bar{X})^2$
39	−0.60	0.36
29	−10.60	112.36
43	3.40	11.56
52	12.40	153.76
39	−0.60	0.36
44	4.40	19.36
40	0.40	0.16
31	−8.60	73.96
44	4.40	19.36
35	−4.60	21.16
	Step 3: **Sum:**	***Step 4:*** **Divide by $(n - 1)$:**
	412.40	45.82

You can also compute the variance by substituting values for the terms in Equation (3.6):

$$S^2 = \frac{\sum_{i=1}^{n}(X_i - \bar{X})^2}{n - 1}$$

$$= \frac{(39 - 39.6)^2 + (29 - 39.6)^2 + \cdots + (35 - 39.6)^2}{10 - 1}$$

$$= \frac{412.4}{9}$$

$$= 45.82$$

Because the variance is in squared units (in squared minutes, for these data), to compute the standard deviation, you take the square root of the variance. Using Equation (3.7) on page 103, the sample standard deviation, S, is

$$S = \sqrt{S^2} = \sqrt{\frac{\sum_{i=1}^{n}(X_i - \bar{X})^2}{n - 1}} = \sqrt{45.82} = 6.77$$

This indicates that the getting-ready times in this sample are clustering within 6.77 minutes around the mean of 39.6 minutes (i.e., clustering between $\bar{X} - 1S = 32.83$ and $\bar{X} + 1S = 46.37$). In fact, 7 out of 10 getting-ready times lie within this interval.

Using the second column of Table 3.1, you can also compute the sum of the differences between each value and the mean to be zero. For any set of data, this sum will always be zero:

$$\sum_{i=1}^{n}(X_i - \bar{X}) = 0 \text{ for all sets of data}$$

This property is one of the reasons that the mean is used as the most common measure of central tendency.

EXAMPLE 3.7

Computing the Variance and Standard Deviation of the Number of Calories in Cereals

Nutritional data about a sample of seven breakfast cereals (stored in **Cereals**) includes the number of calories per serving (see Example 3.1 on page 98). Compute the variance and standard deviation of the calories in the cereals.

SOLUTION Table 3.2 illustrates the computation of the variance and standard deviation for the calories in the cereals.

TABLE 3.2

Computing the Variance of the Calories in the Cereals

$\bar{X} = 130$

Calories	*Step 1:* $(X_i - \bar{X})$	*Step 2:* $(X_i - \bar{X})^2$
80	−50	2,500
100	−30	900
100	−30	900
110	−20	400
130	0	0
190	60	3,600
200	70	4,900
	***Step 3:* Sum:**	***Step 4:* Divide by $(n - 1)$:**
	13,200	2,200

Using Equation (3.6) on page 103:

$$S^2 = \frac{\sum_{i=1}^{n}(X_i - \bar{X})^2}{n-1}$$

$$= \frac{(80-130)^2 + (100-130)^2 + \cdots + (200-130)^2}{7-1}$$

$$= \frac{13{,}200}{6}$$

$$= 2{,}200$$

Using Equation (3.7) on page 103, the sample standard deviation, S, is

$$S = \sqrt{S^2} = \sqrt{\frac{\sum_{i=1}^{n}(X_i - \bar{X})^2}{n-1}} = \sqrt{2{,}200} = 46.9042$$

The standard deviation of 46.9042 indicates that the calories in the cereals are clustering within 46.9042 around the mean of 130 (i.e., clustering between $\bar{X} - 1S = 83.0958$ and $\bar{X} + 1S = 176.9042$). In fact, 57.1% (four out of seven) of the calories lie within this interval.

The characteristics of the range, variance, and standard deviation can be summarized as follows:

- The greater the spread or dispersion of the data, the larger the range, variance, and standard deviation.
- The smaller the spread or dispersion of the data, the smaller the range, variance, and standard deviation.

- If the values are all the same (so that there is no variation in the data), the range, variance, and standard deviation will all equal zero.
- None of the measures of variation (the range, variance, and standard deviation) can *ever* be negative.

The Coefficient of Variation

Unlike the measures of variation presented previously, the coefficient of variation is a *relative measure* of variation that is always expressed as a percentage rather than in terms of the units of the particular data. The coefficient of variation, denoted by the symbol CV, measures the scatter in the data relative to the mean.

COEFFICIENT OF VARIATION

The **coefficient of variation** is equal to the standard deviation divided by the mean, multiplied by 100%.

$$CV = \left(\frac{S}{\overline{X}}\right)100\% \qquad \textbf{(3.8)}$$

where

S = sample standard deviation
$\overline{X}$ = sample mean

For the sample of 10 getting-ready times, because $\overline{X} = 39.6$ and $S = 6.77$, the coefficient of variation is

$$CV = \left(\frac{S}{\overline{X}}\right)100\% = \left(\frac{6.77}{39.6}\right)100\% = 17.10\%$$

For the getting-ready times, the standard deviation is 17.1% of the size of the mean.

The coefficient of variation is especially useful when comparing two or more sets of data that are measured in different units, as Example 3.8 illustrates.

EXAMPLE 3.8

Comparing Two Coefficients of Variation When the Two Variables Have Different Units of Measurement

Which varies more from cereal to cereal, the number of calories or the amount of sugar (in grams)?

SOLUTION Because calories and the amount of sugar have different units of measurement, you need to compare the relative variability in the two measurements.

For calories, from Example 3.7 on page 105, the coefficient of variation is

$$CV_{Calories} = \left(\frac{46.9042}{130}\right)100\% = 36.08\%$$

For the amount of sugar in grams, the values for the seven cereals are

6 2 4 4 4 11 10

For these data, $\overline{X} = 5.8571$ and $S = 3.3877$.

Thus, the coefficient of variation is

$$CV_{Sugar} = \left(\frac{3.3877}{5.8571}\right)100\% = 57.84\%$$

Thus, relative to the mean, the amount of sugar is much more variable than the calories.

Z Scores

An **extreme value** or **outlier** is a value located far away from the mean. The ***Z* score**, which is the difference between the value and the mean, divided by the standard deviation, is useful in identifying outliers. Values located far away from the mean will have either very small (negative) *Z* scores or very large (positive) *Z* scores.

Z SCORE

$$Z = \frac{X - \overline{X}}{S} \qquad \textbf{(3.9)}$$

To further analyze the sample of 10 times to get ready in the morning, you can compute the *Z* scores. Because the mean is 39.6 minutes, the standard deviation is 6.77 minutes, and the time to get ready on the first day is 39.0 minutes, you compute the *Z* score for Day 1 by using Equation (3.9):

$$\begin{aligned} Z &= \frac{X - \overline{X}}{S} \\ &= \frac{39.0 - 39.6}{6.77} \\ &= -0.09 \end{aligned}$$

Table 3.3 shows the *Z* scores for all 10 days.

TABLE 3.3

Z Scores for the 10 Getting-Ready Times

	Time (*X*)	*Z* Score
	39	−0.90
	29	−1.57
	43	0.50
	52	1.83
	39	−0.09
	44	0.65
	40	0.06
	31	−1.27
	44	0.65
	35	−0.68
Mean	39.6	
Standard deviation	6.77	

The largest *Z* score is 1.83 for Day 4, on which the time to get ready was 52 minutes. The lowest *Z* score is −1.57 for Day 2, on which the time to get ready was 29 minutes. As a general rule, a *Z* score is considered an outlier if it is less than −3.0 or greater than +3.0. None of the times in this case meet that criterion to be considered outliers.

EXAMPLE 3.9

Computing the *Z* Scores of the Number of Calories in Cereals

Nutritional data about a sample of seven breakfast cereals (stored in **Cereals**) includes the number of calories per serving (see Example 3.1 on page 98). Compute the *Z* scores of the calories in breakfast cereals.

SOLUTION Table 3.4 on page 108 illustrates the *Z* scores of the calories for the cereals. The largest *Z* score is 1.49, for a cereal with 200 calories. The lowest *Z* score is −1.07 for a cereal with 80 calories. There are no apparent outliers in these data because none of the *Z* scores are less than −3.0 or greater than +3.0.

TABLE 3.4

Z Scores of the Number of Calories in Cereals

	Calories	*Z* Scores
	80	−1.07
	100	−0.64
	100	−0.64
	110	−0.43
	130	0.00
	190	1.28
	200	1.49
Mean	130	
Standard deviation	46.9042	

Shape

Shape is the pattern of the distribution of data values throughout the entire range of all the values. A distribution is either symmetrical or skewed. In a **symmetrical** distribution, the values below the mean are distributed in exactly the same way as the values above the mean. In this case, the low and high values balance each other out. In a **skewed** distribution, the values are not symmetrical around the mean. This skewness results in an imbalance of low values or high values.

Shape also can influence the relationship of the mean to the median. In most cases:

- Mean $<$ median: negative, or left-skewed
- Mean $=$ median: symmetric, or zero skewness
- Mean $>$ median: positive, or right-skewed

Figure 3.1 depicts three data sets, each with a different shape.

FIGURE 3.1

A comparison of three data sets that differ in shape

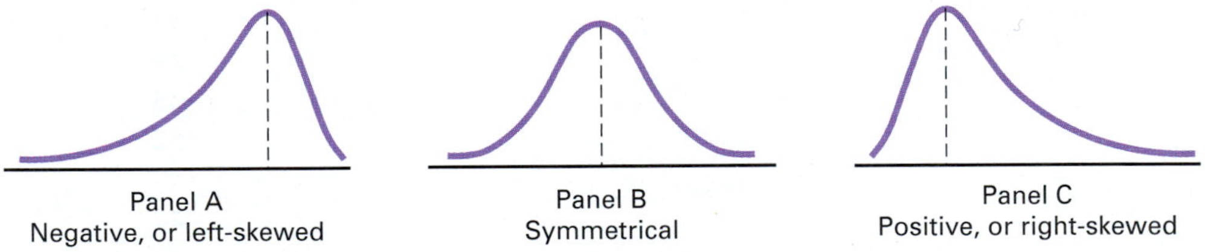

The data in Panel A are negative, or **left-skewed**. In this panel, most of the values are in the upper portion of the distribution. A long tail and distortion to the left is caused by some extremely small values. These extremely small values pull the mean downward so that the mean is less than the median.

The data in Panel B are symmetrical. Each half of the curve is a mirror image of the other half of the curve. The low and high values on the scale balance, and the mean equals the median.

The data in Panel C are positive, or **right-skewed**. In this panel, most of the values are in the lower portion of the distribution. A long tail on the right is caused by some extremely large values. These extremely large values pull the mean upward so that the mean is greater than the median.

Skewness and **kurtosis** are two shape-related statistics. The skewness statistic measures the extent to which a set of data is not symmetric. The kurtosis statistic measures the relative concentration of values in the center of the distribution of a data set, as compared with the tails.

A symmetric distribution has a skewness value of zero. A right-skewed distribution has a positive skewness value, and a left-skewed distribution has a negative skewness value.

A bell-shaped distribution has a kurtosis value of zero. A distribution that is flatter than a bell-shaped distribution has a negative kurtosis value. A distribution with a sharper peak (one that has a higher concentration of values in the center of the distribution than a bell-shaped distribution) has a positive kurtosis value.

EXAMPLE 3.10

Descriptive Statistics for Intermediate Government and Short-Term Corporate Bond Funds

In Part II of the Choice Is Yours scenario, you are interested in comparing the past performance of the intermediate government bond and short-term corporate bond funds. One measure of past performance is the return in 2009. You have already defined the variables to be collected and collected the data from a sample of 184 bond funds. Compute descriptive statistics for the intermediate government and short-term corporate bond funds.

SOLUTION Figure 3.2 presents a table of descriptive summary measures for the two types of bond funds, as computed by Excel (left results) and Minitab (right results). The Excel results include the mean, standard error, median, mode, standard deviation, variance, kurtosis, skewness, range, minimum, maximum, sum (which is meaningless for this example), and count (the sample size). The standard error, discussed in Section 7.4, is the standard deviation divided by the square root of the sample size. The Minitab results also include the coefficient of variation, the first quartile, the third quartile, and the interquartile range (see Section 3.3 on pages 113-115).

FIGURE 3.2

Excel and Minitab Descriptive statistics for the 2009 return for the intermediate government and short-term corporate bond funds

	A	B	C
1	**Descriptive Statistics for Return 2009**		
2		**Intermediate Government**	**Short Term Corporate**
3	Mean	4.4529	9.5959
4	Standard Error	0.5747	0.5774
5	Median	4.4000	9.1000
6	Mode	5.7000	6.8000
7	Standard Deviation	5.3606	5.6867
8	Sample Variance	28.7365	32.3389
9	Kurtosis	4.8953	3.7273
10	Skewness	1.4979	0.9002
11	Range	33.4000	40.8000
12	Minimum	-4.8000	-8.8000
13	Maximum	28.6000	32.0000
14	Sum	387.4000	930.8000
15	Count	87	97

```
Variable     Type                        Count   Mean  StDev  Variance  CoefVar
Return 2009  Intermediate Government        87  4.453  5.361    28.736   120.39
             Short Term Corporate           97  9.596  5.687    32.339    59.26

Variable     Type                      Minimum     Q1  Median      Q3  Maximum
Return 2009  Intermediate Government    -4.800  0.900   4.400   6.500   28.600
             Short Term Corporate       -8.800  5.700   9.100  12.950   32.000

                                                                         N for
Variable     Type                        Range    IQR                Mode   Mode
Return 2009  Intermediate Government    33.400  5.600            3.5, 5.7      3
             Short Term Corporate       40.800  7.250  6, 6.7, 6.8, 7.3      3

Variable     Type                      Skewness  Kurtosis
Return 2009  Intermediate Government       1.50      4.90
             Short Term Corporate          0.90      3.73

The data contain at least five mode values. Only the smallest four are shown.
```

In examining the results, you see that there are large differences in the 2009 return for the intermediate government bond and short-term corporate bond funds. The intermediate government bond funds had a mean 2009 return of 4.4529 and a median return of 4.4. This compares to a mean of 9.5959 and a median of 9.1 for the short-term corporate bond funds. The medians indicate that half of the intermediate government bond funds had returns of 4.4 or better, and half the short-term corporate bond funds had returns of 9.1 or better. You conclude that the short-term corporate bond funds had a much higher return than the intermediate government bond funds.

The intermediate government corporate bond funds had a slightly smaller standard deviation than the short-term corporate bond funds (5.3606, as compared to 5.6867). While both the intermediate government bond funds and the short-term corporate bond funds showed right or positive skewness, the intermediate government bond funds were more skewed. The kurtosis of both the intermediate government and the short-term corporate bond funds was very positive, indicating a distribution that was much more peaked than a bell-shaped distribution.

VISUAL EXPLORATIONS Exploring Descriptive Statistics

Use the Visual Explorations Descriptive Statistics procedure to see the effect of changing data values on measures of central tendency, variation, and shape. Open the **Visual Explorations add-in workbook (Visual Explorations.xla)** and:

1. Select **Add-ins ➔ Visual Explorations ➔ Descriptive Statistics.**
2. Read the instructions in the Descriptive Statistics dialog box and then click **OK** (see the illustration at right).
3. Experiment by entering an extreme value such as 5 into one of the tinted column A cells.

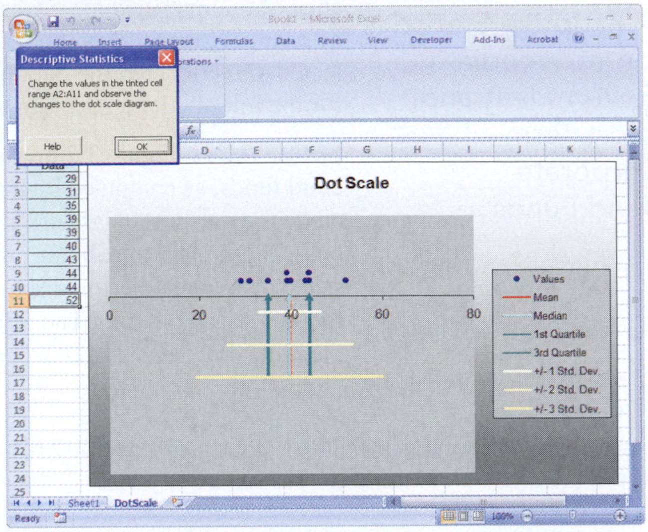

Which measures are affected by this change? Which ones are not? You can switch between the "before" and "after" diagrams by repeatedly pressing **Ctrl+Z** (undo) followed by **Ctrl+Y** (redo) to better see the changes the extreme value has caused in the diagram. (To learn more about Visual Explorations, see Appendix Section D.4.)

Problems for Sections 3.1 and 3.2

LEARNING THE BASICS

3.1 The following set of data is from a sample of $n = 5$:

7 4 9 8 2

a. Compute the mean, median, and mode.
b. Compute the range, variance, standard deviation, and coefficient of variation.
c. Compute the Z scores. Are there any outliers?
d. Describe the shape of the data set.

3.2 The following set of data is from a sample of $n = 6$:

7 4 9 7 3 12

a. Compute the mean, median, and mode.
b. Compute the range, variance, standard deviation, and coefficient of variation.
c. Compute the Z scores. Are there any outliers?
d. Describe the shape of the data set.

3.3 The following set of data is from a sample of $n = 7$:

12 7 4 9 0 7 3

a. Compute the mean, median, and mode.
b. Compute the range, variance, standard deviation, and coefficient of variation.
c. Compute the Z scores. Are there any outliers?
d. Describe the shape of the data set.

3.4 The following set of data is from a sample of $n = 5$:

7 −5 −8 7 9

a. Compute the mean, median, and mode.
b. Compute the range, variance, standard deviation, and coefficient of variation.
c. Compute the Z scores. Are there any outliers?
d. Describe the shape of the data set.

3.5 Suppose that the rate of return for a particular stock during the past two years was 10% and 30%. Compute the geometric rate of return per year. (*Note:* A rate of return of 10% is recorded as 0.10, and a rate of return of 30% is recorded as 0.30.)

3.6 Suppose that the rate of return for a particular stock during the past two years was 20% and −30%. Compute the geometric rate of return per year.

APPLYING THE CONCEPTS

3.7 A survey conducted by the American Statistical Association reported the results at the top of page 111 for the salaries of professors teaching statistics in research universities with four to five years in the rank of associate professor and professor.

Title	Median
Associate professor	82,400
Professor	108,600

Source: Data extracted from K. Crank, "Academic Salary Survey," *AmStat News*, December 2009, p. 34.

Interpret the median salary for the associate professors and professors.

3.8 The operations manager of a plant that manufactures tires wants to compare the actual inner diameters of two grades of tires, each of which is expected to be 575 millimeters. A sample of five tires of each grade was selected, and the results representing the inner diameters of the tires, ranked from smallest to largest, are as follows:

Grade X	Grade Y
568 570 575 578 584	573 574 575 577 578

a. For each of the two grades of tires, compute the mean, median, and standard deviation.
b. Which grade of tire is providing better quality? Explain.
c. What would be the effect on your answers in (a) and (b) if the last value for grade Y were 588 instead of 578? Explain.

3.9 According to the U.S. Census Bureau, in February 2010, the median sales price of new houses was $220,500 and the mean sales price was $282,600 (extracted from **www.census.gov**, March 24, 2010).
a. Interpret the median sales price.
b. Interpret the mean sales price.
c. Discuss the shape of the distribution of the price of new houses.

SELF Test **3.10** The file **FastFood** contains the amount that a sample of nine customers spent for lunch ($) at a fast-food restaurant:

4.20 5.03 5.86 6.45 7.38 7.54 8.46 8.47 9.87

a. Compute the mean and median.
b. Compute the variance, standard deviation, range, and coefficient of variation.
c. Are the data skewed? If so, how?
d. Based on the results of (a) through (c), what conclusions can you reach concerning the amount that customers spent for lunch?

3.11 The file **Sedans** contains the overall miles per gallon (MPG) of 2010 family sedans:

24	21	22	23	24	34	34	34	20	20
22	22	44	32	20	20	22	20	39	20

Source: Data extracted from "Vehicle Ratings," *Consumer Reports*, April 2010, p. 29.

a. Compute the mean, median, and mode.
b. Compute the variance, standard deviation, range, coefficient of variation, and Z scores.
c. Are the data skewed? If so, how?
d. Compare the results of (a) through (c) to those of Problem 3.12 (a) through (c) that refer to the miles per gallon of small SUVs.

3.12 The file **SUV** contains the overall miles per gallon (MPG) of 2010 small SUVs:

24	23	22	21	22	22	18	18	26
26	26	19	19	19	21	21	21	21
21	18	19	21	22	22	16	16	

Source: Data extracted from "Vehicle Ratings," *Consumer Reports*, April 2010, pp. 33–34.

a. Compute the mean, median, and mode.
b. Compute the variance, standard deviation, range, coefficient of variation, and Z scores.
c. Are the data skewed? If so, how?
d. Compare the results of (a) through (c) to those of Problem 3.11 (a) through (c) that refer to the miles per gallon of family sedans.

3.13 The file **ChocolateChip** contains the cost (in cents) per 1-ounce serving for a sample of 13 chocolate chip cookies. The data are as follows:

54 22 25 23 36 43 7 43 25 47 24 45 44

Source: Data extracted from "Chip, Chip, Hooray," *Consumer Reports*, June 2009, p. 7.

a. Compute the mean, median, and mode.
b. Compute the variance, standard deviation, range, coefficient of variation, and Z scores. Are there any outliers? Explain.
c. Are the data skewed? If so, how?
d. Based on the results of (a) through (c), what conclusions can you reach concerning the cost of chocolate chip cookies?

3.14 The file **DarkChocolate** contains the cost per ounce ($) for a sample of 14 dark chocolate bars:

0.68	0.72	0.92	1.14	1.42	0.94	0.77
0.57	1.51	0.57	0.55	0.86	1.41	0.90

Source: Data extracted from "Dark Chocolate: Which Bars Are Best?" *Consumer Reports*, September 2007, p. 8.

a. Compute the mean, median, and mode.
b. Compute the variance, standard deviation, range, coefficient of variation, and Z scores. Are there any outliers? Explain.
c. Are the data skewed? If so, how?
d. Based on the results of (a) through (c), what conclusions can you reach concerning the cost of dark chocolate bars?

3.15 Is there a difference in the variation of the yields of different types of investments? The file **SavingsRate-MMCD** contains the yields for a money market account and a five-year certificate of deposit (CD), for 25 banks in the United States, as of March 29, 2010.

Source: Data extracted from **www.Bankrate.com**, March 29, 2010.

a. For money market accounts and five-year CDs, separately compute the variance, standard deviation, range, and coefficient of variation.

b. Based on the results of (a), do money market accounts or five-year CDs have more variation in the yields offered? Explain.

3.16 The file **HotelUK** contains the room price (in $) paid by U.S. travelers in six British cities in 2009:

185 160 126 116 112 105

Source: Data extracted from **www.hotels.com/press/hotel-price-index-2009-h2.html**.

a. Compute the mean, median, and mode.

b. Compute the range, variance, and standard deviation.

c. Based on the results of (a) and (b), what conclusions can you reach concerning the room price (in $) paid by U.S. travelers in 2009?

d. Suppose that the first value was 85 instead of 185. Repeat (a) through (c), using this value. Comment on the difference in the results.

3.17 A bank branch located in a commercial district of a city has the business objective of developing an improved process for serving customers during the noon-to-1:00 P.M. lunch period. The waiting time, in minutes, is defined as the time the customer enters the line to when he or she reaches the teller window. Data are collected from a sample of 15 customers during this hour. The file **Bank1** contains the results, which are also listed here:

4.21 5.55 3.02 5.13 4.77 2.34 3.54 3.20
4.50 6.10 0.38 5.12 6.46 6.19 3.79

a. Compute the mean and median.

b. Compute the variance, standard deviation, range, coefficient of variation, and Z scores. Are there any outliers? Explain.

c. Are the data skewed? If so, how?

d. As a customer walks into the branch office during the lunch hour, she asks the branch manager how long she can expect to wait. The branch manager replies, "Almost certainly less than five minutes." On the basis of the results of (a) through (c), evaluate the accuracy of this statement.

3.18 Suppose that another bank branch, located in a residential area, is also concerned with the noon-to-1 P.M. lunch hour. The waiting time, in minutes, collected from a sample of 15 customers during this hour, is contained in the file **Bank2** and listed here:

9.66 5.90 8.02 5.79 8.73 3.82 8.01 8.35
10.49 6.68 5.64 4.08 6.17 9.91 5.47

a. Compute the mean and median.

b. Compute the variance, standard deviation, range, coefficient of variation, and Z scores. Are there any outliers? Explain.

c. Are the data skewed? If so, how?

d. As a customer walks into the branch office during the lunch hour, he asks the branch manager how long he can expect to wait. The branch manager replies, "Almost certainly less than five minutes." On the basis of the results of (a) through (c), evaluate the accuracy of this statement.

3.19 General Electric (GE) is one of the world's largest companies; it develops, manufactures, and markets a wide range of products, including medical diagnostic imaging devices, jet engines, lighting products, and chemicals. In 2008, the stock price dropped 53.94%, while in 2009, the stock price rose 0.13%.

Source: Data extracted from **finance.yahoo.com**, March 30, 2010.

a. Compute the geometric mean rate of return per year for the two-year period 2008–2009. (Hint: Denote an increase of 0.13% as $R_2 = 0.0013$.)

b. If you purchased $1,000 of GE stock at the start of 2008, what was its value at the end of 2009?

c. Compare the result of (b) to that of Problem 3.20 (b).

3.20 TASER International, Inc., develops, manufactures, and sells nonlethal self-defense devices known as tasers. Marketing primarily to law enforcement, corrections institutions, and the military, TASER's popularity has enjoyed a roller-coaster ride. The stock price in 2008 decreased by 63.31%, and in 2009, the stock price decreased by 17.05%.

Source: Data extracted from **finance.yahoo.com**, March 30, 2010.

a. Compute the geometric mean rate of return per year for the two-year period 2008–2009. (Hint: Denote a decrease of 63.31% as $R_1 = -0.6331$.)

b. If you purchased $1,000 of TASER stock at the start of 2008, what was its value at the end of 2009?

c. Compare the result of (b) to that of Problem 3.19 (b).

3.21 In 2009, all the major stock market indices increased dramatically as they recovered from the world financial crisis that occurred in 2008. The data in the following table (stored in **Indices**) represent the total rate of return (in percentage) for the Dow Jones Industrial Average (DJIA), the Standard & Poor's 500 (S&P 500), and the technology-heavy NASDAQ Composite (NASDAQ) from 2006 through 2009.

Year	DJIA	S&P 500	NASDAQ
2009	18.8	23.5	43.9
2008	−33.8	−38.5	−40.5
2007	6.4	3.5	9.8
2006	16.3	13.6	9.5

Source: Data extracted from **finance.yahoo.com,** April 1, 2010.

a. Compute the geometric mean rate of return per year for the DJIA, S&P 500, and NASDAQ from 2006 through 2009.

b. What conclusions can you reach concerning the geometric mean rates of return per year of the three market indices?

c. Compare the results of (b) to those of Problem 3.22 (b).

3.22 In 2006–2009, the value of precious metals changed rapidly. The data in the following table (contained in the file **Metals**) represent the total rate of return (in percentage) for platinum, gold, and silver from 2006 through 2009:

Year	Platinum	Gold	Silver
2009	62.7	25.0	56.8
2008	−41.3	4.3	−26.9
2007	36.9	31.9	14.4
2006	15.9	23.2	46.1

Source: Data extracted from **www.kitco.com**, April 1, 2010.

a. Compute the geometric mean rate of return per year for platinum, gold, and silver from 2006 through 2009.

b. What conclusions can you reach concerning the geometric mean rates of return of the three precious metals?

c. Compare the results of (b) to those of Problem 3.21 (b).

3.3 Exploring Numerical Data

Sections 3.1 and 3.2 discuss measures of central tendency, variation, and shape. An additional way of describing numerical data is through an exploratory data analysis that computes the quartiles and the five-number summary and constructs a boxplot. You can also supplement these methods by displaying descriptive statistics across several categorical variables using the multidimensional table technique that Section 2.7 discusses.

Quartiles

Quartiles split a set of data into four equal parts—the **first quartile,** Q_1**,** divides the smallest 25.0% of the values from the other 75.0% that are larger. The **second quartile,** Q_2**,** is the median—50.0% of the values are smaller than or equal to the median and 50.0% are larger than or equal to the median. The **third quartile,** Q_3**,** divides the smallest 75.0% of the values from the largest 25.0%. Equations (3.10) and (3.11) define the first and third quartiles.[1]

[1]The Q_1, median, and Q_3 are also the 25th, 50th, and 75th percentiles, respectively. Equations (3.2), (3.10), and (3.11) can be expressed generally in terms of finding percentiles: $(p \times 100)$th percentile $= p \times (n + 1)$ ranked value, where $p =$ the proportion.

FIRST QUARTILE, Q_1

25.0% of the values are smaller than or equal to Q_1, the first quartile, and 75.0% are larger than or equal to the first quartile, Q_1.

$$Q_1 = \frac{n + 1}{4} \text{ ranked value} \qquad \textbf{(3.10)}$$

THIRD QUARTILE, Q_3

75.0% of the values are smaller than or equal to the third quartile, Q_3, and 25.0% are larger than or equal to the third quartile, Q_3.

$$Q_3 = \frac{3(n + 1)}{4} \text{ ranked value} \qquad \textbf{(3.11)}$$

Use the following rules to compute the quartiles from a set of ranked values:

- **Rule 1** If the ranked value is a whole number, the quartile is equal to the measurement that corresponds to that ranked value. For example, if the sample size $n = 7$, the first quartile, Q_1, is equal to the measurement associated with the $(7 + 1)/4 =$ second ranked value.
- **Rule 2** If the ranked value is a fractional half (2.5, 4.5, etc.), the quartile is equal to the measurement that corresponds to the average of the measurements corresponding to the two ranked values involved. For example, if the sample size $n = 9$, the first quartile,

In Excel, the QUARTILE function uses different rules to compute quartiles. Use the **COMPUTE** *worksheet of the* **Quartiles workbook**, *discussed in Section EG3.3, to compute quartiles using the rules presented in this section.*

Q_1, is equal to the $(9 + 1)/4 = 2.5$ ranked value, halfway between the second ranked value and the third ranked value.

- **Rule 3** If the ranked value is neither a whole number nor a fractional half, you round the result to the nearest integer and select the measurement corresponding to that ranked value. For example, if the sample size $n = 10$, the first quartile, Q_1, is equal to the $(10 + 1)/4 = 2.75$ ranked value. Round 2.75 to 3 and use the third ranked value.

To further analyze the sample of 10 times to get ready in the morning, you can compute the quartiles. To do so, you rank the data from smallest to largest:

Ranked values:	29	31	35	39	39	40	43	44	44	52
Ranks:	1	2	3	4	5	6	7	8	9	10

The first quartile is the $(n + 1)/4 = (10 + 1)/4 = 2.75$ ranked value. Using Rule 3, you round up to the third ranked value. The third ranked value for the time-to-get-ready data is 35 minutes. You interpret the first quartile of 35 to mean that on 25% of the days, the time to get ready is less than or equal to 35 minutes, and on 75% of the days, the time to get ready is greater than or equal to 35 minutes.

The third quartile is the $3(n + 1)/4 = 3(10 + 1)/4 = 8.25$ ranked value. Using Rule 3 for quartiles, you round this down to the eighth ranked value. The eighth ranked value is 44 minutes. Thus, on 75% of the days, the time to get ready is less than or equal to 44 minutes, and on 25% of the days, the time to get ready is greater than or equal to 44 minutes.

EXAMPLE 3.11

Computing the Quartiles

Nutritional data about a sample of seven breakfast cereals (stored in **Cereals**) includes the number of calories per serving (see Example 3.1 on page 98). Compute the first quartile (Q_1) and third quartile (Q_3) numbers of calories for the cereals.

SOLUTION Ranked from smallest to largest, the number of calories for the seven cereals are as follows:

Ranked values:	80	100	100	110	130	190	200
Ranks:	1	2	3	4	5	6	7

For these data

$$Q_1 = \frac{(n + 1)}{4} \text{ ranked value}$$

$$= \frac{7 + 1}{4} \text{ ranked value} = \text{2nd ranked value}$$

Therefore, using Rule 1, Q_1 is the second ranked value. Because the second ranked value is 100, the first quartile, Q_1, is 100.

To compute the third quartile, Q_3,

$$Q_3 = \frac{3(n + 1)}{4} \text{ ranked value}$$

$$= \frac{3(7 + 1)}{4} \text{ ranked value} = \text{6th ranked value}$$

Therefore, using Rule 1, Q_3 is the sixth ranked value. Because the sixth ranked value is 190, Q_3 is 190.

The first quartile of 100 indicates that 25% of the cereals have calories that are below or equal to 100 and 75% are greater than or equal to 100. The third quartile of 190 indicates that 75% of the cereals have calories that are below or equal to 190 and 25% are greater than or equal to 190.

The Interquartile Range

The interquartile range is the difference between the third and first quartiles in a set of data.

INTERQUARTILE RANGE

The **interquartile range** (also called **midspread**) is the difference between the third quartile and the first quartile.

$$\text{Interquartile range} = Q_3 - Q_1 \quad \textbf{(3.12)}$$

The interquartile range measures the spread in the middle 50% of the data. Therefore, it is not influenced by extreme values. To further analyze the sample of 10 times to get ready in the morning, you can compute the interquartile range. You first order the data as follows:

29 31 35 39 39 40 43 44 44 52

You use Equation (3.12) and the earlier results above, $Q_1 = 35$ and $Q_3 = 44$:

$$\text{Interquartile range} = 44 - 35 = 9 \text{ minutes}$$

Therefore, the interquartile range in the time to get ready is 9 minutes. The interval 35 to 44 is often referred to as the *middle fifty*.

EXAMPLE 3.12
Computing the Interquartile Range for the Number of Calories in Cereals

Nutritional data about a sample of seven breakfast cereals (stored in **Cereals**) includes the number of calories per serving (see Example 3.1 on page 98). Compute the interquartile range of the numbers of calories in cereals.

SOLUTION Ranked from smallest to largest, the numbers of calories for the seven cereals are as follows:

80 100 100 110 130 190 200

Using Equation (3.12) and the earlier results from Example 3.11 on page 114, $Q_1 = 100$ and $Q_3 = 190$:

$$\text{Interquartile range} = 190 - 100 = 90$$

Therefore, the interquartile range of the number of calories in cereals is 90 calories.

Because the interquartile range does not consider any value smaller than Q_1 or larger than Q_3, it cannot be affected by extreme values. Descriptive statistics such as the median, Q_1, Q_3, and the interquartile range, which are not influenced by extreme values, are called **resistant measures**.

The Five-Number Summary

A **five-number summary**, which consists of the following, provides a way to determine the shape of a distribution:

$$X_{\text{smallest}} \quad Q_1 \quad \text{Median} \quad Q_3 \quad X_{\text{largest}}$$

Table 3.5 explains how the relationships among these five numbers allows you to recognize the shape of a data set.

TABLE 3.5

Relationships Among the Five-Number Summary and the Type of Distribution

	Type of Distribution		
Comparison	**Left-Skewed**	**Symmetric**	**Right-Skewed**
The distance from $X_{smallest}$ to the median versus the distance from the median to $X_{largest}$.	The distance from $X_{smallest}$ to the median is greater than the distance from the median to $X_{largest}$.	The two distances are the same.	The distance from $X_{smallest}$ to the median is less than the distance from the median to $X_{largest}$.
The distance from $X_{smallest}$ to Q_1 versus the distance from Q_3 to $X_{largest}$.	The distance from $X_{smallest}$ to Q_1 is greater than the distance from Q_3 to $X_{largest}$.	The two distances are the same.	The distance from $X_{smallest}$ to Q_1 is less than the distance from Q_3 to $X_{largest}$.
The distance from Q_1 to the median versus the distance from the median to Q_3.	The distance from Q_1 to the median is greater than the distance from the median to Q_3.	The two distances are the same.	The distance from Q_1 to the median is less than the distance from the median to Q_3.

To further analyze the sample of 10 times to get ready in the morning, you can compute the five-number summary. For these data, the smallest value is 29 minutes, and the largest value is 52 minutes (see page 97). Calculations done on pages 99 and 114 show that the median = 39.5, $Q_1 = 35$, and $Q_3 = 44$. Therefore, the five-number summary is as follows:

$$29 \quad 35 \quad 39.5 \quad 44 \quad 52$$

The distance from $X_{smallest}$ to the median $(39.5 - 29 = 10.5)$ is slightly less than the distance from the median to $X_{largest}$ $(52 - 39.5 = 12.5)$. The distance from $X_{smallest}$ to Q_1 $(35 - 29 = 6)$ is slightly less than the distance from Q_3 to $X_{largest}$ $(52 - 44 = 8)$. The distance from Q_1 to the median $(39.5 - 35 = 4.5)$ is the same as the distance from the median to Q_3 $(44 - 39.5 = 4.5)$. Therefore, the getting-ready times are slightly right-skewed.

EXAMPLE 3.13

Computing the Five-Number Summary of the Number of Calories in Cereals

Nutritional data about a sample of seven breakfast cereals (stored in **Cereals**) includes the number of calories per serving (see Example 3.1 on page 98). Compute the five-number summary of the numbers of calories in cereals.

SOLUTION From previous computations for the calories in cereals (see pages 98 and 114), you know that the median = 110, $Q_1 = 100$, and $Q_3 = 190$.

In addition, the smallest value in the data set is 80, and the largest value is 200. Therefore, the five-number summary is as follows:

$$80 \quad 100 \quad 110 \quad 190 \quad 200$$

The three comparisons listed in Table 3.5 are used to evaluate skewness. The distance from $X_{smallest}$ to the median $(110 - 80 = 30)$ is less than the distance $(200 - 110 = 90)$ from the median to $X_{largest}$. The distance from $X_{smallest}$ to Q_1 $(100 - 80 = 20)$ is the more than the distance from Q_3 to $X_{largest}$ $(200 - 190 = 10)$. The distance from Q_1 to the median $(110 - 100 = 10)$ is less than the distance from the median to Q_3 $(190 - 110 = 80)$. Two comparisons indicate a right-skewed distribution, whereas the other indicates a left-skewed distribution. Therefore, given the small sample size and the conflicting results, the shape is not clearly determined.

The Boxplot

A **boxplot** provides a graphical representation of the data based on the five-number summary. To further analyze the sample of 10 times to get ready in the morning, you can construct a boxplot, as displayed in Figure 3.3.

FIGURE 3.3

Boxplot for the getting-ready times

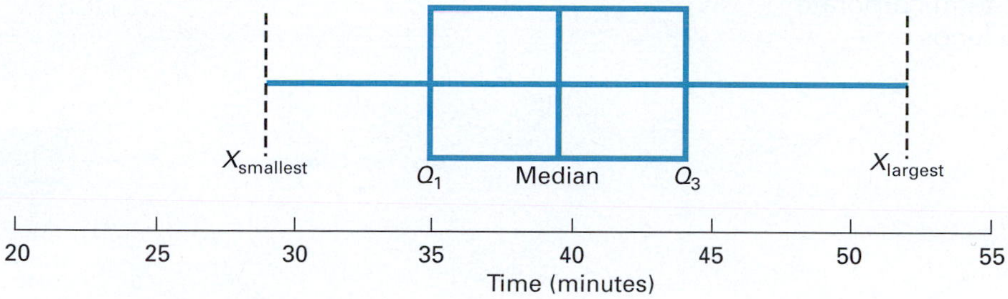

The vertical line drawn within the box represents the median. The vertical line at the left side of the box represents the location of Q_1, and the vertical line at the right side of the box represents the location of Q_3. Thus, the box contains the middle 50% of the values. The lower 25% of the data are represented by a line connecting the left side of the box to the location of the smallest value, $X_{smallest}$. Similarly, the upper 25% of the data are represented by a line connecting the right side of the box to $X_{largest}$.

The boxplot of the getting-ready times in Figure 3.3 indicates slight right-skewness because the distance between the median and the highest value is slightly greater than the distance between the lowest value and the median. Also, the right tail is slightly longer than the left tail.

EXAMPLE 3.14

Boxplots of the 2009 Returns of Intermediate Government and Short-Term Corporate Bond Funds

In Part II of the Choice Is Yours scenario, you are interested in comparing the past performance of the intermediate government bond and short-term corporate bond funds. One measure of past performance is the return in 2009. You have already defined the variables to be collected and collected the data from a sample of 184 bond funds. Construct the boxplot of the 2009 returns for the intermediate government bond and short-term corporate bond funds.

SOLUTION Figure 3.4 contains the five-number summaries and Excel boxplots of the 2009 return for the intermediate government and short-term corporate bond funds. Figure 3.5 displays the Minitab boxplots for the same data. Note that in Figure 3.5 on page 118, several * appear in the boxplots. These indicate outliers that are more than 1.5 times the interquartile range beyond the quartiles.

FIGURE 3.4

Excel five-number summaries and boxplots of the 2009 return for intermediate government bond and short-term corporate bond funds

	A	B	C
1	Five-Number Summary for Return 2009		
2		Intermediate Government	Short Term Corporate
3	Minimum	-4.8	-8.8
4	First Quartile	0.9	5.7
5	Median	4.4	9.1
6	Third Quartile	6.5	12.95
7	Maximum	28.6	32

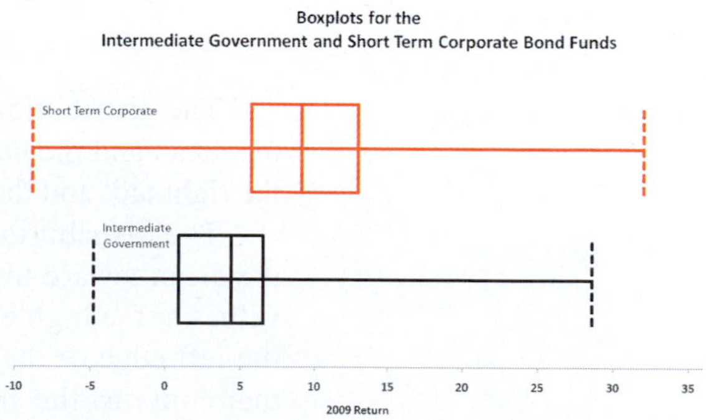

The median return, the quartiles, and the minimum and maximum returns are much higher for the short-term corporate bond funds than for the intermediate government bond funds. The median return for the short-term corporate bond funds is higher than the third quartile return for the intermediate government bond funds. The first quartile return (5.70) for the short-term

FIGURE 3.5

Minitab boxplots of the 2009 return for intermediate government bond and short-term corporate bond funds

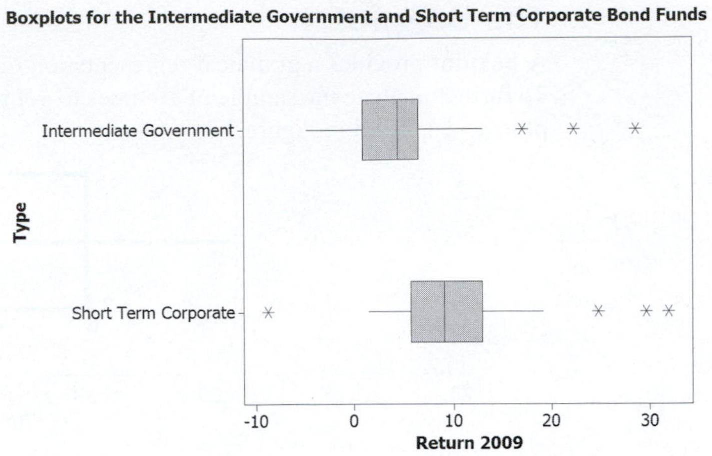

corporate bond funds is higher than the median return (4.40) for the intermediate government bond funds. Both the intermediate government bond and short-term corporate bond funds are right-skewed, with a very long tail in the upper part of the range. These results are consistent with the statistics computed in Figure 3.2 on page 109.

Figure 3.6 demonstrates the relationship between the boxplot and the density curve for four different types of distributions. The area under each density curve is split into quartiles corresponding to the five-number summary for the boxplot.

FIGURE 3.6

Boxplots and corresponding density curves for four distributions

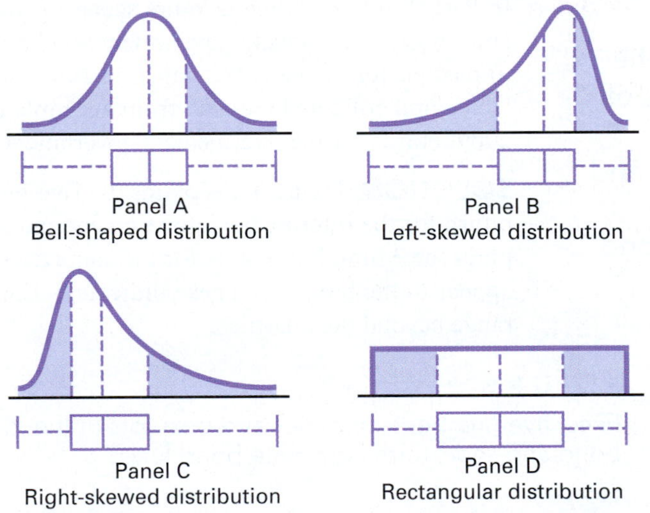

The distributions in Panels A and D of Figure 3.6 are symmetric. In these distributions, the mean and median are equal. In addition, the length of the left tail is equal to the length of the right tail, and the median line divides the box in half.

The distribution in Panel B of Figure 3.6 is left-skewed. The few small values distort the mean toward the left tail. For this left-skewed distribution, there is a heavy clustering of values at the high end of the scale (i.e., the right side); 75% of all values are found between the left edge of the box (Q_1) and the end of the right tail ($X_{largest}$). There is a long left tail that contains the smallest 25% of the values, demonstrating the lack of symmetry in this data set.

The distribution in Panel C of Figure 3.6 is right-skewed. The concentration of values is on the low end of the scale (i.e., the left side of the boxplot). Here, 75% of all values are found between the beginning of the left tail and the right edge of the box (Q_3). There is a long right tail that contains the largest 25% of the values, demonstrating the lack of symmetry in this data set.

Problems for Section 3.3

LEARNING THE BASICS

3.23 The following is a set of data from a sample of $n = 7$:

12 7 4 9 0 7 3

a. Compute the first quartile (Q_1), the third quartile (Q_3), and the interquartile range.
b. List the five-number summary.
c. Construct a boxplot and describe its shape.
d. Compare your answer in (c) with that from Problem 3.3 (d) on page 110. Discuss.

3.24 The following is a set of data from a sample of $n = 6$:

7 4 9 7 3 12

a. Compute the first quartile (Q_1), the third quartile (Q_3), and the interquartile range.
b. List the five-number summary.
c. Construct a boxplot and describe its shape.
d. Compare your answer in (c) with that from Problem 3.2 (d) on page 110. Discuss.

3.25 The following is a set of data from a sample of $n = 5$:

7 4 9 8 2

a. Compute the first quartile (Q_1), the third quartile (Q_3), and the interquartile range.
b. List the five-number summary.
c. Construct a boxplot and describe its shape.
d. Compare your answer in (c) with that from Problem 3.1 (d) on page 110. Discuss.

3.26 The following is a set of data from a sample of $n = 5$:

7 −5 −8 7 9

a. Compute the first quartile (Q_1), the third quartile (Q_3), and the interquartile range.
b. List the five-number summary.
c. Construct a boxplot and describe its shape.
d. Compare your answer in (c) with that from Problem 3.4 (d) on page 110. Discuss.

APPLYING THE CONCEPTS

3.27 The file ChocolateChip contains the cost (in cents) per 1-ounce serving, for a sample of 13 chocolate chip cookies. The data are as follows:

54 22 25 23 36 43 7 43 25 47 24 45 44

Source: Data extracted from "Chip, Chip, Hooray," *Consumer Reports,* June 2009, p. 7.

a. Compute the first quartile (Q_1), the third quartile (Q_3), and the interquartile range.
b. List the five-number summary.
c. Construct a boxplot and describe its shape.

SELF Test **3.28** The file Dark Chocolate contains the cost ($) per ounce for a sample of 14 dark chocolate bars:

0.68 0.72 0.92 1.14 1.42 0.94 0.77 0.57 1.51
0.57 0.55 0.86 1.41 0.90

Source: Data extracted from "Dark Chocolate: Which Bars Are Best?" *Consumer Reports,* September 2007, pp. 8.

a. Compute the first quartile (Q_1), the third quartile (Q_3), and the interquartile range.
b. List the five-number summary.
c. Construct a boxplot and describe its shape.

3.29 The file HotelUK contains the room price (in $) paid by U.S. travelers in six British cities in 2009:

185 160 126 116 112 105

Source: Data extracted from **www.hotels.com/press/hotel-price-index-2009-h2.html**.

a. Compute the first quartile (Q_1), the third quartile (Q_3), and the interquartile range.
b. List the five-number summary.
c. Construct a boxplot and describe its shape.

3.30 The file SUV contains the overall miles per gallon (MPG) of 2010 small SUVs:

24	23	22	21	22	22	18	18	26
26	26	19	19	19	21	21	21	21
21	18	19	21	22	22	16	16	

Source: Data extracted from "Vehicle Ratings," *Consumer Reports,* April 2010, pp. 33–34.

a. Compute the first quartile (Q_1), the third quartile (Q_3), and the interquartile range.
b. List the five-number summary.
c. Construct a boxplot and describe its shape.

3.31 The file SavingsRate-MMCD contains the yields for a money market account and a five-year certificate of deposit (CD), for 25 banks in the United States, as of March 29, 2010.

Source: Data extracted from **www.Bankrate.com**, March 29, 2010.

For each type of account:

a. Compute the first quartile (Q_1), the third quartile (Q_3), and the interquartile range.
b. List the five-number summary.
c. Construct a boxplot and describe its shape.

3.32 A bank branch located in a commercial district of a city has the business objective of developing an improved process for serving customers during the noon-to-1:00 P.M. lunch period. The waiting time, in minutes, is defined as the time the customer enters the line to when he or she reaches the teller window. Data are collected from a sample of 15 customers during this hour. The file Bank1 contains the results, which are listed at the top of page 120:

4.21	5.55	3.02	5.13	4.77	2.34	3.54	3.20
4.50	6.10	0.38	5.12	6.46	6.19	3.79	

Another bank branch, located in a residential area, is also concerned with the noon-to-1 P.M. lunch hour. The waiting times, in minutes, collected from a sample of 15 customers during this hour, are contained in the file **Bank2** and listed here:

9.66	5.90	8.02	5.79	8.73	3.82	8.01	8.35
10.49	6.68	5.64	4.08	6.17	9.91	5.47	

a. List the five-number summaries of the waiting times at the two bank branches.
b. Construct boxplots and describe the shapes of the distributions for the two bank branches.
c. What similarities and differences are there in the distributions of the waiting times at the two bank branches?

3.33 For this problem, use the data in **Bond Funds2008**.
a. Construct a multidimensional table of the mean 2008 return by type and risk.
b. Construct a multidimensional table of the standard deviation of the 2008 return by type and risk.
c. What conclusions can you reach concerning differences between the type of bond funds (intermediate government and short-term corporate) based on risk factor (low, average, and high)?
d. Compare the results in (a)–(c) to the 2009 returns (stored in **Bond Funds**).

3.34 For this problem, use the data in **Bond Funds2008**.
a. Construct a multidimensional table of the mean three-year return by type and risk.
b. Construct a multidimensional table of the standard deviation of the three-year return by type and risk.
c. What conclusions can you reach concerning differences between the type of bond funds (intermediate government and short-term corporate) based on risk factor (low, average, and high)?
d. Compare the results in (a)–(c) to the three-year returns from 2007–2009 (stored in **Bond Funds**).

3.35 For this problem, use the data in **Bond Funds2008**.
a. Construct a multidimensional table of the mean five-year return by type and risk.
b. Construct a multidimensional table of the standard deviation of the five-year return by type and risk.
c. What conclusions can you reach concerning differences between the type of bond funds (intermediate government and short-term corporate) based on risk factor (low, average, and high)?
d. Compare the results in (a)–(c) to the five-year returns from 2005–2009 (stored in **Bond Funds**).

3.36 For this problem, use the data in **Bond Funds2008**.
a. Construct a multidimensional table of the mean 2008 return by type, fees, and risk.
b. Construct a multidimensional table of the standard deviation of the 2008 return by type, fees, and risk.
c. What conclusions can you reach concerning differences between the type of bond funds (intermediate government and short-term corporate) based on fees (yes or no) and risk factor (low, average, and high)?
d. Compare the results in (a)–(c) to the 2009 returns (stored in **Bond Funds**).

3.4 Numerical Descriptive Measures for a Population

Sections 3.1 and 3.2 presented various statistics that described the properties of central tendency and variation for a sample. If your data set represents numerical measurements for an entire population, you need to compute and interpret parameters for a population. In this section, you will learn about three population parameters: the population mean, population variance, and population standard deviation.

To help illustrate these parameters, first review Table 3.6, which contains the one-year returns for the five largest bond funds (in terms of total assets) as of April 27, 2010 (stored in **LargestBonds**).

TABLE 3.6
One-Year Return for the Population Consisting of the Five Largest Bond Funds

Bond Fund	One-Year Return
PIMCO: Total Rtn;Inst	14.8
American Funds Bond;A	16.5
Dodge Cox Income	16.5
Vanguard Tot Bd;Inv	7.6
Vanguard Int-TmTx;Adm	6.6

Source: Data extracted from *The Wall Street Journal*, April 27, 2010, p. C4.

The Population Mean

The population mean is represented by the symbol μ, the Greek lowercase letter mu. Equation (3.13) defines the population mean.

POPULATION MEAN

The **population mean** is the sum of the values in the population divided by the population size, N.

$$\mu = \frac{\sum_{i=1}^{N} X_i}{N} \tag{3.13}$$

where

μ = population mean

X_i = ith value of the variable X

$\sum_{i=1}^{N} X_i$ = summation of all X_i values in the population

N = number of values in the population

To compute the mean one-year return for the population of bond funds given in Table 3.6, use Equation (3.13):

$$\mu = \frac{\sum_{i=1}^{N} X_i}{N} = \frac{14.8 + 16.5 + 16.5 + 7.6 + 6.6}{5} = \frac{62.0}{5} = 12.4$$

Thus, the mean percentage return for these bond funds is 12.4.

The Population Variance and Standard Deviation

The **population variance** and the **population standard deviation** are parameters that measure variation in a population. As was the case for the sample statistics, the population standard deviation is the square root of the population variance. The symbol σ^2, the Greek lowercase letter sigma squared, represents the population variance, and the symbol σ, the Greek lowercase letter sigma, represents the population standard deviation. Equations (3.14) and (3.15) define these parameters. The denominators for the right-side terms in these equations use N and not the $(n - 1)$ term that is used in the equations for the sample variance and standard deviation [see Equations (3.6) and (3.7) on page 103].

POPULATION VARIANCE

The population variance is the sum of the squared differences around the population mean divided by the population size, N.

$$\sigma^2 = \frac{\sum_{i=1}^{N} (X_i - \mu)^2}{N} \tag{3.14}$$

where

μ = population mean

X_i = ith value of the variable X

$\sum_{i=1}^{N} (X_i - \mu)^2$ = summation of all the squared differences between the X_i values and μ

POPULATION STANDARD DEVIATION

$$\sigma = \sqrt{\frac{\sum_{i=1}^{N}(X_i - \mu)^2}{N}} \quad \textbf{(3.15)}$$

To compute the population variance for the data of Table 3.6, you use Equation (3.14):

$$\begin{aligned}
\sigma^2 &= \frac{\sum_{i=1}^{N}(X_i - \mu)^2}{N} \\
&= \frac{(14.8 - 12.4)^2 + (16.5 - 12.4)^2 + (16.5 - 12.4)^2 + (7.6 - 12.4)^2 + (6.6 - 12.4)^2}{5} \\
&= \frac{5.76 + 16.81 + 16.81 + 23.04 + 33.64}{5} \\
&= \frac{96.06}{5} = 19.212
\end{aligned}$$

Thus, the variance of the one-year returns is 19.212 squared percentage return. The squared units make the variance difficult to interpret. You should use the standard deviation that is expressed in the original units of the data (percentage return). From Equation (3.15),

$$\sigma = \sqrt{\sigma^2} = \sqrt{\frac{\sum_{i=1}^{N}(X_i - \mu)^2}{N}} = \sqrt{\frac{96.06}{5}} = 4.3831$$

Therefore, the typical percentage return differs from the mean of 12.4 by approximately 4.3831. This large amount of variation suggests that these large bond funds produce results that differ greatly.

The Empirical Rule

In most data sets, a large portion of the values tend to cluster somewhere near the median. In right-skewed data sets, this clustering occurs to the left of the mean—that is, at a value less than the mean. In left-skewed data sets, the values tend to cluster to the right of the mean—that is, greater than the mean. In symmetric data sets, where the median and mean are the same, the values often tend to cluster around the median and mean, producing a bell-shaped distribution. You can use the **empirical rule** to examine the variability in bell-shaped distributions:

- Approximately 68% of the values are within ± 1 standard deviation from the mean.
- Approximately 95% of the values are within ± 2 standard deviations from the mean.
- Approximately 99.7% of the values are within ± 3 standard deviations from the mean.

The empirical rule helps you measure how the values distribute above and below the mean and can help you identify outliers. The empirical rule implies that for bell-shaped distributions, only about 1 out of 20 values will be beyond two standard deviations from the mean in either direction. As a general rule, you can consider values not found in the interval $\mu \pm 2\sigma$ as potential outliers. The rule also implies that only about 3 in 1,000 will be beyond three standard deviations from the mean. Therefore, values not found in the interval $\mu \pm 3\sigma$ are almost always considered outliers.

EXAMPLE 3.15

Using the Empirical Rule

A population of 2 liter bottles of cola is known to have a mean fill-weight of 2.06 liters and a standard deviation of 0.02 liters. The population is known to be bell-shaped. Describe the distribution of fill-weights. Is it very likely that a bottle will contain less than 2 liters of cola?

SOLUTION

$$\mu \pm \sigma = 2.06 \pm 0.02 = (2.04, 2.08)$$
$$\mu \pm 2\sigma = 2.06 \pm 2(0.02) = (2.02, 2.10)$$
$$\mu \pm 3\sigma = 2.06 \pm 3(0.02) = (2.00, 2.12)$$

Using the empirical rule, you can see that approximately 68% of the bottles will contain between 2.04 and 2.08 liters, approximately 95% will contain between 2.02 and 2.10 liters, and approximately 99.7% will contain between 2.00 and 2.12 liters. Therefore, it is highly unlikely that a bottle will contain less than 2 liters.

For heavily skewed data sets and those not appearing to be bell-shaped, you should use the Chebyshev rule, discussed next, instead of the empirical rule.

The Chebyshev Rule

The **Chebyshev rule** (see reference 1) states that for any data set, regardless of shape, the percentage of values that are found within distances of k standard deviations from the mean must be at least

$$\left(1 - \frac{1}{k^2}\right) \times 100\%$$

You can use this rule for any value of k greater than 1. For example, consider $k = 2$. The Chebyshev rule states that at least $[1 - (1/2)^2] \times 100\% = 75\%$ of the values must be found within ± 2 standard deviations of the mean.

The Chebyshev rule is very general and applies to any distribution. The rule indicates *at least* what percentage of the values fall within a given distance from the mean. However, if the data set is approximately bell-shaped, the empirical rule will more accurately reflect the greater concentration of data close to the mean. Table 3.7 compares the Chebyshev and empirical rules.

TABLE 3.7

How Data Vary Around the Mean

	% of Values Found in Intervals Around the Mean	
Interval	**Chebyshev (any distribution)**	**Empirical Rule (bell-shaped distribution)**
$(\mu - \sigma, \mu + \sigma)$	At least 0%	Approximately 68%
$(\mu - 2\sigma, \mu + 2\sigma)$	At least 75%	Approximately 95%
$(\mu - 3\sigma, \mu + 3\sigma)$	At least 88.89%	Approximately 99.7%

EXAMPLE 3.16

Using the Chebyshev Rule

As in Example 3.15, a population of 2-liter bottles of cola is known to have a mean fill-weight of 2.06 liters and a standard deviation of 0.02 liters. However, the shape of the population is unknown, and you cannot assume that it is bell-shaped. Describe the distribution of fill-weights. Is it very likely that a bottle will contain less than 2 liters of cola?

SOLUTION

$$\mu \pm \sigma = 2.06 \pm 0.02 = (2.04, 2.08)$$
$$\mu \pm 2\sigma = 2.06 \pm 2(0.02) = (2.02, 2.10)$$
$$\mu \pm 3\sigma = 2.06 \pm 3(0.02) = (2.00, 2.12)$$

Because the distribution may be skewed, you cannot use the empirical rule. Using the Chebyshev rule, you cannot say anything about the percentage of bottles containing between 2.04 and 2.08 liters. You can state that at least 75% of the bottles will contain between 2.02 and 2.10 liters and at least 88.89% will contain between 2.00 and 2.12 liters. Therefore, between 0 and 11.11% of the bottles will contain less than 2 liters.

You can use these two rules to understand how data are distributed around the mean when you have sample data. With each rule, you use the value you computed for $\bar{X}$ in place of μ and the value you computed for S in place of σ. The results you compute using the sample statistics are *approximations* because you used sample statistics $(\bar{X}, S)$ and not population parameters (μ, σ).

Problems for Section 3.4

LEARNING THE BASICS

3.37 The following is a set of data for a population with $N = 10$:

7 5 11 8 3 6 2 1 9 8

a. Compute the population mean.
b. Compute the population standard deviation.

3.38 The following is a set of data for a population with $N = 10$:

7 5 6 6 6 4 8 6 9 3

a. Compute the population mean.
b. Compute the population standard deviation.

APPLYING THE CONCEPTS

3.39 The file Tax contains the quarterly sales tax receipts (in thousands of dollars) submitted to the comptroller of the Village of Fair Lake for the period ending March 2010 by all 50 business establishments in that locale:

10.3	11.1	9.6	9.0	14.5
13.0	6.7	11.0	8.4	10.3
13.0	11.2	7.3	5.3	12.5
8.0	11.8	8.7	10.6	9.5
11.1	10.2	11.1	9.9	9.8
11.6	15.1	12.5	6.5	7.5
10.0	12.9	9.2	10.0	12.8
12.5	9.3	10.4	12.7	10.5
9.3	11.5	10.7	11.6	7.8
10.5	7.6	10.1	8.9	8.6

a. Compute the mean, variance, and standard deviation for this population.
b. What percentage of these businesses have quarterly sales tax receipts within ±1, ±2, or ±3 standard deviations of the mean?
c. Compare your findings with what would be expected on the basis of the empirical rule. Are you surprised at the results in (b)?

3.40 Consider a population of 1,024 mutual funds that primarily invest in large companies. You have determined that μ, the mean one-year total percentage return achieved by all the funds, is 8.20 and that σ, the standard deviation, is 2.75.
a. According to the empirical rule, what percentage of these funds are expected to be within ±1 standard deviation of the mean?
b. According to the empirical rule, what percentage of these funds are expected to be within ±2 standard deviations of the mean?
c. According to the Chebyshev rule, what percentage of these funds are expected to be within ±1, ±2, or ±3 standard deviations of the mean?
d. According to the Chebyshev rule, at least 93.75% of these funds are expected to have one-year total returns between what two amounts?

3.41 The file CigaretteTax contains the state cigarette tax ($) for each of the 50 states as of December 31, 2009.
a. Compute the population mean and population standard deviation for the state cigarette tax.
b. Interpret the parameters in (a).

3.42 The file Energy contains the per capita energy consumption, in kilowatt-hours, for each of the 50 states and the District of Columbia during a recent year.
a. Compute the mean, variance, and standard deviation for the population.
b. What proportion of these states has per capita energy consumption within ±1 standard deviation of the mean,

within ±2 standard deviations of the mean, and within ±3 standard deviations of the mean?

c. Compare your findings with what would be expected based on the empirical rule. Are you surprised at the results in (b)?

d. Repeat (a) through (c) with the District of Columbia removed. How have the results changed?

3.43 Thirty companies comprise the DJIA. Just how big are these companies? One common method for measuring the size of a company is to use its market capitalization, which is computed by multiplying the number of stock shares by the price of a share of stock. On March 29, 2010, the market capitalization of these companies ranged from Alcoa's $14.7 billion to ExxonMobil's $318.8 billion. The entire population of market capitalization values is stored in DowMarketCap.

Source: Data extracted from **money.cnn.com**, March 29, 2010.

a. Compute the mean and standard deviation of the market capitalization for this population of 30 companies.

b. Interpret the parameters computed in (a).

3.5 The Covariance and the Coefficient of Correlation

In Section 2.6, you used scatter plots to visually examine the relationship between two numerical variables. This section presents two measures of the relationship between two numerical variables: the covariance and the coefficient of correlation.

The Covariance

The **covariance** measures the strength of the linear relationship between two numerical variables (X and Y). Equation (3.16) defines the **sample covariance**, and Example 3.17 illustrates its use.

SAMPLE COVARIANCE

$$\text{cov}(X, Y) = \frac{\sum_{i=1}^{n}(X_i - \bar{X})(Y_i - \bar{Y})}{n - 1} \tag{3.16}$$

EXAMPLE 3.17

Computing the Sample Covariance

In Figure 2.15 on page 57, you constructed a scatter plot that showed the relationship between the value and the annual revenue of the 30 teams that make up the National Basketball Association (NBA) (extracted from **www.forbes.com/lists/2009/32/basketball-values-09_NBA-Team-Valuations_Rank.html**; stored in NBAValues). Now, you want to measure the association between the value of a franchise and annual revenue by computing the sample covariance.

SOLUTION Table 3.8 on page 126 provides the value and the annual revenue of the 30 teams.

Figure 3.7 on page 126 contains a worksheet that computes the covariance for these data. The Calculations Area section of Figure 3.7 breaks down Equation (3.16) into a set of smaller calculations. From cell F9, or by using Equation (3.16) directly, you find that the covariance is 3,115.7241:

$$\text{cov}(X, Y) = \frac{90{,}356}{30 - 1} = 3{,}115.7241$$

The covariance has a major flaw as a measure of the linear relationship between two numerical variables. Because the covariance can have any value, you are unable to use it to determine the relative strength of the relationship. In other words, you cannot tell whether the value 3,115.7241 indicates a strong relationship or a weak relationship. To better determine the relative strength of the relationship, you need to compute the coefficient of correlation.

TABLE 3.8

Values and Annual Revenues of the 30 NBA Teams (in millions of dollars)

Team	Value	Revenue	Team	Value	Revenue
Atlanta	306	103	Milwaukee	254	91
Boston	433	144	Minnesota	268	96
Charlotte	278	96	New Jersey	269	92
Chicago	511	168	New Orleans	267	95
Cleveland	476	159	New York	586	202
Dallas	446	154	Oklahoma City	310	111
Denver	321	115	Orlando	361	107
Detroit	479	171	Philadelphia	344	115
Golden State	315	113	Phoenix	429	148
Houston	470	160	Portland	338	121
Indiana	281	97	Sacramento	305	109
Los Angeles Clippers	295	102	San Antonio	398	133
Los Angeles Lakers	607	209	Toronto	386	133
Memphis	257	88	Utah	343	118
Miami	364	126	Washington	313	110

FIGURE 3.7

Excel worksheet to compute the covariance between the value and the annual revenue of the 30 NBA teams

	A	B	C	D	E	F
1	Covariance Analysis					
2						
3	Revenue	Value	(X-XBar)(Y-YBar)			
4	103	306	1415.2000		Calculations Area	
5	144	433	1174.8000		XBar	126.2000
6	96	278	2687.8000		YBar	367
7	168	511	6019.2000		*n* -1	29
8	159	476	3575.2000		Σ(X-XBar)(Y-YBar)	90356.0000
9	154	446	2196.2000		**Covariance**	**3115.7241**
10	115	321	515.2000			
11	171	479	5017.6000			
12	113	315	686.4000			
13	160	470	3481.4000			
14	97	281	2511.2000			
15	102	295	1742.4000			
16	209	607	19872.0000			
17	88	257	4202.0000			
18	126	364	0.6000			
19	91	254	3977.6000			
20	96	268	2989.8000			
21	92	269	3351.6000			
22	95	267	3120.0000			
23	202	586	16600.2000			
24	111	310	866.4000			
25	107	361	115.2000			
26	115	344	257.6000			
27	148	429	1351.6000			
28	121	338	150.8000			
29	109	305	1066.4000			
30	133	398	210.8000			
31	133	386	129.2000			
32	118	343	196.8000			
33	110	313	874.8000			

The Coefficient of Correlation

The **coefficient of correlation** measures the relative strength of a linear relationship between two numerical variables. The values of the coefficient of correlation range from -1 for a perfect negative correlation to $+1$ for a perfect positive correlation. *Perfect* in this case means that if the points were plotted on a scatter plot, all the points could be connected with a straight line.

When dealing with population data for two numerical variables, the Greek letter ρ (*rho*) is used as the symbol for the coefficient of correlation. Figure 3.8 illustrates three different types of association between two variables.

FIGURE 3.8
Types of association between variables

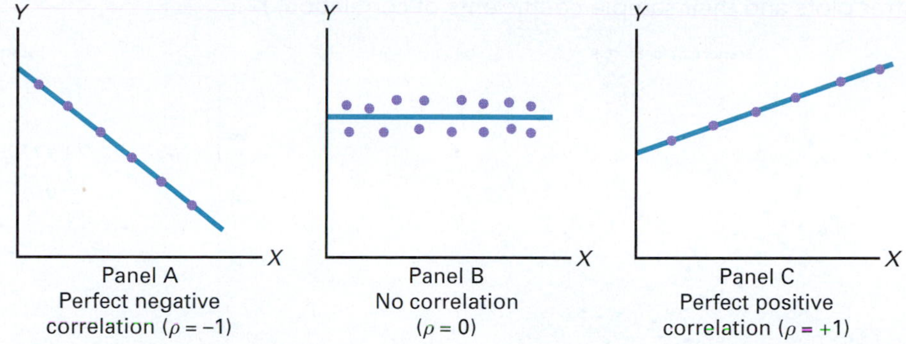

In Panel A of Figure 3.8, there is a perfect negative linear relationship between X and Y. Thus, the coefficient of correlation, ρ, equals -1, and when X increases, Y decreases in a perfectly predictable manner. Panel B shows a situation in which there is no relationship between X and Y. In this case, the coefficient of correlation, ρ, equals 0, and as X increases, there is no tendency for Y to increase or decrease. Panel C illustrates a perfect positive relationship where equals In this case, Y increases in a perfectly predictable manner when X increases.

Correlation alone cannot prove that there is a causation effect—that is, that the change in the value of one variable caused the change in the other variable. A strong correlation can be produced simply by chance, by the effect of a third variable not considered in the calculation of the correlation, or by a cause-and-effect relationship. You would need to perform additional analysis to determine which of these three situations actually produced the correlation. Therefore, you can say that *causation implies correlation, but correlation alone does not imply causation*.

Equation (3.17) defines the **sample coefficient of correlation (r)**.

SAMPLE COEFFICIENT OF CORRELATION

$$r = \frac{\text{cov}(X, Y)}{S_X S_Y} \tag{3.17}$$

where

$$\text{cov}(X, Y) = \frac{\sum_{i=1}^{n}(X_i - \bar{X})(Y_i - \bar{Y})}{n - 1}$$

$$S_X = \sqrt{\frac{\sum_{i=1}^{n}(X_i - \bar{X})^2}{n - 1}}$$

$$S_Y = \sqrt{\frac{\sum_{i=1}^{n}(Y_i - \bar{Y})^2}{n - 1}}$$

When you have sample data, you can compute the sample coefficient of correlation, r. When using sample data, you are unlikely to have a sample coefficient of correlation of exactly $+1$, 0, or -1. Figure 3.9 presents scatter plots along with their respective sample coefficients of correlation, r, for six data sets, each of which contains 100 values of X and Y.

In Panel A, the coefficient of correlation, r, is -0.9. You can see that for small values of X, there is a very strong tendency for Y to be large. Likewise, the large values of X tend to be paired with small values of Y. The data do not all fall on a straight line, so the association between X and Y cannot be described as perfect. The data in Panel B have a coefficient of

FIGURE 3.9

Six scatter plots and their sample coefficients of correlation, r

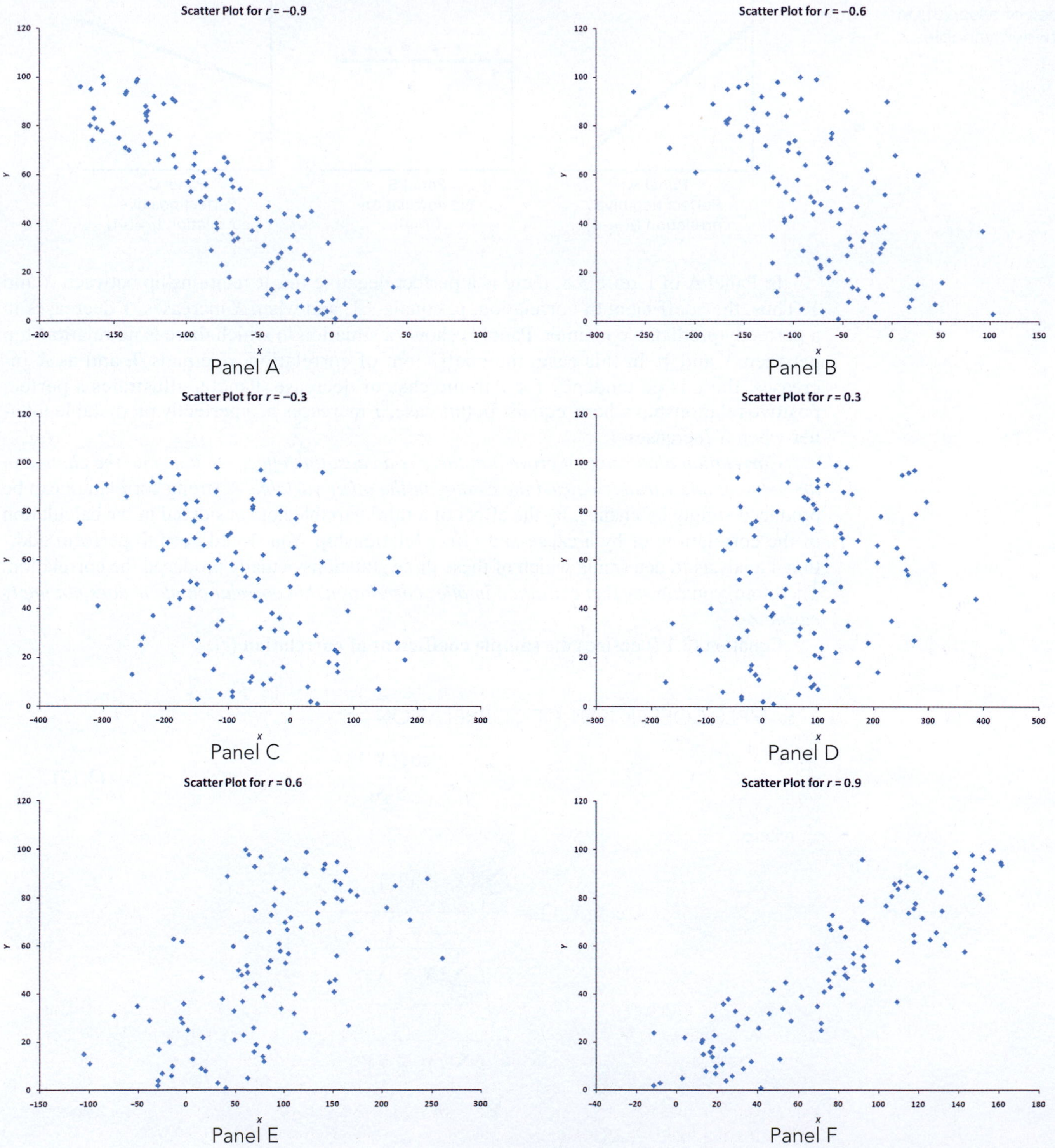

correlation equal to −0.6, and the small values of *X* tend to be paired with large values of *Y*. The linear relationship between *X* and *Y* in Panel B is not as strong as that in Panel A. Thus, the coefficient of correlation in Panel B is not as negative as that in Panel A. In Panel C, the linear relationship between *X* and *Y* is very weak, $r = -0.3$, and there is only a slight tendency for the small values of *X* to be paired with the large values of *Y*. Panels D through F depict data sets that have positive coefficients of correlation because small values of *X* tend to be paired with small values of *Y* and large values of *X* tend to be associated with large values of *Y*. Panel D shows weak positive correlation, with $r = 0.3$. Panel E shows stronger positive correlation with $r = 0.6$. Panel F shows very strong positive correlation, with $r = 0.9$.

EXAMPLE 3.18

Computing the Sample Coefficient of Correlation

In Example 3.17 on page 125, you computed the covariance of the values and revenues of 30 NBA basketball teams. Using Figure 3.10 and Equation (3.17) on page 127, compute the sample coefficient of correlation.

FIGURE 3.10

Excel worksheet to compute the sample coefficient of correlation, *r*, between the values and revenues of 30 NBA basketball teams

	A	B	C	D	E	F
1	Coefficient of Correlation Calculations					
2						
3	Revenue	Value	(X-XBar)(Y-YBar)		Calculations Area	
4	103	306	1415.2000		XBar	126.2000
5	144	433	1174.8000		YBar	367.0000
6	96	278	2687.8000		Σ(X-XBar)^2	30550.8000
7	168	511	6019.2000		Σ(Y-YBar)^2	272410.0000
8	159	476	3575.2000		Σ(X-XBar)(Y-YBar)	90356.0000
9	154	446	2196.2000		*n*-1	29
10	115	321	515.2000			
11	171	479	5017.6000		Results	
12	113	315	686.4000		Covariance	3115.7241
13	160	470	3481.4000		S_X	32.4573
14	97	281	2511.2000		S_Y	96.9198
15	102	295	1742.4000		*r*	0.9905
16	209	607	19872.0000			
17	88	257	4202.0000			
18	126	364	0.6000			
19	91	254	3977.6000			
20	96	268	2989.8000			
21	92	269	3351.6000			
22	95	267	3120.0000			
23	202	586	16600.2000			
24	111	310	866.4000			
25	107	361	115.2000			
26	115	344	257.6000			
27	148	429	1351.6000			
28	121	338	150.8000			
29	109	305	1066.4000			
30	133	398	210.8000			
31	133	386	129.2000			
32	118	343	196.8000			
33	110	313	874.8000			

SOLUTION

$$r = \frac{\text{cov}(X, Y)}{S_X S_Y}$$

$$= \frac{3{,}115.7241}{(32.4573)(96.9198)}$$

$$= 0.9905$$

The value and revenue of the NBA teams are very highly correlated. The teams with the lowest revenues have the lowest values. The teams with the highest revenues have the highest values. This relationship is very strong, as indicated by the coefficient of correlation, $r = 0.9905$.

In general you cannot assume that just because two variables are correlated, changes in one variable caused changes in the other variable. However, for this example, it makes sense to conclude that changes in revenue would cause changes in the value of a team.

In summary, the coefficient of correlation indicates the linear relationship, or association, between two numerical variables. When the coefficient of correlation gets closer to +1 or −1, the linear relationship between the two variables is stronger. When the coefficient of correlation is near 0, little or no linear relationship exists. The sign of the coefficient of correlation indicates whether the data are positively correlated (i.e., the larger values of X are typically paired with the larger values of Y) or negatively correlated (i.e., the larger values of X are typically paired with the smaller values of Y). The existence of a strong correlation does not imply a causation effect. It only indicates the tendencies present in the data.

Problems for Section 3.5

LEARNING THE BASICS

3.44 The following is a set of data from a sample of $n = 11$ items:

X	7	5	8	3	6	10	12	4	9	15	18
Y	21	15	24	9	18	30	36	12	27	45	54

a. Compute the covariance.
b. Compute the coefficient of correlation.
c. How strong is the relationship between X and Y? Explain.

APPLYING THE CONCEPTS

3.45 A study of 218 students at Ohio State University suggests a link between time spent on the social networking site Facebook and grade point average. Students who rarely or never used Facebook had higher grade point averages than students who use Facebook.

Source: Data extracted from M. B. Marklein, "Facebook Use Linked to Less Textbook Time," **www.usatoday.com**, April 14, 2009.

a. Does the study suggest that time spent on Facebook and grade point average are positively correlated or negatively correlated?
b. Do you think that there might be a cause-and-effect relationship between time spent on Facebook and grade point average? Explain.

SELF Test **3.46** The file **Cereals** lists the calories and sugar, in grams, in one serving of seven breakfast cereals:

Cereal	Calories	Sugar
Kellogg's All Bran	80	6
Kellogg's Corn Flakes	100	2
Wheaties	100	4
Nature's Path Organic Multigrain Flakes	110	4
Kellogg Rice Krispies	130	4
Post Shredded Wheat Vanilla Almond	190	11
Kellogg Mini Wheats	200	10

a. Compute the covariance.
b. Compute the coefficient of correlation.
c. Which do you think is more valuable in expressing the relationship between calories and sugar—the covariance or the coefficient of correlation? Explain.
d. Based on (a) and (b), what conclusions can you reach about the relationship between calories and sugar?

3.47 Movie companies need to predict the gross receipts of individual movies after a movie has debuted. The following results, listed in **PotterMovies**, are the first weekend gross, the U.S. gross, and the worldwide gross (in millions of dollars) of the six Harry Potter movies that debuted from 2001 to 2009:

Title	First Weekend	U.S. Gross	Worldwide Gross
Sorcerer's Stone	90.295	317.558	976.458
Chamber of Secrets	88.357	261.988	878.988
Prisoner of Azkaban	93.687	249.539	795.539
Goblet of Fire	102.335	290.013	896.013
Order of the Phoenix	77.108	292.005	938.469
Half-Blood Prince	77.836	301.460	934.601

Source: Data extracted from **www.the-numbers.com/interactive/comp-Harry-Potter.php.**

a. Compute the covariance between first weekend gross and U.S. gross, first weekend gross and worldwide gross, and U.S. gross and worldwide gross.
b. Compute the coefficient of correlation between first weekend gross and U.S. gross, first weekend gross and worldwide gross, and U.S. gross and worldwide gross.
c. Which do you think is more valuable in expressing the relationship between first weekend gross, U.S. gross, and worldwide gross—the covariance or the coefficient of correlation? Explain.
d. Based on (a) and (b), what conclusions can you reach about the relationship between first weekend gross, U.S. gross, and worldwide gross?

3.48 College basketball is big business, with coaches' salaries, revenues, and expenses in millions of dollars. The file **College Basketball** contains the coaches' salaries and revenues for college basketball at 60 of the 65 schools that played in the 2009 NCAA men's basketball tournament (data extracted from "Compensation for Division 1 Men's Basketball Coaches," *USA Today*, April 2, 2010, p. 8C; and C. Isadore, "Nothing but Net: Basketball Dollars by School," **money.cnn.com/2010/03/18/news/companies/basketball_profits/**).

a. Compute the covariance.
b. Compute the coefficient of correlation.
c. Based on (a) and (b), what conclusions can you reach about the relationship between coaches' salaries and revenues?

3.49 College football players trying out for the NFL are given the Wonderlic standardized intelligence test. The file **Wonderlic** contains the average Wonderlic score of football players trying out for the NFL and the graduation rate for football players at selected schools.

Source: Data extracted from S. Walker, "The NFL's Smartest Team," *The Wall Street Journal,* September 30, 2005, pp. W1, W10.

a. Compute the covariance.
b. Compute the coefficient of correlation.
c. Based on (a) and (b), what conclusions can you reach about the relationship between the average Wonderlic score and graduation rate?

3.6 Descriptive Statistics: Pitfalls and Ethical Issues

This chapter describes how a set of numerical data can be characterized by the statistics that measure the properties of central tendency, variation, and shape. In business, descriptive statistics such as the ones you have learned about are frequently included in summary reports that are prepared periodically.

The volume of information available on the Internet, in newspapers, and in magazines has produced much skepticism about the objectivity of data. When you are reading information that contains descriptive statistics, you should keep in mind the quip often attributed to the famous nineteenth-century British statesman Benjamin Disraeli: "There are three kinds of lies: lies, damned lies, and statistics."

For example, in examining statistics, you need to compare the mean and the median. Are they similar, or are they very different? Or, is only the mean provided? The answers to these questions will help you determine whether the data are skewed or symmetrical and whether the median might be a better measure of central tendency than the mean. In addition, you should look to see whether the standard deviation or interquartile range for a very skewed set of data has been included in the statistics provided. Without this, it is impossible to determine the amount of variation that exists in the data.

Ethical considerations arise when you are deciding what results to include in a report. You should document both good and bad results. In addition, when making oral presentations and presenting written reports, you need to give results in a fair, objective, and neutral manner. Unethical behavior occurs when you selectively fail to report pertinent findings that are detrimental to the support of a particular position.

USING STATISTICS @ Choice Is Yours, Part II Revisited

In Part II of the Choice Is Yours scenario, you were hired by the Choice Is Yours investment company to assist investors interested in bond mutual funds. A sample of 184 bond mutual funds included 87 intermediate government funds and 97 short-term corporate bond funds. By comparing these two categories, you were able to provide investors with valuable insights.

The 2009 returns for both the intermediate government funds and the short-term corporate bond funds were right-skewed, as indicated by the boxplots (see Figures 3.4 and 3.5 on pages 117 and 118). The descriptive statistics (see Figure 3.2 on page 109) allowed you to compare the central tendency and variability of returns of the intermediate government funds and the short-term corporate bond funds. The mean indicated that the intermediate government funds returned an average of 4.4529, and the median indicated that half of the funds had returns of 4.4 or more. The short-term corporate bond funds' central tendencies were much higher than those of the intermediate government funds—they had an average of 9.5959, and half the funds had returns above 9.1. The intermediate government funds showed slightly less variability than the short-term corporate funds with a standard deviation of 5.36 as compared to 5.69. An interesting insight is that while 25% of the intermediate government funds had returns of 6.5 or higher ($Q_3 = 6.5$), 75% of the short-term corporate bond funds had returns of 5.7 or higher ($Q_1 = 5.7$). Although past performance is no assurance of future performance, in 2009, the short-term corporate funds greatly outperformed the intermediate government funds. (To see a situation where the opposite was true, open the **Bond Funds2008** file.)

SUMMARY

In this chapter and the previous chapter, you studied descriptive statistics—how you can visualize data through tables and charts and how you can use different statistics to help analyze the data and reach conclusions. In Chapter 2, you were able to visualize data by constructing bar and pie charts, histograms, and other charts. In this chapter, you learned how descriptive statistics such as the mean, median, quartiles, range, and standard deviation are used to describe the characteristics of central tendency, variability, and shape. In addition, you constructed boxplots to visualize the distribution of the data. You also learned how the coefficient of correlation is used to describe the relationship between two numerical variables. Table 3.9 provides a list of the descriptive statistics covered in this chapter.

In the next chapter, the basic principles of probability are presented in order to bridge the gap between the subject of descriptive statistics and the subject of inferential statistics.

TABLE 3.9

Summary of Descriptive Statistics

Type of Analysis	Numerical Data
Describing central tendency, variation, and shape of a numerical variable	Mean, median, mode, quartiles, range, interquartile range, variance, standard deviation, coefficient of variation, Z scores, boxplot (Sections 3.1 through 3.4)
Describing the relationship between two numerical variables	Covariance, coefficient of correlation (Section 3.5)

KEY EQUATIONS

Sample Mean

$$\bar{X} = \frac{\sum_{i=1}^{n} X_i}{n} \quad \textbf{(3.1)}$$

Median

$$\text{Median} = \frac{n+1}{2} \text{ ranked value} \quad \textbf{(3.2)}$$

Geometric Mean

$$\bar{X}_G = (X_1 \times X_2 \times \cdots \times X_n)^{1/n} \quad \textbf{(3.3)}$$

Geometric Mean Rate of Return

$$\bar{R}_G = [(1 + R_1) \times (1 + R_2) \times \cdots \times (1 + R_n)]^{1/n} - 1 \quad \textbf{(3.4)}$$

Range

$$\text{Range} = X_{\text{largest}} - X_{\text{smallest}} \quad \textbf{(3.5)}$$

Sample Variance

$$S^2 = \frac{\sum_{i=1}^{n} (X_i - \bar{X})^2}{n-1} \quad \textbf{(3.6)}$$

Sample Standard Deviation

$$S = \sqrt{S^2} = \sqrt{\frac{\sum_{i=1}^{n} (X_i - \bar{X})^2}{n-1}} \quad \textbf{(3.7)}$$

Coefficient of Variation

$$CV = \left(\frac{S}{\bar{X}}\right) 100\% \quad \textbf{(3.8)}$$

Z Score

$$Z = \frac{X - \bar{X}}{S} \quad \textbf{(3.9)}$$

First Quartile, Q_1

$$Q_1 = \frac{n+1}{4} \text{ ranked value} \quad (3.10)$$

Third Quartile, Q_3

$$Q_3 = \frac{3(n+1)}{4} \text{ ranked value} \quad (3.11)$$

Interquartile Range

$$\text{Interquartile range} = Q_3 - Q_1 \quad (3.12)$$

Population Mean

$$\mu = \frac{\sum_{i=1}^{N} X_i}{N} \quad (3.13)$$

Population Variance

$$\sigma^2 = \frac{\sum_{i=1}^{N} (X_i - \mu)^2}{N} \quad (3.14)$$

Population Standard Deviation

$$\sigma = \sqrt{\frac{\sum_{i=1}^{N} (X_i - \mu)^2}{N}} \quad (3.15)$$

Sample Covariance

$$\text{cov}(X, Y) = \frac{\sum_{i=1}^{n} (X_i - \bar{X})(Y_i - \bar{Y})}{n-1} \quad (3.16)$$

Sample Coefficient of Correlation

$$r = \frac{\text{cov}(X, Y)}{S_X S_Y} \quad (3.17)$$

KEY TERMS

CHAPTER REVIEW PROBLEMS

CHECKING YOUR UNDERSTANDING

3.50 What are the properties of a set of numerical data?

3.51 What is meant by the property of central tendency?

3.52 What are the differences among the mean, median, and mode, and what are the advantages and disadvantages of each?

3.53 How do you interpret the first quartile, median, and third quartile?

3.54 What is meant by the property of variation?

3.55 What does the Z score measure?

3.56 What are the differences among the various measures of variation, such as the range, interquartile range, variance, standard deviation, and coefficient of variation, and what are the advantages and disadvantages of each?

3.57 How does the empirical rule help explain the ways in which the values in a set of numerical data cluster and distribute?

3.58 How do the empirical rule and the Chebyshev rule differ?

3.59 What is meant by the property of shape?

3.60 How do the covariance and the coefficient of correlation differ?

APPLYING THE CONCEPTS

3.61 The American Society for Quality (ASQ) conducted a salary survey of all its members. ASQ members work in all areas of manufacturing and service-related institutions, with a common theme of an interest in quality. For the survey, emails were sent to 58,614 members, and 7,869 valid responses were received. The two most common job titles were manager and quality engineer. Another title is Master Black Belt, who is a person who takes a leadership role as the keeper of the Six Sigma process (see Section 17.8). An additional title is Green Belt, someone who works on Six Sigma projects part-time. Descriptive statistics concerning salaries for these four titles are given in the following table:

Title	Sample Size	Minimum	Maximum	Standard Deviation	Mean	Median
Green Belt	34	33,000	106,000	18,137	65,679	64,750
Manager	2,128	22,568	182,000	25,078	86,349	84,000
Quality Engineer	1,262	24,000	186,000	19,256	74,314	72,100
Master Black Belt	132	33,000	201,000	24,988	109,481	106,000

Source: Data extracted from J. D. Conklin, "Salary Survey: Seeing Green," *Quality Progress*, December 2009, p. 29.

Compare the salaries of Green Belts, managers, quality engineers, and Master Black Belts.

3.62 In New York State, savings banks are permitted to sell a form of life insurance called savings bank life insurance (SBLI). The approval process consists of underwriting, which includes a review of the application, a medical information bureau check, possible requests for additional medical information and medical exams, and a policy compilation stage, during which the policy pages are generated and sent to the bank for delivery. The ability to deliver approved policies to customers in a timely manner is critical to the profitability of this service to the bank. During a period of one month, a random sample of 27 approved policies was selected, and the following were the total processing times (stored in **Insurance**):

73 19 16 64 28 28 31 90 60 56 31 56 22 18
45 48 17 17 17 91 92 63 50 51 69 16 17

a. Compute the mean, median, first quartile, and third quartile.
b. Compute the range, interquartile range, variance, standard deviation, and coefficient of variation.
c. Construct a boxplot. Are the data skewed? If so, how?
d. What would you tell a customer who enters the bank to purchase this type of insurance policy and asks how long the approval process takes?

3.63 One of the major measures of the quality of service provided by an organization is the speed with which it responds to customer complaints. A large family-held department store selling furniture and flooring, including carpet, had undergone a major expansion in the past several years. In particular, the flooring department had expanded from 2 installation crews to an installation supervisor, a measurer, and 15 installation crews. The business objective of the company was to reduce the time between when the complaint is received and when it is resolved. During a recent year, the company received 50 complaints concerning carpet installation. The data from the 50 complaints, organized in **Furniture**, represent the number of days between the receipt of a complaint and the resolution of the complaint:

54 5 35 137 31 27 152 2 123 81 74 27 11
19 126 110 110 29 61 35 94 31 26 5 12 4
165 32 29 28 29 26 25 1 14 13 13 10 5
27 4 52 30 22 36 26 20 23 33 68

a. Compute the mean, median, first quartile, and third quartile.
b. Compute the range, interquartile range, variance, standard deviation, and coefficient of variation.
c. Construct a boxplot. Are the data skewed? If so, how?
d. On the basis of the results of (a) through (c), if you had to tell the president of the company how long a customer should expect to wait to have a complaint resolved, what would you say? Explain.

3.64 A manufacturing company produces steel housings for electrical equipment. The main component part of the housing is a steel trough that is made of a 14-gauge steel coil. It is produced using a 250-ton progressive punch press with a wipe-down operation and two 90-degree forms placed in the flat steel to make the trough. The distance from one side of the form to the other is critical because of weatherproofing in outdoor applications. The company requires that the width of the trough is between 8.31 inches and 8.61 inches. Data are collected from a sample of 49 troughs and stored in **Trough**, which contains the widths of the troughs in inches as shown here:

8.312 8.343 8.317 8.383 8.348 8.410 8.351 8.373 8.481 8.422
8.476 8.382 8.484 8.403 8.414 8.419 8.385 8.465 8.498 8.447
8.436 8.413 8.489 8.414 8.481 8.415 8.479 8.429 8.458 8.462
8.460 8.444 8.429 8.460 8.412 8.420 8.410 8.405 8.323 8.420
8.396 8.447 8.405 8.439 8.411 8.427 8.420 8.498 8.409

a. Compute the mean, median, range, and standard deviation for the width. Interpret these measures of central tendency and variability.

b. List the five-number summary.
c. Construct a boxplot and describe its shape.
d. What can you conclude about the number of troughs that will meet the company's requirement of troughs being between 8.31 and 8.61 inches wide?

3.65 The manufacturing company in Problem 3.64 also produces electric insulators. If the insulators break when in use, a short circuit is likely to occur. To test the strength of the insulators, destructive testing is carried out to determine how much force is required to break the insulators. Force is measured by observing how many pounds must be applied to an insulator before it breaks. Data are collected from a sample of 30 insulators. The file **Force** contains the strengths, as follows:

1,870	1,728	1,656	1,610	1,634	1,784	1,522	1,696	1,592	1,662
1,866	1,764	1,734	1,662	1,734	1,774	1,550	1,756	1,762	1,866
1,820	1,744	1,788	1,688	1,810	1,752	1,680	1,810	1,652	1,736

a. Compute the mean, median, range, and standard deviation for the force needed to break the insulator.
b. Interpret the measures of central tendency and variability in (a).
c. Construct a boxplot and describe its shape.
d. What can you conclude about the strength of the insulators if the company requires a force measurement of at least 1,500 pounds before breakage?

3.66 The file **VeggieBurger** contains data on the calories and total fat (in grams per serving) for a sample of 12 veggie burgers.

Source: Data extracted from "Healthful Burgers That Taste Good," *Consumer Reports*, June 2008, p 8.

a. For each variable, compute the mean, median, first quartile, and third quartile.
b. For each variable, compute the range, interquartile range, variance, standard deviation, and coefficient of variation.
c. For each variable, construct a boxplot. Are the data skewed? If so, how?
d. Compute the coefficient of correlation between calories and total fat.
e. What conclusions can you reach concerning calories and total fat?

3.67 A quality characteristic of interest for a tea-bag-filling process is the weight of the tea in the individual bags. If the bags are underfilled, two problems arise. First, customers may not be able to brew the tea to be as strong as they wish. Second, the company may be in violation of the truth-in-labeling laws. For this product, the label weight on the package indicates that, on average, there are 5.5 grams of tea in a bag. If the mean amount of tea in a bag exceeds the label weight, the company is giving away product. Getting an exact amount of tea in a bag is problematic because of variation in the temperature and humidity inside the factory, differences in the density of the tea, and the extremely fast filling operation of the machine (approximately 170 bags per minute). The file **Teabags**, as shown below, contains the weights, in grams, of a sample of 50 tea bags produced in one hour by a single machine:

5.65	5.44	5.42	5.40	5.53	5.34	5.54	5.45	5.52	5.41
5.57	5.40	5.53	5.54	5.55	5.62	5.56	5.46	5.44	5.51
5.47	5.40	5.47	5.61	5.53	5.32	5.67	5.29	5.49	5.55
5.77	5.57	5.42	5.58	5.58	5.50	5.32	5.50	5.53	5.58
5.61	5.45	5.44	5.25	5.56	5.63	5.50	5.57	5.67	5.36

a. Compute the mean, median, first quartile, and third quartile.
b. Compute the range, interquartile range, variance, standard deviation, and coefficient of variation.
c. Interpret the measures of central tendency and variation within the context of this problem. Why should the company producing the tea bags be concerned about the central tendency and variation?
d. Construct a boxplot. Are the data skewed? If so, how?
e. Is the company meeting the requirement set forth on the label that, on average, there are 5.5 grams of tea in a bag? If you were in charge of this process, what changes, if any, would you try to make concerning the distribution of weights in the individual bags?

3.68 The manufacturer of Boston and Vermont asphalt shingles provides its customers with a 20-year warranty on most of its products. To determine whether a shingle will last as long as the warranty period, accelerated-life testing is conducted at the manufacturing plant. Accelerated-life testing exposes a shingle to the stresses it would be subject to in a lifetime of normal use via an experiment in a laboratory setting that takes only a few minutes to conduct. In this test, a shingle is repeatedly scraped with a brush for a short period of time, and the shingle granules removed by the brushing are weighed (in grams). Shingles that experience low amounts of granule loss are expected to last longer in normal use than shingles that experience high amounts of granule loss. In this situation, a shingle should experience no more than 0.8 gram of granule loss if it is expected to last the length of the warranty period. The file **Granule** contains a sample of 170 measurements made on the company's Boston shingles and 140 measurements made on Vermont shingles.

a. List the five-number summaries for the Boston shingles and for the Vermont shingles.
b. Construct side-by-side boxplots for the two brands of shingles and describe the shapes of the distributions.
c. Comment on the ability of each type of shingle to achieve a granule loss of 0.8 gram or less.

3.69 The file **Restaurants** contains the cost per meal and the ratings of 50 city and 50 suburban restaurants on their food, décor, and service (and their summated ratings). Complete the following for the urban and suburban restaurants.

Source: Data extracted from *Zagat Survey 2009 New York City Restaurants* and *Zagat Survey 2009–2010 Long Island Restaurants*.

a. Construct the five-number summary of the cost of a meal.

b. Construct a boxplot of the cost of a meal. What is the shape of the distribution?
c. Compute and interpret the correlation coefficient of the summated rating and the cost of a meal.

3.70 The file **Protein** contains calories, protein, and cholesterol of popular protein foods (fresh red meats, poultry, and fish).

Source: U.S. Department of Agriculture.

a. Compute the correlation coefficient between calories and protein.
b. Compute the correlation coefficient between calories and cholesterol.
c. Compute the correlation coefficient between protein and cholesterol.
d. Based on the results of (a) through (c), what conclusions can you reach concerning calories, protein, and cholesterol?

3.71 The file **HotelPrices** contains the average price of a room at two-star, three-star, and four-star hotels in cities around the world in 2009 in English pounds (about US$1.57 as of October 2010). Complete the following for two-star, three-star, and four-star hotels.

Source: Data extracted from **www.hotels.com/press/hotel-price-index-2009-h2.html**.

a. Compute the mean, median, first quartile, and third quartile.
b. Compute the range, interquartile range, variance, standard deviation, and coefficient of variation.
c. Interpret the measures of central tendency and variation within the context of this problem.
d. Construct a boxplot. Are the data skewed? If so, how?
e. Compute the covariance between the average price at two-star and three-star hotels, between two-star and four-star hotels, and between three-star and four-star hotels.
f. Compute the coefficient of correlation between the average price at two-star and three-star hotels, between two-star and four-star hotels, and between three-star and four-star hotels.
g. Which do you think is more valuable in expressing the relationship between the average price of a room at two-star, three-star, and four-star hotels—the covariance or the coefficient of correlation? Explain.
h. Based on (f), what conclusions can you reach about the relationship between the average price of a room at two-star, three-star, and four-star hotels?

3.72 The file **PropertyTaxes** contains the property taxes per capita for the 50 states and the District of Columbia.
a. Compute the mean, median, first quartile, and third quartile.
b. Compute the range, interquartile range, variance, standard deviation, and coefficient of variation.
c. Construct a boxplot. Are the data skewed? If so, how?
d. Based on the results of (a) through (c), what conclusions can you reach concerning property taxes per capita, in thousands of dollars, for each state and the District of Columbia?

3.73 The file **CEO-Compensation** includes the total compensation (in millions of $) of CEOs of 197 large public companies and the investment return in 2009. Complete the following for the total compensation (in $).

Source: Data extracted from D. Leonard, "Bargains in the Boardroom," *The New York Times*, April 4, 2010, pp. BU1, BU7, BU10, BU11.

a. Compute the mean, median, first quartile, and third quartile.
b. Compute the range, interquartile range, variance, standard deviation, and coefficient of variation.
c. Construct a boxplot. Are the data skewed? If so, how?
d. Based on the results of (a) through (c), what conclusions can you reach concerning the total compensation (in $millions) of CEOs?
e. Compute the correlation coefficient between compensation and the investment return in 2009.
f. What conclusions can you reach from the results of (e)?

3.74 You are planning to study for your statistics examination with a group of classmates, one of whom you particularly want to impress. This individual has volunteered to use Excel or Minitab to get the needed summary information, tables, and charts for a data set containing several numerical and categorical variables assigned by the instructor for study purposes. This person comes over to you with the printout and exclaims, "I've got it all—the means, the medians, the standard deviations, the boxplots, the pie charts—for all our variables. The problem is, some of the output looks weird—like the boxplots for gender and for major and the pie charts for grade point index and for height. Also, I can't understand why Professor Krehbiel said we can't get the descriptive stats for some of the variables; I got them for everything! See, the mean for height is 68.23, the mean for grade point index is 2.76, the mean for gender is 1.50, the mean for major is 4.33." What is your reply?

REPORT WRITING EXERCISES

3.75 The file **DomesticBeer** contains the percentage of alcohol, number of calories per 12 ounces, and number of carbohydrates (in grams) per 12 ounces for 139 of the best-selling domestic beers in the United States.

Your task is to write a report based on a complete descriptive evaluation of each of the numerical variables—percentage of alcohol, number of calories per 12 ounces, and number of carbohydrates (in grams) per 12 ounces. Appended to your report should be all appropriate tables, charts, and numerical descriptive measures.

Source: Data extracted from **www.Beer100.com**, March 18, 2010.

TEAM PROJECTS

The file **Bond Funds** contains information regarding nine variables from a sample of 184 bond funds:

Fund number—Identification number for each bond fund
Type—Type of bonds comprising the bond fund (intermediate government or short-term corporate)

Assets—In millions of dollars
Fees—Sales charges (no or yes)
Expense ratio—Ratio of expenses to net assets
Return 2009—Twelve-month return in 2009
Three-year return—Annualized return, 2007–2009
Five-year return—Annualized return, 2005–2009
Risk—Risk-of-loss factor of the mutual fund (low, average, or high)

3.76 Complete the following for expense ratio in percentage, three-year return, and five-year return.

a. Compute the mean, median, first quartile, and third quartile.
b. Compute the range, interquartile range, variance, standard deviation, and coefficient of variation.
c. Construct a boxplot. Are the data skewed? If so, how?
d. Based on the results of (a) through (c), what conclusions can you reach concerning these variables?

3.77 You want to compare bond funds that have fees to those that do not have fees. For each of these two groups, use the variables expense ratio, return 2009, three-year return, and five-year return and complete the following.

a. Compute the mean, median, first quartile, and third quartile.
b. Compute the range, interquartile range, variance, standard deviation, and coefficient of variation.
c. Construct a boxplot. Are the data skewed? If so, how?
d. Based on the results of (a) through (c), what conclusions can you reach about differences between bond funds that have fees and those that do not have fees?

3.78 You want to compare intermediate government to the short-term corporate bond funds. For each of these two groups, use the variables expense ratio, three-year return, and five-year return and complete the following.

a. Compute the mean, median, first quartile, and third quartile.
b. Compute the range, interquartile range, variance, standard deviation, and coefficient of variation.
c. Construct a boxplot. Are the data skewed? If so, how?
d. Based on the results of (a) through (c), what conclusions can you reach about differences between intermediate government and short-term corporate bond funds?

3.79 You want to compare bond funds based on risk. For each of these three levels of risk (below average, average, above average), use the variables expense ratio, return 2009, three-year return, and five-year return and complete the following.

a. Compute the mean, median, first quartile, and third quartile.
b. Compute the range, interquartile range, variance, standard deviation, and coefficient of variation.
c. Construct a boxplot. Are the data skewed? If so, how?
d. Based on the results of (a) through (c), what conclusions can you reach about differences between bond funds based on risk?

STUDENT SURVEY DATABASE

3.80 Problem 1.27 on page 14 describes a survey of 62 undergraduate students (stored in UndergradSurvey). For these data, for each numerical variable, complete the following.

a. Compute the mean, median, first quartile, and third quartile.
b. Compute the range, interquartile range, variance, standard deviation, and coefficient of variation.
c. Construct a boxplot. Are the data skewed? If so, how?
d. Write a report summarizing your conclusions.

3.81 Problem 1.27 on page 14 describes a survey of 62 undergraduate students (stored in UndergradSurvey).

a. Select a sample of undergraduate students at your school and conduct a similar survey for those students.
b. For the data collected in (a), repeat (a) through (d) of Problem 3.80.
c. Compare the results of (b) to those of Problem 3.80.

3.82 Problem 1.28 on page 15 describes a survey of 44 MBA students (stored in GradSurvey). For these data, for each numerical variable, complete the following.

a. Compute the mean, median, first quartile, and third quartile.
b. Compute the range, interquartile range, variance, standard deviation, and coefficient of variation.
c. Construct a boxplot. Are the data skewed? If so, how?
d. Write a report summarizing your conclusions.

3.83 Problem 1.28 on page 15 describes a survey of 44 MBA students (stored in GradSurvey).

a. Select a sample of graduate students from your MBA program and conduct a similar survey for those students.
b. For the data collected in (a), repeat (a) through (d) of Problem 3.82.
c. Compare the results of (b) to those of Problem 3.82.

MANAGING ASHLAND MULTICOMM SERVICES

For what variable in the Chapter 2 "Managing Ashland MultiComm Services" case (see page 74) are numerical descriptive measures needed?

1. For the variable you identify, compute the appropriate numerical descriptive measures and construct a boxplot.
2. For the variable you identify, construct a graphical display. What conclusions can you reach from this other plot that cannot be made from the boxplot?
3. Summarize your findings in a report that can be included with the task force's study.

DIGITAL CASE

Apply your knowledge about the proper use of numerical descriptive measures in this continuing Digital Case from Chapter 2.

Open **EndRunGuide.pdf**, the EndRun Financial Services "Guide to Investing." Reexamine EndRun's supporting data for the "More Winners Than Losers" and "The Big Eight Difference" and then answer the following:

1. Can descriptive measures be computed for any variables? How would such summary statistics support EndRun's claims? How would those summary statistics affect your perception of EndRun's record?
2. Evaluate the methods EndRun used to summarize the results presented on the "Customer Survey Results" page. Is there anything you would do differently to summarize these results?
3. Note that the last question of the survey has fewer responses than the other questions. What factors may have limited the number of responses to that question?

REFERENCES

1. Kendall, M. G., A. Stuart, and J. K. Ord, *Kendall's Advanced Theory of Statistics, Volume 1: Distribution Theory*, 6th ed. (New York: Oxford University Press, 1994).
2. *Microsoft Excel 2010* (Redmond, WA: Microsoft Corporation, 2010).
3. *Minitab Release 16* (State College, PA: Minitab, Inc., 2010).

CHAPTER 3 EXCEL GUIDE

EG3.1 CENTRAL TENDENCY

The Mean, Median, and Mode

In-Depth Excel Use the **AVERAGE** (for the mean), **MEDIAN**, or **MODE** functions in worksheet formulas to compute measures of central tendency. Enter these functions in the form ***FUNCTION(cell range of the variable)***. See Section EG3.2 for an example of their use.

Analysis ToolPak Use **Descriptive Statistics** to create a list that includes measures of central tendency. (Section EG3.2 fully explains this procedure.)

The Geometric Mean

In-Depth Excel Use the **GEOMEAN** function in a worksheet formula in the form **=GEOMEAN((1 + (R_1)), (1 + (R_2)), ...(1 + (R_n))) − 1** to compute the geometric mean rate of return. For example, to compute this statistic for Example 3.5 on page 101, enter the formula **=GEOMEAN((1 + (−0.3379)), (1 + (0.2717))) − 1** in any cell.

EG3.2 VARIATION and SHAPE

The Range, Variance, Standard Deviation, Coefficient of Variation, and Shape

In-Depth Excel Use the **COMPUTE worksheet** of the **Descriptive workbook** as a model for computing measures of central tendency, variation, and shape. This worksheet, shown in Figure 3.2 on page 109, computes the descriptive statistics for the 2009 return variable for the intermediate government and short-term corporate bond funds using data found in columns A and B of the **DATA worksheet**. The worksheet uses the **VAR** (sample variance), **STDEV** (sample standard deviation), **MIN** (minimum value), and **MAX** (maximum value) functions to compute measures of variation for a variable of interest. In row 11, the worksheet takes the difference between **MAX** and **MIN** to compute the range. In row 4, the worksheet uses the **COUNT** function to determine the sample size and then divides the sample standard deviation by the square root (**SQRT**) of the sample size to compute the standard error. (See Section 7.4 to learn more about the standard error.)

To add the coefficient of variation to the **COMPUTE worksheet**, first enter **Coefficient of variation** in cell **A16**. Then, enter the formula **=B7/B3** in cell **B16** and then copy it to cell **C16**. Finally, format cells B16 and C16 for percentage display.

Analysis ToolPak Use **Descriptive Statistics** to create a list that contains measures of variation and shape along with central tendency.

For example, to create a worksheet similar to the Figure 3.2 worksheet on page 109 that presents descriptive statistics for the 2009 return for the intermediate government and short-term corporate bond funds (see page 109), open to the **RETURN2009 worksheet** of the **Bond Funds workbook** and:

1. Select **Data → Data Analysis**.
2. In the Data Analysis dialog box, select **Descriptive Statistics** from the **Analysis Tools** list and then click **OK**.

In the Descriptive Statistics dialog box (shown below):

3. Enter **A1:B98** as the **Input Range**. Click **Columns** and check **Labels in First Row**.
4. Click **New Worksheet Ply**, check **Summary statistics**, and then click **OK**.

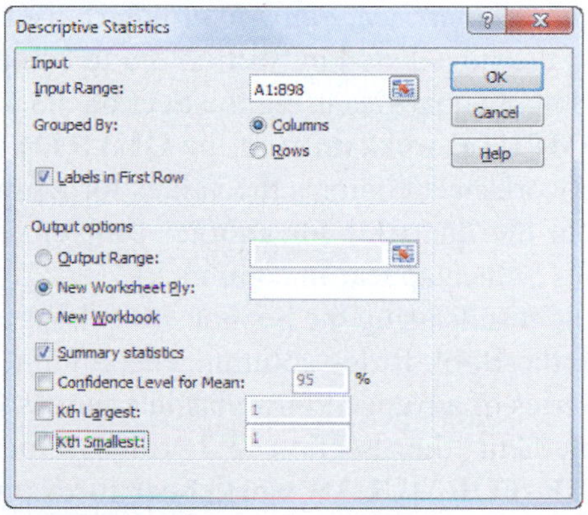

In the new worksheet:

5. Select column C, right-click, and click **Delete** in the shortcut menu (to eliminate the duplicate row labels).
6. Adjust the column headings and cell formatting, using Figure 3.2 as a guide. (See Appendix B for help with these adjustments.)

To add the coefficient of variation to this worksheet, first enter **Coefficient of variation** in cell **A16**. Then, enter the formula **=B7/B3** in cell **B16** and then copy it to cell **C16**. Finally, format cells B16 and C16 for percentage display.

Z Scores

In-Depth Excel Use the **STANDARDIZE** function to compute *Z* scores. Enter the function in the form **STANDARDIZE*(value, mean, standard deviation)*,** where ***value*** is an *X* value. Use the **TABLE_3.4 worksheet** of the

Descriptive workbook as a model for computing Z scores. The worksheet uses the AVERAGE and STDEV functions to compute the mean and standard deviation values used in the STANDARDIZE function.

Shape

In-Depth Excel Use the **SKEW** and **KURT** functions to compute skewness and kurtosis, respectively. Enter these functions in the form ***FUNCTION(cell range of the variable)***. Use the **COMPUTE worksheet** of the **Descriptive workbook** (discussed earlier in this section) as a model for computing these statistics.

Analysis ToolPak Use **Descriptive Statistics** to compute skewness and kurtosis. The *Analysis ToolPak* instructions given earlier in this section will compute these statistics as well.

EG3.3 EXPLORING NUMERICAL DATA

Quartiles

In-Depth Excel As noted on page 114, the Excel **QUARTILE** function, entered as **QUARTILE*(cell range of data to be summarized, quartile number)***, uses rules that differ from the rules listed in Section 3.3 to compute quartiles. To compute quartiles using the Section 3.3 rules, open to the **COMPUTE worksheet** of the **QUARTILES workbook**. The worksheet contains the values for Example 3.11. To compute the quartiles for another problem, overwrite those values (which appear in column A).

Quartile results using the Section 3.3 rules are shown in column D, the Book Rules column. The column D results rely on a series of advanced formulas in columns G through I to implement the Section 3.3 rules. Open to the **COMPUTE_FORMULAS worksheet** to examine these formulas. (A full explanation of the formulas used in that worksheet is beyond the scope of this book.)

The Interquartile Range

In-Depth Excel Use a worksheet formula that subtracts the first quartile from the third quartile to compute the interquartile range. For example, to compute this statistic for Example 3.12 on page 115, open to the **COMPUTE worksheet** of the **Quartiles workbook** and enter the formula **=D5 – D3** into an empty cell.

The Five-Number Summary and the Boxplot

PHStat2 Use **Boxplot** to create a five-number summary and boxplot. For example, to create the Figure 3.4 five-number summary and boxplot on page 117, open to the **DATA worksheet** of the **Bond Funds workbook**. Select **PHStat → Descriptive Statistics → Boxplot**. In the procedure's dialog box (shown below):

1. Enter **F1:F185** as the **Raw Data Cell Range** and check **First cell contains label.**
2. Click **Multiple Groups-Stacked** and enter **B1:B185** as the **Grouping Variable Cell Range**.
3. Enter a **Title**, check **Five-Number Summary**, and click **OK**.

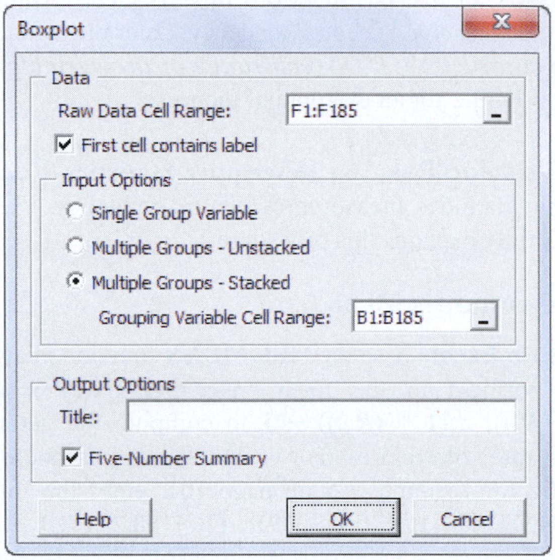

The boxplot appears on its own chart sheet, separate from the worksheet that contains the five-number summary.

In-Depth Excel Use the worksheets of the **Boxplot workbook** as templates for creating a five-number summary and boxplot. Use the **PLOT_DATA worksheet** as a template for creating a five-number summary and a boxplot in one worksheet from unsummarized data. Use the **PLOT worksheet** as a template for constructing a boxplot from a known five-number summary.

Because Excel does not include a boxplot as one of its chart types, creating a boxplot requires the advanced and creative "misuse" of Excel charting features. Open to the **PLOT_FORMULAS worksheet** to examine this "misuse." (A full explanation is beyond the scope of this book.)

EG3.4 NUMERICAL DESCRIPTIVE MEASURES for a POPULATION

The Population Mean, Population Variance, and Population Standard Deviation

In-Depth Excel Use the **AVERAGE** function to compute the population mean. Use the **VARP** and **STDEVP** functions to compute the population variance and standard deviation, respectively. Enter these functions in the form **AVERAGE*(cell range of the population)***, **VARP*(cell range of the population)***, and **STDEVP*(cell range of the population)***.

The Empirical Rule and the Chebyshev Rule

In-Depth Excel Use the **COMPUTE worksheet** of the **Variability workbook** as a template that uses arithmetic formulas to examine the variability in a distribution.

EG3.5 THE COVARIANCE and the COEFFICIENT of CORRELATION

The Covariance

In-Depth Excel Use the **COMPUTE worksheet** of the **Covariance workbook** as a template for covariance analysis. The worksheet contains the Table 3.8 set of 30 values and annual revenues (see page 126). For other problems, overwrite these values and follow the instructions in the worksheet for modifying the worksheet, when you have less than or more than 30 values. (The **COMPUTE_FORMULAS worksheet** shows the formulas used in the COMPUTE worksheet.)

The Coefficient of Correlation

In-Depth Excel Use the **CORREL** function to compute the coefficient of correlation. Enter this function in the form **CORREL(*cell range of the* X *values, cell range of the* Y *values*)**.

Use the **COMPUTE worksheet** of the **Correlation workbook** as a template for the correlation analysis shown in Figure 3.10 on page 129. In this worksheet, the cell F15 formula **=CORREL(A4:A33, B4:B33)** computes the coefficient of correlation.

CHAPTER 3 MINITAB GUIDE

MG3.1 CENTRAL TENDENCY

The Mean, Median, and Mode

Use **Descriptive Statistics** to compute the mean, the median, the mode, and selected measures of variation and shape. For example, to create results similar to Figure 3.2 on page 109 that presents descriptive statistics for the 2009 return for the intermediate government and short-term corporate bond funds, open to the **Bond Funds worksheet**. Select **Stat → Basic Statistics → Display Descriptive Statistics**. In the Display Descriptive Statistics dialog box (shown below):

1. Double-click **C6 Return 2009** in the variables list to add **'Return 2009'** to the **Variables** box and then press **Tab**.
2. Double-click **C2 Type** in the variables list to add **Type** to the **By variables (optional)** box.
3. Click **Statistics**.

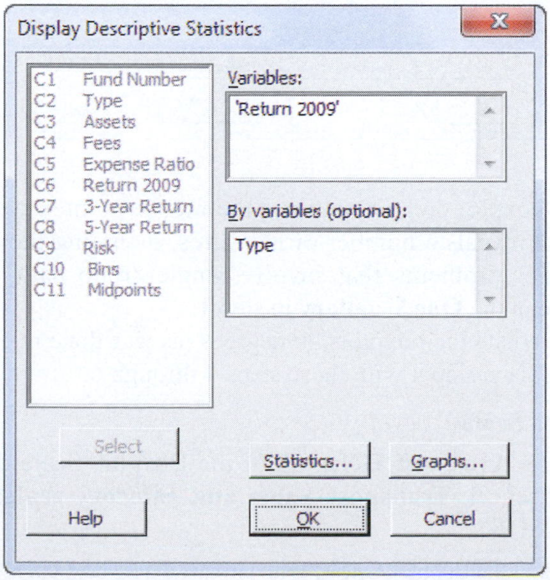

In the Display Descriptive Statistics-Statistics dialog box (shown below):

4. Check **Mean**, **Standard deviation**, **Variance**, **Coefficient of variation**, **First quartile**, **Median**, **Third quartile**, **Interquartile range**, **Mode**, **Minimum**, **Maximum**, **Range**, **Skewness**, **Kurtosis**, and **N total**.
5. Click **OK**.

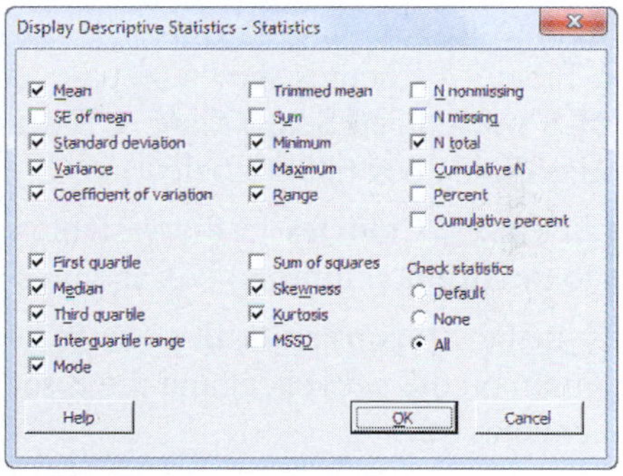

6. Back in the Display Descriptive Statistics dialog box, click **OK**.

The Geometric Mean

Use **Calculator** to compute the geometric mean or the geometric mean rate of return. For example, to compute the geometric mean rate of return for Example 3.5 on page 101, open to the **Investments worksheet**. Select **Calc → Calculator**. In the Calculator dialog box (shown at the top of page 142):

1. Enter **C2** in the **Store result in variable** box and then press **Tab**. (C2 is the first empty column on the worksheet and the result will be placed in row 1 of column C2.)
2. Double-click **Geometric mean** in the **Functions** scrollable list to add **GMEAN(number)** to the **Expression** box.

3. Double-click **C1 Rates of Return** in the variables list to alter the expression to **GMEAN('Rates of Return')**. (If you prefer, you can directly edit the expression as part of the next step.)
4. Edit the expression so that it reads **GMEAN('Rates of Return') – 1**.
5. Click **OK**.

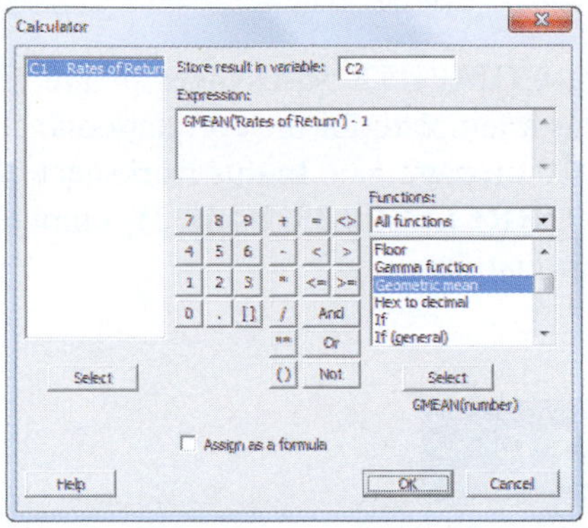

MG3.2 VARIATION and SHAPE

The Range, Variance, Standard Deviation, and Coefficient of Variation

Use **Descriptive Statistics** to compute these measures of variation and shape. The instructions in Section MG3.1 for computing the mean, median, and mode also compute these measures.

Z Scores

Use **Standardize** to compute *Z* scores. For example, to compute the Table 3.4 *Z* scores shown on page 108, open to the **CEREALS worksheet**. Select **Calc ➔ Standardize**. In the Standardize dialog box (shown below):

1. Double-click **C2 Calories** in the variables list to add **Calories** to the **Input column(s)** box and press **Tab**.
2. Enter C5 in the **Store results in** box. (C5 is the first empty column on the worksheet and the *Z* scores will be placed in column C5.)
3. Click **Subtract mean and divide by standard deviation**.
4. Click **OK**.
5. In the new column C5, enter **Z Scores** as the name of the column.

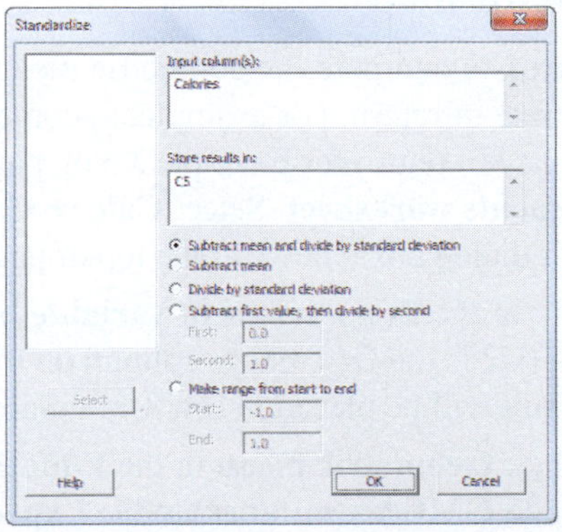

Shape

Use **Descriptive Statistics** to compute skewness and kurtosis. The instructions in Section MG3.1 for computing the mean, median, and mode also compute these measures.

MG3.3 EXPLORING NUMERICAL DATA

Quartiles, the Interquartile Range, and the Five-Number Summary

Use **Descriptive Statistics** to compute these measures. The instructions in Section MG3.1 for computing the mean, median, and mode also compute these measures.

The Boxplot

Use **Boxplot** to create a boxplot. For example, to create the Figure 3.5 boxplots on page 118, open to the **Bond Funds worksheet**. Select **Graph ➔ Boxplot**. In the Boxplots dialog box:

1. Click **With Groups** in the **One Y gallery** and then click **OK**.

In the Boxplot-One Y, With Groups dialog box (shown below):

2. Double-click **C6 Return 2009** in the variables list to add **'Return 2009'** to the **Graph variables** box and then press **Tab**.
3. Double-click **C2 Type** in the variables list to add **Type** in the **Categorical variables** box.
4. Click **OK**.

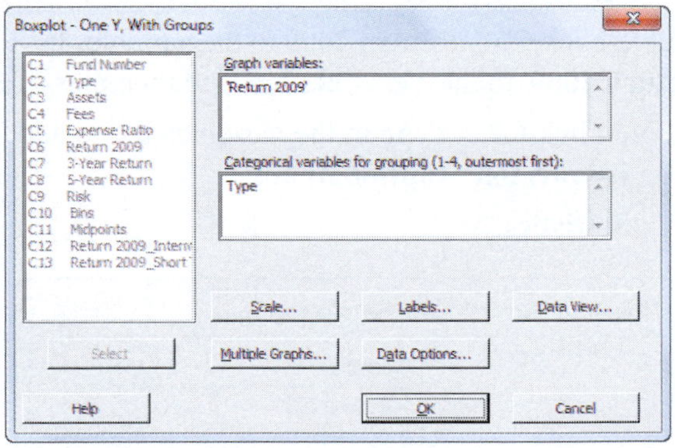

In the boxplot created, pausing the mouse pointer over the boxplot reveals a number of measures, including the quartiles. For problems that involve single-group data, click **Simple** in the **One Y gallery** in step 1.

To rotate the boxplots 90 degrees (as was done in Figure 3.5), replace step 4 with these steps 4 through 6:

4. Click **Scale**.
5. In the **Axes and Ticks** tab of the Boxplot–Scale dialog box, check **Transpose value and category scales** and click **OK**.
6. Back in the Boxplot-One Y, With Groups dialog box, click **OK**.

MG3.4 NUMERICAL DESCRIPTIVE MEASURES for a POPULATION

The Population Mean, Population Variance, and Population Standard Deviation

Minitab does not contain commands that compute these population parameters directly.

The Empirical Rule and the Chebyshev Rule

Manually compute the values needed to apply these rules using the statistics computed in the Section MG3.1 instructions.

MG3.5 THE COVARIANCE and the COEFFICIENT of CORRELATION

The Covariance

Use **Covariance** to compute the covariance. For example, to compute the covariance for the Table 3.8 set of 30 values and annual revenues, open to the **NBAValues worksheet**. Select **Stat ➔ Basic Statistics ➔ Covariance**. In the Covariance dialog box (shown below):

1. Double-click **C2 Revenue** in the variables list to add **Revenue** to the **Variables** box.
2. Double-click **C3 Value** in the variables list to add **Value** to the **Variables** box.

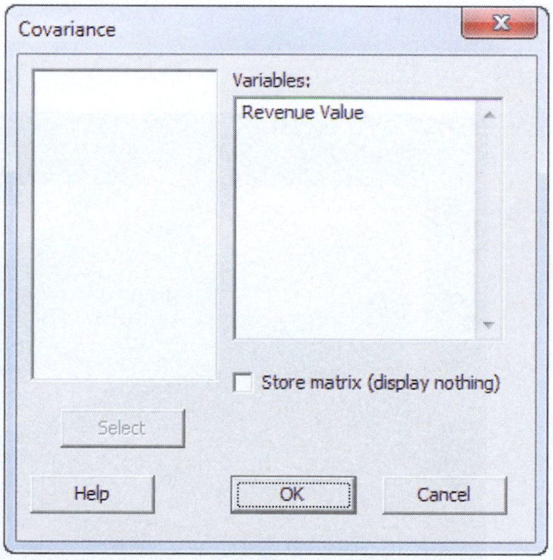

3. Click **OK**.

In the table of numbers produced, the covariance is the number that appears in the cell position that is the intersection of the two variables (the lower-left cell).

The Coefficient of Correlation

Use **Correlation** to compute the coefficient of correlation. For example, to compute the coefficient of correlation for the set of 30 values and annual revenues shown in Figure 3.10 on page 129, open to the **NBAValues worksheet**. Select **Stat ➔ Basic Statistics ➔ Correlation**. In the Correlation dialog box (similar to the Covariance dialog box):

1. Double-click **C2 Revenue** in the variables list to add **Revenue** to the **Variables** box.
2. Double-click **C3 Value** in the variables list to add **Value** to the **Variables** box.
3. Click **OK**.

4 Basic Probability

Learning Objectives

In this chapter, you learn:

- Basic probability concepts
- Conditional probability
- Bayes' theorem to revise probabilities
- Various counting rules

USING STATISTICS

@ M&R Electronics World

As the marketing manager for M&R Electronics World, you are analyzing the survey results of an intent-to-purchase study. This study asked the heads of 1,000 households about their intentions to purchase a big-screen television sometime during the next 12 months. As a follow-up, you plan to survey the same people 12 months later to see whether they purchased televisions. In addition, for households purchasing big-screen televisions, you would like to know whether the television they purchased had a faster refresh rate (120 Hz or higher) or a standard refresh rate (60 Hz), whether they also purchased a Blu-ray disc (BD) player in the past 12 months, and whether they were satisfied with their purchase of the big-screen television.

You are expected to use the results of this survey to plan a new marketing strategy that will enhance sales and better target those households likely to purchase multiple or more expensive products. What questions can you ask in this survey? How can you express the relationships among the various intent-to-purchase responses of individual households?

In previous chapters, you learned descriptive methods to summarize categorical and numerical variables. In this chapter, you will learn about probability to answer questions such as the following:

- What is the probability that a household is planning to purchase a big-screen television in the next year?
- What is the probability that a household will actually purchase a big-screen television?
- What is the probability that a household is planning to purchase a big-screen television and actually purchases the television?
- Given that the household is planning to purchase a big-screen television, what is the probability that the purchase is made?
- Does knowledge of whether a household *plans* to purchase the television change the likelihood of predicting whether the household *will* purchase the television?
- What is the probability that a household that purchases a big-screen television will purchase a television with a faster refresh rate?
- What is the probability that a household that purchases a big-screen television with a faster refresh rate will also purchase a Blu-ray disc player?
- What is the probability that a household that purchases a big-screen television will be satisfied with the purchase?

With answers to questions such as these, you can begin to make decisions about your marketing strategy. Should your strategy for selling more big-screen televisions target those households that have indicated an intent to purchase? Should you concentrate on selling televisions that have faster refresh rates? Is it likely that households that purchase big-screen televisions with faster refresh rates can be easily persuaded to also purchase Blu-ray disc players?

The principles of probability help bridge the worlds of descriptive statistics and inferential statistics. Reading this chapter will help you learn about different types of probabilities, how to compute probabilities, and how to revise probabilities in light of new information. Probability principles are the foundation for the probability distribution, the concept of mathematical expectation, and the binomial, Poisson, and hypergeometric distributions, topics that are discussed in Chapter 5.

4.1 Basic Probability Concepts

What is meant by the word *probability*? A **probability** is the numeric value representing the chance, likelihood, or possibility that a particular event will occur, such as the price of a stock increasing, a rainy day, a defective product, or the outcome five dots in a single toss of a die. In all these instances, the probability involved is a proportion or fraction whose value ranges between 0 and 1, inclusive. An event that has no chance of occurring (the **impossible event**) has a probability of 0. An event that is sure to occur (the **certain event**) has a probability of 1.

There are three types of probability:

- *A priori*
- Empirical
- Subjective

In ***a priori*** **probability**, the probability of an occurrence is based on prior knowledge of the process involved. In the simplest case, where each outcome is equally likely, the chance of occurrence of the event is defined in Equation (4.1).

PROBABILITY OF OCCURRENCE

$$\text{Probability of occurrence} = \frac{X}{T} \tag{4.1}$$

where

X = number of ways in which the event occurs

T = total number of possible outcomes

Consider a standard deck of cards that has 26 red cards and 26 black cards. The probability of selecting a black card is $26/52 = 0.50$ because there are $X = 26$ black cards and $T = 52$ total cards. What does this probability mean? If each card is replaced after it is selected, does it mean that 1 out of the next 2 cards selected will be black? No, because you cannot say for certain what will happen on the next several selections. However, you can say that in the long run, if this selection process is continually repeated, the proportion of black cards selected will approach 0.50. Example 4.1 shows another example of computing an *a priori* probability.

EXAMPLE 4.1

Finding *A Priori* Probabilities

A standard six-sided die has six faces. Each face of the die contains either one, two, three, four, five, or six dots. If you roll a die, what is the probability that you will get a face with five dots?

SOLUTION Each face is equally likely to occur. Because there are six faces, the probability of getting a face with five dots is 1/6.

The preceding examples use the *a priori* probability approach because the number of ways the event occurs and the total number of possible outcomes are known from the composition of the deck of cards or the faces of the die.

In the **empirical probability** approach, the probabilities are based on observed data, not on prior knowledge of a process. Surveys are often used to generate empirical probabilities. Examples of this type of probability are the proportion of individuals in the Using Statistics scenario who actually purchase big-screen televisions, the proportion of registered voters who prefer a certain political candidate, and the proportion of students who have part-time jobs. For example, if you take a survey of students, and 60% state that they have part-time jobs, then there is a 0.60 probability that an individual student has a part-time job.

The third approach to probability, **subjective probability,** differs from the other two approaches because subjective probability differs from person to person. For example, the development team for a new product may assign a probability of 0.60 to the chance of success for the product, while the president of the company may be less optimistic and assign a probability of 0.30. The assignment of subjective probabilities to various outcomes is usually based on a combination of an individual's past experience, personal opinion, and analysis of a particular situation. Subjective probability is especially useful in making decisions in situations in which you cannot use *a priori* probability or empirical probability.

Events and Sample Spaces

The basic elements of probability theory are the individual outcomes of a variable under study. You need the following definitions to understand probabilities.

EVENT

Each possible outcome of a variable is referred to as an **event**.
A **simple event** is described by a single characteristic.

For example, when you toss a coin, the two possible outcomes are heads and tails. Each of these represents a simple event. When you roll a standard six-sided die in which the six faces of the die contain either one, two, three, four, five, or six dots, there are six possible simple events. An event can be any one of these simple events, a set of them, or a subset of all of them. For example, the event of an *even number of dots* consists of three simple events (i.e., two, four, or six dots).

JOINT EVENT

A **joint event** is an event that has two or more characteristics.

Getting two heads when you toss a coin twice is an example of a joint event because it consists of heads on the first toss and heads on the second toss.

COMPLEMENT

The **complement** of event A (represented by the symbol A') includes all events that are not part of A.

The complement of a head is a tail because that is the only event that is not a head. The complement of five dots on a die is not getting five dots. Not getting five dots consists of getting one, two, three, four, or six dots.

SAMPLE SPACE

The collection of all the possible events is called the **sample space**.
The sample space for tossing a coin consists of heads and tails. The sample space when rolling a die consists of one, two, three, four, five, and six dots. Example 4.2 demonstrates events and sample spaces.

EXAMPLE 4.2

Events and Sample Spaces

The Using Statistics scenario on page 145 concerns M&R Electronics World. Table 4.1 presents the results of the sample of 1,000 households in terms of purchase behavior for big-screen televisions.

TABLE 4.1
Purchase Behavior for Big-Screen Televisions

PLANNED TO PURCHASE	ACTUALLY PURCHASED Yes	No	Total
Yes	200	50	250
No	100	650	750
Total	300	700	1,000

What is the sample space? Give examples of simple events and joint events.

SOLUTION The sample space consists of the 1,000 respondents. Simple events are "planned to purchase," "did not plan to purchase," "purchased," and "did not purchase." The complement of the event "planned to purchase" is "did not plan to purchase." The event "planned to purchase and actually purchased" is a joint event because in this joint event the respondent must plan to purchase the television *and* actually purchase it.

Contingency Tables and Venn Diagrams

There are several ways in which you can view a particular sample space. One way involves using a **contingency table** (see Section 2.2) such as the one displayed in Table 4.1. You get the values in the cells of the table by subdividing the sample space of 1,000 households according to whether someone planned to purchase and actually purchased a big-screen television set. For example, 200 of the respondents planned to purchase a big-screen television set and subsequently did purchase the big-screen television set.

A second way to present the sample space is by using a **Venn diagram**. This diagram graphically represents the various events as "unions" and "intersections" of circles. Figure 4.1 presents a typical Venn diagram for a two-variable situation, with each variable having only two events (A and A', B and B'). The circle on the left (the red one) represents all events that are part of A.

The circle on the right (the yellow one) represents all events that are part of B. The area contained within circle A and circle B (center area) is the intersection of A and B (written as $A \cap B$), since it is part of A and also part of B. The total area of the two circles is the union of A and B (written as $A \cup B$) and contains all outcomes that are just part of event A, just part of event B, or part of both A and B. The area in the diagram outside of $A \cup B$ contains outcomes that are neither part of A nor part of B.

You must define A and B in order to develop a Venn diagram. You can define either event as A or B, as long as you are consistent in evaluating the various events. For the big-screen television example, you can define the events as follows:

A = planned to purchase $\qquad B$ = actually purchased

A' = did not plan to purchase $\qquad B'$ = did not actually purchase

In drawing the Venn diagram (see Figure 4.2), you must determine the value of the intersection of A and B so that the sample space can be divided into its parts. $A \cap B$ consists of all 200 households who planned to purchase and actually purchased a big-screen television set.

FIGURE 4.1
Venn diagram for events A and B

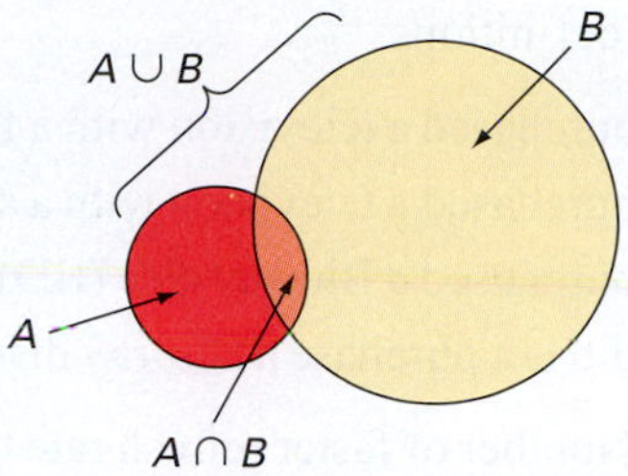

FIGURE 4.2
Venn diagram for the M&R Electronics World example

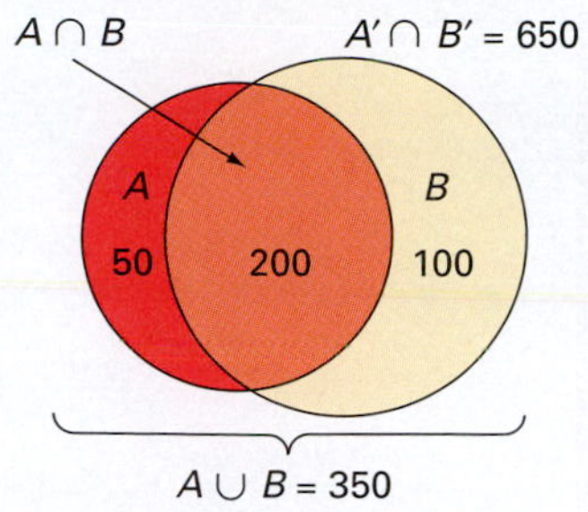

The remainder of event *A* (planned to purchase) consists of the 50 households who planned to purchase a big-screen television set but did not actually purchase one. The remainder of event *B* (actually purchased) consists of the 100 households who did not plan to purchase a big-screen television set but actually purchased one. The remaining 650 households represent those who neither planned to purchase nor actually purchased a big-screen television set.

Simple Probability

Now you can answer some of the questions posed in the Using Statistics scenario. Because the results are based on data collected in a survey (refer to Table 4.1), you can use the empirical probability approach.

As stated previously, the most fundamental rule for probabilities is that they range in value from 0 to 1. An impossible event has a probability of 0, and an event that is certain to occur has a probability of 1.

Simple probability refers to the probability of occurrence of a simple event, $P(A)$. A simple probability in the Using Statistics scenario is the probability of planning to purchase a big-screen television. How can you determine the probability of selecting a household that planned to purchase a big-screen television? Using Equation (4.1) on page 146:

$$\text{Probability of occurrence} = \frac{X}{T}$$

$$P(\text{Planned to purchase}) = \frac{\text{Number who planned to purchase}}{\text{Total number of households}}$$

$$= \frac{250}{1{,}000} = 0.25$$

Thus, there is a 0.25 (or 25%) chance that a household planned to purchase a big-screen television.

Example 4.3 illustrates another application of simple probability.

EXAMPLE 4.3
Computing the Probability That the Big-Screen Television Purchased Had a Faster Refresh Rate

In the Using Statistics follow-up survey, additional questions were asked of the 300 households that actually purchased big-screen televisions. Table 4.2 indicates the consumers' responses to whether the television purchased had a faster refresh rate and whether they also purchased a Blu-ray disc (BD) player in the past 12 months.

Find the probability that if a household that purchased a big-screen television is randomly selected, the television purchased had a faster refresh rate.

TABLE 4.2
Purchase Behavior Regarding Purchasing a Faster Refresh Rate Television and Blu-Ray Disc (BD) Player

REFRESH RATE OF TELEVISION PURCHASED	PURCHASED BD PLAYER		
	Yes	No	Total
Faster	38	42	80
Standard	70	150	220
Total	108	192	300

SOLUTION Using the following definitions:

$$A = \text{purchased a television with a faster refresh rate}$$
$$A' = \text{purchased a television with a standard refresh rate}$$
$$B = \text{purchased a Blu-ray disc (BD) player}$$
$$B' = \text{did not purchase a Blu-ray disc (BD) player}$$

$$P(\text{faster refresh rate}) = \frac{\text{Number of faster refresh rate televisions}}{\text{Total number of televisions}}$$

$$= \frac{80}{300} = 0.267$$

There is a 26.7% chance that a randomly selected big-screen television purchased has a faster refresh rate.

Joint Probability

Whereas simple or marginal probability refers to the probability of occurrence of simple events, **joint probability** refers to the probability of an occurrence involving two or more events. An example of joint probability is the probability that you will get heads on the first toss of a coin and heads on the second toss of a coin.

In Table 4.1 on page 148, the group of individuals who planned to purchase and actually purchased a big-screen television consist only of the outcomes in the single cell "yes—planned to purchase *and* yes—actually purchased." Because this group consists of 200 households, the probability of picking a household that planned to purchase *and* actually purchased a big-screen television is

$$P(\text{Planned to purchase } and \text{ actually purchased}) = \frac{\text{Planned to purchase } and \text{ actually purchased}}{\text{Total number of respondents}}$$

$$= \frac{200}{1{,}000} = 0.20$$

Example 4.4 also demonstrates how to determine joint probability.

EXAMPLE 4.4

Determining the Joint Probability That a Household Purchased a Big-Screen Television with a Faster Refresh Rate and a Blu-ray Disc Player

In Table 4.2, the purchases are cross-classified as having a faster refresh rate or having a standard refresh rate and whether the household purchased a Blu-ray disc player. Find the probability that a randomly selected household that purchased a big-screen television also purchased a television that had a faster refresh rate and purchased a Blu-ray disc player.

SOLUTION Using Equation (4.1) on page 146,

$$P(\text{television with a faster refresh rate } and \text{ Blu-ray disc player}) = \frac{\text{Number that purchased a television with a faster refresh rate } and \text{ a Blu-ray disc player}}{\text{Total number of big-screen television purchasers}}$$

$$= \frac{38}{300} = 0.127$$

Therefore, there is a 12.7% chance that a randomly selected household that purchased a big-screen television purchased a television that had a faster refresh rate and a Blu-ray disc player.

Marginal Probability

The **marginal probability** of an event consists of a set of joint probabilities. You can determine the marginal probability of a particular event by using the concept of joint probability just discussed. For example, if B consists of two events, B_1 and B_2, then $P(A)$, the probability of event A, consists of the joint probability of event A occurring with event B_1 and the joint probability of event A occurring with event B_2. You use Equation (4.2) to compute marginal probabilities.

MARGINAL PROBABILITY

$$P(A) = P(A \textit{ and } B_1) + P(A \textit{ and } B_2) + \cdots + P(A \textit{ and } B_k) \tag{4.2}$$

where $B_1, B_2, \ldots, B_k$ are k mutually exclusive and collectively exhaustive events, defined as follows:

Two events are **mutually exclusive** if both the events cannot occur simultaneously.
A set of events is **collectively exhaustive** if one of the events must occur.

Heads and tails in a coin toss are mutually exclusive events. The result of a coin toss cannot simultaneously be a head and a tail. Heads and tails in a coin toss are also collectively exhaustive events. One of them must occur. If heads does not occur, tails must occur. If tails does not occur, heads must occur. Being male and being female are mutually exclusive and collectively exhaustive events. No person is both (the two are mutually exclusive), and everyone is one or the other (the two are collectively exhaustive).

You can use Equation (4.2) to compute the marginal probability of "planned to purchase" a big-screen television:

$$\begin{aligned} P(\text{Planned to purchase}) &= P(\text{Planned to purchase } \textit{and} \text{ purchased}) \\ &\quad + P(\text{Planned to purchase } \textit{and} \text{ did not purchase}) \\ &= \frac{200}{1{,}000} + \frac{50}{1{,}000} \\ &= \frac{250}{1{,}000} = 0.25 \end{aligned}$$

You get the same result if you add the number of outcomes that make up the simple event "planned to purchase."

General Addition Rule

How do you find the probability of event "*A or B*"? You need to consider the occurrence of either event A or event B or both A and B. For example, how can you determine the probability that a household planned to purchase *or* actually purchased a big-screen television? The event "planned to purchase *or* actually purchased" includes all households that planned to purchase and all households that actually purchased a big-screen television. You examine each cell of the contingency table (Table 4.1 on page 148) to determine whether it is part of this event. From Table 4.1, the cell "planned to purchase *and* did not actually purchase" is part of the event because it includes respondents who planned to purchase. The cell "did not plan to purchase *and* actually purchased" is included because it contains respondents who actually purchased. Finally, the cell "planned to purchase *and* actually purchased" has both characteristics of interest. Therefore, one way to calculate the probability of "planned to purchase *or* actually purchased" is

$$\begin{aligned} P(\text{Planned to purchase } \textit{or} \text{ actually purchased}) &= P(\text{Planned to purchase } \textit{and} \text{ did not actually purchase}) + P(\text{Did not plan to purchase } \textit{and} \text{ actually purchase}) \\ &\quad + P(\text{Planned to purchase } \textit{and} \text{ actually purchased}) \\ &= \frac{50}{1{,}000} + \frac{100}{1{,}000} + \frac{200}{1{,}000} \\ &= \frac{350}{1{,}000} = 0.35 \end{aligned}$$

Often, it is easier to determine $P(A \text{ or } B)$, the probability of the event A *or* B, by using the **general addition rule**, defined in Equation (4.3).

> GENERAL ADDITION RULE
>
> The probability of A *or* B is equal to the probability of A plus the probability of B minus the probability of A *and* B.
>
> $$P(A \text{ or } B) = P(A) + P(B) - P(A \text{ and } B) \quad \textbf{(4.3)}$$

Applying Equation (4.3) to the previous example produces the following result:

$$\begin{aligned} P(\text{Planned to purchase } \textit{or} \text{ actually purchased}) &= P(\text{Planned to purchase}) \\ &\quad + P(\text{Actually purchased}) - P(\text{Planned to purchase } \textit{and} \text{ actually purchased}) \\ &= \frac{250}{1{,}000} + \frac{300}{1{,}000} - \frac{200}{1{,}000} \\ &= \frac{350}{1{,}000} = 0.35 \end{aligned}$$

The general addition rule consists of taking the probability of A and adding it to the probability of B and then subtracting the probability of the joint event A *and* B from this total because the joint event has already been included in computing both the probability of A and the probability of B. Referring to Table 4.1 on page 148, if the outcomes of the event "planned to purchase" are added to those of the event "actually purchased," the joint event "planned to purchase *and* actually purchased" has been included in each of these simple events. Therefore, because this joint event has been double-counted, you must subtract it to provide the correct result. Example 4.5 illustrates another application of the general addition rule.

EXAMPLE 4.5

Using the General Addition Rule for the Households That Purchased Big-Screen Televisions

In Example 4.3 on page 149, the purchases were cross-classified in Table 4.2 as televisions that had a faster refresh rate or televisions that had a standard refresh rate and whether the household purchased a Blu-ray disc (BD) player. Find the probability that among households that purchased a big-screen television, they purchased a television that had a faster refresh rate or a BD player.

SOLUTION Using Equation (4.3),

$$\begin{aligned} P(\text{Television had a faster refresh rate } \textit{or} \text{ purchased a BD player}) &= P(\text{Television had a faster refresh rate}) \\ &\quad + P(\text{purchased a BD player}) - P(\text{Television had a faster refresh rate } \textit{and} \text{ purchased a BD player}) \\ &= \frac{80}{300} + \frac{108}{300} - \frac{38}{300} \\ &= \frac{150}{300} = 0.50 \end{aligned}$$

Therefore, of those households that purchased a big-screen television, there is a 50.0% chance that a randomly selected household purchased a television that had a faster refresh rate or purchased a BD player.

Problems for Section 4.1

LEARNING THE BASICS

4.1 Two coins are tossed.
a. Give an example of a simple event.
b. Give an example of a joint event.
c. What is the complement of a head on the first toss?

4.2 An urn contains 12 red balls and 8 white balls. One ball is to be selected from the urn.
a. Give an example of a simple event.
b. What is the complement of a red ball?

4.3 Consider the following contingency table:

	B	*B'*
A	10	20
A'	20	40

What is the probability of
a. event *A*?
b. event *A'*?
c. event *A and B*?
d. *A or B*?

4.4 Consider the following contingency table:

	B	*B'*
A	10	30
A'	25	35

What is the probability of
a. event *A'*?
b. event *A and B?*
c. event *A' and B'*?
d. event *A' or B'*?

APPLYING THE CONCEPTS

4.5 For each of the following, indicate whether the type of probability involved is an example of *a priori* probability, empirical probability, or subjective probability.
a. The next toss of a fair coin will land on heads.
b. Italy will win soccer's World Cup the next time the competition is held.
c. The sum of the faces of two dice will be seven.
d. The train taking a commuter to work will be more than 10 minutes late.

4.6 For each of the following, state whether the events created are mutually exclusive and collectively exhaustive.
a. Registered voters in the United States were asked whether they are registered as Republicans or Democrats.
b. Each respondent was classified by the type of car he or she drives: sedan, SUV, American, European, Asian, or none.
c. People were asked, "Do you currently live in (i) an apartment or (ii) a house?"
d. A product was classified as defective or not defective.

4.7 Which of the following events occur with a probability of zero? For each, state why or why not.
a. A voter in the United States is registered as a Republican and as a Democrat.
b. A voter in the United States is female and registered as a Republican.
c. An automobile is a Ford and a Toyota.
d. An automobile is a Toyota and was manufactured in the United States.

4.8 Does it take more time to be removed from an email list than it used to take? A study of 100 large online retailers revealed the following:

	NEED THREE OR MORE CLICKS TO BE REMOVED	
YEAR	**Yes**	**No**
2009	39	61
2008	7	93

Source: Data extracted from "More Clicks to Escape an Email List," *The New York Times*, March 29, 2010, p. B2.

a. Give an example of a simple event.
b. Give an example of a joint event.
c. What is the complement of "Needs three or more clicks to be removed from an email list"?
d. Why is "Needs three or more clicks to be removed from an email list in 2009" a joint event?

4.9 Referring to the contingency table in Problem 4.8, if a large online retailer is selected at random, what is the probability that
a. you needed three or more clicks to be removed from an email list?
b. you needed three or more clicks to be removed from an email list in 2009?
c. you needed three or more clicks to be removed from an email list or were a large online retailer surveyed in 2009?
d. Explain the difference in the results in (b) and (c).

4.10 Do people of different age groups differ in their response to email messages? A survey by the Center for the Digital Future of the University of Southern California (data extracted from A. Mindlin, "Older E-mail Users Favor Fast Replies," *The New York Times*, July 14, 2008, p. B3) reported that 70.7% of users over 70 years of age believe that email messages should be answered quickly, as compared to

53.6% of users 12 to 50 years old. Suppose that the survey was based on 1,000 users over 70 years of age and 1,000 users 12 to 50 years old. The following table summarizes the results:

	AGE OF RESPONDENTS		
ANSWERS QUICKLY	**12–50**	**Over 70**	**Total**
Yes	536	707	1,243
No	464	293	757
Total	1,000	1,000	2,000

a. Give an example of a simple event.
b. Give an example of a joint event.
c. What is the complement of a respondent who answers quickly?
d. Why is a respondent who answers quickly and is over 70 years old a joint event?

4.11 Referring to the contingency table in Problem 4.10, if a respondent is selected at random, what is the probability that
a. he or she answers quickly?
b. he or she is over 70 years old?
c. he or she answers quickly *or* is over 70 years old?
d. Explain the difference in the results in (b) and (c).

SELF Test **4.12** According to a Gallup Poll, the extent to which employees are engaged with their workplace varies from country to country. Gallup reports that the percentage of U.S. workers engaged with their workplace is more than twice as high as the percentage of German workers. The study also shows that having more engaged workers leads to increased innovation, productivity, and profitability, as well as reduced employee turnover. The results of the poll are summarized in the following table:

	COUNTRY		
ENGAGEMENT	**United States**	**Germany**	**Total**
Engaged	550	246	796
Not engaged	1,345	1,649	2,994
Total	1,895	1,895	3,790

Source: Data extracted from M. Nink, "Employee Disengagement Plagues Germany," *Gallup Management Journal*, **gmj.gallup.com**, April 9, 2009.

If an employee is selected at random, what is the probability that he or she
a. is engaged with his or her workplace?
b. is a U.S. worker?
c. is engaged with his or her workplace *or* is a U.S. worker?
d. Explain the difference in the results in (b) and (c).

4.13 What is the preferred way for people to order fast food? A survey was conducted in 2009, but the sample sizes were not reported. Suppose the results, based on a sample of 100 males and 100 females, were as follows:

	GENDER		
DINING PREFERENCE	**Male**	**Female**	**Total**
Dine inside	21	12	33
Order inside to go	19	10	29
Order at the drive-through	60	78	138
Total	100	100	200

Source: Data extracted from **www.qsrmagazine.com/reports/drive-thru_time_study/2009/2009_charts/whats_your_preferred_way_to_order_fast_food.html**.

If a respondent is selected at random, what is the probability that he or she
a. prefers to order at the drive-through?
b. is a male *and* prefers to order at the drive-through?
c. is a male *or* prefers to order at the drive-through?
d. Explain the difference in the results in (b) and (c).

4.14 A sample of 500 respondents in a large metropolitan area was selected to study consumer behavior. Among the questions asked was "Do you enjoy shopping for clothing?" Of 240 males, 136 answered yes. Of 260 females, 224 answered yes. Construct a contingency table to evaluate the probabilities. What is the probability that a respondent chosen at random
a. enjoys shopping for clothing?
b. is a female *and* enjoys shopping for clothing?
c. is a female *or* enjoys shopping for clothing?
d. is a male *or* a female?

4.15 Each year, ratings are compiled concerning the performance of new cars during the first 90 days of use. Suppose that the cars have been categorized according to whether a car needs warranty-related repair (yes or no) and the country in which the company manufacturing a car is based (United States or not United States). Based on the data collected, the probability that the new car needs a warranty repair is 0.04, the probability that the car was manufactured by a U.S.-based company is 0.60, and the probability that the new car needs a warranty repair *and* was manufactured by a U.S.-based company is 0.025. Construct a contingency table to evaluate the probabilities of a warranty-related repair. What is the probability that a new car selected at random
a. needs a warranty repair?
b. needs a warranty repair *and* was manufactured by a U.S.-based company?
c. needs a warranty repair *or* was manufactured by a U.S.-based company?
d. needs a warranty repair *or* was not manufactured by a U.S.-based company?

4.2 Conditional Probability

Each example in Section 4.1 involves finding the probability of an event when sampling from the entire sample space. How do you determine the probability of an event if you know certain information about the events involved?

Computing Conditional Probabilities

Conditional probability refers to the probability of event A, given information about the occurrence of another event, B.

CONDITIONAL PROBABILITY

The probability of A given B is equal to the probability of A *and* B divided by the probability of B.

$$P(A|B) = \frac{P(A \text{ and } B)}{P(B)} \quad \textbf{(4.4a)}$$

The probability of B given A is equal to the probability of A *and* B divided by the probability of A.

$$P(B|A) = \frac{P(A \text{ and } B)}{P(A)} \quad \textbf{(4.4b)}$$

where

$P(A \text{ and } B)$ = joint probability of A *and* B

$P(A)$ = marginal probability of A

$P(B)$ = marginal probability of B

Referring to the Using Statistics scenario involving the purchase of big-screen televisions, suppose you were told that a household planned to purchase a big-screen television. Now, what is the probability that the household actually purchased the television? In this example, the objective is to find $P(\text{Actually purchased} \mid \text{Planned to purchase})$. Here you are given the information that the household planned to purchase the big-screen television. Therefore, the sample space does not consist of all 1,000 households in the survey. It consists of only those households that planned to purchase the big-screen television. Of 250 such households, 200 actually purchased the big-screen television. Therefore, based on Table 4.1 on page 148, the probability that a household actually purchased the big-screen television given that he or she planned to purchase is

$$P(\text{Actually purchased}|\text{Planned to purchase}) = \frac{\text{Planned to purchase } and \text{ actually purchased}}{\text{Planned to purchase}}$$

$$= \frac{200}{250} = 0.80$$

You can also use Equation (4.4b) to compute this result:

$$P(B|A) = \frac{P(A \text{ and } B)}{P(A)}$$

where

A = planned to purchase

B = actually purchased

then

$$P(\text{Actually purchased}|\text{Planned to purchase}) = \frac{200/1{,}000}{250/1{,}000}$$

$$= \frac{200}{250} = 0.80$$

Example 4.6 further illustrates conditional probability.

EXAMPLE 4.6

Finding the Conditional Probability of Purchasing a Blu-ray Disc Player

Table 4.2 on page 149 is a contingency table for whether a household purchased a television with a faster refresh rate and whether the household purchased a Blu-ray disc player. If a household purchased a television with a faster refresh rate, what is the probability that it also purchased a Blu-ray disc player?

SOLUTION Because you know that the household purchased a television with a faster refresh rate, the sample space is reduced to 80 households. Of these 80 households, 38 also purchased a Blu-ray disc (BD) player. Therefore, the probability that a household purchased a BD player, given that the household purchased a television with a faster refresh rate, is

$$P(\text{Purchased BD player} \mid \text{Purchased television with faster refresh rate}) = \frac{\text{Number purchasing television with faster refresh rate } \textit{and} \text{ BD player}}{\text{Number purchasing television with faster refresh rate}}$$

$$= \frac{38}{80} = 0.475$$

If you use Equation (4.4b) on page 155:

A = purchased a television with a faster refresh rate

B = purchased a BD player

then

$$P(B|A) = \frac{P(A \text{ and } B)}{P(A)} = \frac{38/300}{80/300} = 0.475$$

Therefore, given that the household purchased a television with a faster refresh rate, there is a 47.5% chance that the household also purchased a Blu-ray disc player. You can compare this conditional probability to the marginal probability of purchasing a Blu-ray disc player, which is $108/300 = 0.36$, or 36%. These results tell you that households that purchased televisions with a faster refresh rate are more likely to purchase a Blu-ray disc player than are households that purchased big-screen televisions that have a standard refresh rate.

Decision Trees

In Table 4.1 on page 148, households are classified according to whether they planned to purchase and whether they actually purchased big-screen televisions. A **decision tree** is an alternative to the contingency table. Figure 4.3 represents the decision tree for this example.

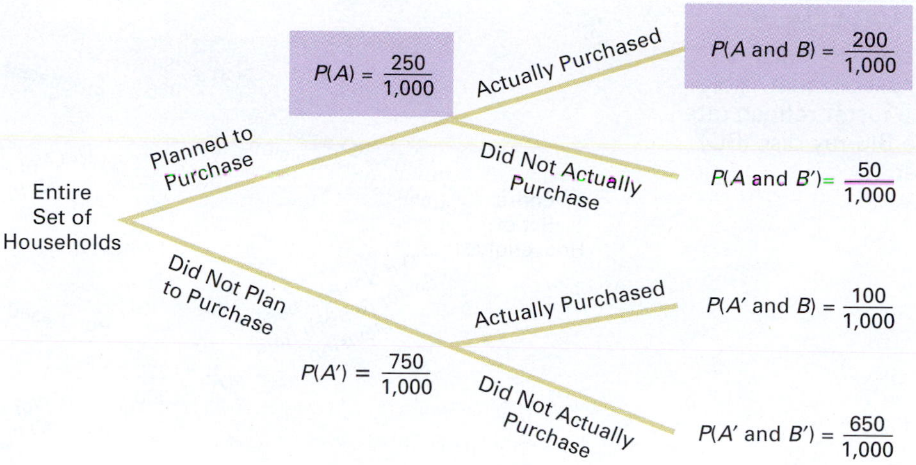

FIGURE 4.3
Decision tree for M&R Electronics World example

In Figure 4.3, beginning at the left with the entire set of households, there are two "branches" for whether or not the household planned to purchase a big-screen television. Each of these branches has two subbranches, corresponding to whether the household actually purchased or did not actually purchase the big-screen television. The probabilities at the end of the initial branches represent the marginal probabilities of A and A'. The probabilities at the end of each of the four subbranches represent the joint probability for each combination of events A and B. You compute the conditional probability by dividing the joint probability by the appropriate marginal probability.

For example, to compute the probability that the household actually purchased, given that the household planned to purchase the big-screen television, you take *P*(Planned to purchase *and* actually purchased) and divide by *P*(Planned to purchase). From Figure 4.3,

$$P(\text{Actually purchased} \mid \text{Planned to purchase}) = \frac{200/1{,}000}{250/1{,}000}$$

$$= \frac{200}{250} = 0.80$$

Example 4.7 illustrates how to construct a decision tree.

EXAMPLE 4.7

Constructing the Decision Tree for the Households That Purchased Big-Screen Televisions

Using the cross-classified data in Table 4.2 on page 149, construct the decision tree. Use the decision tree to find the probability that a household purchased a Blu-ray disc player, given that the household purchased a television with a faster refresh rate.

SOLUTION The decision tree for purchased a Blu-ray disc player and a television with a faster refresh rate is displayed in Figure 4.4 on page 156. Using Equation (4.4b) on page 155 and the following definitions,

A = purchased a television with a faster refresh rate

B = purchased a Blu-ray disc player

$$P(B \mid A) = \frac{P(A \text{ and } B)}{P(A)} = \frac{38/300}{80/300} = 0.475$$

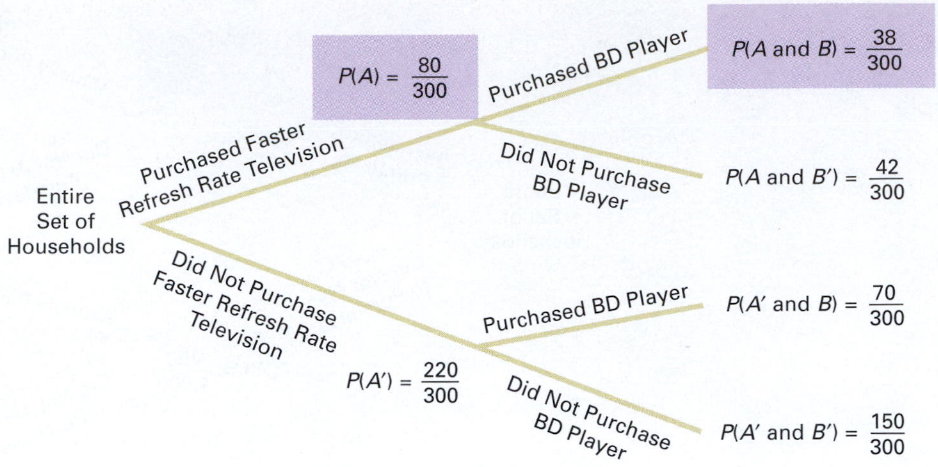

FIGURE 4.4
Decision tree for purchased a television with a faster refresh rate and a Blu-ray disc (BD) player

Independence

In the example concerning the purchase of big-screen televisions, the conditional probability is $200/250 = 0.80$ that the selected household actually purchased the big-screen television, given that the household planned to purchase. The simple probability of selecting a household that actually purchased is $300/1,000 = 0.30$. This result shows that the prior knowledge that the household planned to purchase affected the probability that the household actually purchased the television. In other words, the outcome of one event is *dependent* on the outcome of a second event.

When the outcome of one event does *not* affect the probability of occurrence of another event, the events are said to be independent. **Independence** can be determined by using Equation (4.5).

INDEPENDENCE

Two events, A and B, are independent if and only if

$$P(A \mid B) = P(A) \quad \textbf{(4.5)}$$

where

$P(A \mid B)$ = conditional probability of A given B

$P(A)$ = marginal probability of A

Example 4.8 demonstrates the use of Equation (4.5).

EXAMPLE 4.8

Determining Independence

In the follow-up survey of the 300 households that actually purchased big-screen televisions, the households were asked if they were satisfied with their purchases. Table 4.3 cross-classifies the responses to the satisfaction question with the responses to whether the television had a faster refresh rate.

TABLE 4.3
Satisfaction with Purchase of Big-Screen Televisions

TELEVISION REFRESH RATE	SATISFIED WITH PURCHASE?		
	Yes	No	Total
Faster	64	16	80
Standard	176	44	220
Total	240	60	300

Determine whether being satisfied with the purchase and the refresh rate of the television purchased are independent.

SOLUTION For these data,

$$P(\text{Satisfied}|\text{faster refresh rate}) = \frac{64/300}{80/300} = \frac{64}{80} = 0.80$$

which is equal to

$$P(\text{Satisfied}) = \frac{240}{300} = 0.80$$

Thus, being satisfied with the purchase and the refresh rate of the television purchased are independent. Knowledge of one event does not affect the probability of the other event.

Multiplication Rules

The **general multiplication rule** is derived using Equation (4.4a) on page 155:

$$P(A|B) = \frac{P(A \text{ and } B)}{P(B)}$$

and solving for the joint probability $P(A \text{ and } B)$.

GENERAL MULTIPLICATION RULE

The probability of A and B is equal to the probability of A given B times the probability of B.

$$P(A \text{ and } B) = P(A|B)P(B) \quad \textbf{(4.6)}$$

Example 4.9 demonstrates the use of the general multiplication rule.

EXAMPLE 4.9

Using the General Multiplication Rule

Consider the 80 households that purchased televisions that had a faster refresh rate. In Table 4.3 on page 158 you see that 64 households are satisfied with their purchase, and 16 households are dissatisfied. Suppose 2 households are randomly selected from the 80 households. Find the probability that both households are satisfied with their purchase.

SOLUTION Here you can use the multiplication rule in the following way. If

A = second household selected is satisfied

B = first household selected is satisfied

then, using Equation (4.6),

$$P(A \text{ and } B) = P(A|B)P(B)$$

The probability that the first household is satisfied with the purchase is 64/80. However, the probability that the second household is also satisfied with the purchase depends on the result of the first selection. If the first household is not returned to the sample after the satisfaction level is determined (i.e., sampling without replacement), the number of households remaining is 79. If the first household is satisfied, the probability that the second is also satisfied is 63/79 because 63 satisfied households remain in the sample. Therefore,

$$P(A \text{ and } B) = \left(\frac{63}{79}\right)\left(\frac{64}{80}\right) = 0.6380$$

There is a 63.80% chance that both of the households sampled will be satisfied with their purchase.

The **multiplication rule for independent events** is derived by substituting $P(A)$ for $P(A \mid B)$ in Equation (4.6).

MULTIPLICATION RULE FOR INDEPENDENT EVENTS

If A and B are independent, the probability of A *and* B is equal to the probability of A times the probability of B.

$$P(A \text{ and } B) = P(A)P(B) \quad \textbf{(4.7)}$$

If this rule holds for two events, A and B, then A and B are independent. Therefore, there are two ways to determine independence:

1. Events A and B are independent if, and only if, $P(A \mid B) = P(A)$.
2. Events A and B are independent if, and only if, $P(A \text{ and } B) = P(A)P(B)$.

Marginal Probability Using the General Multiplication Rule

In Section 4.1, marginal probability was defined using Equation (4.2) on page. You can state the equation for marginal probability by using the general multiplication rule. If

$$P(A) = P(A \text{ and } B_1) + P(A \text{ and } B_2) + \cdots + P(A \text{ and } B_k)$$

then, using the general multiplication rule, Equation (4.8) defines the marginal probability.

MARGINAL PROBABILITY USING THE GENERAL MULTIPLICATION RULE

$$P(A) = P(A \mid B_1)P(B_1) + P(A \mid B_2)P(B_2) + \cdots + P(A \mid B_k)P(B_k) \quad \textbf{(4.8)}$$

where $B_1, B_2, \ldots, B_k$ are k mutually exclusive and collectively exhaustive events.

To illustrate Equation (4.8), refer to Table 4.1 on page. Let

$$P(A) = \text{probability of "planned to purchase"}$$
$$P(B_1) = \text{probability of "actually purchased"}$$
$$P(B_2) = \text{probability of "did not actually purchase"}$$

Then, using Equation (4.8), the probability of planned to purchase is

$$\begin{aligned} P(A) &= P(A \mid B_1)P(B_1) + P(A \mid B_2)P(B_2) \\ &= \left(\frac{200}{300}\right)\left(\frac{300}{1{,}000}\right) + \left(\frac{50}{700}\right)\left(\frac{700}{1{,}000}\right) \\ &= \frac{200}{1{,}000} + \frac{50}{1{,}000} = \frac{250}{1{,}000} = 0.25 \end{aligned}$$

Problems for Section 4.2

LEARNING THE BASICS

4.16 Consider the following contingency table:

	B	B'
A	10	20
A'	20	40

What is the probability of

a. $A \mid B$?
b. $A \mid B'$?
c. $A' \mid B'$?
d. Are events A and B independent?

4.17 Consider the following contingency table:

	B	B'
A	10	30
A'	25	35

What is the probability of

a. $A \mid B$?
b. $A' \mid B'$?
c. $A \mid B'$?
d. Are events A and B independent?

4.18 If $P(A \text{ and } B) = 0.4$ and $P(B) = 0.8$, find $P(A \mid B)$.

4.19 If $P(A) = 0.7, P(B) = 0.6$, and A and B are independent, find $P(A \text{ and } B)$.

4.20 If $P(A) = 0.3, P(B) = 0.4$, and $P(A \text{ and } B) = 0.2$, are A and B independent?

APPLYING THE CONCEPTS

4.21 Does it take more time to be removed from an email list than it used to take? A study of 100 large online retailers revealed the following:

	NEED THREE OR MORE CLICKS TO BE REMOVED	
YEAR	**Yes**	**No**
2009	39	61
2008	7	93

Source: Data extracted from "More Clicks to Escape an Email List," *The New York Times*, March 29, 2010, p. B2.

a. Given that three or more clicks are needed to be removed from an email list, what is the probability that this occurred in 2009?
b. Given that the year 2009 is involved, what is the probability that three or more clicks are needed to be removed from an email list?
c. Explain the difference in the results in (a) and (b).
d. Are needing three or more clicks to be removed from an email list and the year independent?

4.22 Do people of different age groups differ in their response to email messages? A survey by the Center for the Digital Future of the University of Southern California (data extracted from A. Mindlin, "Older E-mail Users Favor Fast Replies," *The New York Times*, July 14, 2008, p. B3) reported that 70.7% of users over 70 years of age believe that email messages should be answered quickly, as compared to 53.6% of users 12 to 50 years old. Suppose that the survey was based on 1,000 users over 70 years of age and 1,000 users 12 to 50 years old. The following table summarizes the results:

	ANSWERS QUICKLY		
AGE OF RESPONDENTS	**12–50**	**Over 70**	**Total**
Yes	536	707	1,243
No	464	293	757
Total	1,000	1,000	2,000

a. Suppose you know that the respondent is between 12 and 50 years old. What is the probability that he or she answers quickly?
b. Suppose you know that the respondent is over 70 years old. What is the probability that he or she answers quickly?
c. Are the two events, answers quickly and age of respondents, independent? Explain.

4.23 What is the preferred way for people to order fast food? A survey was conducted in 2009, but the sample sizes were not reported. Suppose the results, based on a sample of 100 males and 100 females, were as follows:

	GENDER		
DINING PREFERENCE	**Male**	**Female**	**Total**
Dine inside	21	12	33
Order inside to go	19	10	29
Order at the drive-through	60	78	138
Total	100	100	200

Source: Data extracted from **www.qsrmagazine.com/reports/drive-thru_time_study/2009/2009_charts/whats_your_preferred_way_to_order_fast_food.html.**

a. Given that a respondent is a male, what is the probability that he prefers to order at the drive-through?
b. Given that a respondent is a female, what is the probability that she prefers to order at the drive-through?
c. Is dining preference independent of gender? Explain.

SELF Test **4.24** According to a Gallup Poll, the extent to which employees are engaged with their workplace varies from country to country. Gallup reports that the percentage of U.S. workers engaged with their workplace is more than twice as high as the percentage of German workers. The study also shows that having more engaged workers leads to increased innovation, productivity, and profitability, as well as reduced employee turnover. The results of the poll are summarized in the following table:

	COUNTRY		
ENGAGEMENT	**United States**	**Germany**	**Total**
Engaged	550	246	796
Not engaged	1,345	1,649	2,994
Total	1,895	1,895	3,790

Source: Data extracted from M. Nink, "Employee Disengagement Plagues Germany," *Gallup Management Journal*, **gmj.gallup.com**, April 9, 2009.

a. Given that a worker is from the United States, what is the probability that the worker is engaged?
b. Given that a worker is from the United States, what is the probability that the worker is not engaged?
c. Given that a worker is from Germany, what is the probability that the worker is engaged?
d. Given that a worker is from Germany, what is the probability that the worker is not engaged?

4.25 A sample of 500 respondents in a large metropolitan area was selected to study consumer behavior, with the following results:

ENJOYS SHOPPING FOR CLOTHING	GENDER		
	Male	**Female**	**Total**
Yes	136	224	360
No	104	36	140
Total	240	260	500

a. Suppose that the respondent chosen is a female. What is the probability that she does not enjoy shopping for clothing?
b. Suppose that the respondent chosen enjoys shopping for clothing. What is the probability that the individual is a male?
c. Are enjoying shopping for clothing and the gender of the individual independent? Explain.

4.26 Each year, ratings are compiled concerning the performance of new cars during the first 90 days of use. Suppose that the cars have been categorized according to whether a car needs warranty-related repair (yes or no) and the country in which the company manufacturing a car is based (United States or not United States). Based on the data collected, the probability that the new car needs a warranty repair is 0.04, the probability that the car is manufactured by a U.S.-based company is 0.60, and the probability that the new car needs a warranty repair *and* was manufactured by a U.S.-based company is 0.025.
a. Suppose you know that a company based in the United States manufactured a particular car. What is the probability that the car needs warranty repair?
b. Suppose you know that a company based in the United States did not manufacture a particular car. What is the probability that the car needs warranty repair?
c. Are need for warranty repair and location of the company manufacturing the car independent?

4.27 In 38 of the 60 years from 1950 through 2009, the S&P 500 finished higher after the first five days of trading. In 33 of those 38 years, the S&P 500 finished higher for the year. Is a good first week a good omen for the upcoming year? The following table gives the first-week and annual performance over this 60-year period:

	S&P 500'S ANNUAL PERFORMANCE	
FIRST WEEK	**Higher**	**Lower**
Higher	33	5
Lower	11	11

a. If a year is selected at random, what is the probability that the S&P 500 finished higher for the year?
b. Given that the S&P 500 finished higher after the first five days of trading, what is the probability that it finished higher for the year?
c. Are the two events "first-week performance" and "annual performance" independent? Explain.
d. Look up the performance after the first five days of 2010 and the 2010 annual performance of the S&P 500 at **finance.yahoo.com**. Comment on the results.

4.28 A standard deck of cards is being used to play a game. There are four suits (hearts, diamonds, clubs, and spades), each having 13 faces (ace, 2, 3, 4, 5, 6, 7, 8, 9, 10, jack, queen, and king), making a total of 52 cards. This complete deck is thoroughly mixed, and you will receive the first 2 cards from the deck, without replacement (the first card is not returned to the deck after it is selected).
a. What is the probability that both cards are queens?
b. What is the probability that the first card is a 10 and the second card is a 5 or 6?

c. If you were sampling with replacement (the first card is returned to the deck after it is selected), what would be the answer in (a)?

d. In the game of blackjack, the face cards (jack, queen, king) count as 10 points, and the ace counts as either 1 or 11 points. All other cards are counted at their face value. Blackjack is achieved if 2 cards total 21 points. What is the probability of getting blackjack in this problem?

4.29 A box of nine gloves contains two left-handed gloves and seven right-handed gloves.

a. If two gloves are randomly selected from the box, without replacement (the first glove is not returned to the box after it is selected), what is the probability that both gloves selected will be right-handed?

b. If two gloves are randomly selected from the box, without replacement (the first glove is not returned to the box after it is selected), what is the probability that there will be one right-handed glove and one left-handed glove selected?

c. If three gloves are selected, with replacement (the gloves are returned to the box after they are selected), what is the probability that all three will be left-handed?

d. If you were sampling with replacement (the first glove is returned to the box after it is selected), what would be the answers to (a) and (b)?

4.3 Bayes' Theorem

Bayes' theorem is used to revise previously calculated probabilities based on new information. Developed by Thomas Bayes in the eighteenth century (see references 1, 2, and 7), Bayes' theorem is an extension of what you previously learned about conditional probability.

You can apply Bayes' theorem to the situation in which M&R Electronics World is considering marketing a new model of televisions. In the past, 40% of the new-model televisions have been successful, and 60% have been unsuccessful. Before introducing the new model television, the marketing research department conducts an extensive study and releases a report, either favorable or unfavorable. In the past, 80% of the successful new-model television(s) had received favorable market research reports, and 30% of the unsuccessful new-model television(s) had received favorable reports. For the new model of television under consideration, the marketing research department has issued a favorable report. What is the probability that the television will be successful?

Bayes' theorem is developed from the definition of conditional probability. To find the conditional probability of B given A, consider Equation (4.4b) (originally presented on page 155 and shown below):

$$P(B \mid A) = \frac{P(A \text{ and } B)}{P(A)} = \frac{P(A \mid B)P(B)}{P(A)}$$

Bayes' theorem is derived by substituting Equation (4.8) on page 160 for $P(A)$ in the denominator of Equation (4.4b).

BAYES' THEOREM

$$P(B_i \mid A) = \frac{P(A \mid B_i)P(B_i)}{P(A \mid B_1)P(B_1) + P(A \mid B_2)P(B_2) + \cdots + P(A \mid B_k)P(B_k)} \quad \textbf{(4.9)}$$

where B_i is the ith event out of k mutually exclusive and collectively exhaustive events.

To use Equation (4.9) for the television-marketing example, let

event S = successful television event F = favorable report
event S' = unsuccessful television event F' = unfavorable report

and

$$P(S) = 0.40 \quad P(F \mid S) = 0.80$$
$$P(S') = 0.60 \quad P(F \mid S') = 0.30$$

Then, using Equation (4.9),

$$
\begin{aligned}
P(S|F) &= \frac{P(F|S)P(S)}{P(F|S)P(S) + P(F|S')P(S')} \\
&= \frac{(0.80)(0.40)}{(0.80)(0.40) + (0.30)(0.60)} \\
&= \frac{0.32}{0.32 + 0.18} = \frac{0.32}{0.50} \\
&= 0.64
\end{aligned}
$$

The probability of a successful television, given that a favorable report was received, is 0.64. Thus, the probability of an unsuccessful television, given that a favorable report was received, is $1 - 0.64 = 0.36$.

Table 4.4 summarizes the computation of the probabilities, and Figure 4.5 presents the decision tree.

TABLE 4.4
Bayes' Theorem Calculations for the Television-Marketing Example

Event S_i	Prior Probability $P(S_i)$	Conditional Probability $P(F\|S_i)$	Joint Probability $P(F\|S_i)P(S_i)$	Revised Probability $P(S_i\|F)$
S = successful television	0.40	0.80	0.32	$P(S\|F) = 0.32/0.50 = 0.64$
S' = unsuccessful television	0.60	0.30	0.18	$P(S'\|F) = 0.18/0.50 = 0.36$
			0.50	

FIGURE 4.5
Decision tree for marketing a new television

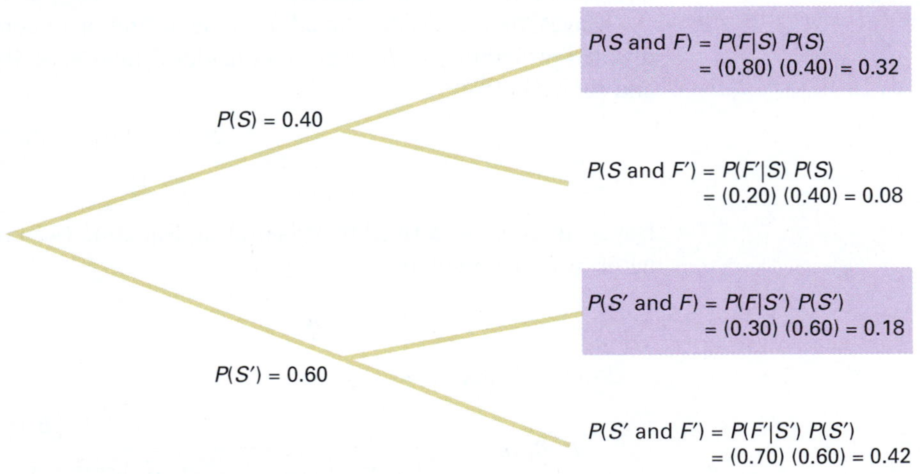

Example 4.10 applies Bayes' theorem to a medical diagnosis problem.

EXAMPLE 4.10

Using Bayes' Theorem in a Medical Diagnosis Problem

The probability that a person has a certain disease is 0.03. Medical diagnostic tests are available to determine whether the person actually has the disease. If the disease is actually present, the probability that the medical diagnostic test will give a positive result (indicating that the disease is present) is 0.90. If the disease is not actually present, the probability of a positive test result (indicating that the disease is present) is 0.02. Suppose that the medical diagnostic test has given a positive result (indicating that the disease is present). What is the probability that the disease is actually present? What is the probability of a positive test result?

SOLUTION Let

event D = has disease event T = test is positive

event D' = does not have disease event T' = test is negative

and

$$P(D) = 0.03 \quad P(T|D) = 0.90$$
$$P(D') = 0.97 \quad P(T|D') = 0.02$$

Using Equation (4.9) on page 163,

$$\begin{aligned} P(D|T) &= \frac{P(T|D)P(D)}{P(T|D)P(D) + P(T|D')P(D')} \\ &= \frac{(0.90)(0.03)}{(0.90)(0.03) + (0.02)(0.97)} \\ &= \frac{0.0270}{0.0270 + 0.0194} = \frac{0.0270}{0.0464} \\ &= 0.582 \end{aligned}$$

The probability that the disease is actually present, given that a positive result has occurred (indicating that the disease is present), is 0.582. Table 4.5 summarizes the computation of the probabilities, and Figure 4.6 presents the decision tree.

TABLE 4.5
Bayes' Theorem Calculations for the Medical Diagnosis Problem

Event D_i	Prior Probability $P(D_i)$	Conditional Probability $P(T \mid D_i)$	Joint Probability $P(T \mid D_i)P(D_i)$	Revised Probability $P(D_i \mid T)$
D = has disease	0.03	0.90	0.0270	$P(D \mid T) = 0.0270/0.0464 = 0.582$
D' = does not have disease	0.97	0.02	0.0194	$P(D' \mid T) = 0.0194/0.0464 = 0.418$
			0.0464	

FIGURE 4.6
Decision tree for the medical diagnosis problem

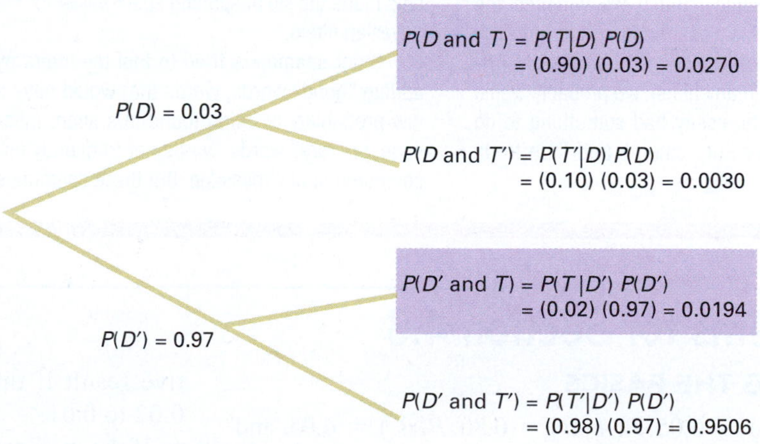

The denominator in Bayes' theorem represents $P(T)$, the probability of a positive test result, which in this case is 0.0464, or 4.64%.

THINK ABOUT THIS Divine Providence and Spam

Would you ever guess that the essays *Divine Benevolence: Or, An Attempt to Prove That the Principal End of the Divine Providence and Government Is the Happiness of His Creatures* and *An Essay Towards Solving a Problem in the Doctrine of Chances* were written by the same person? Probably not, and in doing so, you illustrate a modern-day application of Bayesian statistics: spam, or junk mail, filters.

In not guessing correctly, you probably looked at the words in the titles of the essays and concluded that they were talking about two different things. An implicit rule you used was that word frequencies vary by subject matter. A statistics essay would very likely contain the word *statistics* as well as words such as *chance*, *problem*, and *solving*. An eighteenth-century essay about theology and religion would be more likely to contain the uppercase forms of *Divine* and *Providence*.

Likewise, there are words you would guess to be very unlikely to appear in either book, such as technical terms from finance, and words that are most likely to appear in both—common words such as *a*, *and*, and *the*. That words would either be likely or unlikely suggests an application of probability theory. Of course, likely and unlikely are fuzzy concepts, and we might occasionally misclassify an essay if we kept things too simple, such as relying solely on the occurrence of the words *Divine* and *Providence*.

For example, a profile of the late Harris Milstead, better known as *Divine*, the star of *Hairspray* and other films, visiting Providence (Rhode Island), would most certainly not be an essay about theology. But if we widened the number of words we examined and found such words as *movie* or the name John Waters (Divine's director in many films), we probably would quickly realize the essay had something to do with twentieth-century cinema and little to do with theology and religion.

We can use a similar process to try to classify a new email message in your in-box as either spam or a legitimate message (called "ham," in this context). We would first need to add to your email program a "spam filter" that has the ability to track word frequencies associated with spam and ham messages as you identify them on a day-to-day basis. This would allow the filter to constantly update the prior probabilities necessary to use Bayes' theorem. With these probabilities, the filter can ask, "What is the probability that an email is spam, given the presence of a certain word?"

Applying the terms of Equation (4.9) on page 163, such a Bayesian spam filter would multiply the probability of finding the word in a spam email, $P(A|B)$, by the probability that the email is spam, $P(B)$, and then divide by the probability of finding the word in an email, the denominator in Equation (4.9). Bayesian spam filters also use shortcuts by focusing on a small set of words that have a high probability of being found in a spam message as well as on a small set of other words that have a low probability of being found in a spam message.

As spammers (people who send junk email) learned of such new filters, they tried to outfox them. Having learned that Bayesian filters might be assigning a high $P(A|B)$ value to words commonly found in spam, such as Viagra, spammers thought they could fool the filter by misspelling the word as Vi@gr@ or V1agra. What they overlooked was that the misspelled variants were even *more likely* to be found in a spam message than the original word. Thus, the misspelled variants made the job of spotting spam *easier* for the Bayesian filters.

Other spammers tried to fool the filters by adding "good" words, words that would have a low probability of being found in a spam message, or "rare" words, words not frequently encountered in any message. But these spammers overlooked the fact that the conditional probabilities are constantly updated and that words once considered "good" would be soon discarded from the good list by the filter as their $P(A|B)$ value increased. Likewise, as "rare" words grew more common in spam and yet stayed rare in ham, such words acted like the misspelled variants that others had tried earlier.

Even then, and perhaps after reading about Bayesian statistics, spammers thought that they could "break" Bayesian filters by inserting random words in their messages. Those random words would affect the filter by causing it to see many words whose $P(A|B)$ value would be low. The Bayesian filter would begin to label many spam messages as ham and end up being of no practical use. Spammers again overlooked that conditional probabilities are constantly updated.

Other spammers decided to eliminate all or most of the words in their messages and replace them with graphics so that Bayesian filters would have very few words with which to form conditional probabilities. But this approach failed, too, as Bayesian filters were rewritten to consider things other than words in a message. After all, Bayes' theorem concerns *events*, and "graphics present with no text" is as valid an event as "some word, *X*, present in a message." Other future tricks will ultimately fail for the same reason. (By the way, spam filters use non-Bayesian techniques as well, which makes spammers' lives even more difficult.)

Bayesian spam filters are an example of the unexpected way that applications of statistics can show up in your daily life. You will discover more examples as you read the rest of this book. *By the way, the author of the two essays mentioned earlier was Thomas Bayes, who is a lot more famous for the second essay than the first essay, a failed attempt to use mathematics and logic to prove the existence of God.*

Problems for Section 4.3

LEARNING THE BASICS

4.30 If $P(B) = 0.05$, $P(A|B) = 0.80$, $P(B') = 0.95$, and $P(A|B') = 0.40$, find $P(B|A)$.

4.31 If $P(B) = 0.30$, $P(A|B) = 0.60$, $P(B') = 0.70$, and $P(A|B') = 0.50$, find $P(B|A)$.

APPLYING THE CONCEPTS

4.32 In Example 4.10 on page 164, suppose that the probability that a medical diagnostic test will give a positive result if the disease is not present is reduced from 0.02 to 0.01.

a. If the medical diagnostic test has given a positive result (indicating that the disease is present), what is the probability that the disease is actually present?

b. If the medical diagnostic test has given a negative result (indicating that the disease is not present), what is the probability that the disease is not present?

4.33 An advertising executive is studying television viewing habits of married men and women during prime-time hours.

Based on past viewing records, the executive has determined that during prime time, husbands are watching television 60% of the time. When the husband is watching television, 40% of the time the wife is also watching. When the husband is not watching television, 30% of the time the wife is watching television.

a. Find the probability that if the wife is watching television, the husband is also watching television.

b. Find the probability that the wife is watching television during prime time.

SELF Test **4.34** Olive Construction Company is determining whether it should submit a bid for a new shopping center. In the past, Olive's main competitor, Base Construction Company, has submitted bids 70% of the time. If Base Construction Company does not bid on a job, the probability that Olive Construction Company will get the job is 0.50. If Base Construction Company bids on a job, the probability that Olive Construction Company will get the job is 0.25.

a. If Olive Construction Company gets the job, what is the probability that Base Construction Company did not bid?

b. What is the probability that Olive Construction Company will get the job?

4.35 Laid-off workers who become entrepreneurs because they cannot find meaningful employment with another company are known as *entrepreneurs by necessity*. *The Wall Street Journal* reports that these entrepreneurs by necessity are less likely to grow into large businesses than are *entrepreneurs by choice* (J. Bailey, "Desire—More Than Need—Builds a Business," *The Wall Street Journal*, May 21, 2001, p. B4). This article states that 89% of the entrepreneurs in the United States are entrepreneurs by choice and 11% are entrepreneurs by necessity. Only 2% of entrepreneurs by necessity expect their new business to employ 20 or more people within five years, whereas 14% of entrepreneurs by choice expect to employ at least 20 people within five years.

a. If an entrepreneur is selected at random and that individual expects that his or her new business will employ 20 or more people within five years, what is the probability that this individual is an entrepreneur by choice?

b. Discuss several possible reasons why entrepreneurs by choice are more likely than entrepreneurs by necessity to believe that they will grow their businesses.

4.36 The editor of a textbook publishing company is trying to decide whether to publish a proposed business statistics textbook. Information on previous textbooks published indicates that 10% are huge successes, 20% are modest successes, 40% break even, and 30% are losers. However, before a publishing decision is made, the book will be reviewed. In the past, 99% of the huge successes received favorable reviews, 70% of the moderate successes received favorable reviews, 40% of the break-even books received favorable reviews, and 20% of the losers received favorable reviews.

a. If the proposed textbook receives a favorable review, how should the editor revise the probabilities of the various outcomes to take this information into account?

b. What proportion of textbooks receives favorable reviews?

4.37 A municipal bond service has three rating categories (A, B, and C). Suppose that in the past year, of the municipal bonds issued throughout the United States, 70% were rated A, 20% were rated B, and 10% were rated C. Of the municipal bonds rated A, 50% were issued by cities, 40% by suburbs, and 10% by rural areas. Of the municipal bonds rated B, 60% were issued by cities, 20% by suburbs, and 20% by rural areas. Of the municipal bonds rated C, 90% were issued by cities, 5% by suburbs, and 5% by rural areas.

a. If a new municipal bond is to be issued by a city, what is the probability that it will receive an A rating?

b. What proportion of municipal bonds are issued by cities?

c. What proportion of municipal bonds are issued by suburbs?

4.4 Counting Rules

In Equation (4.1) on page 146, the probability of occurrence of an outcome was defined as the number of ways the outcome occurs, divided by the total number of possible outcomes. Often, there are a large number of possible outcomes, and determining the exact number can be difficult. In such circumstances, rules have been developed for counting the number of possible outcomes. This section presents five different counting rules.

Counting Rule 1

Counting rule 1 determines the number of possible outcomes for a set of mutually exclusive and collectively exhaustive events.

COUNTING RULE 1

If any one of k different mutually exclusive and collectively exhaustive events can occur on each of n trials, the number of possible outcomes is equal to

$$k^n \tag{4.10}$$

For example, using Equation (4.10), the number of different possible outcomes from tossing a two-sided coin five times is $2^5 = 2 \times 2 \times 2 \times 2 \times 2 = 32$.

EXAMPLE 4.11

Rolling a Die Twice

Suppose you roll a die twice. How many different possible outcomes can occur?

SOLUTION If a six-sided die is rolled twice, using Equation (4.10), the number of different outcomes is $6^2 = 36$.

Counting Rule 2

The second counting rule is a more general version of the first and allows the number of possible events to differ from trial to trial.

COUNTING RULE 2

If there are k_1 events on the first trial, k_2 events on the second trial, ... , and k_n events on the nth trial, then the number of possible outcomes is

$$(k_1)(k_2)\ldots(k_n) \tag{4.11}$$

For example, a state motor vehicle department would like to know how many license plate numbers are available if a license plate number consists of three letters followed by three numbers (0 through 9). Using Equation (4.11), if a license plate number consists of three letters followed by three numbers, the total number of possible outcomes is $(26)(26)(26)(10)(10)(10) = 17{,}576{,}000$.

EXAMPLE 4.12

Determining the Number of Different Dinners

A restaurant menu has a price-fixed complete dinner that consists of an appetizer, an entrée, a beverage, and a dessert. You have a choice of 5 appetizers, 10 entrées, 3 beverages, and 6 desserts. Determine the total number of possible dinners.

SOLUTION Using Equation (4.11), the total number of possible dinners is $(5)(10)(3)(6) = 900$.

Counting Rule 3

The third counting rule involves computing the number of ways that a set of items can be arranged in order.

COUNTING RULE 3

The number of ways that all n items can be arranged in order is

$$n! = (n)(n-1)\ldots(1) \tag{4.12}$$

where $n!$ is called n factorial, and $0!$ is defined as 1.

EXAMPLE 4.13

Using Counting Rule 3

If a set of six books is to be placed on a shelf, in how many ways can the six books be arranged?

SOLUTION To begin, you must realize that any of the six books could occupy the first position on the shelf. Once the first position is filled, there are five books to choose from in filling the second position. You continue this assignment procedure until all the positions are occupied. The number of ways that you can arrange six books is

$$n! = 6! = (6)(5)(4)(3)(2)(1) = 720$$

Counting Rule 4

In many instances you need to know the number of ways in which a subset of an entire group of items can be arranged in *order*. Each possible arrangement is called a **permutation**.

COUNTING RULE 4: PERMUTATIONS

The number of ways of arranging x objects selected from n objects in order is

$$_nP_x = \frac{n!}{(n-x)!} \tag{4.13}$$

where

n = total number of objects

x = number of objects to be arranged

$n!$ = n factorial $= n(n-1)\ldots(1)$

P = symbol for permutations[1]

[1]On many scientific calculators, there is a button labeled nPr that allows you to compute permutations. The symbol r is used instead of x.

EXAMPLE 4.14

Using Counting Rule 4

Modifying Example 4.13, if you have six books, but there is room for only four books on the shelf, in how many ways can you arrange these books on the shelf?

SOLUTION Using Equation (4.13), the number of ordered arrangements of four books selected from six books is equal to

$$_nP_x = \frac{n!}{(n-x)!} = \frac{6!}{(6-4)!} = \frac{(6)(5)(4)(3)(2)(1)}{(2)(1)} = 360$$

Counting Rule 5

In many situations, you are not interested in the *order* of the outcomes but only in the number of ways that x items can be selected from n items, *irrespective of order*. Each possible selection is called a **combination**.

COUNTING RULE 5: COMBINATIONS

The number of ways of selecting x objects from n objects, irrespective of order, is equal to

$$_nC_x = \frac{n!}{x!(n-x)!} \quad \textbf{(4.14)}$$

where

n = total number of objects

x = number of objects to be arranged

$n! = n$ factorial $= n(n-1)\ldots(1)$

C = symbol for combinations[2]

[2]On many scientific calculators, there is a button labeled nCr that allows you to compute permutations. The symbol r is used instead of x.

If you compare this rule to counting rule 4, you see that it differs only in the inclusion of a term $x!$ in the denominator. When permutations were used, all of the arrangements of the x objects are distinguishable. With combinations, the $x!$ possible arrangements of objects are irrelevant.

EXAMPLE 4.15
Using Counting Rule 5

Modifying Example 4.14, if the order of the books on the shelf is irrelevant, in how many ways can you arrange these books on the shelf?

SOLUTION Using Equation (4.14), the number of combinations of four books selected from six books is equal to

$$_nC_x = \frac{n!}{x!(n-x)!} = \frac{6!}{4!(6-4)!} = \frac{(6)(5)(4)(3)(2)(1)}{(4)(3)(2)(1)(2)(1)} = 15$$

Problems for Section 4.4

APPLYING THE CONCEPTS

SELF Test **4.38** If there are 10 multiple-choice questions on an exam, each having three possible answers, how many different sequences of answers are there?

4.39 A lock on a bank vault consists of three dials, each with 30 positions. In order for the vault to open, each of the three dials must be in the correct position.

a. How many different possible dial combinations are there for this lock?

b. What is the probability that if you randomly select a position on each dial, you will be able to open the bank vault?

c. Explain why "dial combinations" are not mathematical combinations expressed by Equation (4.14).

4.40 **a.** If a coin is tossed seven times, how many different outcomes are possible?

b. If a die is tossed seven times, how many different outcomes are possible?

c. Discuss the differences in your answers to (a) and (b).

4.41 A particular brand of women's jeans is available in seven different sizes, three different colors, and three different styles. How many different women's jeans does the store manager need to order to have one pair of each type?

4.42 You would like to make a salad that consists of lettuce, tomato, cucumber, and peppers. You go to the supermarket, intending to purchase one variety of each of these ingredients. You discover that there are eight varieties of lettuce, four varieties of tomatoes, three varieties of cucumbers, and three varieties of peppers for sale at the supermarket. If you buy them all, how many different salads can you make?

4.43 A team is being formed that includes four different people. There are four different positions on the teams. How many different ways are there to assign the four people to the four positions??

4.44 In Major League Baseball, there are five teams in the Eastern Division of the National League: Atlanta, Florida,

New York, Philadelphia, and Washington. How many different orders of finish are there for these five teams? (Assume that there are no ties in the standings.) Do you believe that all these orders are equally likely? Discuss.

4.45 Referring to Problem 4.44, how many different orders of finish are possible for the first four positions?

4.46 A gardener has six rows available in his vegetable garden to place tomatoes, eggplant, peppers, cucumbers, beans, and lettuce. Each vegetable will be allowed one and only one row. How many ways are there to position these vegetables in this garden?

4.47 There are eight members of a team. How many ways are there to select a team leader, assistant team leader, and team coordinator?

4.48 Four members of a group of 10 people are to be selected to a team. How many ways are there to select these four members?

4.49 A student has seven books that she would like to place in her backpack. However, there is room for only four books. Regardless of the arrangement, how many ways are there of placing four books into the backpack?

4.50 A daily lottery is conducted in which 2 winning numbers are selected out of 100 numbers. How many different combinations of winning numbers are possible?

4.51 A reading list for a course contains 20 articles. How many ways are there to choose 3 articles from this list?

4.5 Ethical Issues and Probability

Ethical issues can arise when any statements related to probability are presented to the public, particularly when these statements are part of an advertising campaign for a product or service. Unfortunately, many people are not comfortable with numerical concepts (see reference 5) and tend to misinterpret the meaning of the probability. In some instances, the misinterpretation is not intentional, but in other cases, advertisements may unethically try to mislead potential customers.

One example of a potentially unethical application of probability relates to advertisements for state lotteries. When purchasing a lottery ticket, the customer selects a set of numbers (such as 6) from a larger list of numbers (such as 54). Although virtually all participants know that they are unlikely to win the lottery, they also have very little idea of how unlikely it is for them to select all 6 winning numbers from the list of 54 numbers. They have even less of an idea of the probability of winning a consolation prize by selecting either 4 or 5 winning numbers.

Given this background, you might consider a recent commercial for a state lottery that stated, "We won't stop until we have made everyone a millionaire" to be deceptive and possibly unethical. Do you think the state has any intention of ever stopping the lottery, given the fact that the state relies on it to bring millions of dollars into its treasury? Is it possible that the lottery can make everyone a millionaire? Is it ethical to suggest that the purpose of the lottery is to make everyone a millionaire?

Another example of a potentially unethical application of probability relates to an investment newsletter promising a 90% probability of a 20% annual return on investment. To make the claim in the newsletter an ethical one, the investment service needs to (a) explain the basis on which this probability estimate rests, (b) provide the probability statement in another format, such as 9 chances in 10, and (c) explain what happens to the investment in the 10% of the cases in which a 20% return is not achieved (e.g., is the entire investment lost?).

These are serious ethical issues. If you were going to write an advertisement for the state lottery that ethically describes the probability of winning a certain prize, what would you say? If you were going to write an advertisement for the investment newsletter that ethically states the probability of a 20% return on an investment, what would you say?

USING STATISTICS @ M&R Electronics World Revisited

As the marketing manager for M&R Electronics World, you analyzed the survey results of an intent-to-purchase study. This study asked the heads of 1,000 households about their intentions to purchase a big-screen television sometime during the next 12 months, and as a follow-up, M&R surveyed the same people 12 months later to see whether such a television was purchased. In addition, for households purchasing big-screen televisions, the survey asked whether the television they purchased had a faster refresh rate, whether they also purchased a Blu-ray disc (BD) player in the past 12 months, and whether they were satisfied with their purchase of the big-screen television.

By analyzing the results of these surveys, you were able to uncover many pieces of valuable information that will help you plan a marketing strategy to enhance sales and better target those households likely to purchase multiple or more expensive products. Whereas only 30% of the households actually purchased a big-screen television, if a household indicated that it planned to purchase a big-screen television in the next 12 months, there was an 80% chance that the household actually made the purchase. Thus the marketing strategy should target those households that have indicated an intention to purchase.

You determined that for households that purchased a television that had a faster refresh rate, there was a 47.5% chance that the household also purchased a Blu-ray disc player. You then compared this conditional probability to the marginal probability of purchasing a Blu-ray disc player, which was 36%. Thus, households that purchased televisions that had a faster refresh rate are more likely to purchase a Blu-ray disc player than are households that purchased big-screen televisions that have a standard refresh rate.

You were also able to apply Bayes' theorem to M&R Electronics World's market research reports. The reports investigate a potential new television model prior to its scheduled release. If a favorable report was received, then there was a 64% chance that the new television model would be successful. However, if an unfavorable report was received, there is only a 16% chance that the model would be successful. Therefore, the marketing strategy of M&R needs to pay close attention to whether a report's conclusion is favorable or unfavorable.

SUMMARY

This chapter began by developing the basic concepts of probability. You learned that probability is a numeric value from 0 to 1 that represents the chance, likelihood, or possibility that a particular event will occur. In addition to simple probability, you learned about conditional probabilities and independent events. Bayes' theorem was used to revise previously calculated probabilities based on new information. You also learned about several counting rules. Throughout the chapter, contingency tables and decision trees were used to display information. In the next chapter, important discrete probability distributions such as the binomial, Poisson, and hypergeometric distributions are developed.

KEY EQUATIONS

Probability of Occurrence

$$\text{Probability of occurrence} = \frac{X}{T} \tag{4.1}$$

Marginal Probability

$$P(A) = P(A \text{ and } B_1) + P(A \text{ and } B_2) + \cdots + P(A \text{ and } B_k) \tag{4.2}$$

General Addition Rule

$$P(A \text{ or } B) = P(A) + P(B) - P(A \text{ and } B) \tag{4.3}$$

Conditional Probability

$$P(A \mid B) = \frac{P(A \text{ and } B)}{P(B)} \tag{4.4a}$$

$$P(B \mid A) = \frac{P(A \text{ and } B)}{P(A)} \tag{4.4b}$$

Independence

$$P(A \mid B) = P(A) \tag{4.5}$$

General Multiplication Rule

$$P(A \text{ and } B) = P(A \mid B)P(B) \quad \textbf{(4.6)}$$

Multiplication Rule for Independent Events

$$P(A \text{ and } B) = P(A)P(B) \quad \textbf{(4.7)}$$

Marginal Probability Using the General Multiplication Rule

$$P(A) = P(A \mid B_1)P(B_1) + P(A \mid B_2)P(B_2) + \cdots + P(A \mid B_k)P(B_k) \quad \textbf{(4.8)}$$

Bayes' Theorem

$$P(B_i \mid A) = \frac{P(A \mid B_i)P(B_i)}{P(A \mid B_1)P(B_1) + P(A \mid B_2)P(B_2) + \cdots + P(A \mid B_k)P(B_k)} \quad \textbf{(4.9)}$$

Counting Rule 1

$$k^n \quad \textbf{(4.10)}$$

Counting Rule 2

$$(k_1)(k_2)\ldots(k_n) \quad \textbf{(4.11)}$$

Counting Rule 3

$$n! = (n)(n-1)\ldots(1) \quad \textbf{(4.12)}$$

Counting Rule 4: Permutations

$$_nP_x = \frac{n!}{(n-x)!} \quad \textbf{(4.13)}$$

Counting Rule 5: Combinations

$$_nC_x = \frac{n!}{x!(n-x)!} \quad \textbf{(4.14)}$$

KEY TERMS

a priori probability 146
Bayes' theorem 163
certain event 146
collectively exhaustive 151
combination 169
complement 147
conditional probability 155
contingency table 148
decision tree 156
empirical probability 147
event 147
general addition rule 152
general multiplication rule 159
impossible event 146
independence 158
joint event 147
joint probability 150
marginal probability 150
multiplication rule for independent events 160
mutually exclusive 151
permutation 169
probability 146
sample space 148
simple event 147
simple probability 149
subjective probability 147
Venn diagram 148

CHAPTER REVIEW PROBLEMS

CHECKING YOUR UNDERSTANDING

4.52 What are the differences between *a priori* probability, empirical probability, and subjective probability?

4.53 What is the difference between a simple event and a joint event?

4.54 How can you use the general addition rule to find the probability of occurrence of event *A* or *B*?

4.55 What is the difference between mutually exclusive events and collectively exhaustive events?

4.56 How does conditional probability relate to the concept of independence?

4.57 How does the multiplication rule differ for events that are and are not independent?

4.58 How can you use Bayes' theorem to revise probabilities in light of new information?

4.59 In Bayes' theorem, how does the prior probability differ from the revised probability?

APPLYING THE CONCEPTS

4.60 A survey by the Pew Research Center ("Snapshots: Goals of 'Gen Next' vs. 'Gen X,'" *USA Today*, March 27, 2007, p. 1A) indicated that 81% of 18- to 25-year-olds had getting rich as a goal, as compared to 62% of 26- to 40-year-olds. Suppose that the survey was based on 500 respondents from each of the two groups.

a. Construct a contingency table.
b. Give an example of a simple event and a joint event.
c. What is the probability that a randomly selected respondent has a goal of getting rich?
d. What is the probability that a randomly selected respondent has a goal of getting rich *and* is in the 26- to 40-year-old group?
e. Are the events "age group" and "has getting rich as a goal" independent? Explain.

4.61 The owner of a restaurant serving Continental-style entrées was interested in studying ordering patterns of patrons for the Friday-to-Sunday weekend time period.

Records were maintained that indicated the demand for dessert during the same time period. The owner decided to study two other variables, along with whether a dessert was ordered: the gender of the individual and whether a beef entrée was ordered. The results are as follows:

	GENDER		
DESSERT ORDERED	**Male**	**Female**	**Total**
Yes	96	40	136
No	224	240	464
Total	320	280	600

	BEEF ENTRÉE		
DESSERT ORDERED	**Yes**	**No**	**Total**
Yes	71	65	136
No	116	348	464
Total	187	413	600

A waiter approaches a table to take an order for dessert. What is the probability that the first customer to order at the table

a. orders a dessert?
b. orders a dessert *or* has ordered a beef entrée?
c. is a female *and* does not order a dessert?
d. is a female *or* does not order a dessert?
e. Suppose the first person from whom the waiter takes the dessert order is a female. What is the probability that she does not order dessert?
f. Are gender and ordering dessert independent?
g. Is ordering a beef entrée independent of whether the person orders dessert?

4.62 Which meal are people most likely to order at a drive-through? A survey was conducted in 2009, but the sample sizes were not reported. Suppose the results, based on a sample of 100 males and 100 females, were as follows:

	GENDER		
MEAL	**Male**	**Female**	**Total**
Breakfast	18	10	28
Lunch	47	52	99
Dinner	29	29	58
Snack/beverage	6	9	15
Total	100	100	200

Source: Data extracted from **www.qsrmagazine.com/reports/drive-thru_time_study/2009/2009_charts/whats_your_preferred_way_to_order_fast_food.html**.

If a respondent is selected at random, what is the probability that he or she

a. prefers ordering lunch at the drive-through?
b. prefers ordering breakfast or lunch at the drive-through?
c. is a male *or* prefers ordering dinner at the drive-through?
d. is a male *and* prefers ordering dinner at the drive-through?
e. Given that the person selected is a female, what is the probability that she prefers ordering breakfast at the drive-through?

4.63 According to a Gallup Poll, companies with employees who are engaged with their workplace have greater innovation, productivity, and profitability, as well as less employee turnover. A survey of 1,895 workers in Germany found that 13% of the workers were engaged, 67% were not engaged, and 20% were actively disengaged. The survey also noted that 48% of engaged workers strongly agreed with the statement "My current job brings out my most creative ideas." Only 20% of the not engaged workers and 3% of the actively disengaged workers agreed with this statement (data extracted from M. Nink, "Employee Disengagement Plagues Germany," *Gallup Management Journal*, **gmj.gallup.com**, April 9, 2009). If a worker is known to strongly agree with the statement "My current job brings out my most creative ideas," what is the probability that the worker is engaged?

4.64 Sport utility vehicles (SUVs), vans, and pickups are generally considered to be more prone to roll over than cars. In 1997, 24.0% of all highway fatalities involved rollovers; 15.8% of all fatalities in 1997 involved SUVs, vans, and pickups, given that the fatality involved a rollover. Given that a rollover was not involved, 5.6% of all fatalities involved SUVs, vans, and pickups (data extracted from A. Wilde Mathews, "Ford Ranger, Chevy Tracker Tilt in Test," *The Wall Street Journal*, July 14, 1999, p. A2). Consider the following definitions:

A = fatality involved an SUV, van, or pickup
B = fatality involved a rollover

a. Use Bayes' theorem to find the probability that a fatality involved a rollover, given that the fatality involved an SUV, a van, or a pickup.
b. Compare the result in (a) to the probability that a fatality involved a rollover and comment on whether SUVs, vans, and pickups are generally more prone to rollover accidents than other vehicles.

4.65 Enzyme-linked immunosorbent assay (ELISA) is the most common type of screening test for detecting the HIV virus. A positive result from an ELISA indicates that the HIV virus is present. For most populations, ELISA has a high degree of sensitivity (to detect infection) and specificity (to detect noninfection). (See "HIV InSite Gateway to HIV and AIDS Knowledge" at **HIVInsite.ucsf.edu**.) Suppose the probability that a person is infected with the HIV virus for a certain population is 0.015. If the HIV virus is actually present, the probability that the ELISA test will give a positive result is 0.995. If the HIV virus is not actually present, the probability of a positive result from an ELISA is 0.01. If the ELISA has given a positive result, use

Bayes' theorem to find the probability that the HIV virus is actually present.

TEAM PROJECT

The file **Bond Funds** contains information regarding three categorical variables from a sample of 184 bond funds. The variables include

Type—Bond fund type (intermediate government or short-term corporate)
Fees—Sales charges (no or yes)
Risk—Risk-of-loss factor of the bond fund (below average, average, or above average)

4.66 Construct contingency tables of type and fees, type and risk, and fees and risk.

a. For each of these contingency tables, compute all the conditional and marginal probabilities.
b. Based on (a), what conclusions can you reach about whether these variables are independent?

STUDENT SURVEY DATABASE

4.67 Problem 1.27 on page 14 describes a survey of 62 undergraduate students (see the file **UndergradSurvey**). For these data, construct contingency tables of gender and major, gender and graduate school intention, gender and employment status, gender and computer preference, class and graduate school intention, class and employment status, major and graduate school intention, major and employment status, and major and computer preference.

a. For each of these contingency tables, compute all the conditional and marginal probabilities.
b. Based on (a), what conclusions can you reach about whether these variables are independent?

4.68 Problem 1.27 on page 14 describes a survey of 62 undergraduate students (stored in **UndergradSurvey**).

a. Select a sample of undergraduate students at your school and conduct a similar survey for those students.
b. For your data, construct contingency tables of gender and major, gender and graduate school intention, gender and employment status, gender and computer preference, class and graduate school intention, class and employment status, major and graduate school intention, major and employment status, and major and computer preference.
c. Based on (b), what conclusions can you reach about whether these variables are independent?
d. Compare the results of (c) to those of Problem 4.67 (b).

4.69 Problem 1.28 on page 15 describes a survey of 44 MBA students (stored in **GradSurvey**). For these data, construct contingency tables of gender and graduate major, gender and undergraduate major, gender and employment status, gender and computer preference, graduate major and undergraduate major, graduate major and employment status, and graduate major and computer preference.

a. For each of these contingency tables, compute all the conditional and marginal probabilities.
b. Based on (b), what conclusions can you reach about whether these variables are independent?

4.70 Problem 1.28 on page 15 describes a survey of 44 MBA students (stored in **GradSurvey**).

a. Select a sample of MBA students from your MBA program and conduct a similar survey for those students.
b. For your data, construct contingency tables of gender and graduate major, gender and undergraduate major, gender and employment status, gender and computer preference, graduate major and undergraduate major, graduate major and employment status, and graduate major and computer preference.
c. Based on (b), what conclusions can you reach about whether these variables are independent?
d. Compare the results of (c) to those of Problem 4.69 (b).

DIGITAL CASE

Apply your knowledge about contingency tables and the proper application of simple and joint probabilities in this continuing Digital Case from Chapter 3.

Open **EndRunGuide.pdf**, the EndRun Financial Services "Guide to Investing," and read the information about the Guaranteed Investment Package (GIP). Read the claims and examine the supporting data. Then answer the following questions:

1. How accurate is the claim of the probability of success for EndRun's GIP? In what ways is the claim misleading? How would you calculate and state the probability of having an annual rate of return not less than 15%?
2. Using the table found under the "Show Me The Winning Probabilities" subhead, compute the proper probabilities for the group of investors. What mistake was made in reporting the 7% probability claim?
3. Are there any probability calculations that would be appropriate for rating an investment service? Why or why not?

REFERENCES

1. Bellhouse, D. R., "The Reverend Thomas Bayes, FRS: A Biography to Celebrate the Tercentenary of His Birth," *Statistical Science*, 19 (2004), 3–43.
2. Lowd, D., and C. Meek, "Good Word Attacks on Statistical Spam Filters," presented at the Second Conference on Email and Anti-Spam, CEAS 2005.
3. *Microsoft Excel 2010* (Redmond, WA: Microsoft Corp., 2010).
4. *Minitab Release 16* (State College, PA.: Minitab, Inc., 2010).
5. Paulos, J. A., *Innumeracy* (New York: Hill and Wang, 1988).
6. Silberman, S., "The Quest for Meaning," *Wired 8.02*, February 2000.
7. Zeller, T., "The Fight Against V1@gra (and Other Spam)," *The New York Times*, May 21, 2006, pp. B1, B6.

CHAPTER 4 EXCEL GUIDE

EG4.1 BASIC PROBABILITY CONCEPTS

Simple and Joint Probability and the General Addition Rule

PHStat2 Use **Simple & Joint Probabilities** to compute basic probabilities. Select **PHStat → Probability & Prob. Distributions → Simple & Joint Probabilities**. The procedure inserts a worksheet similar to Figure EG4.1 into the current workbook. (Unlike with other procedures, no dialog box is first displayed.) To use the worksheet, fill in the **Sample Space** area with your data.

In-Depth Excel Use the **COMPUTE worksheet** of the **Probabilities workbook** as a template for computing basic probabilities (see Figure EG4.1, below). The worksheet contains the Table 4.1 purchase behavior data shown on page. Overwrite these values when you enter data for other problems.

Open to the **COMPUTE_FORMULAS worksheet** to examine the formulas used in the worksheet, many of which are shown in the inset to Figure EG4.1.

FIGURE EG4.1 COMPUTE worksheet of the Probabilities workbook

	A	B	C	D	E
1	Probabilities				
2					
3	Sample Space		ACTUALLY PURCHASED		
4			Yes	No	Totals
5	PLANNED TO PURCHASE	Yes	200	50	250
6		No	100	650	750
7		Totals	300	700	1000
8					
9	Simple Probabilities				
10	P(Yes)	0.25			
11	P(No)	0.75			
12	P(Yes)	0.30			
13	P(No)	0.70			
14					
15	Joint Probabilities				
16	P(Yes and Yes)	0.20			
17	P(Yes and No)	0.05			
18	P(No and Yes)	0.10			
19	P(No and No)	0.65			
20					
21	Addition Rule				
22	P(Yes or Yes)	0.35			
23	P(Yes or No)	0.90			
24	P(No or Yes)	0.95			
25	P(No or No)	0.80			

Simple Probabilities	
="P(" & B5 & ")"	=E5/E7
="P(" & B6 & ")"	=E6/E7
="P(" & C4 & ")"	=C7/E7
="P(" & D4 & ")"	=D7/E7
Joint Probabilities	
="P(" & B5 & " and " & C4 & ")"	=C5/E7
="P(" & B5 & " and " & D4 & ")"	=D5/E7
="P(" & B6 & " and " & C4 & ")"	=C6/E7
="P(" & B6 & " and " & D4 & ")"	=D6/E7
Addition Rule	
="P(" & B5 & " or " & C4 & ")"	=B10 + B12 - B16
="P(" & B5 & " or " & D4 & ")"	=B10 + B13 - B17
="P(" & B6 & " or " & C4 & ")"	=B11 + B12 - B18
="P(" & B6 & " or " & D4 & ")"	=B11 + B13 - B19

EG4.2 CONDITIONAL PROBABILITY

There is no Excel material for this section.

EG4.3 BAYES' THEOREM

In-Depth Excel Use the **COMPUTE worksheet** of the **Bayes workbook** as a template for computing basic probabilities (see Figure EG4.2, at right). The worksheet contains the television-marketing example of Table 4.4 on page 164. Overwrite these values when you enter data for other problems.

Open to the **COMPUTE_FORMULAS worksheet** to examine the simple arithmetic formulas that compute the probabilities which are also shown in the inset to Figure EG4.2.

	A	B	C	D	E
1	Bayes Theorem Calculations				
2					
3		Probabilities			
4	Event	Prior	Conditional	Joint	Revised
5	S	0.4	0.8	0.32	0.64
6	S'	0.6	0.3	0.18	0.36
7			Total:	0.5	

Joint	Revised
=B5 * C5	=D5/$D$7
=B6 * C6	=D6/$D$7
=D5 + D6	

FIGURE EG4.2 COMPUTE worksheet of the Bayes workbook

EG4.4 COUNTING RULES

Counting Rule 1

In-Depth Excel Use the **POWER(*k*, *n*)** worksheet function in a cell formula to compute the number of outcomes given k events and n trials. For example, the formula **=POWER(6, 2)** computes the answer for Example 4.11 on page 168.

Counting Rule 2

In-Depth Excel Use a formula that takes the product of successive **POWER(*k*, *n*)** functions to solve problems related to counting rule 2. For example, the formula **=POWER(26, 3) * POWER(10, 3)** computes the answer for the state motor vehicle department example on page 168.

Counting Rule 3

In-Depth Excel Use the **FACT(*n*)** worksheet function in a cell formula to compute how many ways n items can be arranged. For example, the formula **=FACT(6)** computes 6!

Counting Rule 4

In-Depth Excel Use the **PERMUT(*n*, *x*)** worksheet function in a cell formula to compute the number of ways of arranging x objects selected from n objects in order. For example, the formula **=PERMUT(6, 4)** computes the answer for Example 4.14 on page 169.

Counting Rule 5

In-Depth Excel Use the **COMBIN(*n*, *x*)** worksheet function in a cell formula to compute the number of ways of arranging x objects selected from n objects, irrespective of order. For example, the formula **=COMBIN(6, 4)** computes the answer for Example 4.15 on page 170.

CHAPTER 4 MINITAB GUIDE

MG4.1 BASIC PROBABILITY CONCEPTS

There is no Minitab material for this section.

MG4.2 CONDITIONAL PROBABILITY

There is no Minitab material for this section.

MG4.3 BAYES' THEOREM

There is no Minitab material for this section.

MG4.4 COUNTING RULES

Use **Calculator** to apply the counting rules. Select **Calc → Calculator**. In the Calculator dialog box (shown at right):

1. Enter the column name of an empty column in the **Store result in variable** box and then press **Tab**.
2. Build the appropriate expression (as discussed later in this section) in the **Expression** box. To apply counting rules 3 through 5, select **Arithmetic** from the **Functions** drop-down list to facilitate the function selection.
3. Click **OK**.

If you have previously used the Calculator during your Minitab session, you may have to clear the contents of the Expression box by selecting the contents and pressing **Del** before you begin step 2.

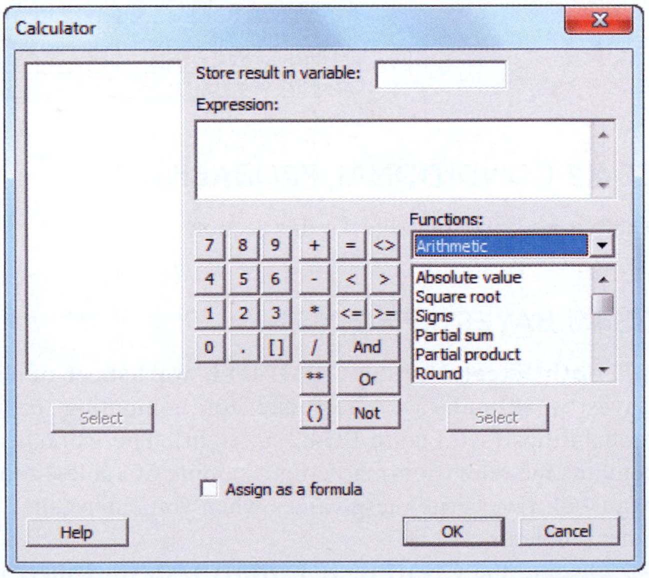

Counting Rule 1

Enter an expression that uses the exponential operator **. For example, the expression **6 ** 2** computes the answer for Example 4.11 on page 168.

Counting Rule 2

Enter an expression that uses the exponential operator **. For example, the expression **26 ** 3 * 10 ** 3** computes the answer for the state motor vehicle department example on page 168.

Counting Rule 3

Enter an expression that uses the **FACTORIAL(*n*)** function to compute how many ways *n* items can be arranged. For example, the expression **FACTORIAL(6)** computes 6!

Counting Rule 4

Enter an expression that uses the **PERMUTATIONS(*n*, *x*)** function to compute the number of ways of arranging *x* objects selected from *n* objects in order. For example, the expression **PERMUTATIONS(6, 4)** computes the answer for Example 4.14 on page 169.

Counting Rule 5

Enter an expression that uses the **COMBINATIONS(*n*, *x*)** function to compute the number of ways of arranging *x* objects selected from *n* objects, irrespective of order. For example, the expression **COMBINATIONS(6, 4)** computes the answer for Example 4.15 on page 170.

5 Discrete Probability Distributions

Learning Objectives

In this chapter, you learn:

- The properties of a probability distribution
- To compute the expected value and variance of a probability distribution
- To calculate the covariance and understand its use in finance
- To compute probabilities from the binomial, Poisson, and hypergeometric distributions
- How the binomial, Poisson, and hypergeometric distributions can be used to solve business problems

USING STATISTICS

@ Saxon Home Improvement

You are an accountant for the Saxon Home Improvement Company, which uses a state-of-the-art accounting information system to manage its accounting and financial operations.

Accounting information systems collect, process, store, transform, and distribute financial information to decision makers both internal and external to a business organization (see reference 7). These systems continuously audit accounting information, looking for errors or incomplete or improbable information. For example, when customers of the Saxon Home Improvement Company submit online orders, the company's accounting information system reviews the order forms for possible mistakes. Any questionable invoices are tagged and included in a daily *exceptions report*. Recent data collected by the company show that the likelihood is 0.10 that an order form will be tagged. Saxon would like to determine the likelihood of finding a certain number of tagged forms in a sample of a specific size. For example, what would be the likelihood that none of the order forms are tagged in a sample of four forms? That one of the order forms is tagged?

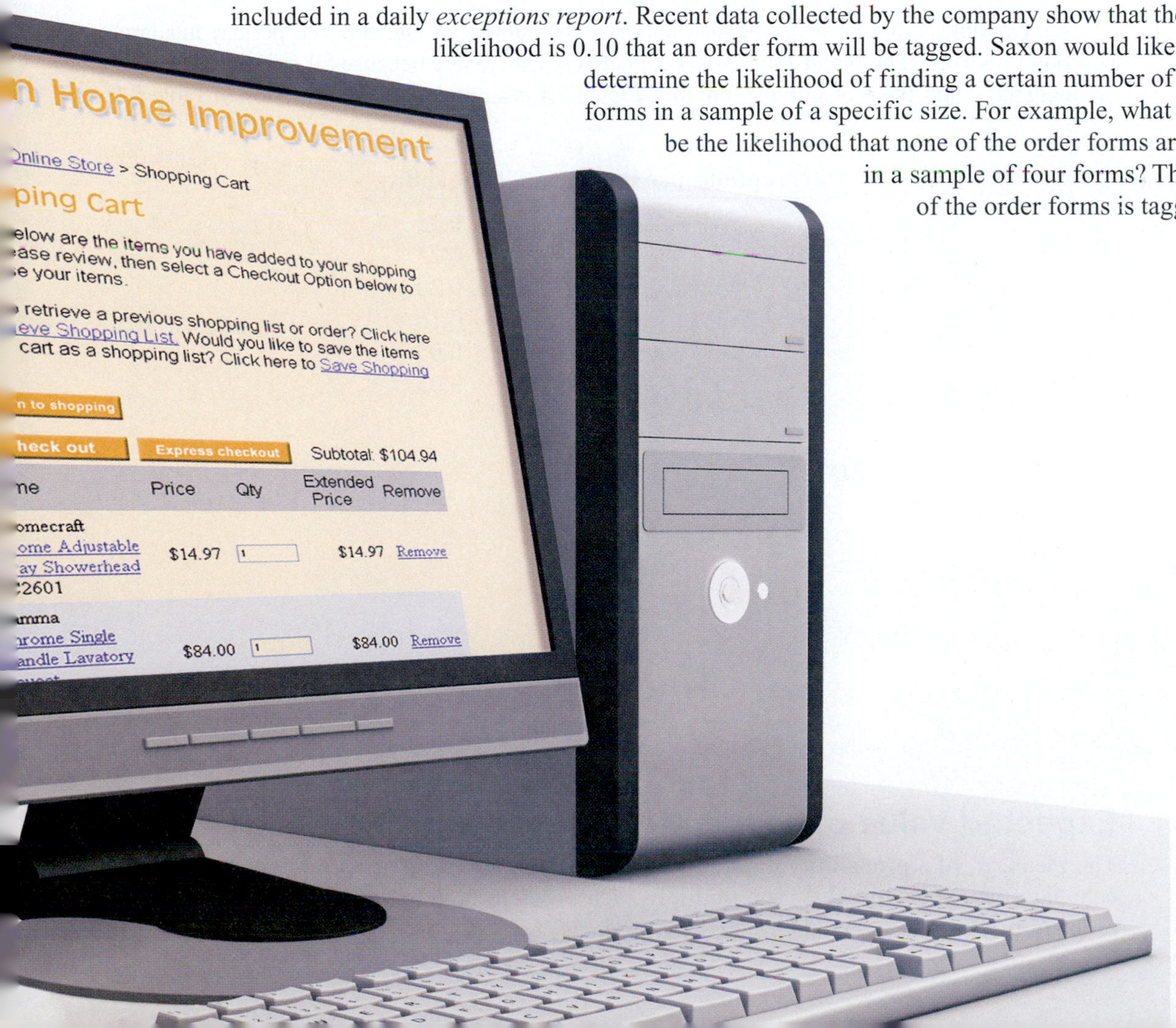

How could the Saxon Home Improvement Company determine the solution to this type of probability problem? One way is to use a model, or small-scale representation, that approximates the process. By using such an approximation, Saxon managers could make inferences about the actual order process. In this case, the Saxon managers can use *probability distributions*, mathematical models suited for solving the type of probability problems the managers are facing.

This chapter introduces you to the concept and characteristics of probability distributions. You will learn how the knowledge about a probability distribution can help you choose between alternative investment strategies. You will also learn how the binomial, Poisson, and hypergeometric distributions can be applied to help solve business problems.

5.1 The Probability Distribution for a Discrete Random Variable

In Section 1.4, a *numerical variable* was defined as a variable that yields numerical responses, such as the number of magazines you subscribe to or your height. Numerical variables are either *discrete* or *continuous*. Continuous numerical variables produce outcomes that come from a measuring process (e.g., your height). Discrete numerical variables produce outcomes that come from a counting process (e.g., the number of magazines you subscribe to). This chapter deals with probability distributions that represent discrete numerical variables.

PROBABILITY DISTRIBUTION FOR A DISCRETE RANDOM VARIABLE

A **probability distribution for a discrete random variable** is a mutually exclusive list of all the possible numerical outcomes along with the probability of occurrence of each outcome.

For example, Table 5.1 gives the distribution of the number of interruptions per day in a large computer network. The list in Table 5.1 is collectively exhaustive because all possible outcomes are included. Thus, the probabilities sum to 1. Figure 5.1 is a graphical representation of Table 5.1.

TABLE 5.1
Probability Distribution of the Number of Interruptions per Day

Interruptions per Day	Probability
0	0.35
1	0.25
2	0.20
3	0.10
4	0.05
5	0.05

FIGURE 5.1
Probability distribution of the number of interruptions per day

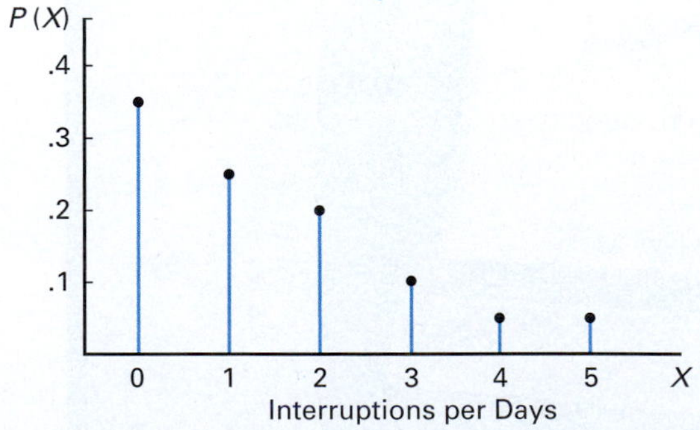

Expected Value of a Discrete Random Variable

The mean, μ, of a probability distribution is the **expected value** of its random variable. To calculate the expected value, you multiply each possible outcome, x, by its corresponding probability, $P(X = x_i)$, and then sum these products.

EXPECTED VALUE, μ, OF A DISCRETE RANDOM VARIABLE

$$\mu = E(X) = \sum_{i=1}^{N} x_i P(X = x_i) \quad \textbf{(5.1)}$$

where

x_i = the ith outcome of the discrete random variable X

$P(X = x_i)$ = probability of occurrence of the ith outcome of X

For the probability distribution of the number of interruptions per day in a large computer network (Table 5.1), the expected value is computed as follows, using Equation (5.1), and is also shown in Table 5.2:

$$\begin{aligned} \mu = E(X) &= \sum_{i=1}^{N} x_i P(X = x_i) \\ &= (0)(0.35) + (1)(0.25) + (2)(0.20) + (3)(0.10) + (4)(0.05) + (5)(0.05) \\ &= 0 + 0.25 + 0.40 + 0.30 + 0.20 + 0.25 \\ &= 1.40 \end{aligned}$$

TABLE 5.2

Computing the Expected Value of the Number of Interruptions per Day

Interruptions per Day (x_i)	$P(X = x_i)$	$x_i P(X = x_i)$
0	0.35	$(0)(0.35) = 0.00$
1	0.25	$(1)(0.25) = 0.25$
2	0.20	$(2)(0.20) = 0.40$
3	0.10	$(3)(0.10) = 0.30$
4	0.05	$(4)(0.05) = 0.20$
5	0.05	$(5)(0.05) = 0.25$
	1.00	$\mu = E(X) = 1.40$

The expected value is 1.40. The expected value of 1.4 for the number of interruptions per day is not a possible outcome because the actual number of interruptions in a given day must be an integer value. The expected value represents the *mean* number of interruptions in a given day.

Variance and Standard Deviation of a Discrete Random Variable

You compute the variance of a probability distribution by multiplying each possible squared difference $[x_i - E(X)]^2$ by its corresponding probability, $P(X = x_i)$, and then summing the resulting products. Equation (5.2) defines the **variance of a discrete random variable**.

VARIANCE OF A DISCRETE RANDOM VARIABLE

$$\sigma^2 = \sum_{i=1}^{N} [x_i - E(X)]^2 P(X = x_i) \quad \textbf{(5.2)}$$

where

x_i = the ith outcome of the discrete random variable X

$P(X = x_i)$ = probability of occurrence of the ith outcome of X

Equation (5.3) defines the **standard deviation of a discrete random variable.**

STANDARD DEVIATION OF A DISCRETE RANDOM VARIABLE

$$\sigma = \sqrt{\sigma^2} = \sqrt{\sum_{i=1}^{N}[x_i - E(X)]^2 P(X = x_i)} \quad \textbf{(5.3)}$$

The variance and the standard deviation of the number of interruptions per day are computed as follows and in Table 5.3, using Equations (5.2) and (5.3):

$$\begin{aligned}\sigma^2 &= \sum_{i=1}^{N}[x_i - E(X)]^2 P(X = x_i)\\ &= (0 - 1.4)^2(0.35) + (1 - 1.4)^2(0.25) + (2 - 1.4)^2(0.20) + (3 - 1.4)^2(0.10)\\ &\quad + (4 - 1.4)^2(0.05) + (5 - 1.4)^2(0.05)\\ &= 0.686 + 0.040 + 0.072 + 0.256 + 0.338 + 0.648\\ &= 2.04\end{aligned}$$

TABLE 5.3

Computing the Variance and Standard Deviation of the Number of Interruptions per Day

Interruptions per Day (x_i)	$P(X = x_i)$	$x_iP(X = x_i)$	$[x_i - E(X)]^2 P(X = x_i)$
0	0.35	$(0)(0.35) = 0.00$	$(0 - 1.4)^2(0.35) = 0.686$
1	0.25	$(1)(0.25) = 0.25$	$(1 - 1.4)^2(0.25) = 0.040$
2	0.20	$(2)(0.20) = 0.40$	$(2 - 1.4)^2(0.20) = 0.072$
3	0.10	$(3)(0.10) = 0.30$	$(3 - 1.4)^2(0.10) = 0.256$
4	0.05	$(4)(0.05) = 0.20$	$(4 - 1.4)^2(0.05) = 0.338$
5	0.05	$(5)(0.05) = 0.25$	$(5 - 1.4)^2(0.05) = 0.648$
	1.00	$\mu = E(X) = 1.40$	$\sigma^2 = 2.04$

and

$$\sigma = \sqrt{\sigma^2} = \sqrt{2.04} = 1.4283$$

Thus, the mean number of interruptions per day is 1.4, the variance is 2.04, and the standard deviation is approximately 1.43 interruptions per day.

Problems for Section 5.1

LEARNING THE BASICS

5.1 Given the following probability distributions:

Distribution *A*		Distribution *B*	
X	$P(X = x_i)$	X	$P(X = x_i)$
0	0.50	0	0.05
1	0.20	1	0.10
2	0.15	2	0.15
3	0.10	3	0.20
4	0.05	4	0.50

a. Compute the expected value for each distribution.
b. Compute the standard deviation for each distribution.
c. Compare the results of distributions *A* and *B*.

APPLYING THE CONCEPTS

SELF Test **5.2** The following table contains the probability distribution for the number of traffic accidents daily in a small city:

Number of Accidents Daily (X)	$P(X = x_i)$
0	0.10
1	0.20
2	0.45
3	0.15
4	0.05
5	0.05

a. Compute the mean number of accidents per day.
b. Compute the standard deviation.

5.3 Recently, a regional automobile dealership sent out fliers to perspective customers, indicating that they had already won one of three different prizes: a Kia Optima valued at $15,000, a $500 gas card, or a $5 Wal-Mart shopping card. To claim his or her prize, a prospective customer needed to present the flier at the dealership's showroom. The fine print on the back of the flier listed the probabilities of winning. The chance of winning the car was 1 out of 31,478, the chance of winning the gas card was 1 out of 31,478, and the chance of winning the shopping card was 31,476 out 31,478.

a. How many fliers do you think the automobile dealership sent out?

b. Using your answer to (a) and the probabilities listed on the flier, what is the expected value of the prize won by a prospective customer receiving a flier?

c. Using your answer to (a) and the probabilities listed on the flier, what is the standard deviation of the value of the prize won by a prospective customer receiving a flier?

d. Do you think this is an effective promotion? Why or why not?

5.4 In the carnival game Under-or-Over-Seven, a pair of fair dice is rolled once, and the resulting sum determines whether the player wins or loses his or her bet. For example, the player can bet $1 that the sum will be under 7—that is, 2, 3, 4, 5, or 6. For this bet, the player wins $1 if the result is under 7 and loses $1 if the outcome equals or is greater than 7. Similarly, the player can bet $1 that the sum will be over 7—that is, 8, 9, 10, 11, or 12. Here, the player wins $1 if the result is over 7 but loses $1 if the result is 7 or under. A third method of play is to bet $1 on the outcome 7. For this bet, the player wins $4 if the result of the roll is 7 and loses $1 otherwise.

a. Construct the probability distribution representing the different outcomes that are possible for a $1 bet on under 7.

b. Construct the probability distribution representing the different outcomes that are possible for a $1 bet on over 7.

c. Construct the probability distribution representing the different outcomes that are possible for a $1 bet on 7.

d. Show that the expected long-run profit (or loss) to the player is the same, no matter which method of play is used.

5.5 The number of arrivals per minute at a bank located in the central business district of a large city was recorded over a period of 200 minutes, with the following results:

Arrivals	Frequency
0	14
1	31
2	47
3	41
4	29
5	21
6	10
7	5
8	2

a. Compute the expected number of arrivals per minute.

b. Compute the standard deviation.

5.6 The manager of the commercial mortgage department of a large bank has collected data during the past two years concerning the number of commercial mortgages approved per week. The results from these two years (104 weeks) indicated the following:

Number of Commercial Mortgages Approved	Frequeny
0	13
1	25
2	32
3	17
4	9
5	6
6	1
7	1

a. Compute the expected number of mortgages approved per week.

b. Compute the standard deviation.

5.2 Covariance and Its Application in Finance

In Section 5.1, the expected value, variance, and standard deviation of a discrete random variable of a probability distribution are discussed. In this section, the covariance between two variables is introduced and applied to portfolio management, a topic of great interest to financial analysts.

Covariance

The **covariance**, σ_{XY}, measures the strength of the relationship between two numerical random variables, X and Y. A positive covariance indicates a positive relationship. A negative covariance indicates a negative relationship. A covariance of 0 indicates that the two variables are independent. Equation (5.4) defines the covariance for a discrete probability distribution.

COVARIANCE

$$\sigma_{XY} = \sum_{i=1}^{N}[x_i - E(X)][y_i - E(Y)]\,P(x_i y_i) \qquad \textbf{(5.4)}$$

where

X = discrete random variable X

x_i = ith outcome of X

Y = discrete random variable Y

y_i = ith outcome of Y

$P(x_i y_i)$ = probability of occurrence of the ith outcome of X and the ith outcome of Y

$i = 1, 2, \ldots, N$ for X and Y

To illustrate the covariance, suppose that you are deciding between two different investments for the coming year. The first investment is a mutual fund that consists of the stocks that comprise the Dow Jones Industrial Average. The second investment is a mutual fund that is expected to perform best when economic conditions are weak. Table 5.4 summarizes your estimate of the returns (per $1,000 investment) under three economic conditions, each with a given probability of occurrence.

TABLE 5.4

Estimated Returns for Each Investment Under Three Economic Conditions

		Investment	
$P(x_i y_i)$	Economic Condition	Dow Jones Fund	Weak-Economy Fund
0.2	Recession	−$300	+$200
0.5	Stable economy	+100	+50
0.3	Expanding economy	+250	−100

The expected value and standard deviation for each investment and the covariance of the two investments are computed as follows:

Let X = Dow Jones fund and Y = weak-economy fund

$$E(X) = \mu_X = (-300)(0.2) + (100)(0.5) + (250)(0.3) = \$65$$

$$E(Y) = \mu_Y = (+200)(0.2) + (50)(0.5) + (-100)(0.3) = \$35$$

$$Var(X) = \sigma_X^2 = (-300 - 65)^2(0.2) + (100 - 65)^2(0.5) + (250 - 65)^2(0.3)$$
$$= 37{,}525$$

$$\sigma_X = \$193.71$$

$$Var(Y) = \sigma_Y^2 = (200 - 35)^2(0.2) + (50 - 35)^2(0.5) + (-100 - 35)^2(0.3)$$
$$= 11{,}025$$

$$\sigma_Y = \$105.00$$

$$\sigma_{XY} = (-300 - 65)(200 - 35)(0.2) + (100 - 65)(50 - 35)(0.5) + (250 - 65)(-100 - 35)(0.3)$$
$$= -12{,}045 + 262.5 - 7{,}492.5$$
$$= -19{,}275$$

Thus, the Dow Jones fund has a higher expected value (i.e., larger expected return) than the weak-economy fund but also has a higher standard deviation (i.e., more risk). The covariance of −19,275 between the two investments indicates a negative relationship in which the two investments are varying in the *opposite* direction. Therefore, when the return on one investment is high, typically, the return on the other is low.

Expected Value, Variance, and Standard Deviation of the Sum of Two Random Variables

Equations (5.1) through (5.3) define the expected value, variance, and standard deviation of a probability distribution, and Equation (5.4) defines the covariance between two variables, X and Y. The **expected value of the sum of two random variables** is equal to the sum of the expected values. The **variance of the sum of two random variables** is equal to the sum of the variances plus twice the covariance. The **standard deviation of the sum of two random variables** is the square root of the variance of the sum of two random variables.

EXPECTED VALUE OF THE SUM OF TWO RANDOM VARIABLES

$$E(X + Y) = E(X) + E(Y) \tag{5.5}$$

VARIANCE OF THE SUM OF TWO RANDOM VARIABLES

$$Var(X + Y) = \sigma_{X+Y}^2 = \sigma_X^2 + \sigma_Y^2 + 2\sigma_{XY} \tag{5.6}$$

STANDARD DEVIATION OF THE SUM OF TWO RANDOM VARIABLES

$$\sigma_{X+Y} = \sqrt{\sigma_{X+Y}^2} \tag{5.7}$$

To illustrate the expected value, variance, and standard deviation of the sum of two random variables, consider the two investments previously discussed. If X = Dow Jones fund and Y = weak-economy fund, using Equations (5.5), (5.6), and (5.7),

$$\begin{aligned} E(X + Y) &= E(X) + E(Y) = 65 + 35 = \$100 \\ \sigma_{X+Y}^2 &= \sigma_X^2 + \sigma_Y^2 + 2\sigma_{XY} \\ &= 37{,}525 + 11{,}025 + (2)(-19{,}275) \\ &= 10{,}000 \\ \sigma_{X+Y} &= \$100 \end{aligned}$$

The expected value of the sum of the Dow Jones fund and the weak-economy fund is \$100, with a standard deviation of \$100. The standard deviation of the sum of the two investments is less than the standard deviation of either single investment because there is a large negative covariance between the investments.

Portfolio Expected Return and Portfolio Risk

Now that the covariance and the expected value and standard deviation of the sum of two random variables have been defined, these concepts can be applied to the study of a group of assets referred to as a **portfolio**. Investors combine assets into portfolios to reduce their risk (see references 1 and 2). Often, the objective is to maximize the return while minimizing the risk. For such portfolios, rather than study the sum of two random variables, the investor weights each investment by the proportion of assets assigned to that investment. Equations (5.8) and (5.9) define the **portfolio expected return** and **portfolio risk**.

PORTFOLIO EXPECTED RETURN

The portfolio expected return for a two-asset investment is equal to the weight assigned to asset X multiplied by the expected return of asset X plus the weight assigned to asset Y multiplied by the expected return of asset Y.

$$E(P) = wE(X) + (1 - w)E(Y) \quad \textbf{(5.8)}$$

where

$E(P)$ = portfolio expected return

w = portion of the portfolio value assigned to asset X

$(1 - w)$ = portion of the portfolio value assigned to asset Y

$E(X)$ = expected return of asset X

$E(Y)$ = expected return of asset Y

PORTFOLIO RISK

$$\sigma_p = \sqrt{w^2\sigma_X^2 + (1 - w)^2\sigma_Y^2 + 2w(1 - w)\sigma_{XY}} \quad \textbf{(5.9)}$$

In the previous section, you evaluated the expected return and risk of two different investments, a Dow Jones fund and a weak-economy fund. You also computed the covariance of the two investments. Now, suppose that you want to form a portfolio of these two investments that consists of an equal investment in each of these two funds. To compute the portfolio expected return and the portfolio risk, using Equations (5.8) and (5.9), with $w = 0.50$, $E(X) = \$65$, $E(Y) = \$35$, $\sigma_X^2 = 37{,}525$, $\sigma_Y^2 = 11{,}025$, and $\sigma_{XY} = -19{,}275$,

$$E(P) = (0.5)(65) + (1 - 0.5)(35) = \$50$$
$$\sigma_p = \sqrt{(0.5)^2(37{,}525) + (1 - 0.5)^2(11{,}025) + 2(0.5)(1 - 0.5)(-19{,}275)}$$
$$= \sqrt{2{,}500} = \$50$$

Thus, the portfolio has an expected return of \$50 for each \$1,000 invested (a return of 5%) and has a portfolio risk of \$50. The portfolio risk here is smaller than the standard deviation of either investment because there is a large negative covariance between the two investments. The fact that each investment performs best under different circumstances reduces the overall risk of the portfolio.

Problems for Section 5.2

LEARNING THE BASICS

5.7 Given the following probability distributions for variables X and Y:

$P(X_iY_i)$	X	Y
0.4	100	200
0.6	200	100

Compute

a. $E(X)$ and $E(Y)$.
b. σ_X and σ_Y.
c. σ_{XY}.
d. $E(X + Y)$.

5.8 Given the following probability distributions for variables X and Y:

$P(X_iY_i)$	X	Y
0.2	−100	50
0.4	50	30
0.3	200	20
0.1	300	20

Compute

a. $E(X)$ and $E(Y)$.
b. σ_X and σ_Y.
c. σ_{XY}.
d. $E(X + Y)$.

5.9 Two investments, X and Y, have the following characteristics:

$$E(X) = \$50, E(Y) = \$100, \sigma_X^2 = 9{,}000,$$

$$\sigma_Y^2 = 15{,}000, \text{ and } \sigma_{XY} = 7{,}500.$$

If the weight of portfolio assets assigned to investment X is 0.4, compute the

a. portfolio expected return.

b. portfolio risk.

APPLYING THE CONCEPTS

5.10 The process of being served at a bank consists of two independent parts—the time waiting in line and the time it takes to be served by the teller. Suppose that the time waiting in line has an expected value of 4 minutes, with a standard deviation of 1.2 minutes, and the time it takes to be served by the teller has an expected value of 5.5 minutes, with a standard deviation of 1.5 minutes. Compute the

a. expected value of the total time it takes to be served at the bank.

b. standard deviation of the total time it takes to be served at the bank.

5.11 In the portfolio example in this section (see page 186), half the portfolio assets are invested in the Dow Jones fund and half in a weak-economy fund. Recalculate the portfolio expected return and the portfolio risk if

a. 30% of the portfolio assets are invested in the Dow Jones fund and 70% in a weak-economy fund.

b. 70% of the portfolio assets are invested in the Dow Jones fund and 30% in a weak-economy fund.

c. Which of the three investment strategies (30%, 50%, or 70% in the Dow Jones fund) would you recommend? Why?

SELF Test **5.12** You are trying to develop a strategy for investing in two different stocks. The anticipated annual return for a $1,000 investment in each stock under four different economic conditions has the following probability distribution:

		Returns	
Probability	**Economic Condition**	**Stock *X***	**Stock *Y***
0.1	Recession	−100	50
0.3	Slow growth	0	150
0.3	Moderate growth	80	−20
0.3	Fast growth	150	−100

Compute the

a. expected return for stock X and for stock Y.

b. standard deviation for stock X and for stock Y.

c. covariance of stock X and stock Y.

d. Would you invest in stock X or stock Y? Explain.

5.13 Suppose that in Problem 5.12 you wanted to create a portfolio that consists of stock X and stock Y. Compute the portfolio expected return and portfolio risk for each of the following percentages invested in stock X:

a. 30%

b. 50%

c. 70%

d. On the basis of the results of (a) through (c), which portfolio would you recommend? Explain.

5.14 You are trying to develop a strategy for investing in two different stocks. The anticipated annual return for a $1,000 investment in each stock under four different economic conditions has the following probability distribution:

		Returns	
Probability	**Economic Condition**	**Stock *X***	**Stock *Y***
0.1	Recession	−50	−100
0.3	Slow growth	20	50
0.4	Moderate growth	100	130
0.2	Fast growth	150	200

Compute the

a. expected return for stock X and for stock Y.

b. standard deviation for stock X and for stock Y.

c. covariance of stock X and stock Y.

d. Would you invest in stock X or stock Y? Explain.

5.15 Suppose that in Problem 5.14 you wanted to create a portfolio that consists of stock X and stock Y. Compute the portfolio expected return and portfolio risk for each of the following percentages invested in stock X:

a. 30%

b. 50%

c. 70%

d. On the basis of the results of (a) through (c), which portfolio would you recommend? Explain.

5.16 You plan to invest $1,000 in a corporate bond fund or in a common stock fund. The following information about the annual return (per $1,000) of each of these investments under different economic conditions is available, along with the probability that each of these economic conditions will occur:

Probability	**Economic Condition**	**Corporate Bond Fund**	**Common Stock Fund**
0.01	Extreme recession	–200	–999
0.09	Recession	–70	–300
0.15	Stagnation	30	–100
0.35	Slow growth	80	100
0.30	Moderate growth	100	150
0.10	High growth	120	350

Compute the

a. expected return for the corporate bond fund and for the common stock fund.

b. standard deviation for the corporate bond fund and for the common stock fund.
c. covariance of the corporate bond fund and the common stock fund.
d. Would you invest in the corporate bond fund or the common stock fund? Explain.
e. If you chose to invest in the common stock fund in (d), what do you think about the possibility of losing $999 of every $1,000 invested if there is an extreme recession?

5.17 Suppose that in Problem 5.16 you wanted to create a portfolio that consists of the corporate bond fund and the common stock fund. Compute the portfolio expected return and portfolio risk for each of the following situations:
a. $300 in the corporate bond fund and $700 in the common stock fund.
b. $500 in each fund.
c. $700 in the corporate bond fund and $300 in the common stock fund.
d. On the basis of the results of (a) through (c), which portfolio would you recommend? Explain.

5.3 Binomial Distribution

The next three sections use mathematical models to solve business problems.

MATHEMATICAL MODEL

A **mathematical model** is a mathematical expression that represents a variable of interest.

When a mathematical expression is available, you can compute the exact probability of occurrence of any particular outcome of the variable.

The **binomial distribution** is one of the most useful mathematical models. You use the binomial distribution when the discrete random variable is the number of events of interest in a sample of n observations. The binomial distribution has four basic properties:

- The sample consists of a fixed number of observations, n.
- Each observation is classified into one of two mutually exclusive and collectively exhaustive categories.
- The probability of an observation being classified as the event of interest, π, is constant from observation to observation. Thus, the probability of an observation being classified as not being the event of interest, $1 - \pi$, is constant over all observations.
- The outcome of any observation is independent of the outcome of any other observation.

Returning to the Saxon Home Improvement scenario presented on page 181 concerning the accounting information system, suppose the event of interest is defined as a tagged order form. You are interested in the number of tagged order forms in a given sample of orders.

What results can occur? If the sample contains four orders, there could be none, one, two, three, or four tagged order forms. No other value can occur because the number of tagged order forms cannot be more than the sample size, n, and cannot be less than zero. Therefore, the range of the binomial random variable is from 0 to n.

Suppose that you observe the following result in a sample of four orders:

First Order	Second Order	Third Order	Fourth Order
Tagged	Tagged	Not tagged	Tagged

What is the probability of having three tagged order forms in a sample of four orders in this particular sequence? Because the historical probability of a tagged order is 0.10, the probability that each order occurs in the sequence is

First Order	Second Order	Third Order	Fourth Order
$\pi = 0.10$	$\pi = 0.10$	$1 - \pi = 0.90$	$\pi = 0.10$

Each outcome is independent of the others because the order forms were selected from an extremely large or practically infinite population and each order form could only be selected once. Therefore, the probability of having this particular sequence is

$$\begin{aligned}\pi\pi(1-\pi)\pi &= \pi^3(1-\pi)^1\\ &= (0.10)^3(0.90)^1\\ &= (0.10)(0.10)(0.10)(0.90)\\ &= 0.0009\end{aligned}$$

This result indicates only the probability of three tagged order forms (events of interest) from a sample of four order forms in a *specific sequence*. To find the number of ways of selecting x objects from n objects, *irrespective of sequence*, you use the **rule of combinations** given in Equation (5.10) and previously defined in Equation (4.14) on page 170.

[1]On many scientific calculators, there is a button labeled ${}_nC_r$ that allows you to compute the number of combinations. On these calculators, the symbol r is used instead of x.

COMBINATIONS

The number of combinations of selecting x objects[1] out of n objects is given by

$$ {}_nC_x = \frac{n!}{x!(n-x)!} \qquad \textbf{(5.10)}$$

where

$n! = (n)(n-1)\cdots(1)$ is called n factorial. By definition, $0! = 1$.

With $n = 4$ and $x = 3$, there are

$$ {}_nC_x = \frac{n!}{x!(n-x)!} = \frac{4!}{3!(4-3)!} = \frac{4\times3\times2\times1}{(3\times2\times1)(1)} = 4$$

such sequences. The four possible sequences are

Sequence 1 = *tagged, tagged, tagged, not tagged*, with probability
$\pi\pi\pi(1-\pi) = \pi^3(1-\pi)^1 = 0.0009$

Sequence 2 = *tagged, tagged, not tagged, tagged*, with probability
$\pi\pi(1-\pi)\pi = \pi^3(1-\pi)^1 = 0.0009$

Sequence 3 = *tagged, not tagged, tagged, tagged*, with probability
$\pi(1-\pi)\pi\pi = \pi^3(1-\pi)^1 = 0.0009$

Sequence 4 = *not tagged, tagged, tagged, tagged*, with probability
$(1-\pi)\pi\pi\pi = \pi^3(1-\pi)^1 = 0.0009$

Therefore, the probability of three tagged order forms is equal to

$$\begin{aligned}&(\text{Number of possible sequences}) \times (\text{Probability of a particular sequence})\\ &= (4)\times(0.0009) = 0.0036\end{aligned}$$

You can make a similar, intuitive derivation for the other possible outcomes of the random variable—zero, one, two, and four tagged order forms. However, as n, the sample size, gets large, the computations involved in using this intuitive approach become time-consuming. Equation

(5.11) is the mathematical model that provides a general formula for computing any probability from the binomial distribution with the number of events of interest, x, given n and π.

BINOMIAL DISTRIBUTION

$$P(X = x \mid n, \pi) = \frac{n!}{x!(n-x)!}\pi^x(1-\pi)^{n-x} \quad \textbf{(5.11)}$$

where

$P(X = x \mid n, \pi)$ = probability that $X = x$ events of interest, given n and π

n = number of observations

π = probability of an event of interest

$1 - \pi$ = probability of not having an event of interest

x = number of events of interest in the sample ($X = 0, 1, 2, \cdots, n$)

$\frac{n!}{x!(n-x)!}$ = the number of combinations of x events of interest out of n observations

Equation (5.11) restates what was intuitively derived previously. The binomial variable X can have any integer value x from 0 through n. In Equation (5.11), the product

$$\pi^x(1-\pi)^{n-x}$$

represents the probability of exactly x events of interest from n observations in a *particular sequence*.

The term

$$\frac{n!}{x!(n-x)!}$$

is the number of *combinations* of the x events of interest from the n observations possible. Hence, given the number of observations, n, and the probability of an event of interest, π, the probability of x events of interest is

$$\begin{aligned} P(X = x \mid n,\pi) &= (\text{Number of combinations}) \times (\text{Probability of a particular combination}) \\ &= \frac{n!}{x!(n-x)!}\pi^x(1-\pi)^{n-x} \end{aligned}$$

Example 5.1 illustrates the use of Equation (5.11).

EXAMPLE 5.1

Determining $P(X = 3)$, Given $n = 4$ and $\pi = 0.1$

If the likelihood of a tagged order form is 0.1, what is the probability that there are three tagged order forms in the sample of four?

SOLUTION Using Equation (5.11), the probability of three tagged orders from a sample of four is

$$\begin{aligned} P(X = 3 \mid n = 4, \pi = 0.1) &= \frac{4!}{3!(4-3)!}(0.1)^3(1-0.1)^{4-3} \\ &= \frac{4!}{3!(1)!}(0.1)^3(0.9)^1 \\ &= 4(0.1)(0.1)(0.1)(0.9) = 0.0036 \end{aligned}$$

Examples 5.2 and 5.3 show the computations for other values of X.

EXAMPLE 5.2

Determining $P(X \geq 3)$, Given $n = 4$ and $\pi = 0.1$

If the likelihood of a tagged order form is 0.1, what is the probability that there are three or more (i.e., at least three) tagged order forms in the sample of four?

SOLUTION In Example 5.1, you found that the probability of *exactly* three tagged order forms from a sample of four is 0.0036. To compute the probability of *at least* three tagged order forms, you need to add the probability of three tagged order forms to the probability of four tagged order forms. The probability of four tagged order forms is

$$P(X = 4 \mid n = 4, \pi = 0.1) = \frac{4!}{4!(4-4)!}(0.1)^4(1-0.1)^{4-4}$$
$$= \frac{4!}{4!(0)!}(0.1)^4(0.9)^0$$
$$= 1(0.1)(0.1)(0.1)(0.1)(1) = 0.0001$$

Thus, the probability of at least three tagged order forms is

$$P(X \geq 3) = P(X = 3) + P(X = 4)$$
$$= 0.0036 + 0.0001$$
$$= 0.0037$$

There is a 0.37% chance that there will be at least three tagged order forms in a sample of four.

EXAMPLE 5.3

Determining $P(X<3)$, Given $n = 4$ and $\pi = 0.1$

If the likelihood of a tagged order form is 0.1, what is the probability that there are fewer than three tagged order forms in the sample of four?

SOLUTION The probability that there are fewer than three tagged order forms is

$$P(X < 3) = P(X = 0) + P(X = 1) + P(X = 2)$$

Using Equation (5.11) on page 192, these probabilities are

$$P(X = 0 \mid n = 4, \pi = 0.1) = \frac{4!}{0!(4-0)!}(0.1)^0(1-0.1)^{4-0} = 0.6561$$
$$P(X = 1 \mid n = 4, \pi = 0.1) = \frac{4!}{1!(4-1)!}(0.1)^1(1-0.1)^{4-1} = 0.2916$$
$$P(X = 2 \mid n = 4, \pi = 0.1) = \frac{4!}{2!(4-2)!}(0.1)^2(1-0.1)^{4-2} = 0.0486$$

Therefore, $P(X < 3) = 0.6561 + 0.2916 + 0.0486 = 0.9963$. $P(X < 3)$ could also be calculated from its complement, $P(X \geq 3)$, as follows:

$$P(X < 3) = 1 - P(X \geq 3)$$
$$= 1 - 0.0037 = 0.9963$$

Computing binomial probabilities become tedious as n gets large. Figure 5.2 shows how binomial probabilities can be computed by Excel (left) and Minitab (right). Binomial probabilities can also be looked up in a table of probabilities, as discussed in the **Binomial** online topic available on this book's companion website. (See Appendix C to learn how to access the online topic files.)

FIGURE 5.2

Excel worksheet and Minitab results for computing binomial probabilities with $n = 4$ and $\pi = 0.1$

	A	B	
1	Binomial Probabilities		
2			
3	Data		
4	Sample size	4	
5	Probability of an event of interest	0.1	
6			
7	Statistics		
8	Mean	0.4	=B4 * B5
9	Variance	0.36	=B8 * (1 - B5)
10	Standard deviation	0.6	=SQRT(B9)
11			
12	Binomial Probabilities Table		
13	X	P(X)	
14	0	0.6561	=BINOMDIST(A14, $B$4, $B$5, FALSE)
15	1	0.2916	=BINOMDIST(A15, $B$4, $B$5, FALSE)
16	2	0.0486	=BINOMDIST(A16, $B$4, $B$5, FALSE)
17	3	0.0036	=BINOMDIST(A17, $B$4, $B$5, FALSE)
18	4	0.0001	=BINOMDIST(A18, $B$4, $B$5, FALSE)

```
Binomial with n = 4 and p = 0.1

x  P( X = x )
0      0.6561
1      0.2916
2      0.0486
3      0.0036
4      0.0001
```

The shape of a binomial probability distribution depends on the values of n and π. Whenever $\pi = 0.5$, the binomial distribution is symmetrical, regardless of how large or small the value of n. When $\pi \neq 0.5$, the distribution is skewed. The closer π is to 0.5 and the larger the number of observations, n, the less skewed the distribution becomes. For example, the distribution of the number of tagged order forms is highly right skewed because $\pi = 0.1$ and $n = 4$ (see Figure 5.3).

FIGURE 5.3

Histogram of the binomial probability distribution with $n = 4$ and $\pi = 0.1$

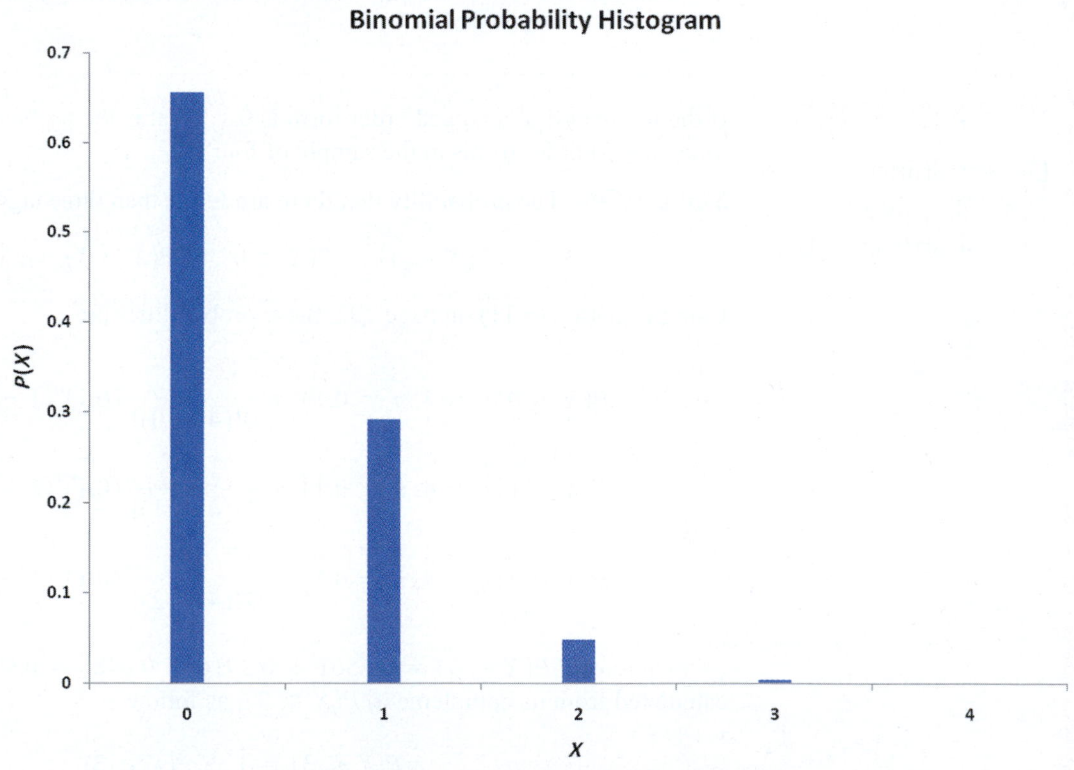

Observe from Figure 5.3 that unlike the histogram for continuous variables in Section 2.6, the bars for the values are very thin, and there is a large gap between each pair of values. That is because the histogram represents a discrete variable. (Theoretically, the bars should have no width. They should be vertical lines.)

The mean (or expected value) of the binomial distribution is equal to the product of n and π. Instead of using Equation (5.1) on page 183 to compute the mean of the probability distribution, you can also use Equation (5.12) to compute the mean for variables that follow the binomial distribution.

MEAN OF THE BINOMIAL DISTRIBUTION

The mean, μ, of the binomial distribution is equal to the sample size, n, multiplied by the probability of an event of interest, π.

$$\mu = E(X) = n\pi \qquad \textbf{(5.12)}$$

On the average, over the long run, you theoretically expect $\mu = E(X) = n\pi = (4)(0.1) = 0.4$ tagged order form in a sample of four orders.

The standard deviation of the binomial distribution can be calculated using Equation (5.13).

STANDARD DEVIATION OF THE BINOMIAL DISTRIBUTION

$$\sigma = \sqrt{\sigma^2} = \sqrt{Var(X)} = \sqrt{n\pi(1 - \pi)} \qquad \textbf{(5.13)}$$

The standard deviation of the number of tagged order forms is

$$\sigma = \sqrt{4(0.1)(0.9)} = 0.60$$

You get the same result if you use Equation (5.3) on page 184.

Example 5.4 applies the binomial distribution to service at a fast-food restaurant.

EXAMPLE 5.4

Computing Binomial Probabilities

Accuracy in taking orders at a drive-through window is important for fast-food chains. Periodically, *QSR Magazine* (data extracted from **http://www.qsrmagazine.com/reports/drive-thru_time_study/2009/2009_charts/whats_your_preferred_way_to_order_fast_food.html**) publishes the results of its surveys. Accuracy is measured as the percentage of orders that are filled correctly. Recently, the percentage of orders filled correctly at Wendy's was approximately 89%. Suppose that you go to the drive-through window at Wendy's and place an order. Two friends of yours independently place orders at the drive-through window at the same Wendy's. What are the probabilities that all three, that none of the three, and that at least two of the three orders will be filled correctly? What are the mean and standard deviation of the binomial distribution for the number of orders filled correctly?

SOLUTION Because there are three orders and the probability of a correct order is 0.89, $n = 3$ and $\pi = 0.89$ Using Equations (5.12) and (5.13),

$$\mu = E(X) = n\pi = 3(0.89) = 2.67$$

$$\begin{aligned}\sigma &= \sqrt{\sigma^2} = \sqrt{Var(X)} = \sqrt{n\pi(1 - \pi)} \\ &= \sqrt{3(0.89)(0.11)} \\ &= \sqrt{0.2937} = 0.5419\end{aligned}$$

Using Equation (5.11) on page 192,

$$\begin{aligned}P(X = 3 \mid n = 3, \pi = 0.89) &= \frac{3!}{3!(3 - 3)!}(0.89)^3(1 - 0.89)^{3-3} \\ &= \frac{3!}{3!(3 - 3)!}(0.89)^3(0.11)^0 \\ &= 1(0.89)(0.89)(0.89)(1) = 0.7050\end{aligned}$$

$$P(X = 0 \mid n = 3, \pi = 0.89) = \frac{3!}{0!(3-0)!}(0.89)^0(1-0.89)^{3-0}$$
$$= \frac{3!}{0!(3-0)!}(0.89)^0(0.11)^3$$
$$= 1(1)(0.11)(0.11)(0.11) = 0.0013$$
$$P(X = 2 \mid n = 3, \pi = 0.89) = \frac{3!}{2!(3-2)!}(0.89)^2(1-0.89)^{3-2}$$
$$= \frac{3!}{2!(3-2)!}(0.89)^2(0.11)^1$$
$$= 3(0.89)(0.89)(0.11) = 0.2614$$
$$P(X \geq 2) = P(X = 2) + P(X = 3)$$
$$= 0.2614 + 0.7050$$
$$= 0.9664$$

The mean number of orders filled correctly in a sample of three orders is 2.67, and the standard deviation is 0.5419. The probability that all three orders are filled correctly is 0.7050, or 70.50%. The probability that none of the orders are filled correctly is 0.0013, or 0.13%. The probability that at least two orders are filled correctly is 0.9664, or 96.64%.

In this section, you have been introduced to the binomial distribution. The binomial distribution is an important mathematical model in many business situations.

Problems for Section 5.3

LEARNING THE BASICS

5.18 If $n = 5$ and $\pi = 0.40$, what is the probability that

a. $X = 4$?
b. $X \leq 3$?
c. $X < 2$?
d. $X > 1$?

5.19 Determine the following:

a. For $n = 4$ and $\pi = 0.12$, what is $P(X = 0)$?
b. For $n = 10$ and $\pi = 0.40$, what is $P(X = 9)$?
c. For $n = 10$ and $\pi = 0.50$, what is $P(X = 8)$?
d. For $n = 6$ and $\pi = 0.83$, what is $P(X = 5)$?

5.20 Determine the mean and standard deviation of the random variable X in each of the following binomial distributions:

a. $n = 4$ and $\pi = 0.10$
b. $n = 4$ and $\pi = 0.40$
c. $n = 5$ and $\pi = 0.80$
d. $n = 3$ and $\pi = 0.50$

APPLYING THE CONCEPTS

5.21 The increase or decrease in the price of a stock between the beginning and the end of a trading day is assumed to be an equally likely random event. What is the probability that a stock will show an increase in its closing price on five consecutive days?

5.22 The U.S. Department of Transportation reported that in 2009, Southwest led all domestic airlines in on-time arrivals for domestic flights, with a rate of 0.825. Using the binomial distribution, what is the probability that in the next six flights

a. four flights will be on time?
b. all six flights will be on time?
c. at least four flights will be on time?
d. What are the mean and standard deviation of the number of on-time arrivals?
e. What assumptions do you need to make in (a) through (c)?

5.23 A student is taking a multiple-choice exam in which each question has four choices. Assume that the student has no knowledge of the correct answers to any of the questions. She has decided on a strategy in which she will place four balls (marked A, B, C, and D) into a box. She randomly selects one ball for each question and replaces the ball in the box. The marking on the ball will determine her answer to the question. There are five multiple-choice questions on the exam. What is the probability that she will get

a. five questions correct?
b. at least four questions correct?
c. no questions correct?
d. no more than two questions correct?

5.24 Investment advisors agree that near-retirees, defined as people aged 55 to 65, should have balanced portfolios. Most advisors suggest that the near-retirees have no more than 50% of their investments in stocks. However, during the huge decline in the stock market in 2008, 22% of near-retirees had 90% or more of their investments in stocks (P. Regnier, "What I Learned from the Crash," *Money*, May 2009, p. 114). Suppose you have a random sample of 10 people who would have been labeled as near-retirees in 2008. What is the probability that during 2008

a. none had 90% or more of their investment in stocks?
b. exactly one had 90% or more of his or her investment in stocks?
c. two or fewer had 90% or more of their investment in stocks?
d. three or more had 90% or more of their investment in stocks?

5.25 When a customer places an order with Rudy's On-Line Office Supplies, a computerized accounting information system (AIS) automatically checks to see if the customer has exceeded his or her credit limit. Past records indicate that the probability of customers exceeding their credit limit is 0.05. Suppose that, on a given day, 20 customers place orders. Assume that the number of customers that the AIS detects as having exceeded their credit limit is distributed as a binomial random variable.

a. What are the mean and standard deviation of the number of customers exceeding their credit limits?
b. What is the probability that zero customers will exceed their limits?
c. What is the probability that one customer will exceed his or her limit?
d. What is the probability that two or more customers will exceed their limits?

SELF Test **5.26** In Example 5.4 on page 195, you and two friends decided to go to Wendy's. Now, suppose that instead you go to Popeye's, which last month filled approximately 84.8% of orders correctly. What is the probability that

a. all three orders will be filled correctly?
b. none of the three will be filled correctly?
c. at least two of the three will be filled correctly?
d. What are the mean and standard deviation of the binomial distribution used in (a) through (c)? Interpret these values.

5.27 In Example 5.4 on page 195, you and two friends decided to go to Wendy's. Now, suppose that instead you go to McDonald's, which last month filled approximately 90.1% of the orders correctly. What is the probability that

a. all three orders will be filled correctly?
b. none of the three will be filled correctly?
c. at least two of the three will be filled correctly?
d. What are the mean and standard deviation of the binomial distribution used in (a) through (c)? Interpret these values.
e. Compare the result of (a) through (d) with those of Popeye's in Problem 5.26 and Wendy's in Example 5.4 on page 195.

5.4 Poisson Distribution

Many studies are based on counts of the times a particular event occurs in a given *area of opportunity*. An **area of opportunity** is a continuous unit or interval of time, volume, or any physical area in which there can be more than one occurrence of an event. Examples of variables that follow the Poisson distribution are the surface defects on a new refrigerator, the number of network failures in a day, the number of people arriving at a bank, and the number of fleas on the body of a dog. You can use the **Poisson distribution** to calculate probabilities in situations such as these if the following properties hold:

- You are interested in counting the number of times a particular event occurs in a given area of opportunity. The area of opportunity is defined by time, length, surface area, and so forth.
- The probability that an event occurs in a given area of opportunity is the same for all the areas of opportunity.
- The number of events that occur in one area of opportunity is independent of the number of events that occur in any other area of opportunity.
- The probability that two or more events will occur in an area of opportunity approaches zero as the area of opportunity becomes smaller.

Consider the number of customers arriving during the lunch hour at a bank located in the central business district in a large city. You are interested in the number of customers who arrive each minute. Does this situation match the four properties of the Poisson distribution given earlier? First, the *event* of interest is a customer arriving, and the *given area of opportunity* is defined as a one-minute interval. Will zero customers arrive, one customer arrive, two customers arrive, and so on? Second, it is reasonable to assume that the probability that a customer arrives during a particular one-minute interval is the same as the probability for all the other one-minute intervals. Third, the arrival of one customer in any one-minute interval has no effect on (i.e., is independent of) the arrival of any other customer in any other one-minute interval. Finally, the probability that two or more customers will arrive in a given time period approaches zero as the time interval becomes small. For example, the probability is virtually zero that two customers will arrive in a time interval of 0.01 second. Thus, you can use the Poisson distribution to determine probabilities involving the number of customers arriving at the bank in a one-minute time interval during the lunch hour.

The Poisson distribution has one characteristic, called λ (the Greek lowercase letter *lambda*), which is the mean or expected number of events per unit. The variance of a Poisson distribution is also equal to λ, and the standard deviation is equal to $\sqrt{\lambda}$. The number of events, X, of the Poisson random variable ranges from 0 to infinity (∞).

Equation (5.14) is the mathematical expression for the Poisson distribution for computing the probability of $X = x$ events, given that λ events are expected.

POISSON DISTRIBUTION

$$P(X = x \mid \lambda) = \frac{e^{-\lambda}\lambda^{x}}{x!} \quad \textbf{(5.14)}$$

where

$P(X = x \mid \lambda) =$ the probability that $X = x$ events in an area of opportunity given λ

$\lambda =$ expected number of events

$e =$ mathematical constant approximated by 2.71828

$x =$ number of events ($x = 0, 1, 2, \ldots, \infty$)

To illustrate an application of the Poisson distribution, suppose that the mean number of customers who arrive per minute at the bank during the noon-to-1 P.M. hour is equal to 3.0. What is the probability that in a given minute, exactly two customers will arrive? And what is the probability that more than two customers will arrive in a given minute?

Using Equation (5.14) and $\lambda = 3$, the probability that in a given minute exactly two customers will arrive is

$$P(X = 2 \mid \lambda = 3) = \frac{e^{-3.0}(3.0)^2}{2!} = \frac{9}{(2.71828)^3(2)} = 0.2240$$

To determine the probability that in any given minute more than two customers will arrive,

$$P(X > 2) = P(X = 3) + P(X = 4) + \cdots + P(X = \infty)$$

Because in a probability distribution, all the probabilities must sum to 1, the terms on the right side of the equation $P(X > 2)$ also represent the complement of the probability that X is less than or equal to 2 [i.e., $1 - P(X \le 2)$]. Thus,

$$P(X > 2) = 1 - P(X \le 2) = 1 - [P(X = 0) + P(X = 1) + P(X = 2)]$$

Now, using Equation (5.14),

$$\begin{aligned} P(X > 2) &= 1 - \left[\frac{e^{-3.0}(3.0)^0}{0!} + \frac{e^{-3.0}(3.0)^1}{1!} + \frac{e^{-3.0}(3.0)^2}{2!}\right] \\ &= 1 - [0.0498 + 0.1494 + 0.2240] \\ &= 1 - 0.4232 = 0.5768 \end{aligned}$$

Thus, there is a 57.68% chance that more than two customers will arrive in the same minute.

Computing Poisson probabilities can be tedious. Figure 5.4 shows how Poisson probabilities can be computed by Excel (left) and Minitab (right). Poisson probabilities can also be looked up in a table of probabilities, as discussed in the **Poisson** online topic available on this book's companion website. (See Appendix C to learn how to access online topics.)

FIGURE 5.4

Excel worksheet and Minitab results for computing Poisson probabilities with $\lambda = 3$

	A	B	C	D	E
1	Poisson Probabilities				
2					
3	Data				
4	Mean/Expected number of events of interest:				3
5					
6	Poisson Probabilities Table				
7	X	P(X)			
8	0	0.0498	=POISSON(A8, $E$4, FALSE)		
9	1	0.1494	=POISSON(A9, $E$4, FALSE)		
10	2	0.2240	=POISSON(A10, $E$4, FALSE)		
11	3	0.2240	=POISSON(A11, $E$4, FALSE)		
12	4	0.1680	=POISSON(A12, $E$4, FALSE)		
13	5	0.1008	=POISSON(A13, $E$4, FALSE)		
14	6	0.0504	=POISSON(A14, $E$4, FALSE)		
15	7	0.0216	=POISSON(A15, $E$4, FALSE)		
16	8	0.0081	=POISSON(A16, $E$4, FALSE)		
17	9	0.0027	=POISSON(A17, $E$4, FALSE)		
18	10	0.0008	=POISSON(A18, $E$4, FALSE)		
19	11	0.0002	=POISSON(A19, $E$4, FALSE)		
20	12	0.0001	=POISSON(A20, $E$4, FALSE)		
21	13	0.0000	=POISSON(A21, $E$4, FALSE)		
22	14	0.0000	=POISSON(A22, $E$4, FALSE)		
23	15	0.0000	=POISSON(A23, $E$4, FALSE)		
24	16	0.0000	=POISSON(A24, $E$4, FALSE)		
25	17	0.0000	=POISSON(A25, $E$4, FALSE)		
26	18	0.0000	=POISSON(A26, $E$4, FALSE)		
27	19	0.0000	=POISSON(A27, $E$4, FALSE)		
28	20	0.0000	=POISSON(A28, $E$4, FALSE)		

```
Poisson with mean = 3

 x   P( X = x )
 0     0.049787
 1     0.149361
 2     0.224042
 3     0.224042
 4     0.168031
 5     0.100819
 6     0.050409
 7     0.021604
 8     0.008102
 9     0.002701
10     0.000810
11     0.000221
12     0.000055
13     0.000013
14     0.000003
15     0.000001
```

EXAMPLE 5.5

Computing Poisson Probabilities

The number of work-related injuries per month in a manufacturing plant is known to follow a Poisson distribution with a mean of 2.5 work-related injuries a month. What is the probability that in a given month, no work-related injuries occur? That at least one work-related injury occurs?

SOLUTION Using Equation (5.14) on page 198 with $\lambda = 2.5$ (or Excel, Minitab, or a Poisson table lookup), the probability that in a given month no work-related injuries occur is

$$P(X = 0 \mid \lambda = 2.5) = \frac{e^{-2.5}(2.5)^0}{0!} = \frac{1}{(2.71828)^{2.5}(1)} = 0.0821$$

The probability that there will be no work-related injuries in a given month is 0.0821, or 8.21%. Thus,

$$\begin{aligned} P(X \geq 1) &= 1 - P(X = 0) \\ &= 1 - 0.0821 \\ &= 0.9179 \end{aligned}$$

The probability that there will be at least one work-related injury is 0.9179, or 91.79%.

Problems for Section 5.4

LEARNING THE BASICS

5.28 Assume a Poisson distribution.
a. If $\lambda = 2.5$, find $P(X = 2)$.
b. If $\lambda = 8.0$, find $P(X = 8)$.
c. If $\lambda = 0.5$, find $P(X = 1)$.
d. If $\lambda = 3.7$, find $P(X = 0)$.

5.29 Assume a Poisson distribution.
a. If $\lambda = 2.0$, find $P(X \geq 2)$.
b. If $\lambda = 8.0$, find $P(X \geq 3)$.
c. If $\lambda = 0.5$, find $P(X \leq 1)$.
d. If $\lambda = 4.0$, find $P(X \geq 1)$.
e. If $\lambda = 5.0$, find $P(X \leq 3)$.

5.30 Assume a Poisson distribution with $\lambda = 5.0$. What is the probability that
a. $X = 1$?
b. $X < 1$?
c. $X > 1$?
d. $X \leq 1$?

APPLYING THE CONCEPTS

5.31 Assume that the number of network errors experienced in a day on a local area network (LAN) is distributed as a Poisson random variable. The mean number of network errors experienced in a day is 2.4. What is the probability that in any given day
a. zero network errors will occur?
b. exactly one network error will occur?
c. two or more network errors will occur?
d. fewer than three network errors will occur?

SELF Test **5.32** The quality control manager of Marilyn's Cookies is inspecting a batch of chocolate-chip cookies that has just been baked. If the production process is in control, the mean number of chip parts per cookie is 6.0. What is the probability that in any particular cookie being inspected
a. fewer than five chip parts will be found?
b. exactly five chip parts will be found?
c. five or more chip parts will be found?
d. either four or five chip parts will be found?

5.33 Refer to Problem 5.32. How many cookies in a batch of 100 should the manager expect to discard if company policy requires that all chocolate-chip cookies sold have at least four chocolate-chip parts?

5.34 The U.S. Department of Transportation maintains statistics for mishandled bags per 1,000 airline passengers. In the first nine months of 2009, airlines had mishandled 3.89 bags per 1,000 passengers. What is the probability that in the next 1,000 passengers, airlines will have
a. no mishandled bags?
b. at least one mishandled bag?
c. at least two mishandled bags?

5.35 The U.S. Department of Transportation maintains statistics for consumer complaints per 100,000 airline passengers. In the first nine months of 2009, consumer complaints were 0.99 per 100,000 passengers. What is the probability that in the next 100,000 passengers, there will be
a. no complaints?
b. at least one complaint?
c. at least two complaints?

5.36 Based on past experience, it is assumed that the number of flaws per foot in rolls of grade 2 paper follows a Poisson distribution with a mean of 1 flaw per 5 feet of paper (0.2 flaw per foot). What is the probability that in a
a. 1-foot roll, there will be at least 2 flaws?
b. 12-foot roll, there will be at least 1 flaw?
c. 50-foot roll, there will be more than or equal to 5 flaws and fewer than or equal to 15 flaws?

5.37 J.D. Power and Associates calculates and publishes various statistics concerning car quality. The initial quality score measures the number of problems per new car sold. For 2009 model cars, Ford had 1.02 problems per car and Dodge had 1.34 problems per car (data extracted from S. Carty, "U.S. Autos Power Forward with Gains in Quality Survey," *USA Today*, June 23, 2009, p. 3B). Let the random variable X be equal to the number of problems with a newly purchased 2009 Ford.
a. What assumptions must be made in order for X to be distributed as a Poisson random variable? Are these assumptions reasonable?
Making the assumptions as in (a), if you purchased a 2009 Ford, what is the probability that the new car will have
b. zero problems?
c. two or fewer problems?
d. Give an operational definition for *problem*. Why is the operational definition important in interpreting the initial quality score?

5.38 Refer to Problem 5.37. If you purchased a 2009 Dodge, what is the probability that the new car will have
a. zero problems?
b. two or fewer problems?
c. Compare your answers in (a) and (b) to those for the Ford in Problem 5.37 (b) and (c).

5.39 Refer to Problem 5.37. Another article reported that in 2008, Ford had 1.12 problems per car and Dodge had 1.41 problems per car (data extracted from S. Carty, "Ford

Moves Up in Quality Survey," *USA Today*, June 5, 2008, p. 3B). If you purchased a 2008 Ford, what is the probability that the new car will have

a. zero problems?

b. two or fewer problems?

c. Compare your answers in (a) and (b) to those for the 2009 Ford in Problem 5.37 (b) and (c).

5.40 Refer to Problem 5.39. If you purchased a 2008 Dodge, what is the probability that the new car will have

a. zero problems?

b. two or fewer problems?

c. Compare your answers in (a) and (b) to those for the 2009 Dodge in Problem 5.38 (a) and (b).

5.41 A toll-free phone number is available from 9 A.M. to 9 P.M. for your customers to register complaints about a product purchased from your company. Past history indicates that an average of 0.8 calls is received per minute.

a. What properties must be true about the situation described here in order to use the Poisson distribution to calculate probabilities concerning the number of phone calls received in a one-minute period?

Assuming that this situation matches the properties discussed in (a), what is the probability that during a one-minute period

b. zero phone calls will be received?

c. three or more phone calls will be received?

d. What is the maximum number of phone calls that will be received in a one-minute period 99.99% of the time?

5.5 Hypergeometric Distribution

Both the binomial distribution and the **hypergeometric distribution** are concerned with the number of events of interest in a sample containing n observations. One of the differences in these two probability distributions is in the way the samples are selected. For the binomial distribution, the sample data are selected *with* replacement from a *finite* population or *without* replacement from an *infinite* population. Thus, the probability of an event of interest, π, is constant over all observations, and the outcome of any particular observation is independent of any other. For the hypergeometric distribution, the sample data are selected *without* replacement from a *finite* population. Thus, the outcome of one observation is dependent on the outcomes of the previous observations.

Consider a population of size N. Let A represent the total number of events of interest in the population. The hypergeometric distribution is then used to find the probability of X events of interest in a sample of size n, selected without replacement. Equation (5.15) represents the mathematical expression of the hypergeometric distribution for finding x events of interest, given a knowledge of n, N, and A.

HYPERGEOMETRIC DISTRIBUTION

$$P(X = x \mid n, N, A) = \frac{\binom{A}{x}\binom{N-A}{n-x}}{\binom{N}{n}} \quad \textbf{(5.15)}$$

where

$P(X = x \mid n, N, A)$ = the probability of x events of interest, given knowledge of n, N, and A

n = sample size

N = population size

A = number of events of interest in the population

$N - A$ = number of events that are not of interest in the population

$$x = \text{number of events of interest in the sample}$$

$$\binom{A}{x} = {}_AC_x \text{ [see Equation (5.10) on page 191]}$$

$$x \leq A$$

$$x \leq n$$

Because the number of events of interest in the sample, represented by x, cannot be greater than the number of events of interest in the population, A, nor can x be greater than the sample size, n, the range of the hypergeometric random variable is limited to the sample size or to the number of events of interest in the population, whichever is smaller.

Equation (5.16) defines the mean of the hypergeometric distribution, and Equation (5.17) defines the standard deviation.

MEAN OF THE HYPERGEOMETRIC DISTRIBUTION

$$\mu = E(X) = \frac{nA}{N} \quad \textbf{(5.16)}$$

STANDARD DEVIATION OF THE HYPERGEOMETRIC DISTRIBUTION

$$\sigma = \sqrt{\frac{nA(N-A)}{N^2}}\sqrt{\frac{N-n}{N-1}} \quad \textbf{(5.17)}$$

In Equation (5.17), the expression $\sqrt{\frac{N-n}{N-1}}$ is a **finite population correction factor** that results from sampling without replacement from a finite population.

To illustrate the hypergeometric distribution, suppose that you are forming a team of 8 managers from different departments within your company. Your company has a total of 30 managers, and 10 of these people are from the finance department. If you are to randomly select members of the team, what is the probability that the team will contain 2 managers from the finance department? Here, the population of $N = 30$ managers within the company is finite. In addition, $A = 10$ are from the finance department. A team of $n = 8$ members is to be selected.

Using Equation (5.15),

$$P(X = 2 \mid n = 8, N = 30, A = 10) = \frac{\binom{10}{2}\binom{20}{6}}{\binom{30}{8}}$$

$$= \frac{\left(\frac{10!}{2!(8)!}\right)\left(\frac{(20)!}{(6)!(14)!}\right)}{\left(\frac{30!}{8!(22)!}\right)}$$

$$= 0.298$$

Thus, the probability that the team will contain two members from the finance department is 0.298, or 29.8%.

Computing hypergeometric probabilities can be tedious, especially as N gets large. Figure 5.5 shows how the hypergeometric probabilities for the team formation example can be computed by Excel (left) and Minitab (right).

FIGURE 5.5

Excel worksheet and Minitab results for the team member example

	A	B	
1	Hypergeometric Probabilities		
2			
3	Data		
4	Sample size	8	
5	No. of events of interest in population	10	
6	Population size	30	
7			
8	Hypergeometric Probabilities Table		
9	X	P(X)	
10	0	0.0215	=HYPGEOMDIST(A10, $B$4, $B$5, $B$6)
11	1	0.1324	=HYPGEOMDIST(A11, $B$4, $B$5, $B$6)
12	2	0.2980	=HYPGEOMDIST(A12, $B$4, $B$5, $B$6)
13	3	0.3179	=HYPGEOMDIST(A13, $B$4, $B$5, $B$6)
14	4	0.1738	=HYPGEOMDIST(A14, $B$4, $B$5, $B$6)
15	5	0.0491	=HYPGEOMDIST(A15, $B$4, $B$5, $B$6)
16	6	0.0068	=HYPGEOMDIST(A16, $B$4, $B$5, $B$6)
17	7	0.0004	=HYPGEOMDIST(A17, $B$4, $B$5, $B$6)
18	8	0.0000	=HYPGEOMDIST(A18, $B$4, $B$5, $B$6)

Probability Density Function

Hypergeometric with N = 30, M = 10, and n = 8

x	P(X = x)
0	0.021523
1	0.132447
2	0.298005
3	0.317872
4	0.173836
5	0.049083
6	0.006817
7	0.000410
8	0.000008

Example 5.6 shows an application of the hypergeometric distribution in portfolio selection.

EXAMPLE 5.6

Computing Hypergeometric Probabilities

You are a financial analyst facing the task of selecting bond mutual funds to purchase for a client's portfolio. You have narrowed the funds to be selected to ten different funds. In order to diversify your client's portfolio, you will recommend the purchase of four different funds. Six of the funds are short-term corporate bond funds. What is the probability that of the four funds selected, three are short-term corporate bond funds?

SOLUTION Using Equation (5.15) with $X = 3, n = 4, N = 10$, and $A = 6$,

$$P(X = 3 \mid n = 4, N = 10, A = 6) = \frac{\binom{6}{3}\binom{4}{1}}{\binom{10}{4}}$$

$$= \frac{\left(\frac{6!}{3!(3)!}\right)\left(\frac{(4)!}{(1)!(3)!}\right)}{\left(\frac{10!}{4!(6)!}\right)}$$

$$= 0.3810$$

The probability that of the four funds selected, three are short-term corporate bond funds is 0.3810, or 38.10%

Problems for Section 5.5

LEARNING THE BASICS

5.42 Determine the following:

a. If $n = 4, N = 10$, and $A = 5$, find $P(X = 3)$.
b. If $n = 4, N = 6$, and $A = 3$, find $P(X = 1)$.
c. If $n = 5, N = 12$, and $A = 3$, find $P(X = 0)$.
d. If $n = 3, N = 10$, and $A = 3$, find $P(X = 3)$.

5.43 Referring to Problem 5.42, compute the mean and standard deviation for the hypergeometric distributions described in (a) through (d).

APPLYING THE CONCEPTS

SELF Test **5.44** An auditor for the Internal Revenue Service is selecting a sample of 6 tax returns for an audit. If 2 or more of these returns are "improper," the entire population of 100 tax returns will be audited. What is the probability that the entire population will be audited if the true number of improper returns in the population is

a. 25?
b. 30?
c. 5?
d. 10?
e. Discuss the differences in your results, depending on the true number of improper returns in the population.

5.45 The dean of a business school wishes to form an executive committee of 5 from among the 40 tenured faculty members at the school. The selection is to be random, and at the school there are 8 tenured faculty members in accounting. What is the probability that the committee will contain

a. none of them?
b. at least 1 of them?
c. not more than 1 of them?
d. What is your answer to (a) if the committee consists of 7 members?

5.46 From an inventory of 30 cars being shipped to a local automobile dealer, 4 are SUVs. What is the probability that if 4 cars arrive at a particular dealership,

a. all 4 are SUVs?
b. none are SUVs?
c. at least 1 is an SUV?
d. What are your answers to (a) through (c) if 6 cars being shipped are SUVs?

5.47 A state lottery is conducted in which 6 winning numbers are selected from a total of 54 numbers. What is the probability that if 6 numbers are randomly selected,

a. all 6 numbers will be winning numbers?
b. 5 numbers will be winning numbers?
c. none of the numbers will be winning numbers?
d. What are your answers to (a) through (c) if the 6 winning numbers are selected from a total of 40 numbers?

5.48 In Example 5.6 on page 203, a financial analyst was facing the task of selecting bond mutual funds to purchase for a client's portfolio. Suppose that the number of funds had been narrowed to 12 funds instead of the ten funds (still with 6 short-term corporate funds) in Example 5.6. What is the probability that of the four funds selected,

a. exactly 1 is a short-term corporate bond funds?
b. at least 1 is a short-term corporate bond fund?
c. three are short-term corporate bond funds?
d. Compare the results of (c) to that of Example 5.6.

5.6 *Online Topic:* Using the Poisson Distribution to Approximate the Binomial Distribution

Under certain circumstances, you can use the Poisson distribution to approximate the binomial distribution. To study this topic, read the Section 5.6 online topic file that is available on this book's companion website. (See Appendix C to learn how to access the online topic files.)

USING STATISTICS @ Saxon Home Improvement Revisited

In the Saxon Home Improvement scenario at the beginning of this chapter, you were an accountant for the Saxon Home Improvement Company. The company's accounting information system automatically reviews order forms from online customers for possible mistakes. Any questionable invoices are tagged and included in a daily exceptions report. Knowing that the probability that an order will be tagged is 0.10, you were able to use the binomial distribution to determine the chance of finding a certain number of tagged forms in a sample of size four. There was a 65.6% chance that none of the forms would be tagged, a 29.2% chance that one would be tagged, and a 5.2% chance that two or more would be tagged. You were also able to determine that, on average, you would expect 0.4 forms to be tagged, and the standard deviation of the number of tagged order forms would be 0.6. Now that you have learned the mechanics of using the binomial distribution for a known probability of 0.10 and a sample size of four, you will be able to apply the same approach to any given probability and sample size. Thus, you will be able to make inferences about the online ordering process and, more importantly, evaluate any changes or proposed changes to the process.

SUMMARY

In this chapter, you have studied mathematical expectation and three important discrete probability distributions: the binomial, Poisson, and hypergeometric distributions. In the next chapter, you will study several important continuous distributions including the normal distribution.

To help decide what probability distribution to use for a particular situation, you need to ask the following questions:

- Is there a fixed number of observations, n, each of which is classified as an event of interest or not an event of interest? Or is there an area of opportunity? If there is a fixed number of observations, n, each of which is classified as an event of interest or not an event of interest, you use the binomial or hypergeometric distribution. If there is an area of opportunity, you use the Poisson distribution.
- In deciding whether to use the binomial or hypergeometric distribution, is the probability of an event of interest constant over all trials? If yes, you can use the binomial distribution. If no, you can use the hypergeometric distribution.

KEY EQUATIONS

Expected Value, μ, of a Discrete Random Variable

$$\mu = E(X) = \sum_{i=1}^{N} x_i P(X = x_i) \qquad \textbf{(5.1)}$$

Variance of a Discrete Random Variable

$$\sigma^2 = \sum_{i=1}^{N} [x_i - E(X)]^2 P(X = x_i) \qquad \textbf{(5.2)}$$

Standard Deviation of a Discrete Random Variable

$$\sigma = \sqrt{\sigma^2} = \sqrt{\sum_{i=1}^{N} [x_i - E(X)]^2 P(X = x_i)} \qquad \textbf{(5.3)}$$

Covariance

$$\sigma_{XY} = \sum_{i=1}^{N} [x_i - E(X)][y_i - E(Y)]\, P(x_i y_i) \qquad \textbf{(5.4)}$$

Expected Value of the Sum of Two Random Variables

$$E(X + Y) = E(X) + E(Y) \qquad \textbf{(5.5)}$$

Variance of the Sum of Two Random Variables

$$Var(X + Y) = \sigma^2_{X+Y} = \sigma^2_X + \sigma^2_Y + 2\sigma_{XY} \qquad \textbf{(5.6)}$$

Standard Deviation of the Sum of Two Random Variables

$$\sigma_{X+Y} = \sqrt{\sigma^2_{X+Y}} \qquad \textbf{(5.7)}$$

Portfolio Expected Return

$$E(P) = wE(X) + (1 - w)E(Y) \quad \textbf{(5.8)}$$

Portfolio Risk

$$\sigma_p = \sqrt{w^2\sigma_X^2 + (1 - w)^2\sigma_Y^2 + 2w(1 - w)\sigma_{XY}} \quad \textbf{(5.9)}$$

Combinations

$${}_nC_x = \frac{n!}{x!(n - x)!} \quad \textbf{(5.10)}$$

Binomial Distribution

$$P(X = x \mid n,\pi) = \frac{n!}{x!(n - x)!}\pi^x(1 - \pi)^{n-x} \quad \textbf{(5.11)}$$

Mean of the Binomial Distribution

$$\mu = E(X) = n\pi \quad \textbf{(5.12)}$$

Standard Deviation of the Binomial Distribution

$$\sigma = \sqrt{\sigma^2} = \sqrt{Var(X)} = \sqrt{n\pi(1 - \pi)} \quad \textbf{(5.13)}$$

Poisson Distribution

$$P(X = x \mid \lambda) = \frac{e^{-\lambda}\lambda^x}{x!} \quad \textbf{(5.14)}$$

Hypergeometric Distribution

$$P(X = x \mid n, N, A) = \frac{\binom{A}{x}\binom{N - A}{n - x}}{\binom{N}{n}} \quad \textbf{(5.15)}$$

Mean of the Hypergeometric Distribution

$$\mu = E(X) = \frac{nA}{N} \quad \textbf{(5.16)}$$

Standard Deviation of the Hypergeometric Distribution

$$\sigma = \sqrt{\frac{nA(N - A)}{N^2}}\sqrt{\frac{N - n}{N - 1}} \quad \textbf{(5.17)}$$

KEY TERMS

area of opportunity 197
binomial distribution 190
covariance, σ_{XY} 185
expected value 182
expected value, μ, of a discrete random variable 182
expected value of the sum of two random variables 187
finite population correction factor 202
hypergeometric distribution 201
mathematical model 190
Poisson distribution 197
portfolio 187
portfolio expected return 187
portfolio risk 187
probability distribution for a discrete random variable 182
rule of combinations 191
standard deviation of a discrete random variable 184
standard deviation of the sum of two random variables 187
variance of a discrete random variable 183
variance of the sum of two random variables 187

CHAPTER REVIEW PROBLEMS

CHECKING YOUR UNDERSTANDING

5.49 What is the meaning of the expected value of a probability distribution?

5.50 What are the four properties that must be present in order to use the binomial distribution?

5.51 What are the four properties that must be present in order to use the Poisson distribution?

5.52 When do you use the hypergeometric distribution instead of the binomial distribution?

APPLYING THE CONCEPTS

5.53 Darwin Head, a 35-year-old sawmill worker, won \$1 million and a Chevrolet Malibu Hybrid by scoring 15 goals within 24 seconds at the Vancouver Canucks National Hockey League game (B. Ziemer, "Darwin Evolves into an Instant Millionaire," *Vancouver Sun*, February 28, 2008, p. 1). Head said he would use the money to pay off his mortgage and provide for his children, and he had no plans to quit his job. The contest was part of the Chevrolet Malibu Million Dollar Shootout, sponsored by General Motors Canadian Division. Did GM-Canada risk the \$1 million?

No! GM-Canada purchased event insurance from a company specializing in promotions at sporting events such as a half-court basketball shot or a hole-in-one giveaway at the local charity golf outing. The event insurance company estimates the probability of a contestant winning the contest, and for a modest charge, insures the event. The promoters pay the insurance premium but take on no added risk as the insurance company will make the large payout in the unlikely event that a contestant wins. To see how it works, suppose that the insurance company estimates that the probability a contestant would win a Million Dollar Shootout is 0.001, and that the insurance company charges $4,000.

a. Calculate the expected value of the profit made by the insurance company.

b. Many call this kind of situation a win–win opportunity for the insurance company and the promoter. Do you agree? Explain.

5.54 Between 1896 when the Dow Jones Index was created and 2009, the index rose in 64% of the years (data extracted from M. Hulbert, "What the Past Can't Tell Investors," *The New York Times*, January 3, 2010, p. BU2). Based on this information, and assuming a binomial distribution, what do you think is the probability that the stock market will rise

a. next year?

b. the year after next?

c. in four of the next five years?

d. in none of the next five years?

e. For this situation, what assumption of the binomial distribution might not be valid?

5.55 In late 2007, it was reported that 79% of U.S. adults owned a cell phone (data extracted from E. C. Baig, "Tips Help Navigate Tech-Buying Maze," *USA Today*, November 28, 2007, p. 5B). Suppose that by the end of 2009, that percentage was 85%. If a sample of 10 U.S. adults is selected, what is the probability that

a. 8 own a cell phone?

b. at least 8 own a cell phone?

c. all 10 own a cell phone?

d. If you selected the sample in a particular geographical area and found that none of the 10 respondents owned a cell phone, what conclusion might you reach about whether the percentage of cell phone owners in this area was 85%?

5.56 One theory concerning the Dow Jones Industrial Average is that it is likely to increase during U.S. presidential election years. From 1964 through 2008, the Dow Jones Industrial Average increased in 9 of the 12 U.S. presidential election years. Assuming that this indicator is a random event with no predictive value, you would expect that the indicator would be correct 50% of the time.

a. What is the probability of the Dow Jones Industrial Average increasing in 9 or more of the 12 U.S. presidential election years if the probability of an increase in the Dow Jones Industrial Average is 0.50?

b. What is the probability that the Dow Jones Industrial Average will increase in 9 or more of the 12 U.S. presidential election years if the probability of an increase in the Dow Jones Industrial Average in any year is 0.75?

5.57 Errors in a billing process often lead to customer dissatisfaction and ultimately hurt bottom-line profits. An article in *Quality Progress* (L. Tatikonda, "A Less Costly Billing Process," *Quality Progress*, January 2008, pp. 30–38) discussed a company where 40% of the bills prepared contained errors. If 10 bills are processed, what is the probability that

a. 0 bills will contain errors?

b. exactly 1 bill will contain an error?

c. 2 or more bills will contain errors?

d. What are the mean and the standard deviation of the probability distribution?

5.58 Refer to Problem 5.57. Suppose that a quality improvement initiative has reduced the percentage of bills containing errors to 20%. If 10 bills are processed, what is the probability that

a. 0 bills will contain errors?

b. exactly 1 bill will contain an error?

c. 2 or more bills will contain errors?

d. What are the mean and the standard deviation of the probability distribution?

e. Compare the results of (a) through (c) to those of Problem 5.57 (a) through (c).

5.59 A study by the Center for Financial Services Innovation showed that only 64% of U.S. income earners aged 15 and older had bank accounts (A. Carrns, "Banks Court a New Client," *The Wall Street Journal*, March 16, 2007, p. D1).

If a random sample of 20 U.S. income earners aged 15 and older is selected, what is the probability that

a. all 20 have bank accounts?

b. no more than 15 have bank accounts?

c. more than 10 have bank accounts?

d. What assumptions did you have to make to answer (a) through (c)?

5.60 One of the biggest frustrations for the consumer electronics industry is that customers are accustomed to returning goods for any reason (C. Lawton, "The War on Returns," *The Wall Street Journal*, May 8, 2008, pp. D1, D6). Recently, it was reported that returns for "no trouble found" were 68% of all the returns. Consider a sample of 20 customers who returned consumer electronics purchases. Use the binomial model to answer the following questions:

a. What is the expected value, or mean, of the binomial distribution?

b. What is the standard deviation of the binomial distribution?

c. What is the probability that 15 of the 20 customers made a return for "no trouble found"?

d. What is the probability that no more than 10 of the customers made a return for "no trouble found"?

e. What is the probability that 10 or more of the customers made a return for "no trouble found"?

5.61 Refer to Problem 5.60. In the same time period, 27% of the returns were for "buyer's remorse."

a. What is the expected value, or mean, of the binomial distribution?

b. What is the standard deviation of the binomial distribution?

c. What is the probability that none of the 20 customers made a return for "buyer's remorse"?

d. What is the probability that no more than 2 of the customers made a return for "buyer's remorse"?

e. What is the probability that 3 or more of the customers made a return for "buyer's remorse"?

5.62 One theory concerning the S&P 500 Index is that if it increases during the first five trading days of the year, it is likely to increase during the entire year. From 1950 through 2009, the S&P 500 Index had these early gains in 38 years. In 33 of these 38 years, the S&P 500 Index increased for the entire year. Assuming that this indicator is a random event with no predictive value, you would expect that the indicator would be correct 50% of the time. What is the probability of the S&P 500 Index increasing in 33 or more years if the true probability of an increase in the S&P 500 Index is

a. 0.50?

b. 0.70?

c. 0.90?

d. Based on the results of (a) through (c), what do you think is the probability that the S&P 500 Index will increase if there is an early gain in the first five trading days of the year? Explain.

5.63 *Spurious correlation* refers to the apparent relationship between variables that either have no true relationship or are related to other variables that have not been measured. One widely publicized stock market indicator in the United States that is an example of spurious correlation is the relationship between the winner of the National Football League Super Bowl and the performance of the Dow Jones Industrial Average in that year. The indicator states that when a team representing the National Football Conference wins the Super Bowl, the Dow Jones Industrial Average will increase in that year. When a team representing the American Football Conference wins the Super Bowl, the Dow Jones Industrial Average will decline in that year. Since the first Super Bowl was held in 1967 through 2009, the indicator has been correct 33 out of 43 times. Assuming that this indicator is a random event with no predictive value, you would expect that the indicator would be correct 50% of the time.

a. What is the probability that the indicator would be correct 33 or more times in 43 years?

b. What does this tell you about the usefulness of this indicator?

5.64 Approximately 300 million golf balls were lost in the United States in 2009. Assume that the number of golf balls lost in an 18-hole round is distributed as a Poisson random variable with a mean of 5 balls.

a. What assumptions need to be made so that the number of golf balls lost in an 18-hole round is distributed as a Poisson random variable?

Making the assumptions given in (a), what is the probability that

b. 0 balls will be lost in an 18-hole round?

c. 5 or fewer balls will be lost in an 18-hole round?

d. 6 or more balls will be lost in an 18-hole round?

5.65 According to a Virginia Tech survey, college students make an average of 11 cell phone calls per day. Moreover, 80% of the students surveyed indicated that their parents pay their cell phone expenses (J. Elliot, "Professor Researches Cell Phone Usage Among Students," **www.physorg.com**, February 26, 2007).

a. What distribution can you use to model the number of calls a student makes in a day?

b. If you select a student at random, what is the probability that he or she makes more than 10 calls in a day? More than 15? More than 20?

c. If you select a random sample of 10 students, what distribution can you use to model the proportion of students who have parents who pay their cell phone expenses?

d. Using the distribution selected in (c), what is the probability that all 10 have parents who pay their cell phone expenses? At least 9? At least 8?

5.66 Mega Millions is one of the most popular lottery games in the United States. Virtually all states participate in Mega Millions. Rules for playing and the list of prizes in most states are given below (see **megamillions.com**).

Rules:

- Select five numbers from a pool of numbers from 1 to 52 and one Mega Ball number from a second pool of numbers from 1 to 52.
- Each wager costs $1.

Prizes:

- Match all five numbers + Mega Ball—win jackpot (minimum of $12,000,000)
- Match all five numbers—win $250,000
- Match four numbers + Mega Ball—win $10,000
- Match four numbers—win $150
- Match three numbers + Mega Ball—win $150
- Match two numbers + Mega Ball—win $10
- Match three numbers—win $7
- Match one number + Mega Ball—win $3
- Match Mega Ball—win $2

Find the probability of winning

a. the jackpot.

b. the $250,000 prize. (Note that this requires matching all five numbers but not matching the Mega Ball.)

c. $10,000.

d. $150.

e. $10.
f. $7.
g. $3.
h. $2.
i. nothing.
j. All stores selling Mega Millions tickets are required to have a brochure that gives complete game rules and probabilities of winning each prize. (The probability of having a losing ticket is not given.) The slogan for all lottery games in the state of Ohio is "Play Responsibly. Odds Are, You'll Have Fun." Do you think Ohio's slogan and the requirement of making available complete game rules and probabilities of winning is an ethical approach to running the lottery system?

MANAGING ASHLAND MULTICOMM SERVICES

The Ashland MultiComm Services (AMS) marketing department wants to increase subscriptions for its *3-For-All* telephone, cable, and Internet combined service. AMS marketing has been conducting an aggressive direct-marketing campaign that includes postal and electronic mailings and telephone solicitations. Feedback from these efforts indicates that including premium channels in this combined service is a very important factor for both current and prospective subscribers. After several brainstorming sessions, the marketing department has decided to add premium cable channels as a no-cost benefit of subscribing to the *3-For-All* service.

The research director, Mona Fields, is planning to conduct a survey among prospective customers to determine how many premium channels need to be added to the *3-For-All* service in order to generate a subscription to the service. Based on past campaigns and on industry-wide data, she estimates the following:

Number of Free Premium Channels	Probability of Subscriptions
0	0.02
1	0.04
2	0.06
3	0.07
4	0.08
5	0.085

1. If a sample of 50 prospective customers is selected and no free premium channels are included in the *3-For-All* service offer, given past results, what is the probability that
a. fewer than 3 customers will subscribe to the *3-For-All* service offer?
b. 0 customers or 1 customers will subscribe to the *3-For- All* service offer?
c. more than 4 customers will subscribe to the *3-For-All* service offer?
Suppose that in the actual survey of 50 prospective customers, 4 customers subscribe to the *3-For-All* service offer.
d. What does this tell you about the previous estimate of the proportion of customers who would subscribe to the *3-For-All* service offer?

2. Instead of offering no premium free channels as in Problem **1**, suppose that two free premium channels are included in the *3-For-All* service offer, Given past results, what is the probability that
a. fewer than 3 customers will subscribe to the *3-For-All* service offer?
b. 0 customers or 1 customer will subscribe to the *3-For-All* service offer?
c. more than 4 customers will subscribe to the *3-For-All* service offer?
d. Compare the results of (a) through (c) to those of **1**.
Suppose that in the actual survey of 50 prospective customers, 6 customers subscribe to the *3-For-All* service offer.
e. What does this tell you about the previous estimate of the proportion of customers who would subscribe to the *3-For-All* service offer?
f. What do the results in (e) tell you about the effect of offering free premium channels on the likelihood of obtaining subscriptions to the *3-For-All* service?

3. Suppose that additional surveys of 50 prospective customers were conducted in which the number of free premium channels was varied. The results were as follows:

Number of Free Premium Channels	Number of Subscriptions
1	5
3	6
4	6
5	7

How many free premium channels should the research director recommend for inclusion in the *3-For-All* service? Explain.

DIGITAL CASE

Apply your knowledge about expected value and the covariance in this continuing Digital Case from Chapters 3 and 4.

Open **BullsAndBears.pdf**, a marketing brochure from EndRun Financial Services. Read the claims and examine the supporting data. Then answer the following:

1. Are there any "catches" about the claims the brochure makes for the rate of return of Happy Bull and Worried Bear Funds?
2. What subjective data influence the rate-of-return analyses of these funds? Could EndRun be accused of making false and misleading statements? Why or why not?
3. The expected-return analysis seems to show that the Worried Bear Fund has a greater expected return than the Happy Bull Fund. Should a rational investor never invest in the Happy Bull Fund? Why or why not?

REFERENCES

1. Bernstein, P. L., *Against the Gods: The Remarkable Story of Risk* (New York: Wiley, 1996).
2. Emery, D. R., J. D. Finnerty, and J. D. Stowe, *Corporate Financial Management*, 3rd ed. (Upper Saddle River, NJ: Prentice Hall, 2007).
3. Kirk, R. L., ed., *Statistical Issues: A Reader for the Behavioral Sciences* (Belmont, CA: Wadsworth, 1972).
4. Levine, D. M., P. Ramsey, and R. Smidt, *Applied Statistics for Engineers and Scientists Using Microsoft Excel and Minitab* (Upper Saddle River, NJ: Prentice Hall, 2001).
5. *Microsoft Excel 2010* (Redmond, WA: Microsoft Corp., 2010).
6. Minitab *Release* 16 (State College, PA.: Minitab, Inc., 2010).
7. Moscove, S. A., M. G. Simkin, and N. A. Bagranoff, *Core Concepts of Accounting Information Systems*, 11th ed. (New York: Wiley, 2010).

CHAPTER 5 EXCEL GUIDE

EG5.1 THE PROBABILITY DISTRIBUTION FOR A DISCRETE RANDOM VARIABLE

In-Depth Excel Use the **COMPUTE worksheet** of the **Discrete Random Variable workbook** as a template for computing the expected value, variance, and standard deviation of a discrete random variable (see Figure EG5.1). The worksheet contains the data for the Section 5.1 example on page 182 involving the number of interruptions per day in a large computer network. For other problems, overwrite the X and $P(X)$ values in columns A and B, respectively. If a problem has more or fewer than six outcomes, select the cell range **A5:E5** and:

If the problem has more than six outcomes:

1. Right-click and click **Insert** from the shortcut menu.
2. If a dialog box appears, click **Shift cells down** and then click **OK**.
3. Repeat steps 1 and 2 as many times as necessary.
4. Select the formulas in cell range **C4:E4** and copy them down through the new table rows.
5. Enter the new X and $P(X)$ values in columns **A** and **B**.

If the problem has fewer than six outcomes, right-click and click **Delete** from the shortcut menu. If a dialog box appears, click **Shift cells up** and then click **OK**. Repeat as many times as necessary and then enter the new X and $P(X)$ values in columns **A** and **B**.

FIGURE EG5.1

Discrete random variable probability worksheet

	A	B	C	D	E	F	G	H	
1	Discrete Random Variable Probability Distribution								
2							Statistics		
3	X	P(X)	X*P(X)	[X-E(X)]^2	[X-E(X)]^2*P(X)		Expected value	1.4	=SUM(C:C)
4	0	0.35	0	1.96	0.686		Variance	2.04	=SUM(E:E)
5	1	0.25	0.25	0.16	0.04		Standard deviation	1.43	=SQRT(H4)
6	2	0.20	0.4	0.36	0.072				
7	3	0.10	0.3	2.56	0.256				
8	4	0.05	0.2	6.76	0.338				
9	5	0.05	0.25	12.96	0.648				

X*P(X)	[X-E(X)]^2	[X-E(X)]^2*P(X)
=A4 * B4	=(A4 - $H$3)^2	=D4 * B4
=A5 * B5	=(A5 - $H$3)^2	=D5 * B5
=A6 * B6	=(A6 - $H$3)^2	=D6 * B6
=A7 * B7	=(A7 - $H$3)^2	=D7 * B7
=A8 * B8	=(A8 - $H$3)^2	=D8 * B8
=A9 * B9	=(A9 - $H$3)^2	=D9 * B9

EG5.2 COVARIANCE AND ITS APPLICATION IN FINANCE

PHStat2 Use **Covariance and Portfolio Analysis** to perform portfolio analysis. For example, to create the portfolio analysis for the Section 5.2 investment example on page 186, select **PHStat → Decision-Making → Covariance and Portfolio Analysis**. In the procedure's dialog box (shown below):

1. Enter **5** as the **Number of Outcomes**.
2. Enter a **Title**, check **Portfolio Management Analysis**, and click **OK**.

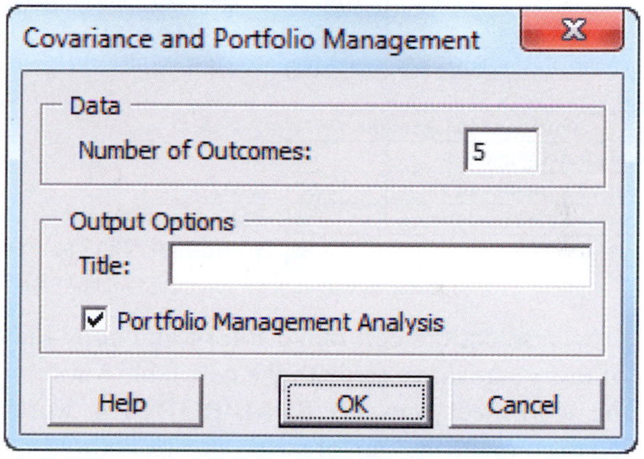

In the new worksheet (shown in Figure EG5.2 on page 212):

3. Enter the probabilities and outcomes in the table that begins in cell B3.
4. Enter **0.5** as the **Weight assigned to X**.

In-Depth Excel Use the **COMPUTE worksheet** of the **Portfolio workbook**, shown in Figure EG5.2, as a template for performing portfolio analysis. The worksheet contains the data for the Section 5.2 investment example on page 186. Overwrite the X and $P(X)$ values and the weight assigned to the X value when you enter data for other problems. If a problem has more or fewer than three outcomes, first select row **5**, right-click, and click **Insert** (or **Delete**) in the shortcut menu to insert (or delete) rows one at a time. If you

FIGURE EG5.2

Portfolio analysis worksheet

	A	B	C	D	
1	Portfolio Expected Return and Risk				
2					
3	Probabilities & Outcomes:	P	X	Y	
4		0.2	-300	200	
5		0.5	100	50	
6		0.3	250	-100	
7					
8	Weight Assigned to X	0.5			
9					
10	Statistics				
11	E(X)	65	=SUMPRODUCT(B4:B6, C4:C6)		
12	E(Y)	35	=SUMPRODUCT(B4:B6, D4:D6)		
13	Variance(X)	37525	=SUMPRODUCT(B4:B6, H4:H6)		
14	Standard Deviation(X)	193.71	=SQRT(B13)		
15	Variance(Y)	11025	=SUMPRODUCT(B4:B6, I4:I6)		
16	Standard Deviation(Y)	105	=SQRT(B15)		
17	Covariance(XY)	-19275	=SUMPRODUCT(B4:B6, J4:J6)		
18	Variance(X+Y)	10000	=B13 + B15 + 2 * B17		
19	Standard Deviation(X+Y)	100	=SQRT(B18)		
20					
21	Portfolio Management				
22	Weight Assigned to X	0.5	=B8		
23	Weight Assigned to Y	0.5	=1-B22		
24	Portfolio Expected Return	50	=B22 * B11 + B23 * B12		
25	Portfolio Risk	50	=SQRT(B22^2 * B13 + B23^2 * B15 + 2 * B22 * B23 * B17)		

insert rows, select the cell range **B4:J4** and copy the contents of this range down through the new table rows.

The worksheet uses the **SUMPRODUCT** worksheet function to compute the sum of the products of corresponding elements of two cell ranges. The worksheet also contains a Calculations Area that contains various intermediate calculations. Open the **COMPUTE_FORMULAS worksheet** to examine all the formulas used in this area.

EG5.3 BINOMIAL DISTRIBUTION

PHStat2 Use **Binomial** to compute binomial probabilities. For example, to create a binomial probabilities table and histogram for Example 5.3 on page 193, similar to those in Figures 5.2 and 5.3, select **PHStat ➔ Probability & Prob. Distributions ➔ Binomial**. In the procedure's dialog box (shown in next column):

1. Enter **4** as the **Sample Size**.
2. Enter **0.1** as the **Prob. of an Event of Interest**.
3. Enter **0** as the **Outcomes From** value and enter **4** as the (Outcomes) **To** value.
4. Enter a **Title**, check **Histogram**, and click **OK**.

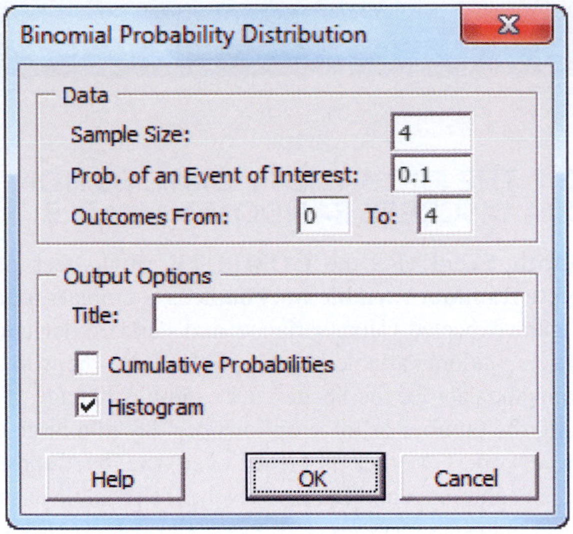

To add columns to the binomial probabilities table for $P(<=X)$, $P(<X)$, $P(>X)$, and $P(\geq X)$, check **Cumulative Probabilities** before clicking **OK** in step 4.

In-Depth Excel Use the **BINOMDIST** worksheet function to compute binomial probabilities. Enter the function as **BINOMDIST** (***X, sample size,*** π**,** ***cumulative***), where ***X*** is the number of events of interest, π is the probability of an event of interest, and ***cumulative*** is a **True** or **False** value. (When ***cumulative*** is **True**, the function computes the probability of ***X*** or fewer events of interest; when ***cumulative*** is **False**, the function computes the probability of exactly ***X*** events of interest.)

Use the **COMPUTE worksheet** of the **Binomial workbook**, shown in Figure 5.2 on page 194, as a template for computing binomial probabilities. The worksheet contains the data for the Section 5.3 tagged orders example. Overwrite these values and adjust the table of probabilities for other problems. To create a histogram of the probability distribution, use the instructions in Appendix Section F.5.

EG5.4 POISSON DISTRIBUTION

PHStat2 Use **Poisson** to compute Poisson probabilities. For example, to create a Poisson probabilities table similar to Figure 5.4 on page 199, select **PHStat ➔ Probability & Prob. Distributions ➔ Poisson**. In this procedure's dialog box (shown the top of the next page):

1. Enter **3** as the **Mean/Expected No. of Events of Interest**.
2. Enter a **Title** and click **OK**.

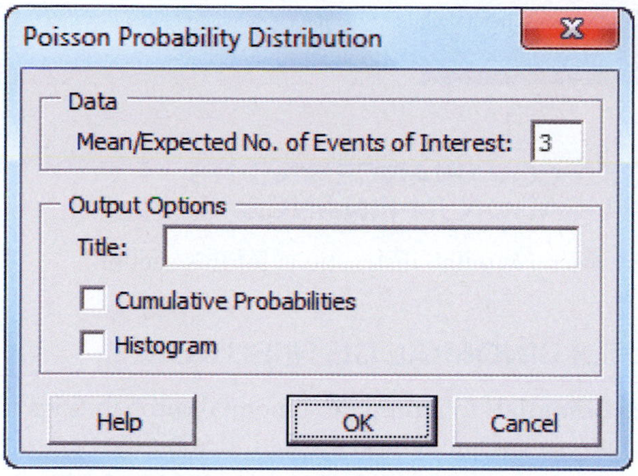

To add columns to the Poisson probabilities table for $P(<=X), P(<X), P(>X)$, and $P(\geq X)$, check **Cumulative Probabilities** before clicking **OK** in step 2. To create a histogram of the probability distribution on a separate chart sheet, check **Histogram** before clicking **OK** in step 2.

In-Depth Excel Use the **POISSON** worksheet function to compute Poisson probabilities. Enter the function as **POISSON(*X, lambda, cumulative*)**, where *X* is the number of events of interest, ***lambda*** is the average or expected number of events of interest, and ***cumulative*** is a **True** or **False** value. (When ***cumulative*** is **True**, the function computes the probability of *X* or fewer events of interest; when ***cumulative*** is **False**, the function computes the probability of exactly *X* events of interest.)

Use the **COMPUTE worksheet** of the **Poisson workbook**, shown in Figure 5.4 on page 199, as a template for computing Poisson probabilities. The worksheet contains the entries for the bank customer arrivals problem of Section 5.4. To adapt this worksheet to other problems, change the **Mean/Expected number of events of interest value** in cell **E4**. To create a histogram of the probability distribution, use the instructions in Appendix Section F.5.

EG5.5 HYPERGEOMETRIC DISTRIBUTION

PHStat2 Use **Hypergeometric** to compute hypergeometric probabilities. For example, to create a hypergeometric probabilities table similar to Figure 5.5 on page 203, select **PHStat → Probability & Prob. Distributions → Hypergeometric**. In this procedure's dialog box (shown in the next column):

1. Enter **8** as the **Sample Size**.
2. Enter **10** as the **No. of Events of Interest in Pop.** (population).
3. Enter **30** as the **Population Size**.
4. Enter a **Title** and click **OK**.

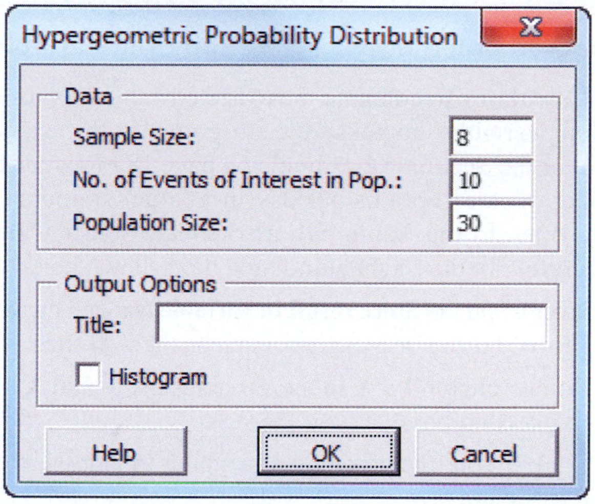

To create a histogram of the probability distribution on a separate chart sheet, check **Histogram** before clicking **OK** in step 4.

In-Depth Excel Use the **HYPGEOMDIST** function to compute hypergeometric probabilities. Enter the function as **HYPGEOMDIST(*X, sample size, A, population size*)**, where *X* is the number of events of interest and *A* is the number of events of interest in the population.

Use the **COMPUTE worksheet** of the **Hypergeometric workbook**, shown in Figure 5.5 on page 203, as a template for computing hypergeometric probabilities. The worksheet contains the data for the Section 5.5 team-formation example. To create a histogram of the probability distribution, use the instructions in Appendix Section F.5.

To adapt this worksheet to other problems, change the sample size, the number of events of interest, and population size values in cells **B4**, **B5**, and **B6**, respectively. If a problem has a sample size other than 8, select row **11**, right-click, and click **Insert** (or **Delete**) in the shortcut menu to insert (or delete) rows one at a time. Then edit the *X* values in column A and if you inserted rows, select the cell **B10** formula, and copy it down through the new table rows.

CHAPTER 5 MINITAB GUIDE

MG5.1 THE PROBABILITY DISTRIBUTION FOR A DISCRETE RANDOM VARIABLE

Expected Value of a Discrete Random Variable

Use **Calculator** to compute the expected value of a discrete random variable. For example, to compute the expected value for the Section 5.1 example on page 182 involving the number of interruptions per day in a large computer network, open to the **Table_5.1 worksheet**. Select **Calc → Calculator**. In the Calculator dialog box (shown below):

1. Enter **C3** in the **Store result in variable** box and then press **Tab**. (C3 is the first empty column on the worksheet.)
2. Double-click **C1 X** in the variables list to add **X** to the **Expression** box.
3. Click * on the simulated keypad to add * to the **Expression** box.
4. Double-click **C2 P(X)** in the variables list to form the expression **X * 'P(X)'** in the **Expression** box.
5. Check **Assign as a formula**.
6. Click **OK**.

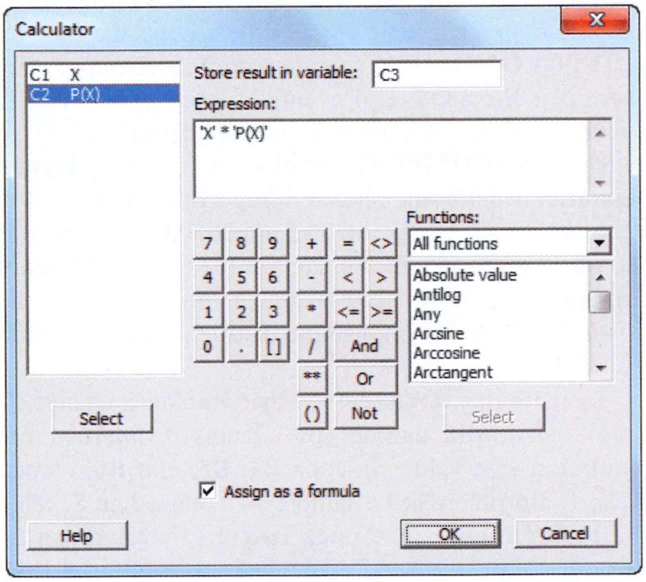

7. Enter **X*P(X)** as the name for column **C3**.
8. Reselect **Calc → Calculator**.

In the Calculator dialog box:

9. Enter **C4** in the **Store result in variable** box and then press **Tab**. (C4 is the first empty column on the worksheet.)
10. Enter **SUM(C3)** in the **Expression** box.
11. If necessary, clear **Assign as a formula**.
12. Click **OK**.

MG5.2 COVARIANCE AND ITS APPLICATION IN FINANCE

There are no Minitab instructions for this section.

MG5.3 BINOMIAL DISTRIBUTION

Use **Binomial** to compute binomial probabilities. For example, to compute these probabilities for the Section 5.3 tagged orders example on page 193, open to a new, blank worksheet and:

1. Enter **X** as the name of column **C1**.
2. Enter **0**, **1**, **2**, **3**, and **4** in rows 1 to 5 of column **C1**.
3. Enter **P(X)** as the name of column **C2**.
4. Select **Calc → Probability Distributions → Binomial**.

In the Binomial Distribution dialog box (shown below):

5. Click **Probability** (to compute the probabilities of exactly *X* events of interest for all values of X).
6. Enter **4** (the sample size) in the **Number of trials** box.
7. Enter **0.1** in the **Event probability** box.
8. Click **Input column** and enter **C1** in its box.
9. Enter **C2** in the first **Optional storage** box.
10. Click **OK**.

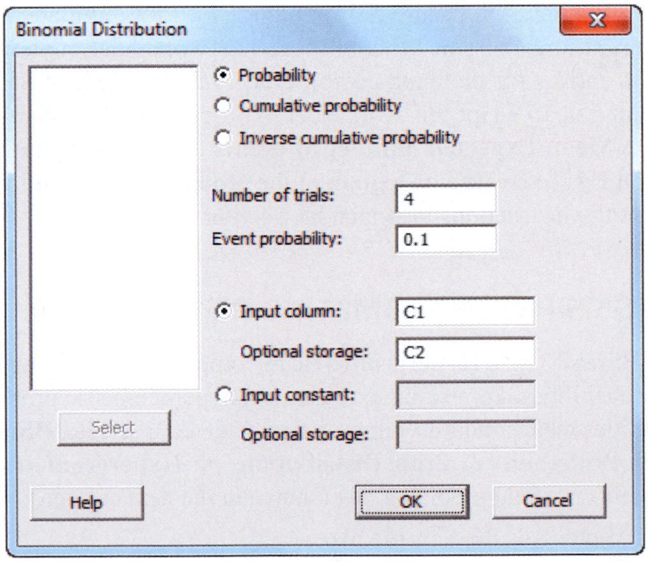

Skip step 9 to create the results shown in Figure 5.2 on page 194.

MG5.4 POISSON DISTRIBUTION

Use **Poisson** to compute Poisson probabilities. For example, to compute these probabilities for the Section 5.4 bank customer arrivals example on page 198, open to a new, blank worksheet and:

1. Enter **X** as the name of column **C1**.
2. Enter values **0** through **15** in rows 1 to 16 of column **C1**.
3. Enter **P(X)** as the name of column **C2**.
4. Select **Calc → Probability Distributions → Poisson**.

In the Poisson Distribution dialog box (shown below):

5. Click **Probability** (to compute the probabilities of exactly *X* events of interest for all values of X).
6. Enter **3** (the value) in the **Mean** box.
7. Click **Input column** and enter **C1** in its box.
8. Enter **C2** in the first **Optional storage** box.
9. Click **OK**.

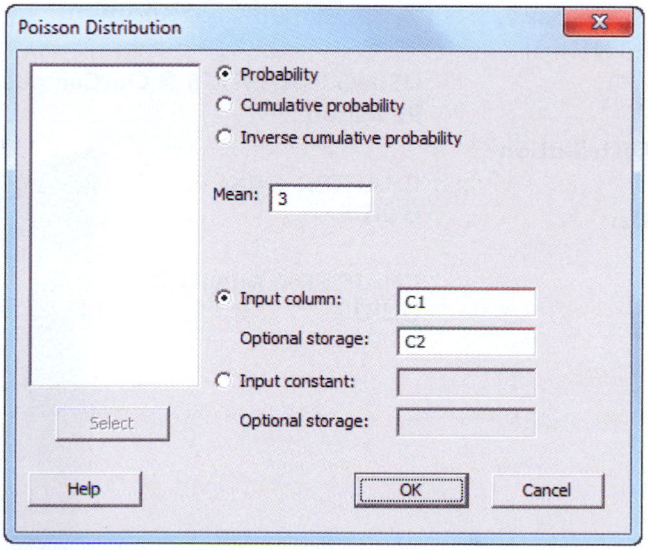

Skip step 8 to create the results shown in Figure 5.4 on page 199.

MG5.5 HYPERGEOMETRIC DISTRIBUTION

Use **Hypergeometric** to compute hypergeometric probabilities. For example, to compute these probabilities for the Section 5.5 team-formation example on page 202, open to a new, blank worksheet and:

1. Enter **X** as the name of column **C1**.
2. Enter the values **0** through **8** in rows 1 to 9 of column **C1**.
3. Enter **P(X)** as the name of column **C2**.
4. Select **Calc → Probability Distributions → Hypergeometric**.

In the Hypergeometric Distribution dialog box (shown below):

5. Click **Probability**.
6. Enter **30** in the **Population size (N)** box.
7. Enter **10** in the **Event count in population (M)** box.
8. Enter **8** in the **Sample size (n)** box.
9. Click **Input column** and enter **C1** in its box.
10. Enter **C2** in the first **Optional storage** box.
11. Click **OK**.

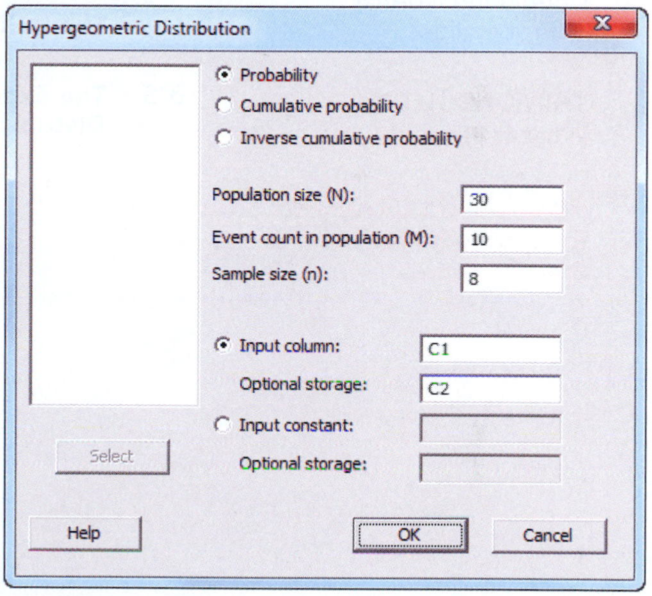

Skip step 10 to create the results shown in Figure 5.5 on page 203.

6 The Normal Distribution and Other Continuous Distributions

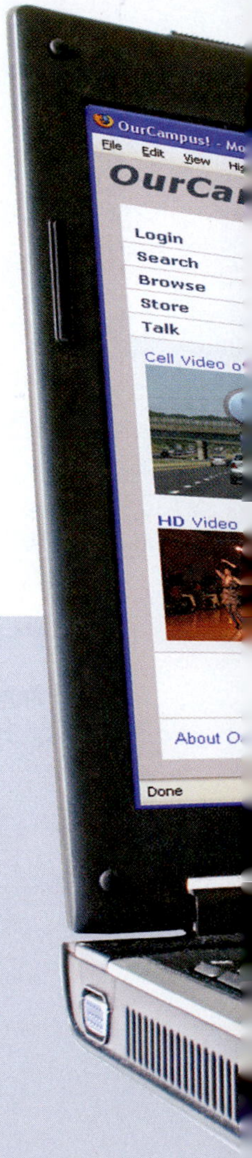

Learning Objectives

In this chapter, you learn:

- To compute probabilities from the normal distribution
- How to use the normal distribution to solve business problems
- To use the normal probability plot to determine whether a set of data is approximately normally distributed
- To compute probabilities from the uniform distribution
- To compute probabilities from the exponential distribution

USING STATISTICS
@ OurCampus!

You are a designer for the OurCampus! website, a social networking site that targets college students. To attract and retain visitors to the site, you need to make sure that the exclusive-content daily videos can be quickly downloaded and played in a user's browser. Download time, the amount of time, in seconds, that passes from the first linking to the website home page until the first video is ready to play, is both a function of the streaming media technology used and the number of simultaneous users of the website.

To check how fast a video downloads, you open a web browser on a PC at the corporate offices of OurCampus! and measure the download time. Past data indicate that the mean download time is 7 seconds, and that the standard deviation is 2 seconds. Approximately two-thirds of the download times are between 5 and 9 seconds, and about 95% of the download times are between 3 and 11 seconds. In other words, the download times are distributed as a bell-shaped curve, with a clustering around the mean of 7 seconds. How could you use this information to answer questions about the download times of the first video?

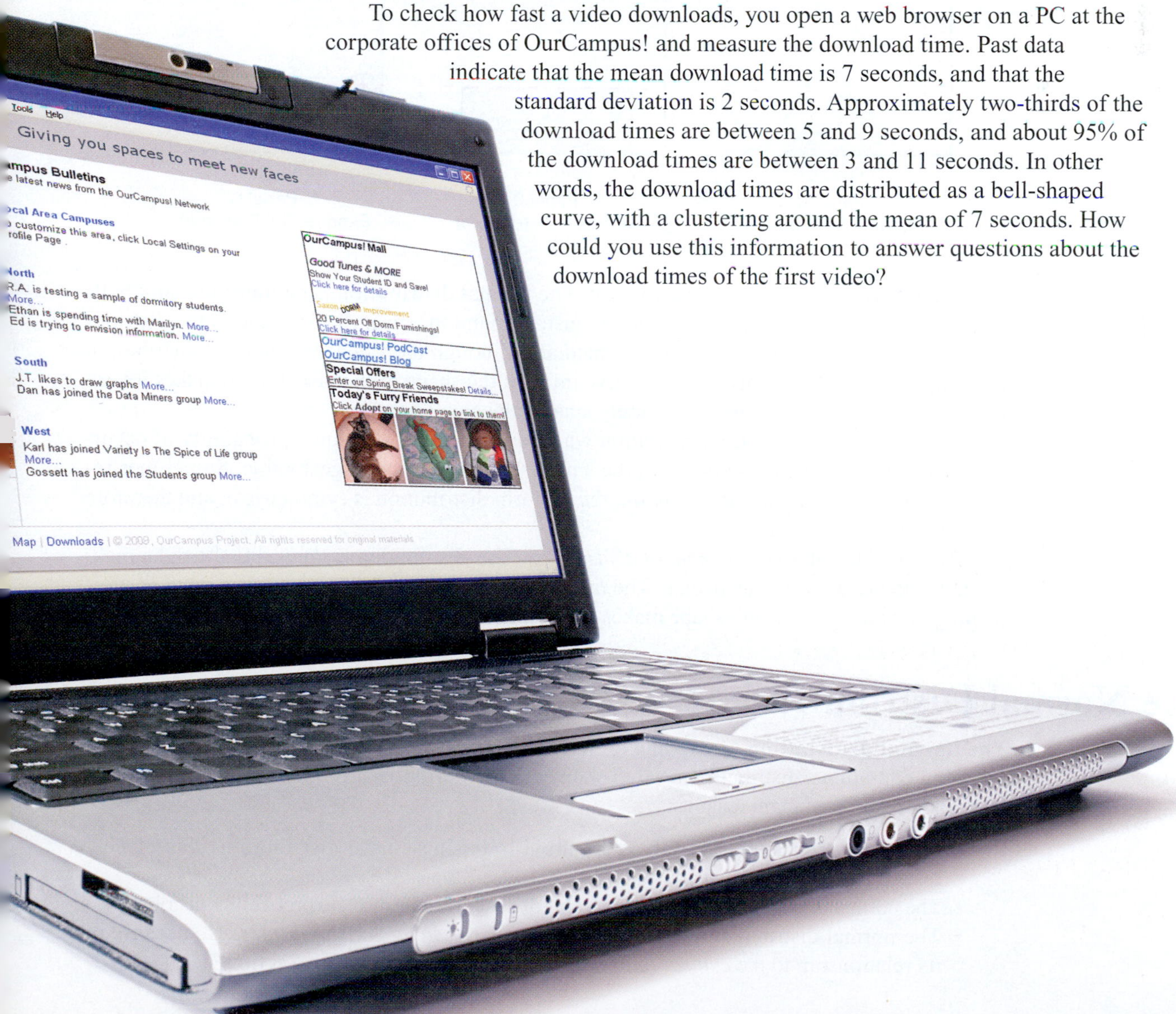

In Chapter 5, Saxon Home Improvement Company managers wanted to be able to answer questions about the number of tagged items in a given sample size. As an OurCampus! web designer, you face a different task, one that involves a continuous measurement because a download time could be any value and not just a whole number. How can you answer questions, such as the following, about this *continuous numerical variable*:

- What proportion of the video downloads take more than 9 seconds?
- How many seconds elapse before 10% of the downloads are complete?
- How many seconds elapse before 99% of the downloads are complete?
- How would enhancing the streaming media technology used affect the answers to these questions?

As in Chapter 5, you can use a probability distribution as a model. Reading this chapter will help you learn about characteristics of continuous probability distributions and how to use the normal, uniform, and exponential distributions to solve business problems.

6.1 Continuous Probability Distributions

A **probability density function** is a mathematical expression that defines the distribution of the values for a continuous random variable. Figure 6.1 graphically displays three probability density functions.

FIGURE 6.1
Three continuous probability distributions

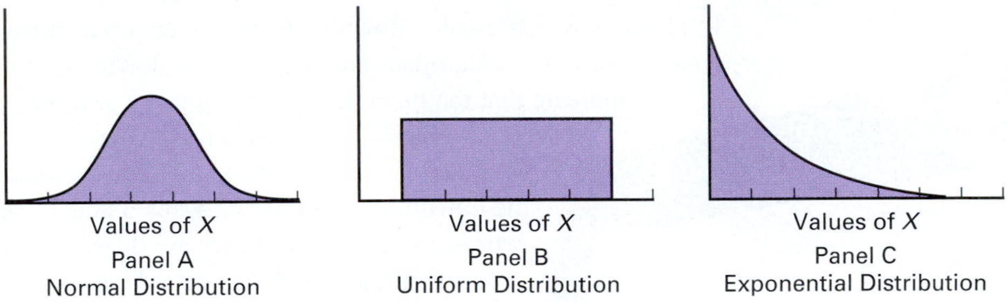

Panel A depicts a *normal* distribution. The normal distribution is symmetrical and bell-shaped, implying that most values tend to cluster around the mean, which, due to the distribution's symmetrical shape, is equal to the median. Although the values in a normal distribution can range from negative infinity to positive infinity, the shape of the distribution makes it very unlikely that extremely large or extremely small values will occur.

Panel B shows a *uniform distribution* where each value has an equal probability of occurrence anywhere in the range between the smallest value and the largest value. Sometimes referred to as the *rectangular distribution*, the uniform distribution is symmetrical, and therefore the mean equals the median.

Panel C illustrates an *exponential distribution*. This distribution is skewed to the right, making the mean larger than the median. The range for an exponential distribution is zero to positive infinity, but the distribution's shape makes the occurrence of extremely large values unlikely.

6.2 The Normal Distribution

The **normal distribution** (sometimes referred to as the *Gaussian distribution*) is the most common continuous distribution used in statistics. The normal distribution is vitally important in statistics for three main reasons:

- Numerous continuous variables common in business have distributions that closely resemble the normal distribution.
- The normal distribution can be used to approximate various discrete probability distributions.
- The normal distribution provides the basis for *classical statistical inference* because of its relationship to the *central limit theorem* (which is discussed in Section 7.4).

The normal distribution is represented by the classic bell shape shown in Panel A of Figure 6.1. In the normal distribution, you can calculate the probability that values occur within certain ranges or intervals. However, because probability for continuous variables is measured as an area under the curve, the *exact* probability of a *particular value* from a continuous distribution such as the normal distribution is zero. As an example, time (in seconds) is measured and not counted. Therefore, you can determine the probability that the download time for a video on a web browser is between 7 and 10 seconds, or the probability that the download time is between 8 and 9 seconds, or the probability that the download time is between 7.99 and 8.01 seconds. However, the probability that the download time is *exactly* 8 seconds is zero.

The normal distribution has several important theoretical properties:

- It is symmetrical, and its mean and median are therefore equal.
- It is bell-shaped in appearance.
- Its interquartile range is equal to 1.33 standard deviations. Thus, the middle 50% of the values are contained within an interval of two-thirds of a standard deviation below the mean and two-thirds of a standard deviation above the mean.
- It has an infinite range ($-\infty < X < \infty$).

In practice, many variables have distributions that closely resemble the theoretical properties of the normal distribution. The data in Table 6.1 represent the amount of soft drink in 10,000 1-liter bottles filled on a recent day. The continuous variable of interest, the amount of soft drink filled, can be approximated by the normal distribution. The measurements of the amount of soft drink in the 10,000 bottles cluster in the interval 1.05 to 1.055 liters and distribute symmetrically around that grouping, forming a bell-shaped pattern.

TABLE 6.1

Amount of Fill in 10,000 Bottles of a Soft Drink

Amount of Fill (liters)	Relative Frequency
< 1.025	$48/10{,}000 = 0.0048$
$1.025 < 1.030$	$122/10{,}000 = 0.0122$
$1.030 < 1.035$	$325/10{,}000 = 0.0325$
$1.035 < 1.040$	$695/10{,}000 = 0.0695$
$1.040 < 1.045$	$1{,}198/10{,}000 = 0.1198$
$1.045 < 1.050$	$1{,}664/10{,}000 = 0.1664$
$1.050 < 1.055$	$1{,}896/10{,}000 = 0.1896$
$1.055 < 1.060$	$1{,}664/10{,}000 = 0.1664$
$1.060 < 1.065$	$1{,}198/10{,}000 = 0.1198$
$1.065 < 1.070$	$695/10{,}000 = 0.0695$
$1.070 < 1.075$	$325/10{,}000 = 0.0325$
$1.075 < 1.080$	$122/10{,}000 = 0.0122$
1.080 or above	$48/10{,}000 = 0.0048$
Total	1.0000

Figure 6.2 shows the relative frequency histogram and polygon for the distribution of the amount filled in 10,000 bottles.

FIGURE 6.2

Relative frequency histogram and polygon of the amount filled in 10,000 bottles of a soft drink

Source: Data are taken from Table 6.1.

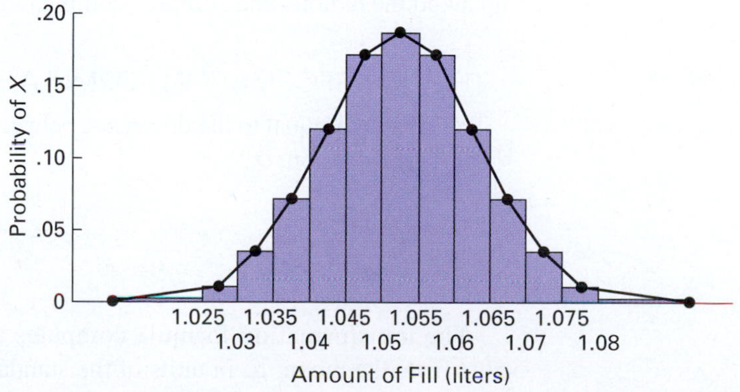

For these data, the first three theoretical properties of the normal distribution are approximately satisfied. However, the fourth one, having an infinite range, is not. The amount filled in a bottle cannot possibly be zero or below, nor can a bottle be filled beyond its capacity. From Table 6.1, you see that only 48 out of every 10,000 bottles filled are expected to contain 1.08 liters or more, and an equal number are expected to contain less than 1.025 liters.

The symbol $f(X)$ is used to represent a probability density function. The **probability density function for the normal distribution** is given in Equation (6.1).

NORMAL PROBABILITY DENSITY FUNCTION

$$f(X) = \frac{1}{\sqrt{2\pi}\sigma} e^{-(1/2)[(X-\mu)/\sigma]^2} \quad \textbf{(6.1)}$$

where

e = mathematical constant approximated by 2.71828

π = mathematical constant approximated by 3.14159

μ = mean

σ = standard deviation

X = any value of the continuous variable, where $-\infty < X < \infty$

Although Equation (6.1) may look complicated, because e and π are mathematical constants, the probabilities of the random variable X are dependent only on the two parameters of the normal distribution—the mean, μ, and the standard deviation, σ. Every time you specify particular values of μ and σ, a *different* normal probability distribution is generated. Figure 6.3 illustrates this principle. The distributions labeled A and B have the same mean (μ) but have different standard deviations. Distributions A and C have the same standard deviation (σ) but have different means. Distributions B and C have different values for both μ and σ.

FIGURE 6.3
Three normal distributions

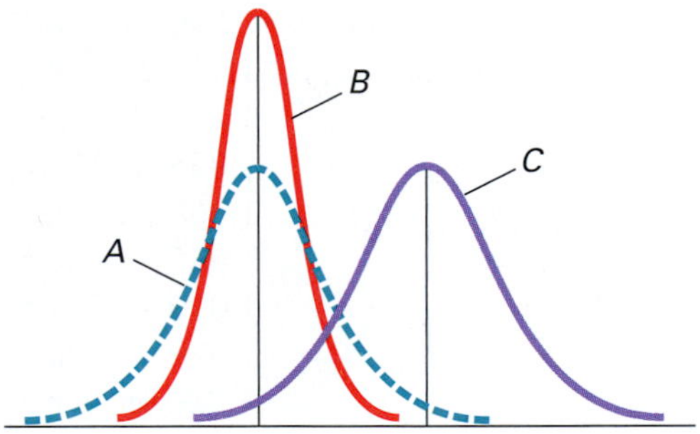

Computing Normal Probabilities

To compute normal probabilities, you first convert a normally distributed random variable, X, to a **standardized normal random variable**, Z, using the **transformation formula**, shown in Equation (6.2). Applying this formula allows you to look up values in a normal probability table and avoid the tedious and complex computations that Equation (6.1) would otherwise require.

THE TRANSFORMATION FORMULA

The Z value is equal to the difference between X and the mean, μ, divided by the standard deviation, σ.

$$Z = \frac{X - \mu}{\sigma} \quad \textbf{(6.2)}$$

The transformation formula computes a Z value that expresses the difference of the X value from the mean, μ, in units of the standard deviation (see Section 3.2 on page 101) called *standardized units*. While a random variable, X, has mean, μ, and standard deviation, σ, the standardized random variable, Z, always has mean $\mu = 0$ and standard deviation $\sigma = 1$.

Then you can determine the probabilities by using Table E.2, the **cumulative standardized normal distribution**. For example, recall from the Using Statistics scenario on page 217 that past data indicate that the time to download a video is normally distributed, with a mean $\mu = 7$ seconds and a standard deviation $\sigma = 2$ seconds. From Figure 6.4, you see that every measurement X has a corresponding standardized measurement Z, computed from Equation (6.2), the transformation formula. Therefore, a download time of 9 seconds is equivalent to 1 standardized unit (1 standard deviation) above the mean because

$$Z = \frac{9 - 7}{2} = +1$$

FIGURE 6.4
Transformation of scales

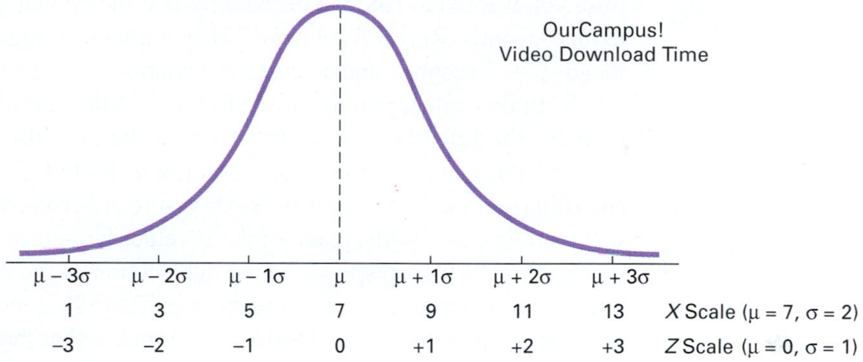

A download time of 1 second is equivalent to –3 standardized units (3 standard deviations) below the mean because

$$Z = \frac{1 - 7}{2} = -3$$

Figure 6.4 illustrates that the standard deviation is the unit of measurement. In other words, a time of 9 seconds is 2 seconds (1 standard deviation) higher, or *slower*, than the mean time of 7 seconds. Similarly, a time of 1 second is 6 seconds (3 standard deviations) lower, or *faster*, than the mean time.

To further illustrate the transformation formula, suppose that another website has a download time for a video that is normally distributed, with a mean $\mu = 4$ seconds and a standard deviation $\sigma = 1$ second. Figure 6.5 shows this distribution.

FIGURE 6.5
A different transformation of scales

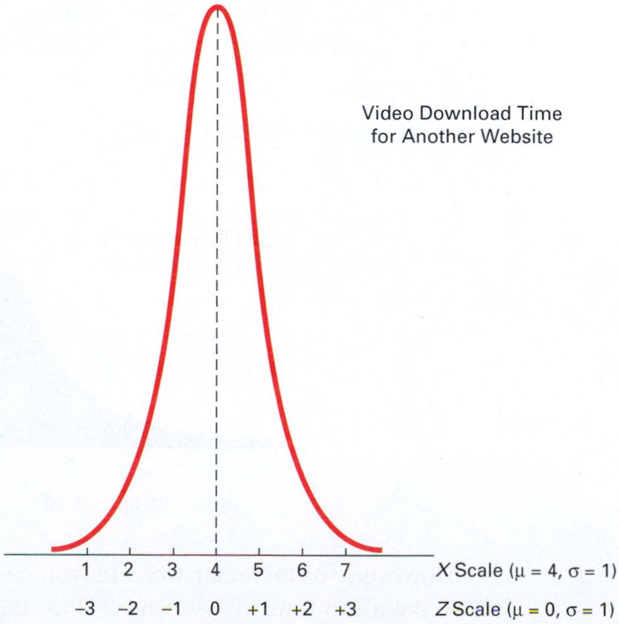

Comparing these results with those of the OurCampus! website, you see that a download time of 5 seconds is 1 standard deviation above the mean download time because

$$Z = \frac{5 - 4}{1} = +1$$

A time of 1 second is 3 standard deviations below the mean download time because

$$Z = \frac{1 - 4}{1} = -3$$

With the Z value computed, you look up the normal probability using a table of values from the cumulative standardized normal distribution, such as Table E.2 in Appendix E. Suppose you wanted to find the probability that the download time for the OurCampus! site is less than 9 seconds. Recall from page 221 that transforming $X = 9$ to standardized Z units, given a mean $\mu = 7$ seconds and a standard deviation $\sigma = 2$ seconds, leads to a Z value of $+1.00$.

With this value, you use Table E.2 to find the cumulative area under the normal curve less than (to the left of) $Z = +1.00$. To read the probability or area under the curve less than $Z = +1.00$, you scan down the Z column in Table E.2 until you locate the Z value of interest (in 10ths) in the Z row for 1.0. Next, you read across this row until you intersect the column that contains the 100ths place of the Z value. Therefore, in the body of the table, the probability for $Z = 1.00$ corresponds to the intersection of the row $Z = 1.0$ with the column $Z = .00$. Table 6.2, which reproduces a portion of Table E.2, shows this intersection. The probability listed at the intersection is 0.8413, which means that there is an 84.13% chance that the download time will be less than 9 seconds. Figure 6.6 graphically shows this probability.

TABLE 6.2

Finding a Cumulative Area Under the Normal Curve

Cumulative Probabilities

Z	.00	.01	.02	.03	.04	.05	.06	.07	.08	.09
0.0	.5000	.5040	.5080	.5120	.5160	.5199	.5239	.5279	.5319	.5359
0.1	.5398	.5438	.5478	.5517	.5557	.5596	.5636	.5675	.5714	.5753
0.2	.5793	.5832	.5871	.5910	.5948	.5987	.6026	.6064	.6103	.6141
0.3	.6179	.6217	.6255	.6293	.6331	.6368	.6406	.6443	.6480	.6517
0.4	.6554	.6591	.6628	.6664	.6700	.6736	.6772	.6808	.6844	.6879
0.5	.6915	.6950	.6985	.7019	.7054	.7088	.7123	.7157	.7190	.7224
0.6	.7257	.7291	.7324	.7357	.7389	.7422	.7454	.7486	.7518	.7549
0.7	.7580	.7612	.7642	.7673	.7704	.7734	.7764	.7794	.7823	.7852
0.8	.7881	.7910	.7939	.7967	.7995	.8023	.8051	.8078	.8106	.8133
0.9	.8159	.8186	.8212	.8238	.8264	.8289	.8315	.8340	.8365	.8389
1.0 →	.8413	.8438	.8461	.8485	.8508	.8531	.8554	.8577	.8599	.8621

Source: Extracted from Table E.2.

FIGURE 6.6

Determining the area less than Z from a cumulative standardized normal distribution

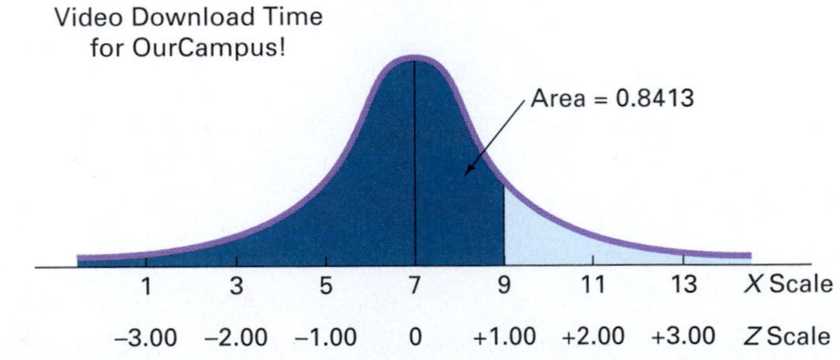

However, for the other website, you see that a time of 5 seconds is 1 standardized unit above the mean time of 4 seconds. Thus, the probability that the download time will be less

than 5 seconds is also 0.8413. Figure 6.7 shows that regardless of the value of the mean, μ, and standard deviation, σ, of a normally distributed variable, Equation (6.2) can transform the X value to a Z value.

FIGURE 6.7

Demonstrating a transformation of scales for corresponding cumulative portions under two normal curves

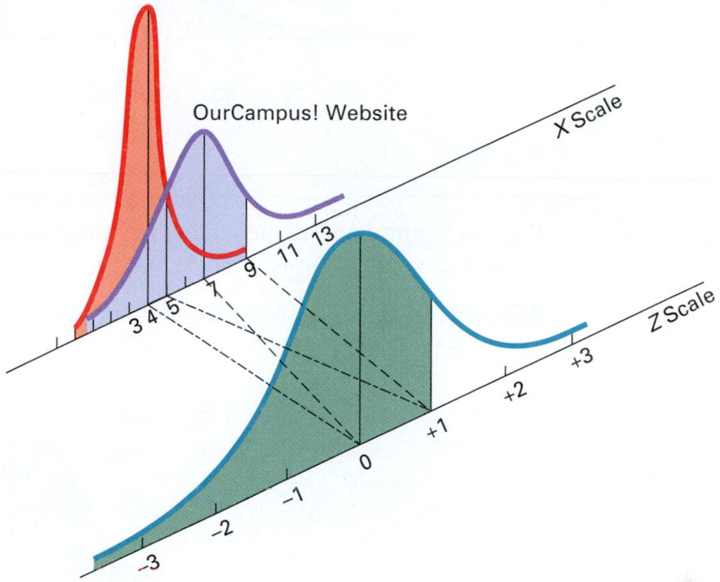

Now that you have learned to use Table E.2 with Equation (6.2), you can answer many questions related to the OurCampus! video download, using the normal distribution.

EXAMPLE 6.1

Finding $P(X > 9)$

What is the probability that the video download time for the OurCampus! website will be more than 9 seconds?

SOLUTION The probability that the download time will be less than 9 seconds is 0.8413 (see Figure 6.6 on page 222). Thus, the probability that the download time will be at least 9 seconds is the *complement* of less than 9 seconds, $1 - 0.8413 = 0.1587$. Figure 6.8 illustrates this result.

FIGURE 6.8

Finding $P(X > 9)$

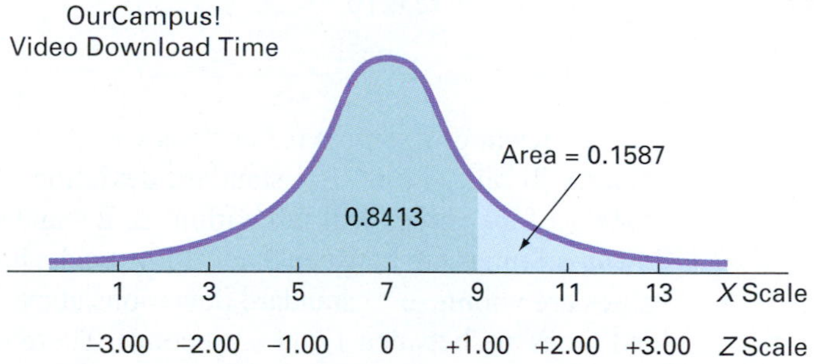

EXAMPLE 6.2

Finding $P(X < 7 \text{ or } X > 9)$

What is the probability that the video download time for the OurCampus! website will be under 7 seconds or over 9 seconds?

SOLUTION To find this probability, you separately calculate the probability of a download time less than 7 seconds and the probability of a download time greater than 9 seconds and then add these two probabilities together. Figure 6.9 on page 224 illustrates this result. Because the mean is 7 seconds, 50% of download times are under 7 seconds. From Example 6.1, you know that the probability that the download time is greater than 9 seconds is 0.1587. Therefore, the probability that a download time is under 7 or over 9 seconds, $P(X < 7 \text{ or } X > 9)$, is $0.5000 + 0.1587 = 0.6587$.

FIGURE 6.9
Finding $P(X < 7 \text{ or } X > 9)$

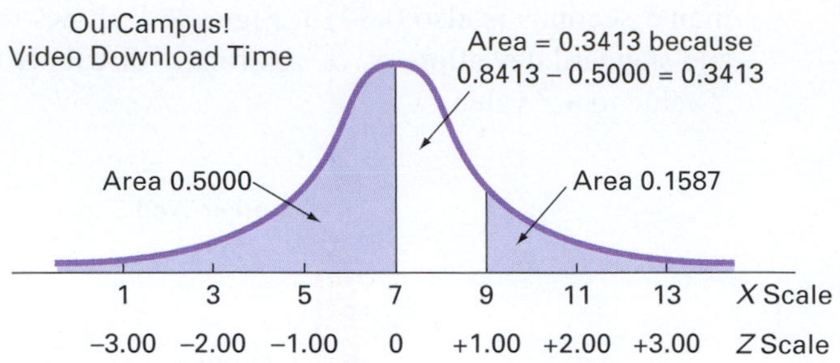

EXAMPLE 6.3

Finding $P(5 < X < 9)$

What is the probability that video download time for the OurCampus! website will be between 5 and 9 seconds—that is, $P(5 < X < 9)$?

SOLUTION In Figure 6.10, you can see that the area of interest is located between two values, 5 and 9.

FIGURE 6.10
Finding $P(5 < X < 9)$

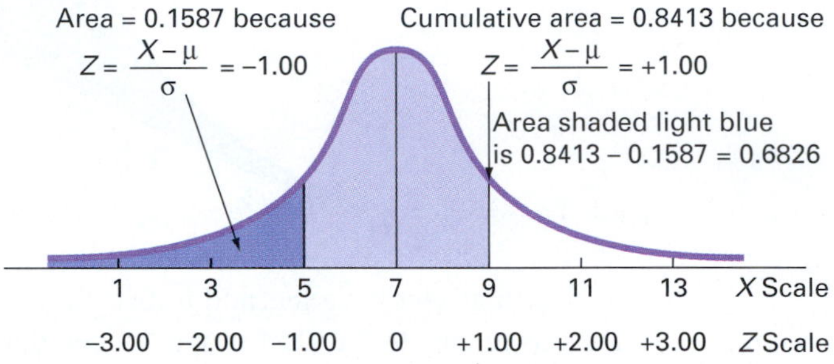

In Example 6.1 on page 223, you already found that the area under the normal curve less than 9 seconds is 0.8413. To find the area under the normal curve less than 5 seconds,

$$Z = \frac{5 - 7}{2} = -1.00$$

Using Table E.2, you look up $Z = -1.00$ and find 0.1587. Therefore, the probability that the download time will be between 5 and 9 seconds is $0.8413 - 0.1587 = 0.6826$, as displayed in Figure 6.10.

The result of Example 6.3 enables you to state that for any normal distribution, 68.26% of the values will fall within $\pm$ 1 standard deviation of the mean. From Figure 6.11, you can see that 95.44% of the values will fall within $\pm$ 2 standard deviations of the mean. Thus, 95.44% of the download times are between 3 and 11 seconds. From Figure 6.12, you can see that 99.73% of the values are within $\pm$ 3 standard deviations above or below the mean. Thus, 99.73% of the download times are between 1 and 13 seconds. Therefore, it is unlikely (0.0027, or only 27 in 10,000) that a download time will be so fast or so slow that it will take under 1 second or more than 13 seconds. In general, you can use 6σ (that is, 3 standard deviations below the mean to 3 standard deviations above the mean) as a practical approximation of the range for normally distributed data.

FIGURE 6.11
Finding $P(3 < X < 11)$

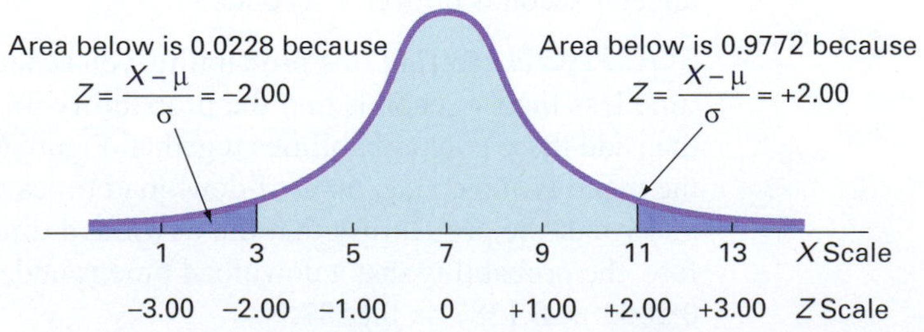

FIGURE 6.12
Finding $P(1 < X < 13)$

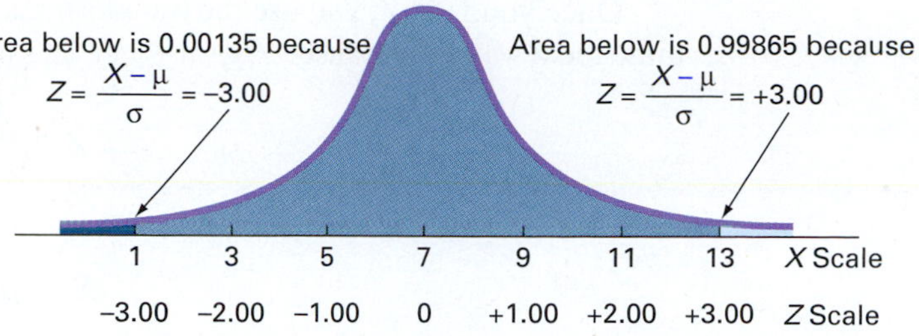

Figures 6.10, 6.11, and 6.12 illustrate that for any normal distribution,

- Approximately 68.26% of the values fall within ± 1 standard deviation of the mean.
- Approximately 95.44% of the values fall within ± 2 standard deviations of the mean
- Approximately 99.73% of the values fall within ± 3 standard deviations of the mean.

This result is the justification for the empirical rule presented on page 122. The accuracy of the empirical rule improves as a data set follows the normal distribution more closely.

Examples 6.1 through 6.3 require you to use the normal distribution Table E.2 to find an area under the normal curve that corresponds to a specific *X* value. There are many circumstances in which you want to find the *X* value that corresponds to a specific area. Examples 6.4 and 6.5 illustrate such situations.

EXAMPLE 6.4

Finding the *X* Value for a Cumulative Probability of 0.10

How much time (in seconds) will elapse before the fastest 10% of the downloads of an OurCampus! video are complete?

SOLUTION Because 10% of the videos are expected to download in under *X* seconds, the area under the normal curve less than this value is 0.1000. Using the body of Table E.2, you search for the area or probability of 0.1000. The closest result is 0.1003, as shown in Table 6.3 (which is extracted from Table E.2).

TABLE 6.3
Finding a *Z* Value Corresponding to a Particular Cumulative Area (0.10) Under the Normal Curve

Cumulative Probabilities

Z	.00	.01	.02	.03	.04	.05	.06	.07	.08	.09
⋮	⋮	⋮	⋮	⋮	⋮	⋮	⋮	⋮	⋮	⋮
−1.5	.0668	.0655	.0643	.0630	.0618	.0606	.0594	.0582	.0571	.0559
−1.4	.0808	.0793	.0778	.0764	.0749	.0735	.0721	.0708	.0694	.0681
−1.3	.0968	.0951	.0934	.0918	.0901	.0885	.0869	.0853	.0838	.0823
−1.2	.1151	.1131	.1112	.1093	.1075	.0156	.0138	.1020	.1003	.0985

Source: Extracted from Table E.2.

Working from this area to the margins of the table, you find that the *Z* value corresponding to the particular *Z* row (−1.2) and *Z* column (.08) is −1.28 (see Figure 6.13).

FIGURE 6.13
Finding *Z* to determine *X*

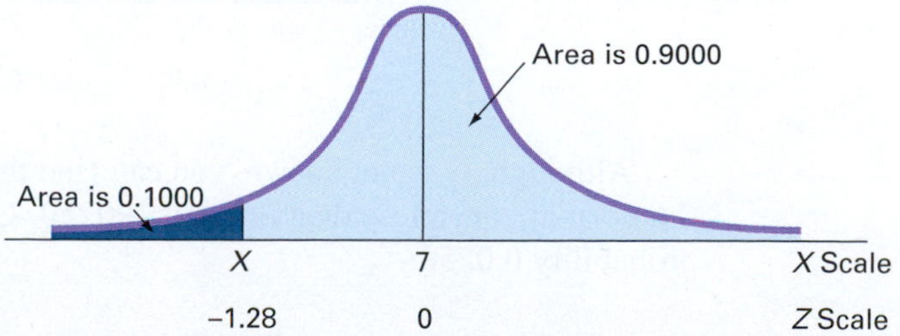

Once you find Z, you use the transformation formula Equation (6.2) on page 220 to determine the X value. Because

$$Z = \frac{X - \mu}{\sigma}$$

then

$$X = \mu + Z\sigma$$

Substituting $\mu = 7, \sigma = 2$, and $Z = -1.28$,

$$X = 7 + (-1.28)(2) = 4.44 \text{ seconds}$$

Thus, 10% of the download times are 4.44 seconds or less.

In general, you use Equation (6.3) for finding an X value.

FINDING AN X VALUE ASSOCIATED WITH A KNOWN PROBABILITY

The X value is equal to the mean, μ, plus the product of the Z value and the standard deviation, σ.

$$X = \mu + Z\sigma \tag{6.3}$$

To find a *particular* value associated with a known probability, follow these steps:

1. Sketch the normal curve and then place the values for the mean and X on the X and Z scales.
2. Find the cumulative area less than X.
3. Shade the area of interest.
4. Using Table E.2, determine the Z value corresponding to the area under the normal curve less than X.
5. Using Equation (6.3), solve for X:

$$X = \mu + Z\sigma$$

EXAMPLE 6.5

Finding the X Values That Include 95% of the Download Times

What are the lower and upper values of X, symmetrically distributed around the mean, that include 95% of the download times for a video at the OurCampus! website?

SOLUTION First, you need to find the lower value of X (called X_L). Then, you find the upper value of X (called X_U). Because 95% of the values are between X_L and X_U, and because X_L and X_U are equally distant from the mean, 2.5% of the values are below X_L (see Figure 6.14).

FIGURE 6.14

Finding Z to determine X_L

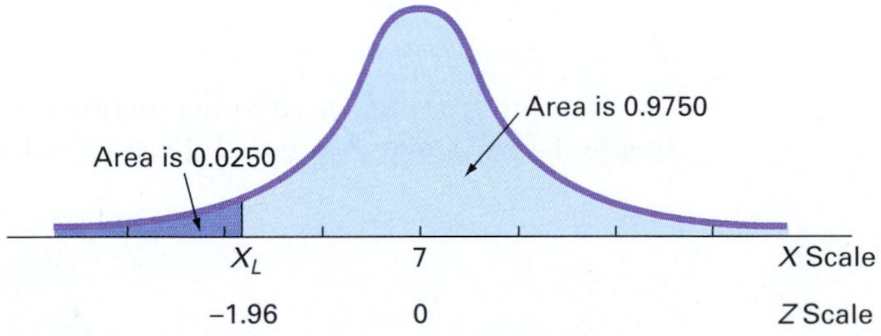

Although X_L is not known, you can find the corresponding Z value because the area under the normal curve less than this Z is 0.0250. Using the body of Table 6.4, you search for the probability 0.0250.

TABLE 6.4

Finding a Z Value Corresponding to a Cumulative Area of 0.025 Under the Normal Curve

Cumulative Area										
Z	**.00**	**.01**	**.02**	**.03**	**.04**	**.05**	**.06**	**.07**	**.08**	**.09**
⋮	⋮	⋮	⋮	⋮	⋮	⋮	↑	⋮	⋮	⋮
−2.0	.0228	.0222	.0217	.0212	.0207	.0202	.0197	.0192	.0188	.0183
−1.9	.0287	.0281	.0274	.0268	.0262	.0256	.0250	.0244	.0239	.0233
−1.8	.0359	.0351	.0344	.0336	.0329	.0232	.0314	.0307	.0301	.0294

Source: Extracted from Table E.2.

Working from the body of the table to the margins of the table, you see that the Z value corresponding to the particular Z row (-1.9) and Z column (.06) is -1.96.

Once you find Z, the final step is to use Equation (6.3) on page 226 as follows:

$$\begin{aligned} X &= \mu + Z\sigma \\ &= 7 + (-1.96)(2) \\ &= 7 - 3.92 \\ &= 3.08 \text{ seconds} \end{aligned}$$

You use a similar process to find X_U. Because only 2.5% of the video downloads take longer than X_U seconds, 97.5% of the video downloads take less than X_U seconds. From the symmetry of the normal distribution, you find that the desired Z value, as shown in Figure 6.15, is $+1.96$ (because Z lies to the right of the standardized mean of 0). You can also extract this Z value from Table 6.5. You can see that 0.975 is the area under the normal curve less than the Z value of $+1.96$.

FIGURE 6.15

Finding Z to determine X_U

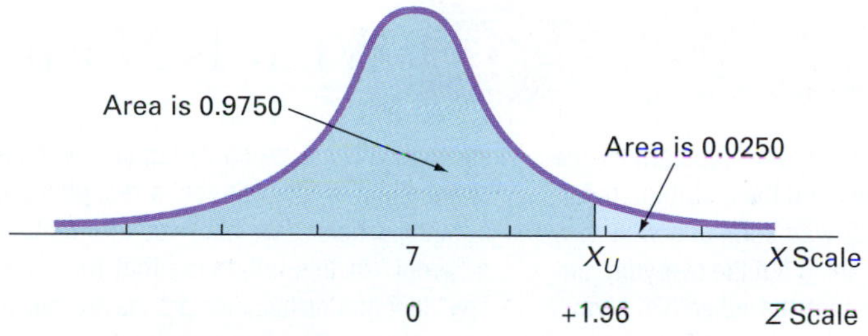

TABLE 6.5

Finding a Z Value Corresponding to a Cumulative Area of 0.975 Under the Normal Curve

Cumulative Area										
Z	**.00**	**.01**	**.02**	**.03**	**.04**	**.05**	**.06**	**.07**	**.08**	**.09**
⋮	⋮	⋮	⋮	⋮	⋮	⋮	↑	⋮	⋮	⋮
+1.8	.9641	.9649	.9656	.9664	.9671	.9678	.9686	.9693	.9699	.9706
+1.9	.9713	.9719	.9726	.9732	.9738	.9744	.9750	.9756	.9761	.9767
+2.0	.9772	.9778	.9783	.9788	.9793	.9798	.9803	.9808	.9812	.9817

Source: Extracted from Table E.2.

Using Equation (6.3) on page 226,

$$\begin{aligned} X &= \mu + Z\sigma \\ &= 7 + (+1.96)(2) \\ &= 7 + 3.92 \\ &= 10.92 \text{ seconds} \end{aligned}$$

Therefore, 95% of the download times are between 3.08 and 10.92 seconds.

Instead of looking up cumulative probabilities in a table, you can use Excel or Minitab to compute normal probabilities. Figure 6.16 is an Excel worksheet that computes normal probabilities for problems similar to Examples 6.1 through 6.4. Figure 6.17 shows Minitab results for Examples 6.1 and 6.4.

FIGURE 6.16
Excel worksheet for computing normal probabilities

	A	B	
1	**Normal Probabilities**		
2			
3	**Common Data**		
4	Mean	7	
5	Standard Deviation	2	
6			
7	**Probability for X <=**		
8	X Value	7	
9	Z Value	0	=STANDARDIZE(B8,B4,B5)
10	P(X<=7)	0.5000	=NORMDIST(B8,B4,B5,TRUE)
11			
12	**Probability for X >**		
13	X Value	9	
14	Z Value	1	=STANDARDIZE(B13,B4,B5)
15	P(X>9)	0.1587	=1-NORMDIST(B13,B4,B5,TRUE)
16			
17	**Probability for X<7 or X >9**		
18	P(X<7 or X >9)	0.6587	=B10+B15

	D	E	
1			
2			
3			
4			
5			
6	**Probability for a Range**		
7	From X Value	5	
8	To X Value	9	
9	Z Value for 5	-1	=STANDARDIZE(E7,B4,B5)
10	Z Value for 9	1	=STANDARDIZE(E8,B4,B5)
11	P(X<=5)	0.1587	=NORMDIST(E7,B4,B5,TRUE)
12	P(X<=9)	0.8413	=NORMDIST(E8,B4,B5,TRUE)
13	P(5<=X<=9)	0.6827	=ABS(E12-E11)
14			
15	**Find X and Z Given Cum. Pctage.**		
16	Cumulative Percentage	10.00%	
17	Z Value	-1.2816	=NORMSINV(E16)
18	X Value	4.4369	=NORMINV(E16,B4,B5)

FIGURE 6.17
Minitab results for Examples 6.1 and 6.4

Cumulative Distribution Function

```
Normal with mean = 7 and standard deviation = 2

x  P( X <= x )
9     0.841345
```

Inverse Cumulative Distribution Function

```
Normal with mean = 7 and standard deviation = 2

P( X <= x )        x
        0.1  4.43690
```

THINK ABOUT THIS What Is Normal?

Ironically, the statistician who popularized the use of "normal" to describe the distribution discussed in Section 6.2 was someone who saw the distribution as anything but the everyday, anticipated occurrence that the adjective *normal* usually suggests.

Starting with an 1894 paper, Karl Pearson argued that measurements of phenomena do not naturally, or "normally," conform to the classic bell shape. While this principle underlies statistics today, Pearson's point of view was radical to contemporaries who saw the world as standardized and normal. Pearson changed minds by showing that some populations are naturally *skewed* (coining that term in passing), and he helped put to rest the notion that the normal distribution underlies all phenomena.

Today, unfortunately, people still make the type of mistake that Pearson refuted. As a student, you are probably familiar with discussions about grade inflation, a real phenomenon at many schools. But, have you ever realized that a "proof" of this inflation—that there are "too few" low grades because grades are skewed toward A's and B's—wrongly implies that grades should be "normally" distributed. By the time you finish reading this book, you may realize that because college students represent small nonrandom samples, there are plenty of reasons to suspect that the distribution of grades would not be "normal."

Misunderstandings about the normal distribution have occurred both in business and in the public sector through the years. These misunderstandings have caused a number of business blunders and have sparked several public policy debates, including the causes of the collapse of large financial institutions in 2008. According to one theory, the investment banking industry's application of the normal distribution to assess risk may have contributed to the global collapse (see "A Finer Formula for Assessing Risks," *The New York Times*, May 11, 2010, p. B2). Using the normal distribution led these banks to overestimate the probability of having stable market conditions and underestimate the chance of unusually large market losses. According to this theory, the use of other distributions that have less area in the middle of their curves, and, therefore, more in the "tails" that represent unusual market outcomes, may have led to less serious losses.

As you study this chapter, make sure you understand the assumptions that must hold for the proper use of the "normal" distribution, assumptions that were not explicitly verified by the investment bankers. And, most importantly, always remember that the name *normal* distribution does not mean to suggest normal in the everyday (dare we say "normal"?!) sense of the word.

VISUAL EXPLORATIONS Exploring the Normal Distribution

Use the Visual Explorations Normal Distribution procedure to see the effects of changes in the mean and standard deviation on the area under a normal distribution curve. Open the **Visual Explorations add-in workbook** (see Appendix Section D.4). Select **Add-ins ➔ VisualExplorations ➔ Normal Distribution.**

The add-in displays a normal curve for the OurCampus! download example and a floating control panel (see illustration at right). Use the control panel spinner buttons to change the values for the mean, standard deviation, and *X* value and note the effects of these changes on the probability of $X <$ value and the corresponding shaded area under the curve (see illustration at right). If you prefer to see the normal curve labeled with *Z* values, click **Z Values.**

Click the **Reset** button to reset the control panel values or click **Help** for additional information about the problem. Click **Finish** when you are done exploring.

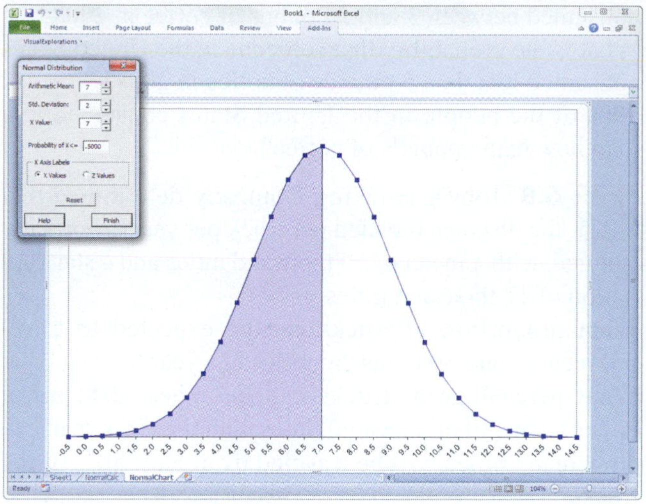

Problems for Section 6.2

LEARNING THE BASICS

6.1 Given a standardized normal distribution (with a mean of 0 and a standard deviation of 1, as in Table E.2), what is the probability that

a. *Z* is less than 1.57?
b. *Z* is greater than 1.84?
c. *Z* is between 1.57 and 1.84?
d. *Z* is less than 1.57 or greater than 1.84?

6.2 Given a standardized normal distribution (with a mean of 0 and a standard deviation of 1, as in Table E.2), what is the probability that

a. *Z* is between -1.57 and 1.84?
b. *Z* is less than -1.57 or greater than 1.84?
c. What is the value of *Z* if only 2.5% of all possible *Z* values are larger?
d. Between what two values of *Z* (symmetrically distributed around the mean) will 68.26% of all possible *Z* values be contained?

6.3 Given a standardized normal distribution (with a mean of 0 and a standard deviation of 1, as in Table E.2), what is the probability that

a. *Z* is less than 1.08?
b. *Z* is greater than -0.21?
c. *Z* is less than -0.21 or greater than the mean?
d. *Z* is less than -0.21 or greater than 1.08?

6.4 Given a standardized normal distribution (with a mean of 0 and a standard deviation of 1, as in Table E.2), determine the following probabilities:

a. $P(Z > 1.08)$
b. $P(Z < -0.21)$
c. $P(-1.96 < Z < -0.21)$
d. What is the value of *Z* if only 15.87% of all possible *Z* values are larger?

6.5 Given a normal distribution with $\mu = 100$ and $\sigma = 10$, what is the probability that

a. $X > 75$?
b. $X < 70$?
c. $X < 80$ or $X > 110$?
d. Between what two *X* values (symmetrically distributed around the mean) are 80% of the values?

6.6 Given a normal distribution with $\mu = 50$ and $\sigma = 4$, what is the probability that

a. $X > 43$?
b. $X < 42$?
c. 5% of the values are less than what *X* value?
d. Between what two *X* values (symmetrically distributed around the mean) are 60% of the values?

APPLYING THE CONCEPTS

6.7 In 2008, the per capita consumption of coffee in the United States was reported to be 4.2 kg, or 9.24 pounds (data extracted from **en.wikipedia.org/wiki/List_of_countries_by_coffee_consumption_per_capita**). Assume that the per capita consumption of coffee in the United States is approximately distributed as a normal random variable, with a mean of 9.24 pounds and a standard deviation of 3 pounds.

a. What is the probability that someone in the United States consumed more than 10 pounds of coffee in 2008?
b. What is the probability that someone in the United States consumed between 3 and 5 pounds of coffee in 2008?
c. What is the probability that someone in the United States consumed less than 5 pounds of coffee in 2008?
d. 99% of the people in the United States consumed less than how many pounds of coffee?

SELF Test **6.8** Toby's Trucking Company determined that the distance traveled per truck per year is normally distributed, with a mean of 50 thousand miles and a standard deviation of 12 thousand miles.
a. What proportion of trucks can be expected to travel between 34 and 50 thousand miles in a year?
b. What percentage of trucks can be expected to travel either below 30 or above 60 thousand miles in a year?
c. How many miles will be traveled by at least 80% of the trucks?
d. What are your answers to (a) through (c) if the standard deviation is 10 thousand miles?

6.9 Consumers spend an average of \$21 per week in cash without being aware of where it goes (data extracted from "Snapshots: A Hole in Our Pockets," *USA Today*, January 18, 2010, p. 1A). Assume that the amount of cash spent without being aware of where it goes is normally distributed and that the standard deviation is \$5.
a. What is the probability that a randomly selected person will spend more than \$25?
b. What is the probability that a randomly selected person will spend between \$10 and \$20?
c. Between what two values will the middle 95% of the amounts of cash spent fall?

6.10 A set of final examination grades in an introductory statistics course is normally distributed, with a mean of 73 and a standard deviation of 8.
a. What is the probability that a student scored below 91 on this exam?
b. What is the probability that a student scored between 65 and 89?
c. The probability is 5% that a student taking the test scores higher than what grade?
d. If the professor grades on a curve (i.e., gives A's to the top 10% of the class, regardless of the score), are you better off with a grade of 81 on this exam or a grade of 68 on a different exam, where the mean is 62 and the standard deviation is 3? Show your answer statistically and explain.

6.11 A statistical analysis of 1,000 long-distance telephone calls made from the headquarters of the Bricks and Clicks Computer Corporation indicates that the length of these calls is normally distributed, with $\mu = 240$ seconds and $\sigma = 40$ seconds.
a. What is the probability that a call lasted less than 180 seconds?
b. What is the probability that a call lasted between 180 and 300 seconds?
c. What is the probability that a call lasted between 110 and 180 seconds?
d. 1% of all calls will last less than how many seconds?

6.12 In 2008, the per capita consumption of coffee in Sweden was reported to be 8.2 kg, or 18.04 pounds (data extracted from **en.wikipedia.org/wiki/List_of_countries_by_coffee_consumption_per_capita**). Assume that the per capita consumption of coffee in Sweden is approximately distributed as a normal random variable, with a mean of 18.04 pounds and a standard deviation of 5 pounds.
a. What is the probability that someone in Sweden consumed more than 10 pounds of coffee in 2008?
b. What is the probability that someone in Sweden consumed between 3 and 5 pounds of coffee in 2008?
c. What is the probability that someone in Sweden consumed less than 5 pounds of coffee in 2008?
d. 99% of the people in Sweden consumed less than how many pounds of coffee?

6.13 Many manufacturing problems involve the matching of machine parts, such as shafts that fit into a valve hole. A particular design requires a shaft with a diameter of 22.000 mm, but shafts with diameters between 21.990 mm and 22.010 mm are acceptable. Suppose that the manufacturing process yields shafts with diameters normally distributed, with a mean of 22.002 mm and a standard deviation of 0.005 mm. For this process, what is
a. the proportion of shafts with a diameter between 21.99 mm and 22.00 mm?
b. the probability that a shaft is acceptable?
c. the diameter that will be exceeded by only 2% of the shafts?
d. What would be your answers in (a) through (c) if the standard deviation of the shaft diameters were 0.004 mm?

6.3 Evaluating Normality

As discussed in Section 6.2, many continuous variables used in business closely follow a normal distribution. To determine whether a set of data can be approximated by the normal distribution, you either compare the characteristics of the data with the theoretical properties of the normal distribution or construct a normal probability plot.

Comparing Data Characteristics to Theoretical Properties

The normal distribution has several important theoretical properties:

- It is symmetrical; thus, the mean and median are equal.
- It is bell-shaped; thus, the empirical rule applies.
- The interquartile range equals 1.33 standard deviations.
- The range is approximately equal to 6 standard deviations.

Many continuous variables have characteristics that approximate these theoretical properties. However, other continuous variables are often neither normally distributed nor approximately normally distributed. For such variables, the descriptive characteristics of the data are inconsistent with the properties of a normal distribution. One approach that you can use to determine whether a variable follows a normal distribution is to compare the observed characteristics of the variable with what would be expected if the variable followed a normal distribution. To do so, you can

- Construct charts and observe their appearance. For small- or moderate-sized data sets, create a stem-and-leaf display or a boxplot. For large data sets, in addition, plot a histogram or polygon.
- Compute descriptive statistics and compare these statistics with the theoretical properties of the normal distribution. Compare the mean and median. Is the interquartile range approximately 1.33 times the standard deviation? Is the range approximately 6 times the standard deviation?
- Evaluate how the values are distributed. Determine whether approximately two-thirds of the values lie between the mean and ± 1 standard deviation. Determine whether approximately four-fifths of the values lie between the mean and ± 1.28 standard deviations. Determine whether approximately 19 out of every 20 values lie between the mean and ± 2 standard deviations.

For example, you can use these techniques to determine whether the returns in 2009 discussed in Chapters 2 and 3 (stored in **Bond Funds**) follow a normal distribution. Figures 6.18 and 6.19 display relevant Excel results for these data, and Figure 6.20 displays a Minitab boxplot for the same data.

FIGURE 6.18
Descriptive statistics for the 2009 returns

Return 2009	
Mean	7.1641
Standard Error	0.4490
Median	6.4000
Mode	6.0000
Standard Deviation	6.0908
Sample Variance	37.0984
Kurtosis	2.4560
Skewness	0.9085
Range	40.8000
Minimum	-8.8000
Maximum	32.0000
Sum	1318.2000
Count	184

FIGURE 6.19
Five-number summary and boxplot for the 2009 returns

Five-Number Summary	
Minimum	-8.8
First Quartile	3.4
Median	6.4
Third Quartile	10.8
Maximum	32

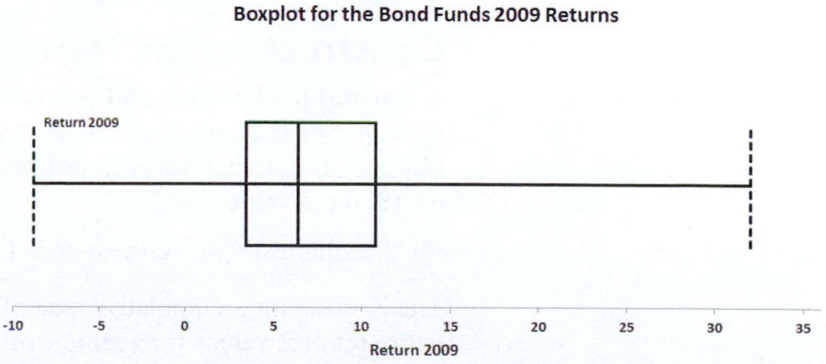

FIGURE 6.20
Minitab boxplot

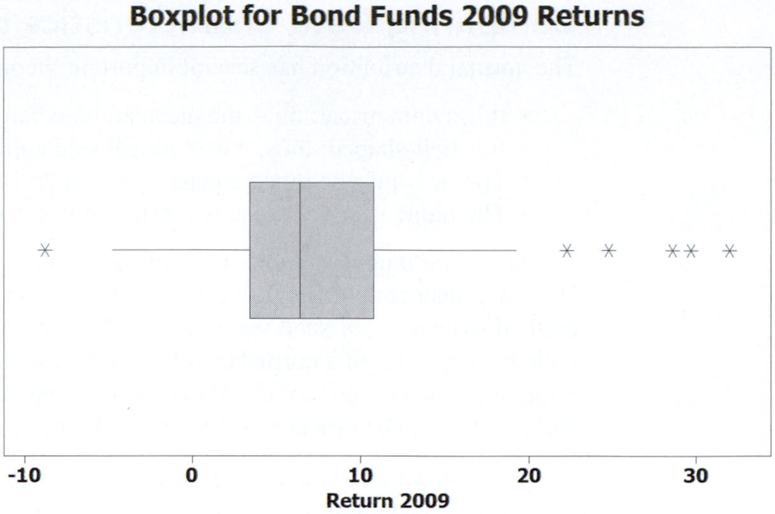

From Figures 6.18 through 6.20, and from an ordered array of the returns (not shown here), you can make the following statements:

- The mean of 7.1641 is greater than the median of 6.4. (In a normal distribution, the mean and median are equal.)
- The boxplot is very right-skewed, with a long tail on the right. (The normal distribution is symmetrical.)
- The interquartile range of 7.4 is approximately 1.21 standard deviations. (In a normal distribution, the interquartile range is 1.33 standard deviations.)
- The range of 40.8 is equal to 6.70 standard deviations. (In a normal distribution, the range is approximately 6 standard deviations.)
- 73.91% of the returns are within ± 1 standard deviation of the mean. (In a normal distribution, 68.26% of the values lie within ± 1 standard deviation of the mean.)
- 85.33% of the returns are within ± 1.28 standard deviations of the mean. (In a normal distribution, 80% of the values lie within ± 1.28 standard deviations of the mean.)
- 96.20% of the returns are within ± 2 standard deviations of the mean. (In a normal distribution, 95.44% of the values lie within ± 2 standard deviations of the mean.)
- The skewness statistic is 0.9085 and the kurtosis statistic is 2.456. (In a normal distribution, each of these statistics equals zero.)

Based on these statements and the criteria given on page 231, you can conclude that the 2009 returns are highly right-skewed and have somewhat more values within ± 1 standard deviation of the mean than expected. The range is higher than what would be expected in a normal distribution, but this is mostly due to the single outlier at 32. Primarily because of the skewness, you can conclude that the data characteristics of the 2009 returns differ from the theoretical properties of a normal distribution.

Constructing the Normal Probability Plot

A **normal probability plot** is a visual display that helps you evaluate whether the data are normally distributed. One common plot is called the **quantile–quantile plot**. To create this plot, you first transform each ordered value to a Z value. For example, if you have a sample of $n = 19$, the Z value

for the smallest value corresponds to a cumulative area of $\dfrac{1}{n+1} = \dfrac{1}{19+1} = \dfrac{1}{20} = 0.05$.

The Z value for a cumulative area of 0.05 (from Table E.2) is -1.65. Table 6.6 illustrates the entire set of Z values for a sample of $n = 19$.

TABLE 6.6
Ordered Values and Corresponding Z Values for a Sample of $n = 19$

Ordered Value	Z Value	Ordered Value	Z Value
1	−1.65	11	0.13
2	−1.28	12	0.25
3	−1.04	13	0.39
4	−0.84	14	0.52
5	−0.67	15	0.67
6	−0.52	16	0.84
7	−0.39	17	1.04
8	−0.25	18	1.28
9	−0.13	19	1.65
10	−0.00		

In a quantile–quantile plot, the Z values are plotted on the X axis, and the corresponding values of the variable are plotted on the Y axis. If the data are normally distributed, the values will plot along an approximately straight line.

Figure 6.21 illustrates the typical shape of the quantile–quantile normal probability plot for a left-skewed distribution (Panel A), a normal distribution (Panel B), and a right-skewed distribution (Panel C). If the data are left-skewed, the curve will rise more rapidly at first and then level off. If the data are normally distributed, the points will plot along an approximately straight line. If the data are right-skewed, the data will rise more slowly at first and then rise at a faster rate for higher values of the variable being plotted.

FIGURE 6.21
Normal probability plots for a left-skewed distribution, a normal distribution, and a right-skewed distribution

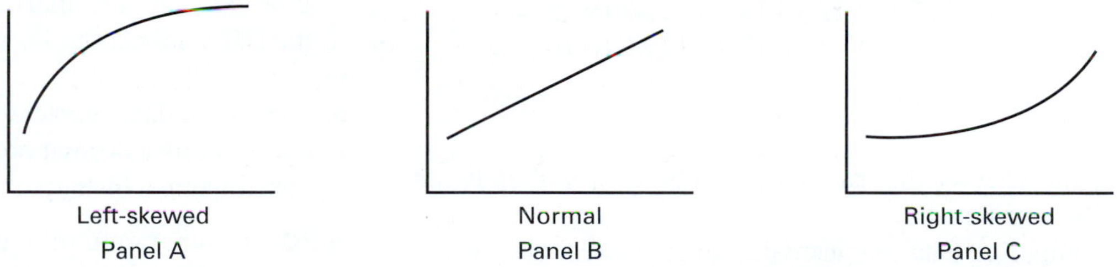

Figure 6.22 shows a normal probability plot for the 2009 returns as created using Excel (left results, a quantile–quantile plot) and Minitab (right results). The Excel quantile–quantile

FIGURE 6.22
Excel (quantile–quantile) and Minitab normal probability plots for 2009 returns

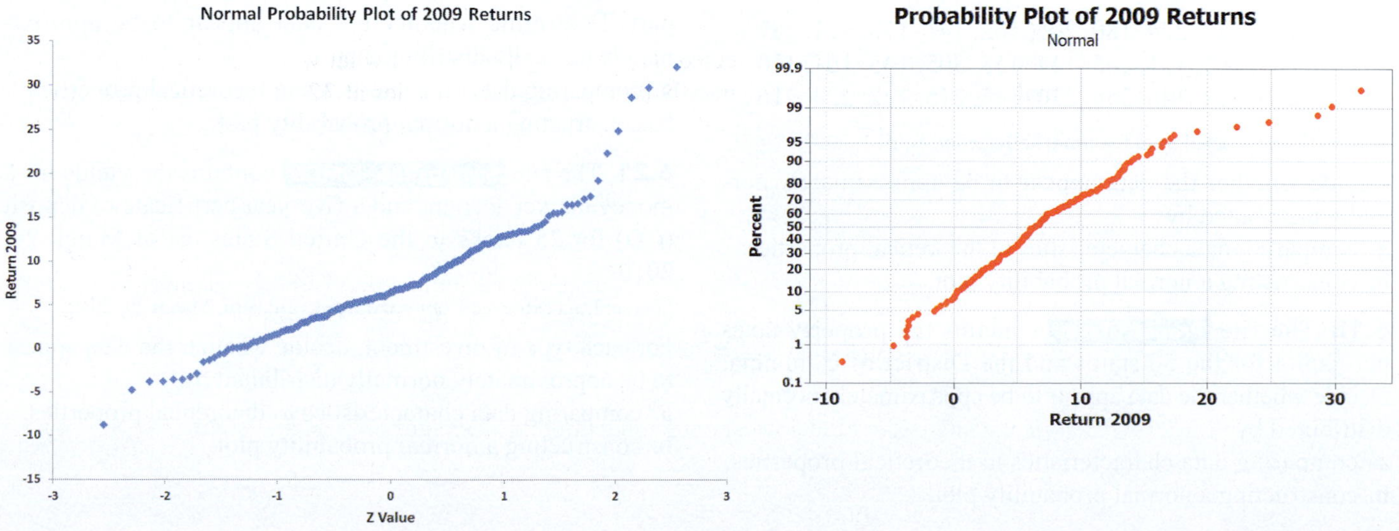

plot shows that the 2009 returns rise slowly at first and then rise more rapidly. Therefore, you can conclude that the 2009 returns are right-skewed.

The Minitab normal probability plot has the Return 2009 variable on the X axis and the cumulative percentage for a normal distribution on the Y axis. As is the case with the quantile–quantile plot, if the data are normally distributed, the points will plot along an approximately straight line. However, if the data are right-skewed, the curve will rise more rapidly at first and then level off. If the data are left-skewed, the data will rise more slowly at first and then rise at a faster rate for higher values of the variable being plotted. Observe that the values rise more rapidly at first and then level off, indicating a right-skewed distribution.

Problems for Section 6.3

LEARNING THE BASICS

6.14 Show that for a sample of $n = 39$, the smallest and largest Z values are -1.96 and $+1.96$, and the middle (i.e., 20th) Z value is 0.00.

6.15 For a sample of $n = 6$, list the six Z values.

APPLYING THE CONCEPTS

SELF Test **6.16** The file **SUV** contains the overall miles per gallon (MPG) of 2010 small SUVs ($n-26$):

24 23 22 21 22 22 18 18 26 26 26 19 19
19 21 21 21 21 21 18 19 21 22 22 16 16

Source: Data extracted from "Vehicle Ratings," *Consumer Reports*, April 2010, pp. 33–34.

Decide whether the data appear to be approximately normally distributed by

a. comparing data characteristics to theoretical properties.
b. constructing a normal probability plot.

6.17 As player salaries have increased, the cost of attending baseball games has increased dramatically. The file **BBCost** contains the cost of four tickets, two beers, four soft drinks, four hot dogs, two game programs, two baseball caps, and the parking fee for one car for each of the 30 Major League Baseball teams in 2009:

164, 326, 224, 180, 205, 162, 141, 170, 411, 187
185, 165, 151, 166, 114, 158, 305, 145, 161, 170
210, 222, 146, 259, 220, 135, 215, 172, 223, 216

Source: Data extracted from **teammarketing.com**, April 1, 2009.

Decide whether the data appear to be approximately normally distributed by

a. comparing data characteristics to theoretical properties.
b. constructing a normal probability plot.

6.18 The file **PropertyTaxes** contains the property taxes per capita for the 50 states and the District of Columbia. Decide whether the data appear to be approximately normally distributed by

a. comparing data characteristics to theoretical properties.
b. constructing a normal probability plot.

6.19 Thirty companies comprise the DJIA. Just how big are these companies? One common method for measuring the size of a company is to use its market capitalization, which is computed by multiplying the number of stock shares by the price of a share of stock. On March 29, 2010, the market capitalization of these companies ranged from Alcoa's \$14.7 billion to ExxonMobil's \$318.8 billion. The entire population of market capitalization values is stored in **DowMarketCap**.

Source: Data extracted from **money.cnn.com**, March 29, 2010.

Decide whether the market capitalization of companies in the DJIA appears to be approximately normally distributed by

a. comparing data characteristics to theoretical properties.
b. constructing a normal probability plot.
c. constructing a histogram.

6.20 One operation of a mill is to cut pieces of steel into parts that will later be used as the frame for front seats in an automotive plant. The steel is cut with a diamond saw, and the resulting parts must be within ± 0.005 inch of the length specified by the automobile company. The data come from a sample of 100 steel parts and are stored in **Steel**. The measurement reported is the difference, in inches, between the actual length of the steel part, as measured by a laser measurement device, and the specified length of the steel part. Determine whether the data appear to be approximately normally distributed by

a. comparing data characteristics to theoretical properties.
b. constructing a normal probability plot.

6.21 The file **SavingsRate-MMCD** contains the yields for a money market account and a five-year certificate of deposit (CD) for 25 banks in the United States, as of March 29, 2010.

Source: Data extracted from **www.Bankrate.com**, March 29, 2010.

For each type of investment, decide whether the data appear to be approximately normally distributed by

a. comparing data characteristics to theoretical properties.
b. constructing a normal probability plot.

6.22 The file **Utility** contains the electricity costs, in dollars, during July 2010 for a random sample of 50 one-bedroom apartments in a large city:

96	171	202	178	147	102	153	197	127	82
157	185	90	116	172	111	148	213	130	165
141	149	206	175	123	128	144	168	109	167
95	163	150	154	130	143	187	166	139	149
108	119	183	151	114	135	191	137	129	158

Decide whether the data appear to be approximately normally distributed by

a. comparing data characteristics to theoretical properties.
b. constructing a normal probability plot.

6.4 The Uniform Distribution

In the **uniform distribution**, a value has the same probability of occurrence anywhere in the range between the smallest value, a, and the largest value, b. Because of its shape, the uniform distribution is sometimes called the **rectangular distribution** (see Panel B of Figure 6.1 on page 218). Equation (6.4) defines the probability density function for the uniform distribution.

UNIFORM PROBABILITY DENSITY FUNCTION

$$f(X) = \frac{1}{b - a} \text{ if } a \le X \le b \text{ and 0 elsewhere} \quad \textbf{(6.4)}$$

where

a = minimum value of X

b = maximum value of X

Equation (6.5) defines the mean of the uniform distribution.

MEAN OF THE UNIFORM DISTRIBUTION

$$\mu = \frac{a + b}{2} \quad \textbf{(6.5)}$$

Equation (6.6) defines the variance and standard deviation of the uniform distribution.

VARIANCE AND STANDARD DEVIATION OF THE UNIFORM DISTRIBUTION

$$\sigma^2 = \frac{(b - a)^2}{12} \quad \textbf{(6.6a)}$$

$$\sigma = \sqrt{\frac{(b - a)^2}{12}} \quad \textbf{(6.6b)}$$

One of the most common uses of the uniform distribution is in the selection of random numbers. When you use simple random sampling (see Section 7.1), you assume that each random number comes from a uniform distribution that has a minimum value of 0 and a maximum value of 1.

Figure 6.23 illustrates the uniform distribution with $a = 0$ and $b = 1$. The total area inside the rectangle is equal to the base (1.0) times the height (1.0). Thus, the resulting area of 1.0 satisfies the requirement that the area under any probability density function equals 1.0.

FIGURE 6.23

Probability density function for a uniform distribution with $a = 0$ and $b = 1$

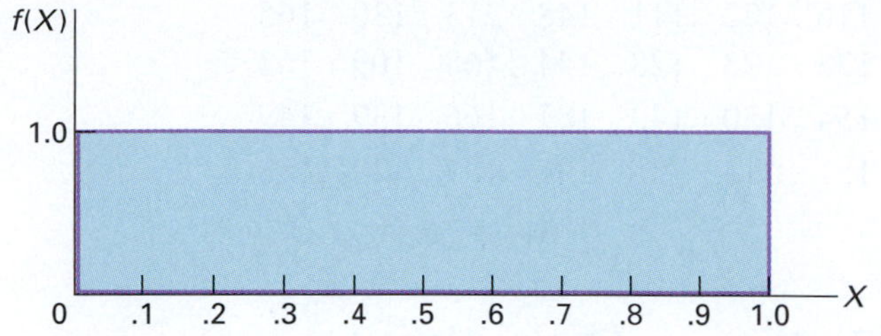

In this uniform distribution, what is the probability of getting a random number between 0.10 and 0.30? The area between 0.10 and 0.30, depicted in Figure 6.24, is equal to the base (which is $0.30 - 0.10 = 0.20$) times the height (1.0). Therefore,

$$P(0.10 < X < 0.30) = (\text{Base})(\text{Height}) = (0.20)(1.0) = 0.20$$

FIGURE 6.24

Finding $P(0.10 < X < 0.30)$ for a uniform distribution with $a = 0$ and $b = 1$

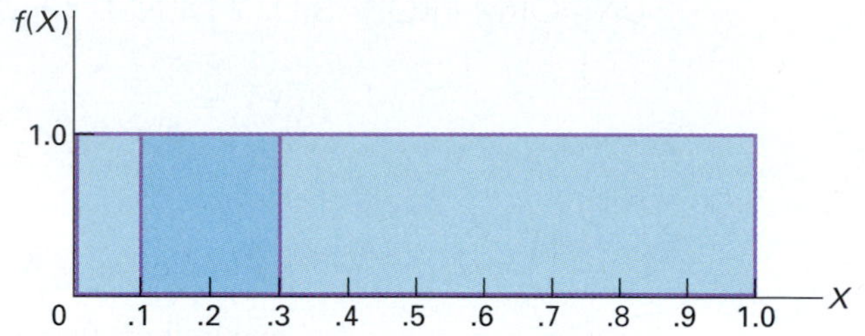

From Equations (6.5) and (6.6), the mean and standard deviation of the uniform distribution for $a = 0$ and $b = 1$ are computed as follows:

$$\mu = \frac{a + b}{2}$$

$$= \frac{0 + 1}{2} = 0.5$$

and

$$\sigma^2 = \frac{(b - a)^2}{12}$$

$$= \frac{(1 - 0)^2}{12}$$

$$= \frac{1}{12} = 0.0833$$

$$\sigma = \sqrt{0.0833} = 0.2887$$

Thus, the mean is 0.5, and the standard deviation is 0.2887.

Example 6.6 provides another application of the uniform distribution.

EXAMPLE 6.6

Computing Uniform Probabilities

In the Using Statistics scenario on page 217, the download time of videos was assumed to be normally distributed with a mean of 7 seconds. Suppose that the download time follows a uniform (instead of a normal) distribution between 4.5 and 9.5 seconds. What is the probability that a download time will take more than 9 seconds?

SOLUTION The download time is uniformly distributed from 4.5 to 9.5 seconds. The area between 9 and 9.5 seconds is equal to 0.5 seconds, and the total area in the distribution is 9.5 – 4.5 = 5 seconds. Therefore, the probability of a download time between 9 and 9.5 seconds is the portion of the area greater than 9, which is equal to 0.5/5.0 = 0.10. Because 9.5 is the maximum value in this distribution, the probability of a download time above 9 seconds is 0.10. In comparison, if the download time is normally distributed with a mean of 7 seconds and a standard deviation of 2 seconds (see Example 6.1 on page 223), the probability of a download time above 9 seconds is 0.1587.

Problems for Section 6.4

LEARNING THE BASICS

6.23 Suppose you select one value from a uniform distribution with $a = 0$ and $b = 10$. What is the probability that the value will be

a. between 5 and 7?
b. between 2 and 3?
c. What is the mean?
d. What is the standard deviation?

APPLYING THE CONCEPTS

SELF Test **6.24** The time between arrivals of customers at a bank during the noon-to-1 P.M. hour has a uniform distribution between 0 to 120 seconds. What is the probability that the time between the arrival of two customers will be

a. less than 20 seconds?
b. between 10 and 30 seconds?
c. more than 35 seconds?
d. What are the mean and standard deviation of the time between arrivals?

6.25 A study of the time spent shopping in a supermarket for a market basket of 20 specific items showed an approximately uniform distribution between 20 minutes and 40 minutes. What is the probability that the shopping time will be

a. between 25 and 30 minutes?
b. less than 35 minutes?
c. What are the mean and standard deviation of the shopping time?

6.26 How long does it take you to download a game for your iPod? According to Apple's technical support site, **www.apple.com/support/itunes**, downloading an iPod game using a broadband connection should take 3 to 6 minutes. Assume that the download times are uniformly distributed between 3 and 6 minutes. If you download a game, what is the probability that the download time will be

a. less than 3.3 minutes?
b. less than 4 minutes?
c. between 4 and 5 minutes?
d. What are the mean and standard deviation of the download times?

6.27 The scheduled commuting time on the Long Island Railroad from Glen Cove to New York City is 65 minutes. Suppose that the actual commuting time is uniformly distributed between 64 and 74 minutes. What is the probability that the commuting time will be

a. less than 70 minutes?
b. between 65 and 70 minutes?
c. greater than 65 minutes?
d. What are the mean and standard deviation of the commuting time?

6.5 The Exponential Distribution

The **exponential distribution** is a continuous distribution that is right-skewed and ranges from zero to positive infinity (see Panel C of Figure 6.1 on page 218). The exponential distribution is widely used in waiting-line (i.e., queuing) theory to model the length of time between arrivals in processes such as customers arriving at a bank's ATM, patients entering a hospital emergency room, and hits on a website.

The exponential distribution is defined by a single parameter, λ, the mean number of arrivals per unit of time. The probability density function for the length of time between arrivals is given by Equation (6.7).

EXPONENTIAL PROBABILITY DENSITY FUNCTION

$$f(X) = \lambda e^{-\lambda x} \text{ for } X > 0 \quad \textbf{(6.7)}$$

where

e = mathematical constant approximated by 2.71828

λ = mean number of arrivals per unit

X = any value of the continuous variable where $0 < X < \infty$

The mean time between arrivals, μ, is given by Equation (6.8).

MEAN TIME BETWEEN ARRIVALS

$$\mu = \frac{1}{\lambda} \quad \textbf{(6.8)}$$

The standard deviation of the time between arrivals, σ, is given by Equation (6.9).

STANDARD DEVIATION OF THE TIME BETWEEN ARRIVALS

$$\sigma = \frac{1}{\lambda} \quad \textbf{(6.9)}$$

The value $1/\lambda$ is equal to the mean time between arrivals. For example, if the mean number of arrivals in a minute is $\lambda = 4$, then the mean time between arrivals is $1/\lambda = 0.25$ minutes, or 15 seconds. Equation (6.10) defines the cumulative probability that the length of time before the next arrival is less than or equal to X.

CUMULATIVE EXPONENTIAL PROBABILITY

$$P(\text{arrival time} \leq X) = 1 - e^{-\lambda x} \quad \textbf{(6.10)}$$

To illustrate the exponential distribution, suppose that customers arrive at a bank's ATM at a rate of 20 per hour. If a customer has just arrived, what is the probability that the next customer will arrive within 6 minutes (i.e., 0.1 hour)? For this example, $\lambda = 20$ and $X = 0.1$. Using Equation (6.10),

$$\begin{aligned} P(\text{Arrival time} \leq 0.1) &= 1 - e^{-20(0.1)} \\ &= 1 - e^{-2} \\ &= 1 - 0.1353 = 0.8647 \end{aligned}$$

Thus, the probability that a customer will arrive within 6 minutes is 0.8647, or 86.47%. Figure 6.25 shows this probability as computed by Excel (left results) and Minitab (right results).

FIGURE 6.25

Excel and Minitab results for finding exponential probabilities (mean = $1/\lambda$)

	A	B	
1	Exponential Probability		
2			
3	Data		
4	Mean	20	
5	X Value	0.1	
6			
7	Results		
8	P(<=X)	0.8647	=EXPONDIST(B5,B4,TRUE)

Cumulative Distribution Function

```
Exponential with mean = 0.05

  x    P( X <= x )
0.1       0.864665
```

EXAMPLE 6.6

Computing Exponential Probabilities

In the ATM example, what is the probability that the next customer will arrive within 3 minutes (i.e., 0.05 hour)?

SOLUTION For this example, $\lambda = 20$ and $X = 0.05$. Using Equation (6.10),

$$\begin{aligned} P(\text{Arrival time} \leq 0.05) &= 1 - e^{-20(0.05)} \\ &= 1 - e^{-1} \\ &= 1 - 0.3679 = 0.6321 \end{aligned}$$

Thus, the probability that a customer will arrive within 3 minutes is 0.6321, or 63.21%.

Problems for Section 6.5

LEARNING THE BASICS

6.28 Given an exponential distribution with $\lambda = 10$, what is the probability that the arrival time is

a. less than $X = 0.1$?
b. greater than $X = 0.1$?
c. between $X = 0.1$ and $X = 0.2$?
d. less than $X = 0.1$ or greater than $X = 0.2$?

6.29 Given an exponential distribution with $\lambda = 30$, what is the probability that the arrival time is

a. less than $X = 0.1$?
b. greater than $X = 0.1$?
c. between $X = 0.1$ and $X = 0.2$?
d. less than $X = 0.1$ or greater than $X = 0.2$?

6.30 Given an exponential distribution with $\lambda = 5$, what is the probability that the arrival time is

a. less than $X = 0.3$?
b. greater than $X = 0.3$?
c. between $X = 0.3$ and $X = 0.5$?
d. less than $X = 0.3$ or greater than $X = 0.5$?

APPLYING THE CONCEPTS

6.31 Autos arrive at a toll plaza located at the entrance to a bridge at a rate of 50 per minute during the 5:00-to-6:00 P.M. hour. If an auto has just arrived,

a. what is the probability that the next auto will arrive within 3 seconds (0.05 minute)?
b. what is the probability that the next auto will arrive within 1 second (0.0167 minute)?
c. What are your answers to (a) and (b) if the rate of arrival of autos is 60 per minute?
d. What are your answers to (a) and (b) if the rate of arrival of autos is 30 per minute?

SELF Test **6.32** Customers arrive at the drive-up window of a fast-food restaurant at a rate of 2 per minute during the lunch hour.

a. What is the probability that the next customer will arrive within 1 minute?
b. What is the probability that the next customer will arrive within 5 minutes?
c. During the dinner time period, the arrival rate is 1 per minute. What are your answers to (a) and (b) for this period?

6.33 Telephone calls arrive at the information desk of a large computer software company at a rate of 15 per hour.

a. What is the probability that the next call will arrive within 3 minutes (0.05 hour)?
b. What is the probability that the next call will arrive within 15 minutes (0.25 hour)?
c. Suppose the company has just introduced an updated version of one of its software programs, and telephone calls are now arriving at a rate of 25 per hour. Given this information, what are your answers to (a) and (b)?

6.34 An on-the-job injury occurs once every 10 days on average at an automobile plant. What is the probability that the next on-the-job injury will occur within

a. 10 days?
b. 5 days?
c. 1 day?

6.35 The time between unplanned shutdowns of a power plant has an exponential distribution with a mean of 20 days. Find the probability that the time between two unplanned shutdowns is

a. less than 14 days.
b. more than 21 days.
c. less than 7 days.

6.36 Golfers arrive at the starter's booth of a public golf course at a rate of 8 per hour during the Monday-to-Friday midweek period. If a golfer has just arrived,

a. what is the probability that the next golfer will arrive within 15 minutes (0.25 hour)?
b. what is the probability that the next golfer will arrive within 3 minutes (0.05 hour)?
c. The actual arrival rate on Fridays is 15 per hour. What are your answers to (a) and (b) for Fridays?

6.37 Some Internet companies sell a service that will boost a website's traffic by delivering additional unique visitors. Assume that one such company claims it can deliver 1,000 visitors a day. If this amount of website traffic is experienced, then the time between visitors has a mean of 1.44 minutes (or 0.6944 per minute). Assume that your website gets 1,000 visitors a day and that the time between visitors has an exponential distribution. What is the probability that the time between two visitors is

a. less than 1 minute?
b. less than 2 minutes?
c. more than 3 minutes?
d. Do you think it is reasonable to assume that the time between visitors has an exponential distribution?

6.6 *Online Topic:* The Normal Approximation to the Binomial Distribution

In many circumstances, you can use the normal distribution to approximate the binomial distribution. To study this topic, read the Section 6.6 online topic file that is available on this book's companion website. (See Appendix C to learn how to access the online topic files.)

USING STATISTICS @ OurCampus! Revisited

In the OurCampus! scenario, you were a designer for a social networking website. You sought to ensure that a video could be downloaded quickly for playback in the web browsers of site visitors. (Quick playback of videos would help attract and retain those visitors.) By running experiments in the corporate offices, you determined that the amount of time, in seconds, that passes from first linking to the website until a video is fully displayed is a bell-shaped distribution with a mean download time of 7 seconds and standard deviation of 2 seconds. Using the normal distribution, you were able to calculate that approximately 84% of the download times are 9 seconds or less, and 95% of the download times are between 3.08 and 10.92 seconds.

Now that you understand how to calculate probabilities from the normal distribution, you can evaluate download times of a video using different web page designs. For example, if the standard deviation remained at 2 seconds, lowering the mean to 6 seconds would shift the entire distribution lower by 1 second. Thus, approximately 84% of the download times would be 8 seconds or less, and 95% of the download times would be between 2.08 and 9.92 seconds. Another change that could reduce long download times would be reducing the variation. For example, consider the case where the mean remained at the original 7 seconds but the standard deviation was reduced to 1 second. Again, approximately 84% of the download times would be 8 seconds or less, and 95% of the download times would be between 5.04 and 8.96 seconds.

SUMMARY

In this and the previous chapter, you have learned about mathematical models called probability distributions and how they can be used to solve business problems. In Chapter 5, you used discrete probability distributions in situations where the outcomes come from a counting process (e.g., the number of courses you are enrolled in, the number of tagged order forms in a report generated by an accounting information system). In this chapter, you learned about continuous probability distributions where the outcomes come from a measuring process (e.g., your height, the download time of a video). Continuous probability distributions come in various shapes, but the most common and most important in business is the normal distribution. The normal distribution is symmetrical; thus, its mean and median are equal. It is also bell-shaped, and approximately 68.26% of its observations are within 1 standard deviation of the mean, approximately 95.44% of its observations are within 2 standard deviations of the mean, and approximately 99.73% of its observations are within 3 standard deviations of the mean. Although many data sets in business are closely approximated by the normal distribution, do not think that all data can be approximated using the normal distribution. In Section 6.3, you learned about various methods for evaluating normality in order to determine whether the normal distribution is a reasonable mathematical model to use in specific situations. In Sections 6.4 and 6.5, you studied continuous distributions that were not normally distributed—in particular, the uniform and exponential distributions.

Chapter 7 uses the normal distribution to develop the subject of statistical inference.

KEY EQUATIONS

Normal Probability Density Function

$$f(X) = \frac{1}{\sqrt{2\pi}\sigma} e^{-(1/2)[(X-\mu)/\sigma]^2} \quad \textbf{(6.1)}$$

Transformation Formula

$$Z = \frac{X - \mu}{\sigma} \quad \textbf{(6.2)}$$

Finding an *X* Value Associated with a Known Probability

$$X = \mu + Z\sigma \quad \textbf{(6.3)}$$

Uniform Probability Density Function

$$f(X) = \frac{1}{b - a} \quad \textbf{(6.4)}$$

Mean of the Uniform Distribution

$$\mu = \frac{a + b}{2} \quad \textbf{(6.5)}$$

Variance and Standard Deviation of the Uniform Distribution

$$\sigma^2 = \frac{(b - a)^2}{12} \quad \textbf{(6.6a)}$$

$$\sigma = \sqrt{\frac{(b - a)^2}{12}} \quad \textbf{(6.6b)}$$

Exponential Probability Density Function

$$f(X) = \lambda e^{-\lambda x} \text{ for } X > 0 \quad \textbf{(6.7)}$$

Mean Time Between Arrivals

$$\mu = \frac{1}{\lambda} \quad \textbf{(6.8)}$$

Standard Deviation of the Time Between Arrivals

$$\sigma = \frac{1}{\lambda} \quad \textbf{(6.9)}$$

Cumulative Exponential Probability

$$P(\text{arrival time} \leq X) = 1 - e^{-\lambda x} \quad \textbf{(6.10)}$$

KEY TERMS

CHAPTER REVIEW PROBLEMS

CHECKING YOUR UNDERSTANDING

6.38 Why is only one normal distribution table such as Table E.2 needed to find any probability under the normal curve?

6.39 How do you find the area between two values under the normal curve?

6.40 How do you find the X value that corresponds to a given percentile of the normal distribution?

6.41 What are some of the distinguishing properties of a normal distribution?

6.42 How does the shape of the normal distribution differ from the shapes of the uniform and exponential distributions?

6.43 How can you use the normal probability plot to evaluate whether a set of data is normally distributed?

6.44 Under what circumstances can you use the exponential distribution?

APPLYING THE CONCEPTS

6.45 An industrial sewing machine uses ball bearings that are targeted to have a diameter of 0.75 inch. The lower and upper specification limits under which the ball bearings can operate are 0.74 inch and 0.76 inch, respectively. Past experience has indicated that the actual diameter of the ball bearings is approximately normally distributed, with a mean of 0.753 inch and a standard deviation of 0.004 inch. What is the probability that a ball bearing is

a. between the target and the actual mean?
b. between the lower specification limit and the target?
c. above the upper specification limit?
d. below the lower specification limit?
e. Of all the ball bearings, 93% of the diameters are greater than what value?

6.46 The fill amount in 2-liter soft drink bottles is normally distributed, with a mean of 2.0 liters and a standard deviation of 0.05 liter. If bottles contain less than 95% of the listed net content (1.90 liters, in this case), the manufacturer may be subject to penalty by the state office of consumer affairs. Bottles that have a net content above 2.10 liters may cause excess spillage upon opening. What proportion of the bottles will contain

a. between 1.90 and 2.0 liters?
b. between 1.90 and 2.10 liters?
c. below 1.90 liters or above 2.10 liters?
d. At least how much soft drink is contained in 99% of the bottles?
e. 99% of the bottles contain an amount that is between which two values (symmetrically distributed) around the mean?

6.47 In an effort to reduce the number of bottles that contain less than 1.90 liters, the bottler in Problem 6.46 sets the filling machine so that the mean is 2.02 liters. Under these circumstances, what are your answers in Problem 6.46 (a) through (e)?

6.48 An orange juice producer buys all his oranges from a large orange grove. The amount of juice squeezed from each of these oranges is approximately normally distributed, with a mean of 4.70 ounces and a standard deviation of 0.40 ounce.

a. What is the probability that a randomly selected orange will contain between 4.70 and 5.00 ounces of juice?
b. What is the probability that a randomly selected orange will contain between 5.00 and 5.50 ounces of juice?
c. At least how many ounces of juice will 77% of the oranges contain?
d. 80% of the oranges contain between what two values (in ounces of juice), symmetrically distributed around the population mean?

6.49 The file DomesticBeer contains the percentage alcohol, number of calories per 12 ounces, and number of carbohydrates (in grams) per 12 ounces for 139 of the best-selling domestic beers in the United States. For each of the three variables, decide whether the data appear to be approximately normally distributed. Support your decision through the use of appropriate statistics and graphs.

Source: Data extracted from **www.Beer100.com**, March 18, 2010.

6.50 The evening manager of a restaurant was very concerned about the length of time some customers were waiting in line to be seated. She also had some concern about the seating times—that is, the length of time between when a customer is seated and the time he or she leaves the restaurant. Over the course of one week, 100 customers (no more than 1 per party) were randomly selected, and their waiting and seating times (in minutes) were recorded in Wait.

a. Think about your favorite restaurant. Do you think waiting times more closely resemble a uniform, an exponential, or a normal distribution?
b. Again, think about your favorite restaurant. Do you think seating times more closely resemble a uniform, an exponential, or a normal distribution?
c. Construct a histogram and a normal probability plot of the waiting times. Do you think these waiting times more closely resemble a uniform, an exponential, or a normal distribution?
d. Construct a histogram and a normal probability plot of the seating times. Do you think these seating times more closely resemble a uniform, an exponential, or a normal distribution?

6.51 All the major stock market indexes posted strong gains in 2009. The mean one-year return for stocks in the S&P 500, a group of 500 very large companies, was 23.45%. The mean one-year return for the NASDAQ, a group of 3,200 small and medium-sized companies, was 43.89%. Historically, the one-year returns are approximately normally distributed, the standard deviation in the S&P 500 is approximately 20%, and the standard deviation in the NASDAQ is approximately 30%.

a. What is the probability that a stock in the S&P 500 gained value in 2009?
b. What is the probability that a stock in the S&P 500 gained 10% or more?
c. What is the probability that a stock in the S&P 500 lost 20% or more in 2009?
d. What is the probability that a stock in the S&P 500 lost 40% or more?
e. Repeat (a) through (d) for a stock in the NASDAQ.
f. Write a short summary on your findings. Be sure to include a discussion of the risks associated with a large standard deviation.

6.52 The speed in which the home page of a website is downloaded is an important quality characteristic of that website. Suppose that the mean time to download the home page for the Internal Revenue Service is 1.2 seconds. Suppose that the download time is normally distributed, with a standard deviation of 0.2 second. What is the probability that a download time is

a. less than 2 seconds?
b. between 1.5 and 2.5 seconds?
c. above 1.8 seconds?
d. 99% of the download times are slower (higher) than how many seconds ?
e. 95% of the download times are between what two values, symmetrically distributed around the mean?
f. Suppose that the download times are uniformly distributed between 0.45 and 1.95 seconds. What are your answers to (a) through (e)?

6.53 Suppose that the mean download time for a commercial tax preparation site is 2.0 seconds. Suppose that the download time is normally distributed, with a standard deviation of 0.5 second. What is the probability that a download time is

a. less than 2 seconds?
b. between 1.5 and 2.5 seconds?
c. above 1.8 seconds?
d. 99% of the download times are slower (higher) than how many seconds ?
e. Suppose that the download times are uniformly distributed between 1.5 and 2.5 seconds. What are your answers to (a) through (e)?
f. Compare the results for the IRS site computed in Problem 6.52 to those of the commercial site.

6.54 (Class Project) According to Burton G. Malkiel, the daily changes in the closing price of stock follow a *random walk*—that is, these daily events are independent of each other and move upward or downward in a random manner—and can be approximated by a normal distribution. To test this theory, use either a newspaper or the Internet to select one company traded on the NYSE, one company traded on the American Stock Exchange, and one company traded on the NASDAQ and then do the following:

1. Record the daily closing stock price of each of these companies for six consecutive weeks (so that you have 30 values per company).
2. Record the daily changes in the closing stock price of each of these companies for six consecutive weeks (so that you have 30 values per company).

For each of your six data sets, decide whether the data are approximately normally distributed by

a. constructing the stem-and-leaf display, histogram or polygon, and boxplot.
b. comparing data characteristics to theoretical properties.
c. constructing a normal probability plot.
d. Discuss the results of (a) through (c). What can you say about your three stocks with respect to daily closing prices and daily changes in closing prices? Which, if any, of the data sets are approximately normally distributed?

Note: *The random-walk theory pertains to the daily changes in the closing stock price, not the daily closing stock price.*

TEAM PROJECT

The file **Bond Funds** contains information regarding eight variables from a sample of 184 bond mutual funds:

Type—Type of bonds comprising the bond mutual fund (intermediate government or short-term corporate)
Assets—In millions of dollars
Fees—Sales charges (no or yes)
Expense ratio—Ratio of expenses to net assets in percentage
Return 2009—Twelve-month return in 2009
Three-year return—Annualized return, 2007–2009
Five-year return—Annualized return, 2005–2009
Risk—Risk-of-loss factor of the mutual fund (below average, average, or above average)

6.55 For the expense ratio, three-year return, and five-year return, decide whether the data are approximately normally distributed by

a. comparing data characteristics to theoretical properties.
b. constructing a normal probability plot.

STUDENT SURVEY DATABASE

6.56 Problem 1.27 on page 14 describes a survey of 62 undergraduate students (stored in **UndergradSurvey**). For these data, for each numerical variable, decide whether the data are approximately normally distributed by

a. comparing data characteristics to theoretical properties.
b. constructing a normal probability plot.

6.57 Problem 1.27 on page 14 describes a survey of 62 undergraduate students (stored in **UndergradSurvey**).

a. Select a sample of undergraduate students and conduct a similar survey for those students.
b. For the data collected in (a), repeat (a) and (b) of Problem 6.56.
c. Compare the results of (b) to those of Problem 6.56.

6.58 Problem 1.28 on page 15 describes a survey of 44 MBA students (stored in **GradSurvey**). For these data, for each numerical variable, decide whether the data are approximately normally distributed by

a. comparing data characteristics to theoretical properties.
b. constructing a normal probability plot.

6.59 Problem 1.28 on page 15 describes a survey of 44 MBA students (stored in **GradSurvey**).

a. Select a sample of graduate students and conduct a similar survey for those students.
b. For the data collected in (a), repeat (a) and (b) of Problem 6.58.
c. Compare the results of (b) to those of Problem 6.58.

MANAGING ASHLAND MULTICOMM SERVICES

The AMS technical services department has embarked on a quality improvement effort. Its first project relates to maintaining the target upload speed for its Internet service subscribers. Upload speeds are measured on a standard scale in which the target value is 1.0. Data collected over the past year indicate that the upload speed is approximately normally distributed, with a mean of 1.005 and a standard deviation of 0.10. Each day, one upload speed is measured. The upload speed is considered acceptable if the measurement on the standard scale is between 0.95 and 1.05.

EXERCISES

1. Assuming that the distribution has not changed from what it was in the past year, what is the probability that the upload speed is
a. less than 1.0?
b. between 0.95 and 1.0?
c. between 1.0 and 1.05?
d. less than 0.95 or greater than 1.05?

2. The objective of the operations team is to reduce the probability that the upload speed is below 1.0. Should the team focus on process improvement that increases the mean upload speed to 1.05 or on process improvement that reduces the standard deviation of the upload speed to 0.075? Explain.

DIGITAL CASE

Apply your knowledge about the normal distribution in this Digital Case, which extends the Using Statistics scenario from this chapter.

To satisfy concerns of potential customers, the management of OurCampus! has undertaken a research project to learn the amount of time it takes users to load a complex video features page. The research team has collected data and has made some claims based on the assertion that the data follow a normal distribution.

Open **OC_QRTStudy.pdf**, which documents the work of a quality response team at OurCampus! Read the internal report that documents the work of the team and their conclusions. Then answer the following:

1. Can the collected data be approximated by the normal distribution?

2. Review and evaluate the conclusions made by the OurCampus! research team. Which conclusions are correct? Which ones are incorrect?

3. If OurCampus! could improve the mean time by five seconds, how would the probabilities change?

REFERENCES

1. Gunter, B., "Q-Q Plots," *Quality Progress* (February 1994), 81–86.
2. Levine, D. M., P. Ramsey, and R. Smidt, *Applied Statistics for Engineers and Scientists Using Microsoft Excel and Minitab* (Upper Saddle River, NJ: Prentice Hall, 2001).
3. *Microsoft Excel 2010* (Redmond, WA: Microsoft Corp., 2010).
4. Miller, J., "Earliest Known Uses of Some of the Words of Mathematics," **http://jeff560.tripod.com/mathword.html**.
5. *Minitab Release 16* (State College, PA: Minitab Inc., 2010).
6. Pearl, R., "Karl Pearson, 1857–1936," *Journal of the American Statistical Association*, 31 (1936), 653–664.
7. Pearson, E. S., "Some Incidents in the Early History of Biometry and Statistics, 1890–94," *Biometrika*, 52 (1965), 3–18.
8. Walker, H., "The Contributions of Karl Pearson," *Journal of the American Statistical Association*, 53 (1958), 11–22.

CHAPTER 6 EXCEL GUIDE

EG6.1 CONTINUOUS PROBABILITY DISTRIBUTIONS

There are no Excel Guide instructions for this section.

EG6.2 THE NORMAL DISTRIBUTION

PHStat2 Use **Normal** to compute normal probabilities. For example, to create the Figure 6.16 worksheet (see page 228) that computes probabilities for several Chapter 6 examples, select **PHStat → Probability & Prob. Distributions → Normal**. In this procedure's dialog box (shown below):

1. Enter **7** as the **Mean** and **2** as the **Standard Deviation**.
2. Check **Probability for:** X< = and enter **7** in its box.
3. Check **Probability for:** X > and enter **9** in its box.
4. Check **X for Cumulative Percentage** and enter **10** in its box.
5. Enter a **Title** and click **OK**.

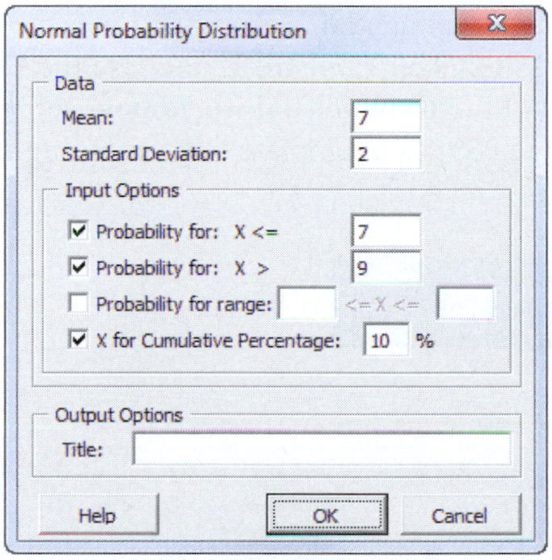

In-Depth Excel Use the **NORMDIST** worksheet function to compute normal probabilities. Enter the function as **NORMDIST(*X value*, *mean*, *standard deviation*, True)** to return the cumulative probability for less than or equal to the specified *X* value.

Use the **COMPUTE worksheet** of the **Normal workbook**, shown in Figure 6.16 on page 228, as a template for computing normal probabilities. The worksheet contains the data for solving the problems in Examples 6.1 through 6.4. Change the values for the **Mean**, **Standard Deviation**, **X Value**, **From X Value**, **To X Value**, and/or **Cumulative Percentage** to solve similar problems. To solve a problem that is similar to Example 6.5 on page 226, change the **Cumulative Percentage** cell twice, once to determine the lower value of *X* and the other time to determine the upper value of *X*.

The COMPUTE worksheet also uses the **STANDARDIZE** worksheet function to compute *Z* values, **NORMDIST** to compute the probability of less than or equal to the *X* value given, **NORMSINV** to compute the *Z* value for the cumulative percentage, and **NORMINV** to compute the *X* value for the given cumulative probability, mean, and standard deviation.

The worksheet also includes formulas that update probability labels when an *X* value is changed. Open to the **COMPUTE_FORMULAS worksheet** to examine all formulas.

EG6.3 EVALUATING NORMALITY

Comparing Data Characteristics to Theoretical Properties

Use instructions in Sections EG3.1 through EG3.3 in the Chapter 3 Excel Guide to compare data characteristics to theoretical properties.

Constructing the Normal Probability Plot

PHStat2 Use **Normal Probability Plot** to create a normal probability plot. For example, to create the Figure 6.22 normal probability plot for the 2009 returns on page 233, open to the **DATA worksheet** of the **Bond Funds workbook**. Select **PHStat → Probability & Prob. Distributions → Normal Probability Plot**. In the procedure's dialog box (shown below):

1. Enter **F1:F185** as the **Variable Cell Range**.
2. Check **First cell contains label**.
3. Enter a **Title** and click **OK**.

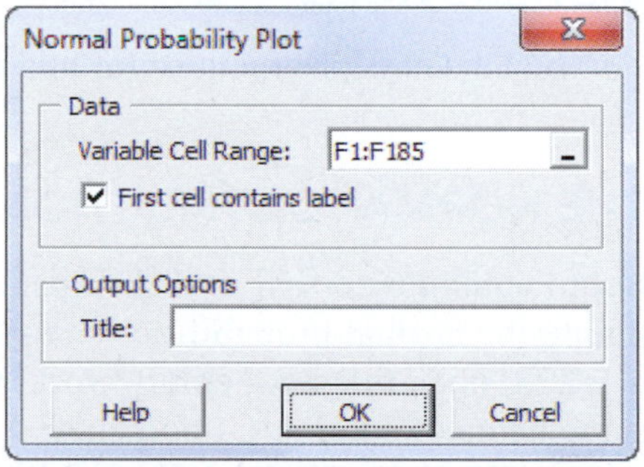

In addition to the chart sheet containing the normal probability plot, the procedure creates a worksheet of plot data that uses the **NORMSINV** function to compute the *Z* values used in the plot.

In-Depth Excel Create a normal probability plot by first creating a worksheet that computes *Z* values for the data to be plotted and then by creating a chart from that worksheet. Use the **PLOT_DATA worksheet** of the **NPP workbook** as a model for computing *Z* values. This worksheet contains columns for the rank, proportion, *Z* value, and the **Return 2009** variable and is the source of the data for the **NORMAL_PLOT chart sheet** that contains the Figure 6.22 normal probability plot (see page 233). For other problems, paste sorted variable data in column D, update the number of ranks in column A, and adjust the formulas in columns B and C. Column B formulas divide the column A cell by the quantity $n + 1$ (185 for the 2009 returns data) to compute cumulative percentages and column C formulas use the NORMSINV function to compute the *Z* values for those cumulative percentages. (Open to the **PLOT_FORMULAS worksheet** in the same workbook to examine these formulas.)

If you have fewer than 184 values, delete rows from the bottom up. If you have more than 184 values, insert rows from somewhere inside the body of the table to ensure that the normal probability plot is properly updated. To create your own normal probability plot for the Return 2009 variable, select the cell range **C1:D185**. Then select **Insert → Scatter** and select the first **Scatter** gallery choice (**Scatter with only Markers**). Relocate the chart to a chart sheet and adjust the chart formatting by using the instructions in Appendix F.

EG6.4 THE UNIFORM DISTRIBUTION

There are no Excel Guide instructions for this section.

EG6.5 THE EXPONENTIAL DISTRIBUTION

PHStat2 Use **Exponential** to compute an exponential probability. For example, to create the Figure 6.25 worksheet that computes the exponential probability for the bank ATM example (see page 239), select **PHStat → Probability & Prob. Distributions → Exponential**. In the procedure's dialog box (shown below):

1. Enter **20** as the **Mean per unit (Lambda)** and **0.1** as the **X Value**.
2. Enter a **Title** and click **OK**.

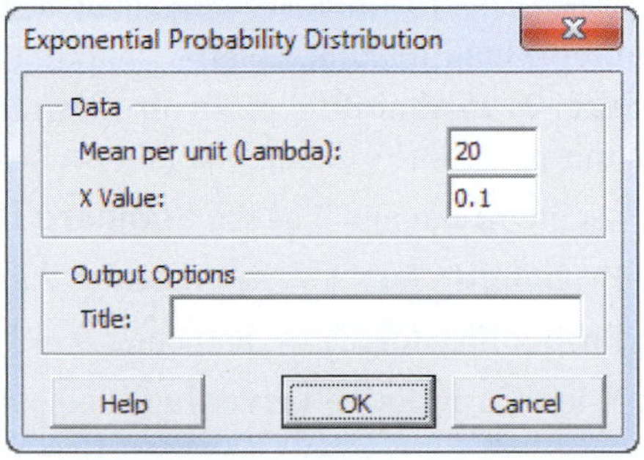

In-Depth Excel Use the **EXPONDIST** worksheet function to compute an exponential probability. Enter the function as **EXPONDIST(*X Value*, *mean*, True)**. Use the **COMPUTE worksheet** of the **Exponential workbook**, shown in Figure 6.25 on page 239, as a template for computing exponential probabilities.

CHAPTER 6 MINITAB GUIDE

MG6.1 CONTINUOUS PROBABILITY DISTRIBUTIONS

There are no Minitab Guide instructions for this section.

MG6.2 THE NORMAL DISTRIBUTION

Use **Normal** to compute normal probabilities. For example, to compute the normal probabilities shown in Figure 6.17 on page 228, open to a new, empty worksheet. Enter **X Value** as the name of column **C1** and enter **9** in the row 1 cell of column **C1**. Select **Calc → Probability Distributions → Normal**. In the Normal Distribution dialog box (shown in the next column):

1. Click **Cumulative probability**.
2. Enter **7** in the **Mean** box.
3. Enter **2** in the **Standard deviation** box.
4. Click **Input column** and enter **C1** in its box.
5. Click **OK**.

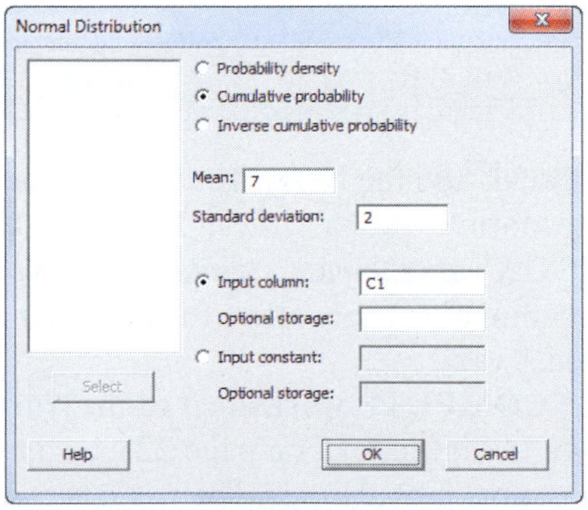

Minitab displays the Example 6.1 probability for a download time that is less than 9 seconds with $\mu = 7$ and $\sigma = 2$ (see in the left portion of Figure 6.17). To compute the normal probability for Example 6.4, enter **Cumulative Percentage** as the name of column **C2** and enter **0.1** in the row 1 cell of column **C2**. Again select **Calc → Probability Distributions → Normal**. In the Normal Distribution dialog box:

1. Click **Inverse cumulative probability**.
2. Enter **7** in the **Mean** box.

3. Enter **2** in the **Standard deviation** box.
4. Click **Input column** and enter **C2** in its box.
5. Click **OK**.

Minitab displays the Example 6.4 *Z* value corresponding to a cumulative area of 0.10 (see the right portion of Figure 6.17).

MG6.3 EVALUATING NORMALITY

Comparing Data Characteristics to Theoretical Properties

Use instructions in Sections MG3.1 through MG3.3 in the Chapter 3 Minitab Guide to compare data characteristics to theoretical properties.

Constructing the Normal Probability Plot

Use **Probability Plot** to create a normal probability plot. For example, to create the Figure 6.22 plot for the 2009 returns on page 233, open to the **Bond Funds worksheet**. Select **Graph ➔ Probability Plot** and:

1. In the Probability Plots dialog box, click **Single** and then click **OK**.

In the Probability Plot - Single dialog box (shown below):

2. Double-click **C6 Return2009** in the variables list to add **'Return 2009'** to the **Graph variables** box.
3. Click **Distribution**.

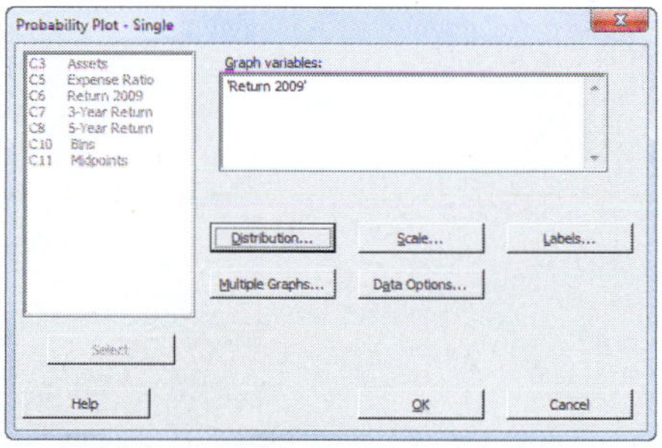

In the Probability Plot - Distribution dialog box:

4. Click the **Distribution** tab (shown at the top of the next column) and select **Normal** from the **Distribution** drop-down list.
5. Click the **Data Display** tab. Click **Symbols only** and clear the **Show confidence interval** check box.
6. Click **OK**.

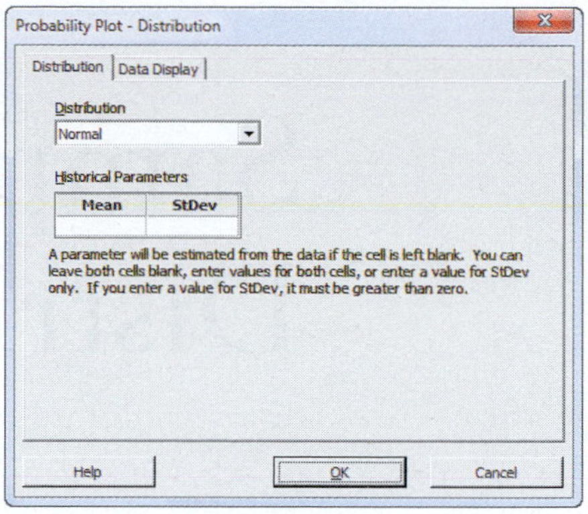

7. Back in the Probability Plot - Single dialog box, click **OK**.

MG6.4 THE UNIFORM DISTRIBUTION

There are no Minitab instructions for this section

MG6.5 THE EXPONENTIAL DISTRIBUTION

Use **Exponential** to compute an exponential probability. For example, to compute the exponential probability for the bank ATM example shown in Figure 6.25 worksheet on page 239, open to a new, blank worksheet. Enter **X Value** as the name of column **C1** and enter **0.1** in the row 1 cell of column **C1**. Select **Calc ➔ Probability Distributions ➔ Exponential**. In the Exponential Distribution dialog box (shown below):

1. Click **Cumulative probability**.
2. Enter **0.05** in the **Scale** box. (Minitab defines scale as the mean time *between* arrivals, $1/\lambda = 1/20 = 0.05$, not the mean number of arrivals, $\lambda = 20$.)
3. Leave the **Threshold** value as **0.0**.
4. Click **Input column** and enter **C1** in its box.
5. Click **OK**.

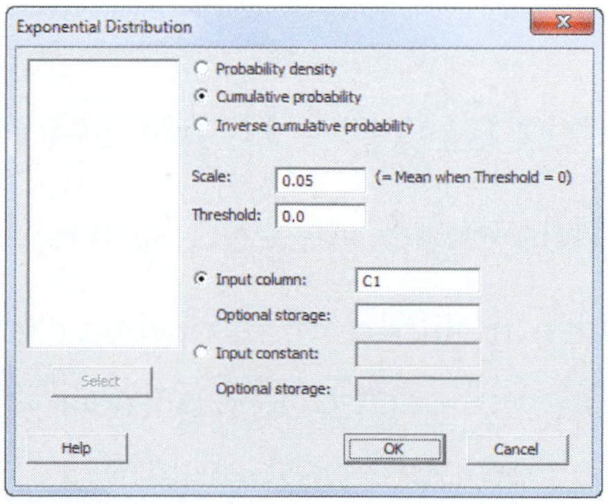

7 Sampling and Sampling Distributions

Learning Objectives

In this chapter, you learn:

- About different sampling methods
- The concept of the sampling distribution
- To compute probabilities related to the sample mean and the sample proportion
- The importance of the Central Limit Theorem

USING STATISTICS

@ Oxford Cereals

Oxford Cereals fills thousands of boxes of cereal during an eight-hour shift. As the plant operations manager, you are responsible for monitoring the amount of cereal placed in each box. To be consistent with package labeling, boxes should contain a mean of 368 grams of cereal. Because of the speed of the process, the cereal weight varies from box to box, causing some boxes to be underfilled and others overfilled. If the process is not working properly, the mean weight in the boxes could vary too much from the label weight of 368 grams to be acceptable.

Because weighing every single box is too time-consuming, costly, and inefficient, you must take a sample of boxes. For each sample you select, you plan to weigh the individual boxes and calculate a sample mean. You need to determine the probability that such a sample mean could have been randomly selected from a population whose mean is 368 grams. Based on your analysis, you will have to decide whether to maintain, alter, or shut down the cereal-filling process.

In Chapter 6, you used the normal distribution to study the distribution of video download times from the OurCampus! website. In this chapter, you need to make a decision about the cereal-filling process, based on the weights of a sample of cereal boxes packaged at Oxford Cereals. You will learn different methods of sampling and about sampling distributions and how to use them to solve business problems.

7.1 Types of Sampling Methods

In Section 1.3, a sample is defined as the portion of a population that has been selected for analysis. Rather than selecting every item in the population, statistical sampling procedures focus on collecting a small representative portion of the larger population. The results of the sample are then used to estimate characteristics of the entire population. There are three main reasons for selecting a sample:

- Selecting a sample is less time-consuming than selecting every item in the population.
- Selecting a sample is less costly than selecting every item in the population.
- Analyzing a sample is less cumbersome and more practical than analyzing the entire population.

The sampling process begins by defining the **frame**, a listing of items that make up the population. Frames are data sources such as population lists, directories, or maps. Samples are drawn from frames. Inaccurate or biased results can occur if a frame excludes certain portions of the population. Using different frames to generate data can lead to different conclusions.

After you select a frame, you draw a sample from the frame. As illustrated in Figure 7.1, there are two types of samples: nonprobability samples and probability samples.

FIGURE 7.1
Types of samples

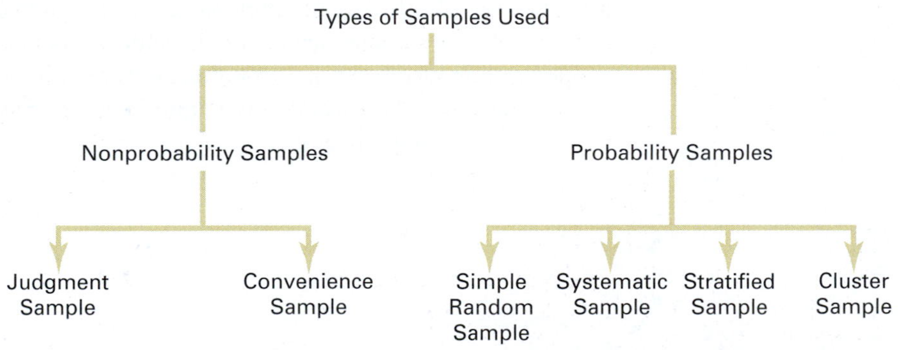

In a **nonprobability sample**, you select the items or individuals without knowing their probabilities of selection. Because of this, the theory of statistical inference that has been developed for probability sampling cannot be applied to nonprobability samples. A common type of nonprobability sampling is **convenience sampling**. In convenience sampling, items selected are easy, inexpensive, or convenient to sample. For example, if you were sampling tires stacked in a warehouse, it would be much more convenient to sample tires at the top of a stack than tires at the bottom of a stack. In many cases, participants in the sample select themselves. For example, many companies conduct surveys by giving visitors to their website the opportunity to complete survey forms and submit them electronically. The responses to these surveys can provide large amounts of data quickly and inexpensively, but the sample consists of self-selected web users. For many studies, only a nonprobability sample such as a judgment sample is available. In a **judgment sample**, you get the opinions of preselected experts in the subject matter. Although the experts may be well informed, you cannot generalize their results to the population.

Nonprobability samples can have certain advantages, such as convenience, speed, and low cost. However, their lack of accuracy due to selection bias and the fact that the results cannot be used for statistical inference more than offset these advantages.

In a **probability sample**, you select items based on known probabilities. Whenever possible, you should use probability sampling methods. Probability samples allow you to make inferences about the population of interest. The four types of probability samples most commonly used are simple random, systematic, stratified, and cluster samples. These sampling methods vary in their cost, accuracy, and complexity.

Simple Random Samples

In a **simple random sample**, every item from a frame has the same chance of selection as every other item. In addition, every sample of a fixed size has the same chance of selection as every other sample of that size. Simple random sampling is the most elementary random sampling technique. It forms the basis for the other random sampling techniques.

With simple random sampling, you use n to represent the sample size and N to represent the frame size. You number every item in the frame from 1 to N. The chance that you will select any particular member of the frame on the first selection is $1/N$.

You select samples with replacement or without replacement. **Sampling with replacement** means that after you select an item, you return it to the frame, where it has the same probability of being selected again. Imagine that you have a fishbowl containing N business cards, one card for each person. On the first selection, you select the card for Judy Craven. You record pertinent information and replace the business card in the bowl. You then mix up the cards in the bowl and select a second card. On the second selection, Judy Craven has the same probability of being selected again, $1/N$. You repeat this process until you have selected the desired sample size, n.

However, usually you do not want the same item to be selected again. **Sampling without replacement** means that once you select an item, you cannot select it again. The chance that you will select any particular item in the frame—for example, the business card for Judy Craven—on the first selection is $1/N$. The chance that you will select any card not previously chosen on the second selection is now 1 out of $N - 1$. This process continues until you have selected the desired sample of size n.

Regardless of whether you have sampled with or without replacement, "fishbowl" methods of sample selection have a major drawback—the ability to thoroughly mix the cards and randomly select the sample. As a result, fishbowl methods are not very useful. You need to use less cumbersome and more scientific methods of selection.

One such method uses a **table of random numbers** (see Table E.1 in Appendix E) for selecting the sample. A table of random numbers consists of a series of digits listed in a randomly generated sequence (see reference 8). Because the numeric system uses 10 digits $(0, 1, 2, \ldots, 9)$, the chance that you will randomly generate any particular digit is equal to the probability of generating any other digit. This probability is 1 out of 10. Hence, if you generate a sequence of 800 digits, you would expect about 80 to be the digit 0, 80 to be the digit 1, and so on. Because every digit or sequence of digits in the table is random, the table can be read either horizontally or vertically. The margins of the table designate row numbers and column numbers. The digits themselves are grouped into sequences of five in order to make reading the table easier.

To use Table E.1 instead of a fishbowl for selecting the sample, you first need to assign code numbers to the individual items of the frame. Then you generate the random sample by reading the table of random numbers and selecting those individuals from the frame whose assigned code numbers match the digits found in the table. You can better understand the process of sample selection by studying Example 7.1.

EXAMPLE 7.1

Selecting a Simple Random Sample by Using a Table of Random Numbers

A company wants to select a sample of 32 full-time workers from a population of 800 full-time employees in order to collect information on expenditures concerning a company-sponsored dental plan. How do you select a simple random sample?

SOLUTION The company decides to conduct an e-mail survey. Assuming that not everyone will respond to the survey, you need to send more than 32 surveys to get the necessary 32 responses. Assuming that 8 out of 10 full-time workers will respond to such a survey (i.e., a response rate of 80%), you decide to send 40 surveys. Because you want to send the 40 surveys to 40 different individuals, you should sample without replacement.

The frame consists of a listing of the names and e-mail addresses of all $N = 800$ full-time employees taken from the company personnel files. Thus, the frame is a complete listing of the population. To select the random sample of 40 employees from this frame, you use a table of random numbers. Because the frame size (800) is a three-digit number, each assigned code number must also be three digits so that every full-time worker has an equal chance of selection. You assign a code of 001 to the first full-time employee in the population listing, a code of 002 to the second full-time employee in the population listing, and so on, until a code of 800 is assigned to the Nth full-time worker in the listing. Because $N = 800$ is the largest possible coded value, you discard all three-digit code sequences greater than 800 (i.e., 801 through 999 and 000).

To select the simple random sample, you choose an arbitrary starting point from the table of random numbers. One method you can use is to close your eyes and strike the table of random numbers with a pencil. Suppose you used this procedure and you selected row 06, column 05 of Table 7.1 (which is extracted from Table E.1) as the starting point. Although you can go in any direction, in this example you read the table from left to right, in sequences of three digits, without skipping.

TABLE 7.1
Using a Table of Random Numbers

		Column							
		00000	**00001**	**11111**	**11112**	**22222**	**22223**	**33333**	**33334**
	Row	**12345**	**67890**	**12345**	**67890**	**12345**	**67890**	**12345**	**67890**
	01	49280	88924	35779	00283	81163	07275	89863	02348
	02	61870	41657	07468	08612	98083	97349	20775	45091
	03	43898	65923	25078	86129	78496	97653	91550	08078
	04	62993	93912	30454	84598	56095	20664	12872	64647
	05	33850	58555	51438	85507	71865	79488	76783	31708
Begin selection (row 06, column 05)	06	97340	03364	88472	04334	63919	36394	11095	92470
	07	70543	29776	10087	10072	55980	64688	68239	20461
	08	89382	93809	00796	95945	34101	81277	66090	88872
	09	37818	72142	67140	50785	22380	16703	53362	44940
	10	60430	22834	14130	96593	23298	56203	92671	15925
	11	82975	66158	84731	19436	55790	69229	28661	13675
	12	39087	71938	40355	54324	08401	26299	49420	59208
	13	55700	24586	93247	32596	11865	63397	44251	43189
	14	14756	23997	78643	75912	83832	32768	18928	57070
	15	32166	53251	70654	92827	63491	04233	33825	69662
	16	23236	73751	31888	81718	06546	83246	47651	04877
	17	45794	26926	15130	82455	78305	55058	52551	47182
	18	09893	20505	14225	68514	46427	56788	96297	78822
	19	54382	74598	91499	14523	68479	27686	46162	83554
	20	94750	89923	37089	20048	80336	94598	26940	36858
	21	70297	34135	53140	33340	42050	82341	44104	82949
	22	85157	47954	32979	26575	57600	40881	12250	73742
	23	11100	02340	12860	74697	96644	89439	28707	25815
	24	36871	50775	30592	57143	17381	68856	25853	35041
	25	23913	48357	63308	16090	51690	54607	72407	55538

Source: Data extracted from Rand Corporation, *A Million Random Digits with 100,000 Normal Deviates* (Glencoe, IL: The Free Press, 1955) and contained in Table E.1.

The individual with code number 003 is the first full-time employee in the sample (row 06 and columns 05–07), the second individual has code number 364 (row 06 and columns 08–10), and the third individual has code number 884. Because the highest code for any employee is 800, you discard the number 884. Individuals with code numbers 720, 433, 463, 363, 109, 592, 470, and 705 are selected third through tenth, respectively.

You continue the selection process until you get the required sample size of 40 full-time employees. If any three-digit sequence repeats during the selection process, you discard the repeating sequence because you are sampling without replacement.

Systematic Samples

In a **systematic sample**, you partition the N items in the frame into n groups of k items, where

$$k = \frac{N}{n}$$

You round k to the nearest integer. To select a systematic sample, you choose the first item to be selected at random from the first k items in the frame. Then, you select the remaining $n - 1$ items by taking every kth item thereafter from the entire frame.

If the frame consists of a listing of prenumbered checks, sales receipts, or invoices, taking a systematic sample is faster and easier than taking a simple random sample. A systematic sample is also a convenient mechanism for collecting data from telephone books, class rosters, and consecutive items coming off an assembly line.

To take a systematic sample of $n = 40$ from the population of $N = 800$ full-time employees, you partition the frame of 800 into 40 groups, each of which contains 20 employees. You then select a random number from the first 20 individuals and include every twentieth individual after the first selection in the sample. For example, if the first random number you select is 008, your subsequent selections are 028, 048, 068, 088, 108, . . . , 768, and 788.

Simple random sampling and systematic sampling are simpler than other, more sophisticated, probability sampling methods, but they generally require a larger sample size. In addition, systematic sampling is prone to selection bias. When using systematic sampling, if there is a pattern in the frame, you could have severe selection biases. To overcome the inefficiency of simple random sampling and the potential selection bias involved with systematic sampling, you can use either stratified sampling methods or cluster sampling methods.

Stratified Samples

In a **stratified sample**, you first subdivide the N items in the frame into separate subpopulations, or **strata**. A stratum is defined by some common characteristic, such as gender or year in school. You select a simple random sample within each of the strata and combine the results from the separate simple random samples. Stratified sampling is more efficient than either simple random sampling or systematic sampling because you are ensured of the representation of items across the entire population. The homogeneity of items within each stratum provides greater precision in the estimates of underlying population parameters.

EXAMPLE 7.2
Selecting a Stratified Sample

A company wants to select a sample of 32 full-time workers from a population of 800 full-time employees in order to estimate expenditures from a company-sponsored dental plan. Of the full-time employees, 25% are managers and 75% are nonmanagerial workers. How do you select the stratified sample in order for the sample to represent the correct percentage of managers and nonmanagerial workers?

SOLUTION If you assume an 80% response rate, you need to send 40 surveys to get the necessary 32 responses. The frame consists of a listing of the names and e-mail addresses of all $N = 800$ full-time employees included in the company personnel files. Because 25% of the full-time employees are managers, you first separate the frame into two strata: a subpopulation listing of all 200 managerial-level personnel and a separate subpopulation listing of all 600 full-time nonmanagerial workers. Because the first stratum consists of a listing of 200 managers, you assign three-digit code numbers from 001 to 200. Because the second stratum contains a listing of 600 nonmanagerial workers, you assign three-digit code numbers from 001 to 600.

To collect a stratified sample proportional to the sizes of the strata, you select 25% of the overall sample from the first stratum and 75% of the overall sample from the second stratum. You take two separate simple random samples, each of which is based on a distinct random starting point from a table of random numbers (Table E.1). In the first sample, you select 10 managers from the listing of 200 in the first stratum, and in the second sample, you select 30 nonmanagerial workers from the listing of 600 in the second stratum. You then combine the results to reflect the composition of the entire company.

Cluster Samples

In a **cluster sample**, you divide the N items in the frame into clusters that contain several items. **Clusters** are often naturally occurring designations, such as counties, election districts, city blocks, households, or sales territories. You then take a random sample of one or more clusters and study all items in each selected cluster.

Cluster sampling is often more cost-effective than simple random sampling, particularly if the population is spread over a wide geographic region. However, cluster sampling often requires a larger sample size to produce results as precise as those from simple random sampling or stratified sampling. A detailed discussion of systematic sampling, stratified sampling, and cluster sampling procedures can be found in reference 1.

Problems for Section 7.1

LEARNING THE BASICS

7.1 For a population containing $N = 902$ individuals, what code number would you assign for

a. the first person on the list?
b. the fortieth person on the list?
c. the last person on the list?

7.2 For a population of $N = 902$, verify that by starting in row 05, column 01 of the table of random numbers (Table E.1), you need only six rows to select a sample of $N = 60$ *without* replacement.

7.3 Given a population of $N = 93$, starting in row 29, column 01 of the table of random numbers (Table E.1), and reading across the row, select a sample of $N = 15$

a. *without* replacement.
b. *with* replacement.

APPLYING THE CONCEPTS

7.4 For a study that consists of personal interviews with participants (rather than mail or phone surveys), explain why simple random sampling might be less practical than some other sampling methods.

7.5 You want to select a random sample of $n = 1$ from a population of three items (which are called A, B, and C). The rule for selecting the sample is as follows: Flip a coin; if it is heads, pick item A; if it is tails, flip the coin again; this time, if it is heads, choose B; if it is tails, choose C. Explain why this is a probability sample but not a simple random sample.

7.6 A population has four members (called A, B, C, and D). You would like to select a random sample of $n = 2$, which you decide to do in the following way: Flip a coin; if it is heads, the sample will be items A and B; if it is tails, the sample will be items C and D. Although this is a random sample, it is not a simple random sample. Explain why. (Compare the procedure described in Problem 7.5 with the procedure described in this problem.)

7.7 The registrar of a college with a population of $N = 4{,}000$ full-time students is asked by the president to conduct a survey to measure satisfaction with the quality of life on campus. The following table contains a breakdown of the 4,000 registered full-time students, by gender and class designation:

	Class Designation				
Gender	**Fr.**	**So.**	**Jr.**	**Sr.**	**Total**
Female	700	520	500	480	2,200
Male	560	460	400	380	1,800
Total	1,260	980	900	860	4,000

The registrar intends to take a probability sample of $n = 200$ students and project the results from the sample to the entire population of full-time students.

a. If the frame available from the registrar's files is an alphabetical listing of the names of all $N = 4{,}000$ registered full-time students, what type of sample could you take? Discuss.
b. What is the advantage of selecting a simple random sample in (a)?
c. What is the advantage of selecting a systematic sample in (a)?
d. If the frame available from the registrar's files is a listing of the names of all $N = 4{,}000$ registered full-time students compiled from eight separate alphabetical lists, based on the gender and class designation breakdowns shown in the class designation table, what type of sample should you take? Discuss.
e. Suppose that each of the $N = 4{,}000$ registered full-time students lived in one of the 10 campus dormitories. Each dormitory accommodates 400 students. It is college policy to fully integrate students by gender and class designation in each dormitory. If the registrar is able to compile a listing of all students by dormitory, explain how you could take a cluster sample.

SELF Test **7.8** Prenumbered sales invoices are kept in a sales journal. The invoices are numbered from 0001 to 5000.

a. Beginning in row 16, column 01, and proceeding horizontally in Table E.1, select a simple random sample of 50 invoice numbers.
b. Select a systematic sample of 50 invoice numbers. Use the random numbers in row 20, columns 05–07, as the starting point for your selection.

c. Are the invoices selected in (a) the same as those selected in (b)? Why or why not?

7.9 Suppose that 5,000 sales invoices are separated into four strata. Stratum 1 contains 50 invoices, stratum 2 contains 500 invoices, stratum 3 contains 1,000 invoices, and stratum 4 contains 3,450 invoices. A sample of 500 sales invoices is needed.

a. What type of sampling should you do? Why?

b. Explain how you would carry out the sampling according to the method stated in (a).

c. Why is the sampling in (a) not simple random sampling?

7.2 Evaluating Survey Worthiness

Surveys are used to collect data. Nearly every day, you read or hear about survey or opinion poll results in newspapers, on the Internet, or on radio or television. To identify surveys that lack objectivity or credibility, you must critically evaluate what you read and hear by examining the worthiness of the survey. First, you must evaluate the purpose of the survey, why it was conducted, and for whom it was conducted.

The second step in evaluating the worthiness of a survey is to determine whether it was based on a probability or nonprobability sample (as discussed in Section 7.1). You need to remember that the only way to make valid statistical inferences from a sample to a population is through the use of a probability sample. Surveys that use nonprobability sampling methods are subject to serious, perhaps unintentional, biases that may make the results meaningless.

Survey Error

Even when surveys use random probability sampling methods, they are subject to potential errors. There are four types of survey errors:

- Coverage error
- Nonresponse error
- Sampling error
- Measurement error

Well-designed surveys reduce or minimize these four types of errors, often at considerable cost.

Coverage Error The key to proper sample selection is having an adequate frame. Remember that a frame is an up-to-date list of all the items from which you will select the sample. **Coverage error** occurs if certain groups of items are excluded from the frame so that they have no chance of being selected in the sample. Coverage error results in a **selection bias**. If the frame is inadequate because certain groups of items in the population were not properly included, any random probability sample selected will provide only an estimate of the characteristics of the frame, not the *actual* population.

Nonresponse Error Not everyone is willing to respond to a survey. In fact, research has shown that individuals in the upper and lower economic classes tend to respond less frequently to surveys than do people in the middle class. **Nonresponse error** arises from failure to collect data on all items in the sample and results in a **nonresponse bias**. Because you cannot always assume that persons who do not respond to surveys are similar to those who do, you need to follow up on the nonresponses after a specified period of time. You should make several attempts to convince such individuals to complete the survey. The follow-up responses are then compared to the initial responses in order to make valid inferences from the survey (see reference 1). The mode of response you use affects the rate of response. Personal interviews and telephone interviews usually produce a higher response rate than do mail surveys—but at a higher cost.

Sampling Error As discussed earlier, a sample is selected because it is simpler, less costly, and more efficient to examine than an entire population. However, chance dictates which individuals or items will or will not be included in the sample. **Sampling error** reflects the variation, or "chance differences," from sample to sample, based on the probability of particular individuals or items being selected in the particular samples.

When you read about the results of surveys or polls in newspapers or magazines, there is often a statement regarding a margin of error, such as "the results of this poll are expected to be within ±4 percentage points of the actual value." This **margin of error** is the sampling error. You can reduce sampling error by using larger sample sizes, although doing so increases the cost of conducting the survey.

Measurement Error In the practice of good survey research, you design a questionnaire with the intention of gathering meaningful information. But you have a dilemma here: Getting meaningful measurements is often easier said than done. Consider the following proverb:

> A person with one watch always knows what time it is;
>
> A person with two watches always searches to identify the correct one;
>
> A person with ten watches is always reminded of the difficulty in measuring time.

Unfortunately, the process of measurement is often governed by what is convenient, not what is needed. The measurements you get are often only a proxy for the ones you really desire. Much attention has been given to measurement error that occurs because of a weakness in question wording (see reference 2). A question should be clear, not ambiguous. Furthermore, in order to avoid *leading questions*, you need to present questions in a neutral manner.

Three sources of **measurement error** are ambiguous wording of questions, the Hawthorne effect, and respondent error. As an example of ambiguous wording, several years ago, the U.S. Department of Labor reported that the unemployment rate in the United States had been underestimated for more than a decade because of poor questionnaire wording in the Current Population Survey. In particular, the wording had led to a significant undercount of women in the labor force. Because unemployment rates are tied to benefit programs such as state unemployment compensation, survey researchers had to rectify the situation by adjusting the questionnaire wording.

The *Hawthorne effect* occurs when a respondent feels obligated to please the interviewer. Proper interviewer training can minimize the Hawthorne effect.

Respondent error occurs as a result of an overzealous or underzealous effort by the respondent. You can minimize this error in two ways: (1) by carefully scrutinizing the data and then recontacting those individuals whose responses seem unusual and (2) by establishing a program of recontacting a small number of randomly chosen individuals in order to determine the reliability of the responses.

Ethical Issues

Ethical considerations arise with respect to the four types of potential errors that can occur when designing surveys: coverage error, nonresponse error, sampling error, and measurement error. Coverage error can result in selection bias and becomes an ethical issue if particular groups or individuals are *purposely* excluded from the frame so that the survey results are more favorable to the survey's sponsor. Nonresponse error can lead to nonresponse bias and becomes an ethical issue if the sponsor knowingly designs the survey so that particular groups or individuals are less likely than others to respond. Sampling error becomes an ethical issue if the findings are purposely presented without reference to sample size and margin of error so that the sponsor can promote a viewpoint that might otherwise be inappropriate. Measurement error becomes an ethical issue in one of three ways: (1) a survey sponsor chooses leading questions that guide the responses in a particular direction; (2) an interviewer, through mannerisms and tone, purposely creates a Hawthorne effect or otherwise guides the responses in a particular direction; or (3) a respondent willfully provides false information.

Ethical issues also arise when the results of nonprobability samples are used to form conclusions about the entire population. When you use a nonprobability sampling method, you need to explain the sampling procedures and state that the results cannot be generalized beyond the sample.

THINK ABOUT THIS New Media Surveys/Old Sampling Problems

Imagine that you are a software distributor and you decide to create a "customer experience improvement program" that records how your customers are using your products, with the goal of using the collected data to improve your products. Or say that you're the moderator of an opinion blog who decides to create an instant poll to ask your readers about important political issues. Or you're a marketer of products aimed at a specific demographic and decide to create a page in a social networking site through which you plan to collect consumer feedback. What might you have in common with a *dead-tree* publication that went out of business over 70 years ago?

By 1932, before there was ever an Internet—or even commercial television—a "straw poll" conducted by the magazine *Literary Digest* had successfully predicted five U.S. presidential elections in a row. For the 1936 election, the magazine promised its largest poll ever and sent about 10 million ballots to people all across the country. After receiving and tabulating more than 2.3 million ballots, the *Digest* confidently proclaimed that Alf Landon would be an easy winner over Franklin D. Roosevelt. As things turned out, FDR won in a landslide, with Landon receiving the fewest electoral votes in U.S. history. The reputation of the *Literary Digest* was ruined; the magazine would cease publication less than two years later.

The failure of the *Literary Digest* poll was a watershed event in the history of sample surveys and polls. This failure refuted the notion that the larger the sample is, the better. (Remember this the next time someone complains about a political survey's "small" sample size.) The failure opened the door to new and more modern methods of sampling—the theory and concepts this book discusses in Sections 7.1 and 7.2. Today's Gallup polls of political opinion (**www.gallup.com**) or Roper (now GfK Roper) Reports about consumer behavior (**www.gfkamerica.com/practice_areas/roper_consulting/roper_reports**) arose, in part, due to this failure. George Gallup, the "Gallup" of the poll, and Elmo Roper, of the eponymous reports, both first gained widespread public notice for their correct "scientific" predictions of the 1936 election.

The failed *Literary Digest* poll became fodder for several postmortems, and the reason for the failure became almost an urban legend. Typically, the explanation is coverage error: The ballots were sent mostly to "rich people," and this created a frame that excluded poorer citizens (presumably more inclined to vote for the Democrat Roosevelt than the Republican Landon). However, later analyses suggest that this was not true; instead, low rates of response (2.3 million ballots represented less than 25% of the ballots distributed) and/or nonresponse error (Roosevelt voters were less likely to mail in a ballot than Landon voters) were significant reasons for the failure (see reference 8).

When Microsoft introduced its new Office Ribbon interface with Office 2007, a program manager explained how Microsoft had applied data collected from its "Customer Experience Improvement Program" to the redesign of the user interface. This led others to speculate that the data were biased toward beginners—who might be less likely to *decline* participation in the program—and that, in turn, had led Microsoft to make decisions that ended up perplexing more experienced users. This was another case of nonresponse error!

The blog moderator's instant poll mentioned earlier is targeted to the moderator's community, and the social network–based survey is aimed at "friends" of a product; such polls can also suffer from nonresponse error, and this fact is often overlooked by users of these new media. Often, marketers extol how much they "know" about survey respondents, thanks to information that can be "mined" (see Sections 2.7 and 15.7) from a social network community. But no amount of information about the respondents can tell marketers who the nonresponders are. Therefore, new media surveys fall prey to the same old type of error that may have been fatal to *Literary Digest* way back when.

Today, companies establish formal surveys based on probability sampling and go to great lengths—and spend large sums—to deal with coverage error, nonresponse error, sampling error, and measurement error. Instant polling and tell-a-friend surveys can be interesting and fun, but they are not replacements for the methods discussed in this chapter.

Problems for Section 7.2

APPLYING THE CONCEPTS

7.10 A survey indicates that the vast majority of college students own their own personal computers. What information would you want to know before you accepted the results of this survey?

7.11 A simple random sample of $n = 300$ full-time employees is selected from a company list containing the names of all $N = 5{,}000$ full-time employees in order to evaluate job satisfaction.

a. Give an example of possible coverage error.
b. Give an example of possible nonresponse error.
c. Give an example of possible sampling error.
d. Give an example of possible measurement error.

SELF Test **7.12** Business Professor Thomas Callarman traveled to China more than a dozen times from 2000 to 2005. He warns people about believing everything they read about surveys conducted in China and gives two specific reasons: "First, things are changing so rapidly that what you hear today may not be true tomorrow. Second, the people who answer the surveys may tell you what they think you want to hear, rather than what they really believe" (T. E. Callarman, "Some Thoughts on China," *Decision Line*, March 2006, pp. 1, 43–44).

a. List the four types of survey error discussed in the paragraph above.
b. Which of the types of survey error in (a) are the basis for Professor Callarman's two reasons to question the surveys being conducted in China?

7.13 A recent survey of college freshmen investigated the amount of involvement their parents have with decisions concerning their education. When asked about the decision to go to college, 84% said their parents' involvement was about right, 10.3% said it was too much, and 5.7% said it was too little. When it came to selecting individual courses, 72.5% said their parents' involvement was about right, 3.5% said it was too much, and 24.0% said it was too little (M. B. Marklein, "Study: Colleges Shouldn't Fret Over Hands-on Parents," **www.usatoday.com**, January 23, 2008). What additional information would you want to know about the survey before you accepted the results of the study?

7.14 Recruiters are finding a wealth of unfiltered information about candidates on social-networking websites. A recent survey found that 83% of recruiters use search engines to learn more about candidates, and 43% eliminated candidates based on information they found (I. Phaneuf, "Who's Googling You?" *Job Postings*, Spring 2009, pp. 12–13). What additional information would you want to know about a survey before you accepted the results of the study?

7.3 Sampling Distributions

In many applications, you want to make inferences that are based on statistics calculated from samples to estimate the values of population parameters. In the next two sections, you will learn about how the sample mean (a statistic) is used to estimate the population mean (a parameter) and how the sample proportion (a statistic) is used to estimate the population proportion (a parameter). Your main concern when making a statistical inference is reaching conclusions about a population, *not* about a sample. For example, a political pollster is interested in the sample results only as a way of estimating the actual proportion of the votes that each candidate will receive from the population of voters. Likewise, as plant operations manager for Oxford Cereals, you are only interested in using the sample mean weight calculated from a sample of cereal boxes for estimating the mean weight of a population of boxes.

In practice, you select a single random sample of a predetermined size from the population. Hypothetically, to use the sample statistic to estimate the population parameter, you could examine *every* possible sample of a given size that could occur. A **sampling distribution** is the distribution of the results if you actually selected all possible samples. The single result you obtain in practice is just one of the results in the sampling distribution.

7.4 Sampling Distribution of the Mean

In Chapter 3, several measures of central tendency, including the mean, median, and mode, were discussed. Undoubtedly, the mean is the most widely used measure of central tendency. The sample mean is often used to estimate the population mean. The **sampling distribution of the mean** is the distribution of all possible sample means if you select all possible samples of a given size.

The Unbiased Property of the Sample Mean

The sample mean is **unbiased** because the mean of all the possible sample means (of a given sample size, n) is equal to the population mean, μ. A simple example concerning a population of four administrative assistants demonstrates this property. Each assistant is asked to apply the same set of updates to a human resources database. Table 7.2 presents the number of errors made by each of the administrative assistants. This population distribution is shown in Figure 7.2.

TABLE 7.2
Number of Errors Made by Each of Four Administrative Assistants

Administrative Assistant	Number of Errors
Ann	$X_1 = 3$
Bob	$X_2 = 2$
Carla	$X_3 = 1$
Dave	$X_4 = 4$

FIGURE 7.2
Number of errors made by a population of four administrative assistants

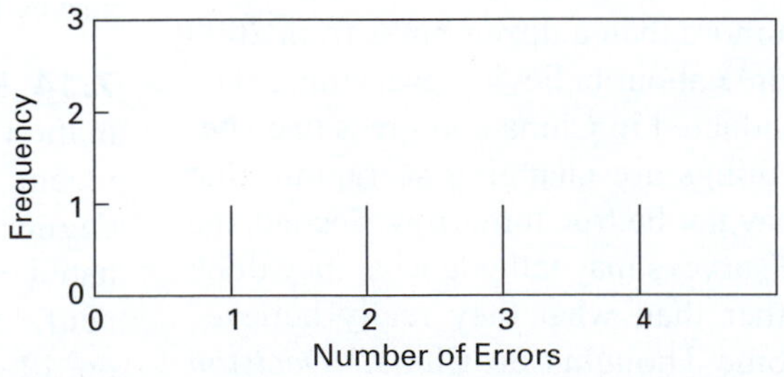

When you have the data from a population, you compute the mean by using Equation (7.1).

POPULATION MEAN

The population mean is the sum of the values in the population divided by the population size, N.

$$\mu = \frac{\sum_{i=1}^{N} X_i}{N} \quad \textbf{(7.1)}$$

You compute the population standard deviation, σ, by using Equation (7.2).

POPULATION STANDARD DEVIATION

$$\sigma = \sqrt{\frac{\sum_{i=1}^{N} (X_i - \mu)^2}{N}} \quad \textbf{(7.2)}$$

Thus, for the data of Table 7.2,

$$\mu = \frac{3 + 2 + 1 + 4}{4} = 2.5 \text{ errors}$$

and

$$\sigma = \sqrt{\frac{(3 - 2.5)^2 + (2 - 2.5)^2 + (1 - 2.5)^2 + (4 - 2.5)^2}{4}} = 1.12 \text{ errors}$$

If you select samples of two administrative assistants *with* replacement from this population, there are 16 possible samples ($N^n = 4^2 = 16$). Table 7.3 lists the 16 possible sample outcomes. If you average all 16 of these sample means, the mean of these values, is equal to 2.5, which is also the mean of the population, μ.

TABLE 7.3

All 16 Samples of $n = 2$ Administrative Assistants from a Population of $N = 4$ Administrative Assistants When Sampling with Replacement

Sample	Administrative Assistants	Sample Outcomes	Sample Mean
1	Ann, Ann	3, 3	$\overline{X}_1 = 3$
2	Ann, Bob	3, 2	$\overline{X}_2 = 2.5$
3	Ann, Carla	3, 1	$\overline{X}_3 = 2$
4	Ann, Dave	3, 4	$\overline{X}_4 = 3.5$
5	Bob, Ann	2, 3	$\overline{X}_5 = 2.5$
6	Bob, Bob	2, 2	$\overline{X}_6 = 2$
7	Bob, Carla	2, 1	$\overline{X}_7 = 1.5$
8	Bob, Dave	2, 4	$\overline{X}_8 = 3$
9	Carla, Ann	1, 3	$\overline{X}_9 = 2$
10	Carla, Bob	1, 2	$\overline{X}_{10} = 1.5$
11	Carla, Carla	1, 1	$\overline{X}_{11} = 1$
12	Carla, Dave	1, 4	$\overline{X}_{12} = 2.5$
13	Dave, Ann	4, 3	$\overline{X}_{13} = 3.5$
14	Dave, Bob	4, 2	$\overline{X}_{14} = 3$
15	Dave, Carla	4, 1	$\overline{X}_{15} = 2.5$
16	Dave, Dave	4, 4	$\overline{X}_{16} = 4$
			$\mu_{\overline{X}} = 2.5$

Because the mean of the 16 sample means is equal to the population mean, the sample mean is an unbiased estimator of the population mean. Therefore, although you do not know how close the sample mean of any particular sample selected comes to the population mean, you are assured that the mean of all the possible sample means that could have been selected is equal to the population mean.

Standard Error of the Mean

Figure 7.3 illustrates the variation in the sample means when selecting all 16 possible samples.

FIGURE 7.3

Sampling distribution of the mean, based on all possible samples containing two administrative assistants

Source: Data are from Table 7.3.

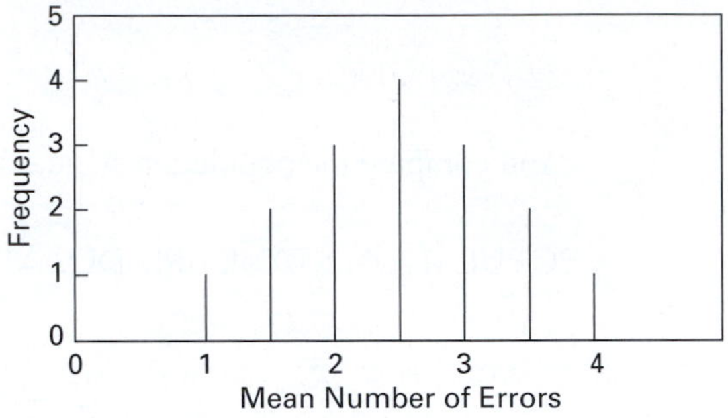

In this small example, although the sample means vary from sample to sample, depending on which two administrative assistants are selected, the sample means do not vary as much as the individual values in the population. That the sample means are less variable than the individual values in the population follows directly from the fact that each sample mean averages together all the values in the sample. A population consists of individual outcomes that can take on a wide range of values, from extremely small to extremely large. However, if a sample contains an extreme value, although this value will have an effect on the sample mean, the effect is reduced because the value is averaged with all the other values in the sample. As the sample size increases, the effect of a single extreme value becomes smaller because it is averaged with more values.

The value of the standard deviation of all possible sample means, called the **standard error of the mean**, expresses how the sample means vary from sample to sample. As the sample size increases, the standard error of the mean decreases by a factor equal to the square root of the sample size.

STANDARD ERROR OF THE MEAN

The standard error of the mean, $\sigma_{\overline{X}}$, is equal to the standard deviation in the population, σ, divided by the square root of the sample size, n.

$$\sigma_{\overline{X}} = \frac{\sigma}{\sqrt{n}} \tag{7.3}$$

Equation (7.3) defines the standard error of the mean when sampling *with* replacement or sampling *without* replacement from large or infinite populations.

Example 7.3 computes the standard error of the mean when the sample selected without replacement contains less than 5% of the entire population.

EXAMPLE 7.3

Computing the Standard Error of the Mean

Returning to the cereal-filling process described in the Using Statistics scenario on page 249, if you randomly select a sample of 25 boxes without replacement from the thousands of boxes filled during a shift, the sample contains much less than 5% of the population. Given that the standard deviation of the cereal-filling process is 15 grams, compute the standard error of the mean.

SOLUTION Using Equation (7.3) with $n = 25$ and $\sigma = 15$, the standard error of the mean is

$$\sigma_{\overline{X}} = \frac{\sigma}{\sqrt{n}} = \frac{15}{\sqrt{25}} = \frac{15}{5} = 3$$

The variation in the sample means for samples of $n = 25$ is much less than the variation in the individual boxes of cereal (i.e., $\sigma_{\overline{X}} = 3$, while $\sigma = 15$).

Sampling from Normally Distributed Populations

Now that the concept of a sampling distribution has been introduced and the standard error of the mean has been defined, what distribution will the sample mean, $\overline{X}$, follow? If you are sampling from a population that is normally distributed with mean, μ, and standard deviation, σ, then regardless of the sample size, n, the sampling distribution of the mean is normally distributed, with mean, $\mu_{\overline{X}} = \mu$, and standard error of the mean, $\sigma_{\overline{X}} = \sigma/\sqrt{n}$.

In the simplest case, if you take samples of size $n = 1$, each possible sample mean is a single value from the population because

$$\overline{X} = \frac{\sum_{i=1}^{n} X_i}{n} = \frac{X_1}{1} = X_1$$

Therefore, if the population is normally distributed, with mean μ and standard deviation σ, the sampling distribution $\overline{X}$ for samples of $n = 1$ must also follow the normal distribution, with mean $\mu_{\overline{X}} = \mu$ and standard error of the mean $\sigma_{\overline{X}} = \sigma/\sqrt{1} = \sigma$. In addition, as the sample size increases, the sampling distribution of the mean still follows a normal distribution, with $\mu_{\overline{X}} = \mu$, but the standard error of the mean decreases, so that a larger proportion of sample means are closer to the population mean. Figure 7.4 illustrates this reduction in variability. Note that 500 samples of size 1, 2, 4, 8, 16, and 32 were randomly selected from a normally distributed population. From the polygons in Figure 7.4, you can see that, although the sampling distribution of the mean is approximately[1] normal for each sample size, the sample means are distributed more tightly around the population mean as the sample size increases.

[1]Remember that "only" 500 samples out of an infinite number of samples have been selected, so that the sampling distributions shown are only approximations of the population distributions.

FIGURE 7.4

Sampling distributions of the mean from 500 samples of sizes $n = 1, 2, 4, 8, 16$, and 32 selected from a normal population

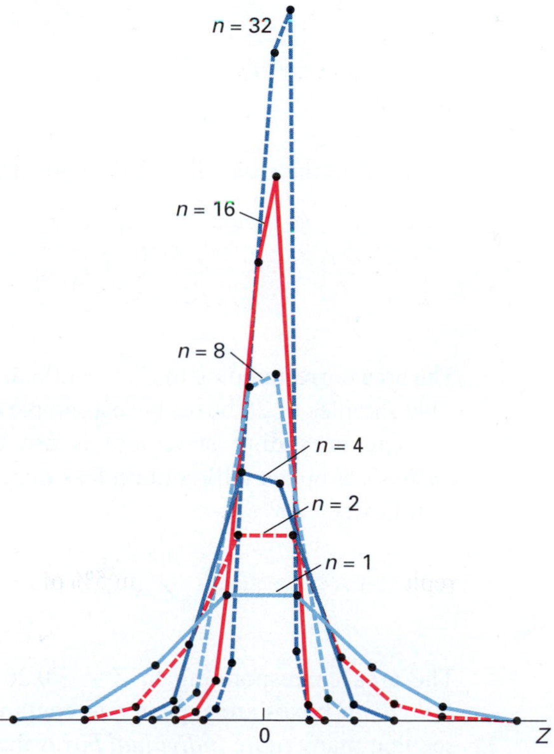

To further examine the concept of the sampling distribution of the mean, consider the Using Statistics scenario described on page 249. The packaging equipment that is filling 368-gram boxes of cereal is set so that the amount of cereal in a box is normally distributed, with a mean of 368 grams. From past experience, you know the population standard deviation for this filling process is 15 grams.

If you randomly select a sample of 25 boxes from the many thousands that are filled in a day and the mean weight is computed for this sample, what type of result could you expect? For example, do you think that the sample mean could be 368 grams? 200 grams? 365 grams?

The sample acts as a miniature representation of the population, so if the values in the population are normally distributed, the values in the sample should be approximately normally distributed. Thus, if the population mean is 368 grams, the sample mean has a good chance of being close to 368 grams.

How can you determine the probability that the sample of 25 boxes will have a mean below 365 grams? From the normal distribution (Section 6.2), you know that you can find the area below any value X by converting to standardized Z values:

$$Z = \frac{X - \mu}{\sigma}$$

In the examples in Section 6.2, you studied how any single value, X, differs from the population mean. Now, in this example, you want to study how a sample mean, $\overline{X}$, differs from the population mean. Substituting $\overline{X}$ for X, $\mu_{\overline{X}}$ for μ, and $\sigma_{\overline{X}}$ for σ in the equation above results in Equation (7.4).

FINDING Z FOR THE SAMPLING DISTRIBUTION OF THE MEAN

The Z value is equal to the difference between the sample mean, $\overline{X}$, and the population mean, μ, divided by the standard error of the mean, $\sigma_{\overline{X}}$.

$$Z = \frac{\overline{X} - \mu_{\overline{X}}}{\sigma_{\overline{X}}} = \frac{\overline{X} - \mu}{\dfrac{\sigma}{\sqrt{n}}} \qquad \textbf{(7.4)}$$

To find the area below 365 grams, from Equation (7.4),

$$Z = \frac{\overline{X} - \mu_{\overline{X}}}{\sigma_{\overline{X}}} = \frac{365 - 368}{\dfrac{15}{\sqrt{25}}} = \frac{-3}{3} = -1.00$$

The area corresponding to $Z = -1.00$ in Table E.2 is 0.1587. Therefore, 15.87% of all the possible samples of 25 boxes have a sample mean below 365 grams.

The preceding statement is not the same as saying that a certain percentage of *individual* boxes will contain less than 365 grams of cereal. You compute that percentage as follows:

$$Z = \frac{X - \mu}{\sigma} = \frac{365 - 368}{15} = \frac{-3}{15} = -0.20$$

The area corresponding to $Z = -0.20$ in Table E.2 is 0.4207. Therefore, 42.07% of the *individual* boxes are expected to contain less than 365 grams. Comparing these results, you see that many more *individual boxes* than *sample means* are below 365 grams. This result is explained by the fact that each sample consists of 25 different values, some small and some large. The averaging process dilutes the importance of any individual value, particularly when the sample size is large. Thus, the chance that the sample mean of 25 boxes is far away from the population mean is less than the chance that a *single* box is far away.

Examples 7.4 and 7.5 show how these results are affected by using different sample sizes.

EXAMPLE 7.4

The Effect of Sample Size, *n*, on the Computation of $\sigma_{\overline{X}}$

How is the standard error of the mean affected by increasing the sample size from 25 to 100 boxes?

SOLUTION If $n = 100$ boxes, then using Equation (7.3) on page 260:

$$\sigma_{\overline{X}} = \frac{\sigma}{\sqrt{n}} = \frac{15}{\sqrt{100}} = \frac{15}{10} = 1.5$$

The fourfold increase in the sample size from 25 to 100 reduces the standard error of the mean by half—from 3 grams to 1.5 grams. This demonstrates that taking a larger sample results in less variability in the sample means from sample to sample.

EXAMPLE 7.5

The Effect of Sample Size, *n*, on the Clustering of Means in the Sampling Distribution

If you select a sample of 100 boxes, what is the probability that the sample mean is below 365 grams?

SOLUTION Using Equation (7.4) on page 263,

$$Z = \frac{\overline{X} - \mu_{\overline{X}}}{\sigma_{\overline{X}}} = \frac{365 - 368}{\frac{15}{\sqrt{100}}} = \frac{-3}{1.5} = -2.00$$

From Table E.2, the area less than $Z = -2.00$ is 0.0228. Therefore, 2.28% of the samples of 100 boxes have means below 365 grams, as compared with 15.87% for samples of 25 boxes.

Sometimes you need to find the interval that contains a fixed proportion of the sample means. To do so, determine a distance below and above the population mean containing a specific area of the normal curve. From Equation (7.4) on page 262,

$$Z = \frac{\overline{X} - \mu}{\frac{\sigma}{\sqrt{n}}}$$

Solving for $\overline{X}$ results in Equation (7.5).

FINDING $\overline{X}$ FOR THE SAMPLING DISTRIBUTION OF THE MEAN

$$\overline{X} = \mu + Z\frac{\sigma}{\sqrt{n}} \quad \textbf{(7.5)}$$

Example 7.6 illustrates the use of Equation (7.5).

EXAMPLE 7.6

Determining the Interval That Includes a Fixed Proportion of the Sample Means

In the cereal-filling example, find an interval symmetrically distributed around the population mean that will include 95% of the sample means, based on samples of 25 boxes.

SOLUTION If 95% of the sample means are in the interval, then 5% are outside the interval. Divide the 5% into two equal parts of 2.5%. The value of Z in Table E.2 corresponding to an area of 0.0250 in the lower tail of the normal curve is -1.96, and the value of Z corresponding to a cumulative area of 0.9750 (i.e., 0.0250 in the upper tail of the normal curve) is $+1.96$. The lower value of $\overline{X}$ (called $\overline{X}_L$) and the upper value of $\overline{X}$ (called $\overline{X}_U$) are found by using Equation (7.5):

$$\overline{X}_L = 368 + (-1.96)\frac{15}{\sqrt{25}} = 368 - 5.88 = 362.12$$

$$\overline{X}_U = 368 + (1.96)\frac{15}{\sqrt{25}} = 368 + 5.88 = 373.88$$

Therefore, 95% of all sample means, based on samples of 25 boxes, are between 362.12 and 373.88 grams.

Sampling from Non-Normally Distributed Populations—The Central Limit Theorem

Thus far in this section, only the sampling distribution of the mean for a normally distributed population has been considered. However, in many instances, either you know that the population is not normally distributed or it is unrealistic to assume that the population is normally distributed. An important theorem in statistics, the Central Limit Theorem, deals with this situation.

THE CENTRAL LIMIT THEOREM

The **Central Limit Theorem** states that as the sample size (i.e., the number of values in each sample) gets *large enough*, the sampling distribution of the mean is approximately normally distributed. This is true regardless of the shape of the distribution of the individual values in the population.

What sample size is large enough? A great deal of statistical research has gone into this issue. As a general rule, statisticians have found that for many population distributions, when the sample size is at least 30, the sampling distribution of the mean is approximately normal. However, you can apply the Central Limit Theorem for even smaller sample sizes if the population distribution is approximately bell-shaped. In the case in which the distribution of a variable is extremely skewed or has more than one mode, you may need sample sizes larger than 30 to ensure normality in the sampling distribution of the mean.

Figure 7.5 illustrates the application of the Central Limit Theorem to different populations. The sampling distributions from three different continuous distributions (normal, uniform, and exponential) for varying sample sizes ($n = 2, 5, 30$) are displayed.

FIGURE 7.5

Sampling distribution of the mean for different populations for samples of $n = 2, 5$, and 30

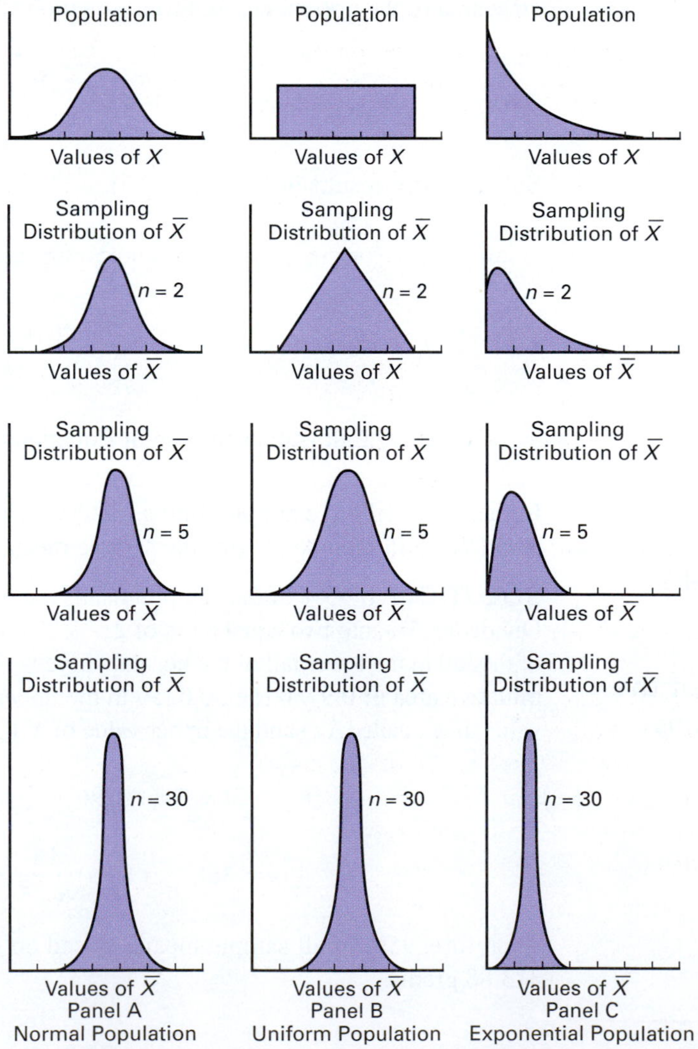

In each of the panels, because the sample mean is an unbiased estimator of the population mean, the mean of any sampling distribution is always equal to the mean of the population.

Panel A of Figure 7.5 shows the sampling distribution of the mean selected from a normal population. As mentioned earlier in this section, when the population is normally distributed, the sampling distribution of the mean is normally distributed for any sample size. [You can measure the variability by using the standard error of the mean, Equation (7.3), on page 260.]

Panel B of Figure 7.5 depicts the sampling distribution from a population with a uniform (or rectangular) distribution (see Section 6.4). When samples of size $n = 2$ are selected, there is a peaking, or *central limiting*, effect already working. For $n = 5$, the sampling distribution is bell-shaped and approximately normal. When $n = 30$, the sampling distribution looks very similar to a normal distribution. In general, the larger the sample size, the more closely the sampling distribution will follow a normal distribution. As with all other cases, the mean of each sampling distribution is equal to the mean of the population, and the variability decreases as the sample size increases.

Panel C of Figure 7.5 presents an exponential distribution (see Section 6.5). This population is extremely right-skewed. When $n = 2$, the sampling distribution is still highly right-skewed but less so than the distribution of the population. For $n = 5$, the sampling distribution is slightly right-skewed. When $n = 30$, the sampling distribution looks approximately normal. Again, the mean of each sampling distribution is equal to the mean of the population, and the variability decreases as the sample size increases.

Using the results from the normal, uniform, and exponential distributions, you can reach the following conclusions regarding the Central Limit Theorem:

- For most population distributions, regardless of shape, the sampling distribution of the mean is approximately normally distributed if samples of at least size 30 are selected.
- If the population distribution is fairly symmetrical, the sampling distribution of the mean is approximately normal for samples as small as size 5.
- If the population is normally distributed, the sampling distribution of the mean is normally distributed, regardless of the sample size.

The Central Limit Theorem is of crucial importance in using statistical inference to reach conclusions about a population. It allows you to make inferences about the population mean without having to know the specific shape of the population distribution.

VISUAL EXPLORATIONS Exploring Sampling Distributions

Use the Visual Explorations **Two Dice Probability** procedure to observe the effects of simulated throws on the frequency distribution of the sum of the two dice. Open the **Visual Explorations add-in workbook** (see Appendix Section D.4) and:

1. Select **Add-Ins ➔ VisualExplorations ➔ Two Dice Probability**
2. Click the **Tally** button to tally a set of throws in the frequency distribution table and histogram. Optionally, click the spinner buttons to adjust the number of throws per tally (round).
3. Repeat step 2 as many times as necessary.
4. Click **Finish** to end the simulation.

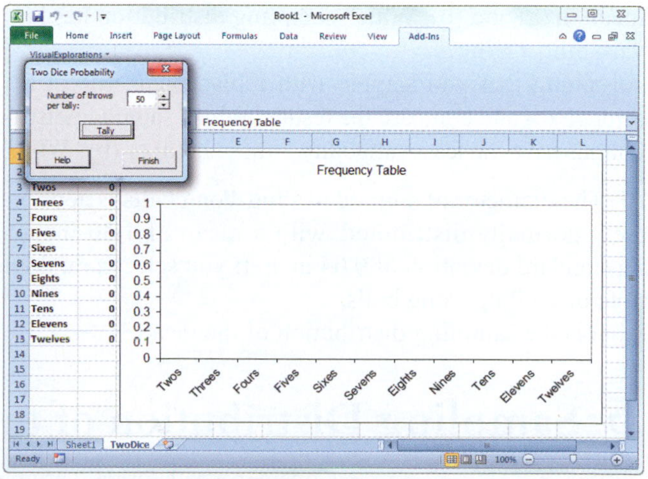

Problems for Section 7.4

LEARNING THE BASICS

7.15 Given a normal distribution with $\mu = 100$ and $\sigma = 10$, if you select a sample of $n = 25$, what is the probability that $\bar{X}$ is

a. less than 95?
b. between 95 and 97.5?
c. above 102.2?
d. There is a 65% chance that $\bar{X}$ is above what value?

7.16 Given a normal distribution with $\mu = 50$ and $\sigma = 5$, if you select a sample of $n = 100$, what is the probability that $\bar{X}$ is

a. less than 47?
b. between 47 and 49.5?
c. above 51.1?
d. There is a 35% chance that $\bar{X}$ is above what value?

APPLYING THE CONCEPTS

7.17 For each of the following three populations, indicate what the sampling distribution for samples of 25 would consist of:

a. Travel expense vouchers for a university in an academic year
b. Absentee records (days absent per year) in 2010 for employees of a large manufacturing company.
c. Yearly sales (in gallons) of unleaded gasoline at service stations located in a particular state.

7.18 The following data represent the number of days absent per year in a population of six employees of a small company:

1 3 6 7 9 10

a. Assuming that you sample without replacement, select all possible samples of $n = 2$ and construct the sampling distribution of the mean. Compute the mean of all the sample means and also compute the population mean. Are they equal? What is this property called?
b. Repeat (a) for all possible samples of $n = 3$.
c. Compare the shape of the sampling distribution of the mean in (a) and (b). Which sampling distribution has less variability? Why?
d. Assuming that you sample with replacement, repeat (a) through (c) and compare the results. Which sampling distributions have the least variability—those in (a) or (b)? Why?

7.19 The diameter of a brand of Ping-Pong balls is approximately normally distributed, with a mean of 1.30 inches and a standard deviation of 0.04 inch. If you select a random sample of 16 Ping-Pong balls,

a. what is the sampling distribution of the mean?
b. what is the probability that the sample mean is less than 1.28 inches?
c. what is the probability that the sample mean is between 1.31 and 1.33 inches?
d. The probability is 60% that the sample mean will be between what two values, symmetrically distributed around the population mean?

7.20 The U.S. Census Bureau announced that the median sales price of new houses sold in 2009 was \$215,600, and the mean sales price was \$270,100 (**www.census.gov/newhomesales**, March 30, 2010). Assume that the standard deviation of the prices is \$90,000.

a. If you select samples of $n = 2$, describe the shape of the sampling distribution of $\bar{X}$.
b. If you select samples of $n = 100$, describe the shape of the sampling distribution of $\bar{X}$.
c. If you select a random sample of $n = 100$, what is the probability that the sample mean will be less than \$300,000?
d. If you select a random sample of $n = 100$, what is the probability that the sample mean will be between \$275,000 and \$290,000?

7.21 Time spent using e-mail per session is normally distributed, with $\mu = 8$ minutes and $\sigma = 2$ minutes. If you select a random sample of 25 sessions,

a. what is the probability that the sample mean is between 7.8 and 8.2 minutes?
b. what is the probability that the sample mean is between 7.5 and 8 minutes?
c. If you select a random sample of 100 sessions, what is the probability that the sample mean is between 7.8 and 8.2 minutes?
d. Explain the difference in the results of (a) and (c).

SELF Test **7.22** The amount of time a bank teller spends with each customer has a population mean, μ, = 3.10 minutes and a standard deviation, σ, = 0.40 minute. If you select a random sample of 16 customers,

a. what is the probability that the mean time spent per customer is at least 3 minutes?
b. there is an 85% chance that the sample mean is less than how many minutes?
c. What assumption must you make in order to solve (a) and (b)?
d. If you select a random sample of 64 customers, there is an 85% chance that the sample mean is less than how many minutes?

7.5 Sampling Distribution of the Proportion

Consider a categorical variable that has only two categories, such as the customer prefers your brand or the customer prefers the competitor's brand. You are interested in the proportion of items belonging to one of the categories—for example, the proportion of customers that prefer your brand. The population proportion, represented by π, is the proportion of items in the entire population with the characteristic of interest. The sample proportion, represented by p, is the proportion of items in the sample with the characteristic of interest. The sample proportion, a statistic, is used to estimate the population proportion, a parameter. To calculate the sample proportion, you assign one of two possible values, 1 or 0, to represent the presence or absence of the characteristic. You then sum all the 1 and 0 values and divide by n, the sample size. For example, if, in a sample of five customers, three preferred your brand and two did not, you have three 1s and two 0s. Summing the three 1s and two 0s and dividing by the sample size of 5 results in a sample proportion of 0.60.

SAMPLE PROPORTION

$$p = \frac{X}{n} = \frac{\text{Number of items having the characteristic of interest}}{\text{Sample size}} \qquad \textbf{(7.6)}$$

The sample proportion, p, will be between 0 and 1. If all items have the characteristic, you assign each a score of 1, and p is equal to 1. If half the items have the characteristic, you assign half a score of 1 and assign the other half a score of 0, and p is equal to 0.5. If none of the items have the characteristic, you assign each a score of 0, and p is equal to 0.

In Section 7.4, you learned that the sample mean, $\overline{X}$ is an unbiased estimator of the population mean, μ. Similarly, the statistic p is an unbiased estimator of the population proportion, π. By analogy to the sampling distribution of the mean, whose standard error is $\sigma_{\overline{X}} = \frac{\sigma}{\sqrt{n}}$, the **standard error of the proportion**, σ_p, is given in Equation (7.7).

STANDARD ERROR OF THE PROPORTION

$$\sigma_p = \sqrt{\frac{\pi(1 - \pi)}{n}} \qquad \textbf{(7.7)}$$

The **sampling distribution of the proportion** follows the binomial distribution, as discussed in Section 5.3 when sampling with replacement (or without replacement from extremely large populations). However, you can use the normal distribution to approximate the binomial distribution when $n\pi$ and $n(1-\pi)$ are each at least 5. In most cases in which inferences are made about the proportion, the sample size is substantial enough to meet the conditions for using the normal approximation (see reference 1). Therefore, in many instances, you can use the normal distribution to estimate the sampling distribution of the proportion.

Substituting p for $\overline{X}$, π for μ, and $\sqrt{\frac{\pi(1 - \pi)}{n}}$ for $\frac{\sigma}{\sqrt{n}}$ in Equation (7.4) on page 262 results in Equation (7.8).

FINDING Z FOR THE SAMPLING DISTRIBUTION OF THE PROPORTION

$$Z = \frac{p - \pi}{\sqrt{\frac{\pi(1 - \pi)}{n}}} \qquad \textbf{(7.8)}$$

To illustrate the sampling distribution of the proportion, suppose that the manager of the local branch of a bank determines that 40% of all depositors have multiple accounts at the bank. If you select a random sample of 200 depositors, because $n\pi = 200(0.40) = 80 \geq 5$ and

$n(1 - \pi) = 200(0.60) = 120 \geq 5$, the sample size is large enough to assume that the sampling distribution of the proportion is approximately normally distributed. Then, you can calculate the probability that the sample proportion of depositors with multiple accounts is less than 0.30 by using Equation (7.8):

$$Z = \frac{p - \pi}{\sqrt{\frac{\pi(1 - \pi)}{n}}}$$

$$= \frac{0.30 - 0.40}{\sqrt{\frac{(0.40)(0.60)}{200}}} = \frac{-0.10}{\sqrt{\frac{0.24}{200}}} = \frac{-0.10}{0.0346}$$

$$= -2.89$$

Using Table E.2, the area under the normal curve less than −2.89 is 0.0019. Therefore, if the population proportion of items of interest is 0.40, only 0.19% of the samples of $n = 200$ would be expected to have sample proportions less than 0.30.

Problems for Section 7.5

LEARNING THE BASICS

7.23 In a random sample of 64 people, 48 are classified as "successful."

a. Determine the sample proportion, p, of "successful" people.
b. If the population proportion is 0.70, determine the standard error of the proportion.

7.24 A random sample of 50 households was selected for a telephone survey. The key question asked was, "Do you or any member of your household own a cellular telephone that you can use to access the Internet?" Of the 50 respondents, 20 said yes and 30 said no.

a. Determine the sample proportion, p, of households with cellular telephones that can be used to access the Internet.
b. If the population proportion is 0.45, determine the standard error of the proportion.

7.25 The following data represent the responses (Y for yes and N for no) from a sample of 40 college students to the question "Do you currently own shares in any stocks?"

N N Y N N Y N Y N Y N N Y N Y Y N N N Y
N Y N N N N Y N N Y Y N N N Y N N Y N N

a. Determine the sample proportion, p, of college students who own shares of stock.
b. If the population proportion is 0.30, determine the standard error of the proportion.

APPLYING THE CONCEPTS

SELF Test **7.26** A political pollster is conducting an analysis of sample results in order to make predictions on election night. Assuming a two-candidate election, if a specific candidate receives at least 55% of the vote in the sample, that candidate will be forecast as the winner of the election. If you select a random sample of 100 voters, what is the probability that a candidate will be forecast as the winner when

a. the population percentage of her vote is 50.1%?
b. the population percentage of her vote is 60%?
c. the population percentage of her vote is 49% (and she will actually lose the election)?
d. If the sample size is increased to 400, what are your answers to (a) through (c)? Discuss.

7.27 You plan to conduct a marketing experiment in which students are to taste one of two different brands of soft drink. Their task is to correctly identify the brand tasted. You select a random sample of 200 students and assume that the students have no ability to distinguish between the two brands. (Hint: If an individual has no ability to distinguish between the two soft drinks, then the two brands are equally likely to be selected.)

a. What is the probability that the sample will have between 50% and 60% of the identifications correct?
b. The probability is 90% that the sample percentage is contained within what symmetrical limits of the population percentage?
c. What is the probability that the sample percentage of correct identifications is greater than 65%?
d. Which is more likely to occur—more than 60% correct identifications in the sample of 200 or more than 55% correct identifications in a sample of 1,000? Explain.

7.28 In a recent survey of full-time female workers ages 22 to 35 years, 46% said that they would rather give up some of their salary for more personal time. (Data extracted from "I'd Rather Give Up," *USA Today*, March 4, 2010, p. 1B.) Suppose you select a sample of 100 full-time female workers 22 to 35 years old.

a. What is the probability that in the sample, fewer than 50% would rather give up some of their salary for more personal time?
b. What is the probability that in the sample, between 40% and 50% would rather give up some of their salary for more personal time?
c. What is the probability that in the sample, more than 40% would rather give up some of their salary for more personal time?
d. If a sample of 400 is taken, how does this change your answers to (a) through (c)?

7.29 Companies often make flextime scheduling available to help recruit and keep female employees who have children. Other workers sometimes view these flextime schedules as unfair. An article in *USA Today* indicates that 25% of male employees state that they have to pick up the slack for moms working flextime schedules. (Data extracted from D. Jones, "Poll Finds Resentment of Flextime," **www.usatoday.com**, May 11, 2007.) Suppose you select a random sample of 100 male employees working for companies offering flextime.

a. What is the probability that 25% or fewer male employees will indicate that they have to pick up the slack for moms working flextime?
b. What is the probability that 20% or fewer male employees will indicate that they have to pick up the slack for moms working flextime?
c. If a random sample of 500 is taken, how does this change your answers to (a) and (b)?

7.30 According to Gallup's poll on consumer behavior, 36% of Americans say they will consider only cars manufactured by an American company when purchasing a new car. (Data extracted from *The Gallup Poll*, **www.gallup.com**, March 31, 2010.) If you select a random sample of 200 Americans,

a. what is the probability that the sample will have between 30% and 40% who say they will consider only cars manufactured by an American company when purchasing a new car?
b. the probability is 90% that the sample percentage will be contained within what symmetrical limits of the population percentage?
c. the probability is 95% that the sample percentage will be contained within what symmetrical limits of the population percentage?

7.31 The Agency for Healthcare Research and Quality reports that medical errors are responsible for injury to 1 out of every 25 hospital patients in the United States. (Data extracted from M. Ozan-Rafferty, "Hospitals: Never Have a Never Event," *The Gallup Management Journal*, **gmj.gallup.com**, May 7, 2009.) These errors are tragic and expensive. Preventable health care–related errors cost an estimated $29 billion each year in the United States. Suppose that you select a sample of 100 U.S. hospital patients.

a. What is the probability that the sample percentage reporting injury due to medical errors will be between 5% and 10%?
b. The probability is 90% that the sample percentage will be within what symmetrical limits of the population percentage?
c. The probability is 95% that the sample percentage will be within what symmetrical limits of the population percentage?
d. Suppose you selected a sample of 400 U.S. hospital patients. How does this change your answers in (a) through (c)?

7.32 A survey of 2,250 American adults reported that 59% got news both online and offline in a typical day. (Data extracted from "How Americans Get News in a Typical Day," *USA Today*, March 10, 2010, p. 1A.)

a. Suppose that you take a sample of 100 American adults. If the population proportion of American adults who get news both online and offline in a typical day is 0.59, what is the probability that fewer than half in your sample will get news both online and offline in a typical day?
b. Suppose that you take a sample of 500 American adults. If the population proportion of American adults who get news both online and offline in a typical day is 0.59, what is the probability that fewer than half in your sample will get news both online and offline in a typical day?
c. Discuss the effect of sample size on the sampling distribution of the proportion in general and the effect on the probabilities in (a) and (b).

7.6 *Online Topic*: Sampling from Finite Populations

In this section, sampling without replacement from finite populations is discussed. To study this topic, read the Section 7.6 online topic file that is available on this book's companion website. (See Appendix C to learn how to access the online topic files.)

USING STATISTICS @ Oxford Cereals Revisited

As the plant operations manager for Oxfords Cereals, you were responsible for monitoring the amount of cereal placed in each box. To be consistent with package labeling, boxes should contain a mean of 368 grams of cereal. Thousands of boxes are produced during a shift, and weighing every single box was determined to be too time-consuming, costly, and inefficient. Instead, a sample of boxes was selected. Based on your analysis of the sample, you had to decide whether to maintain, alter, or shut down the process.

Using the concept of the sampling distribution of the mean, you were able to determine probabilities that such a sample mean could have been randomly selected from a population with a mean of 368 grams. Specifically, if a sample of size $n = 25$ is selected from a population with a mean of 368 and standard deviation of 15, you calculated the probability of selecting a sample with a mean of 365 grams or less to be 15.87%. If a larger sample size is selected, the sample mean should be closer to the population mean. This result was illustrated when you calculated the probability if the sample size were increased to $n = 100$. Using the larger sample size, you determined the probability of selecting a sample with a mean of 365 grams or less to be 2.28%.

SUMMARY

You have learned that in many business situations, the population is so large that you cannot gather information on every item. Instead, statistical sampling procedures focus on selecting a small representative group of the larger population. The results of the sample are then used to estimate characteristics of the entire population. Selecting a sample is less time-consuming, less costly, and more practical than analyzing the entire population.

In this chapter, you studied four common probability sampling methods—simple random, systematic, stratified, and cluster sampling. You also studied the sampling distribution of the sample mean and the sampling distribution of the sample proportion and their relationship to the Central Limit Theorem. You learned that the sample mean is an unbiased estimator of the population mean, and the sample proportion is an unbiased estimator of the population proportion. In the next five chapters, the techniques of confidence intervals and tests of hypotheses commonly used for statistical inference are discussed.

KEY EQUATIONS

Population Mean

$$\mu = \frac{\sum_{i=1}^{N} X_i}{N} \tag{7.1}$$

Population Standard Deviation

$$\sigma = \sqrt{\frac{\sum_{i=1}^{N} (X_i - \mu)^2}{N}} \tag{7.2}$$

Standard Error of the Mean

$$\sigma_{\overline{X}} = \frac{\sigma}{\sqrt{n}} \tag{7.3}$$

Finding Z for the Sampling Distribution of the Mean

$$Z = \frac{\overline{X} - \mu_{\overline{X}}}{\sigma_{\overline{X}}} = \frac{\overline{X} - \mu}{\dfrac{\sigma}{\sqrt{n}}} \tag{7.4}$$

Finding $\overline{X}$ for the Sampling Distribution of the Mean

$$\overline{X} = \mu + Z\frac{\sigma}{\sqrt{n}} \tag{7.5}$$

Sample Proportion

$$p = \frac{X}{n} \tag{7.6}$$

Standard Error of the Proportion

$$\sigma_p = \sqrt{\frac{\pi(1 - \pi)}{n}} \tag{7.7}$$

Finding Z for the Sampling Distribution of the Proportion

$$Z = \frac{p - \pi}{\sqrt{\dfrac{\pi(1 - \pi)}{n}}} \tag{7.8}$$

KEY TERMS

CHAPTER REVIEW PROBLEMS

CHECKING YOUR UNDERSTANDING

7.33 Why is the sample mean an unbiased estimator of the population mean?

7.34 Why does the standard error of the mean decrease as the sample size, n, increases?

7.35 Why does the sampling distribution of the mean follow a normal distribution for a large enough sample size, even though the population may not be normally distributed?

7.36 What is the difference between a population distribution and a sampling distribution?

7.37 Under what circumstances does the sampling distribution of the proportion approximately follow the normal distribution?

7.38 What is the difference between probability sampling and nonprobability sampling?

7.39 What are some potential problems with using "fishbowl" methods to select a simple random sample?

7.40 What is the difference between sampling *with* replacement versus sampling *without* replacement?

7.41 What is the difference between a simple random sample and a systematic sample?

7.42 What is the difference between a simple random sample and a stratified sample?

7.43 What is the difference between a stratified sample and a cluster sample?

APPLYING THE CONCEPTS

7.44 An industrial sewing machine uses ball bearings that are targeted to have a diameter of 0.75 inch. The lower and upper specification limits under which the ball bearing can operate are 0.74 inch (lower) and 0.76 inch (upper). Past experience has indicated that the actual diameter of the ball bearings is approximately normally distributed, with a mean of 0.753 inch and a standard deviation of 0.004 inch. If you select a random sample of 25 ball bearings, what is the probability that the sample mean is

a. between the target and the population mean of 0.753?
b. between the lower specification limit and the target?
c. greater than the upper specification limit?
d. less than the lower specification limit?
e. The probability is 93% that the sample mean diameter will be greater than what value?

7.45 The fill amount of bottles of a soft drink is normally distributed, with a mean of 2.0 liters and a standard deviation of 0.05 liter. If you select a random sample of 25 bottles, what is the probability that the sample mean will be

a. between 1.99 and 2.0 liters?
b. below 1.98 liters?
c. greater than 2.01 liters?
d. The probability is 99% that the sample mean amount of soft drink will be at least how much?
e. The probability is 99% that the sample mean amount of soft drink will be between which two values (symmetrically distributed around the mean)?

7.46 An orange juice producer buys oranges from a large orange grove that has one variety of orange. The amount of juice squeezed from these oranges is approximately normally distributed, with a mean of 4.70 ounces and a standard deviation of 0.40 ounce. Suppose that you select a sample of 25 oranges.

a. What is the probability that the sample mean amount of juice will be at least 4.60 ounces?
b. The probability is 70% that the sample mean amount of juice will be contained between what two values symmetrically distributed around the population mean?
c. The probability is 77% that the sample mean amount of juice will be greater than what value?

7.47 In Problem 7.46, suppose that the mean amount of juice squeezed is 5.0 ounces.

a. What is the probability that the sample mean amount of juice will be at least 4.60 ounces?

b. The probability is 70% that the sample mean amount of juice will be contained between what two values symmetrically distributed around the population mean?

c. The probability is 77% that the sample mean amount of juice will be greater than what value?

7.48 Junk bonds reported strong returns in 2009. The population of junk bonds earned a mean return of 57.5% in 2009. (Data extracted from *The Wall Street Journal*, January 4, 2010, p. R1.) Assume that the returns for junk bonds were distributed as a normal random variable, with a mean of 57.5 and a standard deviation of 20. If you selected a random sample of 16 junk bonds from this population, what is the probability that the sample would have a mean return

a. less than 50?

b. between 40 and 60?

c. greater than 40?

7.49 The article mentioned in Problem 7.48 reported that Treasury bonds had a mean return of −9.3% in 2009. Assume that the returns for the Treasury bonds were distributed as a normal random variable, with a mean of −9.3 and a standard deviation of 10. If you select an individual Treasury bond from this population, what is the probability that it would have a return

a. less than 0 (i.e., a loss)?

b. between −10 and −20?

c. greater than 5?

If you selected a random sample of four Treasury bonds from this population, what is the probability that the sample would have a mean return

d. less than 0—that is, a loss?

e. between −10 and −20?

f. greater than 5?

g. Compare your results in parts (d) through (f) to those in (a) through (c).

7.50 (Class Project) The table of random numbers is an example of a uniform distribution because each digit is equally likely to occur. Starting in the row corresponding to the day of the month in which you were born, use the table of random numbers (Table E.1) to take one digit at a time.

Select five different samples each of $n = 2, n = 5$, and $n = 10$. Compute the sample mean of each sample. Develop a frequency distribution of the sample means for the results of the entire class, based on samples of sizes $n = 2, n = 5$, and $n = 10$.

What can be said about the shape of the sampling distribution for each of these sample sizes?

7.51 (Class Project) Toss a coin 10 times and record the number of heads. If each student performs this experiment five times, a frequency distribution of the number of heads can be developed from the results of the entire class. Does this distribution seem to approximate the normal distribution?

7.52 (Class Project) The number of cars waiting in line at a car wash is distributed as follows:

Number of Cars	Probability
0	0.25
1	0.40
2	0.20
3	0.10
4	0.04
5	0.01

You can use the table of random numbers (Table E.1) to select samples from this distribution by assigning numbers as follows:

1. Start in the row corresponding to the day of the month in which you were born.
2. Select a two-digit random number.
3. If you select a random number from 00 to 24, record a length of 0; if from 25 to 64, record a length of 1; if from 65 to 84, record a length of 2; if from 85 to 94, record a length of 3; if from 95 to 98, record a length of 4; if 99, record a length of 5.

Select samples of $n = 2, n = 5$, and $n = 10$. Compute the mean for each sample. For example, if a sample of size 2 results in the random numbers 18 and 46, these would correspond to lengths 0 and 1, respectively, producing a sample mean of 0.5. If each student selects five different samples for each sample size, a frequency distribution of the sample means (for each sample size) can be developed from the results of the entire class. What conclusions can you reach concerning the sampling distribution of the mean as the sample size is increased?

7.53 (Class Project) Using Table E.1, simulate the selection of different-colored balls from a bowl, as follows:

1. Start in the row corresponding to the day of the month in which you were born.
2. Select one-digit numbers.
3. If a random digit between 0 and 6 is selected, consider the ball white; if a random digit is a 7, 8, or 9, consider the ball red.

Select samples of $n = 10, n = 25$, and $n = 50$ digits. In each sample, count the number of white balls and compute the proportion of white balls in the sample. If each student in the class selects five different samples for each sample size, a frequency distribution of the proportion of white balls (for each sample size) can be developed from the results of the entire class. What conclusions can you reach about the sampling distribution of the proportion as the sample size is increased?

7.54 (Class Project) Suppose that step 3 of Problem 7.53 uses the following rule: "If a random digit between 0 and 8 is selected, consider the ball to be white; if a random digit of 9 is selected, consider the ball to be red." Compare and contrast the results in this problem and those in Problem 7.53.

MANAGING ASHLAND MULTICOMM SERVICES

Continuing the quality improvement effort first described in the Chapter 6 Managing Ashland MultiComm Services case, the target upload speed for AMS Internet service subscribers has been monitored. As before, upload speeds are measured on a standard scale in which the target value is 1.0. Data collected over the past year indicate that the upload speeds are approximately normally distributed, with a mean of 1.005 and a standard deviation of 0.10.

EXERCISE

1. Each day, at 25 random times, the upload speed is measured. Assuming that the distribution has not changed from what it was in the past year, what is the probability that the upload speed is
   a. less than 1.0?
   b. between 0.95 and 1.0?
   c. between 1.0 and 1.05?
   d. less than 0.95 or greater than 1.05?
   e. Suppose that the mean upload speed of today's sample of 25 is 0.952. What conclusion can you reach about the upload speed today based on this result? Explain.
2. Compare the results of AMS1 (a) through (d) to those of AMS1. in Chapter 6 on page 244. What conclusions can you reach concerning the differences?

DIGITAL CASE

Apply your knowledge about sampling distributions in this Digital Case, which reconsiders the Oxford Cereals Using Statistics scenario.

The advocacy group Consumers Concerned About Cereal Cheaters (CCACC) suspects that cereal companies, including Oxford Cereals, are cheating consumers by packaging cereals at less than labeled weights. Recently, the group investigated the package weights of two popular Oxford brand cereals. Open **CCACC.pdf** to examine the group's claims and supporting data, and then answer the following questions:

1. Are the data collection procedures that the CCACC uses to form its conclusions flawed? What procedures could the group follow to make its analysis more rigorous?
2. Assume that the two samples of five cereal boxes (one sample for each of two cereal varieties) listed on the CCACC website were collected randomly by organization members. For each sample, do the following:
   a. Calculate the sample mean.
   b. Assume that the standard deviation of the process is 15 grams and the population mean is 368 grams. Calculate the percentage of all samples for each process that have a sample mean less than the value you calculated in (a).
   c. Again, assuming that the standard deviation is 15 grams, calculate the percentage of individual boxes of cereal that have a weight less than the value you calculated in (a).
3. What, if any, conclusions can you form by using your calculations about the filling processes for the two different cereals?
4. A representative from Oxford Cereals has asked that the CCACC take down its page discussing shortages in Oxford Cereals boxes. Is that request reasonable? Why or why not?
5. Can the techniques discussed in this chapter be used to prove cheating in the manner alleged by the CCACC? Why or why not?

REFERENCES

1. Cochran, W. G., *Sampling Techniques*, 3rd ed. (New York: Wiley, 1977).
2. Gallup, G. H., *The Sophisticated Poll-Watcher's Guide* (Princeton, NJ: Princeton Opinion Press, 1972).
3. Goleman, D., "Pollsters Enlist Psychologists in Quest for Unbiased Results," *The New York Times*, September 7, 1993, pp. C1, C11.
4. Hahn, G., and W. Meeker, *Statistical Intervals: A Guide for Practitioners* (New York: John Wiley and Sons, Inc., 1991).
5. "Landon in a Landslide: The Poll That Changed Polling," *History Matters: The U.S. Survey Course on the Web*, New York: American Social History Productions, 2005, downloaded at **http://historymatters.gmu.edu/d/5168/.**
6. *Microsoft Excel 2010* (Redmond, WA: Microsoft Corp., 2010).
7. *Minitab Release 16* (State College, PA: Minitab, Inc., 2010).
8. Rand Corporation, *A Million Random Digits with 100,000 Normal Deviates* (New York: The Free Press, 1955).
9. Squire, P., "Why the 1936 *Literary Digest* Poll Failed," *Public Opinion Quarterly 52*, 1988, pp.125–133.

CHAPTER 7 EXCEL GUIDE

EG7.1 TYPES OF SAMPLING METHODS

Simple Random Samples

PHStat2 Use **Random Sample Generation** to create a random sample *without replacement*. For example, to select the Example 7.1 sample of 40 workers on page 251, select **PHStat ➔ Sampling ➔ Random Sample Generation**. In the procedure's dialog box (shown below):

1. Enter **40** as the **Sample Size**.
2. Click **Generate list of random numbers** and enter **800** as the **Population Size**.
3. Enter a **Title** and click **OK**.

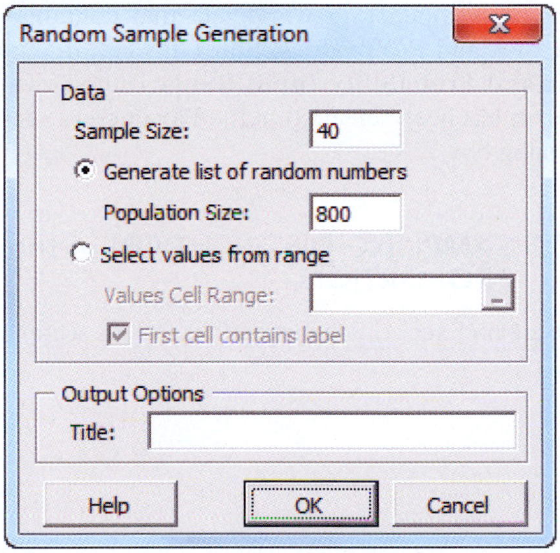

In-Depth Excel Use the **RANDBETWEEN** worksheet function to select a random integer that can be used to select an item from a frame. Enter the function as **RANDBETWEEN(1, *population size*)**.

Use the **COMPUTE worksheet** of the **Random workbook** as a template for creating a random sample. This worksheet contains 40 copies of the formula **=RANDBETWEEN(1, 800)** in column B and provides an alternative way to selecting the sample desired in Example 7.1 on page 251. Because the RANDBETWEEN function samples *with replacement*, add additional copies of the formula in new column B rows until you have the sample size *without replacement* that Example 7.1 needs.

Analysis ToolPak Use **Sampling** to create a random sample *with replacement*. For example, to select a random sample of $n = 20$ from a cell range A1:A201 of 200 values that contains a column heading in cell A1, select **Data ➔ Data Analysis**. In the Data Analysis dialog box, select **Sampling** from the **Analysis Tools** list and then click **OK**. In the procedure's dialog box (see below):

1. Enter **A1:A201** as the **Input Range** and check **Labels**.
2. Click **Random** and enter **20** as the **Number of Samples**.
3. Click **New Worksheet Ply** and then click **OK**.

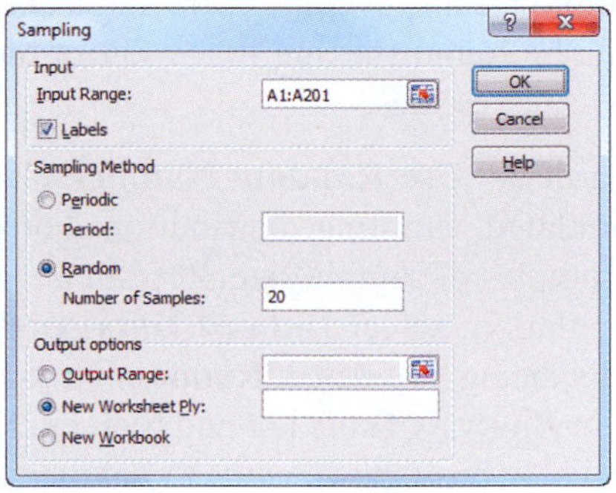

EG7.2 EVALUATING SURVEY WORTHINESS

There are no Excel Guide instructions for this section.

EG7.3 SAMPLING DISTRIBUTIONS

There are no Excel Guide instructions for this section.

EG7.4 SAMPLING DISTRIBUTION of the MEAN

PHStat2 Use **Sampling Distributions Simulation** to create a simulated sampling distribution. For example, to create 100 samples of $n = 30$ from a uniformly distributed population, select **PHStat ➔ Sampling ➔ Sampling Distributions Simulation**. In the procedure's dialog box (shown at the top of page 276):

1. Enter **100** as the **Number of Samples**.
2. Enter **30** as the **Sample Size**.
3. Click **Uniform**.
4. Enter a **Title** and click **OK**.

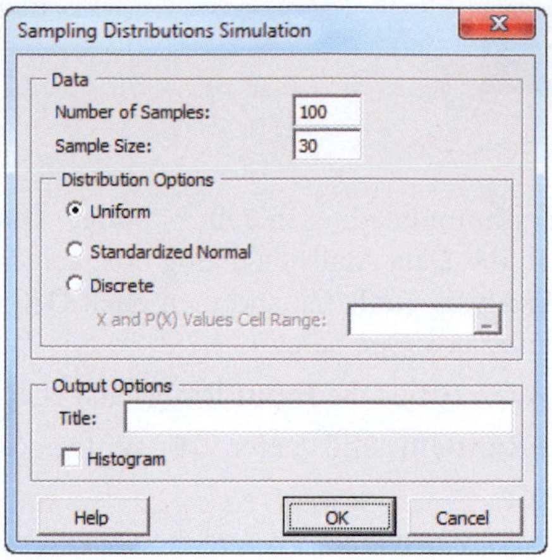

The sample means, overall mean, and standard error of the mean can be found starting in row 34 of the worksheet that the procedure creates.

Analysis ToolPak Use **Random Number Generation** to create a simulated sampling distribution. For example, to create 100 samples of sample size 30 from a uniformly distributed population, select **Data → Data Analysis**. In the Data Analysis dialog box, select **Random Number Generation** from the **Analysis Tools** list and then click **OK**. In the procedure's dialog box (shown at the top of the next column):

1. Enter **100** as the **Number of Variables**
2. Enter **30** as the **Number of Random Numbers**.
3. Select **Uniform** from the **Distribution** drop-down list.
4. Keep the **Parameters** values as is.
5. Click **New Worksheet Ply** and then click **OK**.

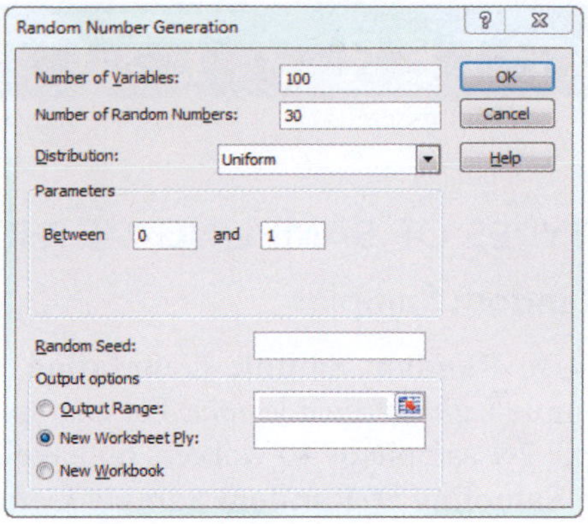

Use the formulas that appear in rows 35 through 39 in the **SDS_FORMULAS worksheet** of the **SDS workbook** as models if you want to compute sample means, the overall mean, and the standard error of the mean.

If, for other problems, you select **Discrete** in step 3, you must be open to a worksheet that contains a cell range of X and $P(X)$ values. Enter this cell range as the **Value and Probability Input Range** (not shown when **Uniform** has been selected) in the **Parameters** section of the dialog box.

EG7.5 SAMPLING DISTRIBUTION of the PROPORTION

There are no Excel Guide instructions for this section.

CHAPTER 7 MINITAB GUIDE

MG7.1 TYPES OF SAMPLING METHODS

Simple Random Samples

Use **Sample From Columns** to create a random sample *with* or *without replacement*. For example, to select the Example 7.1 sample of 40 workers on page 251, first create the list of 800 employee numbers in column **C1**. Select **Calc → Make Patterned Data → Simple Set of Numbers**. In the Simple Set of Numbers dialog box (shown at right):

1. Enter **C1** in the **Store patterned data in** box.
2. Enter **1** in the **From first value** box.
3. Enter **800** in the **To last value** box.
4. Click **OK**.

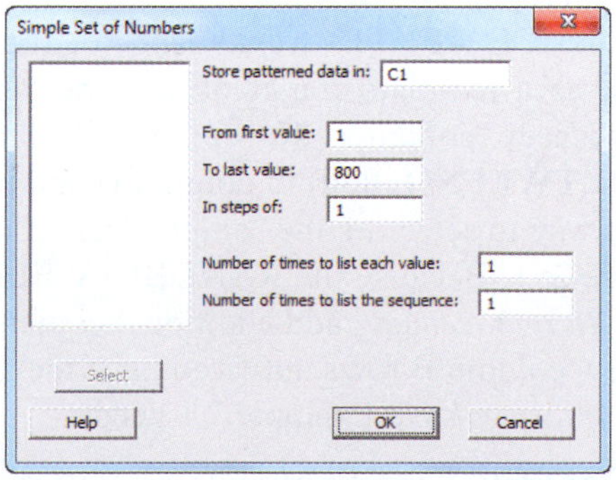

With the worksheet containing the column C1 list still open:

5. Select **Calc → Random Data → Sample from Columns**.

In the Sample From Columns dialog box (shown below):

6. Enter **40** in the **Number of rows to sample** box.
7. Enter **C1** in the **From columns** box.
8. Enter **C2** in the **Store samples in** box.
9. Click **OK**.

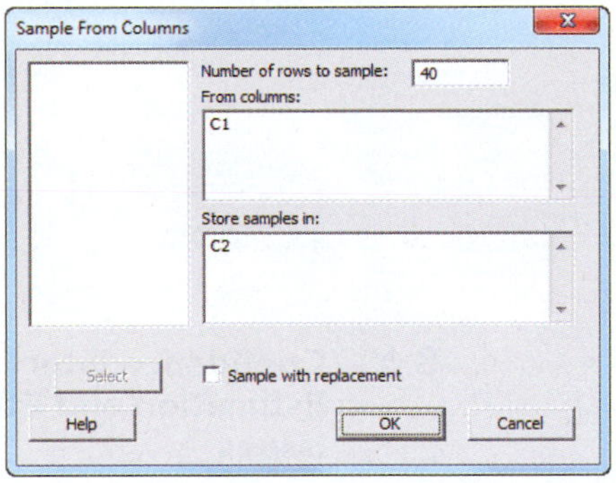

MG7.2 EVALUATING SURVEY WORTHINESS

There are no Minitab Guide instructions for this section.

MG7.3 SAMPLING DISTRIBUTIONS

There are no Minitab Guide instructions for this section.

MG7.4 SAMPLING DISTRIBUTION of the MEAN

Use **Uniform** to create a simulated sampling distribution from a uniformly distributed population. For example, to create 100 samples of $n = 30$ from a uniformly distributed population, open to a new, empty worksheet. Select **Calc ➔ Random Data ➔ Uniform**. In the Uniform Distribution dialog box (shown below):

1. Enter **100** in the **Number of rows of data to generate** box.
2. Enter **C1-C30** in the **Store in column(s)** box (to store the results in the first 30 columns).
3. Enter **0.0** in the **Lower endpoint** box.
4. Enter **1.0** in the **Upper endpoint** box.
5. Click **OK**.

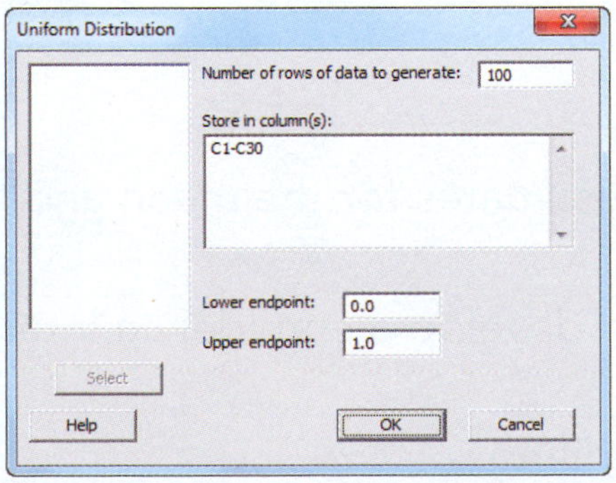

The 100 samples of $n = 30$ are entered *row-wise* in columns C1 through C30, an exception to the rule used in this book to enter data column-wise. (Row-wise data facilitates the computation of means.) While still opened to the worksheet with the 100 samples, enter **Sample Means** as the name of column **C31**. Select **Calc ➔ Row Statistics**. In the Row Statistics dialog box (shown below):

6. Click **Mean**.
7. Enter **C1-C30** in the **Input variables** box.
8. Enter **C31** in the **Store result in** box.
9. Click **OK**.

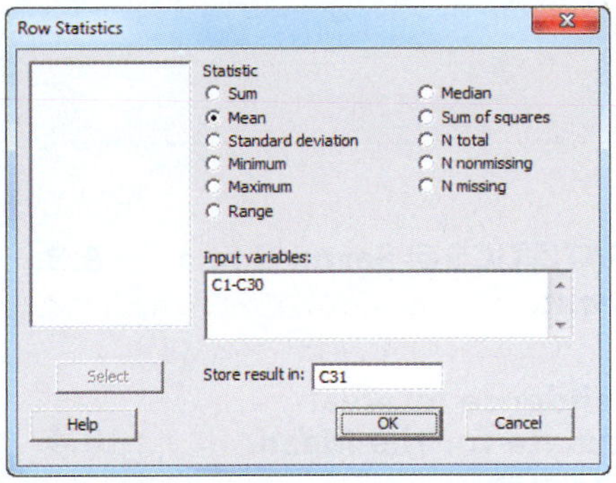

10. With the mean for each of the 100 row-wise samples in column C31, select **Stat ➔ Basic Statistics ➔ Display Descriptive Statistics**.
11. In the Display Descriptive Statistics dialog box, enter **C31** in the **Variables** box and click **Statistics**.
12. In the Display Descriptive Statistics - Statistics dialog box, select **Mean** and **Standard deviation** and then click **OK**.
13. Back in the Display Descriptive Statistics dialog box, click **OK**.

While still open to the worksheet created in steps 1 through 13, select **Graph ➔ Histogram** and in the Histograms dialog box, click **Simple** and then click **OK**. In the Histogram - Simple dialog box:

1. Enter **C31** in the **Graph variables** box.
2. Click **OK**.

Sampling from Normally Distributed Populations

Use **Normal** to create a simulated sampling distribution from a normally distributed population. For example, to create 100 samples of $n = 30$ from a normally distributed population, open to a new, empty worksheet. Select **Calc ➔ Random Data ➔ Normal**. In the Normal Distribution dialog box:

1. Enter **100** in the **Number of rows of data to generate** box.
2. Enter **C1-C30** in the **Store in column(s)** box (to store the results in the first 30 columns).
3. Enter a value for μ in the **Mean** box.
4. Enter a value for σ in the **Standard deviation** box.
5. Click **OK**.

The 100 samples of $n = 30$ are entered row-wise in columns C1 through C30. To compute statistics, select **Calc ➔ Row Statistics** and follow steps 6 through 13 from the set of instructions for a uniformly distributed population.

8 Confidence Interval Estimation

Learning Objectives

In this chapter, you learn:

- To construct and interpret confidence interval estimates for the mean and the proportion
- How to determine the sample size necessary to develop a confidence interval estimate for the mean or proportion
- How to use confidence interval estimates in auditing

USING STATISTICS

@ Saxon Home Improvement

Saxon Home Improvement distributes home improvement supplies in the northeastern United States. As a company accountant, you are responsible for the accuracy of the integrated inventory management and sales information system. You could review the contents of each and every record to check the accuracy of this system, but such a detailed review would be time-consuming and costly. A better approach is to use statistical inference techniques to draw conclusions about the population of all records from a relatively small sample collected during an audit. At the end of each month, you could select a sample of the sales invoices to estimate the following:

- The mean dollar amount listed on the sales invoices for the month
- The proportion of invoices that contain errors that violate the internal control policy of the warehouse
- The total dollar amount listed on the sales invoices for the month
- Any differences between the dollar amounts on the sales invoices and the amounts entered into the sales information system

How accurate are the results from the sample, and how do you use this information? Is the sample size large enough to give you the information you need?

In Section 7.4, you used the Central Limit Theorem and knowledge of the population distribution to determine the percentage of sample means that are within certain distances of the population mean. For instance, in the cereal-filling example used throughout Chapter 7 (see Example 7.6 on page 263), you can conclude that 95% of all sample means are between 362.12 and 373.88 grams. This is an example of *deductive* reasoning because the conclusion is based on taking something that is true in general (for the population) and applying it to something specific (the sample means).

Getting the results that Saxon Home Improvement needs requires *inductive* reasoning. Inductive reasoning lets you use some specifics to make broader generalizations. You cannot guarantee that the broader generalizations are absolutely correct, but with a careful choice of the specifics and a rigorous methodology, you can get useful conclusions. As a Saxon accountant, you need to use inferential statistics, which uses sample results (the "some specifics") to *estimate* (the making of "broader generalizations") unknown population parameters such as a population mean or a population proportion. Note that statisticians use the word *estimate* in the same sense of the everyday usage: something you are reasonably certain about but cannot flatly say is absolutely correct.

You estimate population parameters by using either point estimates or interval estimates. A **point estimate** is the value of a single sample statistic, such as a sample mean. A **confidence interval estimate** is a range of numbers, called an *interval*, constructed around the point estimate. The confidence interval is constructed such that the probability that the interval includes the population parameter is known.

Suppose you want to estimate the mean GPA of all the students at your university. The mean GPA for all the students is an unknown population mean, denoted by μ. You select a sample of students and compute the sample mean, denoted by $\bar{X}$, to be 2.80. As a *point estimate* of the population mean, μ, you ask how accurate is the 2.80 value as an estimate of the population mean, μ? By taking into account the variability from sample to sample (see Section 7.4, concerning the sampling distribution of the mean), you can construct a confidence interval estimate for the population mean to answer this question.

When you construct a confidence interval estimate, you indicate the confidence of correctly estimating the value of the population parameter, μ. This allows you to say that there is a specified confidence that μ is somewhere in the range of numbers defined by the interval.

After studying this chapter, you might find that a 95% confidence interval for the mean GPA at your university is $(2.75 \le \mu \le 2.85)$. You can interpret this interval estimate by stating that you are 95% confident that the mean GPA at your university is between 2.75 and 2.85.

In this chapter, you learn to construct a confidence interval for both the population mean and population proportion. You also learn how to determine the sample size that is necessary to construct a confidence interval of a desired width.

8.1 Confidence Interval Estimate for the Mean (σ Known)

In Section 7.4, you used the Central Limit Theorem and knowledge of the population distribution to determine the percentage of sample means that are within certain distances of the population mean. Suppose that in the cereal-filling example, you wished to estimate the population mean, using the information from a single sample. Thus, rather than taking $\mu \pm (1.96)(\sigma/\sqrt{n})$ to find the upper and lower limits around μ, as in Section 7.4, you substitute the sample mean, $\bar{X}$, for the unknown μ and use $\bar{X} \pm (1.96)(\sigma/\sqrt{n})$ as an interval to estimate the unknown μ. Although in practice you select a single sample of n values and compute the mean, $\bar{X}$, in order to understand the full meaning of the interval estimate, you need to examine a hypothetical set of all possible samples of n values.

Suppose that a sample of $n = 25$ boxes has a mean of 362.3 grams. The interval developed to estimate μ is $362.3 \pm (1.96)(15)/(\sqrt{25})$ or 362.3 ± 5.88. The estimate of μ is

$$356.42 \le \mu \le 368.18$$

Because the population mean, μ (equal to 368), is included within the interval, this sample results in a correct statement about μ (see Figure 8.1).

FIGURE 8.1
Confidence interval estimates for five different samples of $n = 25$ taken from a population where $\mu = 368$ and $\sigma = 15$

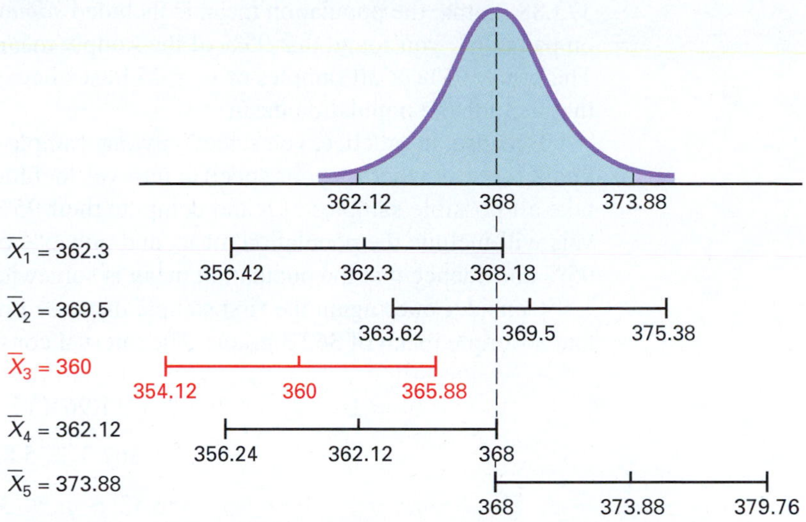

To continue this hypothetical example, suppose that for a different sample of $n = 25$ boxes, the mean is 369.5. The interval developed from this sample is

$$369.5 \pm (1.96)(15)/(\sqrt{25})$$

or 369.5 ± 5.88. The estimate is

$$363.62 \leq \mu \leq 375.38$$

Because the population mean, μ (equal to 368), is also included within this interval, this statement about μ is correct.

Now, before you begin to think that correct statements about μ are always made by developing a confidence interval estimate, suppose a third hypothetical sample of $n = 25$ boxes is selected and the sample mean is equal to 360 grams. The interval developed here is $360 \pm (1.96)(15)/(\sqrt{25})$, or 360 ± 5.88. In this case, the estimate of μ is

$$354.12 \leq \mu \leq 365.88$$

This estimate is *not* a correct statement because the population mean, μ, is not included in the interval developed from this sample (see Figure 8.1). Thus, for some samples, the interval estimate for μ is correct, but for others it is incorrect. In practice, only one sample is selected, and because the population mean is unknown, you cannot determine whether the interval estimate is correct. To resolve this problem of sometimes having an interval that provides a correct estimate and sometimes having an interval that does not, you need to determine the proportion of samples producing intervals that result in correct statements about the population mean, μ. To do this, consider two other hypothetical samples: the case in which $\bar{X} = 362.12$ grams and the case in which $\bar{X} = 373.88$ grams. If $\bar{X} = 362.12$, the interval is $362.12 \pm (1.96)(15)/(\sqrt{25})$, or 362.12 ± 5.88. This leads to the following interval:

$$356.24 \leq \mu \leq 368.00$$

Because the population mean of 368 is at the upper limit of the interval, the statement is correct (see Figure 8.1).

When $\bar{X} = 373.88$, the interval is $373.88 \pm (1.96)(15)/(\sqrt{25})$, or 373.88 ± 5.88. The interval estimate for the mean is

$$368.00 \leq \mu \leq 379.76$$

In this case, because the population mean of 368 is included at the lower limit of the interval, the statement is correct.

In Figure 8.1, you see that when the sample mean falls somewhere between 362.12 and 373.88 grams, the population mean is included *somewhere* within the interval. In Example 7.6 on page 263, you found that 95% of the sample means are between 362.12 and 373.88 grams. Therefore, 95% of all samples of $n = 25$ boxes have sample means that will result in intervals that include the population mean.

Because, in practice, you select only one sample of size n, and $\alpha/2$ is unknown, you never know for sure whether your specific interval includes the population mean. However, if you take all possible samples of n and compute their 95% confidence intervals, 95% of the intervals will include the population mean, and only 5% of them will not. In other words, you have 95% confidence that the population mean is somewhere in your interval.

Consider once again the first sample discussed in this section. A sample of $n = 25$ boxes had a sample mean of 362.3 grams. The interval constructed to estimate μ is

$$362.3 \pm (1.96)(15)/(\sqrt{25})$$

$$362.3 \pm 5.88$$

$$356.42 \le \mu \le 368.18$$

The interval from 356.42 to 368.18 is referred to as a *95% confidence interval*. The following contains an interpretation of the interval that most business professionals will understand. (For a technical discussion of different ways to interpret confidence intervals, see reference 3.)

"I am 95% confident that the mean amount of cereal in the population of boxes is somewhere between 356.42 and 368.18 grams."

To assist in your understanding of the meaning of the confidence interval, the following example concerns the order-filling process at a website. Filling orders consists of several steps, including receiving an order, picking the parts of the order, checking the order, packing, and shipping the order. The file **Order** contains the time, in minutes, to fill orders for a population of $N = 200$ orders on a recent day. Although in practice the population characteristics are rarely known, for this population of orders, the mean, μ, is known to be equal to 69.637 minutes, and the standard deviation, σ, is known to be equal to 10.411 minutes and the population is normally distributed. To illustrate how the sample mean and sample standard deviation can vary from one sample to another, 20 different samples of $n = 10$ were selected from the population of 200 orders, and the sample mean and sample standard deviation (and other statistics) were calculated for each sample. Figure 8.2 shows these results.

FIGURE 8.2

Sample statistics and 95% confidence intervals for 20 samples of $n = 10$ randomly selected from the population of $N = 200$ orders

Variable	Count	Mean	StDev	Minimum	Median	Maximum	Range	95% CI
Sample 1	10	74.15	13.39	56.10	76.85	97.70	41.60	(67.6973, 80.6027)
Sample 2	10	61.10	10.60	46.80	61.35	79.50	32.70	(54.6473, 67.5527)
Sample 3	10	74.36	6.50	62.50	74.50	84.00	21.50	(67.9073, 80.8127)
Sample 4	10	70.40	12.80	47.20	70.95	84.00	36.80	(63.9473, 76.8527)
Sample 5	10	62.18	10.85	47.10	59.70	84.00	36.90	(55.7273, 68.6327)
Sample 6	10	67.03	9.68	51.10	69.60	83.30	32.20	(60.5773, 73.4827)
Sample 7	10	69.03	8.81	56.60	68.85	83.70	27.10	(62.5773, 75.4827)
Sample 8	10	72.30	11.52	54.20	71.35	87.00	32.80	(65.8473, 78.7527)
Sample 9	10	68.18	14.10	50.10	69.95	86.20	36.10	(61.7273, 74.6327)
Sample 10	10	66.67	9.08	57.10	64.65	86.10	29.00	(60.2173, 73.1227)
Sample 11	10	72.42	9.76	59.60	74.65	86.10	26.50	(65.9673, 78.8727)
Sample 12	10	76.26	11.69	50.10	80.60	87.00	36.90	(69.8073, 82.7127)
Sample 13	10	65.74	12.11	47.10	62.15	86.10	39.00	(59.2873, 72.1927)
Sample 14	10	69.99	10.97	51.00	73.40	84.60	33.60	(63.5373, 76.4427)
Sample 15	10	75.76	8.60	61.10	75.05	87.80	26.70	(69.3073, 82.2127)
Sample 16	10	67.94	9.19	56.70	67.70	87.80	31.10	(61.4873, 74.3927)
Sample 17	10	71.05	10.48	50.10	71.15	86.20	36.10	(64.5973, 77.5027)
Sample 18	10	71.68	7.96	55.60	72.35	82.60	27.00	(65.2273, 78.1327)
Sample 19	10	70.97	9.83	54.40	70.05	84.60	30.20	(64.5173, 77.4227)
Sample 20	10	74.48	8.80	62.00	76.25	85.70	23.70	(68.0273, 80.9327)

From Figure 8.2, you can see the following:

- The sample statistics differ from sample to sample. The sample means vary from 61.10 to 76.26 minutes, the sample standard deviations vary from 6.50 to 14.10 minutes, the sample medians vary from 59.70 to 80.60 minutes, and the sample ranges vary from 21.50 to 41.60 minutes.
- Some of the sample means are greater than the population mean of 69.637 minutes, and some of the sample means are less than the population mean.
- Some of the sample standard deviations are greater than the population standard deviation of 10.411 minutes, and some of the sample standard deviations are less than the population standard deviation.
- The variation in the sample ranges is much more than the variation in the sample standard deviations.

The variation of sample statistics from sample to sample is called *sampling error*. Sampling error is the variation that occurs due to selecting a single sample from the population. The size of the sampling error is primarily based on the amount of variation in the population and on the sample size. Large samples have less sampling error than small samples, but large samples cost more to select.

The last column of Figure 8.2 contains 95% confidence interval estimates of the population mean order-filling time, based on the results of those 20 samples of $n = 10$. Begin by examining the first sample selected. The sample mean is 74.15 minutes, and the interval estimate for the population mean is 67.6973 to 80.6027 minutes. In a typical study, you would not know for sure whether this interval estimate is correct because you rarely know the value of the population mean. However, for this example *concerning the order-filling times*, the population mean is known to be 69.637 minutes. If you examine the interval 67.6973 to 80.6027 minutes, you see that the population mean of 69.637 minutes is located *between* these lower and upper limits. Thus, the first sample provides a correct estimate of the population mean in the form of an interval estimate. Looking over the other 19 samples, you see that similar results occur for all the other samples *except* for samples 2, 5, and 12. For each of the intervals generated (other than samples 2, 5, and 12), the population mean of 69.637 minutes is located *somewhere* within the interval.

For sample 2, the sample mean is 61.10 minutes, and the interval is 54.6473 to 67.5527 minutes; for sample 5, the sample mean is 62.18, and the interval is between 55.7273 and 68.6327; for sample 12, the sample mean is 76.26, and the interval is between 69.8073 and 82.7127 minutes. The population mean of 69.637 minutes is *not* located within any of these intervals, and the estimate of the population mean made using these intervals is incorrect. Although 3 of the 20 intervals did not include the population mean, if you had selected all the possible samples of $n = 10$ from a population of $N = 200$, 95% of the intervals would include the population mean.

In some situations, you might want a higher degree of confidence of including the population mean within the interval (such as 99%). In other cases, you might accept less confidence (such as 90%) of correctly estimating the population mean. In general, the **level of confidence** is symbolized by $(1 - \alpha) \times 100\%$, where α is the proportion in the tails of the distribution that is outside the confidence interval. The proportion in the upper tail of the distribution is $\alpha/2$, and the proportion in the lower tail of the distribution is $\alpha/2$. You use Equation (8.1) to construct a $(1 - \alpha) \times 100\%$ confidence interval estimate for the mean with σ known.

CONFIDENCE INTERVAL FOR THE MEAN (σ KNOWN)

$$\bar{X} \pm Z_{\alpha/2}\frac{\sigma}{\sqrt{n}}$$

or

$$\bar{X} - Z_{\alpha/2}\frac{\sigma}{\sqrt{n}} \le \mu \le \bar{X} + Z_{\alpha/2}\frac{\sigma}{\sqrt{n}} \quad \textbf{(8.1)}$$

where $Z_{\alpha/2}$ is the value corresponding to an upper-tail probability of $\alpha/2$ from the standardized normal distribution (i.e., a cumulative area of $1 - \alpha/2$).

The value of $Z_{\alpha/2}$ needed for constructing a confidence interval is called the **critical value** for the distribution. 95% confidence corresponds to an α value of 0.05. The critical Z value corresponding to a cumulative area of 0.975 is 1.96 because there is 0.025 in the upper tail of the distribution, and the cumulative area less than $Z = 1.96$ is 0.975.

There is a different critical value for each level of confidence, $1 - \alpha$. A level of confidence of 95% leads to a Z value of 1.96 (see Figure 8.3). 99% confidence corresponds to an α value of 0.01. The Z value is approximately 2.58 because the upper-tail area is 0.005 and the cumulative area less than $Z = 2.58$ is 0.995 (see Figure 8.4).

FIGURE 8.3
Normal curve for determining the Z value needed for 95% confidence

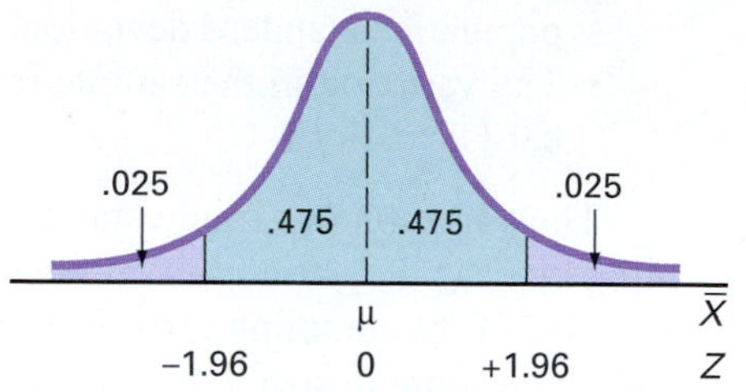

FIGURE 8.4
Normal curve for determining the Z value needed for 99% confidence

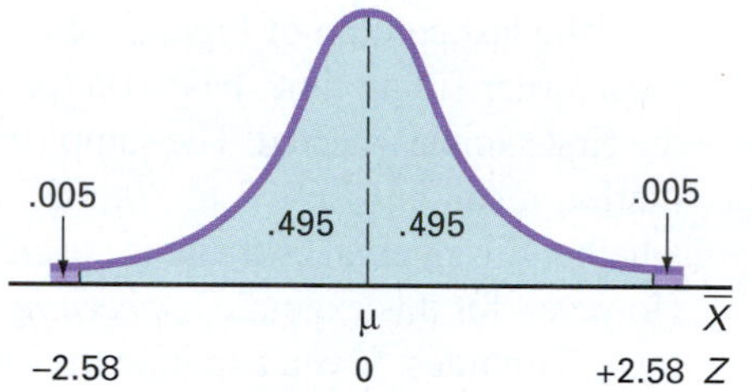

Now that various levels of confidence have been considered, why not make the confidence level as close to 100% as possible? Before doing so, you need to realize that any increase in the level of confidence is achieved only by widening (and making less precise) the confidence interval. There is no "free lunch" here. You would have more confidence that the population mean is within a broader range of values; however, this might make the interpretation of the confidence interval less useful. The trade-off between the width of the confidence interval and the level of confidence is discussed in greater depth in the context of determining the sample size in Section 8.4. Example 8.1 illustrates the application of the confidence interval estimate.

EXAMPLE 8.1

Estimating the Mean Paper Length with 95% Confidence

A paper manufacturer has a production process that operates continuously throughout an entire production shift. The paper is expected to have a mean length of 11 inches, and the standard deviation of the length is 0.02 inch. At periodic intervals, a sample is selected to determine whether the mean paper length is still equal to 11 inches or whether something has gone wrong in the production process to change the length of the paper produced. You select a random sample of 100 sheets, and the mean paper length is 10.998 inches. Construct a 95% confidence interval estimate for the population mean paper length.

SOLUTION Using Equation (8.1) on page 283, with $Z_{\alpha/2} = 1.96$ for 95% confidence,

$$\bar{X} \pm Z_{\alpha/2}\frac{\sigma}{\sqrt{n}} = 10.998 \pm (1.96)\frac{0.02}{\sqrt{100}}$$

$$= 10.998 \pm 0.0039$$

$$10.9941 \leq \mu \leq 11.0019$$

Thus, with 95% confidence, you conclude that the population mean is between 10.9941 and 11.0019 inches. Because the interval includes 11, the value indicating that the production process is working properly, you have no reason to believe that anything is wrong with the production process.

To see the effect of using a 99% confidence interval, examine Example 8.2.

EXAMPLE 8.2

Estimating the Mean Paper Length with 99% Confidence

Construct a 99% confidence interval estimate for the population mean paper length.

SOLUTION Using Equation (8.1) on page 283, with $Z_{\alpha/2} = 2.58$ for 99% confidence,

$$\bar{X} \pm Z_{\alpha/2}\frac{\sigma}{\sqrt{n}} = 10.998 \pm (2.58)\frac{0.02}{\sqrt{100}}$$

$$= 10.998 \pm 0.00516$$

$$10.9928 \leq \mu \leq 11.0032$$

Once again, because 11 is included within this wider interval, you have no reason to believe that anything is wrong with the production process.

As discussed in Section 7.4, the sampling distribution of the sample mean, $\bar{X}$, is normally distributed if the population for your characteristic of interest, X, follows a normal distribution. And, if the population of X does not follow a normal distribution, the Central Limit Theorem almost always ensures that $\bar{X}$ is approximately normally distributed when n is large. However, when dealing with a small sample size and a population that does not follow a normal distribution, the sampling distribution of $\bar{X}$ is not normally distributed, and therefore the confidence interval discussed in this section is inappropriate. In practice, however, as long as the sample size is large enough and the population is not very skewed, you can use the confidence interval defined in Equation (8.1) to estimate the population mean when σ is known. To assess the assumption of normality, you can evaluate the shape of the sample data by constructing a histogram, stem-and-leaf display, boxplot, or normal probability plot.

Can You Ever Know the Population Standard Deviation?

To solve Equation 8.1, you must know the value for σ, the population standard deviation. To know σ implies that you know all the values in the entire population. (How else would you know the value of this population parameter?) If you knew all the values in the entire population, you could directly compute the population mean. There would be no need to use the *inductive* reasoning of inferential statistics to *estimate* the population mean. In other words, if you knew σ, you really do not have a need to use Equation 8.1 to construct a "confidence interval estimate of the mean (σ known)."

More significantly, in virtually all real-world business situations, you would never know the standard deviation of the population. In business situations, populations are often too large to examine all the values. So why study the confidence interval estimate of the mean (σ known) at all? This method serves as an important introduction to the concept of a confidence interval because it uses the normal distribution, which has already been thoroughly discussed in Chapters 6 and 7. In the next section, you will see that constructing a confidence interval estimate when σ is not known requires another distribution (the t distribution) not previously mentioned in this book.

Because the confidence interval concept is a very important concept to understand when reading the rest of this book, review this section carefully to understand the underlying concept—even if you never have a practical reason to use the confidence interval estimate of the mean (σ known).

Problems for Section 8.1

LEARNING THE BASICS

8.1 If $\bar{X} = 85$, $\sigma = 8$, and $n = 64$, construct a 95% confidence interval estimate for the population mean, μ.

8.2 If $\bar{X} = 125$, $\sigma = 24$, and $n = 36$, construct a 99% confidence interval estimate for the population mean, μ.

8.3 Why is it not possible in Example 8.1 on page 284 to have 100% confidence? Explain.

8.4 Is it true in Example 8.1 on page 284 that you do not know for sure whether the population mean is between 10.9941 and 11.0019 inches? Explain.

APPLYING THE CONCEPTS

8.5 A market researcher selects a simple random sample of $n = 100$ customers from a population of 2 million customers. After analyzing the sample, she states that she has 95% confidence that the mean annual income of the 2 million customers is between \$70,000 and \$85,000. Explain the meaning of this statement.

8.6 Suppose that you are going to collect a set of data, either from an entire population or from a random sample taken from that population.

a. Which statistical measure would you compute first: the mean or the standard deviation? Explain.

b. What does your answer to (a) tell you about the "practicality" of using the confidence interval estimate formula given in Equation (8.1)?

8.7 Consider the confidence interval estimate discussed in Problem 8.5. Suppose that the population mean annual income is \$71,000. Is the confidence interval estimate stated in Problem 8.5 correct? Explain.

8.8 You are working as an assistant to the dean of institutional research at your university. The dean wants to survey members of the alumni association who obtained their baccalaureate degrees 5 years ago to learn what their starting salaries were in their first full-time job after receiving their degrees. A sample of 100 alumni is to be randomly selected from the list of 2,500 graduates in that class. If the dean's goal is to construct a 95% confidence interval estimate for the population mean starting salary, why is it not possible that you will be able to use Equation (8.1) on page 283 for this purpose? Explain.

8.9 The manager of a paint supply store wants to estimate the actual amount of paint contained in 1-gallon cans purchased from a nationally known manufacturer. The manufacturer's specifications state that the standard deviation of the amount of paint is equal to 0.02 gallon. A random sample of 50 cans is selected, and the sample mean amount of paint per 1-gallon can is 0.995 gallon.

a. Construct a 99% confidence interval estimate for the population mean amount of paint included in a 1-gallon can.

b. On the basis of these results, do you think that the manager has a right to complain to the manufacturer? Why?

c. Must you assume that the population amount of paint per can is normally distributed here? Explain.

d. Construct a 95% confidence interval estimate. How does this change your answer to (b)?

SELF Test **8.10** The quality control manager at a light bulb factory needs to estimate the mean life of a large shipment of light bulbs. The standard deviation is 100 hours. A random sample of 64 light bulbs indicated a sample mean life of 350 hours.

a. Construct a 95% confidence interval estimate for the population mean life of light bulbs in this shipment.

b. Do you think that the manufacturer has the right to state that the light bulbs have a mean life of 400 hours? Explain.

c. Must you assume that the population light bulb life is normally distributed? Explain.

d. Suppose that the standard deviation changes to 80 hours. What are your answers in (a) and (b)?

8.2 Confidence Interval Estimate for the Mean (σ Unknown)

In the previous section, you learned that in most business situations, you do not know σ, the population standard deviation. This section discusses a method of constructing a confidence interval estimate of μ that uses the sample statistic S as an estimate of the population parameter σ.

Student's t Distribution

At the start of the twentieth century, William S. Gosset was working at Guinness in Ireland, trying to help brew better beer less expensively (see reference 4). As he had only small samples to study, he needed to find a way to make inferences about means without having to know σ. Writing under the pen name "Student,"[1] Gosset solved this problem by developing what today is known as the **Student's *t* distribution**, or the *t* distribution, for short.

If the random variable X is normally distributed, then the following statistic:

$$t = \frac{\bar{X} - \mu}{\dfrac{S}{\sqrt{n}}}$$

has a t distribution with $n - 1$ **degrees of freedom**. This expression has the same form as the Z statistic in Equation (7.4) on page 262, except that S is used to estimate the unknown σ.

[1] Guinness considered all research conducted to be proprietary and a trade secret. The firm prohibited its employees from publishing their results. Gosset circumvented this ban by using the pen name "Student" to publish his findings.

Properties of the t Distribution

The t distribution is very similar in appearance to the standardized normal distribution. Both distributions are symmetrical and bell-shaped, with the mean and the median equal to zero. However, the t distribution has more area in the tails and less in the center than does the standardized normal distribution (see Figure 8.5). This is due to the fact that because S is used to estimate the unknown σ, the values of t are more variable than those for Z.

FIGURE 8.5

Standardized normal distribution and t distribution for 5 degrees of freedom

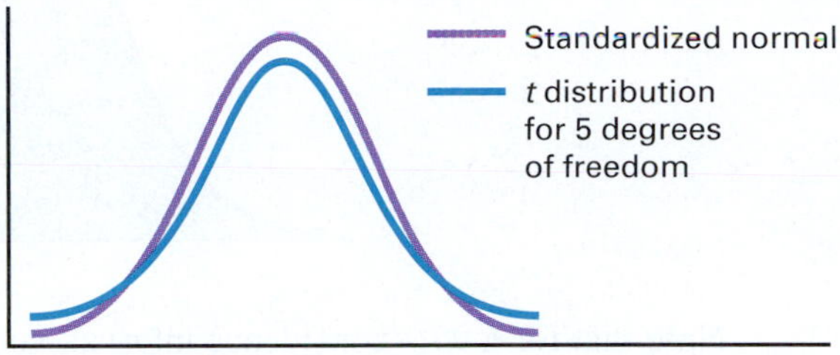

The degrees of freedom, $n - 1$, are directly related to the sample size, n. The concept of *degrees of freedom* is discussed further on page 288. As the sample size and degrees of freedom increase, S becomes a better estimate of σ, and the t distribution gradually approaches the standardized normal distribution, until the two are virtually identical. With a sample size of about 120 or more, S estimates σ closely enough so that there is little difference between the t and Z distributions.

As stated earlier, the t distribution assumes that the random variable X is normally distributed. In practice, however, when the sample size is large enough and the population is not very skewed, in most cases you can use the t distribution to estimate the population mean when σ is unknown. When dealing with a small sample size and a skewed population distribution, the confidence interval estimate may not provide a valid estimate of the population mean. To assess the assumption of normality, you can evaluate the shape of the sample data by constructing a histogram, stem-and-leaf display, boxplot, or normal probability plot. However, the ability of any of these graphs to help you evaluate normality is limited when you have a small sample size.

You find the critical values of t for the appropriate degrees of freedom from the table of the t distribution (see Table E.3). The columns of the table present the most commonly used cumulative probabilities and corresponding upper-tail areas. The rows of the table represent the degrees of freedom. The critical t values are found in the cells of the table. For example, with 99 degrees of freedom, if you want 95% confidence, you find the appropriate value of t, as shown in Table 8.1. The 95% confidence level means that 2.5% of the values (an area of 0.025) are in

TABLE 8.1

Determining the Critical Value from the t Table for an Area of 0.025 in Each Tail with 99 Degrees of Freedom

	Cumulative Probabilities					
	.75	.90	.95	.975	.99	.995
	Upper-Tail Areas					
Degrees of Freedom	.25	.10	.05	.025	.01	.005
1	1.0000	3.0777	6.3138	12.7062	31.8207	63.6574
2	0.8165	1.8856	2.9200	4.3027	6.9646	9.9248
3	0.7649	1.6377	2.3534	3.1824	4.5407	5.8409
4	0.7407	1.5332	2.1318	2.7764	3.7469	4.6041
5	0.7267	1.4759	2.0150	2.5706	3.3649	4.0322
.	.	.	.	.	.	.
.	.	.	.	.	.	.
.	.	.	.	.	.	.
96	0.6771	1.2904	1.6609	1.9850	2.3658	2.6280
97	0.6770	1.2903	1.6607	1.9847	2.3654	2.6275
98	0.6770	1.2902	1.6606	1.9845	2.3650	2.6269
99	0.6770	1.2902	1.6604	1.9842	2.3646	2.6264
100	0.6770	1.2901	1.6602	1.9840	2.3642	2.6259

Source: Extracted from Table E.3.

each tail of the distribution. Looking in the column for a cumulative probability of 0.975 and an upper-tail area of 0.025 in the row corresponding to 99 degrees of freedom gives you a critical value for t of 1.9842 (see Figure 8.6). Because t is a symmetrical distribution with a mean of 0, if the upper-tail value is $+1.9842$, the value for the lower-tail area (lower 0.025) is -1.9842. A t value of -1.9842 means that the probability that t is less than -1.9842 is 0.025, or 2.5%.

FIGURE 8.6
t distribution with 99 degrees of freedom

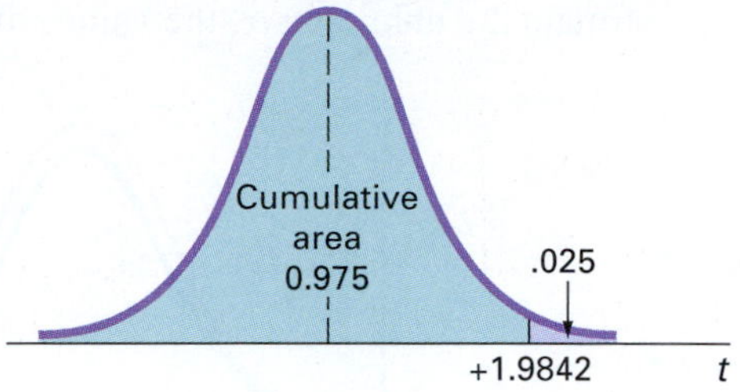

Note that for a 95% confidence interval, you will always have a cumulative probability of 0.975 and an upper-tail area of 0.025. Similarly, for a 99% confidence interval, you will have 0.995 and 0.005, and for a 90% confidence interval you will have 0.95 and 0.05.

The Concept of Degrees of Freedom

In Chapter 3, you learned that the numerator of the sample variance, S^2 [see Equation (3.6) on page 103], requires the computation

$$\sum_{i=1}^{n}(X_i - \overline{X})^2$$

In order to compute S^2, you first need to know $\overline{X}$. Therefore, only $n - 1$ of the sample values are free to vary. This means that you have $n - 1$ degrees of freedom. For example, suppose a sample of five values has a mean of 20. How many values do you need to know before you can determine the remainder of the values? The fact that $n = 5$ and $\overline{X} = 20$ also tells you that

$$\sum_{i=1}^{n} X_i = 100$$

because

$$\frac{\sum_{i=1}^{n} X_i}{n} = \overline{X}$$

Thus, when you know four of the values, the fifth one is *not* free to vary because the sum must be 100. For example, if four of the values are 18, 24, 19, and 16, the fifth value must be 23 so that the sum is 100.

The Confidence Interval Statement

Equation (8.2) defines the $(1 - \alpha) \times 100\%$ confidence interval estimate for the mean with σ unknown.

CONFIDENCE INTERVAL FOR THE MEAN (σ UNKNOWN)

$$\overline{X} \pm t_{\alpha/2}\frac{S}{\sqrt{n}}$$

or

$$\overline{X} - t_{\alpha/2}\frac{S}{\sqrt{n}} \le \mu \le \overline{X} + t_{\alpha/2}\frac{S}{\sqrt{n}} \qquad \textbf{(8.2)}$$

where $t_{\alpha/2}$ is the critical value corresponding to an upper-tail probability of $\alpha/2$ (i.e., a cumulative area of $1 - \alpha/2$) from the t distribution with $n - 1$ degrees of freedom.

To illustrate the application of the confidence interval estimate for the mean when the standard deviation is unknown, recall the Saxon Home Improvement scenario presented on page 279. Using the Define, Collect, Organize, Visualize, and Analyze steps first discussed in Chapter 2, you define the variable of interest as the dollar amount listed on the sales invoices for the month. Your business objective is to estimate the mean dollar amount. Then, you collect the data by selecting a sample of 100 sales invoices from the population of sales invoices during the month. Once you have collected the data, you organize the data in a worksheet. You can construct various graphs (not shown here) to better visualize the distribution of the dollar amounts. To analyze the data, you compute the sample mean of the 100 sales invoices to be equal to \$110.27 and the sample standard deviation to be equal to \$28.95. For 95% confidence, the critical value from the t distribution (as shown in Table 8.1 on page 287) is 1.9842. Using Equation (8.2),

$$\bar{X} \pm t_{\alpha/2}\frac{S}{\sqrt{n}}$$

$$= 110.27 \pm (1.9842)\frac{28.95}{\sqrt{100}}$$

$$= 110.27 \pm 5.74$$

$$104.53 \leq \mu \leq 116.01$$

Figure 8.7 shows this confidence interval estimate of the mean dollar amount as computed by Excel (left results) and Minitab (right results).

FIGURE 8.7

Excel worksheet and Minitab confidence interval estimate for the mean sales invoice amount for the Saxon Home Improvement Company

	A	B	
1	Estimate for the Mean Sales Invoice Amount		
2			
3	Data		
4	Sample Standard Deviation	28.95	
5	Sample Mean	110.27	
6	Sample Size	100	
7	Confidence Level	95%	
8			
9	Intermediate Calculations		
10	Standard Error of the Mean	2.8950	=B4/SQRT(B6)
11	Degrees of Freedom	99	=B6 - 1
12	*t* Value	1.9842	=TINV(1 - B7, B11)
13	Interval Half Width	5.7443	=B12 * B10
14			
15	Confidence Interval		
16	Interval Lower Limit	104.53	=B5 - B13
17	Interval Upper Limit	116.01	=B5 + B13

One-Sample T

N	Mean	StDev	SE Mean	95% CI
100	110.27	28.95	2.90	(104.53, 116.01)

Thus, with 95% confidence, you conclude that the mean amount of all the sales invoices is between \$104.53 and \$116.01. The 95% confidence level indicates that if you selected all possible samples of 100 (something that is never done in practice), 95% of the intervals developed would include the population mean somewhere within the interval. The validity of this confidence interval estimate depends on the assumption of normality for the distribution of the amount of the sales invoices. With a sample of 100, the normality assumption is not overly restrictive (see the Central Limit Theorem on page 264), and the use of the t distribution is likely appropriate. Example 8.3 further illustrates how you construct the confidence interval for a mean when the population standard deviation is unknown.

EXAMPLE 8.3

Estimating the Mean Force Required to Break Electric Insulators

A manufacturing company produces electric insulators. Using the Define, Collect, Organize, Visualize, and Analyze steps first discussed in Chapter 2, you define the variable of interest as the strength of the insulators. If the insulators break when in use, a short circuit is likely. To test the strength of the insulators, you carry out destructive testing to determine how much force is required to break the insulators. You measure force by observing how many pounds are applied to the insulator before it breaks. You collect the data by selecting 30 insulators to be used in the experiment. You organize the data collected in a worksheet. Table 8.2 lists 30 values from this experiment, which are stored in **Force**. To analyze the data, you need to construct a 95% confidence interval estimate for the population mean force required to break the insulator.

TABLE 8.2

Force (in Pounds) Required to Break Insulators

1,870	1,728	1,656	1,610	1,634	1,784	1,522	1,696	1,592	1,662
1,866	1,764	1,734	1,662	1,734	1,774	1,550	1,756	1,762	1,866
1,820	1,744	1,788	1,688	1,810	1,752	1,680	1,810	1,652	1,736

SOLUTION To visualize the data, you construct a boxplot of the force, as displayed in Figure 8.8, and a normal probability plot, as shown in Figure 8.9. To analyze the data, you construct the confidence interval estimate shown in Figure 8.10. In each figure, Excel results are on the left and Minitab results are on the right.

FIGURE 8.8

Boxplots for the amount of force required to break electric insulators

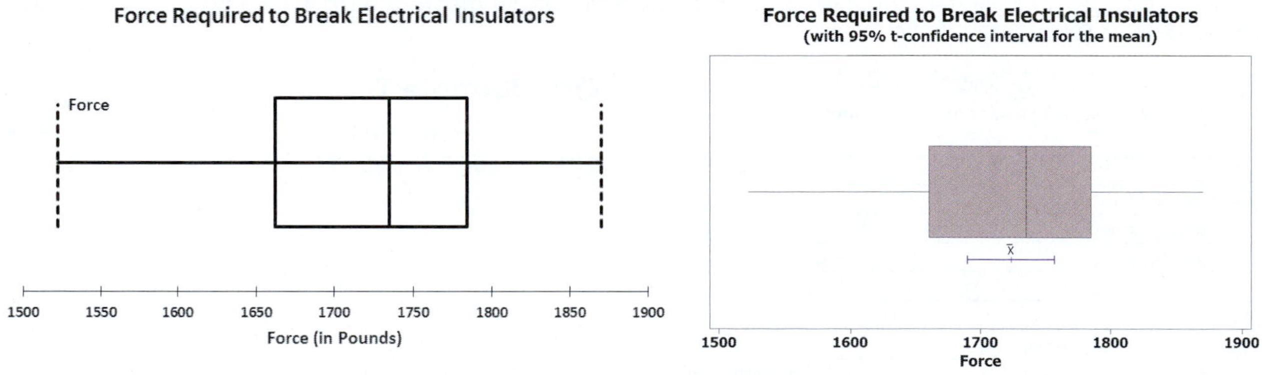

FIGURE 8.9

Normal probability plots for the amount of force required to break electric insulators

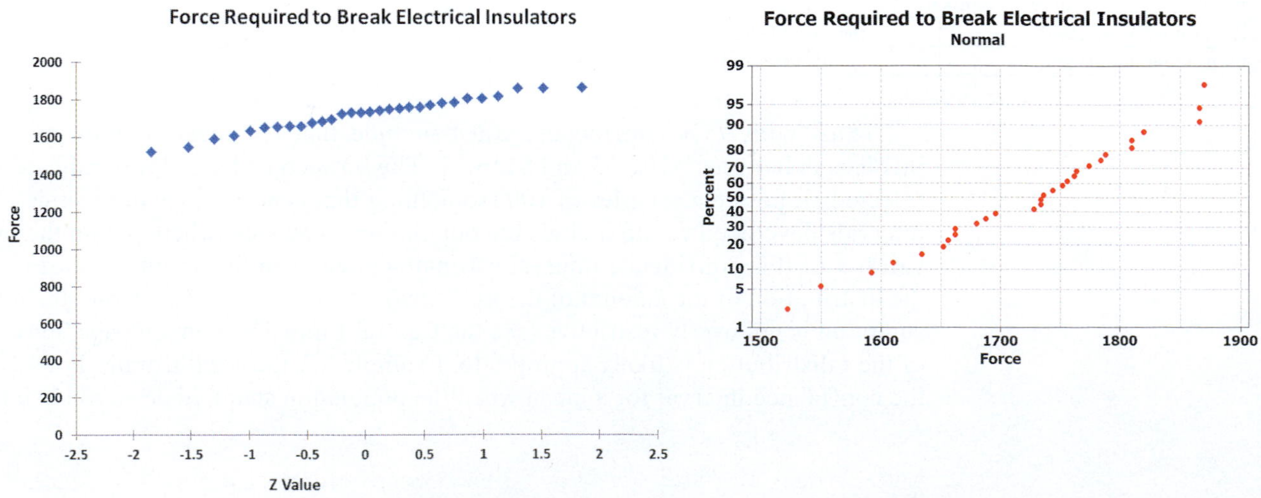

FIGURE 8.10

Confidence interval estimate for the mean amount of force required to break electric insulators

	A	B	
1	Estimate for the Mean Amount of Force Required		
2			
3	Data		
4	Sample Standard Deviation	89.55	
5	Sample Mean	1723.4	
6	Sample Size	30	
7	Confidence Level	95%	
8			
9	Intermediate Calculations		
10	Standard Error of the Mean	16.3495	=B4/SQRT(B6)
11	Degrees of Freedom	29	=B6 - 1
12	*t* Value	2.0452	=TINV(1 - B7, B11)
13	Interval Half Width	33.4385	=B12 * B10
14			
15	Confidence Interval		
16	Interval Lower Limit	1689.96	=B5 - B13
17	Interval Upper Limit	1756.84	=B5 + B13

One-Sample T: Force

Variable	N	Mean	StDev	SE Mean	95% CI
Force	30	1723.4	89.6	16.3	(1690.0, 1756.8)

Figure 8.10 shows that the sample mean is $\bar{X} = 1{,}723.4$ pounds and the sample standard deviation is $S = 89.55$ pounds. Using Equation (8.2) on page 288 to construct the confidence interval, you need to determine the critical value from the *t* table, using the row for 29 degrees of freedom. For 95% confidence, you use the column corresponding to an upper-tail area of 0.025 and a cumulative probability of 0.975. From Table E.3, you see that $t_{\alpha/2} = 2.0452$. Thus, using $\bar{X} = 1{,}723.4$, $S = 89.55$, $n = 30$, and $t_{\alpha/2} = 2.0452$,

$$\bar{X} \pm t_{\alpha/2}\frac{S}{\sqrt{n}}$$

$$= 1{,}723.4 \pm (2.0452)\frac{89.55}{\sqrt{30}}$$

$$= 1{,}723.4 \pm 33.44$$

$$1{,}689.96 \le \mu \le 1{,}756.84$$

You conclude with 95% confidence that the mean breaking force required for the population of insulators is between 1,689.96 and 1,756.84 pounds. The validity of this confidence interval estimate depends on the assumption that the force required is normally distributed. Remember, however, that you can slightly relax this assumption for large sample sizes. Thus, with a sample of 30, you can use the *t* distribution even if the amount of force required is only slightly left-skewed. From the boxplot displayed in Figure 8.8 and the normal probability plot shown in Figure 8.9, the amount of force required appears only slightly left-skewed. Thus, the *t* distribution is appropriate for these data.

The interpretation of the confidence interval when σ is unknown is the same as when σ is known. To illustrate the fact that the confidence interval for the mean varies more when σ is unknown, return to the example concerning the order-filling times discussed in Section 8.1 on pages 282–283. Suppose that, in this case, you do *not* know the population standard deviation and instead use the sample standard deviation to construct the confidence interval estimate of the mean. Figure 8.11 on page 292 shows the results for each of 20 samples of $n = 10$ orders.

In Figure 8.11, observe that the standard deviation of the samples varies from 6.25 (sample 17) to 14.83 (sample 3). Thus, the width of the confidence interval developed varies from 8.94 in sample 17 to 21.22 in sample 3. Because you know that the population mean order time $\mu = 69.637$ minutes, you can see that the interval for sample 8(69.68 − 85.48) and the interval for sample 10(56.41 − 68.69) do not correctly estimate the population mean. All the other

FIGURE 8.11
Confidence interval estimates of the mean for 20 samples of $n = 10$, randomly selected from the population of $N = 200$ orders with σ unknown

Variable	N	Mean	Std Dev	SE Mean	95% CI
Sample 1	10	71.64	7.58	2.40	(66.22, 77.06)
Sample 2	10	67.22	10.95	3.46	(59.39, 75.05)
Sample 3	10	67.97	14.83	4.69	(57.36, 78.58)
Sample 4	10	73.90	10.59	3.35	(66.33, 81.47)
Sample 5	10	67.11	11.12	3.52	(59.15, 75.07)
Sample 6	10	68.12	10.83	3.43	(60.37, 75.87)
Sample 7	10	65.80	10.85	3.43	(58.03, 73.57)
Sample 8	10	77.58	11.04	3.49	(69.68, 85.48)
Sample 9	10	66.69	11.45	3.62	(58.50, 74.88)
Sample 10	10	62.55	8.58	2.71	(56.41, 68.69)
Sample 11	10	71.12	12.82	4.05	(61.95, 80.29)
Sample 12	10	70.55	10.52	3.33	(63.02, 78.08)
Sample 13	10	65.51	8.16	2.58	(59.67, 71.35)
Sample 14	10	64.90	7.55	2.39	(59.50, 70.30)
Sample 15	10	66.22	11.21	3.54	(58.20, 74.24)
Sample 16	10	70.43	10.21	3.23	(63.12, 77.74)
Sample 17	10	72.04	6.25	1.96	(67.57, 76.51)
Sample 18	10	73.91	11.29	3.57	(65.83, 81.99)
Sample 19	10	71.49	9.76	3.09	(64.51, 78.47)
Sample 20	10	70.15	10.84	3.43	(62.39, 77.91)

intervals correctly estimate the population mean. Once again, remember that in practice you select only one sample, and you are unable to know for sure whether your one sample provides a confidence interval that includes the population mean.

Problems for Section 8.2

LEARNING THE BASICS

8.11 If $\bar{X} = 75, S = 24$, and $n = 36$, and assuming that the population is normally distributed, construct a 95% confidence interval estimate for the population mean, μ.

8.12 Determine the critical value of t in each of the following circumstances:

a. $1 - \alpha = 0.95, n = 10$
b. $1 - \alpha = 0.99, n = 10$
c. $1 - \alpha = 0.95, n = 32$
d. $1 - \alpha = 0.95, n = 65$
e. $1 - \alpha = 0.90, n = 16$

8.13 Assuming that the population is normally distributed, construct a 95% confidence interval estimate for the population mean for each of the following samples:

Sample A: 1 1 1 1 8 8 8 8
Sample B: 1 2 3 4 5 6 7 8

Explain why these two samples produce different confidence intervals even though they have the same mean and range.

8.14 Assuming that the population is normally distributed, construct a 95% confidence interval for the population mean, based on the following sample of size $n = 7$:

1, 2, 3, 4, 5, 6, 20

Change the number 20 to 7 and recalculate the confidence interval. Using these results, describe the effect of an outlier (i.e., an extreme value) on the confidence interval.

APPLYING THE CONCEPTS

8.15 A stationery store wants to estimate the mean retail value of greeting cards that it has in its inventory. A random sample of 100 greeting cards indicates a mean value of \$2.55 and a standard deviation of \$0.44.

a. Assuming a normal distribution, construct a 95% confidence interval estimate for the mean value of all greeting cards in the store's inventory.
b. Suppose there are 2,500 greeting cards in the store's inventory. How are the results in (a) useful in assisting the store owner to estimate the total value of the inventory?

SELF Test **8.16** Southside Hospital in Bay Shore, New York, commonly conducts stress tests to study the heart muscle after a person has a heart attack. Members of the diagnostic imaging department conducted a quality improvement project with the objective of reducing the turnaround time for stress tests. Turnaround time is defined as the time from when a test is ordered to when the radiologist signs off on the test results. Initially, the mean turnaround time for a stress test was 68 hours. After incorporating changes into the stress-test process, the quality improvement team collected a sample of 50 turnaround times. In this sample, the mean turnaround time was 32 hours, with a standard deviation of 9 hours. (Data extracted from E. Godin, D. Raven, C. Sweetapple, and F. R. Del Guidice, "Faster Test Results," *Quality Progress*, January 2004, 37(1), pp. 33–39.)

a. Construct a 95% confidence interval estimate for the population mean turnaround time.
b. Interpret the interval constructed in (a).
c. Do you think the quality improvement project was a success?

8.17 The U.S. Department of Transportation requires tire manufacturers to provide tire performance information on the sidewall of a tire to better inform prospective customers as they make purchasing decisions. One very important measure of tire performance is the tread wear index, which indicates the tire's resistance to tread wear compared with a tire graded with a base of 100. A tire with a grade of 200 should last twice as long, on average, as a tire graded with a base of 100. A consumer organization wants to estimate the actual tread wear index of a brand name of tires that claims "graded 200" on the sidewall of the tire. A random sample of $n = 18$ indicates a sample mean tread wear index of 195.3 and a sample standard deviation of 21.4.

a. Assuming that the population of tread wear indexes is normally distributed, construct a 95% confidence interval estimate for the population mean tread wear index for tires produced by this manufacturer under this brand name.
b. Do you think that the consumer organization should accuse the manufacturer of producing tires that do not meet the performance information provided on the sidewall of the tire? Explain.
c. Explain why an observed tread wear index of 210 for a particular tire is not unusual, even though it is outside the confidence interval developed in (a).

8.18 The file **FastFood** contains the amount that a sample of nine customers spent for lunch ($) at a fast-food restaurant

4.20 5.03 5.86 6.45 7.38 7.54 8.46 8.47 9.87

a. Construct a 95% confidence interval estimate for the population mean amount spent for lunch ($) at a fast-food restaurant, assuming a normal distribution.
b. Interpret the interval constructed in (a).

8.19 The file **Sedans** contains the overall miles per gallon (MPG) of 2010 family sedans.

24 21 22 23 24 34 34 34 20 20
22 22 44 32 20 20 22 20 39 20

Source: Data extracted from "Vehicle Ratings," *Consumer Reports*, April 2010, p. 29.

a. Construct a 95% confidence interval estimate for the population mean MPG of 2010 family sedans, assuming a normal distribution.
b. Interpret the interval constructed in (a).
c. Compare the results in (a) to those in Problem 8.20(a).

8.20 The file **SUV** contains the overall miles per gallon (MPG) of 2010 small SUVs.

24 23 22 21 22 22 18 18 26 26 26 19 19
19 21 21 21 21 21 18 19 21 22 22 16 16

Source: Data extracted from "Vehicle Ratings," *Consumer Reports*, April 2010, pp. 33–34.

a. Construct a 95% confidence interval estimate for the population mean MPG of 2010 small SUVs, assuming a normal distribution.
b. Interpret the interval constructed in (a).
c. Compare the results in (a) to those in Problem 8.19(a).

8.21 Is there a difference in the yields of different types of investments? The file **SavingsRate-MMCD** contains the yields for a money market account and a five-year certificate of deposit (CD) for 25 banks in the United States, as of March 29, 2010.

Source: Data extracted from **www.Bankrate.com**, March 29, 2010.

a. Construct a 95% confidence interval estimate for the mean yield of money market accounts.
b. Construct a 95% confidence interval estimate for the mean yield of five-year certificates of deposits.
c. Compare the results of (a) and (b).

8.22 One of the major measures of the quality of service provided by any organization is the speed with which it responds to customer complaints. A large family-held department store selling furniture and flooring, including carpet, had undergone a major expansion in the past several years. In particular, the flooring department had expanded from 2 installation crews to an installation supervisor, a measurer, and 15 installation crews. The store had the business objective of improving its response to complaints. The variable of interest was defined as the number of days between when the complaint was made and when it was resolved. Data were collected from 50 complaints that were made in the last year. The data were stored in **Furniture**, and are as follows:

54	5	35	137	31	27	152	2	123	81	74	27
11	19	126	110	110	29	61	35	94	31	26	5
12	4	165	32	29	28	29	26	25	1	14	13
13	10	5	27	4	52	30	22	36	26	20	23
33	68										

a. Construct a 95% confidence interval estimate for the population mean number of days between the receipt of a complaint and the resolution of the complaint.
b. What assumption must you make about the population distribution in order to construct the confidence interval estimate in (a)?
c. Do you think that the assumption needed in order to construct the confidence interval estimate in (a) is valid? Explain.
d. What effect might your conclusion in (c) have on the validity of the results in (a)?

8.23 In New York State, savings banks are permitted to sell a form of life insurance called savings bank life insurance (SBLI). The approval process consists of underwriting, which includes a review of the application, a medical information bureau check, possible requests for additional medical information and medical exams, and a policy compilation stage in which the policy pages are generated and sent to the bank for delivery. The ability to deliver approved policies to customers in a timely manner is critical to the profitability of this service to the bank. During a period of one month, a random sample of 27 approved policies was selected, and the total processing time, in days, was as shown below and stored in **Insurance**:

73	19	16	64	28	28	31	90	60	56	31	56	22	18
45	48	17	17	17	91	92	63	50	51	69	16	17	

a. Construct a 95% confidence interval estimate for the population mean processing time.
b. What assumption must you make about the population distribution in order to construct the confidence interval estimate in (a)?
c. Do you think that the assumption needed in order to construct the confidence interval estimate in (a) is valid? Explain.

8.24 The file **DarkChocolate** contains the cost per ounce ($) for a sample of 14 dark chocolate bars:

0.68	0.72	0.92	1.14	1.42	0.94	0.77
0.57	1.51	0.57	0.55	0.86	1.41	0.90

Source: Data extracted from "Dark Chocolate: Which Bars Are Best?" *Consumer Reports*, September 2007, p. 8.

a. Construct a 95% confidence interval estimate for the population cost per ounce ($) of dark chocolate bars.
b. What assumption do you need to make about the population distribution to construct the interval in (a)?
c. Given the data presented, do you think the assumption needed in (a) is valid? Explain.

8.25 One operation of a mill is to cut pieces of steel into parts that are used in the frame for front seats in an automobile. The steel is cut with a diamond saw, and the resulting parts must be cut to be within ±0.005 inch of the length specified by the automobile company. The measurement reported from a sample of 100 steel parts (stored in **Steel**) is the difference, in inches, between the actual length of the steel part, as measured by a laser measurement device, and the specified length of the steel part. For example, the first observation, −0.002, represents a steel part that is 0.002 inch shorter than the specified length.
a. Construct a 95% confidence interval estimate for the population mean difference between the actual length of the steel part and the specified length of the steel part.
b. What assumption must you make about the population distribution in order to construct the confidence interval estimate in (a)?
c. Do you think that the assumption needed in order to construct the confidence interval estimate in (a) is valid? Explain.
d. Compare the conclusions reached in (a) with those of Problem 2.41 on page 55.

8.3 Confidence Interval Estimate for the Proportion

The concept of a confidence interval also applies to categorical data. With categorical data, you want to estimate the proportion of items in a population having a certain characteristic of interest. The unknown population proportion is represented by the Greek letter π. The point estimate for π is the sample proportion, $p = X/n$, where n is the sample size and X is the number of items in the sample having the characteristic of interest. Equation (8.3) defines the confidence interval estimate for the population proportion.

CONFIDENCE INTERVAL ESTIMATE FOR THE PROPORTION

$$p \pm Z_{\alpha/2}\sqrt{\frac{p(1-p)}{n}}$$

or

$$p - Z_{\alpha/2}\sqrt{\frac{p(1-p)}{n}} \le \pi \le p + Z_{\alpha/2}\sqrt{\frac{p(1-p)}{n}} \qquad \textbf{(8.3)}$$

where

$$p = \text{sample proportion} = \frac{X}{n} = \frac{\text{Number of items having the characteristic}}{\text{sample size}}$$

π = population proportion

$Z_{\alpha/2}$ = critical value from the standardized normal distribution

n = sample size

Note: To use this equation for the confidence interval, the sample size n must be large enough to ensure that both X and $n - X$ are greater than 5.

You can use the confidence interval estimate for the proportion defined in Equation (8.3) to estimate the proportion of sales invoices that contain errors (see the Saxon Home Improvement scenario on page 279). Using the Define, Collect, Organize, Visualize, and Analyze steps, you define the variable of interest as whether the invoice contains errors (yes or no). Then, you collect the data from a sample of 100 sales invoices. The results, which you organize and store in a worksheet, show that 10 invoices contain errors. To analyze the data, you compute, for these data, $p = X/n = 10/100 = 0.10$. Since both X and $n - X$ are > 5, using Equation (8.3) and $Z_{\alpha/2} = 1.96$, for 95% confidence,

$$p \pm Z_{\alpha/2}\sqrt{\frac{p(1-p)}{n}}$$

$$= 0.10 \pm (1.96)\sqrt{\frac{(0.10)(0.90)}{100}}$$

$$= 0.10 \pm (1.96)(0.03)$$

$$= 0.10 \pm 0.0588$$

$$0.0412 \le \pi \le 0.1588$$

Therefore, you have 95% confidence that the population proportion of all sales invoices containing errors is between 0.0412 and 0.1588. This means that between 4.12% and 15.88% of all the sales invoices contain errors. Figure 8.12 shows a confidence interval estimate for this example. (Excel results are on the left and Minitab results are on the right.)

FIGURE 8.12

Confidence interval estimate for the proportion of sales invoices that contain errors

	A	B	
1	Proportion of In-Error Sales Invoices		
2			
3	Data		
4	Sample Size	100	
5	Number of Successes	10	
6	Confidence Level	95%	
7			
8	Intermediate Calculations		
9	Sample Proportion	0.1	=B5/B4
10	Z Value	-1.9600	=NORMSINV((1 - B6)/2)
11	Standard Error of the Proportion	0.03	=SQRT(B9 * (1 - B9)/B4)
12	Interval Half Width	0.0588	=ABS(B10 * B11)
13			
14	Confidence Interval		
15	Interval Lower Limit	0.0412	=B9 - B12
16	Interval Upper Limit	0.1588	=B9 + B12

Test and CI for One Proportion

```
Sample   X    N  Sample p        95% CI
1       10  100  0.100000  (0.041201, 0.158799)

Using the normal approximation.
```

Example 8.4 illustrates another application of a confidence interval estimate for the proportion.

EXAMPLE 8.4

Estimating the Proportion of Nonconforming Newspapers Printed

The operations manager at a large newspaper wants to estimate the proportion of newspapers printed that have a nonconforming attribute. Using the Define, Collect, Organize, Visualize, and Analyze steps, you define the variable of interest as whether the newspaper has excessive ruboff, improper page setup, missing pages, or duplicate pages. You collect the data by selecting a random sample of $n = 200$ newspapers from all the newspapers printed during a single day. You organize the results, which show that 35 newspapers contain some type of nonconformance, in a worksheet. To analyze the data, you need to construct and interpret a 90% confidence interval for the proportion of newspapers printed during the day that have a nonconforming attribute.

SOLUTION Using Equation (8.3),

$$p = \frac{X}{n} = \frac{35}{200} = 0.175, \text{ and with a 90\% level of confidence } Z_{\alpha/2} = 1.645$$

$$\begin{aligned} & p \pm Z_{\alpha/2}\sqrt{\frac{p(1-p)}{n}} \\ &= 0.175 \pm (1.645)\sqrt{\frac{(0.175)(0.825)}{200}} \\ &= 0.175 \pm (1.645)(0.0269) \\ &= 0.175 \pm 0.0442 \\ & 0.1308 \le \pi \le 0.2192 \end{aligned}$$

You conclude with 90% confidence that the population proportion of all newspapers printed that day with nonconformities is between 0.1308 and 0.2192. This means that between 13.08% and 21.92% of the newspapers printed on that day have some type of nonconformance.

Equation (8.3) contains a Z statistic because you can use the normal distribution to approximate the binomial distribution when the sample size is sufficiently large. In Example 8.4, the confidence interval using Z provides an excellent approximation for the population proportion because both X and $n - X$ are greater than 5. However, if you do not have a sufficiently large sample size, you should use the binomial distribution rather than Equation (8.3) (see references 1, 2, and 7). The exact confidence intervals for various sample sizes and proportions of successes have been tabulated by Fisher and Yates (reference 2).

Problems for Section 8.3

LEARNING THE BASICS

8.26 If $n = 200$ and $X = 50$, construct a 95% confidence interval estimate for the population proportion.

8.27 If $n = 400$ and $X = 25$, construct a 99% confidence interval estimate for the population proportion.

APPLYING THE CONCEPTS

8.28 The telephone company has the business objective of wanting to estimate the proportion of households that would purchase an additional telephone line if it were made available at a substantially reduced installation cost. Data are collected from a random sample of 500 households. The results indicate that 135 of the households would purchase the additional telephone line at a reduced installation cost.

a. Construct a 99% confidence interval estimate for the population proportion of households that would purchase the additional telephone line.

b. How would the manager in charge of promotional programs concerning residential customers use the results in (a)?

8.29 In a survey of 1,200 social media users, 76% said it is okay to friend co-workers, but 56% said it is not okay to friend your boss. (Data extracted from "Facebook Etiquette at Work," *USA Today*, March 24, 2010, p. 1B.)

a. Construct a 95% confidence interval estimate for the population proportion of social media users who would say it is okay to friend co-workers.

b. Construct a 95% confidence interval estimate for the population proportion of social media users who would say it is not okay to friend their boss.

c. Write a short summary of the information derived from (a) and (b).

8.30 Have you ever negotiated a pay raise? According to an Accenture survey, 52% of U.S. workers have (J. Yang and K. Carter, "Have You Ever Negotiated a Pay Raise?" **www.usatoday.com**, May 22, 2009).

a. Suppose that the survey had a sample size of $n = 500$. Construct a 95% confidence interval for the proportion of all U.S. workers who have negotiated a pay raise.

b. Based on (a), can you claim that more than half of all U.S. workers have negotiated a pay raise?

c. Repeat parts (a) and (b), assuming that the survey had a sample size of $n = 5{,}000$.

d. Discuss the effect of sample size on confidence interval estimation.

8.31 In a survey of 1,000 airline travelers, 760 responded that the airline fee that is most unreasonable is additional charges to redeem points/miles. (Data extracted from "Which Airline Fee Is Most Unreasonable?" *USA Today*, December 2, 2008, p. B1.) Construct a 95% confidence interval estimate for the population proportion of airline travelers who think that the airline fee that is most unreasonable is additional charges to redeem points/miles.

8.32 In a survey of 2,395 adults, 1,916 reported that e-mails are easy to misinterpret, but only 1,269 reported that telephone conversations are easy to misinterpret. (Data extracted from "Open to Misinterpretation," *USA Today*, July 17, 2007, p. 1D.)

a. Construct a 95% confidence interval estimate for the population proportion of adults who report that e-mails are easy to misinterpret.

b. Construct a 95% confidence interval estimate for the population proportion of adults who report that telephone conversations are easy to misinterpret.

c. Compare the results of (a) and (b).

8.33 What are the most preferred forms of recognition in the workplace? In a survey by Office Arrow, 163 of 388 administrative professionals responded that verbal recognition is the most preferred form of recognition, and 74 responded that cash bonuses are most preferred. (Data extracted from "Most Preferred Forms of Recognition at Workplace," *USA Today*, May 4, 2009, p. 1B.)

a. Construct a 95% confidence interval estimate for the population proportion of administrative professionals who prefer verbal recognition.

b. Construct a 95% confidence interval estimate for the population proportion of administrative professionals who prefer cash bonuses.

c. Interpret the intervals in (a) and (b).

d. Explain the difference in the results in (a) and (b).

8.4 Determining Sample Size

In each confidence interval developed so far in this chapter, the sample size was reported along with the results, with little discussion of the width of the resulting confidence interval. In the business world, sample sizes are determined prior to data collection to ensure that the confidence interval is narrow enough to be useful in making decisions. Determining the proper sample size is a complicated procedure, subject to the constraints of budget, time, and the amount of acceptable sampling error. In the Saxon Home Improvement example, if you want to estimate the mean dollar amount of the sales invoices, you must determine in advance how large a sampling error to allow in estimating the population mean. You must also determine, in advance, the level of confidence (i.e., 90%, 95%, or 99%) to use in estimating the population parameter.

Sample Size Determination for the Mean

To develop an equation for determining the appropriate sample size needed when constructing a confidence interval estimate for the mean, recall Equation (8.1) on page 283:

$$\bar{X} \pm Z_{\alpha/2}\frac{\sigma}{\sqrt{n}}$$

The amount added to or subtracted from $\bar{X}$ is equal to half the width of the interval. This quantity represents the amount of imprecision in the estimate that results from sampling error.[2] The **sampling error**, e, is defined as

$$e = Z_{\alpha/2}\frac{\sigma}{\sqrt{n}}$$

[2] In this context, some statisticians refer to e as the **margin of error**.

Solving for n gives the sample size needed to construct the appropriate confidence interval estimate for the mean. "Appropriate" means that the resulting interval will have an acceptable amount of sampling error.

SAMPLE SIZE DETERMINATION FOR THE MEAN

The sample size, n, is equal to the product of the $Z_{\alpha/2}$ value squared and the standard deviation, σ, squared, divided by the square of the sampling error, e.

$$n = \frac{Z_{\alpha/2}^2 \sigma^2}{e^2} \quad \textbf{(8.4)}$$

To compute the sample size, you must know three factors:

1. The desired confidence level, which determines the value of $Z_{\alpha/2}$, the critical value from the standardized normal distribution[3]
2. The acceptable sampling error, e
3. The standard deviation, σ

[3]You use Z instead of t because, to determine the critical value of t, you need to know the sample size, but you do not know it yet. For most studies, the sample size needed is large enough that the standardized normal distribution is a good approximation of the t distribution.

In some business-to-business relationships that require estimation of important parameters, legal contracts specify acceptable levels of sampling error and the confidence level required. For companies in the food and drug sectors, government regulations often specify sampling errors and confidence levels. In general, however, it is usually not easy to specify the three factors needed to determine the sample size. How can you determine the level of confidence and sampling error? Typically, these questions are answered only by a subject matter expert (i.e., an individual very familiar with the variables under study). Although 95% is the most common confidence level used, if more confidence is desired, then 99% might be more appropriate; if less confidence is deemed acceptable, then 90% might be used. For the sampling error, you should think not of how much sampling error you would like to have (you really do not want any error) but of how much you can tolerate when reaching conclusions from the confidence interval.

In addition to specifying the confidence level and the sampling error, you need an estimate of the standard deviation. Unfortunately, you rarely know the population standard deviation, σ. In some instances, you can estimate the standard deviation from past data. In other situations, you can make an educated guess by taking into account the range and distribution of the variable. For example, if you assume a normal distribution, the range is approximately equal to 6σ (i.e., $\pm 3\sigma$ around the mean) so that you estimate σ as the range divided by 6. If you cannot estimate σ in this way, you can conduct a small-scale study and estimate the standard deviation from the resulting data.

To explore how to determine the sample size needed for estimating the population mean, consider again the audit at Saxon Home Improvement. In Section 8.2, you selected a sample of 100 sales invoices and constructed a 95% confidence interval estimate for the population mean sales invoice amount. How was this sample size determined? Should you have selected a different sample size?

Suppose that, after consulting with company officials, you determine that a sampling error of no more than $\pm\$5$ is desired, along with 95% confidence. Past data indicate that the standard deviation of the sales amount is approximately \$25. Thus, $e = \$5, \sigma = \$25$, and $Z_{\alpha/2} = 1.96$ (for 95% confidence). Using Equation (8.4),

$$n = \frac{Z_{\alpha/2}^2 \sigma^2}{e^2} = \frac{(1.96)^2(25)^2}{(5)^2}$$

$$= 96.04$$

Because the general rule is to slightly oversatisfy the criteria by rounding the sample size up to the next whole integer, you should select a sample of size 97. Thus, the sample of size $n = 100$ used on page 289 is slightly more than what is necessary to satisfy the needs of the company, based on the estimated standard deviation, desired confidence level, and sampling error. Because the calculated sample standard deviation is slightly higher than expected, \$28.95 compared to \$25.00, the confidence interval is slightly wider than desired. Figure 8.13 shows a worksheet solution for determining the sample size.

FIGURE 8.13

Worksheet for determining sample size for estimating the mean sales invoice amount for the Saxon Home Improvement Company

	A	B	
1	**For the Mean Sales Invoice Amount**		
2			
3	**Data**		
4	Population Standard Deviation	25	
5	Sampling Error	5	
6	Confidence Level	95%	
7			
8	Intemediate Calculations		
9	Z Value	-1.9600	=NORMSINV((1 - B6)/2)
10	Calculated Sample Size	96.0365	=((B9 * B4)/B5)^2
11			
12	**Result**		
13	Sample Size Needed	97	=ROUNDUP(B10, 0)

Example 8.5 illustrates another application of determining the sample size needed to develop a confidence interval estimate for the mean.

EXAMPLE 8.5

Determining the Sample Size for the Mean

Returning to Example 8.3 on page 290, suppose you want to estimate, with 95% confidence, the population mean force required to break the insulator to within ±25 pounds. On the basis of a study conducted the previous year, you believe that the standard deviation is 100 pounds. Determine the sample size needed.

SOLUTION Using Equation (8.4) on page 298 and $e = 25$, $\sigma = 100$, and $Z_{\alpha/2} = 1.96$ for 95% confidence,

$$n = \frac{Z_{\alpha/2}^2\sigma^2}{e^2} = \frac{(1.96)^2(100)^2}{(25)^2}$$
$$= 61.47$$

Therefore, you should select a sample of 62 insulators because the general rule for determining sample size is to always round up to the next integer value in order to slightly oversatisfy the criteria desired. An actual sampling error slightly larger than 25 will result if the sample standard deviation calculated in this sample of 62 is greater than 100 and slightly smaller if the sample standard deviation is less than 100.

Sample Size Determination for the Proportion

So far in this section, you have learned how to determine the sample size needed for estimating the population mean. Now suppose that you want to determine the sample size necessary for estimating a population proportion.

To determine the sample size needed to estimate a population proportion, π, you use a method similar to the method for a population mean. Recall that in developing the sample size for a confidence interval for the mean, the sampling error is defined by

$$e = Z_{\alpha/2}\frac{\sigma}{\sqrt{n}}$$

When estimating a proportion, you replace σ with $\sqrt{\pi(1 - \pi)}$. Thus, the sampling error is

$$e = Z_{\alpha/2}\sqrt{\frac{\pi(1 - \pi)}{n}}$$

Solving for n, you have the sample size necessary to develop a confidence interval estimate for a proportion.

SAMPLE SIZE DETERMINATION FOR THE PROPORTION

The sample size n is equal to the product of $Z_{\alpha/2}$ squared, the population proportion, π, and 1 minus the population proportion, π, divided by the square of the sampling error, e.

$$n = \frac{Z^2_{\alpha/2}\pi(1 - \pi)}{e^2} \quad \textbf{(8.5)}$$

To determine the sample size, you must know three factors:

1. The desired confidence level, which determines the value of $Z_{\alpha/2}$, the critical value from the standardized normal distribution
2. The acceptable sampling error (or margin of error), e
3. The population proportion, π

In practice, selecting these quantities requires some planning. Once you determine the desired level of confidence, you can find the appropriate $Z_{\alpha/2}$ value from the standardized normal distribution. The sampling error, e, indicates the amount of error that you are willing to tolerate in estimating the population proportion. The third quantity, π, is actually the population parameter that you want to estimate! Thus, how do you state a value for what you are trying to determine?

Here you have two alternatives. In many situations, you may have past information or relevant experience that provides an educated estimate of π. Or, if you do not have past information or relevant experience, you can try to provide a value for π that would never *underestimate* the sample size needed. Referring to Equation (8.5), you can see that the quantity $\pi(1 - \pi)$ appears in the numerator. Thus, you need to determine the value of π that will make the quantity $\pi(1 - \pi)$ as large as possible. When $\pi = 0.5$, the product $\pi(1 - \pi)$ achieves its maximum value. To show this result, consider the following values of π, along with the accompanying products of $\pi(1 - \pi)$:

When $\pi = 0.9$, then $\pi(1 - \pi) = (0.9)(0.1) = 0.09$.

When $\pi = 0.7$, then $\pi(1 - \pi) = (0.7)(0.3) = 0.21$.

When $\pi = 0.5$, then $\pi(1 - \pi) = (0.5)(0.5) = 0.25$.

When $\pi = 0.3$, then $\pi(1 - \pi) = (0.3)(0.7) = 0.21$.

When $\pi = 0.1$, then $\pi(1 - \pi) = (0.1)(0.9) = 0.09$.

Therefore, when you have no prior knowledge or estimate for the population proportion, π, you should use $\pi = 0.5$ for determining the sample size. Using $\pi = 0.5$ produces the largest possible sample size and results in the narrowest and most precise confidence interval. This increased precision comes at the cost of spending more time and money for an increased sample size. Also, note that if you use $\pi = 0.5$ and the proportion is different from 0.5, you will overestimate the sample size needed, because you will get a confidence interval narrower than originally intended.

Returning to the Saxon Home Improvement scenario on page 279, suppose that the auditing procedures require you to have 95% confidence in estimating the population proportion of sales invoices with errors to within ±0.07. The results from past months indicate that the largest proportion has been no more than 0.15. Thus, using Equation (8.5) with $e = 0.07$, $\pi = 0.15$, and $Z_{\alpha/2} = 1.96$ for 95% confidence,

$$n = \frac{Z^2_{\alpha/2}\pi(1-\pi)}{e^2}$$

$$= \frac{(1.96)^2(0.15)(0.85)}{(0.07)^2}$$

$$= 99.96$$

Because the general rule is to round the sample size up to the next whole integer to slightly oversatisfy the criteria, a sample size of 100 is needed. Thus, the sample size needed to satisfy the requirements of the company, based on the estimated proportion, desired confidence level, and sampling error, is equal to the sample size taken on page 295. The actual confidence interval is narrower than required because the sample proportion is 0.10, whereas 0.15 was used for π in Equation (8.5). Figure 8.14 shows a worksheet solution for determining the sample size.

FIGURE 8.14

Worksheet for determining sample size for estimating the proportion of sales invoices with errors for the Saxon Home Improvement Company

	A	B	
1	**For the Proportion of In-Error Sales Invoices**		
2			
3	**Data**		
4	Estimate of True Proportion	0.15	
5	Sampling Error	0.07	
6	Confidence Level	95%	
7			
8	Intermediate Calculations		
9	Z Value	-1.9600	=NORMSINV((1 - B6)/2)
10	Calculated Sample Size	99.9563	=(B9^2 * B4 * (1 - B4))/B5^2
11			
12	**Result**		
13	Sample Size Needed	100	=ROUNDUP(B10, 0)

Example 8.6 provides another application of determining the sample size for estimating the population proportion.

EXAMPLE 8.6

Determining the Sample Size for the Population Proportion

You want to have 90% confidence of estimating the proportion of office workers who respond to e-mail within an hour to within ±0.05. Because you have not previously undertaken such a study, there is no information available from past data. Determine the sample size needed.

SOLUTION Because no information is available from past data, assume that $\pi = 0.50$. Using Equation (8.5) on page 300 and $e = 0.05$, $\pi = 0.50$, and $Z_{\alpha/2} = 1.645$ for 90% confidence,

$$n = \frac{Z^2_{\alpha/2}\pi(1-\pi)}{e^2}$$

$$= \frac{(1.645)^2(0.50)(0.50)}{(0.05)^2}$$

$$= 270.6$$

Therefore, you need a sample of 271 office workers to estimate the population proportion to within ±0.05 with 90% confidence.

Problems for Section 8.4

LEARNING THE BASICS

8.34 If you want to be 95% confident of estimating the population mean to within a sampling error of ±5 and the standard deviation is assumed to be 15, what sample size is required?

8.35 If you want to be 99% confident of estimating the population mean to within a sampling error of ±20 and the standard deviation is assumed to be 100, what sample size is required?

8.36 If you want to be 99% confident of estimating the population proportion to within a sampling error of ±0.04, what sample size is needed?

8.37 If you want to be 95% confident of estimating the population proportion to within a sampling error of ±0.02 and there is historical evidence that the population proportion is approximately 0.40, what sample size is needed?

APPLYING THE CONCEPTS

SELF Test **8.38** A survey is planned to determine the mean annual family medical expenses of employees of a large company. The management of the company wishes to be 95% confident that the sample mean is correct to within ±$50 of the population mean annual family medical expenses. A previous study indicates that the standard deviation is approximately $400.

a. How large a sample is necessary?
b. If management wants to be correct to within ±$25, how many employees need to be selected?

8.39 If the manager of a paint supply store wants to estimate, with 95% confidence, the mean amount of paint in a 1-gallon can to within ±0.004 gallon and also assumes that the standard deviation is 0.02 gallon, what sample size is needed?

8.40 If a quality control manager wants to estimate, with 95% confidence, the mean life of light bulbs to within ±20 hours and also assumes that the population standard deviation is 100 hours, how many light bulbs need to be selected?

8.41 If the inspection division of a county weights and measures department wants to estimate the mean amount of soft-drink fill in 2-liter bottles to within ±0.01 liter with 95% confidence and also assumes that the standard deviation is 0.05 liter, what sample size is needed?

8.42 A consumer group wants to estimate the mean electric bill for the month of July for single-family homes in a large city. Based on studies conducted in other cities, the standard deviation is assumed to be $25. The group wants to estimate, with 99% confidence, the mean bill for July to within ±$5.

a. What sample size is needed?
b. If 95% confidence is desired, how many homes need to be selected?

8.43 An advertising agency that serves a major radio station wants to estimate the mean amount of time that the station's audience spends listening to the radio daily. From past studies, the standard deviation is estimated as 45 minutes.

a. What sample size is needed if the agency wants to be 90% confident of being correct to within ±5 minutes?
b. If 99% confidence is desired, how many listeners need to be selected?

8.44 A growing niche in the restaurant business is gourmet-casual breakfast, lunch, and brunch. Chains in this group include EggSpectation and Panera Bread. Suppose that the mean per-person check for EggSpectation is approximately $12.50, and the mean per-person check for Panera Bread is $7.50.

a. Assuming a standard deviation of $2.00, what sample size is needed to estimate, with 95% confidence, the mean per-person check for EggSpectation to within ±$0.25?
b. Assuming a standard deviation of $2.50, what sample size is needed to estimate, with 95% confidence, the mean per-person check for EggSpectation to within ±$0.25?
c. Assuming a standard deviation of $3.00, what sample size is needed to estimate, with 95% confidence, the mean per-person check for EggSpectation to within ±$0.25?
d. Discuss the effect of variation on the sample size needed.

8.45 What proportion of Americans get most of their news from the Internet? According to a poll conducted by Pew Research Center, 40% get most of their news from the Internet. (Data extracted from "Drill Down," *The New York Times*, January 5, 2009, p. B3.)

a. To conduct a follow-up study that would provide 95% confidence that the point estimate is correct to within ±0.04 of the population proportion, how large a sample size is required?
b. To conduct a follow-up study that would provide 99% confidence that the point estimate is correct to within ±0.04 of the population proportion, how many people need to be sampled?
c. To conduct a follow-up study that would provide 95% confidence that the point estimate is correct to within ±0.02 of the population proportion, how large a sample size is required?
d. To conduct a follow-up study that would provide 99% confidence that the point estimate is correct to within ±0.02 of the population proportion, how many people need to be sampled?
e. Discuss the effects on sample size requirements of changing the desired confidence level and the acceptable sampling error.

8.46 A survey of 1,000 adults was conducted in March 2009 concerning "green practices." In response to the question of what was the most beneficial thing to do for the environment, 28% said buying renewable energy, 19% said using greener transportation, and 7% said selecting minimal or reduced packaging. (Data extracted from "Environmentally Friendly Choices," *USA Today*, March 31, 2009, p. D1.) Construct a 95% confidence interval estimate of the population proportion of who said that the most beneficial thing to do for the environment was

a. buy renewable energy.

b. use greener transportation.

c. select minimal or reduced packaging.

d. You have been asked to update the results of this study. Determine the sample size necessary to estimate, with 95% confidence, the population proportions in (a) through (c) to within ± 0.02.

8.47 In a study of 500 executives, 315 stated that their company informally monitored social networking sites to stay on top of information related to their company. (Data extracted from "Checking Out the Buzz," *USA Today*, June 26, 2009, p. 1B.)

a. Construct a 95% confidence interval for the proportion of companies that informally monitored social networking sites to stay on top of information related to their company.

b. Interpret the interval constructed in (a).

c. If you wanted to conduct a follow-up study to estimate the population proportion of companies that informally monitored social networking sites to stay on top of information related to their company to within ± 0.01 with 95% confidence, how many executives would you survey?

8.48 In response to the question "How do you judge a company?" 84% said the most important way was how a company responded to a crisis. (Data extracted from "How Do You Judge a Company?" *USA Today*, December 22, 2008, p. 1B.)

a. If you conduct a follow-up study to estimate the population proportion of individuals who said that the most important way to judge a company was how the company responded to a crisis, would you use a π of 0.84 or 0.50 in the sample size formula? Discuss.

b. Using your answer to (a), find the sample size necessary to estimate, with 95% certainty, the population proportion to within ± 0.03.

8.49 There are many reasons adults use credit cards. A recent survey ("Why Adults Use Credit Cards," *USA Today*, October 18, 2007, p. 1D) found that 66% of adults used credit cards for convenience.

a. To conduct a follow-up study that would provide 99% confidence that the point estimate is correct to within ± 0.03 of the population proportion, how many people need to be sampled?

b. To conduct a follow-up study that would provide 99% confidence that the point estimate is correct to within ± 0.05 of the population proportion, how many people need to be sampled?

c. Compare the results of (a) and (b).

8.5 Applications of Confidence Interval Estimation in Auditing

Auditing is one of the areas in business that makes widespread use of probability sampling methods in order to construct confidence interval estimates.

AUDITING

Auditing is the collection and evaluation of evidence about information related to an economic entity, such as a sole business proprietor, a partnership, a corporation, or a government agency, in order to determine and report on how well the information corresponds to established criteria.

Auditors rarely examine a complete population of information. Instead, they rely on estimation techniques based on the probability sampling methods you have studied in this text. The following list contains some of the reasons sampling is used in auditing:

- Sampling is less time-consuming.
- Sampling is less costly.
- Sampling provides an objective way of estimating the sample size in advance.
- Sampling provides results that are objective and defensible. Because the sample size is based on demonstrable statistical principles, the audit is defensible before one's superiors and in a court of law.
- Sampling provides an estimate of the sampling error and therefore allows auditors to generalize their findings to the population with a known sampling error.

- Sampling is often more accurate than other methods for drawing conclusions about large populations. Examining every item in large populations is time-consuming and therefore often subject to more nonsampling error than is statistical sampling.
- Sampling allows auditors to combine, and then evaluate collectively, samples from different individuals.

Estimating the Population Total Amount

In auditing applications, you are often more interested in developing estimates of the population **total amount** than in the population mean. Equation (8.6) shows how to estimate a population total amount.

ESTIMATING THE POPULATION TOTAL

The point estimate for the population total is equal to the population size, N, times the sample mean.

$$\text{Total} = N\overline{X} \qquad \textbf{(8.6)}$$

Equation (8.7) defines the confidence interval estimate for the population total.

CONFIDENCE INTERVAL ESTIMATE FOR THE TOTAL

$$N\overline{X} \pm N(t_{\alpha/2})\frac{S}{\sqrt{n}}\sqrt{\frac{N-n}{N-1}} \qquad \textbf{(8.7)}$$

where $t_{\alpha/2}$ is the critical value corresponding to an upper-tail probability of $\alpha/2$ from the t distribution with $n - 1$ degrees of freedom (i.e., a cumulative area of $1 - \alpha/2$).

To demonstrate the application of the confidence interval estimate for the population total amount, return to the Saxon Home Improvement scenario on page 279. In addition to estimating the mean dollar amount in Section 8.2 on page 289, one of the auditing tasks defined in the business problem is to estimate the total dollar amount of all sales invoices for the month. If there are 5,000 invoices for that month and $\overline{X} = \$110.27$, then using Equation (8.6),

$$N\overline{X} = (5{,}000)(\$110.27) = \$551{,}350$$

Since $n = 100$ and $S = \$28.95$, then using Equation (8.7) with $t_{\alpha/2} = 1.9842$ for 95% confidence and 99 degrees of freedom,

$$N\overline{X} \pm N(t_{\alpha/2})\frac{S}{\sqrt{n}}\sqrt{\frac{N-n}{N-1}} = 551{,}350 \pm (5{,}000)(1.9842)\frac{28.95}{\sqrt{100}}\sqrt{\frac{5{,}000-100}{5{,}000-1}}$$

$$= 551{,}350 \pm 28{,}721.295(0.99005)$$

$$= 551{,}350 \pm 28{,}435.72$$

$$\$522{,}914.28 \le \text{Population total} \le \$579{,}785.72$$

Therefore, with 95% confidence, you estimate that the total amount of sales invoices is between \$522,914.28 and \$579,785.72. Figure 8.15 shows a worksheet solution for constructing this confidence interval estimate.

Example 8.7 further illustrates the population total.

FIGURE 8.15

Worksheet for the confidence interval estimate of the total amount of all invoices for the Saxon Home Improvement Company

	A	B	
1	**Total Amount of All Sales Invoices**		
2			
3	**Data**		
4	Population Size	5000	
5	Sample Mean	110.27	
6	Sample Size	100	
7	Sample Standard Deviation	28.95	
8	Confidence Level	95%	
9			
10	Intermediate Calculations		
11	Population Total	551350.00	=B4 * B5
12	FPC Factor	0.9900	=SQRT((B4 - B6)/(B4 - 1))
13	Standard Error of the Total	14330.9521	=(B4 * B7 * B12)/SQRT(B6)
14	Degrees of Freedom	99	=B6 - 1
15	*t* Value	1.9842	=TINV(1 - B8, B14)
16	Interval Half Width	28435.72	=B15 * B13
17			
18	**Confidence Interval**		
19	Interval Lower Limit	522914.28	=B11 - B16
20	Interval Upper Limit	579785.72	=B11 + B16

EXAMPLE 8.7

Developing a Confidence Interval Estimate for the Population Total

An auditor is faced with a population of 1,000 vouchers and wants to estimate the total value of the population of vouchers. A sample of 50 vouchers is selected, with the following results:

$$\text{Mean voucher amount } (\bar{X}) = \$1{,}076.39$$
$$\text{Standard deviation } (S) = \$273.62$$

Construct a 95% confidence interval estimate of the total amount for the population of vouchers.

SOLUTION Using Equation (8.6) on page 304, the point estimate of the population total is

$$N\bar{X} = (1{,}000)(1{,}076.39) = \$1{,}076{,}390$$

From Equation (8.7) on page 304 a 95% confidence interval estimate of the population total amount is

$$(1{,}000)(1{,}076.39) \pm (1{,}000)(2.0096)\frac{273.62}{\sqrt{50}}\sqrt{\frac{1{,}000 - 50}{1{,}000 - 1}}$$
$$= 1{,}076{,}390 \pm 77{,}762.878\,(0.97517)$$
$$= 1{,}076{,}390 \pm 75{,}832$$
$$\$1{,}000{,}558 \le \text{Population total} \le \$1{,}152{,}222$$

Therefore, with 95% confidence, you estimate that the total amount of the vouchers is between $1,000,558 and $1,152,222.

Difference Estimation

An auditor uses **difference estimation** when he or she believes that errors exist in a set of items and he or she wants to estimate the magnitude of the errors based only on a sample. The following steps are used in difference estimation:

1. Determine the sample size required.
2. Calculate the differences between the values reached during the audit and the original values recorded. The difference in value i, denoted D_i, is equal to 0 if the auditor finds that the original value is correct, is a positive value when the audited value is larger than the original value, and is negative when the audited value is smaller than the original value.
3. Compute the mean difference in the sample, $\bar{D}$, by dividing the total difference by the sample size, as shown in Equation (8.8).

MEAN DIFFERENCE

$$\bar{D} = \frac{\sum_{i=1}^{n} D_i}{n} \quad \textbf{(8.8)}$$

where D_i = Audited value − Original value

4. Compute the standard deviation of the differences, S_D, as shown in Equation (8.9). *Remember that any item that is not in error has a difference value of 0.*

STANDARD DEVIATION OF THE DIFFERENCE

$$S_D = \sqrt{\frac{\sum_{i=1}^{n}(D_i - \bar{D})^2}{n - 1}} \quad \textbf{(8.9)}$$

5. Use Equation (8.10) to construct a confidence interval estimate of the total difference in the population.

CONFIDENCE INTERVAL ESTIMATE FOR THE TOTAL DIFFERENCE

$$N\bar{D} \pm N(t_{\alpha/2})\frac{S_D}{\sqrt{n}}\sqrt{\frac{N - n}{N - 1}} \quad \textbf{(8.10)}$$

where $t_{\alpha/2}$ is the critical value corresponding to an upper-tail probability of $\alpha/2$ from the t distribution with $n - 1$ degrees of freedom (i.e., a cumulative area of $1 - \alpha/2$).

The auditing procedures for Saxon Home Improvement require a 95% confidence interval estimate of the difference between the audited dollar amounts on the sales invoices and the amounts originally entered into the integrated inventory and sales information system. The data are collected by taking a sample of 100 sales invoices. The results of the sample are organized and stored in the PlumbInv workbook. There are 12 invoices in which the audited dollar amount on the sales invoice and the amount originally entered into the integrated inventory management and sales information system are different. These 12 differences are

\$9.03 \$7.47 \$17.32 \$8.30 \$5.21 \$10.80 \$6.22 \$5.63 \$4.97 \$7.43 \$2.99 \$4.63

The other 88 invoices are not in error. Each of their *differences* is 0. Thus, to analyze the data, you compute

$$\bar{D} = \frac{\sum_{i=1}^{n} D_i}{n} = \frac{90}{100} = 0.90$$

and[4]

$$S_D = \sqrt{\frac{\sum_{i=1}^{n}(D_i - \bar{D})^2}{n - 1}}$$

[4]In the numerator, there are 100 differences. Each of the last 88 is equal to $(0 - 0.9)^2$.

$$= \sqrt{\frac{(9.03 - 0.9)^2 + (7.47 - 0.9)^2 + \cdots + (0 - 0.9)^2}{100 - 1}}$$

$$S_D = 2.752$$

Using Equation (8.10), you construct the 95% confidence interval estimate for the total difference in the population of 5,000 sales invoices, as follows:

$$(5{,}000)(0.90) \pm (5{,}000)(1.9842)\frac{2.752}{\sqrt{100}}\sqrt{\frac{5{,}000 - 100}{5{,}000 - 1}}$$

$$= 4{,}500 \pm 2{,}702.91$$

$$\$1{,}797.09 \le \text{Total difference} \le \$7{,}202.91$$

Thus, the auditor estimates with 95% confidence that the total difference between the sales invoices, as determined during the audit, and the amount originally entered into the accounting system is between $1,797.09 and $7,202.91. Figure 8.16 shows the worksheet results for these data.

FIGURE 8.16

Worksheet for the total difference between the invoice amounts found during audit and the amounts entered into the accounting system for the Saxon Home Improvement Company

	A	B	
1	**Total Difference In Actual and Entered**		
2			
3	**Data**		
4	Population Size	5000	
5	Sample Size	100	
6	Confidence Level	95%	
7			
8	Intermediate Calculations		
9	Sum of Differences	90	=SUM(DIFFERENCES!A:A)
10	Average Difference in Sample	0.9	=B9/B5
11	Total Difference	4500	=B4 * B10
12	Standard Deviation of Differences	2.7518	=SQRT(E15)
13	FPC Factor	0.9900	=SQRT((B4 - B5)/(B4 - 1))
14	Standard Error of the Total Diff.	1362.2064	=(B4 * B12 * B13)/SQRT(B5)
15	Degrees of Freedom	99	=B5 - 1
16	*t* Value	1.9842	=TINV(1 - B6, B15)
17	Interval Half Width	2702.9129	=B16 * B14
18			
19	**Confidence Interval**		
20	Interval Lower Limit	1797.09	=B11 - B17
21	Interval Upper Limit	7202.91	=B11 + B17

In the previous example, all 12 differences are positive because the audited amount on the sales invoice is more than the amount originally entered into the accounting system. In some circumstances, you could have negative errors. Example 8.8 illustrates such a situation.

EXAMPLE 8.8

Difference Estimation

Returning to Example 8.7 on page 305, suppose that 14 vouchers in the sample of 50 vouchers contain errors. The values of the 14 errors are listed below and stored in **DiffTest**. Observe that two differences are negative:

$75.41	$38.97	$108.54	−$37.18	$62.75	$118.32	−$88.84
$127.74	$55.42	$39.03	$29.41	$47.99	$28.73	$84.05

Construct a 95% confidence interval estimate for the total difference in the population of 1,000 vouchers.

SOLUTION For these data,

$$\bar{D} = \frac{\sum_{i=1}^{n} D_i}{n} = \frac{690.34}{50} = 13.8068$$

and

$$S_D = \sqrt{\frac{\sum_{i=1}^{n}(D_i - \bar{D})^2}{n - 1}}$$

$$= \sqrt{\frac{(75.41 - 13.8068)^2 + (38.97 - 13.8068)^2 + \cdots + (0 - 13.8068)^2}{50 - 1}}$$

$$= 37.427$$

Using Equation (8.10) on page 306, construct the confidence interval estimate for the total difference in the population, as follows:

$$(1{,}000)(13.8068) \pm (1{,}000)(2.0096)\frac{37.427}{\sqrt{50}}\sqrt{\frac{1{,}000 - 50}{1{,}000 - 1}}$$

$$= 13{,}806.8 \pm 10{,}372.4$$

$$\$3{,}434.40 \leq \text{Total difference} \leq \$24{,}179.20$$

Therefore, with 95% confidence, you estimate that the total difference in the population of vouchers is between \$3,434.40 and \$24,179.20.

One-Sided Confidence Interval Estimation of the Rate of Noncompliance with Internal Controls

Organizations use internal control mechanisms to ensure that individuals act in accordance with company guidelines. For example, Saxon Home Improvement requires that an authorized warehouse-removal slip be completed before goods are removed from the warehouse. During the monthly audit of the company, the auditing team is charged with the task of estimating the proportion of times goods were removed without proper authorization. This is referred to as the *rate of noncompliance with the internal control*. To estimate the rate of noncompliance, auditors take a random sample of sales invoices and determine how often merchandise was shipped without an authorized warehouse-removal slip. The auditors then compare their results with a previously established tolerable exception rate, which is the maximum allowable proportion of items in the population not in compliance. When estimating the rate of noncompliance, it is commonplace to use a **one-sided confidence interval**. That is, the auditors estimate an upper bound on the rate of noncompliance. Equation (8.11) defines a one-sided confidence interval for a proportion.

ONE-SIDED CONFIDENCE INTERVAL FOR A PROPORTION

$$\text{Upper bound} = p + Z_\alpha\sqrt{\frac{p(1 - p)}{n}}\sqrt{\frac{N - n}{N - 1}} \quad \textbf{(8.11)}$$

where Z_α = the value corresponding to a cumulative area of $(1 - \alpha)$ from the standardized normal distribution (i.e., a right- tail probability of α).

If the tolerable exception rate is higher than the upper bound, the auditor concludes that the company is in compliance with the internal control. If the upper bound is higher than the tolerable exception rate, the auditor has failed to prove that the company is in compliance. The auditor may then request a larger sample.

Suppose that in the monthly audit, you select 400 sales invoices from a population of 10,000 invoices. In the sample of 400 sales invoices, 20 are in violation of the internal control.

If the tolerable exception rate for this internal control is 6%, what should you conclude? Use a 95% level of confidence.

The one-sided confidence interval is computed using $p = 20/400 = 0.05$ and $Z_\alpha = 1.645$. Using Equation (8.11),

$$\text{Upper bound} = p + Z_\alpha\sqrt{\frac{p(1-p)}{n}}\sqrt{\frac{N-n}{N-1}} = 0.05 + 1.645\sqrt{\frac{0.05(1-0.05)}{400}}\sqrt{\frac{10{,}000-400}{10{,}000-1}}$$

$$= 0.05 + 1.645(0.0109)(0.98) = 0.05 + 0.0176 = 0.0676$$

Thus, you have 95% confidence that the rate of noncompliance is less than 6.76%. Because the tolerable exception rate is 6%, the rate of noncompliance may be too high for this internal control. In other words, it is possible that the noncompliance rate for the population is higher than the rate deemed tolerable. Therefore, you should request a larger sample.

In many cases, the auditor is able to conclude that the rate of noncompliance with the company's internal controls is acceptable. Example 8.9 illustrates such an occurrence.

EXAMPLE 8.9

Estimating the Rate of Noncompliance

A large electronics firm writes 1 million checks a year. An internal control policy for the company is that the authorization to sign each check is granted only after an invoice has been initialed by an accounts payable supervisor. The company's tolerable exception rate for this control is 4%. If control deviations are found in 8 of the 400 invoices sampled, what should the auditor do? To solve this, use a 95% level of confidence.

SOLUTION The auditor constructs a 95% one-sided confidence interval for the proportion of invoices in noncompliance and compares this to the tolerable exception rate. Using Equation (8.11) on page 308, $p = 8/400 = 0.02$, and $Z_\alpha = 1.645$ for 95% confidence,

$$\text{Upper bound} = p + Z_\alpha\sqrt{\frac{p(1-p)}{n}}\sqrt{\frac{N-n}{N-1}} = 0.02 + 1.645\sqrt{\frac{0.02(1-0.02)}{400}}\sqrt{\frac{1{,}000{,}000-400}{1{,}000{,}000-1}}$$

$$= 0.02 + 1.645(0.007)(0.9998) = 0.02 + 0.0115 = 0.0315$$

The auditor concludes with 95% confidence that the rate of noncompliance is less than 3.15%. Because this is less than the tolerable exception rate, the auditor concludes that the internal control compliance is adequate. In other words, the auditor is more than 95% confident that the rate of noncompliance is less than 4%.

Problems for Section 8.5

LEARNING THE BASICS

8.50 A sample of 25 is selected from a population of 500 items. The sample mean is 25.7, and the sample standard deviation is 7.8. Construct a 99% confidence interval estimate for the population total.

8.51 Suppose that a sample of 200 (stored in ItemErr) is selected from a population of 10,000 items. Of these, 10 items are found to have the following errors:

13.76	42.87	34.65	11.09	14.54
22.87	25.52	9.81	10.03	15.49

Construct a 95% confidence interval estimate for the total difference in the population.

8.52 If $p = 0.04$, $n = 300$, and $N = 5{,}000$, calculate the upper bound for a one-sided confidence interval estimate for the population proportion, π, using the following levels of confidence:

a. 90%
b. 95%
c. 99%

APPLYING THE CONCEPTS

8.53 A stationery store wants to estimate the total retail value of the 1,000 greeting cards it has in its inventory. Construct a 95% confidence interval estimate for the population total value of all greeting cards that are in inventory if a random sample of 100 greeting cards indicates a mean value of \$2.55 and a standard deviation of \$0.44.

SELF Test **8.54** The personnel department of a large corporation employing 3,000 workers wants to estimate the family dental expenses of its employees to determine the feasibility of providing a dental insurance plan. A random sample of 10 employees (stored in the file **Dental**) reveals the following family dental expenses (in dollars) for the preceding year:

110 362 246 85 510 208 173 425 316 179

Construct a 90% confidence interval estimate for the total family dental expenses for all employees in the preceding year.

8.55 A branch of a chain of large electronics stores is conducting an end-of-month inventory of the merchandise in stock. There were 1,546 items in inventory at that time. A sample of 50 items was randomly selected, and an audit was conducted, with the following results:

Value of Merchandise

$\bar{X} = \$252.28 \qquad S = \$93.67$

Construct a 95% confidence interval estimate for the total value of the merchandise in inventory at the end of the month.

8.56 A customer in the wholesale garment trade is often entitled to a discount for a cash payment for goods. The amount of discount varies by vendor. A sample of 150 items selected from a population of 4,000 invoices at the end of a period of time (stored in **Discount**) revealed that in 13 cases, the customer failed to take the discount to which he or she was entitled. The amounts (in dollars) of the 13 discounts that were not taken were as follows:

6.45 15.32 97.36 230.63 104.18 84.92 132.76
66.12 26.55 129.43 88.32 47.81 89.01

Construct a 99% confidence interval estimate for the population total amount of discounts not taken.

8.57 Econe Dresses is a small company that manufactures women's dresses for sale to specialty stores. It has 1,200 inventory items, and the historical cost is recorded on a first-in, first-out (FIFO) basis. In the past, approximately 15% of the inventory items were incorrectly priced. However, any misstatements were usually not significant. A sample of 120 items was selected (see the **Fifo** file), and the historical cost of each item was compared with the audited value. The results indicated that 15 items differed in their historical costs and audited values. These values were as follows:

Sample Number	Historical Cost ($)	Audited Value ($)	Sample Number	Historical Cost ($)	Audited Value ($)
5	261	240	60	21	210
9	87	105	73	140	152
17	201	276	86	129	112
18	121	110	95	340	216
28	315	298	96	341	402
35	411	356	107	135	97
43	249	211	119	228	220
51	216	305			

Construct a 95% confidence interval estimate for the total population difference in the historical cost and audited value.

8.58 Tom and Brent's Alpine Outfitters conducts an annual audit of its financial records. An internal control policy for the company is that a check can be issued only after the accounts payable manager initials the invoice. The tolerable exception rate for this internal control is 0.04. During an audit, a sample of 300 invoices is examined from a population of 10,000 invoices, and 11 invoices are found to violate the internal control.

a. Calculate the upper bound for a 95% one-sided confidence interval estimate for the rate of noncompliance.

b. Based on (a), what should the auditor conclude?

8.59 An internal control policy for Rhonda's Online Fashion Accessories requires a quality assurance check before a shipment is made. The tolerable exception rate for this internal control is 0.05. During an audit, 500 shipping records were sampled from a population of 5,000 shipping records, and 12 were found that violated the internal control.

a. Calculate the upper bound for a 95% one-sided confidence interval estimate for the rate of noncompliance.

b. Based on (a), what should the auditor conclude?

8.6 Confidence Interval Estimation and Ethical Issues

Ethical issues related to the selection of samples and the inferences that accompany them can occur in several ways. The major ethical issue relates to whether confidence interval estimates are provided along with the point estimates. Providing a point estimate without also including the confidence interval limits (typically set at 95%), the sample size used, and an interpretation of the meaning of the confidence interval in terms that a person untrained in statistics can understand raises ethical issues. Failure to include a confidence interval estimate might mislead the user of the results into thinking that the point estimate is all that is needed to predict the population characteristic with certainty.

When media outlets publicize the results of a political poll, they often overlook including this information. Sometimes, the results of a poll include the sampling error, but the sampling error is often presented in fine print or as an afterthought to the story being reported. A fully ethical presentation of poll results would give equal prominence to the confidence levels, sample size, sampling error, and confidence limits of the poll.

When you prepare your own point estimates, always state the interval estimate in a prominent place and include a brief explanation of the meaning of the confidence interval. In addition, make sure you highlight the sample size and sampling error.

8.7 *Online Topic:* Estimation and Sample Size Determination for Finite Populations

In this section, confidence intervals are developed and the sample size is determined for situations in which sampling is done without replacement from a finite population. To study this topic, read the Section 8.7 online topic file that is available on this book's companion website. (See Appendix C to learn how to access the online topic files from the companion website.)

USING STATISTICS @ Saxon Home Improvement Revisited

In the Saxon Home Improvement scenario, you were an accountant for a distributor of home improvement supplies in the northeastern United States. You were responsible for the accuracy of the integrated inventory management and sales information system. You used confidence interval estimation techniques to draw conclusions about the population of all records from a relatively small sample collected during an audit.

At the end of the month, you collected a random sample of 100 sales invoices and made the following inferences:

- With 95% confidence, you concluded that the mean amount of all the sales invoices is between \$104.53 and \$116.01.
- With 95% confidence, you concluded that between 4.12% and 15.88% of all the sales invoices contain errors.
- With 95% confidence, you concluded that the total amount of all the sales invoices is between \$522,914 and \$579,786.
- With 95% confidence, you concluded that the total difference between the actual and audited amounts of sales invoices was between \$1,797.09 and \$7,202.91.

These estimates provide an interval of values that you believe contain the true population parameters. If these intervals are too wide (i.e., the sampling error is too large) for the types of decisions Saxon Home Improvement needs to make, you will need to take a larger sample. You can use the sample size formulas in Section 8.4 to determine the number of sales invoices to sample to ensure that the size of the sampling error is acceptable.

SUMMARY

This chapter discusses confidence intervals for estimating the characteristics of a population, along with how you can determine the necessary sample size. You learned how to apply these methods to numerical and categorical data. Table 8.3 on page 312 provides a list of topics covered in this chapter.

To determine what equation to use for a particular situation, you need to answer these questions:

- Are you constructing a confidence interval, or are you determining sample size?
- Do you have a numerical variable, or do you have a categorical variable?
- If you are constructing confidence intervals in auditing, are you trying to estimate the population total, the difference between an audited value and an actual value, or the rate of noncompliance?

The next four chapters develop a hypothesis-testing approach to making decisions about population parameters.

TABLE 8.3
Summary of Topics in Chapter 8

Type of Analysis	Type of Data: Numerical	Type of Data: Categorical
Confidence interval for a population parameter	Confidence interval estimate for the mean (Sections 8.1 and 8.2) Confidence interval estimate for the total and mean difference (Section 8.5)	Confidence interval estimate for the proportion (Section 8.3) One-sided confidence interval estimate for the proportion (Section 8.5)
Determining sample size	Sample size determination for the mean (Section 8.4)	Sample size determination for the proportion (Section 8.4)

KEY EQUATIONS

Confidence Interval for the Mean (σ Known)

$$\overline{X} \pm Z_{\alpha/2}\frac{\sigma}{\sqrt{n}}$$

or

$$\overline{X} - Z_{\alpha/2}\frac{\sigma}{\sqrt{n}} \le \mu \le \overline{X} + Z_{\alpha/2}\frac{\sigma}{\sqrt{n}} \quad (8.1)$$

Confidence Interval for the Mean (σ Unknown)

$$\overline{X} \pm t_{\alpha/2}\frac{S}{\sqrt{n}}$$

or

$$\overline{X} - t_{\alpha/2}\frac{S}{\sqrt{n}} \le \mu \le \overline{X} + t_{\alpha/2}\frac{S}{\sqrt{n}} \quad (8.2)$$

Confidence Interval Estimate for the Proportion

$$p \pm Z_{\alpha/2}\sqrt{\frac{p(1-p)}{n}}$$

or

$$p - Z_{\alpha/2}\sqrt{\frac{p(1-p)}{n}} \le \pi \le p + Z_{\alpha/2}\sqrt{\frac{p(1-p)}{n}} \quad (8.3)$$

Sample Size Determination for the Mean

$$n = \frac{Z_{\alpha/2}^2\sigma^2}{e^2} \quad (8.4)$$

Sample Size Determination for the Proportion

$$n = \frac{Z_{\alpha/2}^2\pi(1-\pi)}{e^2} \quad (8.5)$$

Estimating the Population Total

$$\text{Total} = N\overline{X} \quad (8.6)$$

Confidence Interval Estimate for the Total

$$N\overline{X} \pm N(t_{\alpha/2})\frac{S}{\sqrt{n}}\sqrt{\frac{N-n}{N-1}} \quad (8.7)$$

Mean Difference

$$\overline{D} = \frac{\sum_{i=1}^{n} D_i}{n} \quad (8.8)$$

Standard Deviation of the Difference

$$S_D = \sqrt{\frac{\sum_{i=1}^{n}(D_i - \overline{D})^2}{n-1}} \quad (8.9)$$

Confidence Interval Estimate for the Total Difference

$$N\overline{D} \pm N(t_{\alpha/2})\frac{S_D}{\sqrt{n}}\sqrt{\frac{N-n}{N-1}} \quad (8.10)$$

One-Sided Confidence Interval for a Proportion

$$\text{Upper bound} = p + Z_{\alpha}\sqrt{\frac{p(1-p)}{n}}\sqrt{\frac{N-n}{N-1}} \quad (8.11)$$

KEY TERMS

CHAPTER REVIEW PROBLEMS

CHECKING YOUR UNDERSTANDING

8.60 Why can you never really have 100% confidence of correctly estimating the population characteristic of interest?

8.61 When are you able to use the t distribution to develop the confidence interval estimate for the mean?

8.62 Why is it true that for a given sample size, n, an increase in confidence is achieved by widening (and making less precise) the confidence interval?

8.63 Under what circumstances do you use a one-sided confidence interval instead of a two-sided confidence interval?

8.64 When would you want to estimate the population total instead of the population mean?

8.65 How does difference estimation differ from estimation of the mean?

APPLYING THE CONCEPTS

8.66 You work in the corporate office for a nationwide convenience store franchise that operates nearly 10,000 stores. The per-store daily customer count has been steady, at 900, for some time (i.e., the mean number of customers in a store in one day is 900). To increase the customer count, the franchise is considering cutting coffee prices by approximately half. The 12-ounce size will now be \$0.59 instead of \$0.99, and the 16-ounce size will be \$0.69 instead of \$1.19. Even with this reduction in price, the franchise will have a 40% gross margin on coffee. To test the new initiative, the franchise has reduced coffee prices in a sample of 34 stores, where customer counts have been running almost exactly at the national average of 900. After four weeks, the sample stores stabilize at a mean customer count of 974 and a standard deviation of 96. This increase seems like a substantial amount to you, but it also seems like a pretty small sample. Is there some way to get a feel for what the mean per-store count in all the stores will be if you cut coffee prices nationwide? Do you think reducing coffee prices is a good strategy for increasing the mean customer count?

8.67 What do Americans do to conserve energy? A survey of 500 adults (data extracted from "Going on an Energy Diet," *USA Today*, April 16, 2009, p. 1A) found the following percentages:

Turn off lights, power strips, unplug things: 73%
Recycle aluminum, plastic, newspapers, cardboard: 47%
Recycle harder-to-recycle products: 36%
Buy products with least packaging: 34%
Ride a bike or walk: 23%

a. Construct 95% confidence interval estimates for the population proportion of what adults do to conserve energy.
b. What conclusions can you reach concerning what adults do to conserve energy?

8.68 A market researcher for a consumer electronics company wants to study the television viewing habits of residents of a particular area. A random sample of 40 respondents is selected, and each respondent is instructed to keep a detailed record of all television viewing in a particular week. The results are as follows:

- Viewing time per week: $\bar{X} = 15.3$ hours, $S = 3.8$ hours.
- 27 respondents watch the evening news on at least three weeknights.

a. Construct a 95% confidence interval estimate for the mean amount of television watched per week in this area.
b. Construct a 95% confidence interval estimate for the population proportion who watch the evening news on at least three weeknights per week.

Suppose that the market researcher wants to take another survey in a different location. Answer these questions:

c. What sample size is required to be 95% confident of estimating the population mean viewing time to within ± 2 hours assuming that the population standard deviation is equal to five hours?
d. How many respondents need to be selected to be 95% confident of being within ± 0.035 of the population proportion who watch the evening news on at least three weeknights if no previous estimate is available?
e. Based on (c) and (d), how many respondents should the market researcher select if a single survey is being conducted?

8.69 The real estate assessor for a county government wants to study various characteristics of single-family houses in the county. A random sample of 70 houses reveals the following:

- Heated area of the houses (in square feet): $\bar{X} = 1{,}759$, $S = 380$.
- 42 houses have central air-conditioning.

a. Construct a 99% confidence interval estimate for the population mean heated area of the houses.
b. Construct a 95% confidence interval estimate for the population proportion of houses that have central air-conditioning.

8.70 The personnel director of a large corporation wishes to study absenteeism among clerical workers at the corporation's central office during the year. A random sample of 25 clerical workers reveals the following:

- Absenteeism: $\bar{X} = 9.7$ days, $S = 4.0$ days.
- 12 clerical workers were absent more than 10 days.

a. Construct a 95% confidence interval estimate for the mean number of absences for clerical workers during the year.
b. Construct a 95% confidence interval estimate for the population proportion of clerical workers absent more than 10 days during the year.

Suppose that the personnel director also wishes to take a survey in a branch office. Answer these questions:

c. What sample size is needed to have 95% confidence in estimating the population mean absenteeism to within ± 1.5 days if the population standard deviation is estimated to be 4.5 days?
d. How many clerical workers need to be selected to have 90% confidence in estimating the population proportion to within ± 0.075 if no previous estimate is available?
e. Based on (c) and (d), what sample size is needed if a single survey is being conducted?

8.71 The market research director for Dotty's Department Store wants to study women's spending on cosmetics. A survey of the store's customers is designed in order to estimate the proportion of women who purchase their cosmetics primarily from Dotty's Department Store and the mean yearly amount that women spend on cosmetics. A previous survey found that the standard deviation of the amount women spend on cosmetics in a year is approximately \$18.

a. What sample size is needed to have 99% confidence of estimating the population mean amount spent to within $\pm\$5$?
b. How many of the store's credit card holders need to be selected to have 90% confidence of estimating the population proportion to within ± 0.045?

8.72 The branch manager of a nationwide bookstore chain (located near a college campus) wants to study characteristics of her store's customers. She decides to focus on two variables: the amount of money spent by customers (on items other than textbooks) and whether the customers would consider purchasing educational DVDs related to graduate preparation exams, such as the GMAT, GRE, or LSAT. The results from a sample of 70 customers are as follows:

- Amount spent: $\bar{X} = \$28.52$, $S = \$11.39$.
- 28 customers stated that they would consider purchasing the educational DVDs.

a. Construct a 95% confidence interval estimate for the population mean amount spent in the bookstore.
b. Construct a 90% confidence interval estimate for the population proportion of customers who would consider purchasing educational DVDs.

Assume that the branch manager of another store in the chain (also located close to a college campus) wants to conduct a similar survey in his store. Answer the following questions:

c. What sample size is needed to have 95% confidence of estimating the population mean amount spent in this store to within $\pm\$2$ if the standard deviation is assumed to be \$10?
d. How many customers need to be selected to have 90% confidence of estimating the population proportion who would consider purchasing the educational DVDs to within ± 0.04?
e. Based on your answers to (c) and (d), how large a sample should the manager take?

8.73 The branch manager of an outlet (Store 1) of a nationwide chain of pet supply stores wants to study characteristics of her customers. In particular, she decides to focus on two variables: the amount of money spent by customers and whether the customers own only one dog, only one cat, or more than one dog and/or cat. The results from a sample of 70 customers are as follows:

- Amount of money spent: $\bar{X} = \$21.34$, $S = \$9.22$.
- 37 customers own only a dog.
- 26 customers own only a cat.
- 7 customers own more than one dog and/or cat.

a. Construct a 95% confidence interval estimate for the population mean amount spent in the pet supply store.
b. Construct a 90% confidence interval estimate for the population proportion of customers who own only a cat.

The branch manager of another outlet (Store 2) wishes to conduct a similar survey in his store. The manager does not have access to the information generated by the manager of Store 1. Answer the following questions:

c. What sample size is needed to have 95% confidence of estimating the population mean amount spent in this store to within $\pm\$1.50$ if the standard deviation is estimated to be \$10?
d. How many customers need to be selected to have 90% confidence of estimating the population proportion of customers who own only a cat to within ± 0.045?
e. Based on your answers to (c) and (d), how large a sample should the manager take?

8.74 Scarlett and Heather, the owners of an upscale restaurant in Dayton, Ohio, want to study the dining characteristics of their customers. They decide to focus on two variables: the amount of money spent by customers and whether customers order dessert. The results from a sample of 60 customers are as follows:

- Amount spent: $\bar{X} = \$38.54$, $S = \$7.26$.
- 18 customers purchased dessert.

a. Construct a 95% confidence interval estimate for the population mean amount spent per customer in the restaurant.
b. Construct a 90% confidence interval estimate for the population proportion of customers who purchase dessert.

Jeanine, the owner of a competing restaurant, wants to conduct a similar survey in her restaurant. Jeanine does not have access to the information that Scarlett and Heather have obtained from the survey they conducted. Answer the following questions:
c. What sample size is needed to have 95% confidence of estimating the population mean amount spent in her restaurant to within ±\$1.50, assuming that the standard deviation is estimated to be \$8?
d. How many customers need to be selected to have 90% confidence of estimating the population proportion of customers who purchase dessert to within ±0.04?
e. Based on your answers to (c) and (d), how large a sample should Jeanine take?

8.75 The manufacturer of Ice Melt claims that its product will melt snow and ice at temperatures as low as 0¡ Fahrenheit. A representative for a large chain of hardware stores is interested in testing this claim. The chain purchases a large shipment of 5-pound bags for distribution. The representative wants to know, with 95% confidence and within ±0.05, what proportion of bags of Ice Melt perform the job as claimed by the manufacturer.
a. How many bags does the representative need to test? What assumption should be made concerning the population proportion? (This is called *destructive testing*; i.e., the product being tested is destroyed by the test and is then unavailable to be sold.)
b. Suppose that the representative tests 50 bags, and 42 of them do the job as claimed. Construct a 95% confidence interval estimate for the population proportion that will do the job as claimed.
c. How can the representative use the results of (b) to determine whether to sell the Ice Melt product?

8.76 An auditor needs to estimate the percentage of times a company fails to follow an internal control procedure. A sample of 50 from a population of 1,000 items is selected, and in 7 instances, the internal control procedure was not followed.
a. Construct a 90% one-sided confidence interval estimate for the population proportion of items in which the internal control procedure was not followed.
b. If the tolerable exception rate is 0.15, what should the auditor conclude?

8.77 An auditor for a government agency needs to evaluate payments for doctors' office visits paid by Medicare in a particular zip code during the month of June. A total of 25,056 visits occurred during June in this area. The auditor wants to estimate the total amount paid by Medicare to within ±\$5 with 95% confidence. On the basis of past experience, she believes that the standard deviation is approximately \$30.
a. What sample size should she select?

Using the sample size selected in (a), an audit is conducted, with the following results:

Amount of Reimbursement

$\bar{X} = \$93.70 \qquad S = \$34.55$

In 12 of the office visits, an incorrect amount of reimbursement was provided. For the 12 office visits in which there was an incorrect reimbursement, the differences between the amount reimbursed and the amount that the auditor determined should have been reimbursed were as follows (and stored in **Medicare**):

\$17 \$25 \$14 −\$10 \$20 \$40 \$35 \$30 \$28 \$22 \$15 \$5

b. Construct a 90% confidence interval estimate for the population proportion of reimbursements that contain errors.
c. Construct a 95% confidence interval estimate for the population mean reimbursement per office visit.
d. Construct a 95% confidence interval estimate for the population total amount of reimbursements for this geographic area in June.
e. Construct a 95% confidence interval estimate for the total difference between the amount reimbursed and the amount that the auditor determined should have been reimbursed.

8.78 A home furnishings store that sells bedroom furniture is conducting an end-of-month inventory of the beds (mattress, bed spring, and frame) in stock. An auditor for the store wants to estimate the mean value of the beds in stock at that time. She wants to have 99% confidence that her estimate of the mean value is correct to within ±\$100. On the basis of past experience, she estimates that the standard deviation of the value of a bed is \$200.
a. How many beds should she select?
b. Using the sample size selected in (a), an audit was conducted, with the following results:

$\bar{X} = \$1{,}654.27 \qquad S = \$184.62$

Construct a 99% confidence interval estimate for the total value of the beds in stock at the end of the month if there were 258 beds in stock.

8.79 A quality characteristic of interest for a tea-bag-filling process is the weight of the tea in the individual bags. In this example, the label weight on the package indicates that the mean amount is 5.5 grams of tea in a bag. If the bags are underfilled, two problems arise. First, customers may not be able to brew the tea to be as strong as they wish. Second, the company may be in violation of the truth-in-labeling laws. On the other hand, if the mean amount of tea in a bag exceeds the label weight, the company is giving away product. Getting an exact amount of tea in a bag is problematic because of variation in the temperature and humidity inside the factory, differences in the density of the tea, and the extremely fast filling operation of the machine (approximately 170 bags per minute). The following data (stored in **Teabags**) are the weights, in grams, of a sample of 50 tea bags produced in one hour by a single machine:

5.65	5.44	5.42	5.40	5.53	5.34	5.54	5.45	5.52	5.41
5.57	5.40	5.53	5.54	5.55	5.62	5.56	5.46	5.44	5.51
5.47	5.40	5.47	5.61	5.53	5.32	5.67	5.29	5.49	5.55
5.77	5.57	5.42	5.58	5.58	5.50	5.32	5.50	5.53	5.58
5.61	5.45	5.44	5.25	5.56	5.63	5.50	5.57	5.67	5.36

a. Construct a 99% confidence interval estimate for the population mean weight of the tea bags.
b. Is the company meeting the requirement set forth on the label that the mean amount of tea in a bag is 5.5 grams?
c. Do you think the assumption needed to construct the confidence interval estimate in (a) is valid?

8.80 A manufacturing company produces steel housings for electrical equipment. The main component part of the housing is a steel trough that is made from a 14-gauge steel coil. It is produced using a 250-ton progressive punch press with a wipe-down operation that puts two 90-degree forms in the flat steel to make the trough. The distance from one side of the form to the other is critical because of weatherproofing in outdoor applications. The widths (in inches), shown below and stored in **Trough**, are from a sample of 49 troughs:

8.312	8.343	8.317	8.383	8.348	8.410	8.351	8.373	8.481	8.422
8.476	8.382	8.484	8.403	8.414	8.419	8.385	8.465	8.498	8.447
8.436	8.413	8.489	8.414	8.481	8.415	8.479	8.429	8.458	8.462
8.460	8.444	8.429	8.460	8.412	8.420	8.410	8.405	8.323	8.420
8.396	8.447	8.405	8.439	8.411	8.427	8.420	8.498	8.409	

a. Construct a 95% confidence interval estimate for the mean width of the troughs.
b. Interpret the interval developed in (a).
c. Do you think the assumption needed to construct the confidence interval estimate in (a) in valid?

8.81 The manufacturer of Boston and Vermont asphalt shingles knows that product weight is a major factor in a customer's perception of quality. The last stage of the assembly line packages the shingles before they are placed on wooden pallets. Once a pallet is full (a pallet for most brands holds 16 squares of shingles), it is weighed, and the measurement is recorded. The file **Pallet** contains the weight (in pounds) from a sample of 368 pallets of Boston shingles and 330 pallets of Vermont shingles.
a. For the Boston shingles, construct a 95% confidence interval estimate for the mean weight.
b. For the Vermont shingles, construct a 95% confidence interval estimate for the mean weight.
c. Do you think the assumption needed to construct the confidence interval estimates in (a) and (b) is valid?
d. Based on the results of (a) and (b), what conclusions can you reach concerning the mean weight of the Boston and Vermont shingles?

8.82 The manufacturer of Boston and Vermont asphalt shingles provides its customers with a 20-year warranty on most of its products. To determine whether a shingle will last the entire warranty period, accelerated-life testing is conducted at the manufacturing plant. Accelerated-life testing exposes the shingle to the stresses it would be subject to in a lifetime of normal use via a laboratory experiment that takes only a few minutes to conduct. In this test, a shingle is repeatedly scraped with a brush for a short period of time, and the shingle granules removed by the brushing are weighed (in grams). Shingles that experience low amounts of granule loss are expected to last longer in normal use than shingles that experience high amounts of granule loss. In this situation, a shingle should experience no more than 0.8 grams of granule loss if it is expected to last the length of the warranty period. The file **Granule** contains a sample of 170 measurements made on the company's Boston shingles and 140 measurements made on Vermont shingles.
a. For the Boston shingles, construct a 95% confidence interval estimate for the mean granule loss.
b. For the Vermont shingles, construct a 95% confidence interval estimate for the mean granule loss.
c. Do you think the assumption needed to construct the confidence interval estimates in (a) and (b) is valid?
d. Based on the results of (a) and (b), what conclusions can you reach concerning the mean granule loss of the Boston and Vermont shingles?

REPORT WRITING EXERCISE

8.83 Referring to the results in Problem 8.80 concerning the width of a steel trough, write a report that summarizes your conclusions.

TEAM PROJECT

8.84 Refer to the team project on page 73 that uses the data in **Bond Funds**. Construct all appropriate confidence interval estimates of the population characteristics of below-average-risk, average-risk, and above-average-risk bond funds. Include these estimates in a report to the vice president for research at the financial investment service.

STUDENT SURVEY DATABASE

8.85 Problem 1.27 on page 14 describes a survey of 62 undergraduate students (stored in **UndergradSurvey**).
a. For these data, for each variable, construct a 95% confidence interval estimate for the population characteristic.
b. Write a report that summarizes your conclusions.

8.86 Problem 1.27 on page 14 describes a survey of 62 undergraduate students (stored in **UndergradSurvey**).
a. Select a sample of undergraduate students at your school and conduct a similar survey for those students.
b. For the data collected in (a), repeat (a) and (b) of Problem 8.85.
c. Compare the results of (b) to those of Problem 8.85.

8.87 Problem 1.28 on page 15 describes a survey of 44 MBA students (stored in **GradSurvey**).
a. For these data, for each variable, construct a 95% confidence interval estimate for the population characteristic.
b. Write a report that summarizes your conclusions.

8.88 Problem 1.28 on page 15 describes a survey of 44 MBA students (stored in GradSurvey).

a. Select a sample of graduate students in your MBA program and conduct a similar survey for those students.

b. For the data collected in (a), repeat (a) and (b) of Problem 8.87.

c. Compare the results of (b) to those of Problem 8.87.

MANAGING ASHLAND MULTICOMM SERVICES

The marketing department has been considering ways to increase the number of new subscriptions to the *3-For-All* cable/phone/Internet service. Following the suggestion of Assistant Manager Lauren Adler, the department staff designed a survey to help determine various characteristics of households who subscribe to cable television service from Ashland. The survey consists of the following 10 questions:

1. Does your household subscribe to telephone service from Ashland?
   (1) Yes (2) No
2. Does your household subscribe to Internet service from Ashland?
   (1) Yes (2) No
3. What type of cable television service do you have?
   (1) Basic
   (2) Enhanced
   (If Basic, skip to question 5.)
4. How often do you watch the cable television stations that are only available with enhanced service?
   (1) Every day
   (2) Most days
   (3) Occasionally or never
5. How often do you watch premium or on-demand services that require an extra fee?
   (1) Almost every day
   (2) Several times a week
   (3) Rarely
   (4) Never
6. Which method did you use to obtain your current AMS subscription?
   (1) AMS toll-free phone number
   (2) AMS website
   (3) Direct mail reply card
   (4) Good Tunes & More promotion
   (5) Other
7. Would you consider subscribing to the *3-For-All* cable/phone/Internet service for a trial period if a discount were offered?
   (1) Yes (2) No
   (If no, skip to question 9.)
8. If purchased separately, cable, Internet, and phone services would currently cost $24.99 per week. How much would you be willing to pay per week for the *3-For-All* cable/phone/Internet service?
9. Does your household use another provider of telephone service?
   (1) Yes (2) No
10. AMS may distribute Ashland Gold Cards that would provide discounts at selected Ashland-area restaurants for subscribers who agree to a two-year subscription contract to the *3-For-All* service. Would being eligible to receive a Gold Card cause you to agree to the two-year term?
   (1) Yes (2) No

Of the 500 households selected that subscribe to cable television service from Ashland, 82 households either refused to participate, could not be contacted after repeated attempts, or had telephone numbers that were not in service. The summary results are as follows:

Household has AMS Telephone Service	**Frequency**
Yes	83
No	335
Household has AMS Internet Service	**Frequency**
Yes	262
No	156
Type of Cable Service	**Frequency**
Basic	164
Enhanced	254
Watches Enhanced Programming	**Frequency**
Every day	50
Most days	144
Occasionally or never	60
Watches Premium or On-Demand Services	**Frequency**
Almost every day	14
Several times a week	35
Almost never	313
Never	56
Method Used to Obtain Current AMS Subscription	**Frequency**
Toll-free phone number	230
AMS website	106
Direct mail	46
Good Tunes & More	10
Other	26
Would Consider Discounted Trial Offer	**Frequency**
Yes	40
No	378

Trial Weekly Rate ($) Willing to Pay (stored in AMS8)

23.00	20.00	22.75	20.00	20.00	24.50	17.50	22.25	18.00	21.00
18.25	21.00	18.50	20.75	21.25	22.25	22.75	21.75	19.50	20.75
16.75	19.00	22.25	21.00	16.75	19.00	22.25	21.00	19.50	22.75
23.50	19.50	21.75	22.00	24.00	23.25	19.50	20.75	18.25	21.50

Uses Another Phone Service Provider	Frequency
Yes	354
No	64

Gold Card Leads to Two-Year Agreement	Frequency
Yes	38
No	380

EXERCISE

1. Analyze the results of the survey of Ashland households that receive AMS cable television service. Write a report that discusses the marketing implications of the survey results for Ashland MultiComm Services.

DIGITAL CASE

Apply your knowledge about confidence interval estimation in this Digital Case, which extends the OurCampus! Digital Case from Chapter 6.

Among its other features, the OurCampus! website allows customers to purchase OurCampus! LifeStyles merchandise online. To handle payment processing, the management of OurCampus! has contracted with the following firms:

- **PayAFriend (PAF)** This is an online payment system with which customers and businesses such as OurCampus! register in order to exchange payments in a secure and convenient manner, without the need for a credit card.
- **Continental Banking Company (Conbanco)** This processing services provider allows OurCampus! customers to pay for merchandise using nationally recognized credit cards issued by a financial institution.

To reduce costs, management is considering eliminating one of these two payment systems. However, Lorraine Hildick of the sales department suspects that customers use the two forms of payment in unequal numbers and that customers display different buying behaviors when using the two forms of payment. Therefore, she would like to first determine the following:

- The proportion of customers using PAF and the proportion of customers using a credit card to pay for their purchases.
- The mean purchase amount when using PAF and the mean purchase amount when using a credit card.

Assist Ms. Hildick by preparing an appropriate analysis. Open **PaymentsSample.pdf**, read Ms. Hildick's comments, and use her random sample of 50 transactions as the basis for your analysis. Summarize your findings to determine whether Ms. Hildick's conjectures about OurCampus! customer purchasing behaviors are correct. If you want the sampling error to be no more than $3 when estimating the mean purchase amount, is Ms. Hildick's sample large enough to perform a valid analysis?

REFERENCES

1. Cochran, W. G., *Sampling Techniques*, 3rd ed. (New York: Wiley, 1977).
2. Fisher, R. A., and F. Yates, *Statistical Tables for Biological, Agricultural and Medical Research*, 5th ed. (Edinburgh: Oliver & Boyd, 1957).
3. Hahn, G., and W. Meeker, *Statistical Intervals, A Guide for Practitioners* (New York: John Wiley and Sons, Inc., 1991).
4. Kirk, R. E., ed., *Statistical Issues: A Reader for the Behavioral Sciences* (Belmont, CA: Wadsworth, 1972).
5. Larsen, R. L., and M. L. Marx, *An Introduction to Mathematical Statistics and Its Applications*, 4th ed. (Upper Saddle River, NJ: Prentice Hall, 2006).
6. *Microsoft Excel 2010* (Redmond, WA: Microsoft Corp., 2010).
7. *Minitab Release16* (State College, PA.: Minitab Inc., 2010).
8. Snedecor, G. W., and W. G. Cochran, *Statistical Methods*, 7th ed. (Ames, IA: Iowa State University Press, 1980).

CHAPTER 8 EXCEL GUIDE

EG8.1 CONFIDENCE INTERVAL ESTIMATE for the MEAN (σ KNOWN)

PHStat2 Use **Estimate for the Mean, sigma known** to compute the confidence interval estimate for the mean when σ is known. For example, to compute the estimate for the Example 8.1 mean paper length problem on page 284, select **PHStat → Confidence Intervals → Estimate for the Mean, sigma known.** In the procedure's dialog box (shown below):

1. Enter **0.02** as the **Population Standard Deviation**.
2. Enter **95** as the **Confidence Level** percentage.
3. Click **Sample Statistics Known** and enter **100** as the **Sample Size** and **10.998** as the **Sample Mean**.
4. Enter a **Title** and click **OK**.

For problems that use unsummarized data, click **Sample Statistics Unknown** and enter the **Sample Cell Range** in step 3.

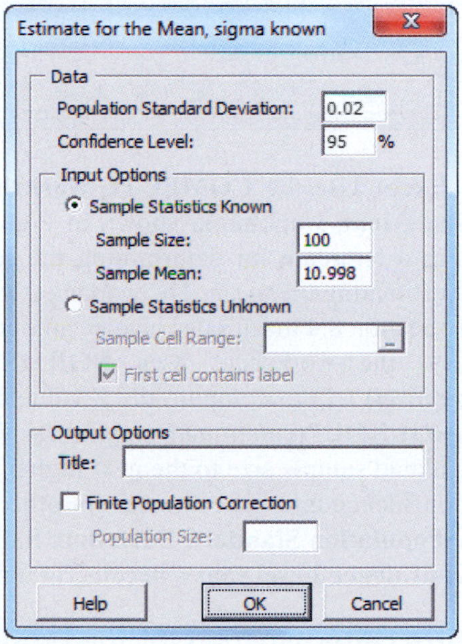

In-Depth Excel Use the **CONFIDENCE** worksheet function to compute the half-width of a confidence interval. Enter the function as **CONFIDENCE(1 – *confidence level*, *population standard deviation*, *sample size*)**.

Use the **COMPUTE worksheet** of the **CIE sigma known workbook** as a template for computing confidence interval estimates when σ is known. The worksheet also uses **NORMSINV(*cumulative percentage*)** to compute the Z value in cell B11 for one-half of the $(1 - \alpha)$ value.

The worksheet contains the data for the Example 8.1 mean paper length problem. To compute confidence interval estimates for other problems, change the **Population Standard Deviation, Sample Mean, Sample Size**, and **Confidence Level** values in cells B4 through B7, respectively. To examine all the formulas in the worksheet, open to the **COMPUTE_FORMULAS worksheet**.

EG8.2 CONFIDENCE INTERVAL ESTIMATE for the MEAN (σ UNKNOWN)

PHStat2 Use **Estimate for the Mean, sigma unknown** to compute the confidence interval estimate for the mean when σ is unknown. For example, to compute the Figure 8.7 estimate for the mean sales invoice amount (see page 289), select **PHStat → Confidence Intervals → Estimate for the Mean, sigma unknown.** In the procedure's dialog box (shown below):

1. Enter **95** as the **Confidence Level** percentage.
2. Click **Sample Statistics Known** and enter **100** as the **Sample Size**, **110.27** as the **Sample Mean**, and **28.95** as the **Sample Std. Deviation**.
3. Enter a **Title** and click **OK**.

For problems that use unsummarized data, click **Sample Statistics Unknown** and enter the **Sample Cell Range** in step 3.

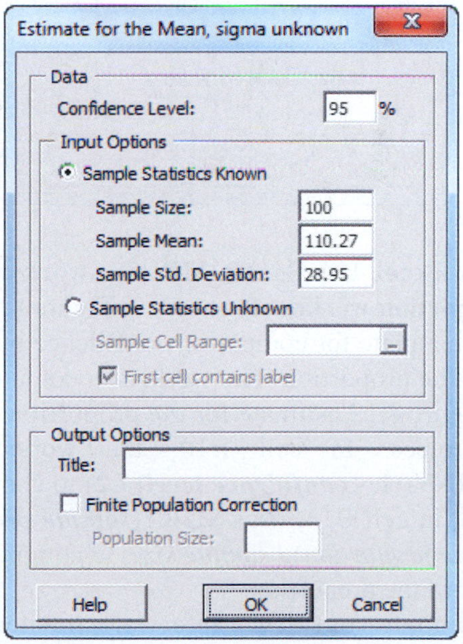

In-Depth Excel Use the **COMPUTE worksheet** of the **CIE sigma unknown workbook**, shown in Figure 8.7 on page 289, as a template for computing confidence interval estimates when σ is unknown. The worksheet contains the data for the Section 8.2 example for estimating the mean sales invoice amount. In cell B12, the worksheet uses **TINV(1 – *confidence level*, *degrees of freedom*)** to determine the critical value from the *t* distribution.

To compute confidence interval estimates for other problems, change the **Sample Standard Deviation**, **Sample Mean**, **Sample Size**, and **Confidence Level** values in cells B4 through B7, respectively.

EG8.3 CONFIDENCE INTERVAL ESTIMATE for the PROPORTION

PHStat2 Use **Estimate for the Proportion** to compute the confidence interval estimate for the proportion. For example, to compute the Figure 8.12 estimate for the proportion of in-error sales invoices (see page 295), select **PHStat → Confidence Intervals → Estimate for the Proportion.** In the procedure's dialog box (shown below):

1. Enter **100** as the **Sample Size**.
2. Enter **10** as the **Number of Successes**.
3. Enter **95** as the **Confidence Level** percentage.
4. Enter a **Title** and click **OK**.

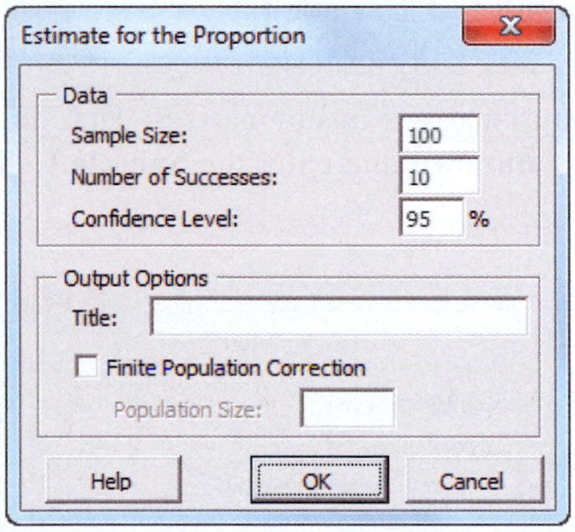

In-Depth Excel Use the **COMPUTE worksheet** of the **CIE Proportion workbook**, shown in Figure 8.12 on page 295, as a template for computing confidence interval estimates for the proportion. The worksheet contains the data for the Figure 8.12 estimate for the proportion of in-error sales invoices. In cell B10, the worksheet uses **NORMSINV((1 – *confidence level*) / 2)** to compute the *Z* value and, in cell B11, uses **SQRT(*sample proportion* * (1 – *sample proportion*) / *sample size*)** to compute the standard error of the proportion.

To compute confidence interval estimates for other problems, change the **Sample Size**, **Number of Successes**, and **Confidence Level** values in cells B4 through B6.

EG8.4 DETERMINING SAMPLE SIZE

Sample Size Determination for the Mean

PHStat2 Use **Determination for the Mean** to compute the sample size needed for estimating the mean. For example, to determine the sample size for the mean sales invoice amount, shown in Figure 8.13 on page 299, select **PHStat → Sample Size → Determination for the Mean.** In the procedure's dialog box (shown below):

1. Enter **25** as the **Population Standard Deviation**.
2. Enter **5** as the **Sampling Error**.
3. Enter **95** as the **Confidence Level** percentage.
4. Enter a **Title** and click **OK**.

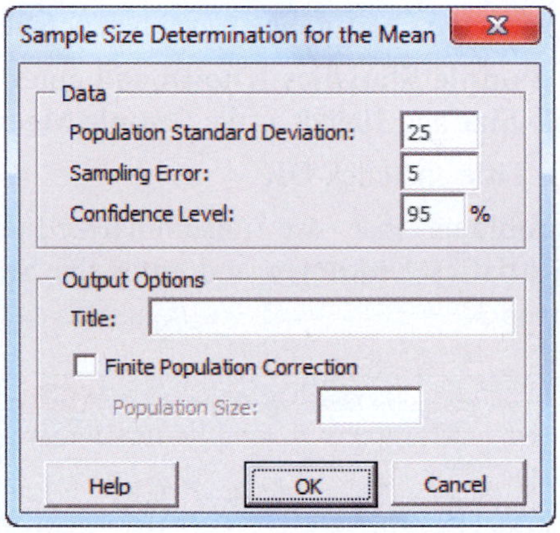

In-Depth Excel Use the **COMPUTE worksheet** of the **Sample Size Mean workbook**, shown in Figure 8.13 on page 299, as a template for determining the sample size needed for estimating the mean. The worksheet contains the data for the Section 8.4 mean sales invoice amount problem. In cell B9, the worksheet uses **NORMSINV((1 – *confidence level*) / 2)** to compute the *Z* value and, in cell B13, uses **ROUNDUP(*calculated sample size*, 0)** to round up the calculated sample size to the next higher integer. To compute confidence interval estimates for other problems, change the **Population Standard Deviation**, **Sampling Error**, and **Confidence Level** values in cells B4 through B6.

Sample Size Determination for the Proportion

PHStat2 Use **Determination for the Proportion** to compute the sample size needed for estimating the proportion. For example, to determine the sample size for the proportion of in-error sales invoices, shown in Figure 8.14 on page 301, select **PHStat → Sample Size → Determination for the Proportion.** In the procedure's dialog box (shown on page 321):

1. Enter **0.15** as the **Estimate of True Proportion**.
2. Enter **0.07** as the **Sampling Error**.
3. Enter **95** as the **Confidence Level** percentage.
4. Enter a **Title** and click **OK**.

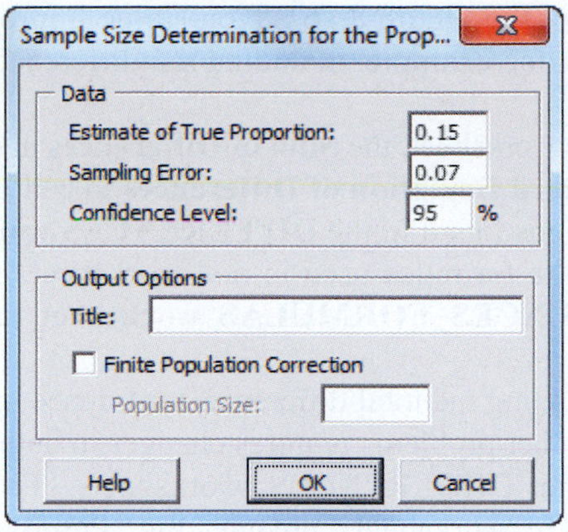

In-Depth Excel Use the **NORMSINV** and **ROUNDUP** functions to help determine the sample size needed for estimating the proportion. Enter **NORMSINV((1 – *confidence level*)/2)** to compute the *Z* value and enter **ROUNDUP(*calculated sample size*, 0)** to round up the calculated sample size to the next higher integer.

Use the **COMPUTE worksheet** of the **Sample Size Proportion workbook**, shown in Figure 8.14 on page 301, as a template for determining the sample size needed for estimating the proportion. The worksheet contains the data for the Section 8.4 in-error sales invoice problem. The worksheet uses the **NORMSINV** and **ROUNDUP** functions in the same way as discussed in the "Sample Size Determination for the Mean" *In-Depth Excel* instructions. To compute confidence interval estimates for other problems, change the **Estimate of True Proportion**, **Sampling Error**, and **Confidence Level** in cells B4 through B6.

EG8.5 APPLICATIONS of CONFIDENCE INTERVAL ESTIMATION in AUDITING

Estimating the Population Total Amount

PHStat2 Use **Estimate for the Population Total** to compute the confidence interval estimate for the population total. For example, to compute the Figure 8.15 estimate for the total of all sales invoices (see page 305), select **PHStat → Confidence Intervals → Estimate for the Population Total.** In the procedure's dialog box (shown in the right column):

1. Enter **5000** as the **Population Size**.
2. Enter **95** as the **Confidence Level** percentage.
3. Click **Sample Statistics Known** and enter **100** as the **Sample Size**, **110.27** as the **Sample Mean**, and **28.95** as the **Sample Standard Deviation**.
4. Enter a **Title** and click **OK**.

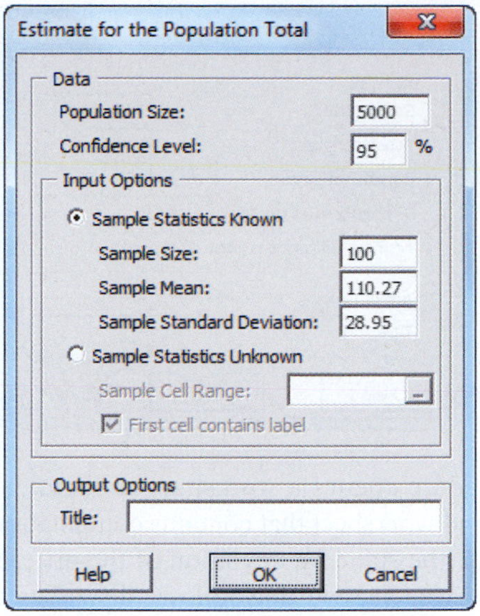

In-Depth Excel Use the **COMPUTE worksheet** of the **CIE Total workbook**, shown in Figure 8.15 on page 305, as a template for computing confidence interval estimates for the population total. The worksheet contains the data for the Figure 8.15 estimate for the total amount of all sales invoices. In cell B15, the worksheet uses **TINV(1 – *confidence level*, *degrees of freedom*)** to determine the *t* value. To compute confidence interval estimates for other problems, change the **Population Size**, **Sample Mean**, **Sample Size**, **Sample Standard Deviation**, and **Confidence Level** values in cells B4 through B8.

Difference Estimation

PHStat2 Use **Estimate for the Total Difference** to compute the confidence interval estimate for the total difference. For example, to compute the Figure 8.16 estimate for the total difference in the Saxon Home Improvement invoice auditing example (see page 307), open to the **DATA worksheet** of the **PlumbInv workbook**. Select **PHStat → Confidence Intervals → Estimate for the Total Difference.** In the procedure's dialog box (shown on page 322):

1. Enter **100** as the **Sample Size**.
2. Enter **5000** as the **Population Size**.
3. Enter **95** as the **Confidence Level** percentage.
4. Enter **A1:A13** as the **Differences Cell Range** and check **First cell contains label**.
5. Enter a **Title** and click **OK**.

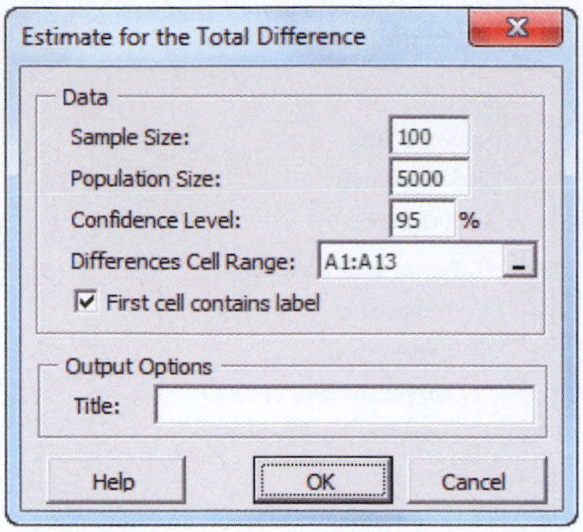

This procedure creates a worksheet containing the results and a second worksheet that contains computations that help to calculate the standard deviation of the differences. (The *In-Depth Excel* section that follows discusses contents of the second worksheet.)

In-Depth Excel Use the **COMPUTE worksheet** of the **CIE Total Difference workbook,** shown in Figure 8.16 on page 307, as a template for computing confidence interval estimates for the total difference. The worksheet contains the data for the Figure 8.16 Saxon Home Improvement invoice auditing example, including the difference data from **PlumbInv**.

In the worksheet, the **Sum of Differences** in cell B9 and the **Standard Deviation of Differences** in cell B12 rely on computations found in the **DIFFERENCES worksheet**. To examine the formulas used in that worksheet, open to the **DIFFERENCES_FORMULAS worksheet** in the same workbook.

Computing the total difference confidence interval estimate for other problems requires changes to both the COMPUTE and DIFFERENCES worksheets. First, in the COMPUTE worksheet, change the **Population Size**, **Sample Size**, and **Confidence Level** in cells B4 through B6, respectively. Then, in the DIFFERENCES worksheet, enter the differences in column A and adjust the column B formulas so that there is a column B formula for each difference listed. If there are more than 12 differences, select cell B13 and copy down through all the rows. If there are fewer than 12 differences, delete formulas in column B from the bottom up, starting with cell B13, until there are as many formulas as there are difference values.

CHAPTER 8 MINITAB GUIDE

MG8.1 CONFIDENCE INTERVAL ESTIMATE for the MEAN (σ KNOWN)

Use **1-Sample Z** to compute a confidence interval estimate for the mean when σ is known. For example, to compute the estimate for the Example 8.1 mean paper length problem on page 284, select **Stat ➔ Basic Statistics ➔ 1-Sample Z.** In the 1-Sample Z (Test and Confidence Interval) dialog box (shown below):

1. Click **Summarized data**.
2. Enter **100** in the **Sample size** box and **10.998** in the **Mean** box.
3. Enter **0.02** in the **Standard deviation** box.
4. Click **Options**.

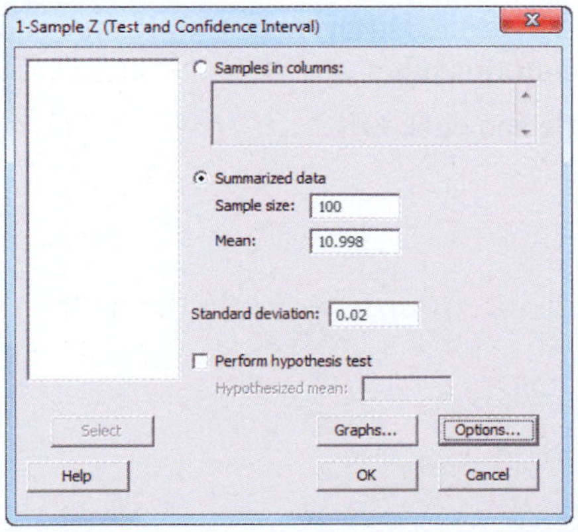

In the 1-Sample Z – Options dialog box (shown below):

5. Enter **95.0** in the **Confidence level** box.
6. Select **not equal** from the **Alternative** drop-down list.
7. Click **OK**.

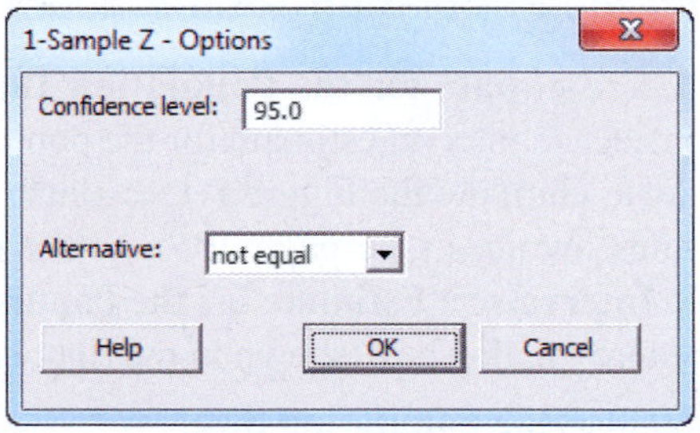

8. Back in the original dialog box, click **OK**.

For problems that use unsummarized data, click **Samples in columns** in step 1 and, in step 2, enter the name of the column that contains the data in the **Samples in columns** box.

MG8.2 CONFIDENCE INTERVAL ESTIMATE for the MEAN (σ UNKNOWN)

Use **1-Sample t** to compute a confidence interval estimate for the mean when σ is unknown. For example, to compute the Figure 8.7 estimate for the mean sales invoice amount (see page 289), select **Stat → Basic Statistics → 1-Sample t.** In the 1-Sample t (Test and Confidence Interval) dialog box (shown below):

1. Click **Summarized data**.
2. Enter **100** in the **Sample size** box, **110.27** in the **Mean** box, and **28.95** in the **Standard deviation** box.
3. Click **Options**.

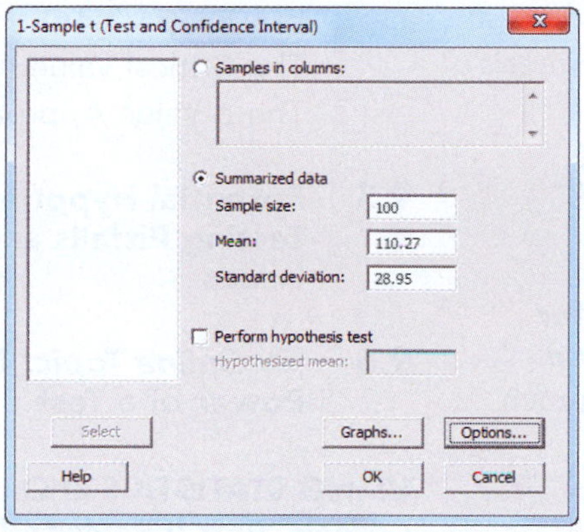

In the 1-Sample t - Options dialog box (similar to the 1-Sample Z - Options dialog box on page 322):

4. Enter **95.0** in the **Confidence level** box.
5. Select **not equal** from the **Alternative** drop-down list.
6. Click **OK**.
7. Back in the original dialog box, click **OK**.

For problems that use unsummarized data, click **Samples in columns** in step 1 and, in step 2, enter the name of the column that contains the data. To create a boxplot of the type shown in Figure 8.9 on page 290, replace step 7 with these steps 7 through 9:

7. Back in the original dialog box, click **Graphs**.
8. In the 1-Sample t - Graphs dialog box, check **Boxplot of data** and then click **OK**.
9. Back in the original dialog box, click **OK**.

MG8.3 CONFIDENCE INTERVAL ESTIMATE for the PROPORTION

Use **1 Proportion** to compute the confidence interval estimate for the population proportion. For example, to compute the Figure 8.12 estimate for the proportion of in-error sales invoices (see page 295), select **Stat → Basic Statistics → 1 Proportion.** In the 1 Proportion dialog box (shown below):

1. Click **Summarized data**.
2. Enter **10** in the **Number of events** box and **100** in the **Number of trials** box.
3. Click **Options**.

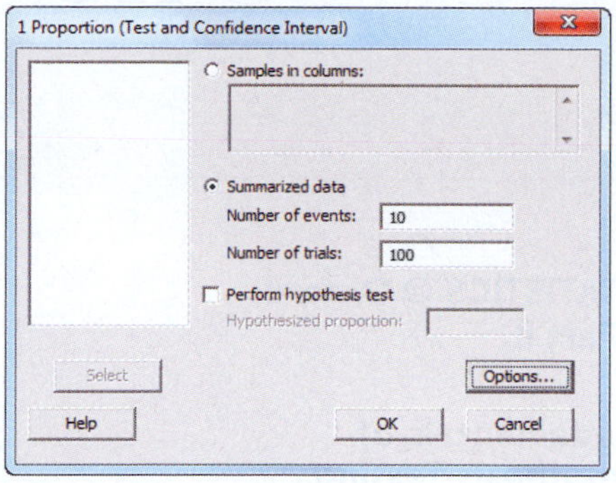

In the 1 Proportion - Options dialog box (shown below):

4. Enter **95.0** in the **Confidence level** box.
5. Select **not equal** from the **Alternative** drop-down list.
6. Check **Use test and interval based on normal distribution**.
7. Click **OK** (to return to the previous dialog box).

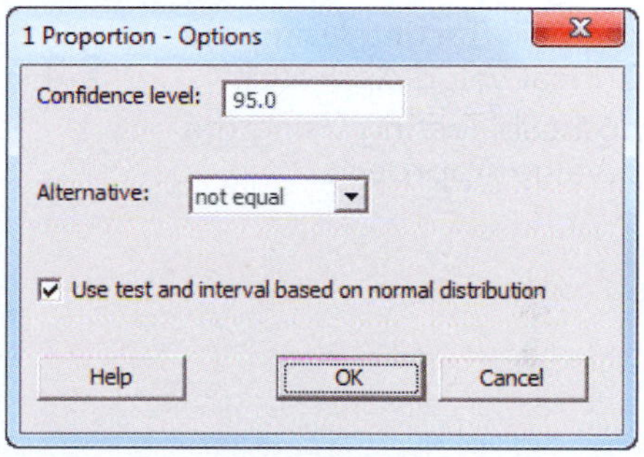

8. Back in the original dialog box, click **OK**.

For problems that use unsummarized data, click **Samples in columns** in step 1 and, in step 2, enter the name of the column that contains the data.

MG8.4 DETERMINING SAMPLE SIZE

There are no Minitab instructions for this section.

MG8.5 APPLICATIONS of CONFIDENCE INTERVAL ESTIMATION in AUDITING

There are no Minitab instructions for this section.

9 Fundamentals of Hypothesis Testing: One-Sample Tests

Learning Objectives

In this chapter, you learn:

- The basic principles of hypothesis testing
- How to use hypothesis testing to test a mean or proportion
- The assumptions of each hypothesis-testing procedure, how to evaluate them, and the consequences if they are seriously violated
- How to avoid the pitfalls involved in hypothesis testing
- Ethical issues involved in hypothesis testing

USING STATISTICS

@ Oxford Cereals, Part II

As in Chapter 7, you again find yourself as plant operations manager for Oxford Cereals. You are responsible for monitoring the amount in each cereal box filled. Company specifications require a mean weight of 368 grams per box. It is your responsibility to adjust the process when the mean fill weight in the population of boxes differs from 368 grams. How can you make the decision about whether to adjust the process when you are unable to weigh every single box as it is being filled? You begin by selecting and weighing a random sample of 25 cereal boxes. After computing the sample mean, how do you proceed?

In Chapter 7, you learned methods to determine whether the value of a sample mean is consistent with a known population mean. In this Oxford Cereals scenario, you want to use a sample mean to validate a claim about the population mean, a somewhat different problem. For this type of problem, you use an inferential method called **hypothesis testing**. Hypothesis testing requires that you state a claim unambiguously. In this scenario, the claim is that the population mean is 368 grams. You examine a sample statistic to see if it better supports the stated claim, called the *null hypothesis*, or the mutually exclusive alternative hypothesis (for this scenario, that the population mean is not 368 grams).

In this chapter, you will learn several applications of hypothesis testing. You will learn how to make inferences about a population parameter by *analyzing differences* between the results observed, the sample statistic, and the results you would expect to get if an underlying hypothesis were actually true. For the Oxford Cereals scenario, hypothesis testing allows you to infer one of the following:

- The mean weight of the cereal boxes in the sample is a value consistent with what you would expect if the mean of the entire population of cereal boxes is 368 grams.
- The population mean is not equal to 368 grams because the sample mean is significantly different from 368 grams.

9.1 Fundamentals of Hypothesis-Testing Methodology

Hypothesis testing typically begins with a theory, a claim, or an assertion about a particular parameter of a population. For example, your initial hypothesis in the cereal example is that the process is working properly, so the mean fill is 368 grams, and no corrective action is needed.

The Null and Alternative Hypotheses

The hypothesis that the population parameter is equal to the company specification is referred to as the null hypothesis. A **null hypothesis** is often one of status quo and is identified by the symbol $\boldsymbol{H_0}$. Here the null hypothesis is that the filling process is working properly, and therefore the mean fill is the 368-gram specification provided by Oxford Cereals. This is stated as

$$H_0 : \mu = 368$$

Even though information is available only from the sample, the null hypothesis is stated in terms of the population parameter because your focus is on the population of all cereal boxes. You use the sample statistic to make inferences about the entire filling process. One inference may be that the results observed from the sample data indicate that the null hypothesis is false. If the null hypothesis is considered false, something else must be true.

Whenever a null hypothesis is specified, an alternative hypothesis is also specified, and it must be true if the null hypothesis is false. The **alternative hypothesis, $\boldsymbol{H_1}$**, is the opposite of the null hypothesis, H_0. This is stated in the cereal example as

$$H_1 : \mu \neq 368$$

The alternative hypothesis represents the conclusion reached by rejecting the null hypothesis. The null hypothesis is rejected when there is sufficient evidence from the sample data that the null hypothesis is false. In the cereal example, if the weights of the sampled boxes are sufficiently above or below the expected 368-gram mean specified by Oxford Cereals, you reject the null hypothesis in favor of the alternative hypothesis that the mean fill is different from 368 grams. You stop production and take whatever action is necessary to correct the problem. If the null hypothesis is not rejected, you should continue to believe that the process is working correctly and therefore no corrective action is necessary. In this second circumstance, you have not proven that the process is working correctly. Rather, you have failed to prove that it is working incorrectly, and therefore you continue your belief (although unproven) in the null hypothesis.

In hypothesis testing, you reject the null hypothesis when the sample evidence suggests that it is far more likely that the alternative hypothesis is true. However, failure to reject the null hypothesis is not proof that it is true. You can never prove that the null hypothesis is correct because the decision is based only on the sample information, not on the entire population. Therefore, if you fail to reject the null hypothesis, you can only conclude that there is insufficient evidence to warrant its rejection. The following key points summarize the null and alternative hypotheses:

- The null hypothesis, H_0, represents the current belief in a situation.
- The alternative hypothesis, H_1, is the opposite of the null hypothesis and represents a research claim or specific inference you would like to prove.
- If you reject the null hypothesis, you have statistical proof that the alternative hypothesis is correct.
- If you do not reject the null hypothesis, you have failed to prove the alternative hypothesis. The failure to prove the alternative hypothesis, however, does not mean that you have proven the null hypothesis.
- The null hypothesis, H_0, always refers to a specified value of the population parameter (such as μ), not a sample statistic (such as $\overline{X}$).
- The statement of the null hypothesis always contains an equal sign regarding the specified value of the population parameter (e.g., $H_0 : \mu = 368$ grams).
- The statement of the alternative hypothesis never contains an equal sign regarding the specified value of the population parameter (e.g., $H_1 : \mu \neq 368$ grams).

EXAMPLE 9.1

The Null and Alternative Hypotheses

You are the manager of a fast-food restaurant. You want to determine whether the waiting time to place an order has changed in the past month from its previous population mean value of 4.5 minutes. State the null and alternative hypotheses.

SOLUTION The null hypothesis is that the population mean has not changed from its previous value of 4.5 minutes. This is stated as

$$H_0 : \mu = 4.5$$

The alternative hypothesis is the opposite of the null hypothesis. Because the null hypothesis is that the population mean is 4.5 minutes, the alternative hypothesis is that the population mean is not 4.5 minutes. This is stated as

$$H_1 : \mu \neq 4.5$$

The Critical Value of the Test Statistic

The logic of hypothesis testing involves determining how likely the null hypothesis is to be true by considering the data collected in a sample. In the Oxford Cereal Company scenario, the null hypothesis is that the mean amount of cereal per box in the entire filling process is 368 grams (the population parameter specified by the company). You select a sample of boxes from the filling process, weigh each box, and compute the sample mean. This statistic is an estimate of the corresponding parameter (the population mean, μ). Even if the null hypothesis is true, the statistic (the sample mean, $\overline{X}$) is likely to differ from the value of the parameter (the population mean, μ) because of variation due to sampling. However, you expect the sample statistic to be close to the population parameter if the null hypothesis is true. If the sample statistic is close to the population parameter, you have insufficient evidence to reject the null hypothesis. For example, if the sample mean is 367.9, you might conclude that the population mean has not changed (i.e., $\mu = 368$) because a sample mean of 367.9 is very close to the hypothesized value of 368. Intuitively, you think that it is likely that you could get a sample mean of 367.9 from a population whose mean is 368.

However, if there is a large difference between the value of the statistic and the hypothesized value of the population parameter, you might conclude that the null hypothesis is false. For example, if the sample mean is 320, you might conclude that the population mean is not 368 (i.e., $\mu \neq 368$) because the sample mean is very far from the hypothesized value of 368.

In such a case, you conclude that it is very unlikely to get a sample mean of 320 if the population mean is really 368. Therefore, it is more logical to conclude that the population mean is not equal to 368. Here you reject the null hypothesis.

However, the decision-making process is not always so clear-cut. Determining what is "very close" and what is "very different" is arbitrary without clear definitions. Hypothesis-testing methodology provides clear definitions for evaluating differences. Furthermore, it enables you to quantify the decision-making process by computing the probability of getting a certain sample result if the null hypothesis is true. You calculate this probability by determining the sampling distribution for the sample statistic of interest (e.g., the sample mean) and then computing the particular **test statistic** based on the given sample result. Because the sampling distribution for the test statistic often follows a well-known statistical distribution, such as the standardized normal distribution or *t* distribution, you can use these distributions to help determine whether the null hypothesis is true.

Regions of Rejection and Nonrejection

The sampling distribution of the test statistic is divided into two regions, a **region of rejection** (sometimes called the critical region) and a **region of nonrejection** (see Figure 9.1). If the test statistic falls into the region of nonrejection, you do not reject the null hypothesis. In the Oxford Cereals scenario, you conclude that there is insufficient evidence that the population mean fill is different from 368 grams. If the test statistic falls into the rejection region, you reject the null hypothesis. In this case, you conclude that the population mean is not 368 grams.

FIGURE 9.1

Regions of rejection and nonrejection in hypothesis testing

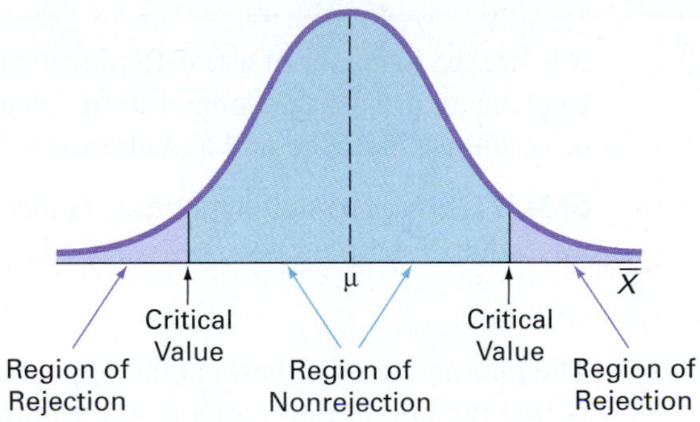

The region of rejection consists of the values of the test statistic that are unlikely to occur if the null hypothesis is true. These values are much more likely to occur if the null hypothesis is false. Therefore, if a value of the test statistic falls into this rejection region, you reject the null hypothesis because that value is unlikely if the null hypothesis is true.

To make a decision concerning the null hypothesis, you first determine the **critical value** of the test statistic. The critical value divides the nonrejection region from the rejection region. Determining the critical value depends on the size of the rejection region. The size of the rejection region is directly related to the risks involved in using only sample evidence to make decisions about a population parameter.

Risks in Decision Making Using Hypothesis Testing

Using hypothesis testing involves the risk of reaching an incorrect conclusion. You might wrongly reject a true null hypothesis, H_0, or, conversely, you might wrongly *not* reject a false null hypothesis, H_0. These types of risk are called Type I and Type II errors.

TYPE I AND TYPE II ERRORS

A **Type I error** occurs if you reject the null hypothesis, H_0, when it is true and should not be rejected. A Type I error is a "false alarm." The probability of a Type I error occurring is α.

A **Type II error** occurs if you do not reject the null hypothesis, H_0, when it is false and should be rejected. A Type II error represents a "missed opportunity" to take some corrective action. The probability of a Type II error occurring is β.

In the Oxford Cereals scenario, you would make a Type I error if you concluded that the population mean fill is *not* 368 when it *is* 368. This error causes you to needlessly adjust the filling process (the "false alarm") even though the process is working properly. In the same scenario, you would make a Type II error if you concluded that the population mean fill *is* 368 when it is *not* 368. In this case, you would allow the process to continue without adjustment, even though an adjustment is needed (the "missed opportunity").

Traditionally, you control the Type I error by determining the risk level, α (the lowercase Greek letter *alpha*) that you are willing to have of rejecting the null hypothesis when it is true. This risk, or probability, of committing a Type I error is called the *level of significance* (α). Because you specify the level of significance before you perform the hypothesis test, you directly control the risk of committing a Type I error. Traditionally, you select a level of 0.01, 0.05, or 0.10. The choice of a particular risk level for making a Type I error depends on the cost of making a Type I error. After you specify the value for α, you can then determine the critical values that divide the rejection and nonrejection regions. You know the size of the rejection region because α is the probability of rejection when the null hypothesis is true. From this, you can then determine the critical value or values that divide the rejection and nonrejection regions.

The probability of committing a Type II error is called the β *risk*. Unlike a Type I error, which you control through the selection of α, the probability of making a Type II error depends on the difference between the hypothesized and actual values of the population parameter. Because large differences are easier to find than small ones, if the difference between the hypothesized and actual value of the population parameter is large, β is small. For example, if the population mean is 330 grams, there is a small chance (β) that you will conclude that the mean has not changed from 368. However, if the difference between the hypothesized and actual value of the parameter is small, β is large. For example, if the population mean is actually 367 grams, there is a large chance (β) that you will conclude that the mean is still 368 grams.

PROBABILITY OF TYPE I AND TYPE II ERRORS

The **level of significance (α)** of a statistical test is the probability of committing a Type I error.

The **β risk** is the probability of committing a Type II error.

The complement of the probability of a Type I error, $(1 - \alpha)$, is called the *confidence coefficient*. The confidence coefficient is the probability that you will not reject the null hypothesis, H_0, when it is true and should not be rejected. In the Oxford Cereals scenario, the confidence coefficient measures the probability of concluding that the population mean fill is 368 grams when it is actually 368 grams.

The complement of the probability of a Type II error, $(1 - \beta)$, is called the *power of a statistical test*. The power of a statistical test is the probability that you will reject the null hypothesis when it is false and should be rejected. In the Oxford Cereals scenario, the power of the test is the probability that you will correctly conclude that the mean fill amount is not 368 grams when it actually is not 368 grams. For an extended discussion of the power of a statistical test, read the **Section 9.6** online topic file that is available in on this book's companion website. (See Appendix C to learn how to access the online topic files.)

COMPLEMENTS OF TYPE I AND TYPE II ERRORS

The **confidence coefficient**, $(1 - \alpha)$, is the probability that you will not reject the null hypothesis, H_0, when it is true and should not be rejected.

The **power of a statistical test**, $(1 - \beta)$, is the probability that you will reject the null hypothesis when it is false and should be rejected.

Risks in Decision Making: A Delicate Balance Table 9.1 illustrates the results of the two possible decisions (do not reject H_0 or reject H_0) that you can make in any hypothesis test. You can make a correct decision or make one of two types of errors.

TABLE 9.1

Hypothesis Testing and Decision Making

	Actual Situation	
Statistical Decision	**H_0 True**	**H_0 False**
Do not reject H_0	Correct decision Confidence = $(1 - \alpha)$	Type II error P(Type II error) = β
Reject H_0	Type I error P(Type I error) = α	Correct decision Power = $(1 - \beta)$

One way to reduce the probability of making a Type II error is by increasing the sample size. Large samples generally permit you to detect even very small differences between the hypothesized values and the actual population parameters. For a given level of α, increasing the sample size decreases β and therefore increases the power of the statistical test to detect that the null hypothesis, H_0, is false.

However, there is always a limit to your resources, and this affects the decision of how large a sample you can select. For any given sample size, you must consider the trade-offs between the two possible types of errors. Because you can directly control the risk of Type I error, you can reduce this risk by selecting a smaller value for α. For example, if the negative consequences associated with making a Type I error are substantial, you could select $\alpha = 0.01$ instead of 0.05. However, when you decrease α, you increase β, so reducing the risk of a Type I error results in an increased risk of a Type II error. However, to reduce β, you could select a larger value for α. Therefore, if it is important to try to avoid a Type II error, you can select α of 0.05 or 0.10 instead of 0.01.

In the Oxford Cereals scenario, the risk of a Type I error occurring involves concluding that the mean fill amount has changed from the hypothesized 368 grams when it actually has not changed. The risk of a Type II error occurring involves concluding that the mean fill amount has not changed from the hypothesized 368 grams when it actually has changed. The choice of reasonable values for α and β depends on the costs inherent in each type of error. For example, if it is very costly to change the cereal-filling process, you would want to be very confident that a change is needed before making any changes. In this case, the risk of a Type I error occurring is more important, and you would choose a small α. However, if you want to be very certain of detecting changes from a mean of 368 grams, the risk of a Type II error occurring is more important, and you would choose a higher level of α.

Now that you have been introduced to hypothesis testing, recall that in the Using Statistics scenario on page 325, the business problem facing Oxford Cereals is to determine whether the cereal-filling process is working properly (i.e., whether the mean fill throughout the entire packaging process remains at the specified 368 grams, and no corrective action is needed). To evaluate the 368-gram requirement, you select a random sample of 25 boxes, weigh each box, compute the sample mean, $\bar{X}$, and then evaluate the difference between this sample statistic and the hypothesized population parameter by comparing the sample mean weight (in grams) to the expected population mean of 368 grams specified by the company. The null and alternative hypotheses are

$$H_0: \mu = 368$$
$$H_1: \mu \neq 368$$

When the standard deviation, σ, is known (which rarely occurs), you use the ***Z* test for the mean** if the population is normally distributed. If the population is not normally distributed, you can still use the Z test if the sample size is large enough for the Central Limit Theorem to take effect (see Section 7.4). Equation (9.1) defines the Z_{STAT} test statistic for determining the difference between the sample mean, $\bar{X}$, and the population mean, μ, when the standard deviation, σ, is known.

Z TEST FOR THE MEAN (σ KNOWN)

$$Z_{STAT} = \frac{\bar{X} - \mu}{\dfrac{\sigma}{\sqrt{n}}} \tag{9.1}$$

In Equation (9.1), the numerator measures the difference between the observed sample mean, $\bar{X}$, and the hypothesized mean, μ. The denominator is the standard error of the mean, so Z_{STAT} represents the difference between $\bar{X}$ and μ in standard error units.

Hypothesis Testing Using the Critical Value Approach

The critical value approach compares the computed Z_{STAT} test statistic value from Equation (9.1) to critical values that divide the normal distribution into regions of rejection and nonrejection. The critical values are expressed as standardized Z values that are determined by the level of significance.

For example, if you use a level of significance of 0.05, the size of the rejection region is 0.05. Because the rejection region is divided into the two tails of the distribution, you divide the 0.05 into two equal parts of 0.025 each. For this **two-tail test**, a rejection region of 0.025 in each tail of the normal distribution results in a cumulative area of 0.025 below the lower critical value and a cumulative area of 0.975 $(1 - 0.025)$ below the upper critical value (which leaves an area of 0.025 in the upper tail). According to the cumulative standardized normal distribution table (Table E.2), the critical values that divide the rejection and nonrejection regions are -1.96 and $+1.96$. Figure 9.2 illustrates that if the mean is actually 368 grams, as H_0 claims, the values of the Z_{STAT} test statistic have a standardized normal distribution centered at $Z = 0$ (which corresponds to an $\bar{X}$ value of 368 grams). Values of Z_{STAT} greater than $+1.96$ or less than -1.96 indicate that $\bar{X}$ is sufficiently different from the hypothesized $\mu = 368$ that it is unlikely that such an $\bar{X}$ value would occur if H_0 were true.

FIGURE 9.2

Testing a hypothesis about the mean (σ known) at the 0.05 level of significance

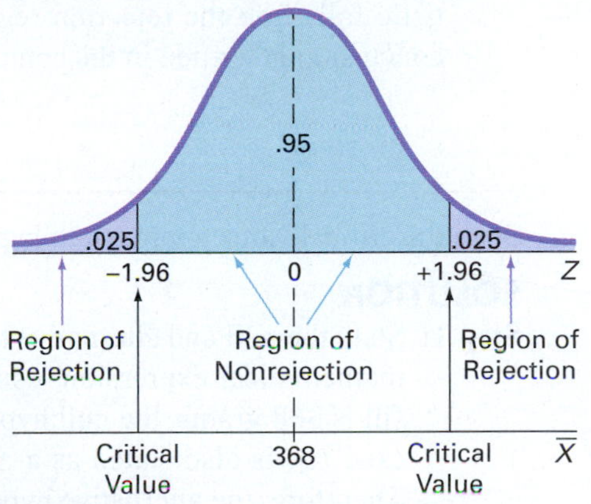

Therefore, the decision rule is

Reject H_0 if $Z_{STAT} > +1.96$

or if $Z_{STAT} < -1.96$;

otherwise, do not reject H_0.

Suppose that the sample of 25 cereal boxes indicates a sample mean, $\bar{X}$ of 372.5 grams, and the population standard deviation, σ, is 15 grams. Using Equation (9.1) on page 330,

$$Z_{STAT} = \frac{\bar{X} - \mu}{\frac{\sigma}{\sqrt{n}}} = \frac{372.5 - 368}{\frac{15}{\sqrt{25}}} = +1.50$$

Because $Z_{STAT} = +1.50$ is between -1.96 and $+1.96$, you do not reject H_0 (see Figure 9.3). You continue to believe that the mean fill amount is 368 grams. To take into account the possibility of a Type II error, you state the conclusion as "there is insufficient evidence that the mean fill is different from 368 grams."

Exhibit 9.1 summarizes the critical value approach to hypothesis testing. Steps 1 though 4 correspond to the Define task, step 5 combines the Collect and Organize tasks, and step 6 corresponds to the Visualize and Analyze tasks of the business problem-solving methodology first introduced in Chapter 2.

FIGURE 9.3

Testing a hypothesis about the mean cereal weight (σ known) at the 0.05 level of significance

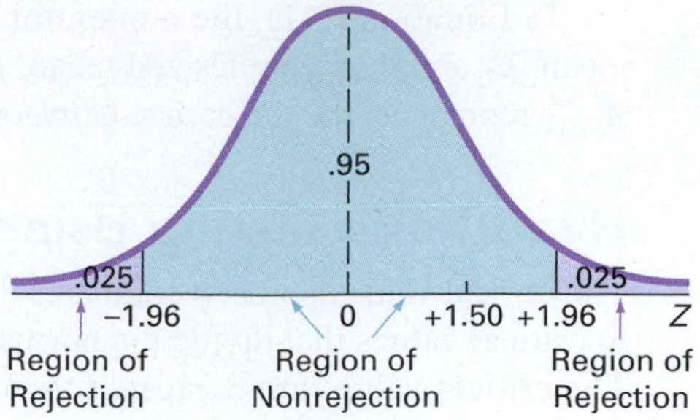

EXHIBIT 9.1 THE CRITICAL VALUE APPROACH TO HYPOTHESIS TESTING

1. State the null hypothesis, H_0, and the alternative hypothesis, H_1.
2. Choose the level of significance, α, and the sample size, n. The level of significance is based on the relative importance of the risks of committing Type I and Type II errors in the problem.
3. Determine the appropriate test statistic and sampling distribution.
4. Determine the critical values that divide the rejection and nonrejection regions.
5. Collect the sample data, organize the results, and compute the value of the test statistic.
6. Make the statistical decision and state the managerial conclusion. If the test statistic falls into the nonrejection region, you do not reject the null hypothesis. If the test statistic falls into the rejection region, you reject the null hypothesis. The managerial conclusion is written in the context of the real-world problem.

EXAMPLE 9.2

Applying the Critical Value Approach to Hypothesis Testing at Oxford Cereals

State the critical value approach to hypothesis testing at Oxford Cereals.

SOLUTION

Step 1: State the null and alternative hypotheses. The null hypothesis, H_0, is always stated as a mathematical expression, using population parameters. In testing whether the mean fill is 368 grams, the null hypothesis states that μ equals 368. The alternative hypothesis, H_1, is also stated as a mathematical expression, using population parameters. Therefore, the alternative hypothesis states that μ is not equal to 368 grams.

Step 2: Choose the level of significance and the sample size. You choose the level of significance, α, according to the relative importance of the risks of committing Type I and Type II errors in the problem. The smaller the value of α, the less risk there is of making a Type I error. In this example, making a Type I error means that you conclude that the population mean is not 368 grams when it is 368 grams. Thus, you will take corrective action on the filling process even though the process is working properly. Here, $\alpha = 0.05$ is selected. The sample size, n, is 25.

Step 3: Select the appropriate test statistic. Because σ is known from information about the filling process, you use the normal distribution and the Z_{STAT} test statistic.

Step 4: Determine the rejection region. Critical values for the appropriate test statistic are selected so that the rejection region contains a total area of α when H_0 is true and the nonrejection region contains a total area of $1 - \alpha$ when H_0 is true. Because $\alpha = 0.05$ in the cereal example, the critical values of the Z_{STAT} test statistic are -1.96 and $+1.96$. The rejection region is therefore $Z_{STAT} < -1.96$ or $Z_{STAT} > +1.96$. The nonrejection region is $-1.96 \leq Z_{STAT} \leq +1.96$.

Step 5: Collect the sample data and compute the value of the test statistic. In the cereal example, $\bar{X} = 372.5$, and the value of the test statistic is $Z_{STAT} = +1.50$.

Step 6: State the statistical decision and the managerial conclusion. First, determine whether the test statistic has fallen into the rejection region or the nonrejection region. For the cereal example, $Z_{STAT} = +1.50$ is in the region of nonrejection because

$-1.96 \le Z_{STAT} = +1.50 \le +1.96$. Because the test statistic falls into the nonrejection region, the statistical decision is to not reject the null hypothesis, H_0. The managerial conclusion is that insufficient evidence exists to prove that the mean fill is different from 368 grams. No corrective action on the filling process is needed.

EXAMPLE 9.3

Testing and Rejecting a Null Hypothesis

You are the manager of a fast-food restaurant. The business problem is to determine whether the population mean waiting time to place an order has changed in the past month from its previous population mean value of 4.5 minutes. From past experience, you can assume that the population is normally distributed, with a population standard deviation of 1.2 minutes. You select a sample of 25 orders during a one-hour period. The sample mean is 5.1 minutes. Use the six-step approach listed in Exhibit 9.1 on page 332 to determine whether there is evidence at the 0.05 level of significance that the population mean waiting time to place an order has changed in the past month from its previous population mean value of 4.5 minutes.

SOLUTION

Step 1: The null hypothesis is that the population mean has not changed from its previous value of 4.5 minutes:

$$H_0: \mu = 4.5$$

The alternative hypothesis is the opposite of the null hypothesis. Because the null hypothesis is that the population mean is 4.5 minutes, the alternative hypothesis is that the population mean is not 4.5 minutes:

$$H_1: \mu \ne 4.5$$

Step 2: You have selected a sample of $n = 25$. The level of significance is 0.05 (i.e., $\alpha = 0.05$).

Step 3: Because σ is assumed known, you use the normal distribution and the Z_{STAT} test statistic.

Step 4: Because $\alpha = 0.05$, the critical values of the Z_{STAT} test statistic are -1.96 and $+1.96$. The rejection region is $Z_{STAT} < -1.96$ or $Z_{STAT} > +1.96$. The nonrejection region is $-1.96 \le Z_{STAT} \le +1.96$

Step 5: You collect the sample data and compute $\bar{X} = 5.1$. Using Equation (9.1) on page 330, you compute the test statistic:

$$Z_{STAT} = \frac{\bar{X} - \mu}{\dfrac{\sigma}{\sqrt{n}}} = \frac{5.1 - 4.5}{\dfrac{1.2}{\sqrt{25}}} = +2.50$$

Step 6: Because $Z_{STAT} = +2.50 > +1.96$, you reject the null hypothesis. You conclude that there is evidence that the population mean waiting time to place an order has changed from its previous value of 4.5 minutes. The mean waiting time for customers is longer now than it was last month. As the manager, you would now want to determine how waiting time could be reduced to improve service.

Hypothesis Testing Using the *p*-Value Approach

Using the *p*-value to determine rejection and nonrejection is another approach to hypothesis testing.

p-VALUE

The ***p*-value** is the probability of getting a test statistic equal to or more extreme than the sample result, given that the null hypothesis, H_0, is true. The *p*-value is also known as the *observed level of significance.*

The decision rules for rejecting H_0 in the *p*-value approach are

- If the *p*-value is greater than or equal to α, do not reject the null hypothesis.
- If the *p*-value is less than α, reject the null hypothesis.

Many people confuse these rules, mistakenly believing that a high p-value is reason for rejection. You can avoid this confusion by remembering the following:

> If the p-value is low, then H_0 must go.

To understand the p-value approach, consider the Oxford Cereals scenario. You tested whether the mean fill was equal to 368 grams. The test statistic resulted in a Z_{STAT} value of $+1.50$, and you did not reject the null hypothesis because $+1.50$ was less than the upper critical value of $+1.96$ and greater than the lower critical value of -1.96.

To use the p-value approach for the *two-tail test*, you find the probability of getting a test statistic Z_{STAT} that is equal to or *more extreme than* 1.50 standard error units from the center of a standardized normal distribution. In other words, you need to compute the probability of a Z_{STAT} value greater than $+1.50$, along with the probability of a Z_{STAT} value less than -1.50. Table E.2 shows that the probability of a Z_{STAT} value below -1.50 is 0.0668. The probability of a value below $+1.50$ is 0.9332, and the probability of a value above $+1.50$ is $1 - 0.9332 = 0.0668$. Therefore, the p-value for this two-tail test is $0.0668 + 0.0668 = 0.1336$ (see Figure 9.4). Thus, the probability of a test statistic equal to or more extreme than the sample result is 0.1336. Because 0.1336 is greater than $\alpha = 0.05$, you do not reject the null hypothesis.

FIGURE 9.4

Finding a p-value for a two-tail test

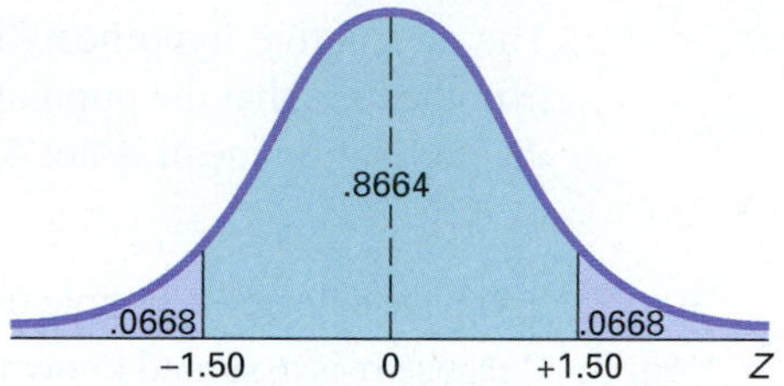

In this example, the observed sample mean is 372.5 grams, 4.5 grams above the hypothesized value, and the p-value is 0.1336. Thus, if the population mean is 368 grams, there is a 13.36% chance that the sample mean differs from 368 grams by at least 4.5 grams (i.e., is ≥ 372.5 grams or ≤ 363.5 grams). Therefore, even though 372.5 is above the hypothesized value of 368, a result as extreme as or more extreme than 372.5 is not highly unlikely when the population mean is 368.

Unless you are dealing with a test statistic that follows the normal distribution, you will only be able to approximate the p-value from the tables of the distribution. However, Excel and Minitab can compute the p-value for any hypothesis test, and this allows you to substitute the p-value approach for the critical value approach when you do hypothesis testing.

Figure 9.5 shows the results for the cereal-filling example discussed in this section, as computed by Excel (left results) and Minitab (right results). These results include the Z_{STAT} test statistic and critical values.

FIGURE 9.5

Excel and Minitab results for the Z test for the mean (σ known) for the cereal-filling example

	A	B	
1	Z Test for the Mean		
2			
3	Data		
4	Null Hypothesis μ=	368	
5	Level of Significance	0.05	
6	Population Standard Deviation	15	
7	Sample Size	25	
8	Sample Mean	372.5	
9			
10	Intermediate Calculations		
11	Standard Error of the Mean	3	=B6/SQRT(B7)
12	Z Test Statistic	1.5	=(B8 - B4)/B11
13			
14	Two-Tail Test		
15	Lower Critical Value	-1.9600	=NORMSINV(B5/2)
16	Upper Critical Value	1.9600	=NORMSINV(1 - B5/2)
17	*p*-Value	0.1336	=2 * (1 - NORMSDIST(ABS(B12)))
18	Do not reject the null hypothesis		=IF(B17 < B5, "Reject the null hypothesis", "Do not reject the null hypothesis")

One-Sample Z

```
Test of mu = 368 vs not = 368
The assumed standard deviation = 15

 N   Mean  SE Mean       95% CI            Z      P
25  372.50    3.00  (366.62, 378.38)  1.50  0.134
```

Exhibit 9.2 summarizes the p-value approach to hypothesis testing.

EXHIBIT 9.2 THE p-VALUE APPROACH TO HYPOTHESIS TESTING

1. State the null hypothesis, H_0, and the alternative hypothesis, H_1.
2. Choose the level of significance, α, and the sample size, n. The level of significance is based on the relative importance of the risks of committing Type I and Type II errors in the problem.
3. Determine the appropriate test statistic and the sampling distribution.
4. Collect the sample data, compute the value of the test statistic, and compute the p-value.
5. Make the statistical decision and state the managerial conclusion. If the p-value is greater than or equal to α, do not reject the null hypothesis. If the p-value is less than α, reject the null hypothesis. The managerial conclusion is written in the context of the real-world problem.

EXAMPLE 9.4

Testing and Rejecting a Null Hypothesis Using the p-Value Approach

You are the manager of a fast-food restaurant. The business problem is to determine whether the population mean waiting time to place an order has changed in the past month from its previous value of 4.5 minutes. From past experience, you can assume that the population standard deviation is 1.2 minutes and the population waiting time is normally distributed. You select a sample of 25 orders during a one-hour period. The sample mean is 5.1 minutes. Use the five-step p-value approach of Exhibit 9.2 to determine whether there is evidence that the population mean waiting time to place an order has changed in the past month from its previous population mean value of 4.5 minutes.

SOLUTION

Step 1: The null hypothesis is that the population mean has not changed from its previous value of 4.5 minutes:

$$H_0: \mu = 4.5$$

The alternative hypothesis is the opposite of the null hypothesis. Because the null hypothesis is that the population mean is 4.5 minutes, the alternative hypothesis is that the population mean is not 4.5 minutes:

$$H_1: \mu \neq 4.5$$

Step 2: You have selected a sample of $n = 25$, and you have chosen a 0.05 level of significance (i.e., $\alpha = 0.05$).

Step 3: Select the appropriate test statistic. Because σ is assumed known, you use the normal distribution and the Z_{STAT} test statistic.

Step 4: You collect the sample data and compute $\bar{X} = 5.1$. Using Equation (9.1) on page 330, you compute the test statistic as follows:

$$Z_{STAT} = \frac{\bar{X} - \mu}{\frac{\sigma}{\sqrt{n}}} = \frac{5.1 - 4.5}{\frac{1.2}{\sqrt{25}}} = +2.50$$

To find the probability of getting a Z_{STAT} test statistic that is equal to or more extreme than 2.50 standard error units from the center of a standardized normal distribution, you compute the probability of a Z_{STAT} value greater than $+2.50$ along with the probability of a Z_{STAT} value less than -2.50. From Table E.2, the probability of a Z_{STAT} value below -2.50 is 0.0062. The probability of a value below $+2.50$ is 0.9938. Therefore, the probability of a value above $+2.50$ is $1 - 0.9938 = 0.0062$. Thus, the p-value for this two-tail test is $0.0062 + 0.0062 = 0.0124$.

Step 5: Because the p-value $= 0.0124 < \alpha = 0.05$, you reject the null hypothesis. You conclude that there is evidence that the population mean waiting time to place an order has changed from its previous population mean value of 4.5 minutes. The mean waiting time for customers is longer now than it was last month.

A Connection Between Confidence Interval Estimation and Hypothesis Testing

This chapter and Chapter 8 discuss confidence interval estimation and hypothesis testing, the two major elements of statistical inference. Although confidence interval estimation and hypothesis testing share the same conceptual foundation, they are used for different purposes. In Chapter 8, confidence intervals estimated parameters. In this chapter, hypothesis testing makes decisions about specified values of population parameters. Hypothesis tests are used when trying to determine whether a parameter is less than, more than, or not equal to a specified value. Proper interpretation of a confidence interval, however, can also indicate whether a parameter is less than, more than, or not equal to a specified value. For example, in this section, you tested whether the population mean fill amount was different from 368 grams by using Equation (9.1) on page 330:

$$Z_{STAT} = \frac{\bar{X} - \mu}{\dfrac{\sigma}{\sqrt{n}}}$$

Instead of testing the null hypothesis that $\mu = 368$ grams, you can reach the same conclusion by constructing a confidence interval estimate of μ. If the hypothesized value of $\mu = 368$ is contained within the interval, you do not reject the null hypothesis because 368 would not be considered an unusual value. However, if the hypothesized value does not fall into the interval, you reject the null hypothesis because $\mu = 368$ grams is then considered an unusual value. Using Equation (8.1) on page 283 and the following data:

$$n = 25, \bar{X} = 372.5 \text{ grams}, \sigma = 15 \text{ grams}$$

for a confidence level of 95% (i.e., $\alpha = 0.05$),

$$\bar{X} \pm Z_{\alpha/2}\frac{\sigma}{\sqrt{n}}$$

$$372.5 \pm (1.96)\frac{15}{\sqrt{25}}$$

$$372.5 \pm 5.88$$

so that

$$366.62 \leq \mu \leq 378.38$$

Because the interval includes the hypothesized value of 368 grams, you do not reject the null hypothesis. There is insufficient evidence that the mean fill amount over the entire filling process is not 368 grams. You reached the same decision by using two-tail hypothesis testing.

Can You Ever Know the Population Standard Deviation?

The end of Section 8.1 on page 285 discussed how learning a confidence interval estimation method that required knowing σ, the population standard deviation, served as an effective introduction to the concept of a confidence interval. That passage then revealed that you would be unlikely to use that procedure for most practical applications for several reasons.

Likewise, for most practical applications, you are unlikely to use a hypothesis-testing method that requires knowing σ. If you knew the population standard deviation, you would also know the population mean and would not need to form a hypothesis about the mean and then test that hypothesis. So why study a hypothesis testing of the mean that requires that σ is known? Using such a test makes it much easier to explain the fundamentals of hypothesis testing. With a known population standard deviation, you can use the normal distribution and compute p-values using the tables of the normal distribution.

Because it is important that you understand the concept of hypothesis testing when reading the rest of this book, review this section carefully—even if you anticipate never having a practical reason to use the test represented by Equation (9.1).

Problems for Section 9.1

LEARNING THE BASICS

9.1 If you use a 0.05 level of significance in a (two-tail) hypothesis test, what will you decide if $Z_{STAT} = -0.76$?

9.2 If you use a 0.05 level of significance in a (two-tail) hypothesis test, what will you decide if $Z_{STAT} = +2.21$?

9.3 If you use a 0.10 level of significance in a (two-tail) hypothesis test, what is your decision rule for rejecting a null hypothesis that the population mean is 500 if you use the Z test?

9.4 If you use a 0.01 level of significance in a (two-tail) hypothesis test, what is your decision rule for rejecting $H_0: \mu = 12.5$ if you use the Z test?

9.5 What is your decision in Problem 9.4 if $Z_{STAT} = -2.61$?

9.6 What is the p-value if, in a two-tail hypothesis test, $Z_{STAT} = +2.00$?

9.7 In Problem 9.6, what is your statistical decision if you test the null hypothesis at the 0.10 level of significance?

9.8 What is the p-value if, in a two-tail hypothesis test, $Z_{STAT} = -1.38$?

APPLYING THE CONCEPTS

9.9 In the U.S. legal system, a defendant is presumed innocent until proven guilty. Consider a null hypothesis, H_0, that the defendant is innocent, and an alternative hypothesis, H_1, that the defendant is guilty. A jury has two possible decisions: Convict the defendant (i.e., reject the null hypothesis) or do not convict the defendant (i.e., do not reject the null hypothesis). Explain the meaning of the risks of committing either a Type I or Type II error in this example.

9.10 Suppose the defendant in Problem 9.9 is presumed guilty until proven innocent, as in some other judicial systems. How do the null and alternative hypotheses differ from those in Problem 9.9? What are the meanings of the risks of committing either a Type I or Type II error here?

9.11 Many consumer groups feel that the U.S. Food and Drug Administration (FDA) drug approval process is too easy and, as a result, too many drugs are approved that are later found to be unsafe. On the other hand, a number of industry lobbyists have pushed for a more lenient approval process so that pharmaceutical companies can get new drugs approved more easily and quickly. Consider a null hypothesis that a new, unapproved drug is unsafe and an alternative hypothesis that a new, unapproved drug is safe.

a. Explain the risks of committing a Type I or Type II error.
b. Which type of error are the consumer groups trying to avoid? Explain.
c. Which type of error are the industry lobbyists trying to avoid? Explain.
d. How would it be possible to lower the chances of both Type I and Type II errors?

9.12 As a result of complaints from both students and faculty about lateness, the registrar at a large university wants to determine whether the scheduled break between classes should be changed and, therefore, is ready to undertake a study. Until now, the registrar has believed that there should be 20 minutes between scheduled classes. State the null hypothesis, H_0, and the alternative hypothesis, H_1.

9.13 Do students at your school study more than, less than, or about the same as students at other business schools? *BusinessWeek* reported that at the top 50 business schools, students studied an average of 14.6 hours per week. (Data extracted from "Cracking the Books," Special Report/Online Extra, **www.businessweek.com**, March 19, 2007.) Set up a hypothesis test to try to prove that the mean number of hours studied at your school is different from the 14.6-hour-per-week benchmark reported by *BusinessWeek*.

a. State the null and alternative hypotheses.
b. What is a Type I error for your test?
c. What is a Type II error for your test?

SELF Test **9.14** The quality-control manager at a light bulb factory needs to determine whether the mean life of a large shipment of light bulbs is equal to 375 hours. The population standard deviation is 100 hours. A random sample of 64 light bulbs indicates a sample mean life of 350 hours.

a. At the 0.05 level of significance, is there evidence that the mean life is different from 375 hours?
b. Compute the p-value and interpret its meaning.
c. Construct a 95% confidence interval estimate of the population mean life of the light bulbs.
d. Compare the results of (a) and (c). What conclusions do you reach?

9.15 Suppose that in Problem 9.14, the standard deviation is 120 hours.

a. Repeat (a) through (d) of Problem 9.14, assuming a standard deviation of 120 hours.
b. Compare the results of (a) to those of Problem 9.14.

9.16 The manager of a paint supply store wants to determine whether the mean amount of paint contained in 1-gallon cans purchased from a nationally known manufacturer is actually 1 gallon. You know from the manufacturer's specifications that the standard deviation of the amount of paint is 0.02 gallon. You select a random sample of 50 cans, and the mean amount of paint per 1-gallon can is 0.995 gallon.

a. Is there evidence that the mean amount is different from 1.0 gallon? (Use $\alpha = 0.01$.)
b. Compute the p-value and interpret its meaning.

c. Construct a 99% confidence interval estimate of the population mean amount of paint.

d. Compare the results of (a) and (c). What conclusions do you reach?

9.17 Suppose that in Problem 9.16, the standard deviation is 0.012 gallon.

a. Repeat (a) through (d) of Problem 9.16, assuming a standard deviation of 0.012 gallon.

b. Compare the results of (a) to those of Problem 9.16.

9.2 *t* Test of Hypothesis for the Mean (σ Unknown)

In virtually all hypothesis-testing situations concerning the population mean, μ, you do not know the population standard deviation, σ. Instead, you use the sample standard deviation, S. If you assume that the population is normally distributed, the sampling distribution of the mean follows a t distribution with $n - 1$ degrees of freedom, and you use the ***t* test for the mean**. If the population is not normally distributed, you can still use the t test if the sample size is large enough for the Central Limit Theorem to take effect (see Section 7.4). Equation (9.2) defines the test statistic for determining the difference between the sample mean, $\bar{X}$, and the population mean, μ, when using the sample standard deviation, S.

t TEST FOR THE MEAN (σ UNKNOWN)

$$t_{STAT} = \frac{\bar{X} - \mu}{\dfrac{S}{\sqrt{n}}} \tag{9.2}$$

where the t_{STAT} test statistic follows a t distribution having $n - 1$ degrees of freedom.

To illustrate the use of the t test for the mean, return to the Chapter 8 Saxon Home Improvement scenario on page 279. The business objective is to determine whether the mean amount per sales invoice is unchanged from the $120 of the past five years. As an accountant for the company, you need to determine whether this amount changes. In other words, the hypothesis test is used to try to determine whether the mean amount per sales invoice is increasing or decreasing.

The Critical Value Approach

To perform this two-tail hypothesis test, you use the six-step method listed in Exhibit 9.1 on page 332.

Step 1 You define the following hypotheses:

$$H_0 : \mu = \$120$$
$$H_1 : \mu \neq \$120$$

The alternative hypothesis contains the statement you are trying to prove. If the null hypothesis is rejected, then there is statistical evidence that the population mean amount per sales invoice is no longer $120. If the statistical conclusion is "do not reject H_0," then you will conclude that there is insufficient evidence to prove that the mean amount differs from the long-term mean of $120.

Step 2 You collect the data from a sample of $n = 12$ sales invoices. You decide to use $\alpha = 0.05$.

Step 3 Because σ is unknown, you use the t distribution and the t_{STAT} test statistic. You must assume that the population of sales invoices is normally distributed because the sample size of 12 is too small for the Central Limit Theorem to take effect. This assumption is discussed on page 340.

Step 4 For a given sample size, n, the test statistic t_{STAT} follows a t distribution with $n - 1$ degrees of freedom. The critical values of the t distribution with $12 - 1 = 11$ degrees of freedom are found in Table E.3, as illustrated in Table 9.2 and Figure 9.6. The alternative hypothesis, $H_1 : \mu \neq \$120$, has two tails. The area in the rejection region of the *t* distribution's left (lower) tail is 0.025, and the area in the rejection region of the *t* distribution's right (upper) tail is also 0.025.

From the *t* table as given in Table E.3, a portion of which is shown in Table 9.2, the critical values are ±2.2010. The decision rule is

$$\text{Reject } H_0 \text{ if } t_{STAT} < -2.2010$$
$$\text{or if } t_{STAT} > +2.2010;$$
$$\text{otherwise, do not reject } H_0.$$

TABLE 9.2

Determining the Critical Value from the *t* Table for an Area of 0.025 in Each Tail, with 11 Degrees of Freedom

	Cumulative Probabilities					
	.75	.90	.95	.975	.99	.995
	Upper-Tail Areas					
Degrees of Freedom	.25	.10	.05	.025	.01	.005
1	1.0000	3.0777	6.3138	12.7062	31.8207	63.6574
2	0.8165	1.8856	2.9200	4.3027	6.9646	9.9248
3	0.7649	1.6377	2.3534	3.1824	4.5407	5.8409
4	0.7407	1.5332	2.1318	2.7764	3.7469	4.6041
5	0.7267	1.4759	2.0150	2.5706	3.3649	4.0322
6	0.7176	1.4398	1.9432	2.4469	3.1427	3.7074
7	0.7111	1.4149	1.8946	2.3646	2.9980	3.4995
8	0.7064	1.3968	1.8595	2.3060	2.8965	3.3554
9	0.7027	1.3830	1.8331	2.2622	2.8214	3.2498
10	0.6998	1.3722	1.8125	2.2281	2.7638	3.1693
11	0.6974	1.3634	1.7959	2.2010	2.7181	3.1058

Source: Extracted from Table E.3.

FIGURE 9.6

Testing a hypothesis about the mean (σ unknown) at the 0.05 level of significance with 11 degrees of freedom

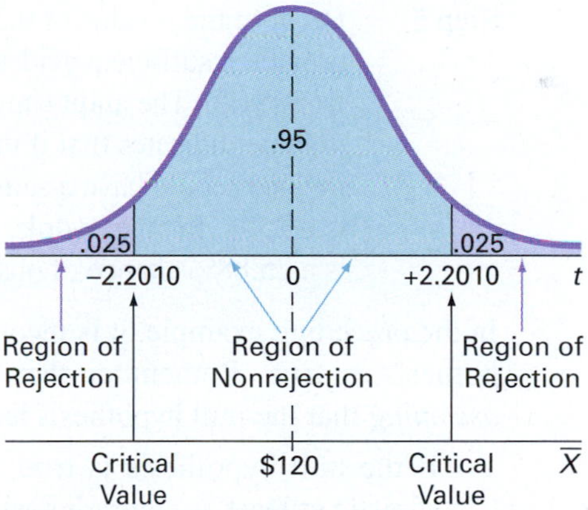

Step 5 You organize and store the data from a random sample of 12 sales invoices in **Invoices**:

108.98 152.22 111.45 110.59 127.46 107.26
93.32 91.97 111.56 75.71 128.58 135.11

Using Equations (3.1) and (3.7) on pages 97 and 103,

$$\bar{X} = \$112.85 \text{ and } S = \$20.80$$

From Equation (9.2) on page 338,

$$t_{STAT} = \frac{\bar{X} - \mu}{\dfrac{S}{\sqrt{n}}} = \frac{112.85 - 120}{\dfrac{20.80}{\sqrt{12}}} = -1.1908$$

Figure 9.7 shows the results for this test of hypothesis, as computed by Excel and Minitab.

FIGURE 9.7

Excel and Minitab results for the t test of sales invoices

	A	B	
1	t Test for the Hypothesis of the Mean		
2			
3	Data		
4	Null Hypothesis μ=	120	
5	Level of Significance	0.05	
6	Sample Size	12	
7	Sample Mean	112.85	
8	Sample Standard Deviation	20.8	
9			
10	Intermediate Calculations		
11	Standard Error of the Mean	6.0044	=B8/SQRT(B6)
12	Degrees of Freedom	11	=B6 - 1
13	t Test Statistic	-1.1908	=(B7 - B4)/B11
14			
15	Two-Tail Test		
16	Lower Critical Value	-2.2010	=-TINV(B5, B12)
17	Upper Critical Value	2.2010	=TINV(B5, B12)
18	p-Value	0.2588	=TDIST(ABS(B13), B12, 2)
19	Do not reject the null hypothesis		=IF(B18 < B5, "Reject the null hypothesis", "Do not reject the null hypothesis")

One-Sample T

```
Test of mu = 120 vs not = 120

 N    Mean  StDev  SE Mean          95% CI              T      P
12  112.85  20.80     6.00  (99.63, 126.07)  -1.19  0.259
```

Step 6 Because $-2.2010 < t_{STAT} = -1.1908 < 2.2010$, you do not reject H_0. You have insufficient evidence to conclude that the mean amount per sales invoice differs from \$120. The audit suggests that the mean amount per invoice has not changed.

The *p*-Value Approach

To perform this two-tail hypothesis test, you use the five-step method listed in Exhibit 9.2 on page 335.

Step 1–3 These steps are the same as in the critical value approach.

Step 4 From the Figure 9.7 results, the $t_{STAT} = -1.19$ and p-value $= 0.2588$.

Step 5 Because the p-value of 0.2588 is greater than $\alpha = 0.05$, you do not reject H_0. The data provide insufficient evidence to conclude that the mean amount per sales invoice differs from \$120. The audit suggests that the mean amount per invoice has not changed. The p-value indicates that if the null hypothesis is true, the probability that a sample of 12 invoices could have a sample mean that differs by \$7.15 or more from the stated \$120 is 0.2588. In other words, if the mean amount per sales invoice is truly \$120, then there is a 25.88% chance of observing a sample mean below \$112.85 or above \$127.15.

In the preceding example, it is incorrect to state that there is a 25.88% chance that the null hypothesis is true. Remember that the p-value is a conditional probability, calculated by *assuming* that the null hypothesis is true. In general, it is proper to state the following:

> If the null hypothesis is true, there is a (p-value) $\times$ 100% chance of observing a test statistic at least as contradictory to the null hypothesis as the sample result.

Checking the Normality Assumption

You use the t test when the population standard deviation, σ, is not known and is estimated using the sample standard deviation, S. To use the t test, you assume that the data represent a random sample from a population that is normally distributed. In practice, as long as the sample size is not very small and the population is not very skewed, the t distribution provides a good approximation of the sampling distribution of the mean when σ is unknown.

There are several ways to evaluate the normality assumption necessary for using the t test. You can examine how closely the sample statistics match the normal distribution's theoretical properties. You can also construct a histogram, stem-and-leaf display, boxplot, or normal probability plot to visualize the distribution of the sales invoice amounts. For details on evaluating normality, see Section 6.3 on pages 230–234.

Figures 9.8 through 9.10 show the descriptive statistics, boxplot, and normal probability plot for the sales invoice data.

FIGURE 9.8

Excel and Minitab descriptive statistics for the sales invoice data

	A	B
1	*Invoice Amount*	
2		
3	Mean	112.8508
4	Standard Error	6.0039
5	Median	111.02
6	Mode	#N/A
7	Standard Deviation	20.7980
8	Sample Variance	432.5565
9	Kurtosis	0.1727
10	Skewness	0.1336
11	Range	76.51
12	Minimum	75.71
13	Maximum	152.22
14	Sum	1354.21
15	Count	12

Descriptive Statistics: Invoice Amount

```
                 Total
Variable         Count    Mean  StDev  Variance  CoefVar  Minimum     Q1  Median
Invoice Amount      12  112.85  20.80    432.56    18.43    75.71  96.80  111.02

Variable             Q3  Maximum  Range     IQR  Skewness  Kurtosis
Invoice Amount   128.30   152.22  76.51   31.50      0.13      0.17
```

FIGURE 9.9

Excel and Minitab boxplots for the sales invoice data

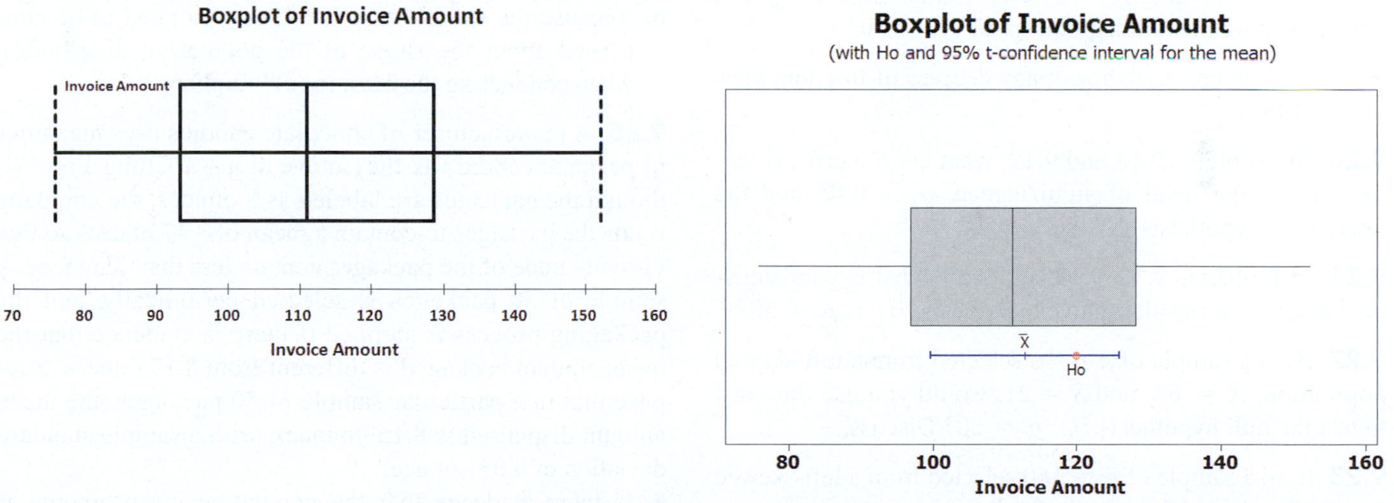

The mean is very close to the median, and the points on the normal probability plots on page 342 appear to be increasing approximately in a straight line. The boxplots appear to be approximately symmetrical. Thus, you can assume that the population of sales invoices is approximately normally distributed. The normality assumption is valid, and therefore the auditor's results are valid.

The t test is a **robust** test. A robust test does not lose power if the shape of the population departs somewhat from a normal distribution, particularly when the sample size is large enough to enable the test statistic t to be influenced by the Central Limit Theorem (see Section 7.4). However, you can reach erroneous conclusions and can lose statistical power if you use the t test incorrectly. If the sample size, n, is small (i.e., less than 30) and you cannot easily make the assumption that the underlying population is at least approximately normally distributed, then *nonparametric* testing procedures are more appropriate (see references 1 and 2).

FIGURE 9.10
Excel and Minitab normal probability plots for the sales invoice data

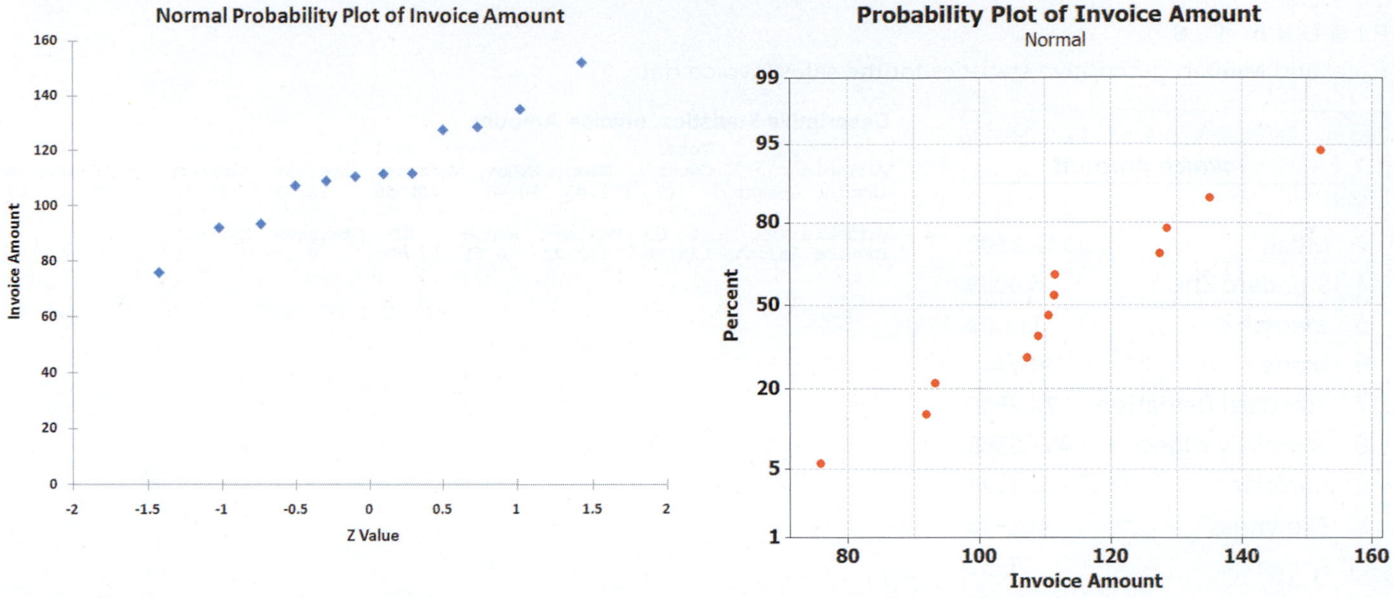

Problems for Section 9.2

LEARNING THE BASICS

9.18 If, in a sample of $n = 16$ selected from a normal population, $\bar{X} = 56$ and $S = 12$, what is the value of t_{STAT} if you are testing the null hypothesis $H_0 : \mu = 50$?

9.19 In Problem 9.18, how many degrees of freedom does the t test have?

9.20 In Problems 9.18 and 9.19, what are the critical values of t if the level of significance, α, is 0.05 and the alternative hypothesis, H_1, is $\mu \neq 50$?

9.21 In Problems 9.18, 9.19, and 9.20, what is your statistical decision if the alternative hypothesis, H_1, is $\mu \neq 50$?

9.22 If, in a sample of $n = 16$ selected from a left-skewed population, $\bar{X} = 65$, and $S = 21$, would you use the t test to test the null hypothesis $H_0 : \mu = 60$? Discuss.

9.23 If, in a sample of $n = 160$ selected from a left-skewed population, $\bar{X} = 65$, and $S = 21$, would you use the t test to test the null hypothesis $H_0 : \mu = 60$? Discuss.

APPLYING THE CONCEPTS

SELF Test **9.24** You are the manager of a restaurant for a fast-food franchise. Last month, the mean waiting time at the drive-through window for branches in your geographical region, as measured from the time a customer places an order until the time the customer receives the order, was 3.7 minutes. You select a random sample of 64 orders. The sample mean waiting time is 3.57 minutes, with a sample standard deviation of 0.8 minute.

a. At the 0.05 level of significance, is there evidence that the population mean waiting time is different from 3.7 minutes?
b. Because the sample size is 64, do you need to be concerned about the shape of the population distribution when conducting the t test in (a)? Explain.

9.25 A manufacturer of chocolate candies uses machines to package candies as they move along a filling line. Although the packages are labeled as 8 ounces, the company wants the packages to contain a mean of 8.17 ounces so that virtually none of the packages contain less than 8 ounces. A sample of 50 packages is selected periodically, and the packaging process is stopped if there is evidence that the mean amount packaged is different from 8.17 ounces. Suppose that in a particular sample of 50 packages, the mean amount dispensed is 8.159 ounces, with a sample standard deviation of 0.051 ounce.

a. Is there evidence that the population mean amount is different from 8.17 ounces? (Use a 0.05 level of significance.)
b. Determine the p-value and interpret its meaning.

9.26 A stationery store wants to estimate the mean retail value of greeting cards that it has in its inventory. A random sample of 100 greeting cards indicates a mean value of $2.55 and a standard deviation of $0.44.

a. Is there evidence that the population mean retail value of the greeting cards is different from $2.50? (Use a 0.05 level of significance.)
b. Determine the p-value and interpret its meaning.

9.27 The U.S. Department of Transportation requires tire manufacturers to provide performance information on tire sidewalls to help prospective buyers make their purchasing decisions. One very important piece of information is the tread wear index, which indicates the tire's resistance to tread wear. A tire with a grade of 200 should last twice as long, on average, as a tire with a grade of 100.

A consumer organization wants to test the actual tread wear index of a brand name of tires that claims "graded 200" on the sidewall of the tire. A random sample of $n = 18$ indicates a sample mean tread wear index of 195.3 and a sample standard deviation of 21.4.

a. Is there evidence that the population mean tread wear index is different from 200? (Use a 0.05 level of significance.)
b. Determine the p-value and interpret its meaning.

9.28 The file **FastFood** contains the amount that a sample of nine customers spent for lunch ($) at a fast-food restaurant:

4.20 5.03 5.86 6.45 7.38 7.54 8.46 8.47 9.87

a. At the 0.05 level of significance, is there evidence that the mean amount spent for lunch is different from $6.50?
b. Determine the p-value in (a) and interpret its meaning.
c. What assumption must you make about the population distribution in order to conduct the t test in (a) and (b)?
d. Because the sample size is 9, do you need to be concerned about the shape of the population distribution when conducting the t test in (a)? Explain.

9.29 In New York State, savings banks are permitted to sell a form of life insurance called savings bank life insurance (SBLI). The approval process consists of underwriting, which includes a review of the application, a medical information bureau check, possible requests for additional medical information and medical exams, and a policy compilation stage in which the policy pages are generated and sent to the bank for delivery. The ability to deliver approved policies to customers in a timely manner is critical to the profitability of this service. During a period of one month, a random sample of 27 approved policies is selected, and the total processing time, in days, is recorded (and stored in **Insurance**):

73 19 16 64 28 28 31 90 60 56 31 56 22 18
45 48 17 17 17 91 92 63 50 51 69 16 17

a. In the past, the mean processing time was 45 days. At the 0.05 level of significance, is there evidence that the mean processing time has changed from 45 days?
b. What assumption about the population distribution is needed in order to conduct the t test in (a)?
c. Construct a boxplot or a normal probability plot to evaluate the assumption made in (b).
d. Do you think that the assumption needed in order to conduct the t test in (a) is valid? Explain.

9.30 The following data (in **Drink**) represent the amount of soft-drink filled in a sample of 50 consecutive 2-liter bottles. The results, listed horizontally in the order of being filled, were

2.109 2.086 2.066 2.075 2.065 2.057 2.052 2.044 2.036 2.038
2.031 2.029 2.025 2.029 2.023 2.020 2.015 2.014 2.013 2.014
2.012 2.012 2.012 2.010 2.005 2.003 1.999 1.996 1.997 1.992
1.994 1.986 1.984 1.981 1.973 1.975 1.971 1.969 1.966 1.967
1.963 1.957 1.951 1.951 1.947 1.941 1.941 1.938 1.908 1.894

a. At the 0.05 level of significance, is there evidence that the mean amount of soft drink filled is different from 2.0 liters?
b. Determine the p-value in (a) and interpret its meaning.
c. In (a), you assumed that the distribution of the amount of soft drink filled was normally distributed. Evaluate this assumption by constructing a boxplot or a normal probability plot.
d. Do you think that the assumption needed in order to conduct the t test in (a) is valid? Explain.
e. Examine the values of the 50 bottles in their sequential order, as given in the problem. Does there appear to be a pattern to the results? If so, what impact might this pattern have on the validity of the results in (a)?

9.31 One of the major measures of the quality of service provided by any organization is the speed with which it responds to customer complaints. A large family-held department store selling furniture and flooring, including carpet, had undergone a major expansion in the past several years. In particular, the flooring department had expanded from 2 installation crews to an installation supervisor, a measurer, and 15 installation crews. The store had the business objective of improving its response to complaints. The variable of interest was defined as the number of days between when the complaint was made and when it was resolved. Data were collected from 50 complaints that were made in the past year. The data, stored in **Furniture**, are as follows:

54 5 35 137 31 27 152 2 123 81 74 27
11 19 126 110 110 29 61 35 94 31 26 5
12 4 165 32 29 28 29 26 25 1 14 13
13 10 5 27 4 52 30 22 36 26 20 23
33 68

a. The installation supervisor claims that the mean number of days between the receipt of a complaint and the resolution of the complaint is 20 days. At the 0.05 level of significance, is there evidence that the claim is not true (i.e., that the mean number of days is different from 20)?
b. What assumption about the population distribution is needed in order to conduct the t test in (a)?
c. Construct a boxplot or a normal probability plot to evaluate the assumption made in (b).
d. Do you think that the assumption needed in order to conduct the t test in (a) is valid? Explain.

9.32 A manufacturing company produces steel housings for electrical equipment. The main component part of the housing is a steel trough that is made out of a 14-gauge steel coil. It is produced using a 250-ton progressive punch press with a wipe-down operation that puts two 90-degree forms in the flat steel to make the trough. The distance from one side of the form to the other is critical because of weather-proofing in outdoor applications. The company requires that the width of the trough be between 8.31 inches and 8.61 inches. The file **Trough** contains the widths of the troughs, in inches, for a sample of $n = 49$:

8.312	8.343	8.317	8.383	8.348	8.410	8.351	8.373	8.481	8.422
8.476	8.382	8.484	8.403	8.414	8.419	8.385	8.465	8.498	8.447
8.436	8.413	8.489	8.414	8.481	8.415	8.479	8.429	8.458	8.462
8.460	8.444	8.429	8.460	8.412	8.420	8.410	8.405	8.323	8.420
8.396	8.447	8.405	8.439	8.411	8.427	8.420	8.498	8.409	

a. At the 0.05 level of significance, is there evidence that the mean width of the troughs is different from 8.46 inches?
b. What assumption about the population distribution is needed in order to conduct the t test in (a)?
c. Evaluate the assumption made in (b).
d. Do you think that the assumption needed in order to conduct the t test in (a) is valid? Explain.

9.33 One operation of a steel mill is to cut pieces of steel into parts that are used in the frame for front seats in an automobile. The steel is cut with a diamond saw and requires the resulting parts must be cut to be within $\pm$ 0.005 inch of the length specified by the automobile company. The file **Steel** contains a sample of 100 steel parts. The measurement reported is the difference, in inches, between the actual length of the steel part, as measured by a laser measurement device, and the specified length of the steel part. For example, a value of –0.002 represents a steel part that is 0.002 inch shorter than the specified length.
a. At the 0.05 level of significance, is there evidence that the mean difference is not equal to 0.0 inches?
b. Construct a 95% confidence interval estimate of the population mean. Interpret this interval.
c. Compare the conclusions reached in (a) and (b).
d. Because $n = 100$, do you have to be concerned about the normality assumption needed for the t test and t interval?

9.34 In Problem 3.67 on page 135, you were introduced to a tea-bag-filling operation. An important quality characteristic of interest for this process is the weight of the tea in the individual bags. The file **Teabags** contains an ordered array of the weight, in grams, of a sample of 50 tea bags produced during an eight-hour shift.
a. Is there evidence that the mean amount of tea per bag is different from 5.5 grams? (Use $\alpha = 0.01$.)
b. Construct a 99% confidence interval estimate of the population mean amount of tea per bag. Interpret this interval.
c. Compare the conclusions reached in (a) and (b).

9.35 Although many people think they can put a meal on the table in a short period of time, an article reported that they end up spending about 40 minutes doing so. (Data extracted from N. Hellmich, "Americans Go for the Quick Fix for Dinner," *USA Today*, February 14, 2006.) Suppose another study is conducted to test the validity of this statement. A sample of 25 people is selected, and the length of time to prepare and cook dinner (in minutes) is recorded, with the following results (in **Dinner**):

44.0	51.9	49.7	40.0	55.5	33.0	43.4	41.3	45.2	40.7	41.1	49.1	30.9
45.2	55.3	52.1	55.1	38.8	43.1	39.2	58.6	49.8	43.2	47.9	46.6	

a. Is there evidence that the population mean time to prepare and cook dinner is different from 40 minutes? Use the p-value approach and a level of significance of 0.05.
b. What assumption about the population distribution is needed in order to conduct the t test in (a)?
c. Make a list of the various ways you could evaluate the assumption noted in (b).
d. Evaluate the assumption noted in (b) and determine whether the t test in (a) is valid.

9.3 One-Tail Tests

In Section 9.1, hypothesis testing was used to examine the question of whether the population mean amount of cereal filled is 368 grams. The alternative hypothesis ($H_1: \mu \neq 368$) contains two possibilities: Either the mean is less than 368 grams or the mean is more than 368 grams. For this reason, the rejection region is divided into the two tails of the sampling distribution of the mean. In Section 9.2, a two-tail test was used to determine whether the mean amount per invoice had changed from \$120.

In contrast to these two examples, many situations require an alternative hypothesis that focuses on a *particular direction*. For example, the population mean is *less than* a specified value. One such situation involves the business problem concerning the service time at the drive-through window of a fast-food restaurant. The speed with which customers are served is of critical importance to the success of the service (see **www.qsrmagazine.com/reports/drive-thru_time_study**). In one past study, McDonald's had a mean service time of 174.22 seconds, which was only ninth best in the industry. Suppose that McDonald's began a quality improvement effort to reduce the service time by deploying an improved drive-through service process in a sample of 25 stores. Because McDonald's would want to institute the new process in all of its stores only if the test sample saw a *decreased* drive-through time, the entire rejection region is located in the lower tail of the distribution.

The Critical Value Approach

You wish to determine whether the new drive-through process has a mean that is less than 174.22 seconds. To perform this one-tail hypothesis test, you use the six-step method listed in Exhibit 9.1 on page 332.

Step 1 You define the null and alternative hypotheses:

$$H_0: \mu \geq 174.22$$
$$H_1: \mu < 174.22$$

The alternative hypothesis contains the statement for which you are trying to find evidence. If the conclusion of the test is "reject H_0," there is statistical evidence that the mean drive-through time is less than the drive-through time in the old process. This would be reason to change the drive-through process for the entire population of stores. If the conclusion of the test is "do not reject H_0," then there is insufficient evidence that the mean drive-through time in the new process is significantly less than the drive-through time in the old process. If this occurs, there would be insufficient reason to institute the new drive-through process in the population of stores.

Step 2 You collect the data by selecting a drive-through time sample of $n = 25$ stores. You decide to use $\alpha = 0.05$.

Step 3 Because σ is unknown, you use the t distribution and the t_{STAT} test statistic. You need to assume that the service time is normally distributed because only a sample of 25 drive-through times is selected.

Step 4 The rejection region is entirely contained in the lower tail of the sampling distribution of the mean because you want to reject H_0 only when the sample mean is significantly less than 174.22 seconds. When the entire rejection region is contained in one tail of the sampling distribution of the test statistic, the test is called a **one-tail test**, or **directional test**. If the alternative hypothesis includes the *less than* sign, the critical value of t is negative. As shown in Table 9.3 and Figure 9.11, because the entire rejection region is in the lower tail of the t distribution and contains an area of 0.05, due to the symmetry of the t distribution, the critical value of the t test statistic with $25 - 1 = 24$ degrees of freedom is -1.7109. The decision rule is

$$\text{Reject } H_0 \text{ if } t_{STAT} < -1.7109;$$
$$\text{otherwise, do not reject } H_0.$$

TABLE 9.3

Determining the Critical Value from the t Table for an Area of 0.05 in the Lower Tail, with 24 Degrees of Freedom

	Cumulative Probabilities					
	.75	.90	.95	.975	.99	.995
	Upper-Tail Areas					
Degrees of Freedom	.25	.10	.05	.025	.01	.005
1	1.0000	3.0777	6.3138	12.7062	31.8207	63.6574
2	0.8165	1.8856	2.9200	4.3027	6.9646	9.9248
3	0.7649	1.6377	2.3534	3.1824	4.5407	5.8409
.	.	.	.	.	.	.
.	.	.	.	.	.	.
.	.	.	.	.	.	.
23	0.6853	1.3195	1.7139	2.0687	2.4999	2.8073
24	0.6848	1.3178	1.7109	2.0639	2.4922	2.7969
25	0.6844	1.3163	1.7081	2.0595	2.4851	2.7874

Source: Extracted from Table E.3.

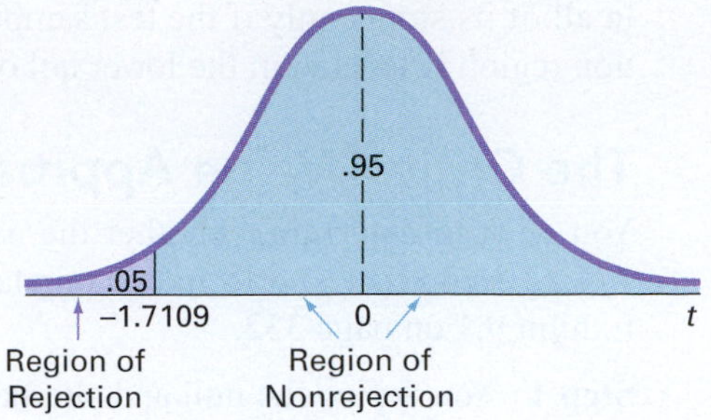

FIGURE 9.11
One-tail test of hypothesis for a mean (σ unknown) at the 0.05 level of significance

Step 5 From the sample of 25 stores you selected, you find that the sample mean service time at the drive-through equals 162.96 seconds and the sample standard deviation equals 20.2 seconds. Using $n = 25$, $\bar{X} = 162.96$, $S = 20.2$, and Equation (9.2) on page 338,

$$t_{STAT} = \frac{\bar{X} - \mu}{\frac{S}{\sqrt{n}}} = \frac{162.96 - 174.22}{\frac{20.2}{\sqrt{25}}} = -2.7871$$

Step 6 Because $t_{STAT} = -2.7871 < -1.7109$, you reject the null hypothesis (see Figure 9.11). You conclude that the mean service time at the drive-through is less than 174.22 seconds. There is sufficient evidence to change the drive-through process for the entire population of stores.

The *p*-Value Approach

Use the five steps listed in Exhibit 9.2 on page 335 to illustrate the t test for the drive-through time study using the p-value approach.

Step 1–3 These steps are the same as in the critical value approach on page 332.

Step 4 $t_{STAT} = -2.7871$ (see step 5 of the critical value approach). Because the alternative hypothesis indicates a rejection region entirely in the lower tail of the sampling distribution, to compute the p-value, you need to find the probability that the t_{STAT} test statistic will be less than –2.7871. Figure 9.12 shows that the p-value is 0.0051.

FIGURE 9.12
Excel and Minitab t test results for the drive-through time study

	A	B	
1	t Test for the Hypothesis of the Mean		
2			
3	Data		
4	Null Hypothesis μ=	174.22	
5	Level of Significance	0.05	
6	Sample Size	25	
7	Sample Mean	162.96	
8	Sample Standard Deviation	20.2	
9			
10	Intermediate Calculations		
11	Standard Error of the Mean	4.0400	=B8/SQRT(B6)
12	Degrees of Freedom	24	=B6 - 1
13	t Test Statistic	-2.7871	=(B7 - B4)/B11
14			
15	Lower-Tail Test		
16	Lower Critical Value	-1.7109	=-TINV(2 * B5, B12)
17	p-Value	0.0051	=IF(B13 < 0, E22, E23)
18	Reject the null hypothesis		=IF(B17 < B5, "Reject the null hypothesis", "Do not reject the null hypothesis")

Not shown
Cell E22: =TDIST(ABS(B13), B12, 1)
Cell E23: =1 - E22

One-Sample T

```
Test of mu = 174.22 vs < 174.22

                                 95% Upper
 N    Mean  StDev  SE Mean      Bound      T      P
25  162.96  20.20     4.04     169.87  -2.79  0.005
```

Step 5 The p-value of 0.0051 is less than $\alpha = 0.05$ (see Figure 9.13). You reject H_0 and conclude that the mean service time at the drive-through is less than 174.22 seconds. There is sufficient evidence to change the drive-through process for the entire population of stores.

FIGURE 9.13
Determining the p-value for a one-tail test

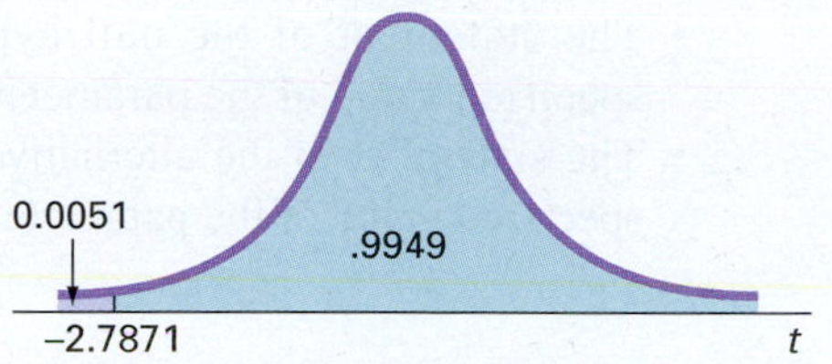

EXAMPLE 9.5
A One-Tail Test for the Mean

A company that manufactures chocolate bars is particularly concerned that the mean weight of a chocolate bar is not greater than 6.03 ounces. A sample of 50 chocolate bars is selected; the sample mean is 6.034 ounces, and the sample standard deviation is 0.02 ounces. Using the $\alpha = 0.01$ level of significance, is there evidence that the population mean weight of the chocolate bars is greater than 6.03 ounces?

SOLUTION Using the critical value approach, listed in Exhibit 9.1 on page 332,

Step 1 First, you define your hypotheses:

$$H_0: \mu \leq 6.03$$
$$H_1: \mu > 6.03$$

Step 2 You collect the data from a sample of $n = 50$. You decide to use $\alpha = 0.01$.

Step 3 Because σ is unknown, you use the t distribution and the t_{STAT} test statistic.

Step 4 The rejection region is entirely contained in the upper tail of the sampling distribution of the mean because you want to reject H_0 only when the sample mean is significantly greater than 6.03 ounces. Because the entire rejection region is in the upper tail of the t distribution and contains an area of 0.01, the critical value of the t distribution with $50 - 1 = 49$ degrees of freedom is 2.4049 (see Table E.3).

The decision rule is

Reject H_0 if $t_{STAT} > 2.4049$;
otherwise, do not reject H_0.

Step 5 From your sample of 50 chocolate bars, you find that the sample mean weight is 6.034 ounces, and the sample standard deviation is 0.02 ounces. Using $n = 50$, $\bar{X} = 6.034$, $S = 0.02$, and Equation (9.2) on page 338,

$$t_{STAT} = \frac{\bar{X} - \mu}{\frac{S}{\sqrt{n}}} = \frac{6.034 - 6.03}{\frac{0.02}{\sqrt{50}}} = 1.414$$

Step 6 Because $t_{STAT} = 1.414 < 2.4049$, or using Microsoft Excel or Minitab, the p-value is $0.0818 > 0.01$, you do not reject the null hypothesis. There is insufficient evidence to conclude that the population mean weight is greater than 6.03 ounces.

To perform one-tail tests of hypotheses, you must properly formulate H_0 and H_1. A summary of the null and alternative hypotheses for one-tail tests is as follows:

- The null hypothesis, H_0, represents the status quo or the current belief in a situation.
- The alternative hypothesis, H_1, is the opposite of the null hypothesis and represents a research claim or specific inference you would like to prove.
- If you reject the null hypothesis, you have statistical proof that the alternative hypothesis is correct.
- If you do not reject the null hypothesis, you have failed to prove the alternative hypothesis. The failure to prove the alternative hypothesis, however, does not mean that you have proven the null hypothesis.
- The null hypothesis always refers to a specified value of the *population parameter* (such as μ), not to a *sample statistic* (such as $\bar{X}$).

- The statement of the null hypothesis *always* contains an equal sign regarding the specified value of the parameter (e.g., $H_0 : \mu \geq 174.22$).
- The statement of the alternative hypothesis *never* contains an equal sign regarding the specified value of the parameter (e.g., $H_1 : \mu < 174.22$).

Problems for Section 9.3

LEARNING THE BASICS

9.36 In a one-tail hypothesis test where you reject H_0 only in the *upper* tail, what is the *p*-value if $Z_{STAT} = +2.00$?

9.37 In Problem 9.36, what is your statistical decision if you test the null hypothesis at the 0.05 level of significance?

9.38 In a one-tail hypothesis test where you reject H_0 only in the *lower* tail, what is the *p*-value if $Z_{STAT} = -1.38$?

9.39 In Problem 9.38, what is your statistical decision if you test the null hypothesis at the 0.01 level of significance?

9.40 In a one-tail hypothesis test where you reject H_0 only in the *lower* tail, what is the *p*-value if $Z_{STAT} = +1.38$?

9.41 In Problem 9.40, what is the statistical decision if you test the null hypothesis at the 0.01 level of significance?

9.42 In a one-tail hypothesis test where you reject H_0 only in the *upper* tail, what is the critical value of the *t*-test statistic with 10 degrees of freedom at the 0.01 level of significance?

9.43 In Problem 9.42, what is your statistical decision if $t_{STAT} = +2.39$?

9.44 In a one-tail hypothesis test where you reject H_0 only in the *lower* tail, what is the critical value of the t_{STAT} test statistic with 20 degrees of freedom at the 0.01 level of significance?

9.45 In Problem 9.44, what is your statistical decision if $t_{STAT} = -1.15$?

APPLYING THE CONCEPTS

9.46 In a recent year, the Federal Communications Commission reported that the mean wait for repairs for Verizon customers was 36.5 hours. In an effort to improve this service, suppose that a new repair service process was developed. This new process, used for a sample of 100 repairs, resulted in a sample mean of 34.5 hours and a sample standard deviation of 11.7 hours.

a. Is there evidence that the population mean amount is less than 36.5 hours? (Use a 0.05 level of significance.)
b. Determine the *p*-value and interpret its meaning.

9.47 In a recent year, the Federal Communications Commission reported that the mean wait for repairs for AT&T customers was 25.3 hours. In an effort to improve this service, suppose that a new repair service process was developed. This new process, used for a sample of 100 repairs, resulted in a sample mean of 22.3 hours and a sample standard deviation of 8.3 hours.

a. Is there evidence that the population mean amount is less than 25.3 hours? (Use a 0.05 level of significance.)
b. Determine the *p*-value and interpret its meaning.

SELF Test **9.48** Southside Hospital in Bay Shore, New York, commonly conducts stress tests to study the heart muscle after a person has a heart attack. Members of the diagnostic imaging department conducted a quality improvement project with the objective of reducing the turnaround time for stress tests. Turnaround time is defined as the time from when a test is ordered to when the radiologist signs off on the test results. Initially, the mean turnaround time for a stress test was 68 hours. After incorporating changes into the stress-test process, the quality improvement team collected a sample of 50 turnaround times. In this sample, the mean turnaround time was 32 hours, with a standard deviation of 9 hours. (Data extracted from E. Godin, D. Raven, C. Sweetapple, and F. R. Del Guidice, "Faster Test Results," *Quality Progress*, January 2004, 37(1), pp. 33–39.)

a. If you test the null hypothesis at the 0.01 level of significance, is their evidence that the new process has reduced turnaround time?
b. Interpret the meaning of the *p*-value in this problem.

9.49 You are the manager of a restaurant that delivers pizza to college dormitory rooms. You have just changed your delivery process in an effort to reduce the mean time between the order and completion of delivery from the current 25 minutes. A sample of 36 orders using the new delivery process yields a sample mean of 22.4 minutes and a sample standard deviation of 6 minutes.

a. Using the six-step critical value approach, at the 0.05 level of significance, is there evidence that the population mean delivery time has been reduced below the previous population mean value of 25 minutes?
b. At the 0.05 level of significance, use the five-step *p*-value approach.
c. Interpret the meaning of the *p*-value in (b).
d. Compare your conclusions in (a) and (b).

9.50 The per-store daily customer count (i.e., the mean number of customers in a store in one day) for a nationwide convenience store chain that operates nearly 10,000 stores has been steady, at 900, for some time. To increase the customer count, the chain is considering cutting prices for coffee beverages by approximately half. The small size will now be \$0.59 instead of \$0.99, and the medium size will be \$0.69 instead of \$1.19. Even with this reduction in price, the chain will have a 40% gross margin on coffee. To test the new initiative, the chain has reduced coffee prices in a sample of 34 stores, where customer counts have been running almost exactly at the national average of 900. After four weeks, the sample stores stabilize at a mean customer count of 974 and a standard deviation of 96. This increase seems like a substantial amount to you, but it also seems like a pretty small sample. Do you think reducing coffee prices is a good strategy for increasing the mean customer count?

a. State the null and alternative hypotheses.
b. Explain the meaning of the Type I and Type II errors in the context of this scenario.
c. At the 0.01 level of significance, is there evidence that reducing coffee prices is a good strategy for increasing the mean customer count?
d. Interpret the meaning of the p-value in (c).

9.51 The population mean waiting time to check out of a supermarket has been 10.73 minutes. Recently, in an effort to reduce the waiting time, the supermarket has experimented with a system in which there is a single waiting line with multiple checkout servers. A sample of 100 customers was selected, and their mean waiting time to check out was 9.52 minutes, with a sample standard deviation of 5.8 minutes.

a. At the 0.05 level of significance, using the critical value approach to hypothesis testing, is there evidence that the population mean waiting time to check out is less than 10.73 minutes?
b. At the 0.05 level of significance, using the p-value approach to hypothesis testing, is there evidence that the population mean waiting time to check out is less than 10.73 minutes?
c. Interpret the meaning of the p-value in this problem.
d. Compare your conclusions in (a) and (b).

9.4 *Z* Test of Hypothesis for the Proportion

In some situations, you want to test a hypothesis about the proportion of events of interest in the population, π, rather than test the population mean. To begin, you select a random sample and compute the **sample proportion**, $p = X/n$. You then compare the value of this statistic to the hypothesized value of the parameter, π, in order to decide whether to reject the null hypothesis. If the number of events of interest (X) and the number of events that are not of interest ($n - X$) are each at least five, the sampling distribution of a proportion approximately follows a normal distribution. You use the ***Z* test for the proportion** given in Equation (9.3) to perform the hypothesis test for the difference between the sample proportion, p, and the hypothesized population proportion, π.

Z TEST FOR THE PROPORTION

$$Z_{STAT} = \frac{p - \pi}{\sqrt{\dfrac{\pi(1-\pi)}{n}}} \qquad \textbf{(9.3)}$$

where

$$p = \text{Sample proportion} = \frac{X}{n} = \frac{\text{Number of events of interest in the sample}}{\text{Sample size}}$$

$$\pi = \text{Hypothesized proportion of events of interest in the population}$$

The Z_{STAT} test statistic approximately follows a standardized normal distribution when X and $(n - X)$ are each at least 5.

Alternatively, by multiplying the numerator and denominator by n, you can write the Z_{STAT} test statistic in terms of the number of events of interest, X, as shown in Equation (9.4).

Z TEST FOR THE PROPORTION IN TERMS OF THE NUMBER OF EVENTS OF INTEREST

$$Z_{STAT} = \frac{X - n\pi}{\sqrt{n\pi(1-\pi)}} \qquad \textbf{(9.4)}$$

The Critical Value Approach

To illustrate the Z test for a proportion, consider a survey conducted for American Express that sought to determine the reasons adults wanted Internet access while on vacation. (Data extracted from "Wired Vacationers," *USA Today*, June 4, 2010, p. 1A.) Of 2,000 adults, 1,540 said that they wanted Internet access so they could check personal e-mail while on vacation. A survey conducted in the previous year indicated that 75% of adults wanted Internet access so they could check personal e-mail while on vacation. Is there evidence that the percentage of adults who wanted Internet access to check personal e-mail while on vacation has changed from the previous year? To investigate this question, the null and alternative hypotheses are follows:

$H_0: \pi = 0.75$ (i.e., the proportion of adults who want Internet access to check personal email while on vacation has not changed from the previous year)

$H_1: \pi \neq 0.75$ (i.e., the proportion of adults who want Internet access to check personal email while on vacation has changed from the previous year)

Because you are interested in determining whether the population proportion of adults who want Internet access to check personal email while on vacation has changed from 0.75 in the previous year, you use a two-tail test. If you select the $\alpha = 0.05$ level of significance, the rejection and nonrejection regions are set up as in Figure 9.14, and the decision rule is

Reject H_0 if $Z_{STAT} < -1.96$ or if $Z_{STAT} > +1.96$;

otherwise, do not reject H_0.

FIGURE 9.14

Two-tail test of hypothesis for the proportion at the 0.05 level of significance

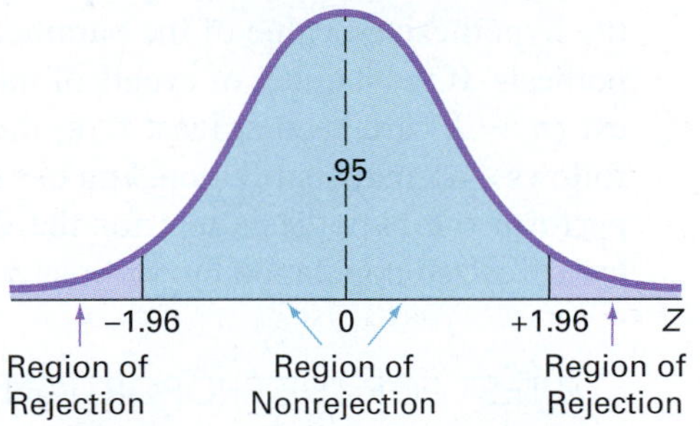

Because 1,540 of the 2,000 adults stated that they wanted Internet access to check personal email while on vacation,

$$p = \frac{1{,}540}{2{,}000} = 0.77$$

Since $X = 1{,}540$ and $n - X = 460$, each > 5, using Equation (9.3),

$$Z_{STAT} = \frac{p - \pi}{\sqrt{\dfrac{\pi(1 - \pi)}{n}}} = \frac{0.77 - 0.75}{\sqrt{\dfrac{0.75(1 - 0.75)}{2{,}000}}} = \frac{0.02}{0.0097} = 2.0656$$

or, using Equation (9.4),

$$Z_{STAT} = \frac{X - n\pi}{\sqrt{n\pi(1 - \pi)}} = \frac{1{,}540 - (2{,}000)(0.75)}{\sqrt{2{,}000(0.75)(0.25)}} = \frac{40}{19.3649} = 2.0656$$

Because $Z_{STAT} = 2.0656 > 1.96$, you reject H_0. There is evidence that the population proportion of all adults who want Internet access to check personal e-mail while on vacation has changed from 0.75 in the previous year. Figure 9.15 presents results for these data, as computed by Excel and Minitab.

FIGURE 9.15

Excel and Minitab results for the Z test for whether the proportion of adults who want Internet access to check personal email while on vacation has changed from the previous year

	A	B	
1	Z Test of Hypothesis for the Proportion		
2			
3	Data		
4	Null Hypothesis *p* =	0.75	
5	Level of Significance	0.05	
6	Number of Items of Interest	1540	
7	Sample Size	2000	
8			
9	Intermediate Calculations		
10	Sample Proportion	0.7700	=B6/B7
11	Standard Error	0.0097	=SQRT(B4*(1 - B4)/B7)
12	Z Test Statistic	2.0656	=(B10 - B4)/B11
13			
14	Two-Tail Test		
15	Lower Critical Value	-1.9600	=NORMSINV(B5/2)
16	Upper Critical Value	1.9600	=NORMSINV(1 - B5/2)
17	*p*-Value	0.0389	=2 * (1 - NORMSDIST(ABS(B12)))
18	Reject the null hypothesis		=IF(B17 < B5, "Reject the null hypothesis", "Do not reject the null hypothesis")

Test and CI for One Proportion

```
Test of p = 0.75 vs p not = 0.75

Sample     X     N  Sample p            95% CI             Z-Value  P-Value
1       1540  2000  0.770000  (0.751557, 0.788443)           2.07    0.039

Using the normal approximation.
```

The *p*-Value Approach

As an alternative to the critical value approach, you can compute the *p*-value. For this two-tail test in which the rejection region is located in the lower tail and the upper tail, you need to find the area below a Z value of –2.0656 and above a Z value of +2.0656. Figure 9.15 reports a *p*-value of 0.0389. Because this value is less than the selected level of significance ($\alpha = 0.05$), you reject the null hypothesis.

EXAMPLE 9.6

Testing a Hypothesis for a Proportion

A fast-food chain has developed a new process to ensure that orders at the drive-through are filled correctly. The business problem is defined as determining whether the new process can increase the percentage of orders processed correctly. The previous process filled orders correctly 85% of the time. Data are collected from a sample of 100 orders using the new process. The results indicate that 94 orders were filled correctly. At the 0.01 level of significance, can you conclude that the new process has increased the proportion of orders filled correctly?

SOLUTION The null and alternative hypotheses are

$H_0: \pi \leq 0.85$ (i.e., the population proportion of orders filled correctly using the new process is less than or equal to 0.85)
$H_1: \pi > 0.85$ (i.e., the population proportion of orders filled correctly using the new process is greater than 0.85)

Since $X = 94$ and $n - X = 6$, both > 5, using Equation (9.3) on page 349,

$$p = \frac{X}{n} = \frac{94}{100} = 0.94$$

$$Z_{STAT} = \frac{p - \pi}{\sqrt{\dfrac{\pi(1 - \pi)}{n}}} = \frac{0.94 - 0.85}{\sqrt{\dfrac{0.85(1 - 0.85)}{100}}} = \frac{0.09}{0.0357} = 2.52$$

The *p*-value for $Z_{STAT} > 2.52$ is 0.0059.

Using the critical value approach, you reject H_0 if $Z_{STAT} > 2.33$. Using the *p*-value approach, you reject H_0 if *p*-value < 0.01. Because $Z_{STAT} = 2.52 > 2.33$ or the *p-value* $= 0.0059 < 0.01$, you reject H_0. You have evidence that the new process has increased the proportion of correct orders above 0.85.

Problems for Section 9.4

LEARNING THE BASICS

9.52 If, in a random sample of 400 items, 88 are defective, what is the sample proportion of defective items?

9.53 In Problem 9.52, if the null hypothesis is that 20% of the items in the population are defective, what is the value of Z_{STAT}?

9.54 In Problems 9.52 and 9.53, suppose you are testing the null hypothesis $H_0: \pi = 0.20$ against the two-tail alternative hypothesis $H_1: \pi \neq 0.20$ and you choose the level of significance $\alpha = 0.05$. What is your statistical decision?

APPLYING THE CONCEPTS

9.55 The U.S. Department of Education reports that 46% of full-time college students are employed while attending college. (Data extracted from "The Condition of Education 2009," *National Center for Education Statistics*, **nces.ed.gov**.) A recent survey of 60 full-time students at Miami University found that 29 were employed.

a. Use the five-step *p*-value approach to hypothesis testing and a 0.05 level of significance to determine whether the proportion of full-time students at Miami University is different from the national norm of 0.46.

b. Assume that the study found that 36 of the 60 full-time students were employed and repeat (a). Are the conclusions the same?

9.56 Online magazines make it easy for readers to link to an advertiser's website directly from an advertisement placed in the digital magazine. A recent survey indicated that 56% of online magazine readers have clicked on an advertisement and linked directly to the advertiser's website. The survey was based on a sample size of $n = 6{,}403$. (Data extracted from "Metrics," *EContent*, January/February, 2007, p. 20.)

a. Use the five-step *p*-value approach to try to determine whether there is evidence that more than half of all the readers of online magazines have linked to an advertiser's website. (Use the 0.05 level of significance.)

b. Suppose that the sample size was only $n = 100$, and, as before, 56% of the online magazine readers indicated that they had clicked on an advertisement to link directly to the advertiser's website. Use the five-step *p*-value approach to try to determine whether there is evidence that more than half of all the readers of online magazines have linked to an advertiser's website. (Use the 0.05 level of significance.)

c. Discuss the effect that sample size has on hypothesis testing.

d. What do you think are your chances of rejecting any null hypothesis concerning a population proportion if a sample size of $n = 20$ is used?

9.57 One of the issues facing organizations is increasing diversity throughout the organization. One of the ways to evaluate an organization's success at increasing diversity is to compare the percentage of employees in the organization in a particular position with a specific background to the percentage in a particular position with that specific background in the general workforce. Recently, a large academic medical center determined that 9 of 17 employees in a particular position were female, whereas 55% of the employees for this position in the general workforce were female. At the 0.05 level of significance, is there evidence that the proportion of females in this position at this medical center is different from what would be expected in the general workforce?

SELF Test **9.58** Of 1,000 respondents aged 24 to 35, 65% reported that they preferred to "look for a job in a place where I would like to live" rather than "look for the best job I can find, the place where I live is secondary." (Data extracted from L. Belkin, "What Do Young Jobseekers Want? (Something Other Than a Job)," *The New York Times*, September 6, 2007, p. G2.) At the 0.05 level of significance, is there evidence that the proportion of all young jobseekers aged 24 to 35 who preferred to "look for a job in a place where I would like to live" rather than "look for the best job I can find, the place where I live is secondary" is different from 60%?

9.59 The telephone company wants to investigate the desirability of beginning a marketing campaign that would offer customers the right to purchase an additional telephone line at a substantially reduced installation cost. The campaign will be initiated if there is evidence that more than 20% of the customers would consider purchasing an additional telephone line if it were made available at a substantially reduced installation cost. A random sample of 500 households is selected. The results indicate that 135 of the households would purchase the additional telephone line at a reduced installation cost.

a. At the 0.05 level of significance, is there evidence that more than 20% of the customers would purchase the additional telephone line?

b. How would the manager in charge of promotional programs concerning residential customers use the results in (a)?

9.60 A study by the Pew Internet and American Life Project (**pewinternet.org**) found that Americans had a complex and ambivalent attitude toward technology. (Data extracted from M. Himowitz, "How to Tell What Kind of Tech User You Are," *Newsday*, May 27, 2007, p. F6.) The study reported that 8% of the respondents were "Omnivores" who are gadget lovers, text messengers, and online gamers (often with their own blogs or web pages), video makers, and YouTube posters. You believe that the percentage of students at your school who are Omnivores is greater than 8%, and you plan to carry out a study to prove that this is so.

a. State the null and alternative hypotheses.

b. You select a sample of 200 students at your school and find that 30 students can be classified as Omnivores. Use either the six-step critical value hypothesis-testing approach or the five-step *p*-value approach to determine at the 0.05 level of significance whether there is evidence that the percentage of Omnivores at your school is greater than 8%.

9.5 Potential Hypothesis-Testing Pitfalls and Ethical Issues

To this point, you have studied the fundamental concepts of hypothesis testing. You have used hypothesis testing to analyze differences between sample statistics and hypothesized population parameters in order to make business decisions concerning the underlying population characteristics. You have also learned how to evaluate the risks involved in making these decisions.

When planning to carry out a hypothesis test based on a survey, research study, or designed experiment, you must ask several questions to ensure that you use proper methodology. You need to raise and answer questions such as the following in the planning stage:

- What is the goal of the survey, study, or experiment? How can you translate the goal into a null hypothesis and an alternative hypothesis?
- Is the hypothesis test a two-tail test or one-tail test?
- Can you select a random sample from the underlying population of interest?
- What types of data will you collect in the sample? Are the variables numerical or categorical?
- At what level of significance should you conduct the hypothesis test?
- Is the intended sample size large enough to achieve the desired power of the test for the level of significance chosen?
- What statistical test procedure should you use and why?
- What conclusions and interpretations can you reach from the results of the hypothesis test?

Failing to consider these questions early in the planning process can lead to biased or incomplete results. Proper planning can help ensure that the statistical study will provide objective information needed to make good business decisions.

Statistical Significance Versus Practical Significance

You need to make a distinction between the existence of a statistically significant result and its practical significance in a field of application. Sometimes, due to a very large sample size, you may get a result that is statistically significant but has little practical significance. For example, suppose that prior to a national marketing campaign focusing on a series of expensive television commercials, you believe that the proportion of people who recognize your brand is 0.30. At the completion of the campaign, a survey of 20,000 people indicates that 6,168 recognized your brand. A one-tail test trying to prove that the proportion is now greater than 0.30 results in a *p*-value of 0.0047, and the correct statistical conclusion is that the proportion of consumers recognizing your brand name has now increased. Was the campaign successful? The result of the hypothesis test indicates a statistically significant increase in brand awareness, but is this increase practically important? The population proportion is now estimated at $6{,}168/20{,}000 = 0.3084$, or 30.84%. This increase is less than 1% more than the hypothesized value of 30%. Did the large expenses associated with the marketing campaign produce a result with a meaningful increase in brand awareness? Because of the minimal real-world impact that an increase of less than 1% has on the overall marketing strategy and the huge expenses associated with the marketing campaign, you should conclude that the campaign was not successful. On the other hand, if the campaign increased brand awareness from 30% to 50%, you could conclude that the campaign was successful.

Reporting of Findings

In conducting research, you should document both good and bad results. You should not just report the results of hypothesis tests that show statistical significance but omit those for which there is insufficient evidence in the findings. In instances in which there is insufficient evidence to reject H_0, you must make it clear that this does not prove that the null hypothesis is true. What the result does indicate is that with the sample size used, there is not enough information to *disprove* the null hypothesis.

Ethical Issues

You need to distinguish between poor research methodology and unethical behavior. Ethical considerations arise when the hypothesis-testing process is manipulated. Some of the areas where ethical issues can arise include the use of human subjects in experiments, the data collection method, the type of test (one-tail or two-tail test), the choice of the level of significance, the cleansing and discarding of data, and the failure to report pertinent findings.

9.6 *Online Topic:* The Power of a Test

Section 9.1 defines Type I and Type II errors and the power of a test. To examine the power of a test in greater depth, read the **Section 9.6** online topic file that is available on this book's companion website. (See Appendix C to learn how to access the online topic files.)

USING STATISTICS @ Oxford Cereals, Part II Revisited

As the plant operations manager for Oxford Cereals, you were responsible for the cereal-filling process. It was your responsibility to adjust the process when the mean fill weight in the population of boxes deviated from the company specification of 368 grams. Because weighing all the cereal boxes would be too time-consuming and impractical, you needed to select and weigh a sample of boxes and conduct a hypothesis test.

You determined that the null hypothesis should be that the population mean fill was 368 grams. If the mean weight of the sampled boxes were sufficiently above or below the expected 368-gram mean specified by Oxford Cereals, you would reject the null hypothesis in favor of the alternative hypothesis that the mean fill was different from 368 grams. If this happened, you would stop production and take whatever action is necessary to correct the problem. If the null hypothesis was not rejected, you would continue to believe in the status quo—that the process was working correctly—and therefore take no corrective action.

Before proceeding, you considered the risks involved with hypothesis tests. If you rejected a true null hypothesis, you would make a Type I error and conclude that the population mean fill was not 368 when it actually was 368. This error would result in adjusting the filling process even though the process was working properly. If you did not reject a false null hypothesis, you would make a Type II error and conclude that the population mean fill was 368 when it actually was not 368. Here, you would allow the process to continue without adjustment even though the process was not working properly.

After collecting a random sample of 25 cereal boxes, you used the six-step critical value approach to hypothesis testing. Because the test statistic fell into the nonrejection region, you did not reject the null hypothesis. You concluded that there was insufficient evidence to prove that the mean fill differed from 368 grams. No corrective action on the filling process was needed.

SUMMARY

This chapter presented the foundation of hypothesis testing. You learned how to perform tests on the population mean and on the population proportion. The chapter developed both the critical value approach and the p-value approach to hypothesis testing.

In deciding which test to use, you should ask the following question: Does the test involve a numerical variable or a categorical variable? If the test involves a numerical variable, use the t test for the mean. If the test involves a categorical variable, use the Z test for the proportion. Table 9.4 provides a list of hypothesis tests covered in the chapter.

TABLE 9.4

Summary of Topics in Chapter 9

	Type of Data	
Type of Analysis	**Numerical**	**Categorical**
Hypothesis test concerning a single parameter	t test of hypothesis for the mean (Section 9.2)	Z test of hypothesis for the proportion (Section 9.4)

KEY EQUATIONS

***Z* Test for the Mean (σ Known)**

$$Z_{STAT} = \frac{\bar{X} - \mu}{\dfrac{\sigma}{\sqrt{n}}} \quad \textbf{(9.1)}$$

***t* Test for the Mean (σ Unknown)**

$$t_{STAT} = \frac{\bar{X} - \mu}{\dfrac{S}{\sqrt{n}}} \quad \textbf{(9.2)}$$

***Z* Test for the Proportion**

$$Z_{STAT} = \frac{p - \pi}{\sqrt{\dfrac{\pi(1 - \pi)}{n}}} \quad \textbf{(9.3)}$$

***Z* Test for the Proportion in Terms of the Number of Events of Interest**

$$Z_{STAT} = \frac{X - n\pi}{\sqrt{n\pi(1 - \pi)}} \quad \textbf{(9.4)}$$

KEY TERMS

alternative hypothesis (H_1) 326
β risk 329
confidence coefficient 329
critical value 328
directional test 345
hypothesis testing 326
level of significance (α) 329
null hypothesis (H_0) 326
one-tail test 345
p-value 333
power of a statistical test 329
region of nonrejection 328
region of rejection 328
robust 341
sample proportion 349
t test for the mean 338
test statistic 328
two-tail test 331
Type I error 328
Type II error 328
Z test for the mean 330
Z test for the proportion 349

CHAPTER REVIEW PROBLEMS

CHECKING YOUR UNDERSTANDING

9.61 What is the difference between a null hypothesis, H_0, and an alternative hypothesis, H_1?

9.62 What is the difference between a Type I error and a Type II error?

9.63 What is meant by the power of a test?

9.64 What is the difference between a one-tail test and a two-tail test?

9.65 What is meant by a p-value?

9.66 How can a confidence interval estimate for the population mean provide conclusions for the corresponding two-tail hypothesis test for the population mean?

9.67 What is the six-step critical value approach to hypothesis testing?

9.68 What is the five-step p-value approach to hypothesis testing?

APPLYING THE CONCEPTS

9.69 An article in *Marketing News* (T. T. Semon, "Consider a Statistical Insignificance Test," *Marketing News*, February 1, 1999) argued that the level of significance used when comparing two products is often too low—that is, sometimes you should be using an α value greater than 0.05. Specifically, the article recounted testing the proportion of potential customers with a preference for product 1 over product 2. The null hypothesis was that the population proportion of potential customers preferring product 1 was 0.50, and the alternative hypothesis was that it was not equal to 0.50. The p-value for the test was 0.22. The article suggested that, in some cases, this should be enough evidence to reject the null hypothesis.

a. State, in statistical terms, the null and alternative hypotheses for this example.
b. Explain the risks associated with Type I and Type II errors in this case.
c. What would be the consequences if you rejected the null hypothesis for a p-value of 0.22?
d. Why do you think the article suggested raising the value of α?
e. What would you do in this situation?
f. What is your answer in (e) if the p-value equals 0.12? What if it equals 0.06?

9.70 La Quinta Motor Inns developed a computer model to help predict the profitability of sites that are being considered as locations for new hotels. If the computer model predicts large profits, La Quinta buys the proposed site and builds a new hotel. If the computer model predicts small or moderate profits, La Quinta chooses not to proceed with that site. (Data extracted from S. E. Kimes and J. A. Fitzsimmons, "Selecting Profitable Hotel Sites at La Quinta Motor Inns," *Interfaces*, Vol. 20, March–April 1990, pp. 12–20.) This decision-making procedure can be expressed in the hypothesis-testing framework. The null hypothesis is that the site is not a profitable location. The alternative hypothesis is that the site is a profitable location.

a. Explain the risks associated with committing a Type I error in this case.
b. Explain the risks associated with committing a Type II error in this case.
c. Which type of error do you think the executives at La Quinta Motor Inns want to avoid? Explain.
d. How do changes in the rejection criterion affect the probabilities of committing Type I and Type II errors?

9.71 Webcredible, a UK-based consulting firm specializing in websites, intranets, mobile devices, and applications, conducted a survey of 1,132 mobile phone users between February and April 2009. The survey found that 52% of mobile phone users are now using the mobile Internet. (Data extracted from "Email and Social Networking Most Popular Mobile Internet Activities," **www.webcredible.co.uk**, May 13, 2009.) The authors of the article imply that the survey proves that more than half of all mobile phone users are now using the mobile Internet.

a. Use the five-step p-value approach to hypothesis testing and a 0.05 level of significance to try to prove that more than half of all mobile phone users are now using the mobile Internet.
b. Based on your result in (a), is the claim implied by the authors valid?
c. Suppose the survey found that 53% of mobile phone users are now using the mobile Internet. Repeat parts (a) and (b).
d. Compare the results of (b) and (c).

9.72 The owner of a gasoline station wants to study gasoline purchasing habits of motorists at his station. He selects a random sample of 60 motorists during a certain week, with the following results:

- The amount purchased was $\bar{X} = 11.3$ gallons, $S = 3.1$ gallons.
- Eleven motorists purchased premium-grade gasoline.

a. At the 0.05 level of significance, is there evidence that the population mean purchase was different from 10 gallons?
b. Determine the p-value in (a).
c. At the 0.05 level of significance, is there evidence that less than 20% of all the motorists at the station purchased premium-grade gasoline?
d. What is your answer to (a) if the sample mean equals 10.3 gallons?
e. What is your answer to (c) if 7 motorists purchased premium-grade gasoline?

9.73 An auditor for a government agency is assigned the task of evaluating reimbursement for office visits to physicians paid by Medicare. The audit was conducted on a sample of 75 of the reimbursements, with the following results:

- In 12 of the office visits, there was an incorrect amount of reimbursement.
- The amount of reimbursement was $\bar{X} = \$93.70$, $S = \$34.55$.

a. At the 0.05 level of significance, is there evidence that the population mean reimbursement was less than \$100?
b. At the 0.05 level of significance, is there evidence that the proportion of incorrect reimbursements in the population was greater than 0.10?
c. Discuss the underlying assumptions of the test used in (a).
d. What is your answer to (a) if the sample mean equals \$90?
e. What is your answer to (b) if 15 office visits had incorrect reimbursements?

9.74 A bank branch located in a commercial district of a city had the business objective of improving the process for serving customers during the noon-to-1:00 P.M. lunch period. The waiting time (defined as the time the customer enters the line until he or she reaches the teller window) of all customers during this hour is recorded over a period of a week. Data were collected from a random sample of 15 customers, and the results are organized (and stored in **Bank1**) as follows:

4.21	5.55	3.02	5.13	4.77	2.34	3.54	3.20
4.50	6.10	0.38	5.12	6.46	6.19	3.79	

a. At the 0.05 level of significance, is there evidence that the population mean waiting time is less than 5 minutes?
b. What assumption about the population distribution is needed in order to conduct the t test in (a)?
c. Construct a boxplot or a normal probability plot to evaluate the assumption made in (b).
d. Do you think that the assumption needed in order to conduct the t test in (a) is valid? Explain.
e. As a customer walks into the branch office during the lunch hour, she asks the branch manager how long she can expect to wait. The branch manager replies, "Almost certainly not longer than 5 minutes." On the basis of the results of (a), evaluate this statement.

9.75 A manufacturing company produces electrical insulators. If the insulators break when in use, a short circuit is likely to occur. To test the strength of the insulators, destructive testing is carried out to determine how much force is required to break the insulators. Force is measured by observing the number of pounds of force applied to the insulator before it breaks. The following data (stored in **Force**) are from 30 insulators subjected to this testing:

1,870	1,728	1,656	1,610	1,634	1,784	1,522	1,696	1,592	1,662
1,866	1,764	1,734	1,662	1,734	1,774	1,550	1,756	1,762	1,866
1,820	1,744	1,788	1,688	1,810	1,752	1,680	1,810	1,652	1,736

a. At the 0.05 level of significance, is there evidence that the population mean force is greater than 1,500 pounds?
b. What assumption about the population distribution is needed in order to conduct the t test in (a)?
c. Construct a histogram, boxplot, or normal probability plot to evaluate the assumption made in (b).
d. Do you think that the assumption needed in order to conduct the t test in (a) is valid? Explain.

9.76 An important quality characteristic used by the manufacturer of Boston and Vermont asphalt shingles is the amount of moisture the shingles contain when they are packaged. Customers may feel that they have purchased a product lacking in quality if they find moisture and wet shingles inside the packaging. In some cases, excessive moisture can cause the granules attached to the shingle for texture and coloring purposes to fall off the shingle, resulting in appearance problems. To monitor the amount of moisture present, the company conducts moisture tests. A shingle is weighed and then dried. The shingle is then reweighed, and, based on the amount of moisture taken out of the product, the pounds of moisture per 100 square feet are calculated. The company would like to show that the mean moisture content is less than 0.35 pound per 100 square feet. The file **Moisture** includes 36 measurements (in pounds per 100 square feet) for Boston shingles and 31 for Vermont shingles.

a. For the Boston shingles, is there evidence at the 0.05 level of significance that the population mean moisture content is less than 0.35 pound per 100 square feet?
b. Interpret the meaning of the p-value in (a).
c. For the Vermont shingles, is there evidence at the 0.05 level of significance that the population mean moisture content is less than 0.35 pound per 100 square feet?
d. Interpret the meaning of the p-value in (c).
e. What assumption about the population distribution is needed in order to conduct the t tests in (a) and (c)?
f. Construct histograms, boxplots, or normal probability plots to evaluate the assumption made in (a) and (c).
g. Do you think that the assumption needed in order to conduct the t tests in (a) and (c) is valid? Explain.

9.77 Studies conducted by the manufacturer of Boston and Vermont asphalt shingles have shown product weight to be a major factor in the customer's perception of quality. Moreover, the weight represents the amount of raw materials being used and is therefore very important to the company from a cost standpoint. The last stage of the assembly line packages the shingles before the packages are placed on wooden pallets. Once a pallet is full (a pallet for most brands holds 16 squares of shingles), it is weighed, and the measurement is recorded. The file **Pallet** contains the weight (in pounds) from a sample of 368 pallets of Boston shingles and 330 pallets of Vermont shingles.

a. For the Boston shingles, is there evidence that the population mean weight is different from 3,150 pounds?
b. Interpret the meaning of the p-value in (a).
c. For the Vermont shingles, is there evidence that the population mean weight is different from 3,700 pounds?
d. Interpret the meaning of the p-value in (c).
e. In (a) through (d), do you have to worry about the normality assumption? Explain.

9.78 The manufacturer of Boston and Vermont asphalt shingles provides its customers with a 20-year warranty on most of its products. To determine whether a shingle will last through the warranty period, accelerated-life testing is conducted at the manufacturing plant. Accelerated-life testing exposes the shingle to the stresses it would be subject to in a lifetime of normal use in a laboratory setting via an experiment that takes only a few minutes to conduct. In this test, a shingle is repeatedly scraped with a brush for a short period of time, and the shingle granules removed by the brushing are weighed (in grams). Shingles that experience low amounts of granule loss are expected to last longer in normal use than shingles that experience high amounts of granule loss. The file Granule contains a sample of 170 measurements made on the company's Boston shingles and 140 measurements made on Vermont shingles.

a. For the Boston shingles, is there evidence that the population mean granule loss is different from 0.50 grams?

b. Interpret the meaning of the *p*-value in (a).

c. For the Vermont shingles, is there evidence that the population mean granule loss is different from 0.50 grams?

d. Interpret the meaning of the *p*-value in (c).

e. In (a) through (d), do you have to worry about the normality assumption? Explain.

REPORT WRITING EXERCISE

9.79 Referring to the results of Problems 9.76 through 9.78 concerning Boston and Vermont shingles, write a report that evaluates the moisture level, weight, and granule loss of the two types of shingles.

MANAGING ASHLAND MULTICOMM SERVICES

Continuing its monitoring of the upload speed first described in the Chapter 6 Managing Ashland MultiComm Services case on page 244, the technical operations department wants to ensure that the mean target upload speed for all Internet service subscribers is at least 0.97 on a standard scale in which the target value is 1.0. Each day, upload speed was measured 50 times, with the following results (stored in AMS9).

0.854	1.023	1.005	1.030	1.219	0.977	1.044	0.778	1.122	1.114
1.091	1.086	1.141	0.931	0.723	0.934	1.060	1.047	0.800	0.889
1.012	0.695	0.869	0.734	1.131	0.993	0.762	0.814	1.108	0.805
1.223	1.024	0.884	0.799	0.870	0.898	0.621	0.818	1.113	1.286
1.052	0.678	1.162	0.808	1.012	0.859	0.951	1.112	1.003	0.972

Calculate the sample statistics and determine whether there is evidence that the population mean upload speed is less than 0.97. Write a memo to management that summarizes your conclusions.

DIGITAL CASE

Apply your knowledge about hypothesis testing in this Digital Case, which continues the cereal-fill-packaging dispute first discussed in the Digital Case from Chapter 7.

In response to the negative statements made by the Concerned Consumers About Cereal Cheaters (CCACC) in the Chapter 7 Digital Case, Oxford Cereals recently conducted an experiment concerning cereal packaging. The company claims that the results of the experiment refute the CCACC allegations that Oxford Cereals has been cheating consumers by packaging cereals at less than labeled weights.

Open **OxfordCurrentNews.pdf**, a portfolio of current news releases from Oxford Cereals. Review the relevant press releases and supporting documents. Then answer the following questions:

1. Are the results of the experiment valid? Why or why not? If you were conducting the experiment, is there anything you would change?
2. Do the results support the claim that Oxford Cereals is not cheating its customers?
3. Is the claim of the Oxford Cereals CEO that many cereal boxes contain *more* than 368 grams surprising? Is it true?
4. Could there ever be a circumstance in which the results of the Oxford Cereals experiment *and* the CCACC's results are both correct? Explain

REFERENCES

1. Bradley, J. V., *Distribution-Free Statistical Tests* (Upper Saddle River, NJ: Prentice Hall, 1968).
2. Daniel, W., *Applied Nonparametric Statistics*, 2nd ed. (Boston: Houghton Mifflin, 1990).
3. *Microsoft Excel 2010* (Redmond, WA: Microsoft Corp., 2007).
4. *Minitab Release 16* (State College, PA: Minitab Inc., 2010).

CHAPTER 9 EXCEL GUIDE

EG9.1 FUNDAMENTALS of HYPOTHESIS-TESTING METHODOLOGY

PHStat2 Use **Z Test for the Mean, sigma known** to perform the *Z* test for the mean when σ is known. For example, to perform the *Z* test for the Figure 9.5 cereal-filling example on page 334, select **PHStat → One-Sample Tests → Z Test for the Mean, sigma known**. In the procedure's dialog box (shown below):

1. Enter **368** as the **Null Hypothesis**.
2. Enter **0.05** as the **Level of Significance**.
3. Enter **15** as the **Population Standard Deviation**.
4. Click **Sample Statistics Known** and enter **25** as the **Sample Size** and **372.5** as the **Sample Mean**.
5. Click **Two-Tail Test**.
6. Enter a **Title** and click **OK**.

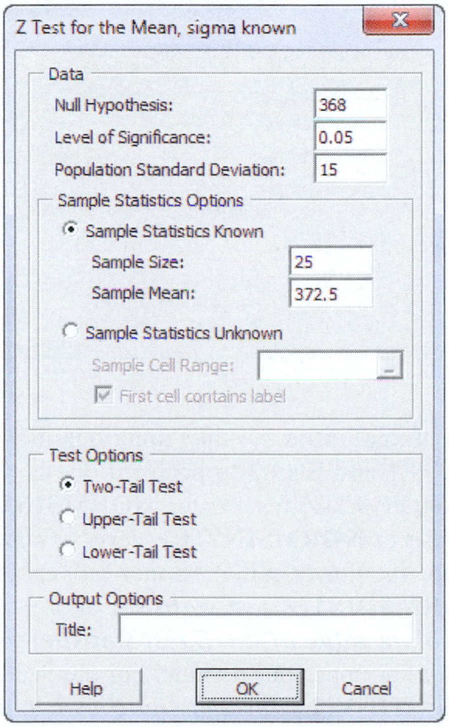

For problems that use unsummarized data, click **Sample Statistics Unknown** in step 4 and enter the cell range of the unsummarized data as the **Sample Cell Range**.

In-Depth Excel Use the **COMPUTE worksheet** of the **Z Mean workbook**, shown in Figure 9.5 on page 334, as a template for performing the two-tail *Z* test. The worksheet contains the data for the Section 9.1 cereal-filling example. For other problems, change the values in cells B4 through B8 as necessary.

In cells B15 and B16, **NORMSINV(*level of significance* / 2)** and **NORMSINV(1 - *level of significance* / 2)** computes the lower and upper critical values. The expression **2 * (1 − NORMSDIST (*absolute value of the Z test statistic*))** computes the *p*-value for the two-tail test in cell B17. In cell A18, **IF(*p-value* < *level of significance*, *display reject message*, *display do not reject message*)** determines which message to display in the cell.

EG9.2 *t* TEST of HYPOTHESIS for the MEAN (σ UNKNOWN)

PHStat2 Use ***t* Test for the Mean, sigma unknown** to perform the *t* test for the mean when σ is unknown. For example, to perform the *t* test for the Figure 9.7 sales invoice example on page 340, select **PHStat → One-Sample Tests → t Test for the Mean, sigma unknown**. In the procedure's dialog box (shown on the top of page 360):

1. Enter **120** as the **Null Hypothesis**.
2. Enter **0.05** as the **Level of Significance**.
3. Click **Sample Statistics Known** and enter **12** as the **Sample Size**, **112.85** as the **Sample Mean**, and **20.8** as the **Sample Standard Deviation**.
4. Click **Two-Tail Test**.
5. Enter a **Title** and click **OK**.

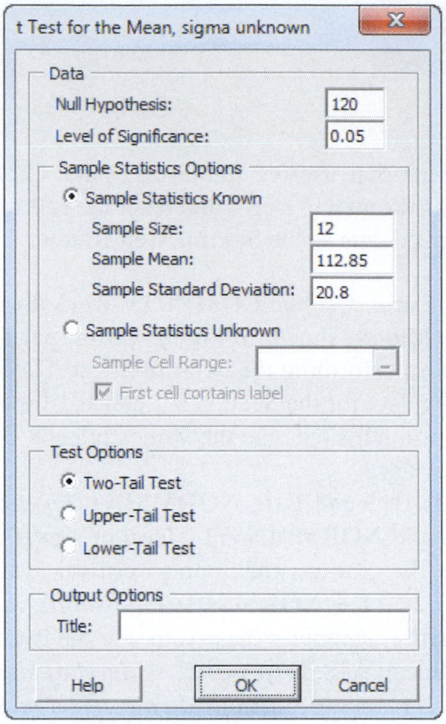

For problems that use unsummarized data, click **Sample Statistics Unknown** in step 3 and enter the cell range of the unsummarized data as the **Sample Cell Range**.

In-Depth Excel Use the **COMPUTE worksheet** of the **T mean workbook**, shown in Figure 9.7 on page 340, as a template for performing the two-tail *t* test. The worksheet contains the data for the Section 9.2 sales invoice example. For other problems, change the values in cells B4 through B8 as necessary.

In cells B16 and B17, the worksheet uses the expressions **-TINV(*level of significance*, *degrees of freedom*)** and **TINV(*level of significance*, *degrees of freedom*)** to compute the lower and upper critical values, respectively. In cell B18, the worksheet uses **TDIST(*absolute value of the t test statistic*, *degrees of freedom*, 2)** to compute the *p*-value. The worksheet also uses an **IF** function to determine which message to display in cell A19.

EG9.3 ONE-TAIL TESTS

PHStat2 Click either **Lower-Tail Test** or **Upper-Tail Test** in the procedure dialog boxes discussed in Sections EG9.1 and EG9.2 to perform a one-tail test. For example, to perform the Figure 9.12 one-tail test for the drive-through time study example on page 346, select **PHStat → One-Sample Tests → t Test for the Mean, sigma unknown**. In the procedure's dialog box (shown below):

1. Enter **174.22** as the **Null Hypothesis**.
2. Enter **0.05** as the **Level of Significance**.
3. Click **Sample Statistics Known** and enter **25** as the **Sample Size**, **162.96** as the **Sample Mean**, and **20.2** as the **Sample Standard Deviation**.
4. Click **Lower-Tail Test**.
5. Enter a **Title** and click **OK**.

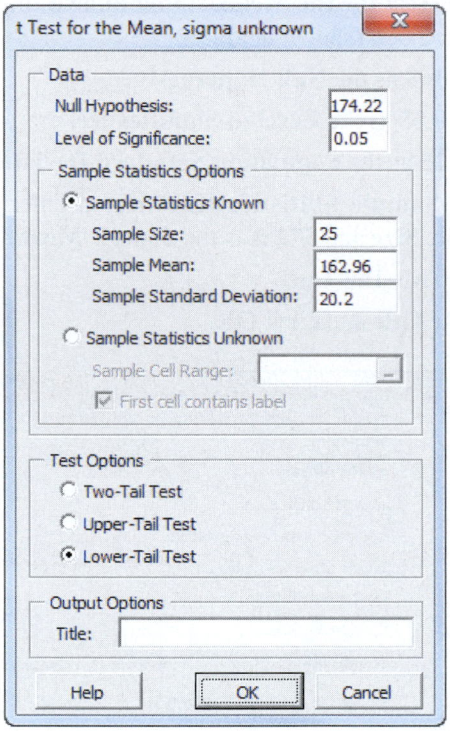

In-Depth Excel Modify the functions discussed in Section EG9.1 and EG9.2 to perform one-tail tests. For the Section EG9.1 *Z* test, enter **NORMSINV(*level of significance*)** or **NORMSINV(1 − *level of significance*)** to compute the lower-tail or upper-tail critical value. Enter **NORMSDIST(*Z test statistic*)** or **1 − NORMSDIST(*absolute value of the Z test statistic*)** to compute the lower-tail or upper-tail *p*-value. For the Section EG9.2 *t* test, enter **-TINV(2 * *level of significance*, *degrees of freedom*)** or **TINV(2 * *level of significance*, *degrees of freedom*)** to compute the lower-tail or upper-tail critical values.

Computing *p*-values is more complex. If the *t* test statistic is less than zero, the lower-tail *p*-value is equal to **TDIST(*absolute value of the t test statistic*, *degrees of***

***freedom*, 1)**, and the upper-tail p-value is equal to **1 − TDIST(*absolute value of the t test statistic*, *degrees of freedom*, 1)**. If the t test statistic is greater than or equal to zero, the values are reversed.

Use the **COMPUTE_LOWER worksheet** or the **COMPUTE_UPPER worksheet** of the **Z Mean workbook** or the **T mean workbook** as a template for performing one-tail t tests. Open the **COMPUTE_ALL_FORMULAS worksheet** of either workbook to examine all formulas.

EG9.4 Z TEST of HYPOTHESIS for the PROPORTION

PHStat2 Use **Z Test for the Proportion** to perform the Z test of hypothesis for the proportion. For example, to perform the Z test for the Figure 9.15 vacation Internet access study example on page 351, select **PHStat → One-Sample Tests → Z Test for the Proportion**. In the procedure's dialog box (shown in the right column):

1. Enter **0.75** as the **Null Hypothesis**.
2. Enter **0.05** as the **Level of Significance**.
3. Enter **1540** as the **Number of Items of Interest**.
4. Enter **2000** as the **Sample Size**.
5. Click **Two-Tail Test**.
6. Enter a **Title** and click **OK**.

In-Depth Excel Use the **COMPUTE worksheet** of the **Z Proportion workbook**, shown in Figure 9.15 on page 351, as a template for performing the two-tail Z test. The worksheet contains the data for the Section 9.4 vacation Internet access study example. For other problems, change the values in cells B4 through B7 as necessary.

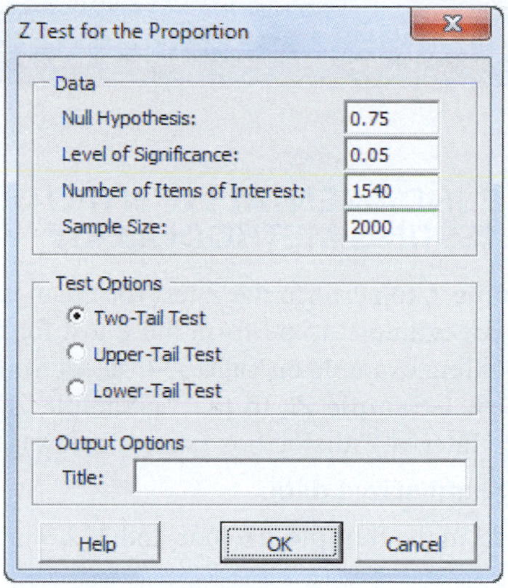

The worksheet uses **NORMSINV(*level of significance* / 2)** and **NORMSINV(1 - *level of significance* / 2)** to compute the lower and upper critical values in cells B15 and B16. In cell B17, the worksheet uses the expression **2 * (1 − NORMSDIST(*absolute value of the Z test statistic*)**) to compute the p-value. The worksheet also uses an **IF** function to determine which message to display in cell A18.

Use the **COMPUTE_LOWER worksheet** or **COMPUTE_UPPER worksheet** as a template for performing one-tail tests. Open to the **COMPUTE_ALL_FORMULAS worksheet** to examine all formulas in the one-tail test worksheets.

CHAPTER 9 MINITAB GUIDE

MG9.1 FUNDAMENTALS of HYPOTHESIS-TESTING METHODOLOGY

Use **1-Sample Z** to perform the *Z* test for the mean when σ is known. For example, to perform the *Z* test for the Figure 9.5 cereal-filling example on page 334, select **Stat → Basic Statistics → 1-Sample Z**. In the "1-Sample *Z* (Test and Confidence Interval)" dialog box (shown below):

1. Click **Summarized data.**
2. Enter **25** in the **Sample size** box and **372.5** in the **Mean** box.
3. Enter **15** in the **Standard deviation** box.
4. Check **Perform hypothesis test** and enter **368** in the **Hypothesized mean** box.
5. Click **Options**.

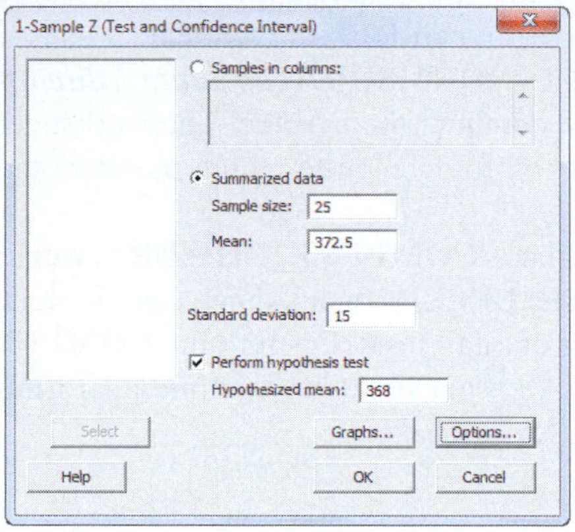

In the 1-Sample Z - Options dialog box:

6. Enter **95.0** in the **Confidence level** box.
7. Select **not equal** from the **Alternative** drop-down list.
8. Click **OK**.
9. Back in the original dialog box, click **OK**.

For problems that use unsummarized data, open the worksheet that contains the data and replace steps 1 and 2 with these steps:

1. Click **Samples in columns**.
2. Enter the name of the column containing the unsummarized data in the **Samples in column** box.

MG9.2 *t* TEST of HYPOTHESIS for the MEAN (σ UNKNOWN)

Use ***t* Test for the Mean, sigma unknown** to perform the *t* test for the mean when σ is unknown. For example, to perform the *t* test for the Figure 9.7 sales invoice example on page 340, select **Stat → Basic Statistics → 1-Sample t**. In the 1-Sample t (Test and Confidence Interval) dialog box (shown below):

1. Click **Summarized data**.
2. Enter **12** in the **Sample size** box, **112.85** in the **Mean** box, and **20.8** in the **Standard deviation** box.
3. Check **Perform hypothesis test** and enter **120** in the **Hypothesized mean** box.
4. Click **Options**.

In the 1-Sample t - Options dialog box:

5. Enter **95.0** in the **Confidence level** box.
6. Select **not equal** from the **Alternative** drop-down list.
7. Click **OK**.
8. Back in the original dialog box, click **OK**.

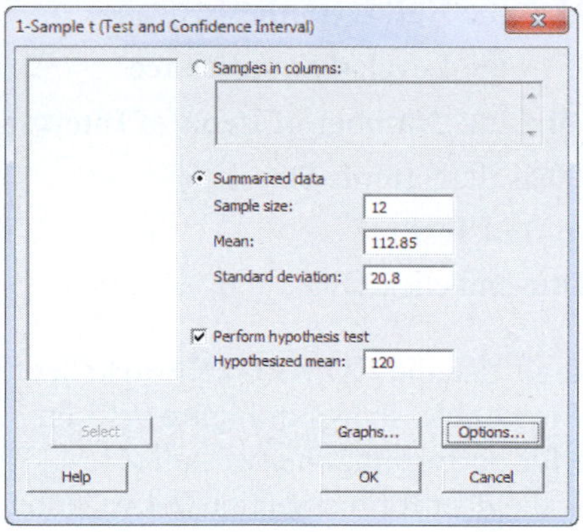

For problems that use unsummarized data, open the worksheet that contains the data and replace steps 1 and 2 with these steps:

1. Click **Samples in columns**.
2. Enter the name of the column containing the unsummarized in the **Samples in column** box.

To create a boxplot of the unsummarized data, replace step 8 with the following steps 8 through 10:

8. Back in the original dialog box, click **Graphs**.
9. In the 1-Sample t - Graphs dialog box, check **Boxplot of data** and then click **OK**.
10. Back in the original dialog box, click **OK.**

MG9.3 ONE-TAIL TESTS

To perform a one-tail test for **1-Sample Z**, select **less than** or **greater than** from the drop-down list in step 7 of the Section MG9.1 instructions.

To perform a one-tail test for **1-Sample t**, select **less than** or **greater than** from the drop-down list in step 6 of the Section MG9.2 instructions.

MG9.4 *Z* TEST of HYPOTHESIS for the PROPORTION

Use **1 Proportion** to perform the *Z* test of hypothesis for the proportion. For example, to perform the *Z* test for the Figure 9.15 vacation Internet access study example on page 351, select **Stat → Basic Statistics → 1 Proportion**. In the 1 Proportion (Test and Confidence Interval) dialog box (shown below):

1. Click **Summarized data**.
2. Enter **1540** in the **Number of events** box and **2000** in the **Number of trials** box.
3. Check **Perform hypothesis test** and enter **0.75** in the **Hypothesized proportion** box.
4. Click **Options**.

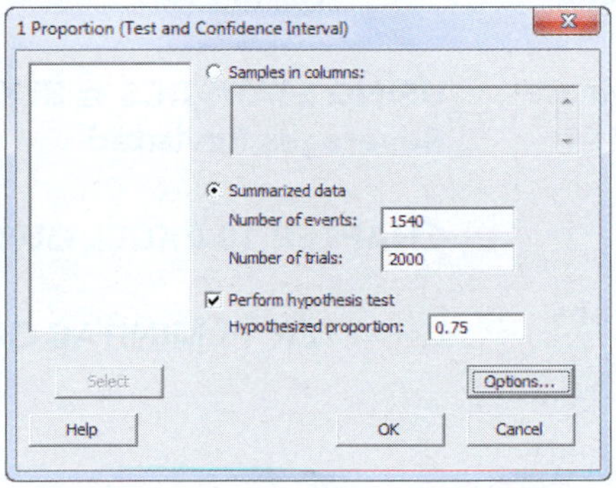

In the 1-Proportion - Options dialog box (shown in right column):

5. Enter **95.0** in the **Confidence level** box.
6. Select **not equal** from the **Alternative** drop-down list.
7. Check **Use test and interval based on normal distribution**.
8. Click **OK**.

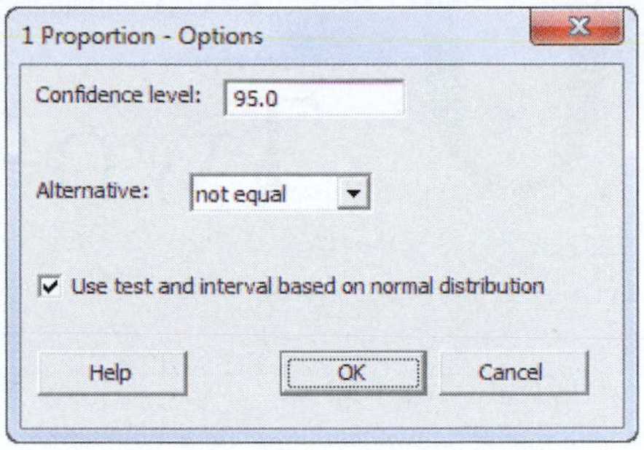

9. Back in the original dialog box, click **OK**.

To perform a one-tail test, select **less than** or **greater than** from the drop-down list in step 6. For problems that use unsummarized data, open the worksheet that contains the data and replace steps 1 and 2 with these steps:

1. Click **Samples in columns**.
2. Enter the name of the column containing the unsummarized in the **Samples in column** box.

10 Two-Sample Tests

Learning Objectives

In this chapter, you learn how to use hypothesis testing for comparing the difference between:

- The means of two independent populations
- The means of two related populations
- The proportions of two independent populations
- The variances of two independent populations

USING STATISTICS

@ BLK Beverages

Does the type of display used in a supermarket affect the sales of products? As the regional sales manager for BLK Beverages, you want to compare the sales volume of BLK Cola when the product is placed in the normal shelf location to the sales volume when the product is featured in a special end-aisle display. To test the effectiveness of the end-aisle displays, you select 20 stores from the Food Pride supermarket chain that all experience similar storewide sales volumes. You then randomly assign 10 of the 20 stores to sample 1 and 10 stores to sample 2. The managers of the 10 stores in sample 1 place the BLK Cola in the normal shelf location, alongside the other cola products. The 10 stores in sample 2 use the special end-aisle promotional display. At the end of one week, the sales of BLK Cola are recorded. How can you determine whether sales of BLK Cola using the end-aisle displays are the same as those when the cola is placed in the normal shelf location? How can you decide if the variability in BLK Cola sales from store to store is the same for the two types of displays? How could you use the answers to these questions to improve sales of BLK Cola?

Hypothesis testing provides a *confirmatory* approach to data analysis. In Chapter 9, you learned a variety of commonly used hypothesis-testing procedures that relate to a single sample of data selected from a single population. In this chapter, you learn how to extend hypothesis testing to **two-sample tests** that compare statistics from samples of data selected from two populations. One such test for the BLK Beverages scenario would be "Are the mean weekly sales of BLK Cola when using the normal shelf location (one population) equal to the mean weekly sales of BLK Cola when using an end-aisle display (a second population)?"

10.1 Comparing the Means of Two Independent Populations

Worksheet data for samples taken from two independent populations can be stored either in stacked or unstacked format, as discussed in Section 2.3. Examples throughout this chapter use unstacked data, although by using the techniques discussed in either Section EG2.3 (for Excel) or MG2.3 (for Minitab), you can rearrange unstacked data as stacked data or rearrange stacked data as unstacked data.

In Sections 8.1 and 9.1, you learned that in almost all cases, you would not know the population standard deviation of the population under study. Likewise, when you take a random sample from each of two independent populations, you almost always do not know the standard deviations of either population. However, you also need to know whether you can assume that the variances in the two populations are equal because the method you use to compare the means of each population depends on whether you can assume that the variances of the two populations are equal.

Pooled-Variance t Test for the Difference Between Two Means

If you assume that the random samples are independently selected from two populations and that the populations are normally distributed and have equal variances, you can use a **pooled-variance *t* test** to determine whether there is a significant difference between the means of the two populations. If the populations are not normally distributed, the pooled-variance *t* test can still be used if the sample sizes are large enough (typically ≥ 30 for each sample[1]).

Using subscripts to distinguish between the population mean of the first population, μ_1, and the population mean of the second population, μ_2, the null hypothesis of no difference in the means of two independent populations can be stated as

$$H_0: \mu_1 = \mu_2 \text{ or } \mu_1 - \mu_2 = 0$$

and the alternative hypothesis, that the means are not the same, can be stated as

$$H_1: \mu_1 \neq \mu_2 \text{ or } \mu_1 - \mu_2 \neq 0$$

To test the null hypothesis, use the pooled-variance *t* test statistic t_{STAT} shown in Equation (10.1). The pooled-variance *t* test gets its name from the fact that the test statistic pools, or combines, the two sample variances S_1^2 and S_2^2 to compute S_p^2, the best estimate of the variance common to both populations, under the assumption that the two population variances are equal.[2]

[1] Review the Section 7.4 discussion about the Central Limit Theorem on page 264 to understand more about "large enough" sample sizes.

[2] When the two sample sizes are equal (i.e., $n_1 = n_2$), the equation for the pooled variance can be simplified to

$$S_p^2 = \frac{S_1^2 + S_2^2}{2}$$

POOLED-VARIANCE *t* TEST FOR THE DIFFERENCE BETWEEN TWO MEANS

$$t_{STAT} = \frac{(\bar{X}_1 - \bar{X}_2) - (\mu_1 - \mu_2)}{\sqrt{S_p^2\left(\frac{1}{n_1} + \frac{1}{n_2}\right)}} \quad \textbf{(10.1)}$$

where

$$S_p^2 = \frac{(n_1 - 1)S_1^2 + (n_2 - 1)S_2^2}{(n_1 - 1) + (n_2 - 1)}$$

and

S_p^2 = pooled variance

$\bar{X}_1$ = mean of the sample taken from population 1

S_1^2 = variance of the sample taken from population 1

n_1 = size of the sample taken from population 1

$\bar{X}_2$ = mean of the sample taken from population 2

S_2^2 = variance of the sample taken from population 2

n_2 = size of the sample taken from population 2

The t_{STAT} test statistic follows a t distribution with $n_1 + n_2 - 2$ degrees of freedom.

For a given level of significance, α, in a two-tail test, you reject the null hypothesis if the computed t_{STAT} test statistic is greater than the upper-tail critical value from the t distribution or if the computed t_{STAT} test statistic is less than the lower-tail critical value from the t distribution. Figure 10.1 displays the regions of rejection.

FIGURE 10.1

Regions of rejection and nonrejection for the pooled-variance t test for the difference between the means (two-tail test)

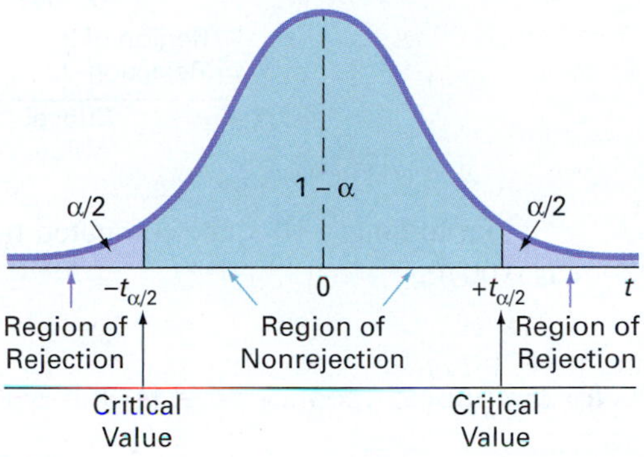

In a one-tail test in which the rejection region is in the lower tail, you reject the null hypothesis if the computed t_{STAT} test statistic is less than the lower-tail critical value from the t distribution. In a one-tail test in which the rejection region is in the upper tail, you reject the null hypothesis if the computed t_{STAT} test statistic is greater than the upper-tail critical value from the t distribution.

To demonstrate the pooled-variance t test, return to the BLK Beverages scenario on page 365. You define the business objective as determining whether the mean weekly sales of BLK Cola are the same when using a normal shelf location and when using an end-aisle display. There are two populations of interest. The first population is the set of all possible weekly sales of BLK Cola if all the Food Pride Supermarkets used the normal shelf location. The second population is the set of all possible weekly sales of BLK Cola if all the Food Pride Supermarkets used the end-aisle displays. You collect the data from a sample of 10 Food Pride Supermarkets that have been assigned a normal shelf location and another sample of 10 Food Pride Supermarkets that have been assigned an end-aisle display. You organize and store the results in Cola. Table 10.1 contains the BLK Cola sales (in number of cases) for the two samples.

TABLE 10.1

Comparing BLK Cola Weekly Sales from Two Different Display Locations (in number of cases)

Display Location									
Normal					**End-Aisle**				
22	34	52	62	30	52	71	76	54	67
40	64	84	56	59	83	66	90	77	84

The null and alternative hypotheses are

$$H_0: \mu_1 = \mu_2 \text{ or } \mu_1 - \mu_2 = 0$$

$$H_1: \mu_1 \neq \mu_2 \text{ or } \mu_1 - \mu_2 \neq 0$$

Assuming that the samples are from normal populations having equal variances, you can use the pooled-variance t test. The t_{STAT} test statistic follows a t distribution with $10 + 10 - 2 = 18$

degrees of freedom. Using an $\alpha = 0.05$ level of significance, you divide the rejection region into the two tails for this two-tail test (i.e., two equal parts of 0.025 each). Table E.3 shows that the critical values for this two-tail test are +2.1009 and −2.1009. As shown in Figure 10.2, the decision rule is

$$\text{Reject } H_0 \text{ if } t_{STAT} > +2.1009$$
$$\text{or if } t_{STAT} < -2.1009;$$
$$\text{otherwise do not reject } H_0.$$

FIGURE 10.2

Two-tail test of hypothesis for the difference between the means at the 0.05 level of significance with 18 degrees of freedom

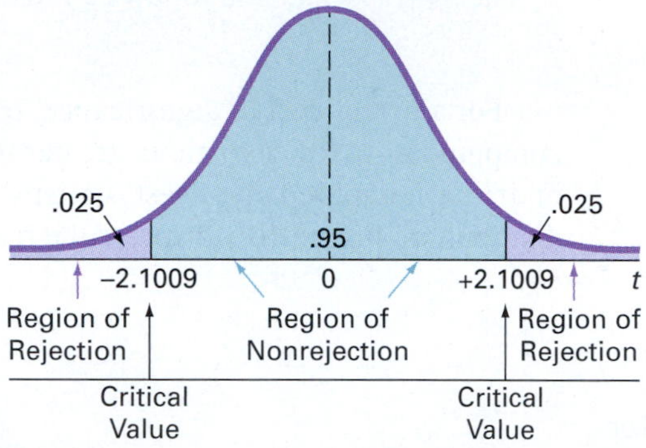

From Figure 10.3, the computed t_{STAT} test statistic for this test is −3.0446 and the p-value is 0.0070.

FIGURE 10.3

Excel and Minitab results for the pooled-variance t test for the BLK Cola display locations

	A	B	
1	Pooled-Variance *t* Test for the Difference Between Two Means		
2	(assumes equal population variances)		
3	**Data**		
4	Hypothesized Difference	0	
5	Level of Significance	0.05	
6	**Population 1 Sample**		
7	Sample Size	10	=COUNT(DATACOPY!$A:$A)
8	Sample Mean	50.3	=AVERAGE(DATACOPY!$A:$A)
9	Sample Standard Deviation	18.7264	=STDEV(DATACOPY!$A:$A)
10	**Population 2 Sample**		
11	Sample Size	10	=COUNT(DATACOPY!$B:$B)
12	Sample Mean	72	=AVERAGE(DATACOPY!$B:$B)
13	Sample Standard Deviation	12.5433	=STDEV(DATACOPY!$B:$B)
14			
15	Intermediate Calculations		
16	Population 1 Sample Degrees of Freedom	9	=B7 - 1
17	Population 2 Sample Degrees of Freedom	9	=B11 - 1
18	Total Degrees of Freedom	18	=B16 + B17
19	Pooled Variance	254.0056	=((B16 * B9^2) + (B17 * B13^2))/B18
20	Standard Error	7.1275	=SQRT(B19 * (1/B7 + 1/B11))
21	Difference in Sample Means	-21.7	=B8 - B12
22	*t* Test Statistic	-3.0446	=(B21 - B4)/B20
23			
24	**Two-Tail Test**		
25	Lower Critical Value	-2.1009	=-TINV(B5, B18)
26	Upper Critical Value	2.1009	=TINV(B5, B18)
27	*p*-Value	0.0070	=TDIST(ABS(B22), B18, 2)
28	Reject the null hypothesis		=IF(B27 < B5, "Reject the null hypothesis", "Do not reject the null hypothesis")

Two-Sample T-Test and CI: Normal, End-Aisle

```
Two-sample T for Normal vs End-Aisle

            N  Mean  StDev  SE Mean
Normal     10  50.3   18.7      5.9
End-Aisle  10  72.0   12.5      4.0

Difference = mu (Normal) - mu (End-Aisle)
Estimate for difference:  -21.70
95% CI for difference:  (-36.67, -6.73)
T-Test of difference = 0 (vs not =): T-Value = -3.04  P-Value = 0.007  DF = 18
Both use Pooled StDev = 15.9376
```

Using Equation (10.1) on page 366 and the descriptive statistics provided in Figure 10.3,

$$t_{STAT} = \frac{(\bar{X}_1 - \bar{X}_2) - (\mu_1 - \mu_2)}{\sqrt{S_p^2\left(\dfrac{1}{n_1} + \dfrac{1}{n_2}\right)}}$$

where

$$S_p^2 = \frac{(n_1 - 1)S_1^2 + (n_2 - 1)S_2^2}{(n_1 - 1) + (n_2 - 1)}$$
$$= \frac{9(18.7264)^2 + 9(12.5433)^2}{9 + 9} = 254.0056$$

Therefore,

$$t_{STAT} = \frac{(50.3 - 72.0) - 0.0}{\sqrt{254.0056\left(\frac{1}{10} + \frac{1}{10}\right)}} = \frac{-21.7}{\sqrt{50.801}} = -3.0446$$

You reject the null hypothesis because $t_{STAT} = -3.0446 < -2.1009$ and the p-value is 0.0070. In other words, the probability that $t_{STAT} > 3.0446$ or $t_{STAT} < -3.0446$ is equal to 0.0070. This p-value indicates that if the population means are equal, the probability of observing a difference this large or larger in the two sample means is only 0.0070. Because the p-value is less than $\alpha = 0.05$, there is sufficient evidence to reject the null hypothesis. You can conclude that the mean sales are different for the normal shelf location and the end-aisle location. Based on these results, the sales are lower for the normal location (i.e., higher for the end-aisle location).

In testing for the difference between the means, you assume that the populations are normally distributed, with equal variances. For situations in which the two populations have equal variances, the pooled-variance t test is **robust** (i.e., not sensitive) to moderate departures from the assumption of normality, provided that the sample sizes are large. In such situations, you can use the pooled-variance t test without serious effects on its power. However, if you cannot assume that both populations are normally distributed, you have two choices. You can use a nonparametric procedure, such as the Wilcoxon rank sum test (see Section 12.6), that does not depend on the assumption of normality for the two populations, or you can use a normalizing transformation (see reference 6) on each of the outcomes and then use the pooled-variance t test.

To check the assumption of normality in each of the two populations, construct the boxplot of the sales for the two display locations shown in Figure 10.4. For these two small samples, there appears to be only moderate departure from normality, so the assumption of normality needed for the t test is not seriously violated.

FIGURE 10.4

Excel and Minitab boxplots of the sales for the two display locations

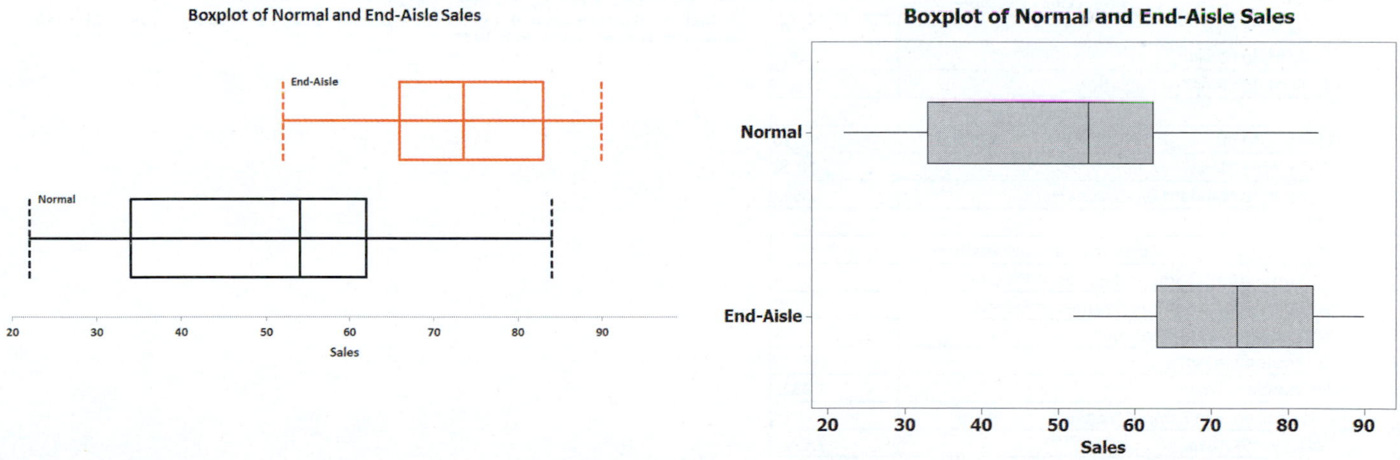

Example 10.1 provides another application of the pooled-variance t test.

EXAMPLE 10.1

Testing for the Difference in the Mean Delivery Times

You and some friends have decided to test the validity of an advertisement by a local pizza restaurant, which says it delivers to the dormitories faster than a local branch of a national chain. Both the local pizza restaurant and national chain are located across the street from your college campus. You define the variable of interest as the delivery time, in minutes, from the time the pizza is ordered to when it is delivered. You collect the data by ordering 10 pizzas from the local pizza restaurant and 10 pizzas from the national chain at different times. You organize and store the data in **PizzaTime**. Table 10.2 shows the delivery times.

TABLE 10.2

Delivery Times (in minutes) for Local Pizza Restaurant and National Pizza Chain

Local		Chain	
16.8	18.1	22.0	19.5
11.7	14.1	15.2	17.0
15.6	21.8	18.7	19.5
16.7	13.9	15.6	16.5
17.5	20.8	20.8	24.0

At the 0.05 level of significance, is there evidence that the mean delivery time for the local pizza restaurant is less than the mean delivery time for the national pizza chain?

SOLUTION Because you want to know whether the mean is *lower* for the local pizza restaurant than for the national pizza chain, you have a one-tail test with the following null and alternative hypotheses:

$H_0: \mu_1 \geq \mu_2$ (The mean delivery time for the local pizza restaurant is equal to or greater than the mean delivery time for the national pizza chain.)

$H_1: \mu_1 < \mu_2$ (The mean delivery time for the local pizza restaurant is less than the mean delivery time for the national pizza chain.)

Figure 10.5 displays the results for the pooled-variance *t* test for these data.

FIGURE 10.5

Excel and Minitab results for the pooled-variance *t* test for the pizza delivery time data

	A	B
1	Pooled-Variance *t* Test for the Difference Between Two Means	
2	(assumes equal population variances)	
3	Data	
4	Hypothesized Difference	0
5	Level of Significance	0.05
6	Population 1 Sample	
7	Sample Size	10
8	Sample Mean	16.7
9	Sample Standard Deviation	3.0955
10	Population 2 Sample	
11	Sample Size	10
12	Sample Mean	18.88
13	Sample Standard Deviation	2.8662
14		
15	Intermediate Calculations	
16	Population 1 Sample Degrees of Freedom	9
17	Population 2 Sample Degrees of Freedom	9
18	Total Degrees of Freedom	18
19	Pooled Variance	8.8987
20	Standard Error	1.3341
21	Difference in Sample Means	-2.18
22	*t* Test Statistic	-1.6341
23		
24	Lower-Tail Test	
25	Lower Critical Value	-1.7341
26	*p*-Value	0.0598
27	Do not reject the null hypothesis	

Two-Sample T-Test and CI: Local, Chain

```
Two-sample T for Local vs Chain

       N   Mean  StDev  SE Mean
Local  10  16.70   3.10     0.98
Chain  10  18.88   2.87     0.91

Difference = mu (Local) - mu (Chain)
Estimate for difference:  -2.18
95% upper bound for difference:  0.13
T-Test of difference = 0 (vs <): T-Value = -1.63  P-Value = 0.060  DF = 18
Both use Pooled StDev = 2.9831
```

To illustrate the computations, using Equation (10.1) on page 366,

$$t_{STAT} = \frac{(\bar{X}_1 - \bar{X}_2) - (\mu_1 - \mu_2)}{\sqrt{S_p^2\left(\frac{1}{n_1} + \frac{1}{n_2}\right)}}$$

where

$$S_p^2 = \frac{(n_1 - 1)S_1^2 + (n_2 - 1)S_2^2}{(n_1 - 1) + (n_2 - 1)}$$

$$= \frac{9(3.0955)^2 + 9(2.8662)^2}{9 + 9} = 8.8987$$

Therefore,

$$t_{STAT} = \frac{(16.7 - 18.88) - 0.0}{\sqrt{8.8987\left(\frac{1}{10} + \frac{1}{10}\right)}} = \frac{-2.18}{\sqrt{1.7797}} = -1.6341$$

You do not reject the null hypothesis because $t_{STAT} = -1.6341 > -1.7341$. The p-value (as computed in Figure 10.5) is 0.0598. This p-value indicates that the probability that $t_{STAT} < -1.6341$ is equal to 0.0598. In other words, if the population means are equal, the probability that the sample mean delivery time for the local pizza restaurant is at least 2.18 minutes faster than the national chain is 0.0598. Because the p-value is greater than $\alpha = 0.05$, there is insufficient evidence to reject the null hypothesis. Based on these results, there is insufficient evidence for the local pizza restaurant to make the advertising claim that it has a faster delivery time.

Confidence Interval Estimate for the Difference Between Two Means

Instead of, or in addition to, testing for the difference in the means of two independent populations, you can use Equation (10.2) to develop a confidence interval estimate of the difference in the means.

CONFIDENCE INTERVAL ESTIMATE FOR THE DIFFERENCE IN THE MEANS OF TWO INDEPENDENT POPULATIONS

$$(\bar{X}_1 - \bar{X}_2) \pm t_{\alpha/2}\sqrt{S_p^2\left(\frac{1}{n_1} + \frac{1}{n_2}\right)}$$

or

$$(\bar{X}_1 - \bar{X}_2) - t_{\alpha/2}\sqrt{S_p^2\left(\frac{1}{n_1} + \frac{1}{n_2}\right)} \leq \mu_1 - \mu_2 \leq (\bar{X}_1 - \bar{X}_2) + t_{\alpha/2}\sqrt{S_p^2\left(\frac{1}{n_1} + \frac{1}{n_2}\right)} \quad \textbf{(10.2)}$$

where $t_{\alpha/2}$ is the critical value of the t distribution, with $n_1 + n_2 - 2$ degrees of freedom, for an area of $\alpha/2$ in the upper tail.

For the sample statistics pertaining to the two aisle locations reported in Figure 10.3 on page 368, using 95% confidence, and Equation (10.2),

$\bar{X}_1 = 50.3, n_1 = 10, \bar{X}_2 = 72.0, n_2 = 10, S_p^2 = 254.0056$, and with $10 + 10 - 2$

$= 18$ degrees of freedom, $t_{0.025} = 2.1009$

$$(50.3 - 72.0) \pm (2.1009)\sqrt{254.0056\left(\frac{1}{10} + \frac{1}{10}\right)}$$

$$-21.7 \pm (2.1009)(7.1275)$$

$$-21.7 \pm 14.97$$

$$-36.67 \leq \mu_1 - \mu_2 \leq -6.73$$

Therefore, you are 95% confident that the difference in mean sales between the normal aisle location and the end-aisle location is between −36.67 cases of cola and −6.73 cases of cola. In other words, the end-aisle location sells, on average, 6.73 to 36.67 cases more than the normal aisle location. From a hypothesis-testing perspective, because the interval does not include zero, you reject the null hypothesis of no difference between the means of the two populations.

t Test for the Difference Between Two Means, Assuming Unequal Variances

If you cannot make the assumption that the two independent populations have equal variances, you cannot pool the two sample variances into the common estimate S_p^2 and therefore cannot use the pooled-variance t test. Instead, you use the **separate-variance t test** developed by Satterthwaite (see reference 5). Equation (10.3) defines the test statistic for the separate-variance t test.

SEPARATE-VARIANCE t TEST FOR THE DIFFERENCE BETWEEN TWO MEANS

$$t_{STAT} = \frac{(\overline{X}_1 - \overline{X}_2) - (\mu_1 - \mu_2)}{\sqrt{\dfrac{S_1^2}{n_1} + \dfrac{S_2^2}{n_2}}} \tag{10.3}$$

where

$\overline{X}_1$ = mean of the sample taken from population 1

S_1^2 = variance of the sample taken from population 1

n_1 = size of the sample taken from population 1

$\overline{X}_2$ = mean of the sample taken from population 2

S_2^2 = variance of the sample taken from population 2

n_2 = size of the sample taken from population 2

The separate-variance t test statistic approximately follows a t distribution with V degrees of freedom equal to the integer portion of the following computation.

COMPUTING DEGREES OF FREEDOM IN THE SEPARATE-VARIANCE t TEST

$$V = \frac{\left(\dfrac{S_1^2}{n_1} + \dfrac{S_2^2}{n_2}\right)^2}{\dfrac{\left(\dfrac{S_1^2}{n_1}\right)^2}{n_1 - 1} + \dfrac{\left(\dfrac{S_2^2}{n_2}\right)^2}{n_2 - 1}} \tag{10.4}$$

For a given level of significance α, you reject the null hypothesis if the computed t test statistic is greater than the upper-tail critical value $t_{a/2}$ from the t distribution with V degrees of freedom or if the computed t test statistic is less than the lower-tail critical value $-t_{a/2}$ from the t distribution with V degrees of freedom. Thus, the decision rule is

$$\text{Reject } H_0 \text{ if } t > t_{a/2}$$
$$\text{or if } t < -t_{a/2};$$
$$\text{otherwise, do not reject } H_0.$$

Recall the Using Statistics scenario for this chapter that concerned the display location of BLK Cola. Using Equation (10.4), the separate-variance t test statistic t_{STAT} is approximated by a t distribution with $V = 15$ degrees of freedom, the integer portion of the following computation:

$$V = \frac{\left(\dfrac{S_1^2}{n_1} + \dfrac{S_2^2}{n_2}\right)^2}{\dfrac{\left(\dfrac{S_1^2}{n_1}\right)^2}{n_1 - 1} + \dfrac{\left(\dfrac{S_2^2}{n_2}\right)^2}{n_2 - 1}}$$

$$= \frac{\left(\frac{350.6778}{10} + \frac{157.3333}{10}\right)^2}{\frac{\left(\frac{350.6778}{10}\right)^2}{9} + \frac{\left(\frac{157.3333}{10}\right)^2}{9}} = 15.72$$

Using $\alpha = 0.05$, the upper and lower critical values for this two-tail test found in Table E.3 are +2.1315 and −2.1315. As depicted in Figure 10.6, the decision rule is

Reject H_0 if $t_{STAT} > +2.1315$

or if $t_{STAT} < -2.1315$;

otherwise do not reject H_0.

FIGURE 10.6

Two-tail test of hypothesis for the difference between the means at the 0.05 level of significance with 15 degrees of freedom

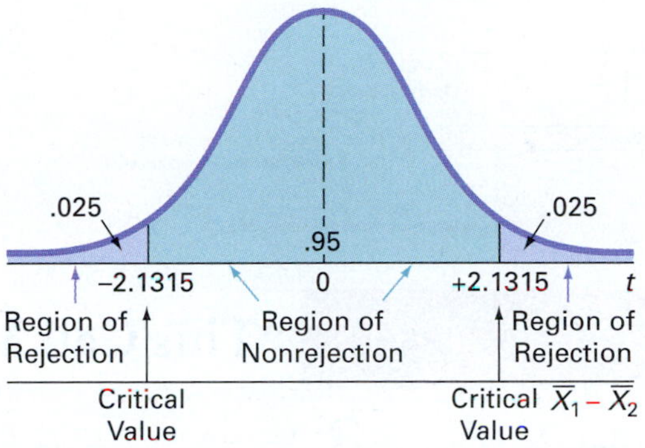

Using Equation (10.3) on page 372 and the descriptive statistics provided in Figure 10.3,

$$t_{STAT} = \frac{(\bar{X}_1 - \bar{X}_2) - (\mu_1 - \mu_2)}{\sqrt{\frac{S_1^2}{n_1} + \frac{S_2^2}{n_2}}}$$

$$= \frac{50.3 - 72}{\sqrt{\left(\frac{350.6778}{10} + \frac{157.3333}{10}\right)}} = \frac{-21.7}{\sqrt{50.801}} = -3.04$$

Using a 0.05 level of significance, you reject the null hypothesis because $t = -3.04 < -2.1315$. Figure 10.7 on page 374 displays the separate-variance t test results for the display location data.

In Figure 10.7, the test statistic $t_{STAT} = -3.0446$ and the p-value is $0.0082 < 0.05$. Thus, the results for the separate-variance t test are almost exactly the same as those of the pooled-variance t test. The assumption of equality of population variances had no appreciable effect on the results. Sometimes, however, the results from the pooled-variance and separate-variance t tests conflict because the assumption of equal variances is violated. Therefore, it is important that you evaluate the assumptions and use those results as a guide in selecting a test procedure. In Section 10.4, the F test for the ratio of two variances is used to determine whether there is evidence of a difference in the two population variances. The results of that test can help you determine which of the t tests—pooled-variance or separate-variance—is more appropriate.

FIGURE 10.7

Excel and Minitab results for the separate-variance *t* test for the display location data

	A	B	
1	Separate-Variances *t* Test for the Difference Between Two Means		
2	(assumes unequal population variances)		
3	Data		
4	Hypothesized Difference	0	
5	Level of Significance	0.05	
6	Population 1 Sample		
7	Sample Size	10	=COUNT(DATACOPY!$A:$A)
8	Sample Mean	50.3	=AVERAGE(DATACOPY!$A:$A)
9	Sample Standard Deviation	18.7264	=STDEV(DATACOPY!$A:$A)
10	Population 2 Sample		
11	Sample Size	10	=COUNT(DATACOPY!$B:$B)
12	Sample Mean	72	=AVERAGE(DATACOPY!$B:$B)
13	Sample Standard Deviation	12.5433	=STDEV(DATACOPY!$B:$B)
14			
15	Intermediate Calculations		
16	Numerator of Degrees of Freedom	2580.7529	=(E18 + E19)^2
17	Denominator of Degrees of Freedom	164.1430	=(E18^2)/(B7 - 1) + (E19^2)/(B11 - 1)
18	Total Degrees of Freedom	15.7226	=B16/B17
19	Degrees of Freedom	15	=INT(B18)
20	Standard Error	7.1275	=SQRT(E18 + E19)
21	Difference in Sample Means	-21.7	=B8 - B12
22	Separate-Variance *t* Test Statistic	-3.0446	=B21/B20
23			
24	Two-Tail Test		
25	Lower Critical Value	-2.1314	=-TINV(B5, B19)
26	Upper Critical Value	2.1314	=TINV(B5, B19)
27	*p*-Value	0.0082	=TDIST(ABS(B22), B19, 2)
28	Reject the null hypothesis		=IF(B27 < B5, "Reject the null hypothesis", "Do not reject the null hypothesis")

Not shown
The Calculations Area in cell range D15:E22

Two-Sample T-Test and CI: Normal, End-Aisle

```
Two-sample T for Normal vs End-Aisle

             N  Mean  StDev  SE Mean
Normal      10  50.3   18.7      5.9
End-Aisle   10  72.0   12.5      4.0

Difference = mu (Normal) - mu (End-Aisle)
Estimate for difference:  -21.70
95% CI for difference:  (-36.89, -6.51)
T-Test of difference = 0 (vs not =): T-Value = -3.04  P-Value = 0.008  DF = 15
```

THINK ABOUT THIS "This Call May Be Monitored ... "

When talking with a customer service representative by phone, you may have heard a "This call may be monitored ... " message. Typically, the message explains that the monitoring is for "quality assurance purposes," but do companies really monitor your calls to improve quality?

From a past student, we've discovered that at least one large financial services company really does monitor the quality of calls. This student was asked to develop an improved training program for a call center that was hiring people to answer phone calls customers make about outstanding loans. For feedback and evaluation, she planned to randomly select phone calls received by each new employee and rate the employee on 10 aspects of the call, including whether the employee maintained a pleasant tone with the customer.

Who You Gonna Call?

The former student presented her plan to her boss for approval, but her boss, quoting a famous statistician, said, "In God we trust, all others must bring data." *Her boss wanted proof that her new training program would improve customer service.* Faced with this request, who would you call? She called her business statistics professor, one of the co-authors of this book. "Hey, Professor, you'll never believe why I called. I work for a large company, and in the project I am currently working on, I have to put some of the statistics you taught us to work! Can you help?" Together they formulated this test:

- Randomly assign the 60 most recent hires to two training programs. Assign half to the preexisting training program and the other half to the new training program.
- At the end of the first month, compare the mean score for the 30 employees in the new training program against the mean score for the 30 employees in the preexisting training program.

She listened as her professor explained, "What you are trying to show is that the mean score from the new training program is higher than the mean score from the current program. You can make the null hypothesis that the means are equal and see if you can reject it in favor of the alternative that the mean score from the new program is higher."

"Or, as you used to say, 'if the *p*-value is low, H_0 must go!'—yes, I do remember!" she replied. Her professor chuckled and added, "If you can reject H_0, you will have the evidence to present to your boss." She thanked him for his help and got back to work, with the newfound confidence that she would be able to successfully apply the *t* test that compares the means of two independent populations.

Problems for Section 10.1

LEARNING THE BASICS

10.1 If you have samples of $n_1 = 12$ and $n_2 = 15$, in performing the pooled-variance *t* test, how many degrees of freedom do you have?

10.2 Assume that you have a sample of $n_1 = 8$, with the sample mean $\bar{X}_1 = 42$, and a sample standard deviation $S_1 = 4$, and you have an independent sample of $n_2 = 15$ from another population with a sample mean of $\bar{X}_2 = 34$ and a sample standard deviation $S_2 = 5$.

a. What is the value of the pooled-variance t_{STAT} test statistic for testing $H_0: \mu_1 = \mu_2$?

b. In finding the critical value, how many degrees of freedom are there?

c. Using the level of significance $\alpha = 0.01$, what is the critical value for a one-tail test of the hypothesis $H_0: \mu_1 \leq \mu_2$ against the alternative, $H_1: \mu_1 > \mu_2$?

d. What is your statistical decision?

10.3 What assumptions about the two populations are necessary in Problem 10.2?

10.4 Referring to Problem 10.2, construct a 95% confidence interval estimate of the population mean difference between μ_1 and μ_2.

10.5 Referring to Problem 10.2, if $n_1 = 5$ and $n_2 = 4$, how many degrees of freedom do you have?

10.6 Referring to Problem 10.2, if $n_1 = 5$ and $n_2 = 4$, at the 0.01 level of significance, is there evidence that $\mu_1 > \mu_2$?

APPLYING THE CONCEPTS

10.7 According to a recent study, when shopping online for luxury goods, men spend a mean of $2,401, whereas women spend a mean of $1,527. (Data extracted from R. A. Smith, "Fashion Online: Retailers Tackle the Gender Gap," *The Wall Street Journal*, March 13, 2008, pp. D1, D10.) Suppose that the study was based on a sample of 600 men and 700 females, and the standard deviation of the amount spent was $1,200 for men and $1,000 for women.

a. State the null and alternative hypothesis if you want to determine whether the mean amount spent is higher for men than for women.

b. In the context of this study, what is the meaning of the Type I error?

c. In the context of this study, what is the meaning of the Type II error?

d. At the 0.01 level of significance, is there evidence that the mean amount spent is higher for men than for women?

10.8 A recent study ("Snack Ads Spur Children to Eat More," *The New York Times*, July 20, 2009, p. B3) found that children who watched a cartoon with food advertising ate, on average, 28.5 grams of Goldfish crackers as compared to an average of 19.7 grams of Goldfish crackers for children who watched a cartoon without food advertising. Although there were 118 children in the study, neither the sample size in each group nor the sample standard deviations were reported. Suppose that there were 59 children in each group, and the sample standard deviation for those children who watched the food ad was 8.6 grams and the sample standard deviation for those children who did not watch the food ad was 7.9 grams.

a. Assuming that the population variances are equal and $\alpha = 0.05$, is there evidence that the mean amount of Goldfish crackers eaten was significantly higher for the children who watched food ads?

b. Assuming that the population variances are equal, construct a 95% confidence interval estimate of the difference between the mean amount of Goldfish crackers eaten by the children who watched and did not watch the food ad.

c. Compare the results of (a) and (b) and discuss.

10.9 A problem with a telephone line that prevents a customer from receiving or making calls is upsetting to both the customer and the telephone company. The file **Phone** contains samples of 20 problems reported to two different offices of a telephone company and the time to clear these problems (in minutes) from the customers' lines:

Central Office I Time to Clear Problems (minutes)

1.48	1.75	0.78	2.85	0.52	1.60	4.15	3.97	1.48	3.10
1.02	0.53	0.93	1.60	0.80	1.05	6.32	3.93	5.45	0.97

Central Office II Time to Clear Problems (minutes)

7.55	3.75	0.10	1.10	0.60	0.52	3.30	2.10	0.58	4.02
3.75	0.65	1.92	0.60	1.53	4.23	0.08	1.48	1.65	0.72

a. Assuming that the population variances from both offices are equal, is there evidence of a difference in the mean waiting time between the two offices? (Use $\alpha = 0.05$.)

b. Find the p-value in (a) and interpret its meaning.

c. What other assumption is necessary in (a)?

d. Assuming that the population variances from both offices are equal, construct and interpret a 95% confidence interval estimate of the difference between the population means in the two offices.

SELF Test **10.10** The Computer Anxiety Rating Scale (CARS) measures an individual's level of computer anxiety, on a scale from 20 (no anxiety) to 100 (highest level of anxiety). Researchers at Miami University administered CARS to 172 business students. One of the objectives of the study was to determine whether there is a difference in the level of computer anxiety experienced by female and male business students. They found the following:

	Males	Females
$\bar{X}$	40.26	36.85
S	13.35	9.42
n	100	72

Source: Data extracted from T. Broome and D. Havelka, "Determinants of Computer Anxiety in Business Students," *The Review of Business Information Systems*, Spring 2002, 6(2), pp. 9–16.

a. At the 0.05 level of significance, is there evidence of a difference in the mean computer anxiety experienced by female and male business students?

b. Determine the p-value and interpret its meaning.

c. What assumptions do you have to make about the two populations in order to justify the use of the t test?

10.11 An important feature of digital cameras is battery life, the number of shots that can be taken before the battery needs to be recharged. The file **DigitalCameras** contains the battery life of 29 subcompact cameras and 16 compact cameras. (Data extracted from "Digital Cameras," *Consumer Reports*, July 2009, pp. 28–29.)

a. Assuming that the population variances from both types of digital cameras are equal, is there evidence of a difference in the mean battery life between the two types of digital cameras ($\alpha = 0.05$)?

b. Determine the p-value in (a) and interpret its meaning.

c. Assuming that the population variances from both types of digital cameras are equal, construct and interpret a 95% confidence interval estimate of the difference between the population mean battery life of the two types of digital cameras.

10.12 A bank with a branch located in a commercial district of a city has the business objective of developing an improved process for serving customers during the noon-to-1 P.M. lunch period. Management decides to first study the waiting time in the current process. The waiting time is defined as the time that elapses from when the customer enters the line until he or she reaches the teller window. Data are collected from a random sample of 15 customers, and the results (in minutes) are as follows (and stored in **Bank1**):

4.21 5.55 3.02 5.13 4.77 2.34 3.54 3.20
4.50 6.10 0.38 5.12 6.46 6.19 3.79

Suppose that another branch, located in a residential area, is also concerned with improving the process of serving customers in the noon-to-1 P.M. lunch period. Data are collected from a random sample of 15 customers, and the results are as follows (and stored in **Bank2**):

9.66 5.90 8.02 5.79 8.73 3.82 8.01 8.35
10.49 6.68 5.64 4.08 6.17 9.91 5.47

a. Assuming that the population variances from both banks are equal, is there evidence of a difference in the mean waiting time between the two branches? (Use $\alpha = 0.05$.)

b. Determine the p-value in (a) and interpret its meaning.

c. In addition to equal variances, what other assumption is necessary in (a)?

d. Construct and interpret a 95% confidence interval estimate of the difference between the population means in the two branches.

10.13 Repeat Problem 10.12 (a), assuming that the population variances in the two branches are not equal. Compare the results with those of Problem 10.12 (a).

10.14 In intaglio printing, a design or figure is carved beneath the surface of hard metal or stone. The business objective of an intaglio printing company is to determine whether there are differences in the mean surface hardness of steel plates, based on two different surface conditions—untreated and treated by lightly polishing with emery paper. An experiment is designed in which 40 steel plates are randomly assigned—20 plates are untreated and 20 plates are treated. The results of the experiment (stored in **Intaglio**) are as follows:

Untreated		Treated	
164.368	177.135	158.239	150.226
159.018	163.903	138.216	155.620
153.871	167.802	168.006	151.233
165.096	160.818	149.654	158.653
157.184	167.433	145.456	151.204
154.496	163.538	168.178	150.869
160.920	164.525	154.321	161.657
164.917	171.230	162.763	157.016
169.091	174.964	161.020	156.670
175.276	166.311	167.706	147.920

a. Assuming that the population variances from both conditions are equal, is there evidence of a difference in the mean surface hardness between untreated and treated steel plates? (Use $\alpha = 0.05$.)

b. Determine the p-value in (a) and interpret its meaning.

c. In addition to equal variances, what other assumption is necessary in (a)?

d. Construct and interpret a 95% confidence interval estimate of the difference between the population means from treated and untreated steel plates.

10.15 Repeat Problem 10.14 (a), assuming that the population variances from untreated and treated steel plates are not equal. Compare the results with those of Problem 10.14 (a).

10.16 Do young children use cell phones? Apparently so, according to a recent study (A. Ross, "Message to Santa; Kids Want a Phone," *Palm Beach Post*, December 16, 2008, pp. 1A, 4A), which stated that cell phone users under 12 years of age averaged 137 calls per month as compared to 231 calls per month for cell phone users 13 to 17 years of age. No sample sizes were reported. Suppose that the results were based on samples of 50 cell phone users in each group and that the sample standard deviation for cell phone users under 12 years of age was 51.7 calls per month and the sample standard deviation for cell phone users 13 to 17 years of age was 67.6 calls per month.

a. Assuming that the variances in the populations of cell phone users are equal, is there evidence of a difference in the mean cell phone usage between cell phone users under 12 years of age and cell phone users 13 to 17 years of age? (Use a 0.05 level of significance.)

b. In addition to equal variances, what other assumption is necessary in (a)?

10.17 Nondestructive evaluation is a method that is used to describe the properties of components or materials without causing any permanent physical change to the units. It includes the determination of properties of materials and the classification of flaws by size, shape, type, and location. This method is most effective for detecting surface flaws and characterizing surface properties of electrically conductive materials. Data were collected that classified each component as having a flaw or not, based on manual inspection and operator judgment, and the data also reported the size of the crack in the material. Do the components classified as unflawed have a smaller mean crack size than components classified as flawed? The results in terms of crack size (in inches) are stored in **Crack**. (Data extracted from B. D. Olin and W. Q. Meeker, "Applications of Statistical Methods to Nondestructive Evaluation," *Technometrics*, 38, 1996, p. 101.)

a. Assuming that the population variances are equal, is there evidence that the mean crack size is smaller for the unflawed specimens than for the flawed specimens? (Use $\alpha = 0.05$.)

b. Repeat (a), assuming that the population variances are not equal.

c. Compare the results of (a) and (b).

10.2 Comparing the Means of Two Related Populations

The hypothesis-testing procedures presented in Section 10.1 enable you to make comparisons and examine differences in the means of two *independent* populations. In this section, you will learn about a procedure for analyzing the difference between the means of two populations when you collect sample data from populations that are related—that is, when results of the first population are *not* independent of the results of the second population.

There are two situations that involve related data between populations. Either you take repeated measurements from the same set of items or individuals or you match items or individuals according to some characteristic. In either situation, you are interested in the *difference between the two related values* rather than the *individual values* themselves.

When you take **repeated measurements** on the same items or individuals, you assume that the same items or individuals will behave alike if treated alike. Your objective is to show that any differences between two measurements of the same items or individuals are due to different treatment conditions. For example, when performing a taste-testing experiment comparing two beverages, you can use each person in the sample as his or her own control so that you can have *repeated measurements* on the same individual.

Another example of repeated measurements involves the pricing of the same goods from two different vendors. For example, have you ever wondered whether new textbook prices at a local college bookstore are different from the prices offered at a major online retailer? You could take two independent samples, that is, select two different sets of textbooks, and then use the hypothesis tests discussed in Section 10.1.

However, by random chance, the first sample may have many large-format hardcover textbooks and the second sample may have many small trade paperback books. This would imply that the first set of textbooks will always be more expensive than the second set of textbooks, regardless of where they are purchased. That observation means that using the Section 10.1 tests would not be a good choice. The better choice would be to use two related samples, that is, to determine the price of the same sample of textbooks at both the local bookstore and the online retailer.

The second situation that involves related data between populations is when you have **matched samples**. Here items or individuals are paired together according to some characteristic of interest. For example, in test marketing a product in two different advertising campaigns, a sample of test markets can be *matched* on the basis of the test market population size and/or demographic variables. By accounting for the differences in test market population size and/or demographic variables, you are better able to measure the effects of the two different advertising campaigns.

Regardless of whether you have matched samples or repeated measurements, the objective is to study the difference between two measurements by reducing the effect of the variability that is due to the items or individuals themselves. Table 10.3 shows the differences in the individual values for two related populations. To read this table, let $X_{11}, X_{12}, \ldots, X_{1n}$ represent the n values from a sample. And let $X_{21}, X_{22}, \ldots, X_{2n}$ represent either the corresponding n matched values from a second sample or the corresponding n repeated measurements from the initial sample. Then, $D_1, D_2, \ldots, D_n$ will represent the corresponding set of n difference *scores* such that

$$D_1 = X_{11} - X_{21}, D_2 = X_{12} - X_{22}, \ldots, \text{and } D_n = X_{1n} - X_{2n}.$$

To test for the mean difference between two related populations, you treat the difference scores, each D_i, as values from a single sample.

TABLE 10.3

Determining the Difference Between Two Related Samples

	Sample		
Value	1	2	Difference
1	X_{11}	X_{21}	$D_1 = X_{11} - X_{21}$
2	X_{12}	X_{22}	$D_2 = X_{12} - X_{22}$
.	.	.	.
.	.	.	.
.	.	.	.
i	X_{1i}	X_{2i}	$D_i = X_{1i} - X_{2i}$
.	.	.	.
.	.	.	.
.	.	.	.
n	X_{1n}	X_{2n}	$D_n = X_{1n} - X_{2n}$

Paired t Test

If you assume that the difference scores are randomly and independently selected from a population that is normally distributed, you can use the **paired *t* test for the mean difference** in related populations to determine if there is a significant population mean difference. As with the one-sample t test developed in Section 9.2 [see Equation (9.2) on page 338], the paired t test statistic follows the t distribution with $n - 1$ degrees of freedom. Although the paired t test assumes that the population is normally distributed, you can use this test as long as the sample size is not very small and the population is not highly skewed.

To test the null hypothesis that there is no difference in the means of two related populations:

$$H_0\colon \mu_D = 0 \text{ (where } \mu_D = \mu_1 - \mu_2)$$

against the alternative that the means are not the same:

$$H_1\colon \mu_D \neq 0$$

you compute the t_{STAT} test statistic using Equation (10.5).

PAIRED t TEST FOR THE MEAN DIFFERENCE

$$t_{STAT} = \frac{\overline{D} - \mu_D}{\dfrac{S_D}{\sqrt{n}}} \qquad \textbf{(10.5)}$$

where

$$\mu_D = \text{hypothesized mean difference}$$

$$\overline{D} = \frac{\sum_{i=1}^{n} D_i}{n}$$

$$S_D = \sqrt{\frac{\sum_{i=1}^{n}(D_i - \overline{D})^2}{n - 1}}$$

The t_{STAT} test statistic follows a t distribution with $n - 1$ degrees of freedom.

For a two-tail test with a given level of significance, α, you reject the null hypothesis if the computed t_{STAT} test statistic is greater than the upper-tail critical value $t_{\alpha/2}$ from the t distribution, or if the computed t_{STAT} test statistic is less than the lower-tail critical value $-t_{\alpha/2}$ from the t distribution. The decision rule is

$$\text{Reject } H_0 \text{ if } t_{STAT} > t_{\alpha/2}$$
$$\text{or if } t_{STAT} < -t_{\alpha/2};$$
$$\text{otherwise, do not reject } H_0.$$

You can use the paired t test for the mean difference to investigate a question raised earlier in this section: Are new textbook prices at a local college bookstore different from the prices offered at a major online retailer?

In this repeated-measurements experiment, you use one set of textbooks. For each textbook, you determine the price at the local bookstore and the price at the online retailer. By determining the two prices for the same textbooks, you can reduce the variability in the prices compared with what would occur if you used two independent sets of textbooks. This approach focuses on the differences between the prices of the same textbooks offered by the two retailers.

You collect data by conducting an experiment from a sample of $n = 19$ textbooks used primarily in business school courses during the summer 2010 semester at a local college. You determine the college bookstore price and the online price (which includes shipping costs, if any). You organize and store the data in **BookPrices**. Table 10.4 shows the results.

TABLE 10.4

Prices of Textbooks at the College Bookstore and at an Online Retailer

Author	Title	Bookstore	Online
Pride	Business 10/e	132.75	136.91
Carroll	Business and Society	201.50	178.58
Quinn	Ethics for the Information Age	80.00	65.00
Bade	Foundations of Microeconomics 5/e	153.50	120.43
Case	Principles of Macroeconomics 9/e	153.50	217.99
Brigham	Financial Management 13/e	216.00	197.10
Griffin	Organizational Behavior 9/e	199.75	168.71
George	Understanding and Managing Organizational Behavior 5/e	147.00	178.63
Grewal	Marketing 2/e	132.00	95.89
Barlow	Abnormal Psychology	182.25	145.49
Foner	Give Me Liberty: Seagull Ed. (V2) 2/e	45.50	37.60
Federer	Mathematical Interest Theory 2/e	89.95	91.69
Hoyle	Advanced Accounting 9/e	123.02	148.41
Haviland	Talking About People 4/e	57.50	53.93
Fuller	Information Systems Project Management	88.25	83.69
Pindyck	Macroeconomics 7/e	189.25	133.32
Mankiw	Macroeconomics 7/e	179.25	151.48
Shapiro	Multinational Financial Management 9/e	210.25	147.30
Losco	American Government 2010 Edition	66.75	55.16

Your objective is to determine whether there is any difference in the mean textbook price between the college bookstore and the online retailer. In other words, is there evidence that the mean price is different between the two sellers of textbooks? Thus, the null and alternative hypotheses are

$H_0: \mu_D = 0$ (There is no difference in the mean price between the college bookstore and the online retailer.)

$H_1: \mu_D \neq 0$ (There is a difference in the mean price between the college bookstore and online retailer.)

Choosing the level of significance $\alpha = 0.05$ and assuming that the differences are normally distributed, you use the paired t test [Equation (10.5)]. For a sample of $n = 19$ textbooks, there are $n - 1 = 18$ degrees of freedom. Using Table E.3, the decision rule is

$$\text{Reject } H_0 \text{ if } t_{STAT} > 2.1009$$
$$\text{or if } t_{STAT} < -2.1009;$$
$$\text{otherwise, do not reject } H_0.$$

For the $n = 19$ differences (see Table 10.4), the sample mean difference is

$$\overline{D} = \frac{\sum_{i=1}^{n} D_i}{n} = \frac{240.66}{19} = 12.6663$$

and

$$S_D = \sqrt{\frac{\sum_{i=1}^{n}(D_i - \overline{D})^2}{n-1}} = 30.4488$$

From Equation (10.5) on page 378,

$$t_{STAT} = \frac{\overline{D} - \mu_D}{\dfrac{S_D}{\sqrt{n}}} = \frac{12.6663 - 0}{\dfrac{30.4488}{\sqrt{19}}} = 1.8132$$

Because $-2.1009 < t_{STAT} = 1.8132 < 2.1009$, you do not reject the null hypothesis, H_0 (see Figure 10.8). There is insufficient evidence of a difference in the mean price of textbooks purchased at the college bookstore and the online retailer.

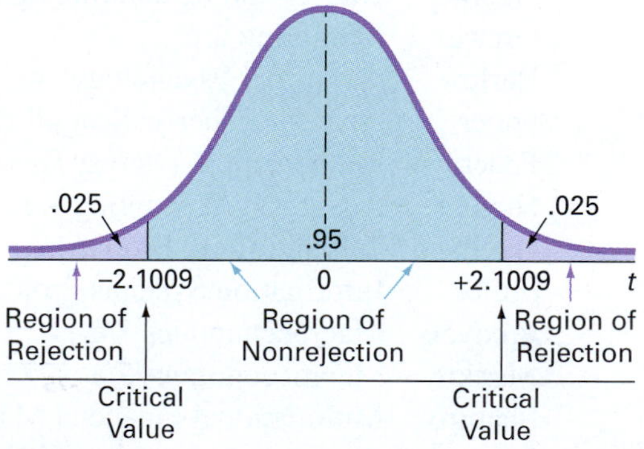

FIGURE 10.8
Two-tail paired t test at the 0.05 level of significance with 18 degrees of freedom

Figure 10.9 presents the results for this example, computing both the t test statistic and the p-value. Because the p-value $= 0.0865 > \alpha = 0.05$, you do not reject H_0. The p-value indicates that if the two sources for textbooks have the same population mean price, the probability that one source would have a sample mean \$12.67 more than the other is 0.0865. Because this probability is greater than $\alpha = 0.05$, you conclude that there is insufficient evidence to reject the null hypothesis.

FIGURE 10.9

Excel and Minitab paired *t* test results for the textbook price data

	A	B	
1	**Paired *t* Test**		
2			
3	**Data**		
4	Hypothesized Mean Diff.	0	
5	Level of significance	0.05	
6			
7	Intermediate Calculations		
8	Sample Size	19	=COUNT(PtCalcs!A:A)
9	DBar	12.6663	=AVERAGE(PtCalcs!C:C)
10	degrees of freedom	18	=B8 - 1
11	S_D	30.4488	=SQRT(SUM(PtCalcs!D:D)/B10)
12	Standard Error	6.9854	=B11/SQRT(A7)
13	*t* Test Statistic	1.8132	=(B9 - B4)/B12
14			
15	**Two-Tail Test**		
16	Lower Critical Value	-2.1009	=-TINV(B5, B10)
17	Upper Critical Value	2.1009	=TINV(B5, B10)
18	*p*-Value	0.0865	=TDIST(ABS(B13), B10, 2)
19	Do not reject the null hypothesis		=IF(B18 < B5, D27, D28)

Not shown
Cell D27: Reject the null hypothesis
Cell D28: Do not reject the null hypothesis

Paired T-Test and CI: Bookstore, Online

```
Paired T for Bookstore - Online

             N   Mean  StDev  SE Mean
Bookstore   19  139.4   55.0     12.6
Online      19  126.7   52.0     11.9
Difference  19  12.67  30.45     6.99

95% CI for mean difference: (-2.01, 27.34)
T-Test of mean difference = 0 (vs not = 0): T-Value = 1.81  P-Value = 0.087
```

To evaluate the validity of the assumption of normality, you construct a boxplot of the differences, as shown in Figure 10.10.

FIGURE 10.10

Excel and Minitab boxplots for the textbook price data

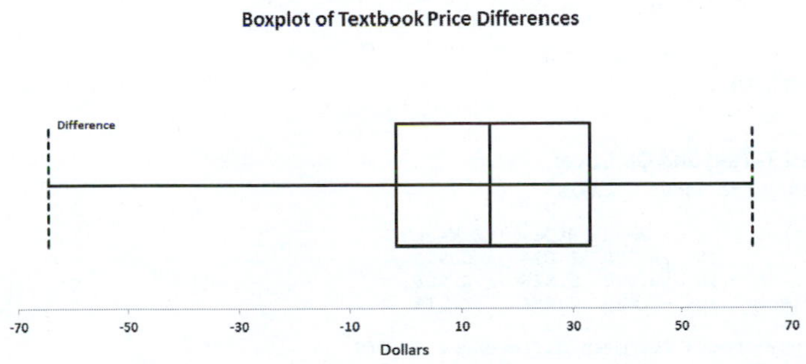

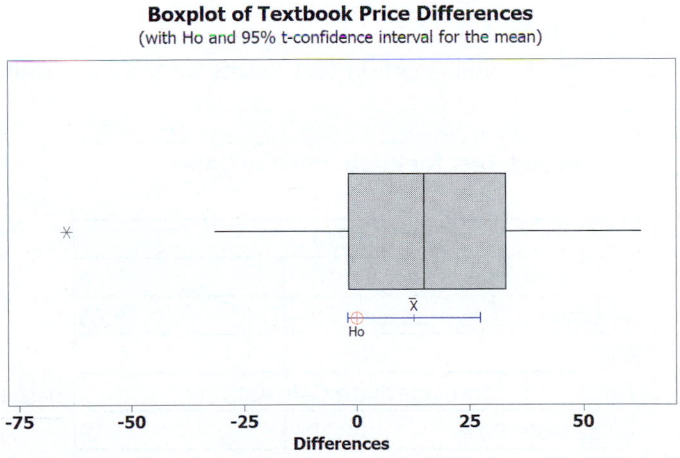

For an Excel boxplot of the differences, use column C of the **PtCalcs worksheet**, *discussed in the Section EG10.2 In-Depth Excel instructions.*

The Figure 10.10 boxplots show approximate symmetry except for one extreme value. Thus, the data do not greatly contradict the underlying assumption of normality. If a boxplot, histogram, or normal probability plot reveals that the assumption of underlying normality in the population is severely violated, then the *t* test may be inappropriate, especially if the sample size is small. If you believe that the *t* test is inappropriate, you can use either a *nonparametric* procedure that does not make the assumption of underlying normality (see Section 12.8) or make a data transformation (see reference 6) and then recheck the assumptions to determine whether you should use the *t* test.

EXAMPLE 10.2

Paired *t* Test of Pizza Delivery Times

Recall from Example 10.1 on page 369 that a local pizza restaurant situated across the street from your college campus advertises that it delivers to the dormitories faster than the local branch of a national pizza chain. In order to determine whether this advertisement is valid, you and some friends have decided to order 10 pizzas from the local pizza restaurant and 10 pizzas from the national chain. In fact, each time you ordered a pizza from the local pizza restaurant, at the same time, your friends ordered a pizza from the national pizza chain. Thus, you have matched samples. For each of the 10 times that pizzas were ordered, you have one measurement from the local pizza restaurant and one from the national chain. At the 0.05 level of significance, is the mean delivery time for the local pizza restaurant less than the mean delivery time for the national pizza chain?

SOLUTION Use the paired *t* test to analyze the Table 10.5 data (stored in **PizzaTime**). Figure 10.11 shows the paired *t* test results for the pizza delivery data.

TABLE 10.5

Delivery Times for Local Pizza Restaurant and National Pizza Chain

Time	Local	Chain	Difference
1	16.8	22.0	−5.2
2	11.7	15.2	−3.5
3	15.6	18.7	−3.1
4	16.7	15.6	1.1
5	17.5	20.8	−3.3
6	18.1	19.5	−1.4
7	14.1	17.0	−2.9
8	21.8	19.5	2.3
9	13.9	16.5	−2.6
10	20.8	24.0	−3.2
			−21.8

FIGURE 10.11

Excel and Minitab paired *t* test results for the pizza delivery data

	A	B
1	Paired *t* Test for Pizza Delivery Data	
2		
3	Data	
4	Hypothesized Mean Diff.	0
5	Level of significance	0.05
6		
7	Intermediate Calculations	
8	Sample Size	10
9	DBar	-2.1800
10	degrees of freedom	9
11	S_D	2.2641
12	Standard Error	0.7160
13	*t* Test Statistic	-3.0448
14		
15	Lower-Tail Test	
16	Lower Critical Value	-1.8331
17	*p*-Value	0.0070
18	Reject the null hypothesis	

Paired T-Test and CI: Local, Chain

```
Paired T for Local - Chain

             N     Mean   StDev   SE Mean
Local       10   16.700   3.096     0.979
Chain       10   18.880   2.866     0.906
Difference  10   -2.180   2.264     0.716

95% upper bound for mean difference: -0.868
T-Test of mean difference = 0 (vs < 0): T-Value = -3.04   P-Value = 0.007
```

The null and alternative hypotheses are

H_0: $\mu_D \geq 0$ (Mean delivery time for the local pizza restaurant is greater than or equal to the mean delivery time for the national pizza chain.)

H_1: $\mu_D < 0$ (Mean delivery time for the local pizza restaurant is less than the mean delivery time for the national pizza chain.)

Choosing the level of significance $\alpha = 0.05$ and assuming that the differences are normally distributed, you use the paired t test [Equation (10.5) on page 378]. For a sample of $n = 10$ delivery times, there are $n - 1 = 9$ degrees of freedom. Using Table E.3, the decision rule is

Reject H_0 if $t_{STAT} < -t_{0.05} = -1.8331$;

otherwise, do not reject H_0.

To illustrate the computations, for $n = 10$ differences (see Table 10.5), the sample mean difference is

$$\overline{D} = \frac{\sum_{i=1}^{n} D_i}{n} = \frac{-21.8}{10} = -2.18$$

and the sample standard deviation of the difference is

$$S_D = \sqrt{\frac{\sum_{i=1}^{n}(D_i - \overline{D})^2}{n-1}} = 2.2641$$

From Equation (10.5) on page 378,

$$t_{STAT} = \frac{\overline{D} - \mu_D}{\dfrac{S_D}{\sqrt{n}}} = \frac{-2.18 - 0}{\dfrac{2.2641}{\sqrt{10}}} = -3.0448$$

Because $t_{STAT} = -3.0448$ is less than -1.8331, you reject the null hypothesis, H_0 (the p-value is $0.0070 < 0.05$). There is evidence that the mean delivery time is lower for the local pizza restaurant than for the national pizza chain.

This conclusion is different from the one you reached in Example 10.1 on page 369 when you used the pooled-variance t test for these data. By pairing the delivery times, you are able to focus on the differences between the two pizza delivery services and not the variability created by ordering pizzas at different times of day. The paired t test is a more powerful statistical procedure that is better able to detect the difference between the two pizza delivery services because you are controlling for the time of day they were ordered.

Confidence Interval Estimate for the Mean Difference

Instead of, or in addition to, testing for the difference between the means of two related populations, you can use Equation (10.6) to construct a confidence interval estimate for the mean difference.

CONFIDENCE INTERVAL ESTIMATE FOR THE MEAN DIFFERENCE

$$\overline{D} \pm t_{\alpha/2}\frac{S_D}{\sqrt{n}}$$

or

$$\overline{D} - t_{\alpha/2}\frac{S_D}{\sqrt{n}} \leq \mu_D \leq \overline{D} + t_{\alpha/2}\frac{S_D}{\sqrt{n}} \qquad \textbf{(10.6)}$$

where $t_{\alpha/2}$ is the critical value of the t distribution, with $n - 1$ degrees of freedom, for an area of $\alpha/2$ in the upper tail.

Recall the example comparing textbook prices on page 379. Using Equation (10.6), $\overline{D} = 12.6663$, $S_D = 30.4488$, $n = 19$, and $t_{\alpha/2} = 2.1009$ (for 95% confidence and $n - 1 = 18$ degrees of freedom),

$$12.6663 \pm (2.1009)\frac{30.4488}{\sqrt{19}}$$

$$12.6663 \pm 14.6757$$

$$-2.0094 \leq \mu_D \leq 27.342$$

Thus, with 95% confidence, the mean difference in textbook prices between the college bookstore and the online retailer is between –\$2.0094 and \$27.342. Because the interval estimate contains zero, you can conclude that there is insufficient evidence of a difference in the population means. There is insufficient evidence of a difference in the mean prices of textbooks at the college bookstore and the online retailer.

Problems for Section 10.2

LEARNING THE BASICS

10.18 An experimental design for a paired t test has 20 pairs of identical twins. How many degrees of freedom are there in this t test?

10.19 Fifteen volunteers are recruited to participate in an experiment. A measurement is made (such as blood pressure) before each volunteer is asked to read a particularly upsetting passage from a book and after each volunteer reads the passage from the book. In the analysis of the data collected from this experiment, how many degrees of freedom are there in the test?

APPLYING THE CONCEPTS

SELF Test **10.20** Nine experts rated two brands of Colombian coffee in a taste-testing experiment. A rating on a 7-point scale (1 = extremely unpleasing, 7 = extremely pleasing) is given for each of four characteristics: taste, aroma, richness, and acidity. The following data (stored in Coffee) display the ratings accumulated over all four characteristics.

	Brand	
Expert	**A**	**B**
C.C.	24	26
S.E.	27	27
E.G.	19	22
B.L.	24	27
C.M.	22	25
C.N.	26	27
G.N.	27	26
R.M.	25	27
P.V.	22	23

a. At the 0.05 level of significance, is there evidence of a difference in the mean ratings between the two brands?
b. What assumption is necessary about the population distribution in order to perform this test?
c. Determine the p-value in (a) and interpret its meaning.
d. Construct and interpret a 95% confidence interval estimate of the difference in the mean ratings between the two brands.

10.21 In industrial settings, alternative methods often exist for measuring variables of interest. The data in Measurement (coded to maintain confidentiality) represent measurements in-line that were collected from an analyzer during the production process and from an analytical lab. (Data extracted from M. Leitnaker, "Comparing Measurement Processes: In-line Versus Analytical Measurements," *Quality Engineering*, 13, 2000–2001, pp. 293–298.)
a. At the 0.05 level of significance, is there evidence of a difference in the mean measurements in-line and from an analytical lab?
b. What assumption is necessary about the population distribution in order to perform this test?
c. Use a graphical method to evaluate the validity of the assumption in (a).
d. Construct and interpret a 95% confidence interval estimate of the difference in the mean measurements in-line and from an analytical lab.

10.22 Is there a difference in the prices at a warehouse club such as Costco and store brands? To investigate this, a random sample of 10 purchases was selected, and the prices were compared. (Data extracted from "Shop Smart and Save Big," *Consumer Reports*, May 2009, p. 17.) The prices for the products are stored in Shopping1.
a. At the 0.05 level of significance, is there evidence of a difference between the mean price of Costco purchases and store-brand purchases?
b. What assumption is necessary about the population distribution in order to perform this test?

c. Construct a 95% confidence interval estimate of the mean difference in price between Costco and store brands. Interpret the interval.

d. Compare the results of (a) and (c).

10.23 In tough economic times, the business staff at magazines are challenged to sell advertising space in their publications. Thus, one indicator of a weak economy is the decline in the number of "ad pages" that magazines have sold. The file **Ad Pages** contains the number of ad pages found in the May 2008 and May 2009 issues of 12 men's magazines. (Data extracted from W. Levith, "Magazine Monitor," *Mediaweek*, April 20, 2009, p. 53.)

a. At the 0.05 level of significance, is there evidence that the mean number of ad pages was higher in May 2008 than in May 2009?

b. What assumption is necessary about the population distribution in order to perform this test?

c. Use a graphical method to evaluate the validity of the assumption in (b).

d. Construct and interpret a 95% confidence interval estimate of the difference in the mean number of ad pages in men's magazines between May 2008 and May 2009.

10.24 Multiple myeloma, or blood plasma cancer, is characterized by increased blood vessel formulation (angiogenesis) in the bone marrow that is a predictive factor in survival. One treatment approach used for multiple myeloma is stem cell transplantation with the patient's own stem cells. The following data (stored in **Myeloma**) represent the bone marrow microvessel density for patients who had a complete response to the stem cell transplant (as measured by blood and urine tests). The measurements were taken immediately prior to the stem cell transplant and at the time the complete response was determined.

Patient	Before	After
1	158	284
2	189	214
3	202	101
4	353	227
5	416	290
6	426	176
7	441	290

Source: Data extracted from S. V. Rajkumar, R. Fonseca, T. E. Witzig, M. A. Gertz, and P. R. Greipp, "Bone Marrow Angiogenesis in Patients Achieving Complete Response After Stem Cell Transplantation for Multiple Myeloma," *Leukemia*, 1999, 13, pp. 469–472.

a. At the 0.05 level of significance, is there evidence that the mean bone marrow microvessel density is higher before the stem cell transplant than after the stem cell transplant?

b. Interpret the meaning of the p-value in (a).

c. Construct and interpret a 95% confidence interval estimate of the mean difference in bone marrow microvessel density before and after the stem cell transplant.

d. What assumption is necessary about the population distribution in order to perform the test in (a)?

10.25 Over the past year, the vice president for human resources at a large medical center has run a series of three-month workshops aimed at increasing worker motivation and performance. To check the effectiveness of the workshops, she selected a random sample of 35 employees from the personnel files. She collected the employee performance ratings recorded before and after workshop attendance and stored the paired ratings, along with descriptive statistics and the results of a paired t test in the **Perform Excel workbook (Perform.xls)** and in the **Perform Minitab project (Perform.mpj)**. Review her results and state your findings and conclusions in a report to the vice president for human resources.

10.26 The data in **Concrete1** represent the compressive strength, in thousands of pounds per square inch (psi), of 40 samples of concrete taken two and seven days after pouring.

Source: Data extracted from O. Carrillo-Gamboa and R. F. Gunst, "Measurement-Error-Model Collinearities," *Technometrics*, 34, 1992, pp. 454–464.

a. At the 0.01 level of significance, is there evidence that the mean strength is lower at two days than at seven days?

b. What assumption is necessary about the population distribution in order to perform this test?

c. Find the p-value in (a) and interpret its meaning.

10.3 Comparing the Proportions of Two Independent Populations

Often, you need to make comparisons and analyze differences between two population proportions. You can perform a test for the difference between two proportions selected from independent populations by using two different methods. This section presents a procedure whose test statistic, Z_{STAT}, is approximated by a standardized normal distribution. In Section 12.1, a procedure whose test statistic, χ^2_{STAT}, is approximated by a chi-square distribution is used. As you will see when you read that section, the results from these two tests are equivalent.

Z Test for the Difference Between Two Proportions

In evaluating differences between two population proportions, you can use a ***Z* test for the difference between two proportions**. The Z_{STAT} test statistic is based on the difference between two sample proportions $(p_1 - p_2)$. This test statistic, given in Equation (10.7), approximately follows a standardized normal distribution for large enough sample sizes.

Z TEST FOR THE DIFFERENCE BETWEEN TWO PROPORTIONS

$$Z_{STAT} = \frac{(p_1 - p_2) - (\pi_1 - \pi_2)}{\sqrt{\bar{p}(1 - \bar{p})\left(\frac{1}{n_1} + \frac{1}{n_2}\right)}} \tag{10.7}$$

with

$$\bar{p} = \frac{X_1 + X_2}{n_1 + n_2} \quad p_1 = \frac{X_1}{n_1} \quad p_2 = \frac{X_2}{n_2}$$

where

p_1 = proportion of items of interest in sample 1

X_1 = number of items of interest in sample 1

n_1 = sample size of sample 1

π_1 = proportion of items of interest in population 1

p_2 = proportion of items of interest in sample 2

X_2 = number of items of interest in sample 2

n_2 = sample size of sample 2

π_2 = proportion of items of interest in population 2

$\bar{p}$ = pooled estimate of the population proportion of items of interest

The Z_{STAT} test statistic approximately follows a standardized normal distribution.

Under the null hypothesis in the Z test for the difference between two proportions, you assume that the two population proportions are equal $(\pi_1 = \pi_2)$. Because the pooled estimate for the population proportion is based on the null hypothesis, you combine, or pool, the two sample proportions to compute $\bar{p}$, an overall estimate of the common population proportion. This estimate is equal to the number of items of interest in the two samples combined $(X_1 + X_2)$ divided by the total sample size from the two samples combined $(n_1 + n_2)$.

As shown in the following table, you can use this Z test for the difference between population proportions to determine whether there is a difference in the proportion of items of interest in the two populations (two-tail test) or whether one population has a higher proportion of items of interest than the other population (one-tail test):

Two-Tail Test	One-Tail Test	One-Tail Test
$H_0: \pi_1 = \pi_2$ $H_1: \pi_1 \neq \pi_2$	$H_0: \pi_1 \geq \pi_2$ $H_1: \pi_1 < \pi_2$	$H_0: \pi_1 \leq \pi_2$ $H_1: \pi_1 > \pi_2$

where

π_1 = proportion of items of interest in population 1

π_2 = proportion of items of interest in population 2

To test the null hypothesis that there is no difference between the proportions of two independent populations:

$$H_0: \pi_1 = \pi_2$$

against the alternative that the two population proportions are not the same:

$$H_1: \pi_1 \neq \pi_2$$

You use the Z_{STAT} test statistic, given by Equation (10.7). For a given level of significance, α, you reject the null hypothesis if the computed Z_{STAT} test statistic is greater than the upper-tail critical value from the standardized normal distribution or if the computed Z_{STAT} test statistic is less than the lower-tail critical value from the standardized normal distribution.

To illustrate the use of the Z test for the equality of two proportions, suppose that you are the manager of T.C. Resort Properties, a collection of five upscale resort hotels located on two tropical islands. On one of the islands, T.C. Resort Properties has two hotels, the Beachcomber and the Windsurfer. You have defined the business objective as improving the return rate of guests at the Beachcomber and the Windsurfer hotels. On the questionnaire completed by hotel guests upon their departure, one question asked is whether the guest is likely to return to the hotel. Responses to this and other questions were collected from 227 guests at the Beachcomber and 262 guests at the Windsurfer. The results for this question indicated that 163 of 227 guests at the Beachcomber responded yes, they were likely to return to the hotel and 154 of 262 guests at the Windsurfer responded yes, they were likely to return to the hotel. At the 0.05 level of significance, is there evidence of a significant difference in guest satisfaction (as measured by the likelihood to return to the hotel) between the two hotels?

The null and alternative hypotheses are

$$H_0: \pi_1 = \pi_2 \text{ or } \pi_1 - \pi_2 = 0$$
$$H_1: \pi_1 \neq \pi_2 \text{ or } \pi_1 - \pi_2 \neq 0$$

Using the 0.05 level of significance, the critical values are −1.96 and +1.96 (see Figure 10.12), and the decision rule is

$$\text{Reject } H_0 \text{ if } Z_{STAT} < -1.96$$
$$\text{or if } Z_{STAT} > +1.96;$$
$$\text{otherwise, do not reject } H_0.$$

FIGURE 10.12
Regions of rejection and nonrejection when testing a hypothesis for the difference between two proportions at the 0.05 level of significance

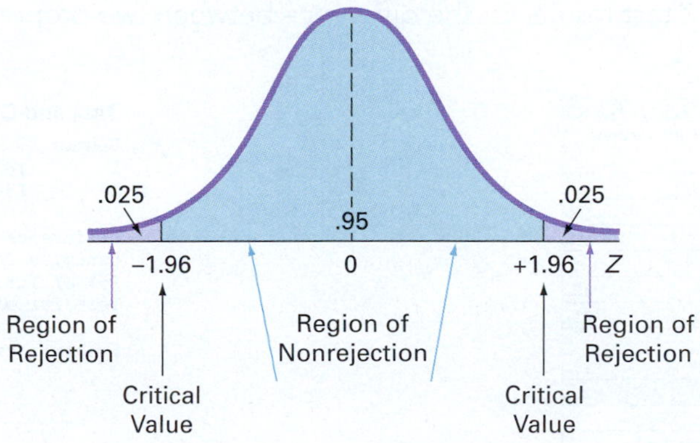

Using Equation (10.7) on page 386,

$$Z_{STAT} = \frac{(p_1 - p_2) - (\pi_1 - \pi_2)}{\sqrt{\bar{p}(1 - \bar{p})\left(\frac{1}{n_1} + \frac{1}{n_2}\right)}}$$

where

$$p_1 = \frac{X_1}{n_1} = \frac{163}{227} = 0.7181 \quad p_2 = \frac{X_2}{n_2} = \frac{154}{262} = 0.5878$$

and

$$\bar{p} = \frac{X_1 + X_2}{n_1 + n_2} = \frac{163 + 154}{227 + 262} = \frac{317}{489} = 0.6483$$

so that

$$Z_{STAT} = \frac{(0.7181 - 0.5878) - (0)}{\sqrt{0.6483(1 - 0.6483)\left(\frac{1}{227} + \frac{1}{262}\right)}}$$

$$= \frac{0.1303}{\sqrt{(0.228)(0.0082)}}$$

$$= \frac{0.1303}{\sqrt{0.00187}}$$

$$= \frac{0.1303}{0.0432} = +3.0088$$

Using the 0.05 level of significance, you reject the null hypothesis because $Z_{STAT} = +3.0088 > +1.96$. The p-value is 0.0026 (computed using Table E.2 or from Figure 10.13) and indicates that if the null hypothesis is true, the probability that a Z_{STAT} test statistic is less than -3.0088 is 0.0013, and, similarly, the probability that a Z_{STAT} test statistic is greater than $+3.0088$ is 0.0013. Thus, for this two-tail test, the p-value is $0.0013 + 0.0013 = 0.0026$. Because $0.0026 < \alpha = 0.05$, you reject the null hypothesis. There is evidence to conclude that the two hotels are significantly different with respect to guest satisfaction; a greater proportion of guests are willing to return to the Beachcomber than to the Windsurfer.

FIGURE 10.13

Excel and Minitab Z test results for the difference between two proportions for the hotel guest satisfaction problem

	A	B	
1	Z Test for Differences in Two Proportions		
2			
3	Data		
4	Hypothesized Difference	0	
5	Level of Significance	0.05	
6	Group 1		
7	Number of Items of Interest	163	
8	Sample Size	227	
9	Group 2		
10	Number of Items of Interest	154	
11	Sample Size	262	
12			
13	Intermediate Calculations		
14	Group 1 Proportion	0.7181	=B7/B8
15	Group 2 Proportion	0.5878	=B10/B11
16	Difference in Two Proportions	0.1303	=B14 - B15
17	Average Proportion	0.6483	=(B7 + B10)/(B8 + B11)
18	Z Test Statistic	3.0088	=(B16 - B4)/SQRT(B17 * (1 - B17) * (1/B8 + 1/B11)
19			
20	Two-Tail Test		
21	Lower Critical Value	-1.9600	=NORMSINV(B5/2)
22	Upper Critical Value	1.9600	=NORMSINV(1 - B5/2)
23	p-Value	0.0026	=2 * (1 - NORMSDIST(ABS(B18)))
24	Reject the null hypothesis		=IF(B23 < B5, "Reject the null hypothesis", "Do not reject the null hypothesis")

Test and CI for Two Proportions

```
Sample    X    N  Sample p
1       163  227  0.718062
2       154  262  0.587786

Difference = p (1) - p (2)
Estimate for difference:  0.130275
95% CI for difference:  (0.0467379, 0.213813)
Test for difference = 0 (vs not = 0):  Z = 3.01  P-Value = 0.003

Fisher's exact test: P-Value = 0.003
```

EXAMPLE 10.3

Testing for the Difference Between Two Proportions

A growing concern about privacy on the Internet has led more people to monitor their online identities. (Data extracted from Drilling Down, "Managing Reputations on Social Sites," *The New York Times*, June 14, 2010, pp. B2B.) The survey reported that 44% of Internet users ages 18 to 29 have taken steps to restrict the amount of information available about themselves online as compared to 20% of Internet users older than 65 who have done the same thing. The sample size in each group was not reported. Suppose that the survey consisted of 100 individuals in each age group. At the 0.05 level of significance, is the proportion of Internet users ages 18 to 29 who have taken steps to restrict the amount of information available about themselves online greater than the proportion of Internet users older than 65 who have done the same thing?

SOLUTION Because you want to know whether there is evidence that the proportion in the 18-to-29 age group is *greater* than in the over-65 age group, you have a one-tail test. The null and alternative hypotheses are

H_0: $\pi_1 \leq \pi_2$ (The proportion of Internet users ages 18 to 29 who have taken steps to restrict the amount of information available about themselves online is less than or equal to the proportion of Internet users older than 65 who have done the same thing.)

H_1: $\pi_1 > \pi_2$ (The proportion of Internet users ages 18 to 29 who have taken steps to restrict the amount of information available about themselves online is greater than the proportion of Internet users older than 65 who have done the same thing.)

Using the 0.05 level of significance, for the one-tail test in the upper tail, the critical value is +1.645. The decision rule is

$$\text{Reject } H_0 \text{ if } Z_{STAT} > +1.645;$$
$$\text{otherwise, do not reject } H_0.$$

Using Equation (10.7) on page 386,

$$Z_{STAT} = \frac{(p_1 - p_2) - (\pi_1 - \pi_2)}{\sqrt{\bar{p}(1 - \bar{p})\left(\frac{1}{n_1} + \frac{1}{n_2}\right)}}$$

where

$$p_1 = \frac{X_1}{n_1} = \frac{44}{100} = 0.44 \quad p_2 = \frac{X_2}{n_2} = \frac{20}{100} = 0.20$$

and

$$\bar{p} = \frac{X_1 + X_2}{n_1 + n_2} = \frac{44 + 20}{100 + 100} = \frac{64}{200} = 0.32$$

so that

$$Z_{STAT} = \frac{(0.44 - 0.20) - (0)}{\sqrt{0.32(1 - 0.32)\left(\frac{1}{100} + \frac{1}{100}\right)}}$$

$$= \frac{0.24}{\sqrt{(0.2176)(0.02)}}$$

$$= \frac{0.24}{\sqrt{0.004352}}$$

$$= \frac{0.24}{0.06597} = +3.638$$

Using the 0.05 level of significance, you reject the null hypothesis because $Z_{STAT} = +3.638 > +1.645$. The p-value is approximately 0.0001. Therefore, if the null hypothesis is true, the probability that a Z_{STAT} test statistic is greater than +3.638 is approximately 0.0001 (which is less than $\alpha = 0.05$). You conclude that there is evidence that the proportion of Internet users ages 18 to 29 who have taken steps to restrict the amount of information available about themselves online is greater than the proportion of Internet users older than 65 who have done the same thing.

Confidence Interval Estimate for the Difference Between Two Proportions

Instead of, or in addition to, testing for the difference between the proportions of two independent populations, you can construct a confidence interval estimate for the difference between the two proportions using Equation (10.8).

CONFIDENCE INTERVAL ESTIMATE FOR THE DIFFERENCE BETWEEN TWO PROPORTIONS

$$(p_1 - p_2) \pm Z_{\alpha/2}\sqrt{\frac{p_1(1 - p_1)}{n_1} + \frac{p_2(1 - p_2)}{n_2}}$$

or

$$(p_1 - p_2) - Z_{\alpha/2}\sqrt{\frac{p_1(1 - p_1)}{n_1} + \frac{p_2(1 - p_2)}{n_2}} \le (\pi_1 - \pi_2)$$

$$\le (p_1 - p_2) + Z_{\alpha/2}\sqrt{\frac{p_1(1 - p_1)}{n_1} + \frac{p_2(1 - p_2)}{n_2}} \quad \textbf{(10.8)}$$

To construct a 95% confidence interval estimate for the population difference between the proportion of guests who would return to the Beachcomber and who would return to the Windsurfer, you use the results on page 387 or from Figure 10.13 on page 388:

$$p_1 = \frac{X_1}{n_1} = \frac{163}{227} = 0.7181 \qquad p_2 = \frac{X_2}{n_2} = \frac{154}{262} = 0.5878$$

Using Equation (10.8),

$$(0.7181 - 0.5878) \pm (1.96)\sqrt{\frac{0.7181(1 - 0.7181)}{227} + \frac{0.5878(1 - 0.5878)}{262}}$$

$$0.1303 \pm (1.96)(0.0426)$$

$$0.1303 \pm 0.0835$$

$$0.0468 \le (\pi_1 - \pi_2) \le 0.2138$$

Thus, you have 95% confidence that the difference between the population proportion of guests who would return to the Beachcomber and the Windsurfer is between 0.0468 and 0.2138. In percentages, the difference is between 4.68% and 21.38%. Guest satisfaction is higher at the Beachcomber than at the Windsurfer.

Problems for Section 10.3

LEARNING THE BASICS

10.27 Let $n_1 = 100, X_1 = 50, n_2 = 100$, and $X_2 = 30$.

a. At the 0.05 level of significance, is there evidence of a significant difference between the two population proportions?

b. Construct a 95% confidence interval estimate for the difference between the two population proportions.

10.28 Let $n_1 = 100, X_1 = 45, n_2 = 50$, and $X_2 = 25$.

a. At the 0.01 level of significance, is there evidence of a significant difference between the two population proportions?

b. Construct a 99% confidence interval estimate for the difference between the two population proportions.

APPLYING THE CONCEPTS

10.29 A survey of 500 shoppers was taken in a large metropolitan area to determine various information about consumer behavior. Among the questions asked was, "Do you enjoy shopping for clothing?" Of 240 males, 136 answered yes. Of 260 females, 224 answered yes.

a. Is there evidence of a significant difference between males and females in the proportion who enjoy shopping for clothing at the 0.01 level of significance?

b. Find the *p*-value in (a) and interpret its meaning.

c. Construct and interpret a 99% confidence interval estimate for the difference between the proportion of males and females who enjoy shopping for clothing.

d. What are your answers to (a) through (c) if 206 males enjoyed shopping for clothing?

10.30 Does it take more effort to be removed from an email list than it used to? A study of 100 large online retailers revealed the following:

	NEED THREE OR MORE CLICKS TO BE REMOVED	
YEAR	**Yes**	**No**
2009	39	61
2008	7	93

Source: Data extracted from "More Clicks to Escape an Email List," *The New York Times,* March 29, 2010, p. B2.

a. Set up the null and alternative hypotheses to try to determine whether it takes more effort to be removed from an email list than it used to.

b. Conduct the hypothesis test defined in (a), using the 0.05 level of significance.

c. Does the result of your test in (b) make it appropriate to claim that it takes more effort to be removed from an email list than it used to?

10.31 Some people enjoy the *anticipation* of an upcoming product or event and prefer to pay in advance and delay the actual consumption/delivery date. In other cases, people do not want a delay. An article in the *Journal of Marketing Research* reported on an experiment in which 50 individuals were told that they had just purchased a ticket to a concert and 50 were told that they had just purchased a personal digital assistant (PDA). The participants were then asked to indicate their preferences for attending the concert or receiving the PDA. Did they prefer tonight or tomorrow, or would they prefer to wait two to four weeks? The individuals were told to ignore their schedule constraints in order to better measure their willingness to delay the consumption/delivery of their purchase. The following table gives partial results of the study:

When to Receive Purchase	Concert	PDA
Tonight or tomorrow	28	47
Two to four weeks	22	3
Total	50	50

Source: Data adapted from O. Amir and D. Ariely, "Decisions by Rules: The Case of Unwillingness to Pay for Beneficial Delays," *Journal of Marketing Research,* February 2007, Vol. XLIV, pp. 142–152.

a. What proportion of the participants would prefer to delay the date of the concert?

b. What proportion of the participants would prefer to delay receipt of a new PDA?

c. Using the 0.05 level of significance, is there evidence of a significant difference in the proportion willing to delay the date of the concert and the proportion willing to delay receipt of a new PDA?

SELF Test **10.32** Do people of different age groups differ in their beliefs about response time to email messages? A survey by the Center for the Digital Future of the University of Southern California reported that 70.7% of users over 70 years of age believe that email messages should be answered quickly as compared to 53.6% of users 12 to 50 years old. (Data extracted from A. Mindlin, "Older E-mail Users Favor Fast Replies," *The New York Times*, July 14, 2008, p. B3.) Suppose that the survey was based on 1,000 users over 70 years of age and 1,000 users 12 to 50 years old.

a. At the 0.01 level of significance, is there evidence of a significant difference between the two age groups in the proportion that believe that email messages should be answered quickly?

b. Find the *p*-value in (a) and interpret its meaning.

10.33 A survey was conducted of 665 consumer magazines on the practices of their websites. Of these, 273 magazines reported that online-only content is copy-edited as rigorously as print content; 379 reported that online-only content is fact-checked as rigorously as print content. (Data extracted from S. Clifford, "Columbia Survey Finds a Slack

Editing Process of Magazine Web Sites," *The New York Times*, March 1, 2010, p. B6.) Suppose that a sample of 500 newspapers revealed that 252 reported that online-only content is copy-edited as rigorously as print content and 296 reported that online-only content is fact-checked as rigorously as print content.

a. At the 0.05 level of significance, is there evidence of a difference between consumer magazines and newspapers in the proportion of online-only content that is copy-edited as rigorously as print content ?
b. Find the p-value in (a) and interpret its meaning.
c. At the 0.05 level of significance, is there evidence of a difference between consumer magazines and newspapers in the proportion of online-only content that is fact-checked as rigorously as print content?

10.34 How do Americans feel about ads on websites? A survey of 1,000 adult Internet users found that 670 opposed ads on websites. (Data extracted from S. Clifford, "Tacked for Ads? Many Americans Say No Thanks," *The New York Times*, September 30, 2009, p. B3.). Suppose that a survey of 1,000 Internet users age 12–17 found that 510 opposed ads on websites

a. At the 0.05 level of significance, is there evidence of a difference between adult Internet users and Internet users age 12–17 in the proportion who oppose ads?
b. Find the p-value in (a) and interpret its meaning.

10.35 Where people turn for news is different for various age groups. (Data extracted from "Cellphone Users Who Access News on Their Phones," *USA Today*, March 1, 2010, p. 1A.) A study was conducted on the use of cell phones for accessing news. The study reported that 47% of users under age 50 and 15% of users age 50 and over accessed news on their cell phones. Suppose that the survey consisted of 1,000 users under age 50, of whom 470 accessed news on their cell phones, and 891 users age 50 and over, of whom 134 accessed news on their cell phones.

a. Is there evidence of a significant difference in the proportion of users under age 50 and users 50 years and older that accessed the news on their cell phones? (Use $\alpha = 0.05$.)
b. Determine the p-value in (a) and interpret its meaning.
c. Construct and interpret a 95% confidence interval estimate for the difference between the population proportion of users under 50 years old and those 50 years or older who access the news on their cell phones.

10.4 *F* Test for the Ratio of Two Variances

Often you need to determine whether two independent populations have the same variability. By testing variances, you can detect differences in the variability in two independent populations. One important reason to test for the difference between the variances of two populations is to determine whether to use the pooled-variance t test (which assumes equal variances) or the separate-variance t test (which does not assume equal variances) while comparing the means of two independent populations.

The test for the difference between the variances of two independent populations is based on the ratio of the two sample variances. If you assume that each population is normally distributed, then the ratio S_1^2/S_2^2 follows the F distribution (see Table E.5). The critical values of the ***F* distribution** in Table E.5 depend on the degrees of freedom in the two samples. The degrees of freedom in the numerator of the ratio are for the first sample, and the degrees of freedom in the denominator are for the second sample. The first sample taken from the first population is defined as the sample that has the *larger* sample variance. The second sample taken from the second population is the sample with the *smaller* sample variance. Equation (10.9) defines the ***F* test for the ratio of two variances**.

F TEST STATISTIC FOR TESTING THE RATIO OF TWO VARIANCES

The F_{STAT} test statistic is equal to the variance of sample 1 (the larger sample variance) divided by the variance of sample 2 (the smaller sample variance).

$$F_{STAT} = \frac{S_1^2}{S_2^2} \qquad (10.9)$$

where

S_1^2 = variance of sample 1 (the larger sample variance)

S_2^2 = variance of sample 2 (the smaller sample variance)

n_1 = sample size selected from population 1

n_2 = sample size selected from population 2

$n_1 - 1$ = degrees of freedom from sample 1 (i.e., the numerator degrees of freedom)

$n_2 - 1$ = degrees of freedom from sample 2 (i.e., the denominator degrees of freedom)

The F_{STAT} test statistic follows an F distribution with $n_1 - 1$ and $n_2 - 1$ degrees of freedom.

For a given level of significance, α, to test the null hypothesis of equality of population variances:

$$H_0: \sigma_1^2 = \sigma_2^2$$

against the alternative hypothesis that the two population variances are not equal:

$$H_1: \sigma_1^2 \neq \sigma_2^2$$

you reject the null hypothesis if the computed F_{STAT} test statistic is greater than the upper-tail critical value, $F_{\alpha/2}$, from the F distribution, with $n_1 - 1$ degrees of freedom in the numerator and $n_2 - 1$ degrees of freedom in the denominator. Thus, the decision rule is

Reject H_0 if $F_{STAT} > F_{\alpha/2}$;

otherwise, do not reject H_0.

To illustrate how to use the F test to determine whether the two variances are equal, return to the BLK Beverages scenario on page 365 concerning the sales of BLK Cola in two different display locations. To determine whether to use the pooled-variance t test or the separate-variance t test in Section 10.1, you can test the equality of the two population variances. The null and alternative hypotheses are

$$H_0: \sigma_1^2 = \sigma_2^2$$
$$H_1: \sigma_1^2 \neq \sigma_2^2$$

Because you are defining sample 1 as the group with the larger sample variance, the rejection region in the upper tail of the F distribution contains $\alpha/2$. Using the level of significance $\alpha = 0.05$, the rejection region in the upper tail contains 0.025 of the distribution.

Because there are samples of 10 stores for each of the two display locations, there are $10-1 = 9$ degrees of freedom in the numerator (the sample with the larger variance) and also in the denominator (the sample with the smaller variance). $F_{\alpha/2}$, the upper-tail critical value of the F distribution, is found directly from Table E.5, a portion of which is presented in Table 10.6. Because there are 9 degrees of freedom in the numerator and 9 degrees of freedom in the denominator, you find the upper-tail critical value, $F_{\alpha/2}$, by looking in the column labeled 9 and the row labeled 9. Thus, the upper-tail critical value of this F distribution is 4.03. Therefore, the decision rule is

Reject H_0 if $F_{STAT} > F_{0.025} = 4.03$;

otherwise, do not reject H_0.

TABLE 10.6

Finding the Upper-Tail Critical Value of F with 9 and 9 Degrees of Freedom for an Upper-Tail Area of 0.025

	Cumulative Probabilities = 0.975 Upper-Tail Area = 0.025 Numerator df_1						
Denominator df_2	**1**	**2**	**3**	**...**	**7**	**8**	**9**
1	647.80	799.50	864.20	...	948.20	956.70	963.30
2	38.51	39.00	39.17	...	39.36	39.37	39.39
3	17.44	16.04	15.44	...	14.62	14.54	14.47
.	.	.	.	.	.	.	.
.	.	.	.	.	.	.	.
.	.	.	.	.	.	.	.
7	8.07	6.54	5.89	...	4.99	4.90	4.82
8	7.57	6.06	5.42	...	4.53	4.43	4.36
9	7.21	5.71	5.08	...	4.20	4.10	4.03

Source: Extracted from Table E.5.

Using Equation (10.9) on page 392 and the cola sales data (see Table 10.1 on page 367),

$$S_1^2 = (18.7264)^2 = 350.6778 \quad S_2^2 = (12.5433)^2 = 157.3333$$

so that

$$F_{STAT} = \frac{S_1^2}{S_2^2}$$

$$= \frac{350.6778}{157.3333} = 2.2289$$

Because $F_{STAT} = 2.2289 < 4.03$, you do not reject H_0. Figure 10.14 shows the results for this test, including the p-value, 0.248. Because $0.248 > 0.05$, you conclude that there is no evidence of a significant difference in the variability of the sales of cola for the two display locations.

FIGURE 10.14

Excel and Minitab F test results for the BLK Cola sales data

	A	B	
1	F Test for Differences in Two Variances		
2			
3	Data		
4	Level of Significance	0.05	
5	Larger-Variance Sample		
6	Sample Size	10	=COUNT(DATACOPY!$A:$A)
7	Sample Variance	350.6778	=VAR(DATACOPY!$A:$A)
8	Smaller-Variance Sample		
9	Sample Size	10	=COUNT(DATACOPY!$B:$B)
10	Sample Variance	157.3333	=VAR(DATACOPY!$B:$B)
11			
12	Intermediate Calculations		
13	F Test Statistic	2.2289	=B7/B10
14	Population 1 Sample Degrees of Freedom	9	=B6 - 1
15	Population 2 Sample Degrees of Freedom	9	=B9 - 1
16			
17	Two-Tail Test		
18	Upper Critical Value	4.0260	=FINV(B4/2, B14, B15)
19	p-Value	0.2482	=2 * E17
20	Do not reject the null hypothesis		=IF(B19 < B4, "Reject the null hypothesis", "Do not reject the null hypothesis")

Not shown
Cell E17: =FDIST(B13, B14, B15)

Test and CI for Two Variances: Normal, End-Aisle

```
Method
Null hypothesis          Sigma(Normal) / Sigma(End-Aisle) = 1
Alternative hypothesis   Sigma(Normal) / Sigma(End-Aisle) not = 1
Significance level       Alpha = 0.05


Statistics
Variable    N   StDev  Variance
Normal     10  18.726   350.678
End-Aisle  10  12.543   157.333

Ratio of standard deviations = 1.493
Ratio of variances = 2.229


95% Confidence Intervals
                                    CI for
Distribution   CI for StDev        Variance
of Data           Ratio              Ratio
Normal        (0.744, 2.996)   (0.554, 8.973)
Continuous    (0.664, 3.082)   (0.441, 9.497)


Tests
                                                Test
Method                           DF1  DF2  Statistic  P-Value
F Test (normal)                    9    9       2.23    0.248
Levene's Test (any continuous)     1   18       1.27    0.275
```

In testing for a difference between two variances using the F test described in this section, you assume that each of the two populations is normally distributed. The F test is very sensitive to the normality assumption. If boxplots or normal probability plots suggest even a mild departure from normality for either of the two populations, you should not use the F test.

If this happens, you should use the Levene test (see Section 11.1) or a nonparametric approach (see references 1 and 2).

In testing for the equality of variances as part of assessing the validity of the pooled-variance t test procedure, the F test is a two-tail test with $\alpha/2$ in the upper tail. However, when you are interested in examining the variability in situations other than the pooled-variance t test, the F test is often a one-tail test. Example 10.4 illustrates a one-tail test.

EXAMPLE 10.4

A One-Tail Test for the Difference Between Two Variances

A professor in the accounting department of a business school would like to determine whether there is more variability in the final exam scores of students taking the introductory accounting course who are not majoring in accounting than for students taking the course who are majoring in accounting. Random samples of 13 non-accounting majors and 10 accounting majors are selected from the professor's class roster in his large lecture, and the following results are computed based on the final exam scores:

$$\text{Non-accounting}: \quad n_1 = 13 \quad S_1^2 = 210.2$$
$$\text{Accounting}: \quad n_2 = 10 \quad S_2^2 = 36.5$$

At the 0.05 level of significance, is there evidence that there is more variability in the final exam scores of students taking the introductory accounting course who are not majoring in accounting than for students taking the course who are majoring in accounting? Assume that the population final exam scores are normally distributed.

SOLUTION The null and alternative hypotheses are

$$H_0: \sigma_{NA}^2 \le \sigma_A^2$$
$$H_1: \sigma_{NA}^2 > \sigma_A^2$$

The F_{STAT} test statistic is given by Equation (10.9) on page 392:

$$F_{STAT} = \frac{S_1^2}{S_2^2}$$

You use Table E.5 to find the upper critical value of the F distribution. With $n_1 - 1 = 13 - 1 = 12$ degrees of freedom in the numerator, $n_2 - 1 = 10 - 1 = 9$ degrees of freedom in the denominator, and $\alpha = 0.05$, the upper-tail critical value, $F_{0.05}$, is 3.07. The decision rule is

$$\text{Reject } H_0 \text{ if } F_{STAT} > 3.07;$$
$$\text{otherwise, do not reject } H_0.$$

From Equation (10.9) on page 392,

$$F_{STAT} = \frac{S_1^2}{S_2^2} = \frac{210.2}{36.5} = 5.7589$$

Because $F_{STAT} = 5.7589 > 3.07$, you reject H_0. Using a 0.05 level of significance, you conclude that there is evidence that there is more variability in the final exam scores of students taking the introductory accounting course who are not majoring in accounting than for students taking the course who are majoring in accounting.

Problems for Section 10.4

LEARNING THE BASICS

10.36 Determine the upper-tail critical values of F in each of the following two-tail tests.

a. $\alpha = 0.10, n_1 = 16, n_2 = 21$
b. $\alpha = 0.05, n_1 = 16, n_2 = 21$
c. $\alpha = 0.01, n_1 = 16, n_2 = 21$

10.37 Determine the upper-tail critical value of F in each of the following one-tail tests.

a. $\alpha = 0.05, n_1 = 16, n_2 = 21$
b. $\alpha = 0.01, n_1 = 16, n_2 = 21$

10.38 The following information is available for two samples selected from independent normally distributed populations:

$$\text{Population A}: \ n_1 = 25 \quad S_1^2 = 16$$
$$\text{Population B}: \ n_2 = 25 \quad S_2^2 = 25$$

a. Which sample variance do you place in the numerator of F_{STAT}?
b. What is the value of F_{STAT}?

10.39 The following information is available for two samples selected from independent normally distributed populations:

$$\text{Population A}: \ n_1 = 25 \quad S_1^2 = 161.9$$
$$\text{Population B}: \ n_2 = 25 \quad S_2^2 = 133.7$$

What is the value of F_{STAT} if you are testing the null hypothesis $H_0: \sigma_1^2 = \sigma_2^2$?

10.40 In Problem 10.39, how many degrees of freedom are there in the numerator and denominator of the F test?

10.41 In Problems 10.39 and 10.40, what is the upper-tail critical value for F if the level of significance, α, is 0.05 and the alternative hypothesis is $H_1: \sigma_1^2 \neq \sigma_2^2$?

10.42 In Problems 10.39 through 10.41, what is your statistical decision?

10.43 The following information is available for two samples selected from independent but very right-skewed populations:

$$\text{Population A}: \ n_1 = 16 \quad S_1^2 = 47.3$$
$$\text{Population B}: \ n_2 = 13 \quad S_2^2 = 36.4$$

Should you use the F test to test the null hypothesis of equality of variances? Discuss.

10.44 In Problem 10.43, assume that two samples are selected from independent normally distributed populations.

a. At the 0.05 level of significance, is there evidence of a difference between σ_1^2 and σ_2^2?
b. Suppose that you want to perform a one-tail test. At the 0.05 level of significance, what is the upper-tail critical value of F to determine whether there is evidence that $\sigma_1^2 > \sigma_2^2$? What is your statistical decision?

APPLYING THE CONCEPTS

10.45 Shipments of meat, meat by-products, and other ingredients are mixed together in several filling lines at a pet food canning factory. Operations managers suspect that, although the mean amount filled per can of pet food is usually stable, the variability of the cans filled in line A is greater than that of line B. The following data from a sample of 8-ounce cans is as follows:

	Line A	Line B
$\bar{X}$	8.005	7.997
S	0.012	0.005
n	11	16

a. At the 0.05 level of significance, is there evidence that the variance in line A is greater than the variance in line B?
b. Interpret the p-value.
c. What assumption do you need to make in (a) about the two populations in order to justify your use of the F test?

SELF Test **10.46** The Computer Anxiety Rating Scale (CARS) measures an individual's level of computer anxiety, on a scale from 20 (no anxiety) to 100 (highest level of anxiety). Researchers at Miami University administered CARS to 172 business students. One of the objectives of the study was to determine whether there is a difference between the level of computer anxiety experienced by female students and male students. They found the following:

	Males	Females
$\bar{X}$	40.26	36.85
S	13.35	9.42
n	100	72

Source: Data extracted from T. Broome and D. Havelka, "Determinants of Computer Anxiety in Business Students," *The Review of Business Information Systems,* Spring 2002, 6(2), pp. 9–16.

a. At the 0.05 level of significance, is there evidence of a difference in the variability of the computer anxiety experienced by males and females?
b. Interpret the p-value.
c. What assumption do you need to make about the two populations in order to justify the use of the F test?
d. Based on (a) and (b), which t test defined in Section 10.1 should you use to test whether there is a significant difference in mean computer anxiety for female and male students?

10.47 A bank with a branch located in a commercial district of a city has the business objective of improving the process for serving customers during the noon-to-1 P.M. lunch period. To do so, the waiting time (defined as the time elapsed from when the customer enters the line until he or she reaches the teller window) needs to be shortened to increase customer satisfaction. A random sample of 15 customers is selected (and stored in **Bank1**), and the results (in minutes) are as follows:

4.21	5.55	3.02	5.13	4.77	2.34	3.54	3.20
4.50	6.10	0.38	5.12	6.46	6.19	3.79	

Suppose that another branch, located in a residential area, is also concerned with the noon-to-1 P.M. lunch period. A random sample of 15 customers is selected (and stored in **Bank2**), and the results (in minutes) are as follows:

9.66	5.90	8.02	5.79	8.73	3.82	8.01	8.35
10.49	6.68	5.64	4.08	6.17	9.91	5.47	

a. Is there evidence of a difference in the variability of the waiting time between the two branches? (Use $\alpha = 0.05$.)
b. Determine the p-value in (a) and interpret its meaning.
c. What assumption about the population distribution of the two banks is necessary in (a)? Is the assumption valid for these data?
d. Based on the results of (a), is it appropriate to use the pooled-variance t test to compare the means of the two branches?

10.48 An important feature of digital cameras is battery life, the number of shots that can be taken before the battery needs to be recharged. The file **DigitalCameras** contains battery life information for 29 subcompact cameras and 16 compact cameras. (Data extracted from "Digital Cameras," *Consumer Reports*, July 2009, pp. 28–29.)
a. Is there evidence of a difference in the variability of the battery life between the two types of digital cameras? (Use $\alpha = 0.05$.)
b. Determine the p-value in (a) and interpret its meaning.
c. What assumption about the population distribution of the two types of cameras is necessary in (a)? Is the assumption valid for these data?
d. Based on the results of (a), which t test defined in Section 10.1 should you use to compare the mean battery life of the two types of cameras?

10.49 Do young children use cell phones? Apparently so, according to a recent study (A. Ross, "Message to Santa; Kids Want a Phone," *Palm Beach Post*, December 16, 2008, pp. 1A, 4A), which stated that cell phone users under 12 years of age averaged 137 calls per month as compared to 231 calls per month for cell phone users 13 to 17 years of age. No sample sizes were reported. Suppose that the results were based on samples of 50 cell phone users in each group and that the sample standard deviation for cell phone users under 12 years of age was 51.7 calls per month and the sample standard deviation for cell phone users 13 to 17 years of age was 67.6 calls per month.
a. Using a 0.05 level of significance, is there evidence of a difference in the variances of cell phone usage between cell phone users under 12 years of age and cell phone users 13 to 17 years of age?
b. On the basis of the results in (a), which t test defined in Section 10.1 should you use to compare the means of the two groups of cell phone users? Discuss.

10.50 Is there a difference in the variation of the yield of five-year CDs at different times? The file **CD-FiveYear** contains the yields for a five-year certificate of deposit (CD) for 25 banks in the United States, as of March 29, 2010 and August 23, 2010. (Data extracted from **www.Bankrate.com**, March 29, 2010 and August 23, 2010.) At the 0.05 level of significance, is there evidence of a difference in the variance of the yield of five-year CDs on March 29, 2010 and August 23, 2010? Assume that the population yields are normally distributed.

USING STATISTICS @ BLK Beverages Revisited

In the Using Statistics scenario, you were the regional sales manager for BLK Beverages. You compared the sales volume of BLK Cola when the product is placed in the normal shelf location to the sales volume when the product is featured in a special end-aisle display. An experiment was performed in which 10 stores used the normal shelf location and 10 stores used the end-aisle displays. Using a t test for the difference between two means, you were able to conclude that the mean sales using end-aisle location are higher than the mean sales for the normal shelf location. A confidence interval allowed you to infer with 95% confidence that the end-aisle location sells, on average, 6.73 to 36.67 cases more than the normal shelf location. You also performed the F test for the difference between two variances to see if the store-to-store variability in sales in stores using the end-aisle location differed from the store-to-store variability in sales in stores using the normal shelf location. You concluded that there was no significant difference in the variability of the sales of cola for the two display locations. As regional sales manager, your next step in increasing sales is to convince more stores to use the special end-aisle display.

SUMMARY

In this chapter, you were introduced to a variety of two-sample tests. For situations in which the samples are independent, you learned statistical test procedures for analyzing possible differences between means, variances, and proportions. In addition, you learned a test procedure that is frequently used when analyzing differences between the means of two related samples. Remember that you need to select the test that is most appropriate for a given set of conditions and to critically investigate the validity of the assumptions underlying each of the hypothesis-testing procedures.

Table 10.7 provides a list of topics covered in this chapter. The roadmap in Figure 10.15 illustrates the steps needed in determining which two-sample test of hypothesis to use. The following are the questions you need to consider:

1. What type of data do you have? If you are dealing with categorical variables, use the Z test for the difference between two proportions. (This test assumes independent samples.)
2. If you have a numerical variable, determine whether you have independent samples or related samples. If you have related samples, and you can assume approximate normality, use the paired t test.
3. If you have independent samples, is your focus on variability or central tendency? If the focus is on variability, and you can assume approximate normality, use the F test.
4. If your focus is central tendency and you can assume approximate normality, determine whether you can assume that the variances of the two populations are equal. (This assumption can be tested using the F test.)
5. If you can assume that the two populations have equal variances, use the pooled-variance t test. If you cannot assume that the two populations have equal variances, use the separate-variance t test.

TABLE 10.7
Summary of Topics in Chapter 10

	Types of Data	
Type of Analysis	**Numerical**	**Categorical**
Comparing two populations	t tests for the difference in the means of two independent populations (Section 10.1)	Z test for the difference between two proportions (Section 10.3)
	Paired t test (Section 10.2)	
	F test for the ratio of two variances (Section 10.4)	

FIGURE 10.15
Roadmap for selecting a two-sample test of hypothesis

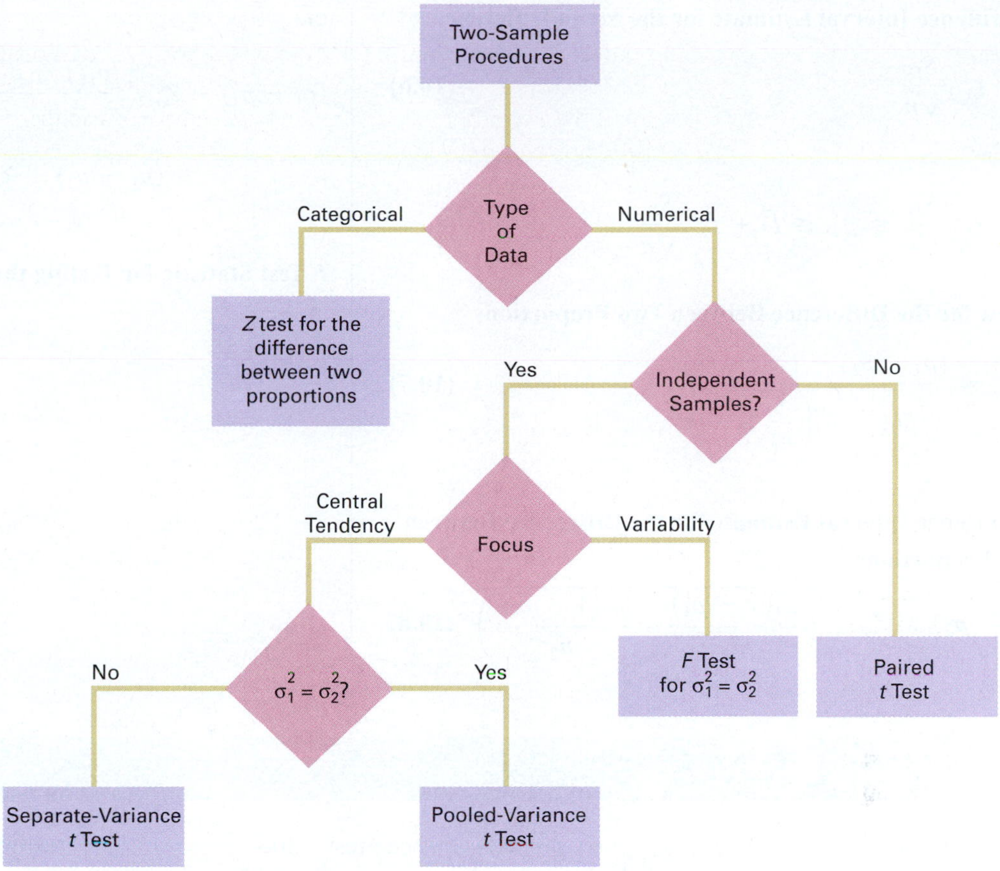

KEY EQUATIONS

Pooled-Variance *t* Test for the Difference Between Two Means

$$t_{STAT} = \frac{(\bar{X}_1 - \bar{X}_2) - (\mu_1 - \mu_2)}{\sqrt{S_p^2\left(\frac{1}{n_1} + \frac{1}{n_2}\right)}} \quad \textbf{(10.1)}$$

Confidence Interval Estimate for the Difference in the Means of Two Independent Populations

$$(\bar{X}_1 - \bar{X}_2) \pm t_{\alpha/2}\sqrt{S_p^2\left(\frac{1}{n_1} + \frac{1}{n_2}\right)} \quad \textbf{(10.2)}$$

or

$$(\bar{X}_1 - \bar{X}_2) - t_{\alpha/2}\sqrt{S_p^2\left(\frac{1}{n_1} + \frac{1}{n_2}\right)} \le \mu_1 - \mu_2 \le (\bar{X}_1 - \bar{X}_2) + t_{\alpha/2}\sqrt{S_p^2\left(\frac{1}{n_1} + \frac{1}{n_2}\right)}$$

Separate-Variance *t* Test for the Difference Between Two Means

$$t_{STAT} = \frac{(\bar{X}_1 - \bar{X}_2) - (\mu_1 - \mu_2)}{\sqrt{\frac{S_1^2}{n_1} + \frac{S_2^2}{n_2}}} \quad \textbf{(10.3)}$$

Computing Degrees of Freedom in the Separate-Variance *t* Test

$$V = \frac{\left(\frac{S_1^2}{n_1} + \frac{S_2^2}{n_2}\right)^2}{\frac{\left(\frac{S_1^2}{n_1}\right)^2}{n_1 - 1} + \frac{\left(\frac{S_2^2}{n_2}\right)^2}{n_2 - 1}} \quad \textbf{(10.4)}$$

Paired *t* Test for the Mean Difference

$$t_{STAT} = \frac{\bar{D} - \mu_D}{\frac{S_D}{\sqrt{n}}} \quad \textbf{(10.5)}$$

Confidence Interval Estimate for the Mean Difference

$$\bar{D} \pm t_{\alpha/2}\frac{S_D}{\sqrt{n}} \quad (10.6)$$

or

$$\bar{D} - t_{\alpha/2}\frac{S_D}{\sqrt{n}} \le \mu_D \le \bar{D} + t_{\alpha/2}\frac{S_D}{\sqrt{n}}$$

Z **Test for the Difference Between Two Proportions**

$$Z_{STAT} = \frac{(p_1 - p_2) - (\pi_1 - \pi_2)}{\sqrt{\bar{p}(1-\bar{p})\left(\frac{1}{n_1} + \frac{1}{n_2}\right)}} \quad (10.7)$$

Confidence Interval Estimate for the Difference Between Two Proportions

$$(p_1 - p_2) \pm Z_{\alpha/2}\sqrt{\left(\frac{p_1(1-p_1)}{n_1} + \frac{p_2(1-p_2)}{n_2}\right)} \quad (10.8)$$

or

$$(p_1 - p_2) - Z_{\alpha/2}\sqrt{\frac{p_1(1-p_1)}{n_1} + \frac{p_2(1-p_2)}{n_1}} \le (\pi_1 - \pi_2)$$
$$\le (p_1 - p_2) + Z_{\alpha/2}\sqrt{\frac{p_1(1-p_1)}{n_1} + \frac{p_2(1-p_2)}{n_2}}$$

F **Test Statistic for Testing the Ratio of Two Variances**

$$F_{STAT} = \frac{S_1^2}{S_2^2} \quad (10.9)$$

KEY TERMS

CHAPTER REVIEW PROBLEMS

CHECKING YOUR UNDERSTANDING

10.51 What are some of the criteria used in the selection of a particular hypothesis-testing procedure?

10.52 Under what conditions should you use the pooled-variance *t* test to examine possible differences in the means of two independent populations?

10.53 Under what conditions should you use the *F* test to examine possible differences in the variances of two independent populations?

10.54 What is the distinction between two independent populations and two related populations?

10.55 What is the distinction between repeated measurements and matched items?

10.56 When you have two independent populations, explain the similarities and differences between the test of hypothesis for the difference between the means and the confidence interval estimate for the difference between the means.

10.57 Under what conditions should you use the paired *t* test for the mean difference between two related populations?

APPLYING THE CONCEPTS

10.58 The per-store daily customer count (i.e., the mean number of customers in a store in one day) for a nationwide convenience store chain that operates nearly 10,000 stores has been steady, at 900, for some time. To increase the customer count, the chain is considering cutting prices for coffee beverages. The small size will now be \$0.59 instead of \$0.99, and medium size will be \$0.69 instead of \$1.19. Even with this reduction in price, the chain will have a 40% gross margin on coffee. The question to be determined is how much to cut prices to increase the daily customer count without reducing the gross margin on coffee sales too much. The chain decides to carry out an experiment in a sample of 30 stores where customer counts have been running almost exactly at the national average of 900. In 15 of the stores, the price of a small coffee will now be \$0.59 instead of \$0.99, and in 15 other stores, the price of a small coffee will now be \$0.79. After four weeks, the 15 stores that priced the small coffee at \$0.59 had a mean daily customer count of 964 and a standard deviation of 88, and the 15 stores that priced the small coffee at \$0.79 had a mean daily customer count of 941 and a standard deviation of 76. Analyze these data (use the 0.05 level of significance) and answer the following questions.

a. Does reducing the price of a small coffee to either \$0.59 or \$0.79 increase the mean per-store daily customer count?

b. If reducing the price of a small coffee to either \$0.59 or \$0.79 increases the mean per-store daily customer count, is there any difference in the mean per-store daily customer count between stores in which a small coffee was priced at \$0.59 and stores in which a small coffee was priced at \$0.79?

c. What price do you recommend that a small coffee should be sold for?

10.59 A study conducted in March 2009 found that about half of U.S. adults trusted the U.S. government more than U.S. business to solve the economic problems of the United States. However, when the population is subdivided by political party affiliation, the results are very different. The study showed that 72% of Democrats trusted the government more, but only 29% of Republicans trusted the government more. Suppose that you are in charge of updating the study. You will take a national sample of Democrats and a national sample of Republicans and then try to use the results to show statistical evidence that the proportion of Democrats trusting the government more than business is greater than the proportion of Republicans trusting the government more than business.

a. What are the null and alternative hypotheses?

b. What is a Type I error in the context of this study?

c. What is a Type II error in the context of this study?

10.60 The American Society for Quality (ASQ) conducted a salary survey of all its members. ASQ members work in all areas of manufacturing and service-related institutions, with a common theme of an interest in quality. Two job titles are black belt and green belt. (See Section 17.8, for a description of these titles in a Six Sigma quality improvement initiative.) Descriptive statistics concerning salaries for these two job titles are given in the following table:

Job Title	Sample Size	Mean	Standard Deviation
Black Belt	219	87,342	20,955
Green belt	34	65,679	18,137

Source: Data extracted from J. D. Conklin, "Salary Survey: Holding Steady," *Quality Progress*, December 2009, pp. 20–53.

a. Using a 0.05 level of significance, is there a difference in the variability of salaries between black belts and green belts?

b. Based on the result of (a), which *t* test defined in Section 10.1 is appropriate for comparing mean salaries?

c. Using a 0.05 level of significance, is there a difference between the mean salary of black belts and green belts?

10.61 Do male and female students study the same amount per week? In 2007, 58 sophomore business students were surveyed at a large university that has more than 1,000 sophomore business students each year. The file **StudyTime** contains the gender and the number of hours spent studying in a typical week for the sampled students.

a. At the 0.05 level of significance, is there a difference in the variance of the study time for male students and female students?

b. Using the results of (a), which *t* test is appropriate for comparing the mean study time for male and female students?

c. At the 0.05 level of significance, conduct the test selected in (b).

d. Write a short summary of your findings.

10.62 Two professors wanted to study how students from their two universities compared in their capabilities of using Excel spreadsheets in undergraduate information systems courses. (Data extracted from H. Howe and M. G. Simkin, "Factors Affecting the Ability to Detect Spreadsheet Errors," *Decision Sciences Journal of Innovative Education*, January 2006, pp. 101–122.) A comparison of the student demographics was also performed. One school is a state university in the western United States, and the other school is a state university in the eastern United States. The following table contains information regarding the ages of the students:

School	Sample Size	Mean	Standard Deviation
Western	93	23.28	6.29
Eastern	135	21.16	1.32

a. Using a 0.01 level of significance, is there evidence of a difference in the variances of the age of students at the western school and at the eastern school?

b. Discuss the practical implications of the test performed in (a). Address, specifically, the impact equal (or unequal) variances in age has on teaching an undergraduate information systems course.

c. To test for a difference in the mean age of students, is it most appropriate to use the pooled-variance *t* test or the separate-variance *t* test?

School	Sample Size	Mean	Standard Deviation
Western	93	2.6	2.4
Eastern	135	4.0	2.1

The following table contains information regarding the years of spreadsheet usage of the students:

d. Using a 0.01 level of significance, is there evidence of a difference in the variances of the years of spreadsheet usage of students at the western school and at the eastern school?

e. Based on the results of (d), use the most appropriate test to determine, at the 0.01 level of significance, whether there is evidence of a difference in the mean years of spreadsheet usage of students at the western school and at the eastern school.

10.63 The file **Restaurants** contains the ratings for food, décor, service, and the price per person for a sample of 50 restaurants located in a city and 50 restaurants located in a suburb. Completely analyze the differences between city and suburban restaurants for the variables food rating, décor rating, service rating, and cost per person, using $\alpha = 0.05$.

Source: Data extracted from *Zagat Survey 2010: New York City Restaurants* and *Zagat Survey 2009–2010: Long Island Restaurants.*

10.64 A computer information systems professor is interested in studying the amount of time it takes students enrolled in the introduction to computers course to write and run a program in Visual Basic. The professor hires you to analyze the following results (in minutes) from a random sample of nine students (the data are stored in the **VB** file):

10 13 9 15 12 13 11 13 12

a. At the 0.05 level of significance, is there evidence that the population mean amount is greater than 10 minutes? What will you tell the professor?

b. Suppose that the professor, when checking her results, realizes that the fourth student needed 51 minutes rather than the recorded 15 minutes to write and run the Visual Basic program. At the 0.05 level of significance, reanalyze the question posed in (a), using the revised data. What will you tell the professor now?

c. The professor is perplexed by these paradoxical results and requests an explanation from you regarding the justification for the difference in your findings in (a) and (b). Discuss.

d. A few days later, the professor calls to tell you that the dilemma is completely resolved. The original number 15 (the fourth data value) was correct, and therefore your findings in (a) are being used in the article she is writing for a computer journal. Now she wants to hire you to compare the results from that group of introduction to computers students against those from a sample of 11 computer majors in order to determine whether there is evidence that computer majors can write a Visual Basic program in less time than introductory students. For the computer majors, the sample mean is 8.5 minutes, and the sample standard deviation is 2.0 minutes. At the 0.05 level of significance, completely analyze these data. What will you tell the professor?

e. A few days later, the professor calls again to tell you that a reviewer of her article wants her to include the *p*-value for the "correct" result in (a). In addition, the professor inquires about an unequal-variances problem, which the reviewer wants her to discuss in her article. In your own words, discuss the concept of *p*-value and also describe the unequal-variances problem. Then, determine the *p*-value in (a) and discuss whether the unequal-variances problem had any meaning in the professor's study.

10.65 An article (A. Jennings, "What's Good for a Business Can Be Hard on Friends," *The New York Times*, August 4, 2007, pp. C1–C2) reported that according to a poll, the mean number of cell phone calls per month was 290 for 18- to 24-year-olds and 194 for 45- to 54-year-olds, whereas the mean number of text messages per month was 290 for 18- to 24-year-olds and 57 for 45- to 54-year-olds. Suppose that the poll was based on a sample of 100 18- to 24-year-olds and 100 45- to 54-year-olds and that the standard deviation of the number of cell phone calls per month was 100 for 18- to 24-year-olds and 90 for 45- to 54-year-olds, whereas the standard deviation of the number of text messages per month was 90 for 18- to 24-year-olds and 77 for 45- to 54-year-olds. Assume a level of significance of 0.05.

a. Is there evidence of a difference in the variances of the number of cell phone calls per month for 18- to 24-year-olds and for 45- to 54-year-olds?

b. Is there evidence of a difference in the mean number of cell phone calls per month for 18- to 24-year-olds and for 45- to 54-year-olds?

c. Construct and interpret a 95% confidence interval estimate for the difference in the mean number of cell phone calls per month for 18- to 24-year-olds and 45- to 54-year-olds.

d. Is there evidence of a difference in the variances of the number of text messages per month for 18- to 24-year-olds and 45- to 54-year-olds?

e. Is there evidence of a difference in the mean number of text messages per month for 18- to 24-year-olds and 45- to 54-year-olds?

f. Construct and interpret a 95% confidence interval estimate for the difference in the mean number of text messages per month for 18- to 24-year-olds and 45- to 54-year-olds.

g. Based on the results of (a) through (f), what conclusions can you make concerning cell phone and text message usage between 18- to 24-year-olds and 45- to 54-year-olds?

10.66 The lengths of life (in hours) of a sample of 40 100-watt light bulbs produced by manufacturer A and a sample of 40 100-watt light bulbs produced by manufacturer B are stored in **Bulbs**. Completely analyze the differences between the lengths of life of the bulbs produced by the two manufacturers. (Use $\alpha = 0.05$.)

10.67 A hotel manager looks to enhance the initial impressions that hotel guests have when they check in. Contributing to initial impressions is the time it takes to deliver a guest's luggage to the room after check-in. A random sample of 20 deliveries on a particular day were selected in Wing A of the hotel, and a random sample of 20 deliveries were selected in Wing B. The results are stored in **Luggage**. Analyze the data and determine whether there is a difference in the mean delivery time in the two wings of the hotel. (Use $\alpha = 0.05$.)

10.68 According to Census estimates, there are about 20 million children between 8 and 12 years old (referred to as *tweens*) in the United States in 2009. A recent survey of 1,223 8- to 12-year-old children (S. Jayson, "It's Cooler Than Ever to Be a Tween," *USA Today*, February 4, 2009, pp. 1A, 2A) reported the following results. Suppose the survey was based on 600 boys and 623 girls.

What Tweens Did in the Past Week	Boys	Girls
Played a game on a video game system	498	243
Read a book for fun	276	324
Gave product advice to parents	186	181
Shopped at a mall	144	262

For *each type of activity*, determine whether there is a difference between boys and girls at the 0.05 level of significance.

10.69 The manufacturer of Boston and Vermont asphalt shingles knows that product weight is a major factor in the customer's perception of quality. Moreover, the weight represents the amount of raw materials being used and is therefore very important to the company from a cost standpoint. The last stage of the assembly line packages the shingles before they are placed on wooden pallets. Once a pallet is full (a pallet for most brands holds 16 squares of shingles), it is weighed, and the measurement is recorded. The file **Pallet** contains the weight (in pounds) from a sample of 368 pallets of Boston shingles and 330 pallets of Vermont shingles. Completely analyze the differences in the weights of the Boston and Vermont shingles, using $\alpha = 0.05$.

10.70 The manufacturer of Boston and Vermont asphalt shingles provides its customers with a 20-year warranty on most of its products. To determine whether a shingle will last as long as the warranty period, the manufacturer conducts accelerated-life testing. Accelerated-life testing exposes the shingle to the stresses it would be subject to in a lifetime of normal use in a laboratory setting via an experiment that takes only a few minutes to conduct. In this test, a shingle is repeatedly scraped with a brush for a short period of time, and the shingle granules removed by the brushing are weighed (in grams). Shingles that experience low amounts of granule loss are expected to last longer in normal use than shingles that experience high amounts of granule loss. In this situation, a shingle should experience no more than 0.8 grams of granule loss if it is expected to last the length of the warranty period. The file **Granule** contains a sample of 170 measurements made on the company's Boston shingles and 140 measurements made on Vermont shingles. Completely analyze the differences in the granule loss of the Boston and Vermont shingles, using $\alpha = 0.05$.

10.71 There are a tremendous number of mutual funds from which an investor can choose. Each mutual fund has its own mix of different types of investments. The data in **BestFunds** present the 3-year annualized return, 5-year annualized return, 10-year annualized return, and expense ratio (in %) for the 10 best mutual funds according to the *U.S. News & World Report* score for large cap value and large cap growth mutual funds. (Data extracted from K. Shinkle, "The Best Funds for the Long Term, *U.S. News & World Report*, Summer 2010, pp. 52–56.) Analyze the data and determine whether any differences exist between large cap value and large cap growth mutual funds. (Use the 0.05 level of significance.)

REPORT WRITING EXERCISE

10.72 Referring to the results of Problems 10.69 and 10.70 concerning the weight and granule loss of Boston and Vermont shingles, write a report that summarizes your conclusions.

TEAM PROJECT

The file **Bond Funds** contains information regarding eight variables from a sample of 184 bond mutual funds:

Type—Type of bonds comprising the bond fund (intermediate government or short-term corporate)
Assets—In millions of dollars
Fees—Sales charges (no or yes)
Expense ratio—Ratio of expenses to net assets, in percentage
Return 2009—Twelve-month return in 2009
Three-year return—Annualized return, 2007–2009
Five-year return—Annualized return, 2005–2009
Risk—Risk-of-loss factor of the mutual fund (below average, average, or above average)

10.73 Completely analyze the differences between bond mutual funds without fees and bond mutual funds with fees in terms of 2009 return, three-year return, five-year return, and expense ratio. Write a report summarizing your findings.

10.74 Completely analyze the difference between intermediate government bond mutual funds and short-term corporate bond mutual funds in terms of 2009 return, three-year return, five-year return, and expense ratio. Write a report summarizing your findings.

STUDENT SURVEY DATABASE

10.75 Problem 1.27 on page 14 describes a survey of 62 undergraduate students (stored in **UndergradSurvey**).

a. At the 0.05 level of significance, is there evidence of a difference between males and females in grade point average, expected starting salary, number of social networking sites registered for, age, spending on textbooks and supplies, text messages sent in a week, and the wealth needed to feel rich?

b. At the 0.05 level of significance, is there evidence of a difference between students who plan to go to graduate school and those who do not plan to go to graduate school in grade point average, expected starting salary, number of social networking sites registered for, age, spending on textbooks and supplies, text messages sent in a week, and the wealth needed to feel rich?

10.76 Problem 1.27 on page 14 describes a survey of 62 undergraduate students (stored in **UndergradSurvey**).

a. Select a sample of undergraduate students at your school and conduct a similar survey for them.

b. For the data collected in (a), repeat (a) and (b) of Problem 10.75.

c. Compare the results of (b) to those of Problem 10.75.

10.77 Problem 1.28 on page 15 describes a survey of 44 MBA students (stored in **GradSurvey**). For these data, at the 0.05 level of significance, is there evidence of a difference between males and females in age, undergraduate grade point average, graduate grade point average, expected salary upon graduation, spending on textbooks and supplies, text messages sent in a week, and the wealth needed to feel rich?

10.78 Problem 1.28 on page 15 describes a survey of 44 MBA students (stored in **GradSurvey**).

a. Select a sample of graduate students in your MBA program and conduct a similar survey for those students.

b. For the data collected in (a), repeat Problem 10.77.

c. Compare the results of (b) to those of Problem 10.77.

MANAGING ASHLAND MULTICOMM SERVICES

AMS communicates with customers who subscribe to cable television services through a special secured email system that sends messages about service changes, new features, and billing information to in-home digital set-top boxes for later display. To enhance customer service, the operations department established the business objective of reducing the amount of time to fully update each subscriber's set of messages. The department selected two candidate messaging systems and conducted an experiment in which 30 randomly chosen cable subscribers were assigned one of the two systems (15 assigned to each system). Update times were measured, and the results are organized in Table AMS10.1 (and stored in **AMS10**).

EXERCISES

1. Analyze the data in Table AMS10.1 and write a report to the computer operations department that indicates your findings. Include an appendix in which you discuss the reason you selected a particular statistical test to compare the two independent groups of callers.

2. Suppose that instead of the research design described in the case, there were only 15 subscribers sampled, and the update process for each subscriber e-mail was measured for each of the two messaging systems. Suppose the results were organized in Table AMS10.1—making each row in the table a pair of values for an individual subscriber. Using these suppositions, reanalyze the Table AMS10.1 data and write a report for presentation to the team that indicates your findings.

TABLE AMS10.1
Download Time for Two Different E-mail Interfaces

Email Interface 1	Email Interface 2
4.13	3.71
3.75	3.89
3.93	4.22
3.74	4.57
3.36	4.24
3.85	3.90
3.26	4.09
3.73	4.05
4.06	4.07
3.33	3.80
3.96	4.36
3.57	4.38
3.13	3.49
3.68	3.57
3.63	4.74

DIGITAL CASE

Apply your knowledge about hypothesis testing in this Digital Case, which continues the cereal-fill packaging dispute Digital Case from Chapters 7 and 9.

Even after the recent public experiment about cereal box weights, Consumers Concerned About Cereal Cheaters (CCACC) remains convinced that Oxford Cereals has misled the public. The group has created and circulated **MoreCheating.pdf,** a document in which it claims that cereal boxes produced at Plant Number 2 in Springville weigh less than the claimed mean of 368 grams. Review this document and then answer the following questions:

1. Do the CCACC's results prove that there is a statistically significant difference in the mean weights of cereal boxes produced at Plant Numbers 1 and 2?
2. Perform the appropriate analysis to test the CCACC's hypothesis. What conclusions can you reach based on the data?

REFERENCES

1. Conover, W. J., *Practical Nonparametric Statistics*, 3rd ed. (New York: Wiley, 2000).
2. Daniel, W., *Applied Nonparametric Statistics*, 2nd ed. (Boston: Houghton Mifflin, 1990).
3. *Microsoft Excel 2010* (Redmond, WA: Microsoft Corp., 2010).
4. *Minitab Release 16* (State College, PA: Minitab, Inc., 2010).
5. Satterthwaite, F. E., "An Approximate Distribution of Estimates of Variance Components," *Biometrics Bulletin*, 2(1946): 110–114.
6. Snedecor, G. W., and W. G. Cochran, *Statistical Methods*, 8th ed. (Ames, IA: Iowa State University Press, 1989).
7. Winer, B. J., D. R. Brown, and K. M. Michels, *Statistical Principles in Experimental Design*, 3rd ed. (New York: McGraw-Hill, 1989).

EG10.1 COMPARING the MEANS of TWO INDEPENDENT POPULATIONS

Pooled-Variance t Test for the Difference Between Two Means

PHStat2 Use **Pooled-Variance t Test** to perform the pooled-variance *t* test. For example, to perform the Figure 10.3 pooled-variance *t* test for the BLK Cola data shown on page 365, open to the **DATA worksheet** of the **COLA workbook**. Select **PHStat ➔ Two-Sample Tests (Unsummarized Data) ➔ Pooled-Variance t Test**. In the procedure's dialog box (shown below):

1. Enter **0** as the **Hypothesized Difference**.
2. Enter **0.05** as the **Level of Significance**.
3. Enter **A1:A11** as the **Population 1 Sample Cell Range**.
4. Enter **B1:B11** as the **Population 2 Sample Cell Range**.
5. Check **First cells in both ranges contain label**.
6. Click **Two-Tail Test**.
7. Enter a **Title** and click **OK**.

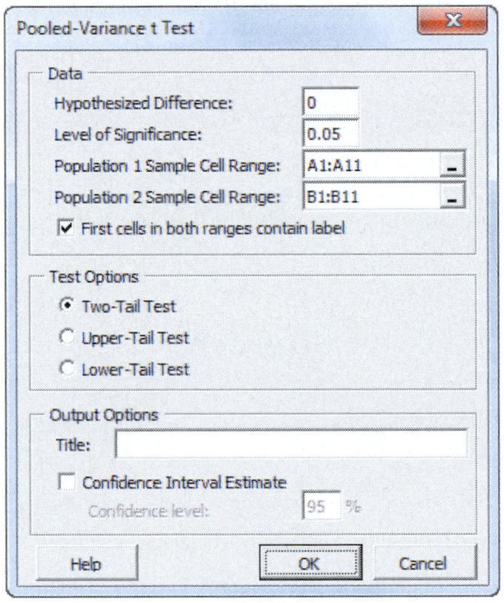

For problems that use summarized data, select **PHStat ➔ Two-Sample Tests (Summarized Data) ➔ Pooled-Variance t Test**. In that procedure's dialog box, enter the hypothesized difference and level of significance, as well as the sample size, sample mean, and sample standard deviation for each sample.

In-Depth Excel Use the **COMPUTE worksheet** of the **Pooled-Variance T workbook**, shown in Figure 10.3 on page 368, as a template for performing the two-tail pooled-variance *t* test. The worksheet contains data and formulas to use the unsummarized data for the BLK Cola example. In cell B24 and B25, respectively, the worksheet uses the expressions **-TINV(*level of significance, degrees of freedom*)** and **TINV(*level of significance, degrees of freedom*)** to compute the lower and upper critical values. In cell B26, **TDIST(*absolute value of the t test statistic, degrees of freedom*, 2)** computes the *p*-value.

For other problems, use the COMPUTE worksheet with either unsummarized or summarized data. For unsummarized data, keep the formulas that calculate the sample size, sample mean, and sample standard deviation in cell ranges B7:B9 and B11:B13 and change the data in columns A and B in the **DATACOPY worksheet**. For summarized data, replace the formulas in cell ranges B7:B9 and B11:B13 with the sample statistics and ignore the DATACOPY worksheet.

Use the similar **COMPUTE_LOWER** or **COMPUTE_UPPER worksheets** in the same workbook as templates for performing one-tail pooled-variance *t* tests. These worksheets can also use either unsummarized or summarized data.

Analysis ToolPak Use **t-Test: Two-Sample Assuming Equal Variances** to perform the pooled-variance *t* test for unsummarized data. For example, to create results equivalent to those in the Figure 10.3 pooled-variance *t* test for the BLK Cola example on page 368, open to the **DATA worksheet** of the **COLA workbook** and:

1. Select **Data ➔ Data Analysis**.
2. In the Data Analysis dialog box, select **t-Test: Two-Sample Assuming Equal Variances** from the **Analysis Tools** list and then click **OK**.

In the procedure's dialog box (shown below):

3. Enter **A1:A11** as the **Variable 1 Range** and enter **B1:B11** as the **Variable 2 Range**.
4. Enter **0** as the **Hypothesized Mean Difference**.
5. Check **Labels** and enter **0.05** as **Alpha**.
6. Click **New Worksheet Ply**.
7. Click **OK**.

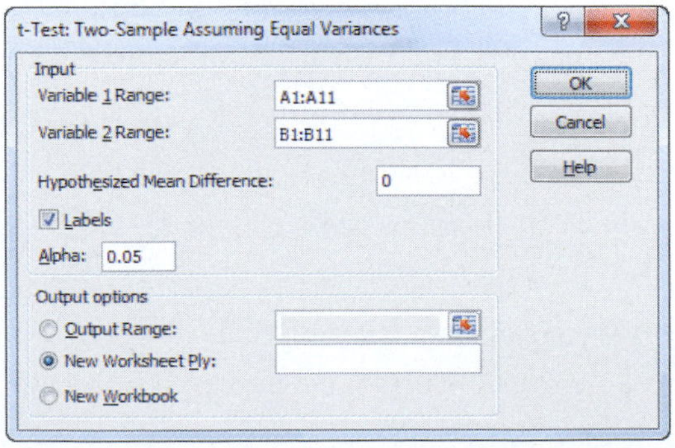

Results (shown below) appear in a new worksheet that contains both two-tail and one-tail test critical values and *p*-values. Unlike Figure 10.3, only the positive (upper) critical value is listed for the two-tail test.

	A	B	C
1	t-Test: Two-Sample Assuming Equal Variances		
2			
3		*Normal*	*EndAisle*
4	Mean	50.3	72
5	Variance	350.6778	157.3333
6	Observations	10	10
7	Pooled Variance	254.0056	
8	Hypothesized Mean Difference	0	
9	df	18	
10	t Stat	-3.04455	
11	P(T<=t) one-tail	0.003487	
12	t Critical one-tail	1.734064	
13	P(T<=t) two-tail	0.006975	
14	t Critical two-tail	2.100922	

Confidence Interval Estimate for the Difference Between Two Means

PHStat2 Use the *PHStat2* instructions for the pooled-variance *t* test. In step 7, also check **Confidence Interval Estimate** and enter a **Confidence Level** in its box, in addition to entering a **Title** and clicking **OK**.

In-Depth Excel Use the *In-Depth Excel* instructions for the pooled-variance *t* test. The worksheets in the **Pooled-Variance T workbook** include a confidence interval estimate for the difference between two means in the cell range D3:E16.

t Test for the Difference Between Two Means Assuming Unequal Variances

PHStat2 Use **Separate-Variance t Test** to perform this *t* test. For example, to perform the Figure 10.7 separate-variance *t* test for the BLK Cola data on page 374, open to the **DATA worksheet** of the **COLA workbook**. Select **PHStat → Two-Sample Tests (Unsummarized Data) → Separate-Variance t Test**. In the procedure's dialog box (shown at the top of the right column):

1. Enter **0** as the **Hypothesized Difference**.
2. Enter **0.05** as the **Level of Significance**.
3. Enter **A1:A11** as the **Population 1 Sample Cell Range**.
4. Enter **B1:B11** as the **Population 2 Sample Cell Range**.
5. Check **First cells in both ranges contain label**.
6. Click **Two-Tail Test**.
7. Enter a **Title** and click **OK**.

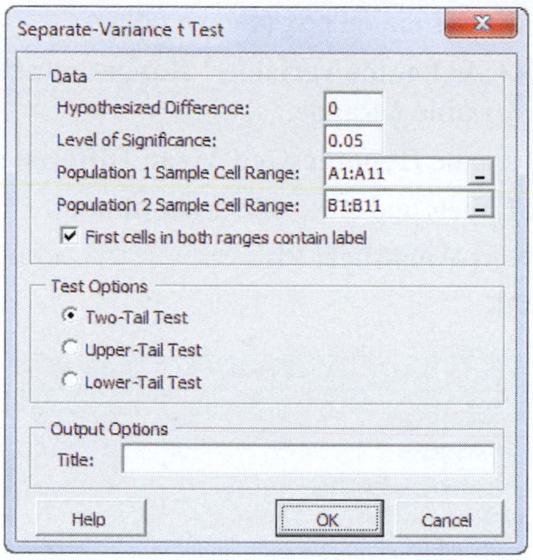

For problems that use summarized data, select **PHStat → Two-Sample Tests (Summarized Data) → Separate-Variance t Test**. In that procedure's dialog box, enter the hypothesized difference and the level of significance, as well as the sample size, sample mean, and sample standard deviation for each group.

In-Depth Excel Use the **COMPUTE worksheet** of the **Separate-Variance T workbook**, shown in Figure 10.7 on page 374, as a template for performing the two-tail separate-variance *t* test. The worksheet contains data and formulas to use the unsummarized data for the BLK Cola example. In cells B25 and B26, respectively, **-TINV(*level of significance, degrees of freedom*)** and **TINV(*level of significance, degrees of freedom*)** computes the lower and upper critical values. In cell B27, the worksheet uses **TDIST(*absolute value of the t test statistic, degrees of freedom*, 2)** to compute the *p*-value.

For other problems, use the COMPUTE worksheet with either unsummarized or summarized data. For unsummarized data, keep the formulas that calculate the sample size, sample mean, and sample standard deviation in cell ranges B7:B9 and B11:B13 and change the data in columns A and B in the **DATACOPY worksheet**. For summarized data, replace the formulas in cell ranges B7:B9 and B11:B13 with the sample statistics and ignore the DATACOPY worksheet. Use the similar **COMPUTE_LOWER** or **COMPUTE_UPPER worksheets** in the same workbook as templates for performing one-tail *t* tests.

Analysis ToolPak Use **t-Test: Two-Sample Assuming Unequal Variances** to perform the separate-variance *t* test for unsummarized data. For example, to create results equivalent to those in the Figure 10.7 separate-variance *t* test for the BLK Cola data on page 374, open to the **DATA worksheet** of the **COLA workbook** and:

1. Select **Data → Data Analysis**.
2. In the Data Analysis dialog box, select **t-Test: Two-Sample Assuming Unequal Variances** from the **Analysis Tools** list and then click **OK**.

In the procedure's dialog box (shown below):

3. Enter **A1:A11** as the **Variable 1 Range** and enter **B1:B11** as the **Variable 2 Range**.
4. Enter **0** as the **Hypothesized Mean Difference**.
5. Check **Labels** and enter **0.05** as **Alpha**.
6. Click **New Worksheet Ply**.
7. Click **OK**.

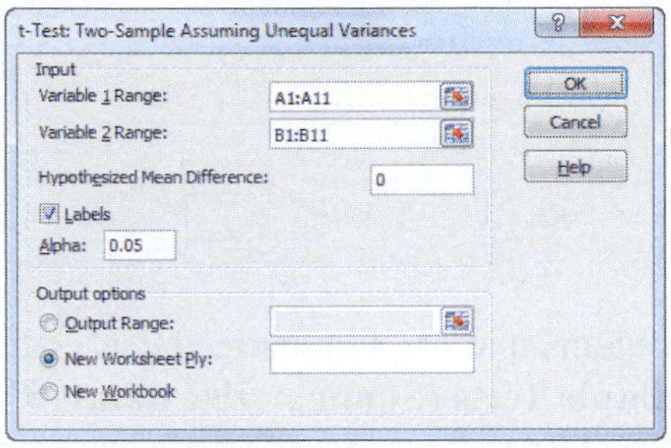

Results (shown below) appear in a new worksheet that contains both two-tail and one-tail test critical values and *p*-values. Unlike Figure 10.7, only the positive (upper) critical value is listed for the two-tail test. Because the Analysis ToolPak uses table lookups to approximate the critical values and the *p*-value, the results will differ slightly from the values shown in Figure 10.7.

	A	B	C
1	t-Test: Two-Sample Assuming Unequal Variances		
2			
3		*Normal*	*EndAisle*
4	Mean	50.3	72
5	Variance	350.6778	157.3333
6	Observations	10	10
7	Hypothesized Mean Difference	0	
8	df	16	
9	t Stat	-3.04455	
10	P(T<=t) one-tail	0.003863	
11	t Critical one-tail	1.745884	
12	P(T<=t) two-tail	0.007726	
13	t Critical two-tail	2.119905	

EG10.2 COMPARING the MEANS of TWO RELATED POPULATIONS

Paired t Test

PHStat2 Use **Paired t Test** to perform the paired *t* test. For example, to perform the Figure 10.9 paired *t* test for the textbook price data on page 381, open to the **DATA worksheet** of the **BookPrices workbook**. Select **PHStat → Two-Sample Tests (Unsummarized Data) → Paired t Test**. In the procedure's dialog box (shown in the right column):

1. Enter **0** as the **Hypothesized Mean Difference**.
2. Enter **0.05** as the **Level of Significance**.
3. Enter **C1:C20** as the **Population 1 Sample Cell Range**.
4. Enter **D1:D20** as the **Population 2 Sample Cell Range**.
5. Check **First cells in both ranges contain label**.
6. Click **Two-Tail Test**.
7. Enter a **Title** and click **OK**.

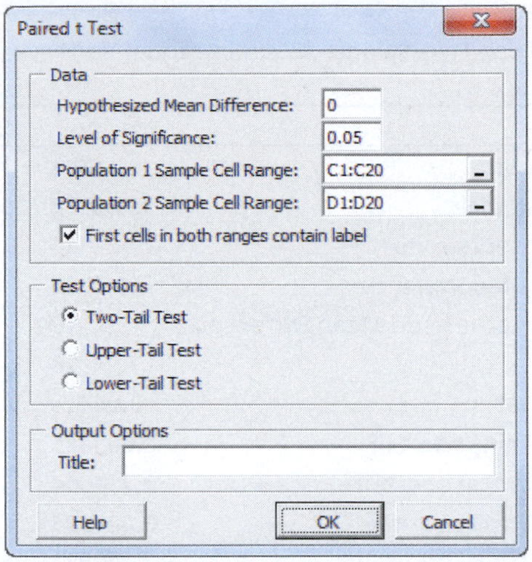

The procedure creates two worksheets, one of which is similar to the PtCalcs worksheet discussed in the following *In-Depth Excel* section. For problems that use summarized data, select **PHStat → Two-Sample Tests (Summarized Data) → Paired t Test**. In that procedure's dialog box, enter the hypothesized mean difference and the level of significance, as well as the sample size, sample mean, and sample standard deviation for each sample.

In-Depth Excel Use the **COMPUTE** and **PtCalcs worksheets** of the **Paired T workbook**, as a template for performing the two-tail paired *t* test. The PtCalcs worksheet contains the differences and other intermediate calculations that allow the COMPUTE worksheet, shown in Figure 10.9 on page 381, to compute the sample size, $\overline{D}$, and S_D.

The COMPUTE and PtCalcs worksheets contain the data and formulas for the unsummarized data for the textbook prices example. In cells B16 and B17, respectively, the COMPUTE worksheet uses **-TINV(*level of significance*, *degrees of freedom*)** and **TINV(*level of significance*, *degrees of freedom*)** to compute the lower and upper critical values. In cell B18, the worksheet uses **TDIST(*absolute value of the t test statistic*, *degrees of freedom*, 2)** to compute the *p*-value.

For other problems, paste the unsummarized data into columns A and B of the PtCalcs worksheet. For sample sizes greater than 19, select the cell range C20:D20 and copy the formulas in those cells down through the last data row. For sample sizes less than 19, delete the column C and D formulas for which there are no column A and B values. If you know the sample size, $\overline{D}$, and S_D values, you can ignore the PtCalcs worksheet and enter the values in cells B8, B9, and B11 of the COMPUTE worksheet, overwriting the formulas that those cells contain. Use the **COMPUTE_LOWER** or **COMPUTE_UPPER worksheets** in the same workbook as templates for performing one-tail tests.

Analysis ToolPak Use **t-Test: Paired Two Sample for Means** to perform the paired *t* test for unsummarized data. For example, to create results equivalent to those in the Figure 10.9 paired *t* test for the textbook price data on page 381, open to the **DATA worksheet** of the **BookPrices workbook** and:

1. Select **Data → Data Analysis**.
2. In the Data Analysis dialog box, select **t-Test: Paired Two Sample for Means** from the **Analysis Tools** list and then click **OK**.

In the procedure's dialog box (shown below):

3. Enter **C1:C20** as the **Variable 1 Range** and enter **D1:D20** as the **Variable 2 Range**.
4. Enter **0** as the **Hypothesized Mean Difference**.
5. Check **Labels** and enter **0.05** as **Alpha**.
6. Click **New Worksheet Ply**.
7. Click **OK**.

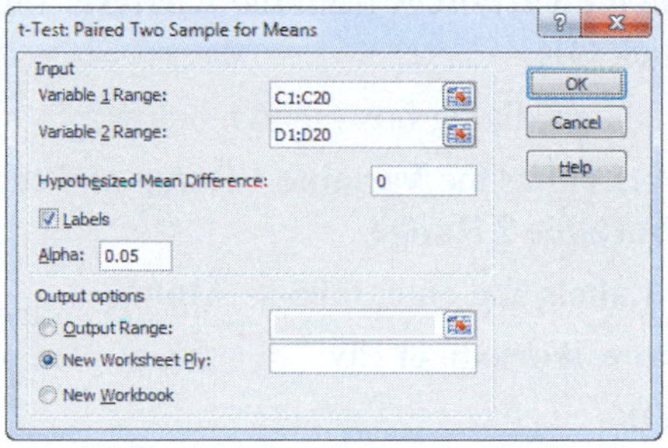

Results (shown below) appear in a new worksheet that contains both two-tail and one-tail test critical values and *p*-values. Unlike Figure 10.9, only the positive (upper) critical value is listed for the two-tail test.

	A	B	C
1	t-Test: Paired Two Sample for Means		
2			
3		*Bookstore*	*Online*
4	Mean	139.3668	126.7005
5	Variance	3028.359	2704.292
6	Observations	19	19
7	Pearson Correlation	0.839615	
8	Hypothesized Mean Difference	0	
9	df	18	
10	t Stat	1.813248	
11	P(T<=t) one-tail	0.043252	
12	t Critical one-tail	1.734064	
13	P(T<=t) two-tail	0.086504	
14	t Critical two-tail	2.100922	

EG10.3 COMPARING the PROPORTIONS of TWO INDEPENDENT POPULATIONS

Z Test for the Difference Between Two Proportions

PHStat2 Use ***Z* Test for Differences in Two Proportions** to perform this *Z* test. For example, to perform the Figure 10.13 *Z* test for the hotel guest satisfaction survey on page 388, select **PHStat → Two-Sample Tests (Summarized Data) → *Z* Test for Differences in Two Proportions**. In the procedure's dialog box (shown below):

1. Enter **0** as the **Hypothesized Difference**.
2. Enter **0.05** as the **Level of Significance**.
3. For the Population 1 Sample, enter **163** as the **Number of Items of Interest** and **227** as the **Sample Size**.
4. For the Population 2 Sample, enter **154** as the **Number of Items of Interest** and **262** as the **Sample Size**.
5. Click **Two-Tail Test**.
6. Enter a **Title** and click **OK**.

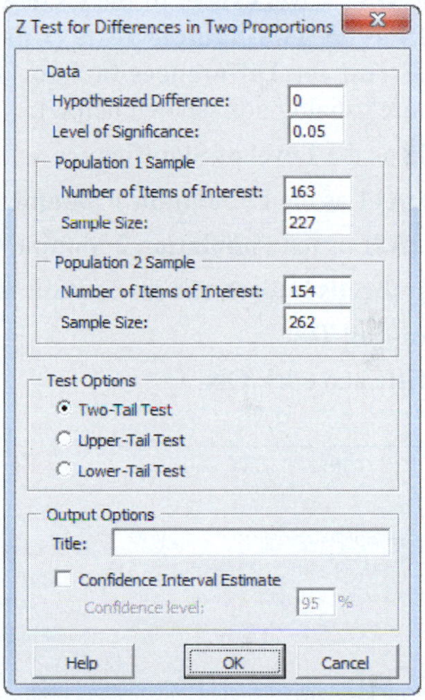

In-Depth Excel Use the **COMPUTE worksheet** of the ***Z* Two Proportions workbook**, shown in Figure 10.13 on page 388, as a template for performing the two-tail *Z* test for the difference between two proportions. The worksheet contains data for the hotel guest satisfaction survey. In cells B21 and B22 respectively, the worksheet uses **NORMSINV (*level of significance*/2)** and **NORMSINV(1 - *level of significance*/2)** to compute the lower and upper critical values. In cell B23, the worksheet uses the expression **2 * (1 - NORMSDIST(*absolute value of the Z test statistic*))** to compute the *p*-value.

For other problems, change the values in cells B4, B5, B7, B8, B10, and B11 as necessary. Use the similar **COMPUTE_LOWER** or **COMPUTE_UPPER worksheets** in the same workbook as templates for performing one-tail separate-variance *t* tests.

Confidence Interval Estimate for the Difference Between Two Proportions

PHStat2 Use the *PHStat2* instructions for the *Z* test for the difference between two proportions. In step 6, also check

Confidence Interval Estimate and enter a **Confidence Level** in its box, in addition to entering a **Title** and clicking **OK**.

In-Depth Excel Use the *In-Depth Excel* instructions for the Z test for the difference between two proportions. The worksheets in the **Z Two Proportions workbook** include a confidence interval estimate for the difference between two means in the cell range D3:E16.

EG10.4 *F* TEST for the RATIO of TWO VARIANCES

PHStat2 Use **F Test for Differences in Two Variances** to perform this F test. For example, to perform the Figure 10.14 F test for the BLK Cola sales data on page 394, open to the **DATA worksheet** of the **COLA workbook**. Select **PHStat → Two-Sample Tests (Unsummarized Data) → F Test for Differences in Two Variances**. In the procedure's dialog box (shown below):

1. Enter **0.05** as the **Level of Significance**.
2. Enter **A1:A11** as the **Population 1 Sample Cell Range**.
3. Enter **B1:B11** as the **Population 2 Sample Cell Range**.
4. Check **First cells in both ranges contain label**.
5. Click **Two-Tail Test**.
6. Enter a **Title** and click **OK**.

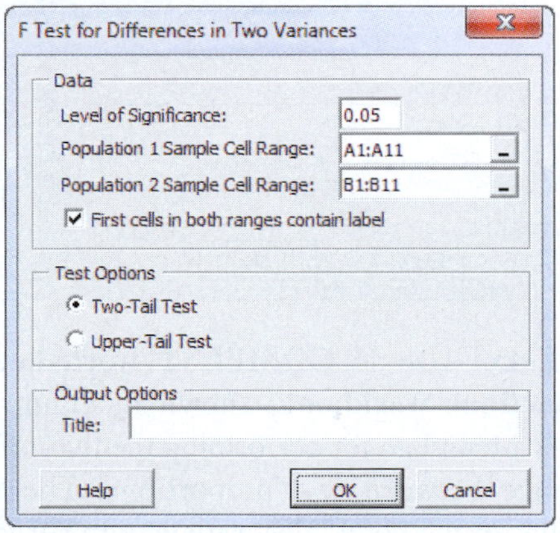

For problems that use summarized data, select **PHStat → Two-Sample Tests (Summarized Data) → F Test for Differences in Two Variances**. In that procedure's dialog box, enter the level of significance and the sample size and sample variance for each sample.

In-Depth Excel Use the **COMPUTE worksheet** of the **F Two Variances workbook**, shown in Figure 10.14 on page 394, as a template for performing the two-tail F test for the ratio of two variances. The worksheet contains data and formulas for using the unsummarized data for the BLK Cola example. In cell B18, the worksheet uses **FINV(*level of significance* / 2, *population 1 sample degrees of freedom, population 2 sample degrees of freedom*)** to compute the upper critical value and in cell B19 uses the equivalent of the expression **2 * FDIST(*F test statistic, population 1 sample degrees of freedom, population 2 sample degrees of freedom*)** to compute the p-value.

For other problems using unsummarized data, paste the unsummarized data into columns A and B of the **DATACOPY worksheet**. For summarized data, replace the COMPUTE worksheet formulas in cell ranges B6:B7 and B9:B10 with the sample statistics and ignore the DATACOPY worksheet. Use the similar **COMPUTE_UPPER worksheet** in the same workbook as a template for performing the upper-tail test.

Analysis ToolPak Use the **F-Test Two-Sample for Variances** procedure to perform the F test for the difference between two variances for unsummarized data. For example, to create results equivalent to those in the Figure 10.14 F test for the BLK Cola sales data on page 394, open to the **DATA worksheet** of the **COLA workbook** and:

1. Select **Data → Data Analysis**.
2. In the Data Analysis dialog box, select **F-Test Two-Sample for Variances** from the **Analysis Tools** list and then click **OK**.

In the procedure's dialog box (shown below):

3. Enter **A1:A11** as the **Variable 1 Range** and enter **B1:B11** as the **Variable 2 Range**.
4. Check **Labels** and enter **0.05** as **Alpha**.
5. Click **New Worksheet Ply**.
6. Click **OK**.

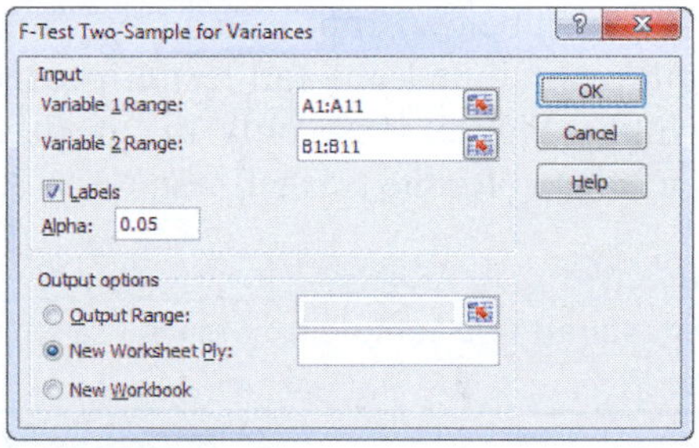

Results (shown below) appear in a new worksheet and include only the one-tail test p-value (0.124104), which must be doubled for the two-tail test shown in Figure 10.14 on page 394.

	A	B	C
1	F-Test Two-Sample for Variances		
2			
3		*Normal*	*End-Aisle*
4	Mean	50.3	72
5	Variance	350.6778	157.3333
6	Observations	10	10
7	df	9	9
8	F	2.228884	
9	P(F<=f) one-tail	0.124104	
10	F Critical one-tail	3.178893	

CHAPTER 10 MINITAB GUIDE

MG10.1 COMPARING the MEANS of TWO INDEPENDENT POPULATIONS

Pooled-Variance *t* Test for the Difference Between Two Means

Use **2-Sample t** to perform the pooled-variance *t* test. For example, to perform the Figure 10.3 pooled-variance *t* test for the BLK Cola data shown on page xx, open to the **Cola worksheet**. Select **Stat ➔ Basic Statistics ➔ 2-Sample t**. In the 2-Sample t (Test and Confidence Interval) dialog box (shown below):

1. Click **Samples in different columns** and press **Tab**.
2. Double-click **C1 Normal** in the variables list to add **Normal** to the **First** box.
3. Double-click **C2 End-Aisle** in the variables list to add **'End-Aisle'** to the **Second** box.
4. Check **Assume equal variances**.
5. Click **Graphs**.

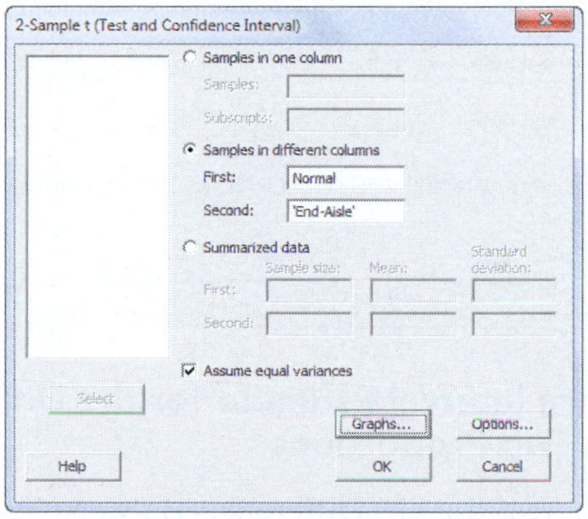

In the 2-Sample t - Graphs dialog box (not shown):

6. Check **Boxplots of data** and then click **OK**.
7. Back in the 2-Sample t (Test and Confidence Interval) dialog box, click **OK**.

For stacked data, use these replacement steps 1 through 3:

1. Click **Samples in one column**.
2. Enter the name of the column that contains the measurement in the **Samples** box.
3. Enter the name of the column that contains the sample names in the **Subscripts** box.

Confidence Interval Estimate for the Difference Between Two Means

Use the instructions for the pooled-variance *t* test, replacing step 7 with these steps 7 through 12:

7. Back in the 2-Sample t (Test and Confidence Interval) dialog box, click **Options**.

In the 2-Sample t - Options dialog box (shown below):

8. Enter **95.0** in the **Confidence level** box.
9. Enter **0.0** in the **Test difference** box.
10. Select **not equal** from the **Alternative** drop-down list (to perform the two-tail test).
11. Click **OK**.
12. Back in the 2-Sample t (Test and Confidence Interval) dialog box, click **OK**.

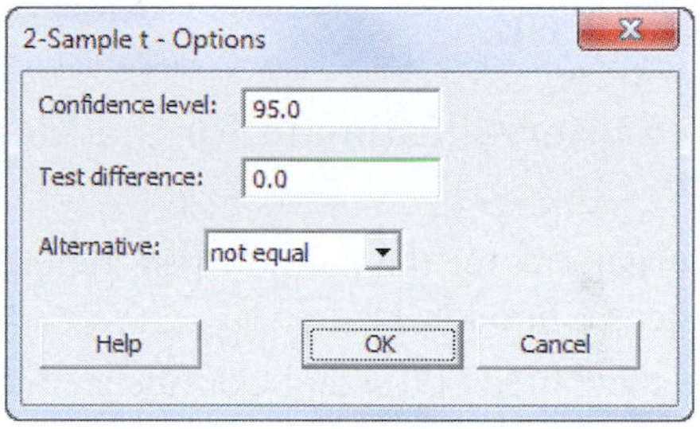

To perform a one-tail test, select **less than** or **greater than** in step 10.

t Test for the Difference Between Two Means, Assuming Unequal Variances

Use the instructions for the pooled-variance *t* test with this replacement step 4:

4. Clear **Assume equal variances.**

MG10.2 COMPARING the MEANS of TWO RELATED POPULATIONS

Paired *t* Test

Use **Paired t** to perform the paired *t* test. For example, to perform the Figure 10.9 paired *t* test for the textbook price data on page 381, open to the **BookPrices worksheet**. Select **Stat ➔ Basic Statistics ➔ Paired t**. In the Paired *t* (Test and Confidence Interval) dialog box (shown on the top of page 412):

1. Click **Samples in columns** and press **Tab**.
2. Double-click **C3 Bookstore** in the variables list to enter **Bookstore** in the **First sample** box.
3. Double-click **C4 Online** in the variables list to enter **Online** in the **Second sample** box.
4. Click **Graphs**.

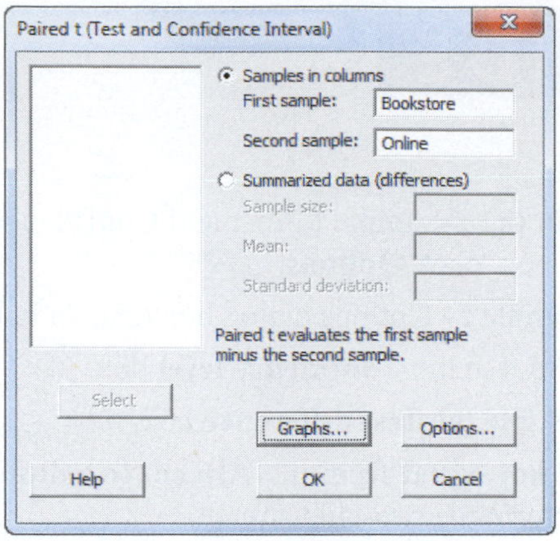

In the Paired t - Graphs dialog box (not shown):

5. Check **Boxplots of differences** and then click **OK**.
6. Back in the Paired *t* (Test and Confidence Interval) dialog box, click **OK**.

Confidence Interval Estimate for the Mean Difference

Use the instructions for the paired *t* test, replacing step 6 with these steps 6 through 11:

6. Back in the Paired *t* (Test and Confidence Interval) dialog box, click **Options**.

In the Paired t - Options dialog box (not shown):

7. Enter **95.0** in the **Confidence level** box.
8. Enter **0.0** in the **Test difference** box.
9. Select **not equal** from the **Alternative** drop-down list (to perform the two-tail test).
10. Click **OK**.
11. Back in the Paired *t* (Test and Confidence Interval) dialog box, click **OK**.

To perform a one-tail test, select **less than** or **greater than** in step 9.

MG10.3 COMPARING the PROPORTIONS of TWO INDEPENDENT POPULATIONS

Z Test for the Difference Between Two Proportions

Use **2 Proportions** to perform this *Z* test. For example, to perform the Figure 10.13 *Z* test for the hotel guest satisfaction survey on page 388, select **Stat → Basic Statistics → 2 Proportions**. In the 2 Proportions (Test and Confidence Interval) dialog box (shown at the top of the right column):

1. Click **Summarized data**.
2. In the **First** row, enter **163** in the **Events** box and **227** in the **Trials** box.
3. In the **Second** row, enter **154** in the **Events** box and **262** in the **Trials** box.
4. Click **Options**.

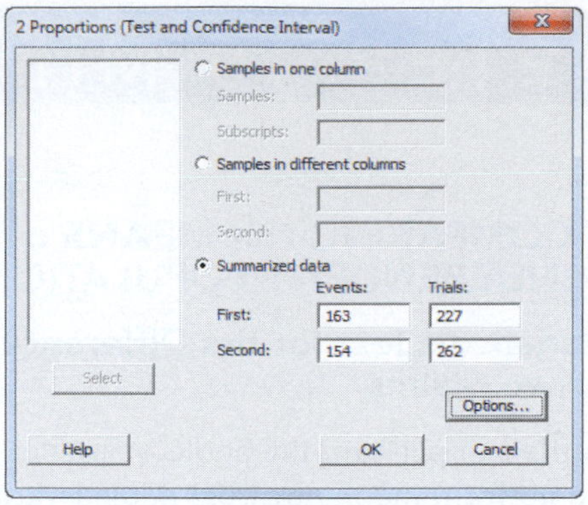

In the 2 Proportions - Options dialog box (shown below):

5. Enter **95.0** in the **Confidence level** box.
6. Enter **0.0** in the **Test difference** box.
7. Select **not equal** from the **Alternative** drop-down list.
8. Check **Use pooled estimate of p for test**.
9. Click **OK**.
10. Back in the 2 Proportions (Test and Confidence Interval) dialog box, click **OK**.

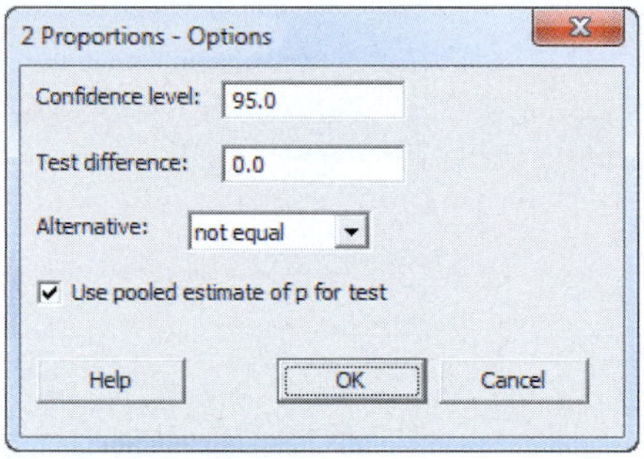

Confidence Interval Estimate for the Difference Between Two Proportions

Use the "*Z* Test for the Difference Between Two Proportions" instructions above to compute the confidence interval estimate.

MG10.4 *F* TEST for the RATIO of TWO VARIANCES

Use **2 Variances** to perform this *F* test. For example, to perform the Figure 10.14 *F* test for the BLK Cola sales data on page 394, open to the **COLA worksheet**. Select **Stat → Basic Statistics → 2 Variances**. In the 2 Variances (Test and Confidence) dialog box (shown on page 413):

1. Select **Samples in different columns** from the **Data** drop-down list and press **Tab**.
2. Double-click **C1 Normal** in the variables list to add **Normal** to the **First** box.
3. Double-click **C2 End-Aisle** in the variables list to add **'End-Aisle'** to the **Second** box.
4. Click **Graphs**.

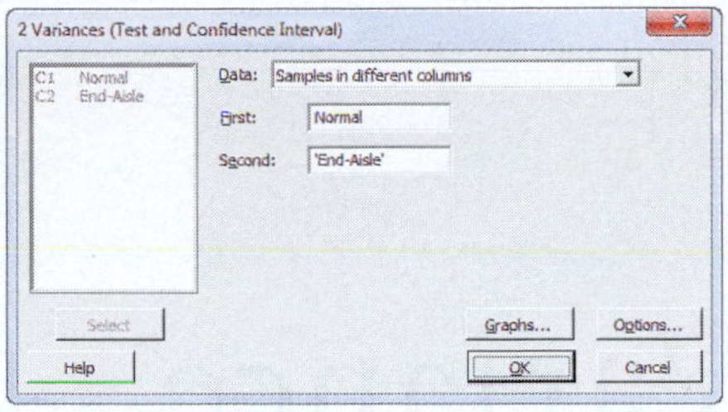

In the 2 Variances - Graph dialog box (not shown):

5. Clear all check boxes
6. Click **OK**.
7. Back in the 2 Variances (Test and Confidence) dialog box, click **OK**.

For summarized data, select **Sample standard deviations** or **Sample variances** in step 1 and enter the sample size and the sample statistics for the two variables in lieu of steps 2 and 3. For stacked data, use these replacement steps 1 through 3:

1. Select **Samples in one column** from the **Data** drop-down list.
2. Enter the name of the column that contains the measurement in the **Samples** box.
3. Enter the name of the column that contains the sample names in the **Subscripts** box.

If you use an older version of Minitab, you will see a 2 Variances dialog box instead of the 2 Variances (Test and Confidence) dialog box shown and described in this section. This older dialog box is similar to the dialog boxes shown in the preceding three sections: You click either **Samples in different columns** or **Summarized data** and then make entries similar to the ones described in the previous sections. The results created using older versions differ slightly from the Minitab results shown in Figure 10.14.

11 Analysis of Variance

Learning Objectives

In this chapter, you learn:

- The basic concepts of experimental design
- How to use the one-way analysis of variance to test for differences among the means of several groups
- When and how to use a randomized block design
- How to use the two-way analysis of variance and interpret the interaction effect
- How to perform multiple comparisons in a one-way analysis of variance, a randomized block design, and a two-way analysis of variance

USING STATISTICS

@ Perfect Parachutes

You are the production manager at the Perfect Parachutes Company. Parachutes are woven in your factory using a synthetic fiber purchased from one of four different suppliers. Strength of these fibers is an important characteristic that ensures quality parachutes. You need to decide whether the synthetic fibers from each of your four suppliers result in parachutes of equal strength. Furthermore, your factory uses two types of looms to produce parachutes, the Jetta and the Turk. You need to establish that the parachutes woven on both types of looms are equally strong. You also want to know if any differences in the strength of the parachute that can be attributed to the four suppliers are dependent on the type of loom used. How would you go about finding this information?

In Chapter 10, you used hypothesis testing to reach conclusions about possible differences between two populations. As a manager at Perfect Parachutes, you need to design an experiment to test the strength of parachutes woven from the synthetic fibers from the *four* suppliers. That is, you need to evaluate differences among *more than two* populations, or groups. (Populations are called *groups* in this chapter.)

This chapter begins by examining a *completely randomized design* that has one *factor* (which supplier to use) and several groups (the four suppliers). The randomized block design, which is an extension of the paired t test of Section 10.2, is discussed next. Then the completely randomized design is extended to the *factorial design*, in which more than one factor is simultaneously studied in a single experiment. For example, an experiment incorporating the four suppliers and the two types of looms would help you determine which supplier and type of loom to use in order to manufacture the strongest parachutes. Throughout the chapter, emphasis is placed on the assumptions behind the use of the various testing procedures.

11.1 The Completely Randomized Design: One-Way Analysis of Variance

In many situations, you need to examine differences among more than two **groups**. The groups involved are classified according to **levels** of a **factor** of interest. For example, a factor such as the price for which a product is sold may have several groups defined by *numerical levels* such as $0.59, $0.79, and $0.99, and a factor such as preferred supplier for a parachute manufacturer may have several groups defined by *categorical levels* such as Supplier 1, Supplier 2, Supplier 3, and Supplier 4. When there is only one factor, the experimental design is called a **completely randomized design**.

Organize multiple-sample data as unstacked data, one column per group, in order to make best use of the Excel and Minitab procedures that support the methods discussed in this chapter. For more information about unstacked (and stacked) data, review Section 2.3.

One-Way ANOVA *F* Test for Differences Among More Than Two Means

When you are analyzing a numerical variable and certain assumptions are met, you use the **analysis of variance (ANOVA)** to compare the means of the groups. The ANOVA procedure used for the completely randomized design is referred to as the **one-way ANOVA**, and it is an extension of the pooled variance t test for the difference between two means discussed in Section 10.1. Although ANOVA is an acronym for *analysis of variance*, the term is misleading because the objective in ANOVA is to analyze differences among the group means, *not* the variances. However, by analyzing the variation among and within the groups, you can reach conclusions about possible differences in group means. In ANOVA, the total variation is subdivided into variation that is due to differences *among* the groups and variation that is due to differences *within* the groups (see Figure 11.1). **Within-group variation** measures random variation. **Among-group variation** is due to differences from group to group. The symbol c is used to indicate the number of groups.

FIGURE 11.1
Partitioning the total variation in a completely randomized design

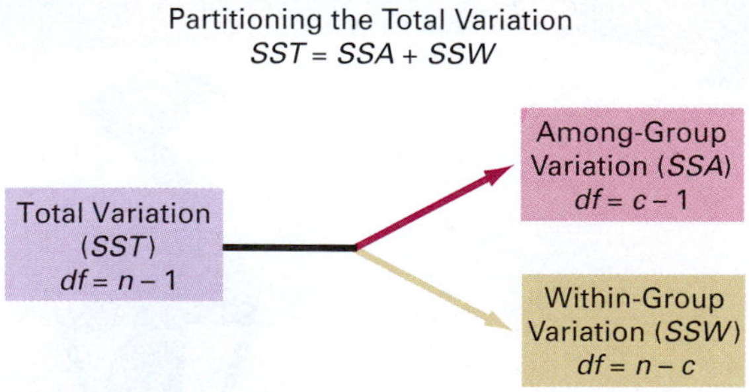

Assuming that the c groups represent populations whose values are randomly and independently selected, follow a normal distribution, and have equal variances, the null hypothesis of no differences in the population means:

$$H_0: \mu_1 = \mu_2 = \cdots = \mu_c$$

is tested against the alternative that not all the c population means are equal:

$$H_1: \text{Not all } \mu_j \text{ are equal (where } j = 1, 2, \ldots, c).$$

To perform an ANOVA test of equality of population means, you subdivide the total variation in the values into two parts—that which is due to variation among the groups and that which is due to variation within the groups. The **total variation** is represented by the **sum of squares total (*SST*)**. Because the population means of the c groups are assumed to be equal under the null hypothesis, you compute the total variation among all the values by summing the squared differences between each individual value and the **grand mean**, $\bar{\bar{X}}$. The grand mean is the mean of all the values in all the groups combined. Equation (11.1) shows the computation of the total variation.

TOTAL VARIATION IN ONE-WAY ANOVA

$$SST = \sum_{j=1}^{c}\sum_{i=1}^{n_j}(X_{ij} - \bar{\bar{X}})^2 \quad \textbf{(11.1)}$$

where

$$\bar{\bar{X}} = \frac{\sum_{j=1}^{c}\sum_{i=1}^{n_j} X_{ij}}{n} = \text{Grand mean}$$

X_{ij} = ith value in group j

n_j = number of values in group j

n = total number of values in all groups combined (that is, $n = n_1 + n_2 + \cdots + n_c$)

c = number of groups

You compute the among-group variation, usually called the **sum of squares among groups (*SSA*)**, by summing the squared differences between the sample mean of each group, $\bar{X}_j$, and the grand mean, $\bar{\bar{X}}$, weighted by the sample size, n_j, in each group. Equation (11.2) shows the computation of the among-group variation.

AMONG-GROUP VARIATION IN ONE-WAY ANOVA

$$SSA = \sum_{j=1}^{c} n_j(\bar{X}_j - \bar{\bar{X}})^2 \quad \textbf{(11.2)}$$

where

c = number of groups

n_j = number of values in group j

$\bar{X}_j$ = sample mean of group j

$\bar{\bar{X}}$ = grand mean

The within-group variation, usually called the **sum of squares within groups (*SSW*)**, measures the difference between each value and the mean of its own group and sums the squares of these differences over all groups. Equation (11.3) shows the computation of the within-group variation.

WITHIN-GROUP VARIATION IN ONE-WAY ANOVA

$$SSW = \sum_{j=1}^{c}\sum_{i=1}^{n_j}(X_{ij} - \bar{X}_j)^2 \quad \textbf{(11.3)}$$

where

$$X_{ij} = i\text{th value in group } j$$
$$\bar{X}_j = \text{sample mean of group } j$$

Because you are comparing c groups, there are $c - 1$ degrees of freedom associated with the sum of squares among groups. Because each of the c groups contributes $n_j - 1$ degrees of freedom, there are $n - c$ degrees of freedom associated with the sum of squares within groups. In addition, there are $n - 1$ degrees of freedom associated with the sum of squares total because you are comparing each value, X_{ij}, to the grand mean, $\bar{\bar{X}}$, based on all n values.

If you divide each of these sums of squares by its respective degrees of freedom, you have three variances, which in ANOVA are called **mean square** terms: *MSA* (mean square among), *MSW* (mean square within), and *MST* (mean square total).

MEAN SQUARES IN ONE-WAY ANOVA

$$MSA = \frac{SSA}{c - 1} \quad \textbf{(11.4a)}$$

$$MSW = \frac{SSW}{n - c} \quad \textbf{(11.4b)}$$

$$MST = \frac{SST}{n - 1} \quad \textbf{(11.4c)}$$

Although you want to compare the means of the c groups to determine whether a difference exists among them, the name ANOVA comes from the fact that you are comparing variances. If the null hypothesis is true and there are no differences in the c group means, all three mean squares (or *variances*)—*MSA*, *MSW*, and *MST*—provide estimates of the overall variance in the data. Thus, to test the null hypothesis:

$$H_0: \mu_1 = \mu_2 = \cdots = \mu_c$$

against the alternative:

$$H_1: \text{Not all } \mu_j \text{ are equal (where } j = 1, 2, \ldots, c)$$

you compute the one-way ANOVA F_{STAT} test statistic as the ratio of *MSA* to *MSW*, as in Equation (11.5).

ONE-WAY ANOVA F_{STAT} TEST STATISTIC

$$F_{STAT} = \frac{MSA}{MSW} \quad \textbf{(11.5)}$$

The F_{STAT} test statistic follows an ***F* distribution**, with $c - 1$ degrees of freedom in the numerator and $n - c$ degrees of freedom in the denominator. For a given level of significance, α, you reject the null hypothesis if the F_{STAT} test statistic computed in Equation (11.5) is greater than the upper-tail critical value, F_α, from the F distribution with $c - 1$ degrees of freedom in the numerator and $n - c$ in the denominator (see Table E.5). Thus, as shown in Figure 11.2, the decision rule is

$$\text{Reject } H_0 \text{ if } F_{STAT} > F_\alpha;$$
$$\text{otherwise, do not reject } H_0.$$

FIGURE 11.2

Regions of rejection and nonrejection when using ANOVA

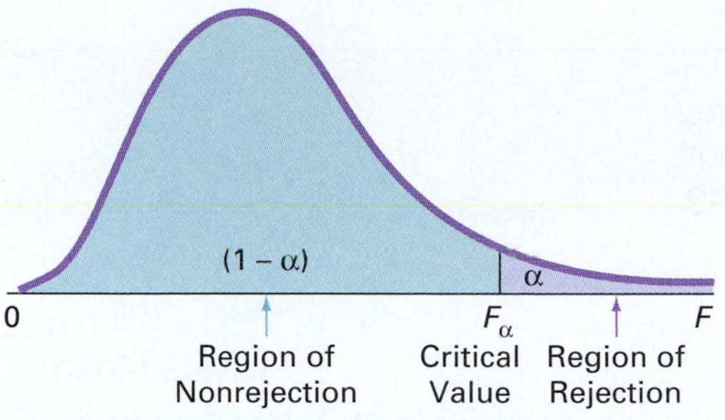

If the null hypothesis is true, the computed F_{STAT} test statistic is expected to be approximately equal to 1 because both the numerator and denominator mean square terms are estimating the overall variance in the data. If H_0 is false (and there are differences in the group means), the computed F_{STAT} test statistic is expected to be larger than 1 because the numerator, MSA, is estimating the differences among groups in addition to the overall variability in the values, while the denominator, MSW, is measuring only the overall variability in the values. Thus, when you use the ANOVA procedure, you reject the null hypothesis at a selected level of significance, α, only if the computed F_{STAT} test statistic is greater than F_α, the upper-tail critical value of the F distribution having $c - 1$ and $n - c$ degrees of freedom, as illustrated in Figure 11.2.

The results of an analysis of variance are usually displayed in an **ANOVA summary table**, as shown in Table 11.1. The entries in this table include the sources of variation (i.e., among-groups, within-groups, and total), the degrees of freedom, the sums of squares, the mean squares (i.e., the variances), and the computed F_{STAT} test statistic. The p-value, the probability of having an F_{STAT} value as large as or larger than the one computed, given that the null hypothesis is true, usually appears also. The p-value allows you to reach conclusions about the null hypothesis without needing to refer to a table of critical values of the F distribution. If the p-value is less than the chosen level of significance, α, you reject the null hypothesis.

TABLE 11.1

Analysis-of-Variance Summary Table

Source	Degrees of Freedom	Sum of Squares	Mean Square (Variance)	F
Among groups	$c - 1$	SSA	$MSA = \dfrac{SSA}{c - 1}$	$F_{STAT} = \dfrac{MSA}{MSW}$
Within groups	$n - c$	SSW	$MSW = \dfrac{SSW}{n - c}$	
Total	$n - 1$	SST		

To illustrate the one-way ANOVA F test, return to the Perfect Parachutes scenario (see page 415). You define the business problem as whether significant differences exist in the strength of parachutes woven using synthetic fiber purchased from each of the four suppliers. The strength of the parachutes is measured by placing them in a testing device that pulls on both ends of a parachute until it tears apart. The amount of force required to tear the parachute is measured on a tensile-strength scale, where the larger the value, the stronger the parachute.

Five parachutes are woven using the fiber supplied by each group—Supplier 1, Supplier 2, Supplier 3, and Supplier 4. You perform the experiment of testing the strength of each of the 20 parachutes by collecting the tensile strength measurement of each parachute. Results are organized by group and stored in **Parachute**. Those results, along with the sample mean and the sample standard deviation of each group are shown in Figure 11.3.

FIGURE 11.3

Tensile strength for parachutes woven with synthetic fibers from four different suppliers, along with the sample mean and sample standard deviation

	Supplier 1	Supplier 2	Supplier 3	Supplier 4
	18.5	26.3	20.6	25.4
	24.0	25.3	25.2	19.9
	17.2	24.0	20.8	22.6
	19.9	21.2	24.7	17.5
	18.0	24.5	22.9	20.4
Sample Mean	19.52	24.26	22.84	21.16
Sample Standard Deviation	2.69	1.92	2.13	2.98

In Figure 11.3, observe that there are differences in the sample means for the four suppliers. For Supplier 1, the mean tensile strength is 19.52. For Supplier 2, the mean tensile strength is 24.26. For Supplier 3, the mean tensile strength is 22.84, and for Supplier 4, the mean tensile strength is 21.16. What you need to determine is whether these sample results are sufficiently different to conclude that the *population* means are not all equal.

A scatter plot or main effects plot enables you to visualize the data and see how the measurements of tensile strength distribute. You can also observe differences among the groups as well as within groups. If the sample sizes in each group were larger, you could construct stem-and-leaf displays, boxplots, and normal probability plots.

Figure 11.4 shows an Excel scatter plot and a Minitab main effects plot for the four suppliers.

FIGURE 11.4

Excel scatter plot and Minitab main effects plot of tensile strengths for four different suppliers

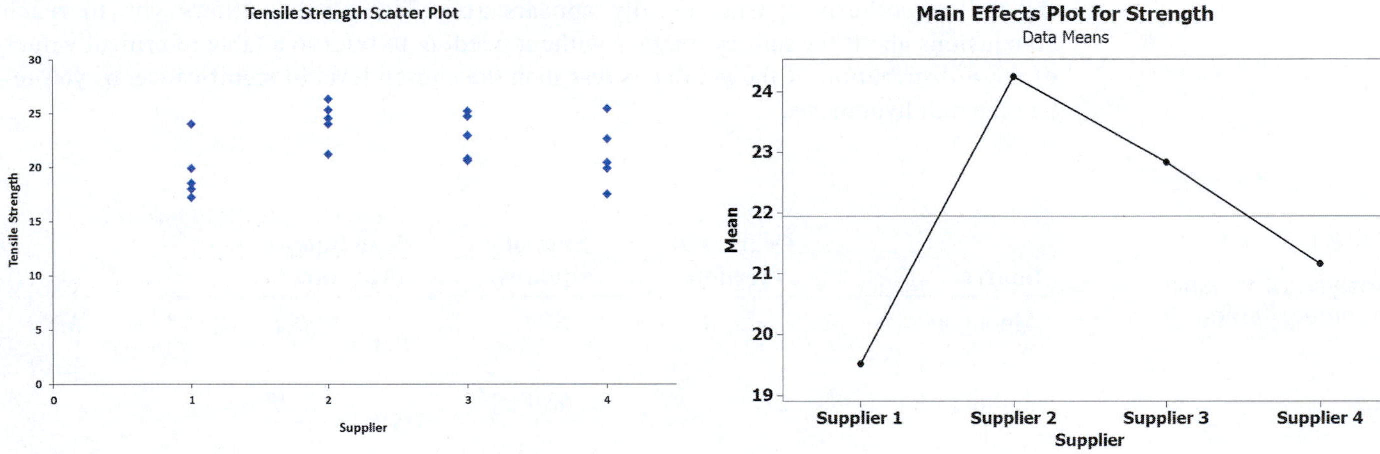

The null hypothesis states that there is no difference in mean tensile strength among the four suppliers:

$$H_0: \mu_1 = \mu_2 = \mu_3 = \mu_4$$

The alternative hypothesis states that at least one of the suppliers differs with respect to the mean tensile strength:

$$H_1: \text{Not all the means are equal.}$$

To construct the ANOVA summary table, you first compute the sample means in each group (see Figure 11.3 above). Then you compute the grand mean by summing all 20 values and dividing by the total number of values:

$$\bar{\bar{X}} = \frac{\sum_{j=1}^{c}\sum_{i=1}^{n_j} X_{ij}}{n} = \frac{438.9}{20} = 21.945$$

Then, using Equations (11.1) through (11.3) on page 417, you compute the sum of squares:

$$SSA = \sum_{j=1}^{c} n_j(\bar{X}_j - \bar{\bar{X}})^2 = (5)(19.52 - 21.945)^2 + (5)(24.26 - 21.945)^2$$
$$+ (5)(22.84 - 21.945)^2 + (5)(21.16 - 21.945)^2$$
$$= 63.2855$$

$$SSW = \sum_{j=1}^{c}\sum_{i=1}^{n_j}(X_{ij} - \bar{X}_j)^2$$
$$= (18.5 - 19.52)^2 + \cdots + (18 - 19.52)^2 + (26.3 - 24.26)^2 + \cdots + (24.5 - 24.26)^2$$
$$+ (20.6 - 22.84)^2 + \cdots + (22.9 - 22.84)^2 + (25.4 - 21.16)^2 + \cdots + (20.4 - 21.16)^2$$
$$= 97.5040$$

$$SST = \sum_{j=1}^{c}\sum_{i=1}^{n_j}(X_{ij} - \bar{\bar{X}})^2$$
$$= (18.5 - 21.945)^2 + (24 - 21.945)^2 + \cdots + (20.4 - 21.945)^2$$
$$= 160.7895$$

You compute the mean squares by dividing the sum of squares by the corresponding degrees of freedom [see Equation (11.4) on page 418]. Because $c = 4$ and $n = 20$,

$$MSA = \frac{SSA}{c - 1} = \frac{63.2855}{4 - 1} = 21.0952$$

$$MSW = \frac{SSW}{n - c} = \frac{97.5040}{20 - 4} = 6.0940$$

so that using Equation (11.5) on page 418,

$$F_{STAT} = \frac{MSA}{MSW} = \frac{21.0952}{6.0940} = 3.4616$$

For a selected level of significance, α, you find the upper-tail critical value, F_α, from the F distribution using Table E.5. A portion of Table E.5 is presented in Table 11.2. In the parachute supplier example, there are 3 degrees of freedom in the numerator and 16 degrees of freedom in the denominator. F_α, the upper-tail critical value at the 0.05 level of significance, is 3.24.

TABLE 11.2

Finding the Critical Value of F with 3 and 16 Degrees of Freedom at the 0.05 Level of Significance

Cumulative Probabilities = 0.95
Upper-Tail Area = 0.05
Numerator df_1

Denominator df_2	1	2	3	4	5	6	7	8	9
.	.	.	.	.	.	.	.	.	.
.	.	.	.	.	.	.	.	.	.
.	.	.	.	.	.	.	.	.	.
11	4.84	3.98	3.59	3.36	3.20	3.09	3.01	2.95	2.90
12	4.75	3.89	3.49	3.26	3.11	3.00	2.91	2.85	2.80
13	4.67	3.81	3.41	3.18	3.03	2.92	2.83	2.77	2.71
14	4.60	3.74	3.34	3.11	2.96	2.85	2.76	2.70	2.65
15	4.54	3.68	3.29	3.06	2.90	2.79	2.71	2.64	2.59
16	4.49	3.63	3.24	3.01	2.85	2.74	2.66	2.59	2.54

Source: Extracted from Table E.5.

Because $F_{STAT} = 3.4616$ is greater than $F_\alpha = 3.24$, you reject the null hypothesis (see Figure 11.5). You conclude that there is a significant difference in the mean tensile strength among the four suppliers.

FIGURE 11.5

Regions of rejection and nonrejection for the one-way ANOVA at the 0.05 level of significance, with 3 and 16 degrees of freedom

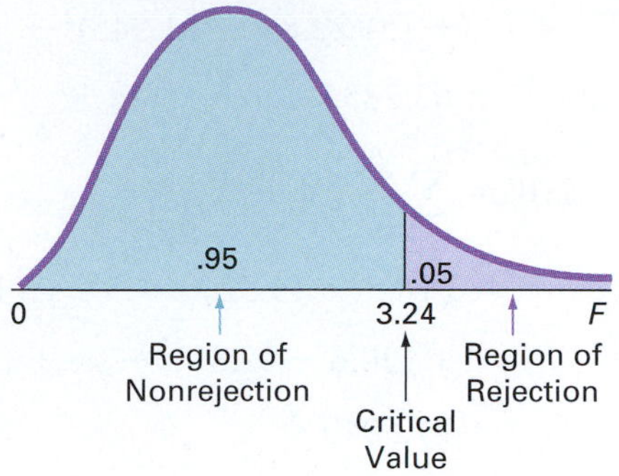

Figure 11.6 shows the ANOVA results for the parachute experiment, including the p-value. In Figure 11.6, what Table 11.1 (see page 419) labels Among Groups is labeled Between Groups in the Excel results and Factor in the Minitab results. What Table 11.1 labels Within Groups is labeled Error in the Minitab results.

FIGURE 11.6

Excel and Minitab ANOVA results for the parachute experiment

	A	B	C	D	E	F	G
1	ANOVA: Single Factor						
2							
3	**SUMMARY**						
4	*Groups*	*Count*	*Sum*	*Average*	*Variance*		
5	Supplier 1	5	97.6	19.52	7.237		
6	Supplier 2	5	121.3	24.26	3.683		
7	Supplier 3	5	114.2	22.84	4.553		
8	Supplier 4	5	105.8	21.16	8.903		
9							
10							
11	**ANOVA**						
12	*Source of Variation*	*SS*	*df*	*MS*	*F*	*P-value*	*F crit*
13	Between Groups	63.2855	3	21.0952	3.4616	0.0414	3.2389
14	Within Groups	97.504	16	6.0940			
15							
16	Total	160.7895	19				
17					Level of significance		0.05

One-way ANOVA: Supplier 1, Supplier 2, Supplier 3, Supplier 4

```
Source  DF      SS     MS     F      P
Factor   3   63.29  21.10  3.46  0.041
Error   16   97.50   6.09
Total   19  160.79

S = 2.469   R-Sq = 39.36%   R-Sq(adj) = 27.99%

                              Individual 95% CIs For Mean Based on Pooled StDev
Level       N    Mean  StDev  -+---------+---------+---------+--------
Supplier 1  5  19.520  2.690  (--------*--------)
Supplier 2  5  24.260  1.919                    (--------*--------)
Supplier 3  5  22.840  2.134              (---------*---------)
Supplier 4  5  21.160  2.984        (---------*--------)
                              -+---------+---------+---------+--------
                              17.5      20.0      22.5      25.0

Pooled StDev = 2.469
```

The p-value, or probability of getting a computed F_{STAT} statistic of 3.4616 or larger when the null hypothesis is true, is 0.0414. Because this p-value is less than the specified α of 0.05, you reject the null hypothesis. The p-value 0.0414 indicates that there is a 4.14% chance of observing differences this large or larger if the population means for the four suppliers are all equal. After performing the one-way ANOVA and finding a significant difference among the suppliers, you still do not know *which* suppliers differ. All you know is that there is sufficient evidence to state that the population means are not all the same. In other words, one or more population means are significantly different. To determine which suppliers differ, you can use a multiple comparisons procedure such as the Tukey-Kramer procedure.

Multiple Comparisons: The Tukey-Kramer Procedure

In the Perfect Parachutes scenario on page 415, you used the one-way ANOVA F test to determine that there was a difference among the suppliers. The next step is to construct **multiple comparisons** to determine which suppliers are different.

Although many procedures are available (see references 5, 6, and 10), this text uses the **Tukey-Kramer multiple comparisons procedure for one-way ANOVA** to determine which of the c means are significantly different. The Tukey-Kramer procedure enables you to simultaneously make comparisons between *all* pairs of groups. You use the following four steps to construct the comparisons:

1. Compute the absolute mean differences, $|\bar{X}_j - \bar{X}_{j'}|$ (where $j \neq j'$), among all $c(c - 1)/2$ pairs of sample means.
2. Compute the **critical range** for the Tukey-Kramer procedure, using Equation (11.6).

CRITICAL RANGE FOR THE TUKEY-KRAMER PROCEDURE

$$\text{Critical range} = Q_\alpha \sqrt{\frac{MSW}{2}\left(\frac{1}{n_j} + \frac{1}{n_{j'}}\right)} \quad \textbf{(11.6)}$$

where Q_α is the upper-tail critical value from a **Studentized range distribution** having c degrees of freedom in the numerator and $n - c$ degrees of freedom in the denominator. (Values for the Studentized range distribution are found in Table E.7.)

If the sample sizes differ, you compute a critical range for each pairwise comparison of sample means.

3. Compare each of the $c(c - 1)/2$ pairs of means against its corresponding critical range. You declare a specific pair significantly different if the absolute difference in the sample means, $|\bar{X}_j - \bar{X}_{j'}|$, is greater than the critical range.
4. Interpret the results.

In the parachute example, there are four suppliers. Thus, there are $4(4 - 1)/2 = 6$ pairwise comparisons. To apply the Tukey-Kramer multiple comparisons procedure, you first compute the absolute mean differences for all six pairwise comparisons. *Multiple comparisons* refer to the fact that you are simultaneously making an inference about all six of these comparisons:

1. $|\bar{X}_1 - \bar{X}_2| = |19.52 - 24.26| = 4.74$
2. $|\bar{X}_1 - \bar{X}_3| = |19.52 - 22.84| = 3.32$
3. $|\bar{X}_1 - \bar{X}_4| = |19.52 - 21.16| = 1.64$
4. $|\bar{X}_2 - \bar{X}_3| = |24.26 - 22.84| = 1.42$
5. $|\bar{X}_2 - \bar{X}_4| = |24.26 - 21.16| = 3.10$
6. $|\bar{X}_3 - \bar{X}_4| = |22.84 - 21.16| = 1.68$

You need to compute only one critical range because the sample sizes in the four groups are equal. From the ANOVA summary table (Figure 11.6 on page 422), $MSW = 6.094$ and $n_j = n_{j'} = 5$. From Table E.7, for $\alpha = 0.05, c = 4$, and $n - c = 20 - 4 = 16, Q_\alpha$, the upper-tail critical value of the test statistic, is 4.05 (see Table 11.3).

TABLE 11.3

Finding the Studentized Range, Q_α, Statistic for $\alpha = 0.05$, with 4 and 16 Degrees of Freedom

Cumulative Probabilities = 0.95
Upper-Tail Area = 0.05
Numerator df_1

Denominator df_2	**2**	**3**	**4**	**5**	**6**	**7**	**8**	**9**
.	.	.	.	.	.	.	.	.
.	.	.	.	.	.	.	.	.
.	.	.	.	.	.	.	.	.
11	3.11	3.82	4.26	4.57	4.82	5.03	5.20	5.35
12	3.08	3.77	4.20	4.51	4.75	4.95	5.12	5.27
13	3.06	3.73	4.15	4.45	4.69	4.88	5.05	5.19
14	3.03	3.70	4.11	4.41	4.64	4.83	4.99	5.13
15	3.01	3.67	4.08	4.37	4.60	4.78	4.94	5.08
16	3.00	3.65	4.05	4.33	4.56	4.74	4.90	5.03

Source: Extracted from Table E.7.

From Equation (11.6),

$$\text{Critical range} = 4.05\sqrt{\left(\frac{6.094}{2}\right)\left(\frac{1}{5}+\frac{1}{5}\right)} = 4.4712$$

Because 4.74 > 4.4712, there is a significant difference between the means of Suppliers 1 and 2. All other pairwise differences are less than 4.4712. With 95% confidence, you can conclude that parachutes woven using fiber from Supplier 1 have a lower mean tensile strength than those from Supplier 2, but there are no statistically significant differences between Suppliers 1 and 3, Suppliers 1 and 4, Suppliers 2 and 3, Suppliers 2 and 4, and Suppliers 3 and 4. Note that by using $\alpha = 0.05$, you are able to make all six of the comparisons with an overall error rate of only 5%. These results are shown in Figure 11.7.

FIGURE 11.7

Excel and Minitab Tukey-Kramer procedure results for the parachute experiment

	A	B	C	D	E	F	G	H	I
1	Tukey Kramer Multiple Comparisons								
2									
3		Sample	Sample			Absolute	Std. Error	Critical	
4	Group	Mean	Size		Comparison	Difference	of Difference	Range	Results
5	1: Supplier 1	19.52	5		Group 1 to Group 2	4.74	1.103992754	4.4712	Means are different
6	2: Supplier 2	24.26	5		Group 1 to Group 3	3.32	1.103992754	4.4712	Means are not different
7	3: Supplier 3	22.84	5		Group 1 to Group 4	1.64	1.103992754	4.4712	Means are not different
8	4: Supplier 4	21.16	5		Group 2 to Group 3	1.42	1.103992754	4.4712	Means are not different
9					Group 2 to Group 4	3.1	1.103992754	4.4712	Means are not different
10	Other Data				Group 3 to Group 4	1.68	1.103992754	4.4712	Means are not different
11	Level of significance	0.05							
12	Numerator d.f.	4							
13	Denominator d.f.	16							
14	MSW	6.094							
15	Q Statistic	4.05							

```
Grouping Information Using Tukey Method
             N    Mean  Grouping
Supplier 2   5  24.260  A
Supplier 3   5  22.840  A B
Supplier 4   5  21.160  A B
Supplier 1   5  19.520    B

Means that do not share a letter are significantly different.

Tukey 95% Simultaneous Confidence Intervals
All Pairwise Comparisons
Individual confidence level = 98.87%

Supplier 1 subtracted from:
             Lower  Center   Upper  -----+---------+---------+---------+----
Supplier 2   0.269   4.740   9.211              (--------*--------)
Supplier 3  -1.151   3.320   7.791          (--------*--------)
Supplier 4  -2.831   1.640   6.111      (--------*--------)
                                    -----+---------+---------+---------+----
                                      -5.0       0.0       5.0      10.0

Supplier 2 subtracted from:
             Lower  Center   Upper  -----+---------+---------+---------+----
Supplier 3  -5.891  -1.420   3.051     (--------*--------)
Supplier 4  -7.571  -3.100   1.371  (--------*--------)
                                    -----+---------+---------+---------+----
                                      -5.0       0.0       5.0      10.0

Supplier 3 subtracted from:
             Lower  Center   Upper  -----+---------+---------+---------+----
Supplier 4  -6.151  -1.680   2.791     (--------*--------)
                                    -----+---------+---------+---------+----
                                      -5.0       0.0       5.0      10.0
```

The Figure 11.7 Excel results follow the steps used on page 423 for evaluating the comparisons. Each mean is computed, and the absolute differences are determined, the critical range is computed, and then each comparison is declared significant (means are different) or not significant (means are not different). The Minitab results show the comparisons in the form of interval estimates. Each interval is computed. Any interval that does not include 0 is considered significant. Thus, the only significant comparison is supplier 1 versus supplier 2 since its interval 0.269 to 9.211 does not include 0.

Online Topic: The Analysis of Means (ANOM)

The analysis of means (ANOM) provides an alternative approach that allows you to determine which, if any, of the *c* groups has a mean significantly different from the overall mean of all the group means combined. To study this topic, download the **ANOM** online topic file that is available in MyStatLab and on this book's companion website. (Visit www.mystatlab.com, or see Appendix C to learn how to access the online topic files from the companion website.)

ANOVA Assumptions

In Chapters 9 and 10, you learned about the assumptions required in order to use each hypothesis-testing procedure and the consequences of departures from these assumptions. To use the one-way ANOVA *F* test, you must make the following assumptions about the populations:

- Randomness and independence
- Normality
- Homogeneity of variance

The first assumption, **randomness and independence**, is critically important. The validity of any experiment depends on random sampling and/or the randomization process. To avoid biases in the outcomes, you need to select random samples from the c groups or use the randomization process to randomly assign the items to the c levels of the factor. Selecting a random sample, or randomly assigning the levels, ensures that a value from one group is independent of any other value in the experiment. Departures from this assumption can seriously affect inferences from the ANOVA. These problems are discussed more thoroughly in references 5 and 10.

The second assumption, **normality**, states that the sample values in each group are from a normally distributed population. Just as in the case of the t test, the one-way ANOVA F test is fairly robust against departures from the normal distribution. As long as the distributions are not extremely different from a normal distribution, the level of significance of the ANOVA F test is usually not greatly affected, particularly for large samples. You can assess the normality of each of the c samples by constructing a normal probability plot or a boxplot.

The third assumption, **homogeneity of variance**, states that the variances of the c groups are equal (i.e., $\sigma_1^2 = \sigma_2^2 = \cdots = \sigma_c^2$). If you have equal sample sizes in each group, inferences based on the F distribution are not seriously affected by unequal variances. However, if you have unequal sample sizes, unequal variances can have a serious effect on inferences from the ANOVA procedure. Thus, when possible, you should have equal sample sizes in all groups. You can use the Levene test for homogeneity of variance presented next to test whether the variances of the c groups are equal.

When only the normality assumption is violated, you can use the Kruskal-Wallis rank test, a nonparametric procedure discussed in Section 12.7. When only the homogeneity-of-variance assumption is violated, you can use procedures similar to those used in the separate-variance t test of Section 10.1 (see references 1 and 2). When both the normality and homogeneity-of-variance assumptions have been violated, you need to use an appropriate data transformation that both normalizes the data and reduces the differences in variances (see reference 6) or use a more general nonparametric procedure (see references 2 and 3).

Levene Test for Homogeneity of Variance

Although the one-way ANOVA F test is relatively robust with respect to the assumption of equal group variances, large differences in the group variances can seriously affect the level of significance and the power of the F test. One powerful yet simple procedure for testing the equality of the variances is the modified **Levene test** (see references 1 and 7). To test for the homogeneity of variance, you use the following null hypothesis:

$$H_0: \sigma_1^2 = \sigma_2^2 = \cdots = \sigma_c^2$$

against the alternative hypothesis:

$$H_1: \text{Not all } \sigma_j^2 \text{ are equal } (j = 1, 2, 3, \ldots, c)$$

To test the null hypothesis of equal variances, you first compute the absolute value of the difference between each value and the median of the group. Then you perform a one-way ANOVA on these *absolute differences*. Most statisticians suggest using a level of significance of $\alpha = 0.05$ when performing the ANOVA. To illustrate the modified Levene test, return to the Perfect Parachutes scenario concerning the tensile strength of parachutes first presented in Table 11.2 on page 421. Table 11.4 summarizes the absolute differences from the median of each supplier.

TABLE 11.4

Absolute Differences from the Median Tensile Strength for Four Suppliers

Supplier 1 (Median = 18.5)	Supplier 2 (Median = 24.5)	Supplier 3 (Median = 22.9)	Supplier 4 (Median = 20.4)
$\lvert 18.5 - 18.5 \rvert = 0.0$	$\lvert 26.3 - 24.5 \rvert = 1.8$	$\lvert 20.6 - 22.9 \rvert = 2.3$	$\lvert 25.4 - 20.4 \rvert = 5.0$
$\lvert 24.0 - 18.5 \rvert = 5.5$	$\lvert 25.3 - 24.5 \rvert = 0.8$	$\lvert 25.2 - 22.9 \rvert = 2.3$	$\lvert 19.9 - 20.4 \rvert = 0.5$
$\lvert 17.2 - 18.5 \rvert = 1.3$	$\lvert 24.0 - 24.5 \rvert = 0.5$	$\lvert 20.8 - 22.9 \rvert = 2.1$	$\lvert 22.6 - 20.4 \rvert = 2.2$
$\lvert 19.9 - 18.5 \rvert = 1.4$	$\lvert 21.2 - 24.5 \rvert = 3.3$	$\lvert 24.7 - 22.9 \rvert = 1.8$	$\lvert 17.5 - 20.4 \rvert = 2.9$
$\lvert 18.0 - 18.5 \rvert = 0.5$	$\lvert 24.5 - 24.5 \rvert = 0.0$	$\lvert 22.9 - 22.9 \rvert = 0.0$	$\lvert 20.4 - 20.4 \rvert = 0.0$

Using the absolute differences given in Table 11.4, you perform a one-way ANOVA (see Figure 11.8).

FIGURE 11.8

Excel and Minitab Levene test results for the absolute differences for the parachute experiment

	A	B	C	D	E	F	G	H	I	J
1	ANOVA: Levene Test								Calculations	
2									c	4
3	SUMMARY								n	20
4	*Groups*	*Count*	*Sum*	*Average*	*Variance*					
5	Supplier 1	5	8.7	1.74	4.753					
6	Supplier 2	5	6.4	1.28	1.707					
7	Supplier 3	5	8.5	1.7	0.945					
8	Supplier 4	5	10.6	2.12	4.007					
9										
10										
11	ANOVA									
12	*Source of Variation*	*SS*	*df*	*MS*	*F*	*P-value*	*F crit*			
13	Between Groups	1.77	3	0.5900	0.2068	0.8902	3.2389			
14	Within Groups	45.648	16	2.8530						
15										
16	Total	47.418	19							
17					Level of significance		0.05			

Test for Equal Variances: Strength versus Supplier

```
Levene's Test (Any Continuous Distribution)
Test statistic = 0.21, p-value = 0.890
```

From the Figure 11.8 Excel results, observe that $F_{STAT} = 0.2068$. (Excel labels this value F. Minitab labels the value Test statistic and reports a value of 0.21.) Because $F_{STAT} = 0.2068 < 3.2389$ (or the p-value $= 0.8902 > 0.05$), you do not reject H_0. There is no evidence of a significant difference among the four variances. In other words, it is reasonable to assume that the materials from the four suppliers produce parachutes with an equal amount of variability. Therefore, the homogeneity-of-variance assumption for the ANOVA procedure is justified.

Example 11.1 illustrates another example of the one way ANOVA.

EXAMPLE 11.1

ANOVA of the Speed of Drive-Through Service at Fast-Food Chains

For fast-food restaurants, the drive-through window is an increasing source of revenue. The chain that offers the fastest service is likely to attract additional customers. Each month *QSR Magazine*, **www.qsrmagazine.com**, publishes its results of drive-through service times (from menu board to departure) at fast-food chains. In a recent month, the mean time was 134.09 seconds for Wendy's, 163.17 seconds for Taco Bell, 166.65 seconds for Burger King, 174.22 seconds for McDonald's, and 194.58 seconds for KFC. Suppose the study was based on 20 customers for each fast-food chain. Table 11.5 contains the ANOVA table for this problem.

TABLE 11.5

ANOVA Summary Table of Drive-Through Service Times at Fast-Food Chains

Source	Degrees of Freedom	Sum of Squares	Mean Squares	F	p-value
Among chains	4	38,191.9096	9,547.9774	73.1086	0.0000
Within chains	95	12,407.00	130.60		

At the 0.05 level of significance, is there evidence of a difference in the mean drive-through service times of the five chains?

SOLUTION

$H_0: \mu_1 = \mu_2 = \mu_3 = \mu_4 = \mu_5$ where 1 = Wendy s, 2 = Taco Bell, 3 = Burger King, 4 = McDonalds, 5 = KFC

H_1: Not all μ_j are equal where $j = 1, 2, 3, 4, 5$

Decision rule: If p-value < 0.05, reject H_0. Because the p-value is virtually 0, which is less than $\alpha = 0.05$, reject H_0.

You have sufficient evidence to conclude that the mean drive-through times of the five chains are not all equal.

To determine which of the means are significantly different from one another, use the Tukey-Kramer procedure [Equation (11.6) on page 423] to establish the critical range:

$$\text{Critical value of } Q \text{ with 5 and 95 degrees of freedom} \approx 3.92$$

$$\text{Critical range} = Q_{\alpha}\sqrt{\left(\frac{MSW}{2}\right)\left(\frac{1}{n_j} + \frac{1}{n_{j'}}\right)} = (3.92)\sqrt{\left(\frac{130.6}{2}\right)\left(\frac{1}{20} + \frac{1}{20}\right)}$$

$$= 10.02$$

Any observed difference greater than 10.02 is considered significant. The mean drive-through service times are different between Wendy's (mean of 134.09 seconds) and each of the other four chains and between KFC (mean of 194.58 seconds) and the other four chains. In addition, the mean drive-through service time is different between McDonald's and Taco Bell. Thus, with 95% confidence, you can conclude that the mean drive-through service time for Wendy's is faster than those of Burger King, Taco Bell, McDonald's, and KFC. The mean drive-through service time for KFC is slower than those of Wendy's, Burger King, Taco Bell, McDonald's. In addition, the mean drive-through service time for McDonald's is slower than for Taco Bell.

Problems for Section 11.1

LEARNING THE BASICS

11.1 An experiment has a single factor with five groups and seven values in each group.

a. How many degrees of freedom are there in determining the among-group variation?
b. How many degrees of freedom are there in determining the within-group variation?
c. How many degrees of freedom are there in determining the total variation?

11.2 You are working with the same experiment as in Problem 11.1.

a. If $SSA = 60$ and $SST = 210$, what is SSW?
b. What is MSA?
c. What is MSW?
d. What is the value of F_{STAT}?

11.3 You are working with the same experiment as in Problems 11.1 and 11.2.

a. Construct the ANOVA summary table and fill in all values in the table.
b. At the 0.05 level of significance, what is the upper-tail critical value from the F distribution?
c. State the decision rule for testing the null hypothesis that all five groups have equal population means.
d. What is your statistical decision?

11.4 Consider an experiment with three groups, with seven values in each.

a. How many degrees of freedom are there in determining the among-group variation?
b. How many degrees of freedom are there in determining the within-group variation?
c. How many degrees of freedom are there in determining the total variation?

11.5 Consider an experiment with four groups, with eight values in each. For the ANOVA summary table below, fill in all the missing results:

Source	Degrees of Freedom	Sum of Squares	Mean Square (Variance)	F
Among groups	$c - 1 = ?$	$SSA = ?$	$MSA = 80$	$F_{STAT} = ?$
Within groups	$n - c = ?$	$SSW = 560$	$MSW = ?$	
Total	$n - 1 = ?$	$SST = ?$		

11.6 You are working with the same experiment as in Problem 11.5.

a. At the 0.05 level of significance, state the decision rule for testing the null hypothesis that all four groups have equal population means.
b. What is your statistical decision?
c. At the 0.05 level of significance, what is the upper-tail critical value from the Studentized range distribution?
d. To perform the Tukey-Kramer procedure, what is the critical range?

APPLYING THE CONCEPTS

11.7 The Computer Anxiety Rating Scale (CARS) measures an individual's level of computer anxiety, on a scale from 20 (no anxiety) to 100 (highest level of anxiety). Researchers at Miami University administered CARS to 172 business students. One of the objectives of the study was to determine whether there are differences in the amount of computer anxiety experienced by students with different majors. They found the following:

Source	Degrees of Freedom	Sum of Squares	Mean Squares	F
Among majors	5	3,172		
Within majors	166	21,246		
Total	171	24,418		

Major	n	Mean
Marketing	19	44.37
Management	11	43.18
Other	14	42.21
Finance	45	41.80
Accountancy	36	37.56
MIS	47	32.21

Source: Data Extracted from T. Broome and D. Havelka, "Determinants of Computer Anxiety in Business Students," *The Review of Business Information Systems,* Spring 2002, 6(2), pp. 9–16.

a. Complete the ANOVA summary table.
b. At the 0.05 level of significance, is there evidence of a difference in the mean computer anxiety experienced by different majors?
c. If the results in (b) indicate that it is appropriate, use the Tukey-Kramer procedure to determine which majors differ in mean computer anxiety. Discuss your findings.

SELF Test **11.8** Students in a business statistics course performed a completely randomized design to test the strength of four brands of trash bags. One-pound weights were placed into a bag, one at a time, until the bag broke. A total of 40 bags, 10 for each brand, were used. The data in **Trashbags** give the weight (in pounds) required to break the trash bags.
a. At the 0.05 level of significance, is there evidence of a difference in the mean strength of the four brands of trash bags?
b. If appropriate, determine which brands differ in mean strength.
c. At the 0.05 level of significance, is there evidence of a difference in the variation in strength among the four brands of trash bags?
d. Which brand(s) should you buy, and which brand(s) should you avoid? Explain.

11.9 A hospital conducted a study of the waiting time in its emergency room. The hospital has a main campus and three satellite locations. Management had a business objective of reducing waiting time for emergency room cases that did not require immediate attention. To study this, a random sample of 15 emergency room cases that did not require immediate attention at each location were selected on a particular day, and the waiting time (measured from check-in to when the patient was called into the clinic area) was measured. The results are stored in **ERWaiting**.
a. At the 0.05 level of significance, is there evidence of a difference in the mean waiting times in the four locations?
b. If appropriate, determine which locations differ in mean waiting time.
c. At the 0.05 level of significance, is there evidence of a difference in the variation in waiting time among the four locations?

11.10 A manufacturer of pens has hired an advertising agency to develop an advertising campaign for the upcoming holiday season. To prepare for this project, the research director decides to initiate a study of the effect of advertising on product perception. An experiment is designed to compare five different advertisements. Advertisement A greatly undersells the pen's characteristics. Advertisement B slightly undersells the pen's characteristics. Advertisement C slightly oversells the pen's characteristics. Advertisement D greatly oversells the pen's characteristics. Advertisement E attempts to correctly state the pen's characteristics. A sample of 30 adult respondents, taken from a larger focus group, is randomly assigned to the five advertisements (so that there are 6 respondents to each). After reading the advertisement and developing a sense of "product expectation," all respondents unknowingly receive the same pen to evaluate. The respondents are permitted to test the pen and the plausibility of the advertising copy. The respondents are then asked to rate the pen from 1 to 7 (lowest to highest) on the product characteristic scales of appearance, durability, and writing performance. The *combined* scores of three ratings (appearance, durability, and writing performance) for the 30 respondents (stored in **Pen**) are as follows:

A	B	C	D	E
15	16	8	5	12
18	17	7	6	19
17	21	10	13	18
19	16	15	11	12
19	19	14	9	17
20	17	14	10	14

a. At the 0.05 level of significance, is there evidence of a difference in the mean rating of the pens following exposure to five advertisements?
b. If appropriate, determine which advertisements differ in mean ratings.
c. At the 0.05 level of significance, is there evidence of a difference in the variation in ratings among the five advertisements?
d. Which advertisement(s) should you use, and which advertisement(s) should you avoid? Explain.

11.11 The per-store daily customer count (i.e., the mean number of customers in a store in one day) for a nationwide convenience store chain that operates nearly 10,000 stores has been steady, at 900, for some time. To increase the customer count, the chain is considering cutting prices for coffee beverages. The question to be determined is how much to cut prices to increase the daily customer count without reducing the gross margin on coffee sales too much. You decide to carry out an experiment in a sample of 24 stores where customer counts have been running almost exactly at the national average of 900. In 6 of the stores, the price of a small coffee will now be $0.59, in 6 stores the price of a small coffee will now be $0.69, in 6 stores, the price of a small coffee will now be $0.79, and in 6 stores, the price of a small coffee will now be $0.89. After four weeks of selling the coffee at the new price, the daily customer count in the stores was recorded and stored in **CoffeeSales**.

a. At the 0.05 level of significance, is there evidence of a difference in the daily customer count based on the price of a small coffee?

b. If appropriate, determine which prices differ in daily customer counts.

c. At the 0.05 level of significance, is there evidence of a difference in the variation in daily customer count among the different prices?

d. What effect does your result in (c) have on the validity of the results in (a) and (b)?

11.12 Integrated circuits are manufactured on silicon wafers through a process that involves a series of steps. An experiment was carried out to study the effect on the yield of using three methods in the cleansing step (coded to maintain confidentiality). The results (stored in **Yield-OneWay**) are as follows:

New1	New2	Standard
38	29	31
34	35	23
38	34	38
34	20	29
19	35	32
28	37	30

Source: Data Extracted from J. Ramirez and W. Taam, "An Autologistic Model for Integrated Circuit Manufacturing," *Journal of Quality Technology*, 2000, 32, pp. 254–262.

a. At the 0.05 level of significance, is there evidence of a difference in the mean yield among the methods used in the cleansing steps?

b. If appropriate, determine which methods differ in mean yields.

c. At the 0.05 level of significance, is there evidence of a difference in the variation in yields among the different methods?

d. What effect does your result in (c) have on the validity of the results in (a) and (b)?

11.13 A pet food company has a business objective of expanding its product line beyond its current kidney- and shrimp-based cat foods. The company developed two new products, one based on chicken livers and the other based on salmon. The company conducted an experiment to compare the two new products with its two existing ones, as well as a generic beef-based product sold in a supermarket chain.

For the experiment, a sample of 50 cats from the population at a local animal shelter was selected. Ten cats were randomly assigned to each of the five products being tested. Each of the cats was then presented with 3 ounces of the selected food in a dish at feeding time. The researchers defined the variable to be measured as the number of ounces of food that the cat consumed within a 10-minute time interval that began when the filled dish was presented. The results for this experiment are summarized in the following table and stored in **CatFood**.

Kidney	Shrimp	Chicken Liver	Salmon	Beef
2.37	2.26	2.29	1.79	2.09
2.62	2.69	2.23	2.33	1.87
2.31	2.25	2.41	1.96	1.67
2.47	2.45	2.68	2.05	1.64
2.59	2.34	2.25	2.26	2.16
2.62	2.37	2.17	2.24	1.75
2.34	2.22	2.37	1.96	1.18
2.47	2.56	2.26	1.58	1.92
2.45	2.36	2.45	2.18	1.32
2.32	2.59	2.57	1.93	1.94

a. At the 0.05 level of significance, is there evidence of a difference in the mean amount of food eaten among the various products?

b. If appropriate, which products appear to differ significantly in the mean amount of food eaten?

c. At the 0.05 level of significance, is there evidence of a significant difference in the variation in the amount of food eaten among the various products?

d. What should the pet food company conclude? Fully describe the pet food company's options with respect to the products.

11.14 A sporting goods manufacturing company wanted to compare the distance traveled by golf balls produced using four different designs. Ten balls were manufactured with each design and were brought to the local golf course for the club professional to test. The order in which the balls were hit with the same club from the first tee was randomized so that the pro did not know which type of ball was being hit. All 40 balls were hit in a short period of time, during which the environmental conditions were essentially the same. The results (distance traveled in yards) for the four designs are stored in **Golfball** and shown in the following table.

Design			
1	2	3	4
206.32	217.08	226.77	230.55
207.94	221.43	224.79	227.95
206.19	218.04	229.75	231.84
204.45	224.13	228.51	224.87
209.65	211.82	221.44	229.49
203.81	213.90	223.85	231.10
206.75	221.28	223.97	221.53
205.68	229.43	234.30	235.45
204.49	213.54	219.50	228.35
210.86	214.51	233.00	225.09

a. At the 0.05 level of significance, is there evidence of a difference in the mean distances traveled by the golf balls with different designs?

b. If the results in (a) indicate that it is appropriate, use the Tukey-Kramer procedure to determine which designs differ in mean distances.

c. What assumptions are necessary in (a)?

d. At the 0.05 level of significance, is there evidence of a difference in the variation of the distances traveled by the golf balls with different designs?

e. What golf ball design should the manufacturing manager choose? Explain.

11.2 The Randomized Block Design

Section 11.1 discussed how to use the one-way ANOVA F test to evaluate differences among the means of more than two independent groups. Section 10.2 discussed how to use the paired t test to evaluate the difference between the means of two groups when you had repeated measurements or matched samples. The **randomized block design** evaluates differences among more than two groups that contain matched samples or repeated measures that have been placed in **blocks**. Blocks are heterogeneous sets of items or individuals that have been either matched or on whom repeated measurements have been taken. Blocking removes as much variability as possible from the measure of random error so that the differences among the groups are more evident.

Although blocks are used in a randomized block design, the focus of the analysis is on the differences among the different groups. As is the case in completely randomized designs, groups are often different levels pertaining to a factor of interest. A randomized block design is often more efficient statistically than a completely randomized design and therefore produces more precise results (see references 5, 6, and 10). For example, if the factor of interest is advertising medium, three groups could be subject to the following different levels: television, radio, and newspaper. Different cities could be used as blocks. The variability among the different cities is therefore removed from the random error in order to better detect differences among the three advertising mediums.

To compare a completely randomized design with a randomized block design, return to the Perfect Parachutes scenario on page 415. Suppose that a completely randomized design is used with 12 parachutes woven during a 24-hour period. Any variability among the shifts of workers becomes part of the random error, and therefore differences among the four suppliers might be difficult to detect. To reduce the random error, a randomized block experiment is designed, in which three shifts of workers are used and four parachutes are woven during each shift (one parachute using fibers from Supplier 1, one parachute using fibers from Supplier 2, etc.). The three shifts are considered blocks, but the factor of interest is still the four suppliers. The advantage of the randomized block design is that the variability among the three shifts is removed from the random error. Therefore, this design should provide more precise results concerning differences among the four suppliers.

Testing for Factor and Block Effects

Recall from Figure 11.1 on page 416 that, in the completely randomized design, the total variation (SST) is subdivided into variation due to differences *among* the c groups (SSA) and variation due to differences *within* the c groups (SSW). Within-group variation is considered random variation, and among-group variation is due to differences from group to group.

To remove the effects of the blocking from the random variation component in the randomized block design, the within-group variation (SSW) is subdivided into variation due to differences among the blocks ($SSBL$) and random variation (SSE). Therefore, as presented in Figure 11.9, in a randomized block design, the total variation is the sum of three components: among-group variation (SSA), among-block variation ($SSBL$), and random variation (SSE).

FIGURE 11.9
Partitioning the total variation in a randomized block model

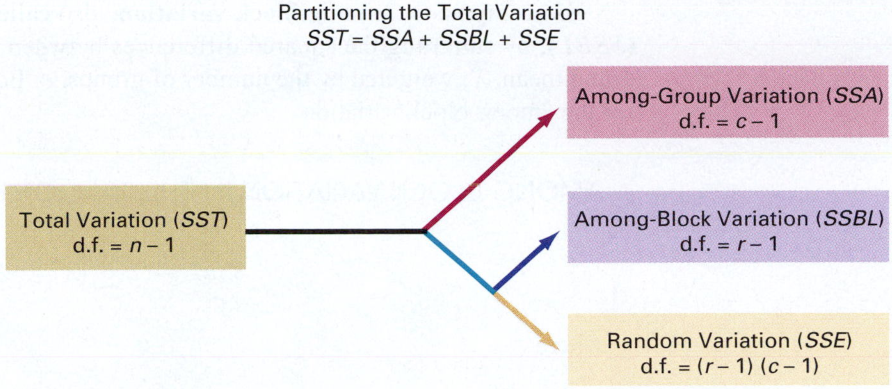

The following definitions are needed to develop the ANOVA procedure for the randomized block design:

r = number of blocks
c = number of groups
n = total number of values (where $n = rc$)
X_{ij} = value in the ith block for the jth group
$\bar{X}_{i.}$ = mean of all the values in block i
$\bar{X}_{.j}$ = mean of all the values for group j

$$\sum_{j=1}^{c}\sum_{i=1}^{r} X_{ij} = \text{grand total}$$

The total variation, also called sum of squares total (SST), is a measure of the variation among all the values. You compute SST by summing the squared differences between each individual value and the grand mean, $\bar{\bar{X}}$, that is based on all n values. Equation (11.7) shows the computation for total variation.

TOTAL VARIATION IN THE RANDOMIZED BLOCK DESIGN

$$SST = \sum_{j=1}^{c}\sum_{i=1}^{r}(X_{ij} - \bar{\bar{X}})^2 \quad \textbf{(11.7)}$$

where

$$\bar{\bar{X}} = \frac{\sum_{j=1}^{c}\sum_{i=1}^{r} X_{ij}}{rc} \quad \text{(i.e., the grand mean)}$$

You compute the among-group variation, also called the sum of squares among groups (SSA), by summing the squared differences between the sample mean of each group, $\bar{X}_{.j}$, and the grand mean, $\bar{\bar{X}}$, weighted by the number of blocks, r. Equation (11.8) shows the computation for the among-group variation.

AMONG-GROUP VARIATION IN THE RANDOMIZED BLOCK DESIGN

$$SSA = r\sum_{j=1}^{c}(\bar{X}_{.j} - \bar{\bar{X}})^2 \quad \textbf{(11.8)}$$

where

$$\bar{X}_{.j} = \frac{\sum_{i=1}^{r} X_{ij}}{r}$$

You compute the **among-block variation**, also called the **sum of squares among blocks ($SSBL$)**, by summing the squared differences between the mean of each block, $\bar{X}_{i.}$, and the grand mean, $\bar{\bar{X}}$, weighted by the number of groups, c. Equation (11.9) shows the computation for the among-block variation.

AMONG-BLOCK VARIATION IN THE RANDOMIZED BLOCK DESIGN

$$SSBL = c\sum_{i=1}^{r}(\bar{X}_{i.} - \bar{\bar{X}})^2 \qquad \textbf{(11.9)}$$

where

$$\bar{X}_{i.} = \frac{\sum_{j=1}^{c} X_{ij}}{c}$$

You compute the random variation, also called the **sum of squares error (SSE)**, by summing the squared differences among all the values after the effect of the groups and blocks have been accounted for. Equation (11.10) shows the computation for random variation.

RANDOM VARIATION IN THE RANDOMIZED BLOCK DESIGN

$$SSE = \sum_{j=1}^{c}\sum_{i=1}^{r}(X_{ij} - \bar{X}_{.j} - \bar{X}_{i.} + \bar{\bar{X}})^2 \qquad \textbf{(11.10)}$$

Because you are comparing c groups, there are $c - 1$ degrees of freedom associated with the sum of squares among groups (SSA). Similarly, because there are r blocks, there are $r - 1$ degrees of freedom associated with the sum of squares among blocks ($SSBL$). Moreover, there are $n - 1$ degrees of freedom associated with the sum of squares total (SST) because you are comparing each value, X_{ij}, to the grand mean, $\bar{\bar{X}}$, based on all n values. Therefore, because the degrees of freedom for each source of variation must add to the degrees of freedom for the total variation, you compute the degrees of freedom for the sum of squares error (SSE) component by subtraction and algebraic manipulation. Thus, the degrees of freedom associated with the sum of squares error is $(r - 1)(c - 1)$.

If you divide each of the sum of squares by its associated degrees of freedom, you have the three *variances*, or mean square terms (MSA, $MSBL$, and MSE). Equations (11.11a–c) provide the mean square terms needed for the ANOVA table.

MEAN SQUARES IN THE RANDOMIZED BLOCK DESIGN

$$MSA = \frac{SSA}{c - 1} \qquad \textbf{(11.11a)}$$

$$MSBL = \frac{SSBL}{r - 1} \qquad \textbf{(11.11b)}$$

$$MSE = \frac{SSE}{(r - 1)(c - 1)} \qquad \textbf{(11.11c)}$$

In a randomized block design you first test for a factor effect—that is, you test for any differences among the c group means. If the assumptions of the analysis of variance are valid, the null hypothesis of no differences in the c group means:

$$H: \mu_{.1} = \mu_{.2} = \ldots = \mu_{.c}$$

is tested against the alternative that not all the c group means are equal:

$$H_1\text{: Not all } \mu_{.j} \text{ are equal (where } j = 1, 2, \ldots, c)$$

by computing the F_{STAT} test statistic given in Equation (11.12).

F_{STAT} STATISTIC FOR FACTOR EFFECT

$$F_{STAT} = \frac{MSA}{MSE} \tag{11.12}$$

The F_{STAT} test statistic follows an F distribution with $c - 1$ degrees of freedom for the MSA term and $(r - 1)(c - 1)$ degrees of freedom for the MSE term. For a given level of significance α, you reject the null hypothesis if the computed F_{STAT} test statistic is greater than the upper-tail critical value, F_α, from the F distribution with $c - 1$ and $(r - 1)(c - 1)$ degrees of freedom (see Table E.5). The decision rule is:

$$\text{Reject } H_0 \text{ if } F_{STAT} > F_\alpha;$$

$$\text{otherwise, do not reject } H_0.$$

To examine whether the randomized block design was advantageous to use as compared to a completely randomized design, some statisticians suggest that you perform the F test for block effects. The null hypothesis of no block effects:

$$H_0: \mu_{1.} = \mu_{2.} = \cdots = \mu_{r.}$$

is tested against the alternative:

$$H_1\text{: Not all } \mu_{i.} \text{ are equal (where } i = 1, 2, \ldots, r)$$

using the F_{STAT} test statistic for block effect given in Equation (11.13).

F_{STAT} STATISTIC FOR BLOCK EFFECT

$$F_{STAT} = \frac{MSBL}{MSE} \tag{11.13}$$

You reject the null hypothesis at the α level of significance if the computed F_{STAT} test statistic is greater than the upper-tail critical value F_α from the F distribution with $r - 1$ and $(r - 1)(c - 1)$ degrees of freedom (see Table E.5). That is, the decision rule is

$$\text{Reject } H_0 \text{ if } F_{STAT} > F_\alpha;$$

$$\text{otherwise, do not reject } H_0.$$

The results of the analysis-of-variance procedure are usually displayed in an ANOVA summary table, as shown in Table 11.6.

TABLE 11.6

Analysis-of-Variance Table for the Randomized Block Design

Source	**Degrees of Freedom**	**Sum of Squares**	**Mean Square (Variance)**	**F**
Among groups (A)	$c - 1$	SSA	$MSA = \frac{SSA}{c - 1}$	$F_{STAT} = \frac{MSA}{MSE}$
Among blocks (BL)	$r - 1$	$SSBL$	$MSBL = \frac{SSBL}{r - 1}$	$F_{STAT} = \frac{MSBL}{MSE}$
Error	$(r - 1)(c - 1)$	SSE	$MSE = \frac{SSE}{(r - 1)(c - 1)}$	
Total	$rc - 1$	SST		

To illustrate the randomized block design, suppose that the customer service director for a fast-food chain has the business objective of wanting to improve service at four restaurants in the chain. The customer service director hires six evaluators with varied experiences in food-service evaluations to act as raters of service at the four restaurants. To reduce the effect of the variability from rater to rater, you use a randomized block design, with raters serving as the blocks. The four restaurants are the groups of interest.

The six raters evaluate the service at each of the four restaurants in a random order. A rating scale from 0 (low) to 100 (high) is used. Table 11.7 summarizes the results (stored in **FFChain**), along with the group totals, group means, block totals, block means, grand total, and grand mean.

TABLE 11.7

Ratings at Four Restaurants of a Fast-Food Chain

	RESTAURANTS					
RATERS	**A**	**B**	**C**	**D**	**Totals**	**Means**
1	70	61	82	74	287	71.75
2	77	75	88	76	316	79.00
3	76	67	90	80	313	78.25
4	80	63	96	76	315	78.75
5	84	66	92	84	326	81.50
6	78	68	98	86	330	82.50
Totals	465	400	546	476	1,887	
Means	77.50	66.67	91.00	79.33	78.625	

In addition, from Table 11.7,

$$r = 6 \quad c = 4 \quad n = rc = 24$$

and

$$\bar{\bar{X}} = \frac{\sum_{j=1}^{c}\sum_{i=1}^{r} X_{ij}}{rc} = \frac{1,887}{24} = 78.625$$

Figure 11.10 shows the results for this randomized block design.

FIGURE 11.10

Excel and Minitab randomized block design results for the fast-food chain study

	A	B	C	D	E	F	G
1	ANOVA: Two-Factor Without Replication						
2							
3	*SUMMARY*	*Count*	*Sum*	*Average*	*Variance*		
4	Rater 1	4	287	71.7500	76.2500		
5	Rater 2	4	316	79.0000	36.6667		
6	Rater 3	4	313	78.2500	90.9167		
7	Rater 4	4	315	78.7500	184.9167		
8	Rater 5	4	326	81.5000	121.0000		
9	Rater 6	4	330	82.5000	161.0000		
10							
11	Restaurant A	6	465	77.5000	21.5000		
12	Restaurant B	6	400	66.6667	23.4667		
13	Restaurant C	6	546	91.0000	33.2000		
14	Restaurant D	6	476	79.3333	23.4667		
15							
16							
17	ANOVA						
18	*Source of Variation*	*SS*	*df*	*MS*	*F*	*P-value*	*F crit*
19	Rows	283.3750	5	56.6750	3.7818	0.0205	2.9013
20	Columns	1787.4583	3	595.8194	39.7581	0.0000	3.2874
21	Error	224.7917	15	14.9861			
22							
23	Total	2295.6250	23				
24					Level of significance		0.05

Two-way ANOVA: Rating versus Rater, Restaurant

```
Source      DF       SS       MS      F      P
Rater        5   283.38   56.675   3.78  0.020
Restaurant   3  1787.46  595.819  39.76  0.000
Error       15   224.79   14.986
Total       23  2295.63

S = 3.871   R-Sq = 90.21%   R-Sq(adj) = 84.99%

                  Individual 95% CIs For Mean Based on
                  Pooled StDev
Rater    Mean     -----+---------+---------+---------+----
1       71.75     (--------*-------)
2       79.00                   (-------*-------)
3       78.25                 (--------*-------)
4       78.75                  (--------*-------)
5       81.50                        (-------*-------)
6       82.50                          (-------*-------)
                  -----+---------+---------+---------+----
                      70.0      75.0      80.0      85.0

                         Individual 95% CIs For Mean Based on Pooled StDev
Restaurant      Mean     -+---------+---------+---------+--------
A            77.5000                (---*---)
B            66.6667      (---*----)
C            91.0000                               (---*---)
D            79.3333                  (---*---)
                         -+---------+---------+---------+--------
                         64.0      72.0      80.0      88.0
```

Using the 0.05 level of significance to test for differences among the restaurants, you reject the null hypothesis (H_0: $\mu_{.1} = \mu_{.2} = \mu_{.3} = \mu_{.4}$) if the computed F_{STAT} test statistic is greater than 3.29, the upper-tail critical value from the F distribution with 3 and 15 degrees of freedom in the numerator and denominator, respectively (see Figure 11.11).

FIGURE 11.11

Regions of rejection and nonrejection for the fast-food chain study at the 0.05 level of significance with 3 and 15 degrees of freedom

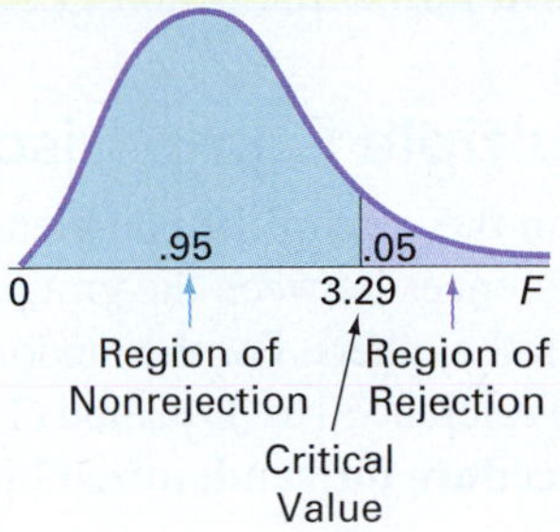

Because $F_{STAT} = 39.7581 > F_{\alpha} = 3.29$, or because the p-value $= 0.000 < 0.05$, you reject H_0 and conclude that there is evidence of a difference in the mean ratings among the different restaurants. The extremely small p-value indicates that if the means from the four restaurants are equal, there is virtually no chance that you will get differences as large or larger among the sample means, as observed in this study. You conclude that the mean ratings among the four restaurants are different.

As a check on the effectiveness of blocking, you can test for a difference among the raters. The decision rule, using the 0.05 level of significance, is to reject the null hypothesis (H_0: $\mu_{1.} = \mu_{2.} = \cdots = \mu_{6.}$) if the computed F_{STAT} test statistic is greater than 2.90, the upper-tail critical value from the F distribution with 5 and 15 degrees of freedom (see Figure 11.12).

FIGURE 11.12

Regions of rejection and nonrejection for the fast-food chain study at the 0.05 level of significance with 5 and 15 degrees of freedom

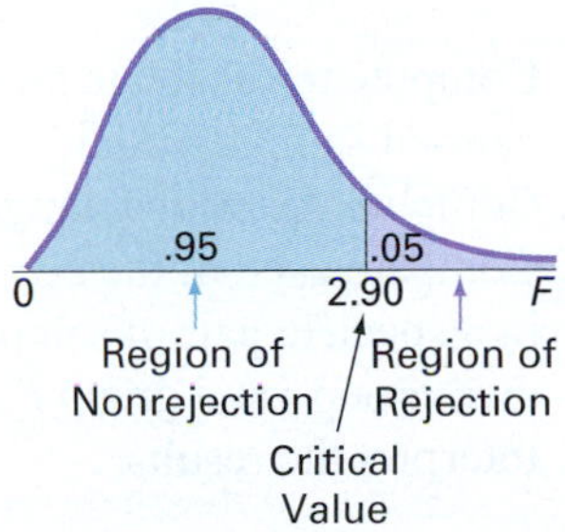

Because $F_{STAT} = 3.7818 > F_{\alpha} = 2.90$ or because the p-value $= 0.0205 < 0.05$, you reject H_0 and conclude that there is evidence of a difference among the raters. Thus, you conclude that the blocking has been advantageous in reducing the random error.

To measure the increase in precision from blocking, you use Equation (11.14) to calculate the **estimated relative efficiency (*RE*)** of the randomized block design as compared with the completely randomized design.

ESTIMATED RELATIVE EFFICIENCY

$$RE = \frac{(r-1)MSBL + r(c-1)MSE}{(rc-1)MSE} \tag{11.14}$$

Using Figure 11.12,

$$RE = \frac{(5)(56.675) + (6)(3)(14.986)}{(23)(14.986)} = 1.60$$

A relative efficiency of 1.6 means that it would take 1.6 times as many observations in a one-way ANOVA design as compared to the randomized block design in order to have the same precision in comparing the restaurants.

The assumptions of the one-way analysis of variance (randomness and independence, normality, and homogeneity of variance) also apply to the randomized block design. If the normality assumption is violated, you can use the Friedman rank test (see Online Section 12.9). In addition, you need to assume that there is no *interacting effect* between the groups and the blocks. In other words, you need to assume that any differences between the groups (the restaurants) are consistent across the entire set of blocks (the raters). The concept of *interaction* is discussed further in Section 11.3.

Multiple Comparisons: The Tukey Procedure

As in the case of the completely randomized design, once you reject the null hypothesis of no differences between the groups, you need to determine *which* groups are significantly different from the others. For the randomized block design, you can use a procedure developed by Tukey (see reference 10). Equation (11.15) gives the critical range for the **Tukey multiple comparisons procedure for randomized block designs**.

CRITICAL RANGE FOR THE RANDOMIZED BLOCK DESIGN

$$\text{Critical range} = Q_{\alpha}\sqrt{\frac{MSE}{r}} \qquad \textbf{(11.15)}$$

where Q_{α} is the upper-tail critical value from a Studentized range distribution having c degrees of freedom in the numerator and $(r - 1)(c - 1)$ degrees of freedom in the denominator. Values for the Studentized range distribution are found in Table E.7.

To perform the multiple comparisons, you do the following:

1. Compute the absolute mean differences, $|\bar{X}_{.j} - \bar{X}_{.j'}|$ (where $j \neq j'$), among all $c(c - 1)/2$ pairs of sample means.
2. Compute the critical range for the Tukey procedure using Equation (11.15).
3. Compare each of the $c(c - 1)/2$ pairs against the critical range. If the absolute difference in a specific pair of sample means, such as $|\bar{X}_{.j} - \bar{X}_{.j'}|$, is greater than the critical range, then group j and group j' are significantly different.
4. Interpret the results.

To apply the Tukey procedure, return to the fast-food chain study. Because there are four restaurants, there are $4(4 - 1)/2 = 6$ possible pairwise comparisons. From Figure 11.10 on page 434, the absolute mean differences are

1. $|\bar{X}_{.1} - \bar{X}_{.2}| = |77.50 - 66.67| = 10.83$
2. $|\bar{X}_{.1} - \bar{X}_{.3}| = |77.50 - 91.00| = 13.50$
3. $|\bar{X}_{.1} - \bar{X}_{.4}| = |77.50 - 79.33| = 1.83$
4. $|\bar{X}_{.2} - \bar{X}_{.3}| = |66.67 - 91.00| = 24.33$
5. $|\bar{X}_{.2} - \bar{X}_{.4}| = |66.67 - 79.33| = 12.66$
6. $|\bar{X}_{.3} - \bar{X}_{.4}| = |91.00 - 79.33| = 11.67$

Locate $MSE = 14.986$ and $r = 6$ in Figure 11.10 to determine the critical range. From Table E.7 [for $\alpha = .05, c = 4$, and $(r - 1)(c - 1) = 15$], Q_{α}, the upper-tail critical value of the test statistic with 4 and 15 degrees of freedom, is 4.08. Using Equation (11.15),

$$\text{Critical range} = 4.08\sqrt{\frac{14.986}{6}} = 6.448$$

All pairwise comparisons except $|\bar{X}_{.1} - \bar{X}_{.4}|$ are greater than the critical range. Therefore, you conclude with 95% confidence that there is evidence of a significant difference in the mean rating between all pairs of restaurant branches except for branches *A* and *D*. In addition, branch *C* has the highest ratings (i.e., is most preferred), and branch *B* has the lowest (i.e., is least preferred).

Problems for Section 11.2

LEARNING THE BASICS

11.15 Given a randomized block experiment with five groups and seven blocks, answer the following:

a. How many degrees of freedom are there in determining the among-group variation?

b. How many degrees of freedom are there in determining the among-block variation?

c. How many degrees of freedom are there in determining the random variation?

d. How many degrees of freedom are there in determining the total variation?

11.16 From Problem 11.15, if $SSA = 60$, $SSBL = 75$, and $SST = 210$,

a. what is *SSE*?

b. what are *MSA*, *MSBL*, and *MSE*?

c. what is the value of the F_{STAT} test statistic for the factor effect?

d. what is the value of the F_{STAT} test statistic for the block effect?

11.17 From Problems 11.15 and 11.16,

a. construct the ANOVA summary table and fill in all values in the body of the table.

b. at the 0.05 level of significance, is there evidence of a difference in the group means?

c. at the 0.05 level of significance, is there evidence of a difference due to blocks?

11.18 From Problems 11.15, 11.16, and 11.17,

a. to perform the Tukey procedure, how many degrees of freedom are there in the numerator, and how many degrees of freedom are there in the denominator of the Studentized range distribution?

b. at the 0.05 level of significance, what is the upper-tail critical value from the Studentized range distribution?

c. to perform the Tukey procedure, what is the critical range?

11.19 Given a randomized block experiment with three groups and seven blocks,

a. how many degrees of freedom are there in determining the among-group variation?

b. how many degrees of freedom are there in determining the among-block variation?

c. how many degrees of freedom are there in determining the random variation?

d. how many degrees of freedom are there in determining the total variation?

11.20 From Problem 11.19, if $SSA = 36$ and the randomized block F_{STAT} statistic is 6.0,

a. what are *MSE* and *SSE*?

b. what is *SSBL* if the F_{STAT} test statistic for block effect is 4.0?

c. what is *SST*?

d. at the 0.01 level of significance, is there evidence of an effect due to groups, and is there evidence of an effect due to blocks?

11.21 Given a randomized block experiment with four groups and eight blocks, in the following ANOVA summary table, fill in all the missing results.

Source	Degrees of Freedom	Sum of Squares	Mean Square (Variance)	F
Among groups	$c - 1 = ?$	$SSA = ?$	$MSA = 80$	$F_{STAT} = ?$
Among blocks	$r - 1 = ?$	$SSBL = 540$	$MSBL = ?$	$F_{STAT} = 5.0$
Error	$(r - 1)(c - 1)$	$SSE = ?$	$MSE = ?$	
Total	$rc - 1 = ?$	$SST = ?$		

11.22 From Problem 11.21,

a. at the 0.05 level of significance, is there evidence of a difference among the four group means?

b. at the 0.05 level of significance, is there evidence of an effect due to blocks?

APPLYING THE CONCEPTS

11.23 Nine experts rated four brands of Colombian coffee in a taste-testing experiment. A rating on a 7-point scale (1 = extremely unpleasing, 7 = extremely pleasing) is given for each of four characteristics: taste, aroma, richness, and acidity. The following data (stored in **Coffee**) display the summated ratings, accumulated over all four characteristics.

	BRAND			
EXPERT	A	B	C	D
C.C.	24	26	25	22
S.E.	27	27	26	24
E.G.	19	22	20	16
B.L.	24	27	25	23
C.M.	22	25	22	21
C.N.	26	27	24	24
G.N.	27	26	22	23
R.M.	25	27	24	21
P.V.	22	23	20	19

At the 0.05 level of significance, completely analyze the data to determine whether there is evidence of a difference in the summated ratings of the four brands of Colombian coffee and, if so, which of the brands are rated highest (i.e., best). What can you conclude?

SELF Test **11.24** Which cell phone service has the highest rating? The data in **CellRating** represent the mean ratings for Verizon, AT&T, T-Mobile, and Sprint in 19 different cities.

Source: Data extracted from "Best Cell-Phone Service," *Consumer Reports*, January 2009, pp. 28–32.

a. At the 0.05 level of significance, determine whether there is evidence of a difference in the mean cell rating for the four cell phone services.

b. If appropriate, use the Tukey procedure to determine which cell phone services' mean ratings differ. Again, use a 0.05 level of significance.

11.25 How different are the rates of return of money market accounts and certificates of deposit that vary in length of their term? The data in **MMCD Rate** contain these rates for banks in a suburban area. (Data extracted from "Consumer Money Rates," *Newsday*, June 24, 2010, p. A43.)

a. At the 0.05 level of significance, determine whether there is evidence of a difference in the mean rates for these investments.

b. What assumptions are necessary to perform this test?

c. If appropriate, use the Tukey procedure to determine which investments differ. (Use $\alpha = 0.05$.)

d. Do you think that there was a significant block effect in this experiment? Explain.

11.26 Is there a difference in the prices if you shop as an impulsive shopper, if you shop as a savvy shopper, if you shop at a warehouse club such as Costco, or if you purchase store brands? To investigate this, a random sample of 10 purchases was selected, and the prices were compared. (Data extracted from "Shop Smart and Save Big," *Consumer Reports*, May 2009, p. 17.) The prices for the products are stored in **Shopping2**.

a. At the 0.05 level of significance, is there evidence of a difference between the mean price of an impulsive shopper, a savvy shopper, a shopper at a warehouse club such as Costco, or a purchaser of store brands?

b. What assumptions are necessary to perform this test?

c. If appropriate, use the Tukey procedure to determine which types of shopping differ. (Use $\alpha = 0.05$.)

d. Do you think that there was a significant block effect in this experiment? Explain.

11.27 Philips Semiconductors is a leading European manufacturer of integrated circuits. Integrated circuits are produced on silicon wafers, which are ground to target thickness early in the production process. The wafers are positioned in different locations on a grinder and kept in place using vacuum decompression. One of the goals of process improvement is to reduce the variability in the thickness of the wafers in different positions and in different batches. Data were collected from a sample of 30 batches. In each batch, the thickness of the wafers on positions 1 and 2 (outer circle), 18 and 19 (middle circle), and 28 (inner circle) was measured and stored in **Circuits**. At the 0.01 level of significance, completely analyze the data to determine whether there is evidence of a difference in the mean thickness of the wafers for the five positions and, if so, which of the positions are different. What can you conclude?

Source: Data extracted from K. C. B. Roes and R. J. M. M. Does, "Shewhart-Type Charts in Nonstandard Situations," *Technometrics*, 37, 1995, pp. 15–24.

11.28 The data in **Concrete2** represent the compressive strength in thousands of pounds per square inch of 40 samples of concrete taken 2, 7, and 28 days after pouring.

Source: Data extracted from O. Carrillo-Gamboa and R. F. Gunst, "Measurement-Error-Model Collinearities," *Technometrics*, 34, 1992, pp. 454–464.

a. At the 0.05 level of significance, is there evidence of a difference in the mean compressive strength after 2, 7, and 28 days?

b. If appropriate, use the Tukey procedure to determine the days that differ in mean compressive strength. (Use $\alpha = 0.05$.)

c. Determine the relative efficiency of the randomized block design as compared with the completely randomized (one-way ANOVA) design.

d. Construct boxplots of the compressive strength for the different time periods.

e. Based on the results of (a), (b), and (d), is there a pattern in the compressive strength over the three time periods?

11.3 The Factorial Design: Two-Way Analysis of Variance

In Section 11.1, you learned about the completely randomized design. In this section, the single-factor completely randomized design is extended to the **two-factor factorial design**, in which two factors are simultaneously evaluated. Each factor is evaluated at two or more levels. For example, in the Perfect Parachutes scenario on page 415, the company faces the business problem of simultaneously evaluating four suppliers and two types of looms to determine which supplier and which loom produce the strongest parachutes. Although this section uses only two factors, factorial designs for three or more factors are also possible (see references 4, 5, 6, 7, and 10).

To analyze data from a two-factor factorial design, you use **two-way ANOVA**. The following definitions are needed to develop the two-way ANOVA procedure:

r = number of levels of factor A

c = number of levels of factor B

n' = number of values (replicates) for each cell (combination of a particular level of factor A and a particular level of factor B)

n = number of values in the entire experiment (where $n = rcn'$)

X_{ijk} = value of the kth observation for level i of factor A and level j of factor B

$$\bar{\bar{X}} = \frac{\sum_{i=1}^{r}\sum_{j=1}^{c}\sum_{k=1}^{n'} X_{ijk}}{rcn'} = \text{grand mean}$$

$$\bar{X}_{i..} = \frac{\sum_{j=1}^{c}\sum_{k=1}^{n'} X_{ijk}}{cn'} = \text{mean of the } i\text{th level of factor } A \text{ (where } i = 1, 2, \ldots, r)$$

$$\bar{X}_{.j.} = \frac{\sum_{i=1}^{r}\sum_{k=1}^{n'} X_{ijk}}{rn'} = \text{mean of the } j\text{th level of factor } B \text{ (where } j = 1, 2, \ldots, c)$$

$$\bar{X}_{ij.} = \frac{\sum_{k=1}^{n'} X_{ijk}}{n'} = \text{mean of the cell } ij\text{, the combination of the } i\text{th level of factor } A \text{ and the } j\text{th level of factor } B$$

Because of the complexity of these computations, you should use only computerized methods when performing this analysis. However, to help explain the two-way ANOVA, the decomposition of the total variation is illustrated. In this discussion, only cases in which there are an equal number of **replicates** (sample sizes n') for each combination of the levels of factor A with those of factor B are considered. (See references 1 and 6 for a discussion of two-factor factorial designs with unequal sample sizes.)

Testing for Factor and Interaction Effects

There is an **interaction** between factors A and B if the effect of factor A is dependent on the level of factor B. Thus, when dividing the total variation into different sources of variation, you need to account for a possible interaction effect, as well as for factor A, factor B, and random error. To accomplish this, the total variation (SST) is subdivided into sum of squares due to factor A (or SSA), sum of squares due to factor B (or SSB), sum of squares due to the interaction effect of A and B (or $SSAB$), and sum of squares due to random variation (or SSE). This decomposition of the total variation (SST) is displayed in Figure 11.13.

FIGURE 11.13
Partitioning the total variation in a two-factor factorial design

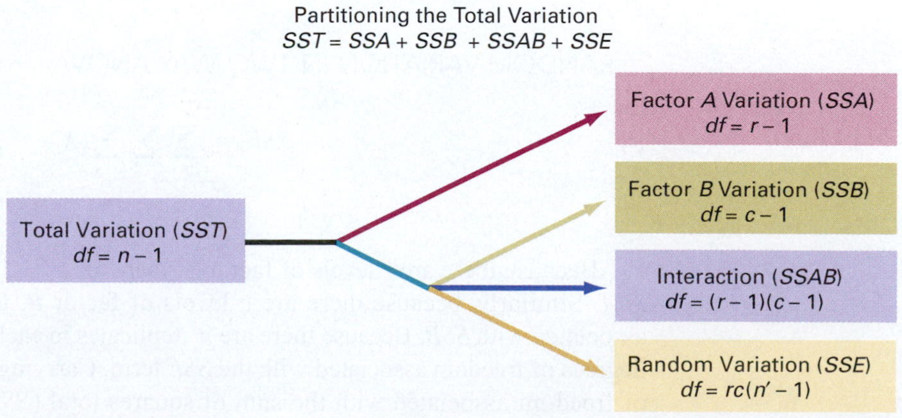

The sum of squares total (SST) represents the total variation among all the values around the grand mean. Equation (11.16) shows the computation for total variation.

TOTAL VARIATION IN TWO-WAY ANOVA

$$SST = \sum_{i=1}^{r}\sum_{j=1}^{c}\sum_{k=1}^{n'}(X_{ijk} - \bar{\bar{X}})^2 \tag{11.16}$$

The **sum of squares due to factor *A* (*SSA*)** represents the differences among the various levels of factor A and the grand mean. Equation (11.17) shows the computation for factor A variation.

FACTOR A VARIATION

$$SSA = cn'\sum_{i=1}^{r}(\bar{X}_{i..} - \bar{\bar{X}})^2 \tag{11.17}$$

The **sum of squares due to factor *B* (*SSB*)** represents the differences among the various levels of factor B and the grand mean. Equation (11.18) shows the computation for factor B variation.

FACTOR *B* VARIATION

$$SSB = rn'\sum_{j=1}^{c}(\bar{X}_{.j.} - \bar{\bar{X}})^2 \tag{11.18}$$

The **sum of squares due to interaction (*SSAB*)** represents the interacting effect of specific combinations of factor A and factor B. Equation (11.19) shows the computation for interaction variation.

INTERACTION VARIATION

$$SSAB = n'\sum_{i=1}^{r}\sum_{j=1}^{c}(\bar{X}_{ij.} - \bar{X}_{i..} - \bar{X}_{.j.} + \bar{\bar{X}})^2 \tag{11.19}$$

The sum of squares error (SSE) represents random variation—that is, the differences among the values within each cell and the corresponding cell mean. Equation (11.20) shows the computation for random variation.

RANDOM VARIATION IN TWO-WAY ANOVA

$$SSE = \sum_{i=1}^{r}\sum_{j=1}^{c}\sum_{k=1}^{n'}(X_{ijk} - \bar{X}_{ij.})^2 \tag{11.20}$$

Because there are r levels of factor A, there are $r - 1$ degrees of freedom associated with SSA. Similarly, because there are c levels of factor B, there are $c - 1$ degrees of freedom associated with SSB. Because there are n' replicates in each of the rc cells, there are $rc(n' - 1)$ degrees of freedom associated with the SSE term. Carrying this further, there are $n - 1$ degrees of freedom associated with the sum of squares total (SST) because you are comparing each value, X_{ijk}, to the grand mean, $\bar{\bar{X}}$, based on all n values. Therefore, because the degrees of freedom for each of the sources of variation must add to the degrees of freedom for the total variation (SST), you can calculate the degrees of freedom for the interaction component ($SSAB$) by subtraction. The degrees of freedom for interaction are $(r - 1)(c - 1)$.

If you divide each sum of squares by its associated degrees of freedom, you have the four variances or mean square terms (MSA, MSB, $MSAB$, and MSE). Equations (11.21a–d) give the mean square terms needed for the two-way ANOVA table.

MEAN SQUARES IN TWO-WAY ANOVA

$$MSA = \frac{SSA}{r - 1} \quad \textbf{(11.21a)}$$

$$MSB = \frac{SSB}{c - 1} \quad \textbf{(11.21b)}$$

$$MSAB = \frac{SSAB}{(r - 1)(c - 1)} \quad \textbf{(11.21c)}$$

$$MSE = \frac{SSE}{rc(n' - 1)} \quad \textbf{(11.21d)}$$

There are three different tests to perform in a two-way ANOVA:

1. To test the hypothesis of no difference due to factor A:

$$H_0: \mu_{1..} = \mu_{2..} = \cdots = \mu_{r..}$$

against the alternative:

$$H_1: \text{Not all } \mu_{i..} \text{ are equal}$$

you use the F_{STAT} test statistic in Equation (11.22).

F TEST FOR FACTOR A EFFECT

$$F_{STAT} = \frac{MSA}{MSE} \quad \textbf{(11.22)}$$

You reject the null hypothesis at the α level of significance if

$$F_{STAT} = \frac{MSA}{MSE} > F_\alpha$$

where F_α is the upper-tail critical value from an F distribution with $r - 1$ and $rc(n' - 1)$ degrees of freedom.

2. To test the hypothesis of no difference due to factor B:

$$H_0: \mu_{.1.} = \mu_{.2.} = \cdots = \mu_{.c.}$$

against the alternative:

$$H_1: \text{Not all } \mu_{.j.} \text{ are equal}$$

you use the F_{STAT} test statistic in Equation (11.23).

F TEST FOR FACTOR B EFFECT

$$F_{STAT} = \frac{MSB}{MSE} \quad \textbf{(11.23)}$$

You reject the null hypothesis at the α level of significance if

$$F_{STAT} = \frac{MSB}{MSE} > F_\alpha$$

where F_α is the upper-tail critical value from an F distribution with $c - 1$ and $rc(n' - 1)$ degrees of freedom.

3. To test the hypothesis of no interaction of factors A and B:

$$H_0\text{: The interaction of } A \text{ and } B \text{ is equal to zero}$$

against the alternative:

$$H_1\text{: The interaction of } A \text{ and } B \text{ is not equal to zero}$$

you use the F_{STAT} test statistic in Equation (11.24).

F TEST FOR INTERACTION EFFECT

$$F_{STAT} = \frac{MSAB}{MSE} \quad \textbf{(11.24)}$$

You reject the null hypothesis at the α level of significance if

$$F_{STAT} = \frac{MSAB}{MSE} > F_\alpha$$

where F_α is the upper-tail critical value from an F distribution with $(r - 1)(c - 1)$ and $rc(n' - 1)$ degrees of freedom.

Table 11.8 presents the entire two-way ANOVA table.

TABLE 11.8

Analysis of Variance Table for the Two-Factor Factorial Design

Source	Degrees of Freedom	Sum of Squares	Mean Square (Variance)	F
A	$r - 1$	SSA	$MSA = \frac{SSA}{r-1}$	$F_{STAT} = \frac{MSA}{MSE}$
B	$c - 1$	SSB	$MSB = \frac{SSB}{c-1}$	$F_{STAT} = \frac{MSB}{MSE}$
AB	$(r - 1)(c - 1)$	$SSAB$	$MSAB = \frac{SSAB}{(r-1)(c-1)}$	$F_{STAT} = \frac{MSAB}{MSE}$
Error	$rc(n' - 1)$	SSE	$MSE = \frac{SSE}{rc(n'-1)}$	
Total	$n - 1$	SST		

The Excel version of ***Parachute2*** *contains unstacked data, while the Minitab version contains stacked data.*

To illustrate a two-way ANOVA, return to the Perfect Parachutes scenario on page 415. As production manager at Perfect Parachutes, the business problem you decided to examine involved not just the different suppliers but also whether parachutes woven on the Jetta looms are as strong as those woven on the Turk looms. In addition, you need to determine whether any differences among the four suppliers in the strength of the parachutes are dependent on the type of loom being used. Thus, you have decided to collect the data by performing an experiment in which five different parachutes from each supplier are manufactured on each of the two different looms. The results are organized in Table 11.9 and stored in **Parachute2**.

TABLE 11.9

Tensile Strengths of Parachutes Woven by Two Types of Looms, Using Synthetic Fibers from Four Suppliers

	SUPPLIER			
LOOM	**1**	**2**	**3**	**4**
Jetta	20.6	22.6	27.7	21.5
Jetta	18.0	24.6	18.6	20.0
Jetta	19.0	19.6	20.8	21.1
Jetta	21.3	23.8	25.1	23.9
Jetta	13.2	27.1	17.7	16.0
Turk	18.5	26.3	20.6	25.4
Turk	24.0	25.3	25.2	19.9
Turk	17.2	24.0	20.8	22.6
Turk	19.9	21.2	24.7	17.5
Turk	18.0	24.5	22.9	20.4

Figure 11.14 presents the results for this example. In the Excel results, the A, B, and Error sources of variation in Table 11.8 on page 442 are labeled Sample, Columns, and Within, respectively. In the Minitab results, factor names are used to label the A and B sources of variation.

FIGURE 11.14

Excel and Minitab two-way ANOVA results for the parachute loom and supplier experiment

	A	B	C	D	E	F	G
1	ANOVA: Two-Factor With Replication						
2							
3	SUMMARY	Supplier 1	Supplier 2	Supplier 3	Supplier 4	Total	
4	*Jetta*						
5	Count	5	5	5	5	20	
6	Sum	92.1	117.7	109.9	102.5	422.2	
7	Average	18.42	23.54	21.98	20.5	21.11	
8	Variance	10.2020	7.5680	18.3970	8.3550	13.1283	
9							
10	*Turk*						
11	Count	5	5	5	5	20	
12	Sum	97.6	121.3	114.2	105.8	438.9	
13	Average	19.52	24.26	22.84	21.16	21.945	
14	Variance	7.2370	3.6830	4.5530	8.9030	8.4626	
15							
16	*Total*						
17	Count	10	10	10	10		
18	Sum	189.7	239	224.1	208.3		
19	Average	18.97	23.9	22.41	20.83		
20	Variance	8.0868	5.1444	10.4054	7.7912		
21							
22							
23	ANOVA						
24	*Source of Variation*	*SS*	*df*	*MS*	*F*	*P-value*	*F crit*
25	Sample	6.9722	1	6.9722	0.8096	0.3750	4.1491
26	Columns	134.3488	3	44.7829	5.1999	0.0049	2.9011
27	Interaction	0.2868	3	0.0956	0.0111	0.9984	2.9011
28	Within	275.5920	32	8.6123			
29							
30	Total	417.1998	39				
31					Level of significance	0.05	

Two-way ANOVA: Strength versus Loom, Supplier

```
Source       DF       SS       MS     F      P
Loom          1    6.972   6.9722  0.81  0.375
Supplier      3  134.349  44.7829  5.20  0.005
Interaction   3    0.287   0.0956  0.01  0.998
Error        32  275.592   8.6123
Total        39  417.200

S = 2.935   R-Sq = 33.94%   R-Sq(adj) = 19.49%

                   Individual 95% CIs For Mean Based on
                   Pooled StDev
Loom     Mean      --+---------+---------+---------+-------
jetta  21.110       (-----------*-----------)
turk   21.945                 (------------*------------)
                   --+---------+---------+---------+-------
                   20.0      21.0      22.0      23.0

                      Individual 95% CIs For Mean Based on
                      Pooled StDev
Supplier   Mean    --+---------+---------+---------+-------
1         18.97     (-------*------)
2         23.90                           (-------*------)
3         22.41                     (-------*------)
4         20.83             (------*-------)
                   --+---------+---------+---------+-------
                   17.5      20.0      22.5      25.0
```

To interpret the results, you start by testing whether there is an interaction effect between factor A (loom) and factor B (supplier). If the interaction effect is significant, further analysis will focus on this interaction. If the interaction effect is not significant, you can focus on the **main effects**—potential differences in looms (factor A) and potential differences in suppliers (factor B).

Using the 0.05 level of significance, to determine whether there is evidence of an interaction effect, you reject the null hypothesis of no interaction between loom and supplier if the computed F_{STAT} statistic is greater than 2.9011, the upper-tail critical value from the F distribution, with 3 and 32 degrees of freedom (see Figures 11.14 and 11.15).[1]

FIGURE 11.15
Regions of rejection and nonrejection at the 0.05 level of significance, with 3 and 32 degrees of freedom

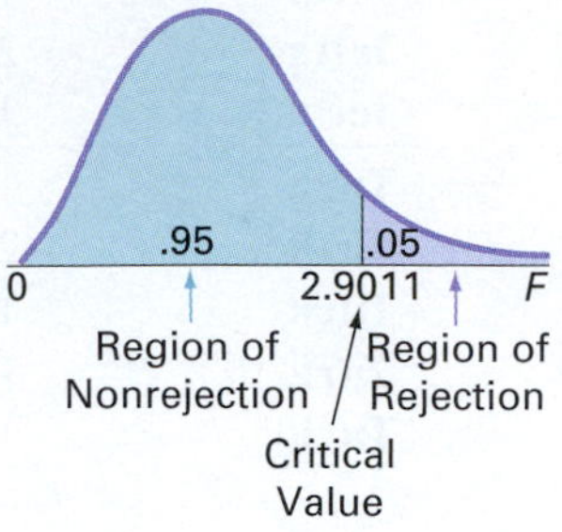

[1]Table E.5 does not provide the upper-tail critical values from the F distribution with 32 degrees of freedom in the denominator. When the desired degrees of freedom are not provided in the table, use the p-value computed by Excel or Minitab.

Because $F_{STAT} = 0.0111 < 2.9011$ or the p-value $= 0.9984 > 0.05$, you do not reject H_0. You conclude that there is insufficient evidence of an interaction effect between loom and supplier. You can now focus on the main effects.

Using the 0.05 level of significance and testing for a difference between the two looms (factor A), you reject the null hypothesis if the computed F_{STAT} test statistic is greater than 4.1491, the (approximate) upper-tail critical value from the F distribution with 1 and 32 degrees of freedom (see Figures 11.14 and 11.16). Because $F_{STAT} = 0.8096 < 4.1491$ or the p-value $= 0.3750 > 0.05$, you do not reject H_0. You conclude that there is insufficient evidence of a difference in the mean tensile strengths of the parachutes manufactured between the two looms.

FIGURE 11.16
Regions of rejection and nonrejection at the 0.05 level of significance, with 1 and 32 degrees of freedom

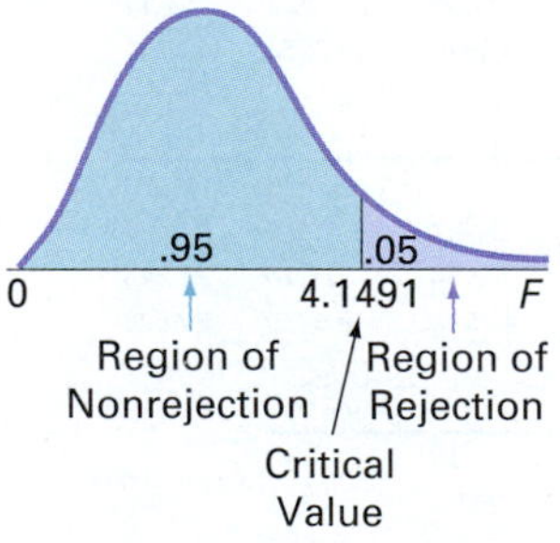

Using the 0.05 level of significance and testing for a difference among the suppliers (factor B), you reject the null hypothesis of no difference if the computed F_{STAT} test statistic is greater than 2.9011, the upper-tail critical value from the F distribution with 3 degrees of freedom in the numerator and 32 degrees of freedom in the denominator (see Figures 11.14 and 11.15). Because $F_{STAT} = 5.1999 > 2.9011$ or the p-value $= 0.0049 < 0.05$, reject H_0. You conclude that there is evidence of a difference in the mean tensile strength of the parachutes among the suppliers.

Multiple Comparisons: The Tukey Procedure

If one or both of the factor effects are significant and there is no significant interaction effect, when there are more than two levels of a factor, you can determine the particular levels that are significantly different by using the **Tukey multiple comparisons procedure for two-way ANOVA** (see references 6 and 10). Equation (11.25) gives the critical range for factor A.

CRITICAL RANGE FOR FACTOR A

$$\text{Critical range} = Q_{\alpha}\sqrt{\frac{MSE}{cn'}} \quad \textbf{(11.25)}$$

where Q_{α} is the upper-tail critical value from a Studentized range distribution having r and $rc(n' - 1)$ degrees of freedom. (Values for the Studentized range distribution are found in Table E.7.)

Equation (11.26) gives the critical range for factor B.

CRITICAL RANGE FOR FACTOR B

$$\text{Critical range} = Q_{\alpha}\sqrt{\frac{MSE}{rn'}} \quad \textbf{(11.26)}$$

where Q_{α} is the upper-tail critical value from a Studentized range distribution having c and $rc(n' - 1)$ degrees of freedom. (Values for the Studentized range distribution are found in Table E.7.)

To use the Tukey procedure, return to the parachute manufacturing data of Table 11.9 on page 443. In the ANOVA summary table in Figure 11.14 on page 443, the interaction effect is not significant. Using $\alpha = 0.05$, there is no evidence of a significant difference between the two looms (Jetta and Turk) that comprise factor A, but there is evidence of a significant difference among the four suppliers that comprise factor B. Thus, you can use the Tukey multiple comparisons procedure to determine which of the four suppliers differ.

Because there are four suppliers, there are $4(4 - 1)/2 = 6$ pairwise comparisons. Using the calculations presented in Figure 11.14, the absolute mean differences are as follows:

1. $|\bar{X}_{.1.} - \bar{X}_{.2.}| = |18.97 - 23.90| = 4.93$
2. $|\bar{X}_{.1.} - \bar{X}_{.3.}| = |18.97 - 22.41| = 3.44$
3. $|\bar{X}_{.1.} - \bar{X}_{.4.}| = |18.97 - 20.83| = 1.86$
4. $|\bar{X}_{.2.} - \bar{X}_{.3.}| = |23.90 - 22.41| = 1.49$
5. $|\bar{X}_{.2.} - \bar{X}_{.4.}| = |23.90 - 20.83| = 3.07$
6. $|\bar{X}_{.3.} - \bar{X}_{.4.}| = |22.41 - 20.83| = 1.58$

To determine the critical range, refer to Figure 11.14 to find $MSE = 8.6123, r = 2, c = 4$, and $n' = 5$. From Table E.7 [for $\alpha = 0.05, c = 4$, and $rc(n' - 1) = 32$], Q_{α}, the upper-tail critical value of the Studentized range distribution with 4 and 32 degrees of freedom is approximately 3.84. Using Equation (11.26),

$$\text{Critical range} = 3.84\sqrt{\frac{8.6123}{10}} = 3.56$$

Because $4.93 > 3.56$, only the means of Suppliers 1 and 2 are different. You can conclude that the mean tensile strength is lower for Supplier 1 than for Supplier 2, but there are no statistically significant differences between Suppliers 1 and 3, Suppliers 1 and 4, Suppliers 2 and 3, Suppliers 2 and 4, and Suppliers 3 and 4. Note that by using $\alpha = 0.05$, you are able to make all six comparisons with an overall error rate of only 5%.

Visualizing Interaction Effects: The Cell Means Plot

You can get a better understanding of the interaction effect by plotting the **cell means**, the means of all possible factor-level combinations. Figure 11.17 presents a cell means plot that uses the cell means for the loom/supplier combinations shown in Figure 11.14 on page 443. From the plot of the mean tensile strength for each combination of loom and supplier, observe that the two lines (representing the two looms) are roughly parallel. This indicates that the *difference* between the mean tensile strengths of the two looms is virtually the same for the four suppliers. In other words, there is no *interaction* between these two factors, as was indicated by the F test.

FIGURE 11.17
Excel cell means plot of tensile strength based on loom and supplier

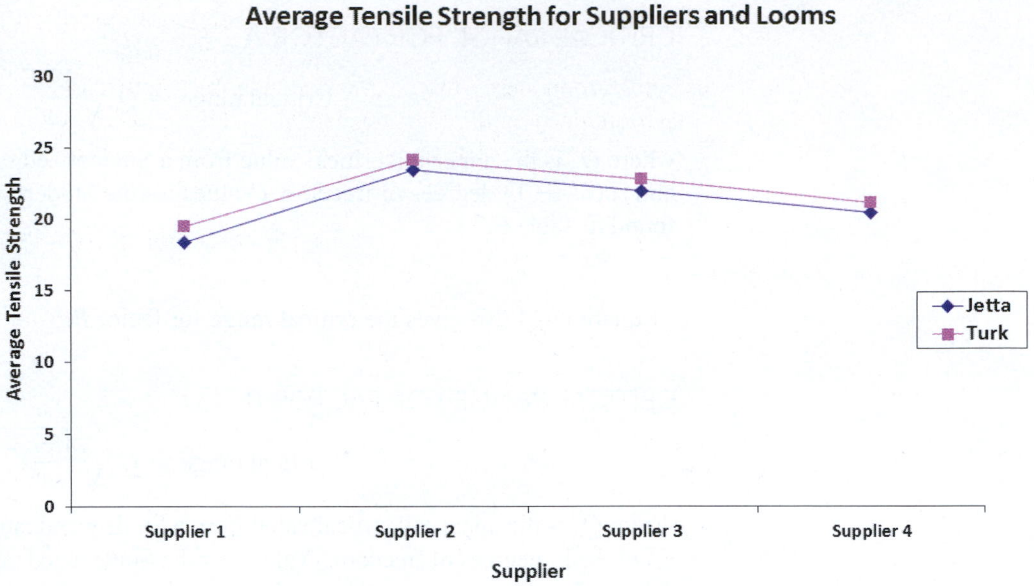

Interpreting Interaction Effects

What is the interpretation if there is an interaction? In such a situation, some levels of factor A would respond better with certain levels of factor B. For example, with respect to tensile strength, suppose that some suppliers were better for the Jetta loom and other suppliers were better for the Turk loom. If this were true, the lines of Figure 11.17 would not be nearly as parallel, and the interaction effect might be statistically significant. In such a situation, the difference between the looms is no longer the same for all suppliers. Such an outcome would also complicate the interpretation of the *main effects* because differences in one factor (the loom) would not be consistent across the other factor (the supplier).

Example 11.2 illustrates a situation with a significant interaction effect.

EXAMPLE 11.2

Interpreting Significant Interaction Effects

A nationwide company specializing in preparing students for college and graduate school entrance exams, such as the SAT, ACT, and LSAT, had the business objective of improving its ACT preparatory course. Two factors of interest to the company are the length of the course (a condensed 10-day period or a regular 30-day period) and the type of course (traditional classroom or online distance learning). The company collected data by randomly assigning 10 clients to each of the four cells that represent a combination of length of the course and type of course. The results are organized in the file **ACT** and presented in Table 11.10.

What are the effects of the type of course and the length of the course on ACT scores?

TABLE 11.10
ACT Scores for Different Types and Lengths of Courses

	LENGTH OF COURSE			
TYPE OF COURSE	Condensed		Regular	
Traditional	26	18	34	28
Traditional	27	24	24	21
Traditional	25	19	35	23
Traditional	21	20	31	29
Traditional	21	18	28	26
Online	27	21	24	21
Online	29	32	16	19
Online	30	20	22	19
Online	24	28	20	24
Online	30	29	23	25

SOLUTION The cell means plot presented in Figure 11.18 shows a strong interaction between the type of course and the length of the course. The nonparallel lines indicate that the effect of condensing the course depends on whether the course is taught in the traditional classroom or by online distance learning. The online mean score is higher when the course is condensed to a 10-day period, whereas the traditional mean score is higher when the course takes place over the regular 30-day period.

FIGURE 11.18
Cell means plot of ACT scores

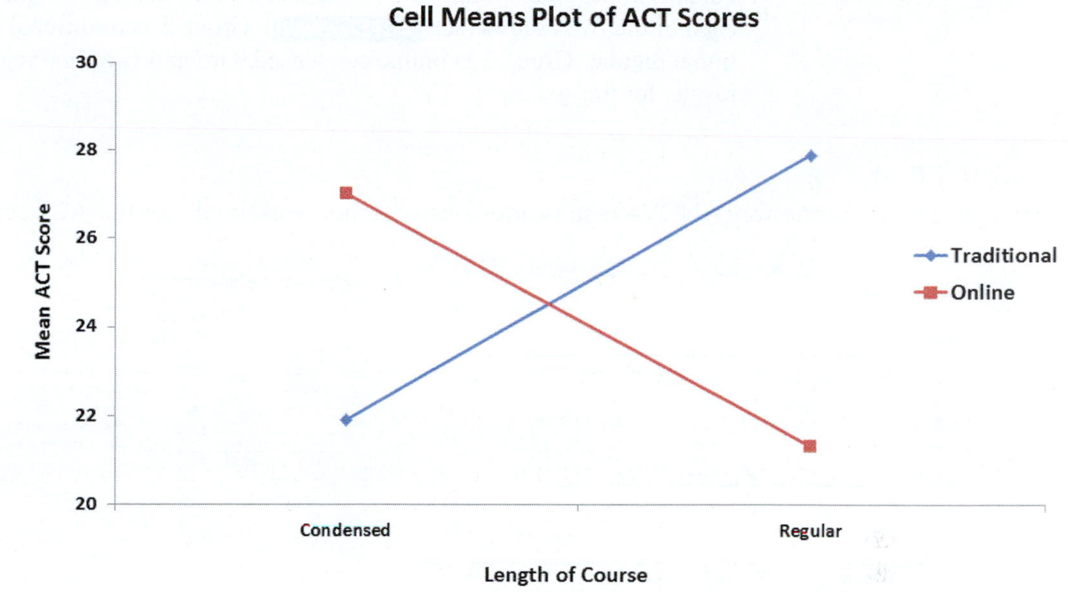

To verify the somewhat subjective analysis provided by interpreting the cell means plot, you begin by testing whether there is a statistically significant interaction between factor A (length of course) and factor B (type of course). Using a 0.05 level of significance, you reject the null hypothesis because $F_{STAT} = 24.2569 > 4.1132$ or the p-value equals $0.000 < 0.05$

FIGURE 11.19
Excel and Minitab two-way ANOVA results for ACT scores

	A	B	C	D	E	F	G
1	ANOVA: Two-Factor With Replication						
2							
3	SUMMARY	Condensed	Regular	Total			
4	*traditional*						
5	Count	10	10	20			
6	Sum	219	279	498			
7	Average	21.9	27.9	24.9			
8	Variance	11.2111	20.9889	24.7263			
9							
10	*online*						
11	Count	10	10	20			
12	Sum	270	213	483			
13	Average	27	21.3	24.15			
14	Variance	16.2222	8.0111	20.0289			
15							
16	*Total*						
17	Count	20	20				
18	Sum	489	492				
19	Average	24.45	24.6				
20	Variance	19.8395	25.2000				
21							
22							
23	ANOVA						
24	*Source of Variation*	*SS*	*df*	*MS*	*F*	*P-value*	*F crit*
25	Sample	5.6250	1	5.6250	0.3987	0.5318	4.1132
26	Columns	0.2250	1	0.2250	0.0159	0.9002	4.1132
27	Interaction	342.2250	1	342.2250	24.2569	0.0000	4.1132
28	Within	507.9000	36	14.1083			
29							
30	Total	855.9750	39				
31				*Level of significance*			0.05

Two-way ANOVA: Score versus Method, Course Length

```
Source          DF       SS       MS      F      P
Method           1    5.625    5.625   0.40  0.532
Course Length    1    0.225    0.225   0.02  0.900
Interaction      1  342.225  342.225  24.26  0.000
Error           36  507.900   14.108
Total           39  855.975

S = 3.756   R-Sq = 40.66%   R-Sq(adj) = 35.72%

                       Individual 95% CIs For Mean Based on
                       Pooled StDev
Method          Mean   ---+---------+---------+---------+------
online         24.15   (-------------*-------------)
traditional    24.90         (-------------*-------------)
                       ---+---------+---------+---------+------
                         22.8      24.0      25.2      26.4

                         Individual 95% CIs For Mean Based on
                         Pooled StDev
Course Length   Mean     ---+---------+---------+---------+------
Condensed      24.45     (----------------*----------------)
Regular        24.60       (----------------*----------------)
                         ---+---------+---------+---------+------
                           23.0      24.0      25.0      26.0
```

(see Figure 11.19). Thus, the hypothesis test confirms the interaction evident in the cell means plot. The existence of this significant interaction effect complicates the interpretation of the hypothesis tests concerning the two main effects. You cannot directly conclude that there is no effect with respect to length of course and type of course, even though both have p-values > 0.05.

Given that the interaction is significant, you can reanalyze the data with the two factors collapsed into four groups of a single factor rather than a two-way ANOVA with two levels of each of the two factors (see **ACT-OneWay**). Group 1 is traditional condensed. Group 2 is traditional regular. Group 3 is online condensed. Group 4 is online regular. Figure 11.20 shows the results for this example.

FIGURE 11.20

Excel and Minitab one-way ANOVA results and Tukey-Kramer worksheets for the ACT scores

	A	B	C	D	E	F	G
1	ANOVA: Single Factor						
2							
3	SUMMARY						
4	*Groups*	*Count*	*Sum*	*Average*	*Variance*		
5	Group 1	10	219	21.9	11.2111		
6	Group 2	10	279	27.9	20.9889		
7	Group 3	10	270	27	16.2222		
8	Group 4	10	213	21.3	8.0111		
9							
10							
11	ANOVA						
12	*Source of Variation*	*SS*	*df*	*MS*	*F*	*P-value*	*F crit*
13	Between Groups	348.0750	3	116.0250	8.2239	0.0003	2.8663
14	Within Groups	507.9	36	14.1083			
15							
16	Total	855.9750	39				
17					Level of significance		0.05

	A	B	C	D	E	F	G	H	I
1	**Tukey Kramer Multiple Comparisons**								
2									
3		Sample	Sample			Absolute	Std. Error	Critical	
4	Group	Mean	Size		**Comparison**	Difference	of Difference	Range	**Results**
5	1: Group 1	21.9	10		Group 1 to Group 2	6	1.187785054	4.5017	Means are different
6	2: Group 2	27.9	10		Group 1 to Group 3	5.1	1.187785054	4.5017	Means are different
7	3: Group 3	27	10		Group 1 to Group 4	0.6	1.187785054	4.5017	Means are not different
8	4: Group 4	21.3	10		Group 2 to Group 3	0.9	1.187785054	4.5017	Means are not different
9					Group 2 to Group 4	6.6	1.187785054	4.5017	Means are different
10	**Other Data**				Group 3 to Group 4	5.7	1.187785054	4.5017	Means are different
11	Level of significance	0.05							
12	Numerator d.f.	4							
13	Denominator d.f.	36							
14	MSW	14.1083							
15	Q Statistic	3.79							

One-way ANOVA: Group 1, Group 2, Group 3, Group 4

```
Source  DF     SS     MS     F      P
Factor   3  348.1  116.0  8.22  0.000
Error   36  507.9   14.1
Total   39  856.0

S = 3.756   R-Sq = 40.66%   R-Sq(adj) = 35.72%

                                Individual 95% CIs For Mean Based on
                                Pooled StDev
Level     N    Mean  StDev  -------+---------+---------+---------+--
Group 1  10  21.900  3.348    (-------*-------)
Group 2  10  27.900  4.581                       (-------*-------)
Group 3  10  27.000  4.028                    (-------*-------)
Group 4  10  21.300  2.830  (-------*-------)
                            -------+---------+---------+---------+--
                                 21.0      24.0      27.0      30.0
Pooled StDev = 3.756

Grouping Information Using Tukey Method
          N    Mean  Grouping
Group 2  10  27.900  A
Group 3  10  27.000  A
Group 1  10  21.900    B
Group 4  10  21.300    B

Means that do not share a letter are significantly different.
```

```
Tukey 95% Simultaneous Confidence Intervals
All Pairwise Comparisons

Individual confidence level = 98.93%

Group 1 subtracted from:
          Lower  Center   Upper  ---------+---------+---------+---------+
Group 2   1.475   6.000  10.525                      (-------*-------)
Group 3   0.575   5.100   9.625                     (-------*------)
Group 4  -5.125  -0.600   3.925           (-------*-------)
                                 ---------+---------+---------+---------+
                                       -6.0       0.0       6.0      12.0

Group 2 subtracted from:
           Lower  Center   Upper  ---------+---------+---------+---------+
Group 3   -5.425  -0.900   3.625            (-------*------)
Group 4  -11.125  -6.600  -2.075  (-------*-------)
                                  ---------+---------+---------+---------+
                                        -6.0       0.0       6.0      12.0

Group 3 subtracted from:
           Lower  Center   Upper  ---------+---------+---------+---------+
Group 4  -10.225  -5.700  -1.175    (-------*------)
                                  ---------+---------+---------+---------+
                                        -6.0       0.0       6.0      12.0
```

From Figure 11.20, because $F_{STAT} = 8.2239 > 2.8663$ or p-value $= 0.0003 < 0.05$, there is evidence of a significant difference in the four groups (traditional condensed, traditional regular, online condensed, and online regular). Traditional condensed is different from traditional regular and from online condensed. Traditional regular is also different from online regular, and online condensed is also different from online regular. Thus, whether condensing a course is a good idea depends on whether the course is offered in a traditional classroom or as an online distance learning course. To ensure the highest mean ACT scores, the company should use the traditional approach for courses that are given over a 30-day period but use the online approach for courses that are condensed into a 10-day period.

Problems for Section 11.3

LEARNING THE BASICS

11.29 Consider a two-factor factorial design with three levels in factor A, three levels in factor B, and four replicates in each of the nine cells.

a. How many degrees of freedom are there in determining the factor A variation and the factor B variation?
b. How many degrees of freedom are there in determining the interaction variation?
c. How many degrees of freedom are there in determining the random variation?
d. How many degrees of freedom are there in determining the total variation?

11.30 Assume that you are working with the results from Problem 11.29, if $SSA = 120$, $SSB = 110$, $SSE = 270$, and $SST = 540$.

a. What is $SSAB$?
b. What are MSA and MSB?
c. What is $MSAB$?
d. What is MSE?

11.31 Assume that you are working with the results from Problems 11.29 and 11.30.

a. What is the value of the F_{STAT} test statistic for the interaction effect?
b. What is the value of the F_{STAT} test statistic for the factor A effect?
c. What is the value of the F_{STAT} test statistic for the factor B effect?
d. Form the ANOVA summary table and fill in all values in the body of the table.

11.32 Given the results from Problems 11.29 through 11.31,

a. at the 0.05 level of significance, is there an effect due to factor A?
b. at the 0.05 level of significance, is there an effect due to factor B?
c. at the 0.05 level of significance, is there an interaction effect?

11.33 Given a two-way ANOVA with two levels for factor A, five levels for factor B, and four replicates in each of the 10 cells, with $SSA = 18$, $SSB = 64$, $SSE = 60$, and $SST = 150$,

a. form the ANOVA summary table and fill in all values in the body of the table.
b. at the 0.05 level of significance, is there an effect due to factor A?
c. at the 0.05 level of significance, is there an effect due to factor B?
d. at the 0.05 level of significance, is there an interaction effect?

11.34 Given a two-factor factorial experiment and the ANOVA summary table that follows, fill in all the missing results:

Source	Degrees of Freedom	Sum of Squares	Mean Square (Variance)	F
A	$r - 1 = 2$	$SSA = ?$	$MSA = 80$	$F_{STAT} = ?$
B	$c - 1 = ?$	$SSB = 220$	$MSB = ?$	$F_{STAT} = 11.0$
AB	$(r - 1)(c - 1) = 8$	$SSAB = ?$	$MSAB = 10$	$F_{STAT} = ?$
Error	$rc(n' - 1) = 30$	$SSE = ?$	$MSE = ?$	
Total	$n - 1 = ?$	$SST = ?$		

11.35 Given the results from Problem 11.34,

a. at the 0.05 level of significance, is there an effect due to factor A?
b. at the 0.05 level of significance, is there an effect due to factor B?
c. at the 0.05 level of significance, is there an interaction effect?

APPLYING THE CONCEPTS

11.36 The effects of developer strength (factor A) and development time (factor B) on the density of photographic plate film were being studied. Two strengths and two development times were used, and four replicates in each of the four cells were evaluated. The results (with larger being best) are stored in **Photo** and shown in the following table:

	DEVELOPMENT TIME (MINUTES)	
DEVELOPER STRENGTH	**10**	**14**
1	0	1
1	5	4
1	2	3
1	4	2
2	4	6
2	7	7
2	6	8
2	5	7

At the 0.05 level of significance,

a. is there an interaction between developer strength and development time?
b. is there an effect due to developer strength?
c. is there an effect due to development time?
d. Plot the mean density for each developer strength for each development time.
e. What can you conclude about the effect of developer strength and development time on density?

11.37 A chef in a restaurant that specializes in pasta dishes was experiencing difficulty in getting brands of pasta to be *al dente*—that is, cooked enough so as not to feel starchy or hard but still feel firm when bitten into. She decided to conduct an experiment in which two brands of pasta, one American and one Italian, were cooked for either 4 or 8 minutes. The variable of interest was weight of the pasta because cooking the pasta enables it to absorb water. A pasta with a faster rate of water absorption may provide a shorter interval in which the pasta is *al dente*, thereby increasing the chance that it might be overcooked. The experiment was conducted by using 150 grams of uncooked pasta. Each trial began by bringing a pot containing 6 quarts of cold, unsalted water to a moderate boil. The 150 grams of uncooked pasta was added and then weighed after a given period of time by lifting the pasta from the pot via a built-in strainer. The results (in terms of weight in grams) for two replicates of each type of pasta and cooking time are stored in **Pasta** and are as follows:

	COOKING TIME (MINUTES)	
TYPE OF PASTA	4	8
American	265	310
American	270	320
Italian	250	300
Italian	245	305

At the 0.05 level of significance,

a. is there an interaction between type of pasta and cooking time?
b. is there an effect due to type of pasta?
c. is there an effect due to cooking time?
d. Plot the mean weight for each type of pasta for each cooking time.
e. What conclusions can you reach concerning the importance of each of these two factors on the weight of the pasta?

SELF Test **11.38** A student team in a business statistics course performed a factorial experiment to investigate the time required for pain-relief tablets to dissolve in a glass of water. The two factors of interest were brand name (Equate, Kroger, or Alka-Seltzer) and water temperature (hot or cold). The experiment consisted of four replicates for each of the six factor combinations. The following data (stored in **PainRelief**) show the time a tablet took to dissolve (in seconds) for the 24 tablets used in the experiment:

	BRAND OF PAIN-RELIEF TABLET		
WATER	Equate	Kroger	Alka-Seltzer
Cold	85.87	75.98	100.11
Cold	78.69	87.66	99.65
Cold	76.42	85.71	100.83
Cold	74.43	86.31	94.16
Hot	21.53	24.10	23.80
Hot	26.26	25.83	21.29
Hot	24.95	26.32	20.82
Hot	21.52	22.91	23.21

At the 0.05 level of significance,

a. is there an interaction between brand of pain reliever and water temperature?
b. is there an effect due to brand?
c. is there an effect due to water temperature?
d. Plot the mean dissolving time for each brand for each water temperature.
e. Discuss the results of (a) through (d).

11.39 Integrated circuits are manufactured on silicon wafers through a process that involves a series of steps. An experiment was carried out to study the effect of the cleansing and etching steps on the yield (coded to maintain confidentiality). The results (stored in **Yield**) are as follows:

	ETCHING STEP	
CLEANSING STEP	New	Standard
New 1	38	34
New 1	34	19
New 1	38	28
New 2	29	20
New 2	35	35
New 2	34	37
Standard	31	29
Standard	23	32
Standard	38	30

Source: *Extracted from J. Ramirez and W. Taam, "An Autologistic Model for Integrated Circuit Manufacturing,"* Journal of Quality Technology, *2000, 32, pp. 254–262.*

At the 0.05 level of significance,

a. is there an interaction between the cleansing step and the etching step?
b. is there an effect due to the cleansing step?
c. is there an effect due to the etching step?
d. Plot the mean yield for each cleansing step for each etching step.
e. Discuss the results of (a) through (d).

11.40 An experiment was conducted to try to resolve a problem of brake discs overheating at high speed on construction equipment. Five different brake discs were measured by two different temperature gauges. The temperature of each brake disc and gauge combination was measured at eight different times and the results stored in **Brakes**

Source: Data extracted from M. Awad, T. P. Erdmann, V. Shansal, and B. Barth, "A Measurement System Analysis Approach for Hard-to-Repeat Events," *Quality Engineering,* 21, 2009, pp. 300–305.

At the 0.05 level of significance,

a. is there an interaction between the brake discs and the gauges?
b. is there an effect due to brake discs?
c. is there an effect due to the gauges?
d. Plot the mean temperature for each brake disc for each gauge.
e. Discuss the results of (a) through (d).

USING STATISTICS @ Perfect Parachutes Revisited

In the Using Statistics scenario, you were the production manager at the Perfect Parachutes Company. You performed an experiment to determine whether there was a difference in the strength of parachutes woven from synthetic fibers from four different suppliers. Using the one-way ANOVA, you were able to determine that there was a difference in the mean strength of the parachutes from the different suppliers. You then were able to conclude that the mean strength of parachutes woven from synthetic fibers from supplier 1 was less than for supplier 2. Further experimentation was carried out to study the effect of the loom. You determined that there was no interaction between the supplier and loom and there was no difference in mean strength between the looms. Your next step as production manager is to investigate reasons the mean strength of parachutes woven from synthetic fibers from supplier 1 was less than for supplier 2 and possibly reduce the number of suppliers.

SUMMARY

In this chapter, various statistical procedures were used to analyze the effect of one or two factors of interest. The assumptions required for using these procedures were discussed in detail. Remember that you need to critically investigate the validity of the assumptions underlying the hypothesis-testing procedures. Table 11.11 summarizes the topics covered in this chapter.

TABLE 11.11
Summary of Topics in Chapter 11

Type of Analysis (numerical data only)	Number of Factors
Comparing more than two groups	One-way analysis of variance (Section 11.1)
	Randomized block design (Section 11.2)
	Two-way analysis of variance (Section 11.3)

KEY EQUATIONS

Total Variation in One-Way ANOVA

$$SST = \sum_{j=1}^{c}\sum_{i=1}^{n_j}(X_{ij} - \bar{\bar{X}})^2 \quad \textbf{(11.1)}$$

Among-Group Variation in One-Way ANOVA

$$SSA = \sum_{j=1}^{c} n_j(\bar{X}_j - \bar{\bar{X}})^2 \quad \textbf{(11.2)}$$

Within-Group Variation in One-Way ANOVA

$$SSW = \sum_{j=1}^{c}\sum_{i=1}^{n_j}(X_{ij} - \bar{X}_j)^2 \quad \textbf{(11.3)}$$

Mean Squares in One-Way ANOVA

$$MSA = \frac{SSA}{c - 1} \quad \textbf{(11.4a)}$$

$$MSW = \frac{SSW}{n - c} \quad \textbf{(11.4b)}$$

$$MST = \frac{SST}{n - 1} \quad \textbf{(11.4c)}$$

One-Way ANOVA F_{STAT} Test Statistic

$$F_{STAT} = \frac{MSA}{MSW} \quad \textbf{(11.5)}$$

Critical Range for the Tukey-Kramer Procedure

$$\text{Critical range} = Q_{\alpha}\sqrt{\frac{MSW}{2}\left(\frac{1}{n_j} + \frac{1}{n_{j'}}\right)} \quad \textbf{(11.6)}$$

Total Variation in the Randomized Block Design

$$SST = \sum_{j=1}^{c}\sum_{i=1}^{r}(X_{ij} - \bar{\bar{X}})^2 \quad \textbf{(11.7)}$$

Among-Group Variation in the Randomized Block Design

$$SSA = r\sum_{j=1}^{c}(\bar{X}_{.j} - \bar{\bar{X}})^2 \quad \textbf{(11.8)}$$

Among-Block Variation in the Randomized Block Design

$$SSBL = c\sum_{i=1}^{r}(\bar{X}_{i.} - \bar{\bar{X}})^2 \quad \textbf{(11.9)}$$

Random Variation in the Randomized Block Design

$$SSE = \sum_{j=1}^{c}\sum_{i=1}^{r}(X_{ij} - \bar{X}_{.j} - \bar{X}_{i.} + \bar{\bar{X}})^2 \quad \textbf{(11.10)}$$

Mean Squares in the Randomized Block Design

$$MSA = \frac{SSA}{c - 1} \quad \textbf{(11.11a)}$$

$$MSBL = \frac{SSBL}{r - 1} \quad \textbf{(11.11b)}$$

$$MSE = \frac{SSE}{(r - 1)(c - 1)} \quad \textbf{(11.11c)}$$

F_{STAT} Statistic for Factor Effect

$$F_{STAT} = \frac{MSA}{MSE} \quad \textbf{(11.12)}$$

F_{STAT} Statistic for Block Effects

$$F_{STAT} = \frac{MSBL}{MSE} \quad \textbf{(11.13)}$$

Estimated Relative Efficiency

$$RE = \frac{(r - 1)MSBL + r(c - 1)MSE}{(rc - 1)MSE} \quad \textbf{(11.14)}$$

Critical Range for the Randomized Block Design

$$\text{Critical range} = Q_{\alpha}\sqrt{\frac{MSE}{r}} \quad \textbf{(11.15)}$$

Total Variation in Two-Way ANOVA

$$SST = \sum_{i=1}^{r}\sum_{j=1}^{c}\sum_{k=1}^{n'}(X_{ijk} - \bar{\bar{X}})^2 \quad \textbf{(11.16)}$$

Factor *A* Variation

$$SSA = cn'\sum_{i=1}^{r}(\bar{X}_{i..} - \bar{\bar{X}})^2 \quad \textbf{(11.17)}$$

Factor *B* Variation

$$SSB = rn'\sum_{j=1}^{c}(\bar{X}_{.j.} - \bar{\bar{X}})^2 \quad \textbf{(11.18)}$$

Interaction Variation

$$SSAB = n'\sum_{i=1}^{r}\sum_{j=1}^{c}(\bar{X}_{ij.} - \bar{X}_{i..} - \bar{X}_{.j.} + \bar{\bar{X}})^2 \quad \textbf{(11.19)}$$

Random Variation in Two-Way ANOVA

$$SSE = \sum_{i=1}^{r}\sum_{j=1}^{c}\sum_{k=1}^{n'}(X_{ijk} - \bar{X}_{ij.})^2 \quad \textbf{(11.20)}$$

Mean Squares in Two-Way ANOVA

$$MSA = \frac{SSA}{r - 1} \quad \textbf{(11.21a)}$$

$$MSB = \frac{SSB}{c - 1} \quad \textbf{(11.21b)}$$

$$MSAB = \frac{SSAB}{(r - 1)(c - 1)} \quad \textbf{(11.21c)}$$

$$MSE = \frac{SSE}{rc(n' - 1)} \quad \textbf{(11.21d)}$$

***F* Test for Factor *A* Effect**

$$F_{STAT} = \frac{MSA}{MSE} \quad \textbf{(11.22)}$$

***F* Test for Factor *B* Effect**

$$F_{STAT} = \frac{MSB}{MSE} \quad \textbf{(11.23)}$$

***F* Test for Interaction Effect**

$$F_{STAT} = \frac{MSAB}{MSE} \quad \textbf{(11.24)}$$

Critical Range for Factor *A*

$$\text{Critical range} = Q_{\alpha}\sqrt{\frac{MSE}{cn'}} \quad \textbf{(11.25)}$$

Critical Range for Factor *B*

$$\text{Critical range} = Q_{\alpha}\sqrt{\frac{MSE}{rn'}} \quad \textbf{(11.26)}$$

KEY TERMS

CHAPTER REVIEW PROBLEMS

CHECKING YOUR UNDERSTANDING

11.41 In a one-way ANOVA, what is the difference between the among-groups variance *MSA* and the within-groups variance *MSW*?

11.42 What is the difference between the completely randomized one-way ANOVA design and the randomized block design?

11.43 What are the distinguishing features of the completely randomized design, randomized block design, and two-factor factorial designs?

11.44 What are the assumptions of ANOVA?

11.45 Under what conditions should you use the one-way ANOVA *F* test to examine possible differences among the means of *c* independent populations?

11.46 When and how should you use multiple comparison procedures for evaluating pairwise combinations of the group means?

11.47 What is the difference between the randomized block design and the two-factor factorial design?

11.48 What is the difference between the one-way ANOVA *F* test and the Levene test?

11.49 Under what conditions should you use the two-way ANOVA *F* test to examine possible differences among the means of each factor in a factorial design?

11.50 What is meant by the concept of interaction in a two-factor factorial design?

11.51 How can you determine whether there is an interaction in the two-factor factorial design?

APPLYING THE CONCEPTS

11.52 The operations manager for an appliance manufacturer wants to determine the optimal length of time for the washing cycle of a household clothes washer. An experiment is designed to measure the effect of detergent brand and washing cycle time on the amount of dirt removed from standard household laundry loads. Four brands of detergent (A, B, C, and D) and four levels of washing cycle (18, 20, 22, and 24 minutes) are specifically selected for analysis. In order to run the experiment, 32 standard household laundry loads (having equal weight and dirt) are randomly assigned, 2 each, to the 16 detergent/washing cycle time combinations. The results, in pounds of dirt removed (stored in **Laundry**), are as follows:

	WASHING CYCLE TIME (IN MINUTES)			
DETERGENT BRAND	**18**	**20**	**22**	**24**
A	0.11	0.13	0.17	0.17
A	0.09	0.13	0.19	0.18
B	0.12	0.14	0.17	0.19
B	0.10	0.15	0.18	0.17
C	0.08	0.16	0.18	0.20
C	0.09	0.13	0.17	0.16
D	0.11	0.12	0.16	0.15
D	0.13	0.13	0.17	0.17

At the 0.05 level of significance,

a. is there an interaction between detergent brand and washing cycle time?

b. is there an effect due to detergent brand?

c. is there an effect due to washing cycle time?

d. Plot the mean amount of dirt removed (in pounds) for each detergent brand for each washing cycle time.

e. If appropriate, use the Tukey procedure to determine differences between detergent brands and between washing cycle times.

f. What washing cycle time should be used for this type of household clothes washer?

g. Repeat the analysis, using washing cycle time as the only factor. Compare your results to those of (c), (e), and (f).

11.53 The quality control director for a clothing manufacturer wants to study the effect of operators and machines on the breaking strength (in pounds) of wool serge material. A batch of the material is cut into square-yard pieces, and these pieces are randomly assigned, 3 each, to each of the 12 combinations of 4 operators and 3 machines chosen specifically for the experiment. The results (stored in **Breakstw**) are as follows:

	MACHINE		
OPERATOR	I	II	III
A	115	111	109
A	115	108	110
A	119	114	107
B	117	105	110
B	114	102	113
B	114	106	114
C	109	100	103
C	110	103	102
C	106	101	105
D	112	105	108
D	115	107	111
D	111	107	110

At the 0.05 level of significance,

a. is there an interaction between operator and machine?

b. is there an effect due to operator?

c. is there an effect due to machine?

d. Plot the mean breaking strength for each operator for each machine.

e. If appropriate, use the Tukey procedure to examine differences among operators and among machines.

f. What can you conclude about the effects of operators and machines on breaking strength? Explain.

g. Repeat the analysis, using machines as the only factor. Compare your results to those of (c), (e), and (f).

11.54 An operations manager wants to examine the effect of air-jet pressure (in pounds per square inch [psi]) on the breaking strength of yarn. Three different levels of air-jet pressure are to be considered: 30 psi, 40 psi, and 50 psi. A random sample of 18 yarns are selected from the same batch, and the yarns are randomly assigned, 6 each, to the 3 levels of air-jet pressure. The breaking strength scores are in the file **Yarn**.

a. Is there evidence of a significant difference in the variances of the breaking strengths for the three air-jet pressures? (Use $\alpha = 0.05$.)

b. At the 0.05 level of significance, is there evidence of a difference among mean breaking strengths for the three air-jet pressures?

c. If appropriate, use the Tukey-Kramer procedure to determine which air-jet pressures significantly differ with respect to mean breaking strength. (Use $\alpha = 0.05$.)

d. What should the operations manager conclude?

11.55 Suppose that, when setting up his experiment in Problem 11.54, the operations manager had access to only six samples of yarn from the batch but was able to divide each yarn sample into three parts and randomly assign them, one each, to the three air-jet pressure levels. Thus, instead of the one-factor completely randomized design model in Problem 11.54, he used a randomized block design with the six yarn samples being the blocks and one yarn part each assigned to the three air-jet pressure levels. The breaking-strength scores are stored in **Yarn**.

a. At the 0.05 level of significance, is there evidence of a difference in the mean breaking strengths for the three air-jet pressures?

b. If appropriate, use the Tukey procedure to determine the air-jet pressures that differ in mean breaking strength. (Use $\alpha = 0.05$.)

c. At the 0.05 level of significance, is there evidence of a blocking effect?

d. Determine the relative efficiency of the randomized block design as compared with the completely randomized design.

e. Compare your result in (a) with your result in Problem 11.54 (b). Given your results in (c) and (d), what do you think happened? What can you conclude about the "impact of blocking" when the blocks themselves are not really different from each other?

11.56 Suppose that, when setting up the experiment in Problem 11.54, the operations manager is able to study the effect of side-to-side aspect in addition to air-jet pressure. Thus, instead of the one-factor completely randomized design in Problem 11.54, a two-factor factorial design was used, with the first factor, side-to-side aspect, having two levels (nozzle and opposite) and the second factor, air-jet pressure, having three levels (30 psi, 40 psi, and 50 psi). A sample of 18 yarns is randomly assigned, 3 to each of the 6 side-to-side aspect and pressure level combinations. The breaking-strength scores (stored in **Yarn**) are as follows:

	AIR-JET PRESSURE		
SIDE-TO-SIDE ASPECT	30 psi	40 psi	50 psi
Nozzle	25.5	24.8	23.2
Nozzle	24.9	23.7	23.7
Nozzle	26.1	24.4	22.7
Opposite	24.7	23.6	22.6
Opposite	24.2	23.3	22.8
Opposite	23.6	21.4	24.9

At the 0.05 level of significance,

a. is there an interaction between side-to-side aspect and air-jet pressure?
b. is there an effect due to side-to-side aspect?
c. is there an effect due to air-jet pressure?
d. Plot the mean yarn breaking strength for each level of side-to-side aspect for each level of air-jet pressure.
e. If appropriate, use the Tukey procedure to study differences among the air-jet pressures.
f. On the basis of the results of (a) through (e), what conclusions can you reach concerning yarn breaking strength? Discuss.
g. Compare your results in (a) through (f) with those from the completely randomized design in Problem 11.55. Discuss fully.

11.57 A pet food company has the business objective of having the weight of a can of cat food come as close to the specified weight as possible. Realizing that the size of the pieces of meat contained in a can and the can fill height could impact the weight of a can, a team studying the weight of canned cat food wondered whether the current larger chunk size produced higher can weight and more variability. The team decided to study the effect on weight of a cutting size that was finer than the current size. In addition, the team slightly lowered the target for the sensing mechanism that determines the fill height in order to determine the effect of the fill height on can weight.

Twenty cans were filled for each of the four combinations of piece size (fine and current) and fill height (low and current). The contents of each can were weighed, and the amount above or below the label weight of 3 ounces was recorded as the variable coded weight. For example, a can containing 2.90 ounces was given a coded weight of −0.10. Results were stored in **CatFood2**.

Analyze these data and write a report for presentation to the team. Indicate the importance of the piece size and the fill height on the weight of the canned cat food. Be sure to include a recommendation for the level of each factor that will come closest to meeting the target weight and the limitations of this experiment, along with recommendations for future experiments that might be undertaken.

11.58 A hotel wanted to develop a new system for delivering room service breakfasts. In the current system, an order form is left on the bed in each room. If the customer wishes to receive a room service breakfast, he or she places the order form on the doorknob before 11 P.M. The current system requires customers to select a 15-minute interval for desired delivery time (6:30–6:45 A.M., 6:45–7:00 A.M., etc.). The new system is designed to allow the customer to request a specific delivery time. The hotel wants to measure the difference between the actual delivery time and the requested delivery time of room service orders for breakfast. (A negative time means that the order was delivered before the requested time. A positive time means that the order was delivered after the requested time.) The factors included were the menu choice (American or Continental) and the desired time period in which the order was to be delivered (Early Time Period [6:30–8:00 A.M.] or Late Time Period [8:00–9:30 A.M.]). Ten orders for each combination of menu choice and desired time period were studied on a particular day. The data (stored in **Breakfast**) are as follows:

	DESIRED TIME	
TYPE OF BREAKFAST	Early Time Period	Late Time Period
Continental	1.2	−2.5
Continental	2.1	3.0
Continental	3.3	−0.2
Continental	4.4	1.2
Continental	3.4	1.2
Continental	5.3	0.7
Continental	2.2	−1.3
Continental	1.0	0.2
Continental	5.4	−0.5
Continental	1.4	3.8
American	4.4	6.0
American	1.1	2.3
American	4.8	4.2
American	7.1	3.8
American	6.7	5.5
American	5.6	1.8
American	9.5	5.1
American	4.1	4.2
American	7.9	4.9
American	9.4	4.0

At the 0.05 level of significance,

a. is there an interaction between type of breakfast and desired time?
b. is there an effect due to type of breakfast?
c. is there an effect due to desired time?
d. Plot the mean delivery time difference for each desired time for each type of breakfast.
e. On the basis of the results of (a) through (d), what conclusions can you reach concerning delivery time difference? Discuss.

11.59 Refer to the room service experiment in Problem 11.58. Now suppose that the results are as follows (and stored in **Breakfast2**). Repeat (a) through (e), using these data, and compare the results to those of (a) through (e) of Problem 11.58.

	DESIRED TIME	
TYPE OF BREAKFAST	Early	Late
Continental	1.2	−0.5
Continental	2.1	5.0
Continental	3.3	1.8
Continental	4.4	3.2
Continental	3.4	3.2
Continental	5.3	2.7
Continental	2.2	0.7
Continental	1.0	2.2
Continental	5.4	1.5
Continental	1.4	5.8
American	4.4	6.0
American	1.1	2.3
American	4.8	4.2
American	7.1	3.8
American	6.7	5.5
American	5.6	1.8
American	9.5	5.1
American	4.1	4.2
American	7.9	4.9
American	9.4	4.0

11.60 There are a tremendous number of mutual funds from which an investor can choose. Each mutual fund has its own mix of different types of investments. The data in **BestFunds2** represent the 3-year annualized return, 5-year annualized return, 10-year annualized return, and expense ratio (in %) for the 10 mutual funds rated best by the *U.S. News & World Report* for foreign large-cap blend, small-cap blend, mid-cap blend, large-cap blend, and diversified emerging markets categories. (Data extracted from K. Shinkle, "The Best Funds for the Long Term, *U.S. News & World Report*, Summer 2010, pp. 52–56.) Analyze the data and determine whether any differences exist between foreign large-cap blend, small-cap blend, mid-cap blend, large-cap blend, and diversified emerging market mutual funds. (Use the 0.05 level of significance.)

11.61 The data in **BestFunds3** represent the 3-year annualized return, 5-year annualized return, 10-year annualized return, and expense ratio (in %) for the 10 mutual funds rated best by the *U.S. News & World Report* for intermediate municipal bond, short-term bond, and intermediate-term bond categories. (Data extracted from K. Shinkle, "The Best Funds for the Long Term, *U.S. News & World Report*, Summer 2010, pp. 52–56.) Analyze the data and determine whether any differences exist between intermediate municipal bond, short-term bond, and intermediate-term bond mutual funds. (Use the 0.05 level of significance.)

11.62 In a recent wine tasting held by the J. S. Wine Club, club members rated eight wines. Information concerning the country of origin and the price were not known to the club members until after the tasting took place. The wines rated (and the prices paid for them) were

- French white, \$10.59
- Italian white, \$8.50
- Italian red, \$8.50
- French burgundy (red), \$10.69
- French burgundy (red), \$11.75
- California Beaujolais (red), \$10.50
- French white, \$9.75
- California white, \$13.59

The summated ratings over several characteristics for the 12 club members are in the data file **Wine**

a. At the 0.01 level of significance, is there evidence of a difference in the mean rating scores among the wines?

b. What assumptions are necessary in order to do (a) of this problem? Comment on the validity of these assumptions.

c. If appropriate, use the Tukey procedure to determine the wines that differ in mean rating. (Use $\alpha = 0.01$.)

d. Based upon your results in (c), do you think that country of origin, type of wine, or price has had an effect on the ratings?

e. Determine the relative efficiency of the randomized block design as compared with the completely randomized design.

11.63 Ignore the blocking variable in Problem 11.62.

a. "Erroneously" reanalyze the data as a one-factor completely randomized design where the one factor brands of wines has eight levels, and each level contains a sample of 12 independent values.

b. Compare the *SSBL* and *SSE* terms in Problem 11.62 (a) to the *SSW* term in (a). Discuss.

c. Using the results in Problem 11.62 (a) and this problem, describe the issues that can arise when analyzing data if the wrong procedures are applied.

TEAM PROJECT

The file **Bond Funds** contains information regarding eight variables from a sample of 184 bond mutual funds:

Type—Type of bonds comprising the bond mutual fund (intermediate government or short-term corporate)
Assets—In millions of dollars
Fees—Sales charges (no or yes)
Expense ratio—Ratio of expenses to net assets in percentage
Return 2009—Twelve-month return in 2009
Three-year return—Annualized return, 2007–2009
Five-year return—Annualized return, 2005–2009
Risk—Risk-of-loss factor of the bond mutual fund (below average, average, or above average)

11.64 Completely analyze the difference between below-average-risk, average-risk, and above-average-risk bond mutual funds in terms of 2009 return, three-year return, five-year return, and expense ratio. Write a report summarizing your findings.

STUDENT SURVEY DATABASE

11.65 Problem 1.27 on page 14 describes a survey of 62 undergraduate students (stored in UndergradSurvey). For these data,

a. at the 0.05 level of significance, is there evidence of a difference based on academic major in grade point average, expected starting salary, age, number of social networking sites registered for, spending on textbooks and supplies, number of text messages sent in a typical week, and the wealth needed to feel rich?

b. at the 0.05 level of significance, is there evidence of a difference based on graduate school intention in grade point average, expected starting salary, age, number of social networking sites registered for, spending on textbooks and supplies, number of text messages sent in a typical week, and the wealth needed to feel rich?

c. at the 0.05 level of significance, is there evidence of a difference based on employment status in grade point average, expected starting salary, age, number of social networking sites registered for, spending on textbooks and supplies, number of text messages sent in a typical week, and the wealth needed to feel rich?

11.66 Problem 1.27 on page 14 describes a survey of 62 undergraduate students (stored in UndergradSurvey).

a. Select a sample of undergraduate students at your school and conduct a similar survey for those students.

b. For the data collected in (a), repeat (a) through (c) of Problem 11.65.

c. Compare the results of (b) to those of Problem 11.65.

11.67 Problem 1.28 on page 15 describes a survey of 44 MBA students (stored in GradSurvey). For these data, at the 0.05 level of significance,

a. is there evidence of a difference, based on undergraduate major, in age, undergraduate grade point average, graduate grade point average, expected salary upon graduation, number of text messages sent in a typical week, spending on textbooks and supplies, and the wealth needed to feel rich?

b. is there evidence of a difference, based on graduate major, in age, undergraduate grade point average, graduate grade point average, expected salary upon graduation, number of text messages sent in a typical week, spending on textbooks and supplies, and the wealth needed to feel rich?

c. is there evidence of a difference, based on employment status, in age, undergraduate grade point average, graduate grade point average, expected salary upon graduation, number of text messages sent in a typical week, spending on textbooks and supplies, and the wealth needed to feel rich?

11.68 Problem 1.28 on page 15 describes a survey of 44 MBA students (stored in GradSurvey).

a. Select a sample of graduate students in your MBA program and conduct a similar survey for those students.

b. For the data collected in (a), repeat (a) through (c) of Problem 11.67.

c. Compare the results of (b) to those of Problem 11.67.

MANAGING ASHLAND MULTICOMM SERVICES

Phase 1

The computer operations department had a business objective of reducing the amount of time to fully update each subscriber's set of messages in a special secured e-mail system. An experiment was conducted in which 24 subscribers were selected and three different messaging systems were used. Eight subscribers were assigned to each system, and the update times were measured. The results (stored in AMS11-1) are presented in Table AMS11.1.

TABLE AMS11.1

Update Times for Three Different Systems

System1	System2	System3
38.8	41.8	32.9
42.1	36.4	36.1
45.2	39.1	39.2
34.8	28.7	29.3
48.3	36.4	41.9
37.8	36.1	31.7
41.1	35.8	35.2
43.6	33.7	38.1

EXERCISE

1. Analyze the data in Table AMS11.1 and write a report to the computer operations department that indicates your findings. Include an appendix in which you discuss the reason you selected a particular statistical test to compare the three e-mail interfaces.

DO NOT CONTINUE UNTIL THE PHASE 1 EXERCISE HAS BEEN COMPLETED.

Phase 2

After analyzing the data in Table AMS11.1, the computer operations department team decided to also study the effect of the connection media used (cable or fiber).

The team designed a study in which a total of 30 subscribers were chosen. The subscribers were randomly assigned to one of the three messaging systems so that there were five subscribers in each of the six combinations of the two factors—messaging system and media used. Measurements were taken on the updated time. Table AMS11.2 summarizes the results (stored in AMS11-2).

TABLE AMS11.2

Update Times (in seconds), Based on Messaging System and Media Used

	INTERFACE		
MEDIA	**System1**	**System2**	**System3**
Cable	4.56	4.17	3.53
	4.90	4.28	3.77
	4.18	4.00	4.10
	3.56	3.96	2.87
	4.34	3.60	3.18
Fiber	4.41	3.79	4.33
	4.08	4.11	4.00
	4.69	3.58	4.31
	5.18	4.53	3.96
	4.85	4.02	3.32

EXERCISE

2. Completely analyze these data and write a report to the team that indicates the importance of each of the two factors and/or the interaction between them on the length of the call. Include recommendations for future experiments to perform.

DIGITAL CASE

Apply your knowledge about ANOVA in this Digital Case, which continues the cereal-fill packaging dispute Digital Case from Chapters 7, 9, and 10.

After reviewing CCACC's latest document (see the Digital Case for Chapter 10 on page 405), Oxford Cereals has released **SecondAnalysis.pdf**, a press kit that Oxford Cereals has assembled to refute the claim that it is guilty of using selective data. Review the Oxford Cereals press kit and then answer the following questions.

1. Does Oxford Cereals have a legitimate argument? Why or why not?
2. Assuming that the samples Oxford Cereals has posted were randomly selected, perform the appropriate analysis to resolve the ongoing weight dispute.
3. What conclusions can you reach from your results? If you were called as an expert witness, would you support the claims of the CCACC or the claims of Oxford Cereals? Explain.

REFERENCES

1. Berenson, M. L., D. M. Levine, and M. Goldstein, *Intermediate Statistical Methods and Applications: A Computer Package Approach* (Upper Saddle River, NJ: Prentice Hall, 1983).
2. Conover, W. J., *Practical Nonparametric Statistics*, 3rd ed. (New York: Wiley, 2000).
3. Daniel, W. W., *Applied Nonparametric Statistics*, 2nd ed. (Boston: PWS Kent, 1990).
4. Gitlow, H. S., and D. M. Levine, *Six Sigma for Green Belts and Champions: Foundations, DMAIC, Tools, Cases, and Certification* (Upper Saddle River, NJ: Financial Times/Prentice Hall, 2005).
5. Hicks, C. R., and K. V. Turner, *Fundamental Concepts in the Design of Experiments*, 5th ed. (New York: Oxford University Press, 1999).
6. Kutner, M. H, J. Neter, C. Nachtsheim, and W. Li, *Applied Linear Statistical Models*, 5th ed. (New York: McGraw-Hill-Irwin, 2005).
7. Levine, D. M., *Statistics for Six Sigma Green Belts* (Upper Saddle River, NJ: Financial Times/Prentice Hall, 2006).
8. *Microsoft Excel 2010* (Redmond, WA: Microsoft Corp., 2010).
9. *Minitab Release 16* (State College, PA: Minitab, Inc., 2010).
10. Montgomery, D. M., *Design and Analysis of Experiments*, 6th ed. (New York: Wiley, 2005).

CHAPTER 11 EXCEL GUIDE

EG11.1 The COMPLETELY RANDOMIZED DESIGN: ONE-WAY ANALYSIS of VARIANCE

One-Way ANOVA *F* Test for Differences Among More Than Two Means

PHStat2 Use **One-Way ANOVA** to perform the one-way ANOVA *F* test. For example, to perform the Figure 11.6 one-way ANOVA for the parachute experiment on page 422, open to the **DATA worksheet** of the **Parachute workbook**. Select **PHStat → Multiple-Sample Tests → One-Way ANOVA**. In the procedure's dialog box (shown below):

1. Enter **0.05** as the **Level of Significance**.
2. Enter **A1:D6** as the **Group Data Cell Range**.
3. Check **First cells contain label**.
4. Enter a **Title**, clear the **Tukey-Kramer Procedure** check box, and click **OK**.

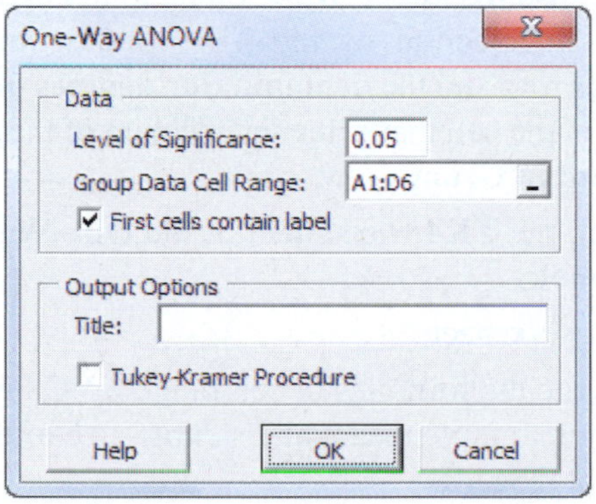

In addition to the worksheet shown in Figure 11.6, this procedure creates an **ASFData worksheet** to hold the data used for the test. See the following *In-Depth Excel* section for a complete description of this worksheet.

In-Depth Excel Use the **COMPUTE worksheet** of the **One-Way ANOVA workbook**, shown in Figure 11.6 on page 422, as a template for performing the one-way ANOVA *F* test. The worksheet performs the test for the Section 11.1 parachute experiment, using the data in the **ASFData worksheet**. The *SSA* in cell B13 is labeled **Between Groups** (not Among Groups) for consistency with the Analysis ToolPak results.

In cell B16, the worksheet uses **DEVSQ(*cell range of data of all groups*)** to compute *SST*, the total variation, and uses an expression in the form ***SST* − DEVSQ(*group 1 data cell range*) − DEVSQ(*group 2 data cell range*) . . . − DEVSQ(*group n data cell range*)** to compute *SSA*, the sum of squares among groups in cell B13. The worksheet also uses the FINV and FDIST worksheet functions to compute the *F* critical value and the *p*-value in cells F13 and G13, respectively.

Modifying the One-Way ANOVA workbook for use with other problems is a bit more difficult than modifications discussed in the Excel Guide in previous chapters, but it can be done using these steps:

1. Paste the data for the problem into the **ASFData worksheet**, overwriting the parachute experiment data.

In the COMPUTE worksheet (see Figure 11.6):

2. Edit the *SST* formula **=DEVSQ(ASFData!A1:D6)** in cell B16 to use the cell range of the new data just pasted into the ASFData worksheet.
3. Edit the cell B13 *SSA* formula so there are as many **DEVSQ(*group n data cell range*)** terms as there are groups.
4. Change the level of significance in cell G17, if necessary.
5. If the problem contains three groups, select **row 8**, right-click, and select **Delete** from the shortcut menu.
6. If the problem contains more than four groups, select **row 8**, right-click, and click **Insert** from the shortcut menu. Repeat this step as many times as necessary.
7. If the problem contains more than four groups, cut and paste the formulas in columns B through E of the new last row of the summary table to the cell range **B8:E8**. (These formulas were in row 8 before you inserted new rows.) For each new row inserted, enter formulas in columns B through E that refer to the next subsequent column in the ASFData worksheet.
8. Adjust table formatting as necessary.

Open to the **COMPUTE_FORMULAS worksheet** of the **One-Way ANOVA workbook** to examine the details of other formulas used in the COMPUTE worksheet. Of note is the expression **COUNTA(ASFData!1:1)**, a novel way to determine the number of groups by counting the number of column heading entries found in row 1 of the ASFData worksheet.

Analysis ToolPak Use **Anova: Single Factor** to perform the one-way ANOVA *F* test. For example, to perform the Figure 11.6 one-way ANOVA for the parachute experiment on page 422, open to the **DATA worksheet** of the **Parachute workbook** and:

1. Select **Data → Data Analysis**.
2. In the Data Analysis dialog box, select **Anova: Single Factor** from the **Analysis Tools** list and then click **OK**.

In the procedure's dialog box (shown below):

3. Enter **A1:D6** as the **Input Range**.
4. Click **Columns**, check **Labels in First Row**, and enter **0.05** as **Alpha**.
5. Click **New Worksheet Ply**.
6. Click **OK**.

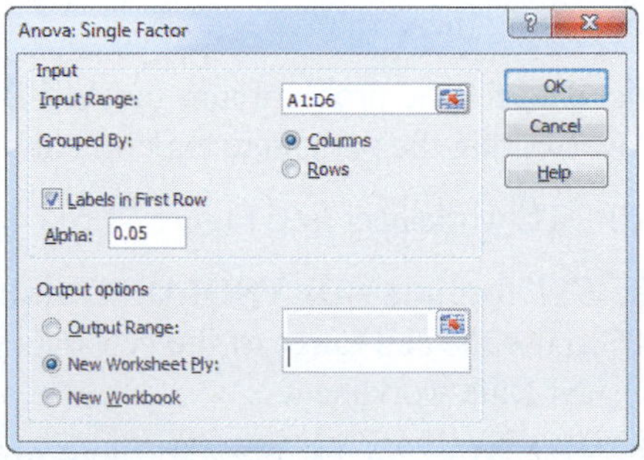

The Analysis ToolPak creates a worksheet that is visually similar to Figure 11.6 but a worksheet that does not include any cell formulas. The ToolPak worksheet also does not contain the level of significance in row 17.

Multiple Comparisons: The Tukey-Kramer Procedure

PHStat2 Use the *PHStat2* instructions for the one-way ANOVA *F* test to perform the Tukey-Kramer procedure, but in step 4, check **Tukey-Kramer Procedure** instead of clearing this check box. The procedure creates a worksheet identical to the one shown in Figure 11.7 on page 424 and discussed in the following *In-Depth Excel* section. To complete the worksheet, enter the **Studentized Range *Q* statistic** (look up the value using Table E.7 on pages 809–810) for the level of significance and the numerator and denominator degrees of freedom that are given in the worksheet.

In-Depth Excel To perform the Tukey-Kramer procedure, first use the *In-Depth Excel* instructions for the one-way ANOVA *F* test. Then open to the appropriate **"TK" worksheet** in the **One-Way ANOVA workbook** and enter the **Studentized Range *Q* statistic** (look up the value using Table E.7 on pages 809–810) for the level of significance and the numerator and denominator degrees of freedom that are given in the worksheet.

For example, to create the Figure 11.7 Tukey-Kramer worksheet for the parachute experiment on page 424, use the one-way ANOVA instructions and then open to the **TK4 worksheet**. Enter the **Studentized Range *Q* statistic** (look up the value using Table E.7 on pages 809–810) in cell B15 for the level of significance and the numerator and denominator degrees of freedom that are given in cells B11 through B13.

Other TK worksheets can be used for problems using three (**TK3**), four (**TK4**), five (**TK5**), six (**TK6**), or seven (**TK7**) groups. When you use either the **TK5**, **TK6**, and **TK7** worksheets, you must also enter the name, sample mean, and sample size for the fifth and, if applicable, sixth and seventh groups. Open to the **TK4_FORMULAS worksheet** of the **One-Way ANOVA workbook** to examine the details of all the formulas found in a TK worksheet.

Analysis ToolPak Adapt the previous *In-Depth Excel* instructions to perform the Tukey-Kramer procedure in conjunction with using the **Anova: Single Factor** procedure. Transfer selected values from the ToolPak results worksheet to one of the TK worksheets in the **One-Way ANOVA workbook.** For example, to perform the Figure 11.7 Tukey-Kramer procedure for the parachute experiment on page 424:

1. Use the **Anova: Single Factor** procedure, as described earlier in this section to create a worksheet that contains ANOVA results for the parachute experiment.
2. Record the name, **sample size** (in the **Count** column), and **sample mean** (in the **Average** column) of each group. Also record the ***MSW*** value, found in the cell that is the intersection of the **MS** column and **Within Groups** row, and the **denominator degrees of freedom**, found in the cell that is the intersection of the **df** column and **Within Groups** row.
3. Open to the **TK4 worksheet** of the **One-Way ANOVA workbook**.

In the TK4 worksheet:

4. Overwrite the formulas in cell range A5:C8 by entering the name, sample mean, and sample size of each group into that range.
5. Enter **0.05** in cell B11 (the level of significance used in the Anova: Single Factor procedure).
6. Enter **4** in cell B12 as the **Numerator d.f.** (equal to the number of groups).
7. Enter **16** in cell B13 as the **Denominator d.f.**
8. Enter **6.094** in cell B14 as the **MSW**.
9. Enter **4.05** in cell B15 as the **Q Statistic**. (Look up the **Studentized Range *Q* statistic** using Table E.7 on pages 809–810.)

Levene Test for Homogeneity of Variance

PHStat2 Use **Levene Test** to perform this test. For example, to perform the Figure 11.8 Levene test for the parachute experiment on page 426, open to the **DATA worksheet** of the **Parachute workbook**. Select **PHStat → Multiple-Sample Tests → Levene Test**. In the procedure's dialog box (shown on page 461):

1. Enter **0.05** as the **Level of Significance**.
2. Enter **A1:D6** as the **Sample Data Cell Range**.

3. Check **First cells contain label.**
4. Enter a **Title** and click **OK**.

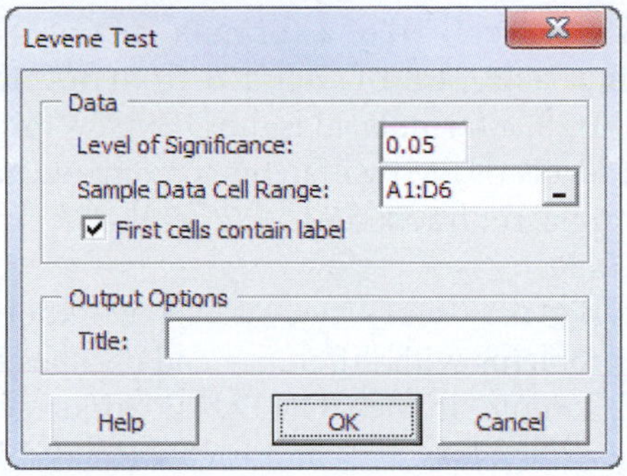

This procedure works only with data in which the sample sizes of each group are equal. The procedure creates a worksheet that performs the Table 11.4 absolute differences computations (see page 425) as well as the worksheet shown in Figure 11.8 (see page 426). (See the following *In-Depth Excel* section for a description of these worksheets.)

In-Depth Excel Use the **COMPUTE worksheet** of the **Levene workbook**, shown in Figure 11.8 on page 426, as a template for performing the Levene test. The worksheet performs the test using the data in the **AbsDiffs worksheet**, which computes absolute differences based on values in the **DATA worksheet**.

The COMPUTE worksheet shares its design with the COMPUTE worksheet of the **One-Way ANOVA workbook.** For other problems in which the absolute differences are already known, paste the absolute differences into the AbsDiffs worksheet. Otherwise, paste the problem data into the DATA worksheet, add formulas to compute the median for each group, and adjust the AbsDiffs worksheet as necessary. For example, for the parachute experiment data, the following steps 1 through 7 were done with the workbook open to the DATA worksheet.

1. Enter the label **Medians** in cell **A7**, the first empty cell in column A.
2. Enter the formula **=MEDIAN(A2:A6)** in cell **A8**. (Cell range A2:A6 contains the data for the first group, Supplier 1.)
3. Copy the cell A8 formula across through column **D**.
4. Open to the **AbsDiffs** worksheet.

In the AbsDiffs worksheet:

5. Enter row 1 column headings **AbsDiff1**, **AbsDiff2**, **AbsDiff3**, and **AbsDiff4** in columns A through D.
6. Enter the formula **=ABS(DATA!A2 – DATA!A8)** in cell A2. Copy this formula down through row 6. This formula computes the absolute difference of the first data value (DATA!A2) and the median of the Supplier 1 group data (DATA!A8).
7. Copy the formulas now in cell range A2:A6 across through column D. Absolute differences now appear in the cell range A2:D6.

Analysis ToolPak Use **Anova: Single Factor** with absolute difference data to perform the Levene test. If the absolute differences have not already been computed, use steps 1 through 7 of the preceding *In-Depth Excel* instructions to compute them.

EG11.2 The RANDOMIZED BLOCK DESIGN

In-Depth Excel Use the **COMPUTE worksheet** of the **Randomized Block workbook**, shown in Figure 11.10 on page 434, as a model for analyzing randomized block designs. The worksheet uses the data for the fast-food chain study example of Section 11.2 that is in the **Data worksheet**. In the ANOVA summary table of this worksheet, the source labeled **Among groups (*A*)** in Table 11.6 on page 433 is labeled **Columns**, and the source **Among blocks (*BL*)** is labeled **Rows**.

In cell B23, the worksheet uses **DEVSQ(*cell range of all data*)** to compute *SST*. In cell B19, a formula subtracts the list of DEVSQs for each group from *SST* to compute *SSA*. In cell B20, a formula subtracts the list of DEVSQs for each block from *SST* to compute *SSBL*. In cell B21, a formula subtracts *SSA* and *SSBL* from *SST* to compute *SSE*.

Open to the **COMPUTE_FORMULAS worksheet** to examine the formulas used in the COMPUTE worksheet. Modifying the COMPUTE worksheet workbook for use with other problems is both challenging and beyond the scope of this book. To attempt a modification, study and then modify the Section EG11.3 *In-Depth Excel* instructions or, better, use the *Analysis ToolPak* instructions to create the worksheet results.

Analysis ToolPak Use **Anova: Two-Factor Without Replication** to analyze a randomized block design. This procedure requires that the labels that identify blocks appear stacked in column A and that group names appear in row 1, starting with cell B1.

For example, to create a worksheet similar to Figure 11.10 on page 434 that analyzes the randomized block design for the fast-food chain study example of Section 11.2, open to the **DATA worksheet** of the **FFChain workbook** and:

1. Select **Data → Data Analysis**.
2. In the Data Analysis dialog box, select **Anova: Two-Factor Without Replication** from the **Analysis Tools** list and then click **OK**.

In the procedure's dialog box (shown on page 462):

3. Enter **A1:E7** as the **Input Range**.
4. Check **Labels** and enter **0.05** as **Alpha**.
5. Click **New Worksheet Ply**.
6. Click **OK**.

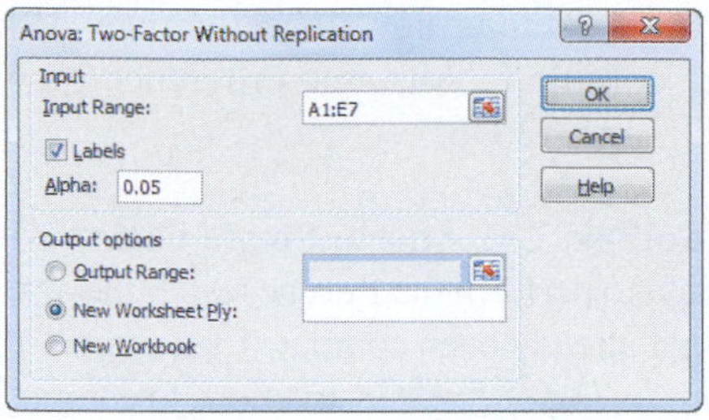

The Analysis ToolPak creates a worksheet that is visually similar to Figure 11.10 but contains only values and does not include any cell formulas. The ToolPak worksheet also does not contain the level of significance in row 24.

EG11.3 The FACTORIAL DESIGN: TWO-WAY ANALYSIS of VARIANCE

PHStat2 Use **Two-Way ANOVA with replication** to perform a two-way ANOVA. This procedure requires that the labels that identify factor *A* appear stacked in column A, followed by columns for factor *B*. For example, to perform the Figure 11.14 two-way ANOVA for the supplier and loom parachute example on page 443, open to the **DATA worksheet** of the **Parachute2 workbook**. Select **PHStat → Multiple-Sample Tests → Two-Way ANOVA**. In the procedure's dialog box (shown below):

1. Enter **0.05** as the **Level of Significance**.
2. Enter **A1:E11** as the **Sample Data Cell Range**.
3. Check **First cells contain label**.
4. Enter a **Title** and click **OK**.

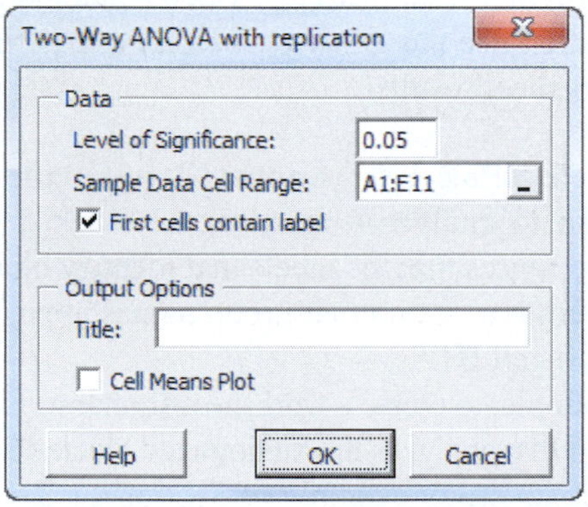

See the following *In-Depth Excel* section for a complete description of the worksheets.

In-Depth Excel Use the **COMPUTE worksheet** of the **Two-Way ANOVA workbook**, shown in Figure 11.14 on page 443, as a model for performing a two-way ANOVA. The worksheet performs the test for the supplier and loom parachute example of Section 11.3. In the ANOVA summary table of this worksheet, the source labeled *A* in Table 11.8 on page 442 is labeled **Sample**, source *B* is labeled **Columns**, source *AB* is labeled **Interaction**, and source *Error* is labeled **Within**.

In cell B30, the worksheet uses **DEVSQ(*cell range of all data*)** to compute *SST*. In cell B25, a formula subtracts the list of DEVSQs for each level of Factor *A* from *SST* to compute *SSA*. In cell B26, a formula subtracts the list of DEVSQs for each level of Factor *B* from *SST* to compute *SSB*. In cell B28, a formula adds the DEVSQs for each combination of levels of the two factors to compute *SSE*. In cell B27, a formula subtracts *SSA, SSB,* and *SSE* from *SST* to compute *SSAB*.

Modifying the Two-Way ANOVA workbook for use with other problems with different r and c values can be difficult. For example, in the COMPUTE worksheet, because Factor *A* has 2 levels ($r = 2$) and Factor B has 4 levels ($c = 4$), the formula for *SSE* in cell B28 contains 8 (r times c) different DEVSQ terms. For another problem in which $r = 4$ and $c = 4$, the formula would expand to 16 different DEVSQ terms—quite a lot to enter correctly! You should use PHStat2 or the Analysis ToolPak for such complicated problems.

For problems similar to the supplier and loom parachute example of Section 11.3, use the following steps to modify the Two-Way ANOVA workbook:

1. Paste the data for the problem into the **TWAData worksheet**, overwriting the parachute experiment data.

In the COMPUTE worksheet (see Figure 11.14 on page 443):

2. Select the cell range **E1:E20** (the current Supplier 4 column).
3. For problems in which $c > 4$, right-click and select **Insert** from the shortcut menu. In the Insert dialog box, click **Shift cells right** and click **OK**. Repeat this step as many times as necessary.
4. For problems in which $c < 4$, right-click and select **Delete** from the shortcut menu. In the Delete dialog box, click **Shift cells left** and click **OK**.
5. For problems in which $c = 2$, select cell range **D1:D20**, right-click, and select **Delete** from the shortcut menu. In the Delete dialog box, again click **Shift cells left** and click **OK**.
6. For problems in which $r > 2$, select the cell range **A10:G15** (which includes the current Turk rows). Right-click and select **Insert** from the shortcut menu. In the Insert dialog box, click **Shift cells down** and click **OK**. Repeat the previous sentence as many times as necessary. Enter new row labels in the new column A cells as necessary.
7. Edit the formulas in the top table area. Remember that each cell range in every formula in this area refers to a cell range on the TWAData worksheet that contains the range that hold the n' number of cells for a unique combination of a Factor *A* level and a Factor *B* level.
8. Edit the column B formulas for *SSA*, *SSB*, *SSE*, and *SST* that appear in the ANOVA summary table at the bottom

of the worksheet. (The formula for *SSAB* does not need to be edited.) As noted earlier, this step becomes harder as the product of *r* and *c* increases.

Open to the **COMPUTE_FORMULAS worksheet** of the **Two-Way ANOVA workbook** to examine the formulas used in the COMPUTE worksheet. Of special note is the complex expression **INT(COUNTA(TWAData!A:A) / COUNTIF(TWAData!A:A, TWAData!A2)) - 1** in cell C25 that computes $r - 1$.

Analysis ToolPak Use **Anova: Two-Factor With Replication** to perform a two-way ANOVA. This procedure requires that the labels that identify factor *A* appear stacked in column A, followed by columns for factor *B*. For example, to create a worksheet that performs the two-way ANOVA for the supplier and loom parachute example of Section 11.3, similar to Figure 11.14 on page 443, open to the **DATA worksheet** of the **Parachute2 workbook** and:

1. Select **Data ➔ Data Analysis**.
2. In the Data Analysis dialog box, select **Anova: Two-Factor With Replication** from the **Analysis Tools** list and then click **OK**.

In the procedure's dialog box (shown below):

3. Enter **A1:E11** as the **Input Range**.
4. Enter **5** as the **Rows per sample**.
5. Enter **0.05** as **Alpha**.
6. Click **New Worksheet Ply**.
7. Click **OK**.

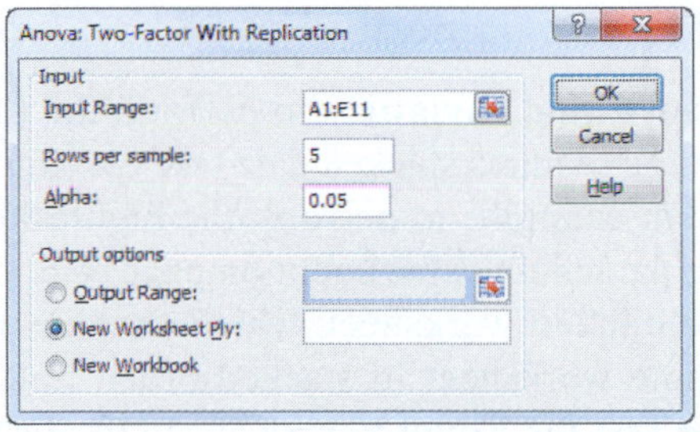

The Analysis ToolPak creates a worksheet that is visually similar to Figure 11.14 on page 443 but contains only values and does not include any cell formulas. This worksheet also does not contain the level of significance in row 31.

Visualizing Interaction Effects: The Cell Means Plot

PHStat2 Use the *PHStat2* instructions for the two-way ANOVA. In step 4, check **Cell Means Plot** before clicking **OK**.

In-Depth Excel Create a cell means plot from a two-way ANOVA results worksheet. To organize the data, insert a new worksheet and first copy and paste the Factor *B* level names to row 1 of the new worksheet and then copy and use Paste Special to transfer the values in the **Average** rows data for each Factor *B* level to the new worksheet. (See Appendix Section F.6 to learn more about the Paste Special command.)

For example, to create the Figure 11.17 cell means plot for the mean tensile strength for suppliers and looms on page 446, open to the **COMPUTE worksheet** of the **Two-Way ANOVA** workbook (shown in Figure 11.14 on page 443) and:

1. Insert a new worksheet.
2. Copy and paste the cell range **B3:E3** of the COMPUTE worksheet (the Factor *B* level names) to cell **B1** of the new worksheet.
3. Copy the cell range **B7:E7** of the COMPUTE worksheet (the AVERAGE row for the *Jetta* level of Factor *A*) and paste to cell **B2** of the new worksheet, using the Paste Special **Values** option.
4. Copy the cell range **B13:E13** of the COMPUTE worksheet (the AVERAGE row for the *Turk* level of Factor *A*) and paste to cell **B3** of a new worksheet, using the Paste Special **Values** option.
5. Enter **Jetta** in cell **B3** and **Turk** in cell **A3** of the new worksheet as labels for the Factor *A* levels.
6. Select the cell range **A1:E3**.
7. Select **Insert ➔ Line** and select the fourth **2-D Line** gallery choice (**Line with Markers**).
8. Relocate the chart to a chart sheet and adjust the chart formatting by using the instructions in Appendix Section F.4.

Analysis ToolPak Use the *In-Depth Excel* instructions for creating a cell means plot.

CHAPTER 11 MINITAB GUIDE

MG11.1 The COMPLETELY RANDOMIZED DESIGN: ONE-WAY ANALYSIS of VARIANCE

Use **Main Effects Plot** to create a main effects plot and use **One-Way (Unstacked)** or **One-Way** to perform the one-way ANOVA *F* test. (**Main Effects Plot** requires stacked data.)

For example, to create the Figure 11.4 main effect plot for the Section 11.1 parachute experiment on page 420, open to the **ParachuteStacked** worksheet. Select **Stat → ANOVA → Main Effects Plot**. In the Main Effects Plot dialog box (shown below):

1. Double-click **C2 Strength** in the variables list to add **Strength** to the **Responses** box and press **Tab.**
2. Double-click **C1 Supplier** in the variables list to add **Supplier** to the **Factors** box.
3. Click **OK.**

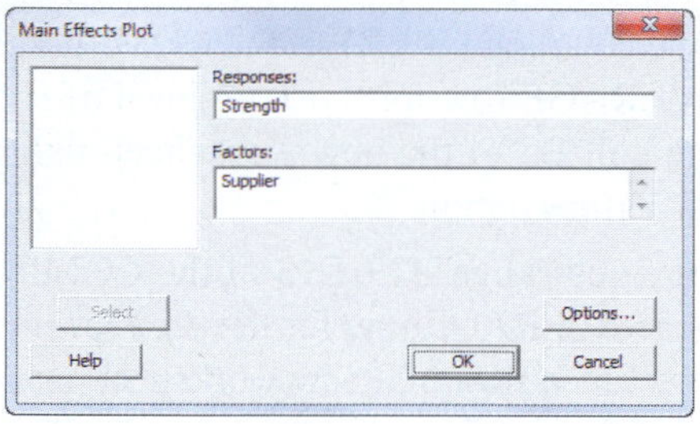

To perform the Figure 11.6 one-way ANOVA for the parachute experiment on page xx, open to the **PARACHUTE worksheet**. Select **Stat → ANOVA → One-Way (Unstacked).** In the One-Way Analysis of Variance dialog box (shown below):

1. Enter **'Supplier 1'-'Supplier 4'** in the **Responses (in separate columns)** box.
2. Enter **95.0** in the **Confidence level** box.
3. Click **Comparisons**.

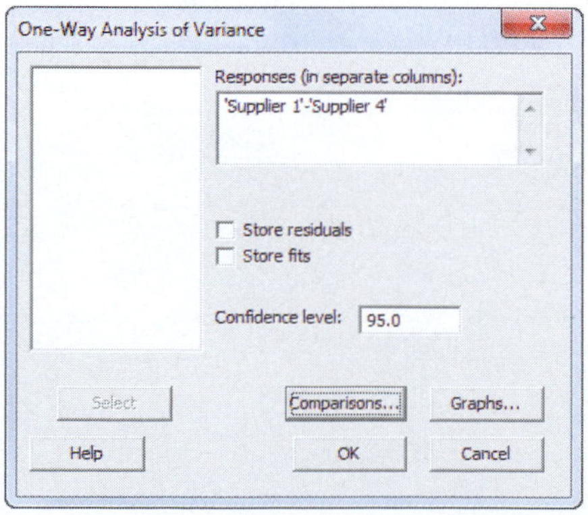

In the One-Way Multiple Comparisons dialog box (not shown):

4. Clear all check boxes.
5. Click **OK**.
6. Back in the original dialog box, click **Graphs.**

In the One-Way Analysis of Variance - Graphs dialog box (not shown):

7. Check **Boxplots of data**.
8. Click **OK**.
9. Back in the original dialog box, click **OK**.

For problems that use stacked data, select **Stat → ANOVA → One-Way** and in step 1 enter the name of the column that contains the measurements in the **Response** box and enter the name of the column that contains the factor names in the **Factor** box.

Multiple Comparisons: The Tukey-Kramer Procedure

Use the previous set of instructions to perform the Tukey-Kramer procedure, replacing step 4 with:

4. Check **Tukey's, family error rate** and enter **5** in its box. (A family error rate of 5 produces comparisons with an overall confidence level of 95%.)

Levene Test for Homogeneity of Variance

Use **Test for Equal Variances** to perform the Levene test. The procedure requires stacked data (see Section MG2.3 on page 87). For example, to perform the Figure 11.8 Levene test for the parachute experiment on page 426, open to the **ParachuteStacked** worksheet, which contains the data of the Parachute worksheet in stacked order. Select **Stat → ANOVA → Test for Equal Variances**. In the Test for Equal Variances dialog box (shown at the top of page 465):

1. Double-click **C2 Strength** in the variables list to add **Strength** to the **Response** box
2. Double-click **C1 Supplier** in the variables list to add **Supplier** to the **Factor** box.
3. Enter **95.0** in the **Confidence level** box.
4. Click **OK**.

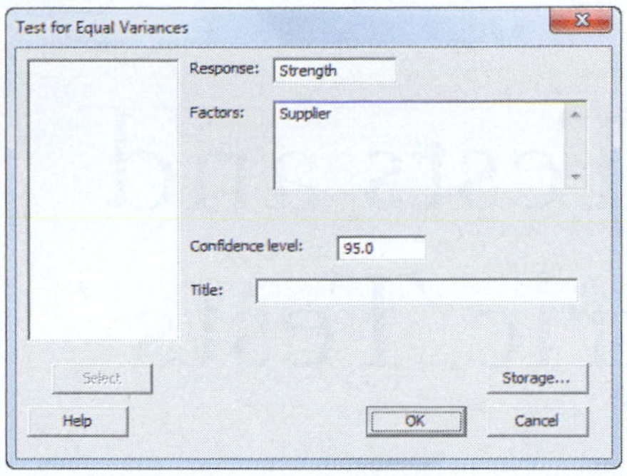

The Levene test results shown in Figure 11.8 on page 426 will be part of the results of this procedure.

MG11.2 The RANDOMIZED BLOCK DESIGN

Use **Two-Way** to analyze a randomized block design. For example, to create a worksheet similar to Figure 11.10 on page 434 that analyzes the randomized block design for the fast-food chain study example of Section 11.2, open to the **FFChain worksheet**. Select **Stat ➔ ANOVA ➔ Two-Way**. In the Two-Way Analysis of Variance dialog box (shown below):

1. Double-click **C3 Rating** in the variables list to add **Rating** to the **Response** box.
2. Double-click **C1 Rater** in the variables list to add **Rater** to the **Row factor** box.
3. Double-click **C2 Restaurant** in the variables list to add **Restaurant** to the **Column factor** box.
4. Check **Display means** for both the row and column factors.
5. Check **Fit Additive Model**.
6. Enter **95.0** in the **Confidence level** box.
7. Click **OK**.

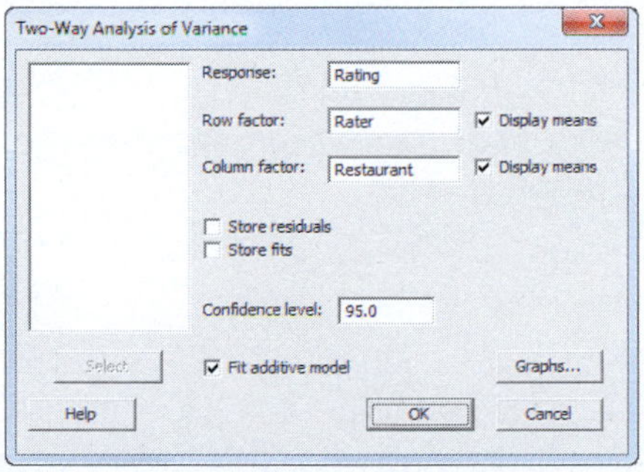

MG11.3 The FACTORIAL DESIGN: TWO-WAY ANALYSIS of VARIANCE

Use **Two-Way** to perform a two-way ANOVA. This procedure requires stacked data. For example, to perform the Figure 11.14 two-way ANOVA for the supplier and loom parachute example on page 443, open to the **Parachute2 worksheet**. Select **Stat ➔ ANOVA ➔ Two-Way.** In the Two-Way Analysis of Variance dialog box (shown below):

1. Double-click **C3 Strength** in the variables list to add **Strength** to the **Response** box.
2. Double-click **C1 Loom** in the variables list to add **Loom** to the **Row factor** box.
3. Double-click **C2 Supplier** in the variables list to add **Supplier** to the **Column factor** box.
4. Check **Display Means** for both the row and column factors.
5. Enter **95.0** in the **Confidence level** box.
6. Click **OK**.

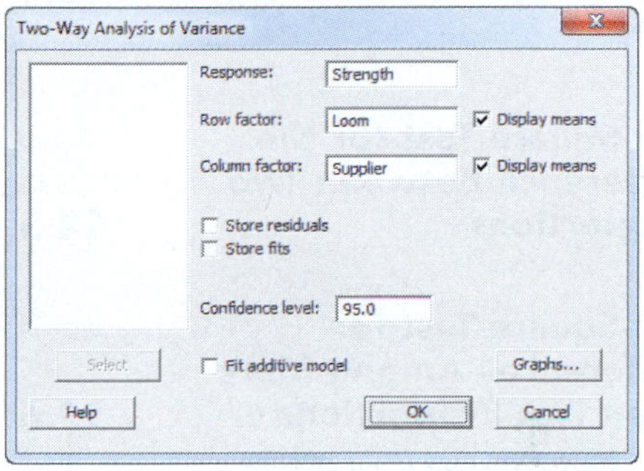

Visualizing Interaction Effects: The Cell Means Plot

Use **Interactions Plot** to create a cell means plot. This procedure requires stacked data. For example, to create a plot similar to the Figure 11.17 cell means plot of tensile strength based on loom and supplier on page 446, open to the **Parachute2 worksheet**. Select **Stat ➔ ANOVA ➔ Interactions Plot**. In the Interactions Plot dialog box (shown below):

1. Double-click **C3 Strength** in the variables list to add **Strength** to the **Responses** box and press **Tab**.
2. Double-click **C1 Loom** in the variables list to add **Loom** to the **Factors** box.
3. Double-click **C2 Supplier** in the variables list to add **Supplier** to the **Factors** box.
4. Clear **Display full interaction plot matrix**.
5. Click **OK**.

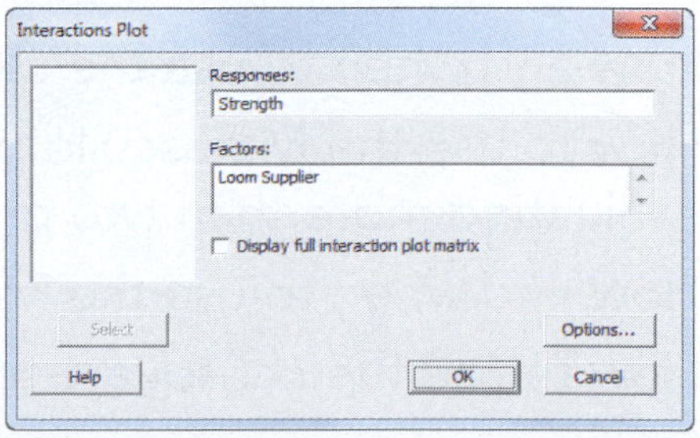

12 Chi-Square Tests and Nonparametric Tests

Learning Objectives

In this chapter, you learn:

- How and when to use the chi-square test for contingency tables
- How to use the Marascuilo procedure for determining pairwise differences when evaluating more than two proportions
- How and when to use the McNemar test
- How to use the chi-square test for a variance or standard deviation
- How and when to use nonparametric tests

USING STATISTICS @ T.C. Resort Properties

You are the manager of T.C. Resort Properties, a collection of five upscale hotels located on two tropical islands. Guests who are satisfied with the quality of services during their stay are more likely to return on a future vacation and to recommend the hotel to friends and relatives. You have defined the business objective as improving the return rate at the hotels. To assess the quality of services being provided by your hotels, guests are encouraged to complete a satisfaction survey when they check out. You need to analyze the data from these surveys to determine the overall satisfaction with the services provided, the likelihood that the guests will return to the hotel, and the reasons some guests indicate that they will not return. For example, on one island, T.C. Resort Properties operates the Beachcomber and Windsurfer hotels. Is the perceived quality at the Beachcomber Hotel the same as at the Windsurfer Hotel? If there is a difference, how can you use this information to improve the overall quality of service at T.C. Resort Properties? Furthermore, if guests indicate that they are not planning to return, what are the most common reasons given for this decision? Are the reasons given unique to a certain hotel or common to all hotels operated by T.C. Resort Properties?

In the preceding three chapters, you used hypothesis-testing procedures to analyze both numerical and categorical data. Chapter 9 presented some one-sample tests, and Chapter 10 developed several two-sample tests. Chapter 11 discussed the analysis of variance (ANOVA), which you use to study one or two factors of interest. This chapter extends hypothesis testing to analyze differences between population proportions based on two or more samples, to test the hypothesis of *independence* in the joint responses to two categorical variables, and to test for a population variance or standard deviation. The chapter concludes with nonparametric tests as alternatives to several hypothesis tests considered in Chapters 10 and 11.

12.1 Chi-Square Test for the Difference Between Two Proportions

In Section 10.3, you studied the Z test for the difference between two proportions. In this section, the data are examined from a different perspective. The hypothesis-testing procedure uses a test statistic that is approximated by a chi-square (χ^2) distribution. The results of this χ^2 test are equivalent to those of the Z test described in Section 10.3.

If you are interested in comparing the counts of categorical responses between two independent groups, you can develop a two-way **contingency table** (see Section 2.2) to display the frequency of occurrence of items of interest and items not of interest for each group. In Chapter 4, contingency tables were used to define and study probability.

To illustrate the contingency table, return to the Using Statistics scenario concerning T.C. Resort Properties. On one of the islands, T.C. Resort Properties has two hotels (the Beachcomber and the Windsurfer). You define the business objective as improving the quality of service at T.C. Resort Properties. You collect data from customer satisfaction surveys and focus on the responses to the single question "Are you likely to choose this hotel again?" You organize the results of the survey and determine that 163 of 227 guests at the Beachcomber responded yes to "Are you likely to choose this hotel again?" and 154 of 262 guests at the Windsurfer responded yes to "Are you likely to choose this hotel again?" You want to analyze the results to determine whether, at the 0.05 level of significance, there is evidence of a significant difference in guest satisfaction (as measured by likelihood to return to the hotel) between the two hotels.

The contingency table displayed in Table 12.1, which has two rows and two columns, is called a **2 × 2 contingency table**. The cells in the table indicate the frequency for each row and column combination.

TABLE 12.1
Layout of a 2 × 2 Contingency Table

	COLUMN VARIABLE (GROUP)		
ROW VARIABLE	**1**	**2**	**Totals**
Items of interest	X_1	X_2	X
Items not of interest	$n_1 - X_1$	$n_2 - X_2$	$n - X$
Totals	n_1	n_2	n

where

$$X_1 = \text{number of items of interest in group 1}$$
$$X_2 = \text{number of items of interest in group 2}$$
$$n_1 - X_1 = \text{number of items that are not of interest in group 1}$$
$$n_2 - X_2 = \text{number of items that are not of interest in group 2}$$
$$X = X_1 + X_2, \text{ the total number of items of interest}$$
$$n - X = (n_1 - X_1) + (n_2 - X_2), \text{ the total number of items that are not of interest}$$
$$n_1 = \text{sample size in group 1}$$
$$n_2 = \text{sample size in group 2}$$
$$n = n_1 + n_2 = \text{total sample size}$$

Table 12.2 contains the contingency table for the hotel guest satisfaction study. The contingency table has two rows, indicating whether the guests would return to the hotel or would not return to the hotel, and two columns, one for each hotel. The cells in the table indicate the frequency of each row and column combination. The row totals indicate the number of guests who would return to the hotel and those who would not return to the hotel. The column totals are the sample sizes for each hotel location.

TABLE 12.2

2 × 2 Contingency Table for the Hotel Guest Satisfaction Survey

	HOTEL		
CHOOSE HOTEL AGAIN?	**Beachcomber**	**Windsurfer**	**Total**
Yes	163	154	317
No	64	108	172
Total	227	262	489

To test whether the population proportion of guests who would return to the Beachcomber, π_1, is equal to the population proportion of guests who would return to the Windsurfer, π_2, you can use the **χ^2 test for the difference between two proportions**. To test the null hypothesis that there is no difference between the two population proportions:

$$H_0: \pi_1 = \pi_2$$

against the alternative that the two population proportions are not the same:

$$H_1: \pi_1 \neq \pi_2$$

you use the χ^2_{STAT} test statistic, shown in Equation (12.1).

χ^2 TEST FOR THE DIFFERENCE BETWEEN TWO PROPORTIONS

The χ^2_{STAT} test statistic is equal to the squared difference between the observed and expected frequencies, divided by the expected frequency in each cell of the table, summed over all cells of the table.

$$\chi^2_{STAT} = \sum_{all\ cells} \frac{(f_o - f_e)^2}{f_e} \quad \textbf{(12.1)}$$

where

f_o = **observed frequency** in a particular cell of a contingency table

f_e = **expected frequency** in a particular cell if the null hypothesis is true

The χ^2_{STAT} test statistic approximately follows a chi-square distribution with 1 degree of freedom.[1]

[1]In general, the degrees of freedom in a contingency table are equal to (number of rows − 1) multiplied by (number of columns − 1).

To compute the expected frequency, f_e, in any cell, you need to understand that if the null hypothesis is true, the proportion of items of interest in the two populations will be equal. Then the sample proportions you compute from each of the two groups would differ from each other only by chance. Each would provide an estimate of the common population parameter, π. A statistic that combines these two separate estimates together into one overall estimate of the population parameter provides more information than either of the two separate estimates could provide by itself. This statistic, given by the symbol $\bar{p}$, represents the estimated overall proportion of items of interest for the two groups combined (i.e., the total number of items of interest divided by the total sample size). The complement of $\bar{p}$, $1 - \bar{p}$, represents the estimated overall proportion of items that are not of interest in the two groups. Using the notation presented in Table 12.1 on page 468, Equation (12.2) defines $\bar{p}$.

COMPUTING THE ESTIMATED OVERALL PROPORTION FOR TWO GROUPS

$$\bar{p} = \frac{X_1 + X_2}{n_1 + n_2} = \frac{X}{n} \quad \textbf{(12.2)}$$

To compute the expected frequency, f_e, for cells that involve items of interest (i.e., the cells in the first row in the contingency table), you multiply the sample size (or column total) for a group by $\bar{p}$. To compute the expected frequency, f_e, for cells that involve items that are not of interest (i.e., the cells in the second row in the contingency table), you multiply the sample size (or column total) for a group by $1 - \bar{p}$.

The χ^2_{STAT} test statistic shown in Equation (12.1) on page 469 approximately follows a **chi-square (χ^2) distribution** (see Table E.4) with 1 degree of freedom. Using a level of significance α, you reject the null hypothesis if the computed χ^2_{STAT} test statistic is greater than χ^2_α, the upper-tail critical value from the χ^2 distribution with 1 degree of freedom. Thus, the decision rule is

$$\text{Reject } H_0 \text{ if } \chi^2_{STAT} > \chi^2_\alpha;$$
$$\text{otherwise, do not reject } H_0.$$

Figure 12.1 illustrates the decision rule.

FIGURE 12.1
Regions of rejection and nonrejection when using the chi-square test for the difference between two proportions, with level of significance α

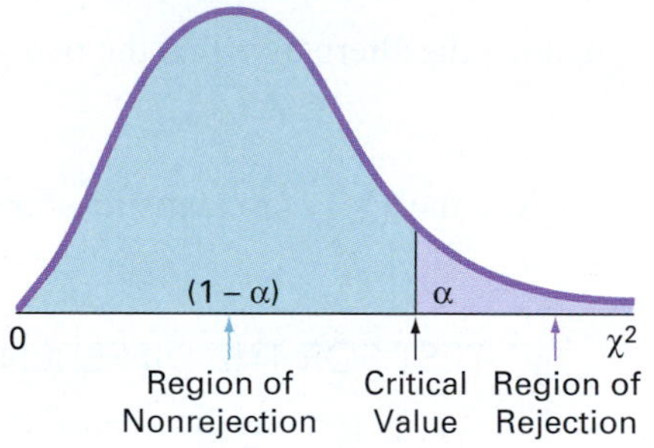

If the null hypothesis is true, the computed χ^2_{STAT} test statistic should be close to zero because the squared difference between what is actually observed in each cell, f_o, and what is theoretically expected, f_e, should be very small. If H_0 is false, then there are differences in the population proportions, and the computed χ^2_{STAT} test statistic is expected to be large. However, what is a large difference in a cell is relative. The same actual difference between f_o and f_e from a cell with a small number of expected frequencies contributes more to the χ^2_{STAT} test statistic than a cell with a large number of expected frequencies.

To illustrate the use of the chi-square test for the difference between two proportions, return to the Using Statistics scenario concerning T.C. Resort Properties on page 467 and the corresponding contingency table displayed in Table 12.2 on page 469. The null hypothesis (H_0: $\pi_1 = \pi_2$) states that there is no difference between the proportion of guests who are likely to choose either of these hotels again. To begin,

$$\bar{p} = \frac{X_1 + X_2}{n_1 + n_2} = \frac{163 + 154}{227 + 262} = \frac{317}{489} = 0.6483$$

$\bar{p}$ is the estimate of the common parameter π, the population proportion of guests who are likely to choose either of these hotels again if the null hypothesis is true. The estimated proportion of guests who are *not* likely to choose these hotels again is the complement of $\bar{p}$, $1 - 0.6483 = 0.3517$. Multiplying these two proportions by the sample size for the Beachcomber Hotel gives the number of guests expected to choose the Beachcomber again and the number not expected to choose this hotel again. In a similar manner, multiplying the two proportions by the Windsurfer Hotel's sample size yields the corresponding expected frequencies for that group.

EXAMPLE 12.1

Computing the Expected Frequencies

Compute the expected frequencies for each of the four cells of Table 12.2 on page 469.

SOLUTION

Yes—Beachcomber: $\bar{p} = 0.6483$ and $n_1 = 227$, so $f_e = 147.16$

Yes—Windsurfer: $\bar{p} = 0.6483$ and $n_2 = 262$, so $f_e = 169.84$

No—Beachcomber: $1 - \bar{p} = 0.3517$ and $n_1 = 227$, so $f_e = 79.84$

No—Windsurfer: $1 - \bar{p} = 0.3517$ and $n_2 = 262$, so $f_e = 92.16$

Table 12.3 presents these expected frequencies next to the corresponding observed frequencies.

TABLE 12.3

Comparing the Observed (f_o) and Expected (f_e) Frequencies

	HOTEL				
	BEACHCOMBER		WINDSURFER		
CHOOSE HOTEL AGAIN?	**Observed**	**Expected**	**Observed**	**Expected**	**Total**
Yes	163	147.16	154	169.84	317
No	64	79.84	108	92.16	172
Total	227	227.00	262	262.00	489

To test the null hypothesis that the population proportions are equal:

$$H_0: \pi_1 = \pi_2$$

against the alternative that the population proportions are not equal:

$$H_1: \pi_1 \neq \pi_2$$

you use the observed and expected frequencies from Table 12.3 to compute the χ^2_{STAT} test statistic given by Equation (12.1) on page 469. Table 12.4 presents the calculations.

TABLE 12.4

Computing the χ^2_{STAT} Test Statistic for the Hotel Guest Satisfaction Survey

f_o	f_e	$(f_o - f_e)$	$(f_o - f_e)^2$	$(f_o - f_e)^2/f_e$
163	147.16	15.84	250.91	1.71
154	169.84	−15.84	250.91	1.48
64	79.84	−15.84	250.91	3.14
108	92.16	15.84	250.91	2.72
				9.05

The chi-square (χ^2) distribution is a right-skewed distribution whose shape depends solely on the number of degrees of freedom. You find the critical value for the χ^2 test from Table E.4, a portion of which is presented as Table 12.5.

TABLE 12.5

Finding the Critical Value from the Chi-Square Distribution with 1 Degree of Freedom, Using the 0.05 Level of Significance

	Cumulative Probabilities						
	.005	**.01**	**...**	**.95**	**.975**	**.99**	**.995**
	Upper-Tail Area						
Degrees of Freedom	**.995**	**.99**	**...**	**.05**	**.025**	**.01**	**.005**
1			...	3.841	5.024	6.635	7.879
2	0.010	0.020	...	5.991	7.378	9.210	10.597
3	0.072	0.115	...	7.815	9.348	11.345	12.838
4	0.207	0.297	...	9.488	11.143	13.277	14.860
5	0.412	0.554	...	11.071	12.833	15.086	16.750

The values in Table 12.5 refer to selected upper-tail areas of the χ^2 distribution. A 2×2 contingency table has $(2 - 1)(2 - 1) = 1$ degree of freedom. Using $\alpha = 0.05$, with 1 degree of freedom, the critical value of χ^2 from Table 12.5 is 3.841. You reject H_0 if the computed χ^2_{STAT} test statistic is greater than 3.841 (see Figure 12.2). Because $\chi^2_{STAT} = 9.05 > 3.841$, you reject H_0. You conclude that the proportion of guests who would return to the Beachcomber is different from the proportion of guests who would return to the Windsurfer.

FIGURE 12.2
Regions of rejection and nonrejection when finding the χ^2 critical value with 1 degree of freedom, at the 0.05 level of significance

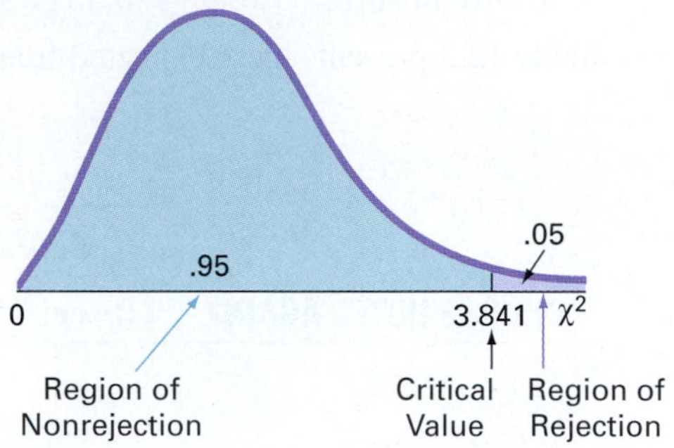

Figure 12.3 shows the results for the Table 12.2 guest satisfaction contingency table on page 469.

FIGURE 12.3
Excel and Minitab chi-square test results for the two-hotel guest satisfaction data

	A	B	C	D	E	F	G
1	Chi-Square Test						
2							
3	Observed Frequencies						
4		Hotel				Calculations	
5	Choose Again?	Beachcomber	Windsurfer	Total		fo-fe	
6	Yes	163	154	317		15.8446	-15.8446
7	No	64	108	172		-15.8446	15.8446
8	Total	227	262	489			
9							
10	Expected Frequencies						
11		Hotel					
12	Choose Again?	Beachcomber	Windsurfer	Total		(fo-fe)^2/fe	
13	Yes	147.1554	169.8446	317		1.7060	1.4781
14	No	79.8446	92.1554	172		3.1442	2.7242
15	Total	227	262	489			
16							
17	Data						
18	Level of Significance	0.05					
19	Number of Rows	2					
20	Number of Columns	2					
21	Degrees of Freedom	1	=(B19 - 1) * (B20 -1)				
22							
23	Results						
24	Critical Value	3.8415	=CHIINV(B18, B21)				
25	Chi-Square Test Statistic	9.0526	=SUM(F13:G14)				
26	*p*-Value	0.0026	=CHIDIST(B25, B21)				
27	Reject the null hypothesis		=IF(B26 < B18, "Reject the null hypothesis",				
28			"Do not reject the null hypothesis")				
29	*Expected frequency assumption*						
30	*is met.*		=IF(OR(B13 < 5, C13 < 5, B14 < 5, C14 < 5), " is violated.", " is met.")				

Chi-Square Test: Beachcomber, Windsurfer

```
Expected counts are printed below observed counts
Chi-Square contributions are printed below expected counts

       Beachcomber  Windsurfer  Total
   1           163         154    317
            147.16      169.84
             1.706       1.478

   2            64         108    172
             79.84       92.16
             3.144       2.724

Total          227         262    489

Chi-Sq = 9.053, DF = 1, P-Value = 0.003
```

These results include the expected frequencies, χ^2_{STAT}, degrees of freedom, and *p*-value. The computed χ^2_{STAT} test statistic is 9.0526, which is greater than the critical value of 3.8415 (or the *p*-value $= 0.0026 < 0.05$), so you reject the null hypothesis that there is no difference in guest satisfaction between the two hotels. The *p*-value, equal to 0.0026, is the probability of observing sample proportions as different as or more different from the actual difference between the Beachcomber and Windsurfer $(0.718 - 0.588 = 0.13)$ observed in the sample data, if the population proportions for the Beachcomber and Windsurfer hotels are equal. Thus, there is strong evidence to conclude that the two hotels are significantly different with respect to guest satisfaction, as measured by whether a guest is likely to return to the hotel again. From Table 12.3 on page 471 you can see that a greater proportion of guests are likely to return to the Beachcomber than to the Windsurfer.

For the χ^2 test to give accurate results for a 2 $\times$ 2 table, you must assume that each expected frequency is at least 5. If this assumption is not satisfied, you can use alternative procedures, such as Fisher's exact test (see references 1, 2, and 4).

In the hotel guest satisfaction survey, both the Z test based on the standardized normal distribution (see Section 10.3) and the χ^2 test based on the chi-square distribution provide the same conclusion. You can explain this result by the interrelationship between the standardized normal distribution and a chi-square distribution with 1 degree of freedom. For such situations, the χ^2_{STAT} test statistic is the square of the Z_{STAT} test statistic. For instance, in the guest satisfaction study, the computed Z_{STAT} test statistic is $+3.0088$ and the computed χ^2_{STAT} test statistic is 9.0526. Except for rounding error, this 9.0526 value is the square of $+3.0088$ [i.e., $(+3.0088)^2 \cong 9.0526$]. Also, if you compare the critical values of the test statistics from the two distributions, at the 0.05 level of significance, the χ^2 value of 3.841 with 1 degree of freedom is the square of the Z value of ± 1.96. Furthermore, the p-values for both tests are equal. Therefore, when testing the null hypothesis of equality of proportions:

$$H_0: \pi_1 = \pi_2$$

against the alternative that the population proportions are not equal:

$$H_1: \pi_1 \neq \pi_2$$

the Z test and the χ^2 test are equivalent.

If you are interested in determining whether there is evidence of a *directional* difference, such as $\pi_1 > \pi_2$, you must use the Z test, with the entire rejection region located in one tail of the standardized normal distribution.

In Section 12.2, the χ^2 test is extended to make comparisons and evaluate differences between the proportions among more than two groups. However, you cannot use the Z test if there are more than two groups.

Problems for Section 12.1

LEARNING THE BASICS

12.1 Determine the critical value of χ^2 with 1 degree of freedom in each of the following circumstances:

a. $\alpha = 0.01$
b. $\alpha = 0.005$
c. $\alpha = 0.10$

12.2 Determine the critical value of χ^2 with 1 degree of freedom in each of the following circumstances:

a. $\alpha = 0.05$
b. $\alpha = 0.025$
c. $\alpha = 0.01$

12.3 Use the following contingency table:

	A	B	Total
1	20	30	50
2	30	45	75
Total	50	75	125

a. Compute the expected frequency for each cell.
b. Compare the observed and expected frequencies for each cell.
c. Compute χ^2_{STAT}. Is it significant at $\alpha = 0.05$?

12.4 Use the following contingency table:

	A	B	Total
1	20	30	50
2	30	20	50
Total	50	50	100

a. Compute the expected frequency for each cell.
b. Compute χ^2_{STAT}. Is it significant at $\alpha = 0.05$?

APPLYING THE CONCEPTS

12.5 A sample of 500 shoppers was selected in a large metropolitan area to determine various information concerning consumer behavior. Among the questions asked was, "Do you enjoy shopping for clothing?" The results are summarized in the following contingency table:

ENJOY SHOPPING FOR CLOTHING	GENDER		
	Male	Female	Total
Yes	136	224	360
No	104	36	140
Total	240	260	500

a. Is there evidence of a significant difference between the proportion of males and females who enjoy shopping for clothing at the 0.01 level of significance?
b. Determine the p-value in (a) and interpret its meaning.
c. What are your answers to (a) and (b) if 206 males enjoyed shopping for clothing and 34 did not?
d. Compare the results of (a) through (c) to those of Problem 10.29 (a), (b), and (d) on page 391.

12.6 Has the ease of removing your name from an e-mail list changed? A study of 100 large online retailers revealed the following:

YEAR	NEED THREE OR MORE CLICKS TO BE REMOVED	
	Yes	No
2009	39	61
2008	7	93

Source: Data extracted from "More Clicks to Escape an Email List," *The New York Times,* March 29, 2010, p. B2.

a. Set up the null and alternative hypotheses to try to determine whether the effort it takes to be removed from an e-mail list has changed.
b. Conduct the hypothesis test defined in (a), using the 0.05 level of significance.
c. Why shouldn't you compare the results in (a) to those of Problem 10.30 (b) on page 391?

12.7 A survey was conducted of 665 consumer magazines on the practices of their websites. Of these, 273 magazines reported that online-only content is copy-edited as rigorously as print content; 379 reported that online-only content is fact-checked as rigorously as print content. (Data extracted from S. Clifford, "Columbia Survey Finds a Slack Editing Process of Magazine Web Sites," *The New York Times*, March 1, 2010, p. B6.) Suppose that a sample of 500 newspapers revealed that 252 reported that online-only content is copy-edited as rigorously as print content and 296 reported that online-only content is fact-checked as rigorously as print content.
a. At the 0.05 level of significance, is there evidence of a difference between consumer magazines and newspapers in the proportion of online-only content that is copy-edited as rigorously as print content ?
b. Find the p-value in (a) and interpret its meaning.
c. At the 0.05 level of significance, is there evidence of a difference between consumer magazines and newspapers in the proportion of online-only content that is fact-checked as rigorously as print content?
d. Find the p-value in (c) and interpret its meaning.

SELF Test **12.8** Do people of different age groups differ in their response to e-mail messages? A survey by the Center for the Digital Future of the University of Southern California reported that 70.7% of users over age 70 believe that e-mail messages should be answered quickly, as compared to 53.6% of users 12 to 50 years old. (Data extracted from A. Mindlin, "Older E-mail Users Favor Fast Replies," *The New York Times*, July 14, 2008, p. B3.) Suppose that the survey was based on 1,000 users over age 70 and 1,000 users 12 to 50 years old.
a. At the 0.01 level of significance, is there evidence of a significant difference between the two age groups in their belief that e-mail messages should be answered quickly?
b. Find the p-value in (a) and interpret its meaning.
c. Compare the results of (a) and (b) to those of Problem 10.32 on page 391.

12.9 Different age groups use different media sources for news. A study on this issue explored the use of cell phones for accessing news. The study reported that 47% of users under age 50 and 15% of users age 50 and over accessed news on their cell phones. (Data extracted from "Cellphone Users Who Access News on Their Phones," *USA Today*, March 1, 2010, p. 1A.) Suppose that the survey consisted of 1,000 users under age 50, of whom 470 accessed news on their cell phones, and 891 users age 50 and over, of whom 134 accessed news on their cell phones.
a. Construct a 2×2 contingency table.
b. Is there evidence of a significant difference in the proportion that accessed the news on their cell phones between users under age 50 and users 50 years and older? (Use $\alpha = 0.05$.)
c. Determine the p-value in (b) and interpret its meaning.
d. Compare the results of (b) and (c) to those of Problem 10.35 (a) and (b) on page 392.

12.10 How do Americans feel about ads on websites? A survey of 1,000 adult Internet users found that 670 opposed ads on websites. (Data extracted from S. Clifford, "Tracked for Ads? Many Americans Say No Thanks," *The New York Times*, September 30, 2009, p. B3.) Suppose that a survey of 1,000 Internet users age 12–17 found that 510 opposed ads on websites.
a. At the 0.05 level of significance, is there evidence of a difference between adult Internet users and Internet users age 12–17 in the proportion who oppose ads?
b. Find the p-value in (a) and interpret its meaning.

12.2 Chi-Square Test for Differences Among More Than Two Proportions

In this section, the χ^2 test is extended to compare more than two independent populations. The letter c is used to represent the number of independent populations under consideration. Thus, the contingency table now has two rows and c columns. To test the null hypothesis that there are no differences among the c population proportions:

$$H_0: \pi_1 = \pi_2 = \cdots = \pi_c$$

against the alternative that not all the c population proportions are equal:

$$H_1: \text{Not all } \pi_j \text{ are equal (where } j = 1, 2, \ldots, c)$$

you use Equation (12.1) on page 469:

$$\chi^2_{STAT} = \sum_{all\ cells} \frac{(f_o - f_e)^2}{f_e}$$

where

f_o = observed frequency in a particular cell of a $2 \times c$ contingency table

f_e = expected frequency in a particular cell if the null hypothesis is true

If the null hypothesis is true and the proportions are equal across all c populations, the c sample proportions should differ only by chance. In such a situation, a statistic that combines these c separate estimates into one overall estimate of the population proportion, π, provides more information than any one of the c separate estimates alone. To expand on Equation (12.2) on page 470, the statistic $\bar{p}$ in Equation (12.3) represents the estimated overall proportion for all c groups combined.

COMPUTING THE ESTIMATED OVERALL PROPORTION FOR c GROUPS

$$\bar{p} = \frac{X_1 + X_2 + \cdots + X_c}{n_1 + n_2 + \cdots + n_c} = \frac{X}{n} \quad \textbf{(12.3)}$$

To compute the expected frequency, f_e, for each cell in the first row in the contingency table, multiply each sample size (or column total) by $\bar{p}$. To compute the expected frequency, f_e, for each cell in the second row in the contingency table, multiply each sample size (or column total) by $(1 - \bar{p})$. The test statistic shown in Equation (12.1) on page 469 approximately follows a chi-square distribution, with degrees of freedom equal to the number of rows in the contingency table minus 1, multiplied by the number of columns in the table minus 1. For a **$2 \times c$ contingency table**, there are $c - 1$ degrees of freedom:

$$\text{Degrees of freedom} = (2 - 1)(c - 1) = c - 1$$

Using the level of significance α, you reject the null hypothesis if the computed χ^2_{STAT} test statistic is greater than χ^2_α, the upper-tail critical value from a chi-square distribution with $c - 1$ degrees of freedom. Therefore, the decision rule is

$$\text{Reject } H_0 \text{ if } \chi^2_{STAT} > \chi^2_\alpha;$$

otherwise, do not reject H_0.

Figure 12.4 illustrates this decision rule.

FIGURE 12.4
Regions of rejection and nonrejection when testing for differences among c proportions using the χ^2 test

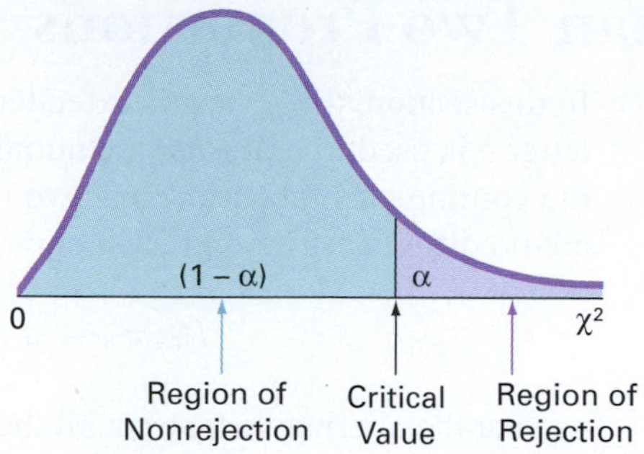

To illustrate the χ^2 test for equality of proportions when there are more than two groups, return to the Using Statistics scenario on page 467 concerning T.C. Resort Properties. Once again, you define the business objective as improving the quality of service, but this time, three hotels located on a different island are to be surveyed. Data are collected from customer satisfaction surveys at these three hotels. You organize the responses into the contingency table shown in Table 12.6.

TABLE 12.6
2 × 3 Contingency Table for Guest Satisfaction Survey

	HOTEL			
CHOOSE HOTEL AGAIN?	**Golden Palm**	**Palm Royale**	**Palm Princess**	**Total**
Yes	128	199	186	513
No	88	33	66	187
Total	216	232	252	700

Because the null hypothesis states that there are no differences among the three hotels in the proportion of guests who would likely return again, you use Equation (12.3) to calculate an estimate of π, the population proportion of guests who would likely return again:

$$\bar{p} = \frac{X_1 + X_2 + \cdots + X_c}{n_1 + n_2 + \cdots + n_c} = \frac{X}{n}$$

$$= \frac{(128 + 199 + 186)}{(216 + 232 + 252)} = \frac{513}{700}$$

$$= 0.733$$

The estimated overall proportion of guests who would *not* be likely to return again is the complement, $(1 - \bar{p})$, or 0.267. Multiplying these two proportions by the sample size for each hotel yields the expected number of guests who would and would not likely return.

EXAMPLE 12.2

Computing the Expected Frequencies

Compute the expected frequencies for each of the six cells in Table 12.6.

SOLUTION

Yes—Golden Palm: $\bar{p} = 0.733$ and $n_1 = 216$, so $f_e = 158.30$
Yes—Palm Royale: $\bar{p} = 0.733$ and $n_2 = 232$, so $f_e = 170.02$
Yes—Palm Princess: $\bar{p} = 0.733$ and $n_3 = 252$, so $f_e = 184.68$
No—Golden Palm: $1 - \bar{p} = 0.267$ and $n_1 = 216$, so $f_e = 57.70$
No—Palm Royale: $1 - \bar{p} = 0.267$ and $n_2 = 232$, so $f_e = 61.98$
No—Palm Princess: $1 - \bar{p} = 0.267$ and $n_3 = 252$, so $f_e = 67.32$

Table 12.7 presents these expected frequencies.

TABLE 12.7

Contingency Table of Expected Frequencies from a Guest Satisfaction Survey of Three Hotels

	HOTEL			
CHOOSE HOTEL AGAIN?	Golden Palm	Palm Royale	Palm Princess	Total
Yes	158.30	170.02	184.68	513
No	57.70	61.98	67.32	187
Total	216.00	232.00	252.00	700

To test the null hypothesis that the proportions are equal:

$$H_0: \pi_1 = \pi_2 = \pi_3$$

against the alternative that not all three proportions are equal:

$$H_1: \text{Not all } \pi_j \text{ are equal (where } j = 1, 2, 3)$$

you use the observed frequencies from Table 12.6 and the expected frequencies from Table 12.7 to compute the χ^2_{STAT} test statistic [given by Equation (12.1) on page 469]. Table 12.8 presents the calculations.

TABLE 12.8

Computing the χ^2_{STAT} Test Statistic for the Guest Satisfaction Survey of Three Hotels

f_o	f_e	$(f_o - f_e)$	$(f_o - f_e)^2$	$(f_o - f_e)^2/f_e$
128	158.30	−30.30	918.09	5.80
199	170.02	28.98	839.84	4.94
186	184.68	1.32	1.74	0.01
88	57.70	30.30	918.09	15.91
33	61.98	−28.98	839.84	13.55
66	67.32	−1.32	1.74	0.02
				40.23

You use Table E.4 to find the critical value of the χ^2 test statistic. In the guest satisfaction survey, because there are three hotels, there are $(2 - 1)(3 - 1) = 2$ degrees of freedom. Using $\alpha = 0.05$, the χ^2 critical value with 2 degrees of freedom is 5.991 (see Figure 12.5). Because the computed χ^2_{STAT} test statistic is 40.23, which is greater than this critical value, you reject the null hypothesis.

FIGURE 12.5

Regions of rejection and nonrejection when testing for differences in three proportions at the 0.05 level of significance, with 2 degrees of freedom

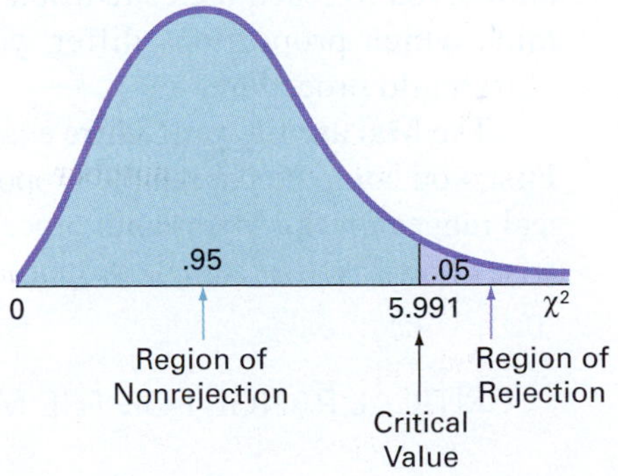

Figure 12.6 shows the results for this problem. The results also report the p-value. Because the p-value is (approximately) 0.0000, less than $\alpha = 0.05$, you reject the null hypothesis. Further, this p-value indicates that there is virtually no chance that there will be differences this large or larger among the three sample proportions, if the population proportions for the three hotels are equal. Thus, there is sufficient evidence to conclude that the hotel properties are different with respect to the proportion of guests who are likely to return.

FIGURE 12.6

Excel and Minitab chi-square test results for the Table 12.6 guest satisfaction data

	A	B	C	D	E	F	G	H	I
1	**Chi-Square Test**								
2									
3		**Observed Frequencies**							
4		Hotel					Calculations		
5	Choose Again?	Golden Palm	Palm Royale	Palm Princess	Total		fo - fe		
6	Yes	128	199	186	513		-30.2971	28.9771	1.3200
7	No	88	33	66	187		30.2971	-28.9771	-1.3200
8	Total	216	232	252	700				
9									
10		Expected Frequencies							
11		Hotel							
12	Choose Again?	Golden Palm	Palm Royale	Palm Princess	Total		(fo - fe)^2/fe		
13	Yes	158.2971	170.0229	184.68	513		5.7987	4.9386	0.0094
14	No	57.7029	61.9771	67.32	187		15.9077	13.5481	0.0259
15	Total	216	232	252	700				
16									
17	**Data**								
18	Level of Significance	0.05							
19	Number of Rows	2							
20	Number of Columns	3							
21	Degrees of Freedom	2	=(B19 - 1) * (B20 - 1)						
22									
23	**Results**								
24	Critical Value	5.9915	=CHIINV(B18, B21)						
25	Chi-Square Test Statistic	40.2284	=SUM(G13:I14)						
26	*p*-Value	0.0000	=CHIDIST(B25, B21)						
27	Reject the null hypothesis		=IF(B26 < B18, "Reject the null hypothesis", "Do not reject the null hypothesis")						
28									
29	***Expected frequency assumption***								
30	***is met.***		=IF(OR(B13 < 1, C13 < 1, D13 < 1, B14 < 1, C14 < 1, D14 < 1), " is violated.", " is met.")						

Chi-Square Test: Golden Palm, Palm Royale, Palm Princess

```
Expected counts are printed below observed counts
Chi-Square contributions are printed below expected counts

        Golden     Palm      Palm
          Palm   Royale   Princess   Total
    1      128      199        186     513
        158.30   170.02     184.68
         5.799    4.939      0.009

    2       88       33         66     187
         57.70    61.98      67.32
        15.908   13.548      0.026

Total      216      232        252     700

Chi-Sq = 40.228, DF = 2, P-Value = 0.000
```

For the χ^2 test to give accurate results when dealing with $2 \times c$ contingency tables, all expected frequencies must be large. The definition of "large" has led to research among statisticians. Some statisticians (see reference 5) have found that the test gives accurate results as long as all expected frequencies are at least 0.5. Other statisticians, more conservative in their approach, believe that no more than 20% of the cells should contain expected frequencies less than 5, and no cells should have expected frequencies less than 1 (see reference 3). As a reasonable compromise between these points of view, to assure the validity of the test, you should make sure that each expected frequency is at least 1. To do this, you may need to collapse two or more low-expected-frequency categories into one category in the contingency table before performing the test. If combining categories is undesirable, you can use one of the available alternative procedures (see references 1, 2, and 7).

The Marascuilo Procedure

Rejecting the null hypothesis in a χ^2 test of equality of proportions in a $2 \times c$ table only allows you to reach the conclusion that not all c population proportions are equal. To determine which proportions differ, you use a multiple comparisons procedure such as the Marascuilo procedure.

The **Marascuilo procedure** enables you to make comparisons between all pairs of groups. First, you compute the sample proportions. Then, you use Equation (12.4) to compute the critical ranges for the Marascuilo procedure. You compute a different critical range for each pairwise comparison of sample proportions.

CRITICAL RANGE FOR THE MARASCUILO PROCEDURE

$$\text{Critical range} = \sqrt{\chi^2_\alpha}\sqrt{\frac{p_j(1 - p_j)}{n_j} + \frac{p_{j'}(1 - p_{j'})}{n_{j'}}} \quad \textbf{(12.4)}$$

Then, you compare each of the $c(c - 1)/2$ pairs of sample proportions against its corresponding critical range. You declare a specific pair significantly different if the absolute difference in the sample proportions, $|p_j - p_{j'}|$, is greater than its critical range.

To apply the Marascuilo procedure, return to the guest satisfaction survey. Using the χ^2 test, you concluded that there was evidence of a significant difference among the population proportions. From Table 12.6 on page 476, the three sample proportions are

$$p_1 = \frac{X_1}{n_1} = \frac{128}{216} = 0.5926$$

$$p_2 = \frac{X_2}{n_2} = \frac{199}{232} = 0.8578$$

$$p_3 = \frac{X_3}{n_3} = \frac{186}{252} = 0.7381$$

Next, you compute the absolute differences in sample proportions and their corresponding critical ranges. Because there are three hotels, there are $(3)(3 - 1)/2 = 3$ pairwise comparisons. Using Table E.4 and an overall level of significance of 0.05, the upper-tail critical value for a chi-square distribution having $(c - 1) = 2$ degrees of freedom is 5.991. Thus,

$$\sqrt{\chi^2_\alpha} = \sqrt{5.991} = 2.4477$$

Absolute Difference in Proportions	**Critical Range**
$\lvert p_j - p_{j'} \rvert$	$2.4477\sqrt{\frac{p_j(1 - p_j)}{n_j} + \frac{p_{j'}(1 - p_{j'})}{n_{j'}}}$
$\lvert p_1 - p_2 \rvert = \lvert 0.5926 - 0.8578 \rvert = 0.2652$	$2.4477\sqrt{\frac{(0.5926)(0.4074)}{216} + \frac{(0.8578)(0.1422)}{232}} = 0.0992$
$\lvert p_1 - p_3 \rvert = \lvert 0.5926 - 0.7381 \rvert = 0.1455$	$2.4477\sqrt{\frac{(0.5926)(0.4074)}{216} + \frac{(0.7381)(0.2619)}{252}} = 0.1063$
$\lvert p_2 - p_3 \rvert = \lvert 0.8578 - 0.7381 \rvert = 0.1197$	$2.4477\sqrt{\frac{(0.8578)(0.1422)}{232} + \frac{(0.7381)(0.2619)}{252}} = 0.0880$

Figure 12.7 shows the Excel results for this example.

FIGURE 12.7

Excel Marascuilo procedure results worksheet for the guest satisfaction survey

Minitab does not contain a command to perform the Marascuilo procedure.

	A	B	C	D
1	Marascuilo Procedure for Guest Satisfaction Analysis			
2				
3	Level of Significance	0.05	=ChiSquare2x3!B18	
4	Square Root of Critical Value	2.4477	=SQRT(ChiSquare2x3!B24)	
5				
6	Group Sample Proportions			
7	1: Golden Palm	0.5926	=ChiSquare2x3!B6/ChiSquare2x3!B8	
8	2: Palm Royale	0.8578	=ChiSquare2x3!C6/ChiSquare2x3!C8	
9	3: Palm Princess	0.7381	=ChiSquare2x3!D6/ChiSquare2x3!D8	
10				
11	MARASCUILO TABLE			
12	Proportions	Absolute Differences	Critical Range	
13	| Group 1 - Group 2 |	0.2652	0.0992	Significant
14	| Group 1 - Group 3 |	0.1455	0.1063	Significant
15				
16	| Group 2 - Group 3 |	0.1197	0.0880	Significant

As the final step, you compare the absolute differences to the critical ranges. If the absolute difference is greater than its critical range, the proportions are significantly different. At the 0.05 level of significance, you can conclude that guest satisfaction is higher at the Palm Royale ($p_2 = 0.858$) than at either the Golden Palm ($p_1 = 0.593$) or the Palm Princess ($p_3 = 0.738$) and that guest satisfaction is also higher at the Palm Princess than at the Golden Palm. These results clearly suggest that you should investigate possible reasons for these differences. In particular, you should try to determine why satisfaction is significantly lower at the Golden Palm than at the other two hotels.

Online Topic: The Analysis of Proportions (ANOP)

The ANOP procedure provides a confidence interval approach that allows you to determine which, if any, of the *c* groups has a proportion significantly different from the overall mean of all the group proportions combined. To study this topic, read the **ANOP** online topic file that is available on this book's companion website. (See Appendix C to learn how to access the online topic files.)

Problems for Section 12.2

LEARNING THE BASICS

12.11 Consider a contingency table with two rows and five columns.

a. How many degrees of freedom are there in the contingency table?
b. Determine the critical value for $\alpha = 0.05$.
c. Determine the critical value for $\alpha = 0.01$.

12.12 Use the following contingency table:

	A	B	C	Total
1	10	30	50	90
2	40	45	50	135
Total	50	75	100	225

a. Compute the expected frequencies for each cell.
b. Compute χ^2_{STAT}. Is it significant at $\alpha = 0.05$?

12.13 Use the following contingency table:

	A	B	C	Total
1	20	30	25	75
2	30	20	25	75
Total	50	50	50	150

a. Compute the expected frequencies for each cell.
b. Compute χ^2_{STAT}. Is it significant at $\alpha = 0.05$?
c. If appropriate, use the Marascuilo procedure and $\alpha = 0.05$ to determine which groups are different.

APPLYING THE CONCEPTS

12.14 How do Americans feel about online ads tailored to their individual interests? A survey of 1,000 adult Internet users found that 55% of the 18 to 24 year olds, 59% of 25 to 34 year olds, 66% of 35 to 49 year olds, 77% of 50 to 64 year olds, and 82% of 65 to 89 year olds opposed such ads. (Data extracted from S. Clifford, "Tracked for Ads? Many Americans Say No Thanks," *The New York Times*, September 30, 2009, p. B3.) Suppose that the survey was based on 200 respondents in each of five age groups: 18 to 24, 25 to 34, 35 to 49, 50 to 64, and 65 to 89.

a. At the 0.05 level of significance, is there evidence of a difference among the age groups in the opposition to ads on web pages tailored to their interests?
b. Determine the *p*-value in (a) and interpret its meaning.
c. If appropriate, use the Marascuilo procedure and $\alpha = 0.05$ to determine which age groups are different.

12.15 How do Americans feel about online discounts tailored to their individual interests? A survey of 1,000 adult Internet users found that 37% of the 18 to 24 year olds, 44% of 25 to 34 year olds, 50% of 35 to 49 year olds, 58% of 50 to 64 year olds, and 70% of 65 to 89 year olds opposed such discounts. (Data extracted from S. Clifford, "Tracked for Ads? Many Americans Say No Thanks," *The New York Times*, September 30, 2009, p. B3.) Suppose that the survey was based on 200 respondents in each of five age groups: 18 to 24, 25 to 34, 35 to 49, 50 to 64, and 65 to 89.

a. At the 0.05 level of significance, is there evidence of a difference among the age groups in the opposition to discounts on web pages tailored to their interests?
b. Compute the *p*-value and interpret its meaning.
c. If appropriate, use the Marascuilo procedure and $\alpha = 0.05$ to determine which age groups are different.

SELF Test **12.16** More shoppers do the majority of their grocery shopping on Saturday than any other day of the week. However, is there a difference in the various age groups in the proportion of people who do the majority of their grocery shopping on Saturday? A study showed the results for the different age groups. (Data extracted from "Major Shopping by Day," *Progressive Grocer Annual*

Report, April 30, 2002.) The data were reported as percentages, and no sample sizes were given:

	AGE		
MAJOR SHOPPING DAY	**Under 35**	**35–54**	**Over 54**
Saturday	24%	28%	12%
A day other than Saturday	76%	72%	88%

Assume that 200 shoppers for each age group were surveyed.

a. Is there evidence of a significant difference among the age groups with respect to major grocery shopping day? (Use $\alpha = 0.05$.)

b. Determine the p-value in (a) and interpret its meaning.

c. If appropriate, use the Marascuilo procedure and $\alpha = 0.05$ to determine which age groups are different.

d. Discuss the managerial implications of (a) and (c). How can grocery stores use this information to improve marketing and sales? Be specific.

12.17 Repeat (a) and (b) of Problem 12.16, assuming that only 50 shoppers for each age group were surveyed. Discuss the implications of sample size on the χ^2 test for differences among more than two populations.

12.18 Is there a generation gap in music? A study reported that 45% of 16 to 29 year olds, 42% of 30 to 49 year olds, and 33% of 50 to 64 year olds often listened to rock music. (Data extracted from A. Tugend, "Bridging the Workplace Generation Gap: It Starts with a Text," *The New York Times*, November 7, 2009, p. B5.) Suppose that the study was based on a sample of 200 respondents in each group.

a. Is there evidence of a significant difference among the age groups with respect to the proportion who often listened to rock music? (Use $\alpha = 0.05$.)

b. Determine the p-value in (a) and interpret its meaning.

c. If appropriate, use the Marascuilo procedure and $\alpha = 0.05$. to determine which age groups are different.

12.19 Is there a generation gap in music? A study reported that 25% of 16 to 29 year olds, 21% of 30 to 49 year olds, and 31% of 50 to 64 year olds often listened to country music. (Data extracted from A. Tugend, "Bridging the Workplace Generation Gap: It Starts with a Text," *The New York Times*, November 7, 2009, p. B5.) Suppose that the study was based on a sample of 200 respondents in each group.

a. Is there evidence of a significant difference among the age groups with respect to the proportion who often listened to country music? (Use $\alpha = 0.05$.)

b. Determine the p-value in (a) and interpret its meaning.

c. If appropriate, use the Marascuilo procedure and $\alpha = 0.05$. to determine which age groups are different.

12.3 Chi-Square Test of Independence

In Sections 12.1 and 12.2, you used the χ^2 test to evaluate potential differences among population proportions. For a contingency table that has r rows and c columns, you can generalize the χ^2 test as a *test of independence* for two categorical variables.

For a test of independence, the null and alternative hypotheses follow:

H_0: The two categorical variables are independent (i.e., there is no relationship between them).

H_1: The two categorical variables are dependent (i.e., there is a relationship between them).

Once again, you use Equation (12.1) on page 469 to compute the test statistic:

$$\chi^2_{STAT} = \sum_{\text{all cells}} \frac{(f_o - f_e)^2}{f_e}$$

You reject the null hypothesis at the α level of significance if the computed value of the χ^2_{STAT} test statistic is greater than χ^2_α, the upper-tail critical value from a chi-square distribution with $(r - 1)(c - 1)$ degrees of freedom (see Figure 12.8 on page 482). Thus, the decision rule is

$$\text{Reject } H_0 \text{ if } \chi^2_{STAT} > \chi^2_\alpha;$$

otherwise, do not reject H_0.

The χ^2 **test of independence** is similar to the χ^2 test for equality of proportions. The test statistics and the decision rules are the same, but the null and alternative hypotheses and conclusions are different. For example, in the guest satisfaction survey of Sections 12.1 and 12.2, there is evidence of a significant difference between the hotels with respect to the proportion

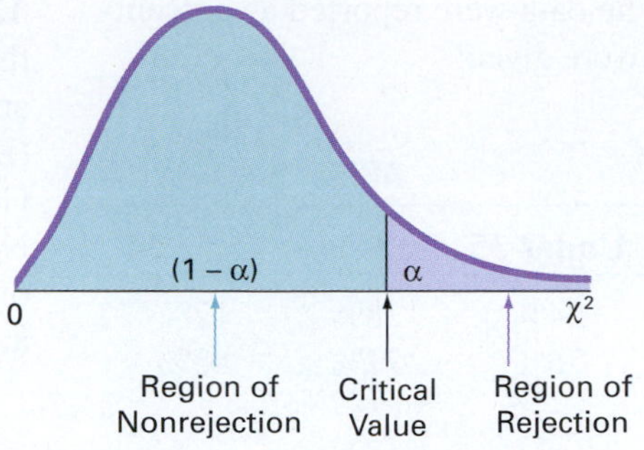

FIGURE 12.8
Regions of rejection and nonrejection when testing for independence in an $r \times c$ contingency table, using the χ^2 test

of guests who would return. From a different viewpoint, you could conclude that there is a significant relationship between the hotels and the likelihood that a guest would return. However, the two types of tests differ in how the samples are selected.

In a test for equality of proportions, there is one factor of interest, with two or more levels. These levels represent samples drawn from independent populations. The categorical responses in each group or level are classified into two categories, such as *item of interest* and *not an item of interest*. The objective is to make comparisons and evaluate differences between the proportions of the *items of interest* among the various levels. However, in a test for independence, there are two factors of interest, each of which has two or more levels. You select one sample and tally the joint responses to the two categorical variables into the cells of a contingency table.

To illustrate the χ^2 test for independence, suppose that, in the survey on hotel guest satisfaction, respondents who stated that they were not likely to return were asked what was the primary reason for their unwillingness to return to the hotel. Table 12.9 presents the resulting 4×3 contingency table.

In Table 12.9, observe that of the primary reasons for not planning to return to the hotel, 67 were due to price, 60 were due to location, 31 were due to room accommodation, and 29 were due to other reasons. As in Table 12.6 on page 476, there were 88 guests at the Golden Palm, 33 guests at the Palm Royale, and 66 guests at the Palm Princess who were not planning

TABLE 12.9
Contingency Table of Primary Reason for Not Returning and Hotel

PRIMARY REASON FOR NOT RETURNING	HOTEL			
	Golden Palm	Palm Royale	Palm Princess	Total
Price	23	7	37	67
Location	39	13	8	60
Room accommodation	13	5	13	31
Other	13	8	8	29
Total	88	33	66	187

to return. The observed frequencies in the cells of the 4×3 contingency table represent the joint tallies of the sampled guests with respect to primary reason for not returning and the hotel where they stayed. The null and alternative hypotheses are

H_0: There is no relationship between the primary reason for not returning and the hotel.

H_1: There is a relationship between the primary reason for not returning and the hotel.

To test this null hypothesis of independence against the alternative that there is a relationship between the two categorical variables, you use Equation (12.1) on page 469 to compute the test statistic:

$$\chi^2_{STAT} = \sum_{all\ cells} \frac{(f_o - f_e)^2}{f_e}$$

where

f_o = observed frequency in a particular cell of the $r \times c$ contingency table

f_e = expected frequency in a particular cell if the null hypothesis of independence is true

To compute the expected frequency, f_e, in any cell, you use the multiplication rule for independent events discussed on page 160 [see Equation (4.7)]. For example, under the null hypothesis of independence, the probability of responses expected in the upper-left-corner cell representing primary reason of price for the Golden Palm is the product of the two separate probabilities $P(\text{Price})$ and $P(\text{Golden Palm})$. Here, the proportion of reasons that are due to price, $P(\text{Price})$, is $67/187 = 0.3583$, and the proportion of all responses from the Golden Palm, $P(\text{Golden Palm})$, is $88/187 = 0.4706$. If the null hypothesis is true, then the primary reason for not returning and the hotel are independent:

$$\begin{aligned} P(\text{Price } \textit{and} \text{ Golden Palm}) &= P(\text{Price}) \times P(\text{Golden Palm}) \\ &= (0.3583) \times (0.4706) \\ &= 0.1686 \end{aligned}$$

The expected frequency is the product of the overall sample size, n, and this probability, $187 \times 0.1686 = 31.53$. The f_e values for the remaining cells are calculated in a similar manner (see Table 12.10).

Equation (12.5) presents a simpler way to compute the expected frequency.

COMPUTING THE EXPECTED FREQUENCY

The expected frequency in a cell is the product of its row total and column total, divided by the overall sample size.

$$f_e = \frac{\text{Row total} \times \text{Column total}}{n} \quad \textbf{(12.5)}$$

where

Row total = sum of the frequencies in the row

Column total = sum of the frequencies in the column

n = overall sample size

For example, using Equation (12.5) for the upper-left-corner cell (price for the Golden Palm),

$$f_e = \frac{\text{Row total} \times \text{Column total}}{n} = \frac{(67)(88)}{187} = 31.53$$

and for the lower-right-corner cell (other reason for the Palm Princess),

$$f_e = \frac{\text{Row total} \times \text{Column total}}{n} = \frac{(29)(66)}{187} = 10.24$$

Table 12.10 lists the entire set of f_e values.

TABLE 12.10

Contingency Table of Expected Frequencies of Primary Reason for Not Returning with Hotel

PRIMARY REASON FOR NOT RETURNING	HOTEL			
	Golden Palm	Palm Royale	Palm Princess	Total
Price	31.53	11.82	23.65	67
Location	28.24	10.59	21.18	60
Room accommodation	14.59	5.47	10.94	31
Other	13.65	5.12	10.24	29
Total	88.00	33.00	66.00	187

To perform the test of independence, you use the χ^2_{STAT} test statistic shown in Equation (12.1) on page 469. The χ^2_{STAT} test statistic approximately follows a chi-square distribution, with degrees of freedom equal to the number of rows in the contingency table minus 1, multiplied by the number of columns in the table minus 1:

$$\text{Degrees of freedom} = (r - 1)(c - 1)$$
$$= (4 - 1)(3 - 1) = 6$$

Table 12.11 illustrates the computations for the χ^2_{STAT} test statistic.

TABLE 12.11

Computing the χ^2_{STAT} Test Statistic for the Test of Independence

Cell	f_o	f_e	$(f_o - f_e)$	$(f_o - f_e)^2$	$(f_o - f_e)^2/f_e$
Price/Golden Palm	23	31.53	−8.53	72.76	2.31
Price/Palm Royale	7	11.82	−4.82	23.23	1.97
Price/Palm Princess	37	23.65	13.35	178.22	7.54
Location/Golden Palm	39	28.24	10.76	115.78	4.10
Location/Palm Royale	13	10.59	2.41	5.81	0.55
Location/Palm Princess	8	21.18	−13.18	173.71	8.20
Room/Golden Palm	13	14.59	−1.59	2.53	0.17
Room/Palm Royale	5	5.47	−0.47	0.22	0.04
Room/Palm Princess	13	10.94	2.06	4.24	0.39
Other/Golden Palm	13	13.65	−0.65	0.42	0.03
Other/Palm Royale	8	5.12	2.88	8.29	1.62
Other/Palm Princess	8	10.24	−2.24	5.02	0.49
					27.41

Using the $\alpha = 0.05$ level of significance, the upper-tail critical value from the chi-square distribution with 6 degrees of freedom is 12.592 (see Table E.4). Because $\chi^2_{STAT} = 27.41 > 12.592$, you reject the null hypothesis of independence (see Figure 12.9).

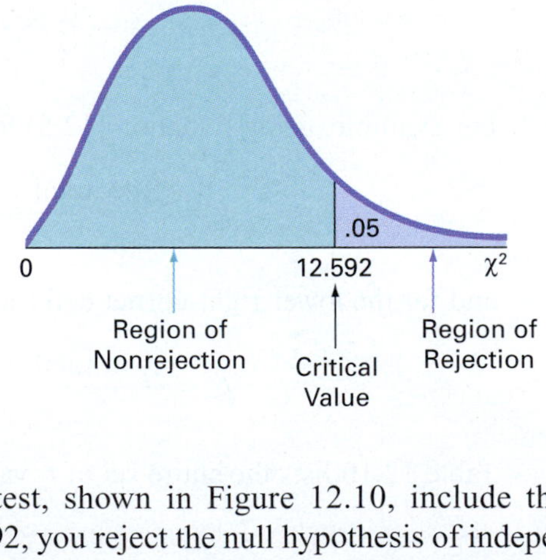

FIGURE 12.9

Regions of rejection and nonrejection when testing for independence in the hotel guest satisfaction survey example at the 0.05 level of significance, with 6 degrees of freedom

The results for this test, shown in Figure 12.10, include the p-value, 0.0001. Since $\chi^2_{STAT} = 27.4104 > 12.592$, you reject the null hypothesis of independence. Using the p-value approach, you reject the null hypothesis of independence because the p-value $= 0.0001 < 0.05$. The p-value indicates that there is virtually no chance of having a relationship this strong or stronger between the hotel and the primary reasons for not returning in a sample, if the primary reasons for not returning are independent of the specific hotels in the entire population. Thus, there is strong evidence of a relationship between primary reason for not returning and the hotel.

Examination of the observed and expected frequencies (see Table 12.11 above) reveals that price is underrepresented as a reason for not returning to the Golden Palm (i.e., $f_o = 23$ and $f_e = 31.53$) but is overrepresented at the Palm Princess. Guests are more satisfied with the

FIGURE 12.10

Excel and Minitab chi-square test results for the Table 12.9 primary reason for not returning and hotel data

	A	B	C	D	E
1	Chi-Square Test of Independence				
2					
3		Observed Frequencies			
4			Hotel		
5	Reason for Not Returning	Golden Palm	Palm Royale	Palm Princess	Total
6	Price	23	7	37	67
7	Location	39	13	8	60
8	Room accommodation	13	5	13	31
9	Other	13	8	8	29
10	Total	88	33	66	187
11					
12		Expected Frequencies			
13			Hotel		
14	Reason for Not Returning	Golden Palm	Palm Royale	Palm Princess	Total
15	Price	31.5294	11.8235	23.6471	67
16	Location	28.2353	10.5882	21.1765	60
17	Room accommodation	14.5882	5.4706	10.9412	31
18	Other	13.6471	5.1176	10.2353	29
19	Total	88	33	66	187
20					
21	Data				
22	Level of Significance	0.05			
23	Number of Rows	4			
24	Number of Columns	3			
25	Degrees of Freedom	6	=(B23 - 1) * (B24 - 1)		
26					
27	Results				
28	Critical Value	12.5916	=CHIINV(B22, B25)		
29	Chi-Square Test Statistic	27.4104	=SUM(G15:I18)		
30	*p*-Value	0.0001	=CHIDIST(B29, B25)		
31	Reject the null hypothesis		=IF(B30 < B22, "Reject the null hypothesis", "Do not reject the null hypothesis")		
32					
33	*Expected frequency assumption*				
34	*is met.*		=IF(OR(B15 < 1, C15 < 1, D15 < 1, B16 < 1, C16 < 1 ,D16 < 1, B17 < 1, C17 < 1, D17 < 1, B18 < 1, C18 < 1, D18 < 1), " is violated."," is met.")		

Chi-Square Test: Golden Palm, Palm Royale, Palm Princess

```
Expected counts are printed below observed counts
Chi-Square contributions are printed below expected counts

     Golden     Palm      Palm
       Palm   Royale  Princess  Total
 1       23        7        37     67
      31.53    11.82     23.65
      2.307    1.968     7.540

 2       39       13         8     60
      28.24    10.59     21.18
      4.104    0.549     8.199

 3       13        5        13     31
      14.59     5.47     10.94
      0.173    0.040     0.387

 4       13        8         8     29
      13.65     5.12     10.24
      0.031    1.623     0.488

Total    88       33        66    187

Chi-Sq = 27.410, DF = 6, P-Value = 0.000
```

price at the Golden Palm than at the Palm Princess. Location is overrepresented as a reason for not returning to the Golden Palm but greatly underrepresented at the Palm Princess. Thus, guests are much more satisfied with the location of the Palm Princess than with that of the Golden Palm.

To ensure accurate results, all expected frequencies need to be large in order to use the χ^2 test when dealing with $r \times c$ contingency tables. As in the case of $2 \times c$ contingency tables in Section 12.2, all expected frequencies should be at least 1. For contingency tables in which one or more expected frequencies are less than 1, you can use the chi-square test after collapsing two or more low-frequency rows into one row (or collapsing two or more low-frequency columns into one column). Merging rows or columns usually results in expected frequencies sufficiently large to assure the accuracy of the χ^2 test.

Problems for Section 12.3

LEARNING THE BASICS

12.20 If a contingency table has three rows and four columns, how many degrees of freedom are there for the χ^2 test of independence?

12.21 When performing a χ^2 test of independence in a contingency table with r rows and c columns, determine the upper-tail critical value of the test statistic in each of the following circumstances:

a. $\alpha = 0.05, r = 4$ rows, $c = 5$ columns
b. $\alpha = 0.01, r = 4$ rows, $c = 5$ columns
c. $\alpha = 0.01, r = 4$ rows, $c = 6$ columns
d. $\alpha = 0.01, r = 3$ rows, $c = 6$ columns
e. $\alpha = 0.01, r = 6$ rows, $c = 3$ columns

APPLYING THE CONCEPTS

12.22 The owner of a restaurant serving Continental-style entrées has the business objective of learning more about the patterns of patron demand during the Friday-to-Sunday weekend time period. Data were collected from 630 customers on the type of entrée ordered and the type of dessert ordered and organized into the following table:

TYPE OF DESSERT	TYPE OF ENTRÉE: Beef	Poultry	Fish	Pasta	Total
Ice cream	13	8	12	14	47
Cake	98	12	29	6	145
Fruit	8	10	6	2	26
None	124	98	149	41	412
Total	243	128	196	63	630

At the 0.05 level of significance, is there evidence of a relationship between type of dessert and type of entrée?

12.23 Is there a generation gap in the type of music that people listen to? The following table represents the type of favorite music for a sample of 1,000 respondents classified according to their age group:

FAVORITE TYPE	AGE: 16–29	30–49	50–64	65 and over	Total
Rock	71	62	51	27	211
Rap or hip-hop	40	21	7	3	71
Rhythm and blues	48	46	46	40	180
Country	43	53	59	79	234
Classical	22	28	33	46	129
Jazz	18	26	36	43	123
Salsa	8	14	18	12	52
Total	250	250	250	250	1000

At the 0.05 level of significance, is there evidence of a relationship between favorite type of music and age group?

SELF Test **12.24** A large corporation is interested in determining whether a relationship exists between the commuting time of its employees and the level of stress-related problems observed on the job. A study of 116 workers reveals the following:

COMMUTING TIME	STRESS LEVEL: High	Moderate	Low	Total
Under 15 min.	9	5	18	32
15–45 min.	17	8	28	53
Over 45 min.	18	6	7	31
Total	44	19	53	116

a. At the 0.01 level of significance, is there evidence of a significant relationship between commuting time and stress level?

b. What is your answer to (a) if you use the 0.05 level of significance?

12.25 Where people turn for news is different for various age groups. A study indicated where different age groups primarily get their news:

MEDIA	AGE GROUP: Under 36	36–50	50 +
Local TV	107	119	133
National TV	73	102	127
Radio	75	97	109
Local newspaper	52	79	107
Internet	95	83	76

At the 0.05 level of significance, is there evidence of a significant relationship between the age group and where people primarily get their news? If so, explain the relationship.

12.26 *USA Today* reported on when the decision of what to have for dinner is made. Suppose the results were based on a survey of 1,000 respondents and considered whether the household included any children under 18 years old. The results are cross-classified in the following table:

WHEN DECISION MADE	TYPE OF HOUSEHOLD: One Adult/No Children	Two or More Adults/ Children	Two or More Adults/No Children
Just before eating	162	54	154
In the afternoon	73	38	69
In the morning	59	58	53
A few days before	21	64	45
The night before	15	50	45
Always eat the same thing on this night	2	16	2
Not sure	7	6	7

Source: Data extracted from "What's for Dinner," **www.usatoday.com**, January 10, 2000.

At the 0.05 level of significance, is there evidence of a significant relationship between when the decision is made of what to have for dinner and the type of household?

12.4 McNemar Test for the Difference Between Two Proportions (Related Samples)

In Section 10.3, you used the Z test, and in Section 12.1, you used the chi-square test to examine whether there was a difference in the proportion of items of interest between two populations. These tests require independent samples from each population. However, sometimes when you are testing differences between the proportion of items of interest, the data are collected from repeated measurements or matched samples. For example, in marketing, these situations can occur when you want to determine whether there has been a change in attitude, perception, or behavior from one time period to another. To test whether there is evidence of a difference between the proportions when the data have been collected from two related samples, you can use the **McNemar test**.

Table 12.12 presents the 2 × 2 table needed for the McNemar test.

TABLE 12.12
2 × 2 Contingency Table for the McNemar Test

	CONDITION (GROUP) 2		
CONDITION (GROUP) 1	**Yes**	**No**	**Totals**
Yes	A	B	$A + B$
No	C	D	$C + D$
Totals	$A + C$	$B + D$	n

where

A = number of respondents who answer yes to condition 1 and yes to condition 2
B = number of respondents who answer yes to condition 1 and no to condition 2
C = number of respondents who answer no to condition 1 and yes to condition 2
D = number of respondents who answer no to condition 1 and no to condition 2
n = number of respondents in the sample

The sample proportions are

$$p_1 = \frac{A + B}{n} = \text{proportion of respondents in the sample who answer yes to condition 1}$$

$$p_2 = \frac{A + C}{n} = \text{proportion of respondents in the sample who answer yes to condition 2}$$

The population proportions are

π_1 = proportion in the population who would answer yes to condition 1

π_2 = proportion in the population who would answer yes to condition 2

When testing differences between the proportions, you can use a two-tail test or a one-tail test. In both cases, you use a test statistic that approximately follows the normal distribution. Equation (12.6) presents the McNemar test statistic used to test $H_0: \pi_1 = \pi_2$.

MCNEMAR TEST STATISTIC

$$Z_{STAT} = \frac{B - C}{\sqrt{B + C}} \quad \textbf{(12.6)}$$

where the Z_{STAT} test statistic is approximately normally distributed.

To illustrate the McNemar test, suppose that the business problem facing a cell phone provider was to determine the effect of a marketing campaign on the brand loyalty of cell phone customers.

Data were collected from $n = 600$ participants. In the study, the participants were initially asked to state their preferences for two competing cell phone providers, Sprint and Verizon. Initially, 282 panelists said they preferred Sprint and 318 said they preferred Verizon. After exposing the set of participants to an intensive marketing campaign strategy for Verizon, the same 600 participants are again asked to state their preferences. Of the 282 panelists who previously preferred Sprint, 246 maintained their brand loyalty, but 36 switched their preference to Verizon. Of the 318 participants who initially preferred Verizon, 306 remained brand loyal, but 12 switched their preference to Sprint. These results are organized into the contingency table presented in Table 12.13.

You use the McNemar test for these data because you have repeated measurements from the same set of panelists. Each participant gave a response about whether he or she preferred Sprint or Verizon before exposure to the intensive marketing campaign and then again after exposure to the campaign.

TABLE 12.13

Brand Loyalty of Cell Phone Providers

	AFTER MARKETING CAMPAIGN		
BEFORE MARKETING CAMPAIGN	**Sprint**	**Verizon**	**Total**
Sprint	246	36	282
Verizon	12	306	318
Total	258	342	600

To determine whether the intensive marketing campaign was effective, you want to investigate whether there is a difference between the population proportion who favor Sprint before the campaign, π_1, versus the proportion who favor Sprint after the campaign, π_2. The null and alternative hypotheses are

$$H_0: \pi_1 = \pi_2$$

$$H_1: \pi_1 \neq \pi_2$$

Using a 0.05 level of significance, the critical values are -1.96 and $+1.96$ (see Figure 12.11), and the decision rule is

$$\text{Reject } H_0 \text{ if } Z_{STAT} < -1.96 \text{ or if } Z_{STAT} > +1.96;$$
$$\text{otherwise, do not reject } H_0.$$

FIGURE 12.11

Two-tail McNemar test at the 0.05 level of significance

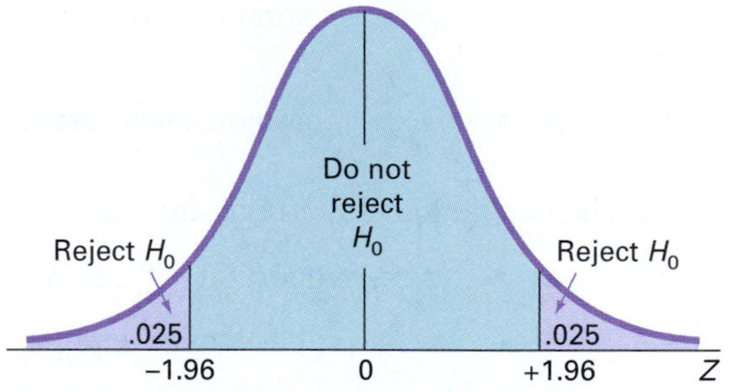

For the data in Table 12.13,

$$A = 246 \quad B = 36 \quad C = 12 \quad D = 306$$

so that

$$p_1 = \frac{A + B}{n} = \frac{246 + 36}{600} = \frac{282}{600} = 0.47 \text{ and } p_2 = \frac{A + C}{n} = \frac{246 + 12}{600} = \frac{258}{600} = 0.43$$

Using Equation (12.6),

$$Z = \frac{B - C}{\sqrt{B + C}} = \frac{36 - 12}{\sqrt{36 + 12}} = \frac{24}{\sqrt{48}} = 3.4641$$

Because $Z_{STAT} = 3.4641 > 1.96$, you reject H_0. Using the p-value approach (see Figure 12.12), the p-value is 0.0005. Because $0.0005 < 0.05$, you reject H_0. You can conclude that the population proportion who prefer Sprint before the intensive marketing campaign is different from the population proportion who prefer Sprint after exposure to the intensive Verizon marketing campaign. In fact, from Figure 12.12, observe that preference for Verizon increased after exposure to the intensive marketing campaign.

FIGURE 12.12

Excel results for the McNemar test for brand loyalty of cell phone providers

Minitab does not contain a command to perform the McNemar test.

	A	B	C	D	
1	**McNemar Test**				
2					
3	**Observed Frequencies**				
4		After Campaign			
5	Before Campaign	Sprint	Verizon	Total	
6	Sprint	246	36	282	
7	Verizon	12	306	318	
8	Total	258	342	600	
9					
10	**Data**				
11	Level of Significance	0.05			
12					
13	Intermediate Calculations				
14	Numerator	24	=C6 - B7		
15	Denominator	6.9282	=SQRT(C6 + B7)		
16	*Z* Test Statistic	3.4641	=B14/B15		
17					
18	**Two-Tail Test**				
19	Lower Critical Value	-1.9600	=NORMSINV(B11/2)		
20	Upper Critical Value	1.9600	=NORMSINV(1 - B11/2)		
21	*p*-Value	0.0005	=2 * (1 - NORMSDIST(ABS(B16)))		
22	Reject the null hypothesis		=IF(B21 < B11, "Reject the null hypothesis", "Do not reject the null hypothesis")		

Problems for Section 12.4

LEARNING THE BASICS

12.27 Given the following table for two related samples:

GROUP 1	GROUP 2: Yes	No	Total
Yes	46	25	71
No	16	59	75
Total	62	84	146

a. Compute the McNemar test statistic.

b. At the 0.05 level of significance, is there evidence of a difference between group 1 and group 2?

APPLYING THE CONCEPTS

SELF Test **12.28** A market researcher wanted to determine whether the proportion of coffee drinkers who preferred Brand *A* increased as a result of an advertising campaign. A random sample of 200 coffee drinkers was selected. The results indicating preference for Brand *A* or Brand *B* prior to the beginning of the advertising campaign and after its completion are shown in the following table:

PREFERENCE PRIOR TO ADVERTISING CAMPAIGN	PREFERENCE AFTER COMPLETION OF ADVERTISING CAMPAIGN: Brand *A*	Brand *B*	Total
Brand *A*	101	9	110
Brand *B*	22	68	90
Total	123	77	200

a. At the 0.05 level of significance, is there evidence that the proportion of coffee drinkers who prefer Brand *A* is lower at the beginning of the advertising campaign than at the end of the advertising campaign?

b. Compute the p-value in (a) and interpret its meaning.

12.29 Two candidates for governor participated in a televised debate. A political pollster recorded the preferences of 500 registered voters in a random sample prior to and after the debate:

PREFERENCE PRIOR TO DEBATE	PREFERENCE AFTER DEBATE		
	Candidate A	Candidate B	Total
Candidate A	269	21	290
Candidate B	36	174	210
Total	305	195	500

a. At the 0.01 level of significance, is there evidence of a difference in the proportion of voters who favored Candidate A prior to and after the debate?

b. Compute the p-value in (a) and interpret its meaning.

12.30 A taste-testing experiment compared two brands of Chilean merlot wines. After the initial comparison, 60 preferred Brand A, and 40 preferred Brand B. The 100 respondents were then exposed to a very professional and powerful advertisement promoting Brand A. The 100 respondents were then asked to taste the two wines again and declare which brand they preferred. The results are shown in the following table:

PREFERENCE PRIOR TO ADVERTISING	PREFERENCE AFTER ADVERTISING		
	Brand A	Brand B	Total
Brand A	55	5	60
Brand B	15	25	40
Total	70	30	100

a. At the 0.05 level of significance, is there evidence that the proportion who preferred Brand A was lower before the advertising than after the advertising?

b. Compute the p-value in (a) and interpret its meaning.

12.31 The CEO of a large metropolitan health-care facility would like to assess the effect of the recent implementation of the Six Sigma management approach on customer satisfaction. A random sample of 100 patients is selected from a list of patients who were at the facility the past week and also a year ago:

SATISFIED LAST YEAR	SATISFIED NOW		
	Yes	No	Total
Yes	67	5	72
No	20	8	28
Total	87	13	100

a. At the 0.05 level of significance, is there evidence that satisfaction was lower last year, prior to introduction of Six Sigma management?

b. Compute the p-value in (a) and interpret its meaning.

12.32 The personnel director of a large department store wants to reduce absenteeism among sales associates. She decides to institute an incentive plan that provides financial rewards for sales associates who are absent fewer than five days in a given calendar year. A sample of 100 sales associates selected at the end of the second year reveals the following:

YEAR 1	YEAR 2		
	$<$ 5 Days Absent	$\geq$ 5 Days Absent	Total
$<$ 5 Days Absent	32	4	36
$\geq$ 5 Days Absent	25	39	64
Total	57	43	100

a. At the 0.05 level of significance, is there evidence that the proportion of employees absent fewer than five days was lower in year 1 than in year 2?

b. Compute the p-value in (a) and interpret its meaning.

12.5 Chi-Square Test for the Variance or Standard Deviation

When analyzing numerical data, sometimes you need to test a hypothesis about the population variance or standard deviation. For example, in the cereal-filling process described in Section 9.1, you assumed that the population standard deviation, σ, was equal to 15 grams. To determine whether the variability of the process has changed, you need to test whether the standard deviation has changed from the previously specified level of 15 grams.

Assuming that the data are normally distributed, you use the χ^2 **test for the variance or standard deviation** defined in Equation (12.7) to test whether the population variance or standard deviation is equal to a specified value.

χ^2 TEST FOR THE VARIANCE OR STANDARD DEVIATION

$$\chi^2_{STAT} = \frac{(n-1)S^2}{\sigma^2} \tag{12.7}$$

where

n = sample size

S^2 = sample variance

σ^2 = hypothesized population variance

The test statistic χ^2_{STAT} follows a chi-square distribution with $n - 1$ degrees of freedom.

To apply the test of hypothesis, return to the cereal-filling example. You are interested in determining whether the standard deviation has changed from the previously specified level of 15 grams. Thus, you use a two-tail test with the following null and alternative hypotheses:

$$H_0: \sigma^2 = 225 \text{ (that is, } \sigma = 15 \text{ grams)}$$
$$H_1: \sigma^2 \neq 225 \text{ (that is, } \sigma \neq 15 \text{ grams)}$$

If you select a sample of 25 cereal boxes, you reject the null hypothesis if the computed χ^2_{STAT} test statistic falls into either the lower or upper tail of a chi-square distribution with $25 - 1 = 24$ degrees of freedom, as shown in Figure 12.13. From Equation (12.7), observe that the χ^2_{STAT} test statistic falls into the lower tail of the chi-square distribution if the sample standard deviation (S) is sufficiently smaller than the hypothesized σ of 15 grams, and it falls into the upper tail if S is sufficiently larger than 15 grams. From Table 12.14 (or Table E.4), if you select a level of significance of 0.05, the lower and upper critical values are 12.401 and 39.364, respectively. Therefore, the decision rule is

$$\text{Reject } H_0 \text{ if } \chi^2_{STAT} < 12.401 \text{ or if } \chi^2_{STAT} > 39.364;$$
$$\text{otherwise, do not reject } H_0.$$

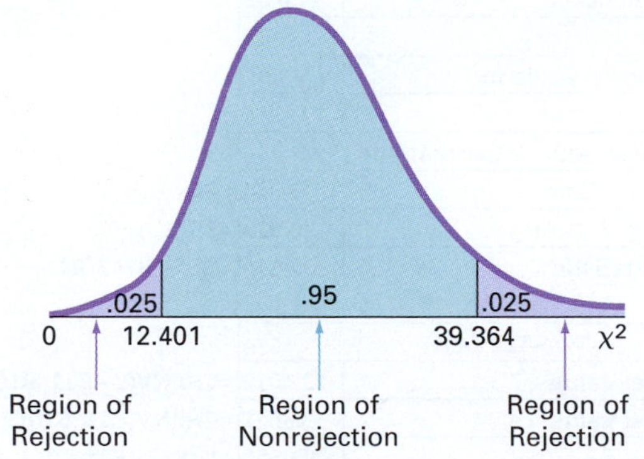

FIGURE 12.13
Determining the lower and upper critical values of a chi-square distribution with 24 degrees of freedom corresponding to a 0.05 level of significance for a two-tail test of hypothesis about a population variance or standard deviation

TABLE 12.14

Finding the Critical Values Corresponding to a 0.05 Level of Significance for a Two-Tail Test from the Chi-Square Distribution with 24 Degrees of Freedom

	Cumulative Area							
	.005	.01	**.025**	.05	.10	.90	.95	**.975**
	Upper-Tail Areas							
Degrees of Freedom	.995	.99	**.975**	.95	.90	.10	.05	**.025**
1	...	...	0.001	0.004	0.016	2.706	3.841	5.024
2	0.010	0.020	0.051	0.103	0.211	4.605	5.991	7.378
3	0.072	0.115	0.216	0.352	0.584	6.251	7.815	9.348
.	.	.	.	.	.	.	.	.
.	.	.	.	.	.	.	.	.
.	.	.	.	.	.	.	.	.
23	9.260	10.196	11.689	13.091	14.848	32.007	35.172	38.076
24	9.886	10.856	**12.401**	13.848	15.659	33.196	36.415	**39.364**
25	10.520	11.524	13.120	14.611	16.473	34.382	37.652	40.646

Source: Extracted from Table E.4.

Suppose that in the sample of 25 cereal boxes, the standard deviation, S, is 17.7 grams. Using Equation (12.7),

$$\chi^2_{STAT} = \frac{(n-1)S^2}{\sigma^2} = \frac{(25-1)(17.7)^2}{(15)^2} = 33.42$$

Because $12.401 < \chi^2_{STAT} = 33.42 < 39.364$, or because the p-value $= 0.0956 > 0.05$ (see Figure 12.14), you do not reject H_0. You conclude that there is insufficient evidence that the population standard deviation is different from 15 grams.

FIGURE 12.14

Excel results for the chi-square test for the standard deviation of the cereal-filling process

Minitab does not contain a command that directly performs this test.

	A	B	
1	**Cereal-Filling Analysis**		
2			
3	**Data**		
4	Null Hypothesis σ^2=	225	
5	Level of Significance	0.05	
6	Sample Size	25	
7	Sample Standard Deviation	17.7	
8			
9	Intermediate Calculations		
10	Degrees of Freedom	24	=B6 - 1
11	Half Area	0.025	=B5/2
12	Chi-Square Statistic	33.4176	=B10 * B7^2/B4
13			
14	**Two-Tail Test**		
15	Lower Critical Value	12.4012	=CHIINV(1 - B11, B10)
16	Upper Critical Value	39.3641	=CHIINV(B11, B10)
17	*p*-Value	0.0956	=IF(B12 - B15 < 0, 1 - CHIDIST(B12, B10), CHIDIST(B12, B10))
18	Do not reject the null hypothesis		=IF(B17 < B5/2, "Reject the null hypothesis", "Do not reject the null hypothesis")

In testing a hypothesis about a population variance or standard deviation, you assume that the values in the population are normally distributed. However, the chi-square test statistic for the variance or standard deviation is very sensitive to departures from this assumption (i.e., it is not a robust test). Thus, if the population is not normally distributed, particularly for small sample sizes, the accuracy of the test can be seriously affected.

Problems for Section 12.5

LEARNING THE BASICS

12.33 Determine the lower- and upper-tail critical values of χ^2 for each of the following two-tail tests:

a. $\alpha = 0.01, n = 26$
b. $\alpha = 0.05, n = 17$
c. $\alpha = 0.10, n = 14$

12.34 Determine the lower- and upper-tail critical values of χ^2 for each of the following two-tail tests:

a. $\alpha = 0.01, n = 24$
b. $\alpha = 0.05, n = 20$
c. $\alpha = 0.10, n = 16$

12.35 You are working with a sample of $n = 25$ selected from an underlying normal population, $S = 150$. What is the value of χ^2_{STAT} if you are testing the null hypothesis H_0: $\sigma = 100$?

12.36 You are working with a sample of $n = 16$ selected from an underlying normal population, $S = 10$. What is the value of χ^2_{STAT} if you are testing the null hypothesis H_0: $\sigma = 12$?

12.37 In Problem 12.36, how many degrees of freedom are there in the hypothesis test?

12.38 In Problems 12.36 and 12.37, what are the critical values from Table E.4 if the level of significance is $\alpha = 0.05$ and H_1 is as follows:

a. $\sigma \neq 12$?
b. $\sigma < 12$?

12.39 In Problems 12.36, 12.37, and 12.38, what is your statistical decision if H_1 is

a. $\sigma \neq 12$?
b. $\sigma < 12$?

12.40 If, in a sample of size $n = 16$ selected from a very left-skewed population, the sample standard deviation is $S = 24$, would you use the hypothesis test given in Equation (12.7) to test H_0: $\sigma = 20$? Discuss.

APPLYING THE CONCEPTS

12.41 A manufacturer of candy must monitor the temperature at which the candies are baked. Too much variation will cause inconsistency in the taste of the candy. Past records show that the standard deviation of the temperature has been 1.2°F. A random sample of 30 batches of candy is selected, and the sample standard deviation of the temperature is 2.1°F.

a. At the 0.05 level of significance, is there evidence that the population standard deviation has increased above 1.2°F?
b. What assumption do you need to make in order to perform this test?
c. Compute the p-value in (a) and interpret its meaning.

SELF Test **12.42** A market researcher for an automobile manufacturer intends to conduct a nationwide survey concerning car repairs. Among the questions included in the survey is the following: "What was the cost of all repairs performed on your car last year?" In order to determine the sample size necessary, the researcher needs to provide an estimate of the standard deviation. Using his past experience and judgment, he estimates that the standard deviation of the amount of repairs is \$200. Suppose that a small-scale study of 25 auto owners selected at random indicates a sample standard deviation of \$237.52.

a. At the 0.05 level of significance, is there evidence that the population standard deviation is different from \$200?
b. What assumption do you need to make in order to perform this test?
c. Compute the p-value in part (a) and interpret its meaning.

12.43 The marketing manager of a branch office of a local telephone operating company wants to study characteristics of residential customers served by her office. In particular, she wants to estimate the mean monthly cost of calls within the local calling region. In order to determine the sample size necessary, she needs an estimate of the standard deviation. On the basis of her past experience and judgment, she estimates that the standard deviation is equal to \$12. Suppose that a small-scale study of 15 residential customers indicates a sample standard deviation of \$9.25.

a. At the 0.10 level of significance, is there evidence that the population standard deviation is different from \$12?
b. What assumption do you need to make in order to perform this test?
c. Compute the p-value in (a) and interpret its meaning.

12.44 A manufacturer of doorknobs has a production process that is designed to provide a doorknob with a target diameter of 2.5 inches. In the past, the standard deviation of the diameter has been 0.035 inch. In an effort to reduce the variation in the process, various studies have resulted in a redesigned process. A sample of 25 doorknobs produced under the new process indicates a sample standard deviation of 0.025 inch.

a. At the 0.05 level of significance, is there evidence that the population standard deviation is less than 0.035 inch in the new process?
b. What assumption do you need to make in order to perform this test?
c. Compute the p-value in (a) and interpret its meaning.

12.45 A manufacturing company produces steel housings for electrical equipment. The main component part of the housing is a steel trough that is made out of a 14-gauge steel coil. It is produced using a 250-ton progressive punch press with a wipe-down operation that puts two 90-degree forms in the flat steel to make the trough. The distance from one side of the form to the other is critical because of weatherproofing in outdoor applications. The company requires that the width of the trough must be between 8.31 inches and 8.61 inches. In the past, the standard deviation of the width of the trough has been 0.05 inch. The file **Trough2** contains the widths of the troughs, in inches, for a sample of $n = 25$:

8.312 8.343 8.317 8.383 8.348 8.410 8.351 8.373 8.481
8.422 8.476 8.382 8.484 8.403 8.414 8.419 8.385 8.465
8.498 8.447 8.436 8.413 8.489 8.414 8.481

a. At the 0.05 level of significance, is there evidence that the standard deviation of the width of the troughs is different from 0.05 inch?

b. What assumption about the population distribution is needed in order to conduct the test in (a)?

12.46 An important quality characteristic of interest in a teabag filling process is the weight of the tea in the individual bags. The weight of the teabags should be as consistent as possible. In the past, the standard deviation of the weight of the teabags has been 0.05 grams. The file **Teabags2** contains an ordered array of the weight, in grams, of a sample of 20 tea bags produced during an eight-hour shift. Is there evidence that the standard deviation of the amount of tea per bag is greater than 0.05 grams? (Use $\alpha = 0.01$.)

12.6 Wilcoxon Rank Sum Test: Nonparametric Analysis for Two Independent Populations

"A nonparametric procedure is a statistical procedure that has (certain) desirable properties that hold under relatively mild assumptions regarding the underlying population(s) from which the data are obtained."

—Myles Hollander and Douglas A. Wolfe (reference 4, p. 1)

In Section 10.1, you used the t test for the difference between the means of two independent populations. If sample sizes are small and you cannot assume that the data in each sample are from normally distributed populations, you have two choices:

- Use a nonparametric procedure such as the Wilcoxon rank sum test, which does not depend on the assumption of normality for the two populations.
- Use the pooled-variance t test, following a *normalizing transformation* on the data (see reference 10).

This section introduces the **Wilcoxon rank sum test** for testing whether there is a difference between two *medians*. The Wilcoxon rank sum test is almost as powerful as the pooled-variance and separate-variance t tests discussed in Section 10.1 under conditions appropriate to these tests and is likely to be more powerful when the assumptions of those t tests are not met. In addition, you can use the Wilcoxon rank sum test when you have only ordinal data, as often happens in consumer behavior and marketing research.

To perform the Wilcoxon rank sum test, you replace the values in the two samples of size n_1 and n_2 with their combined ranks (unless the data contained the ranks initially). You begin by defining $n = n_1 + n_2$ as the total sample size. Next, you assign the ranks so that rank 1 is given to the smallest of the n combined values, rank 2 is given to the second smallest, and so on, until rank n is given to the largest. If several values are tied, you assign each value the average of the ranks that otherwise would have been assigned had there been no ties.

Whenever the two sample sizes are unequal, n_1 represents the smaller sample and n_2 the larger sample. The Wilcoxon rank sum test statistic, T_1, is defined as the sum of the ranks assigned to the n_1 values in the smaller sample. (For equal-sized samples, either sample may be used for determining T_1.) For any integer value n, the sum of the first n consecutive integers is $n(n + 1)/2$. Therefore, T_1 plus T_2, the sum of the ranks assigned to the n_2 items in the second sample, must equal $n(n + 1)/2$. You can use Equation (12.8) to check the accuracy of your rankings.

CHECKING THE RANKINGS

$$T_1 + T_2 = \frac{n(n+1)}{2} \quad \textbf{(12.8)}$$

When n_1 and n_2 are both ≤ 10, you use Table E.6 to find the critical values of the test statistic T_1. For a two-tail test, you reject the null hypothesis (see Panel A of Figure 12.15) if the computed value of T_1 is greater than or equal to the upper critical value, or if T_1 is less than or equal to the lower critical value. For one-tail tests having the alternative hypothesis $H_1: M_1 < M_2$ [i.e., the median of population 1 (M_1) is less than the median of population 2 (M_2)], you reject the null hypothesis if the observed value of T_1 is less than or equal to the lower critical value (see Panel B of Figure 12.15). For one-tail tests having the alternative hypothesis $H_1: M_1 > M_2$, you reject the null hypothesis if the observed value of T_1 equals or is greater than the upper critical value (see Panel C of Figure 12.15).

FIGURE 12.15
Regions of rejection and nonrejection using the Wilcoxon rank sum test

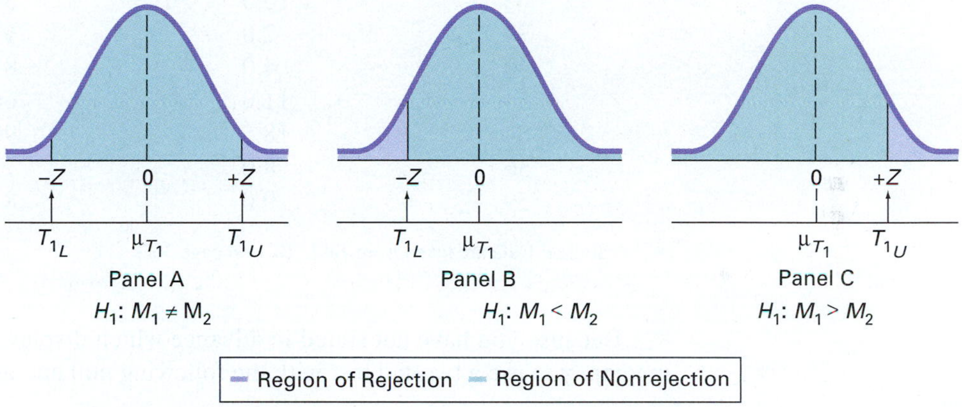

For large sample sizes, the test statistic T_1 is approximately normally distributed, with the mean, μ_{T_1}, equal to

$$\mu_{T_1} = \frac{n_1(n+1)}{2}$$

and the standard deviation, σ_{T_1}, equal to

$$\sigma_{T_1} = \sqrt{\frac{n_1 n_2 (n+1)}{12}}$$

Therefore, Equation (12.9) defines the standardized Z test statistic.

LARGE SAMPLE WILCOXON RANK SUM TEST

$$Z_{STAT} = \frac{T_1 - \dfrac{n_1(n+1)}{2}}{\sqrt{\dfrac{n_1 n_2 (n+1)}{12}}} \quad \textbf{(12.9)}$$

where the test statistic Z_{STAT} approximately follows a standardized normal distribution.

You use Equation (12.9) for testing the null hypothesis when the sample sizes are outside the range of Table E.6. Based on α, the level of significance selected, you reject the null hypothesis if the Z_{STAT} test statistic falls in the rejection region.

To study an application of the Wilcoxon rank sum test, return to the Using Statistics scenario of Chapter 10 concerning sales of BLK Cola for the normal shelf display and end-aisle locations (see page 365). If you cannot assume that the populations are normally distributed, you can use the Wilcoxon rank sum test to evaluate possible differences in the median sales for the two display locations.[2] The data (stored in Cola) and the combined ranks are shown in Table 12.15.

[2]To test for differences in the median sales between the two locations, you must assume that the distributions of sales in both populations are identical except for differences in central tendency (i.e., the medians).

TABLE 12.15

Forming the Combined Rankings

Sales			
Normal Display ($n_1 = 10$)	**Combined Ranking**	**End-Aisle Display ($n_2 = 10$)**	**Combined Ranking**
22	1.0	52	5.5
34	3.0	71	14.0
52	5.5	76	15.0
62	10.0	54	7.0
30	2.0	67	13.0
40	4.0	83	17.0
64	11.0	66	12.0
84	18.5	90	20.0
56	8.0	77	16.0
59	9.0	84	18.5

Source: Data are taken from Table 10.1 on page 367.

Because you have not stated in advance which display location is likely to have a higher median, you use a two-tail test with the following null and alternative hypotheses:

$$H_0: M_1 = M_2 \text{ (the median sales are equal)}$$
$$H_1: M_1 \neq M_2 \text{ (the median sales are not equal)}$$

Now you need to compute T_1, the sum of the ranks assigned to the *smaller* sample. When the sample sizes are equal, as in this example, you can define either sample as the group from which to compute T_1. Choosing the normal display as the first sample,

$$T_1 = 1 + 3 + 5.5 + 10 + 2 + 4 + 11 + 18.5 + 8 + 9 = 72$$

As a check on the ranking procedure, you compute T_2 from

$$T_2 = 5.5 + 14 + 15 + 7 + 13 + 17 + 12 + 20 + 16 + 18.5 = 138$$

and then use Equation (12.8) on page 495 to show that the sum of the first $n = 20$ integers in the combined ranking is equal to $T_1 + T_2$:

$$T_1 + T_2 = \frac{n(n+1)}{2}$$

$$72 + 138 = \frac{20(21)}{2} = 210$$

$$210 = 210$$

Next, you use Table E.6 to determine the lower- and upper-tail critical values for the test statistic T_1. From Table 12.16, a portion of Table E.6, observe that for a level of significance of 0.05, the critical values are 78 and 132. The decision rule is

Reject H_0 if $T_1 \leq 78$ or if $T_1 \geq 132$;

otherwise, do not reject H_0.

TABLE 12.16

Finding the Lower- and Upper-Tail Critical Values for the Wilcoxon Rank Sum Test Statistic, T_1, Where $n_1 = 10$, $n_2 = 10$, and $\alpha = 0.05$

	α		n_1						
n_2	One-Tail	Two-Tail	4	5	6	7 (Lower, Upper)	8	9	10
	.05	.10	16,40	24,51	33,63	43,76	54,90	66,105	
9	.025	.05	14,42	22,53	31,65	40,79	51,93	62,109	
	.01	.02	13,43	20,55	28,68	37,82	47,97	59,112	
	.005	.01	11,45	18,57	26,70	35,84	45,99	56,115	
	.05	.10	17,43	26,54	35,67	45,81	56,96	69,111	82,128
10	.025	.05	15,45	23,57	32,70	42,84	53,99	65,115	78,132
	.01	.02	13,47	21,59	29,73	39,87	49,103	61,119	74,136
	.005	.01	12,48	19,61	27,75	37,89	47,105	58,122	71,139

Source: Extracted from Table E.6.

Because the test statistic $T_1 = 72 < 78$, you reject H_0. There is evidence of a significant difference in the median sales for the two display locations. Because the sum of the ranks is lower for the normal display, you conclude that median sales are lower for the normal display.

Figure 12.16 shows the Wilcoxon rank sum test results (Excel) and the Mann-Whitney test results (Minitab) for the BLK Cola sales data. Although the Mann-Whitney test computes a different test statistic, the test is numerically equivalent to the Wilcoxon rank sum test (see references 1, 2, and 9). From the Figure 12.16 Excel results, you reject the null hypothesis because the p-value is 0.0126, which is less than $\alpha = 0.05$. This p-value indicates that if the medians of the two populations are equal, the chance of finding a difference at least this large in the samples is only 0.0126. The Figure 12.16 Minitab results report "The test is significant at 0.0139." The slight difference in the results is due to the fact that Minitab is computing an exact probability and Excel is using the normal approximation. Minitab also computes the p-value adjusted for ties.

FIGURE 12.16

Wilcoxon rank sum test (Excel) and Mann-Whitney test (Minitab) results for the BLK Cola sales data

	A	B	
1	Wilcoxon Rank Sum Test		
2			
3	Data		
4	Level of Significance	0.05	
5			
6	Population 1 Sample		
7	Sample Size	10	=COUNTIF(SortedRanks!A2:A21,"Normal")
8	Sum of Ranks	72	=SUMIF(SortedRanks!A2:A21,"Normal",SortedRanks!C2:C21)
9	Population 2 Sample		
10	Sample Size	10	=COUNTIF(SortedRanks!A2:A21,"End-Aisle")
11	Sum of Ranks	138	=SUMIF(SortedRanks!A2:A21,"End-Aisle",SortedRanks!C2:C21)
12			
13	Intermediate Calculations		
14	Total Sample Size n	20	=B7 + B10
15	T1 Test Statistic	72	=IF(B7 <= B10, B8, B11)
16	T1 Mean	105	=IF(B7 <= B10, B7 * (B14 + 1)/2, B10 * (B14 + 1)/2)
17	Standard Error of T1	13.2288	=SQRT(B7 * B10 * (B14 + 1)/12)
18	Z Test Statistic	-2.4946	=(B15 - B16)/B17
19			
20	Two-Tail Test		
21	Lower Critical Value	-1.9600	=NORMSINV(B4/2)
22	Upper Critical Value	1.9600	=NORMSINV(1 - B4/2)
23	p-Value	0.0126	=2 * (1 - NORMSDIST(ABS(B18)))
24	Reject the null hypothesis		=IF(B23 < B4, "Reject the null hypothesis", "Do not reject the null hypothesis")

Mann-Whitney Test and CI: Normal, End-Aisle

```
             N  Median
Normal      10   54.00
End-Aisle   10   73.50

Point estimate for ETA1-ETA2 is -21.50
95.5 Percent CI for ETA1-ETA2 is (-37.01,-6.00)
W = 72.0
Test of ETA1 = ETA2 vs ETA1 not = ETA2 is significant at 0.0140
The test is significant at 0.0139 (adjusted for ties)
```

Table E.6 shows the lower and upper critical values of the Wilcoxon rank sum test statistic, T_1, but only for situations in which both n_1 and n_2 are less than or equal to 10. If either one or both of the sample sizes are greater than 10, you *must* use the large-sample Z approximation formula [Equation (12.9) on page 495]. However, you can also use this approximation formula for small sample sizes. To demonstrate the large-sample Z approximation formula, consider the BLK Cola sales data. Using Equation (12.9),

$$Z_{STAT} = \frac{T_1 - \dfrac{n_1(n+1)}{2}}{\sqrt{\dfrac{n_1 n_2 (n+1)}{12}}}$$

$$= \frac{72 - \dfrac{(10)(21)}{2}}{\sqrt{\dfrac{(10)(10)(21)}{12}}}$$

$$= \frac{72 - 105}{13.2288} = -2.4946$$

Because $Z_{STAT} = -2.4946 < -1.96$, the critical value of Z at the 0.05 level of significance (or *p-value* $= 0.0126 < 0.05$), you reject H_0.

Problems for Section 12.6

LEARNING THE BASICS

12.47 Using Table E.6, determine the lower- and upper-tail critical values for the Wilcoxon rank sum test statistic, T_1, in each of the following two-tail tests:

a. $\alpha = 0.10, n_1 = 6, n_2 = 8$
b. $\alpha = 0.05, n_1 = 6, n_2 = 8$
c. $\alpha = 0.01, n_1 = 6, n_2 = 8$
d. Given your results in (a) through (c), what do you conclude regarding the width of the region of nonrejection as the selected level of significance, α, gets smaller?

12.48 Using Table E.6, determine the lower-tail critical value for the Wilcoxon rank sum test statistic, T_1, in each of the following one-tail tests:

a. $\alpha = 0.05, n_1 = 6, n_2 = 8$
b. $\alpha = 0.025, n_1 = 6, n_2 = 8$
c. $\alpha = 0.01, n_1 = 6, n_2 = 8$
d. $\alpha = 0.005, n_1 = 6, n_2 = 8$

12.49 The following information is available for two samples selected from independent populations:

Sample 1: $n_1 = 7$ Assigned ranks: 4 1 8 2 5 10 11

Sample 2: $n_2 = 9$ Assigned ranks: 7 16 12 9 3 14 13 6 15

What is the value of T_1 if you are testing the null hypothesis $H_0: M_1 = M_2$?

12.50 In Problem 12.49, what are the lower- and upper-tail critical values for the test statistic T_1 from Table E.6 if you use a 0.05 level of significance and the alternative hypothesis is $H_1: M_1 \neq M_2$?

12.51 In Problems 12.49 and 12.50, what is your statistical decision?

12.52 The following information is available for two samples selected from independent and similarly shaped right-skewed populations:

Sample 1: $n_1 = 5$ 1.1 2.3 2.9 3.6 14.7

Sample 2: $n_2 = 6$ 2.8 4.4 4.4 5.2 6.0 18.5

a. Replace the observed values with the corresponding ranks (where 1 = smallest value; $n = n_1 + n_2 = 11$ = largest value) in the combined samples.
b. What is the value of the test statistic T_1?
c. Compute the value of T_2, the sum of the ranks in the larger sample.
d. To check the accuracy of your rankings, use Equation (12.8) on page 495 to demonstrate that

$$T_1 + T_2 = \frac{n(n+1)}{2}$$

12.53 From Problem 12.52, at the 0.05 level of significance, determine the lower-tail critical value for the Wilcoxon rank sum test statistic, T_1, if you want to test the null hypothesis, $H_0: M_1 \geq M_2$, against the one-tail alternative, $H_1: M_1 < M_2$.

12.54 In Problems 12.52 and 12.53, what is your statistical decision?

APPLYING THE CONCEPTS

12.55 A vice president for marketing recruits 20 college graduates for management training. Each of the 20 individuals is randomly assigned, 10 each, to one of two groups. A "traditional" method of training (*T*) is used in one group, and an "experimental" method (*E*) is used in the other. After the graduates spend six months on the job, the vice president ranks them on the basis of their performance, from 1 (worst) to 20 (best), with the following results (stored in the file **TestRank**):

T:	1	2	3	5	9	10	12	13	14	15
E:	4	6	7	8	11	16	17	18	19	20

Is there evidence of a difference in the median performance between the two methods? (Use $\alpha = 0.05$.)

12.56 Wine experts Gaiter and Brecher use a six-category scale when rating wines: Yech, OK, Good, Very Good, Delicious, and Delicious! (Data extracted from D. Gaiter and J. Brecher, "A Good U.S. Cabernet Is Hard to Find," *The Wall Street Journal*, May 19, 2006, p. W7.) Suppose Gaiter and Brecher tested a random sample of eight inexpensive California Cabernets and a random sample of eight inexpensive Washington Cabernets. *Inexpensive* is defined as a suggested retail value in the United States of under \$20. The data, stored in **Cabernet**, are as follows:

California—Good, Delicious, Yech, OK, OK, Very Good, Yech, OK

Washington—Very Good, OK, Delicious!, Very Good, Delicious, Good, Delicious, Delicious!

a. Are the data collected by rating wines using this scale nominal, ordinal, interval, or ratio?

b. Why is the two-sample *t* test defined in Section 10.1 inappropriate to test the mean rating of California Cabernets versus Washington Cabernets?

c. Is there evidence of a significance difference in the median rating of California Cabernets and Washington Cabernets? (Use $\alpha = 0.05$.)

12.57 A problem with a telephone line that prevents a customer from receiving or making calls is upsetting to both the customer and the telephone company. The file **Phone** contains samples of 20 problems reported to two different offices of a telephone company and the time to clear these problems (in minutes) from the customers' lines:

Central Office I Time to Clear Problems (Minutes)

1.48 1.75 0.78 2.85 0.52 1.60 4.15 3.97 1.48 3.10
1.02 0.53 0.93 1.60 0.80 1.05 6.32 3.93 5.45 0.97

Central Office II Time to Clear Problems (Minutes)

7.55 3.75 0.10 1.10 0.60 0.52 3.30 2.10 0.58 4.02
3.75 0.65 1.92 0.60 1.53 4.23 0.08 1.48 1.65 0.72

a. Is there evidence of a difference in the median time to clear problems between offices? (Use $\alpha = 0.05$.)

b. What assumptions must you make in (a)?

c. Compare the results of (a) with those of Problem 10.9(a) on page 375.

SELF Test **12.58** The management of a hotel has the business objective of increasing the return rate for hotel guests. One aspect of first impressions by guests relates to the time it takes to deliver a guest's luggage to the room after check-in to the hotel. A random sample of 20 deliveries on a particular day were selected in Wing A of the hotel, and a random sample of 20 deliveries were selected in Wing B. The results are stored in **Luggage**.

a. Is there evidence of a difference in the median delivery times in the two wings of the hotel? (Use $\alpha = 0.05$.)

b. Compare the results of (a) with those of Problem 10.67 on page 402.

12.59 The lengths of life (in hours) of a sample of 40 100-watt light bulbs produced by Manufacturer A and a sample of 40 100-watt light bulbs produced by Manufacturer B are stored in **Bulbs**.

a. Using a 0.05 level of significance, is there evidence of a difference in the median life of bulbs produced by the two manufacturers?

b. What assumptions must you make in (a)?

c. Compare the results of (a) with those of Problem 10.66 (a) on page 402. Discuss.

12.60 Nondestructive evaluation is used to measure the properties of components or materials without causing any permanent physical change to the components or materials. It includes the determination of properties of materials and the classification of flaws by size, shape, type, and location. Nondestructive evaluation is very effective for detecting surface flaws and characterizing surface properties of electrically conductive materials. Data were collected that classified each component as having a flaw or not, based on manual inspection and operator judgment, and also reported the size of the crack in the material. The results in terms of crack size (in inches) are stored in **Crack** and shown below. (Data extracted from B. D. Olin and W. Q. Meeker, "Applications of Statistical Methods to Nondestructive Evaluation," *Technometrics*, 38, 1996, p. 101.)

Unflawed

0.003 0.004 0.012 0.014 0.021 0.023 0.024 0.030 0.034
0.041 0.041 0.042 0.043 0.045 0.057 0.063 0.074 0.076

Flawed

0.022 0.026 0.026 0.030 0.031 0.034 0.042 0.043 0.044
0.046 0.046 0.052 0.055 0.058 0.060 0.060 0.070 0.071
0.073 0.073 0.078 0.079 0.079 0.083 0.090 0.095 0.095
0.096 0.100 0.102 0.103 0.105 0.114 0.119 0.120 0.130
0.160 0.306 0.328 0.440

a. Using a 0.05 level of significance, is there evidence that the median crack size is smaller for unflawed components than for flawed components?
b. What assumptions must you make in (a)?
c. Compare the results of (a) with those of Problem 10.17 (a) on page 376. Discuss.

12.61 A bank with a branch located in a commercial district of a city has developed an improved process for serving customers during the noon-to-1 P.M. lunch period. The bank has the business objective of reducing the waiting time (defined as the time elapsed from when the customer enters the line until he or she reaches the teller window) to increase customer satisfaction. A random sample of 15 customers is selected (and stored in Bank1); the results (in minutes) are as follows:

4.21 5.55 3.02 5.13 4.77 2.34 3.54 3.20
4.50 6.10 0.38 5.12 6.46 6.19 3.79

Another branch, located in a residential area, is also concerned with the noon-to-1 P.M. lunch period. A random sample of 15 customers is selected (and stored in the file Bank2); the results (in minutes) are as follows:

9.66 5.90 8.02 5.79 8.73 3.82 8.01 8.35
10.49 6.68 5.64 4.08 6.17 9.91 5.47

a. Is there evidence of a difference in the median waiting time between the two branches? (Use $\alpha = 0.05$.)
b. What assumptions must you make in (a)?
c. Compare the results (a) with those of Problem 10.12 (a) on page 376. Discuss.

12.62 Digital cameras have taken over the majority of the point-and-shoot camera market. One of the important features of a camera is the battery life, as measured by the number of shots taken until the battery needs to be recharged. The file DigitalCameras contains the battery life of 29 subcompact cameras and 16 compact cameras. (Data extracted from "Digital Cameras," *Consumer Reports*, July 2009, pp. 28–29.)
a. Is there evidence of a difference in the median battery life between subcompact cameras and compact cameras? (Use $\alpha = 0.05$.)
b. What assumptions must you make in (a)?
c. Compare the results of (a) with those of Problem 10.11 (a) on page 376. Discuss.

12.7 Kruskal-Wallis Rank Test: Nonparametric Analysis for the One-Way ANOVA

If the normality assumption of the one-way ANOVA F test is violated, you can use the Kruskal-Wallis rank test. The Kruskal-Wallis rank test for differences among c medians (where $c > 2$) is an extension of the Wilcoxon rank sum test for two independent populations, discussed in Section 12.6. Thus, the Kruskal-Wallis test has the same power relative to the one-way ANOVA F test that the Wilcoxon rank sum test has relative to the t test.

You use the **Kruskal-Wallis rank test** to test whether c independent groups have equal medians. The null hypothesis is

$$H_0: M_1 = M_2 = \cdots = M_c$$

and the alternative hypothesis is

$$H_1: \text{Not all } M_j \text{ are equal (where } j = 1, 2, \ldots, c).$$

To use the Kruskal-Wallis rank test, you first replace the values in the c samples with their combined ranks (if necessary). Rank 1 is given to the smallest of the combined values and rank n to the largest of the combined values (where $n = n_1 + n_2 + \cdots + n_c$). If any values are tied, you assign each of them the mean of the ranks they would have otherwise been assigned if ties had not been present in the data.

The Kruskal-Wallis test is an alternative to the one-way ANOVA F test. Instead of comparing each of the c group means against the grand mean, the Kruskal-Wallis test compares the mean rank in each of the c groups against the overall mean rank, based on all n combined values. Equation (12.10) defines the Kruskal-Wallis test statistic, H.

KRUSKAL-WALLIS RANK TEST FOR DIFFERENCES AMONG C MEDIANS

$$H = \left[\frac{12}{n(n+1)}\sum_{j=1}^{c}\frac{T_j^2}{n_j}\right] - 3(n+1) \quad \textbf{(12.10)}$$

where

n = total number of values over the combined samples

n_j = number of values in the jth sample ($j = 1, 2, \ldots, c$)

T_j = sum of the ranks assigned to the jth sample

T_j^2 = square of the sum of the ranks assigned to the jth sample

c = number of groups

If there is a significant difference among the c groups, the mean rank differs considerably from group to group. In the process of squaring these differences, the test statistic H becomes large. If there are no differences present, the test statistic H is small because the mean of the ranks assigned in each group should be very similar from group to group.

As the sample sizes in each group get large (i.e., at least 5), you can approximate the test statistic, H, by the chi-square distribution with $c - 1$ degrees of freedom. Thus, you reject the null hypothesis if the computed value of H is greater than the upper-tail critical value (see Figure 12.17). Therefore, the decision rule is

$$\text{Reject } H_0 \text{ if } H > \chi^2_\alpha;$$

otherwise, do not reject H_0.

FIGURE 12.17
Determining the rejection region for the Kruskal-Wallis test

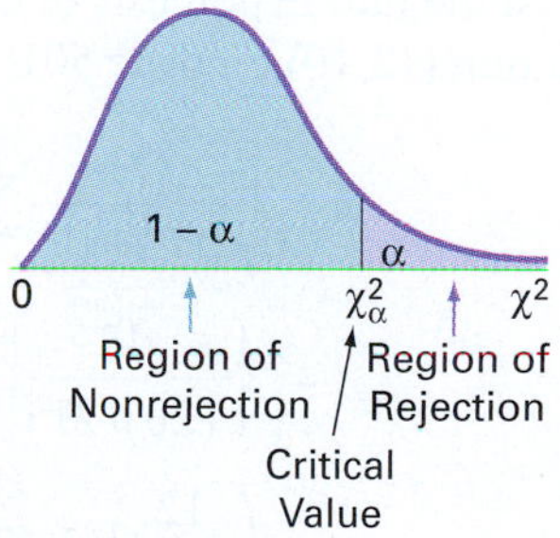

To illustrate the Kruskal-Wallis rank test for differences among c medians, return to the Using Statistics scenario from Chapter 11 on page 415, concerning the strength of parachutes. If you cannot assume that the tensile strength of the parachutes is normally distributed in all c groups, you can use the Kruskal-Wallis rank test.

The null hypothesis is that the median tensile strengths of parachutes for the four suppliers are equal. The alternative hypothesis is that at least one of the suppliers differs from the others:

$$H_0: M_1 = M_2 = M_3 = M_4$$

$$H_1: \text{Not all } M_j \text{ are equal (where } j = 1, 2, 3, 4).$$

Table 12.17 presents the data (stored in the file **Parachute**), along with the corresponding ranks.

TABLE 12.17

Tensile Strength and Ranks of Parachutes Woven from Synthetic Fibers from Four Suppliers

Supplier							
1		2		3		4	
Amount	Rank	Amount	Rank	Amount	Rank	Amount	Rank
18.5	4	26.3	20	20.6	8	25.4	19
24.0	13.5	25.3	18	25.2	17	19.9	5.5
17.2	1	24.0	13.5	20.8	9	22.6	11
19.9	5.5	21.2	10	24.7	16	17.5	2
18.0	3	24.5	15	22.9	12	20.4	7

In converting the 20 tensile strengths to ranks, observe in Table 12.17 that the third parachute for Supplier 1 has the lowest tensile strength, 17.2. It is assigned a rank of 1. The fourth value for Supplier 1 and the second value for Supplier 4 each have a value of 19.9. Because they are tied for ranks 5 and 6, each is assigned the rank 5.5. Finally, the first value for Supplier 2 is the largest value, 26.3, and is assigned a rank of 20.

After all the ranks are assigned, you compute the sum of the ranks for each group:

$$\text{Rank sums: } T_1 = 27 \quad T_2 = 76.5 \quad T_3 = 62 \quad T_4 = 44.5$$

As a check on the rankings, recall from Equation (12.8) on page 495 that for any integer n, the sum of the first n consecutive integers is $n(n + 1)/2$. Therefore,

$$T_1 + T_2 + T_3 + T_4 = \frac{n(n+1)}{2}$$

$$27 + 76.5 + 62 + 44.5 = \frac{(20)(21)}{2}$$

$$210 = 210$$

To test the null hypothesis of equal population medians, you calculate the test statistic H using Equation (12.10) on page 501:

$$H = \left[\frac{12}{n(n+1)} \sum_{j=1}^{c} \frac{T_j^2}{n_j}\right] - 3(n+1)$$

$$= \left\{\frac{12}{(20)(21)}\left[\frac{(27)^2}{5} + \frac{(76.5)^2}{5} + \frac{(62)^2}{5} + \frac{(44.5)^2}{5}\right]\right\} - 3(21)$$

$$= \left(\frac{12}{420}\right)(2{,}481.1) - 63 = 7.8886$$

The test statistic H approximately follows a chi-square distribution with $c - 1$ degrees of freedom. Using a 0.05 level of significance, χ^2_α, the upper-tail critical value of the chi-square distribution with $c - 1 = 3$ degrees of freedom, is 7.815 (see Table 12.18). Because the computed value of the test statistic $H = 7.8886$ is greater than the critical value, you reject the null hypothesis and conclude that the median tensile strength is not the same for all the suppliers. You reach the same conclusion by using the p-value approach, because, as shown in Figure 12.18, $p\text{-value} = 0.0484 < 0.05$. At this point, you could simultaneously compare all pairs of suppliers to determine which ones differ (see reference 2).

TABLE 12.18

Finding χ^2_α, the Upper-Tail Critical Value for the Kruskal-Wallis Rank Test, at the 0.05 Level of Significance with 3 Degrees of Freedom

	Cumulative Area									
	.005	**.01**	**.025**	**.05**	**.10**	**.25**	**.75**	**.90**	**.95**	**.975**
	Upper-Tail Area									
Degrees of Freedom	**.995**	**.99**	**.975**	**.95**	**.90**	**.75**	**.25**	**.10**	**.05**	**.025**
1	—	—	0.001	0.004	0.016	0.102	1.323	2.706	3.841	5.024
2	0.010	0.020	0.051	0.103	0.211	0.575	2.773	4.605	5.991	7.378
3	0.072	0.115	0.216	0.352	0.584	1.213	4.108	6.251	7.815	9.348
4	0.207	0.297	0.484	0.711	1.064	1.923	5.385	7.779	9.488	11.143
5	0.412	0.554	0.831	1.145	1.610	2.675	6.626	9.236	11.071	12.833

Source: Extracted from Table E.4.

FIGURE 12.18

Excel and Minitab Kruskal-Wallis rank test results for differences among the four median tensile strengths of parachutes

	A	B	C	D	E	F	G
1	**Kruskal-Wallis Rank Test**						
2							
3	Data			Calculations			
4	Level of Significance	0.05		Group	Sample Size	Sum of Ranks	Mean Ranks
5				1	5	27	5.4
6	Intermediate Calculations			2	5	76.5	15.3
7	Sum of Squared Ranks/Sample Size	2481.1		3	5	62	12.4
8	Sum of Sample Sizes	20		4	5	44.5	8.9
9	Number of Groups	4					
10							
11	Test Result						
12	*H* Test Statistic	7.8886	=(12/(B8 * (B8 + 1))) * B7 - (3 * (B8 + 1))				
13	Critical Value	7.8147	=CHIINV(B4, B9 - 1)				
14	*p*-Value	0.0484	=CHIDIST(B12, B9 - 1)				
15	Reject the null hypothesis		=IF(B14 < B4, "Reject the null hypothesis", "Do not reject the null hypothesis")				

Also
Cell B7: =(G5 * F5) + (G6 * F6) + (G7 * F7) + (G8 * F8)
Cell B8: =SUM(E5:E8)

Kruskal-Wallis Test: Strength versus Supplier

```
Kruskal-Wallis Test on Strength

Supplier     N  Median  Ave Rank      Z
Supplier 1   5   18.50       5.4  -2.23
Supplier 2   5   24.50      15.3   2.09
Supplier 3   5   22.90      12.4   0.83
Supplier 4   5   20.40       8.9  -0.70
Overall     20              10.5

H = 7.89  DF = 3  P = 0.048
H = 7.90  DF = 3  P = 0.048  (adjusted for ties)
```

The following assumptions are needed to use the Kruskal-Wallis rank test:

- The c samples are randomly and independently selected from their respective populations.
- The underlying variable is continuous.
- The data provide at least a set of ranks, both within and among the c samples.
- The c populations have the same variability.
- The c populations have the same shape.

The Kruskal-Wallis procedure makes less stringent assumptions than does the F test. If you ignore the last two assumptions (variability and shape), you can still use the Kruskal-Wallis rank test to determine whether at least one of the populations differs from the other populations in some characteristic—such as central tendency, variation, or shape.

To use the F test, you must assume that the c samples are from normal populations that have equal variances. When the more stringent assumptions of the F test hold, you should use the F test instead of the Kruskal-Wallis test because it has slightly more power to detect significant differences among groups. However, if the assumptions of the F test do not hold, you should use the Kruskal-Wallis test.

Problems for Section 12.7

LEARNING THE BASICS

12.63 What is the upper-tail critical value from the chi-square distribution if you use the Kruskal-Wallis rank test for comparing the medians in six populations at the 0.01 level of significance?

12.64 For this problem, use the results of Problem 12.63.

a. State the decision rule for testing the null hypothesis that all six groups have equal population medians.

b. What is your statistical decision if the computed value of the test statistic H is 13.77?

APPLYING THE CONCEPTS

12.65 A pet food company has the business objective of expanding its product line beyond its current kidney- and shrimp-based cat foods. The company developed two new products—one based on chicken livers and the other based on salmon. The company conducted an experiment to compare the two new products with its two existing ones as well as a generic beef-based product sold in a supermarket chain.

For the experiment, a sample of 50 cats from the population at a local animal shelter was selected. Ten cats were randomly assigned to each of the five products being tested. Each of the cats was then presented with 3 ounces of the selected food in a dish at feeding time. The researchers defined the variable to be measured as the number of ounces of food that the cat consumed within a 10-minute time interval that began when the filled dish was presented. The results for this experiment are summarized in the following table and stored in **CatFood**:

Kidney	Shrimp	Chicken Liver	Salmon	Beef
2.37	2.26	2.29	1.79	2.09
2.62	2.69	2.23	2.33	1.87
2.31	2.25	2.41	1.96	1.67
2.47	2.45	2.68	2.05	1.64
2.59	2.34	2.25	2.26	2.16
2.62	2.37	2.17	2.24	1.75
2.34	2.22	2.37	1.96	1.18
2.47	2.56	2.26	1.58	1.92
2.45	2.36	2.45	2.18	1.32
2.32	2.59	2.57	1.93	1.94

a. At the 0.05 level of significance, is there evidence of a significant difference in the median amount of food eaten among the various products?

b. Compare the results of (a) with those of Problem 11.13 (a) on page 429.

c. Which test is more appropriate for these data, the Kruskal-Wallis rank test or the one-way ANOVA F test? Explain.

SELF Test **12.66** A hospital conducted a study of the waiting time in its emergency room. The hospital has a main campus, along with three satellite locations. Management had a business objective of reducing waiting time for emergency room cases that did not require immediate attention. To study this, a random sample of 15 emergency room cases at each location were selected on a particular day, and the waiting time (recorded from check-in to when the patient was called into the clinic area) was measured. The results are stored in **ERWaiting**.

a. At the 0.05 level of significance, is there evidence of a difference in the median waiting times in the four locations?

b. Compare the results of (a) with those of Problem 11.9 (a) on page 428.

12.67 The per-store daily customer count (i.e., the mean number of customers in a store in one day) for a nationwide convenience store chain that operates nearly 10,000 stores has been steady, at 900, for some time. To increase the customer count, the chain is considering cutting prices for coffee beverages. Management needs to determine how much prices can be cut in order to increase the daily customer count without reducing the gross margin on coffee sales too much. You decide to carry out an experiment in a sample of 24 stores where customer counts have been running almost exactly at the national average of 900. In 6 of the stores, a small coffee will be \$0.59, in another 6 stores the price will be \$0.69, in a third group of 6 stores, the price will be \$0.79, and in a fourth group of 6 stores, the price will now be \$0.89. After four weeks, the daily customer count in the stores is stored in **CoffeeSales**.

a. At the 0.05 level of significance, is there evidence of a difference in the daily customer count based on the price of a small coffee?

b. Compare the results of (a) with those of Problem 11.11 (a) on page 428.

12.68 An advertising agency has been hired by a manufacturer of pens to develop an advertising campaign for the upcoming holiday season. To prepare for this project, the research director decides to initiate a study of the effect of advertising on product perception. An experiment is designed to compare five different advertisements. Advertisement A greatly undersells the pen's characteristics. Advertisement B slightly undersells the pen's characteristics. Advertisement C slightly oversells the pen's characteristics. Advertisement D greatly oversells the pen's characteristics. Advertisement E attempts to correctly state the pen's characteristics. A sample of 30 adult respondents, taken from a larger focus group, is randomly assigned to the five advertisements (so that there are six respondents to each). After reading the advertisement and developing a sense of product expectation, all respondents unknowingly receive the same pen to evaluate. The respondents are permitted to test the pen and the plausibility of the advertising copy. The respondents are then asked to rate the pen from 1 to 7 on the product characteristic scales of appearance, durability, and writing performance. The *combined* scores of three ratings (appearance, durability, and writing performance) for the 30 respondents (stored in **Pen**) are as follows:

A	B	C	D	E
15	16	8	5	12
18	17	7	6	19
17	21	10	13	18
19	16	15	11	12
19	19	14	9	17
20	17	14	10	14

a. At the 0.05 level of significance, is there evidence of a difference in the median ratings of the five advertisements?

b. Compare the results of (a) with those of Problem 11.10 (a) on page 428.

c. Which test is more appropriate for these data, the Kruskal-Wallis rank test or the one-way ANOVA F test? Explain.

12.69 A sporting goods manufacturing company wanted to compare the distance traveled by golf balls produced using each of four different designs. Ten balls of each design were manufactured and brought to the local golf course for the club professional to test. The order in which the balls were hit with the same club from the first tee was randomized so that the pro did not know which type of ball was being hit. All 40 balls were hit in a short period of time, during which the environmental conditions were essentially the same. The results (distance traveled in yards) for the four designs are stored in **Golfball**:

a. At the 0.05 level of significance, is there evidence of a difference in the median distances traveled by the golf balls with different designs?

b. Compare the results of (a) with those of Problem 11.14 (a) on page 429.

12.70 Students in a business statistics course performed an experiment to test the strength of four brands of trash bags. One-pound weights were placed into a bag, one at a time, until the bag broke. A total of 40 bags were used (10 for each brand). The file **Trashbags** gives the weight (in pounds) required to break the trash bags.

a. At the 0.05 level of significance, is there evidence of a difference in the median strength of the four brands of trash bags?

b. Compare the results in (a) to those in Problem 11.8 (a) on page 428.

12.8 *Online Topic:* Wilcoxon Signed Ranks Test: Nonparametric Analysis for Two Related Populations

In Section 10.2, you used the paired t test to compare the means of two populations when you had repeated measures or matched samples. The paired t test assumes that the data are measured on an interval or a ratio scale and are normally distributed. If you cannot make these assumptions, you can use the nonparametric **Wilcoxon signed ranks test** to test for the median difference. To study this topic, read the **Section 12.8** online topic file that is available on this book's companion website. (See Appendix C to learn how to access the online topic files.)

12.9 *Online Topic:* Friedman Rank Test: Nonparametric Analysis for the Randomized Block Design

When analyzing a randomized block design, sometimes the data consist of only the ranks within each block. Other times, you cannot assume that the data from each of the c groups are from normally distributed populations. In these situations, you can use the **Friedman rank test**. To study this topic, read the **Section 12.9** online topic file that is available on this book's companion website. (See Appendix C to learn how to access the online topic files.)

USING STATISTICS @ T.C. Resort Properties Revisited

In the Using Statistics scenario, you were the manager of T.C. Resort Properties, a collection of five upscale hotels located on two tropical islands. To assess the quality of services being provided by your hotels, guests are encouraged to complete a satisfaction survey when they check out. You analyzed the data from these surveys to determine the overall satisfaction with the services provided, the likelihood that the guests will return to the hotel, and the reasons given by some guests for not wanting to return.

On one island, T.C. Resort Properties operates the Beachcomber and Windsurfer hotels. You performed a chi-square test for the difference in two proportions and concluded that a greater proportion of guests are willing to return to the Beachcomber Hotel than to the Windsurfer. On the other island, T.C. Resort Properties operates the Golden Palm, Palm Royale, and Palm Princess hotels. To see if guest satisfaction was the same among the three hotels, you performed a chi-square test for the differences among more than two proportions. The test confirmed that the three proportions are not equal, and guests are most likely to return to the Palm Royale and least likely to return to the Golden Palm.

In addition, you investigated whether the reasons given for not returning to the Golden Palm, Palm Royale, and Palm Princess were unique to a certain hotel or common to all three hotels. By performing a chi-square test of independence, you determined that the reasons given for wanting to return or not depended on the hotel where the guests had been staying. By examining the observed and expected frequencies, you concluded that guests were more satisfied with the price at the Golden Palm and were much more satisfied with the location of the Palm Princess. Guest satisfaction with room accommodations was not significantly different among the three hotels.

SUMMARY

Figure 12.19 presents a roadmap for this chapter. First, you used hypothesis testing for analyzing categorical response data from two independent samples and from more than two independent samples. In addition, the rules of probability from Section 4.2 were extended to the hypothesis of independence in the joint responses to two categorical variables. You also used the McNemar test to study situations where the samples were not independent. In addition, you used the chi-square distribution to test a variance or standard deviation. You also studied two nonparametric tests. You used the Wilcoxon rank sum test when the assumptions of the t test for two independent samples were violated and the Kruskal-Wallis test when the assumptions of the one-way ANOVA F test were violated.

FIGURE 12.19
Roadmap of Chapter 12

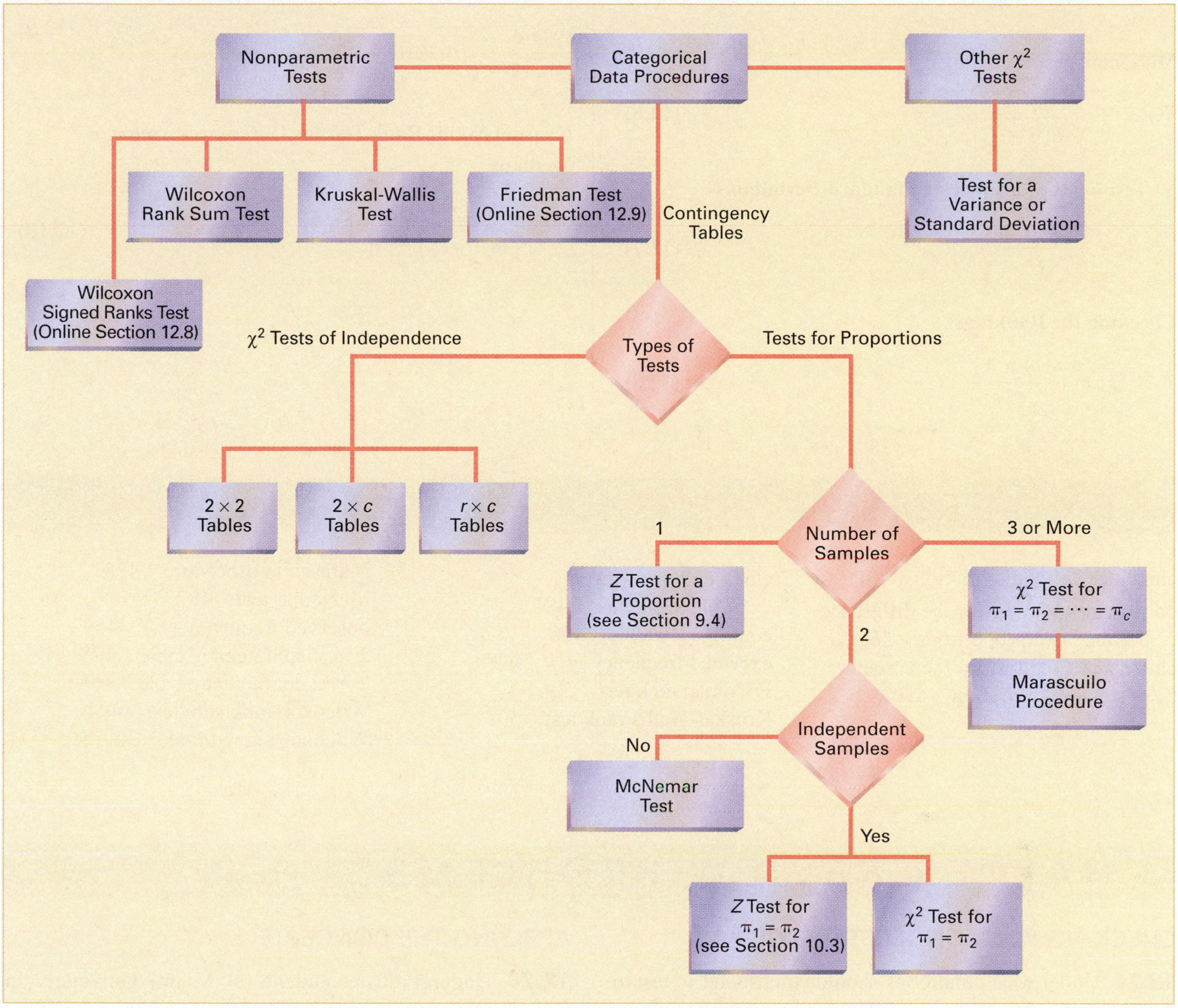

KEY EQUATIONS

χ^2 Test for the Difference Between Two Proportions

$$\chi^2_{STAT} = \sum_{\textit{all cells}} \frac{(f_0 - f_e)^2}{f_e} \tag{12.1}$$

Computing the Estimated Overall Proportion for Two Groups

$$\bar{p} = \frac{X_1 + X_2}{n_1 + n_2} = \frac{X}{n} \tag{12.2}$$

Computing the Estimated Overall Proportion for c Groups

$$\bar{p} = \frac{X_1 + X_2 + \cdots + X_c}{n_1 + n_2 + \cdots + n_c} = \frac{X}{n} \tag{12.3}$$

Critical Range for the Marascuilo Procedure

$$\text{Critical range} = \sqrt{\chi^2_\alpha}\sqrt{\frac{p_j(1 - p_j)}{n_j} + \frac{p_{j'}(1 - p_{j'})}{n_{j'}}} \tag{12.4}$$

Computing the Expected Frequency

$$f_e = \frac{\text{Row total} \times \text{Column total}}{n} \quad (12.5)$$

McNemar Test Statistic

$$Z_{STAT} = \frac{B - C}{\sqrt{B + C}} \quad (12.6)$$

χ^2 Test for the Variance or Standard Deviation

$$\chi^2_{STAT} = \frac{(n - 1)S^2}{\sigma^2} \quad (12.7)$$

Checking the Rankings

$$T_1 + T_2 = \frac{n(n + 1)}{2} \quad (12.8)$$

Large Sample Wilcoxon Rank Sum Test

$$Z_{STAT} = \frac{T_1 - \dfrac{n_1(n + 1)}{2}}{\sqrt{\dfrac{n_1 n_2(n + 1)}{12}}} \quad (12.9)$$

Kruskal-Wallis Rank Test for Differences Among *c* Medians

$$H = \left[\frac{12}{n(n + 1)}\sum_{j=1}^{c}\frac{T_j^2}{n_j}\right] - 3(n + 1) \quad (12.10)$$

KEY TERMS

CHAPTER REVIEW PROBLEMS

CHECKING YOUR UNDERSTANDING

12.71 Under what conditions should you use the χ^2 test to determine whether there is a difference between the proportions of two independent populations?

12.72 Under what conditions should you use the χ^2 test to determine whether there is a difference among the proportions of more than two independent populations?

12.73 Under what conditions should you use the χ^2 test of independence?

12.74 Under what conditions should you use the McNemar test?

12.75 What is a nonparametric procedure?

12.76 Under what conditions should you use the Wilcoxon rank sum test instead of the *t* test for the difference between the means?

12.77 Under what conditions should you use the Kruskal-Wallis rank test instead of the one-way ANOVA?

APPLYING THE CONCEPTS

12.78 Undergraduate students at Miami University in Oxford, Ohio, were surveyed in order to evaluate the effect of gender and price on purchasing a pizza from Pizza Hut. Students were told to suppose that they were planning to have a large two-topping pizza delivered to their residence that evening. The students had to decide between ordering from Pizza Hut at a reduced price of $8.49 (the regular price for a large two-topping pizza from the Oxford Pizza Hut at this time was $11.49) and ordering a pizza from a different pizzeria. The results from this question are summarized in the following contingency table:

	PIZZERIA		
GENDER	**Pizza Hut**	**Other**	**Total**
Female	4	13	17
Male	6	12	18
Total	10	25	35

A subsequent survey evaluated purchase decisions at other prices. These results are summarized in the following contingency table:

	PRICE			
PIZZERIA	**\$8.49**	**\$11.49**	**\$14.49**	**Total**
Pizza Hut	10	5	2	17
Other	25	23	27	75
Total	35	28	29	92

a. Using a 0.05 level of significance and using the data in the first contingency table, is there evidence of a significant difference between males and females in their pizzeria selection?

b. What is your answer to (a) if nine of the male students selected Pizza Hut and nine selected another pizzeria?

c. Using a 0.05 level of significance and using the data in the second contingency table, is there evidence of a difference in pizzeria selection based on price?

d. Determine the *p*-value in (c) and interpret its meaning.

12.79 According to U.S. Census estimates, there were about 20 million children between 8 and 12 years old (referred to as *tweens*) in the United States in 2009. A recent survey of 1,223 8- to 12-year-old children (S. Jayson, "It's Cooler Than Ever to Be a Tween," *USA Today*, February 4, 2009, pp. 1A, 2A) reported the following results. Suppose that the survey was based on 600 boys and 623 girls.

What Tweens Did in the Past Week	Boys	Girls
Played a game on a video game system	498	243
Read a book for fun	276	324
Gave product advice to parents	186	181
Shopped at a mall	144	262

For *each type of activity*, determine whether there is a difference between boys and girls at the 0.05 level of significance.

12.80 A company is considering an organizational change involving the use of self-managed work teams. To assess the attitudes of employees of the company toward this change, a sample of 400 employees is selected and asked whether they favor the institution of self-managed work teams in the organization. Three responses are permitted: favor, neutral, or oppose. The results of the survey, cross-classified by type of job and attitude toward self-managed work teams, are summarized as follows:

	SELF-MANAGED WORK TEAMS			
TYPE OF JOB	**Favor**	**Neutral**	**Oppose**	**Total**
Hourly worker	108	46	71	225
Supervisor	18	12	30	60
Middle management	35	14	26	75
Upper management	24	7	9	40
Total	185	79	136	400

a. At the 0.05 level of significance, is there evidence of a relationship between attitude toward self-managed work teams and type of job?

The survey also asked respondents about their attitudes toward instituting a policy whereby an employee could take one additional vacation day per month without pay. The results, cross-classified by type of job, are as follows:

	VACATION TIME WITHOUT PAY			
TYPE OF JOB	**Favor**	**Neutral**	**Oppose**	**Total**
Hourly worker	135	23	67	225
Supervisor	39	7	14	60
Middle management	47	6	22	75
Upper management	26	6	8	40
Total	247	42	111	400

b. At the 0.05 level of significance, is there evidence of a relationship between attitude toward vacation time without pay and type of job?

12.81 A company that produces and markets continuing education programs on DVDs for the educational testing industry has traditionally mailed advertising to prospective customers. A market research study was undertaken to compare two approaches: mailing a sample DVD upon request that contained highlights of the full DVD and sending an e-mail containing a link to a website from which sample material could be downloaded. Of those who responded to either the mailing or the e-mail, the results were as follows in terms of purchase of the complete DVD:

	TYPE OF MEDIA USED		
PURCHASED	**Mailing**	**E-mail**	**Total**
Yes	26	11	37
No	227	247	474
Total	253	258	511

a. At the 0.05 level of significance, is there evidence of a difference in the proportion of DVDs purchased on the basis of the type of media used?

b. On the basis of the results of (a), which type of media should the company use in the future? Explain the rationale for your decision.

The company also wanted to determine which of three sales approaches should be used to generate sales among those who either requested the sample DVD by mail or downloaded the sample DVD but did not purchase the full DVD: (1) targeted e-mail, (2) a DVD that contained additional features, or (3) a telephone call to prospective customers. The 474 respondents who did not initially purchase the full DVD were randomly assigned to each of the three sales approaches. The results, in terms of purchases of the full-program DVD, are as follows:

	SALES APPROACH			
ACTION	Targeted E-mail	More Complete DVD	Telephone Call	Total
Purchase	5	17	18	40
Don't purchase	153	141	140	434
Total	158	158	158	474

c. At the 0.05 level of significance, is there evidence of a difference in the proportion of DVDs purchased on the basis of the sales strategy used?

d. On the basis of the results of (c), which sales approach do you think the company should use in the future? Explain the rationale for your decision.

12.82 A market researcher investigated consumer preferences for Coca-Cola and Pepsi before a taste test and after a taste test. The following table summarizes the results from a sample of 200 consumers:

	PREFERENCE AFTER TASTE TEST		
PREFERENCE BEFORE TASTE TEST	Coca-Cola	Pepsi	Total
Coca-Cola	104	6	110
Pepsi	14	76	90
Total	118	82	200

a. Is there evidence of a difference in the proportion of respondents who prefer Coca-Cola before and after the taste tests? (Use $\alpha = 0.10$.)

b. Compute the p-value and interpret its meaning.

c. Show how the following table was derived from the table above:

	SOFT DRINK		
PREFERENCE	Coca-Cola	Pepsi	Total
Before taste test	110	90	200
After taste test	118	82	200
Total	228	172	400

d. Using the second table, is there evidence of a difference in preference for Coca-Cola before and after the taste test? (Use $\alpha = 0.05$.)

e. Determine the p-value and interpret its meaning.

f. Explain the difference in the results of (a) and (d). Which method of analyzing the data should you use? Why?

12.83 A market researcher was interested in studying the effect of advertisements on brand preference of people purchasing a new personal computer. Prospective purchasers of new computers were first asked whether they preferred Apple or Dell and then watched video advertisements of comparable models of the two brands. After viewing the ads, the prospective customers again indicated their preferences. The results are summarized in the following table:

	PREFERENCE AFTER ADS		
PREFERENCE BEFORE ADS	Apple	Dell	Total
Apple	97	3	100
Dell	11	89	100
Total	108	92	200

a. Is there evidence of a difference in the proportion of respondents who prefer Apple before and after viewing the ads? (Use $\alpha = 0.05$.)

b. Compute the p-value and interpret its meaning.

c. Show how the following table was derived from the table above:

	MANUFACTURER		
PREFERENCE	Apple	Dell	Total
Before ad	100	100	200
After ad	108	92	200
Total	208	192	400

d. Using the second table, is there evidence of a difference in preference for Apple before and after viewing the ads? (Use $\alpha = 0.05$.)

e. Determine the p-value and interpret its meaning.

f. Explain the difference in the results of (a) and (d). Which method of analyzing the data should you use? Why?

TEAM PROJECT

The file **Bond Funds** contains information regarding eight variables from a sample of 184 bond mutual funds:

Type—Type of bonds comprising the bond mutual fund (intermediate government or short-term corporate)
Assets—In millions of dollars
Fees—Sales charges (no or yes)
Expense ratio—Ratio of expenses to net assets in percentage
Return 2009—Twelve-month return in 2009
Three-year return—Annualized return, 2007–2009
Five-year return—Annualized return, 2005–2009
Risk—Risk-of-loss factor of the bond mutual fund (below average, average, or above average)

12.84 **a.** Construct a 2×2 contingency table, using fees as the row variable and type as the column variable.
b. At the 0.05 level of significance, is there evidence of a significant relationship between the type of bond mutual fund and whether there is a fee?

12.85 **a.** Construct a 2×3 contingency table, using fees as the row variable and risk as the column variable.
b. At the 0.05 level of significance, is there evidence of a significant relationship between the perceived risk of a bond mutual fund and whether there is a fee?

12.86 **a.** Construct a 3×2 contingency table, using risk as the row variable and category as the column variable.
b. At the 0.05 level of significance, is there evidence of a significant relationship between the category of a bond mutual fund and its perceived risk?

STUDENT SURVEY DATABASE

12.87 Problem 1.27 on page 14 describes a survey of 62 undergraduate students (stored in **UndergradSurvey**). For these data, construct contingency tables, using gender, major, plans to go to graduate school, and employment status. (You need to construct six tables, taking two variables at a time.) Analyze the data at the 0.05 level of significance to determine whether any significant relationships exist among these variables.

12.88 Problem 1.27 on page 14 describes a survey of 62 undergraduate students (stored in **UndergradSurvey**).
a. Select a sample of undergraduate students at your school and conduct a similar survey for those students.
b. For the data collected in (a), repeat Problem 12.87.
c. Compare the results of (b) to those of Problem 12.87.

12.89 Problem 1.28 on page 15 describes a survey of 44 MBA students (see the file **GradSurvey**). For these data, construct contingency tables, using gender, undergraduate major, graduate major, and employment status. (You need to construct six tables, taking two variables at a time.) Analyze the data at the 0.05 level of significance to determine whether any significant relationships exist among these variables.

12.90 Problem 1.28 on page 15 describes a survey of 44 MBA students (stored in **GradSurvey**).
a. Select a sample of graduate students in your MBA program and conduct a similar survey for those students.
b. For the data collected in (a), repeat Problem 12.89.
c. Compare the results of (b) to those of Problem 12.89.

MANAGING ASHLAND MULTICOMM SERVICES

Phase 1

Reviewing the results of its research, the marketing department team concluded that a segment of Ashland households might be interested in a discounted trial subscription to the AMS *3-For-All* cable/phone/Internet service. The team decided to test various discounts before determining the type of discount to offer during the trial period. It decided to conduct an experiment using three types of discounts plus a plan that offered no discount during the trial period:

1. No discount for the *3-For-All* cable/phone/Internet service. Subscribers would pay \$24.99 per week for the *3-For-All* cable/phone/Internet service during the 90-day trial period.
2. Moderate discount for the *3-For-All* cable/phone/Internet service. Subscribers would pay \$19.99 per week for the *3-For-All* cable/phone/Internet service during the 90-day trial period.
3. Substantial discount for the *3-For-All* cable/phone/Internet service. Subscribers would pay \$14.99 per week for the *3-For-All* cable/phone/Internet service during the 90-day trial period.
4. Discount restaurant card. Subscribers would be given a card providing a discount of 15% at selected restaurants in Ashland during the trial period.

Each participant in the experiment was randomly assigned to a discount plan. A random sample of 100 subscribers to each plan during the trial period was tracked to determine how many would continue to subscribe to the *3-For-All* service after the trial period. Table AMS12.1 summarizes the results.

TABLE AMS12.1

Number of Subscribers Who Continue Subscriptions After Trial Period with Four Discount Plans

CONTINUE SUBSCRIPTIONS AFTER TRIAL PERIOD	DISCOUNT PLANS				
	No Discount	Moderate Discount	Substantial Discount	Restaurant Card	Total
Yes	24	30	38	51	143
No	76	70	62	49	257
Total	100	100	100	100	400

Exercise

1. Analyze the results of the experiment. Write a report to the team that includes your recommendation for which discount plan to use. Be prepared to discuss the limitations and assumptions of the experiment.

Phase 2

The marketing department team discussed the results of the survey presented in Chapter 8, on pages 317–318. The team realized that the evaluation of individual questions was providing only limited information. In order to further understand the market for the *3-For-All* cable/phone/Internet service, the data were organized in the following contingency tables:

HAS AMS TELEPHONE SERVICE	HAS AMS INTERNET SERVICE		
	Yes	No	Total
Yes	55	28	83
No	207	128	335
Total	262	156	418

TYPE OF SERVICE	DISCOUNT TRIAL		
	Yes	No	Total
Basic	8	156	164
Enhanced	32	222	254
Total	40	378	418

TYPE OF SERVICE	WATCHES PREMIUM OR ON-DEMAND SERVICES				
	Almost Every Day	Several Times a Week	Almost Never	Never	Total
Basic	2	5	127	30	164
Enhanced	12	30	186	26	254
Total	14	35	313	56	418

DISCOUNT	WATCHES PREMIUM OR ON-DEMAND SERVICES				
	Almost Every Day	Several Times a Week	Almost Never	Never	Total
Yes	4	5	27	4	40
No	10	30	286	52	378
Total	14	35	313	56	418

DISCOUNT	METHOD FOR CURRENT SUBSCRIPTION					
	Toll-Free Phone	AMS Website	Direct Mail Reply Card	Good Tunes & More	Other	Total
Yes	11	21	5	1	2	40
No	219	85	41	9	24	378
Total	230	106	46	10	26	418

GOLD CARD	METHOD FOR CURRENT SUBSCRIPTION					
	Toll-Free Phone	AMS Website	Direct Mail Reply Card	Good Tunes & More	Other	Total
Yes	10	20	5	1	2	38
No	220	86	41	9	24	380
Total	230	106	46	10	26	418

Exercise

2. Analyze the results of the contingency tables. Write a report for the marketing department team and discuss the marketing implications of the results for Ashland Multi-Comm Services.

DIGITAL CASE

Apply your knowledge of testing for the difference between two proportions in this Digital Case, which extends the T.C. Resort Properties Using Statistics scenario of this chapter.

As T.C. Resort Properties seeks to improve its customer service, the company faces new competition from SunLow Resorts. SunLow has recently opened resort hotels on the islands where T.C. Resort Properties has its five hotels. SunLow is currently advertising that a random survey of 300 customers revealed that about 60% of the customers preferred its "Concierge Class" travel reward program over the T.C. Resorts "TCRewards Plus" program.

Open and review **ConciergeClass.pdf**, an electronic brochure that describes the Concierge Class program and compares it to the T.C. Resorts program. Then answer the following questions:

1. Are the claims made by SunLow valid?

2. What analyses of the survey data would lead to a more favorable impression about T.C. Resort Properties?

3. Perform one of the analyses identified in your answer to step 2.

4. Review the data about the T.C. Resorts properties customers presented in this chapter. Are there any other questions that you might include in a future survey of travel reward programs? Explain.

REFERENCES

1. Conover, W. J., *Practical Nonparametric Statistics*, 3rd ed. (New York: Wiley, 2000).
2. Daniel, W. W., *Applied Nonparametric Statistics*, 2nd ed. (Boston: PWS Kent, 1990).
3. Dixon, W. J., and F. J. Massey, Jr., *Introduction to Statistical Analysis*, 4th ed. (New York: McGraw-Hill, 1983).
4. Hollander, M., and D. A. Wolfe, *Nonparametric Statistical Methods*, 2nd ed. (New York: Wiley, 1999).
5. Lewontin, R. C., and J. Felsenstein, "Robustness of Homogeneity Tests in 2 $\times$ *n* Tables," *Biometrics* 21 (March 1965): 19–33.
6. Marascuilo, L. A., "Large-Sample Multiple Comparisons," *Psychological Bulletin* 65 (1966): 280–290.
7. Marascuilo, L. A., and M. McSweeney, *Nonparametric and Distribution-Free Methods for the Social Sciences* (Monterey, CA: Brooks/Cole, 1977).
8. *Microsoft Excel 2010* (Redmond, WA: Microsoft Corp., 2010).
9. *Minitab Release16* (State College, PA: Minitab, Inc., 2010).
10. Winer, B. J., D. R. Brown, and K. M. Michels, *Statistical Principles in Experimental Design*, 3rd ed. (New York: McGraw-Hill, 1989).

CHAPTER 12 EXCEL GUIDE

EG12.1 CHI-SQUARE TEST for the DIFFERENCE BETWEEN TWO PROPORTIONS

PHStat2 Use **Chi-Square Test for Differences in Two Proportions** to perform this chi-square test. For example, to perform the Figure 12.3 test for the two-hotel guest satisfaction data on page 472, select **PHStat → Two-Sample Tests (Summarized Data) → Chi-Square Test for Differences in Two Proportions**. In the procedure's dialog box, enter **0.05** as the **Level of Significance**, enter a **Title**, and click **OK**. In the new worksheet:

1. Read the yellow note about entering values and then press the **Delete** key to delete the note.
2. Enter **Hotel** in cell **B4** and **Choose Again?** in cell **A5**.
3. Enter **Beachcomber** in cell **B5** and **Windsurfer** in cell **C5**.
4. Enter **Yes** in cell **A6** and **No** in cell **A7**.
5. Enter **163**, **64**, **154**, and **108** in cells **B6**, **B7**, **C6**, and **C7**, respectively.

In-Depth Excel Use the **COMPUTE worksheet** of the **Chi-Square workbook**, shown in Figure 12.3 on page 472, as a template for performing this test. The worksheet contains the Table 12.3 two-hotel guest satisfaction data. Use the **CHIINV** and **CHIDIST** functions to help perform the chi-square test for the difference between two proportions. In cell B24, the worksheet uses **CHIINV(*level of significance, degrees of freedom*)** to compute the critical value for the test and in cell B26 uses **CHIDIST(*chi-square test statistic, degrees of freedom*)** to compute the *p*-value. Open to the **COMPUTE_FORMULAS worksheet** to examine the other formulas used in the worksheet.

For other problems, change the **Observed Frequencies** cell counts and row and column labels in rows 4 through 7.

EG12.2 CHI-SQUARE TEST for DIFFERENCES AMONG MORE THAN TWO PROPORTIONS

PHStat2 Use **Chi-Square Test** to perform the test for differences among more than two proportions. For example, to perform the Figure 12.6 test for the three-hotel guest satisfaction data on page 478, select **PHStat → Multiple-Sample Tests → Chi-Square Test**. In the procedure's dialog box (shown in the right column):

1. Enter **0.05** as the **Level of Significance**.
2. Enter **2** as the **Number of Rows**.
3. Enter **3** as the **Number of Columns**.
4. Enter a **Title** and click **OK**.

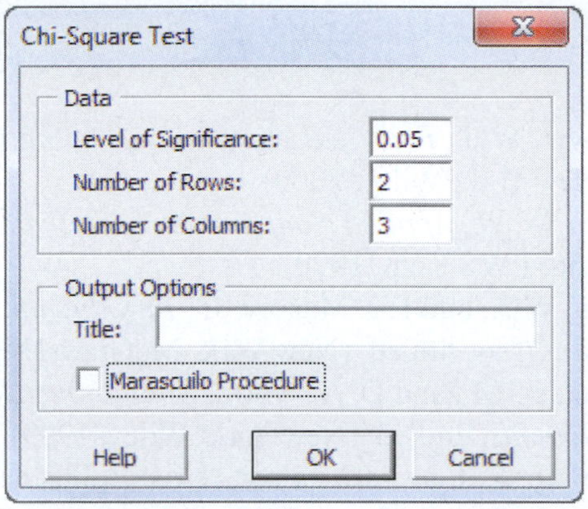

In the new worksheet:

5. Read the yellow note about entering values and then press the **Delete** key to delete the note.
6. Enter the Table 12.6 data on page 476, including row and column labels, in rows 4 through 7.

In-Depth Excel Use the **ChiSquare2x3 worksheet** of the **Chi-Square Worksheets workbook**, shown in Figure 12.6 on page 478, as a model for this chi-square test. The worksheet contains the data for Table 12.6 guest satisfaction data (see page 476). The worksheet uses formulas to compute the expected frequencies and the intermediate results for the chi-square test statistic in much the same way as the COMPUTE worksheet of the Chi-Square workbook discussed in the Section EG12.1 *In-Depth Excel* instructions and shown in Figure 12.3 on page 472. (Open to the **ChiSquare2x3 _FORMULAS worksheet** to examine all the formulas used in the worksheet.)

For other 2 × 3 problems, change the **Observed Frequencies** cell counts and row and column labels in rows 4 through 7. For 2 × 4 problems, use the **ChiSquare2x4 worksheet**. For 2 × 5 problems, use the **ChiSquare2x5 worksheet**. In either case, enter the contingency table data for the problem in the rows 4 through 7 Observed Frequencies area.

The Marascuilo Procedure

PHStat2 Modify the *PHStat2* instructions for the chi-square test to include the Marascuilo procedure to test for the difference among more than two proportions (see page 514). In step 4, enter a **Title**, check **Marascuilo Procedure**, and then click **OK**.

In-Depth Excel Use the Marascuilo worksheet linked to a particular chi-square 2 × *c* worksheet in the **Chi-Square Wooksheets workbook** to perform the Marascuilo procedure.

For example, Figure 12.7 on page 479 shows the **Marascuilo2x3 worksheet**, which is linked to the **ChiSquare2x3 worksheet**. This Marascuilo worksheet uses values from the ChiSquare2x3 worksheet to compute group sample proportions in cells B7 through B9 (shown in Figure 12.7) and to compute the critical range in rows 13, 14, and 16. In column D, the worksheet uses IF functions in the form **IF(*absolute difference > critical range, display "Significant", display "Not significant"*)** to indicate which pairs of groups are significantly different. (Open to the **Marascuilo2x3_ FORMULAS worksheet** to examine all the formulas used in the worksheet.)

EG12.3 CHI-SQUARE TEST of INDEPENDENCE

PHStat2 Use **Chi-Square Test** to perform the chi-square test of independence. For example, to perform the Figure 12.10 test for the survey data concerning three hotels on page 485, select **PHStat → Multiple-Sample Tests → Chi-Square Test**. In the procedure's dialog box (shown below):

1. Enter **0.05** as the **Level of Significance**.
2. Enter **4** as the **Number of Rows**.
3. Enter **3** as the **Number of Columns**.
4. Enter a **Title** and click **OK**.

In the new worksheet:

5. Read the yellow note about entering values and then press the **Delete** key to delete the note.
6. Enter the Table 12.9 data on page 482, including row and column labels, in rows 4 through 9.

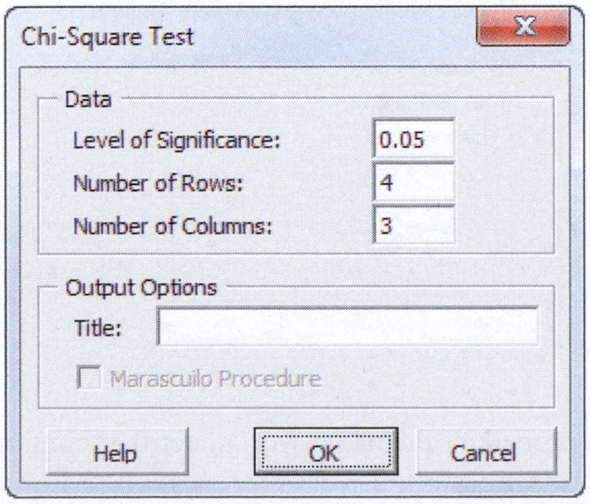

In-Depth Excel Use one of the *r* × *c* worksheets in the **Chi-Square worksheets workbook** to perform the chi-square test of independence. For example, Figure 12.10 on page 485 shows the **ChiSquare4x3 worksheet** that contains the data for Table 12.9 not-returning survey (see page 482). The worksheet computes the expected frequencies and the intermediate results for the chi-square test statistic in much the same way as the COMPUTE worksheet of the Chi-Square workbook discussed in the Section EG12.1 *In-Depth Excel* instructions.

For other 4 × 3 problems, change the **Observed Frequencies** cell counts and row and column labels in rows 4 through 9. For 3 × 4 problems, use the **ChiSquare3x4 worksheet.** For 4 × 3 problems, use the **ChiSquare4x3 worksheet**. For 7 × 3 problems, use the **ChiSquare7x3 worksheet**. For 8 × 3 problems, use the **ChiSquare8x3 worksheet**. In each case, enter the contingency table data for the problem in the Observed Frequencies area.

EG12.4 McNEMAR TEST for the DIFFERENCE BETWEEN TWO PROPORTIONS (RELATED SAMPLES)

PHStat2 Use **McNemar Test** to perform the McNemar test. For example, to perform the Figure 12.12 test for the brand loyalty of cell phone providers (see page 489), select **PHStat → Two-Sample Tests (Summarized Data) → McNemar Test**. In the procedure's dialog box (shown below):

1. Enter **0.05** as the **Level of Significance**.
2. Click **Two-Tail Test**.
3. Enter a **Title** and click **OK**.

In the new worksheet:

4. Read the yellow note about entering values and then press the **Delete** key to delete the note.
5. Enter the Table 12.13 data (see page 488), including row and column labels, in rows 4 through 7.

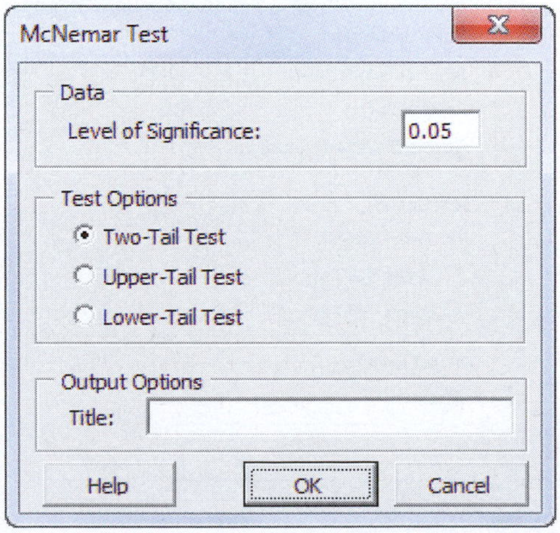

In-Depth Excel Use the **COMPUTE worksheet** of the **McNemar workbook**, shown in Figure 12.12 on page 489, as a template for performing the McNemar test. The worksheet contains the data of Table 12.13 concerning brand loyalty for cell phone providers (see page 488). In cells B20 and B19, respectively, the worksheet uses the expressions **NORMSINV((1 − *level of significance*) / 2)** and **NORMSINV(*level of significance* / 2)** to compute the upper and lower critical values. In cell B21, the expression **2 * (1 − NORMSDIST(*absolute value of the Z test statistic*))** computes the p-value.

To perform the McNemar two-tail test for other problems, change the row 4 through 7 entries in the **Observed Frequencies** area and enter the level of significance for the test in cell B11. For one-tail tests, change the Observed Frequencies area and level of significance in the **COMPUTE_ALL worksheet** in the **McNemar workbook**. (Open to the **COMPUTE_ALL_FORMULAS worksheet** to examine the formulas used in the worksheet.)

EG12.5 CHI-SQUARE TEST for the VARIANCE or STANDARD DEVIATION

PHStat2 Use **Chi-Square Test for the Variance** to perform this chi-square test. For example, to perform the test for the Section 12.5 cereal-filling process example, select **PHStat → One-Sample Tests → Chi-Square Test for the Variance**. In the procedure's dialog box (shown below):

1. Enter **225** as the **Null Hypothesis.**
2. Enter **0.05** as the **Level of Significance**.
3. Enter **25** as the **Sample Size.**
4. Enter **17.7** as the **Sample Standard Deviation**.
5. Select **Two-Tail Test**.
6. Enter a **Title** and click **OK**.

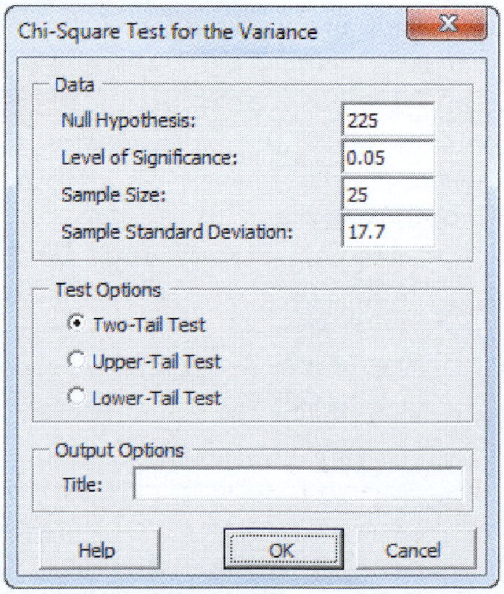

The procedure creates a worksheet similar to Figure 12.14 on page 492.

In-Depth Excel Use the **COMPUTE worksheet** of the **Chi-Square Variance workbook**, shown in Figure 12.14 on page 492, as a template for performing the chi-square test. The worksheet contains the data for the cereal-filling process example. In cells B15 and B16, respectively, the worksheet uses the expressions **CHIINV(1 − *half area, degrees of freedom*)** and enter **CHIINV(*half area, degrees of freedom*)** to compute the lower and upper critical values. In B17, the expression **CHIDIST(χ^2 *test statistic, degrees of freedom*)** helps to compute the p-value.

To perform the test for other problems, change the null hypothesis, level of significance, sample size, and sample standard deviation in the cell range B4:B7. (Open to the **COMPUTE_ FORMULAS worksheet** to examine the details of all formulas used in the COMPUTE worksheet.)

EG12.6 WILCOXON RANK SUM TEST: NONPARAMETRIC ANALYSIS for TWO INDEPENDENT POPULATIONS

PHStat2 Use **Wilcoxon Rank Sum Test** to perform the Wilcoxon rank sum test. For example, to perform the Figure 12.16 test for the BLK Cola sales data on page 498, open to the **DATA worksheet** of the **Cola workbook**. Select **PHStat → Two-Sample Tests (Unsummarized Data) → Wilcoxon Rank Sum Test**. In the procedure's dialog box (shown below):

1. Enter **0.05** as the **Level of Significance**.
2. Enter **A1:A11** as the **Population 1 Sample Cell Range**.
3. Enter **B1:B11** as the **Population 2 Sample Cell Range**.
4. Check **First cells in both ranges contain label**.
5. Click **Two-Tail Test**.
6. Enter a **Title** and click **OK**.

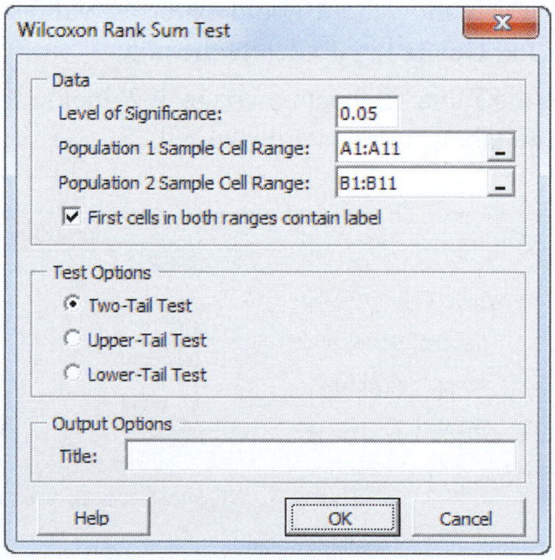

The procedure creates a worksheet that contains sorted ranks in addition to the worksheet shown in Figure 12.16. Both of these worksheets are discussed in the following *In-Depth Excel* instructions.

In-Depth Excel Use the **COMPUTE worksheet** of the **Wilcoxon workbook**, shown in Figure 12.16 on page 498, as a template for performing the two-tail Wilcoxon rank sum test. The worksheet contains data and formulas to use the unsummarized data for the BLK Cola sales example. In cells B22 and B21, respectively, the worksheet uses **NORMSINV((1 − *level of significance*) / 2)** and **NORMSINV(*level of significance* / 2)** to compute the upper and lower critical values. In cell B23, **2 * (1 − NORMSDIST(*absolute value of the Z test statistic*))** computes the *p*-value.

For other problems, use the COMPUTE worksheet with either unsummarized or summarized data. For summarized data, overwrite the formulas that compute the **Sample Size** and **Sum of Ranks** in cells B7, B8, B10, and B11, with the values for these statistics.

For unsummarized data, first open to the **SortedRanks worksheet** and enter the sorted values for both groups in stacked format. Use column A for the sample names and column B for the sorted values. Assign a rank for each value and enter the ranks in column C of the same worksheet. Then open to the COMPUTE worksheet (or the similar COMPUTE_ALL worksheet, if performing a one-tail test) and edit the formulas in cells B7, B8, B10, and B11. Enter **COUNTIF(*cell range for all sample names, sample name to be matched*)** functions to compute the sample size for a sample. Enter **SUMIF(*cell range for all sample names, sample name to be matched, cell range in which to select cells for summing*)** functions to compute the sum of ranks for a sample. For example, in the current COMPUTE worksheet, the formula **=COUNTIF(SortedRanks!A2:A21, "Normal")** in cell B7 counts the number of occurrences of the sample name **"Normal"** in column A to compute the sample size of the **Population 1 Sample**. The formula **=SUMIF(SortedRanks!A2:A21, "Normal", C2:C21)** in cell B8 computes the sum of ranks for the **Population 1 Sample** by summing the column C ranks for rows in which the column A value is **Normal**.

EG12.7 KRUSKAL-WALLIS RANK TEST: NONPARAMETRIC ANALYSIS for the ONE-WAY ANOVA

PHStat2 Use **Kruskal-Wallis Rank Test** to perform the Kruskal-Wallis rank test. For example, to perform the Figure 12.18 Kruskal-Wallis rank test for differences among the four median tensile strengths of parachutes on page 503, open to the **DATA worksheet** of the **Parachute workbook**. Select **PHStat ➔ Multiple-Sample Tests ➔ Kruskal-Wallis Rank Test**. In the procedure's dialog box (shown in the right column):

1. Enter **0.05** as the **Level of Significance**.
2. Enter **A1:D6** as the **Sample Data Cell Range**.
3. Check **First cells contain label**.
4. Enter a **Title** and click **OK**.

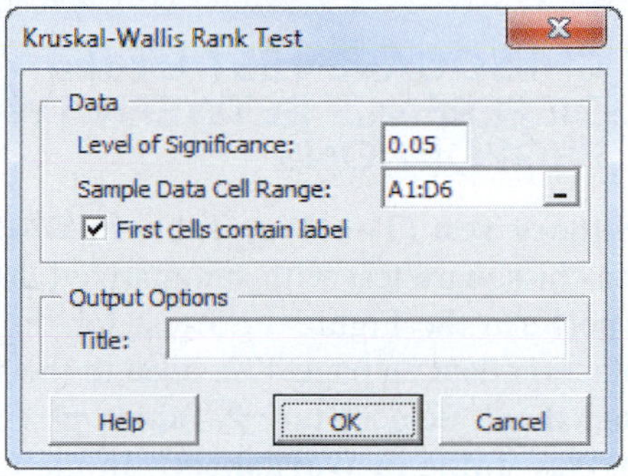

The procedure creates a worksheet that contains sorted ranks in addition to the worksheet shown in Figure 12.18 on page 503. Both of these worksheets are discussed in the following *In-Depth Excel* instructions.

In-Depth Excel Use the **KruskalWallis4 worksheet** of the **Kruskal-Wallis Worksheets workbook**, shown in Figure 12.18 on page 503, as a model for performing the Kruskal-Wallis rank test. The worksheet contains the data and formulas to use the unsummarized data for the Section 12.7 four-supplier parachute example. In cell B13, the worksheet uses **CHIINV(*level of significance, number of groups* - 1)** to compute the critical value and, in cell B14, **CHIDIST(*H test statistic, number of groups* - 1)** computes the *p*-value.

For other problems with four groups, use the KruskalWallis4 worksheet with either unsummarized or summarized data. For summarized data, overwrite the formulas that display the group names and compute the **Sample Size** and **Sum of Ranks** in columns D, E, and F with the values for these statistics.

For unsummarized data, first open to the **SortedRanks worksheet** and enter the sorted values for both groups in stacked format. Use column A for the sample names and column B for the sorted values. Assign ranks for each value and enter the ranks in column C of the same worksheet. Also paste your unsummarized stacked data in columns, starting with Column E. (The row 1 cells, starting with cell E1, are used to identify each group.) Then open to the KruskalWallis4 worksheet (or the similar **KruskalWallis3 worksheet**, if using three groups) and edit the formulas in columns E and F. Enter **COUNTIF(*cell range for all group names, group name to be matched*)** functions to compute the sample size for a group. Enter **SUMIF(*cell range for all group names, group name to be matched, cell range in which to select cells for summing*)** functions to compute the sum of ranks for a group. (Open to the **Kruskal Wallis4_FORMULAS worksheet** to examine all current formulas.)

CHAPTER 12 MINITAB GUIDE

MG12.1 CHI-SQUARE TEST for the DIFFERENCE BETWEEN TWO PROPORTIONS

Use **Chi-Square Test (Two-Way Table in Worksheet)** to perform the chi-square test with summarized data. For example, to perform the Figure 12.3 test for the two-hotel guest satisfaction data on page 472, open to the **Two-Hotel Survey worksheet**. Select **Stat ➔ Tables ➔ Chi-Square Test (Two-Way Table in Worksheet)**. In the Chi-Square Test (Table in Worksheet) dialog box (shown below):

1. Double-click **C2 Beachcomber** in the variables list to add **Beachcomber** to the **Columns containing the table** box.
2. Double-click **C3 Windsurfer** in the variables list to add **Windsurfer** to the **Columns containing the table** box.
3. Click **OK**.

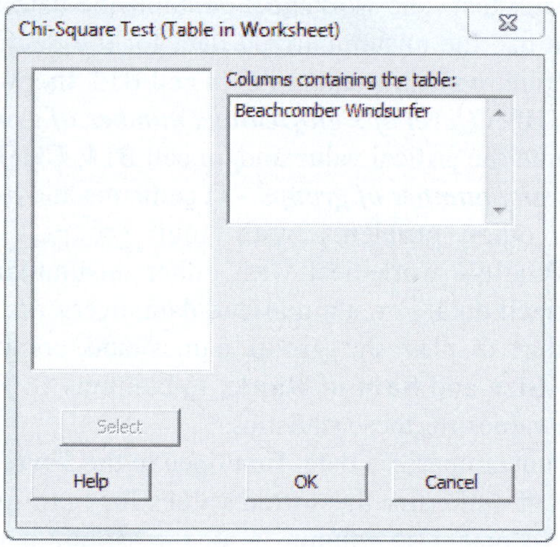

Minitab can also perform a chi-square test for the difference between two proportions using unsummarized data. Use the Section MG2.2 instructions for using **Cross Tabulation and Chi-Square** to create contingency tables (see page 87), replacing step 4 with these steps 4 though 7:

4. Click **Chi-Square**.

In the Cross Tabulation - Chi-Square dialog box:

5. Select **Chi-Square analysis**, **Expected cell counts**, and **Each cell's contribution to the Chi-Square statistic**.
6. Click **OK**.
7. Back in the original dialog box, click **OK**.

MG12.2 CHI-SQUARE TEST for DIFFERENCES AMONG MORE THAN TWO PROPORTIONS

Use **Chi-Square Test (Two-Way Table in Worksheet)** to perform the chi-square test with summarized data. Use modified Section MG2.2 instructions on the page 87 for using **Cross Tabulation and Chi-Square** to perform the chi-square test with unsummarized data. See Section MG12.1 for detailed instructions.

To perform the Figure 12.6 test for the guest satisfaction data concerning three hotels on page 478, open to the **Three-Hotel Survey worksheet**, select **Stat ➔ Tables ➔ Chi-Square Test (Two-Way Table in Worksheet)**, and add the names of columns 2 through 4 to the **Columns containing the table** box.

The Marascuilo Procedure

There are no Minitab Guide instructions for this section.

MG12.3 CHI-SQUARE TEST of INDEPENDENCE

Again, as in Section MG12.2, use either **Chi-Square Test (Two-Way Table in Worksheet)** for summarized data or the modified instructions for using **Cross Tabulation and Chi-Square** for unsummarized data to perform this test.

MG12.4 MCNEMAR TEST for the DIFFERENCE BETWEEN TWO PROPORTIONS (RELATED SAMPLES)

There are no Minitab Guide instructions for this section.

MG12.5 CHI-SQUARE TEST for the VARIANCE or STANDARD DEVIATION

There are no Minitab Guide instructions for this section.

MG12.6 WILCOXON RANK SUM TEST: NONPARAMETRIC ANALYSIS for TWO INDEPENDENT POPULATIONS

Use **Mann-Whitney** to perform a test numerically equivalent to the Wilcoxon rank sum test. For example, to perform the Figure 12.16 test for the BLK Cola sales data on page 498, open to the **Cola worksheet**. Select **Stat ➔ Nonparametrics ➔ Mann-Whitney**. In the Mann-Whitney dialog box (shown below):

1. Double-click **C1 Normal** in the variables list to add **Normal** in the **First Sample** box.
2. Double-click **C2 End-Aisle** in the variables list to add **'EndAisle'** in the **Second Sample** box.
3. Enter **95.0** in the **Confidence level** box.
4. Select **not equal** in the **Alternative** drop-down list.
5. Click **OK**.

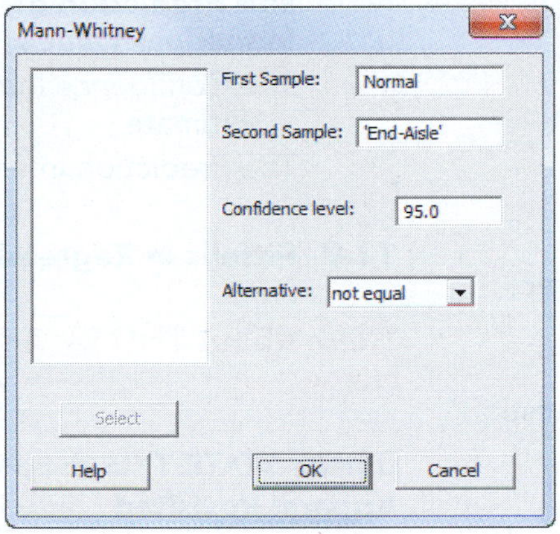

MG12.7 KRUSKAL-WALLIS RANK TEST: NONPARAMETRIC ANALYSIS for the ONE-WAY ANOVA

Use **Kruskal-Wallis** to perform the Kruskal-Wallis rank test. For example, to perform the Figure 12.18 Kruskal-Wallis rank test for differences among the four median tensile strengths of parachutes on page 503, open to the **ParachuteStacked worksheet**. Select **Stat ➔ Nonparametrics ➔ Kruskal-Wallis**. In the Kruskal-Wallis dialog box (shown below):

1. Double-click **C2 Strength** in the variables list to add **Strength** in the **Response** box.
2. Double-click **C1 Supplier** in the variables list to add **Supplier** in the **Factor** box.
3. Click **OK**.

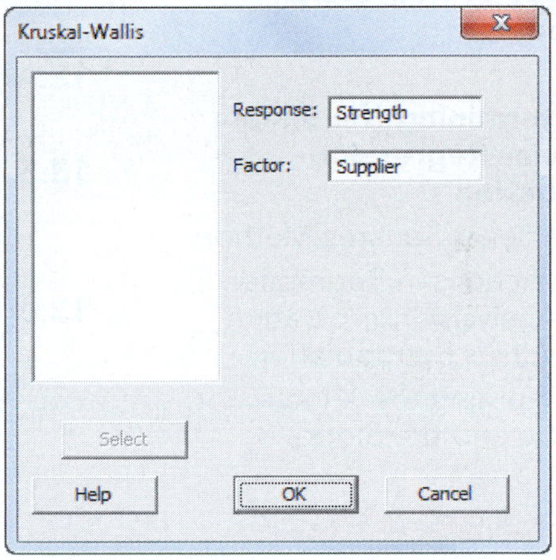

13 Simple Linear Regression

Learning Objectives

In this chapter, you learn:

- How to use regression analysis to predict the value of a dependent variable based on an independent variable
- The meaning of the regression coefficients b_0 and b_1
- How to evaluate the assumptions of regression analysis and know what to do if the assumptions are violated
- How to make inferences about the slope and correlation coefficient
- How to estimate mean values and predict individual values

USING STATISTICS

@ Sunflowers Apparel

The sales for Sunflowers Apparel, a chain of upscale clothing stores for women, have increased during the past 12 years as the chain has expanded the number of stores. Until now, Sunflowers managers selected sites based on subjective factors, such as the availability of a good lease or the perception that a location seemed ideal for an apparel store. As the new director of planning, you need to develop a systematic approach that will lead to making better decisions during the site-selection process. As a starting point, you believe that the size of the store significantly contributes to store sales, and you want to use this relationship in the decision-making process. How can you use statistics so that you can forecast the annual sales of a proposed store based on the size of that store?

In this chapter and the next two chapters, you learn how **regression analysis** enables you to develop a model to predict the values of a numerical variable, based on the value of other variables.

In regression analysis, the variable you wish to predict is called the **dependent variable**. The variables used to make the prediction are called **independent variables**. In addition to predicting values of the dependent variable, regression analysis also allows you to identify the type of mathematical relationship that exists between a dependent variable and an independent variable, to quantify the effect that changes in the independent variable have on the dependent variable, and to identify unusual observations. For example, as the director of planning, you might want to predict sales for a Sunflowers store based on the size of the store. Other examples include predicting the monthly rent of an apartment based on its size and predicting the monthly sales of a product in a supermarket based on the amount of shelf space devoted to the product.

This chapter discusses **simple linear regression**, in which a *single* numerical independent variable, X, is used to predict the numerical dependent variable Y, such as using the size of a store to predict the annual sales of the store. Chapters 14 and 15 discuss *multiple regression models*, which use *several* independent variables to predict a numerical dependent variable, Y. For example, you could use the amount of advertising expenditures, price, and the amount of shelf space devoted to a product to predict its monthly sales.

13.1 Types of Regression Models

In Section 2.6, you used a **scatter plot** (also known as a **scatter diagram**) to examine the relationship between an X variable on the horizontal axis and a Y variable on the vertical axis. The nature of the relationship between two variables can take many forms, ranging from simple to extremely complicated mathematical functions. The simplest relationship consists of a straight-line relationship, or **linear relationship**. Figure 13.1 illustrates a straight-line relationship.

FIGURE 13.1
A straight-line relationship

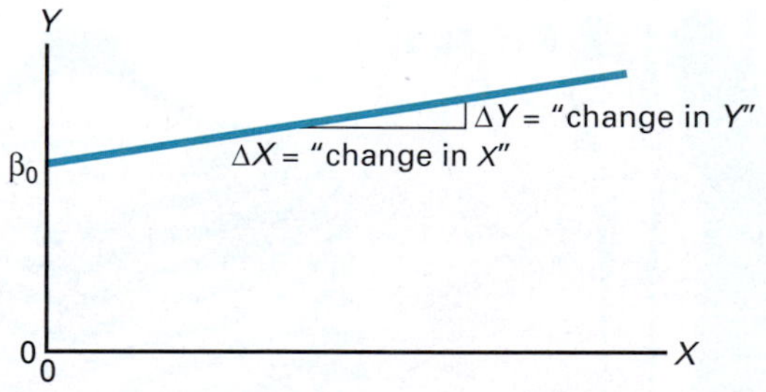

Equation (13.1) represents the straight-line (linear) model.

SIMPLE LINEAR REGRESSION MODEL

$$Y_i = \beta_0 + \beta_1 X_i + \varepsilon_i \qquad \textbf{(13.1)}$$

where

β_0 = Y intercept for the population
β_1 = slope for the population
ε_i = random error in Y for observation i
Y_i = dependent variable (sometimes referred to as the **response variable**) for observation i
X_i = independent variable (sometimes referred to as the predictor, or **explanatory variable**) for observation i

The $Y_i = \beta_0 + \beta_1 X_i$ portion of the simple linear regression model expressed in Equation (13.1) is a straight line. The **slope** of the line, β_1, represents the expected change in Y per unit change in X. It represents the mean amount that Y changes (either positively or negatively) for a one-unit change in X. The ***Y* intercept**, β_0, represents the mean value of Y when X equals 0. The last component of the model, ε_i, represents the random error in Y for each observation, i. In other words, ε_i is the vertical distance of the actual value of Y_i above or below the expected value of Y_i on the line.

The selection of the proper mathematical model depends on the distribution of the X and Y values on the scatter plot. Figure 13.2 illustrates six different types of relationships.

FIGURE 13.2

Six types of relationships found in scatter plots

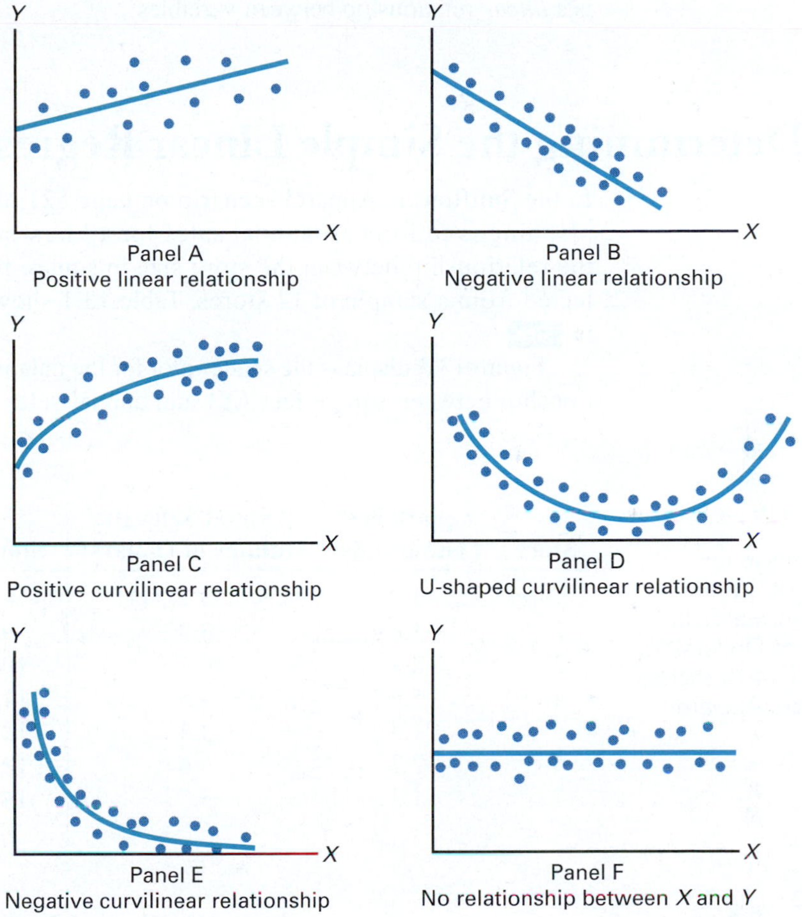

In Panel A, the values of Y are generally increasing linearly as X increases. This panel is similar to Figure 13.3 on page 524, which illustrates the positive relationship between the square footage of the store and the annual sales at branches of the Sunflowers Apparel women's clothing store chain.

Panel B is an example of a negative linear relationship. As X increases, the values of Y are generally decreasing. An example of this type of relationship might be the price of a particular product and the amount of sales.

Panel C shows a positive curvilinear relationship between X and Y. The values of Y increase as X increases, but this increase tapers off beyond certain values of X. An example of a positive curvilinear relationship might be the age and maintenance cost of a machine. As a machine gets older, the maintenance cost may rise rapidly at first but then level off beyond a certain number of years.

Panel D shows a U-shaped relationship between X and Y. As X increases, at first Y generally decreases; but as X continues to increase, Y not only stops decreasing but actually increases above its minimum value. An example of this type of relationship might be the number of errors per hour at a task and the number of hours worked. The number of errors per hour decreases as the individual becomes more proficient at the task, but then it increases beyond a certain point because of factors such as fatigue and boredom.

Panel E illustrates an exponential relationship between X and Y. In this case, Y decreases very rapidly as X first increases, but then it decreases much less rapidly as X increases further. An example of an exponential relationship could be the value of an automobile and its age. The value drops drastically from its original price in the first year, but it decreases much less rapidly in subsequent years.

Finally, Panel F shows a set of data in which there is very little or no relationship between X and Y. High and low values of Y appear at each value of X.

Although scatter plots are useful in visually displaying the mathematical form of a relationship, more sophisticated statistical procedures are available to determine the most appropriate model for a set of variables. The rest of this chapter discusses the model used when there is a *linear* relationship between variables.

13.2 Determining the Simple Linear Regression Equation

In the Sunflowers Apparel scenario on page 521, the business objective of the director of planning is to forecast annual sales for all new stores, based on store size. To examine the relationship between the store size in square feet and its annual sales, data were collected from a sample of 14 stores. Table 13.1 shows the organized data, which are stored in **Site**.

Figure 13.3 displays the scatter plot for the data in Table 13.1. Observe the increasing relationship between square feet (X) and annual sales (Y). As the size of the store increases,

TABLE 13.1

Square Footage (in Thousands of Square Feet) and Annual Sales (in Millions of Dollars) for a Sample of 14 Branches of Sunflowers Apparel

Store	Square Feet (Thousands)	Annual Sales (in Millions of Dollars)	Store	Square Feet (Thousands)	Annual Sales (in Millions of Dollars)
1	1.7	3.7	8	1.1	2.7
2	1.6	3.9	9	3.2	5.5
3	2.8	6.7	10	1.5	2.9
4	5.6	9.5	11	5.2	10.7
5	1.3	3.4	12	4.6	7.6
6	2.2	5.6	13	5.8	11.8
7	1.3	3.7	14	3.0	4.1

FIGURE 13.3

Scatter plot for the Sunflowers Apparel data

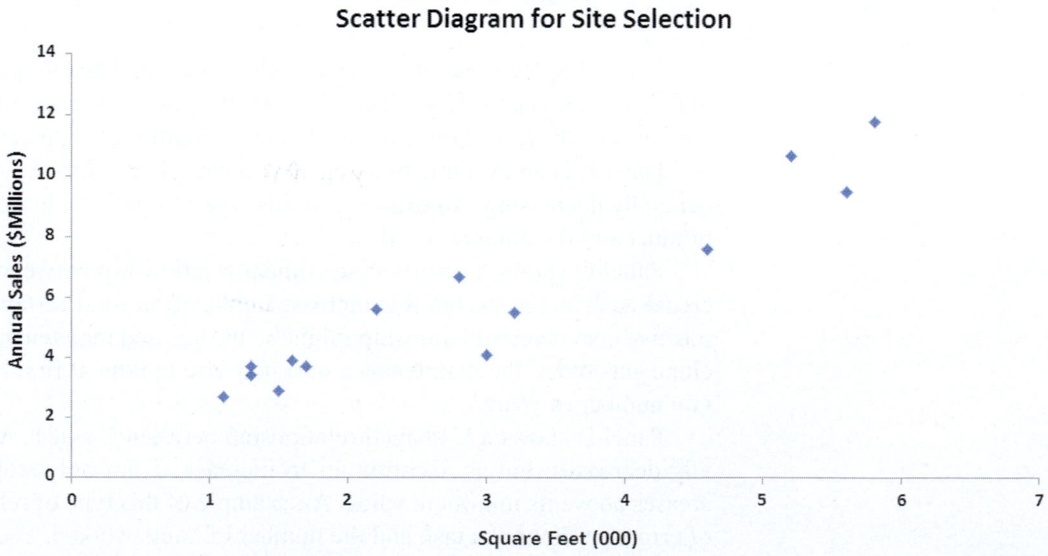

annual sales increase approximately as a straight line. Thus, you can assume that a straight line provides a useful mathematical model of this relationship. Now you need to determine the specific straight line that is the *best* fit to these data.

The Least-Squares Method

In the preceding section, a statistical model is hypothesized to represent the relationship between two variables, square footage and sales, in the entire population of Sunflowers Apparel stores. However, as shown in Table 13.1, the data are collected from a random sample of stores. If certain assumptions are valid (see Section 13.4), you can use the sample Y intercept, b_0, and the sample slope, b_1, as estimates of the respective population parameters, β_0 and β_1. Equation (13.2) uses these estimates to form the **simple linear regression equation**. This straight line is often referred to as the **prediction line**.

SIMPLE LINEAR REGRESSION EQUATION: THE PREDICTION LINE

The predicted value of Y equals the Y intercept plus the slope multiplied by the value of X.

$$\hat{Y}_i = b_0 + b_1X_i \quad \textbf{(13.2)}$$

where

$\hat{Y}_i$ = predicted value of Y for observation i
X_i = value of X for observation i
b_0 = sample Y intercept
b_1 = sample slope

Equation (13.2) requires you to determine two **regression coefficients**—b_0 (the sample Y intercept) and b_1 (the sample slope). The most common approach to finding b_0 and b_1 is using the least-squares method. This method minimizes the sum of the squared differences between the actual values (Y_i) and the predicted values ($\hat{Y}_i$) using the simple linear regression equation [i.e., the prediction line; see Equation (13.2)]. This sum of squared differences is equal to

$$\sum_{i=1}^{n}(Y_i - \hat{Y}_i)^2$$

Because $\hat{Y}_i = b_0 + b_1X_i$,

$$\sum_{i=1}^{n}(Y_i - \hat{Y}_i)^2 = \sum_{i=1}^{n}[Y_i - (b_0 + b_1X_i)]^2$$

Because this equation has two unknowns, b_0 and b_1, the sum of squared differences depends on the sample Y intercept, b_0, and the sample slope, b_1. The **least-squares method** determines the values of b_0 and b_1 that minimize the sum of squared differences around the prediction line. Any values for b_0 and b_1 other than those determined by the least-squares method result in a greater sum of squared differences between the actual values (Y_i) and the predicted values ($\hat{Y}_i$). Figure 13.4[1] presents the simple linear regression model for the Table 13.1 Sunflowers Apparel data.

[1]The equations used to compute these results are shown in Examples 13.3 and 13.4 on pages 528–530 and 535–536. You should use software to do these computations for large data sets, given the complex nature of the computations.

FIGURE 13.4

Excel and Minitab simple linear regression models for the Sunflowers Apparel data

	A	B	C	D	E	F	G	H	I
1	**Simple Linear Regression**								
2									
3	***Regression Statistics***								
4	Multiple R	0.9509							
5	R Square	0.9042							
6	Adjusted R Square	0.8962							
7	Standard Error	0.9664							
8	Observations	14							
9									
10	**ANOVA**								
11		*df*	*SS*	*MS*	*F*	*Significance F*			
12	Regression	1	105.7476	105.7476	113.2335	0.0000			
13	Residual	12	11.2067	0.9339					
14	Total	13	116.9543						
15									
16		*Coefficients*	*Standard Error*	*t Stat*	*P-value*	*Lower 95%*	*Upper 95%*	*Lower 95.0%*	*Upper 95.0%*
17	Intercept	0.9645	0.5262	1.8329	0.0917	-0.1820	2.1110	-0.1820	2.11095
18	Square Feet	1.6699	0.1569	10.6411	0.0000	1.3280	2.0118	1.3280	2.01177

Regression Analysis: Annual Sales versus Square Feet

```
The regression equation is
Annual Sales = 0.964 + 1.67 Square Feet

Predictor       Coef  SE Coef      T      P
Constant      0.9645   0.5262   1.83  0.092
Square Feet   1.6699   0.1569  10.64  0.000

S = 0.966380   R-Sq = 90.4%   R-Sq(adj) = 89.6%

Analysis of Variance
Source          DF      SS      MS       F      P
Regression       1  105.75  105.75  113.23  0.000
Residual Error  12   11.21    0.93
Total           13  116.95

Predicted Values for New Observations
New Obs    Fit  SE Fit        95% CI             95% PI
      1  7.644   0.309  (6.971, 8.317)  (5.433, 9.854)

Values of Predictors for New Observations
          Square
New Obs     Feet
      1     4.00
```

In Figure 13.4, observe that $b_0 = 0.9645$ and $b_1 = 1.6699$. Using Equation (13.2) on page 525, the prediction line for these data is

$$\hat{Y}_i = 0.9645 + 1.6699X_i$$

The slope, b_1, is +1.6699. This means that for each increase of 1 unit in X, the predicted value of Y is estimated to increase by 1.6699 units. In other words, for each increase of 1.0 thousand square feet in the size of the store, the predicted annual sales are estimated to increase by 1.6699 millions of dollars. Thus, the slope represents the portion of the annual sales that are estimated to vary according to the size of the store.

The Y intercept, b_0, is +0.9645. The Y intercept represents the predicted value of Y when X equals 0. Because the square footage of the store cannot be 0, this Y intercept has little or no practical interpretation. Also, the Y intercept for this example is outside the range of the observed values of the X variable, and therefore interpretations of the value of b_0 should be made cautiously. Figure 13.5 displays the actual values and the prediction line. To illustrate a situation in which there is a direct interpretation for the Y intercept, b_0, see Example 13.1.

FIGURE 13.5

Scatter plot and prediction line for Sunflowers Apparel data

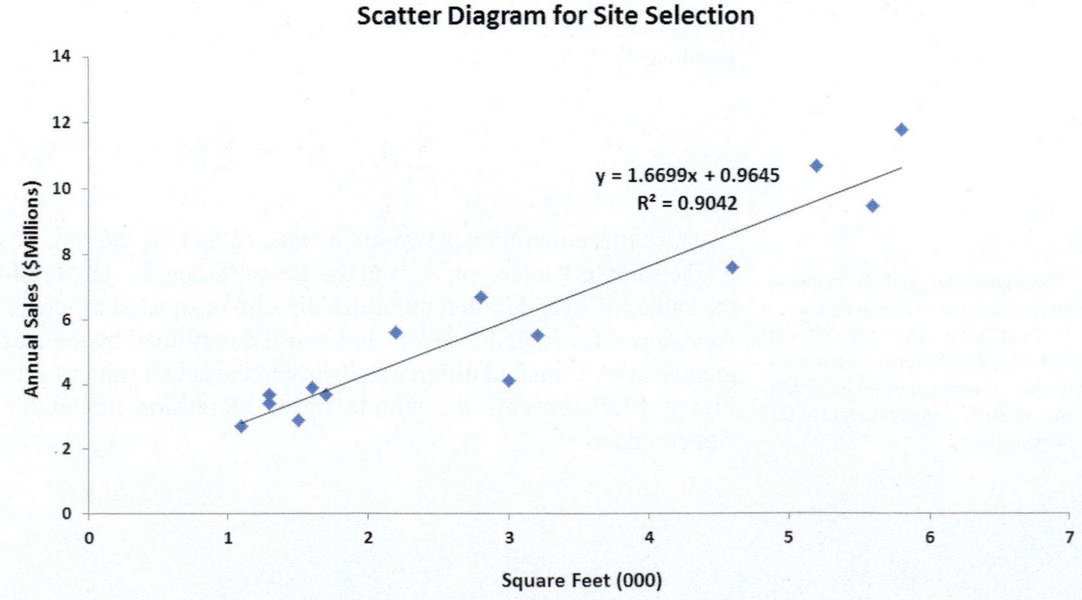

EXAMPLE 13.1

Interpreting the Y Intercept, b_0, and the Slope, b_1

A statistics professor wants to use the number of hours a student studies for a statistics final exam (X) to predict the final exam score (Y). A regression model was fit based on data collected from a class during the previous semester, with the following results:

$$\hat{Y}_i = 35.0 + 3X_i$$

What is the interpretation of the Y intercept, b_0, and the slope, b_1?

SOLUTION The Y intercept $b_0 = 35.0$ indicates that when the student does not study for the final exam, the predicted final exam score is 35.0. The slope $b_1 = 3$ indicates that for each increase of one hour in studying time, the predicted change in the final exam score is +3.0. In other words, the final exam score is predicted to increase by a mean of 3 points for each one-hour increase in studying time.

Return to the Sunflowers Apparel scenario on page 521. Example 13.2 illustrates how you use the prediction line to predict the annual sales.

EXAMPLE 13.2

Predicting Annual Sales Based on Square Footage

Use the prediction line to predict the annual sales for a store with 4,000 square feet.

SOLUTION You can determine the predicted value by substituting $X = 4$ (thousands of square feet) into the simple linear regression equation:

$$\hat{Y}_i = 0.9645 + 1.6699X_i$$

$$\hat{Y}_i = 0.9645 + 1.6699(4) = 7.644 \text{ or } \$7,644,000$$

Thus, a store with 4,000 square feet has predicted annual sales of $7,644,000.

Predictions in Regression Analysis: Interpolation Versus Extrapolation

When using a regression model for prediction purposes, you should consider only the **relevant range** of the independent variable in making predictions. This relevant range includes all values from the smallest to the largest X used in developing the regression model. Hence, when predicting Y for a given value of X, you can interpolate within this relevant range of the X values, but you should not extrapolate beyond the range of X values. When you use the square footage to predict annual sales, the square footage (in thousands of square feet) varies from 1.1 to 5.8 (see Table 13.1 on page 524). Therefore, you should predict annual sales *only* for stores whose size is between 1.1 and 5.8 thousands of square feet. Any prediction of annual sales for stores outside this range assumes that the observed relationship between sales and store size for store sizes from 1.1 to 5.8 thousand square feet is the same as for stores outside this range. For example, you cannot extrapolate the linear relationship beyond 5,800 square feet in Example 13.2. It would be improper to use the prediction line to forecast the sales for a new store containing 8,000 square feet because the relationship between sales and store size may have a point of diminishing returns. If that is true, as square footage increases beyond 5,800 square feet, the effect on sales may become smaller and smaller.

Computing the Y Intercept, b_0, and the Slope, b_1

For small data sets, you can use a hand calculator to compute the least-squares regression coefficients. Equations (13.3) and (13.4) give the values of b_0 and b_1, which minimize

$$\sum_{i=1}^{n}(Y_i - \hat{Y}_i)^2 = \sum_{i=1}^{n}[Y_i - (b_0 + b_1X_i)]^2$$

COMPUTATIONAL FORMULA FOR THE SLOPE, b_1

$$b_1 = \frac{SSXY}{SSX} \tag{13.3}$$

where

$$SSXY = \sum_{i=1}^{n}(X_i - \overline{X})(Y_i - \overline{Y}) = \sum_{i=1}^{n}X_iY_i - \frac{\left(\sum_{i=1}^{n}X_i\right)\left(\sum_{i=1}^{n}Y_i\right)}{n}$$

$$SSX = \sum_{i=1}^{n}(X_i - \overline{X})^2 = \sum_{i=1}^{n}X_i^2 - \frac{\left(\sum_{i=1}^{n}X_i\right)^2}{n}$$

COMPUTATIONAL FORMULA FOR THE Y INTERCEPT, b_0

$$b_0 = \overline{Y} - b_1\overline{X} \tag{13.4}$$

where

$$\overline{Y} = \frac{\sum_{i=1}^{n}Y_i}{n}$$

$$\overline{X} = \frac{\sum_{i=1}^{n}X_i}{n}$$

EXAMPLE 13.3

Computing the Y Intercept, b_0, and the Slope, b_1

Compute the Y intercept, b_0, and the slope, b_1, for the Sunflowers Apparel data.

SOLUTION In Equations (13.3) and (13.4), five quantities need to be computed to determine b_1 and b_0. These are n, the sample size; $\sum_{i=1}^{n}X_i$, the sum of the X values; $\sum_{i=1}^{n}Y_i$, the sum of the Y values; $\sum_{i=1}^{n}X_i^2$, the sum of the squared X values; and $\sum_{i=1}^{n}X_iY_i$, the sum of the product of X and Y. For the Sunflowers Apparel data, the number of square feet (X) is used to predict the annual sales (Y) in a store. Table 13.2 presents the computations of the sums needed for the site selection problem. The table also includes $\sum_{i=1}^{n}Y_i^2$, the sum of the squared Y values that will be used to compute SST in Section 13.3.

TABLE 13.2
Computations for the Sunflowers Apparel Data

Store	Square Feet (X)	Annual Sales (Y)	X^2	Y^2	XY
1	1.7	3.7	2.89	13.69	6.29
2	1.6	3.9	2.56	15.21	6.24
3	2.8	6.7	7.84	44.89	18.76
4	5.6	9.5	31.36	90.25	53.20
5	1.3	3.4	1.69	11.56	4.42
6	2.2	5.6	4.84	31.36	12.32
7	1.3	3.7	1.69	13.69	4.81
8	1.1	2.7	1.21	7.29	2.97
9	3.2	5.5	10.24	30.25	17.60
10	1.5	2.9	2.25	8.41	4.35
11	5.2	10.7	27.04	114.49	55.64
12	4.6	7.6	21.16	57.76	34.96
13	5.8	11.8	33.64	139.24	68.44
14	3.0	4.1	9.00	16.81	12.30
Totals	40.9	81.8	157.41	594.90	302.30

Using Equations (13.3) and (13.4), you can compute b_0 and b_1:

$$SSXY = \sum_{i=1}^{n}(X_i - \overline{X})(Y_i - \overline{Y}) = \sum_{i=1}^{n}X_iY_i - \frac{\left(\sum_{i=1}^{n}X_i\right)\left(\sum_{i=1}^{n}Y_i\right)}{n}$$

$$SSXY = 302.3 - \frac{(40.9)(81.8)}{14}$$

$$= 302.3 - 238.97285$$

$$= 63.32715$$

$$SSX = \sum_{i=1}^{n}(X_i - \overline{X})^2 = \sum_{i=1}^{n}X_i^2 - \frac{\left(\sum_{i=1}^{n}X_i\right)^2}{n}$$

$$= 157.41 - \frac{(40.9)^2}{14}$$

$$= 157.41 - 119.48642$$

$$= 37.92358$$

Therefore,

$$b_1 = \frac{SSXY}{SSX}$$

$$= \frac{63.32715}{37.92358}$$

$$= 1.6699$$

And,

$$\overline{Y} = \frac{\sum_{i=1}^{n}Y_i}{n} = \frac{81.8}{14} = 5.842857$$

$$\overline{X} = \frac{\sum_{i=1}^{n}X_i}{n} = \frac{40.9}{14} = 2.92143$$

Therefore,

$$
\begin{aligned}
b_0 &= \overline{Y} - b_1\overline{X} \\
&= 5.842857 - (1.6699)(2.92143) \\
&= 0.9645
\end{aligned}
$$

VISUAL EXPLORATIONS Exploring Simple Linear Regression Coefficients

Use the Visual Explorations Simple Linear Regression procedure to create a prediction line that is as close as possible to the prediction line defined by the least-squares solution. Open the **Visual Explorations** add-in workbook (see Appendix Section D.4) and select **Add-ins ➔ VisualExplorations ➔ Simple Linear Regression**.

In the Simple Linear Regression dialog box (shown below):

1. Click for the spinner buttons for **b1 slope** (the slope of the prediction line), and **b0 intercept** (the Y intercept of the prediction line) to change the prediction line.
2. Using the visual feedback of the chart, try to create a prediction line that is as close as possible to the prediction line defined by the least-squares estimates. In other words, try to make the **Difference from Target SSE** value as small as possible. (See page 533 for an explanation of SSE.)

At any time, click **Reset** to reset the b_1 and b_0 values or **Solution** to reveal the prediction line defined by the least-squares method. Click **Finish** when you are finished with this exercise.

Using Your Own Regression Data

Select **Simple Linear Regression with your worksheet data** from the **VisualExplorations** menu to explore the simple linear regression coefficients using data you supply from a worksheet. In the procedure's dialog box, enter the cell range of your Y variable as the **Y Variable Cell Range** and the cell range of your X variable as the **X Variable Cell Range**. Click **First cells in both ranges contain a label**, enter a **Title**, and click **OK**. After the scatter plot appears onscreen, continue with the step 1 and step 2 instructions.

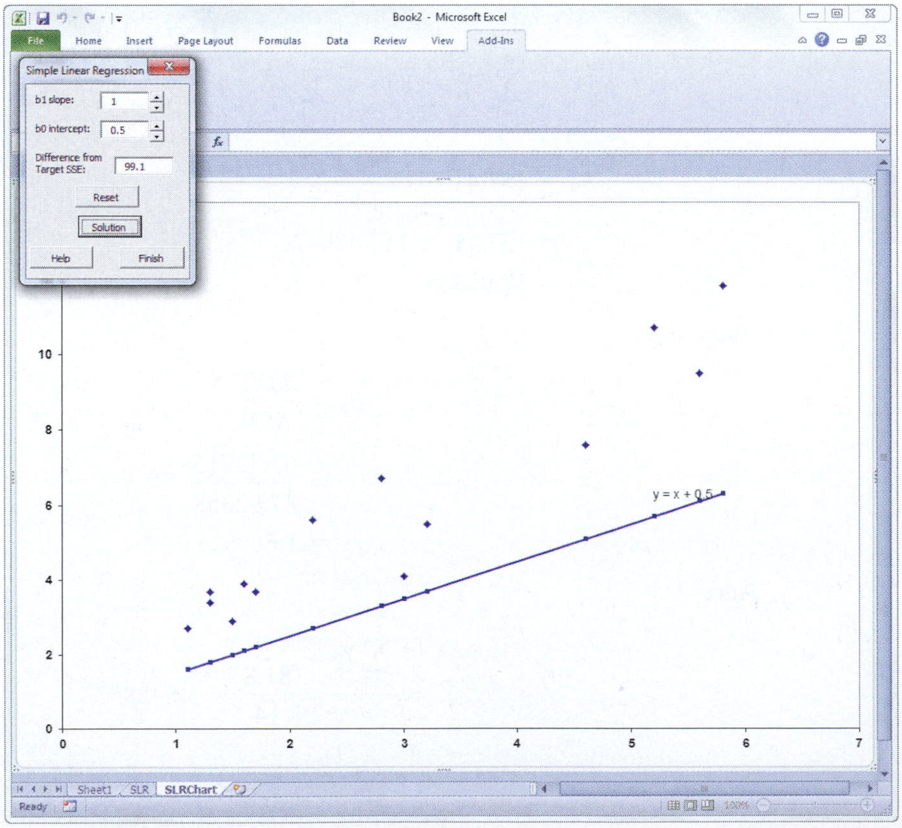

Problems for Section 13.2

LEARNING THE BASICS

13.1 Fitting a straight line to a set of data yields the following prediction line:

$$\hat{Y}_i = 2 + 5X_i$$

a. Interpret the meaning of the Y intercept, b_0.
b. Interpret the meaning of the slope, b_1.
c. Predict the value of Y for $X = 3$.

13.2 If the values of X in Problem 13.1 range from 2 to 25, should you use this model to predict the mean value of Y when X equals
a. 3?
b. −3?
c. 0?
d. 24?

13.3 Fitting a straight line to a set of data yields the following prediction line:

$$\hat{Y}_i = 16 - 0.5X_i$$

a. Interpret the meaning of the Y intercept, b_0.
b. Interpret the meaning of the slope, b_1.
c. Predict the value of Y for $X = 6$.

APPLYING THE CONCEPTS

SELF Test **13.4** The marketing manager of a large supermarket chain would like to use shelf space to predict the sales of pet food. A random sample of 12 equal-sized stores is selected, with the following results (stored in **Petfood**):

Store	Shelf Space (X) (Feet)	Weekly Sales (Y) ($)
1	5	160
2	5	220
3	5	140
4	10	190
5	10	240
6	10	260
7	15	230
8	15	270
9	15	280
10	20	260
11	20	290
12	20	310

a. Construct a scatter plot.
For these data, $b_0 = 145$ and $b_1 = 7.4$.
b. Interpret the meaning of the slope, b_1, in this problem.
c. Predict the weekly sales of pet food for stores with 8 feet of shelf space for pet food.

13.5 Zagat's publishes restaurant ratings for various locations in the United States. The file **Restaurants** contains the Zagat rating for food, décor, service, and the cost per person for a sample of 100 restaurants located in New York City and in a suburb of New York City. Develop a regression model to predict the price per person, based on a variable that represents the sum of the ratings for food, décor, and service.

Sources: Extracted from *Zagat Survey 2010, New York City Restaurants;* and *Zagat Survey 2009–2010, Long Island Restaurants.*

a. Construct a scatter plot.
For these data, $b_0 = -28.1975$ and $b_1 = 1.2409$.
b. Assuming a linear cost relationship, use the least-squares method to compute the regression coefficients b_0 and b_1.
c. Interpret the meaning of the Y intercept, b_0, and the slope, b_1, in this problem.
d. Predict the cost per person for a restaurant with a summated rating of 50.

13.6 The owner of a moving company typically has his most experienced manager predict the total number of labor hours that will be required to complete an upcoming move. This approach has proved useful in the past, but the owner has the business objective of developing a more accurate method of predicting labor hours. In a preliminary effort to provide a more accurate method, the owner has decided to use the number of cubic feet moved as the independent variable and has collected data for 36 moves in which the origin and destination were within the borough of Manhattan in New York City and in which the travel time was an insignificant portion of the hours worked. The data are stored in **Moving**.
a. Construct a scatter plot.
b. Assuming a linear relationship, use the least-squares method to determine the regression coefficients b_0 and b_1.
c. Interpret the meaning of the slope, b_1, in this problem.
d. Predict the labor hours for moving 500 cubic feet.

13.7 A critically important aspect of customer service in a supermarket is the waiting time at the checkout (defined as the time the customer enters the line until he or she is served). Data were collected during time periods in which a constant number of checkout counters were open. The total number of customers in the store and the waiting times (in minutes) were recorded. The results are stored in **Supermarket**.
a. Construct a scatter plot.
b. Assuming a linear relationship, use the least-squares method to determine the regression coefficients b_0 and b_1.
c. Interpret the meaning of the slope, b_1, in this problem.
d. Predict the waiting time when there are 20 customers in the store.

13.8 The value of a sports franchise is directly related to the amount of revenue that a franchise can generate. The file **BBRevenue** represents the value in 2010 (in millions of dollars) and the annual revenue (in millions of dollars) for the 30 major league baseball franchises. (Data extracted from **www.forbes.com/2010/04/07/most-valuable-baseball-teams-business-sportsmoney-baseball-valuations-10_values.html**.) Suppose you want to develop a simple linear regression model to predict franchise value based on annual revenue generated.

a. Construct a scatter plot.
b. Use the least-squares method to determine the regression coefficients b_0 and b_1.
c. Interpret the meaning of b_0 and b_1 in this problem.
d. Predict the value of a baseball franchise that generates $150 million of annual revenue.

13.9 An agent for a residential real estate company in a large city would like to be able to predict the monthly rental cost for apartments, based on the size of an apartment, as defined by square footage. The agent selects a sample of 25 apartments in a particular residential neighborhood and gathers the following data (stored in **Rent**).

Rent ($)	Size (Square Feet)
950	850
1,600	1,450
1,200	1,085
1,500	1,232
950	718
1,700	1,485
1,650	1,136
935	726
875	700
1,150	956
1,400	1,100
1,650	1,285
2,300	1,985
1,800	1,369
1,400	1,175
1,450	1,225
1,100	1,245
1,700	1,259
1,200	1,150
1,150	896
1,600	1,361
1,650	1,040
1,200	755
800	1,000
1,750	1,200

a. Construct a scatter plot.
b. Use the least-squares method to determine the regression coefficients b_0 and b_1.
c. Interpret the meaning of b_0 and b_1 in this problem.
d. Predict the monthly rent for an apartment that has 1,000 square feet.
e. Why would it not be appropriate to use the model to predict the monthly rent for apartments that have 500 square feet?
f. Your friends Jim and Jennifer are considering signing a lease for an apartment in this residential neighborhood. They are trying to decide between two apartments, one with 1,000 square feet for a monthly rent of $1,275 and the other with 1,200 square feet for a monthly rent of $1,425. Based on (a) through (d), which apartment do you think is a better deal?

13.10 A company that holds the DVD distribution rights to movies previously released only in theaters wants to estimate sales revenue of DVDs based on box office success. The box office gross (in $millions) for each of 22 movies in the year that they were released and the DVD revenue (in $millions) in the following year are shown below and stored in **Movie**.

Title	Gross	DVD Revenue
Bolt	109.92	81.60
Madagascar: Escape 2 Africa	177.02	107.54
Quantum of Solace	166.82	44.41
Beverly Hills Chihuahua	93.78	60.21
Marley and Me	106.66	62.82
High School Musical 3 Senior Year	90.22	58.81
Bedtime Stories	85.54	48.79
Role Models	66.70	38.78
Pineapple Express	87.34	44.67
Eagle Eye	101.40	34.88
Fireproof	33.26	31.05
Momma Mia!	144.13	33.14
Seven Pounds	60.15	27.12
Australia	46.69	28.16
Valkyrie	60.73	26.43
Saw V	56.75	26.10
The Curious Case of Benjamin Button	79.30	42.04
Max Payne	40.68	25.03
Body of Lies	39.32	21.45
Nights in Rodanthe	41.80	17.51
Lakeview Terrace	39.26	21.08
The Spirit	17.74	18.78

Sources: Data extracted from **www.the-numbers.com/market/movies2008.php**; and **www.the-numbers.com/dvd/charts/annual/2009.php**.

For these data,

a. construct a scatter plot.
b. assuming a linear relationship, use the least-squares method to determine the regression coefficients b_0 and b_1.
c. interpret the meaning of the slope, b_1, in this problem.
d. predict the sales revenue for a movie DVD that had a box office gross of $75 million.

13.3 Measures of Variation

When using the least-squares method to determine the regression coefficients for a set of data, you need to compute three measures of variation. The first measure, the **total sum of squares (SST)**, is a measure of variation of the Y_i values around their mean, $\bar{Y}$. The **total variation**, or total sum of squares, is subdivided into **explained variation** and **unexplained variation**. The explained variation, or **regression sum of squares (SSR)**, represents variation that is explained by the relationship between X and Y, and the unexplained variation, or **error sum of squares (SSE)**, represents variation due to factors other than the relationship between X and Y. Figure 13.6 shows these different measures of variation.

FIGURE 13.6
Measures of variation

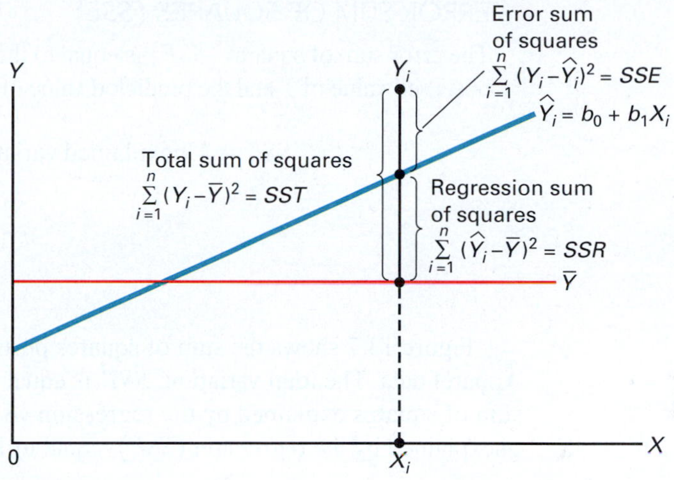

Computing the Sum of Squares

The regression sum of squares (SSR) is based on the difference between $\hat{Y}_i$ (the predicted value of Y from the prediction line) and $\bar{Y}$ (the mean value of Y). The error sum of squares (SSE) represents the part of the variation in Y that is not explained by the regression. It is based on the difference between Y_i and $\hat{Y}_i$ Equations (13.5), (13.6), (13.7), and (13.8) define these measures of variation and the total sum of squares (SST).

MEASURES OF VARIATION IN REGRESSION

The total sum of squares is equal to the regression sum of squares (SSR) plus the error sum of squares (SSE).

$$SST = SSR + SSE \quad \textbf{(13.5)}$$

TOTAL SUM OF SQUARES (SST)

The total sum of squares (SST) is equal to the sum of the squared differences between each observed value of Y and the mean value of Y.

$$SST = \text{Total sum of squares}$$
$$= \sum_{i=1}^{n}(Y_i - \bar{Y})^2 \quad \textbf{(13.6)}$$

REGRESSION SUM OF SQUARES (SSR)

The regression sum of squares (SSR) is equal to the sum of the squared differences between each predicted value of Y and the mean value of Y.

$$SSR = \text{Explained variation or regression sum of squares}$$
$$= \sum_{i=1}^{n}(\hat{Y}_i - \overline{Y})^2 \quad \textbf{(13.7)}$$

ERROR SUM OF SQUARES (SSE)

The error sum of squares (SSE) is equal to the sum of the squared differences between each observed value of Y and the predicted value of Y.

$$SSE = \text{Unexplained variation or error sum of squares}$$
$$= \sum_{i=1}^{n}(Y_i - \hat{Y}_i)^2 \quad \textbf{(13.8)}$$

Figure 13.7 shows the sum of squares portion of the Figure 13.4 results for the Sunflowers Apparel data. The total variation, SST, is equal to 116.9543. This amount is subdivided into the sum of squares explained by the regression (SSR), equal to 105.7476, and the sum of squares unexplained by the regression (SSE), equal to 11.2067. From Equation (13.5) on page 533:

$$SST = SSR + SSE$$

$$116.9543 = 105.7476 + 11.2067$$

FIGURE 13.7

Excel and Minitab sum of squares portion for the Sunflowers Apparel data

	A	B	C	D	E	F
10	ANOVA					
11		*df*	*SS*	*MS*	*F*	*Significance F*
12	Regression	1	105.7476	105.7476	113.2335	0.0000
13	Residual	12	11.2067	0.9339		
14	Total	13	116.9543			

Analysis of Variance

Source	DF	SS	MS	F	P
Regression	1	105.75	105.75	113.23	0.000
Residual Error	12	11.21	0.93		
Total	13	116.95			

The Coefficient of Determination

By themselves, SSR, SSE, and SST provide little information. However, the ratio of the regression sum of squares (SSR) to the total sum of squares (SST) measures the proportion of variation in Y that is explained by the independent variable X in the regression model. This ratio, called the coefficient of determination, r^2, is defined in Equation (13.9).

COEFFICIENT OF DETERMINATION

The coefficient of determination is equal to the regression sum of squares (i.e., explained variation) divided by the total sum of squares (i.e., total variation).

$$r^2 = \frac{\text{Regression sum of squares}}{\text{Total sum of squares}} = \frac{SSR}{SST} \quad \textbf{(13.9)}$$

The **coefficient of determination** measures the proportion of variation in Y that is explained by the variation in the independent variable X in the regression model.

For the Sunflowers Apparel data, with $SSR = 105.7476, SSE = 11.2067$, and $SST = 116.9543$,

$$r^2 = \frac{105.7476}{116.9543} = 0.9042$$

Therefore, 90.42% of the variation in annual sales is explained by the variability in the size of the store as measured by the square footage. This large r^2 indicates a strong linear relationship between these two variables because the regression model has explained 90.42% of the variability in predicting annual sales. Only 9.58% of the sample variability in annual sales is due to factors other than what is accounted for by the linear regression model that uses square footage.

Figure 13.8 presents the regression statistics table portion of the Figure 13.4 results for the Sunflowers Apparel data. This table contains the coefficient of determination (labeled R Square in Excel and R-Sq in Minitab).

FIGURE 13.8 Excel and Minitab regression statistics for the Sunflowers Apparel data

	A	B
3	*Regression Statistics*	
4	Multiple R	0.9509
5	R Square	0.9042
6	Adjusted R Square	0.8962
7	Standard Error	0.9664
8	Observations	14

```
Predictor      Coef  SE Coef      T      P
Constant     0.9645   0.5262   1.83  0.092
Square Feet  1.6699   0.1569  10.64  0.000

S = 0.966380    R-Sq = 90.4%    R-Sq(adj) = 89.6%
```

EXAMPLE 13.4

Computing the Coefficient of Determination

Compute the coefficient of determination, r^2, for the Sunflowers Apparel data.

SOLUTION You can compute SST, SSR, and SSE, which are defined in Equations (13.6), (13.7), and (13.8) on pages 533 and 534, by using Equations (13.10), (13.11), and (13.12).

COMPUTATIONAL FORMULA FOR *SST*

$$SST = \sum_{i=1}^{n}(Y_i - \overline{Y})^2 = \sum_{i=1}^{n}Y_i^2 - \frac{\left(\sum_{i=1}^{n}Y_i\right)^2}{n} \quad \textbf{(13.10)}$$

COMPUTATIONAL FORMULA FOR *SSR*

$$SSR = \sum_{i=1}^{n}(\hat{Y}_i - \overline{Y})^2$$

$$= b_0\sum_{i=1}^{n}Y_i + b_1\sum_{i=1}^{n}X_iY_i - \frac{\left(\sum_{i=1}^{n}Y_i\right)^2}{n} \quad \textbf{(13.11)}$$

COMPUTATIONAL FORMULA FOR *SSE*

$$SSE = \sum_{i=1}^{n}(Y_i - \hat{Y}_i)^2 = \sum_{i=1}^{n}Y_i^2 - b_0\sum_{i=1}^{n}Y_i - b_1\sum_{i=1}^{n}X_iY_i \quad \textbf{(13.12)}$$

Using the summary results from Table 13.2 on page 529,

$$SST = \sum_{i=1}^{n}(Y_i - \overline{Y})^2 = \sum_{i=1}^{n} Y_i^2 - \frac{\left(\sum_{i=1}^{n} Y_i\right)^2}{n}$$

$$= 594.9 - \frac{(81.8)^2}{14}$$

$$= 594.9 - 477.94571$$

$$= 116.95429$$

$$SSR = \sum_{i=1}^{n}(\hat{Y}_i - \overline{Y})^2$$

$$= b_0\sum_{i=1}^{n} Y_i + b_1\sum_{i=1}^{n} X_iY_i - \frac{\left(\sum_{i=1}^{n} Y_i\right)^2}{n}$$

$$= (0.9645)(81.8) + (1.6699)(302.3) - \frac{(81.8)^2}{14}$$

$$= 105.74726$$

$$SSE = \sum_{i=1}^{n}(Y_i - \hat{Y}_i)^2$$

$$= \sum_{i=1}^{n} Y_i^2 - b_0\sum_{i=1}^{n} Y_i - b_1\sum_{i=1}^{n} X_iY_i$$

$$= 594.9 - (0.9645)(81.8) - (1.6699)(302.3)$$

$$= 11.2067$$

Therefore,

$$r^2 = \frac{105.74726}{116.95429} = 0.9042$$

Standard Error of the Estimate

Although the least-squares method produces the line that fits the data with the minimum amount of prediction error, unless all the observed data points fall on a straight line, the prediction line is not a perfect predictor. Just as all data values cannot be expected to be exactly equal to their mean, neither can all the values in a regression analysis be expected to fall exactly on the prediction line. Figure 13.5 on page 526 illustrates the variability around the prediction line for the Sunflowers Apparel data. Observe that many of the actual values of Y fall near the prediction line, but none of the values are exactly on the line.

The **standard error of the estimate** measures the variability of the actual Y values from the predicted Y values in the same way that the standard deviation in Chapter 3 measures the variability of each value around the sample mean. In other words, the standard error of the estimate is the standard deviation *around* the prediction line, whereas the standard deviation in Chapter 3 is the standard deviation *around* the sample mean. Equation (13.13) defines the standard error of the estimate, represented by the symbol S_{YX}.

STANDARD ERROR OF THE ESTIMATE

$$S_{YX} = \sqrt{\frac{SSE}{n-2}} = \sqrt{\frac{\sum_{i=1}^{n}(Y_i - \hat{Y}_i)^2}{n-2}} \quad (13.13)$$

where

Y_i = actual value of Y for a given X_i
$\hat{Y}_i$ = predicted value of Y for a given X_i
SSE = error sum of squares

From Equation (13.8) and Figure 13.4 or Figure 13.7 on pages 526 or 534, $SSE = 11.2067$. Thus,

$$S_{YX} = \sqrt{\frac{11.2067}{14-2}} = 0.9664$$

This standard error of the estimate, equal to 0.9664 millions of dollars (i.e., $966,400), is labeled Standard Error in the Figure 13.8 Excel results and S in the Minitab results. The standard error of the estimate represents a measure of the variation around the prediction line. It is measured in the same units as the dependent variable Y. The interpretation of the standard error of the estimate is similar to that of the standard deviation. Just as the standard deviation measures variability around the mean, the standard error of the estimate measures variability around the prediction line. For Sunflowers Apparel, the typical difference between actual annual sales at a store and the predicted annual sales using the regression equation is approximately $966,400.

Problems for Section 13.3

LEARNING THE BASICS

13.11 How do you interpret a coefficient of determination, r^2, equal to 0.80?

13.12 If $SSR = 36$ and $SSE = 4$, determine SST, then compute the coefficient of determination, r^2, and interpret its meaning.

13.13 If $SSR = 66$ and $SST = 88$, compute the coefficient of determination, r^2, and interpret its meaning.

13.14 If $SSE = 10$ and $SSR = 30$, compute the coefficient of determination, r^2, and interpret its meaning.

13.15 If $SSR = 120$, why is it impossible for SST to equal 110?

APPLYING THE CONCEPTS

SELF Test **13.16** In Problem 13.4 on page 531, the marketing manager used shelf space for pet food to predict weekly sales (stored in **Petfood**). For those data, $SSR = 20{,}535$ and $SST = 30{,}025$.

a. Determine the coefficient of determination, r^2, and interpret its meaning.
b. Determine the standard error of the estimate.
c. How useful do you think this regression model is for predicting sales?

13.17 In Problem 13.5 on page 531, you used the summated rating to predict the cost of a restaurant meal (stored in **Restaurants**). For those data, $SSR = 6{,}951.3963$ and $SST = 15{,}890.11$

a. Determine the coefficient of determination, r^2, and interpret its meaning.
b. Determine the standard error of the estimate.
c. How useful do you think this regression model is for predicting audited sales?

13.18 In Problem 13.6 on page 531, an owner of a moving company wanted to predict labor hours, based on the cubic feet moved (stored in **Moving**). Using the results of that problem,

a. determine the coefficient of determination, r^2, and interpret its meaning.
b. determine the standard error of the estimate.
c. How useful do you think this regression model is for predicting labor hours?

13.19 In Problem 13.7 on page 531, you used the number of customers to predict the waiting time at the checkout line in a supermarket (stored in **Supermarket**). Using the results of that problem,

a. determine the coefficient of determination, r^2, and interpret its meaning.
b. determine the standard error of the estimate.
c. How useful do you think this regression model is for predicting the waiting time at the checkout line in a supermarket?

13.20 In Problem 13.8 on page 531, you used annual revenues to predict the value of a baseball franchise (stored in **BBRevenue**). Using the results of that problem,

a. determine the coefficient of determination, r^2, and interpret its meaning.
b. determine the standard error of the estimate.
c. How useful do you think this regression model is for predicting the value of a baseball franchise?

13.21 In Problem 13.9 on page 532, an agent for a real estate company wanted to predict the monthly rent for apartments, based on the size of the apartment (stored in **Rent**). Using the results of that problem,

a. determine the coefficient of determination, r^2, and interpret its meaning.
b. determine the standard error of the estimate.
c. How useful do you think this regression model is for predicting the monthly rent?
d. Can you think of other variables that might explain the variation in monthly rent?

13.22 In Problem 13.10 on page 532, you used box office gross to predict DVD revenue (stored in **Movie**). Using the results of that problem,

a. determine the coefficient of determination, r^2, and interpret its meaning.
b. determine the standard error of the estimate.
c. How useful do you think this regression model is for predicting DVD revenue?
d. Can you think of other variables that might explain the variation in DVD revenue?

13.4 Assumptions

When hypothesis testing and the analysis of variance were discussed in Chapters 9 through 12, the importance of the assumptions to the validity of any conclusions reached was emphasized. The assumptions necessary for regression are similar to those of the analysis of variance because both are part of the general category of *linear models* (reference 4).

The four **assumptions of regression** (known by the acronym LINE) are as follows:

- **L**inearity
- **I**ndependence of errors
- **N**ormality of error
- **E**qual variance

The first assumption, **linearity**, states that the relationship between variables is linear. Relationships between variables that are not linear are discussed in Chapter 15.

The second assumption, **independence of errors**, requires that the errors (ε_i) are independent of one another. This assumption is particularly important when data are collected over a period of time. In such situations, the errors in a specific time period are sometimes correlated with those of the previous time period.

The third assumption, **normality**, requires that the errors (ε_i) are normally distributed at each value of X. Like the t test and the ANOVA F test, regression analysis is fairly robust against departures from the normality assumption. As long as the distribution of the errors at each level of X is not extremely different from a normal distribution, inferences about β_0 and β_1 are not seriously affected.

The fourth assumption, **equal variance**, or **homoscedasticity**, requires that the variance of the errors (ε_i) be constant for all values of X. In other words, the variability of Y values is the same when X is a low value as when X is a high value. The equal-variance assumption is important when making inferences about β_0 and β_1. If there are serious departures from this assumption, you can use either data transformations or weighted least-squares methods (see reference 4).

13.5 Residual Analysis

Sections 13.2 and 13.3 developed a regression model using the least-squares method for the Sunflowers Apparel data. Is this the correct model for these data? Are the assumptions presented in Section 13.4 valid? **Residual analysis** visually evaluates these assumptions and helps you to determine whether the regression model that has been selected is appropriate.

The **residual**, or estimated error value, e_i, is the difference between the observed (Y_i) and predicted $(\hat{Y}_i)$ values of the dependent variable for a given value of X_i. A residual appears on a scatter plot as the vertical distance between an observed value of Y and the prediction line. Equation (13.14) defines the residual.

RESIDUAL

The residual is equal to the difference between the observed value of Y and the predicted value of Y.

$$e_i = Y_i - \hat{Y}_i \quad \textbf{(13.14)}$$

Evaluating the Assumptions

Recall from Section 13.4 that the four assumptions of regression (known by the acronym LINE) are linearity, independence, normality, and equal variance.

Linearity To evaluate linearity, you plot the residuals on the vertical axis against the corresponding X_i values of the independent variable on the horizontal axis. If the linear model is appropriate for the data, you will not see any apparent pattern in the plot. However, if the linear model is not appropriate, in the residual plot, there will be a relationship between the X_i values and the residuals, e_i.

You can see such a pattern in Figure 13.9. Panel A shows a situation in which, although there is an increasing trend in Y as X increases, the relationship seems curvilinear because the upward trend decreases for increasing values of X. This quadratic effect is highlighted in Panel B, where there is a clear relationship between X_i and e_i. By plotting the residuals, the linear trend of X with Y has been removed, thereby exposing the lack of fit in the simple linear model. Thus, a quadratic model is a better fit and should be used in place of the simple linear model. (See Section 15.1 for further discussion of fitting curvilinear models.)

FIGURE 13.9
Studying the appropriateness of the simple linear regression model

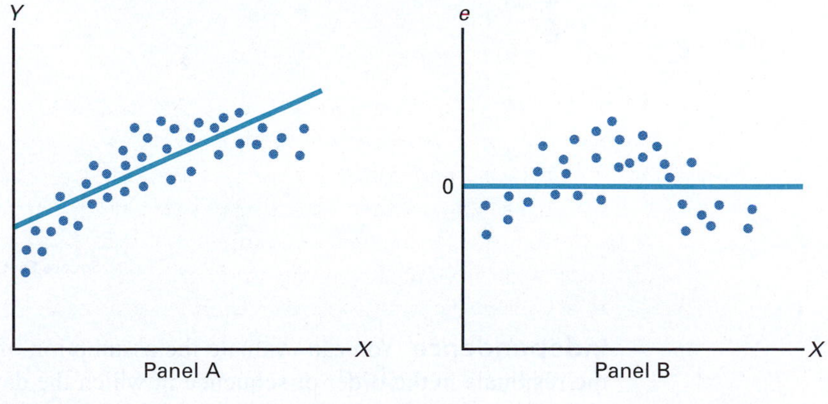

To determine whether the simple linear regression model is appropriate, return to the evaluation of the Sunflowers Apparel data. Figure 13.10 displays the predicted annual sales values and residuals.

FIGURE 13.10
Table of residuals for the Sunflowers Apparel data

	A	B	C	D	E
1	*Observation*	*Square Feet*	*Predicted Annual Sales*	*Annual Sales*	*Residuals*
2	1	1.7	3.803239598	3.7	0.103239598
3	2	1.6	3.636253367	3.9	-0.263746633
4	3	2.8	5.640088147	6.7	-1.059911853
5	4	5.6	10.31570263	9.5	0.815702635
6	5	1.3	3.135294672	3.4	-0.264705328
7	6	2.2	4.638170757	5.6	-0.961829243
8	7	1.3	3.135294672	3.7	-0.564705328
9	8	1.1	2.801322208	2.7	0.101322208
10	9	3.2	6.308033074	5.5	0.808033074
11	10	1.5	3.469267135	2.9	0.569267135
12	11	5.2	9.647757708	10.7	-1.052242292
13	12	4.6	8.645840318	7.6	1.045840318
14	13	5.8	10.6496751	11.8	-1.150324902
15	14	3.0	5.974060611	4.1	1.874060611

To assess linearity, the residuals are plotted against the independent variable (store size, in thousands of square feet) in Figure 13.11. Although there is widespread scatter in the residual plot, there is no clear pattern or relationship between the residuals and X_i. The residuals appear to be evenly spread above and below 0 for different values of X. You can conclude that the linear model is appropriate for the Sunflowers Apparel data.

FIGURE 13.11
Plot of residuals against the square footage of a store for the Sunflowers Apparel data

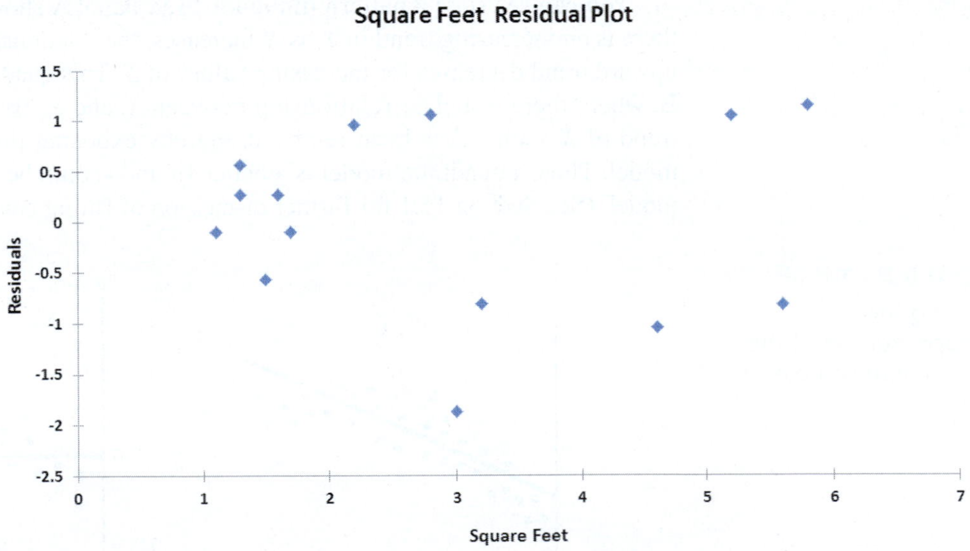

Independence You can evaluate the assumption of independence of the errors by plotting the residuals in the order or sequence in which the data were collected. If the values of Y are part of a time series (see Section 2.6), one residual may sometimes be related to the previous residual. If this relationship exists between consecutive residuals (which violates the assumption of independence), the plot of the residuals versus the time in which the data were collected will often show a cyclical pattern. Because the Sunflowers Apparel data were collected during the same time period, you do not need to evaluate the independence assumption for these data.

Normality You can evaluate the assumption of normality in the errors by organizing the residuals into a frequency distribution as shown in Table 13.3. You cannot construct a meaningful histogram because the sample size is too small. And with such a small sample size ($n = 14$), it can be difficult to evaluate the normality assumption by using a stem-and-leaf display (see Section 2.5), a boxplot (see Section 3.3), or a normal probability plot (see Section 6.3).

TABLE 13.3

Frequency Distribution of 14 Residual Values for the Sunflowers Apparel Data

Residuals	Frequency
−2.25 but less than −1.75	1
−1.75 but less than −1.25	0
−1.25 but less than −0.75	3
−0.75 but less than −0.25	1
−0.25 but less than +0.25	2
+0.25 but less than +0.75	3
+0.75 but less than +1.25	4
	14

From the normal probability plot of the residuals in Figure 13.12, the data do not appear to depart substantially from a normal distribution. The robustness of regression analysis with modest departures from normality enables you to conclude that you should not be overly concerned about departures from this normality assumption in the Sunflowers Apparel data.

FIGURE 13.12

Excel and Minitab normal probability plots of the residuals for the Sunflowers Apparel data

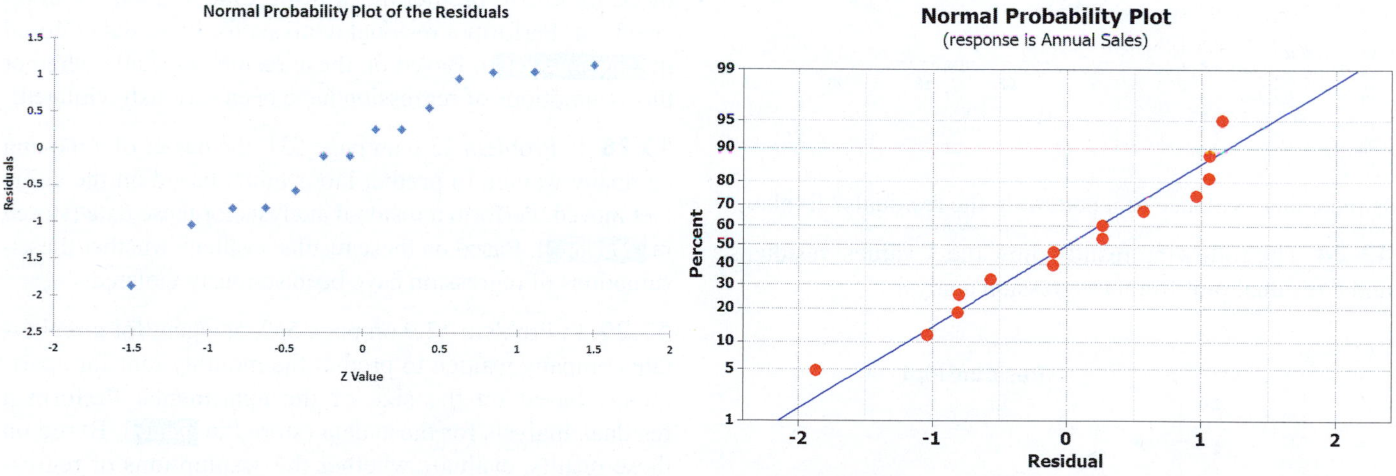

Equal Variance You can evaluate the assumption of equal variance from a plot of the residuals with X_i. For the Sunflowers Apparel data of Figure 13.11 on page 540, there do not appear to be major differences in the variability of the residuals for different X_i values. Thus, you can conclude that there is no apparent violation in the assumption of equal variance at each level of X.

To examine a case in which the equal-variance assumption is violated, observe Figure 13.13, which is a plot of the residuals with X_i for a hypothetical set of data. This plot is fan shaped because the variability of the residuals increases dramatically as X increases. Because this plot shows unequal variances of the residuals at different levels of X, the equal-variance assumption is invalid.

FIGURE 13.13
Violation of equal variance

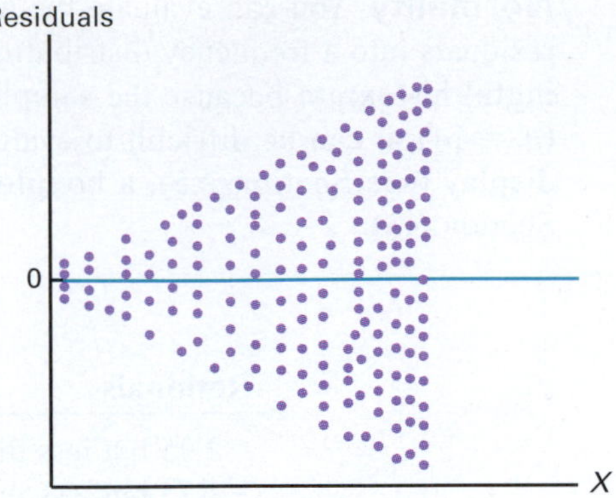

Problems for Section 13.5

LEARNING THE BASICS

13.23 The following results provide the X values, residuals, and a residual plot from a regression analysis:

X	Residuals
1	0.70
2	-0.78
3	1.03
4	0.33
5	2.39
6	-0.67
7	0.16
8	1.65
9	-1.19
10	0.84
11	0.29
12	-1.28
13	1.21
14	-0.37
15	1.02
16	-0.16
17	1.42
18	-0.71
19	-0.63
20	0.67

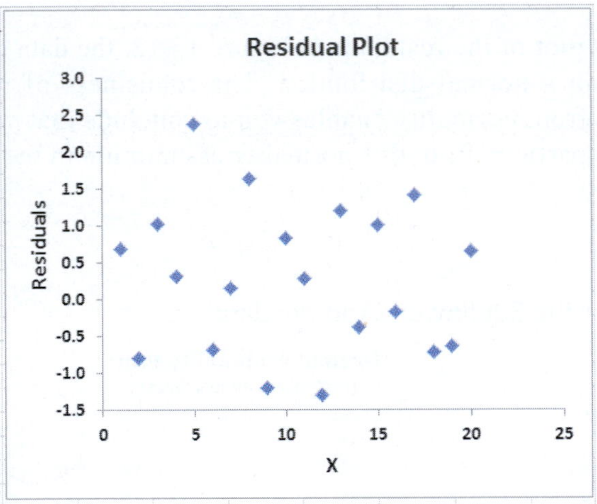

Is there any evidence of a pattern in the residuals? Explain.

13.24 The following results show the X values, residuals, and a residual plot from a regression analysis:

X	Residuals
1	0.70
2	1.58
3	1.03
4	0.33
5	-0.39
6	-0.67
7	-0.56
8	-0.65
9	-1.19
10	-0.84
11	-0.29
12	-1.28
13	-0.21
14	-0.37
15	0.22
16	-0.16
17	0.82

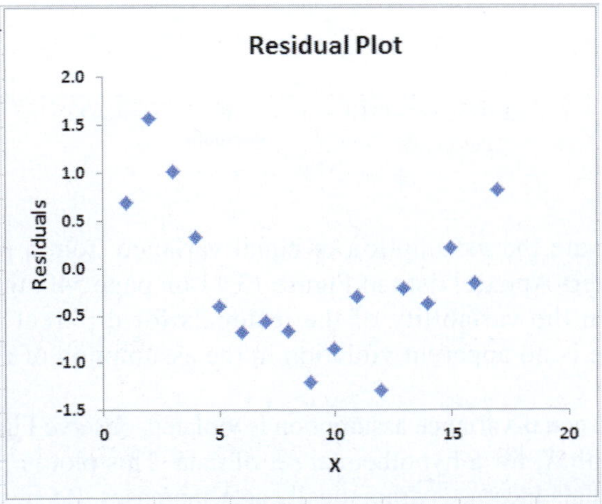

Is there any evidence of a pattern in the residuals? Explain.

APPLYING THE CONCEPTS

13.25 In Problem 13.5 on page 531, you used the summated rating to predict the cost of a restaurant meal. Perform a residual analysis for these data (stored in **Restaurants**). Evaluate whether the assumptions of regression have been seriously violated.

SELF Test **13.26** In Problem 13.4 on page 531, the marketing manager used shelf space for pet food to predict weekly sales. Perform a residual analysis for these data (stored in **Petfood**). Evaluate whether the assumptions of regression have been seriously violated.

13.27 In Problem 13.7 on page 531, you used the number of customers to predict the waiting time at a supermarket checkout. Perform a residual analysis for these data (stored in **Supermarket**). Based on these results, evaluate whether the assumptions of regression have been seriously violated.

13.28 In Problem 13.6 on page 531, the owner of a moving company wanted to predict labor hours based on the cubic feet moved. Perform a residual analysis for these data (stored in **Moving**). Based on these results, evaluate whether the assumptions of regression have been seriously violated.

13.29 In Problem 13.9 on page 532, an agent for a real estate company wanted to predict the monthly rent for apartments, based on the size of the apartments. Perform a residual analysis for these data (stored in **Rent**). Based on these results, evaluate whether the assumptions of regression have been seriously violated.

13.30 In Problem 13.8 on page 531, you used annual revenues to predict the value of a baseball franchise. Perform a residual analysis for these data (stored in **BBRevenue**). Based on these results, evaluate whether the assumptions of regression have been seriously violated.

13.31 In Problem 13.10 on page 532, you used box office gross to predict DVD revenue. Perform a residual analysis for these data (stored in **Movie**). Based on these results, evaluate whether the assumptions of regression have been seriously violated.

13.6 Measuring Autocorrelation: The Durbin-Watson Statistic

One of the basic assumptions of the regression model is the independence of the errors. This assumption is sometimes violated when data are collected over sequential time periods because a residual at any one time period may tend to be similar to residuals at adjacent time periods. This pattern in the residuals is called **autocorrelation**. When a set of data has substantial autocorrelation, the validity of a regression model is in serious doubt.

Residual Plots to Detect Autocorrelation

As mentioned in Section 13.5, one way to detect autocorrelation is to plot the residuals in time order. If a positive autocorrelation effect exists, there will be clusters of residuals with the same sign, and you will readily detect an apparent pattern. If negative autocorrelation exists, residuals will tend to jump back and forth from positive to negative to positive, and so on. This type of pattern is very rarely seen in regression analysis. Thus, the focus of this section is on positive autocorrelation. To illustrate positive autocorrelation, consider the following example.

The business problem faced by the manager of a package delivery store is to predict weekly sales. In approaching this problem, she has decided to develop a regression model to use the number of customers making purchases as an independent variable. Data are collected for a period of 15 weeks. Table 13.4 organizes the data (stored in CustSale).

TABLE 13.4

Customers and Sales for a Period of 15 Consecutive Weeks

Week	Customers	Sales ($Thousands)	Week	Customers	Sales ($Thousands)
1	794	9.33	9	880	12.07
2	799	8.26	10	905	12.55
3	837	7.48	11	886	11.92
4	855	9.08	12	843	10.27
5	845	9.83	13	904	11.80
6	844	10.09	14	950	12.15
7	863	11.01	15	841	9.64
8	875	11.49			

Because the data are collected over a period of 15 consecutive weeks at the same store, you need to determine whether autocorrelation is present. Figure 13.14 presents results for these data.

FIGURE 13.14

Excel and Minitab regression results for the Table 13.4 package delivery store data

	A	B	C	D	E	F	G
1	Package Delivery Store Sales Analysis						
2							
3	*Regression Statistics*						
4	Multiple R	0.8108					
5	R Square	0.6574					
6	Adjusted R Square	0.6311					
7	Standard Error	0.9360					
8	Observations	15					
9							
10	ANOVA						
11		*df*	*SS*	*MS*	*F*	*Significance F*	
12	Regression	1	21.8604	21.8604	24.9501	0.0002	
13	Residual	13	11.3901	0.8762			
14	Total	14	33.2506				
15							
16		*Coefficients*	*Standard Error*	*t Stat*	*P-value*	*Lower 95%*	*Upper 95%*
17	Intercept	-16.0322	5.3102	-3.0192	0.0099	-27.5041	-4.5603
18	Customers	0.0308	0.0062	4.9950	0.0002	0.0175	0.0441

Regression Analysis: Sales versus Customers

```
The regression equation is
Sales = - 16.0 + 0.0308 Customers

Predictor       Coef    SE Coef      T      P
Constant     -16.032      5.310  -3.02  0.010
Customers   0.030760   0.006158   5.00  0.000

S = 0.936037   R-Sq = 65.7%   R-Sq(adj) = 63.1%

Analysis of Variance
Source          DF      SS      MS      F      P
Regression       1  21.860  21.860  24.95  0.000
Residual Error  13  11.390   0.876
Total           14  33.251

Durbin-Watson statistic = 0.883003
```

From Figure 13.14, observe that r^2 is 0.6574, indicating that 65.74% of the variation in sales is explained by variation in the number of customers. In addition, the Y intercept, b_0, is -16.0322, and the slope, b_1, is 0.0308. However, before using this model for prediction, you must perform a residual analysis. Because the data have been collected over a consecutive period of 15 weeks, in addition to checking the linearity, normality, and equal-variance assumptions, you must investigate the independence-of-errors assumption. To do this, you plot the residuals versus time in Figure 13.15 to help examine whether a pattern exists. In Figure 13.15, you can see that the residuals tend to fluctuate up and down in a cyclical pattern. This cyclical pattern provides strong cause for concern about the existence of autocorrelation in the residuals and, therefore, a violation of the independence-of-errors assumption.

FIGURE 13.15
Residual plot for the Table 13.4 package delivery store data

The Durbin-Watson Statistic

The **Durbin-Watson statistic** is used to measure autocorrelation. This statistic measures the correlation between each residual and the residual for the previous time period. Equation (13.15) defines the Durbin-Watson statistic.

DURBIN-WATSON STATISTIC

$$D = \frac{\sum_{i=2}^{n}(e_i - e_{i-1})^2}{\sum_{i=1}^{n} e_i^2} \tag{13.15}$$

where

e_i = residual at the time period i

In Equation (13.15), the numerator, $\sum_{i=2}^{n}(e_i - e_{i-1})^2$, represents the squared difference between two successive residuals, summed from the second value to the nth value and the denominator, $\sum_{i=1}^{n} e_i^2$, represents the sum of the squared residuals. This means that value of the Durbin-Watson statistic, D, will approach 0 if successive residuals are positively autocorrelated. If the residuals are not correlated, the value of D will be close to 2. (If the residuals are negatively autocorrelated, D will be greater than 2 and could even approach its maximum value of 4.) For the package delivery store data, the Durbin-Watson statistic, D, is 0.8830. (See the Figure 13.16 Excel results below or the Figure 13.14 Minitab results on page 543.)

FIGURE 13.16

Excel Durbin-Watson statistic worksheet for the package delivery store data

	A	B	
1	**Durbin-Watson Statistics**		
2			
3	Sum of Squared Difference of Residuals	10.0575	=SUMXMY2(RESIDUALS!E3:E16, RESIDUALS!E2:E15)
4	Sum of Squared Residuals	11.3901	=SUMSQ(RESIDUALS!E2:E16)
5			
6	Durbin-Watson Statistic	0.8830	=B3/B4

Minitab reports the Durbin-Watson statistic as part of its regression results. See Section MG13.6 for more information.

You need to determine when the autocorrelation is large enough to conclude that there is significant positive autocorrelation. After computing D, you compare it to the critical values of the Durbin-Watson statistic found in Table E.8, a portion of which is presented in Table 13.5. The critical values depend on α, the significance level chosen, n, the sample size, and k, the number of independent variables in the model (in simple linear regression, $k = 1$).

TABLE 13.5

Finding Critical Values of the Durbin-Watson Statistic

	$\alpha = .05$									
	$k = 1$		$k = 2$		$k = 3$		$k = 4$		$k = 5$	
n	d_L	d_U	d_L	d_U	d_L	d_U	d_L	d_U	d_L	d_U
15	1.08	1.36	.95	1.54	.82	1.75	.69	1.97	.56	2.21
16	1.10	1.37	.98	1.54	.86	1.73	.74	1.93	.62	2.15
17	1.13	1.38	1.02	1.54	.90	1.71	.78	1.90	.67	2.10
18	1.16	1.39	1.05	1.53	.93	1.69	.82	1.87	.71	2.06

In Table 13.5, two values are shown for each combination of α (level of significance), n (sample size), and k (number of independent variables in the model). The first value, d_L, represents the lower critical value. If D is below d_L, you conclude that there is evidence of positive autocorrelation among the residuals. If this occurs, the least-squares method used in this chapter is inappropriate, and you should use alternative methods (see reference 4). The second value, d_U, represents the upper critical value of D, above which you would conclude that there is no evidence of positive autocorrelation among the residuals. If D is between d_L and d_U, you are unable to arrive at a definite conclusion.

For the package delivery store data, with one independent variable ($k = 1$) and 15 values ($n = 15$), $d_L = 1.08$ and $d_U = 1.36$. Because $D = 0.8830 < 1.08$, you conclude that there is positive autocorrelation among the residuals. The least-squares regression analysis of the data is inappropriate because of the presence of significant positive autocorrelation among the residuals. In other words, the independence-of-errors assumption is invalid. You need to use alternative approaches, discussed in reference 4.

Problems for Section 13.6

LEARNING THE BASICS

13.32 The residuals for 10 consecutive time periods are as follows:

Time Period	Residual	Time Period	Residual
1	−5	6	+1
2	−4	7	+2
3	−3	8	+3
4	−2	9	+4
5	−1	10	+5

a. Plot the residuals over time. What conclusion can you reach about the pattern of the residuals over time?

b. Based on (a), what conclusion can you reach about the autocorrelation of the residuals?

13.33 The residuals for 15 consecutive time periods are as follows:

Time Period	Residual	Time Period	Residual
1	+4	9	+6
2	−6	10	−3
3	−1	11	+1
4	−5	12	+3
5	+2	13	0
6	+5	14	−4
7	−2	15	−7
8	+7		

a. Plot the residuals over time. What conclusion can you reach about the pattern of the residuals over time?

b. Compute the Durbin-Watson statistic. At the 0.05 level of significance, is there evidence of positive autocorrelation among the residuals?

c. Based on (a) and (b), what conclusion can you reach about the autocorrelation of the residuals?

APPLYING THE CONCEPTS

13.34 In Problem 13.4 on page 531 concerning pet food sales, the marketing manager used shelf space for pet food to predict weekly sales.

a. Is it necessary to compute the Durbin-Watson statistic in this case? Explain.

b. Under what circumstances is it necessary to compute the Durbin-Watson statistic before proceeding with the least-squares method of regression analysis?

13.35 What is the relationship between the price of crude oil and the price you pay at the pump for gasoline? The file **Oil & Gas** contains the price ($) for a barrel of crude oil (Cushing, Oklahoma spot price) and a gallon of gasoline (New York Harbor Conventional spot price) for 104 weeks ending June 25, 2010. (Data extracted from Energy Information Administration, U.S. Department of Energy, **www.eia.doe.gov.**)

a. Construct a scatter plot with the price of oil on the horizontal axis and the price of gasoline on the vertical axis.

b. Use the least-squares method to develop a simple linear regression equation to predict the price of a gallon of gasoline using the price of a barrel of crude oil as the independent variable.

c. Interpret the meaning of the slope, b_1, in this problem.

d. Plot the residuals versus the time period.

e. Compute the Durbin-Watson statistic.

f. At the 0.05 level of significance, is there evidence of positive autocorrelation among the residuals?

g. Based on the results of (d) through (f), is there reason to question the validity of the model?

SELF Test **13.36** A mail-order catalog business that sells personal computer supplies, software, and hardware maintains a centralized warehouse for the distribution of products ordered. Management is currently examining the process of distribution from the warehouse and is interested in studying the factors that affect warehouse distribution costs. Currently, a small handling fee is added to the order, regardless of the amount of the order. Data that indicate the warehouse distribution costs and the number of orders received have been collected over the past 24 months and stored in **Warecost**. The results are

Months	Distribution Cost ($Thousands)	Number of Orders
1	52.95	4,015
2	71.66	3,806
3	85.58	5,309
4	63.69	4,262
5	72.81	4,296
6	68.44	4,097
7	52.46	3,213
8	70.77	4,809
9	82.03	5,237
10	74.39	4,732
11	70.84	4,413
12	54.08	2,921
13	62.98	3,977
14	72.30	4,428
15	58.99	3,964
16	79.38	4,582
17	94.44	5,582
18	59.74	3,450
19	90.50	5,079
20	93.24	5,735
21	69.33	4,269
22	53.71	3,708
23	89.18	5,387
24	66.80	4,161

a. Assuming a linear relationship, use the least-squares method to find the regression coefficients b_0 and b_1.
b. Predict the monthly warehouse distribution costs when the number of orders is 4,500.
c. Plot the residuals versus the time period.
d. Compute the Durbin-Watson statistic. At the 0.05 level of significance, is there evidence of positive autocorrelation among the residuals?
e. Based on the results of (c) and (d), is there reason to question the validity of the model?

13.37 A freshly brewed shot of espresso has three distinct components: the heart, body, and crema. The separation of these three components typically lasts only 10 to 20 seconds. To use the espresso shot in making a latte, a cappuccino, or another drink, the shot must be poured into the beverage during the separation of the heart, body, and crema. If the shot is used after the separation occurs, the drink becomes excessively bitter and acidic, ruining the final drink. Thus, a longer separation time allows the drink-maker more time to pour the shot and ensure that the beverage will meet expectations. An employee at a coffee shop hypothesized that the harder the espresso grounds were tamped down into the portafilter before brewing, the longer the separation time would be. An experiment using 24 observations was conducted to test this relationship. The independent variable Tamp measures the distance, in inches, between the espresso grounds and the top of the portafilter (i.e., the harder the tamp, the larger the distance). The dependent variable Time is the number of seconds the heart, body, and crema are separated (i.e., the amount of time after the shot is poured before it must be used for the customer's beverage). The data are stored in **Espresso** and are shown below:

Shot	Tamp (Inches)	Time (Seconds)	Shot	Tamp (Inches)	Time (Seconds)
1	0.20	14	13	0.50	18
2	0.50	14	14	0.50	13
3	0.50	18	15	0.35	19
4	0.20	16	16	0.35	19
5	0.20	16	17	0.20	17
6	0.50	13	18	0.20	18
7	0.20	12	19	0.20	15
8	0.35	15	20	0.20	16
9	0.50	9	21	0.35	18
10	0.35	15	22	0.35	16
11	0.50	11	23	0.35	14
12	0.50	16	24	0.35	16

a. Use the least-squares method to develop a simple regression equation with Time as the dependent variable and Tamp as the independent variable.
b. Predict the separation time for a tamp distance of 0.50 inch.
c. Plot the residuals versus the time order of experimentation. Are there any noticeable patterns?
d. Compute the Durbin-Watson statistic. At the 0.05 level of significance, is there evidence of positive autocorrelation among the residuals?
e. Based on the results of (c) and (d), is there reason to question the validity of the model?

13.38 The owner of a chain of ice cream stores has the business objective of improving the forecast of daily sales so that staffing shortages can be minimized during the summer season. The owner has decided to begin by developing a simple linear regression model to predict daily sales based on atmospheric temperature. A sample of 21 consecutive days is selected, and the results are stored in **IceCream**. (Hint: Determine which are the independent and dependent variables.)
a. Assuming a linear relationship, use the least-squares method to compute the regression coefficients b_0 and b_1.
b. Predict the sales for a day in which the temperature is 83°F.
c. Plot the residuals versus the time period.
d. Compute the Durbin-Watson statistic. At the 0.05 level of significance, is there evidence of positive autocorrelation among the residuals?
e. Based on the results of (c) and (d), is there reason to question the validity of the model?

13.7 Inferences About the Slope and Correlation Coefficient

In Sections 13.1 through 13.3, regression was used solely for descriptive purposes. You learned how the least-squares method determines the regression coefficients and how to predict Y for a given value of X. In addition, you learned how to compute and interpret the standard error of the estimate and the coefficient of determination.

When residual analysis, as discussed in Section 13.5, indicates that the assumptions of a least-squares regression model are not seriously violated and that the straight-line model is appropriate, you can make inferences about the linear relationship between the variables in the population.

t Test for the Slope

To determine the existence of a significant linear relationship between the X and Y variables, you test whether β_1 (the population slope) is equal to 0. The null and alternative hypotheses are as follows:

$$H_0: \beta_1 = 0 \text{ [There is no linear relationship (the slope is zero).]}$$
$$H_1: \beta_1 \neq 0 \text{ [There is a linear relationship (the slope is not zero).]}$$

If you reject the null hypothesis, you conclude that there is evidence of a linear relationship. Equation (13.16) defines the test statistic.

TESTING A HYPOTHESIS FOR A POPULATION SLOPE, β_1, USING THE t TEST

The t_{STAT} test statistic equals the difference between the sample slope and hypothesized value of the population slope divided by the standard error of the slope.

$$t_{STAT} = \frac{b_1 - \beta_1}{S_{b_1}} \quad \textbf{(13.16)}$$

where

$$S_{b_1} = \frac{S_{YX}}{\sqrt{SSX}}$$
$$SSX = \sum_{i=1}^{n}(X_i - \bar{X})^2$$

The t_{STAT} test statistic follows a t distribution with $n - 2$ degrees of freedom.

Return to the Sunflowers Apparel scenario on page 521. To test whether there is a significant linear relationship between the size of the store and the annual sales at the 0.05 level of significance, refer to the t test results shown in Figure 13.17.

FIGURE 13.17
Excel and Minitab t test results for the slope for the Sunflowers Apparel data

	A	B	C	D	E	F	G	H	I
16		*Coefficients*	*Standard Error*	*t Stat*	*P-value*	*Lower 95%*	*Upper 95%*	*Lower 95.0%*	*Upper 95.0%*
17	Intercept	0.9645	0.5262	1.8329	0.0917	-0.1820	2.1110	-0.1820	2.11095
18	Square Feet	1.6699	0.1569	10.6411	0.0000	1.3280	2.0118	1.3280	2.01177

Predictor	Coef	SE Coef	T	P
Constant	0.9645	0.5262	1.83	0.092
Square Feet	1.6699	0.1569	10.64	0.000

From Figure 13.17,

$$b_1 = +1.6699 \quad n = 14 \quad S_{b_1} = 0.1569$$

and

$$t_{STAT} = \frac{b_1 - \beta_1}{S_{b_1}}$$
$$= \frac{1.6699 - 0}{0.1569} = 10.6411$$

Using the 0.05 level of significance, the critical value of t with $n - 2 = 12$ degrees of freedom is 2.1788. Because $t_{STAT} = 10.6411 > 2.1788$ or because the p-value is approximately 0, which is less than $\alpha = 0.05$, you reject H_0 (see Figure 13.18). Hence, you can conclude that there is a significant linear relationship between mean annual sales and the size of the store.

FIGURE 13.18

Testing a hypothesis about the population slope at the 0.05 level of significance, with 12 degrees of freedom

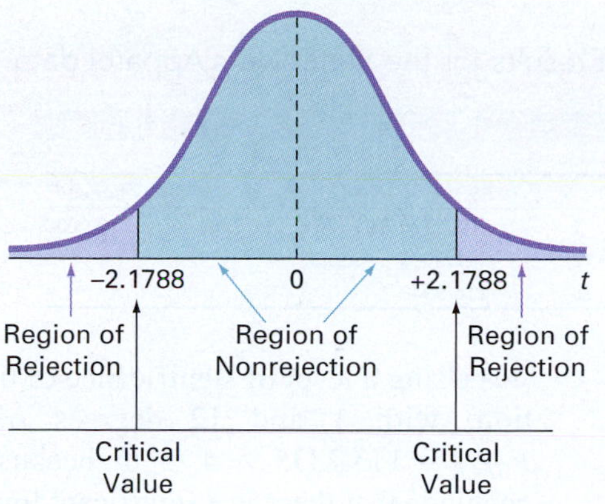

F Test for the Slope

As an alternative to the *t* test, in simple linear regression, you can use an *F* test to determine whether the slope is statistically significant. In Section 10.4, you used the *F* distribution to test the ratio of two variances. Equation (13.17) defines the *F* test for the slope as the ratio of the variance that is due to the regression (MSR) divided by the error variance ($MSE = S_{YX}^2$).

TESTING A HYPOTHESIS FOR A POPULATION SLOPE, β_1, USING THE *F* TEST

The F_{STAT} test statistic is equal to the regression mean square (MSR) divided by the mean square error (MSE).

$$F_{STAT} = \frac{MSR}{MSE} \quad \textbf{(13.17)}$$

where

$$MSR = \frac{SSR}{1} = SSR$$

$$MSE = \frac{SSE}{n-2}$$

The F_{STAT} test statistic follows an *F* distribution with 1 and $n - 2$ degrees of freedom.

Using a level of significance α, the decision rule is

Reject H_0 if $F_{STAT} > F_\alpha$;

otherwise, do not reject H_0.

Table 13.6 organizes the complete set of results into an analysis of variance (ANOVA) table.

TABLE 13.6

ANOVA Table for Testing the Significance of a Regression Coefficient

Source	*df*	Sum of Squares	Mean Square (Variance)	*F*
Regression	1	SSR	$MSR = \frac{SSR}{1} = SSR$	$F_{STAT} = \frac{MSR}{MSE}$
Error	$n - 2$	SSE	$MSE = \frac{SSE}{n-2}$	
Total	$n - 1$	SST		

Figure 13.19, a completed ANOVA table for the Sunflowers sales data, shows that the computed F_{STAT} test statistic is 113.2335 and the *p*-value is approximately 0.

FIGURE 13.19

Excel and Minitab F test results for the Sunflowers Apparel data

	A	B	C	D	E	F
10	**ANOVA**					
11		*df*	*SS*	*MS*	*F*	*Significance F*
12	Regression	1	105.7476	105.7476	113.2335	0.0000
13	Residual	12	11.2067	0.9339		
14	Total	13	116.9543			

Analysis of Variance

Source	DF	SS	MS	F	P
Regression	1	105.75	105.75	113.23	0.000
Residual Error	12	11.21	0.93		
Total	13	116.95			

Using a level of significance of 0.05, from Table E.5, the critical value of the F distribution, with 1 and 12 degrees of freedom, is 4.75 (see Figure 13.20). Because $F_{STAT} = 113.2335 > 4.75$ or because the p-value $= 0.0000 < 0.05$, you reject H_0 and conclude that there is a significant linear relationship between the size of the store and annual sales. Because the F test in Equation (13.17) on page 549 is equivalent to the t test in Equation (13.16) on page 548, you reach the same conclusion.

FIGURE 13.20

Regions of rejection and nonrejection when testing for the significance of the slope at the 0.05 level of significance, with 1 and 12 degrees of freedom

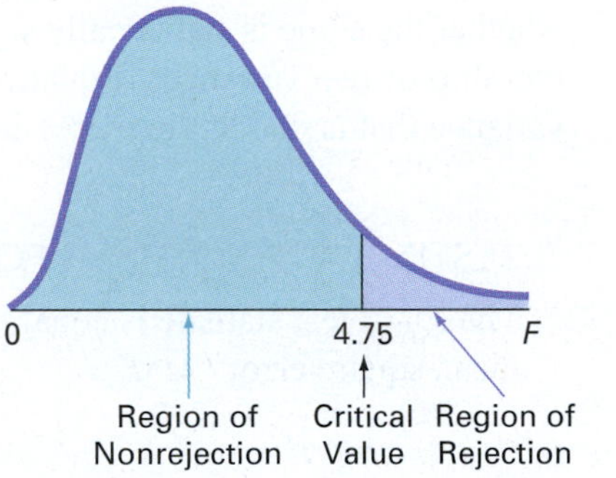

Confidence Interval Estimate for the Slope

As an alternative to testing for the existence of a linear relationship between the variables, you can construct a confidence interval estimate of β_1 using Equation (13.18).

CONFIDENCE INTERVAL ESTIMATE OF THE SLOPE, β_1

The confidence interval estimate for the population slope can be constructed by taking the sample slope, b_1, and adding and subtracting the critical t value multiplied by the standard error of the slope.

$$b_1 \pm t_{\alpha/2} S_{b_1}$$

$$\text{(or)} \quad b_1 - t_{\alpha/2} S_{b_1} \le \beta_1 \le b_1 + t_{\alpha/2} S_{b_1} \tag{13.18}$$

where

$t_{\alpha/2}$ = critical value corresponding to an upper-tail probability of $\alpha/2$ from the t distribution with $n - 2$ degrees of freedom (i.e., a cumulative area of $1 - \alpha/2$).

From the Figure 13.17 results on page 548,

$$b_1 = 1.6699 \quad n = 14 \quad S_{b_1} = 0.1569$$

To construct a 95% confidence interval estimate, $\alpha/2 = 0.025$, and from Table E.3, $t_{\alpha/2} = 2.1788$. Thus,

$$\begin{aligned} b_1 \pm t_{\alpha/2} S_{b_1} &= 1.6699 \pm (2.1788)(0.1569) \\ &= 1.6699 \pm 0.3419 \end{aligned}$$

$$1.3280 \le \beta_1 \le 2.0118$$

Therefore, you estimate with 95% confidence that the population slope is between 1.3280 and 2.0118. Because these values are both above 0, you conclude that there is a significant linear relationship between annual sales and the size of the store. Had the interval included 0, you would have concluded that no significant relationship exists between the variables. The confidence interval indicates that for each increase of 1,000 square feet, predicted annual sales are estimated to increase by at least $1,328,000 but no more than $2,011,800.

t Test for the Correlation Coefficient

In Section 3.5 on page 127, the strength of the relationship between two numerical variables was measured using the **correlation coefficient**, r. The values of the coefficient of correlation range from -1 for a perfect negative correlation to $+1$ for a perfect positive correlation. You can use the correlation coefficient to determine whether there is a statistically significant linear relationship between X and Y. To do so, you hypothesize that the population correlation coefficient, ρ, is 0. Thus, the null and alternative hypotheses are

$$H_0: \rho = 0 \text{ (no correlation)}$$

$$H_1: \rho \neq 0 \text{ (correlation)}$$

Equation (13.19) defines the test statistic for determining the existence of a significant correlation.

TESTING FOR THE EXISTENCE OF CORRELATION

$$t_{STAT} = \frac{r - \rho}{\sqrt{\dfrac{1 - r^2}{n - 2}}} \qquad \textbf{(13.19a)}$$

where

$$r = +\sqrt{r^2} \text{ if } b_1 > 0$$

$$r = -\sqrt{r^2} \text{ if } b_1 < 0$$

The t_{STAT} test statistic follows a t distribution with $n - 2$ degrees of freedom. r is calculated as follows:

$$r = \frac{\text{cov}(X,Y)}{S_X S_Y} \qquad \textbf{(13.19b)}$$

where

$$\text{cov}(X, Y) = \frac{\sum_{i=1}^{n}(X_i - \overline{X})(Y_i - \overline{Y})}{n - 1}$$

$$S_X = \sqrt{\frac{\sum_{i=1}^{n}(X_i - \overline{X})^2}{n - 1}}$$

$$S_Y = \sqrt{\frac{\sum_{i=1}^{n}(Y_i - \overline{Y})^2}{n - 1}}$$

In the Sunflowers Apparel problem, $r^2 = 0.9042$ and $b_1 = +1.6699$ (see Figure 13.4 on page 526). Because $b_1 > 0$, the correlation coefficient for annual sales and store size is the positive square root of r^2, that is, $r = +\sqrt{0.9042} = +0.9509$. Using Equation (13.19a) to test the null hypothesis that there is no correlation between these two variables results in the following observed t statistic:

$$t_{STAT} = \frac{r - 0}{\sqrt{\frac{1 - r^2}{n - 2}}}$$

$$= \frac{0.9509 - 0}{\sqrt{\frac{1 - (0.9509)^2}{14 - 2}}} = 10.6411$$

Using the 0.05 level of significance, because $t_{STAT} = 10.6411 > 2.1788$, you reject the null hypothesis. You conclude that there is a significant association between annual sales and store size. This t_{STAT} test statistic is equivalent to the t_{STAT} test statistic found when testing whether the population slope, β_1, is equal to zero.

Problems for Section 13.7

LEARNING THE BASICS

13.39 You are testing the null hypothesis that there is no linear relationship between two variables, X and Y. From your sample of $n = 10$, you determine that $r = 0.80$.

a. What is the value of the t test statistic t_{STAT}?

b. At the $\alpha = 0.05$ level of significance, what are the critical values?

c. Based on your answers to (a) and (b), what statistical decision should you make?

13.40 You are testing the null hypothesis that there is no linear relationship between two variables, X and Y. From your sample of $n = 18$, you determine that $b_1 = +4.5$ and $S_{b_1} = 1.5$.

a. What is the value of t_{STAT}?

b. At the $\alpha = 0.05$ level of significance, what are the critical values?

c. Based on your answers to (a) and (b), what statistical decision should you make?

d. Construct a 95% confidence interval estimate of the population slope, β_1.

13.41 You are testing the null hypothesis that there is no linear relationship between two variables, X and Y. From your sample of $n = 20$, you determine that $SSR = 60$ and $SSE = 40$.

a. What is the value of F_{STAT}?

b. At the $\alpha = 0.05$ level of significance, what is the critical value?

c. Based on your answers to (a) and (b), what statistical decision should you make?

d. Compute the correlation coefficient by first computing r^2 and assuming that b_1 is negative.

e. At the 0.05 level of significance, is there a significant correlation between X and Y?

APPLYING THE CONCEPTS

SELF Test **13.42** In Problem 13.4 on page 531, the marketing manager used shelf space for pet food to predict weekly sales. The data are stored in **Petfood**. From the results of that problem, $b_1 = 7.4$ and $S_{b_1} = 1.59$.

a. At the 0.05 level of significance, is there evidence of a linear relationship between shelf space and sales?

b. Construct a 95% confidence interval estimate of the population slope, β_1.

13.43 In Problem 13.5 on page 531, you used the summated rating of a restaurant to predict the cost of a meal. The data are stored in **Restaurants**. Using the results of that problem, $b_1 = 1.2409$ and $S_{b_1} = 0.1421$.

a. At the 0.05 level of significance, is there evidence of a linear relationship between the summated rating of a restaurant and the cost of a meal?

b. Construct a 95% confidence interval estimate of the population slope, β_1.

13.44 In Problem 13.6 on page 531, the owner of a moving company wanted to predict labor hours, based on the number of cubic feet moved. The data are stored in **Moving**. Use the results of that problem.

a. At the 0.05 level of significance, is there evidence of a linear relationship between the number of cubic feet moved and labor hours?

b. Construct a 95% confidence interval estimate of the population slope, β_1.

13.45 In Problem 13.7 on page 531, you used the number of customers to predict the waiting time on the checkout line. The data are stored in **Supermarket**. Use the results of that problem.

a. At the 0.05 level of significance, is there evidence of a linear relationship between the number of customers and the waiting time on the checkout line?

b. Construct a 95% confidence interval estimate of the population slope, β_1.

13.46 In Problem 13.8 on page 531, you used annual revenues to predict the value of a baseball franchise. The data are stored in **BBRevenue**. Use the results of that problem.

a. At the 0.05 level of significance, is there evidence of a linear relationship between annual revenue and franchise value?

b. Construct a 95% confidence interval estimate of the population slope, β_1.

13.47 In Problem 13.9 on page 532, an agent for a real estate company wanted to predict the monthly rent for apartments, based on the size of the apartment. The data are stored in **Rent**. Use the results of that problem.

a. At the 0.05 level of significance, is there evidence of a linear relationship between the size of the apartment and the monthly rent?

b. Construct a 95% confidence interval estimate of the population slope, β_1.

13.48 In Problem 13.10 on page 532, you used box office gross to predict DVD revenue. The data are stored in **Movie**. Use the results of that problem.

a. At the 0.05 level of significance, is there evidence of a linear relationship between box office gross and DVD revenue?

b. Construct a 95% confidence interval estimate of the population slope, β_1.

13.49 The volatility of a stock is often measured by its beta value. You can estimate the beta value of a stock by developing a simple linear regression model, using the percentage weekly change in the stock as the dependent variable and the percentage weekly change in a market index as the independent variable. The S&P 500 Index is a common index to use. For example, if you wanted to estimate the beta for Disney, you could use the following model, which is sometimes referred to as a *market model*:

$$(\%\text{ weekly change in Disney}) = \beta_0$$
$$+\beta_1(\%\text{ weekly change in S \& P 500 index}) + \varepsilon$$

The least-squares regression estimate of the slope b_1 is the estimate of the beta value for Disney. A stock with a beta value of 1.0 tends to move the same as the overall market. A stock with a beta value of 1.5 tends to move 50% more than the overall market, and a stock with a beta value of 0.6 tends to move only 60% as much as the overall market. Stocks with negative beta values tend to move in the opposite direction of the overall market. The following table gives some beta values for some widely held stocks as of July 7, 2010:

Company	Ticker Symbol	Beta
Procter & Gamble	PG	0.53
AT&T	T	0.65
Disney	DIS	1.25
Apple	AAPL	1.43
eBay	EBAY	1.75
Ford	F	2.75

Source: Data extracted from **finance.yahoo.com**, July 7, 2010.

a. For each of the six companies, interpret the beta value.

b. How can investors use the beta value as a guide for investing?

13.50 Index funds are mutual funds that try to mimic the movement of leading indexes, such as the S&P 500 or the Russell 2000. The beta values (as described in Problem 13.49) for these funds are therefore approximately 1.0, and the estimated market models for these funds are approximately

$$(\%\text{ weekly change in index fund}) =$$
$$0.0 + 1.0(\%\text{ weekly change in the index})$$

Leveraged index funds are designed to magnify the movement of major indexes. Direxion Funds is a leading provider of leveraged index and other alternative-class mutual fund products for investment advisors and sophisticated investors. Two of the company's funds are shown in the following table. (Data extracted from **www.direxionfunds.com**, July 7, 2010.)

Name	Ticker Symbol	Description
Daily Small Cap 3x Fund	TNA	300% of the Russell 2000 Index
Daily India Bull 2x Fund	INDL	200% of the Indus India Index

The estimated market models for these funds are approximately

$$(\%\text{ weekly change in TNA}) = 0.0 + 3.0$$
$$(\%\text{ weekly change in the Russell 2000})$$
$$(\%\text{ weekly change in INDL}) = 0.0 + 2.0$$
$$(\%\text{ weekly change in the Indus India Index})$$

Thus, if the Russell 2000 Index gains 10% over a period of time, the leveraged mutual fund TNA gains approximately 30%. On the downside, if the same index loses 20%, TNA loses approximately 60%.

a. The objective of the Direxion Funds Large Cap Bull 3x fund, BGU, is 300% of the performance of the Russell 1000 Index. What is its approximate market model?

b. If the Russell 1000 Index gains 10% in a year, what return do you expect BGU to have?

c. If the Russell 1000 Index loses 20% in a year, what return do you expect BGU to have?

d. What type of investors should be attracted to leveraged index funds? What type of investors should stay away from these funds?

13.51 The file **Cereals** contains the calories and sugar, in grams, in one serving of seven breakfast cereals:

Cereal	Calories	Sugar
Kellogg's All Bran	80	6
Kellogg's Corn Flakes	100	2
Wheaties	100	4
Nature's Path Organic Multigrain Flakes	110	4
Kellogg's Rice Krispies	130	4
Post Shredded Wheat Vanilla Almond	190	11
Kellogg Mini Wheats	200	10

a. Compute and interpret the coefficient of correlation, r.

b. At the 0.05 level of significance, is there a significant linear relationship between calories and sugar?

13.52 Movie companies need to predict the gross receipts of an individual movie once the movie has debuted. The following results (stored in **PotterMovies**) are the first weekend gross, the U.S. gross, and the worldwide gross (in $millions) of the six Harry Potter movies that debuted from 2001 to 2009:

Title	First Weekend	U.S. Gross	Worldwide Gross
Sorcerer's Stone	90.295	317.558	976.458
Chamber of Secrets	88.357	261.988	878.988
Prisoner of Azkaban	93.687	249.539	795.539
Goblet of Fire	102.335	290.013	896.013
Order of the Phoenix	77.108	292.005	938.469
Half-Blood Prince	77.836	301.460	934.601

Source: Data extracted from **www.the-numbers.com/interactive/comp-Harry-Potter.php**.

a. Compute the coefficient of correlation between first weekend gross and the U.S. gross, first weekend gross and the worldwide gross, and the U.S. gross and worldwide gross.

b. At the 0.05 level of significance, is there a significant linear relationship between first weekend gross and the U.S. gross, first weekend gross and the worldwide gross, and the U.S. gross and worldwide gross?

13.53 College basketball is big business, with coaches' salaries, revenues, and expenses in millions of dollars. The file **College Basketball** contains the coaches' salary and revenue for college basketball at 60 of the 65 schools that played in the 2009 NCAA men's basketball tournament. (Data extracted from "Compensation for Division I Men's Basketball Coaches," *USA Today*, April 2, 2010, p. 8C; and C. Isadore, "Nothing but Net: Basketball Dollars by School," **money.cnn.com/2010/03/18/news/companies/basketball_profits/**.)

a. Compute and interpret the coefficient of correlation, r.

b. At the 0.05 level of significance, is there a significant linear relationship between a coach's salary and revenue?

13.54 College football players trying out for the NFL are given the Wonderlic standardized intelligence test. The file **Wonderlic** lists the average Wonderlic scores of football players trying out for the NFL and the graduation rates for football players at the schools they attended. (Data extracted from S. Walker, "The NFL's Smartest Team," *The Wall Street Journal*, September 30, 2005, pp. W1, W10.)

a. Compute and interpret the coefficient of correlation, r.

b. At the 0.05 level of significance, is there a significant linear relationship between the average Wonderlic score of football players trying out for the NFL and the graduation rates for football players at selected schools?

c. What conclusions can you reach about the relationship between the average Wonderlic score of football players trying out for the NFL and the graduation rates for football players at selected schools?

13.8 Estimation of Mean Values and Prediction of Individual Values

In Chapter 8, you studied the concept of the confidence interval estimate of the population mean. In Example 13.2 on page 527, you used the prediction line to predict the mean value of Y for a given X. The annual sales for stores with 4,000 square feet was predicted to be 7.644 millions of dollars ($7,644,000). This estimate, however, is a *point estimate* of the population mean. This section presents methods to develop a confidence interval estimate for the mean response for a given X and for developing a prediction interval for an individual response, Y, for a given value of X.

The Confidence Interval Estimate

Equation (13.20) defines the **confidence interval estimate for the mean response** for a given X.

CONFIDENCE INTERVAL ESTIMATE FOR THE MEAN OF Y

$$\hat{Y}_i \pm t_{\alpha/2} S_{YX} \sqrt{h_i}$$

$$\hat{Y}_i - t_{\alpha/2} S_{YX} \sqrt{h_i} \le \mu_{Y|X=X_i} \le - \hat{Y}_i + t_{\alpha/2} S_{YX} \sqrt{h_i} \quad \textbf{(13.20)}$$

where

$$h_i = \frac{1}{n} + \frac{(X_i - \bar{X})^2}{SSX}$$

$\hat{Y}_i$ = predicted value of Y; $\hat{Y}_i = b_0 + b_1 X_i$

S_{YX} = standard error of the estimate

n = sample size

X_i = given value of X

$\mu_{Y|X=X_i}$ = mean value of Y when $X = X_i$

$$SSX = \sum_{i=1}^{n} (X_i - \bar{X})^2$$

$t_{\alpha/2}$ = critical value corresponding to an upper-tail probability of $\alpha/2$ from the t distribution with $n - 2$ degrees of freedom (i.e., a cumulative area of $1 - \alpha/2$).

The width of the confidence interval in Equation (13.20) depends on several factors. Increased variation around the prediction line, as measured by the standard error of the estimate, results in a wider interval. As you would expect, increased sample size reduces the width of the interval. In addition, the width of the interval varies at different values of X. When you predict Y for values of X close to $\bar{X}$, the interval is narrower than for predictions for X values further away from $\bar{X}$.

In the Sunflowers Apparel example, suppose you want to construct a 95% confidence interval estimate of the mean annual sales for the entire population of stores that contain 4,000 square feet ($X = 4$). Using the simple linear regression equation,

$$\begin{aligned} \hat{Y}_i &= 0.9645 + 1.6699 X_i \\ &= 0.9645 + 1.6699(4) = 7.6439 \text{ (millions of dollars)} \end{aligned}$$

Also, given the following:

$$\bar{X} = 2.9214 \quad S_{YX} = 0.9664$$

$$SSX = \sum_{i=1}^{n} (X_i - \bar{X})^2 = 37.9236$$

From Table E.3, $t_{\alpha/2} = 2.1788$. Thus,

$$\hat{Y}_i \pm t_{\alpha/2} S_{YX} \sqrt{h_i}$$

where

$$h_i = \frac{1}{n} + \frac{(X_i - \bar{X})^2}{SSX}$$

so that

$$\begin{aligned} &\hat{Y}_i \pm t_{\alpha/2} S_{YX} \sqrt{\frac{1}{n} + \frac{(X_i - \bar{X})^2}{SSX}} \\ &= 7.6439 \pm (2.1788)(0.9664) \sqrt{\frac{1}{14} + \frac{(4 - 2.9214)^2}{37.9236}} \\ &= 7.6439 \pm 0.6728 \end{aligned}$$

so

$$6.9711 \le \mu_{Y|X=4} \le 8.3167$$

Therefore, the 95% confidence interval estimate is that the mean annual sales are between \$6,971,100 and \$8,316,700 for the population of stores with 4,000 square feet.

The Prediction Interval

In addition to constructing a confidence interval for the mean value of Y, you can also construct a prediction interval for an individual value of Y. Although the form of this interval is similar to that of the confidence interval estimate of Equation (13.20), the prediction interval is predicting an individual value, not estimating a mean. Equation (13.21) defines the **prediction interval for an individual response, Y,** at a given value, X_i, denoted by $Y_{X=X_i}$.

PREDICTION INTERVAL FOR AN INDIVIDUAL RESPONSE, Y

$$\hat{Y}_i \pm t_{\alpha/2} S_{YX} \sqrt{1 + h_i} \quad \textbf{(13.21)}$$

$$\hat{Y}_i - t_{\alpha/2} S_{YX} \sqrt{1 + h_i} \le Y_{X=X_i} \le \hat{Y}_i + t_{\alpha/2} S_{YX} \sqrt{1 + h_i}$$

where

$Y_{X=X_i}$ = future value of Y when $X = X_i$
$t_{\alpha/2}$ = critical value corresponding to an upper-tail probability of $\alpha/2$ from the t distribution with $n - 2$ degrees of freedom (i.e., a cumulative area of $1 - \alpha/2$)

In addition, h_i, $\hat{Y}_i$, S_{YX}, n, and X_i are defined as in Equation (13.20) on page 555.

To construct a 95% prediction interval of the annual sales for an individual store that contains 4,000 square feet ($X = 4$), you first compute $\hat{Y}_i$. Using the prediction line:

$$\begin{aligned} \hat{Y}_i &= 0.9645 + 1.6699X_i \\ &= 0.9645 + 1.6699(4) \\ &= 7.6439 \text{ (millions of dollars)} \end{aligned}$$

Also, given the following:

$$\bar{X} = 2.9214 \quad S_{YX} = 0.9664$$

$$SSX = \sum_{i=1}^{n} (X_i - \bar{X})^2 = 37.9236$$

From Table E.3, $t_{\alpha/2} = 2.1788$. Thus,

$$\hat{Y}_i \pm t_{\alpha/2} S_{YX} \sqrt{1 + h_i}$$

where

$$h_i = \frac{1}{n} + \frac{(X_i - \bar{X})^2}{\sum_{i=1}^{n} (X_i - \bar{X})^2}$$

so that

$$\hat{Y}_i \pm t_{\alpha/2} S_{YX} \sqrt{1 + \frac{1}{n} + \frac{(X_i - \bar{X})^2}{SSX}}$$

$$= 7.6439 \pm (2.1788)(0.9664)\sqrt{1 + \frac{1}{14} + \frac{(4 - 2.9214)^2}{37.9236}}$$

$$= 7.6439 \pm 2.2104$$

so

$$5.4335 \leq Y_{X=4} \leq 9.8543$$

Therefore, with 95% confidence, you predict that the annual sales for an individual store with 4,000 square feet is between \$5,433,500 and \$9,854,300.

Figure 13.21 presents results for the confidence interval estimate and the prediction interval for the Sunflowers Apparel data. If you compare the results of the confidence interval estimate and the prediction interval, you see that the width of the prediction interval for an individual store is much wider than the confidence interval estimate for the mean. Remember that there is much more variation in predicting an individual value than in estimating a mean value.

FIGURE 13.21

Excel and Minitab confidence interval estimate and prediction interval results for the Sunflowers Apparel data

	A	B	
1	Confidence Interval Estimate and Prediction Interval		
2			
3	Data		
4	X Value	4	
5	Confidence Level	95%	
6			
7	Intermediate Calculations		
8	Sample Size	14	=COUNT(SLRData!A:A)
9	Degrees of Freedom	12	=B8 - 2
10	t Value	2.1788	=TINV(1 - B5, B9)
11	Sample Mean	2.9214	=AVERAGE(SLRData!A:A)
12	Sum of Squared Difference	37.9236	=DEVSQ(SLRData!A:A)
13	Standard Error of the Estimate	0.9664	=COMPUTE!B7
14	h Statistic	0.1021	=1/B8 + (B4 - B11)^2/B12
15	Predicted Y (YHat)	7.6439	=TREND(SLRData!B2:B15, SLRData!A2:A15, B4)
16			
17	For Average Y		
18	Interval Half Width	0.6728	=B10 * B13 * SQRT(B14)
19	Confidence Interval Lower Limit	6.9711	=B15 - B18
20	Confidence Interval Upper Limit	8.3167	=B15 + B18
21			
22	For Individual Response Y		
23	Interval Half Width	2.2104	=B10 * B13 * SQRT(1 + B14)
24	Prediction Interval Lower Limit	5.4335	=B15 - B23
25	Prediction Interval Upper Limit	9.8544	=B15 + B23

```
Predicted Values for New Observations
New Obs    Fit  SE Fit        95% CI              95% PI
      1  7.644   0.309  (6.971, 8.317)  (5.433, 9.854)

Values of Predictors for New Observations
          Square
New Obs     Feet
      1     4.00
```

Problems for Section 13.8

LEARNING THE BASICS

13.55 Based on a sample of $n = 20$, the least-squares method was used to develop the following prediction line: $\hat{Y}_i = 5 + 3X_i$. In addition,

$$S_{YX} = 1.0 \quad \bar{X} = 2 \quad \sum_{i=1}^{n}(X_i - \bar{X})^2 = 20$$

a. Construct a 95% confidence interval estimate of the population mean response for $X = 2$.

b. Construct a 95% prediction interval of an individual response for $X = 2$.

13.56 Based on a sample of $n = 20$, the least-squares method was used to develop the following prediction line: $\hat{Y}_i = 5 + 3X_i$. In addition,

$$S_{YX} = 1.0 \quad \bar{X} = 2 \quad \sum_{i=1}^{n}(X_i - \bar{X})^2 = 20$$

a. Construct a 95% confidence interval estimate of the population mean response for $X = 4$.

b. Construct a 95% prediction interval of an individual response for $X = 4$.

c. Compare the results of (a) and (b) with those of Problem 13.55 (a) and (b). Which intervals are wider? Why?

APPLYING THE CONCEPTS

13.57 In Problem 13.5 on page 531, you used the summated rating of a restaurant to predict the cost of a meal. The data are stored in **Restaurants**. For these data, $S_{YX} = 9.5505$ and $h_i = 0.026844$ when $X = 50$.

a. Construct a 95% confidence interval estimate of the mean cost of a meal for restaurants that have a summated rating of 50.

b. Construct a 95% prediction interval of the cost of a meal for an individual restaurant that has a summated rating of 50

c. Explain the difference in the results in (a) and (b).

SELF Test **13.58** In Problem 13.4 on page 531, the marketing manager used shelf space for pet food to predict weekly sales. The data are stored in **Petfood**. For these data, $S_{YX} = 30.81$ and $h_i = 0.1373$ when $X = 8$.

a. Construct a 95% confidence interval estimate of the mean weekly sales for all stores that have 8 feet of shelf space for pet food.

b. Construct a 95% prediction interval of the weekly sales of an individual store that has 8 feet of shelf space for pet food.

c. Explain the difference in the results in (a) and (b).

13.59 In Problem 13.7 on page 531, you used the total number of customers in the store to predict the waiting time at the checkout counter. The data are stored in **Supermarket**.

a. Construct a 95% confidence interval estimate of the mean waiting time for all customers when there are 20 customers in the store.

b. Construct a 95% prediction interval of the waiting time for an individual customer when there are 20 customers in the store.

c. Why is the interval in (a) narrower than the interval in (b)?

13.60 In Problem 13.6 on page 531, the owner of a moving company wanted to predict labor hours based on the number of cubic feet moved. The data are stored in **Moving**.

a. Construct a 95% confidence interval estimate of the mean labor hours for all moves of 500 cubic feet.

b. Construct a 95% prediction interval of the labor hours of an individual move that has 500 cubic feet.

c. Why is the interval in (a) narrower than the interval in (b)?

13.61 In Problem 13.9 on page 532, an agent for a real estate company wanted to predict the monthly rent for apartments, based on the size of an apartment. The data are stored in **Rent**.

a. Construct a 95% confidence interval estimate of the mean monthly rental for all apartments that are 1,000 square feet in size.

b. Construct a 95% prediction interval of the monthly rental for an individual apartment that is 1,000 square feet in size.

c. Explain the difference in the results in (a) and (b).

13.62 In Problem 13.8 on page 531, you predicted the value of a baseball franchise, based on current revenue. The data are stored in **BBRevenue**.

a. Construct a 95% confidence interval estimate of the mean value of all baseball franchises that generate $200 million of annual revenue.

b. Construct a 95% prediction interval of the value of an individual baseball franchise that generates $200 million of annual revenue.

c. Explain the difference in the results in (a) and (b).

13.63 In Problem 13.10 on page 532, you used box office gross to predict DVD revenue. The data are stored in **Movie**. The company is about to release a movie on DVD that had a box office gross of $75 million.

a. What is the predicted DVD revenue?

b. Which interval is more useful here, the confidence interval estimate of the mean or the prediction interval for an individual response? Explain.

c. Construct and interpret the interval you selected in (b).

13.9 Pitfalls in Regression

Some of the pitfalls involved in using regression analysis are as follows:

- Lacking awareness of the assumptions of least-squares regression
- Not knowing how to evaluate the assumptions of least-squares regression
- Not knowing what the alternatives are to least-squares regression if a particular assumption is violated
- Using a regression model without knowledge of the subject matter
- Extrapolating outside the relevant range
- Concluding that a significant relationship identified in an observational study is due to a cause-and-effect relationship

The widespread availability of spreadsheet and statistical applications has made regression analysis much more feasible today than it once was. However, many users with access to such applications do not understand how to use regression analysis properly. Someone who is not familiar with either the assumptions of regression or how to evaluate the assumptions cannot be expected to know what the alternatives to least-squares regression are if a particular assumption is violated.

The data in Table 13.7 (stored in **Anscombe**) illustrate the importance of using scatter plots and residual analysis to go beyond the basic number crunching of computing the Y intercept, the slope, and r^2.

TABLE 13.7

Four Sets of Artificial Data

Data Set A		Data Set B		Data Set C		Data Set D	
X_i	Y_i	X_i	Y_i	X_i	Y_i	X_i	Y_i
10	8.04	10	9.14	10	7.46	8	6.58
14	9.96	14	8.10	14	8.84	8	5.76
5	5.68	5	4.74	5	5.73	8	7.71
8	6.95	8	8.14	8	6.77	8	8.84
9	8.81	9	8.77	9	7.11	8	8.47
12	10.84	12	9.13	12	8.15	8	7.04
4	4.26	4	3.10	4	5.39	8	5.25
7	4.82	7	7.26	7	6.42	19	12.50
11	8.33	11	9.26	11	7.81	8	5.56
13	7.58	13	8.74	13	12.74	8	7.91
6	7.24	6	6.13	6	6.08	8	6.89

Source: Data extracted from F. J. Anscombe, "Graphs in Statistical Analysis," *The American Statistician*, 27 (1973), 17–21.

Anscombe (reference 1) showed that all four data sets given in Table 13.7 have the following identical results:

$$\hat{Y}_i = 3.0 + 0.5X_i$$

$$S_{YX} = 1.237$$

$$S_{b_1} = 0.118$$

$$r^2 = 0.667$$

$$SSR = \text{Explained variation} = \sum_{i=1}^{n}(\hat{Y}_i - \overline{Y})^2 = 27.51$$

$$SSE = \text{Unexplained variation} = \sum_{i=1}^{n}(Y_i - \hat{Y}_i)^2 = 13.76$$

$$SST = \text{Total variation} = \sum_{i=1}^{n}(Y_i - \overline{Y})^2 = 41.27$$

If you stopped the analysis at this point, you would fail to observe the important differences among the four data sets.

From the scatter plots of Figure 13.22 and the residual plots of Figure 13.23 on page 560, you see how different the data sets are. Each has a different relationship between X and Y. The only data set that seems to approximately follow a straight line is data set A. The residual plot for data set A does not show any obvious patterns or outlying residuals. This is certainly not true for data sets B, C, and D. The scatter plot for data set B shows that a curvilinear regression model is more appropriate. This conclusion is reinforced by the residual plot for data set B. The scatter plot and the residual plot for data set C clearly show an outlying observation. In this case, one approach used is to remove the outlier and reestimate the regression model (see reference 4). The scatter plot for data set D represents a situation in which the model is heavily dependent on the outcome of a single data point ($X_8 = 19$ and $Y_8 = 12.50$). Any regression model with this characteristic should be used with caution.

FIGURE 13.22
Scatter plots for four data sets

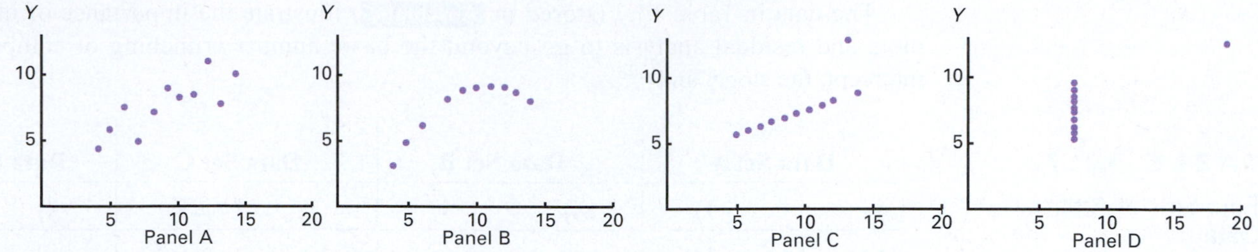

FIGURE 13.23
Residual plots for four data sets

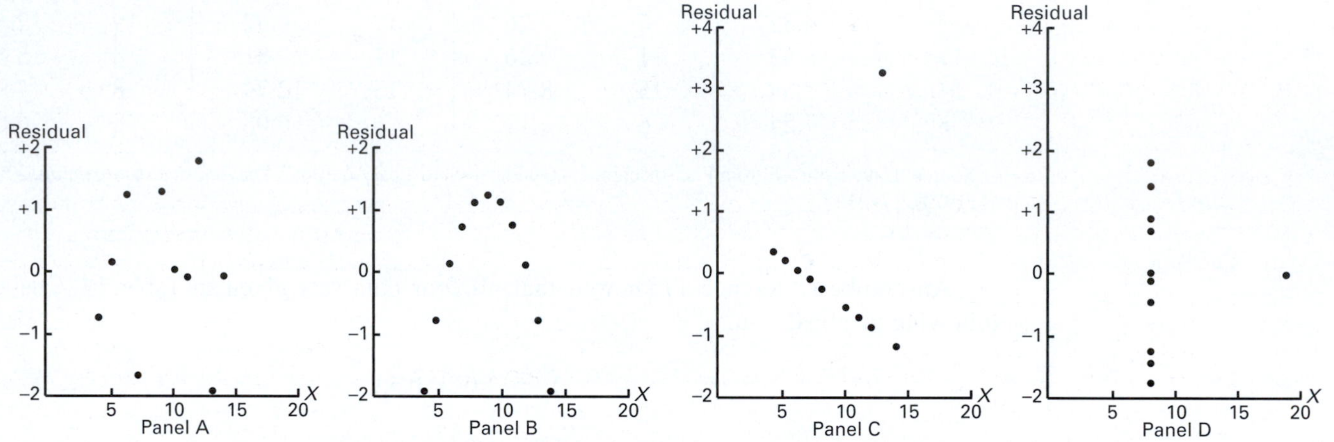

In summary, scatter plots and residual plots are of vital importance to a complete regression analysis. The information they provide is so basic to a credible analysis that you should always include these graphical methods as part of a regression analysis. Thus, a strategy you can use to help avoid the pitfalls of regression is as follows:

1. Start with a scatter plot to observe the possible relationship between X and Y.
2. Check the assumptions of regression (**l**inearity, **i**ndependence, **n**ormality, **e**qual variance) by performing a residual analysis that includes the following:
   a. Plotting the residuals versus the independent variable to determine whether the linear model is appropriate and to check for equal variance
   b. Constructing a histogram, stem-and-leaf display, boxplot, or normal probability plot of the residuals to check for normality
   c. Plotting the residuals versus time to check for independence (this step is necessary only if the data are collected over time)
3. If there are violations of the assumptions, use alternative methods to least-squares regression or alternative least-squares models (see reference 4).
4. If there are no violations of the assumptions, carry out tests for the significance of the regression coefficients and develop confidence and prediction intervals.
5. Avoid making predictions and forecasts outside the relevant range of the independent variable.

6. Keep in mind that the relationships identified in observational studies may or may not be due to cause-and-effect relationships. Remember that, although causation implies correlation, correlation does not imply causation.

THINK ABOUT THIS By Any Other Name

You may not have frequently heard the phrase "regression model" outside a classroom, but the basic concepts of regression can be found under a variety of names in many sectors of the economy:

- **Advertising and marketing** Managers use econometric models (in other words, regression models) to determine the effect of an advertisement on sales, based on a set of factors. In one recent example, the number of tweets that mention specific products was used to make accurate prediction of sales trends. (See H. Rui, A. Whinston, and E. Winkler, "Follow the Tweets," *The Wall Street Journal*, November 30, 2009, p. R4.) Also, managers use data mining to predict patterns of behavior of what customers will buy in the future, based on historic information about the consumer.
- **Finance** Any time you read about a financial "model," you should assume that some type of regression model is being used. For example, a *New York Times* article on June 18, 2006, titled "An Old Formula That Points to New Worry" by Mark Hulbert (p. BU8), discusses a market timing model that predicts the returns of stocks in the next three to five years, based on the dividend yield of the stock market and the interest rate of 90-day Treasury bills.
- **Food and beverage** Enologix, a California consulting company, has developed a "formula" (a regression model) that predicts a wine's quality index, based on a set of chemical compounds found in the wine. (See D. Darlington, "The Chemistry of a 90+ Wine," *The New York Times Magazine*, August 7, 2005, pp. 36–39.)
- **Government** The Bureau of Labor Statistics uses hedonic models, a type of regression model, to adjust and manage its consumer price index ("Hedonic Quality Adjustment in the CPI," *Consumer Price Index*, **stat.bls.gov/cpi/cpihqaitem.htm**).
- **Transportation** Bing Travel uses data mining and predictive technologies to objectively predict airfare pricing. (See C. Elliott, "Bing Travel's Crean: We Save the Average Couple $50 per Trip," *Elliott Blog*, **www.elliott.org/first-person/bing-travel-we-save-the-average-couple-50-per-trip/**.)
- **Real estate** Zillow.com uses information about the features contained in a home and its location to develop estimates about the market value of the home, using a "formula" built with a proprietary model.

In a more general way, regression models are part of the "quants" movement that revolutionized Wall Street investing before moving on to other fields (see S. Baker, "Why Math Will Rock Your World: More Math Geeks Are Calling the Shots in Business. Is Your Industry Next?" *BusinessWeek*, January 23, 2006, pp. 54–62). While the methods, including advanced regression models, that the quants used in Wall Street operations have been seen by some as the cause of the 2007 economic meltdown (see S. Patterson, *The Quants: How a New Breed of Math Whizzes Conquered Wall Street and Nearly Destroyed It*, New York: Crown Business, 2010), the rise of quants reflects a growing use of regression and other statistical techniques in business.

In his landmark 2006 *BusinessWeek* article, Baker predicted that statistics and probability will become core skills for businesspeople and consumers. He claimed that those who would become successful would know how to use statistics, whether they are building financial models or making marketing plans. More recent articles, including S. Lohr's "For Today's Graduate, Just One Word: Statistics" (*The New York Times*, August 6, 2009, pp. A1, A3) confirm Baker's prediction and discussed how statistics is being used to "mine" large data sets to discover patterns, often using regression models. Hal Varian, the chief economist at Google, is quoted in that article as saying, "I keep saying that the sexy job in the next ten years will be statisticians."

USING STATISTICS @Sunflowers Apparel Revisited

In the Sunflowers Apparel scenario, you were the director of planning for a chain of upscale clothing stores for women. Until now, Sunflowers managers selected sites based on factors such as the availability of a good lease or a subjective opinion that a location seemed like a good place for a store. To make more objective decisions, you developed a regression model to analyze the relationship between the size of a store and its annual sales. The model indicated that about 90.4% of the variation in sales was explained by the size of the store. Furthermore, for each increase of 1,000 square feet, mean annual sales were estimated to increase by $1.67 million. You can now use your model to help make better decisions when selecting new sites for stores as well as to forecast sales for existing stores.

SUMMARY

As you can see from the chapter roadmap in Figure 13.24, this chapter develops the simple linear regression model and discusses the assumptions and how to evaluate them. Once you are assured that the model is appropriate, you can predict values by using the prediction line and test for the significance of the slope. In Chapter 14, regression analysis is extended to situations in which more than one independent variable is used to predict the value of a dependent variable.

FIGURE 13.24

Roadmap for simple linear regression

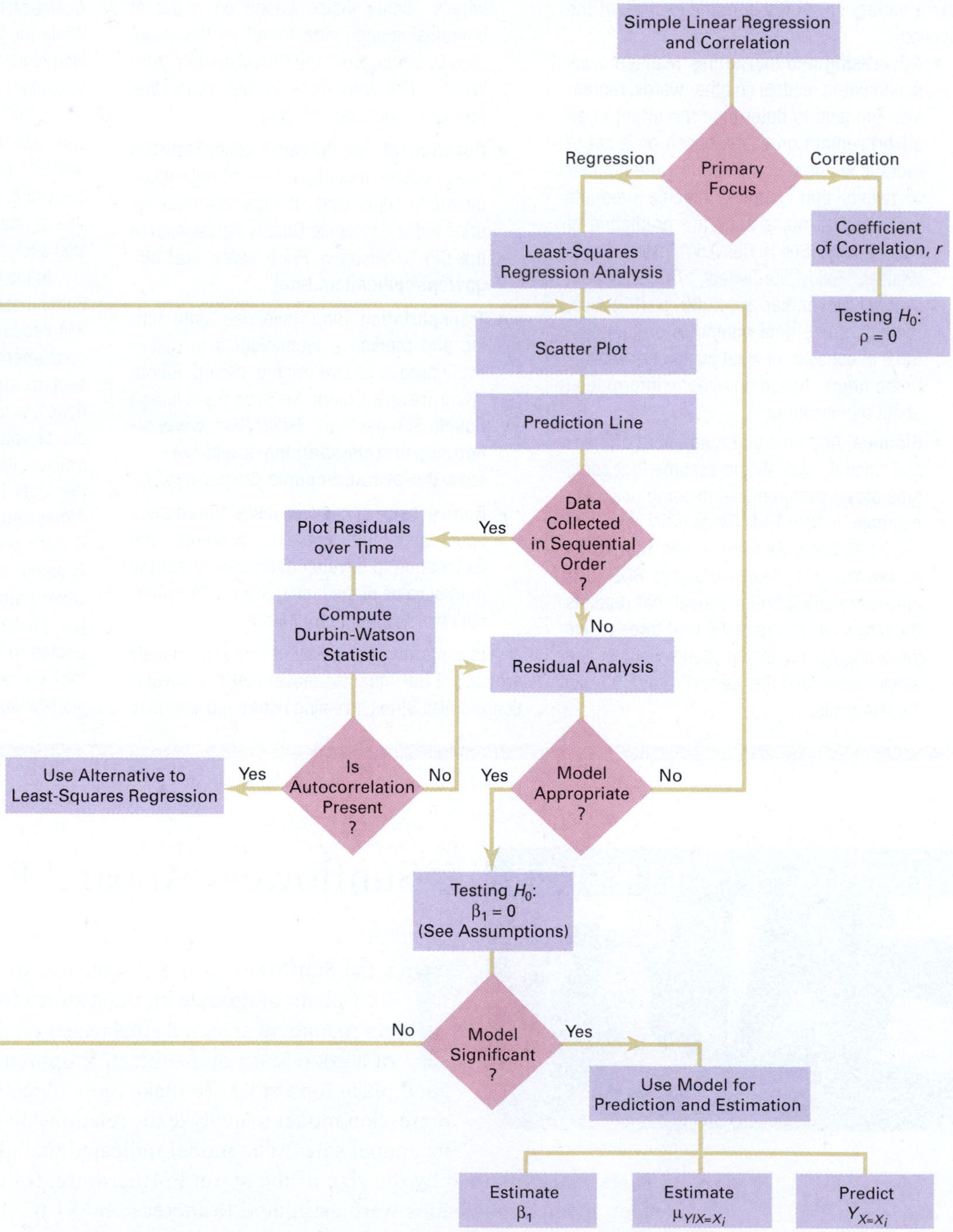

KEY EQUATIONS

Simple Linear Regression Model

$$Y_i = \beta_0 + \beta_1 X_i + \varepsilon_i \quad (13.1)$$

Simple Linear Regression Equation: The Prediction Line

$$\hat{Y}_i = b_0 + b_1 X_i \quad (13.2)$$

Computational Formula for the Slope, b_1

$$b_1 = \frac{SSXY}{SSX} \quad (13.3)$$

Computational Formula for the Y Intercept, b_0

$$b_0 = \bar{Y} - b_1 \bar{X} \quad (13.4)$$

Measures of Variation in Regression

$$SST = SSR + SSE \quad (13.5)$$

Total Sum of Squares (SST)

$$SST = \text{Total sum of squares} = \sum_{i=1}^{n}(Y_i - \bar{Y})^2 \quad (13.6)$$

Regression Sum of Squares (SSR)

$$SSR = \text{Explained variation or regression sum of squares}$$
$$= \sum_{i=1}^{n}(\hat{Y}_i - \bar{Y})^2 \quad (13.7)$$

Error Sum of Squares (SSE)

$$SSE = \text{Unexplained variation or error sum of squares}$$
$$= \sum_{i=1}^{n}(Y_i - \hat{Y}_i)^2 \quad (13.8)$$

Coefficient of Determination

$$r^2 = \frac{\text{Regression sum of squares}}{\text{Total sum of squares}} = \frac{SSR}{SST} \quad (13.9)$$

Computational Formula for SST

$$SST = \sum_{i=1}^{n}(Y_i - \bar{Y})^2 = \sum_{i=1}^{n} Y_i^2 - \frac{\left(\sum_{i=1}^{n} Y_i\right)^2}{n} \quad (13.10)$$

Computational Formula for SSR

$$SSR = \sum_{i=1}^{n}(\hat{Y}_i - \bar{Y})^2$$
$$= b_0 \sum_{i=1}^{n} Y_i + b_1 \sum_{i=1}^{n} X_i Y_i - \frac{\left(\sum_{i=1}^{n} Y_i\right)^2}{n} \quad (13.11)$$

Computational Formula for SSE

$$SSE = \sum_{i=1}^{n}(Y_i - \hat{Y}_i)^2 = \sum_{i=1}^{n} Y_i^2 - b_0 \sum_{i=1}^{n} Y_i - b_1 \sum_{i=1}^{n} X_i Y_i \quad (13.12)$$

Standard Error of the Estimate

$$S_{YX} = \sqrt{\frac{SSE}{n-2}} = \sqrt{\frac{\sum_{i=1}^{n}(Y_i - \hat{Y}_i)^2}{n-2}} \quad (13.13)$$

Residual

$$e_i = Y_i - \hat{Y}_i \quad (13.14)$$

Durbin-Watson Statistic

$$D = \frac{\sum_{i=2}^{n}(e_i - e_{i-1})^2}{\sum_{i=1}^{n} e_i^2} \quad (13.15)$$

Testing a Hypothesis for a Population Slope, β_1, Using the t Test

$$t_{STAT} = \frac{b_1 - \beta_1}{S_{b_1}} \quad (13.16)$$

Testing a Hypothesis for a Population Slope, β_1, Using the F Test

$$F_{STAT} = \frac{MSR}{MSE} \quad (13.17)$$

Confidence Interval Estimate of the Slope, β_1

$$b_1 \pm t_{\alpha/2} S_{b_1}$$
$$b_1 - t_{\alpha/2} S_{b_1} \le \beta_1 \le b_1 + t_{\alpha/2} S_{b_1} \quad (13.18)$$

Testing for the Existence of Correlation

$$t_{STAT} = \frac{r - \rho}{\sqrt{\frac{1 - r^2}{n - 2}}} \quad \textbf{(13.19a)}$$

$$r = \frac{cov(X,Y)}{S_X S_Y} \quad \textbf{(13.19b)}$$

Confidence Interval Estimate for the Mean of *Y*

$$\hat{Y}_i \pm t_{\alpha/2} S_{YX} \sqrt{h_i}$$

$$\hat{Y}_i - t_{\alpha/2} S_{YX} \sqrt{h_i} \le \mu_{Y|X=X_i} \le \hat{Y}_i + t_{\alpha/2} S_{YX} \sqrt{h_i} \quad \textbf{(13.20)}$$

Prediction Interval for an Individual Response, *Y*

$$\hat{Y}_i \pm t_{\alpha/2} S_{YX} \sqrt{1 + h_i}$$

$$\hat{Y}_i - t_{\alpha/2} S_{YX} \sqrt{1 + h_i} \le Y_{X=X_i} \le \hat{Y}_i + t_{\alpha/2} S_{YX} \sqrt{1 + h_i} \quad \textbf{(13.21)}$$

KEY TERMS

CHAPTER REVIEW PROBLEMS

CHECKING YOUR UNDERSTANDING

13.64 What is the interpretation of the *Y* intercept and the slope in the simple linear regression equation?

13.65 What is the interpretation of the coefficient of determination?

13.66 When is the unexplained variation (i.e., error sum of squares) equal to 0?

13.67 When is the explained variation (i.e., regression sum of squares) equal to 0?

13.68 Why should you always carry out a residual analysis as part of a regression model?

13.69 What are the assumptions of regression analysis?

13.70 How do you evaluate the assumptions of regression analysis?

13.71 When and how do you use the Durbin-Watson statistic?

13.72 What is the difference between a confidence interval estimate of the mean response, $\mu_{Y|X=X_i}$, and a prediction interval of $Y_{X=X_i}$?

APPLYING THE CONCEPTS

13.73 Researchers from the Pace University Lubin School of Business conducted a study on Internet-supported courses. In one part of the study, four numerical variables were collected on 108 students in an introductory management course that met once a week for an entire semester. One variable collected was *hit consistency*. To measure hit consistency, the researchers did the following: If a student did not visit the Internet site between classes, the student was given a 0 for that time period. If a student visited the Internet site one or more times between classes, the student was given a 1 for that time period. Because there were 13 time periods, a student's score on hit consistency could range from 0 to 13.

The other three variables included the student's course average, the student's cumulative grade point average (GPA), and the total number of hits the student had on the Internet site supporting the course. The following table gives the correlation coefficient for all pairs of variables. Note that correlations marked with an * are statistically significant, using $\alpha = 0.001$:

Variable	Correlation
Course Average, Cumulative GPA	0.72*
Course Average, Total Hits	0.08
Course Average, Hit Consistency	0.37*
Cumulative GPA, Total Hits	0.12
Cumulative GPA, Hit Consistency	0.32*
Total Hits & Hit Consistency	0.64*

Source: Data extracted from D. Baugher, A. Varanelli, and E. Weisbord, "Student Hits in an Internet-Supported Course: How Can Instructors Use Them and What Do They Mean?" *Decision Sciences Journal of Innovative Education,* 1 (Fall 2003), 159–179.

a. What conclusions can you reach from this correlation analysis?
b. Are you surprised by the results, or are they consistent with your own observations and experiences?

13.74 Management of a soft-drink bottling company has the business objective of developing a method for allocating delivery costs to customers. Although one cost clearly relates to travel time within a particular route, another variable cost reflects the time required to unload the cases of soft drink at the delivery point. To begin, management decided to develop a regression model to predict delivery time based on the number of cases delivered. A sample of 20 deliveries within a territory was selected. The delivery times and the number of cases delivered were organized in the following table (and stored in **Delivery**):

Customer	Number of Cases	Delivery Time (Minutes)	Customer	Number of Cases	Delivery Time (Minutes)
1	52	32.1	11	161	43.0
2	64	34.8	12	184	49.4
3	73	36.2	13	202	57.2
4	85	37.8	14	218	56.8
5	95	37.8	15	243	60.6
6	103	39.7	16	254	61.2
7	116	38.5	17	267	58.2
8	121	41.9	18	275	63.1
9	143	44.2	19	287	65.6
10	157	47.1	20	298	67.3

a. Use the least-squares method to compute the regression coefficients b_0 and b_1.
b. Interpret the meaning of b_0 and b_1 in this problem.
c. Predict the delivery time for 150 cases of soft drink.
d. Should you use the model to predict the delivery time for a customer who is receiving 500 cases of soft drink? Why or why not?
e. Determine the coefficient of determination, r^2, and explain its meaning in this problem.
f. Perform a residual analysis. Is there any evidence of a pattern in the residuals? Explain.
g. At the 0.05 level of significance, is there evidence of a linear relationship between delivery time and the number of cases delivered?
h. Construct a 95% confidence interval estimate of the mean delivery time for 150 cases of soft drink and a 95% prediction interval of the delivery time for a single delivery of 150 cases of soft drink.

13.75 Measuring the height of a California redwood tree is a very difficult undertaking because these trees grow to heights of over 300 feet. People familiar with these trees understand that the height of a California redwood tree is related to other characteristics of the tree, including the diameter of the tree at the breast height of a person. The data in **Redwood** represent the height (in feet) and diameter (in inches) at the breast height of a person for a sample of 21 California redwood trees.

a. Assuming a linear relationship, use the least-squares method to compute the regression coefficients b_0 and b_1. State the regression equation that predicts the height of a tree based on the tree's diameter at breast height of a person.
b. Interpret the meaning of the slope in this equation.
c. Predict the height for a tree that has a breast diameter of 25 inches.
d. Interpret the meaning of the coefficient of determination in this problem.
e. Perform a residual analysis on the results and determine the adequacy of the model.
f. Determine whether there is a significant relationship between the height of redwood trees and the breast height diameter at the 0.05 level of significance.
g. Construct a 95% confidence interval estimate of the population slope between the height of the redwood trees and breast diameter.

13.76 You want to develop a model to predict the selling price of homes based on assessed value. A sample of 30 recently sold single-family houses in a small city is selected to study the relationship between selling price (in thousands of dollars) and assessed value (in thousands of dollars). The houses in the city were reassessed at full value one year prior to the study. The results are in **House1**. (Hint: First, determine which are the independent and dependent variables.)

a. Construct a scatter plot and, assuming a linear relationship, use the least-squares method to compute the regression coefficients b_0 and b_1.
b. Interpret the meaning of the Y intercept, b_0, and the slope, b_1, in this problem.
c. Use the prediction line developed in (a) to predict the selling price for a house whose assessed value is \$170,000.
d. Determine the coefficient of determination, r^2, and interpret its meaning in this problem.
e. Perform a residual analysis on your results and evaluate the regression assumptions.
f. At the 0.05 level of significance, is there evidence of a linear relationship between selling price and assessed value?
g. Construct a 95% confidence interval estimate of the population slope.

13.77 You want to develop a model to predict the assessed value of houses, based on heating area. A sample of 15 single-family houses in a city is selected. The assessed value (in thousands of dollars) and the heating area of the houses (in thousands of square feet) are recorded; the results are stored in **House2**. (Hint: First, determine which are the independent and dependent variables.)

a. Construct a scatter plot and, assuming a linear relationship, use the least-squares method to compute the regression coefficients b_0 and b_1.
b. Interpret the meaning of the Y intercept, b_0, and the slope, b_1, in this problem.
c. Use the prediction line developed in (a) to predict the assessed value for a house whose heating area is 1,750 square feet.
d. Determine the coefficient of determination, r^2, and interpret its meaning in this problem.
e. Perform a residual analysis on your results and evaluate the regression assumptions.
f. At the 0.05 level of significance, is there evidence of a linear relationship between assessed value and heating area?

13.78 The director of graduate studies at a large college of business would like to predict the grade point average (GPA) of students in an MBA program based on Graduate Management Admission Test (GMAT) score. A sample of 20 students who have completed two years in the program is selected. The results are stored in **GPIGMAT**. (Hint: First, determine which are the independent and dependent variables.)

a. Construct a scatter plot and, assuming a linear relationship, use the least-squares method to compute the regression coefficients b_0 and b_1.
b. Interpret the meaning of the Y intercept, b_0, and the slope, b_1, in this problem.
c. Use the prediction line developed in (a) to predict the GPA for a student with a GMAT score of 600.
d. Determine the coefficient of determination, r^2, and interpret its meaning in this problem.
e. Perform a residual analysis on your results and evaluate the regression assumptions.
f. At the 0.05 level of significance, is there evidence of a linear relationship between GMAT score and GPA?
g. Construct a 95% confidence interval estimate of the mean GPA of students with a GMAT score of 600 and a 95% prediction interval of the GPA for a particular student with a GMAT score of 600.
h. Construct a 95% confidence interval estimate of the population slope.

13.79 An accountant for a large department store would like to develop a model to predict the amount of time it takes to process invoices. Data are collected from the past 32 working days, and the number of invoices processed and completion time (in hours) are stored in **Invoice**. (Hint: First, determine which are the independent and dependent variables.)

a. Assuming a linear relationship, use the least-squares method to compute the regression coefficients b_0 and b_1.
b. Interpret the meaning of the Y intercept, b_0, and the slope, b_1, in this problem.
c. Use the prediction line developed in (a) to predict the amount of time it would take to process 150 invoices.
d. Determine the coefficient of determination, r^2, and interpret its meaning.
e. Plot the residuals against the number of invoices processed and also against time.
f. Based on the plots in (e), does the model seem appropriate?
g. Based on the results in (e) and (f), what conclusions can you make about the validity of the prediction made in (c)?

13.80 On January 28, 1986, the space shuttle *Challenger* exploded, and seven astronauts were killed. Prior to the launch, the predicted atmospheric temperature was for freezing weather at the launch site. Engineers for Morton Thiokol (the manufacturer of the rocket motor) prepared charts to make the case that the launch should not take place due to the cold weather. These arguments were rejected, and the launch tragically took place. Upon investigation after the tragedy, experts agreed that the disaster occurred because of leaky rubber O-rings that did not seal properly due to the cold temperature. Data indicating the atmospheric temperature at the time of 23 previous launches and the O-ring damage index are stored in **O-Ring**.

Note: Data from flight 4 is omitted due to unknown O-ring condition.

Sources: Data extracted from *Report of the Presidential Commission on the Space Shuttle Challenger Accident,* Washington, DC, 1986, Vol. II (H1–H3); and Vol. IV (664), and *Post Challenger Evaluation of Space Shuttle Risk Assessment and Management,* Washington, DC, 1988, pp. 135–136.

a. Construct a scatter plot for the seven flights in which there was O-ring damage (O-ring damage index $\neq 0$). What conclusions, if any, can you reach about the relationship between atmospheric temperature and O-ring damage?

b. Construct a scatter plot for all 23 flights.

c. Explain any differences in the interpretation of the relationship between atmospheric temperature and O-ring damage in (a) and (b).

d. Based on the scatter plot in (b), provide reasons why a prediction should not be made for an atmospheric temperature of 31°F, the temperature on the morning of the launch of the *Challenger*.

e. Although the assumption of a linear relationship may not be valid for the set of 23 flights, fit a simple linear regression model to predict O-ring damage, based on atmospheric temperature.

f. Include the prediction line found in (e) on the scatter plot developed in (b).

g. Based on the results in (f), do you think a linear model is appropriate for these data? Explain.

h. Perform a residual analysis. What conclusions do you reach?

13.81 Crazy Dave, a well-known baseball analyst, would like to study various team statistics for the 2009 baseball season to determine which variables might be useful in predicting the number of wins achieved by teams during the season. He has decided to begin by using a team's earned run average (ERA), a measure of pitching performance, to predict the number of wins. The data for the 30 Major League Baseball teams are stored in BB2009. (Hint: First, determine which are the independent and dependent variables.)

a. Assuming a linear relationship, use the least-squares method to compute the regression coefficients b_0 and b_1.

b. Interpret the meaning of the Y intercept, b_0, and the slope, b_1, in this problem.

c. Use the prediction line developed in (a) to predict the number of wins for a team with an ERA of 4.50.

d. Compute the coefficient of determination, r^2, and interpret its meaning.

e. Perform a residual analysis on your results and determine the adequacy of the fit of the model.

f. At the 0.05 level of significance, is there evidence of a linear relationship between the number of wins and the ERA?

g. Construct a 95% confidence interval estimate of the mean number of wins expected for teams with an ERA of 4.50.

h. Construct a 95% prediction interval of the number of wins for an individual team that has an ERA of 4.50.

i. Construct a 95% confidence interval estimate of the population slope.

j. The 30 teams constitute a population. In order to use statistical inference, as in (f) through (i), the data must be assumed to represent a random sample. What "population" would this sample be drawing conclusions about?

k. What other independent variables might you consider for inclusion in the model?

13.82 Can you use the annual revenues generated by National Basketball Association (NBA) franchises to predict franchise values? Figure 2.15 on page 57 shows a scatter plot of revenue with franchise value, and Figure 3.10 on page 129, shows the correlation coefficient. Now, you want to develop a simple linear regression model to predict franchise values based on revenues. (Franchise values and revenues are stored in NBAValues.)

a. Assuming a linear relationship, use the least-squares method to compute the regression coefficients b_0 and b_1.

b. Interpret the meaning of the Y intercept, b_0, and the slope, b_1, in this problem.

c. Predict the value of an NBA franchise that generates $150 million of annual revenue.

d. Compute the coefficient of determination, r^2, and interpret its meaning.

e. Perform a residual analysis on your results and evaluate the regression assumptions.

f. At the 0.05 level of significance, is there evidence of a linear relationship between the annual revenues generated and the value of an NBA franchise?

g. Construct a 95% confidence interval estimate of the mean value of all NBA franchises that generate $150 million of annual revenue.

h. Construct a 95% prediction interval of the value of an individual NBA franchise that generates $150 million of annual revenue.

i. Compare the results of (a) through (h) to those of baseball franchises in Problems 13.8, 13.20, 13.30, 13.46, and 13.62 and European soccer teams in Problem 13.83.

13.83 In Problem 13.82 you used annual revenue to develop a model to predict the franchise value of National Basketball Association (NBA) teams. Can you also use the annual revenues generated by European soccer teams to predict franchise values? (European soccer team values and revenues are stored in SoccerValues.)

a. Repeat Problem 13.82 (a) through (h) for the European soccer teams.

b. Compare the results of (a) to those of baseball franchises in Problems 13.8, 13.20, 13.30, 13.46, and 13.62 and NBA franchises in Problem 13.82.

13.84 During the fall harvest season in the United States, pumpkins are sold in large quantities at farm stands. Often, instead of weighing the pumpkins prior to sale, the farm stand operator will just place the pumpkin in the appropriate circular cutout on the counter. When asked why this was done, one farmer replied, "I can tell the weight of the pumpkin from its circumference." To determine whether this was really true, a sample of 23 pumpkins were measured for circumference and weighed; the results are stored in Pumpkin.

a. Assuming a linear relationship, use the least-squares method to compute the regression coefficients b_0 and b_1.

b. Interpret the meaning of the slope, b_1, in this problem.

c. Predict the weight for a pumpkin that is 60 centimeters in circumference.

d. Do you think it is a good idea for the farmer to sell pumpkins by circumference instead of weight? Explain.

e. Determine the coefficient of determination, r^2, and interpret its meaning.

f. Perform a residual analysis for these data and evaluate the regression assumptions.

g. At the 0.05 level of significance, is there evidence of a linear relationship between the circumference and weight of a pumpkin?

h. Construct a 95% confidence interval estimate of the population slope, β_1.

13.85 Can demographic information be helpful in predicting sales at sporting goods stores? The file **Sporting** contains the monthly sales totals from a random sample of 38 stores in a large chain of nationwide sporting goods stores. All stores in the franchise, and thus within the sample, are approximately the same size and carry the same merchandise. The county or, in some cases, counties in which the store draws the majority of its customers is referred to here as the customer base. For each of the 38 stores, demographic information about the customer base is provided. The data are real, but the name of the franchise is not used, at the request of the company. The data set contains the following variables:

Sales—Latest one-month sales total (dollars)
Age—Median age of customer base (years)
HS—Percentage of customer base with a high school diploma
College—Percentage of customer base with a college diploma
Growth—Annual population growth rate of customer base over the past 10 years
Income—Median family income of customer base (dollars)

a. Construct a scatter plot, using sales as the dependent variable and median family income as the independent variable. Discuss the scatter plot.

b. Assuming a linear relationship, use the least-squares method to compute the regression coefficients b_0 and b_1.

c. Interpret the meaning of the Y intercept, b_0, and the slope, b_1, in this problem.

d. Compute the coefficient of determination, r^2, and interpret its meaning.

e. Perform a residual analysis on your results and determine the adequacy of the fit of the model.

f. At the 0.05 level of significance, is there evidence of a linear relationship between the independent variable and the dependent variable?

g. Construct a 95% confidence interval estimate of the population slope and interpret its meaning.

13.86 For the data of Problem 13.85, repeat (a) through (g), using Age as the independent variable.

13.87 For the data of Problem 13.85, repeat (a) through (g), using HS as the independent variable.

13.88 For the data of Problem 13.85, repeat (a) through (g), using College as the independent variable.

13.89 For the data of Problem 13.85, repeat (a) through (g), using Growth as the independent variable.

13.90 The file **CEO-Compensation** includes the total compensation (in $) of CEOs of 197 large public companies and their investment return in 2009.

Source: Data extracted from D. Leonard, "Bargains in the Boardroom," *The New York Times,* April 4, 2010, pp. BU1, BU7, BU10, BU11.

a. Compute the correlation coefficient between compensation and the investment return in 2009.

b. At the 0.05 level of significance, is the correlation between compensation and the investment return in 2009 statistically significant?

c. Write a short summary of your findings in (a) and (b). Do the results surprise you?

13.91 Refer to the discussion of beta values and market models in Problem 13.49 on page 553. The S&P 500 Index tracks the overall movement of the stock market by considering the stock prices of 500 large corporations. The file **StockPrices** contains 2009 weekly data for the S&P 500 and three companies. The following variables are included:

WEEK—Week ending on date given
S&P—Weekly closing value for the S&P 500 Index
GE—Weekly closing stock price for General Electric
DISC—Weekly closing stock price for Discovery Communications
AAPL—Weekly closing stock price for Apple

Source: Data extracted from **finance.yahoo.com**, June 3, 2010.

a. Estimate the market model for GE. (Hint: Use the percentage change in the S&P 500 Index as the independent variable and the percentage change in GE's stock price as the dependent variable.)

b. Interpret the beta value for GE.

c. Repeat (a) and (b) for Discovery.

d. Repeat (a) and (b) for Apple.

e. Write a brief summary of your findings.

REPORT WRITING EXERCISE

13.92 In Problems 13.85 through 13.89, you developed regression models to predict monthly sales at a sporting goods store. Now, write a report based on the models you developed. Append to your report all appropriate charts and statistical information.

MANAGING ASHLAND MULTICOMM SERVICES

To ensure that as many trial subscriptions to the *3-For-All* service as possible are converted to regular subscriptions, the marketing department works closely with the customer support department to accomplish a smooth initial process for the trial subscription customers. To assist in this effort, the marketing department needs to accurately forecast the monthly total of new regular subscriptions.

A team consisting of managers from the marketing and customer support departments was convened to develop a better method of forecasting new subscriptions. Previously, after examining new subscription data for the prior three months, a group of three managers would develop a subjective forecast of the number of new subscriptions. Livia Salvador, who was recently hired by the company to provide expertise in quantitative forecasting methods, suggested that the department look for factors that might help in predicting new subscriptions.

Members of the team found that the forecasts in the past year had been particularly inaccurate because in some months, much more time was spent on telemarketing than in other months. Livia collected data (stored in AMS13) for the number of new subscriptions and hours spent on telemarketing for each month for the past two years.

EXERCISES

1. What criticism can you make concerning the method of forecasting that involved taking the new subscriptions data for the prior three months as the basis for future projections?
2. What factors other than number of telemarketing hours spent might be useful in predicting the number of new subscriptions? Explain.
3. a. Analyze the data and develop a regression model to predict the number of new subscriptions for a month, based on the number of hours spent on telemarketing for new subscriptions.
   b. If you expect to spend 1,200 hours on telemarketing per month, estimate the number of new subscriptions for the month. Indicate the assumptions on which this prediction is based. Do you think these assumptions are valid? Explain.
   c. What would be the danger of predicting the number of new subscriptions for a month in which 2,000 hours were spent on telemarketing?

DIGITAL CASE

Apply your knowledge of simple linear regression in this Digital Case, which extends the Sunflowers Apparel Using Statistics scenario from this chapter.

Leasing agents from the Triangle Mall Management Corporation have suggested that Sunflowers consider several locations in some of Triangle's newly renovated lifestyle malls that cater to shoppers with higher-than-mean disposable income. Although the locations are smaller than the typical Sunflowers location, the leasing agents argue that higher-than-mean disposable income in the surrounding community is a better predictor than store size of higher sales. The leasing agents maintain that sample data from 14 Sunflowers stores prove that this is true.

Open **Triangle_Sunflower.pdf** and review the leasing agents' proposal and supporting documents. Then answer the following questions:

1. Should mean disposable income be used to predict sales based on the sample of 14 Sunflowers stores?
2. Should the management of Sunflowers accept the claims of Triangle's leasing agents? Why or why not?
3. Is it possible that the mean disposable income of the surrounding area is not an important factor in leasing new locations? Explain.
4. Are there any other factors not mentioned by the leasing agents that might be relevant to the store leasing decision?

REFERENCES

1. Anscombe, F. J., "Graphs in Statistical Analysis," *The American Statistician*, 27 (1973), 17–21.
2. Hoaglin, D. C., and R. Welsch, "The Hat Matrix in Regression and ANOVA," *The American Statistician*, 32 (1978), 17–22.
3. Hocking, R. R., "Developments in Linear Regression Methodology: 1959–1982," *Technometrics*, 25 (1983), 219–250.
4. Kutner, M. H., C. J. Nachtsheim, J. Neter, and W. Li, *Applied Linear Statistical Models*, 5th ed. (New York: McGraw-Hill/Irwin, 2005).
5. *Microsoft Excel 2010* (Redmond, WA: Microsoft Corp., 2010).
6. *Minitab Release 16* (State College, PA: Minitab, Inc., 2010).

CHAPTER 13 EXCEL GUIDE

EG13.1 TYPES of REGRESSION MODELS

There are no Excel Guide instructions for this section.

EG13.2 DETERMINING the SIMPLE LINEAR REGRESSION EQUATION

PHStat2 Use **Simple Linear Regression** to perform a simple linear regression analysis. For example, to perform the Figure 13.4 analysis of the Sunflowers Apparel data on page 526, open to the **DATA worksheet** of the **Site workbook**. Select **PHStat ➔ Regression ➔ Simple Linear Regression**. In the procedure's dialog box (shown below):

1. Enter **C1:C15** as the **Y Variable Cell Range**.
2. Enter **B1:B15** as the **X Variable Cell Range**.
3. Check **First cells in both ranges contain label**.
4. Enter **95** as the **Confidence level for regression coefficients**.
5. Check **Regression Statistics Table** and **ANOVA and Coefficients Table**.
6. Enter a **Title** and click **OK**.

The procedure creates a worksheet that contains a copy of your data as well as the worksheet shown in Figure 13.4.

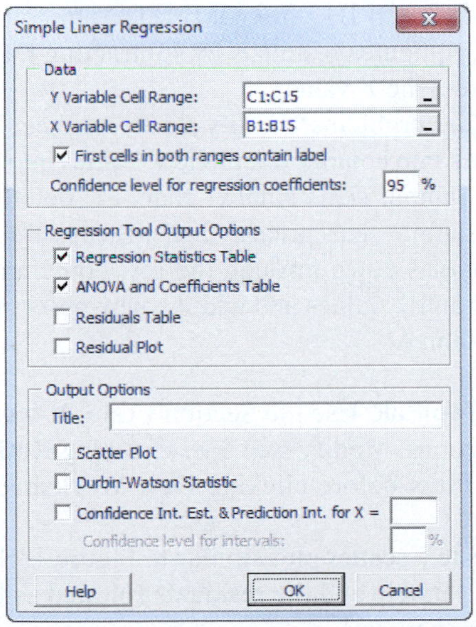

For more information about these worksheets, read the following *In-Depth Excel* section.

To create a scatter plot that contains a prediction line and regression equation similar to Figure 13.5 on page 526, modify step 6 by checking the **Scatter Plot** output option before clicking **OK**.

In-Depth Excel Use the **COMPUTE worksheet** of the **Simple Linear Regression workbook**, shown in Figure 13.4 on page 526, as a template for performing simple linear regression. Columns A through I of this worksheet duplicate the visual design of the Analysis ToolPak regression worksheet. The worksheet uses the regression data in the **SLRDATA worksheet** to perform the regression analysis for the Table 13.1 Sunflowers Apparel data.

Not shown in Figure 13.4 is the Calculations area in columns K through M. This area contains an array formula in the cell range L2:M6 that contains the expression **LINEST(*cell range of Y variable, cell range of X variable,* True, True)** to compute the b_1 and b_0 coefficients in cells L2 and M2, the b_1 and b_0 standard errors in cells L3 and M3, r^2 and the standard error of the estimate in cells L4 and M4, the F test statistic and error df in cells L5 and M5, and SSR and SSE in cells L6 and M6. In cell L9, the expression **TINV(1 − *confidence level, Error degrees of freedom*)** computes the critical value for the t test.

To perform simple linear regression for other data, paste the regression data into the SLRDATA worksheet. Paste the values for the X variable into column A and the values for the Y variable into column B. Open to the COMPUTE worksheet. First, enter the confidence level in cell L8. Then edit the array formula: Select the cell range L2:M6, edit the cell ranges in the formulas, and then, while holding down the **Control** and **Shift** keys (or the **Apple** key on a Mac), press the **Enter** key. (Open the **COMPUTE_FORMULAS worksheet** to examine all the formulas in the worksheet, some of which are discussed in later sections of this Excel Guide.)

To create a scatter plot that contains a prediction line and regression equation similar to Figure 13.5 on page 526, first use the Section EG2.6 *In-Depth Excel* scatter plot instructions with the Table 13.1 Sunflowers Apparel data to create a basic plot. Then select the plot and:

1. Select **Layout ➔ Trendline** and select **More Trendline Options** from the Trendline gallery.

In the Format Trendline dialog box (shown on page 572):

2. Click **Trendline Options** in the left pane. In the Trendline Options pane on the right, click **Linear**, check **Display Equation on chart**, check **Display R-squared value on chart**, and then click **Close**.

For scatter plots of other data, if the X axis does not appear at the bottom of the plot, right-click the **Y axis** and

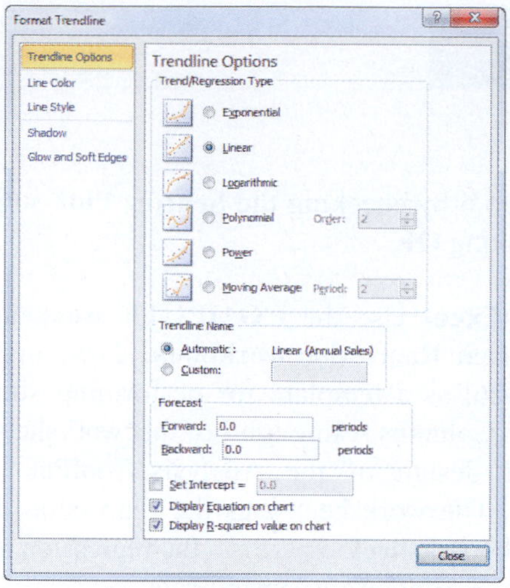

click **Format Axis** from the shortcut menu. In the Format Axis dialog box, click **Axis Options** in the left pane. In the Axis Options pane on the right, click **Axis value** and in its box enter the value shown in the dimmed **Minimum** box at the top of the pane. Then click **Close.**

Analysis ToolPak Use **Regression** to perform simple linear regression. For example, to perform the Figure 13.4 analysis of the Sunflowers Apparel data (see page 526), open to the **DATA worksheet** of the **Site workbook** and:

1. Select **Data → Data Analysis**.
2. In the Data Analysis dialog box, select **Regression** from the **Analysis Tools** list and then click **OK**.

In the Regression dialog box (see below):

3. Enter **C1:C15** as the **Input Y Range** and enter **B1:B15** as the **Input X Range**.
4. Check **Labels** and check **Confidence Level** and enter **95** in its box.
5. Click **New Worksheet Ply** and then click **OK**.

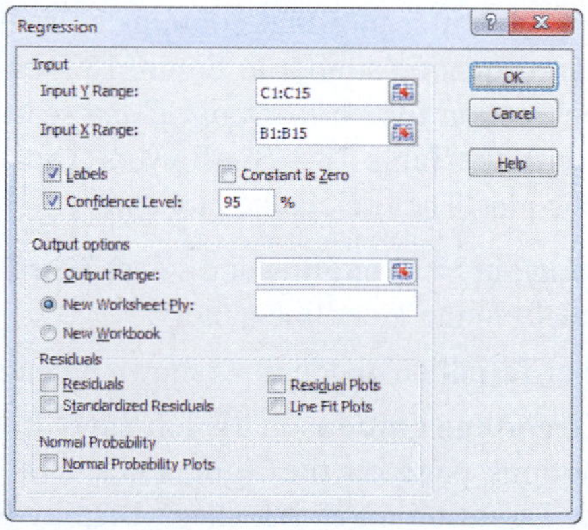

EG13.3 MEASURES of VARIATION

The measures of variation are computed as part of creating the simple linear regression worksheet using the Section EG13.2 instructions.

If you use either Section EG13.2 *PHStat2* or *In-Depth Excel* instructions, formulas used to compute these measures are in the **COMPUTE worksheet** that is created. Formulas in cells B5, B7, B13, C12, C13, D12, and E12 copy values computed by the array formula in cell range L2:M6. The cell F12 formula, in the form **=FDIST(*F test statistic*, 1, *error degrees of freedom*)**, computes the *p*-value for the *F* test for the slope, discussed in Section 13.7.

EG13.4 ASSUMPTIONS

There are no Excel Guide instructions for this section.

EG13.5 RESIDUAL ANALYSIS

PHStat2 Use the Section EG13.2 *PHStat2* instructions. Modify step 5 by checking **Residuals Table** and **Residual Plot** in addition to checking **Regression Statistics Table** and **ANOVA and Coefficients Table.**

In-Depth Excel Use the **RESIDUALS worksheet** of the **Simple Linear Regression workbook**, shown in Figure 13.10 on page 540, as a template for creating a residuals worksheet. This worksheet computes the residuals for the regression analysis for the Table 13.1 Sunflowers Apparel data. In column C, the worksheet computes the predicted *Y* values (labeled Predicted Annual Sales in Figure 13.10) by first multiplying the *X* values by the b_1 coefficient in cell B18 of the **COMPUTE worksheet** and then adding the b_0 coefficient (in cell B17 of COMPUTE). In column E, the worksheet computes residuals by subtracting the predicted *Y* values from the *Y* values.

For other problems, modify this worksheet by pasting the *X* values into column B and the *Y* values into column D. Then, for sample sizes smaller than 14, delete the extra rows. For sample sizes greater than 14, copy the column C and E formulas down through the row containing the last pair and *X* and *Y* values and add the new observation numbers in column A.

Analysis ToolPak Use the Section EG13.2 *Analysis ToolPak* instructions. Modify step 5 by checking **Residuals** and **Residual Plots** before clicking **New Worksheet Ply** and then **OK**.

To create a scatter plot similar to Figure 13.11, use the original *X* variable and the residuals (plotted as the *Y* variable) as the chart data.

EG13.6 MEASURING AUTOCORRELATION: the DURBIN-WATSON STATISTIC

PHStat2 Use the *PHStat2* instructions at the beginning of Section EG13.2. Modify step 6 by checking the **Durbin-Watson Statistic** output option before clicking **OK**.

In-Depth Excel Use the **DURBIN_WATSON worksheet** of the **Simple Linear Regression workbook**, similar to the worksheet shown in Figure 13.16 on page 545, as a template for computing the Durbin-Watson statistic. The worksheet computes the statistic for the package delivery simple linear regression model. In cell B3, the worksheet uses the expression **SUMXMY2(*cell range of the second through last residual, cell range of the first through the second-to-last residual*)** to compute the sum of squared difference of the residuals, the numerator in Equation (13.15) on page 544, and in cell B4 uses **SUMSQ(*cell range of the residuals*)** to compute the sum of squared residuals, the denominator in Equation (13.15).

To compute the Durbin-Watson statistic for other problems, first create the simple linear regression model and the RESIDUALS worksheet for the problem, using the instructions in Sections EG13.2 and EG13.5. Then open the DURBIN_WATSON worksheet and edit the formulas in cell B3 and B4 to point to the proper cell ranges of the new residuals.

EG13.7 INFERENCES ABOUT the SLOPE and CORRELATION COEFFICIENT

The *t* test for the slope and *F* test for the slope are included in the worksheet created by using the Section EG13.2 instructions. The *t* test computations in the worksheets created by using the *PHStat2* and *In-Depth Excel* instructions are discussed in Section EG13.2. The *F* test computations are discussed in Section EG13.3.

EG13.8 ESTIMATION of MEAN VALUES and PREDICTION of INDIVIDUAL VALUES

PHStat2 Use the Section EG13.2 *PHStat2* instructions but replace step 6 with these steps 6 and 7:

6. Check **Confidence Int. Est. & Prediction Int. for X =** and enter **4** in its box. Enter **95** as the percentage for **Confidence level for intervals**.
7. Enter a **Title** and click **OK**.

The additional worksheet created is discussed in the following *In-Depth Excel* instructions.

In-Depth Excel Use the **CIEandPI worksheet** of the **Simple Linear Regression workbook**, shown in Figure 13.21 on page 557, as a template for computing confidence interval estimates and prediction intervals. The worksheet contains the data and formulas for the Section 13.8 examples that use the Table 13.1 Sunflowers Apparel data. The worksheet uses the expression **TINV(1 − *confidence level, degrees of freedom*)** to compute the *t* critical value in cell B10 and the expression **TREND(*Y variable cell range, X variable cell range, X value*)** to compute the predicted *Y* value for the *X* value in cell B15. In cell B12, the expression **DEVSQ(*X variable cell range*)** computes the *SSX* value that is used, in turn, to help compute the *h* statistic.

To compute a confidence interval estimate and prediction interval for other problems:

1. Paste the regression data into the **SLRData worksheet**. Use column A for the *X* variable data and column B for the *Y* variable data.
2. Open to the **CIEandPI worksheet**.

In the CIEandPI worksheet:

3. Change values for the **X Value** and **Confidence Level**, as is necessary.
4. Edit the cell ranges used in the cell B15 formula that uses the TREND function to refer to the new cell ranges for the *Y* and *X* variables.

To create a scatter plot similar to Figure 13.11 on page 540, use the original *X* variable and the residuals (plotted as the *Y* variable) as the chart data.

CHAPTER 13 MINITAB GUIDE

MG13.1 TYPES of REGRESSION MODELS

There are no Minitab Guide instructions for this section.

MG13.2 DETERMINING the SIMPLE LINEAR REGRESSION EQUATION

Use **Regression** to perform a simple linear regression analysis. For example, to perform the Figure 13.4 analysis of the Sunflowers Apparel data on page 526, open to the **Site worksheet**. Select **Stat → Regression → Regression**. In the Regression dialog box (shown below):

1. Double-click **C3 Annual Sales** in the variables list to add '**Annual Sales**' to the **Response** box.
2. Double-click **C2 Square Feet** in the variables list to add '**Square Feet**' to the **Predictors** box.
3. Click **Graphs**.

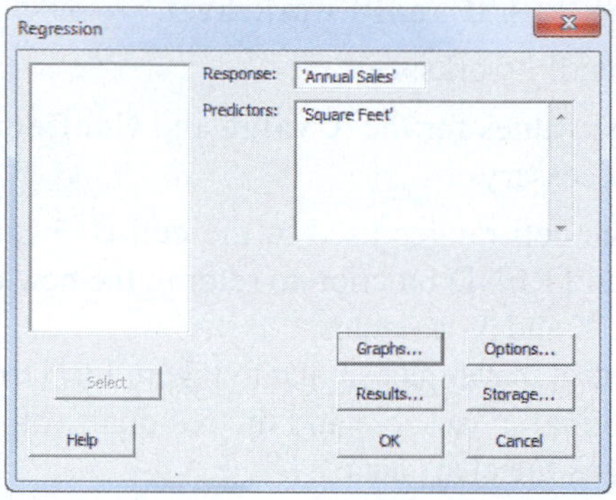

In the Regression - Graphs dialog box (shown below):

4. Click **Regular** (in Residuals for Plots) and **Individual Plots** (in Residual Plots).
5. Check **Histogram of residuals, Normal plot of residuals, Residuals versus fits,** and **Residuals versus order** and then press **Tab**.
6. Double-click **C2 Square Feet** in the variables list to add '**Square Feet**' in the **Residuals versus the variables** box.
7. Click **OK**.

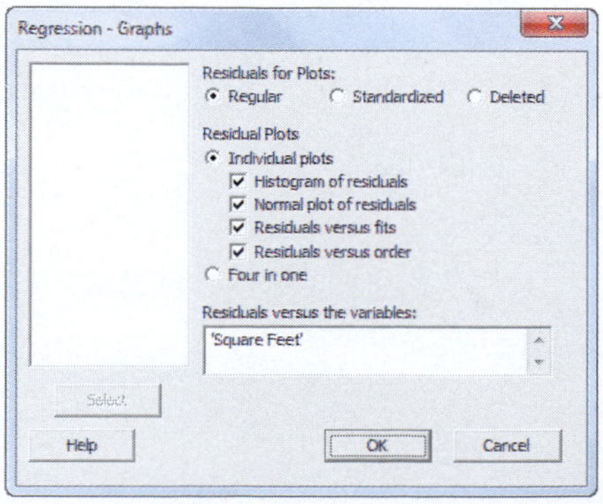

8. Back in the Regression dialog box, click **Results**.

In the Regression - Results dialog box (not shown):

9. Click **Regression equation, table of coefficients, s, R-squared, and basic analysis of variance** and then click **OK**.
10. Back in the Regression dialog box, click **Options**.

In the Regression - Options dialog box (shown below):

11. Check **Fit Intercept**.
12. Clear all the **Display** and **Lack of Fit Test** check boxes.
13. Enter **4** in the **Prediction intervals for new observations** box.
14. Enter **95** in the **Confidence level** box.
15. Click **OK**.
16. Back in the Regression dialog box, click **OK**.

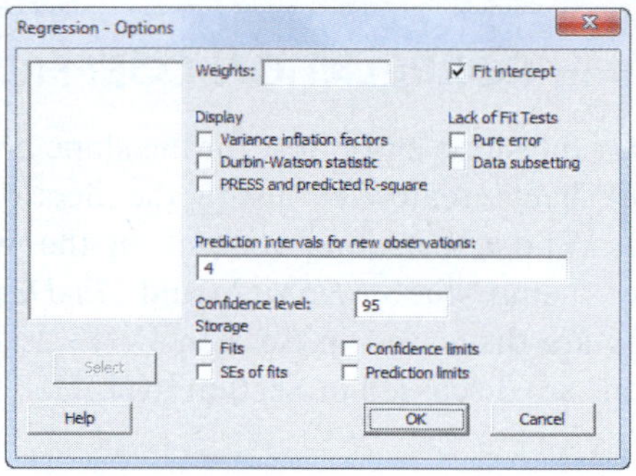

To create a scatter plot that contains a prediction line and regression equation similar to Figure 13.5 on page 526, use the Section MG2.6 scatter plot instructions with the Table 13.1 Sunflowers Apparel data.

MG13.3 MEASURES of VARIATION

The measures of variation are computed in the Analysis of Variance table that is part of the simple linear regression results created using the Section MG13.2 instructions.

MG13.4 ASSUMPTIONS

There are no Minitab Guide instructions for this section.

MG13.5 RESIDUAL ANALYSIS

Selections in step 5 of the Section MG13.2 instructions create the residual plots and normal probability plots necessary for residual analysis. To create the list of residual values similar to column E in Figure 13.10 on page 540, replace step

15 of the Section MG13.2 instructions with these steps 15 through 17:

15. Click **Storage**.

16. In the Regression - Storage dialog box, check **Residuals** and then click **OK**.

17. Back in the Regression dialog box, click **OK**.

MG13.6 MEASURING AUTOCORRELATION: the DURBIN-WATSON STATISTIC

To compute the Durbin-Watson statistic, use the Section MG13.2 instructions but check **Durbin-Watson statistic** (in the Regression - Options dialog box) as part of step 12.

MG13.7 INFERENCES ABOUT the SLOPE and CORRELATION COEFFICIENT

The *t* test for the slope and *F* test for the slope are included in the results created by using the Section MG13.2 instructions.

MG13.8 ESTIMATION of MEAN VALUES and PREDICTION of INDIVIDUAL VALUES

The confidence interval estimate and prediction interval are included in the results created by using the Section MG13.2 instructions.

14 Introduction to Multiple Regression

Learning Objectives

In this chapter, you learn:

- How to develop a multiple regression model
- How to interpret the regression coefficients
- How to determine which independent variables to include in the regression model
- How to determine which independent variables are most important in predicting a dependent variable
- How to use categorical independent variables in a regression model
- How to predict a categorical dependent variable using logistic regression

USING STATISTICS

@ OmniFoods

You are the marketing manager for OmniFoods, a large food products company. The company is planning a nationwide introduction of OmniPower, a new high-energy bar. Originally marketed to runners, mountain climbers, and other athletes, high-energy bars are now popular with the general public. OmniFoods is anxious to capture a share of this thriving market.

Because the marketplace already contains several successful energy bars, you need to develop an effective marketing strategy. In particular, you need to determine the effect that price and in-store promotions will have on sales of OmniPower. Before marketing the bar nationwide, you plan to conduct a test-market study of OmniPower sales, using a sample of 34 stores in a supermarket chain. How can you extend the linear regression methods discussed in Chapter 13 to incorporate the effects of price *and* promotion into the same model? How can you use this model to improve the success of the nationwide introduction of OmniPower?

Chapter 13 focused on simple linear regression models that use *one* numerical independent variable, X, to predict the value of a numerical dependent variable, Y. Often you can make better predictions by using *more than one* independent variable. This chapter introduces you to **multiple regression models** that use two or more independent variables to predict the value of a dependent variable.

14.1 Developing a Multiple Regression Model

The business objective facing the marketing manager at OmniFoods is to develop a model to predict monthly sales volume per store of OmniPower bars and to determine what variables influence sales. Two independent variables are considered here: the price of an OmniPower bar, as measured in cents (X_1), and the monthly budget for in-store promotional expenditures, measured in dollars (X_2). In-store promotional expenditures typically include signs and displays, in-store coupons, and free samples. The dependent variable Y is the number of OmniPower bars sold in a month. Data are collected from a sample of 34 stores in a supermarket chain selected for a test-market study of OmniPower. All the stores selected have approximately the same monthly sales volume. The data are organized and stored in OmniPower and presented in Table 14.1.

TABLE 14.1

Monthly OmniPower Sales, Price, and Promotional Expenditures

Store	Sales	Price	Promotion	Store	Sales	Price	Promotion
1	4,141	59	200	18	2,730	79	400
2	3,842	59	200	19	2,618	79	400
3	3,056	59	200	20	4,421	79	400
4	3,519	59	200	21	4,113	79	600
5	4,226	59	400	22	3,746	79	600
6	4,630	59	400	23	3,532	79	600
7	3,507	59	400	24	3,825	79	600
8	3,754	59	400	25	1,096	99	200
9	5,000	59	600	26	761	99	200
10	5,120	59	600	27	2,088	99	200
11	4,011	59	600	28	820	99	200
12	5,015	59	600	29	2,114	99	400
13	1,916	79	200	30	1,882	99	400
14	675	79	200	31	2,159	99	400
15	3,636	79	200	32	1,602	99	400
16	3,224	79	200	33	3,354	99	600
17	2,295	79	400	34	2,927	99	600

Visualizing Multiple Regression Data

With the special case of two independent variables and one dependent variable, you can visualize your data with a three-dimensional scatter plot. Figure 14.1 on page 579 presents a three-dimensional Minitab plot of the OmniPower data. This figure shows the points plotted at a height equal to their sales with drop lines down to their promotion expense and price values.

Interpreting the Regression Coefficients

When there are several independent variables, you can extend the simple linear regression model of Equation (13.1) on page 522 by assuming a linear relationship between each independent variable and the dependent variable. For example, with k independent variables, the multiple regression model is expressed in Equation (14.1).

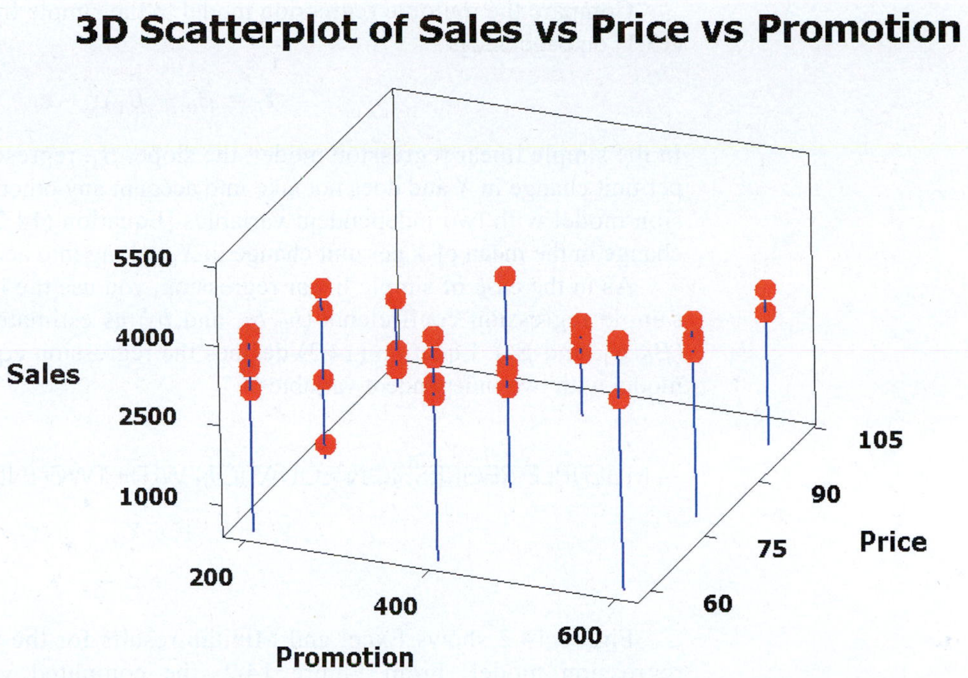

FIGURE 14.1
Minitab three-dimensional plot of monthly OmniPower sales, price, and promotional expenditures

Excel does not include the capability to create three-dimensional scatter plots.

MULTIPLE REGRESSION MODEL WITH k INDEPENDENT VARIABLES

$$Y_i = \beta_0 + \beta_1 X_{1i} + \beta_2 X_{2i} + \beta_3 X_{3i} + \cdots + \beta_k X_{ki} + \varepsilon_i \quad \textbf{(14.1)}$$

where

$\beta_0 = Y$ intercept

$\beta_1 =$ slope of Y with variable X_1, holding variables $X_2, X_3, \ldots, X_k$ constant

$\beta_2 =$ slope of Y with variable X_2, holding variables $X_1, X_3, \ldots, X_k$ constant

$\beta_3 =$ slope of Y with variable X_3, holding variables $X_1, X_2, X_4, \ldots, X_k$ constant

.
.
.

$\beta_k =$ slope of Y with variable X_k, holding variables $X_1, X_2, X_3, \ldots, X_{k-1}$ constant

$\varepsilon_i =$ random error in Y for observation i

Equation (14.2) defines the multiple regression model with two independent variables.

MULTIPLE REGRESSION MODEL WITH TWO INDEPENDENT VARIABLES

$$Y_i = \beta_0 + \beta_1 X_{1i} + \beta_2 X_{2i} + \varepsilon_i \quad \textbf{(14.2)}$$

where

$\beta_0 = Y$ intercept

$\beta_1 =$ slope of Y with variable X_1, holding variable X_2 constant

$\beta_2 =$ slope of Y with variable X_2, holding variable X_1 constant

$\varepsilon_i =$ random error in Y for observation i

Compare the multiple regression model to the simple linear regression model [Equation (13.1) on page 522]:

$$Y_i = \beta_0 + \beta_1 X_i + \varepsilon_i$$

In the simple linear regression model, the slope, β_1, represents the change in the mean of Y per unit change in X and does not take into account any other variables. In the multiple regression model with two independent variables [Equation (14.2)], the slope, β_1, represents the change in the mean of Y per unit change in X_1, taking into account the effect of X_2.

As in the case of simple linear regression, you use the least-squares method to compute sample regression coefficients (b_0, b_1, and b_2) as estimates of the population parameters (β_0, β_1, and β_2). Equation (14.3) defines the regression equation for a multiple regression model with two independent variables.

MULTIPLE REGRESSION EQUATION WITH TWO INDEPENDENT VARIABLES

$$\hat{Y}_i = b_0 + b_1 X_{1i} + b_2 X_{2i} \qquad \textbf{(14.3)}$$

Figure 14.2 shows Excel and Minitab results for the OmniPower sales data multiple regression model. From Figure 14.2, the computed values of the three regression coefficients are

$$b_0 = 5{,}837.5208 \quad b_1 = -53.2173 \quad b_2 = 3.6131$$

Therefore, the multiple regression equation is

$$\hat{Y}_i = 5{,}837.5208 - 53.2173 X_{1i} + 3.6131 X_{2i}$$

where

$\hat{Y}_i$ = predicted monthly sales of OmniPower bars for store i

X_{1i} = price of OmniPower bar (in cents) for store i

X_{2i} = monthly in-store promotional expenditures (in dollars) for store i

FIGURE 14.2

Excel and Minitab results for the OmniPower sales data multiple regression model

	A	B	C	D	E	F	G
1	**Multiple Regression**						
2							
3	*Regression Statistics*						
4	Multiple R	0.8705					
5	R Square	0.7577					
6	Adjusted R Square	0.7421					
7	Standard Error	638.0653					
8	Observations	34					
9							
10	**ANOVA**						
11		*df*	*SS*	*MS*	*F*	*Significance F*	
12	Regression	2	39472730.7730	19736365.3865	48.4771	0.0000	
13	Residual	31	12620946.6682	407127.3119			
14	Total	33	52093677.4412				
15							
16		*Coefficients*	*Standard Error*	*t Stat*	*P-value*	*Lower 95%*	*Upper 95%*
17	Intercept	5837.5208	628.1502	9.2932	0.0000	4556.3999	7118.6416
18	Price	-53.2173	6.8522	-7.7664	0.0000	-67.1925	-39.2421
19	Promotion	3.6131	0.6852	5.2728	0.0000	2.2155	5.0106

Regression Analysis: Sales versus Price, Promotion

```
The regression equation is
Sales = 5838 - 53.2 Price + 3.61 Promotion

Predictor      Coef  SE Coef      T      P
Constant     5837.5    628.2   9.29  0.000
Price       -53.217    6.852  -7.77  0.000
Promotion    3.6131   0.6852   5.27  0.000

S = 638.065   R-Sq = 75.8%   R-Sq(adj) = 74.2%

Analysis of Variance
Source          DF        SS        MS      F      P
Regression       2  39472731  19736365  48.48  0.000
Residual Error  31  12620947    407127
Total           33  52093677

Predicted Values for New Observations
New Obs   Fit  SE Fit      95% CI            95% PI
      1  3079     110  (2854, 3303)  (1758, 4399)

Values of Predictors for New Observations
New Obs  Price  Promotion
      1   79.0        400
```

The sample Y intercept ($b_0 = 5{,}837.5208$) estimates the number of OmniPower bars sold in a month if the price is \$0.00 and the total amount spent on promotional expenditures is also \$0.00. Because these values of price and promotion are outside the range of price and promotion used in the test-market study, and because they make no sense in the context of the problem, the value of b_0 has little or no practical interpretation.

The slope of price with OmniPower sales ($b_1 = -53.2173$) indicates that, for a given amount of monthly promotional expenditures, the predicted sales of OmniPower are estimated to decrease by 53.2173 bars per month for each 1-cent increase in the price. The slope of monthly promotional expenditures with OmniPower sales ($b_2 = 3.6131$) indicates that, for a given price, the estimated sales of OmniPower are predicted to increase by 3.6131 bars for each additional \$1 spent on promotions. These estimates allow you to better understand the likely effect that price and promotion decisions will have in the marketplace. For example, a 10-cent decrease in price is predicted to increase sales by 532.173 bars, with a fixed amount of monthly promotional expenditures. A \$100 increase in promotional expenditures is predicted to increase sales by 361.31 bars, for a given price.

Regression coefficients in multiple regression are called **net regression coefficients**; they estimate the predicted change in Y per unit change in a particular X, *holding constant the effect of the other X variables*. For example, in the study of OmniPower bar sales, for a store with a given amount of promotional expenditures, the estimated sales are predicted to decrease by 53.2173 bars per month for each 1-cent increase in the price of an OmniPower bar. Another way to interpret this "net effect" is to think of two stores with an equal amount of promotional expenditures. If the first store charges 1 cent more than the other store, the net effect of this difference is that the first store is predicted to sell 53.2173 fewer bars per month than the second store. To interpret the net effect of promotional expenditures, you can consider two stores that are charging the same price. If the first store spends \$1 more on promotional expenditures, the net effect of this difference is that the first store is predicted to sell 3.6131 more bars per month than the second store.

Predicting the Dependent Variable *Y*

You can use the multiple regression equation to predict values of the dependent variable. For example, what are the predicted sales for a store charging 79 cents during a month in which promotional expenditures are \$400? Using the multiple regression equation,

$$\hat{Y}_i = 5{,}837.5208 - 53.2173X_{1i} + 3.6131X_{2i}$$

with $X_{1i} = 79$ and $X_{2i} = 400$,

$$\begin{aligned}\hat{Y}_i &= 5{,}837.5208 - 53.2173(79) + 3.6131(400)\\ &= 3{,}078.57\end{aligned}$$

Thus, you predict that stores charging 79 cents and spending \$400 in promotional expenditures will sell 3,078.57 OmniPower bars per month.

After you have developed the regression equation, done a residual analysis (see Section 14.3), and determined the significance of the overall fitted model (see Section 14.2), you can construct a confidence interval estimate of the mean value and a prediction interval for an individual value. You should rely on software to do these computations for you, given the complex nature of the computations. Figure 14.3 presents an Excel worksheet that computes a confidence interval estimate and a prediction interval for the OmniPower sales data. (The Minitab results in Figure 14.2 include these computations.)

FIGURE 14.3

Excel confidence interval estimate and prediction interval worksheet for the OmniPower sales data

	A	B	C	D	
1	Confidence Interval Estimate and Prediction Interval				
2					
3	Data				
4	Confidence Level	95%			
5		1			
6	Price given value	79			
7	Promotion given value	400			
8					
9	X'X	34	2646	13200	
10		2646	214674	1018800	
11		13200	1018800	6000000	
12					
13	Inverse of X'X	0.9692	-0.0094	-0.0005	
14		-0.0094	0.0001	0.0000	
15		-0.0005	0.0000	0.0000	
16					
17	X'G times Inverse of X'X	0.0121	0.0001	0.0000	
18					
19	[X'G times Inverse of X'X] times XG	0.0298			=MMULT(B17:D17, B5:B7)
20	*t* Statistic	2.0395			=TINV(1 - B4, COMPUTE!B13)
21	Predicted Y (YHat)	3078.57			{=MMULT(TRANSPOSE(B5:B7), COMPUTE!B17:B19)}
22					
23	For Average Predicted Y (YHat)				
24	Interval Half Width	224.50			=B20 * SQRT(B19) * COMPUTE!B7
25	Confidence Interval Lower Limit	2854.07			=B21 - B24
26	Confidence Interval Upper Limit	3303.08			=B21 + B24
27					
28	For Individual Response Y				
29	Interval Half Width	1320.57			=B20 * SQRT(1 + B19) * COMPUTE!B7
30	Prediction Interval Lower Limit	1758.01			=B21 - B29
31	Prediction Interval Upper Limit	4399.14			=B21 + B29

Also:

Cell range B9:D11	=MMULT(TRANSPOSE(MRArray!A2:C35), MRArray!A2:C35)
Cell range B13:B15	=MINVERSE(B9:D11)
Cell range B17:D17	=MMULT(TRANSPOSE(B5:B7), B13:D15)

The 95% confidence interval estimate of the mean OmniPower sales for all stores charging 79 cents and spending \$400 in promotional expenditures is 2,854.07 to 3,303.08 bars. The prediction interval for an individual store is 1,758.01 to 4,399.14 bars.

Problems for Section 14.1

LEARNING THE BASICS

14.1 For this problem, use the following multiple regression equation:

$$\hat{Y}_i = 10 + 5X_{1i} + 3X_{2i}$$

a. Interpret the meaning of the slopes.
b. Interpret the meaning of the Y intercept.

14.2 For this problem, use the following multiple regression equation:

$$\hat{Y}_i = 50 - 2X_{1i} + 7X_{2i}$$

a. Interpret the meaning of the slopes.
b. Interpret the meaning of the Y intercept.

APPLYING THE CONCEPTS

14.3 A shoe manufacturer is considering developing a new brand of running shoes. The business problem facing the marketing analyst is to determine which variables should be used to predict durability (i.e., the effect of long-term impact). Two independent variables under consideration are X_1 (FOREIMP), a measurement of the forefoot shock-absorbing capability, and X_2 (MIDSOLE), a measurement of the change in impact properties over time. The dependent variable Y is LTIMP, a measure of the shoe's durability after a repeated impact test. Data are collected from a random sample of 15 types of currently manufactured running shoes, with the following results:

Variable	Coefficients	Standard Error	t Statistic	p-Value
Intercept	−0.02686	0.06905	−0.39	0.7034
Foreimp	0.79116	0.06295	12.57	0.0000
Midsole	0.60484	0.07174	8.43	0.0000

a. State the multiple regression equation.
b. Interpret the meaning of the slopes, b_1 and b_2, in this problem.

SELF Test **14.4** A mail-order catalog business selling personal computer supplies, software, and hardware maintains a centralized warehouse. Management is currently examining the process of distribution from the warehouse. The business problem facing management relates to the factors that affect warehouse distribution costs. Currently, a small handling fee is added to each order, regardless of the amount of the order. Data collected over the past 24 months (stored in **WareCost**) indicate the warehouse distribution costs (in thousands of dollars), the sales (in thousands of dollars), and the number of orders received.
a. State the multiple regression equation.
b. Interpret the meaning of the slopes, b_1 and b_2, in this problem.
c. Explain why the regression coefficient, b_0, has no practical meaning in the context of this problem.
d. Predict the monthly warehouse distribution cost when sales are $400,000 and the number of orders is 4,500.
e. Construct a 95% confidence interval estimate for the mean monthly warehouse distribution cost when sales are $400,000 and the number of orders is 4,500.
f. Construct a 95% prediction interval for the monthly warehouse distribution cost for a particular month when sales are $400,000 and the number of orders is 4,500.
g. Explain why the interval in (e) is narrower than the interval in (f).

14.5 How does horsepower and weight affect the mileage of family sedans? Data from a sample of twenty 2010 family sedans were collected and organized and stored in **Auto2010**. (Data extracted from "Top 2010 Cars," *Consumer Reports*, April 2010, pp. 38–70.) Develop a regression model to predict mileage (as measured by miles per gallon) based on the horsepower of the car's engine and the weight of the car (in pounds).
a. State the multiple regression equation.
b. Interpret the meaning of the slopes, b_1 and b_2, in this problem.
c. Explain why the regression coefficient, b_0, has no practical meaning in the context of this problem.
d. Predict the miles per gallon for cars that have 190 horsepower and weigh 3,500 pounds.
e. Construct a 95% confidence interval estimate for the mean miles per gallon for cars that have 190 horsepower and weigh 3,500 pounds.
f. Construct a 95% prediction interval for the miles per gallon for an individual car that has 190 horsepower and weighs 3,500 pounds.

14.6 The business problem facing a consumer products company is to measure the effectiveness of different types of advertising media in the promotion of its products. Specifically, the company is interested in the effectiveness of radio advertising and newspaper advertising (including the cost of discount coupons). During a one month test period, data were collected from a sample of 22 cities with approximately equal populations. Each city is allocated a specific expenditure level for radio advertising and for newspaper advertising. The sales of the product (in thousands of dollars) and also the levels of media expenditure (in thousands of dollars) during the test month are recorded, with the following results shown below and stored in **Advertise**:

City	Sales ($Thousands)	Radio Adverting ($Thousands)	Newspaper Advertising ($Thousands)
1	973	0	40
2	1,119	0	40
3	875	25	25
4	625	25	25
5	910	30	30
6	971	30	30
7	931	35	35
8	1,177	35	35
9	882	40	25
10	982	40	25
11	1,628	45	45
12	1,577	45	45
13	1,044	50	0
14	914	50	0
15	1,329	55	25
16	1,330	55	25
17	1,405	60	30
18	1,436	60	30
19	1,521	65	35
20	1,741	65	35
21	1,866	70	40
22	1,717	70	40

a. State the multiple regression equation.
b. Interpret the meaning of the slopes, b_1 and b_2, in this problem.
c. Interpret the meaning of the regression coefficient, b_0.
d. Which type of advertising is more effective? Explain.

14.7 The business problem facing the director of broadcasting operations for a television station was the issue of standby hours (i.e., hours in which unionized graphic artists at the station are paid but are not actually involved in any activity) and what factors were related to standby hours. The study included the following variables:

Standby hours (Y)—Total number of standby hours in a week

Total staff present (X_1)—Weekly total of people-days

Remote hours (X_2)—Total number of hours worked by employees at locations away from the central plant

Data were collected for 26 weeks; these data are organized and stored in Standby.

a. State the multiple regression equation.

b. Interpret the meaning of the slopes, b_1 and b_2, in this problem.

c. Explain why the regression coefficient, b_0, has no practical meaning in the context of this problem.

d. Predict the standby hours for a week in which the total staff present have 310 people-days and the remote hours are 400.

e. Construct a 95% confidence interval estimate for the mean standby hours for weeks in which the total staff present have 310 people-days and the remote hours are 400.

f. Construct a 95% prediction interval for the standby hours for a single week in which the total staff present have 310 people-days and the remote hours are 400.

14.8 Nassau County is located approximately 25 miles east of New York City. The data organized and stored in GlenCove include the appraised value, land area of the property in acres, and age, in years, for a sample of 30 single-family homes located in Glen Cove, a small city in Nassau County. Develop a multiple linear regression model to predict appraised value based on land area of the property and age, in years.

a. State the multiple regression equation.

b. Interpret the meaning of the slopes, b_1 and b_2, in this problem.

c. Explain why the regression coefficient, b_0, has no practical meaning in the context of this problem.

d. Predict the appraised value for a house that has a land area of 0.25 acres and is 45 years old.

e. Construct a 95% confidence interval estimate for the mean appraised value for houses that have a land area of 0.25 acres and are 45 years old.

f. Construct a 95% prediction interval estimate for the appraised value for an individual house that has a land area of 0.25 acres and is 45 years old.

14.2 r^2, Adjusted r^2, and the Overall F Test

This section discusses three methods you can use to evaluate the overall multiple regression model: the coefficient of multiple determination, r^2, the adjusted r^2, and the overall F test.

Coefficient of Multiple Determination

Recall from Section 13.3 that the coefficient of determination, r^2, measures the proportion of the variation in Y that is explained by the independent variable X in the simple linear regression model. In multiple regression, the **coefficient of multiple determination** represents the proportion of the variation in Y that is explained by the set of independent variables. Equation (14.4) defines the coefficient of multiple determination for a multiple regression model with two or more independent variables.

COEFFICIENT OF MULTIPLE DETERMINATION

The coefficient of multiple determination is equal to the regression sum of squares (SSR) divided by the total sum of squares (SST).

$$r^2 = \frac{\text{Regression sum of squares}}{\text{Total sum of squares}} = \frac{SSR}{SST} \qquad \textbf{(14.4)}$$

where

SSR = regression sum of squares

SST = total sum of squares

In the OmniPower example, from Figure 14.2 on page 580, $SSR = 39{,}472{,}730.77$ and $SST = 52{,}093{,}677.44$. Thus,

$$r^2 = \frac{SSR}{SST} = \frac{39{,}472{,}730.77}{52{,}093{,}677.44} = 0.7577$$

The coefficient of multiple determination ($r^2 = 0.7577$) indicates that 75.77% of the variation in sales is explained by the variation in the price and in the promotional expenditures. The coefficient of multiple determination also appears in the Figure 14.2 results on page 580, and is labeled R Square in the Excel results and R-Sq in the Minitab results.

Adjusted r^2

When considering multiple regression models, some statisticians suggest that you should use the **adjusted r^2** to take into account both the number of independent variables in the model and the sample size. Reporting the adjusted r^2 is extremely important when you are comparing two or more regression models that predict the same dependent variable but have a different number of independent variables. Equation (14.5) defines the adjusted r^2.

ADJUSTED r^2

$$r^2_{\text{adj}} = 1 - \left[(1 - r^2)\frac{n - 1}{n - k - 1}\right] \tag{14.5}$$

where k is the number of independent variables in the regression equation.

Thus, for the OmniPower data, because $r^2 = 0.7577$, $n = 34$, and $k = 2$,

$$\begin{aligned} r^2_{\text{adj}} &= 1 - \left[(1 - 0.7577)\frac{34 - 1}{34 - 2 - 1}\right] \\ &= 1 - \left[(0.2423)\frac{33}{31}\right] \\ &= 1 - 0.2579 \\ &= 0.7421 \end{aligned}$$

Therefore, 74.21% of the variation in sales is explained by the multiple regression model—adjusted for the number of independent variables and sample size. The adjusted r^2 also appears in the Figure 14.2 results on page 580, and is labeled Adjusted R Square in the Excel results and R-Sq(adj) in the Minitab results.

Test for the Significance of the Overall Multiple Regression Model

You use the **overall F test** to determine whether there is a significant relationship between the dependent variable and the entire set of independent variables (the overall multiple regression model). Because there is more than one independent variable, you use the following null and alternative hypotheses:

$H_0: \beta_1 = \beta_2 = \cdots = \beta_k = 0$ (There is no linear relationship between the dependent variable and the independent variables.)

H_1: At least one $\beta_j \neq 0$, $j = 1, 2, \ldots, k$ (There is a linear relationship between the dependent variable and at least one of the independent variables.)

Equation (14.6) defines the overall F test statistic. Table 14.2 presents the ANOVA summary table.

OVERALL F TEST

The F_{STAT} test statistic is equal to the regression mean square (MSR) divided by the mean square error (MSE).

$$F_{STAT} = \frac{MSR}{MSE} \tag{14.6}$$

where

F_{STAT} = test statistic from an F distribution with k and $n - k - 1$ degrees of freedom

k = number of independent variables in the regression model

TABLE 14.2

ANOVA Summary Table for the Overall F Test

Source	Degrees of Freedom	Sum of Squares	Mean Squares (Variance)	F
Regression	k	SSR	$MSR = \frac{SSR}{k}$	$F_{STAT} = \frac{MSR}{MSE}$
Error	$n - k - 1$	SSE	$MSE = \frac{SSE}{n - k - 1}$	
Total	$n - 1$	SST		

The decision rule is

$$\text{Reject } H_0 \text{ at the } \alpha \text{ level of significance if } F_{STAT} > F_\alpha;$$
$$\text{otherwise, do not reject } H_0.$$

Using a 0.05 level of significance, the critical value of the F distribution with 2 and 31 degrees of freedom found from Table E.5 is approximately 3.32 (see Figure 14.4 below). From Figure 14.2 on page 580, the F_{STAT} test statistic given in the ANOVA summary table is 48.4771. Because $48.4771 > 3.32$, or because the p-value $= 0.000 < 0.05$, you reject H_0 and conclude that at least one of the independent variables (price and/or promotional expenditures) is related to sales.

FIGURE 14.4

Testing for the significance of a set of regression coefficients at the 0.05 level of significance, with 2 and 31 degrees of freedom

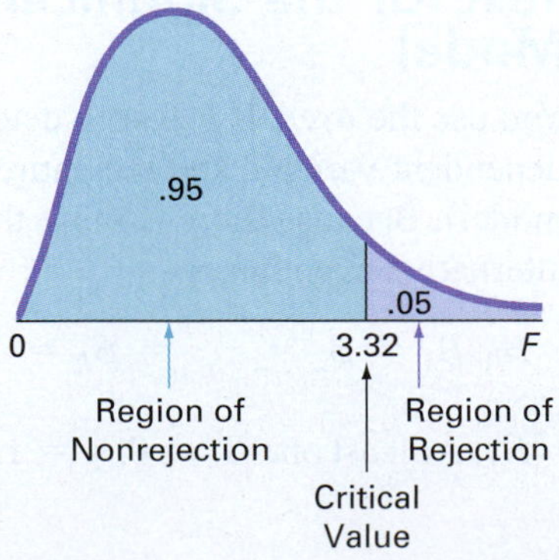

Problems for Section 14.2

LEARNING THE BASICS

14.9 The following ANOVA summary table is for a multiple regression model with two independent variables:

Source	Degrees of Freedom	Sum of Squares	Mean Squares	F
Regression	2	60		
Error	18	120		
Total	20	180		

a. Determine the regression mean square (MSR) and the mean square error (MSE).
b. Compute the overall F_{STAT} test statistic.
c. Determine whether there is a significant relationship between Y and the two independent variables at the 0.05 level of significance.
d. Compute the coefficient of multiple determination, r^2, and interpret its meaning.
e. Compute the adjusted r^2.

14.10 The following ANOVA summary table is for a multiple regression model with two independent variables:

Source	Degrees of Freedom	Sum of Squares	Mean Squares	F
Regression	2	30		
Error	10	120		
Total	12	150		

a. Determine the regression mean square (MSR) and the mean square error (MSE).
b. Compute the overall F_{STAT} test statistic.
c. Determine whether there is a significant relationship between Y and the two independent variables at the 0.05 level of significance.
d. Compute the coefficient of multiple determination, r^2, and interpret its meaning.
e. Compute the adjusted r^2.

APPLYING THE CONCEPTS

14.11 Eileen M. Van Aken and Brian M. Kleiner, professors at Virginia Polytechnic Institute and State University, investigated the factors that contribute to the effectiveness of teams. (Data extracted from "Determinants of Effectiveness for Cross-Functional Organizational Design Teams," *Quality Management Journal*, 4 (1997), 51–79.) The researchers studied 34 independent variables, such as team skills, diversity, meeting frequency, and clarity in expectations. For each of the teams studied, each of the variables was given a value of 1 through 100, based on the results of interviews and survey data, where 100 represents the highest rating. The dependent variable, team performance, was also given a value of 1 through 100, with 100 representing the highest rating. Many different regression models were explored, including the following:

Model 1

$$\text{Team performance} = \beta_0 + \beta_1(\text{Team skills}) + \varepsilon$$
$$r^2_{\text{adj}} = 0.68$$

Model 2

$$\text{Team performance} = \beta_0 + \beta_1(\text{Clarity in expectations}) + \varepsilon$$
$$r^2_{\text{adj}} = 0.78$$

Model 3

$$\text{Team performance} = \beta_0 + \beta_1(\text{Team skills}) + \beta_2(\text{Clarity in expectations}) + \varepsilon$$
$$r^2_{\text{adj}} = 0.97$$

a. Interpret the adjusted r^2 for each of the three models.
b. Which of these three models do you think is the best predictor of team performance?

14.12 In Problem 14.3 on page 582, you predicted the durability of a brand of running shoe, based on the forefoot shock-absorbing capability and the change in impact properties over time. The regression analysis resulted in the following ANOVA summary table:

Source	Degrees of Freedom	Sum of Squares	Mean Squares	F	p-Value
Regression	2	12.61020	6.30510	97.69	0.0001
Error	12	0.77453	0.06454		
Total	14	13.38473			

a. Determine whether there is a significant relationship between durability and the two independent variables at the 0.05 level of significance.
b. Interpret the meaning of the p-value.
c. Compute the coefficient of multiple determination, r^2, and interpret its meaning.
d. Compute the adjusted r^2.

14.13 In Problem 14.5 on page 583, you used horsepower and weight to predict mileage (stored in Auto2010). Using the results from that problem,
a. determine whether there is a significant relationship between mileage and the two independent variables (horsepower and weight) at the 0.05 level of significance.
b. interpret the meaning of the p-value.
c. compute the coefficient of multiple determination, r^2, and interpret its meaning.
d. compute the adjusted r^2.

SELF Test **14.14** In Problem 14.4 on page 583, you used sales and number of orders to predict distribution costs at a mail-order catalog business (stored in WareCost). Use the results from that problem.

a. Determine whether there is a significant relationship between distribution costs and the two independent variables (sales and number of orders) at the 0.05 level of significance.

b. Interpret the meaning of the p-value.

c. Compute the coefficient of multiple determination, r^2, and interpret its meaning.

d. Compute the adjusted r^2.

14.15 In Problem 14.7 on page 584, you used the total staff present and remote hours to predict standby hours (stored in Standby). Use the results from that problem.

a. Determine whether there is a significant relationship between standby hours and the two independent variables (total staff present and remote hours) at the 0.05 level of significance.

b. Interpret the meaning of the p-value.

c. Compute the coefficient of multiple determination, r^2, and interpret its meaning.

d. Compute the adjusted r^2.

14.16 In Problem 14.6 on page 583, you used radio advertising and newspaper advertising to predict sales (stored in Advertise). Use the results from that problem.

a. Determine whether there is a significant relationship between sales and the two independent variables (radio advertising and newspaper advertising) at the 0.05 level of significance.

b. Interpret the meaning of the p-value.

c. Compute the coefficient of multiple determination, r^2, and interpret its meaning.

d. Compute the adjusted r^2.

14.17 In Problem 14.8 on page 584, you used the land area of a property and the age of a house to predict appraised value (stored in GlenCove). Use the results from that problem.

a. Determine whether there is a significant relationship between appraised value and the two independent variables (land area of a property and age of a house) at the 0.05 level of significance.

b. Interpret the meaning of the p-value.

c. Compute the coefficient of multiple determination, r^2, and interpret its meaning.

d. Compute the adjusted r^2.

14.3 Residual Analysis for the Multiple Regression Model

In Section 13.5, you used residual analysis to evaluate the fit of the simple linear regression model. For the multiple regression model with two independent variables, you need to construct and analyze the following residual plots:

1. Residuals versus $\hat{Y}_i$
2. Residuals versus X_{1i}
3. Residuals versus X_{2i}
4. Residuals versus time

The first residual plot examines the pattern of residuals versus the predicted values of Y. If the residuals show a pattern for the predicted values of Y, there is evidence of a possible curvilinear effect (see Section 15.1) in at least one independent variable, a possible violation of the assumption of equal variance (see Figure 13.13 on page 542), and/or the need to transform the Y variable.

The second and third residual plots involve the independent variables. Patterns in the plot of the residuals versus an independent variable may indicate the existence of a curvilinear effect and, therefore, the need to add a curvilinear independent variable to the multiple regression model (see Section 15.1).

The fourth plot is used to investigate patterns in the residuals in order to validate the independence assumption when the data are collected in time order. Associated with this residual plot, as in Section 13.6, you can compute the Durbin-Watson statistic to determine the existence of positive autocorrelation among the residuals.

Figure 14.5 presents the residual plots for the OmniPower sales example. There is very little or no pattern in the relationship between the residuals and the predicted value of Y, the value of X_1 (price), or the value of X_2 (promotional expenditures). Thus, you can conclude that the multiple regression model is appropriate for predicting sales. There is no need to plot the residuals versus time because the data were not collected in time order.

FIGURE 14.5

Residual plots for the OmniPower sales data: Panel A, residuals versus predicted Y; Panel B, residuals versus price; Panel C, residuals versus promotional expenditures

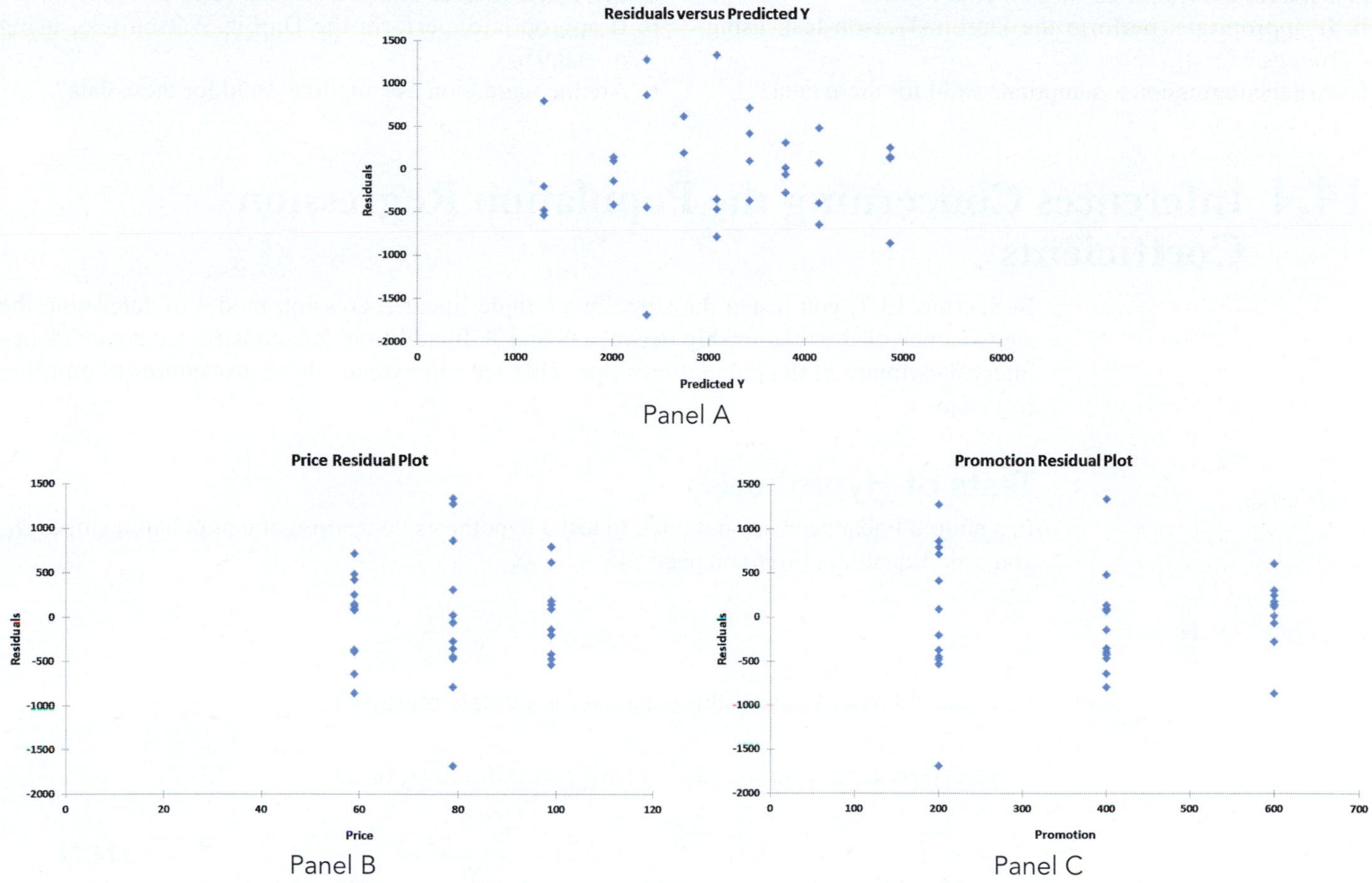

Problems for Section 14.3

APPLYING THE CONCEPTS

14.18 In Problem 14.4 on page 583, you used sales and number of orders to predict distribution costs at a mail-order catalog business (stored in **WareCost**).

a. Plot the residuals versus $\hat{Y}_i$.
b. Plot the residuals versus X_{1i}.
c. Plot the residuals versus X_{2i}.
d. Plot the residuals versus time.
e. In the residual plots created in (a) through (d), is there any evidence of a violation of the regression assumptions? Explain.
f. Determine the Durbin-Watson statistic.
g. At the 0.05 level of significance, is there evidence of positive autocorrelation in the residuals?

14.19 In Problem 14.5 on page 583, you used horsepower and weight to predict mileage (stored in **Auto2010**).

a. Plot the residuals versus $\hat{Y}_i$
b. Plot the residuals versus X_{1i}.
c. Plot the residuals versus X_{2i}.
d. In the residual plots created in (a) through (c), is there any evidence of a violation of the regression assumptions? Explain.
e. Should you compute the Durbin-Watson statistic for these data? Explain.

14.20 In Problem 14.6 on page 583, you used radio advertising and newspaper advertising to predict sales (stored in **Advertise**).

a. Perform a residual analysis on your results.
b. If appropriate, perform the Durbin-Watson test, using $\alpha = 0.05$.
c. Are the regression assumptions valid for these data?

14.21 In Problem 14.7 on page 584, you used the total staff present and remote hours to predict standby hours (stored in **Standby**).

a. Perform a residual analysis on your results.

b. If appropriate, perform the Durbin-Watson test, using $\alpha = 0.05$.

c. Are the regression assumptions valid for these data?

14.22 In Problem 14.8 on page 584, you used the land area of a property and the age of a house to predict appraised value (stored in **GlenCove**).

a. Perform a residual analysis on your results.

b. If appropriate, perform the Durbin-Watson test, using $\alpha = 0.05$.

c. Are the regression assumptions valid for these data?

14.4 Inferences Concerning the Population Regression Coefficients

In Section 13.7, you tested the slope in a simple linear regression model to determine the significance of the relationship between X and Y. In addition, you constructed a confidence interval estimate of the population slope. This section extends those procedures to multiple regression.

Tests of Hypothesis

In a simple linear regression model, to test a hypothesis concerning the population slope, β_1, you used Equation (13.16) on page 548:

$$t_{STAT} = \frac{b_1 - \beta_1}{S_{b_1}}$$

Equation (14.7) generalizes this equation for multiple regression.

TESTING FOR THE SLOPE IN MULTIPLE REGRESSION

$$t_{STAT} = \frac{b_j - \beta_j}{S_{b_j}} \quad \textbf{(14.7)}$$

where

b_j = slope of variable j with Y, holding constant the effects of all other independent variables

S_{b_j} = standard error of the regression coefficient b_j

t_{STAT} = test statistic for a t distribution with $n-k-1$ degrees of freedom

k = number of independent variables in the regression equation

β_j = hypothesized value of the population slope for variable j, holding constant the effects of all other independent variables

To determine whether variable X_2 (amount of promotional expenditures) has a significant effect on sales, taking into account the price of OmniPower bars, the null and alternative hypotheses are

$$H_0: \beta_2 = 0$$
$$H_1: \beta_2 \neq 0$$

From Equation (14.7) and Figure 14.2 on page 580,

$$t_{STAT} = \frac{b_2 - \beta_2}{S_{b_2}}$$
$$= \frac{3.6131 - 0}{0.6852} = 5.2728$$

If you select a level of significance of 0.05, the critical values of t for 31 degrees of freedom from Table E.3 are -2.0395 and $+2.0395$ (see Figure 14.6).

FIGURE 14.6

Testing for significance of a regression coefficient at the 0.05 level of significance, with 31 degrees of freedom

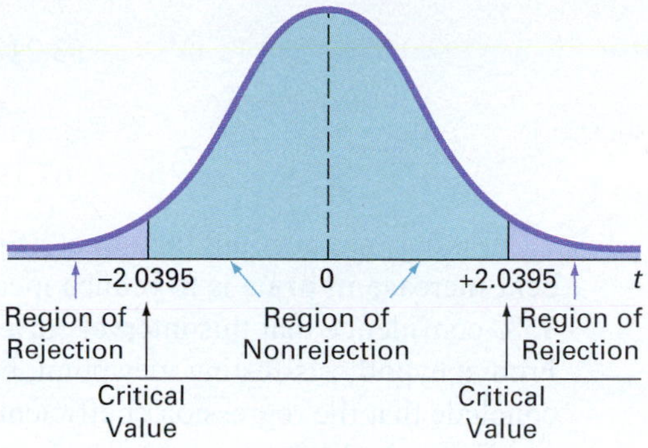

From Figure 14.2 on page 580, observe that the computed t_{STAT} test statistic is 5.2728. Because $t_{STAT} = 5.2728 > 2.0395$ or because the p-value is approximately zero, you reject H_0 and conclude that there is a significant relationship between the variable X_2 (promotional expenditures) and sales, taking into account the price, X_1. The extremely small p-value allows you to strongly reject the null hypothesis that there is no linear relationship between sales and promotional expenditures. Example 14.1 presents the test for the significance of β_1, the slope of sales with price.

EXAMPLE 14.1

Testing for the Significance of the Slope of Sales with Price

At the 0.05 level of significance, is there evidence that the slope of sales with price is different from zero?

SOLUTION From Figure 14.2 on page 580, $t_{STAT} = -7.7664 < -2.0395$ (the critical value for $\alpha = 0.05$) or the p-value $= 0.0000 < 0.05$. Thus, there is a significant relationship between price, X_1, and sales, taking into account the promotional expenditures, X_2.

As shown with these two independent variables, the test of significance for a specific regression coefficient in multiple regression is a test for the significance of adding that variable into a regression model, given that the other variable is included. In other words, the t test for the regression coefficient is actually a test for the contribution of each independent variable.

Confidence Interval Estimation

Instead of testing the significance of a population slope, you may want to estimate the value of a population slope. Equation (14.8) defines the confidence interval estimate for a population slope in multiple regression.

CONFIDENCE INTERVAL ESTIMATE FOR THE SLOPE

$$b_j \pm t_{\alpha/2} S_{b_j} \qquad \textbf{(14.8)}$$

where $t_{\alpha/2}$ is the critical value corresponding to an upper-tail probability of $\alpha/2$ from the t distribution with $n-k-1$ degrees of freedom (i.e., a cumulative area of $1 - \alpha/2$), and k is the number of independent variables.

To construct a 95% confidence interval estimate of the population slope, β_1 (the effect of price, X_1, on sales, Y, holding constant the effect of promotional expenditures, X_2), the critical value of t at the 95% confidence level with 31 degrees of freedom is 2.0395 (see Table E.3). Then, using Equation (14.8) and Figure 14.2 on page 580,

$$b_1 \pm t_{\alpha/2}S_{b_1}$$
$$-53.2173 \pm (2.0395)(6.8522)$$
$$-53.2173 \pm 13.9752$$
$$-67.1925 \le \beta_1 \le -39.2421$$

Taking into account the effect of promotional expenditures, the estimated effect of a 1-cent increase in price is to reduce mean sales by approximately 39.2 to 67.2 bars. You have 95% confidence that this interval correctly estimates the relationship between these variables. From a hypothesis-testing viewpoint, because this confidence interval does not include 0, you conclude that the regression coefficient, β_1, has a significant effect.

Example 14.2 constructs and interprets a confidence interval estimate for the slope of sales with promotional expenditures.

EXAMPLE 14.2

Constructing a Confidence Interval Estimate for the Slope of Sales with Promotional Expenditures

Construct a 95% confidence interval estimate of the population slope of sales with promotional expenditures.

SOLUTION The critical value of t at the 95% confidence level, with 31 degrees of freedom, is 2.0395 (see Table E.3). Using Equation (14.8) and Figure 14.2 on page 580,

$$b_2 \pm t_{\alpha/2}S_{b_2}$$
$$3.6131 \pm (2.0395)(0.6852)$$
$$3.6131 \pm 1.3975$$
$$2.2156 \le \beta_2 \le 5.0106$$

Thus, taking into account the effect of price, the estimated effect of each additional dollar of promotional expenditures is to increase mean sales by approximately 2.22 to 5.01 bars. You have 95% confidence that this interval correctly estimates the relationship between these variables. From a hypothesis-testing viewpoint, because this confidence interval does not include 0, you can conclude that the regression coefficient, β_2, has a significant effect.

Problems for Section 14.4

LEARNING THE BASICS

14.23 Use the following information from a multiple regression analysis:

$$n = 25 \quad b_1 = 5 \quad b_2 = 10 \quad S_{b_1} = 2 \quad S_{b_2} = 8$$

a. Which variable has the largest slope, in units of a t statistic?
b. Construct a 95% confidence interval estimate of the population slope, β_1.
c. At the 0.05 level of significance, determine whether each independent variable makes a significant contribution to the regression model. On the basis of these results, indicate the independent variables to include in this model.

14.24 Use the following information from a multiple regression analysis:

$$n = 20 \quad b_1 = 4 \quad b_2 = 3 \quad S_{b_1} = 1.2 \quad S_{b_2} = 0.8$$

a. Which variable has the largest slope, in units of a t statistic?
b. Construct a 95% confidence interval estimate of the population slope, β_1.
c. At the 0.05 level of significance, determine whether each independent variable makes a significant contribution to the regression model. On the basis of these results, indicate the independent variables to include in this model.

APPLYING THE CONCEPTS

14.25 In Problem 14.3 on page 582, you predicted the durability of a brand of running shoe, based on the forefoot shock-absorbing capability (FOREIMP) and the change in impact properties over time (MIDSOLE) for a sample of 15 pairs of shoes. Use the following results:

Variable	Coefficient	Standard Error	*t* Statistic	*p*-value
Intercept	−0.02686	0.06905	−0.39	0.7034
Foreimp	0.79116	0.06295	12.57	0.0000
Midsole	0.60484	0.07174	8.43	0.0000

a. Construct a 95% confidence interval estimate of the population slope between durability and forefoot shock-absorbing capability.
b. At the 0.05 level of significance, determine whether each independent variable makes a significant contribution to the regression model. On the basis of these results, indicate the independent variables to include in this model.

SELF Test **14.26** In Problem 14.4 on page 583, you used sales and number of orders to predict distribution costs at a mail-order catalog business (stored in WareCost). Use the results from that problem.
a. Construct a 95% confidence interval estimate of the population slope between distribution cost and sales.
b. At the 0.05 level of significance, determine whether each independent variable makes a significant contribution to the regression model. On the basis of these results, indicate the independent variables to include in this model.

14.27 In Problem 14.5 on page 583, you used horsepower and weight to predict mileage (stored in Auto2010). Use the results from that problem.
a. Construct a 95% confidence interval estimate of the population slope between mileage and horsepower.
b. At the 0.05 level of significance, determine whether each independent variable makes a significant contribution to the regression model. On the basis of these results, indicate the independent variables to include in this model.

14.28 In Problem 14.6 on page 583, you used radio advertising and newspaper advertising to predict sales (stored in Advertise). Use the results from that problem.
a. Construct a 95% confidence interval estimate of the population slope between sales and radio advertising.
b. At the 0.05 level of significance, determine whether each independent variable makes a significant contribution to the regression model. On the basis of these results, indicate the independent variables to include in this model.

14.29 In Problem 14.7 on page 584, you used the total number of staff present and remote hours to predict standby hours (stored in Standby). Use the results from that problem.
a. Construct a 95% confidence interval estimate of the population slope between standby hours and total number of staff present.
b. At the 0.05 level of significance, determine whether each independent variable makes a significant contribution to the regression model. On the basis of these results, indicate the independent variables to include in this model.

14.30 In Problem 14.8 on page 584, you used land area of a property and age of a house to predict appraised value (stored in GlenCove). Use the results from that problem.
a. Construct a 95% confidence interval estimate of the population slope between appraised value and land area of a property.
b. At the 0.05 level of significance, determine whether each independent variable makes a significant contribution to the regression model. On the basis of these results, indicate the independent variables to include in this model.

14.5 Testing Portions of the Multiple Regression Model

In developing a multiple regression model, you want to use only those independent variables that significantly reduce the error in predicting the value of a dependent variable. If an independent variable does not improve the prediction, you can delete it from the multiple regression model and use a model with fewer independent variables.

The **partial *F* test** is an alternative method to the *t* test discussed in Section 14.4 for determining the contribution of an independent variable. Using this method, you determine the contribution to the regression sum of squares made by each independent variable after all the other independent variables have been included in the model. The new independent variable is included only if it significantly improves the model.

To conduct partial *F* tests for the OmniPower sales example, you need to evaluate the contribution of promotional expenditures (X_2) after price (X_1) has been included in the model, and also evaluate the contribution of price (X_1) after promotional expenditures (X_2) have been included in the model.

In general, if there are several independent variables, you determine the contribution of each independent variable by taking into account the regression sum of squares of a model that includes all independent variables except the one of interest, j. This regression sum of squares is denoted SSR (all Xs except j). Equation (14.9) determines the contribution of variable j, assuming that all other variables are already included.

DETERMINING THE CONTRIBUTION OF AN INDEPENDENT VARIABLE TO THE REGRESSION MODEL

$$SSR(X_j \mid \text{All } Xs \text{ except } j) = SSR\,(\text{All } Xs) - SSR\,(\text{All } Xs \text{ except } j) \quad \textbf{(14.9)}$$

If there are two independent variables, you use Equations (14.10a) and (14.10b) to determine the contribution of each.

CONTRIBUTION OF VARIABLE X_1, GIVEN THAT X_2 HAS BEEN INCLUDED

$$SSR(X_1 \mid X_2) = SSR(X_1 \text{ and } X_2) - SSR(X_2) \quad \textbf{(14.10a)}$$

CONTRIBUTION OF VARIABLE X_2, GIVEN THAT X_1 HAS BEEN INCLUDED

$$SSR(X_2 \mid X_1) = SSR(X_1 \text{ and } X_2) - SSR(X_1) \quad \textbf{(14.10b)}$$

The term $SSR(X_2)$ represents the sum of squares due to regression for a model that includes only the independent variable X_2 (promotional expenditures). Similarly, $SSR(X_1)$ represents the sum of squares due to regression for a model that includes only the independent variable X_1 (price). Figures 14.7 and 14.8 present results for these two models.

From Figure 14.7, $SSR(X_2) = 14{,}915{,}814.10$ and from Figure 14.2 on page 580, $SSR\ (X_1 \text{ and } X_2) = 39{,}472{,}730.77$. Then, using Equation (14.10a),

$$\begin{aligned} SSR(X_1 \mid X_2) &= SSR(X_1 \text{ and} X_2) - SSR(X_2) \\ &= 39{,}472{,}730.77 - 14{,}915{,}814.10 \\ &= 24{,}556{,}916.67 \end{aligned}$$

FIGURE 14.7

Excel and Minitab regression results for a simple linear regression model of sales with promotional expenditures, $SSR(X_2)$

	A	B	C	D	E	F	G
1	**Sales and Promotional Expenses Analysis**						
2							
3	*Regression Statistics*						
4	Multiple R	0.5351					
5	R Square	0.2863					
6	Adjusted R Square	0.2640					
7	Standard Error	1077.8721					
8	Observations	34					
9							
10	ANOVA						
11		*df*	*SS*	*MS*	*F*	*Significance F*	
12	Regression	1	14915814.1025	14915814.1025	12.8384	0.0011	
13	Residual	32	37177863.3387	1161808.2293			
14	Total	33	52093677.4412				
15							
16		*Coefficients*	*Standard Error*	*t Stat*	*P-value*	*Lower 95%*	*Upper 95%*
17	Intercept	1496.0161	483.9789	3.0911	0.0041	510.1843	2481.8480
18	Promotion	4.1281	1.1521	3.5831	0.0011	1.7813	6.4748

Regression Analysis: Sales versus Promotion

```
The regression equation is
Sales = 1496 + 4.13 Promotion

Predictor     Coef  SE Coef     T      P
Constant    1496.0    484.0  3.09  0.004
Promotion    4.128    1.152  3.58  0.001

S = 1077.87    R-Sq = 28.6%    R-Sq(adj) = 26.4%

Analysis of Variance
Source          DF        SS        MS      F      P
Regression       1  14915814  14915814  12.84  0.001
Residual Error  32  37177863   1161808
Total           33  52093677
```

FIGURE 14.8

Excel and Minitab regression results for a simple linear regression model of sales with price, $SSR(X_1)$

	A	B	C	D	E	F	G
1	**Sales and Price Analysis**						
2							
3	*Regression Statistics*						
4	Multiple R	0.7351					
5	R Square	0.5404					
6	Adjusted R Square	0.5261					
7	Standard Error	864.9457					
8	Observations	34					
9							
10	ANOVA						
11		*df*	*SS*	*MS*	*F*	*Significance F*	
12	Regression	1	28153486.1482	28153486.1482	37.6318	0.0000	
13	Residual	32	23940191.2930	748130.9779			
14	Total	33	52093677.4412				
15							
16		*Coefficients*	*Standard Error*	*t Stat*	*P-value*	*Lower 95%*	*Upper 95%*
17	Intercept	7512.3480	734.6189	10.2262	0.0000	6015.9796	9008.7164
18	Price	-56.7138	9.2451	-6.1345	0.0000	-75.5455	-37.8822

Regression Analysis: Sales versus Price

```
The regression equation is
Sales = 7512 - 56.7 Price

Predictor      Coef  SE Coef      T      P
Constant     7512.3    734.6  10.23  0.000
Price       -56.714    9.245  -6.13  0.000

S = 864.946   R-Sq = 54.0%   R-Sq(adj) = 52.6%

Analysis of Variance
Source          DF        SS        MS      F      P
Regression       1  28153486  28153486  37.63  0.000
Residual Error  32  23940191    748131
Total           33  52093677
```

To determine whether X_1 significantly improves the model after X_2 has been included, you divide the regression sum of squares into two component parts, as shown in Table 14.3.

TABLE 14.3

ANOVA Table Dividing the Regression Sum of Squares into Components to Determine the Contribution of Variable X_1

Source	Degrees of Freedom	Sum of Squares	Mean Square (Variance)	F
Regression	2	39,472,730.77	19,736,365.39	
$\left\{ X_2 \right.$	$\left\{ 1 \right.$	$\left\{ 14,915,814.10 \right.$		
$\left. X_1 \mid X_2 \right\}$	$\left. 1 \right\}$	$\left. 24,556,916.67 \right\}$	24,556,916.67	60.32
Error	31	12,620,946.67	407,127.31	
Total	33	52,093,677.44		

The null and alternative hypotheses to test for the contribution of X_1 to the model are

H_0: Variable X_1 does not significantly improve the model after variable X_2 has been included.

H_1: Variable X_1 significantly improves the model after variable X_2 has been included.

Equation (14.11) defines the partial F test statistic for testing the contribution of an independent variable.

PARTIAL *F* TEST STATISTIC

$$F_{STAT} = \frac{SSR(X_j \mid \text{All } Xs \text{ except } j)}{MSE} \qquad \textbf{(14.11)}$$

The partial F test statistic follows an F distribution with 1 and $n-k-1$ degrees of freedom.

From Table 14.3,

$$F_{STAT} = \frac{24{,}556{,}916.67}{407{,}127.31} = 60.32$$

The partial F_{STAT} test statistic has 1 and $n-k-1 = 34-2-1 = 31$ degrees of freedom. Using a level of significance of 0.05, the critical value from Table E.5 is approximately 4.17 (see Figure 14.9).

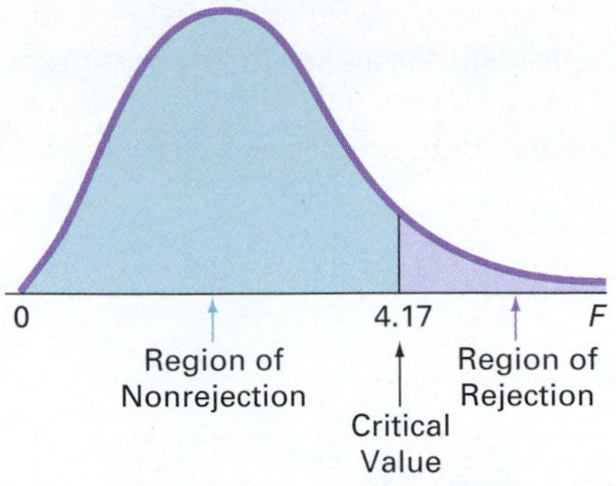

FIGURE 14.9
Testing for the contribution of a regression coefficient to a multiple regression model at the 0.05 level of significance, with 1 and 31 degrees of freedom

Because the computed partial F_{STAT} test statistic (60.32) is greater than this critical F value (4.17), you reject H_0. You can conclude that the addition of variable X_1 (price) significantly improves a regression model that already contains variable X_2 (promotional expenditures).

To evaluate the contribution of variable X_2 (promotional expenditures) to a model in which variable X_1 (price) has been included, you need to use Equation (14.10b). First, from Figure 14.8 on page 595, observe that $SSR(X_1) = 28{,}153{,}486.15$. Second, from Table 14.3, observe that $SSR(X_1 \text{ and } X_2) = 39{,}472{,}730.77$. Then, using Equation (14.10b) on page 594,

$$SSR(X_2 | X_1) = 39{,}472{,}730.77 - 28{,}153{,}486.15 = 11{,}319{,}244.62$$

To determine whether X_2 significantly improves a model after X_1 has been included, you can divide the regression sum of squares into two component parts, as shown in Table 14.4.

TABLE 14.4
ANOVA Table Dividing the Regression Sum of Squares into Components to Determine the Contribution of Variable X_2

Source	Degrees of Freedom	Sum of Squares	Mean Square (Variance)	F
Regression	2	39,472,730.77	19,736,365.39	
$\begin{Bmatrix} X_1 \\ X_2 \| X_1 \end{Bmatrix}$	$\begin{Bmatrix} 1 \\ 1 \end{Bmatrix}$	$\begin{Bmatrix} 28{,}153{,}486.15 \\ 11{,}319{,}244.62 \end{Bmatrix}$	11,319,244.62	27.80
Error	31	12,620,946.67	407,127.31	
Total	33	52,093,677.44		

The null and alternative hypotheses to test for the contribution of X_2 to the model are

H_0: Variable X_2 does not significantly improve the model after variable X_1 has been included.

H_1: Variable X_2 significantly improves the model after variable X_1 has been included.

Using Equation (14.11) and Table 14.4,

$$F_{STAT} = \frac{11{,}319{,}244.62}{407{,}127.31} = 27.80$$

In Figure 14.9, you can see that, using a 0.05 level of significance, the critical value of F, with 1 and 31 degrees of freedom, is approximately 4.17. Because the computed partial F_{STAT} test statistic (27.80) is greater than this critical value (4.17), you reject H_0. You can conclude that the addition of variable X_2 (promotional expenditures) significantly improves the multiple regression model already containing X_1 (price).

Thus, by testing for the contribution of each independent variable after the other has been included in the model, you determine that each of the two independent variables significantly improves the model. Therefore, the multiple regression model should include both price, X_1, and promotional expenditures, X_2.

The partial F-test statistic developed in this section and the t-test statistic of Equation (14.7) on page 590 are both used to determine the contribution of an independent variable to a multiple regression model. The hypothesis tests associated with these two statistics always result in the same decision (i.e., the p-values are identical). The t_{STAT} test statistics for the OmniPower regression model are -7.7664 and $+5.2728$, and the corresponding F_{STAT} test statistics are 60.32 and 27.80. Equation (14.12) states this relationship between t and F.[1]

[1]This relationship holds only when the F_{STAT} statistic has 1 degree of freedom in the numerator.

RELATIONSHIP BETWEEN A t STATISTIC AND AN F STATISTIC

$$t_{STAT}^2 = F_{STAT} \quad \textbf{(14.12)}$$

Coefficients of Partial Determination

Recall from Section 14.2 that the coefficient of multiple determination, r^2, measures the proportion of the variation in Y that is explained by variation in the independent variables. The **coefficients of partial determination** ($r_{Y1.2}^2$ and $r_{Y2.1}^2$) measure the proportion of the variation in the dependent variable that is explained by each independent variable while controlling for, or holding constant, the other independent variable. Equation (14.13) defines the coefficients of partial determination for a multiple regression model with two independent variables.

COEFFICIENTS OF PARTIAL DETERMINATION FOR A MULTIPLE REGRESSION MODEL CONTAINING TWO INDEPENDENT VARIABLES

$$r_{Y1.2}^2 = \frac{SSR(X_1 \mid X_2)}{SST - SSR(X_1\ and\ X_2) + SSR(X_1 \mid X_2)} \quad \textbf{(14.13a)}$$

and

$$r_{Y2.1}^2 = \frac{SSR(X_2 \mid X_1)}{SST - SSR(X_1\ and\ X_2) + SSR(X_2 \mid X_1)} \quad \textbf{(14.13b)}$$

where

$SSR(X_1 \mid X_2)$ = sum of squares of the contribution of variable X_1 to the regression model, given that variable X_2 has been included in the model

SST = total sum of squares for Y

$SSR(X_1 \text{ and } X_2)$ = regression sum of squares when variables X_1 and X_2 are both included in the multiple regression model

$SSR(X_2 \mid X_1)$ = sum of squares of the contribution of variable X_2 to the regression model, given that variable X_1 has been included in the model

For the OmniPower sales example,

$$r_{Y1.2}^2 = \frac{24{,}556{,}916.67}{52{,}093{,}677.44 - 39{,}472{,}730.77 + 24{,}556{,}916.67}$$
$$= 0.6605$$

$$r_{Y2.1}^2 = \frac{11{,}319{,}244.62}{52{,}093{,}677.44 - 39{,}472{,}730.77 + 11{,}319{,}244.62}$$
$$= 0.4728$$

The coefficient of partial determination, $r^2_{Y1.2}$, of variable Y with X_1 while holding X_2 constant is 0.6605. Thus, for a given (constant) amount of promotional expenditures, 66.05% of the variation in OmniPower sales is explained by the variation in the price. The coefficient of partial determination, $r^2_{Y2.1}$, of variable Y with X_2 while holding X_1 constant is 0.4728. Thus, for a given (constant) price, 47.28% of the variation in sales of OmniPower bars is explained by variation in the amount of promotional expenditures.

Equation (14.14) defines the coefficient of partial determination for the jth variable in a multiple regression model containing several (k) independent variables.

COEFFICIENT OF PARTIAL DETERMINATION FOR A MULTIPLE REGRESSION MODEL CONTAINING k INDEPENDENT VARIABLES

$$r^2_{Yj.(\text{All variables } except\ j)} = \frac{SSR(X_j \mid \text{All } Xs\ except\ j)}{SST - SSR(\text{All } Xs) + SSR(X_j \mid \text{All } Xs\ except\ j)} \tag{14.14}$$

Problems for Section 14.5

LEARNING THE BASICS

14.31 The following is the ANOVA summary table for a multiple regression model with two independent variables:

Source	Degrees of Freedom	Sum of Squares	Mean Squares	F
Regression	2	60		
Error	18	120		
Total	20	180		

If $SSR(X_1) = 45$ and $SSR(X_2) = 25$,

a. determine whether there is a significant relationship between Y and each independent variable at the 0.05 level of significance.

b. compute the coefficients of partial determination, $r^2_{Y1.2}$ and $r^2_{Y2.1}$, and interpret their meaning.

14.32 The following is the ANOVA summary table for a multiple regression model with two independent variables:

Source	Degrees of Freedom	Sum of Squares	Mean Squares	F
Regression	2	30		
Error	10	120		
Total	12	150		

If $SSR(X_1) = 20$ and $SSR(X_2) = 15$,

a. determine whether there is a significant relationship between Y and each independent variable at the 0.05 level of significance.

b. compute the coefficients of partial determination, $r^2_{Y1.2}$ and $r^2_{Y2.1}$, and interpret their meaning.

APPLYING THE CONCEPTS

14.33 In Problem 14.5 on page 583, you used horsepower and weight to predict mileage (stored in **Auto2010**). Use the results from that problem.

a. At the 0.05 level of significance, determine whether each independent variable makes a significant contribution to the regression model. On the basis of these results, indicate the most appropriate regression model for this set of data.

b. Compute the coefficients of partial determination, $r^2_{Y1.2}$ and $r^2_{Y2.1}$, and interpret their meaning.

SELF Test **14.34** In Problem 14.4 on page 583, you used sales and number of orders to predict distribution costs at a mail-order catalog business (stored in **WareCost**). Use the results from that problem.

a. At the 0.05 level of significance, determine whether each independent variable makes a significant contribution to the regression model. On the basis of these results, indicate the most appropriate regression model for this set of data.

b. Compute the coefficients of partial determination, $r^2_{Y1.2}$ and $r^2_{Y2.1}$, and interpret their meaning.

14.35 In Problem 14.7 on page 584, you used the total staff present and remote hours to predict standby hours (stored in **Standby**). Use the results from that problem.

a. At the 0.05 level of significance, determine whether each independent variable makes a significant contribution to the regression model. On the basis of these results, indicate the most appropriate regression model for this set of data.

b. Compute the coefficients of partial determination, $r^2_{Y1.2}$ and $r^2_{Y2.1}$, and interpret their meaning.

14.36 In Problem 14.6 on page 583, you used radio advertising and newspaper advertising to predict sales (stored in **Advertise**). Use the results from that problem.

a. At the 0.05 level of significance, determine whether each independent variable makes a significant contribution to the regression model. On the basis of these results, indicate the most appropriate regression model for this set of data.

b. Compute the coefficients of partial determination, $r^2_{Y1.2}$ and $r^2_{Y2.1}$, and interpret their meaning.

14.37 In Problem 14.8 on page 584, you used land area of a property and age of a house to predict appraised value (stored in **GlenCove**). Use the results from that problem.

a. At the 0.05 level of significance, determine whether each independent variable makes a significant contribution to the regression model. On the basis of these results, indicate the most appropriate regression model for this set of data.

b. Compute the coefficients of partial determination, $r^2_{Y1.2}$ and $r^2_{Y2.1}$, and interpret their meaning.

14.6 Using Dummy Variables and Interaction Terms in Regression Models

The multiple regression models discussed in Sections 14.1 through 14.5 assumed that each independent variable is a numerical variable. For example, in Section 14.1, you used price and promotional expenditures, two numerical independent variables, to predict the monthly sales of OmniPower energy bars. However, for some models, you might want to include the effect of a categorical independent variable. For example, to predict the monthly sales of the OmniPower bars, you might want to include the categorical variable shelf location (not end-aisle or end-aisle) in the model.

Dummy Variables

To include a categorical independent variable in a regression model, you use a **dummy variable**. A dummy variable recodes the categories of a categorical variable using the numeric values 0 and 1. Where appropriate, the value of 0 is assigned to the absence of a characteristic and the value 1 is assigned to the presence of the characteristic. If a given categorical independent variable has only two categories, such as shelf location in the previous example, then you can define one dummy variable, X_d, to represent the two categories as

$$X_d = 0 \text{ if the observation is in category 1 (not end-aisle in the example)}$$
$$X_d = 1 \text{ if the observation is in category 2 (end-aisle in the example)}$$

To illustrate using dummy variables in regression, consider a business problem that involves developing a model for predicting the assessed value of houses ($000), based on the size of the house (in thousands of square feet) and whether the house has a fireplace. To include the categorical variable for the presence of a fireplace, the dummy variable X_2 is defined as

$$X_2 = 0 \text{ if the house does not have a fireplace}$$
$$X_2 = 1 \text{ if the house has a fireplace}$$

Data collected from a sample of 15 houses are organized and stored in **House3**. Table 14.5 presents the data. In the last column of Table 14.5, you can see how the categorical values are converted to numerical values.

Assuming that the slope of assessed value with the size of the house is the same for houses that have and do not have a fireplace, the multiple regression model is

$$Y_i = \beta_0 + \beta_1 X_{1i} + \beta_2 X_{2i} + \varepsilon_i$$

TABLE 14.5

Predicting Assessed Value, Based on Size of House and Presence of a Fireplace

Assessed Value	Size	Fireplace	Fireplace Coded
234.4	2.00	Yes	1
227.4	1.71	No	0
225.7	1.45	No	0
235.9	1.76	Yes	1
229.1	1.93	No	0
220.4	1.20	Yes	1
225.8	1.55	Yes	1
235.9	1.93	Yes	1
228.5	1.59	Yes	1
229.2	1.50	Yes	1
236.7	1.90	Yes	1
229.3	1.39	Yes	1
224.5	1.54	No	0
233.8	1.89	Yes	1
226.8	1.59	No	0

where

Y_i = assessed value, in thousands of dollars, for house i

β_0 = Y intercept

X_{1i} = size of the house, in thousands of square feet, for house i

β_1 = slope of assessed value with size of the house, holding constant the presence or absence of a fireplace

X_{2i} = dummy variable representing the absence or presence of a fireplace for house i

β_2 = net effect of the presence of a fireplace on assessed value, holding constant the size of the house

ε_i = random error in Y for house i

Figure 14.10 presents the regression results for this model.

FIGURE 14.10

Excel and Minitab regression results for the model that includes size of house and presence of fireplace

	A	B	C	D	E	F	G
1	Assessed Value Analysis						
2							
3	*Regression Statistics*						
4	Multiple R	0.9006					
5	R Square	0.8111					
6	Adjusted R Square	0.7796					
7	Standard Error	2.2626					
8	Observations	15					
9							
10	ANOVA						
11		*df*	*SS*	*MS*	*F*	*Significance F*	
12	Regression	2	263.7039	131.8520	25.7557	0.0000	
13	Residual	12	61.4321	5.1193			
14	Total	14	325.1360				
15							
16		*Coefficients*	*Standard Error*	*t Stat*	*P-value*	*Lower 95%*	*Upper 95%*
17	Intercept	200.0905	4.3517	45.9803	0.0000	190.6090	209.5719
18	Size	16.1858	2.5744	6.2871	0.0000	10.5766	21.7951
19	FireplaceCoded	3.8530	1.2412	3.1042	0.0091	1.1486	6.5574

Regression Analysis: Value versus Size, FireplaceCoded

```
The regression equation is
Value = 200 + 16.2 Size + 3.85 FireplaceCoded

Predictor          Coef  SE Coef      T      P
Constant        200.090    4.352  45.98  0.000
Size             16.186    2.574   6.29  0.000
FireplaceCoded    3.853    1.241   3.10  0.009

S = 2.26260   R-Sq = 81.1%   R-Sq(adj) = 78.0%

Analysis of Variance
Source          DF      SS      MS      F      P
Regression       2  263.70  131.85  25.76  0.000
Residual Error  12   61.43    5.12
Total           14  325.14
```

From Figure 14.10, the regression equation is

$$\hat{Y}_i = 200.0905 + 16.1858X_{1i} + 3.8530X_{2i}$$

For houses without a fireplace, you substitute $X_2 = 0$ into the regression equation:

$$\begin{aligned}\hat{Y}_i &= 200.0905 + 16.1858X_{1i} + 3.8530X_{2i} \\ &= 200.0905 + 16.1858X_{1i} + 3.8530(0) \\ &= 200.0905 + 16.1858X_{1i}\end{aligned}$$

For houses with a fireplace, you substitute $X_2 = 1$ into the regression equation:

$$\begin{aligned}\hat{Y}_i &= 200.0905 + 16.1858X_{1i} + 3.8530X_{2i} \\ &= 200.0905 + 16.1858X_{1i} + 3.8530(1) \\ &= 203.9435 + 16.1858X_{1i}\end{aligned}$$

In this model, the regression coefficients are interpreted as follows:

- Holding constant whether a house has a fireplace, for each increase of 1.0 thousand square feet in the size of the house, the predicted assessed value is estimated to increase by 16.1858 thousand dollars (i.e., \$16,185.80).
- Holding constant the size of the house, the presence of a fireplace is estimated to increase the predicted assessed value of the house by 3.8530 thousand dollars (i.e., \$3,853).

In Figure 14.10, the t_{STAT} test statistic for the slope of the size of the house with assessed value is 6.2871, and the p-value is approximately 0.000; the t_{STAT} test statistic for presence of a fireplace is 3.1042, and the p-value is 0.0091. Thus, each of the two variables makes a significant contribution to the model at the 0.01 level of significance. In addition, the coefficient of multiple determination indicates that 81.11% of the variation in assessed value is explained by variation in the size of the house and whether the house has a fireplace.

EXAMPLE 14.3

Modeling a Three-Level Categorical Variable

Define a multiple regression model using sales as the dependent variable and package design and price as independent variables. Package design is a three-level categorical variable with designs A, B, or C.

SOLUTION To model the three-level categorical variable package design, two dummy variables, X_1 and X_2, are needed:

$$X_{1i} = 1 \text{ if package design } A \text{ is used in observation } i\text{; 0 otherwise}$$

$$X_{2i} = 1 \text{ if package design } B \text{ is used in observation } i\text{; 0 otherwise}$$

Thus, if observation i uses package design A, then $X_{1i} = 1$ and $X_{2i} = 0$; if observation i uses package design B, then $X_{1i} = 0$ and $X_{2i} = 1$; and if observation i uses package design C, then $X_{1i} = X_{2i} = 0$. A third independent variable is used for price:

$$X_{3i} = \text{price for observation } i$$

Thus, the regression model for this example is

$$Y_i = \beta_0 + \beta_1 X_{1i} + \beta_2 X_{2i} + \beta_3 X_{3i} + \varepsilon_i$$

where

Y_i = sales for observation i

β_0 = Y intercept

β_1 = difference between the predicted sales of design A and the predicted sales of design C, holding price constant

β_2 = difference between the predicted sales of design B and the predicted sales of design C, holding price constant

β_3 = slope of sales with price, holding the package design constant

ε_i = random error in Y for observation i

Interactions

In all the regression models discussed so far, the effect an independent variable has on the dependent variable has been assumed to be independent of the other independent variables in the model. An **interaction** occurs if the effect of an independent variable on the dependent variable changes according to the *value* of a second independent variable. For example, it is possible for advertising to have a large effect on the sales of a product when the price of a product is low. However, if the price of the product is too high, increases in advertising will not dramatically change sales. In this case, price and advertising are said to interact. In other words, you cannot make general statements about the effect of advertising on sales. The effect that advertising has on sales is *dependent* on the price. You use an **interaction term** (sometimes referred to as a **cross-product term**) to model an interaction effect in a regression model.

To illustrate the concept of interaction and use of an interaction term, return to the example concerning the assessed values of homes discussed on pages 599–601. In the regression model, you assumed that the effect the size of the home has on the assessed value is independent of whether the house has a fireplace. In other words, you assumed that the slope of assessed value with size is the same for houses with fireplaces as it is for houses without fireplaces. If these two slopes are different, an interaction exists between the size of the home and the fireplace.

To evaluate whether an interaction exists, you first define an interaction term that is the product of the independent variable X_1 (size of house) and the dummy variable X_2 (FireplaceCoded). You then test whether this interaction variable makes a significant contribution to the regression model. If the interaction is significant, you cannot use the original model for prediction. For the data of Table 14.5 on page 600, you define the following:

$$X_3 = X_1 \times X_2$$

Figure 14.11 presents the results for this regression model, which includes the size of the house, X_1, the presence of a fireplace, X_2, and the interaction of X_1 and X_2 (defined as X_3).

FIGURE 14.11

Excel and Minitab regression results for a model that includes size, presence of fireplace, and interaction of size and fireplace

	A	B	C	D	E	F	G
1	**Assessed Value Analysis**						
2							
3	*Regression Statistics*						
4	Multiple R	0.9179					
5	R Square	0.8426					
6	Adjusted R Square	0.7996					
7	Standard Error	2.1573					
8	Observations	15					
9							
10	**ANOVA**						
11		*df*	*SS*	*MS*	*F*	*Significance F*	
12	Regression	3	273.9441	91.3147	19.6215	0.0001	
13	Residual	11	51.1919	4.6538			
14	Total	14	325.1360				
15							
16		*Coefficients*	*Standard Error*	*t Stat*	*P-value*	*Lower 95%*	*Upper 95%*
17	Intercept	212.9522	9.6122	22.1544	0.0000	191.7959	234.1084
18	Size	8.3624	5.8173	1.4375	0.1784	-4.4414	21.1662
19	FireplaceCoded	-11.8404	10.6455	-1.1122	0.2898	-35.2710	11.5902
20	Size * FireplaceCoded	9.5180	6.4165	1.4834	0.1661	-4.6046	23.6406

Regression Analysis: Value versus Size, FireplaceCoded, Size*FireplaceCo

```
The regression equation is
Value = 213 + 8.36 Size - 11.8 FireplaceCoded + 9.52 Size*FireplaceCoded

Predictor                Coef  SE Coef      T      P
Constant              212.952    9.612  22.15  0.000
Size                    8.362    5.817   1.44  0.178
FireplaceCoded         -11.84    10.65  -1.11  0.290
Size*FireplaceCoded     9.518    6.416   1.48  0.166

S = 2.15727   R-Sq = 84.3%   R-Sq(adj) = 80.0%

Analysis of Variance
Source          DF       SS      MS      F      P
Regression       3  273.944  91.315  19.62  0.000
Residual Error  11   51.192   4.654
Total           14  325.136
```

To test for the existence of an interaction, you use the null hypothesis:

$$H_0: \beta_3 = 0$$

versus the alternative hypothesis:

$$H_1: \beta_3 \neq 0.$$

In Figure 14.11, the t_{STAT} test statistic for the interaction of size and fireplace is 1.4834. Because $t_{STAT} = 1.4834 < 2.201$ or the p-value $= 0.1661 > 0.05$, you do not reject the null hypothesis. Therefore, the interaction does not make a significant contribution to the model, given that size and presence of a fireplace are already included. You can conclude that the slope of assessed value with size is the same for houses with fireplaces and without fireplaces.

Regression models can have several numerical independent variables. Example 14.4 illustrates a regression model in which there are two numerical independent variables and a categorical independent variable.

EXAMPLE 14.4

Studying a Regression Model That Contains a Dummy Variable

The business problem facing a real estate developer involves predicting heating oil consumption in single-family houses. The independent variables considered are atmospheric temperature, X_1, and the amount of attic insulation, X_2. Data are collected from a sample of 15 single-family houses. Of the 15 houses selected, houses 1, 4, 6, 7, 8, 10, and 12 are ranch-style houses. The data are organized and stored in **HeatingOil**. Develop and analyze an appropriate regression model, using these three independent variables X_1, X_2, and X_3 (where X_3 is the dummy variable for ranch-style houses).

SOLUTION Define X_3, a dummy variable for ranch-style house, as follows:

$$X_3 = 0 \text{ if the style is not ranch}$$

$$X_3 = 1 \text{ if the style is ranch}$$

Assuming that the slope between heating oil consumption and atmospheric temperature, X_1, and between heating oil consumption and the amount of attic insulation, X_2, is the same for both styles of houses, the regression model is

$$Y_i = \beta_0 + \beta_1 X_{1i} + \beta_2 X_{2i} + \beta_3 X_{3i} + \varepsilon_i$$

where

Y_i = monthly heating oil consumption, in gallons, for house i

β_0 = Y intercept

β_1 = slope of heating oil consumption with atmospheric temperature, holding constant the effect of attic insulation and the style of the house

β_2 = slope of heating oil consumption with attic insulation, holding constant the effect of atmospheric temperature and the style of the house

β_3 = incremental effect of the presence of a ranch-style house, holding constant the effect of atmospheric temperature and attic insulation

ε_i = random error in Y for house i

Figure 14.12 presents results for this regression model.

FIGURE 14.12

Excel and Minitab results for a regression model that includes temperature, insulation, and ranch-style for the heating oil data

	A	B	C	D	E	F	G
1	Heating Oil Consumption Analysis						
2							
3	*Regression Statistics*						
4	Multiple R	0.9942					
5	R Square	0.9884					
6	Adjusted R Square	0.9853					
7	Standard Error	15.7489					
8	Observations	15					
9							
10	ANOVA						
11		*df*	*SS*	*MS*	*F*	*Significance F*	
12	Regression	3	233406.9094	77802.3031	313.6822	0.0000	
13	Residual	11	2728.3200	248.0291			
14	Total	14	236135.2293				
15							
16		*Coefficients*	*Standard Error*	*t Stat*	*P-value*	*Lower 95%*	*Upper 95%*
17	Intercept	592.5401	14.3370	41.3295	0.0000	560.9846	624.0956
18	Temperature	-5.5251	0.2044	-27.0267	0.0000	-5.9751	-5.0752
19	Insulation	-21.3761	1.4480	-14.7623	0.0000	-24.5632	-18.1891
20	Ranch-style	-38.9727	8.3584	-4.6627	0.0007	-57.3695	-20.5759

Regression Analysis: Gallons versus Temperature, Insulation, Ranch-style

```
The regression equation is
Gallons = 593 - 5.53 Temperature - 21.4 Insulation - 39.0 Ranch-style

Predictor       Coef  SE Coef       T      P
Constant      592.54    14.34   41.33  0.000
Temperature  -5.5251   0.2044  -27.03  0.000
Insulation   -21.376    1.448  -14.76  0.000
Ranch-style  -38.973    8.358   -4.66  0.001

S = 15.7489   R-Sq = 98.8%   R-Sq(adj) = 98.5%

Analysis of Variance
Source          DF      SS     MS       F      P
Regression       3  233407  77802  313.68  0.000
Residual Error  11    2728    248
Total           14  236135
```

From the results in Figure 14.12, the regression equation is

$$\hat{Y}_i = 592.5401 - 5.5251X_{1i} - 21.3761X_{2i} - 38.9727X_{3i}$$

For houses that are not ranch style, because $X_3 = 0$, the regression equation reduces to

$$\hat{Y}_i = 592.5401 - 5.5251X_{1i} - 21.3761X_{2i}$$

For houses that are ranch style, because $X_3 = 1$, the regression equation reduces to

$$\hat{Y}_i = 553.5674 - 5.5251X_{1i} - 21.3761X_{2i}$$

In this model, the regression coefficients are interpreted as follows:

- Holding constant the attic insulation and the house style, for each additional 1°F increase in atmospheric temperature, you estimate that the predicted heating oil consumption decreases by 5.5251 gallons.
- Holding constant the atmospheric temperature and the house style, for each additional 1-inch increase in attic insulation, you estimate that the predicted heating oil consumption decreases by 21.3761 gallons.
- b_3 measures the effect on oil consumption of having a ranch-style house ($X_3 = 1$) compared with having a house that is not ranch style ($X_3 = 0$). Thus, with atmospheric temperature and attic insulation held constant, you estimate that the predicted heating oil consumption is 38.9727 gallons less for a ranch-style house than for a house that is not ranch style.

The three t_{STAT} test statistics representing the slopes for temperature, insulation, and ranch style are −27.0267, −14.7623, and −4.6627. Each of the corresponding *p*-values is extremely small (less than 0.001). Thus, each of the three variables makes a significant contribution to the model. In addition, the coefficient of multiple determination indicates that 98.84% of the variation in oil usage is explained by variation in temperature, insulation, and whether the house is ranch style.

Before you can use the model in Example 14.4, you need to determine whether the independent variables interact with each other. In Example 14.5, three interaction terms are added to the model.

EXAMPLE 14.5

Evaluating a Regression Model with Several Interactions

For the data of Example 14.4, determine whether adding the interaction terms make a significant contribution to the regression model.

SOLUTION To evaluate possible interactions between the independent variables, three interaction terms are constructed as follows: $X_4 = X_1 \times X_2, X_5 = X_1 \times X_3$, and $X_6 = X_2 \times X_3$. The regression model is now

$$Y_i = \beta_0 + \beta_1X_{1i} + \beta_2X_{2i} + \beta_3X_{3i} + \beta_4X_{4i} + \beta_5X_{5i} + \beta_6X_{6i} + \varepsilon_i$$

where X_1 is temperature, X_2 is insulation, X_3 is the dummy variable ranch style, X_4 is the interaction between temperature and insulation, X_5 is the interaction between temperature and ranch style, and X_6 is the interaction between insulation and ranch style. Figure 14.13 presents the results for this regression model.

FIGURE 14.13

Excel and Minitab regression results for a model that includes temperature, X_1; insulation, X_2; the dummy variable ranch-style, X_3; the interaction of temperature and insulation, X_4; the interaction of temperature and ranch-style, X_5; and the interaction of insulation and ranch-style, X_6

	A	B	C	D	E	F	G
1	**Heating Oil Consumption Analysis**						
2							
3	*Regression Statistics*						
4	Multiple R	0.9966					
5	R Square	0.9931					
6	Adjusted R Square	0.9880					
7	Standard Error	14.2506					
8	Observations	15					
9							
10	**ANOVA**						
11		*df*	*SS*	*MS*	*F*	*Significance F*	
12	Regression	6	234510.5818	39085.0970	192.4607	0.0000	
13	Residual	8	1624.6475	203.0809			
14	Total	14	236135.2293				
15							
16		*Coefficients*	*Standard Error*	*t Stat*	*P-value*	*Lower 95%*	*Upper 95%*
17	Intercept	642.8867	26.7059	24.0728	0.0000	581.3027	704.4707
18	Temperature	-6.9263	0.7531	-9.1969	0.0000	-8.6629	-5.1896
19	Insulation	-27.8825	3.5801	-7.7882	0.0001	-36.1383	-19.6268
20	Style	-84.6088	29.9956	-2.8207	0.0225	-153.7788	-15.4389
21	Temperature * Insulation	0.1702	0.0886	1.9204	0.0911	-0.0342	0.3746
22	Temperature * Ranch-style	0.6596	0.4617	1.4286	0.1910	-0.4051	1.7242
23	Insulation * Ranch-style	4.9870	3.5137	1.4193	0.1936	-3.1156	13.0895

Regression Analysis: Gallons versus Temperature, Insulation, ...

```
The regression equation is
Gallons = 643 - 6.93 Temperature - 27.9 Insulation - 84.6 Ranch-style
          + 0.170 Temperature*Insulation + 0.660 Temperature*Ranch-style
          + 4.99 Insulation*Ranch-style

Predictor                     Coef   SE Coef      T      P
Constant                    642.89     26.71  24.07  0.000
Temperature                -6.9263    0.7531  -9.20  0.000
Insulation                 -27.883     3.580  -7.79  0.000
Ranch-style                 -84.61     30.00  -2.82  0.022
Temperature*Insulation     0.17021   0.08863   1.92  0.091
Temperature*Ranch-style     0.6596    0.4617   1.43  0.191
Insulation*Ranch-style       4.987     3.514   1.42  0.194

S = 14.2506   R-Sq = 99.3%   R-Sq(adj) = 98.8%

Analysis of Variance
Source          DF      SS     MS       F      P
Regression       6  234511  39085  192.46  0.000
Residual Error   8    1625    203
Total           14  236135
```

To test whether the three interactions significantly improve the regression model, you use the partial F test. The null and alternative hypotheses are

$$H_0: \beta_4 = \beta_5 = \beta_6 = 0 \text{ (There are no interaction among } X_1, X_2, \text{ and } X_3.)$$

$$H_1: \beta_4 \neq 0 \text{ and/or } \beta_5 \neq 0 \text{ and/or } \beta_6 \neq 0 \text{ (} X_1 \text{ interacts with } X_2, \text{ and/or } X_1 \text{ interacts with } X_3, \text{ and/or } X_2 \text{ interacts with } X_3.)$$

From Figure 14.13,

$$SSR(X_1, X_2, X_3, X_4, X_5, X_6) = 234{,}510.5818 \text{ with 6 degrees of freedom}$$

and from Figure 14.12 on page 603, $SSR\,(X_1, X_2, X_3) = 233{,}406.9094$ with 3 degrees of freedom. Thus,

$$SSR(X_1, X_2, X_3, X_4, X_5, X_6) - SSR(X_1, X_2, X_3) = 234{,}510.5818 - 233{,}406.9094 = 1{,}103.6724.$$

The difference in degrees of freedom is $6 - 3 = 3$.

To use the partial F test for the simultaneous contribution of three variables to a model, you use an extension of Equation (14.11) on page 616.[2] The partial F_{STAT} test statistic is

$$F_{STAT} = \frac{[SSR(X_1, X_2, X_3, X_4, X_5, X_6) - SSR(X_1, X_2, X_3)]/3}{MSE(X_1, X_2, X_3, X_4, X_5, X_6)} = \frac{1{,}103.6724/3}{203.0809} = 1.8115$$

You compare the computed F_{STAT} test statistic to the critical F value for 3 and 8 degrees of freedom. Using a level of significance of 0.05, the critical F value from Table E.5 is 4.07. Because $F_{STAT} = 1.8115 < 4.07$, you conclude that the interactions do not make a significant contribution to the model, given that the model already includes temperature, X_1; insulation, X_2; and whether the house is ranch style, X_3. Therefore, the multiple regression model using X_1, X_2, and X_3 but no interaction terms is the better model. If you rejected this null hypothesis, you would then test the contribution of each interaction separately in order to determine which interaction terms to include in the model.

[2] In general, if a model has several independent variables and you want to test whether additional independent variables contribute to the model, the numerator of the F test is SSR(for all independent variables) minus SSR(for the initial set of variables) divided by the number of independent variables whose contribution is being tested.

Problems for Section 14.6

LEARNING THE BASICS

14.38 Suppose X_1 is a numerical variable and X_2 is a dummy variable and the regression equation for a sample of $n = 20$ is

$$\hat{Y}_i = 6 + 4X_{1i} + 2X_{2i}$$

a. Interpret the regression coefficient associated with variable X_1.
b. Interpret the regression coefficient associated with variable X_2.
c. Suppose that the t_{STAT} test statistic for testing the contribution of variable X_2 is 3.27. At the 0.05 level of significance, is there evidence that variable X_2 makes a significant contribution to the model?

APPLYING THE CONCEPTS

14.39 The chair of the accounting department plans to develop a regression model to predict the grade point average in accounting for those students who are graduating and have completed the accounting major, based on the student's SAT score and whether the student received a grade of B or higher in the introductory statistics course (0 = no and 1 = yes).
a. Explain the steps involved in developing a regression model for these data. Be sure to indicate the particular models you need to evaluate and compare.
b. Suppose the regression coefficient for the variable whether the student received a grade of B or higher in the introductory statistics course is +0.30. How do you interpret this result?

14.40 A real estate association in a suburban community would like to study the relationship between the size of a single-family house (as measured by the number of rooms) and the selling price of the house (in thousands of dollars). Two different neighborhoods are included in the study, one on the east side of the community (=0) and the other on the west side (=1). A random sample of 20 houses was selected, with the results stored in **Neighbor**. For (a) through (k), do not include an interaction term.
a. State the multiple regression equation that predicts the selling price, based on the number of rooms and the neighborhood.
b. Interpret the regression coefficients in (a).
c. Predict the selling price for a house with nine rooms that is located in an east-side neighborhood. Construct a 95% confidence interval estimate and a 95% prediction interval.
d. Perform a residual analysis on the results and determine whether the regression assumptions are valid.
e. Is there a significant relationship between selling price and the two independent variables (rooms and neighborhood) at the 0.05 level of significance?
f. At the 0.05 level of significance, determine whether each independent variable makes a contribution to the regression model. Indicate the most appropriate regression model for this set of data.
g. Construct and interpret a 95% confidence interval estimate of the population slope for the relationship between selling price and number of rooms.
h. Construct and interpret a 95% confidence interval estimate of the population slope for the relationship between selling price and neighborhood.
i. Compute and interpret the adjusted r^2.
j. Compute the coefficients of partial determination and interpret their meaning.
k. What assumption do you need to make about the slope of selling price with number of rooms?
l. Add an interaction term to the model and, at the 0.05 level of significance, determine whether it makes a significant contribution to the model.
m. On the basis of the results of (f) and (l), which model is most appropriate? Explain.

14.41 The marketing manager of a large supermarket chain faced the business problem of determining the effect on the sales of pet food of shelf space and whether the product was placed at the front (=1) or back (=0) of the aisle. Data are collected from a random sample of 12 equal-sized stores. The results are shown in the following table (and organized and stored in **Petfood**):

Store	Shelf Space (Feet)	Location	Weekly Sales ($)
1	5	Back	160
2	5	Front	220
3	5	Back	140
4	10	Back	190
5	10	Back	240
6	10	Front	260
7	15	Back	230
8	15	Back	270
9	15	Front	280
10	20	Back	260
11	20	Back	290
12	20	Front	310

For (a) through (m), do not include an interaction term.
a. State the multiple regression equation that predicts weekly sales based on shelf space and location.
b. Interpret the regression coefficients in (a).
c. Predict the weekly sales of pet food for a store with 8 feet of shelf space situated at the back of the aisle. Construct a 95% confidence interval estimate and a 95% prediction interval.

d. Perform a residual analysis on the results and determine whether the regression assumptions are valid.
e. Is there a significant relationship between sales and the two independent variables (shelf space and aisle position) at the 0.05 level of significance?
f. At the 0.05 level of significance, determine whether each independent variable makes a contribution to the regression model. Indicate the most appropriate regression model for this set of data.
g. Construct and interpret 95% confidence interval estimates of the population slope for the relationship between sales and shelf space and between sales and aisle location.
h. Compare the slope in (b) with the slope for the simple linear regression model of Problem 13.4 on page 531. Explain the difference in the results.
i. Compute and interpret the meaning of the coefficient of multiple determination, r^2.
j. Compute and interpret the adjusted r^2.
k. Compare r^2 with the r^2 value computed in Problem 13.16 (a) on page 537.
l. Compute the coefficients of partial determination and interpret their meaning.
m. What assumption about the slope of shelf space with sales do you need to make in this problem?
n. Add an interaction term to the model and, at the 0.05 level of significance, determine whether it makes a significant contribution to the model.
o. On the basis of the results of (f) and (n), which model is most appropriate? Explain.

14.42 In mining engineering, holes are often drilled through rock, using drill bits. As a drill hole gets deeper, additional rods are added to the drill bit to enable additional drilling to take place. It is expected that drilling time increases with depth. This increased drilling time could be caused by several factors, including the mass of the drill rods that are strung together. The business problem relates to whether drilling is faster using dry drilling holes or wet drilling holes. Using dry drilling holes involves forcing compressed air down the drill rods to flush the cuttings and drive the hammer. Using wet drilling holes involves forcing water rather than air down the hole. Data have been collected from a sample of 50 drill holes that contains measurements of the time to drill each additional 5 feet (in minutes), the depth (in feet), and whether the hole was a dry drilling hole or a wet drilling hole. The data are organized and stored in. Develop a model to predict additional drilling time, based on depth and type of drilling hole (dry or wet). For (a) through (k) do not include an interaction term **Drill**.

Source: Data extracted from R. Penner and D. G. Watts, "Mining Information," *The American Statistician,* 45, 1991, pp. 4–9.

a. State the multiple regression equation.
b. Interpret the regression coefficients in (a).
c. Predict the additional drilling time for a dry drilling hole at a depth of 100 feet. Construct a 95% confidence interval estimate and a 95% prediction interval.
d. Perform a residual analysis on the results and determine whether the regression assumptions are valid.
e. Is there a significant relationship between additional drilling time and the two independent variables (depth and type of drilling hole) at the 0.05 level of significance?
f. At the 0.05 level of significance, determine whether each independent variable makes a contribution to the regression model. Indicate the most appropriate regression model for this set of data.
g. Construct a 95% confidence interval estimate of the population slope for the relationship between additional drilling time and depth.
h. Construct a 95% confidence interval estimate of the population slope for the relationship between additional drilling time and the type of hole drilled.
i. Compute and interpret the adjusted r^2.
j. Compute the coefficients of partial determination and interpret their meaning.
k. What assumption do you need to make about the slope of additional drilling time with depth?
l. Add an interaction term to the model and, at the 0.05 level of significance, determine whether it makes a significant contribution to the model.
m. On the basis of the results of (f) and (l), which model is most appropriate? Explain.

14.43 The owner of a moving company typically has his most experienced manager predict the total number of labor hours that will be required to complete an upcoming move. This approach has proved useful in the past, but the owner has the business objective of developing a more accurate method of predicting labor hours. In a preliminary effort to provide a more accurate method, the owner has decided to use the number of cubic feet moved and whether there is an elevator in the apartment building as the independent variables and has collected data for 36 moves in which the origin and destination were within the borough of Manhattan in New York City and the travel time was an insignificant portion of the hours worked. The data are organized and stored in. For (a) through (k), do not include an interaction term **Moving**.

a. State the multiple regression equation for predicting labor hours, using the number of cubic feet moved and whether there is an elevator.
b. Interpret the regression coefficients in (a).
c. Predict the labor hours for moving 500 cubic feet in an apartment building that has an elevator and construct a 95% confidence interval estimate and a 95% prediction interval.
d. Perform a residual analysis on the results and determine whether the regression assumptions are valid.
e. Is there a significant relationship between labor hours and the two independent variables (cubic feet moved and whether there is an elevator in the apartment building) at the 0.05 level of significance?

f. At the 0.05 level of significance, determine whether each independent variable makes a contribution to the regression model. Indicate the most appropriate regression model for this set of data.
g. Construct a 95% confidence interval estimate of the population slope for the relationship between labor hours and cubic feet moved.
h. Construct a 95% confidence interval estimate for the relationship between labor hours and the presence of an elevator.
i. Compute and interpret the adjusted r^2.
j. Compute the coefficients of partial determination and interpret their meaning.
k. What assumption do you need to make about the slope of labor hours with cubic feet moved?
l. Add an interaction term to the model and, at the 0.05 level of significance, determine whether it makes a significant contribution to the model.
m. On the basis of the results of (f) and (l), which model is most appropriate? Explain.

SELF Test **14.44** In Problem 14.4 on page 583, you used sales and orders to predict distribution cost (stored in WareCost). Develop a regression model to predict distribution cost that includes sales, orders, and the interaction of sales and orders.
a. At the 0.05 level of significance, is there evidence that the interaction term makes a significant contribution to the model?
b. Which regression model is more appropriate, the one used in (a) or the one used in Problem 14.4? Explain.

14.45 Zagat's publishes restaurant ratings for various locations in the United States. The file Restaurants contains the Zagat rating for food, décor, service, and cost per person for a sample of 50 restaurants located in a city and 50 restaurants located in a suburb. Develop a regression model to predict the cost per person, based on a variable that represents the sum of the ratings for food, décor, and service and a dummy variable concerning location (city vs. suburban). For (a) through (m), do not include an interaction term.

Sources: Extracted from *Zagat Survey 2010, New York City Restaurants*; and *Zagat Survey 2009–2010, Long Island Restaurants.*

a. State the multiple regression equation.
b. Interpret the regression coefficients in (a).
c. Predict the cost for a restaurant with a summated rating of 60 that is located in a city and construct a 95% confidence interval estimate and a 95% prediction interval.
d. Perform a residual analysis on the results and determine whether the regression assumptions are satisfied.
e. Is there a significant relationship between price and the two independent variables (summated rating and location) at the 0.05 level of significance?
f. At the 0.05 level of significance, determine whether each independent variable makes a contribution to the regression model. Indicate the most appropriate regression model for this set of data.
g. Construct a 95% confidence interval estimate of the population slope for the relationship between cost and summated rating.
h. Compare the slope in (b) with the slope for the simple linear regression model of Problem 13.5 on page 531. Explain the difference in the results.
i. Compute and interpret the meaning of the coefficient of multiple determination.
j. Compute and interpret the adjusted r^2.
k. Compare r^2 with the r^2 value computed in Problem 13.17 (b) on page 537.
l. Compute the coefficients of partial determination and interpret their meaning.
m. What assumption about the slope of cost with summated rating do you need to make in this problem?
n. Add an interaction term to the model and, at the 0.05 level of significance, determine whether it makes a significant contribution to the model.
o. On the basis of the results of (f) and (n), which model is most appropriate? Explain.

14.46 In Problem 14.6 on page 583, you used radio advertising and newspaper advertising to predict sales (stored in Advertise). Develop a regression model to predict sales that includes radio advertising, newspaper advertising, and the interaction of radio advertising and newspaper advertising.
a. At the 0.05 level of significance, is there evidence that the interaction term makes a significant contribution to the model?
b. Which regression model is more appropriate, the one used in this problem or the one used in Problem 14.6? Explain.

14.47 In Problem 14.5 on page 583, horsepower and weight were used to predict miles per gallon (stored in Auto2010). Develop a regression model that includes horsepower, weight, and the interaction of horsepower and weight to predict miles per gallon.
a. At the 0.05 level of significance, is there evidence that the interaction term makes a significant contribution to the model?
b. Which regression model is more appropriate, the one used in this problem or the one used in Problem 14.5? Explain.

14.48 In Problem 14.7 on page 584, you used total staff present and remote hours to predict standby hours (stored in Standby). Develop a regression model to predict standby hours that includes total staff present, remote hours, and the interaction of total staff present and remote hours.
a. At the 0.05 level of significance, is there evidence that the interaction term makes a significant contribution to the model?
b. Which regression model is more appropriate, the one used in this problem or the one used in Problem 14.7? Explain.

14.49 The director of a training program for a large insurance company has the business objective of determining which training method is best for training underwriters. The three methods to be evaluated are traditional, CD-ROM based, and Web based. The 30 trainees are divided into three randomly assigned groups of 10. Before the start of the training, each trainee is given a proficiency exam that measures mathematics and computer skills. At the end of the training, all students take the same end-of-training exam. The results are organized and stored in **Underwriting**.

Develop a multiple regression model to predict the score on the end-of-training exam, based on the score on the proficiency exam and the method of training used. For (a) through (k), do not include an interaction term.

a. State the multiple regression equation.
b. Interpret the regression coefficients in (a).
c. Predict the end-of-training exam score for a student with a proficiency exam score of 100 who had Web-based training.
d. Perform a residual analysis on your results and determine whether the regression assumptions are valid.
e. Is there a significant relationship between the end-of-training exam score and the independent variables (proficiency score and training method) at the 0.05 level of significance?
f. At the 0.05 level of significance, determine whether each independent variable makes a contribution to the regression model. Indicate the most appropriate regression model for this set of data.
g. Construct and interpret a 95% confidence interval estimate of the population slope for the relationship between the end-of-training exam score and the proficiency exam score.
h. Construct and interpret a 95% confidence interval estimate of the population slope for the relationship between the end-of-training exam score and type of training method.
i. Compute and interpret the adjusted r^2.
j. Compute the coefficients of partial determination and interpret their meaning.
k. What assumption about the slope of proficiency score with end-of-training exam score do you need to make in this problem?
l. Add interaction terms to the model and, at the 0.05 level of significance, determine whether any interaction terms make a significant contribution to the model.
m. On the basis of the results of (f) and (l), which model is most appropriate? Explain.

14.7 Logistic Regression

The discussion of the simple linear regression model in Chapter 13 and the multiple regression models in Sections 14.1 through 14.6 only considered *numerical* dependent variables. However, in many instances, the dependent variable is a *categorical* variable that takes on one of only two possible values such as a customer prefers Brand *A* or a customer prefers Brand *B*. Using a categorical dependent variable violates the normality assumption of least-squares and can also result in predicted *Y* values that are impossible.

An alternative approach to least-squares regression originally applied to survival data in the health sciences (see reference 1), **logistic regression**, enables you to use regression models to predict the probability of a particular categorical response for a given set of independent variables. The logistic regression model uses the **odds ratio**, which represents the probability of an event of interest compared with the probability of not having an event of interest. Equation (14.15) defines the odds ratio.

ODDS RATIO

$$\text{Odds ratio} = \frac{\text{Probability of an event of interest}}{1 - \text{Probability of an event of interest}} \quad \textbf{(14.15)}$$

Using Equation (14.15), if the probability of an event of interest is 0.50, the odds ratio is

$$\text{Odds ratio} = \frac{0.50}{1 - 0.50} = 1.0, \text{ or } 1 \text{ to } 1$$

If the probability of an event of interest is 0.75, the odds ratio is

$$\text{Odds ratio} = \frac{0.75}{1 - 0.75} = 3.0, \text{ or } 3 \text{ to } 1$$

The logistic regression model is based on the natural logarithm (ln) of this odds ratio.[3] Equation (14.16) defines the logistic regression model for k independent variables.

[3]For more information on logarithms, see Appendix Section A.3.

LOGISTIC REGRESSION MODEL

$$\ln(\text{Odds ratio}) = \beta_0 + \beta_1 X_{1i} + \beta_2 X_{2i} + \cdots + \beta_k X_{ki} + \varepsilon_i \quad \textbf{(14.16)}$$

where

k = number of independent variables in the model

ε_i = random error in observation i

In Sections 13.2 and 14.1, the method of least squares was used to develop a regression equation. In logistic regression, a mathematical method called *maximum likelihood estimation* is usually used to develop a regression equation to predict the natural logarithm of this odds ratio. Equation (14.17) defines the logistic regression equation.

LOGISTIC REGRESSION EQUATION

$$\ln(\text{Estimated odds ratio}) = b_0 + b_1 X_{1i} + b_2 X_{2i} + \cdots + b_k X_{ki} \quad \textbf{(14.17)}$$

Once you have determined the logistic regression equation, you use Equation (14.18) to compute the estimated odds ratio.

ESTIMATED ODDS RATIO

$$\text{Estimated odds ratio} = e^{\ln(\text{Estimated odds ratio})} \quad \textbf{(14.18)}$$

Once you have computed the estimated odds ratio, you use Equation (14.19) to find the estimated probability of an event of interest.

ESTIMATED PROBABILITY OF AN EVENT OF INTEREST

$$\text{Estimated probability of an event of interest} = \frac{\text{Estimated odds ratio}}{1 + \text{Estimated odds ratio}} \quad \textbf{(14.19)}$$

To illustrate the logistic regression model, the marketing department for a credit card company wants to organize a campaign to convince existing holders of the company's standard credit card to upgrade to the company's premium card for a nominal annual fee. The marketing department begins with the question "Which of the existing standard credit cardholders should be the target for the campaign?"

The department has access to data from a sample of 30 cardholders who were contacted during last year's campaign. That data indicates whether the cardholder upgraded to a premium card (0= no, 1= yes). The department wants to predict the categorical variable (i.e., did the customer upgrade to a premium card?) using two independent variables: total amount of credit card purchases (in thousands of dollars) in the prior year (X_1), and whether the cardholder ordered additional credit cards (at extra cost) for other members of the household (X_2: 0= no, 1= yes). Figure 14.14 presents results for the logistic regression model, the data for which are stored in **Logpurch**.

FIGURE 14.14
Minitab logistic regression results for the credit card marketing data

Binary Logistic Regression: Upgraded versus Purchases, Extra Cards

```
Link Function: Logit

Response Information
Variable  Value  Count
Upgraded  1         13  (Event)
          0         17
          Total     30

Logistic Regression Table
                                                          Odds      95% CI
Predictor          Coef    SE Coef      Z      P  Ratio  Lower   Upper
Constant       -6.93984    2.94712  -2.35  0.019
Purchases      0.139469  0.0680641   2.05  0.040   1.15   1.01    1.31
Extra Cards
 1              2.77434    1.19267   2.33  0.020  16.03   1.55  165.99

Log-Likelihood = -10.038
Test that all slopes are zero: G = 20.977, DF = 2, P-Value = 0.000

Goodness-of-Fit Tests
Method            Chi-Square  DF      P
Pearson              18.5186  27  0.887
Deviance             20.0769  27  0.828
Hosmer-Lemeshow       6.5174   8  0.589
```

Excel does not contain any logistic regression functions, but logistic regression analysis can be done using the Excel Solver add-in (beyond the scope of this book).

In this model, the regression coefficients are interpreted as follows:

- The regression constant b_0 is -6.940. This means that for a credit cardholder who did not charge any purchases last year and who does not have additional cards, the estimated natural logarithm of the odds ratio of purchasing the premium card is -6.940.
- The regression coefficient b_1 is 0.13947. This means that holding constant the effect of whether the credit cardholder has additional cards for members of the household, for each increase of \$1,000 in annual credit card spending using the company's card, the estimated natural logarithm of the odds ratio of purchasing the premium card increases by 0.13947. Therefore, cardholders who charged more in the previous year are more likely to upgrade to a premium card.
- The regression coefficient b_2 is 2.774. This means that holding constant the annual credit card spending, the estimated natural logarithm of the odds ratio of purchasing the premium card increases by 2.774 for a credit cardholder who has additional cards for members of the household compared with one who does not have additional cards. Therefore, cardholders possessing additional cards for other members of the household are much more likely to upgrade to a premium card.

The regression coefficients suggest that the credit card company should develop a marketing campaign that targets cardholders who tend to charge large amounts to their cards, and to households that possess more than one card.

As was the case with least-squares regression models, a main purpose of performing logistic regression analysis is to provide predictions of a dependent variable. For example, consider a cardholder who charged \$36,000 last year and possesses additional cards for members of the household. What is the probability the cardholder will upgrade to the premium card during the marketing campaign? Using $X_1 = 36, X_2 = 1$, Equation (14.17) on page 610, and the results displayed in Figure 14.14 on page 611,

$$\begin{aligned}\ln(\text{estimated odds of purchasing versus not purchasing}) &= -6.94 + (0.13947)(36) + (2.774)(1)\\ &= 0.85492\end{aligned}$$

Then, using Equation (14.18) on page 610,

$$\text{Estimated odds ratio} = e^{0.85492} = 2.3512$$

Therefore, the odds are 2.3512 to 1 that a credit cardholder who spent $36,000 last year and has additional cards will purchase the premium card during the campaign. Using Equation (14.19) on page 610, you can convert this odds ratio to a probability:

$$\begin{aligned}\text{estimated probability of purchasing premium card} &= \frac{2.3512}{1 + 2.3512}\\ &= 0.7016\end{aligned}$$

Thus, the estimated probability is 0.7016 that a credit cardholder who spent $36,000 last year and has additional cards will purchase the premium card during the campaign. In other words, you predict 70.16% of such individuals will purchase the premium card.

Now that you have used the logistic regression model for prediction, you need to determine whether or not the model is a good-fitting model. The **deviance statistic** is frequently used to determine whether or not the current model provides a good fit to the data. This statistic measures the fit of the current model compared with a model that has as many parameters as there are data points (what is called a *saturated* model). The deviance statistic follows a chi-square distribution with $n-k-1$ degrees of freedom. The null and alternative hypotheses are

H_0: The model is a good-fitting model.

H_1: The model is not a good-fitting model.

When using the deviance statistic for logistic regression, the null hypothesis represents a good-fitting model, which is the opposite of the null hypothesis when using the overall F test for the multiple regression model (see Section 14.2). Using the α level of significance, the decision rule is

Reject H_0 if deviance $> \chi^2_\alpha$

Otherwise, do not reject H_o.

The critical value for a χ^2 statistic with $n-k-1 = 30-2-1 = 27$ degrees of freedom is 40.113 (see Table E.4). From Figure 14.14 on page 611, the deviance $= 20.08 < 40.113$, or the p-value $= 0.828 > 0.05$. Thus, you do not reject H_0, and you conclude that the model is a good-fitting one.

Now that you have concluded that the model is a good-fitting one, you need to evaluate whether each of the independent variables makes a significant contribution to the model in the presence of the others. As was the case with linear regression in Sections 13.7 and 14.4, the test statistic is based on the ratio of the regression coefficient to the standard error of the regression coefficient. In logistic regression, this ratio is defined by the **Wald statistic**, which approximately follows the normal distribution. From Figure 14.14, the Wald statistic (labeled Z) is 2.05 for X_1 and 2.33 for X_2. Each of these is greater than the critical value of +1.96 for the normal distribution at the 0.05 level of significance (the p-values are 0.04 and 0.02). You can conclude that each of the two independent variables makes a contribution to the model in the presence of the other. Therefore, you should include both these independent variables in the model.

Problems for Section 14.7

LEARNING THE BASICS

14.50 Interpret the meaning of a slope coefficient equal to 2.2 in logistic regression.

14.51 Given an estimated odds ratio of 2.5, compute the estimated probability of an event of interest.

14.52 Given an estimated odds ratio of 0.75, compute the estimated probability of an event of interest.

14.53 Consider the following logistic regression equation:

$$\ln(\text{Estimated odds ratio}) = 0.1 + 0.5X_{1i} + 0.2X_{2i}$$

a. Interpret the meaning of the logistic regression coefficients.
b. If $X_1 = 2$ and $X_2 = 1.5$, compute the estimated odds ratio and interpret its meaning.
c. On the basis of the results of (b), compute the estimated probability of an event of interest.

APPLYING THE CONCEPTS

14.54 Refer to Figure 14.14 on page 611.
a. Predict the probability that a cardholder who charged \$36,000 last year and does not have any additional credit cards for members of the household will purchase the premium card during the marketing campaign.
b. Compare the results in (a) with those for a person with additional credit cards.
c. Predict the probability that a cardholder who charged \$18,000 and does not have any additional credit cards for members of the household will purchase the premium card during the marketing campaign.
d. Compare the results of (a) and (c) and indicate what implications these results might have for the strategy for the marketing campaign.

14.55 Undergraduate students at Miami University in Oxford, Ohio, were surveyed in order to evaluate the effect of price on the purchase of a pizza from Pizza Hut. The students were asked to suppose that they were going to have a large two-topping pizza delivered to their residence. Then they were asked to select from either Pizza Hut or another pizzeria of their choice. The price they would have to pay to get a Pizza Hut pizza differed from survey to survey. For example, some surveys used the price \$11.49. Other prices investigated were \$8.49, \$9.49, \$10.49, \$12.49, \$13.49, and \$14.49. The dependent variable for this study is whether or not a student will select Pizza Hut. Possible independent variables are the price of a Pizza Hut pizza and the gender of the student. The data set PizzaHut has 220 observations and three variables:

Gender (1=male, 0=female)

Price (8.49, 9.49, 10.49, 11.49, 12.49, 13.49, or 14.49)

Purchase (1=the student selected Pizza Hut, 0=the student selected another pizzeria)

a. Develop a logistic regression model to predict the probability that a student selects Pizza Hut based on the price of the pizza. Is price an important indicator of purchase selection?
b. Develop a logistic regression model to predict the probability that a student selects Pizza Hut based on the price of the pizza and the gender of the student. Is price an important indicator of purchase selection? Is gender an important indicator of purchase selection?
c. Compare the results from (a) and (b). Which model would you choose? Discuss.
d. Using the model selected in (c), predict the probability that a student will select Pizza Hut if the price is \$8.99.
e. Using the model selected in (c), predict the probability that a student will select Pizza Hut if the price is \$11.49.
f. Using the model selected in (c), predict the probability that a student will select Pizza Hut if the price is \$13.99.

14.56 The director of graduate studies at a college of business wants to predict the success of students in an MBA program using two independent variables, undergraduate grade point average (GPA) and GMAT score. A random sample of 30 students (stored in MBA) indicates that 20 successfully completed the program (coded as 1) and 10 did not (coded as 0).

Success in MBA Program	Undergraduate GPA	GMAT Score	Success in MBA Program	Undergraduate GPA	GMAT Score
0	2.93	617	1	3.17	639
0	3.05	557	1	3.24	632
0	3.11	599	1	3.41	639
0	3.24	616	1	3.37	619
0	3.36	594	1	3.46	665
0	3.41	567	1	3.57	694
0	3.45	542	1	3.62	641
0	3.60	551	1	3.66	594
0	3.64	573	1	3.69	678
0	3.57	536	1	3.70	624
1	2.75	688	1	3.78	654
1	2.81	647	1	3.84	718
1	3.03	652	1	3.77	692
1	3.10	608	1	3.79	632
1	3.06	680	1	3.97	784

a. Develop a logistic regression model to predict the probability of successful completion of the MBA program based on undergraduate grade point average and GMAT score.
b. Explain the meaning of the regression coefficients for the model in (a).
c. Predict the probability of successful completion of the program for a student with an undergraduate grade point average of 3.25 and a GMAT score of 600.
d. At the 0.05 level of significance, is there evidence that a logistic regression model that uses undergraduate grade

point average and GMAT score to predict probability of success in the MBA program is a good-fitting model?

e. At the 0.05 level of significance, is there evidence that undergraduate grade point average and GMAT score each make a significant contribution to the logistic regression model?

f. Develop a logistic regression model that includes only undergraduate grade point average to predict probability of success in the MBA program.

g. Develop a logistic regression model that includes only GMAT score to predict probability of success in the MBA program.

h. Compare the models in (a), (f), and (g). Evaluate the differences among the models.

14.57 A hotel has designed a new system for room service delivery of breakfast that allows the customer to select a specific delivery time. The difference between the actual and requested delivery times was recorded (a negative time means that the breakfast was delivered before the requested time) for 30 deliveries on a particular day along with whether the customer had previously stayed at the hotel. The data are stored in the file **Satisfaction**.

a. Develop a logistic regression model to predict the probability that the customer will be satisfied (0 = unfavorable, 1 = favorable), based on the delivery time difference and whether the customer had previously stayed at the hotel.

b. Explain the meaning of the regression coefficients for the model in (a).

c. Predict the probability that the customer will be satisfied if the delivery time difference is +3 minutes and he or she did not previously stay at the hotel.

d. At the 0.05 level of significance, is there evidence that a logistic regression model that uses delivery time difference and whether the customer had previously stayed at the hotel is a good-fitting model?

e. At the 0.05 level of significance, is there evidence that both independent variables (delivery time difference and whether the customer had previously stayed at the hotel) make a significant contribution to the logistic regression model?

USING STATISTICS @ OmniFoods Revisited

In the Using Statistics scenario, you were the marketing manager for OmniFoods, a large food products company planning a nationwide introduction of a new high-energy bar, OmniPower. You needed to determine the effect that price and in-store promotions would have on sales of OmniPower in order to develop an effective marketing strategy. A sample of 34 stores in a supermarket chain was selected for a test-market study. The stores charged between 59 and 99 cents per bar and were given an in-store promotion budget between $200 and $600.

At the end of the one-month test-market study, you performed a multiple regression analysis on the data. Two independent variables were considered: the price of an OmniPower bar and the monthly budget for in-store promotional expenditures. The dependent variable was the number of OmniPower bars sold in a month. The coefficient of determination indicated that 75.8% of the variation in sales was explained by knowing the price charged and the amount spent on in-store promotions. The model indicated that the predicted sales of OmniPower are estimated to decrease by 532 bars per month for each 10-cent increase in the price, and the predicted sales are estimated to increase by 361 bars for each additional $100 spent on promotions.

After studying the relative effects of price and promotion, OmniFoods needs to set price and promotion standards for a nationwide introduction (obviously, lower prices and higher promotion budgets lead to more sales, but they do so at a lower profit margin). You determined that if stores spend $400 a month for in-store promotions and charge 79 cents, the 95% confidence interval estimate of the mean monthly sales is 2,854 to 3,303 bars. OmniFoods can multiply the lower and upper bounds of this confidence interval by the number of stores included in the nationwide introduction to estimate total monthly sales. For example, if 1,000 stores are in the nationwide introduction, then total monthly sales should be between 2.854 million and 3.308 million bars.

SUMMARY

In this chapter, you learned how multiple regression models allow you to use two or more independent variables to predict the value of a dependent variable. You also learned how to include categorical independent variables and interaction terms in regression models. In addition, you used the logistic regression model to predict a categorical dependent variable. Figure 14.15 presents a roadmap of the chapter.

FIGURE 14.15
Roadmap for multiple regression

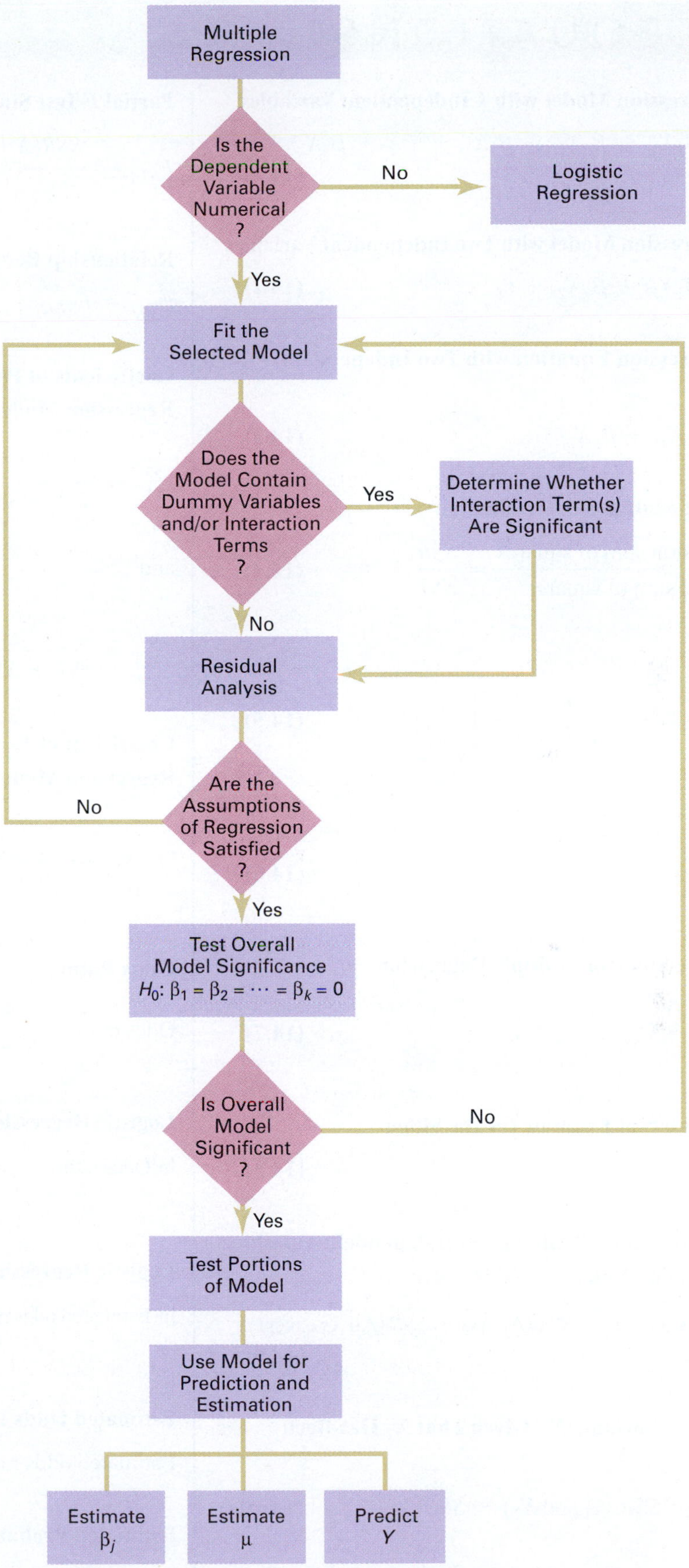

KEY EQUATIONS

Multiple Regression Model with *k* Independent Variables

$$Y_i = \beta_0 + \beta_1 X_{1i} + \beta_2 X_{2i} + \beta_3 X_{3i} + \cdots + \beta_k X_{ki} + \varepsilon_i \qquad \textbf{(14.1)}$$

Multiple Regression Model with Two Independent Variables

$$Y_i = \beta_0 + \beta_1 X_{1i} + \beta_2 X_{2i} + \varepsilon_i \qquad \textbf{(14.2)}$$

Multiple Regression Equation with Two Independent Variables

$$\hat{Y}_i = b_0 + b_1 X_{1i} + b_2 X_{2i} \qquad \textbf{(14.3)}$$

Coefficient of Multiple Determination

$$r^2 = \frac{\text{Regression sum of squares}}{\text{Total sum of squares}} = \frac{SSR}{SST} \qquad \textbf{(14.4)}$$

Adjusted r^2

$$r^2_{\text{adj}} = 1 - \left[(1 - r^2)\frac{n - 1}{n - k - 1}\right] \qquad \textbf{(14.5)}$$

Overall *F* Test

$$F_{STAT} = \frac{MSR}{MSE} \qquad \textbf{(14.6)}$$

Testing for the Slope in Multiple Regression

$$t_{STAT} = \frac{b_j - \beta_j}{S_{b_j}} \qquad \textbf{(14.7)}$$

Confidence Interval Estimate for the Slope

$$b_j \pm t_{\alpha/2} S_{b_j} \qquad \textbf{(14.8)}$$

Determining the Contribution of an Independent Variable to the Regression Model

$$SSR(X_j \mid \text{All } Xs \text{ except } j) = SSR\,(\text{All } Xs) - SSR\,(\text{All } Xs \text{ except } j) \qquad \textbf{(14.9)}$$

Contribution of Variable X_1, Given That X_2 Has Been Included

$$SSR(X_1 \mid X_2) = SSR(X_1 \text{ and } X_2) - SSR(X_2) \qquad \textbf{(14.10a)}$$

Contribution of Variable X_2, Given That X_1 Has Been Included

$$SSR(X_2 \mid X_1) = SSR(X_1 \text{ and } X_2) - SSR(X_1) \qquad \textbf{(14.10b)}$$

Partial *F* Test Statistic

$$F_{STAT} = \frac{SSR(X_j \mid \text{All } Xs \text{ except } j)}{MSE} \qquad \textbf{(14.11)}$$

Relationship Between a *t* Statistic and an *F* Statistic

$$t^2_{STAT} = F_{STAT} \qquad \textbf{(14.12)}$$

Coefficients of Partial Determination for a Multiple Regression Model Containing Two Independent Variables

$$r^2_{Y1.2} = \frac{SSR(X_1 \mid X_2)}{SST - SSR(X_1 \text{ and } X_2) + SSR(X_1 \mid X_2)} \qquad \textbf{(14.13a)}$$

and

$$r^2_{Y2.1} = \frac{SSR(X_2 \mid X_1)}{SST - SSR(X_1 \text{ and } X_2) + SSR(X_2 \mid X_1)} \qquad \textbf{(14.13b)}$$

Coefficient of Partial Determination for a Multiple Regression Model Containing *k* Independent Variables

$$r^2_{Yj.(\text{All variables except } j)} = \frac{SSR(X_j \mid \text{All } Xs \text{ except } j)}{SST - SSR(\text{All } Xs) + SSR(X_j \mid \text{All } Xs \text{ except } j)} \qquad \textbf{(14.14)}$$

Odds Ratio

$$\text{Odds ratio} = \frac{\text{Probability of an event of interest}}{1 - \text{Probability of an event of interest}} \qquad \textbf{(14.15)}$$

Logistic Regression Model

$$\ln(\text{Odds ratio}) = \beta_0 + \beta_1 X_{1i} + \beta_2 X_{2i} + \ldots + \beta_k X_{ki} + \varepsilon_i \qquad \textbf{(14.16)}$$

Logistic Regression Equation

$$\ln(\text{Estimated odds ratio}) = b_0 + b_1 X_{1i} + b_2 X_{2i} + \ldots + b_k X_{ki} \qquad \textbf{(14.17)}$$

Estimated Odds Ratio

$$\text{Estimated odds ratio} = e^{\ln(\text{Estimated odds ratio})} \qquad \textbf{(14.18)}$$

Estimated Probability of an Event of Interest

$$\text{Estimated probability of an event of interest} = \frac{\text{Estimated odds ratio}}{1 + \text{Estimated odds ratio}} \qquad \textbf{(14.19)}$$

KEY TERMS

CHAPTER REVIEW PROBLEMS

CHECKING YOUR UNDERSTANDING

14.58 What is the difference between r^2 and adjusted r^2?

14.59 How does the interpretation of the regression coefficients differ in multiple regression and simple linear regression?

14.60 How does testing the significance of the entire multiple regression model differ from testing the contribution of each independent variable?

14.61 How do the coefficients of partial determination differ from the coefficient of multiple determination?

14.62 Why and how do you use dummy variables?

14.63 How can you evaluate whether the slope of the dependent variable with an independent variable is the same for each level of the dummy variable?

14.64 Under what circumstances do you include an interaction term in a regression model?

14.65 When a dummy variable is included in a regression model that has one numerical independent variable, what assumption do you need to make concerning the slope between the dependent variable, Y, and the numerical independent variable, X?

14.66 When do you use logistic regression?

APPLYING THE CONCEPTS

14.67 Increasing customer satisfaction typically results in increased purchase behavior. For many products, there is more than one measure of customer satisfaction. In many of these instances, purchase behavior can increase dramatically with an increase in any one of the customer satisfaction measures, not necessarily all of them at the same time. Gunst and Barry ("One Way to Moderate Ceiling Effects," *Quality Progress*, October 2003, pp. 83–85) consider a product with two satisfaction measures, X_1 and X_2, that range from the lowest level of satisfaction, 1, to the highest level of satisfaction, 7. The dependent variable, Y, is a measure of purchase behavior, with the highest value generating the most sales. The following regression equation is presented:

$$\hat{Y}_i = -3.888 + 1.449X_{1i} + 1.462X_{2i} - 0.190X_{1i}X_{2i}$$

Suppose that X_1 is the perceived quality of the product and X_2 is the perceived value of the product. (Note: If the customer thinks the product is overpriced, he or she perceives it to be of low value and vice versa.)

a. What is the predicted purchase behavior when $X_1 = 2$ and $X_2 = 2$?
b. What is the predicted purchase behavior when $X_1 = 2$ and $X_2 = 7$?
c. What is the predicted purchase behavior when $X_1 = 7$ and $X_2 = 2$?
d. What is the predicted purchase behavior when $X_1 = 7$ and $X_2 = 7$?
e. What is the regression equation when $X_2 = 2$? What is the slope for X_1 now?
f. What is the regression equation when $X_2 = 7$? What is the slope for X_1 now?
g. What is the regression equation when $X_1 = 2$? What is the slope for X_2 now?
h. What is the regression equation when $X_1 = 7$? What is the slope for X_2 now?
i. Discuss the implications of (a) through (h) within the context of increasing sales for this product with two customer satisfaction measures.

14.68 The owner of a moving company typically has his most experienced manager predict the total number of labor hours that will be required to complete an upcoming move. This approach has proved useful in the past, but the owner has the business objective of developing a more accurate method of predicting labor hours. In a preliminary effort to provide a more accurate method, the owner has decided to use the number of cubic feet moved and the number of pieces of large furniture as the independent variables and has collected data for 36 moves in which the origin and destination were within the borough of Manhattan in New York City and the travel time was an insignificant portion of the hours worked. The data are organized and stored in **Moving**.

a. State the multiple regression equation.
b. Interpret the meaning of the slopes in this equation.
c. Predict the labor hours for moving 500 cubic feet with two large pieces of furniture.
d. Perform a residual analysis on your results and determine whether the regression assumptions are valid.
e. Determine whether there is a significant relationship between labor hours and the two independent variables (the number of cubic feet moved and the number of pieces of large furniture) at the 0.05 level of significance.
f. Determine the p-value in (e) and interpret its meaning.
g. Interpret the meaning of the coefficient of multiple determination in this problem.
h. Determine the adjusted r^2.
i. At the 0.05 level of significance, determine whether each independent variable makes a significant contribution to the regression model. Indicate the most appropriate regression model for this set of data.
j. Determine the p-values in (i) and interpret their meaning.
k. Construct a 95% confidence interval estimate of the population slope between labor hours and the number of cubic feet moved. How does the interpretation of the slope here differ from that in Problem 13.44 on page 552?
l. Compute and interpret the coefficients of partial determination.

14.69 Professional basketball has truly become a sport that generates interest among fans around the world. More and more players come from outside the United States to play in the National Basketball Association (NBA). You want to develop a regression model to predict the number of wins achieved by each NBA team, based on field goal (shots made) percentage for the team and for the opponent. The data are stored in **NBA2010**.
a. State the multiple regression equation.
b. Interpret the meaning of the slopes in this equation.
c. Predict the number of wins for a team that has a field goal percentage of 45% and an opponent field goal percentage of 44%.
d. Perform a residual analysis on your results and determine whether the regression assumptions are valid.
e. Is there a significant relationship between number of wins and the two independent variables (field goal percentage for the team and for the opponent) at the 0.05 level of significance?
f. Determine the p-value in (e) and interpret its meaning.
g. Interpret the meaning of the coefficient of multiple determination in this problem.
h. Determine the adjusted r^2.
i. At the 0.05 level of significance, determine whether each independent variable makes a significant contribution to the regression model. Indicate the most appropriate regression model for this set of data.
j. Determine the p-values in (i) and interpret their meaning.
k. Compute and interpret the coefficients of partial determination.

14.70 A sample of 30 recently sold single-family houses in a small city is selected. Develop a model to predict the selling price (in thousands of dollars), using the assessed value (in thousands of dollars) as well as time (in months since reassessment). The houses in the city had been reassessed at full value one year prior to the study. The results are stored in **House1**.
a. State the multiple regression equation.
b. Interpret the meaning of the slopes in this equation.
c. Predict the selling price for a house that has an assessed value of $170,000 and was sold 12 months after reassessment.
d. Perform a residual analysis on your results and determine whether the regression assumptions are valid.
e. Determine whether there is a significant relationship between selling price and the two independent variables (assessed value and time period) at the 0.05 level of significance.
f. Determine the p-value in (e) and interpret its meaning.
g. Interpret the meaning of the coefficient of multiple determination in this problem.
h. Determine the adjusted r^2.
i. At the 0.05 level of significance, determine whether each independent variable makes a significant contribution to the regression model. Indicate the most appropriate regression model for this set of data.
j. Determine the p-values in (i) and interpret their meaning.
k. Construct a 95% confidence interval estimate of the population slope between selling price and assessed value. How does the interpretation of the slope here differ from that in Problem 13.76 on page 565?
l. Compute and interpret the coefficients of partial determination.

14.71 Measuring the height of a California redwood tree is very difficult because these trees grow to heights over 300 feet. People familiar with these trees understand that the height of a California redwood tree is related to other characteristics of the tree, including the diameter of the tree at the breast height of a person (in inches) and the thickness of the bark of the tree (in inches). The file **Redwood** contains the height, diameter at breast height of a person, and bark thickness for a sample of 21 California redwood trees.
a. State the multiple regression equation that predicts the height of a tree, based on the tree's diameter at breast height and the thickness of the bark.
b. Interpret the meaning of the slopes in this equation.
c. Predict the height for a tree that has a breast height diameter of 25 inches and a bark thickness of 2 inches.
d. Interpret the meaning of the coefficient of multiple determination in this problem.
e. Perform a residual analysis on the results and determine whether the regression assumptions are valid.
f. Determine whether there is a significant relationship between the height of redwood trees and the two independent variables (breast-height diameter and bark thickness) at the 0.05 level of significance.

g. Construct a 95% confidence interval estimate of the population slope between the height of redwood trees and breast-height diameter and between the height of redwood trees and the bark thickness.
h. At the 0.05 level of significance, determine whether each independent variable makes a significant contribution to the regression model. Indicate the independent variables to include in this model.
i. Construct a 95% confidence interval estimate of the mean height for trees that have a breast-height diameter of 25 inches and a bark thickness of 2 inches, along with a prediction interval for an individual tree.
j. Compute and interpret the coefficients of partial determination.

14.72 Develop a model to predict the assessed value (in thousands of dollars), using the size of the houses (in thousands of square feet) and the age of the houses (in years) from the following table (stored in **House2**):

House	Assessed Value ($Thousands)	Size of House (Thousands of Square Feet)	Age (Years)
1	184.4	2.00	3.42
2	177.4	1.71	11.50
3	175.7	1.45	8.33
4	185.9	1.76	0.00
5	179.1	1.93	7.42
6	170.4	1.20	32.00
7	175.8	1.55	16.00
8	185.9	1.93	2.00
9	178.5	1.59	1.75
10	179.2	1.50	2.75
11	186.7	1.90	0.00
12	179.3	1.39	0.00
13	174.5	1.54	12.58
14	183.8	1.89	2.75
15	176.8	1.59	7.17

a. State the multiple regression equation.
b. Interpret the meaning of the slopes in this equation.
c. Predict the assessed value for a house that has a size of 1,750 square feet and is 10 years old.
d. Perform a residual analysis on the results and determine whether the regression assumptions are valid.
e. Determine whether there is a significant relationship between assessed value and the two independent variables (size and age) at the 0.05 level of significance.
f. Determine the p-value in (e) and interpret its meaning.
g. Interpret the meaning of the coefficient of multiple determination in this problem.
h. Determine the adjusted r^2.
i. At the 0.05 level of significance, determine whether each independent variable makes a significant contribution to the regression model. Indicate the most appropriate regression model for this set of data.
j. Determine the p-values in (i) and interpret their meaning.
k. Construct a 95% confidence interval estimate of the population slope between assessed value and size. How does the interpretation of the slope here differ from that of Problem 13.77 on page 566?
l. Compute and interpret the coefficients of partial determination.
m. The real estate assessor's office has been publicly quoted as saying that the age of a house has no bearing on its assessed value. Based on your answers to (a) through (l), do you agree with this statement? Explain.

14.73 Crazy Dave, a well-known baseball analyst, wants to determine which variables are important in predicting a team's wins in a given season. He has collected data related to wins, earned run average (ERA), and runs scored for the 2009 season (stored in **BB2009**). Develop a model to predict the number of wins based on ERA and runs scored.
a. State the multiple regression equation.
b. Interpret the meaning of the slopes in this equation.
c. Predict the number of wins for a team that has an ERA of 4.50 and has scored 750 runs.
d. Perform a residual analysis on the results and determine whether the regression assumptions are valid.
e. Is there a significant relationship between number of wins and the two independent variables (ERA and runs scored) at the 0.05 level of significance?
f. Determine the p-value in (e) and interpret its meaning.
g. Interpret the meaning of the coefficient of multiple determination in this problem.
h. Determine the adjusted r^2.
i. At the 0.05 level of significance, determine whether each independent variable makes a significant contribution to the regression model. Indicate the most appropriate regression model for this set of data.
j. Determine the p-values in (i) and interpret their meaning.
k. Construct a 95% confidence interval estimate of the population slope between wins and ERA.
l. Compute and interpret the coefficients of partial determination.
m. Which is more important in predicting wins—pitching, as measured by ERA, or offense, as measured by runs scored? Explain.

14.74 Referring to Problem 14.73, suppose that in addition to using ERA to predict the number of wins, Crazy Dave wants to include the league (0 = American, 1 = National) as an independent variable. Develop a model to predict wins based on ERA and league. For (a) through (k), do not include an interaction term.
a. State the multiple regression equation.
b. Interpret the slopes in (a).
c. Predict the number of wins for a team with an ERA of 4.50 in the American League. Construct a 95% confidence interval estimate for all teams and a 95% prediction interval for an individual team.
d. Perform a residual analysis on the results and determine whether the regression assumptions are valid.

e. Is there a significant relationship between wins and the two independent variables (ERA and league) at the 0.05 level of significance?

f. At the 0.05 level of significance, determine whether each independent variable makes a contribution to the regression model. Indicate the most appropriate regression model for this set of data.

g. Construct a 95% confidence interval estimate of the population slope for the relationship between wins and ERA.

h. Construct a 95% confidence interval estimate of the population slope for the relationship between wins and league.

i. Compute and interpret the adjusted r^2.

j. Compute and interpret the coefficients of partial determination.

k. What assumption do you have to make about the slope of wins with ERA?

l. Add an interaction term to the model and, at the 0.05 level of significance, determine whether it makes a significant contribution to the model.

m. On the basis of the results of (f) and (l), which model is most appropriate? Explain.

14.75 You are a real estate broker who wants to compare property values in Glen Cove and Roslyn (which are located approximately 8 miles apart). In order to do so, you will analyze the data in GCRoslyn, a file that includes samples of houses from Glen Cove and Roslyn. Making sure to include the dummy variable for location (Glen Cove or Roslyn), develop a regression model to predict appraised value, based on the land area of a property, the age of a house, and location. Be sure to determine whether any interaction terms need to be included in the model.

14.76 A recent article discussed a metal deposition process in which a piece of metal is placed in an acid bath and an alloy is layered on top of it. The business objective of engineers working on the process was to reduce variation in the thickness of the alloy layer. To begin, the temperature and the pressure in the tank holding the acid bath are to be studied as independent variables. Data are collected from 50 samples. The results are organized and stored in Thickness. (Data extracted from J. Conklin, "It's a Marathon, Not a Sprint," *Quality Progress*, June 2009, pp. 46–49.)

Develop a multiple regression model that uses temperature and the pressure in the tank holding the acid bath to predict the thickness of the alloy layer. Be sure to perform a thorough residual analysis. The article suggests that there is a significant interaction between the pressure and the temperature in the tank. Do you agree?

MANAGING ASHLAND MULTICOMM SERVICES

In its continuing study of the *3-For-All* subscription solicitation process, a marketing department team wants to test the effects of two types of structured sales presentations (personal formal and personal informal) and the number of hours spent on telemarketing on the number of new subscriptions. The staff has recorded these data in the file AMS14 for the past 24 weeks.

Analyze these data and develop a multiple regression model to predict the number of new subscriptions for a week, based on the number of hours spent on telemarketing and the sales presentation type. Write a report, giving detailed findings concerning the regression model used.

DIGITAL CASE

Apply your knowledge of multiple regression models in this Digital Case, which extends the OmniFoods Using Statistics scenario from this chapter.

To ensure a successful test marketing of its OmniPower energy bars, the OmniFoods marketing department has contracted with In-Store Placements Group (ISPG), a merchandising consultancy. ISPG will work with the grocery store chain that is conducting the test-market study. Using the same 34-store sample used in the test-market study, ISPG claims that the choice of shelf location and the presence of in-store OmniPower coupon dispensers both increase sales of the energy bars.

Open **Omni_ISPGMemo.pdf** to review the ISPG claims and supporting data. Then answer the following questions:

1. Are the supporting data consistent with ISPG's claims? Perform an appropriate statistical analysis to confirm (or discredit) the stated relationship between sales and the two independent variables of product shelf location and the presence of in-store OmniPower coupon dispensers.
2. If you were advising OmniFoods, would you recommend using a specific shelf location and in-store coupon dispensers to sell OmniPower bars?
3. What additional data would you advise collecting in order to determine the effectiveness of the sales promotion techniques used by ISPG?

REFERENCES

1. Hosmer, D. W., and S. Lemeshow, *Applied Logistic Regression*, 2nd ed. (New York: Wiley, 2001).
2. Kutner, M., C. Nachtsheim, J. Neter, and W. Li, *Applied Linear Statistical Models*, 5th ed. (New York: McGraw-Hill/Irwin, 2005).
3. *Microsoft Excel 2010* (Redmond, WA: Microsoft Corp., 2010).
4. *Minitab Release 16* (State College, PA: Minitab, Inc., 2010).

CHAPTER 14 EXCEL GUIDE

EG14.1 DEVELOPING a MULTIPLE REGRESSION MODEL

Interpreting the Regression Coefficients

PHStat2 Use **Multiple Regression** to perform a multiple regression analysis. For example, to perform the Figure 14.2 analysis of the OmniPower sales data on page 580, open to the **DATA worksheet** of the **OmniPower workbook**. Select **PHStat → Regression → Multiple Regression**, and in the procedure's dialog box (shown below):

1. Enter **A1:A35** as the **Y Variable Cell Range**.
2. Enter **B1:C35** as the **X Variables Cell Range**.
3. Check **First cells in both ranges contain label**.
4. Enter **95** as the **Confidence level for regression coefficients**.
5. Check **Regression Statistics Table** and **ANOVA and Coefficients Table**.
6. Enter a **Title** and click **OK**.

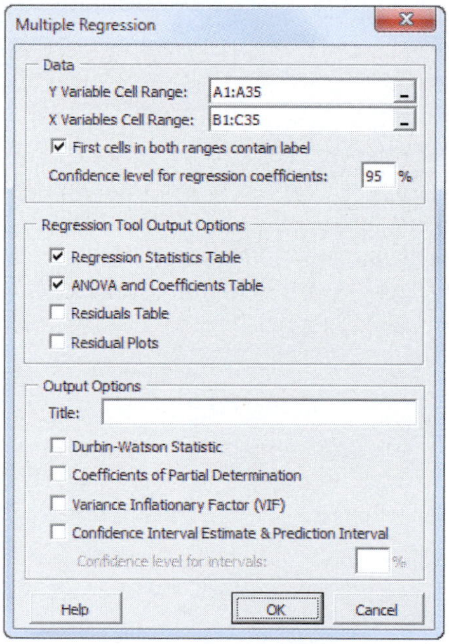

The procedure creates a worksheet that contains a copy of your data in addition to the regression results worksheet shown in Figure 14.2. For more information about these worksheets, read the following *In-Depth Excel* section.

In-Depth Excel Use the **COMPUTE worksheet** of the **Multiple Regression workbook**, partially shown in Figure 14.2 on page 580, as a template for performing multiple regression. Columns A through I of this worksheet duplicate the visual design of the Analysis ToolPak regression worksheet. The worksheet uses the regression data in the **MRData worksheet** to perform the regression analysis for the OmniPower sales data.

Figure 14.2 does not show the columns K through N Calculations area. This area contains a **LINEST(*cell range of Y variable, cell range of X variable,* True, True)** array formula in the cell range L2:N6 and calculations for the t test of the slope (see Section 13.7 on page 548). The array formula computes the b_2, b_1, and b_0 coefficients in cells L2, M2, and N2; the b_2, b_1, and b_0 standard error in cells L3, M3, and N3; r^2 and the standard error of the estimate in cells L4 and M4; the F test statistic and error df in cells L5 and M5; and *SSR* and *SSE* in cells L6 and M6. (The rest of the cell range, N4, N5, and N6, displays the **#N/A** message. This is not an error.)

Open to the **COMPUTE_FORMULAS worksheet** to examine all the formulas in the worksheet, some of which are discussed in the Chapter 13 Excel Guide *In-Depth Excel* sections.

To perform multiple regression analyses for other data, paste the regression data into the MRData worksheet. Paste the values for the Y variable into column A. Paste the values for the X variables into consecutive columns, starting with column B. Open to the COMPUTE worksheet. First, enter the confidence level in cell L8. Then, edit the correct 5-row-by–3-column array of cells that starts with cell L2. First adjust the range of the array, adding a column for each independent variable in excess of two. Then, edit the cell ranges in the array formula, and then, while holding down the **Control** and **Shift** keys (or the **Apple** key on a Mac), press the **Enter** key.

Analysis ToolPak Use **Regression** to perform a multiple regression analysis. For example, to perform the Figure 14.2 analysis of the OmniPower sales data on page 580, open to the **DATA worksheet** of the **OmniPower workbook** and:

1. Select **Data → Data Analysis**.
2. In the Data Analysis dialog box, select **Regression** from the **Analysis Tools** list and then click **OK**.

In the Regression dialog box (shown on page 623):

3. Enter **A1:A35** as the **Input Y Range** and enter **B1:C35** as the **Input X Range**.
4. Check **Labels** and check **Confidence Level** and enter **95** in its box.
5. Click **New Worksheet Ply**.
6. Click **OK**.

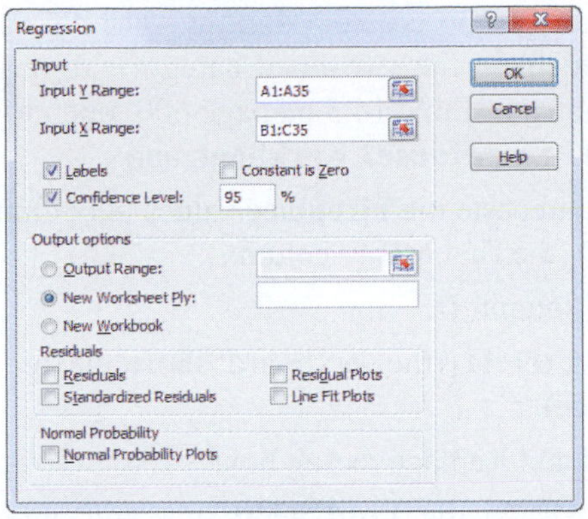

Predicting the Dependent Variable Y

PHStat2 Use the "Interpreting the Regression Coefficients" *PHStat2* instructions but replace step 6 with the following steps 6 through 8:

6. Check **Confidence Interval Estimate & Prediction Interval** and enter **95** as the percentage for **Confidence level for intervals**.
7. Enter a **Title** and click **OK**.
8. In the new worksheet, enter **79** in cell **B6** and enter **400** in cell **B7**.

These steps create a new worksheet that is discussed in the following *In-Depth Excel* instructions.

In-Depth Excel Use the **CIEandPI worksheet** of the **Multiple Regression workbook**, shown in Figure 14.3 on page 582, as a template for computing confidence interval estimates and prediction intervals for a multiple regression model with two independent variables. The worksheet contains the data and formulas for the OmniPower sales example shown in Figure 14.3. The worksheet uses several array formulas to use functions that perform matrix operations to compute the matrix product X′X (in cell range B9:D11), the inverse of the X′X matrix (in cell range B13:D15), the product of X′G multiplied by the inverse of X′X (in cell range B17:D17), and the predicted Y (in cell B21). (Open to the **CIEandPI_FORMULAS worksheet** to examine all formulas.)

Modifying this worksheet for other models with more than two independent variables requires knowledge that is beyond the scope of this book. For other models with two independent variables, paste the data for those variables into columns B and C of the **MRArray worksheet** and adjust the number of entries in column A (all of which are **1**). Then open to the COMPUTE worksheet and edit the array formula in cell range B9:D11 and edit the labels in cells A6 and A7.

EG14.2 r^2, ADJUSTED r^2, and the OVERALL F TEST

The coefficient of multiple determination, r^2, the adjusted r^2, and the overall F test are all computed as part of creating the multiple regression results worksheet using the Section EG14.1 instructions. If you use either the *PHStat2* or *In-Depth Excel* instructions, formulas are used to compute these results in the **COMPUTE worksheet**. Formulas in cells B5, B7, B13, C12, C13, D12, and E12 copy values computed by an array formula in cell range L2:N6 and in cell F12, the expression **FDIST(*F test statistic*, 1, *error degrees of freedom*)** computes the p-value for the overall F test.

EG14.3 RESIDUAL ANALYSIS for the MULTIPLE REGRESSION MODEL

PHStat2 Use the Section EG14.1 "Interpreting the Regression Coefficients" *PHStat2* instructions. Modify step 5 by checking **Residuals Table** and **Residual Plots** in addition to checking **Regression Statistics Table** and **ANOVA and Coefficients Table.**

In-Depth Excel Create a worksheet that calculates residuals and then create a scatter plot of the original X variable and the residuals (plotted as the Y variable).

Use the **RESIDUALS worksheet** of the **Multiple Regression workbook** as a template for creating a residuals worksheet. The formulas in this worksheet compute the residuals for the multiple regression model for the OmniPower sales example by using the regression data in the **MRData worksheet** in the same workbook. In column D, the worksheet computes the predicted Y values by multiplying the X_1 values by the b_1 coefficient and the X_2 values by the b_2 coefficient and adding these products to the b_0 coefficient. In column F, the worksheet computes residuals by subtracting the predicted Y values from the Y values. (Open to the **RESIDUALS_FORMULAS worksheet** to examine all formulas.) For other problems, modify this worksheet as follows:

1. If the number of independent variables is greater than 2, select column D, right-click, and click **Insert** from the shortcut menu. Repeat this step as many times as necessary to create the additional columns to hold all the X variables.
2. Paste the data for the X variables into columns, starting with column B.
3. Paste Y values in column E (or in the second-to-last column if there are more than two X variables).
4. For sample sizes smaller than 34, delete the extra rows. For sample sizes greater than 34, copy the predicted Y and residuals formulas down through the row containing the last pair of X and Y values. Also, add the new observation numbers in column A.

To create residual plots, use copy-and-paste special values (see Appendix Section F.6) to paste data values on a new worksheet in the proper order before applying the Section EG2.6 scatter plot instructions.

Analysis ToolPak Use the Section EG14.1 *Analysis ToolPak* instructions. Modify step 5 by checking **Residuals** and **Residual Plots** before clicking **New Worksheet Ply** and then **OK**. (Note that the **Residuals Plots** option creates residual plots only for each independent variable.)

EG14.4 INFERENCES CONCERNING the POPULATION REGRESSION COEFFICIENTS

The regression results worksheets created by using the EG14.1 instructions include the information needed to make the inferences discussed in Section 14.4.

EG14.5 TESTING PORTIONS of the MULTIPLE REGRESSION MODEL

PHStat2 Use the Section EG14.1 "Interpreting the Regression Coefficients" *PHStat2* instructions but modify step 6 by checking **Coefficients of Partial Determination** before you click **OK**.

In-Depth Excel You compute the coefficients of partial determination by using a two-step process. You first use the Section EG14.1 *In-Depth Excel* instructions to create all possible regression results worksheets in a copy of the **Multiple Regression workbook**. For example, if you have two independent variables, you perform three regression analyses: Y with X_1 and X_2, Y with X_1, and Y with X_2, to create three regression results worksheets. Then open to the **CPD worksheet** for the number of independent variables (**CPD_2, CPD_3**, and **CPD_4 worksheets** are included) and follow the italicized instructions to copy and paste special values from the regression results worksheets. The **CPD_2 worksheet** contains the data to compute the coefficients of partial determination for the OmniPower regression model used as an example in Section 14.5.

EG14.6 USING DUMMY VARIABLES and INTERACTION TERMS in REGRESSION MODELS

Dummy Variables

Use **Find and Replace** to create a dummy variable from a two-level categorical variable. Before using **Find and Replace**, copy and paste the categorical values to another column in order to preserve the original values.

For example, to create a dummy variable named FireplaceCoded from the two-level categorical variable Fireplace as shown in Table 14.5 on page 600, open to the **DATA worksheet** of the **House3 workbook** and:

1. Copy and paste the **Fireplace** values in column **C** to column D (the first empty column).
2. Select column **D**.
3. Press **Ctrl+H** (the keyboard shortcut for **Find and Replace**).

In the Find and Replace dialog box:

4. Enter **Yes** in the **Find what** box and enter **1** in the **Replace with** box.
5. Click **Replace All**. If a message box to confirm the replacement appears, click **OK** to continue.
6. Enter **No** in the **Find what** box and enter **0** in the **Replace with** box.
7. Click **Replace All**. If a message box to confirm the replacement appears, click **OK** to continue.
8. Click **Close**.

Categorical variables that have more than two levels require the use of formulas in multiple columns. For example, to create the dummy variables for Example 14.3 on page 601, two columns are needed. Assume that the three-level categorical variable mentioned in the example is in Column D of the opened worksheet. A first new column that contains formulas in the form **=IF(*column D cell* = *first level*, *1*, *0*)** and a second new column that contains formulas in the form **=IF(*column D cell* = *second level*, *1*, *0*)** would properly create the two dummy variables that the example requires.

Interactions

To create an interaction term, add a column of formulas that multiply one independent variable by another. For example, if the first independent variable appeared in column B and the second independent variable appeared in column C, enter the formula **= B2 * C2** in the row 2 cell of an empty new column and then copy the formula down through all rows of data to create the interaction.

EG14.7 LOGISTIC REGRESSION

There are no Excel Guide instructions for this section.

CHAPTER 14 MINITAB GUIDE

MG14.1 DEVELOPING a MULTIPLE REGRESSION MODEL

Visualizing Multiple Regression Data

Use **3D Scatterplot** to create a three-dimensional plot for the special case of a regression model that contains two independent variables. For example, to create the Figure 14.1 plot on page 579 for the OmniPower sales data, open the **OmniPower worksheet**. Select **Graph ➔ 3D Scatterplot**. In the 3D Scatterplots dialog box, click **Simple** and then click **OK**. In the 3D Scatterplot - Simple dialog box (shown below):

1. Double-click **C1 Sales** in the variables list to add **Sales** to the **Z variable** box.
2. Double-click **C2 Price** in the variables list to add **Price** to the **Y variable** box.
3. Double-click **C3 Promotion** in the variables list to add **Promotion** to the **X variable** box.
4. Click **Data View**.

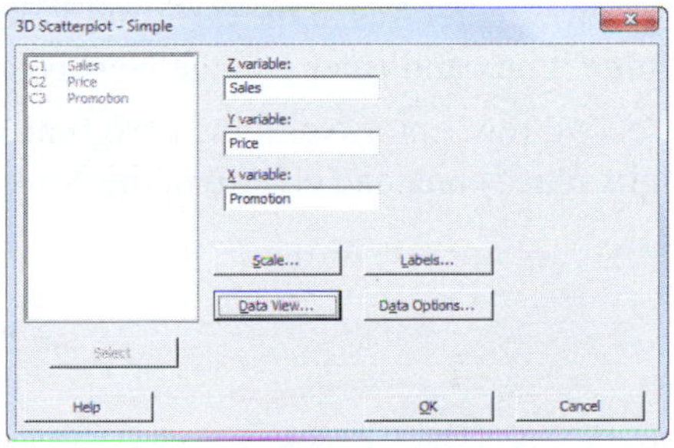

In the 3D Scatterplot - Data View dialog box:

5. Check **Symbols** and **Project lines**.
6. Click **OK**.
7. Back in the 3D Scatterplot - Simple dialog box, click **OK**.

Interpreting the Regression coefficients

Use **Regression** to perform a multiple regression analysis. For example, to perform the Figure 14.2 analysis of the OmniPower sales data on page 580, open to the **OmniPower worksheet**. Select **Stat ➔ Regression ➔ Regression**. In the Regression dialog box (shown at the top of the next column):

1. Double-click **C1 Sales** in the variables list to add **Sales** to the **Response** box.
2. Double-click **C2 Price** in the variables list to add **Price** to the **Predictors** box.
3. Double-click **C3 Promotion** in the variables list to add **Promotion** to the **Predictors** box.
4. Click **Graphs**.

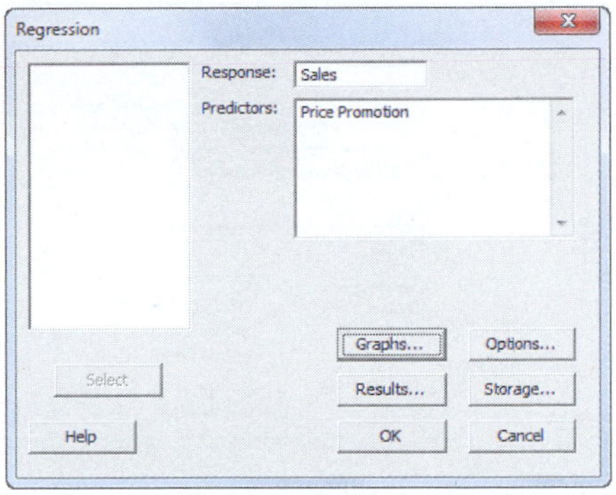

In the Regression - Graphs dialog box (shown below):

5. Click **Regular** and **Individual Plots**.
6. Check **Histogram of residuals** and clear all the other check boxes.
7. Click anywhere inside the **Residuals versus the variables** box.
8. Double-click **C2 Price** in the variables list to add **Price** in the **Residuals versus the variables** box.
9. Double-click **C3 Promotion** in the variables list to add **Promotion** in the **Residuals versus the variables** box.
10. Click **OK**.

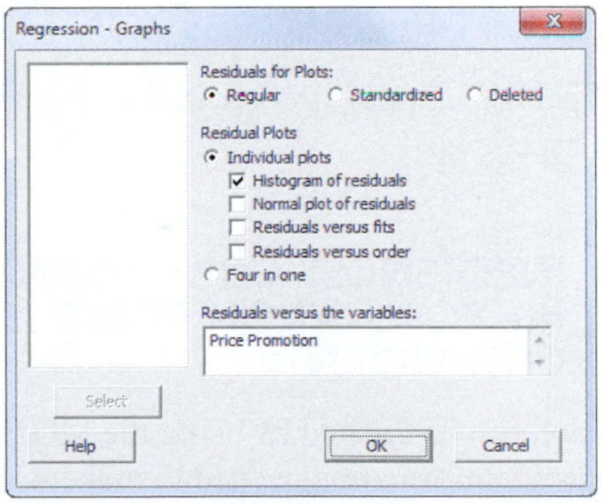

11. Back in the Regression dialog box, click **Results**.

In the Regression - Results dialog box (not shown):

12. Click **In addition, the full table of fits and residuals** and then click **OK**.
13. Back in the Regression dialog box, click **Options**.

In the Regression - Options dialog box (shown below):

14. Check **Fit Intercept**.
15. Clear all the **Display** and **Lack of Fit Test** check boxes.
16. Enter **79** and **400** in the **Prediction intervals for new observations** box.
17. Enter **95** in the **Confidence level** box.
18. Click **OK**.

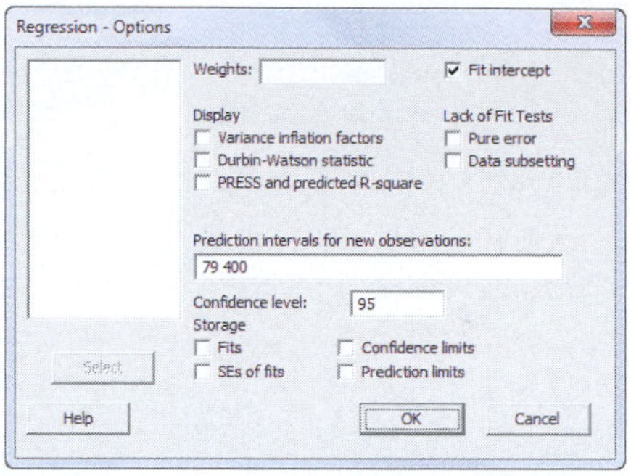

19. Back in the Regression dialog box, click **OK**.

The results in the Session Window will include a table of residuals that is not shown in Figure 14.2.

MG14.2 r^2, ADJUSTED r^2, and the OVERALL F TEST

The coefficient of multiple determination, r^2, the adjusted r^2, and the overall F test are all computed as part of creating the multiple regression results using the Section MG14.1 instructions.

MG14.3 RESIDUAL ANALYSIS for the MULTIPLE REGRESSION MODEL

Residual analysis results are created using the Section MG14.1 instructions.

MG14.4 INFERENCES CONCERNING the POPULATION REGRESSION COEFFICIENTS

The regression results created by using the MG14.1 instructions include the information needed to make the inferences discussed in Section 14.4.

MG14.5 TESTING PORTIONS of the MULTIPLE REGRESSION MODEL

You compute the coefficients of partial determination by using a two-step process. You first use the Section MG14.1 instructions to create all possible regression results in the same project file. For example, if you have two independent variables, you perform three regression analyses—Y with X_1 and X_2, Y with X_1, and Y with X_2—to create three sets of regression results. With those results you can then compute the partial F test and the coefficients of partial determination using the instructions in Section 14.5.

MG14.6 USING DUMMY VARIABLES and INTERACTION TERMS in REGRESSION MODELS

Dummy Variables

Use **Text to Numeric** to create a dummy variable. For example, to create a dummy variable named FireplaceCoded from the categorical variable Fireplace (see Table 14.5 on page 600), open to the **House3 worksheet** and select **Data ➔ Code ➔ Text to Numeric**. In the Code - Text to Numeric dialog box (shown below):

1. Double-click **C3 Fireplace** in the variables list to add **Fireplace** to the **Code data from columns** box and press **Tab**.
2. Enter **C4** in the **Store coded data in columns** box and press **Tab**. (Column C4 is the first empty column in the worksheet.)
3. In the first row, enter **Yes** in the **Original Values (eg, red "light blue")** box and enter **1** in the **New** box.
4. In the second row, enter **No** in the **Original Values (eg, red "light blue")** box and enter **0** in the **New** box.
5. Click **OK**.

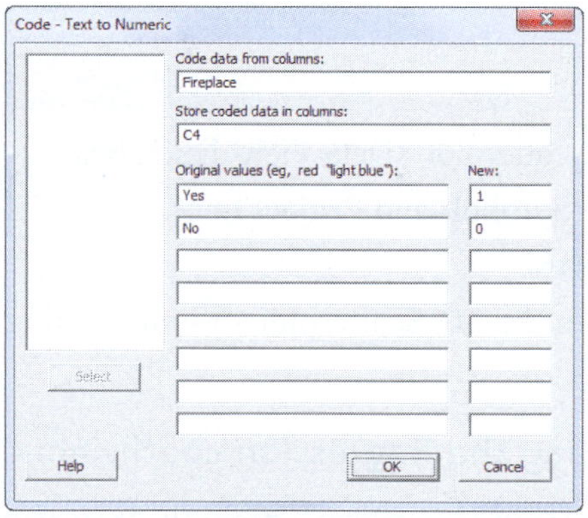

6. Enter **FireplaceCoded** as the name of column **C4**.

Interactions

Use **Calculator** to add a new column that contains the product of multiplying one independent variable by another to create an interaction term. For example, to create an interaction term of size and the dummy variable FireplaceCoded (see Table 14.5 on page 600), open to the **House3 worksheet**. Use the "Dummy Variables" instructions in the preceding part to create the **FireplaceCoded** column in the worksheet. Select **Calc ➔ Calculator**. In the Calculator dialog box (shown below):

1. Enter **C5** in the **Store result in variable** box and press **Tab**.
2. Enter **Size * FireplaceCoded** in the **Expression** box.
3. Click **OK**.

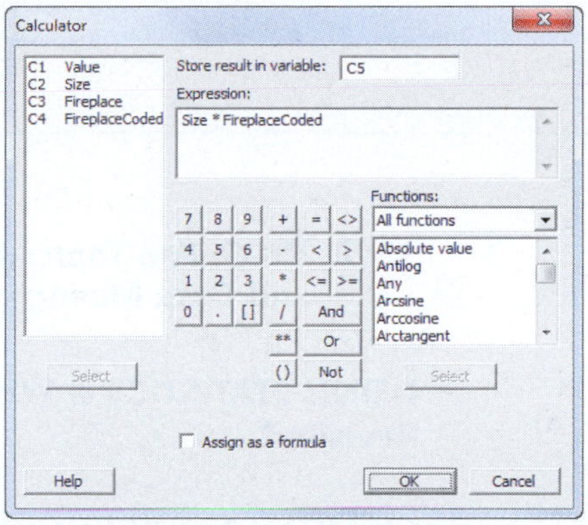

4. Enter **Size*FireplaceCoded** as the name for column **C5**.

MG14.7 LOGISTIC REGRESSION

Use **Binary Logistic Regression** to perform a logistic regression. For example, to perform the Figure 14.14 analysis of the credit card marketing data on page 611, open to **Logpurch worksheet**. Select **Stat ➔ Regression ➔ Binary Logistic Regression**. In the Binary Logistic Regression dialog box (shown below):

1. Click **Response in response/frequency format** and press **Tab**.
2. Double-click **C1 Upgraded** in the variables list to add **Upgraded** in the **Response** box.
3. Click inside the **Model** box.
4. Double-click **C2 Purchases** in the variables list to add **Purchases** to the **Model** box.
5. Double-click **C3 Extra Cards** in the variables list to add **'Extra Cards'** to the **Model** box and press **Tab**.
6. Double-click **C3 Extra Cards** in the variables list to add **'Extra Cards'** to the Factors box (because **Extra Cards** is a categorical variable).
7. Click **OK**.

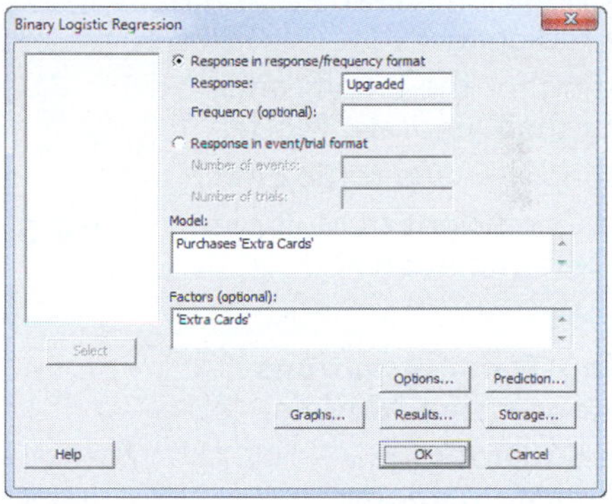

15 Multiple Regression Model Building

Learning Objectives

In this chapter, you learn:

- To use quadratic terms in a regression model
- To use transformed variables in a regression model
- To measure the correlation among independent variables
- To build a regression model using either the stepwise or best-subsets approach
- To avoid the pitfalls involved in developing a multiple regression model

@ WHIT-DT

As part of your job as the operations manager at WHIT-DT, your business objective is to reduce unnecessary labor expenses. Currently, the unionized graphic artists at the television station receive hourly pay for a significant number of hours during which they are idle. These hours are called *standby hours*. You have collected data concerning standby hours and four factors that you suspect are related to the excessive number of standby hours the station is currently experiencing: the total number of staff present, remote hours, Dubner hours, and total labor hours.

You plan to build a multiple regression model to help determine which factors most heavily affect standby hours. You believe that an appropriate model will help you to predict the number of future standby hours, identify the root causes of excessive numbers of standby hours, and allow you to reduce the total number of future standby hours. How do you build the model with the most appropriate mix of independent variables? Are there statistical techniques that can help you identify a "best" model without having to consider all possible models? How do you begin?

Chapter 14 discussed multiple regression models with two independent variables. This chapter extends regression analysis to models containing more than two independent variables. The chapter introduces you to various topics related to model building to help you learn to develop the best model when confronted with a set of data (such as the one described in the WHIT-DT scenario) that has many independent variables. These topics include quadratic independent variables, transformations of the dependent or independent variables, stepwise regression, and best-subsets regression.

15.1 The Quadratic Regression Model

The simple regression model discussed in Chapter 13 and the multiple regression model discussed in Chapter 14 assume that the relationship between Y and each independent variable is linear. However, in Section 13.1, several different types of nonlinear relationships between variables were introduced. One of the most common nonlinear relationships is a quadratic, or curvilinear, relationship between two variables in which Y increases (or decreases) at a changing rate for various values of X (see Figure 13.2, Panels C–E, on page 523). You can use the quadratic regression model defined in Equation (15.1) to analyze this type of relationship between X and Y.

QUADRATIC REGRESSION MODEL

$$Y_i = \beta_0 + \beta_1 X_{1i} + \beta_2 X_{1i}^2 + \varepsilon_i \quad \textbf{(15.1)}$$

where

β_0 = Y intercept
β_1 = coefficient of the linear effect on Y
β_2 = coefficient of the quadratic effect on Y
ε_i = random error in Y for observation i

This **quadratic regression model** is similar to the multiple regression model with two independent variables [see Equation (14.2) on page 579] except that the second independent variable, the **quadratic term**, is the square of the first independent variable. Once again, you use the least-squares method to compute sample regression coefficients (b_0, b_1, and b_2) as estimates of the population parameters (β_0, β_1, and β_2). Equation (15.2) defines the regression equation for the quadratic model with an independent variable (X_1) and a dependent variable (Y).

QUADRATIC REGRESSION EQUATION

$$\hat{Y}_i = b_0 + b_1 X_{1i} + b_2 X_{1i}^2 \quad \textbf{(15.2)}$$

In Equation (15.2), the first regression coefficient, b_0, represents the Y intercept; the second regression coefficient, b_1, represents the linear effect; and the third regression coefficient, b_2, represents the quadratic effect.

Finding the Regression Coefficients and Predicting Y

To illustrate the quadratic regression model, consider a study that examined the business problem facing a concrete supplier of how adding fly ash affects the strength of concrete. (Fly ash is an inexpensive industrial waste by-product that can be used as a substitute for Portland cement, a more expensive ingredient of concrete.) Batches of concrete were prepared in which the percentage of fly ash ranged from 0% to 60%. Data were collected from a sample of 18 batches and organized and stored in FlyAsh. Table 15.1 summarizes the results.

TABLE 15.1

Fly Ash Percentage and Strength of 18 Batches of 28-Day-Old Concrete

Fly Ash %	Strength (psi)	Fly Ash %	Strength (psi)
0	4,779	40	5,995
0	4,706	40	5,628
0	4,350	40	5,897
20	5,189	50	5,746
20	5,140	50	5,719
20	4,976	50	5,782
30	5,110	60	4,895
30	5,685	60	5,030
30	5,618	60	4,648

By creating the scatter plot in Figure 15.1 to visualize these data, you will be better able to select the proper model for expressing the relationship between fly ash percentage and strength.

FIGURE 15.1

Scatter plot of fly ash percentage (X) and strength (Y)

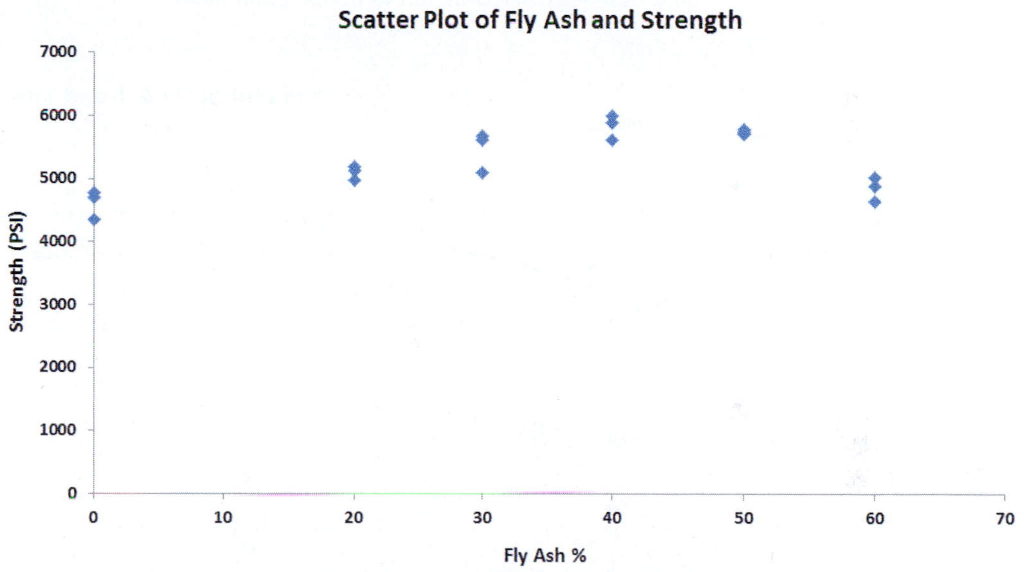

Figure 15.1 indicates an initial increase in the strength of the concrete as the percentage of fly ash increases. The strength appears to level off and then drop after achieving maximum strength at about 40% fly ash. Strength for 50% fly ash is slightly below strength at 40%, but strength at 60% fly ash is substantially below strength at 50%. Therefore, you should fit a quadratic model, not a linear model, to estimate strength based on fly ash percentage.

Figure 15.2 on page 632 shows regression results for these data.

From Figure 15.2,

$$b_0 = 4{,}486.3611 \quad b_1 = 63.0052 \quad b_2 = -0.8765$$

Therefore, the quadratic regression equation is

$$\hat{Y}_i = 4{,}486.3611 + 63.0052X_{1i} - 0.8765X_{1i}^2$$

where

$\hat{Y}_i$ = predicted strength for sample i

X_{1i} = percentage of fly ash for sample i

FIGURE 15.2

Excel and Minitab regression results for the concrete strength data

	A	B	C	D	E	F	G
1	Concrete Strength Analysis						
2							
3	*Regression Statistics*						
4	Multiple R	0.8053					
5	R Square	0.6485					
6	Adjusted R Square	0.6016					
7	Standard Error	312.1129					
8	Observations	18					
9							
10	ANOVA						
11		*df*	*SS*	*MS*	*F*	*Significance F*	
12	Regression	2	2695473.4897	1347736.745	13.8351	0.0004	
13	Residual	15	1461217.0103	97414.4674			
14	Total	17	4156690.5000				
15							
16		*Coefficients*	*Standard Error*	*t Stat*	*P-value*	*Lower 95%*	*Upper 95%*
17	Intercept	4486.3611	174.7531	25.6726	0.0000	4113.8834	4858.8389
18	Fly Ash%	63.0052	12.3725	5.0923	0.0001	36.6338	89.3767
19	Fly Ash% ^2	-0.8765	0.1966	-4.4578	0.0005	-1.2955	-0.4574

Regression Analysis: Strength versus Fly Ash%, Fly Ash%^2

```
The regression equation is
Strength = 4486 + 63.0 Fly Ash% - 0.876 Fly Ash%^2

Predictor      Coef  SE Coef      T      P
Constant     4486.4    174.8  25.67  0.000
Fly Ash%      63.01    12.37   5.09  0.000
Fly Ash%^2  -0.8765   0.1966  -4.46  0.000

S = 312.113   R-Sq = 64.8%   R-Sq(adj) = 60.2%

Analysis of Variance
Source          DF       SS       MS      F      P
Regression       2  2695473  1347737  13.84  0.000
Residual Error  15  1461217    97414
Total           17  4156690
```

Figure 15.3 is a scatter plot of this quadratic regression equation that shows the fit of the quadratic regression model to the original data.

FIGURE 15.3

Scatter plot showing the quadratic relationship between fly ash percentage and strength for the concrete data

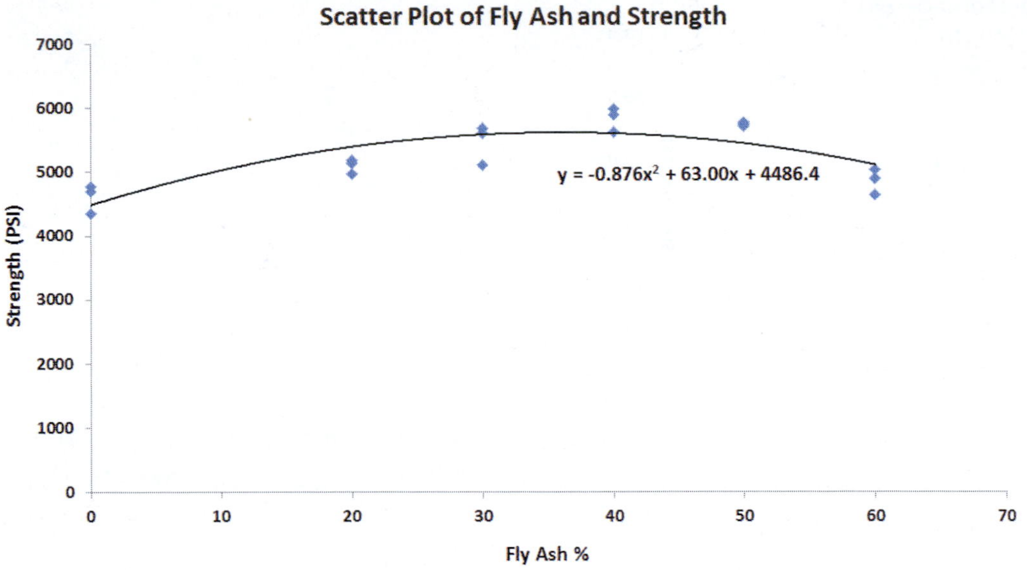

From the quadratic regression equation and Figure 15.3, the Y intercept ($b_0 = 4{,}486.3611$) is the predicted strength when the percentage of fly ash is 0. To interpret the coefficients b_1 and b_2, observe that after an initial increase, strength decreases as fly ash percentage increases. This nonlinear relationship is further demonstrated by predicting the strength for fly ash percentages of 20, 40, and 60. Using the quadratic regression equation,

$$\hat{Y}_i = 4{,}486.3611 + 63.0052X_{1i} - 0.8765X_{1i}^2$$

for $X_{1i} = 20$,

$$\hat{Y}_i = 4{,}486.3611 + 63.0052(20) - 0.8765(20)^2 = 5{,}395.865$$

for $X_{1i} = 40$,

$$\hat{Y}_i = 4{,}486.3611 + 63.0052(40) - 0.8765(40)^2 = 5{,}604.169$$

and for $X_{1i} = 60$,

$$\hat{Y}_i = 4{,}486.3611 + 63.0052(60) - 0.8765(60)^2 = 5{,}111.273$$

Thus, the predicted concrete strength for 40% fly ash is 208.304 psi above the predicted strength for 20% fly ash, but the predicted strength for 60% fly ash is 492.896 psi below the predicted strength for 40% fly ash.

Testing for the Significance of the Quadratic Model

After you calculate the quadratic regression equation, you can test whether there is a significant overall relationship between strength, Y, and fly ash percentage, X_1. The null and alternative hypotheses are as follows:

H_0: $\beta_1 = \beta_2 = 0$ (There is no overall relationship between X_1 and Y.)

H_1: β_1 and/or $\beta_2 \neq 0$ (There is an overall relationship between X_1 and Y.)

Equation (14.6) on page 586 defines the overall F_{STAT} test statistic used for this test:

$$F_{STAT} = \frac{MSR}{MSE}$$

From the Figure 15.2 results on page 632,

$$F_{STAT} = \frac{MSR}{MSE} = \frac{1{,}347{,}736.745}{97{,}414.4674} = 13.8351$$

If you choose a level of significance of 0.05, from Table E.5, the critical value of the F distribution, with 2 and 15 degrees of freedom, is 3.68 (see Figure 15.4). Because $F_{STAT} = 13.8351 > 3.68$, or because the p-value $= 0.0004 < 0.05$, you reject the null hypothesis (H_0) and conclude that there is a significant overall relationship between strength and fly ash percentage.

FIGURE 15.4

Testing for the existence of the overall relationship at the 0.05 level of significance, with 2 and 15 degrees of freedom

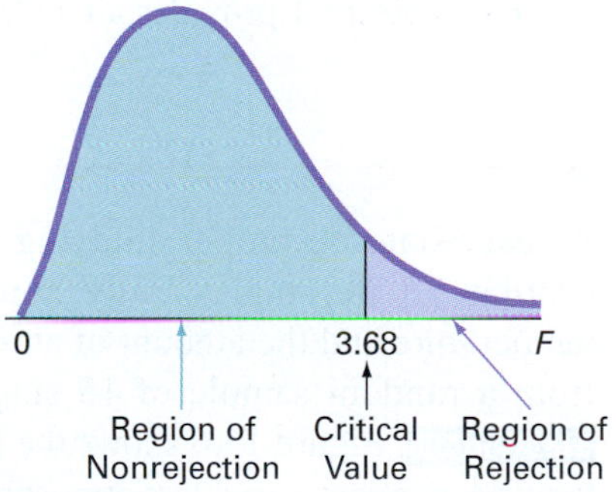

Testing the Quadratic Effect

In using a regression model to examine a relationship between two variables, you want to find not only the most accurate model but also the simplest model that expresses that relationship. Therefore, you need to examine whether there is a significant difference between the quadratic model:

$$Y_i = \beta_0 + \beta_1 X_{1i} + \beta_2 X_{1i}^2 + \varepsilon_i$$

and the linear model:

$$Y_i = \beta_0 + \beta_1 X_{1i} + \varepsilon_i$$

In Section 14.4, you used the t test to determine whether each independent variable makes a significant contribution to the regression model. To test the significance of the contribution of the quadratic effect, you use the following null and alternative hypotheses:

H_0 : Including the quadratic effect does not significantly improve the model ($\beta_2 = 0$).

H_1 : Including the quadratic effect significantly improves the model ($\beta_2 \neq 0$).

The standard error of each regression coefficient and its corresponding t_{STAT} test statistic are part of the regression results (see Figure 15.2 on page 632). Equation (14.7) on page 590 defines the t_{STAT} test statistic:

$$t_{STAT} = \frac{b_2 - \beta_2}{S_{b_2}}$$

$$= \frac{-0.8765 - 0}{0.1966} = -4.4578$$

If you select the 0.05 level of significance, then from Table E.3, the critical values for the t distribution with 15 degrees of freedom are -2.1315 and $+2.1315$ (see Figure 15.5).

FIGURE 15.5

Testing for the contribution of the quadratic effect to a regression model at the 0.05 level of significance, with 15 degrees of freedom

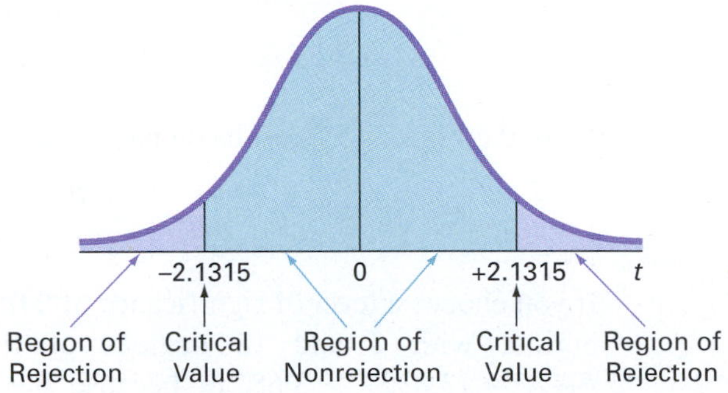

Because $t_{STAT} = -4.4578 < -2.1315$ or because the p-value $= 0.0005 < 0.05$, you reject H_0 and conclude that the quadratic model is significantly better than the linear model for representing the relationship between strength and fly ash percentage.

Example 15.1 provides an additional illustration of a possible quadratic effect.

EXAMPLE 15.1

Studying the Quadratic Effect in a Multiple Regression Model

A real estate developer studying the business problem of estimating the consumption of heating oil by single-family houses has decided to examine the effect of atmospheric temperature and the amount of attic insulation on heating oil consumption. Data are collected from a random sample of 15 single-family houses. The data are organized and stored in **HeatingOil**. Figure 15.6 shows the regression results for a multiple regression model using the two independent variables: atmospheric temperature and attic insulation.

FIGURE 15.6

Excel and Minitab regression results for the multiple linear regression model predicting monthly consumption of heating oil

	A	B	C	D	E	F	G
1	Heating Oil Consumption Analysis						
2							
3	*Regression Statistics*						
4	Multiple R	0.9827					
5	R Square	0.9656					
6	Adjusted R Square	0.9599					
7	Standard Error	26.0138					
8	Observations	15					
9							
10	ANOVA						
11		*df*	*SS*	*MS*	*F*	*Significance F*	
12	Regression	2	228014.6263	114007.3132	168.4712	0.0000	
13	Residual	12	8120.6030	676.7169			
14	Total	14	236135.2293				
15							
16		*Coefficients*	*Standard Error*	*t Stat*	*P-value*	*Lower 95%*	*Upper 95%*
17	Intercept	562.1510	21.0931	26.6509	0.0000	516.1931	608.1089
18	Temperature	-5.4366	0.3362	-16.1699	0.0000	-6.1691	-4.7040
19	Insulation	-20.0123	2.3425	-8.5431	0.0000	-25.1162	-14.9084

Regression Analysis: Gallons versus Temperature, Insulation

```
The regression equation is
Gallons = 562 - 5.44 Temperature - 20.0 Insulation

Predictor        Coef  SE Coef       T      P
Constant       562.15    21.09   26.65  0.000
Temperature   -5.4366   0.3362  -16.17  0.000
Insulation    -20.012    2.343   -8.54  0.000

S = 26.0138   R-Sq = 96.6%   R-Sq(adj) = 96.0%

Analysis of Variance
Source          DF      SS      MS       F      P
Regression       2  228015  114007  168.47  0.000
Residual Error  12    8121     677
Total           14  236135
```

The residual plot for attic insulation (not shown here) contained some evidence of a quadratic effect. Thus, the real estate developer reanalyzed the data by adding a quadratic term for attic insulation to the multiple regression model. At the 0.05 level of significance, is there evidence of a significant quadratic effect for attic insulation?

SOLUTION Figure 15.7 shows the results for this regression model.

FIGURE 15.7

Excel and Minitab results for the multiple regression model with a quadratic term for attic insulation

	A	B	C	D	E	F	G
1	**Quadratic Effect for Insulation Variable?**						
2							
3	*Regression Statistics*						
4	Multiple R	0.9862					
5	R Square	0.9725					
6	Adjusted R Square	0.9650					
7	Standard Error	24.2938					
8	Observations	15					
9							
10	ANOVA						
11		*df*	*SS*	*MS*	*F*	*Significance F*	
12	Regression	3	229643.1645	76547.7215	129.7006	0.0000	
13	Residual	11	6492.0649	590.1877			
14	Total	14	236135.2293				
15							
16		*Coefficients*	*Standard Error*	*t Stat*	*P-value*	*Lower 95%*	*Upper 95%*
17	Intercept	624.5864	42.4352	14.7186	0.0000	531.1872	717.9856
18	Temperature	-5.3626	0.3171	-16.9099	0.0000	-6.0606	-4.6646
19	Insulation	-44.5868	14.9547	-2.9815	0.0125	-77.5019	-11.6717
20	Insulation ^2	1.8667	1.1238	1.6611	0.1249	-0.6067	4.3401

Regression Analysis: Gallons versus Temperature, Insulation, ...

```
The regression equation is
Gallons = 625 - 5.36 Temperature - 44.6 Insulation + 1.87 Insulation^2

Predictor        Coef  SE Coef       T      P
Constant       624.59    42.44   14.72  0.000
Temperature   -5.3626   0.3171  -16.91  0.000
Insulation     -44.59    14.95   -2.98  0.012
Insulation^2    1.867    1.124    1.66  0.125

S = 24.2938   R-Sq = 97.3%   R-Sq(adj) = 96.5%

Analysis of Variance
Source          DF      SS     MS       F      P
Regression       3  229643  76548  129.70  0.000
Residual Error  11    6492    590
Total           14  236135
```

The multiple regression equation is

$$\hat{Y}_i = 624.5864 - 5.3626X_{1i} - 44.5868X_{2i} + 1.8667X_{2i}^2$$

To test for the significance of the quadratic effect,

H_0 : Including the quadratic effect does not significantly improve the model ($\beta_3 = 0$).

H_1 : Including the quadratic effect significantly improves the model ($\beta_3 \neq 0$).

From Figure 15.7 and Table E.3, $-2.2010 < t_{STAT} = 1.6611 < 2.2010$ (or the p-value $= 0.1249 > 0.05$). Therefore, you do not reject the null hypothesis. You conclude that there is insufficient evidence that the quadratic effect for attic insulation is different from zero. In the interest of keeping the model as simple as possible, you should use the multiple regression equation shown in Figure 15.6:

$$\hat{Y}_i = 562.1510 - 5.4366X_{1i} - 20.0123X_{2i}$$

The Coefficient of Multiple Determination

In the multiple regression model, the coefficient of multiple determination, r^2 (see Section 14.2), represents the proportion of variation in Y that is explained by variation in the independent variables. Consider the quadratic regression model you used to predict the strength of concrete using fly ash and fly ash squared. You compute r^2 by using Equation (14.4) on page 616:

$$r^2 = \frac{SSR}{SST}$$

From Figure 15.2 on page 632,

$$SSR = 2{,}695{,}473.897 \quad SST = 4{,}156{,}690.5$$

Thus,

$$r^2 = \frac{SSR}{SST} = \frac{2{,}695{,}473.897}{4{,}156{,}690.5} = 0.6485$$

This coefficient of multiple determination indicates that 64.85% of the variation in strength is explained by the quadratic relationship between strength and the percentage of fly ash. You should also compute r^2_{adj} to account for the number of independent variables and the sample size. In the quadratic regression model, $k = 2$ because there are two independent variables, X_1 and X_1^2. Thus, using Equation (14.5) on page 585,

$$\begin{aligned} r^2_{adj} &= 1 - \left[(1 - r^2)\frac{(n - 1)}{(n - k - 1)}\right] \\ &= 1 - \left[(1 - 0.6485)\frac{17}{15}\right] \\ &= 1 - 0.3984 \\ &= 0.6016 \end{aligned}$$

Problems for Section 15.1

LEARNING THE BASICS

15.1 The following is the quadratic regression equation for a sample of $n = 25$:

$$\hat{Y}_i = 5 + 3X_{1i} + 1.5X_{1i}^2$$

a. Predict Y for $X_1 = 2$.
b. Suppose that the computed t_{STAT} test statistic for the quadratic regression coefficient is 2.35. At the 0.05 level of significance, is there evidence that the quadratic model is better than the linear model?
c. Suppose that the computed t_{STAT} test statistic for the quadratic regression coefficient is 1.17. At the 0.05 level of significance, is there evidence that the quadratic model is better than the linear model?
d. Suppose the regression coefficient for the linear effect is −3.0. Predict Y for $X_1 = 2$.

APPLYING THE CONCEPTS

15.2 Businesses actively recruit business students with well-developed higher-order cognitive skills (HOCS) such as problem identification, analytical reasoning, and content integration skills. Researchers conducted a study to see if improvement in students' HOCS was related to the students' GPA. (Data extracted from R. V. Bradley, C. S. Sankar, H. R. Clayton, V. W. Mbarika, and P. K. Raju, "A Study on the Impact of GPA on Perceived Improvement of Higher-Order Cognitive Skills," *Decision Sciences Journal of Innovative Education*, January 2007, 5(1), pp 151–168.) The researchers conducted a study in which business students were taught using the case study method. Using data collected from 300 business students, the following quadratic regression equation was derived:

$$\text{HOCS} = -3.48 + 4.53(\text{GPA}) - 0.68(\text{GPA})^2$$

where the dependent variable HOCS measured the improvement in higher-order cognitive skills, with 1 being the lowest improvement in HOCS and 5 being the highest improvement in HOCS.

a. Construct a table of predicted HOCS, using GPA equal to 2.0, 2.1, 2.2, . . . , 4.0.
b. Plot the values in the table constructed in (a), with GPA on the horizontal axis and predicted HOCS on the vertical axis.
c. Discuss the curvilinear relationship between students' GPA and their predicted improvement in HOCS.
d. The researchers reported that the model had an r^2 of 0.07 and an adjusted r^2 of 0.06. What does this tell you about the scatter of individual HOCS scores around the curvilinear relationship plotted in (b) and discussed in (c)?

15.3 A national chain of consumer electronics stores had the business objective of determining the effectiveness of newspaper advertising. To promote sales, the chain relies heavily on local newspaper advertising to support its modest exposure in nationwide television commercials. A sample of 20 cities with similar populations and monthly sales totals were assigned different newspaper advertising budgets for one month. The following table (stored in **Advertising**) summarizes the sales (in $millions) and the newspaper advertising budgets (in $thousands) observed during the study:

Sales	Newspaper Advertising	Sales	Newspaper Advertising
6.14	5	6.84	15
6.04	5	6.66	15
6.21	5	6.95	20
6.32	5	6.65	20
6.42	10	6.83	20
6.56	10	6.81	20
6.67	10	7.03	25
6.35	10	6.88	25
6.76	15	6.84	25
6.79	15	6.99	25

a. Construct a scatter plot for newspaper advertising and sales.
b. Fit a quadratic regression model and state the quadratic regression equation.
c. Predict the monthly sales for a city with newspaper advertising of $20,000.
d. Perform a residual analysis on the results and determine whether the regression assumptions are valid.
e. At the 0.05 level of significance, is there a significant quadratic relationship between monthly sales and newspaper advertising?
f. At the 0.05 level of significance, determine whether the quadratic model is a better fit than the linear model.
g. Interpret the meaning of the coefficient of multiple determination.
h. Compute the adjusted r^2.

15.4 Is the number of calories in a beer related to the number of carbohydrates and/or the percentage of alcohol in the beer? Data concerning 139 of the best-selling domestic beers in the United States are stored in **DomesticBeer**. The values for three variables are included: the number of calories per 12 ounces, the alcohol percentage, and the number of carbohydrates (in grams) per 12 ounces. (Data extracted from **www.Beer100.com**, March 18, 2010.)

a. Perform a multiple linear regression analysis, using calories as the dependent variable and percentage alcohol and number of carbohydrates as the independent variables.
b. Add quadratic terms for alcohol percentage and the number of carbohydrates.
c. Which model is better, the one in (a) or (b)?
d. Write a short summary concerning the relationship between the number of calories in a beer and the alcohol percentage and number of carbohydrates.

15.5 The per-store daily customer count (i.e., the mean number of customers in a store in one day) for a nationwide convenience store chain that operates nearly 10,000 stores has been steady, at 900, for some time. To increase the customer count, the chain is considering cutting prices for coffee beverages. The question to be determined is how much prices should be cut to increase the daily customer count without reducing the gross margin on coffee sales too much. You decide to carry out an experiment in a sample of 24 stores where customer counts have been running almost exactly at the national average of 900. In 6 of the stores, the price of a small coffee will now be $0.59, in 6 stores the price of a small coffee will now be $0.69, in 6 stores, the price of a small coffee will now be $0.79, and in 6 stores, the price of a small coffee will now be $0.89. After four weeks at the new prices, the daily customer count in the stores is determined and is stored in **CoffeeSales2**.

a. Construct a scatter plot for price and sales.
b. Fit a quadratic regression model and state the quadratic regression equation.
c. Predict the weekly sales for a small coffee priced at 79 cents.
d. Perform a residual analysis on the results and determine whether the regression model is valid.
e. At the 0.05 level of significance, is there a significant quadratic relationship between weekly sales and price?
f. At the 0.05 level of significance, determine whether the quadratic model is a better fit than the linear model.
g. Interpret the meaning of the coefficient of multiple determination.
h. Compute the adjusted r^2.
i. Compare the results of (a) through (h) to those of Problem 11.11 on page 428.

SELF Test **15.6** An agronomist designed a study in which tomatoes were grown using six different amounts of fertilizer: 0, 20, 40, 60, 80, and 100 pounds per 1,000 square feet. These fertilizer application rates were then randomly assigned to plots of land. The results including the yield of tomatoes (in pounds) are stored in **Tomato** and are listed here:

	Fertilizer Application			Fertilizer Application	
Plot	Rate	Yield	Plot	Rate	Yield
1	0	6	7	60	46
2	0	9	8	60	50
3	20	19	9	80	48
4	20	24	10	80	54
5	40	32	11	100	52
6	40	38	12	100	58

a. Construct a scatter plot for fertilizer application rate and yield.
b. Fit a quadratic regression model and state the quadratic regression equation.
c. Predict the yield for a plot of land fertilized with 70 pounds per 1,000 square feet.
d. Perform a residual analysis on the results and determine whether the regression model is valid.
e. At the 0.05 level of significance, is there a significant overall relationship between the fertilizer application rate and tomato yield?
f. What is the p-value in (e)? Interpret its meaning.
g. At the 0.05 level of significance, determine whether there is a significant quadratic effect.
h. What is the p-value in (g)? Interpret its meaning.
i. Interpret the meaning of the coefficient of multiple determination.
j. Compute the adjusted r^2.

15.7 An auditor for a county government would like to develop a model to predict county taxes, based on the age of single-family houses. She selects a random sample of 19 single-family houses, and the results are stored in **Taxes**.

a. Construct a scatter plot of age and county taxes.
b. Fit a quadratic regression model and state the quadratic regression equation.
c. Predict the county taxes for a house that is 20 years old.
d. Perform a residual analysis on the results and determine whether the regression model is valid.
e. At the 0.05 level of significance, is there a significant overall relationship between age and county taxes?
f. What is the p-value in (e)? Interpret its meaning.
g. At the 0.05 level of significance, determine whether the quadratic model is superior to the linear model.
h. What is the p-value in (g)? Interpret its meaning.
i. Interpret the meaning of the coefficient of multiple determination.
j. Compute the adjusted r^2.

15.2 Using Transformations in Regression Models

This section introduces regression models in which the independent variable, the dependent variable, or both are transformed in order to either overcome violations of the assumptions of regression or to make a model whose form is not linear into a linear model. Among the many transformations available (see reference 1) are the square-root transformation and transformations involving the common logarithm (base 10) and the natural logarithm (base e).[1]

[1]For more information on logarithms, see Appendix Section A.3.

The Square-Root Transformation

The **square-root transformation** is often used to overcome violations of the equal-variance assumption as well as to transform a model whose form is not linear into a linear model. Equation (15.3) shows a regression model that uses a square-root transformation of the independent variable.

REGRESSION MODEL WITH A SQUARE-ROOT TRANSFORMATION

$$Y_i = \beta_0 + \beta_1\sqrt{X_{1i}} + \varepsilon_i \qquad \textbf{(15.3)}$$

Example 15.2 illustrates the use of a square-root transformation.

EXAMPLE 15.2

Using the Square-Root Transformation

Given the following values for Y and X, use a square-root transformation for the X variable:

Y	X	Y	X
42.7	1	100.4	3
50.4	1	104.7	4
69.1	2	112.3	4
79.8	2	113.6	5
90.0	3	123.9	5

Construct a scatter plot for X and Y and for the square root of X and Y.

SOLUTION Figure 15.8 displays both scatter plots.

FIGURE 15.8

Example 15.2 scatter plots of X and Y and the square root of X and Y

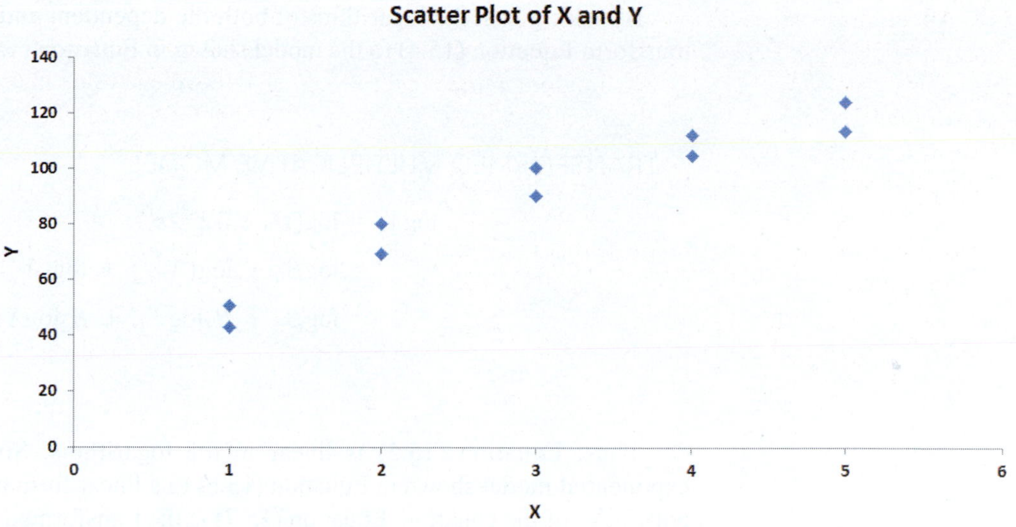

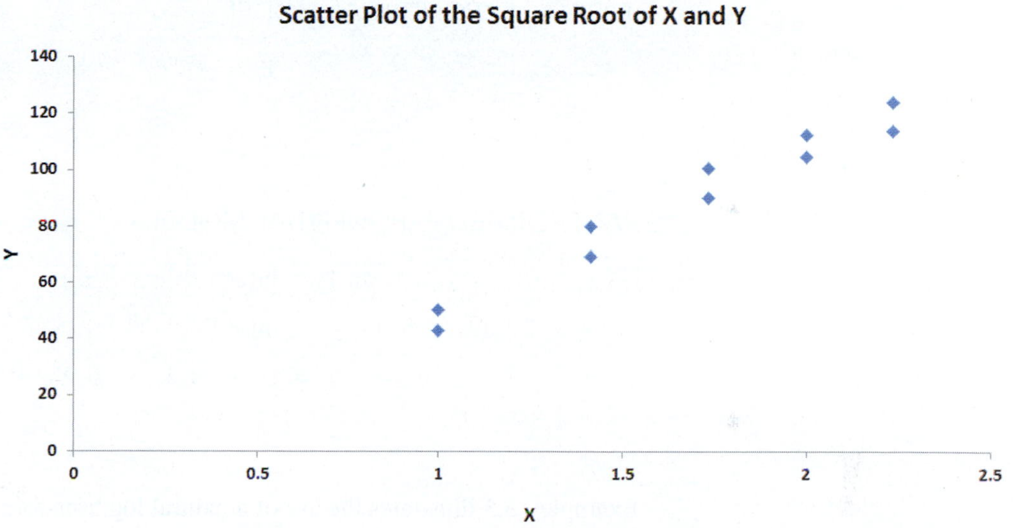

You can see that the square-root transformation has transformed a nonlinear relationship into a linear relationship.

The Log Transformation

The **logarithmic transformation** is often used to overcome violations to the equal-variance assumption. You can also use the logarithmic transformation to change a nonlinear model into a linear model. Equation (15.4) shows a multiplicative model.

ORIGINAL MULTIPLICATIVE MODEL

$$Y_i = \beta_0 X_{1i}^{\beta_1} X_{2i}^{\beta_2} \varepsilon_i \qquad \textbf{(15.4)}$$

By taking base 10 logarithms of both the dependent and independent variables, you can transform Equation (15.4) to the model shown in Equation (15.5).

TRANSFORMED MULTIPLICATIVE MODEL

$$\begin{aligned}\log Y_i &= \log(\beta_0 X_{1i}^{\beta_1} X_{2i}^{\beta_2} \varepsilon_i) \\ &= \log\beta_0 + \log(X_{1i}^{\beta_1}) + \log(X_{2i}^{\beta_2}) + \log \varepsilon_i \\ &= \log\beta_0 + \beta_1 \log X_{1i} + \beta_2 \log X_{2i} + \log \varepsilon_i\end{aligned} \quad \textbf{(15.5)}$$

Thus, Equation (15.5) is linear in the logarithms. Similarly, you can transform the exponential model shown in Equation (15.6) to a linear form by taking the natural logarithm of both sides of the equation. Equation (15.7) is the transformed model.

ORIGINAL EXPONENTIAL MODEL

$$Y_i = e^{\beta_0 + \beta_1 X_{1i} + \beta_2 X_{2i}} \varepsilon_i \quad \textbf{(15.6)}$$

TRANSFORMED EXPONENTIAL MODEL

$$\begin{aligned}\ln Y_i &= \ln(e^{\beta_0 + \beta_1 X_{1i} + \beta_2 X_{2i}} \varepsilon_i) \\ &= \ln(e^{\beta_0 + \beta_1 X_{1i} + \beta_2 X_{2i}}) + \ln \varepsilon_i \\ &= \beta_0 + \beta_1 X_{1i} + \beta_2 X_{2i} + \ln \varepsilon_i\end{aligned} \quad \textbf{(15.7)}$$

Example 15.3 illustrates the use of a natural log transformation.

EXAMPLE 15.3

Using the Natural Log Transformation

Given the following values for Y and X, use a natural logarithm transformation for the Y variable:

Y	X	Y	X
0.7	1	4.8	3
0.5	1	12.9	4
1.6	2	11.5	4
1.8	2	32.1	5
4.2	3	33.9	5

Construct a scatter plot for X and Y and for X and the natural logarithm of Y.

SOLUTION Figure 15.9 displays both scatter plots. The plots show that the natural logarithm transformation has transformed a nonlinear relationship into a linear relationship.

FIGURE 15.9
Example 15.3 scatter plots of X and Y and X and the natural logarithm of Y

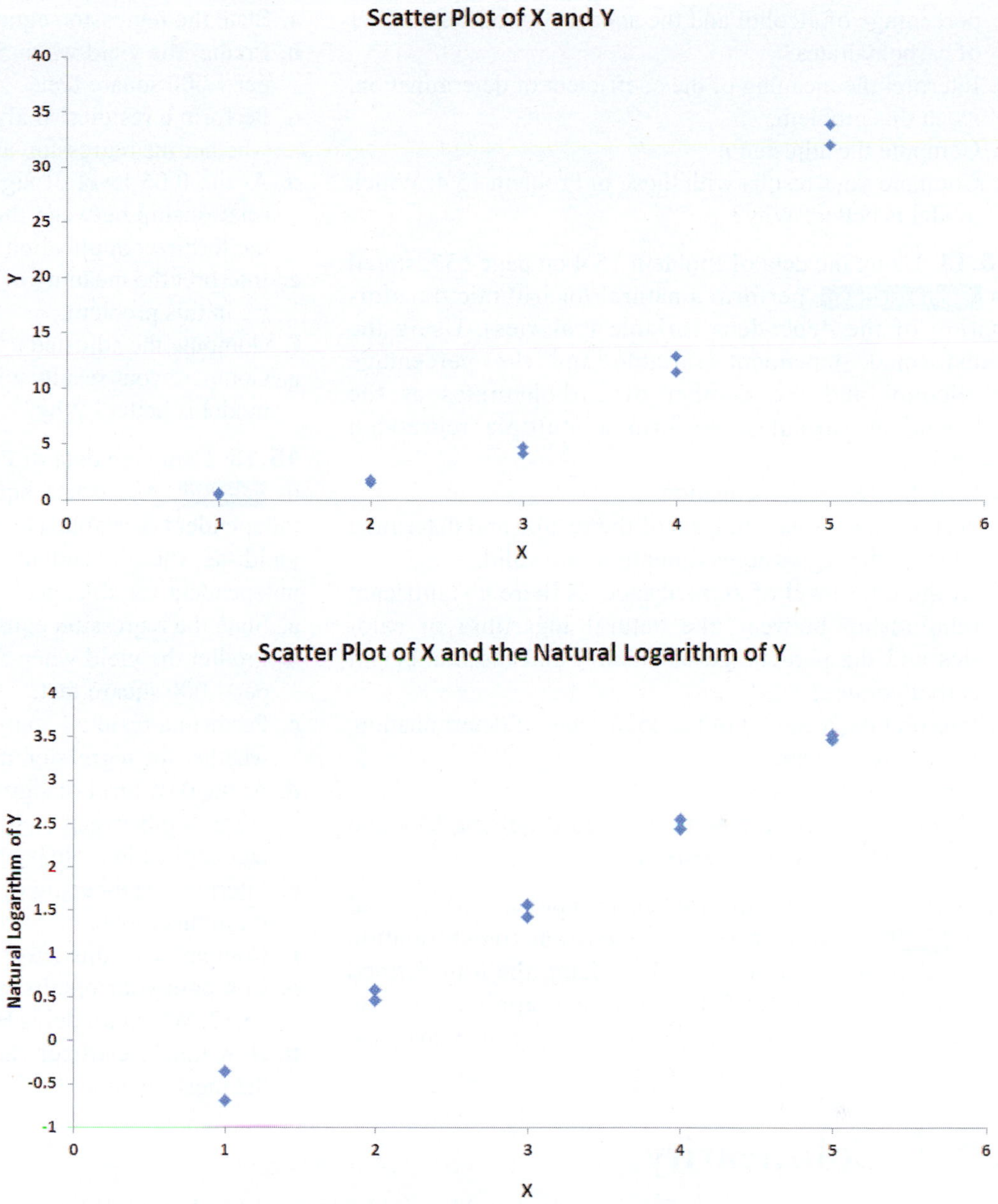

Problems for Section 15.2

LEARNING THE BASICS

15.8 Consider the following regression equation:

$$\log \hat{Y}_i = \log 3.07 + 0.9 \log X_{1i} + 1.41 \log X_{2i}$$

a. Predict the value of Y when $X_1 = 8.5$ and $X_2 = 5.2$.
b. Interpret the meaning of the regression coefficients b_0, b_1, and b_2.

15.9 Consider the following regression equation:

$$\ln \hat{Y}_i = 4.62 + 0.5X_{1i} + 0.7X_{2i}$$

a. Predict the value of Y when $X_1 = 8.5$ and $X_2 = 5.2$.
b. Interpret the meaning of the regression coefficients b_0, b_1, and b_2.

APPLYING THE CONCEPTS

SELF Test **15.10** Using the data of Problem 15.4 on page 637, stored in DomesticBeer, perform a square-root transformation on each of the independent variables (percentage alcohol and number of carbohydrates). Using calories as the dependent variable and the transformed independent variables, perform a multiple regression analysis.
a. State the regression equation.
b. Perform a residual analysis of the results and determine whether the regression model is valid.
c. At the 0.05 level of significance, is there a significant relationship between calories and the square root of the

percentage of alcohol and the square root of the number of carbohydrates?

d. Interpret the meaning of the coefficient of determination, r^2, in this problem.

e. Compute the adjusted r^2.

f. Compare your results with those in Problem 15.4. Which model is better? Why?

15.11 Using the data of Problem 15.4 on page 637, stored in DomesticBeer, perform a natural logarithmic transformation of the dependent variable (calories). Using the transformed dependent variable and the percentage of alcohol and the number of carbohydrates as the independent variables, perform a multiple regression analysis.

a. State the regression equation.

b. Perform a residual analysis of the results and determine whether the regression assumptions are valid.

c. At the 0.05 level of significance, is there a significant relationship between the natural logarithm of calories and the percentage of alcohol and the number of carbohydrates?

d. Interpret the meaning of the coefficient of determination, r^2, in this problem.

e. Compute the adjusted r^2.

f. Compare your results with those in Problems 15.4 and 15.10. Which model is best? Why?

15.12 Using the data of Problem 15.6 on page 637, stored in Tomato, perform a natural logarithm transformation of the dependent variable (yield). Using the transformed dependent variable and the fertilizer application rate as the independent variable, perform a regression analysis.

a. State the regression equation.

b. Predict the yield when 55 pounds of fertilizer is applied per 1,000 square feet.

c. Perform a residual analysis of the results and determine whether the regression assumptions are valid.

d. At the 0.05 level of significance, is there a significant relationship between the natural logarithm of yield and the fertilizer application rate?

e. Interpret the meaning of the coefficient of determination, r^2, in this problem.

f. Compute the adjusted r^2.

g. Compare your results with those in Problem 15.6. Which model is better? Why?

15.13 Using the data of Problem 15.6 on page 637, stored in Tomato, perform a square-root transformation of the independent variable (fertilizer application rate). Using yield as the dependent variable and the transformed independent variable, perform a regression analysis.

a. State the regression equation.

b. Predict the yield when 55 pounds of fertilizer is applied per 1,000 square feet.

c. Perform a residual analysis of the results and determine whether the regression model is valid.

d. At the 0.05 level of significance, is there a significant relationship between yield and the square root of the fertilizer application rate?

e. Interpret the meaning of the coefficient of determination, r^2, in this problem.

f. Compute the adjusted r^2.

g. Compare your results with those of Problems 15.6 and 15.12. Which model is best? Why?

h. How much fertilizer should you apply in order to grow the most tomatoes?

15.3 Collinearity

One important problem in the application of multiple regression analysis involves the possible **collinearity** of the independent variables. This condition refers to situations in which two or more of the independent variables are highly correlated with each other. In such situations, collinear variables do not provide unique information, and it becomes difficult to separate the effects of such variables on the dependent variable. When collinearity exists, the values of the regression coefficients for the correlated variables may fluctuate drastically, depending on which independent variables are included in the model.

One method of measuring collinearity is to determine the **variance inflationary factor (*VIF*)** for each independent variable. Equation (15.8) defines VIF_j, the variance inflationary factor for variable j.

VARIANCE INFLATIONARY FACTOR

$$VIF_j = \frac{1}{1 - R_j^2} \tag{15.8}$$

where

R_j^2 is the coefficient of multiple determination for a regression model, using variable X_j as the dependent variable and all other X variables as independent variables.

If there are only two independent variables, R_1^2 is the coefficient of determination between X_1 and X_2. It is identical to R_2^2, which is the coefficient of determination between X_2 and X_1. If there are three independent variables, then R_1^2 is the coefficient of multiple determination of X_1 with X_2 and X_3; R_2^2 is the coefficient of multiple determination of X_2 with X_1 and X_3; and R_3^2 is the coefficient of multiple determination of X_3 with X_1 and X_2.

If a set of independent variables is uncorrelated, each VIF_j is equal to 1. If the set is highly correlated, then a VIF_j might even exceed 10. Marquardt (see reference 2) suggests that if VIF_j is greater than 10, there is too much correlation between the variable X_j and the other independent variables. However, other statisticians suggest a more conservative criterion. Snee (see reference 5) recommends using alternatives to least-squares regression if the maximum VIF_j exceeds 5.

You need to proceed with extreme caution when using a multiple regression model that has one or more large *VIF* values. You can use the model to predict values of the dependent variable *only* in the case where the values of the independent variables used in the prediction are in the relevant range of the values in the data set. However, you cannot extrapolate to values of the independent variables not observed in the sample data. And because the independent variables contain overlapping information, you should always avoid interpreting the regression coefficient estimates separately because there is no way to accurately estimate the individual effects of the independent variables. One solution to the problem is to delete the variable with the largest *VIF* value. The reduced model (i.e., the model with the independent variable with the largest *VIF* value deleted) is often free of collinearity problems. If you determine that all the independent variables are needed in the model, you can use methods discussed in reference 1.

In the OmniPower sales data (see Section 14.1), the correlation between the two independent variables, price and promotional expenditure, is −0.0968. Because there are only two independent variables in the model, from Equation (15.8) on page 642:

$$VIF_1 = VIF_2 = \frac{1}{1 - (-0.0968)^2} = 1.009$$

Thus, you can conclude that you should not be concerned with collinearity for the OmniPower sales data.

In models containing quadratic and interaction terms, collinearity is usually present. The linear and quadratic terms of an independent variable are usually highly correlated with each other, and an interaction term is often correlated with one or both of the independent variables making up the interaction. Thus, you cannot interpret individual parameter estimates separately. You need to interpret the linear and quadratic parameter estimates together in order to understand the nonlinear relationship. Likewise, you need to interpret an interaction parameter estimate in conjunction with the two parameter estimates associated with the variables comprising the interaction. In summary, large *VIF*s in quadratic or interaction models do not necessarily mean that the model is not a good one. They do, however, require you to carefully interpret the parameter estimates.

Problems for Section 15.3

LEARNING THE BASICS

15.14 If the coefficient of determination between two independent variables is 0.20, what is the *VIF*?

15.15 If the coefficient of determination between two independent variables is 0.50, what is the *VIF*?

APPLYING THE CONCEPTS

SELF Test **15.16** Refer to Problem 14.4 on page 583. Perform a multiple regression analysis using the data in **WareCost** and determine the *VIF* for each independent variable in the model. Is there reason to suspect the existence of collinearity?

15.17 Refer to Problem 14.5 on page 583. Perform a multiple regression analysis using the data in **Auto2010** and determine the *VIF* for each independent variable in the model. Is there reason to suspect the existence of collinearity?

15.18 Refer to Problem 14.6 on page 583. Perform a multiple regression analysis using the data in **Advertise** and determine the *VIF* for each independent variable in the model. Is there reason to suspect the existence of collinearity?

15.19 Refer to Problem 14.7 on page 584. Perform a multiple regression analysis using the data in **Standby** and determine the *VIF* for each independent variable in the model. Is there reason to suspect the existence of collinearity?

15.20 Refer to Problem 14.8 on page 584. Perform a multiple regression analysis using the data in **GlenCove** and determine the *VIF* for each independent variable in the model. Is there reason to suspect the existence of collinearity?

15.4 Model Building

This chapter and Chapter 14 have introduced you to many different topics in regression analysis, including quadratic terms, dummy variables, and interaction terms. In this section, you learn a structured approach to building the most appropriate regression model. As you will see, successful model building incorporates many of the topics you have studied so far.

To begin, refer to the WHIT-DT scenario introduced on page 629, in which four independent variables (total staff present, remote hours, Dubner hours, and total labor hours) are considered in the business problem that involves developing a regression model to predict standby hours of unionized graphic artists. Data are collected over a period of 26 weeks and organized and stored in **Standby**. Table 15.2 summarizes the data.

TABLE 15.2

Predicting Standby Hours Based on Total Staff Present, Remote Hours, Dubner Hours, and Total Labor Hours

Week	Standby Hours	Total Staff Present	Remote Hours	Dubner Hours	Total Labor Hours
1	245	338	414	323	2,001
2	177	333	598	340	2,030
3	271	358	656	340	2,226
4	211	372	631	352	2,154
5	196	339	528	380	2,078
6	135	289	409	339	2,080
7	195	334	382	331	2,073
8	118	293	399	311	1,758
9	116	325	343	328	1,624
10	147	311	338	353	1,889
11	154	304	353	518	1,988
12	146	312	289	440	2,049
13	115	283	388	276	1,796
14	161	307	402	207	1,720
15	274	322	151	287	2,056
16	245	335	228	290	1,890
17	201	350	271	355	2,187
18	183	339	440	300	2,032
19	237	327	475	284	1,856
20	175	328	347	337	2,068
21	152	319	449	279	1,813
22	188	325	336	244	1,808
23	188	322	267	253	1,834
24	197	317	235	272	1,973
25	261	315	164	223	1,839
26	232	331	270	272	1,935

To develop a model to predict the dependent variable, standby hours in the WHIT-DT scenario, you need to be guided by a general problem-solving strategy or *heuristic*. One heuristic appropriate for building regression models uses the principle of parsimony.

Parsimony guides you to select the regression model with the fewest independent variables that can predict the dependent variable adequately. Regression models with fewer independent variables are easier to interpret, particularly because they are less likely to be affected by collinearity problems (described in Section 15.3).

The selection of an appropriate model when many independent variables are under consideration involves complexities that are not present with a model that has only two independent variables. The evaluation of all possible regression models is more computationally complex. And, although you can quantitatively evaluate competing models, there may not be a *uniquely* best model but several *equally appropriate* models.

To begin analyzing the standby-hours data, you compute the variance inflationary factors [see Equation (15.8) on page 642] to measure the amount of collinearity among the independent variables. The values for the four *VIF*s for this model appear in Figure 15.10, along with the results for the model that uses the four independent variables.

FIGURE 15.10

Excel and Minitab regression results for predicting standby hours based on four independent variables (Excel results contain additional worksheets for Durbin-Watson statistic and *VIF* inset)

	A	B	C	D	E
1	Variance Inflationary Factor (*VIF*) Calculations				
2		Regression Model			
3		Total Staff and all other X	Remote and all other X	Dubner and all other X	Total Labor and all other X
4	R Square	0.4143	0.1891	0.3147	0.4998
5	VIF	1.7074	1.2333	1.4592	1.9993

	A	B	C	D	E	F	G
1	Standby Hours Analysis						
2							
3	*Regression Statistics*						
4	Multiple R	0.7894					
5	R Square	0.6231					
6	Adjusted R Square	0.5513					
7	Standard Error	31.8350					
8	Observations	26					
9							
10	ANOVA						
11		*df*	*SS*	*MS*	*F*	*Significance F*	
12	Regression	4	35181.7937	8795.4484	8.6786	0.0003	
13	Residual	21	21282.8217	1013.4677			
14	Total	25	56464.6154				
15							
16		*Coefficients*	*Standard Error*	*t Stat*	*P-value*	*Lower 95%*	*Upper 95%*
17	Intercept	-330.8318	110.8954	-2.9833	0.0071	-561.4514	-100.2123
18	Total Staff	1.2456	0.4121	3.0229	0.0065	0.3887	2.1026
19	Remote	-0.1184	0.0543	-2.1798	0.0408	-0.2314	-0.0054
20	Dubner	-0.2971	0.1179	-2.5189	0.0199	-0.5423	-0.0518
21	Total Labor	0.1305	0.0593	2.2004	0.0391	0.0072	0.2539

	A	B
1	Durbin-Watson Calculations	
2		
3	Sum of Squared Difference of Residuals	47241.6126
4	Sum of Squared Residuals	21282.8217
5		
6	Durbin-Watson Statistic	2.2197

Regression Analysis: Standby versus Total Staff, ...

```
The regression equation is
Standby = - 331 + 1.25 Total Staff - 0.118 Remote
          - 0.297 Dubner + 0.131 Total Labor

Predictor        Coef  SE Coef      T      P    VIF
Constant       -330.8    110.9  -2.98  0.007
Total Staff    1.2456   0.4121   3.02  0.006  1.707
Remote       -0.11842  0.05432  -2.18  0.041  1.233
Dubner        -0.2971   0.1179  -2.52  0.020  1.459
Total Labor   0.13053  0.05932   2.20  0.039  1.999

S = 31.8350   R-Sq = 62.3%   R-Sq(adj) = 55.1%

Analysis of Variance
Source          DF     SS    MS     F      P
Regression       4  35182  8795  8.68  0.000
Residual Error  21  21283  1013
Total           25  56465

Source       DF  Seq SS
Total Staff   1   20667
Remote        1    6995
Dubner        1    2612
Total Labor   1    4907

Durbin-Watson statistic = 2.21971
```

Observe that all the *VIF* values in Figure 15.10 are relatively small, ranging from a high of 1.999 for the total labor hours to a low of 1.233 for remote hours. Thus, on the basis of the criteria developed by Snee that all *VIF* values should be less than 5.0 (see reference 5), there is little evidence of collinearity among the set of independent variables.

The Stepwise Regression Approach to Model Building

You continue your analysis of the standby-hours data by attempting to determine whether a subset of all independent variables yields an adequate and appropriate model. The first approach described here is **stepwise regression**, which attempts to find the "best" regression model without examining all possible models.

The first step of stepwise regression is to find the best model that uses one independent variable. The next step is to find the best of the remaining independent variables to add to the model selected in the first step. An important feature of the stepwise approach is that an independent variable that has entered into the model at an early stage may subsequently be removed after other independent variables are considered. Thus, in stepwise regression, variables are either added to or deleted from the regression model at each step of the model-building process. The *t* test for the slope (see Section 14.4) or the partial F_{STAT} test statistic (see Section 14.5) is used to determine whether variables are added or deleted. The stepwise procedure terminates with the selection of a best-fitting model when no additional variables can be added to or deleted from the last model evaluated. Figure 15.11 shows the Excel (using PHStat2) and Minitab stepwise regression results for the standby-hours data.

FIGURE 15.11

Excel (PHStat2) and Minitab stepwise regression results for the standby-hours data

	A / B	C	D	E	F	G	H
1	**Stepwise Analysis for Standby Hours**						
2	Table of Results for General Stepwise						
3							
4	Total Staff entered.						
5							
6		*df*	*SS*	*MS*	*F*	*Significance F*	
7	Regression	1	20667.3980	20667.3980	13.8563	0.0011	
8	Residual	24	35797.2174	1491.5507			
9	Total	25	56464.6154				
10							
11		*Coefficients*	*Standard Error*	*t Stat*	*P-value*	*Lower 95%*	*Upper 95%*
12	Intercept	-272.3816	124.2402	-2.1924	0.0383	-528.8008	-15.9625
13	Total Staff	1.4241	0.3826	3.7224	0.0011	0.6345	2.2136
14							
15							
16	Remote entered.						
17							
18		*df*	*SS*	*MS*	*F*	*Significance F*	
19	Regression	2	27662.5429	13831.2714	11.0450	0.0004	
20	Residual	23	28802.0725	1252.2640			
21	Total	25	56464.6154				
22							
23		*Coefficients*	*Standard Error*	*t Stat*	*P-value*	*Lower 95%*	*Upper 95%*
24	Intercept	-330.6748	116.4802	-2.8389	0.0093	-571.6322	-89.7175
25	Total Staff	1.7649	0.3790	4.6562	0.0001	0.9808	2.5490
26	Remote	-0.1390	0.0588	-2.3635	0.0269	-0.2606	-0.0173
27							
28							
29	No other variables could be entered into the model. Stepwise ends.						

Stepwise Regression: Standby versus Total Staff, Remote, ...

```
  Alpha-to-Enter: 0.05  Alpha-to-Remove: 0.05

Response is Standby on 4 predictors, with N = 26

Step              1       2
Constant     -272.4  -330.7

Total Staff    1.42    1.76
T-Value        3.72    4.66
P-Value       0.001   0.000

Remote               -0.139
T-Value               -2.36
P-Value               0.027

S              38.6    35.4
R-Sq          36.60   48.99
R-Sq(adj)     33.96   44.56
Mallows Cp     13.3     8.4
```

Figure 15.11 contains an Excel worksheet created by PHStat2. Although manually creating stepwise results in Excel is not impossible to do, the decision making inherent in adding and deleting variables and the need to cut and paste or delete partial regression results in order to report results makes relying on an add-in such as PHStat2 the only practical choice.

For this example, a significance level of 0.05 is used to enter a variable into the model or to delete a variable from the model. The first variable entered into the model is total staff, the variable that correlates most highly with the dependent variable standby hours. Because the *p*-value of 0.0011 is less than 0.05, total staff is included in the regression model.

The next step involves selecting a second independent variable for the model. The second variable chosen is one that makes the largest contribution to the model, given that the first variable has been selected. For this model, the second variable is remote hours. Because the *p*-value of 0.0269 for remote hours is less than 0.05, remote hours is included in the regression model.

After the remote hours variable is entered into the model, the stepwise procedure determines whether total staff is still an important contributing variable or whether it can be eliminated from the model. Because the *p*-value of 0.0001 for total staff is less than 0.05, total staff remains in the regression model.

The next step involves selecting a third independent variable for the model. Because none of the other variables meets the 0.05 criterion for entry into the model, the stepwise procedure terminates with a model that includes total staff present and the number of remote hours.

This stepwise regression approach to model building was originally developed more than four decades ago, when regression computations on computers were time-consuming and costly. Although stepwise regression limited the evaluation of alternative models, the method was deemed a good trade-off between evaluation and cost.

Given the ability of today's computers to perform regression computations at very low cost and high speed, stepwise regression has been superseded to some extent by the best-subsets approach, discussed next, which evaluates a larger set of alternative models. Stepwise regression is not obsolete, however. Today, many businesses use stepwise regression as part of the research technique called **data mining** (see Online Section 15.7), which tries to identify significant statistical relationships in very large data sets that contain extremely large numbers of variables.

The Best-Subsets Approach to Model Building

The **best-subsets approach** evaluates all possible regression models for a given set of independent variables. Figure 15.12 presents best-subsets regression results of all possible regression models for the standby-hours data.

FIGURE 15.12

Excel and Minitab best-subsets regression results for the standby-hours data

	A	B	C	D	E	F
1	**Best-Subsets Analysis for Standby Hours**					
2						
3	Intermediate Calculations					
4	R2T	0.6231				
5	1 - R2T	0.3769				
6	n	26				
7	T	5				
8	n - T	21				
9						
10	Model	Cp	k+1	R Square	Adj. R Square	Std. Error
11	X1	13.3215	2	0.3660	0.3396	38.6206
12	X1X2	8.4193	3	0.4899	0.4456	35.3873
13	X1X2X3	7.8418	4	0.5362	0.4729	34.5029
14	X1X2X3X4	5.0000	5	0.6231	0.5513	31.8350
15	X1X2X4	9.3449	4	0.5092	0.4423	35.4921
16	X1X3	10.6486	3	0.4499	0.4021	36.7490
17	X1X3X4	7.7517	4	0.5378	0.4748	34.4426
18	X1X4	14.7982	3	0.3754	0.3211	39.1579
19	X2	33.2078	2	0.0091	-0.0322	48.2836
20	X2X3	32.3067	3	0.0612	-0.0205	48.0087
21	X2X3X4	12.1381	4	0.4591	0.3853	37.2608
22	X2X4	23.2481	3	0.2238	0.1563	43.6540
23	X3	30.3884	2	0.0597	0.0205	47.0345
24	X3X4	11.8231	3	0.4288	0.3791	37.4466
25	X4	24.1846	2	0.1710	0.1365	44.1619

Best Subsets Regression: Standby versus Total Staff, Remote, ...

Response is Standby

Vars	R-Sq	R-Sq(adj)	Mallows Cp	S	Total Staff	Remote	Dubner	Total Labor
1	36.6	34.0	13.3	38.621	X			
1	17.1	13.7	24.2	44.162				X
1	6.0	2.1	30.4	47.035			X	
2	49.0	44.6	8.4	35.387	X	X		
2	45.0	40.2	10.6	36.749	X		X	
2	42.9	37.9	11.8	37.447			X	X
3	53.8	47.5	7.8	34.443	X		X	X
3	53.6	47.3	7.8	34.503	X	X	X	
3	50.9	44.2	9.3	35.492	X	X		X
4	62.3	55.1	5.0	31.835	X	X	X	X

A criterion often used in model building is the adjusted r^2, which adjusts the r^2 of each model to account for the number of independent variables in the model as well as for the sample size (see Section 14.2). Because model building requires you to compare models with different numbers of independent variables, the adjusted r^2 is more appropriate than r^2. Referring to Figure 15.12, you see that the adjusted r^2 reaches a maximum value of 0.5513 when all four independent variables plus the intercept term (for a total of five estimated parameters) are included in the model.

A second criterion often used in the evaluation of competing models is the C_p statistic developed by Mallows (see reference 1). The $\boldsymbol{C_p}$ **statistic**, defined in Equation (15.9), measures the differences between a fitted regression model and a *true* model, along with random error.

C_p STATISTIC

$$C_p = \frac{(1 - R_k^2)(n - T)}{1 - R_T^2} - [n - 2(k + 1)] \quad \textbf{(15.9)}$$

where

k = number of independent variables included in a regression model
T = total number of parameters (including the intercept) to be estimated in the full regression model
R_k^2 = coefficient of multiple determination for a regression model that has k independent variables
R_T^2 = coefficient of multiple determination for a full regression model that contains all T estimated parameters

Using Equation (15.9) to compute C_p for the model containing total staff and remote hours,

$$n = 26 \qquad k = 2 \qquad T = 4 + 1 = 5 \qquad R_k^2 = 0.4899 \qquad R_T^2 = 0.6231$$

so that

$$C_p = \frac{(1 - 0.4899)(26 - 5)}{1 - 0.6231} - [26 - 2(2 + 1)]$$
$$= 8.4193$$

When a regression model with k independent variables contains only random differences from a *true* model, the mean value of C_p is $k + 1$, the number of parameters. Thus, in evaluating many alternative regression models, the goal is to find models whose C_p is close to or less than $k + 1$. In Figure 15.12, you see that only the model with all four independent variables considered contains a C_p value close to or below $k + 1$. Therefore, using the C_p criterion, you should choose that model.

Although it is not the case here, the C_p statistic often provides several alternative models for you to evaluate in greater depth. Moreover, the best model or models using the C_p criterion might differ from the model selected using the adjusted r^2 and/or the model selected using the stepwise procedure. (Note here that the model selected using stepwise regression has a C_p value of 8.4193, which is substantially above the suggested criterion of $k + 1 = 3$ for that model.) Remember that there may not be a uniquely best model, but there may be several equally appropriate models. Final model selection often involves using subjective criteria, such as parsimony, interpretability, and departure from model assumptions (as evaluated by residual analysis).

When you have finished selecting the independent variables to include in the model, you should perform a residual analysis to evaluate the regression assumptions, and because the data were collected in time order, you also need to compute the Durbin-Watson statistic to determine whether there is autocorrelation in the residuals (see Section 13.6). From Figure 15.10 on page 645, you see that the Durbin-Watson statistic, D, is 2.2197. Because D is greater than 2.0, there is no indication of positive correlation in the residuals. Figure 15.13 presents the plots used in the residual analysis.

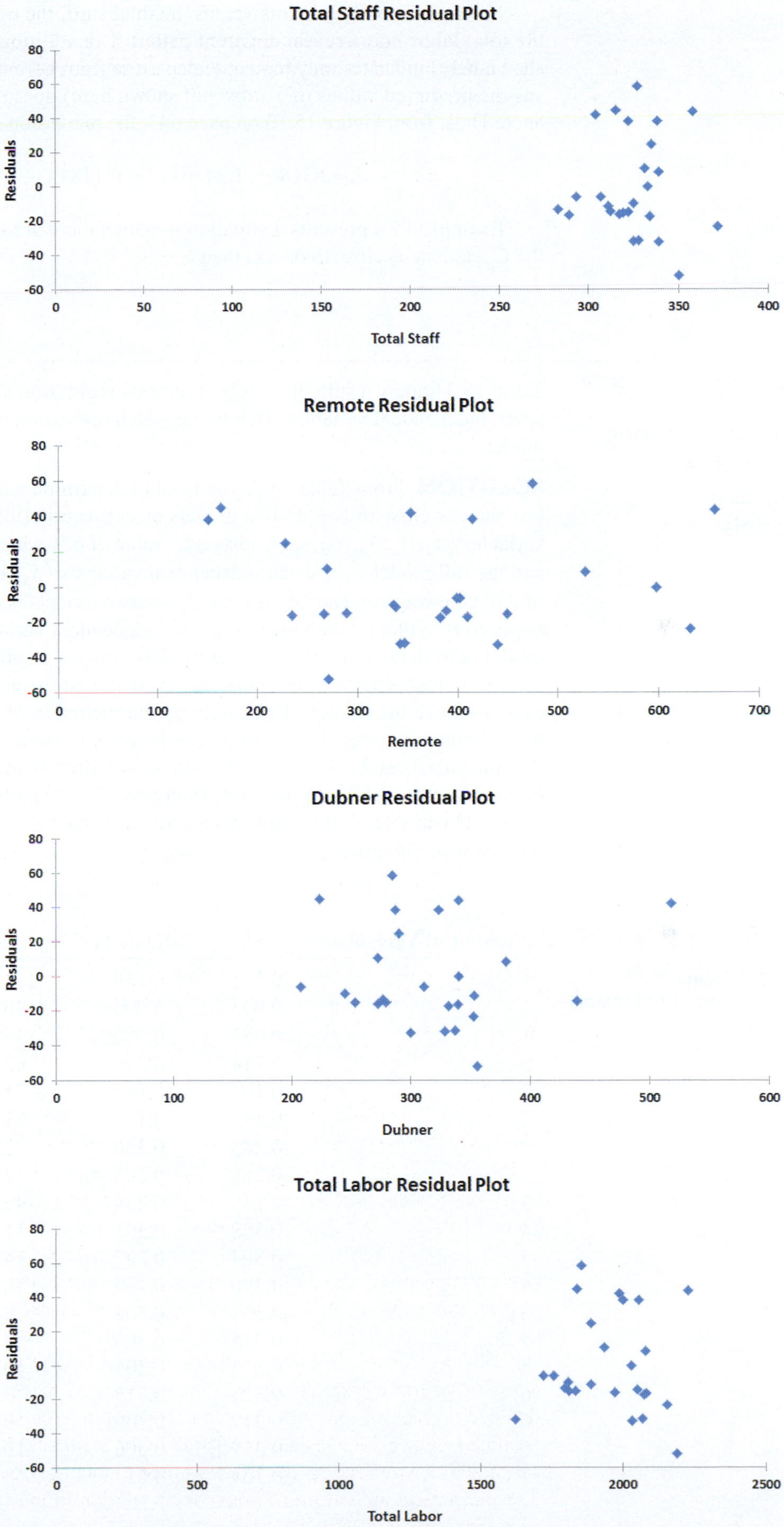

FIGURE 15.13
Residual plots for the standby-hours data

None of the residual plots versus the total staff, the remote hours, the Dubner hours, and the total labor hours reveal apparent patterns. In addition, a histogram of the residuals (not shown here) indicates only moderate departure from normality, and a plot of the residuals versus the predicted values of Y (also not shown here) does not show evidence of unequal variance. Thus, from Figure 15.10 on page 645, the regression equation is

$$\hat{Y}_i = -330.8318 + 1.2456X_{1i} - 0.1184X_{2i} - 0.2971X_{3i} + 0.1305X_{4i}$$

Example 15.4 presents a situation in which there are several alternative models in which the C_p statistic is close to or less than $k + 1$.

EXAMPLE 15.4

Choosing Among Alternative Regression Models

Table 15.3 shows results from a best-subsets regression analysis of a regression model with seven independent variables. Determine which regression model you would choose as the *best* model.

SOLUTION From Table 15.3, you need to determine which models have C_p values that are less than or close to $k + 1$. Two models meet this criterion. The model with six independent variables $(X_1, X_2, X_3, X_4, X_5, X_6)$ has a C_p value of 6.8, which is less than $k + 1 = 6 + 1 = 7$, and the full model with seven independent variables $(X_1, X_2, X_3, X_4, X_5, X_6, X_7)$ has a C_p value of 8.0. One way you can choose among the two models is to select the model with the largest adjusted r^2—that is, the model with six independent variables. Another way to select a final model is to determine whether the models contain a subset of variables that are common. Then you test whether the contribution of the additional variables is significant. In this case, because the models differ only by the inclusion of variable X_7 in the full model, you test whether variable X_7 makes a significant contribution to the regression model, given that the variables X_1, X_2, X_3, X_4, X_5, and X_6 are already included in the model. If the contribution is statistically significant, then you should include variable X_7 in the regression model. If variable X_7 does not make a statistically significant contribution, you should not include it in the model.

TABLE 15.3

Partial Results from Best-Subsets Regression

Number of Variables	r^2	Adjusted r^2	C_p	Variables Included
1	0.121	0.119	113.9	X_4
1	0.093	0.090	130.4	X_1
1	0.083	0.080	136.2	X_3
2	0.214	0.210	62.1	X_3, X_4
2	0.191	0.186	75.6	X_1, X_3
2	0.181	0.177	81.0	X_1, X_4
3	0.285	0.280	22.6	X_1, X_3, X_4
3	0.268	0.263	32.4	X_3, X_4, X_5
3	0.240	0.234	49.0	X_2, X_3, X_4
4	0.308	0.301	11.3	X_1, X_2, X_3, X_4
4	0.304	0.297	14.0	X_1, X_3, X_4, X_6
4	0.296	0.289	18.3	X_1, X_3, X_4, X_5
5	0.317	0.308	8.2	X_1, X_2, X_3, X_4, X_5
5	0.315	0.306	9.6	X_1, X_2, X_3, X_4, X_6
5	0.313	0.304	10.7	X_1, X_3, X_4, X_5, X_6
6	0.323	0.313	6.8	$X_1, X_2, X_3, X_4, X_5, X_6$
6	0.319	0.309	9.0	$X_1, X_2, X_3, X_4, X_5, X_7$
6	0.317	0.306	10.4	$X_1, X_2, X_3, X_4, X_6, X_7$
7	0.324	0.312	8.0	$X_1, X_2, X_3, X_4, X_5, X_6, X_7$

Exhibit 15.1 summarizes the steps involved in model building.

EXHIBIT 15.1
Steps Involved in Model Building

1. Compile a list of all independent variables under consideration.
2. Fit a regression model that includes all the independent variables under consideration and determine the *VIF* for each independent variable. Three possible results can occur:
   a. None of the independent variables has a $VIF > 5$; in this case, proceed to step 3.
   b. One of the independent variables has a $VIF > 5$; in this case, eliminate that independent variable and proceed to step 3.
   c. More than one of the independent variables has a $VIF > 5$; in this case, eliminate the independent variable that has the highest *VIF* and repeat step 2.
3. Perform a best-subsets regression with the remaining independent variables and determine the C_p statistic and/or the adjusted r^2 for each model.
4. List all models that have C_p close to or less than $k + 1$ and/or a high adjusted r^2.
5. From the models listed in step 4, choose a best model.
6. Perform a complete analysis of the model chosen, including a residual analysis.
7. Depending on the results of the residual analysis, add quadratic and/or interaction terms, transform variables, and reanalyze the data.
8. Use the selected model for prediction and inference.

Figure 15.14 represents a roadmap for the steps involved in model building.

FIGURE 15.14
Roadmap for model building

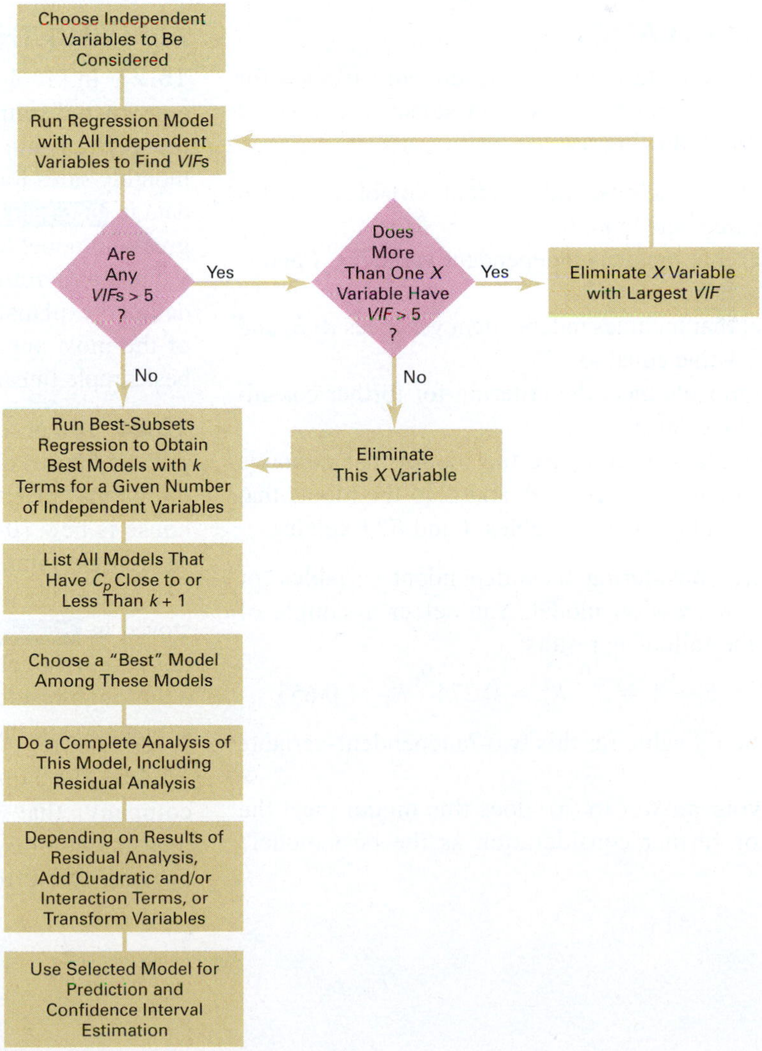

Model Validation

The final step in the model-building process is to validate the selected regression model. This step involves checking the model against data that were not part of the sample analyzed. The following are several ways of validating a regression model:

- Collect new data and compare the results.
- Compare the results of the regression model to previous results.
- If the data set is large, split the data into two parts and cross-validate the results.

Perhaps the best way of validating a regression model is by collecting new data. If the results with new data are consistent with the selected regression model, you have strong reason to believe that the fitted regression model is applicable in a wide set of circumstances.

If it is not possible to collect new data, you can use one of the two other approaches. In one approach, you compare your regression coefficients and predictions to previous results. If the data set is large, you can use **cross-validation**. First, you split the data into two parts. Then you use the first part of the data to develop the regression model. You then use the second part of the data to evaluate the predictive ability of the regression model.

Problems for Section 15.4

LEARNING THE BASICS

15.21 You are considering four independent variables for inclusion in a regression model. You select a sample of $n = 30$, with the following results:

1. The model that includes independent variables A and B has a C_p value equal to 4.6.
2. The model that includes independent variables A and C has a C_p value equal to 2.4.
3. The model that includes independent variables A, B, and C has a C_p value equal to 2.7.

a. Which models meet the criterion for further consideration? Explain.

b. How would you compare the model that contains independent variables A, B, and C to the model that contains independent variables A and B? Explain.

15.22 You are considering six independent variables for inclusion in a regression model. You select a sample of $n = 40$, with the following results:

$$k = 2 \quad T = 6 + 1 = 7 \quad R_k^2 = 0.274 \quad R_T^2 = 0.653$$

a. Compute the C_p value for this two-independent-variable model.

b. Based on your answer to (a), does this model meet the criterion for further consideration as the best model? Explain.

APPLYING THE CONCEPTS

15.23 In Problems 13.85 through 13.89 on page 568, you constructed simple linear regression models to investigate the relationship between demographic information and monthly sales for a chain of sporting goods stores using the data in **Sporting**. Develop the most appropriate multiple regression model to predict a store's monthly sales. Be sure to include a thorough residual analysis. In addition, provide a detailed explanation of the results, including a comparison of the most appropriate multiple regression model to the best simple linear regression model.

15.24 You need to develop a model to predict the selling price of houses in a small city, based on assessed value, time in months since the house was reassessed, and whether the house is new ($0 =$ no, $1 =$ yes). A sample of 30 recently sold single-family houses that were reassessed at full value one year prior to the study is selected and the results are stored in **House1**. Develop the most appropriate multiple regression model to predict selling price. Be sure to perform a thorough residual analysis. In addition, provide a detailed explanation of the results.

15.25 The human resources (HR) director for a large company that produces highly technical industrial instrumentation devices has the business objective of improving recruiting decisions concerning sales managers.

The company has 45 sales regions, each headed by a sales manager. Many of the sales managers have degrees in electrical engineering and, due to the technical nature of the product line, several company officials believe that only applicants with degrees in electrical engineering should be considered. At the time of their application, candidates are asked to take the Strong-Campbell Interest Inventory Test and the Wonderlic Personnel Test. Due to the time and money involved with the testing, some discussion has taken place about dropping one or both of the tests. To start, the HR director gathered information on each of the 45 current sales managers, including years of selling experience, electrical engineering background, and the scores from both the Wonderlic and Strong-Campbell tests. The HR director has decided to use regression modeling to predict a dependent variable of "sales index" score, which is the ratio of the regions' actual sales divided by the target sales. The target values are constructed each year by upper management, in consultation with the sales managers, and are based on past performance and market potential within each region. The file **Managers** contains information on the 45 current sales managers. The following variables are included:

Sales—Ratio of yearly sales divided by the target sales value for that region. The target values were mutually agreed-upon "realistic expectations."

Wonder—Score from the Wonderlic Personnel Test. The higher the score, the higher the applicant's perceived ability to manage.

SC—Score on the Strong-Campbell Interest Inventory Test. The higher the score, the higher the applicant's perceived interest in sales.

Experience—Number of years of selling experience prior to becoming a sales manager.

Engineer—Dummy variable that equals 1 if the sales manager has a degree in electrical engineering and 0 otherwise.

a. Develop the most appropriate regression model to predict sales.

b. Do you think that the company should continue administering both the Wonderlic and Strong-Campbell tests? Explain.

c. Do the data support the argument that electrical engineers outperform the other sales managers? Would you support the idea to hire only electrical engineers? Explain.

d. How important is prior selling experience in this case? Explain.

e. Discuss in detail how the HR director should incorporate the regression model you developed into the recruiting process.

15.5 Pitfalls in Multiple Regression and Ethical Issues

Pitfalls in Multiple Regression

Model building is an art as well as a science. Different individuals may not always agree on the best multiple regression model. To try to construct a best regression model, you should use the process described in Exhibit 15.1 on page 651. In doing so, you must avoid certain pitfalls that can interfere with the development of a useful model. Section 13.9 discussed pitfalls in simple linear regression and strategies for avoiding them. Now that you have studied a variety of multiple regression models, you need to take some additional precautions. To avoid pitfalls in multiple regression, you also need to

- Interpret the regression coefficient for a particular independent variable from a perspective in which the values of all other independent variables are held constant.
- Evaluate residual plots for each independent variable.
- Evaluate interaction and quadratic terms.
- Compute the *VIF* for each independent variable before determining which independent variables to include in the model.
- Examine several alternative models, using best-subsets regression.
- Validate the model before implementing it.

Ethical Issues

Ethical issues arise when a user who wants to make predictions manipulates the development process of the multiple regression model. The key here is intent. In addition to the situations discussed in Section 13.9, unethical behavior occurs when someone uses multiple regression analysis and *willfully fails* to remove from consideration independent variables that exhibit a high collinearity with other independent variables or *willfully fails* to use methods other than least-squares regression when the assumptions necessary for least-squares regression are seriously violated.

15.6 *Online Topic:* Influence Analysis

Influence analysis measures the influence of individual observations on a regression model. To study this topic, read the Section 15.6 online topic file that is available on this book's companion website. (See Appendix C to learn how to access the online topic files.)

15.7 *Online Topic:* Analytics and Data Mining

Analytics and data mining are methods that are used with very large data sets to present summary results and to discern patterns that may exist. To study this topic, read the Section 15.7 online topic file that is available on this book's companion website. (See Appendix C to learn how to access the online topic files.)

USING STATISTICS @ WHIT-DT Revisited

In the Using Statistics scenario, you were the operations manager of WHIT-DT, looking for ways to reduce labor expenses. You needed to determine which variables have an effect on standby hours, the time during which unionized graphic artists are idle but are getting paid. You have collected data concerning standby hours and the total number of staff present, remote hours, Dubner hours, and total labor hours over a period of 26 weeks.

You performed a multiple regression analysis on the data. The coefficient of multiple determination indicated that 62.31% of the variation in standby hours can be explained by variation in the total number of staff present, remote hours, Dubner hours, and total labor hours. The model indicated that standby hours are estimated to increase by 1.2456 hours for each additional staff hour holding constant the other independent variables; to decrease by 0.1184 hour for each additional remote hour holding constant the other independent variables; to decrease by 0.2974 hour for each additional Dubner hour holding constant the other independent variables; and to increase by 0.1305 hour for each additional labor hour holding constant the other independent variables. Each of the four independent variables had a significant effect on standby hours holding constant the other independent variables. This regression model enables you to predict standby hours based on the total number of staff present, remote hours, Dubner hours, and total labor hours. It also enables you to investigate how changing each of these four independent variables could affect standby hours.

SUMMARY

In this chapter, various multiple regression topics were considered (see Figure 15.15), including quadratic regression models, transformations, collinearity, and model building.

FIGURE 15.15

Roadmap for multiple regression

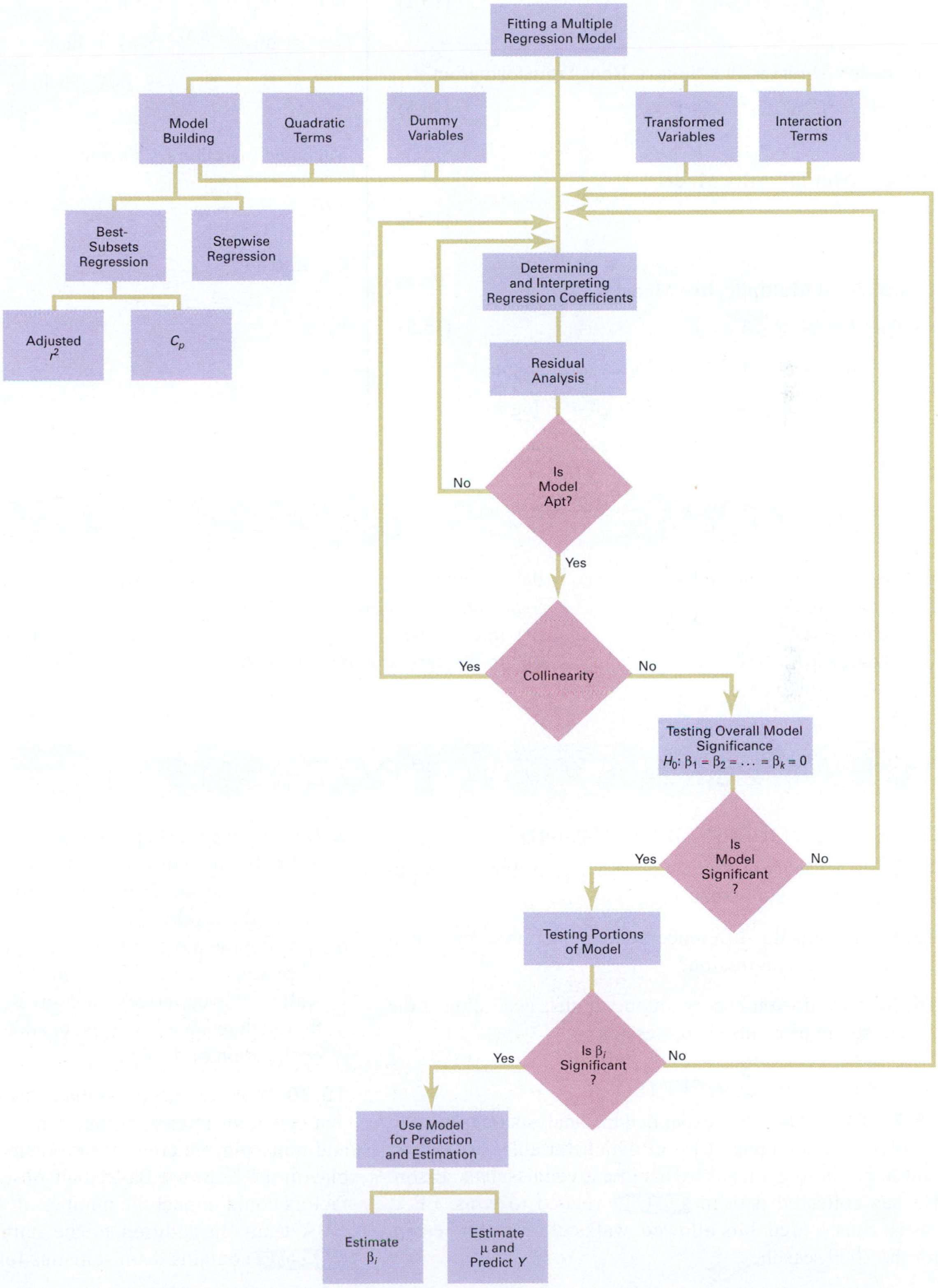

KEY EQUATIONS

Quadratic Regression Model

$$Y_i = \beta_0 + \beta_1 X_{1i} + \beta_2 X_{1i}^2 + \varepsilon_i \tag{15.1}$$

Quadratic Regression Equation

$$\hat{Y}_i = b_0 + b_1 X_{1i} + b_2 X_{1i}^2 \tag{15.2}$$

Regression Model with a Square-Root Transformation

$$Y_i = \beta_0 + \beta_1 \sqrt{X_{1i}} + \varepsilon_i \tag{15.3}$$

Original Multiplicative Model

$$Y_i = \beta_0 X_{1i}^{\beta_1} X_{2i}^{\beta_2} \varepsilon_i \tag{15.4}$$

Transformed Multiplicative Model

$$\begin{aligned} \log Y_i &= \log(\beta_0 X_{1i}^{\beta_1} X_{2i}^{\beta_2} \varepsilon_i) \\ &= \log\beta_0 + \log(X_{1i}^{\beta_1}) + \log(X_{2i}^{\beta_2}) + \log \varepsilon_i \\ &= \log\beta_0 + \beta_1 \log X_{1i} + \beta_2 \log X_{2i} + \log \varepsilon_i \end{aligned} \tag{15.5}$$

Original Exponential Model

$$Y_i = e^{\beta_0 + \beta_1 X_{1i} + \beta_2 X_{2i}} \varepsilon_i \tag{15.6}$$

Transformed Exponential Model

$$\begin{aligned} \ln Y_i &= \ln(e^{\beta_0 + \beta_1 X_{1i} + \beta_2 X_{2i}} \varepsilon_i) \\ &= \ln(e^{\beta_0 + \beta_1 X_{1i} + \beta_2 X_{2i}}) + \ln \varepsilon_i \\ &= \beta_0 + \beta_1 X_{1i} + \beta_2 X_{2i} + \ln \varepsilon_i \end{aligned} \tag{15.7}$$

Variance Inflationary Factor

$$VIF_j = \frac{1}{1 - R_j^2} \tag{15.8}$$

C_p Statistic

$$C_p = \frac{(1 - R_k^2)(n - T)}{1 - R_T^2} - [n - 2(k + 1)] \tag{15.9}$$

KEY TERMS

CHAPTER REVIEW PROBLEMS

CHECKING YOUR UNDERSTANDING

15.26 How can you evaluate whether collinearity exists in a multiple regression model?

15.27 What is the difference between stepwise regression and best-subsets regression?

15.28 How do you choose among models according to the C_p statistic in best-subsets regression?

APPLYING THE CONCEPTS

15.29 Crazy Dave has expanded his analysis, presented in Problem 14.73 on page 619, of which variables are important in predicting a team's wins in a given baseball season. He has collected data in **BB2009** related to wins, ERA, saves, runs scored, hits allowed, walks allowed, and errors for the 2009 season.

a. Develop the most appropriate multiple regression model to predict a team's wins. Be sure to include a thorough residual analysis. In addition, provide a detailed explanation of the results.

b. Develop the most appropriate multiple regression model to predict a team's ERA on the basis of hits allowed, walks allowed, errors, and saves. Be sure to include a thorough residual analysis. In addition, provide a detailed explanation of the results.

15.30 Professional basketball has truly become a sport that generates interest among fans around the world. More and more players come from outside the United States to play in the National Basketball Association (NBA). Many factors could impact the number of wins achieved by each NBA team. In addition to the number of wins, the file **NBA2010** contains team statistics for points per game (for team, opponent, and the difference between team and opponent), field goal (shots made) percentage (for team, opponent, and the difference between team and opponent), steals per game (for team, opponent, and the difference between team and opponent), rebounds per game (for team, opponent, and the difference between team and opponent).

a. Consider team points per game, opponent points per game, team field goal percentage, opponent field goal percentage, steals per game, and rebounds per game as independent variables for possible inclusion in the multiple regression model. Develop the most appropriate multiple regression model to predict the number of wins.

b. Consider the difference between team points and opponent points per game, the difference between team field goal percentage and opponent field goal percentage, the difference in team and opponent steals, and the difference between team and opponent rebounds per game as independent variables for possible inclusion in the multiple regression model. Develop the most appropriate multiple regression model to predict the number of wins.

c. Compare the results of (a) and (b). Which model is better for predicting the number of wins? Explain.

15.31 Hemlock Farms is a community located in the Pocono Mountains area of eastern Pennsylvania. The file **HemlockFarms** contains information on homes that were recently for sale. The variables included were

List Price—Asking price of the house
Hot Tub—Whether the house has a hot tub, with 0 = No and 1 = Yes
Lake View—Whether the house has a lake view, with 0 = No and 1 = Yes
Bathrooms—Number of bathrooms
Bedrooms—Number of bedrooms
Loft/Den—Whether the house has a loft or den, with 0 = No and 1 = Yes
Finished basement—Whether the house has a finished basement, with 0 = No and 1 = Yes
Acres—Number of acres for the property

Develop the most appropriate multiple regression model to predict the asking price. Be sure to perform a thorough residual analysis. In addition, provide a detailed explanation of your results.

15.32 Nassau County is located approximately 25 miles east of New York City. Data in **GlenCove** are from a sample of 30 single-family homes located in Glen Cove. Variables included are the appraised value, land area of the property (acres), interior size of the house (square feet), age (years), number of rooms, number of bathrooms, and number of cars that can be parked in the garage.

a. Develop the most appropriate multiple regression model to predict appraised value.

b. Compare the results in (a) with those of Problems 15.33 (a) and 15.34 (a).

15.33 Data similar to those in Problem 15.32 are available for homes located in Roslyn (approximately 8 miles from Glen Cove) and are stored in **Roslyn**.

a. Perform an analysis similar to that of Problem 15.32.

b. Compare the results in (a) with those of Problems 15.32 (a) and 15.34 (a).

15.34 Data similar to Problem 15.32 are available for homes located in Freeport (located approximately 20 miles from Roslyn) and are stored in **Freeport**.

a. Perform an analysis similar to that of Problem 15.32.

b. Compare the results in (a) with those of Problems 15.32 (a) and 15.33 (a).

15.35 You are a real estate broker who wants to compare property values in Glen Cove and Roslyn (which are located approximately 8 miles apart). Use the data in **GCRoslyn**. Make sure to include the dummy variable for location (Glen Cove or Roslyn) in the regression model.

a. Develop the most appropriate multiple regression model to predict appraised value.

b. What conclusions can you reach concerning the differences in appraised value between Glen Cove and Roslyn?

15.36 You are a real estate broker who wants to compare property values in Glen Cove, Freeport, and Roslyn. Use the data in **GCFreeRoslyn**.

a. Develop the most appropriate multiple regression model to predict appraised value.

b. What conclusions can you reach concerning the differences in appraised value between Glen Cove, Freeport, and Roslyn?

15.37 Over the past 30 years, public awareness and concern about air pollution have escalated dramatically. Venturi scrubbers are used for the removal of submicron particulate matter from smoke stacks. An experiment was conducted to determine the effect of air flow rate, water flow rate (liters/minute), recirculating water flow rate (liters/minute), and orifice size (mm) in the air side of the pneumatic nozzle on the performance of the scrubber, as measured by the number of transfer units. The results are stored in **Scrubber**.

Develop the most appropriate multiple regression model to predict the number of transfer units. Be sure to perform a thorough residual analysis. In addition, provide a detailed explanation of your results.

Source: Data extracted from D. A. Marshall, R. J. Sumner, and C. A. Shook, "Removal of SiO_2 Particles with an Ejector Venturi Scrubber," *Environmental Progress*, 14 (1995), 28–32.

15.38 A recent article (J. Conklin, "It's a Marathon, Not a Sprint," *Quality Progress*, June 2009, pp. 46–49) discussed a metal deposition process in which a piece of metal is placed in an acid bath and an alloy is layered on top of it. The key quality characteristic is the thickness of the alloy layer. The file **Thickness** contains the following variables:

Thickness—Thickness of the alloy layer
Catalyst—Catalyst concentration in the acid bath
pH—pH level of the acid bath
Pressure—Pressure in the tank holding the acid bath
Temp—Temperature in the tank holding the acid bath
Voltage—Voltage applied to the tank holding the acid bath

Develop the most appropriate multiple regression model to predict the thickness of the alloy layer. Be sure to perform a thorough residual analysis. The article suggests that there is a significant interaction between the pressure and the temperature in the tank. Do you agree?

15.39 A headline in *The New York Times* on March 4, 1990, read: "Wine equation puts some noses out of joint." The article explained that Professor Orley Ashenfelter, a Princeton University economist, had developed a multiple regression model to predict the quality of French Bordeaux, based on the amount of winter rain, the average temperature during the growing season, and the harvest rain. The multiple regression equation is

$$Q = -12.145 + 0.00117WR + 0.6164TMP - 0.00386HR$$

where

Q = logarithmic index of quality
WR = winter rain (October through March), in millimeters
TMP = average temperature during the growing season (April through September), in degrees Celsius
HR = harvest rain (August to September), in millimeters

You are at a cocktail party, sipping a glass of wine, when one of your friends mentions to you that she has read the article. She asks you to explain the meaning of the coefficients in the equation and also asks you about analyses that might have been done and were not included in the article. What is your reply?

REPORT WRITING EXERCISE

15.40 In Problem 15.23 on page 652, you developed a multiple regression model to predict monthly sales at sporting goods stores for the data stored in **Sporting**. Now write a report based on the model you developed. Append all appropriate charts and statistical information to your report.

TEAM PROJECT

15.41 The file **Bond Funds** contains information regarding eight variables from a sample of 184 bond mutual funds:

Type—Type of bonds comprising the bond mutual fund (intermediate government or short-term corporate)
Assets—In millions of dollars
Fees—Sales charges (no or yes)
Expense ratio—Ratio of expenses to net assets in percentage
Return 2009—Twelve-month return in 2009
Three-year return—Annualized return, 2007–2009
Five-year return—Annualized return, 2005–2009
Risk—Risk-of-loss factor of the bond mutual fund (below average, average, or above average)

Develop regression models to predict the 2009 return, the three-year return, and the five-year return, based on fees, expense ratio, type, and risk. (For the purpose of this analysis, combine below-average risk and average risk into one category.) Be sure to perform a thorough residual analysis. In addition, provide a detailed explanation of your results. Append all appropriate charts and statistical information to your report.

THE MOUNTAIN STATES POTATO COMPANY

Mountain States Potato Company sells a by-product of its potato-processing operation, called a filter cake, to area feedlots as cattle feed. The business problem faced by the feedlot owners is that the cattle are not gaining weight as quickly as they once were. The feedlot owners believe that the root cause of the problem is that the percentage of solids in the filter cake is too low.

Historically, the percentage of solids in the filter cakes ran slightly above 12%. Lately, however, the solids are running in the 11% range. What is actually affecting the solids is a mystery, but something has to be done quickly. Individuals involved in the process were asked to identify variables that might affect the percentage of solids. This review turned up the six variables (in addition to the percentage of solids) listed in the table on page 659. Data collected by monitoring the process several times daily for 20 days are stored in **Potato**.

Variable	Comments
SOLIDS	Percentage of solids in the filter cake.
PH	Acidity. This measure of acidity indicates bacterial action in the clarifier and is controlled by the amount of downtime in the system. As bacterial action progresses, organic acids are produced that can be measured using pH.
LOWER	Pressure of the vacuum line below the fluid line on the rotating drum.
UPPER	Pressure of the vacuum line above the fluid line on the rotating drum.
THICK	Filter cake thickness, measured on the drum.
VARIDRIV	Setting used to control the drum speed. May differ from DRUMSPD due to mechanical inefficiencies.
DRUMSPD	Speed at which the drum is rotating when collecting the filter cake. Measured with a stopwatch.

1. Thoroughly analyze the data and develop a regression model to predict the percentage of solids.

2. Write an executive summary concerning your findings to the president of the Mountain States Potato Company. Include specific recommendations on how to get the percentage of solids back above 12%.

DIGITAL CASE

Apply your knowledge of multiple regression model building in this Digital Case, which extends the Chapter 14 OmniFoods Using Statistics scenario.

Still concerned about ensuring a successful test marketing of its OmniPower energy bars, the marketing department of OmniFoods has contacted Connect2Coupons (C2C), another merchandising consultancy. C2C suggests that earlier analysis done by In-Store Placements Group (ISPG) was faulty because it did not use the correct type of data. C2C claims that its Internet-based viral marketing will have an even greater effect on OmniPower energy bar sales, as new data from the same 34-store sample will show. In response, ISPG says its earlier claims are valid and has reported to the OmniFoods marketing department that it can discern no simple relationship between C2C's viral marketing and increased OmniPower sales.

Open **OmniPowerForum15.pdf** to review all the claims made in a private online forum and chat hosted on the OmniFoods corporate website. Then answer the following:

1. Which of the claims are true? False? True but misleading? Support your answer by performing an appropriate statistical analysis.

2. If the grocery store chain allowed OmniFoods to use an unlimited number of sales techniques, which techniques should it use? Explain.

3. If the grocery store chain allowed OmniFoods to use only one sales technique, which technique should it use? Explain.

REFERENCES

1. Kutner, M., C. Nachtsheim, J. Neter, and W. Li, *Applied Linear Statistical Models*, 5th ed. (New York: McGraw-Hill/Irwin, 2005).
2. Marquardt, D. W., "You Should Standardize the Predictor Variables in Your Regression Models," discussion of "A Critique of Some Ridge Regression Methods," by G. Smith and F. Campbell, *Journal of the American Statistical Association*, 75 (1980), 87–91.
3. *Microsoft Excel 2010* (Redmond, WA: Microsoft Corp., 2010).
4. *Minitab Release 16* (State College, PA: Minitab, Inc., 2010).
5. Snee, R. D., "Some Aspects of Nonorthogonal Data Analysis, Part I. Developing Prediction Equations," *Journal of Quality Technology*, 5 (1973), 67–79.

CHAPTER 15 EXCEL GUIDE

EG15.1 The QUADRATIC REGRESSION MODEL

To the worksheet that contains your regression data, add a new column of formulas that computes the square of one of the independent variables to create a quadratic term. For example, to create a quadratic term for the Section 15.1 fly ash analysis, open to the **DATA worksheet** of the **FlyAsh workbook**. That worksheet contains the independent variable **FlyAsh%** in column A and the dependent variable **Strength** in column B. While the quadratic term **FlyAsh%^2** could be created in any column, a good practice is to place independent variables in contiguous columns. (You must follow this practice if you are using the Analysis ToolPak Regression procedure.) To do so, first select column B (**Strength**), right-click, and click **Insert** from the shortcut menu to add a new column B. (Strength becomes column C.) Enter the label **FlyAsh%^2** in cell B1 and then enter the formula **=A2^2** in cell **B2**. Copy this formula down the column through all the data rows.

To perform a regression analysis using this new variable, apply the Section EG14.1 instructions on page 622.

EG15.2 USING TRANSFORMATIONS in REGRESSION MODELS

The Square-Root Transformation

To the worksheet that contains your regression data, add a new column of formulas that computes the square root of one of the independent variables to create a square-root transformation. For example, to create a square root transformation in a blank column D for an independent variable in a column C, enter the formula **=SQRT(C2)** in cell D2 of that worksheet and copy the formula down through all data rows. If the rightmost column in the worksheet contains the dependent variable, first select that column, right-click, and click **Insert** from the shortcut menu and place the transformation in that new column.

The Log Transformation

To the worksheet that contains your regression data, add a new column of formulas that compute the common (base 10) logarithm or natural logarithm (base *e*) of one of the independent variables to create a log transformation. For example, to create a common logarithm transformation in a blank column D for an independent variable in a column C, enter the formula **=LOG(C2)** in cell D2 of that worksheet and copy the formula down through all data rows. To create a natural logarithm transformation in a blank column D for an independent variable in a column C, enter the formula **=LN(C2)** in cell D2 of that worksheet and copy the formula down through all data rows.

If the dependent variable appears in a column to the immediate right of the independent variable being transformed, first select the dependent variable column, right-click, and click **Insert** from the shortcut menu and then place the transformation of the independent variable in that new column.

EG15.3 COLLINEARITY

PHStat2 To compute the variance inflationary factor, use the Section EG14.1 "Interpreting the Regression Coefficients" *PHStat2* instructions on page 622 but modify step 6 by checking **Variance Inflationary Factor** (*VIF*) before you click **OK**. The *VIF* will appear in cell B9 of the regression results worksheet, immediately following the Regression Statistics area.

In-Depth Excel To compute the variance inflationary factor, first use the Section EG14.1 "Interpreting the Regression Coefficients" *In-Depth Excel* instructions on page 622 to create regression results worksheets for every combination of independent variables in which one serves as the dependent variable. Then, in each of the regression results worksheets, enter the label *VIF* in cell **A9** and enter the formula **=1/(1 - B5)** in cell **B9** to compute the *VIF*.

EG15.4 MODEL BUILDING

The Stepwise Regression Approach to Model Building

PHStat2 Use **Stepwise Regression** to use the stepwise regression approach to model building. For example, to create the Figure 15.11 stepwise analysis of the standby-hours data on page 646, open to the **DATA worksheet** of the **Standby workbook.** Select **PHStat → Regression → Stepwise Regression**. In the procedure's dialog box (shown on page 661):

1. Enter **A1:A27** as the **Y Variable Cell Range**.
2. Enter **B1:E27** as the **X Variables Cell Range**.
3. Check **First cells in both ranges contain label**.
4. Enter **95** as the **Confidence level for regression coefficients**.
5. Click **p values** as the **Stepwise Criteria**.

6. Click **General Stepwise** and keep the pair of **.05** values as the **p value to enter** and the **p value to remove**.
7. Enter a **Title** and click **OK**.

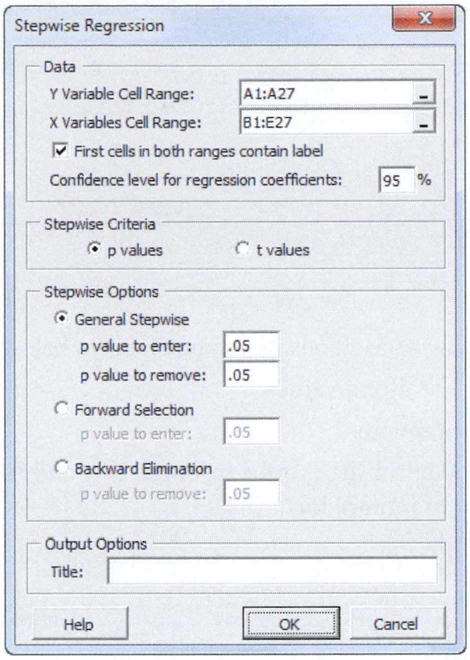

This procedure may take a noticeable amount of time to create its results. The procedure finishes when the statement "Stepwise ends" (as shown in row 29 in the Figure 15.11 Excel results on page 646) is added to the stepwise regression results worksheet.

The Best-Subsets Approach to Model Building

PHStat2 Use **Best Subsets** to use a best-subsets approach to model building. For example, to create the Figure 15.12 best subsets analysis of the standby-hours data on page 647, open to the **DATA worksheet** of the **Standby workbook**. Select **PHStat ➔ Regression ➔ Best Subsets**. In the procedure's dialog box (shown below):

1. Enter **A1:A27** as the **Y Variable Cell Range**.
2. Enter **B1:E27** as the **X Variables Cell Range**.
3. Check **First cells in each range contains label.**
4. Enter **95** as the **Confidence level for regression coefficients**.
5. Enter a **Title** and click **OK**.

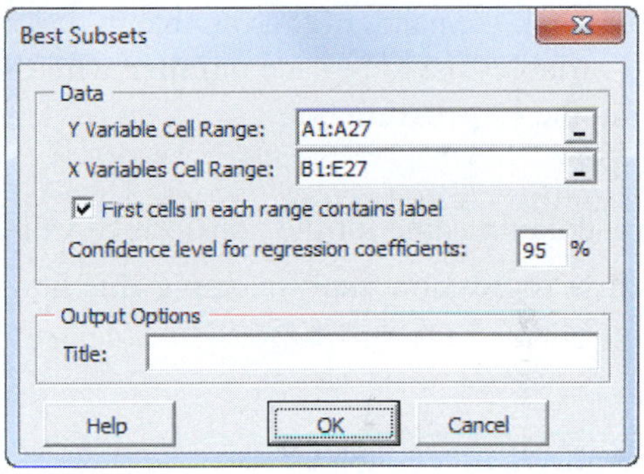

This procedure creates many regression results worksheets (seen as a flickering in the Excel windows) as it evaluates each subset of independent variables.

CHAPTER 15 MINITAB GUIDE

MG15.1 The QUADRATIC REGRESSION MODEL

Use **Calculator** to compute the square of one of the independent variables to create a quadratic term. For example, to create a quadratic term for the Section 15.1 fly ash analysis, open to the **FlyAsh worksheet**. Select **Calc ➔ Calculator**. In the Calculator dialog box (shown in the right column):

1. Enter **C3** in the **Store result in variable** box and press **Tab**.
2. Double-click **C1 Fly Ash%** in the variables list to add **'Fly Ash%'** to the **Expression** box.
3. Click ** and then **2** on the simulated calculator keypad to add ****2** to the **Expression** box.
4. Click **OK**.
5. Enter **Fly Ash%^2** as the name for column **C3**.

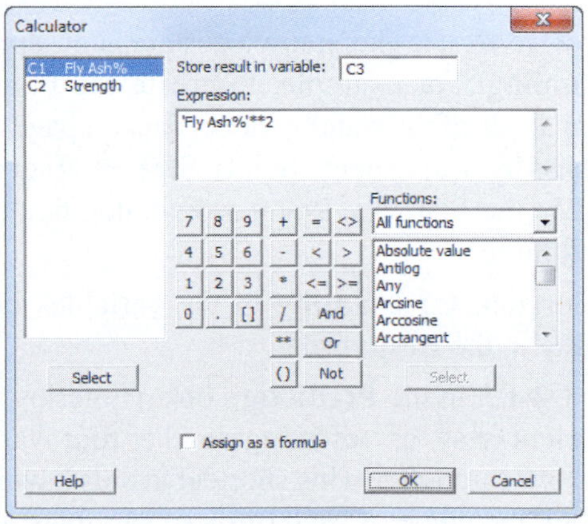

To perform a regression analysis using this new variable, see Section MG14.1 on page 625.

MG15.2 USING TRANSFORMATIONS in REGRESSION MODELS

Use **Calculator** to transform a variable. Open to the worksheet that contains your regression data. Select **Calc → Calculator**. In the Calculator dialog box:

1. Enter the name of the empty column that will contain the transformed values in the **Store result in variable** box and press **Tab**.
2. Select **All functions** from the **Functions** drop-down list.
3. In the list of functions, select one of these choices: **Square root**, **Log base 10**, or **Natural log (log base e)**. Selecting these choices enters **SQRT(number)**, **LOGTEN(number)**, or **LN(number)**, respectively, in the **Expression** box.
4. Double-click the name of the variable to be transformed in the variables list to replace **number** with the variable name in the **Expression** box.
5. Click **OK**.
6. Enter a column name for the transformed values.

To perform a regression analysis using this new variable, see Section MG14.1 on page 625.

MG15.3 COLLINEARITY

To compute the variance inflationary factor, modify the Section MG14.1 "Interpreting the Regression Coefficients" instructions on page 625. In step 15, check **Variance inflation factors** while clearing the other **Display** and **Lack of Fit Test** check boxes in the Regression - Options dialog box.

MG15.4 MODEL BUILDING

The Stepwise Regression Approach to Model Building

Use **Stepwise** to use the stepwise regression approach to model building. For example, to create the Figure 15.11 stepwise analysis of the standby-hours data on page 646, open to the **Standby worksheet**. Select **Stat → Regression → Stepwise**. In the Stepwise Regression dialog box (shown in the right column):

1. Double-click **C1 Standby** in the variables list to add **Standby** in the **Response** box.
2. Enter **C2-C5** in the **Predictors** box. (Entering **C2-C5** is a shortcut way of referring to the four variables in columns 2 through 5. This shortcut avoids having to double-click the name of each of these variables in order to add them to the Predictors box.)
3. Click **Methods**.

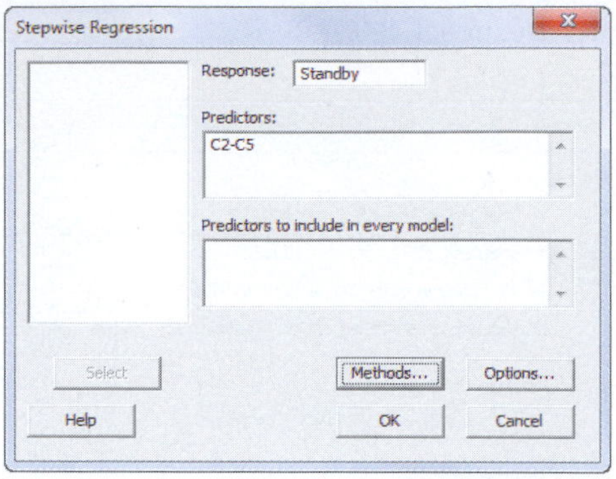

In the Stepwise-Methods dialog box (shown below):

4. Click **Use alpha values**.
5. Click **Stepwise**.
6. Enter **0.05** in the **Alpha to enter** box and **0.05** in the **Alpha to remove** box.
7. Click **OK**.

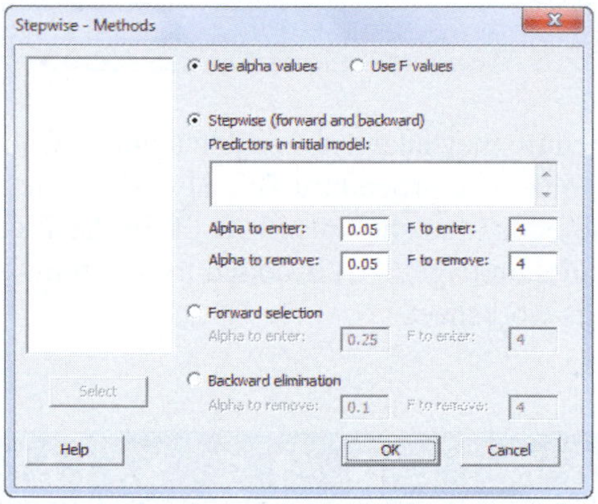

8. Back in the Stepwise Regression dialog box, click **OK**.

The Best-Subsets Approach to Model Building

Use **Best Subsets** to use a best-subsets approach to model building. For example, to create the Figure 15.12 stepwise analysis of the standby-hours data on page 647, open to the **Standby worksheet**. Select **Stat → Regression → Best Subsets**. In the Best Subsets Regression dialog box (shown on page 663):

1. Double-click **C1 Standby** in the variables list to add **Standby** in the **Response** box.
2. Enter **C2-C5** in the **Free Predictors** box. (Entering **C2-C5** is a shortcut way of referring to the four variables in columns 2 through 5 as explained in the previous set of instructions.)

3. Click **Options**.

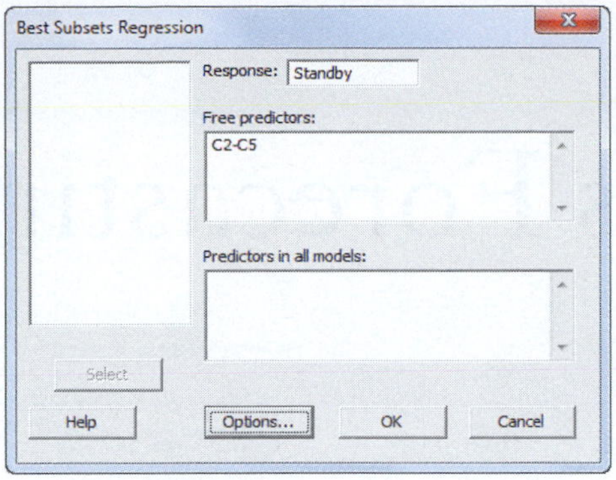

In the Best Subsets Regression - Options dialog box (shown in the right column):

4. Enter **1** in the **Minimum box** and keep the **Maximum** box empty.
5. Enter **3** in the **Models of each size to print** box.
6. Check **Fit intercept**
7. Click **OK**.
8. Back in the Best Subsets Regression dialog box, click **OK**.

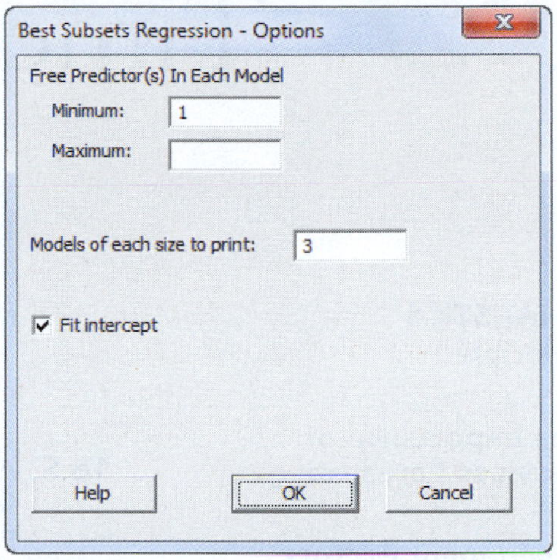

16 Time-Series Forecasting

Learning Objectives

In this chapter, you learn:

- About different time-series forecasting models—moving averages, exponential smoothing, the linear trend, the quadratic trend, the exponential trend—and the autoregressive models and least-squares models for seasonal data
- To choose the most appropriate time-series forecasting model

USING STATISTICS

@ The Principled

You are a financial analyst for The Principled, a large financial services company. You need to better evaluate investment opportunities for your clients. To assist in the forecasting, you have collected time-series data on the three-month U.S. Treasury bill rate and revenues of two large well-known companies, The Coca-Cola Company, and Wal-Mart Stores, Inc. Each time series has unique characteristics. You understand that you can use several different types of forecasting models. How do you decide which type of forecasting is best? How do you use the information gained from the forecasting models to evaluate investment opportunities for your clients?

In Chapters 13 through 15, you used regression analysis as a tool for model building and prediction. In this chapter, regression analysis and other statistical methodologies are applied to time-series data. A **time series** is a set of numerical data collected over time. Due to differences in the features of data for various investments described in the Using Statistics scenario, you need to consider several different approaches to forecasting time-series data.

This chapter begins with an introduction to the importance of business forecasting (see Section 16.1) and a description of the components of time-series models (see Section 16.2). The coverage of forecasting models begins with annual time-series data. Section 16.3 presents moving averages and exponential smoothing methods for smoothing a series. This is followed by least-squares trend fitting and forecasting in Section 16.4 and autoregressive modeling in Section 16.5. Section 16.6 discusses how to choose among alternative forecasting models. Section 16.7 develops models for monthly and quarterly time series.

16.1 The Importance of Business Forecasting

Forecasting is done by monitoring changes that occur over time and projecting into the future. Forecasting is commonly used in both the for-profit and not-for-profit sectors of the economy. For example, marketing executives of a retailing corporation forecast product demand, sales revenues, consumer preferences, inventory, and so on in order to make decisions regarding product promotions and strategic planning. Government officials forecast unemployment, inflation, industrial production, and revenues from income taxes in order to formulate policies. And the administrators of a college or university forecast student enrollment in order to plan for the construction of dormitories and academic facilities, plan for student and faculty recruitment, and make assessments of other needs.

There are two common approaches to forecasting: *qualitative* and *quantitative*. **Qualitative forecasting methods** are especially important when historical data are unavailable. Qualitative forecasting methods are considered to be highly subjective and judgmental.

Quantitative forecasting methods make use of historical data. The goal of these methods is to use past data to predict future values. Quantitative forecasting methods are subdivided into two types: *time series* and *causal*. **Time-series forecasting methods** involve forecasting future values based entirely on the past and present values of a variable. For example, the daily closing prices of a particular stock on the New York Stock Exchange constitute a time series. Other examples of economic or business time series are the consumer price index (CPI), the quarterly gross domestic product (GDP), and the annual sales revenues of a particular company.

Causal forecasting methods involve the determination of factors that relate to the variable you are trying to forecast. These include multiple regression analysis with lagged variables, econometric modeling, leading indicator analysis, and other economic barometers that are beyond the scope of this text (see references 2–4). The primary emphasis in this chapter is on time-series forecasting methods.

16.2 Component Factors of Time-Series Models

Time-series forecasting assumes that the factors that have influenced activities in the past and present will continue to do so in approximately the same way in the future. Time-series forecasting seeks to identify and isolate these component factors in order to make predictions. Typically, the following four factors are examined in time-series models:

- Trend
- Cyclical effect
- Irregular or random effect
- Seasonal effect

A **trend** is an overall long-term upward or downward movement in a time series. Trend is not the only component factor that can influence data in a time series. The **cyclical effect** depicts the up-and-down swings or movements through the series. Cyclical movements vary in length, usually lasting from 2 to 10 years. They differ in intensity and are often correlated with a business cycle. In some time periods, the values are higher than would be predicted by a trend line (i.e., they are at or near the peak of a cycle). In other time periods, the values are lower than would be predicted by a trend line (i.e., they are at or near the bottom of a cycle). Any data that do not follow the trend modified by the cyclical component are considered part of the **irregular effect**, or **random effect**. When you have monthly or quarterly data, an additional component, the **seasonal effect**, is considered, along with the trend, cyclical, and irregular effects.

Your first step in a time-series analysis is to plot the data and observe whether any patterns exist over time. You must determine whether there is a long-term upward or downward movement in the series (i.e., a trend). If there is no obvious long-term upward or downward trend, then you can use moving averages or exponential smoothing to smooth the series (see Section 16.3). If a trend is present, you can consider several time-series forecasting methods. (See Sections 16.4 and 16.5 for forecasting annual data and Section 16.7 for forecasting monthly or quarterly time series.)

16.3 Smoothing an Annual Time Series

One of the investments considered in The Principled scenario is three-month U.S. Treasury bills. Table 16.1 gives the rate for three-month U.S. Treasury bills at the end of the year from 1991 to 2009 (stored in Treasury). Figure 16.1 presents the time-series plot.

TABLE 16.1

Rate for Three-Month U.S. Treasury Bills from 1991 to 2009

Year	Rate	Year	Rate	Year	Rate
1991	5.38	1997	5.06	2003	1.01
1992	3.43	1998	4.78	2004	1.37
1993	3.00	1999	4.64	2005	3.15
1994	4.25	2000	5.82	2006	4.73
1995	5.49	2001	3.40	2007	4.36
1996	5.01	2002	1.61	2008	1.37
				2009	0.15

Source: Board of Governors of the Federal Reserve System, **www.federalreserve.gov**.

FIGURE 16.1

Plot of three-month U.S. Treasury bill rate from 1991 to 2009

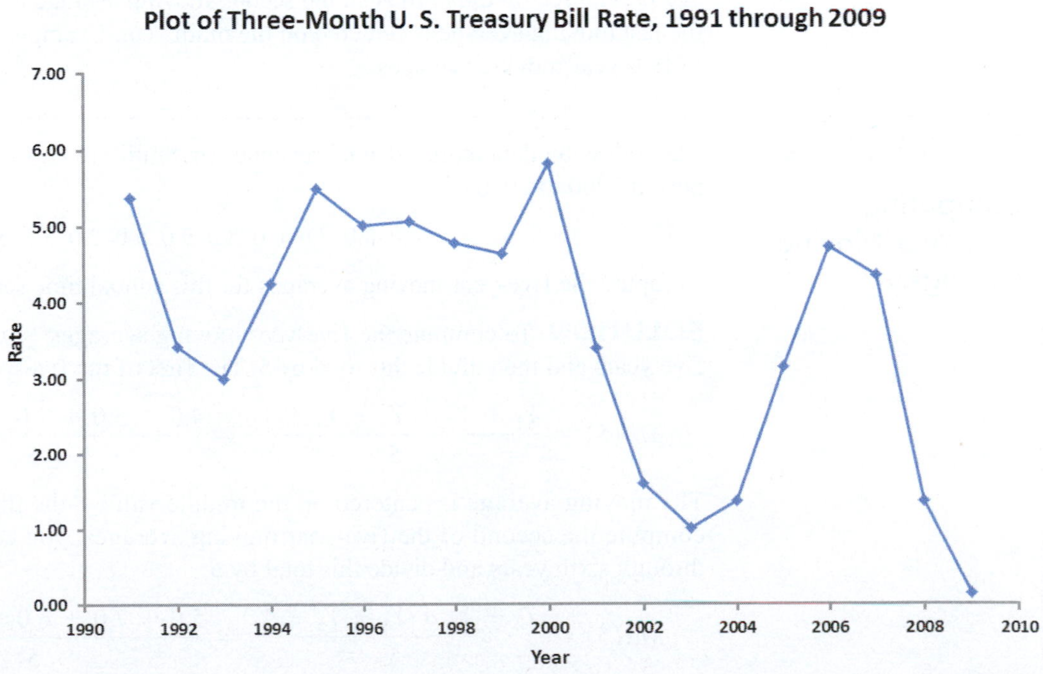

When you examine annual data, your visual impression of the long-term trend in the series is sometimes obscured by the amount of variation from year to year. Often, you cannot judge whether any long-term upward or downward trend exists in the series. To get a better overall impression of the pattern of movement in the data over time, you can use the methods of *moving averages* or *exponential smoothing*.

Moving Averages

Moving averages for a chosen period of length L consist of a series of means, each computed over time for a sequence of L observed values. Moving averages, represented by the symbol $MA(L)$, can be greatly affected by the value chosen for L, which should be an integer value that corresponds to, or is a multiple of, the estimated average length of a cycle in the time series.

To illustrate, suppose you want to compute five-year moving averages from a series that has $n = 11$ years. Because $L = 5$, the five-year moving averages consist of a series of means computed by averaging consecutive sequences of five values. You compute the first five-year moving average by summing the values for the first five years in the series and dividing by 5:

$$MA(5) = \frac{Y_1 + Y_2 + Y_3 + Y_4 + Y_5}{5}$$

You compute the second five-year moving average by summing the values of years 2 through 6 in the series and then dividing by 5:

$$MA(5) = \frac{Y_2 + Y_3 + Y_4 + Y_5 + Y_6}{5}$$

You continue this process until you have computed the last of these five-year moving averages by summing the values of the last 5 years in the series (i.e., years 7 through 11) and then dividing by 5:

$$MA(5) = \frac{Y_7 + Y_8 + Y_9 + Y_{10} + Y_{11}}{5}$$

When you have annual time-series data, L should be an *odd* number of years. By following this rule, you are unable to compute any moving averages for the first $(L - 1)/2$ years or the last $(L - 1)/2$ years of the series. Thus, for a five-year moving average, you cannot make computations for the first two years or the last two years of the series.

When plotting moving averages, you plot each of the computed values against the middle year of the sequence of years used to compute it. If $n = 11$ and $L = 5$, the first moving average is centered on the third year, the second moving average is centered on the fourth year, and the last moving average is centered on the ninth year. Example 16.1 illustrates the computation of five-year moving averages.

EXAMPLE 16.1 Computing Five-Year Moving Averages

The following data represent total revenues (in $millions) for a fast-food store over the 11-year period 2000 to 2010:

4.0 5.0 7.0 6.0 8.0 9.0 5.0 2.0 3.5 5.5 6.5

Compute the five-year moving averages for this annual time series.

SOLUTION To compute the five-year moving averages, you first compute the total for the five years and then divide this total by 5. The first of the five-year moving averages is

$$MA(5) = \frac{Y_1 + Y_2 + Y_3 + Y_4 + Y_5}{5} = \frac{4.0 + 5.0 + 7.0 + 6.0 + 8.0}{5} = \frac{30.0}{5} = 6.0$$

The moving average is centered on the middle value—the third year of this time series. To compute the second of the five-year moving averages, you compute the total of the second through sixth years and divide this total by 5:

$$MA(5) = \frac{Y_2 + Y_3 + Y_4 + Y_5 + Y_6}{5} = \frac{5.0 + 7.0 + 6.0 + 8.0 + 9.0}{5} = \frac{35.0}{5} = 7.0$$

This moving average is centered on the new middle value—the fourth year of the time series. The remaining moving averages are

$$MA(5) = \frac{Y_3 + Y_4 + Y_5 + Y_6 + Y_7}{5} = \frac{7.0 + 6.0 + 8.0 + 9.0 + 5.0}{5} = \frac{35.0}{5} = 7.0$$

$$MA(5) = \frac{Y_4 + Y_5 + Y_6 + Y_7 + Y_8}{5} = \frac{6.0 + 8.0 + 9.0 + 5.0 + 2.0}{5} = \frac{30.0}{5} = 6.0$$

$$MA(5) = \frac{Y_5 + Y_6 + Y_7 + Y_8 + Y_9}{5} = \frac{8.0 + 9.0 + 5.0 + 2.0 + 3.5}{5} = \frac{27.5}{5} = 5.5$$

$$MA(5) = \frac{Y_6 + Y_7 + Y_8 + Y_9 + Y_{10}}{5} = \frac{9.0 + 5.0 + 2.0 + 3.5 + 5.5}{5} = \frac{25.0}{5} = 5.0$$

$$MA(5) = \frac{Y_7 + Y_8 + Y_9 + Y_{10} + Y_{11}}{5} = \frac{5.0 + 2.0 + 3.5 + 5.5 + 6.5}{5} = \frac{22.5}{5} = 4.5$$

These moving averages are centered on their respective middle values—the fifth, sixth, seventh, eighth, and ninth years in the time series. When you use the five-year moving averages, you are unable to compute a moving average for the first two or last two values in the time series.

In practice, you can avoid the tedious computations by using Excel or Minitab to compute moving averages. Figure 16.2 presents the annual three-month U.S. Treasury bill rate data from 1991 through 2009, the computations for three- and seven-year moving averages, and a plot of the original data and the moving averages.

FIGURE 16.2

Excel worksheet with superimposed chart for the three-year and seven-year moving averages for the three-month U.S. Treasury bill rate

Year	Rate	MA 3-Year	MA 7-Year
1991	5.38	#N/A	#N/A
1992	3.43	3.94	#N/A
1993	3.00	3.56	#N/A
1994	4.25	4.25	4.52
1995	5.49	4.92	4.43
1996	5.01	5.19	4.60
1997	5.06	4.95	5.01
1998	4.78	4.83	4.89
1999	4.64	5.08	4.33
2000	5.82	4.62	3.76
2001	3.40	3.61	3.23
2002	1.61	2.01	3.00
2003	1.01	1.33	3.01
2004	1.37	1.84	2.80
2005	3.15	3.08	2.51
2006	4.73	4.08	2.31
2007	4.36	3.49	#N/A
2008	1.37	1.96	#N/A
2009	0.15	#N/A	#N/A

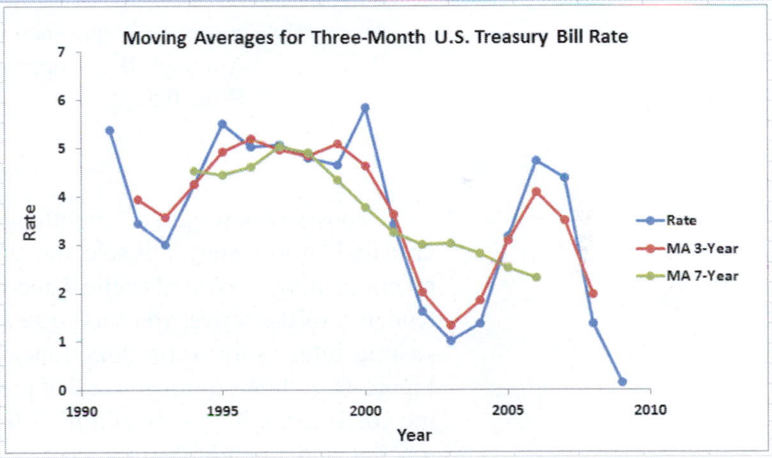

In Figure 16.2, there is no three-year moving average for the first year and the last year, and there is no seven-year moving average for the first three years and last three years. Both the three-year and seven-year moving averages have smoothed out the large amount of variation that exists in the three-month U.S. Treasury bill rates. The seven-year moving average smoothes the series more than the three-year moving average because the period is longer. However, the longer the period, the smaller the number of moving averages you can compute. Therefore, selecting moving averages that are longer than seven years is usually undesirable because too many moving average values are missing at the beginning and end of the series. The selection of L, the length of the period used for constructing the averages, is highly subjective. If cyclical fluctuations are present in the data, choose an integer value of L that corresponds to (or is a multiple of) the estimated length of a cycle in the series. For annual time-series data that has no obvious cyclical fluctuations, most people choose three years, five years, or seven years as the value of L, depending on the amount of smoothing desired and the amount of data available.

Exponential Smoothing

Exponential smoothing consists of a series of *exponentially weighted* moving averages. The weights assigned to the values change so that the most recent value receives the highest weight, the previous value receives the second-highest weight, and so on, with the first value receiving the lowest weight. Throughout the series, each exponentially smoothed value depends on all previous values, which is an advantage of exponential smoothing over the method of moving averages. Exponential smoothing also allows you to compute short-term (one period into the future) forecasts when the presence and type of long-term trend in a time series is difficult to determine.

The equation developed for exponentially smoothing a series in any time period, i, is based on only three terms—the current value in the time series, Y_i; the previously computed exponentially smoothed value, E_{i-1}; and an assigned weight or smoothing coefficient, W. You use Equation (16.1) to exponentially smooth a time series.

Computing an Exponentially Smoothed Value in Time Period i

$$E_1 = Y_1 \qquad \textbf{(16.1)}$$

$$E_i = WY_i + (1 - W)E_{i-1} \quad i = 2, 3, 4, \ldots$$

where

E_i = value of the exponentially smoothed series being computed in time period i

E_{i-1} = value of the exponentially smoothed series already computed in time period $i - 1$

Y_i = observed value of the time series in period i

W = subjectively assigned weight or smoothing coefficient (where $0 < W < 1$). Although W can approach 1.0, in virtually all business applications, $W \leq 0.5$.

Choosing the weight or smoothing coefficient (i.e., W) that you assign to the time series is critical. Unfortunately, this selection is somewhat subjective. If your goal is to smooth a series by eliminating unwanted cyclical and irregular variations in order to see the overall long-term tendency of the series, you should select a small value for W (close to 0). If your goal is forecasting future short-term directions, you should choose a large value for W (close to 0.5). Figure 16.3 shows a worksheet that presents the exponentially smoothed values (with smoothing coefficients $W = 0.50$ and $W = 0.25$), the three-month U.S. Treasury bill rates from 1991 to 2009, and a plot of the original data and the two exponentially smoothed time series.

FIGURE 16.3

Excel worksheet with superimposed chart for the exponentially smoothed series ($W = 0.50$ and $W = 0.25$) of the three-month U.S. Treasury bill rates

	A	B	C	D
1	Year	Rate	ES(W=.50)	ES(W=.25)
2	1991	5.38	5.38	5.38
3	1992	3.43	4.41	4.89
4	1993	3.00	3.70	4.42
5	1994	4.25	3.98	4.38
6	1995	5.49	4.73	4.66
7	1996	5.01	4.87	4.74
8	1997	5.06	4.97	4.82
9	1998	4.78	4.87	4.81
10	1999	4.64	4.76	4.77
11	2000	5.82	5.29	5.03
12	2001	3.40	4.34	4.62
13	2002	1.61	2.98	3.87
14	2003	1.01	1.99	3.16
15	2004	1.37	1.68	2.71
16	2005	3.15	2.42	2.82
17	2006	4.73	3.57	3.30
18	2007	4.36	3.97	3.56
19	2008	1.37	2.67	3.01
20	2009	0.15	1.41	2.30

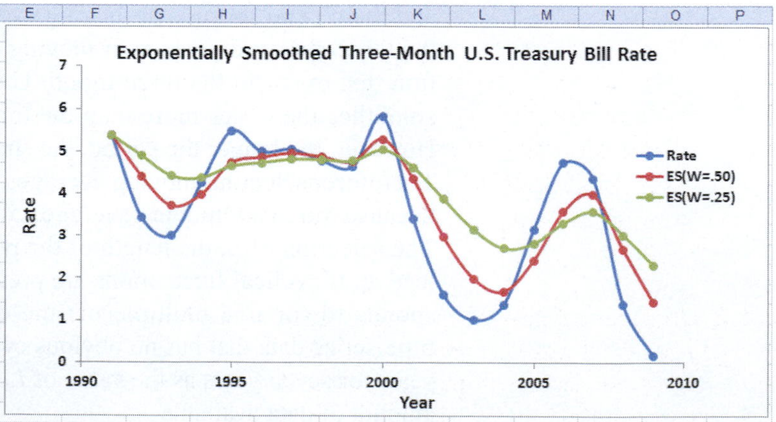

To illustrate these exponential smoothing computations for a smoothing coefficient of $W = 0.25$, you begin with the initial value $Y_{1991} = 5.38$ as the first smoothed value ($E_{1991} = 5.38$). Then, using the value of the time series for 1992 ($Y_{1992} = 3.43$), you smooth the series for 1992 by computing

$$E_{1992} = WY_{1992} + (1 - W)E_{1991}$$
$$= (0.25)(3.43) + (0.75)(5.38) = 4.89$$

To smooth the series for 1993:

$$E_{1993} = WY_{1993} + (1 - W)E_{1992}$$
$$= (0.25)(3.0) + (0.75)(4.89) = 4.42$$

To smooth the series for 1994:

$$E_{1994} = WY_{1994} + (1 - W)E_{1993}$$
$$= (0.25)(4.25) + (0.75)(4.42) = 4.38$$

You continue this process until you have computed the exponentially smoothed values for all 19 years in the series, as shown in Figure 16.3.

To use exponential smoothing for forecasting, you use the smoothed value in the current time period as the forecast of the value in the following period ($\hat{Y}_{i+1}$).

FORECASTING TIME PERIOD $i + 1$

$$\hat{Y}_{i+1} = E_i \qquad \textbf{(16.2)}$$

To forecast the three-month U.S. Treasury bill rates at the end of 2010, using a smoothing coefficient of $W = 0.25$, you use the smoothed value for 2009 as its estimate. Figure 16.3 shows that this value is 2.30. (How close is this forecast? Look up the three-month U.S. Treasury bill rate at **www.federalreserve.gov** to find out.) When the value for 2010 becomes available, you can use Equation (16.1) to make a forecast for 2011 by computing the smoothed value for 2010, as follows:

$$\text{Current smoothed value} = (W)(\text{Current value}) + (1 - W)(\text{Previous smoothest value})$$
$$E_{2010} = WY_{2010} + (1 - W)E_{2009}$$

Or, in terms of forecasting, you compute the following:

$$\text{New forecast} = (W)(\text{Current value}) + (1 - W)(\text{Current forecast})$$
$$\hat{Y}_{2011} = WY_{2010} + (1 - W)\hat{Y}_{2010}$$

Problems for Section 16.3

LEARNING THE BASICS

16.1 If you are using exponential smoothing for forecasting an annual time series of revenues, what is your forecast for next year if the smoothed value for this year is \$32.4 million?

16.2 Consider a nine-year moving average used to smooth a time series that was first recorded in 2002.

a. Which year serves as the first centered value in the smoothed series?

b. How many years of values in the series are lost when computing all the nine-year moving averages?

16.3 You are using exponential smoothing on an annual time series concerning total revenues (in millions of dollars). You decide to use a smoothing coefficient of $W = 0.20$, and the exponentially smoothed value for 2010 is $E_{2010} = (0.20)(12.1) + (0.80)(9.4)$.

a. What is the smoothed value of this series in 2010?

b. What is the smoothed value of this series in 2011 if the value of the series in that year is \$11.5 million?

APPLYING THE CONCEPTS

SELF Test **16.4** The following data (stored in Movie Attendance) represent the yearly movie attendance (in billions) from 2001 to 2009:

Year	Attendance
2001	1.44
2002	1.60
2003	1.52
2004	1.48
2005	1.38
2006	1.40
2007	1.40
2008	1.36
2009	1.42

Source: Data extracted from Motion Picture Association of America, **www.mpaa.org**.

a. Plot the time series.
b. Fit a three-year moving average to the data and plot the results.
c. Using a smoothing coefficient of $W = 0.50$, exponentially smooth the series and plot the results.
d. What is your exponentially smoothed forecast for 2010?
e. Repeat (c) and (d), using $W = 0.25$.
f. Compare the results of (d) and (e).

16.5 The following data, stored in NASCAR, provide the number of accidents in the NASCAR Sprint Cup series from 2001 to 2009:

Year	Accidents
2001	200
2002	186
2003	235
2004	204
2005	253
2006	237
2007	240
2008	211
2009	195

Source: Data extracted from C. Graves, "On-Track Incidents Decrease in Sprint Cup," *USA Today*, December 16, 2008, p. 1C; and **usatoday.com/sports/graphics/2009/nascar-crash-database/flash.htm**.

a. Plot the time series.
b. Fit a three-year moving average to the data and plot the results.
c. Using a smoothing coefficient of $W = 0.50$, exponentially smooth the series and plot the results.
d. What is your exponentially smoothed forecast for 2010?
e. Repeat (c) and (d), using $W = 0.25$.
f. Compare the results of (d) and (e).

16.6 How have stocks performed in the past? The following table presents the data stored in Stock Performance, which show the performance of a broad measure of stock performance (by percentage) for each decade from the 1830s through the 2000s:

Decade	Performance (%)	Decade	Performance (%)
1830s	2.8	1920s	13.3
1840s	12.8	1930s	−2.2
1850s	6.6	1940s	9.6
1860s	12.5	1950s	18.2
1870s	7.5	1960s	8.3
1880s	6.0	1970s	6.6
1890s	5.5	1980s	16.6
1900s	10.9	1990s	17.6
1910s	2.2	2000s*	−0.5

*Through December 15, 2009.

Source: T. Lauricella, "Investors Hope the '10s Beat the '00s," *The Wall Street Journal*, December 21, 2009, pp. C1, C2.

a. Plot the time series.
b. Fit a three-period moving average to the data and plot the results.
c. Using a smoothing coefficient of $W = 0.50$, exponentially smooth the series and plot the results.
d. What is your exponentially smoothed forecast for the 2010s?
e. Repeat (c) and (d), using $W = 0.25$.
f. Compare the results of (d) and (e).
g. What conclusions can you reach concerning how stocks have performed in the past?

16.7 The following data (stored in EuroDollar) represent the sixth-month Eurodollar deposit rate from 2001 to 2009:

Year	EuroDollar Rate
2001	3.65
2002	1.81
2003	1.16
2004	1.72
2005	3.71
2006	5.27
2007	5.27
2008	3.48
2009	1.51

Source: **www.federalreserve.gov/releases/h15/data/Annual/H15_ED_M6.txt**.

a. Plot the data.
b. Fit a three-year moving average to the data and plot the results.
c. Using a smoothing coefficient of $W = 0.50$, exponentially smooth the series and plot the results.
d. What is your exponentially smoothed forecast for 2010?
e. Repeat (c) and (d), using a smoothing coefficient of $W = 0.25$.
f. Compare the results of (d) and (e).

16.8 The file **Audits** contains the number of audits of corporations with assets of more than $250 million conducted by the Internal Revenue Service. (Data extracted from K. McCoy, "IRS Audits Big Firms Less Often," *USA Today*, April 15, 2010, p. 1B.)

a. Plot the data.

b. Fit a three-year moving average to the data and plot the results.

c. Using a smoothing coefficient of $W = 0.50$, exponentially smooth the series and plot the results.

d. What is your exponentially smoothed forecast for 2010?

e. Repeat (c) and (d), using a smoothing coefficient of $W = 0.25$.

f. Compare the results of (d) and (e).

16.4 Least-Squares Trend Fitting and Forecasting

Trend is the component factor of a time series most often used to make intermediate and long-range forecasts. To get a visual impression of the overall long-term movements in a time series, you construct a time-series plot. If a straight-line trend adequately fits the data, you can use a linear trend model [see Equation (16.3) and Section 13.2]. If the time-series data indicate some long-run downward or upward quadratic movement, you can use a quadratic trend model [see Equation (16.4) and Section 15.1]. When the time-series data increase at a rate such that the percentage difference from value to value is constant, you can use an exponential trend model [see Equation (16.5)].

The Linear Trend Model

The **linear trend model**:

$$Y_i = \beta_0 + \beta_1 X_i + \varepsilon_i$$

is the simplest forecasting model. Equation (16.3) defines the linear trend forecasting equation.

LINEAR TREND FORECASTING EQUATION

$$\hat{Y}_i = b_0 + b_1 X_i \quad \textbf{(16.3)}$$

Recall that in linear regression analysis, you use the method of least squares to compute the sample slope, b_1, and the sample Y intercept, b_0. You then substitute the values for X into Equation (16.3) to predict Y.

When using the least-squares method for fitting trends in a time series, you can simplify the interpretation of the coefficients by assigning coded values to the X (time) variable. You assign consecutively numbered integers, starting with 0, as the coded values for the time periods. For example, in time-series data that have been recorded annually for 15 years, you assign the coded value 0 to the first year, the coded value 1 to the second year, the coded value 2 to the third year, and so on, concluding by assigning 14 to the fifteenth year.

In The Principled scenario on page 665, one of the companies of interest is The Coca-Cola Company. Founded in 1886 and headquartered in Atlanta, Georgia, Coca-Cola manufactures, distributes, and markets more than 3,300 beverages in over 200 countries worldwide. Some of its brands include Barq's, Dasani, Full Throttle, Glacéau Vitaminwater, Minute Maid, Powerade, and Sprite in addition to Coca-Cola. According to The Coca-Cola Company's website (**www.thecoca-colacompany.com**), revenues in 2009 topped $31 billion. Table 16.2 lists The Coca-Cola Company's gross revenues (in billions of dollars) from 1995 to 2009 (stored in **Coca-Cola**).

TABLE 16.2

Revenues (in Billions of Dollars) for The Coca-Cola Company (1995–2009)

Year	Revenue	Year	Revenue
1995	18.0	2003	21.0
1996	18.5	2004	21.9
1997	18.9	2005	23.1
1998	18.8	2006	24.1
1999	19.8	2007	28.9
2000	20.5	2008	31.9
2001	20.1	2009	31.0
2002	19.6		

Source: Data extracted from *Mergent's Handbook of Common Stocks,* 2006; and **www.thecoca-colacompany.com**.

Figure 16.4 presents the regression results for the simple linear regression that uses the consecutive coded values 0 through 14 as the X (coded year) variable. These results produce the following linear trend forecasting equation:

$$\hat{Y}_i = 16.0017 + 0.9150X_i$$

where $X_1 = 0$ represents 1995.

FIGURE 16.4

Excel and Minitab regression results for a linear trend model to forecast revenues (in billions of dollars) for The Coca-Cola Company

	A	B	C	D	E	F	G
1	Linear Trend Model for Coca-Cola Company Revenue						
2							
3	*Regression Statistics*						
4	Multiple R	0.8909					
5	R Square	0.7938					
6	Adjusted R Square	0.7779					
7	Standard Error	2.1645					
8	Observations	15					
9							
10	ANOVA						
11		*df*	*SS*	*MS*	*F*	*Significance F*	
12	Regression	1	234.4230	234.4230	50.0358	0.0000	
13	Residual	13	60.9063	4.6851			
14	Total	14	295.3293				
15							
16		*Coefficients*	*Standard Error*	*t Stat*	*P-value*	*Lower 95%*	*Upper 95%*
17	Intercept	16.0017	1.0641	15.0382	0.0000	13.7029	18.3004
18	Coded Year	0.9150	0.1294	7.0736	0.0000	0.6355	1.1945

Regression Analysis: Revenues versus Coded Year

```
The regression equation is
Revenues = 16.0 + 0.915 Coded Year

Predictor     Coef  SE Coef      T      P
Constant    16.002    1.064  15.04  0.000
Coded Year  0.9150   0.1294   7.07  0.000

S = 2.16451   R-Sq = 79.4%   R-Sq(adj) = 77.8%

Analysis of Variance
Source          DF      SS      MS      F      P
Regression       1  234.42  234.42  50.04  0.000
Residual Error  13   60.91    4.69
Total           14  295.33
```

You interpret the regression coefficients as follows:

- The Y intercept, $b_0 = 16.0017$, is the predicted revenues (in billions of dollars) at The Coca-Cola Company during the origin or base year, 1995.
- The slope, $b_1 = 0.9150$, indicates that revenues are predicted to increase by 0.915 billion dollars per year.

To project the trend in the revenues at Coca-Cola to 2010, you substitute $X_{16} = 15$, the code for 2010, into the linear trend forecasting equation:

$$\hat{Y}_i = 16.0017 + 0.9150(15) = 29.7267 \text{ billions of dollars}$$

The trend line is plotted in Figure 16.5, along with the observed values of the time series. There is a strong upward linear trend, and r^2 is 0.7938, indicating that more than 79% of the variation in revenues is explained by the linear trend of the time series. To investigate whether a different trend model might provide a better fit, a *quadratic* trend model and an *exponential* trend model are fitted next.

FIGURE 16.5
Plot of the linear trend forecasting equation for The Coca-Cola Company revenue data

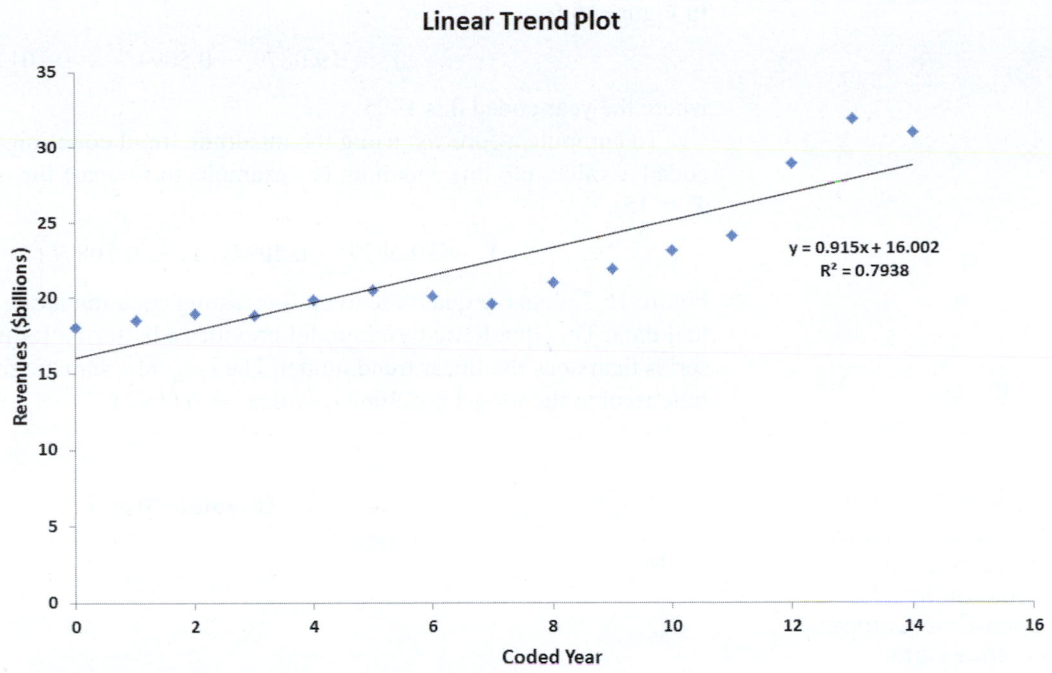

The Quadratic Trend Model

A **quadratic trend model**:

$$\hat{Y}_i = \beta_0 + \beta_1 X_i + \beta_2 X_i^2 + \varepsilon_i$$

is the simplest nonlinear model. Using the least-squares method described in Section 15.1, you can develop a quadratic trend forecasting equation, as presented in Equation (16.4).

QUADRATIC TREND FORECASTING EQUATION

$$\hat{Y}_i = b_0 + b_1 X_i + b_2 X_i^2 \quad \textbf{(16.4)}$$

where

b_0 = estimated Y intercept

b_1 = estimated *linear* effect on Y

b_2 = estimated *quadratic* effect on Y

Figure 16.6 presents the regression results for the quadratic trend model used to forecast revenues at The Coca-Cola Company.

FIGURE 16.6
Excel and Minitab regression results for the quadratic trend model to forecast revenues for The Coca-Cola Company

	A	B	C	D	E	F	G
1	Quadratic Trend Model for Coca-Cola Company Revenues						
2							
3	*Regression Statistics*						
4	Multiple R	0.9687					
5	R Square	0.9384					
6	Adjusted R Square	0.9281					
7	Standard Error	1.2315					
8	Observations	15					
9							
10	ANOVA						
11		*df*	*SS*	*MS*	*F*	*Significance F*	
12	Regression	2	277.1289	138.5644	91.3590	0.0000	
13	Residual	12	18.2004	1.5167			
14	Total	14	295.3293				
15							
16		*Coefficients*	*Standard Error*	*t Stat*	*P-value*	*Lower 95%*	*Upper 95%*
17	Intercept	19.0879	0.8395	22.7363	0.0000	17.2587	20.9171
18	Coded Year	-0.5094	0.2783	-1.8302	0.0922	-1.1159	0.0970
19	Coded Year^2	0.1017	0.0192	5.3063	0.0002	0.0600	0.1435

Regression Analysis: Revenues versus Coded Year, Coded Year^2

```
The regression equation is
Revenues = 19.1 - 0.509 Coded Year + 0.102 Coded Year^2

Predictor         Coef   SE Coef      T      P
Constant       19.0879    0.8395  22.74  0.000
Coded Year     -0.5094    0.2783  -1.83  0.092
Coded Year^2   0.10175   0.01917   5.31  0.000

S = 1.23154   R-Sq = 93.8%   R-Sq(adj) = 92.8%

Analysis of Variance
Source          DF      SS      MS      F      P
Regression       2  277.13  138.56  91.36  0.000
Residual Error  12   18.20    1.52
Total           14  295.33
```

In Figure 16.6,

$$\hat{Y}_i = 19.0879 - 0.5094X_i + 0.1017X_i^2$$

where the year coded 0 is 1995.

To compute a forecast using the quadratic trend equation, you substitute the appropriate coded X value into this equation. For example, to forecast the trend in revenues for 2010 (i.e., $X = 15$),

$$\hat{Y}_i = 19.0879 - 0.5094(15) + 0.1087(15)^2 = 35.9044$$

Figure 16.7 plots the quadratic trend forecasting equation along with the time series for the actual data. This quadratic trend model provides a better fit (adjusted $r^2 = 0.9281$) to the time series than does the linear trend model. The t_{STAT} test statistic for the contribution of the quadratic term to the model is 5.3063 (p-value $= 0.0002$).

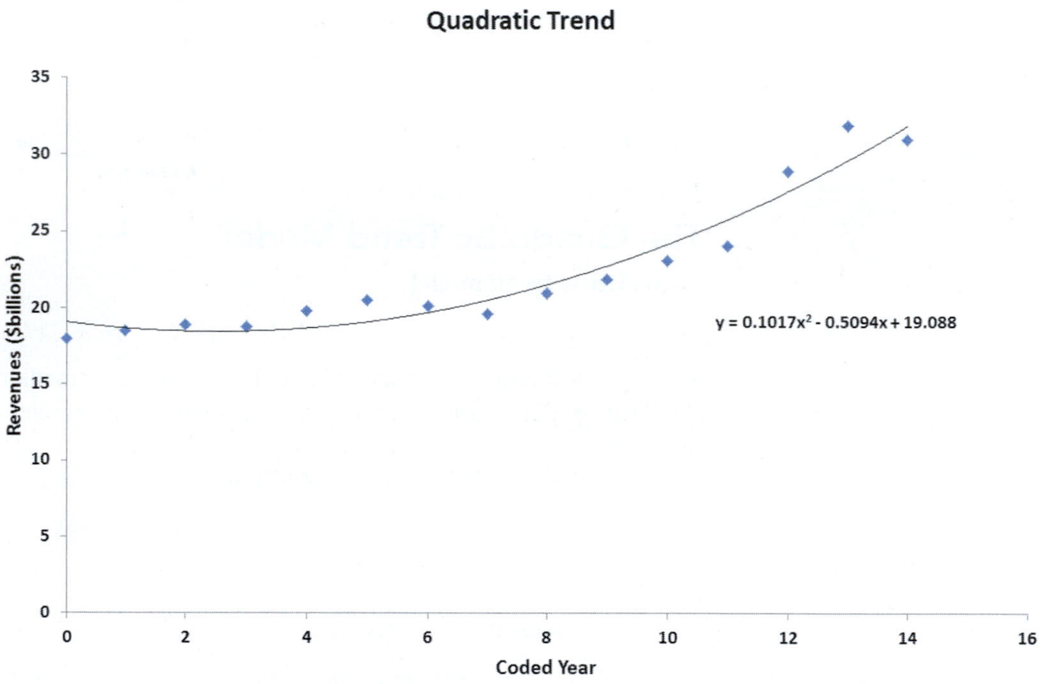

FIGURE 16.7
Plot of the quadratic trend forecasting equation for The Coca-Cola Company revenue data

The Exponential Trend Model

When a time series increases at a rate such that the percentage difference from value to value is constant, an exponential trend is present. Equation (16.5) defines the **exponential trend model**.

EXPONENTIAL TREND MODEL

$$Y_i = \beta_0 \beta_1^{X_i} \varepsilon_i \quad \textbf{(16.5)}$$

where

$\beta_0 = Y$ intercept

$(\beta_1 - 1) \times 100\%$ is the annual compound growth rate (in %)

The model in Equation (16.5) is not in the form of a linear regression model. To transform this nonlinear model to a linear model, you use a base 10 logarithm transformation.[1] Taking the logarithm of each side of Equation (16.5) results in Equation (16.6).

[1]Alternatively, you can use base e logarithms. For more information on logarithms, see Section A.3 in Appendix A.

TRANSFORMED EXPONENTIAL TREND MODEL

$$\begin{aligned}\log(Y_i) &= \log(\beta_0\beta_1^{X_i}\varepsilon_i) \\ &= \log(\beta_0) + \log(\beta_1^{X_i}) + \log(\varepsilon_i) \\ &= \log(\beta_0) + X_i\log(\beta_1) + \log(\varepsilon_i)\end{aligned} \quad \textbf{(16.6)}$$

Equation (16.6) is a linear model you can estimate using the least-squares method, with log (Y_i) as the dependent variable and X_i as the independent variable. This results in Equation (16.7).

EXPONENTIAL TREND FORECASTING EQUATION

$$\log(\hat{Y}_i) = b_0 + b_1X_i \quad \textbf{(16.7a)}$$

where

$$b_0 = \text{estimate of } \log(\beta_0) \text{and thus } 10^{b_0} = \hat{\beta}_0$$

$$b_1 = \text{estimate of } \log(\beta_1) \text{ and thus } 10^{b_1} = \hat{\beta}_1$$

therefore,

$$\hat{Y}_i = \hat{\beta}_0\hat{\beta}_1^{X_i} \quad \textbf{(16.7b)}$$

where

$(\hat{\beta}_1 - 1) \times 100\%$ is the estimated annual compound growth rate (in %)

Figure 16.8 shows the regression results for an exponential trend model of revenues at The Coca-Cola Company.

FIGURE 16.8

Excel and Minitab regression results for an exponential model to forecast revenues for The Coca-Cola Company

	A	B	C	D	E	F	G
1	Exponential Trend Model for Coca-Cola Company Revenue						
2							
3	*Regression Statistics*						
4	Multiple R	0.9165					
5	R Square	0.8400					
6	Adjusted R Square	0.8277					
7	Standard Error	0.0340					
8	Observations	15					
9							
10	ANOVA						
11		*df*	*SS*	*MS*	*F*	*Significance F*	
12	Regression	1	0.0790	0.0790	68.2657	0.0000	
13	Residual	13	0.0150	0.0012			
14	Total	14	0.0940				
15							
16		*Coefficients*	*Standard Error*	*t Stat*	*P-value*	*Lower 95%*	*Upper 95%*
17	Intercept	1.2252	0.0167	73.2614	0.0000	1.1890	1.2613
18	Coded Year	0.0168	0.0020	8.2623	0.0000	0.0124	0.0212

Regression Analysis: Log(Revenues) versus Coded Year

```
The regression equation is
Log(Revenues) = 1.23 + 0.0168 Coded Year

Predictor        Coef    SE Coef      T      P
Constant      1.22517    0.01672  73.26  0.000
Coded Year   0.016797   0.002033   8.26  0.000

S = 0.0340183   R-Sq = 84.0%   R-Sq(adj) = 82.8%

Analysis of Variance
Source          DF        SS        MS      F      P
Regression       1  0.079000  0.079000  68.27  0.000
Residual Error  13  0.015044  0.001157
Total           14  0.094045
```

Using Equation (16.7a) and the results from Figure 16.8,

$$\log(\hat{Y}_i) = 1.2252 + 0.0168X_i$$

where the year coded 0 is 1995.

You compute the values for $\hat{\beta}_0$ and $\hat{\beta}_1$ by taking the antilog of the regression coefficients (b_0 and b_1):

$$\hat{\beta}_0 = \text{antilog}(b_0) = \text{antilog}(1.2252) = 10^{1.2252} = 16.7958$$

$$\hat{\beta}_1 = \text{antilog}(b_1) = \text{antilog}(0.0168) = 10^{0.0168} = 1.0394$$

Thus, using Equation (16.7b), the exponential trend forecasting equation is

$$\hat{Y}_i = (16.7958)(1.0394)^{X_i}$$

where the year coded 0 is 1995.

The Y intercept, $\hat{\beta}_0 = 16.7958$ billions of dollars, is the revenue forecast for the base year 1995. The value $(\hat{\beta}_1 - 1) \times 100\% = 3.94\%$ is the annual compound growth rate in revenues at The Coca-Cola Company.

For forecasting purposes, you substitute the appropriate coded X values into either Equation (16.7a) or Equation (16.7b). For example, to forecast revenues for 2010 (i.e., $X = 15$) using Equation (16.7a),

$$\log(\hat{Y}_i) = 1.2252 + 0.0168(15) = 1.4772$$
$$\hat{Y}_i = \text{antilog}(1.4772) = 10^{1.4772} = 30.0054 \text{ billions of dollars}$$

Figure 16.9 plots the exponential trend forecasting equation, along with the time-series data. The adjusted r^2 for the exponential trend model (0.8277) is greater than the adjusted r^2 for the linear trend model (0.7779) but less than the quadratic model (0.9281).

FIGURE 16.9

Plot of the exponential trend forecasting equation for The Coca-Cola Company revenues

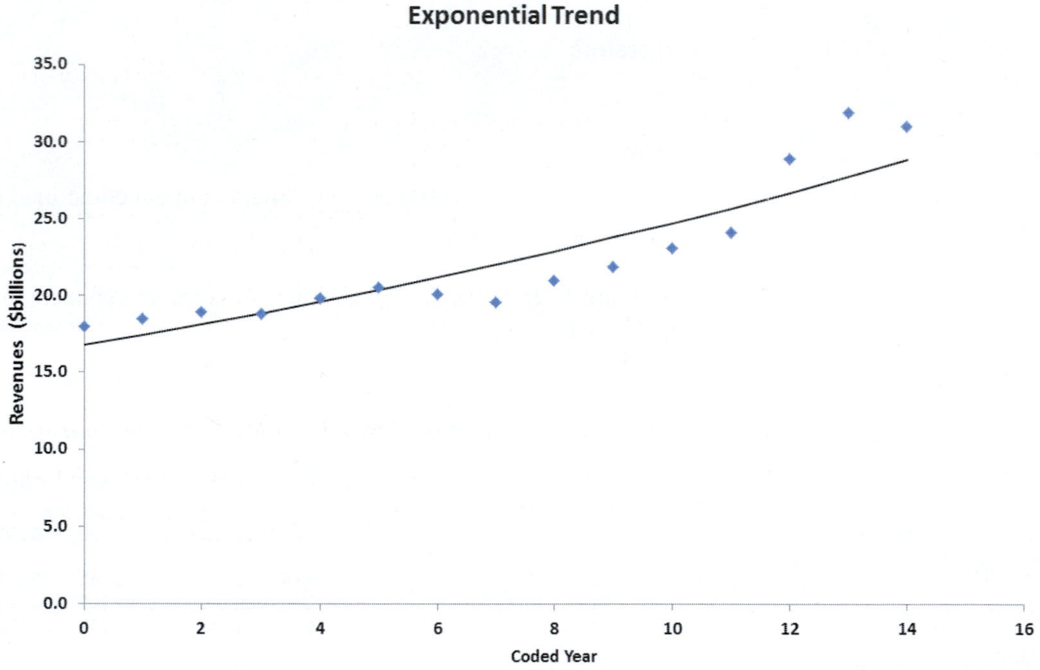

Model Selection Using First, Second, and Percentage Differences

You have used the linear, quadratic, and exponential models to forecast revenues for The Coca-Cola Company. How can you determine which of these models is the most appropriate model? In addition to visually inspecting time-series plots and comparing adjusted r^2 values, you can compute and examine first, second, and percentage differences. The identifying features of linear, quadratic, and exponential trend models are as follows:

- If a linear trend model provides a perfect fit to a time series, then the first differences are constant. Thus,

$$(Y_2 - Y_1) = (Y_3 - Y_2) = \ldots = (Y_n - Y_{n-1})$$

- If a quadratic trend model provides a perfect fit to a time series, then the second differences are constant. Thus,

$$[(Y_3 - Y_2) - (Y_2 - Y_1)] = [(Y_4 - Y_3) - (Y_3 - Y_2)] = \ldots = [(Y_n - Y_{n-1}) - (Y_{n-1} - Y_{n-2})]$$

- If an exponential trend model provides a perfect fit to a time series, then the percentage differences between consecutive values are constant. Thus,

$$\frac{Y_2 - Y_1}{Y_1} \times 100\% = \frac{Y_3 - Y_2}{Y_2} \times 100\% = \cdots = \frac{Y_n - Y_{n-1}}{Y_{n-1}} \times 100\%$$

Although you should not expect a perfectly fitting model for any particular set of time-series data, you can consider the first differences, second differences, and percentage differences as guides in choosing an appropriate model. Examples 16.2, 16.3, and 16.4 illustrate linear, quadratic, and exponential trend models that have perfect (or nearly perfect) fits to their respective data sets.

EXAMPLE 16.2

A Linear Trend Model with a Perfect Fit

The following time series represents the number of passengers per year (in millions) on ABC Airlines:

	Year									
	2001	**2002**	**2003**	**2004**	**2005**	**2006**	**2007**	**2008**	**2009**	**2010**
Passengers	30.0	33.0	36.0	39.0	42.0	45.0	48.0	51.0	54.0	57.0

Using first differences, show that the linear trend model provides a perfect fit to these data.

SOLUTION The following table shows the solution:

	Year									
	2001	**2002**	**2003**	**2004**	**2005**	**2006**	**2007**	**2008**	**2009**	**2010**
Passengers	30.0	33.0	36.0	39.0	42.0	45.0	48.0	51.0	54.0	57.0
First differences		3.0	3.0	3.0	3.0	3.0	3.0	3.0	3.0	3.0

The differences between consecutive values in the series are the same throughout. Thus, ABC Airlines shows a linear growth pattern. The number of passengers increases by 3 million per year.

EXAMPLE 16.3

A Quadratic Trend Model with a Perfect Fit

The following time series represents the number of passengers per year (in millions) on XYZ Airlines:

	Year									
	2001	**2002**	**2003**	**2004**	**2005**	**2006**	**2007**	**2008**	**2009**	**2010**
Passengers	30.0	31.0	33.5	37.5	43.0	50.0	58.5	68.5	80.0	93.0

Using second differences, show that the quadratic trend model provides a perfect fit to these data.

SOLUTION The following table shows the solution:

	Year									
	2001	**2002**	**2003**	**2004**	**2005**	**2006**	**2007**	**2008**	**2009**	**2010**
Passengers	30.0	31.0	33.5	37.5	43.0	50.0	58.5	68.5	80.0	93.0
First differences		1.0	2.5	4.0	5.5	7.0	8.5	10.0	11.5	13.0
Second differences			1.5	1.5	1.5	1.5	1.5	1.5	1.5	1.5

The second differences between consecutive pairs of values in the series are the same throughout. Thus, XYZ Airlines shows a quadratic growth pattern. Its rate of growth is accelerating over time.

EXAMPLE 16.4

An Exponential Trend Model with an Almost Perfect Fit

The following time series represents the number of passengers per year (in millions) for EXP Airlines:

	Year									
	2001	**2002**	**2003**	**2004**	**2005**	**2006**	**2007**	**2008**	**2009**	**2010**
Passengers	30.0	31.5	33.1	34.8	36.5	38.3	40.2	42.2	44.3	46.5

Using percentage differences, show that the exponential trend model provides almost a perfect fit to these data.

SOLUTION The following table shows the solution:

	Year									
	2001	**2002**	**2003**	**2004**	**2005**	**2006**	**2007**	**2008**	**2009**	**2010**
Passengers	30.0	31.5	33.1	34.8	36.5	38.3	40.2	42.2	44.3	46.5
First differences		1.5	1.6	1.7	1.7	1.8	1.9	2.0	2.1	2.2
Percentage differences		5.0	5.1	5.1	4.9	4.9	5.0	5.0	5.0	5.0

The percentage differences between consecutive values in the series are approximately the same throughout. Thus, EXP Airlines shows an exponential growth pattern. Its rate of growth is approximately 5% per year.

Figure 16.10 shows a worksheet that compares the first, second, and percentage differences for the revenues data at The Coca-Cola Company. Neither the first differences, second differences, nor percentage differences are constant across the series. Therefore, other models (including those considered in Section 16.5) may be more appropriate.

FIGURE 16.10

Worksheet that compares first, second, and percentage differences in revenues (in billions of dollars) for The Coca-Cola Company

	A	B	C	D	E
1	Year	Revenues	First Difference	Second Difference	Percentage Difference
2	1995	18.0	#N/A	#N/A	#N/A
3	1996	18.5	0.5	#N/A	2.78%
4	1997	18.9	0.4	-0.1	2.16%
5	1998	18.8	-0.1	-0.5	-0.53%
6	1999	19.8	1.0	1.1	5.32%
7	2000	20.5	0.7	-0.3	3.54%
8	2001	20.1	-0.4	-1.1	-1.95%
9	2002	19.6	-0.5	-0.1	-2.49%
10	2003	21.0	1.4	1.9	7.14%
11	2004	21.9	0.9	-0.5	4.29%
12	2005	23.1	1.2	0.3	5.48%
13	2006	24.1	1.0	-0.2	4.33%
14	2007	28.9	4.8	3.8	19.92%
15	2008	31.9	3.0	-1.8	10.38%
16	2009	31.0	-0.9	-3.9	-2.82%

Problems for Section 16.4

LEARNING THE BASICS

16.9 If you are using the method of least squares for fitting trends in an annual time series containing 25 consecutive yearly values,

a. what coded value do you assign to X for the first year in the series?
b. what coded value do you assign to X for the fifth year in the series?
c. what coded value do you assign to X for the most recent recorded year in the series?
d. what coded value do you assign to X if you want to project the trend and make a forecast five years beyond the last observed value?

16.10 The linear trend forecasting equation for an annual time series containing 22 values (from 1989 to 2010) on total revenues (in millions of dollars) is

$$\hat{Y}_i = 4.0 + 1.5X_i$$

a. Interpret the Y intercept, b_0.
b. Interpret the slope, b_1.
c. What is the fitted trend value for the fifth year?
d. What is the fitted trend value for the most recent year?
e. What is the projected trend forecast three years after the last value?

16.11 The linear trend forecasting equation for an annual time series containing 42 values (from 1969 to 2010) on net sales (in billions of dollars) is

$$\hat{Y}_i = 1.2 + 0.5X_i$$

a. Interpret the Y intercept, b_0.
b. Interpret the slope, b_1.
c. What is the fitted trend value for the tenth year?
d. What is the fitted trend value for the most recent year?
e. What is the projected trend forecast two years after the last value?

APPLYING THE CONCEPTS

SELF Test **16.12** Bed Bath & Beyond is a nationwide chain of retail stores that sell a wide assortment of merchandise, including domestics merchandise and home furnishings, as well as food, giftware, and health and beauty care items. The following data (stored in **Bed & Bath**) show the number of stores open at the end of the fiscal year from 1993 to 2010:

Year	Stores Open	Year	Stores Open
1993	38	2002	396
1994	45	2003	519
1995	61	2004	629
1996	80	2005	721
1997	108	2006	809
1998	141	2007	888
1999	186	2008	971
2000	241	2009	1,037
2001	311	2010	1,100

Source: Data extracted from *Bed Bath & Beyond Annual Report*, 2005, 2007, 2009, 2010.

a. Plot the data.
b. Compute a linear trend forecasting equation and plot the results.
c. Compute a quadratic trend forecasting equation and plot the results.
d. Compute an exponential trend forecasting equation and plot the results.
e. Using the forecasting equations in (b) through (d), what are your annual forecasts of the number of stores open for 2011 and 2012?
f. How can you explain the differences in the three forecasts in (e)? What forecast do you think you should use? Why?

16.13 Gross domestic product (GDP) is a major indicator of a nation's overall economic activity. It consists of personal consumption expenditures, gross domestic investment, net exports of goods and services, and government consumption expenditures. The GDP (in billions of current dollars) for the United States from 1980 to 2009 is stored in **GDP**.

Source: Data extracted from Bureau of Economic Analysis, U.S. Department of Commerce, **www.bea.gov.**

a. Plot the data.
b. Compute a linear trend forecasting equation and plot the trend line.
c. What are your forecasts for 2010 and 2011?
d. What conclusions can you reach concerning the trend in GDP?

16.14 The data in **FedReceipt** represent federal receipts from 1978 through 2009, in billions of current dollars, from individual and corporate income tax, social insurance, excise tax, estate and gift tax, customs duties, and federal reserve deposits.

Source: Data extracted from Tax Policy Center, **www.taxpolicycenter.org.**

a. Plot the series of data.
b. Compute a linear trend forecasting equation and plot the trend line.
c. What are your forecasts of the federal receipts for 2010 and 2011?
d. What conclusions can you reach concerning the trend in federal receipts?

16.15 The data in **Strategic** represent the amount of oil, in billions of barrels, held in the U.S. strategic oil reserve, from 1981 through 2009.

a. Plot the data.
b. Compute a linear trend forecasting equation and plot the trend line.
c. Compute a quadratic trend forecasting equation and plot the results.
d. Compute an exponential trend forecasting equation and plot the results.
e. Which model is the most appropriate?
f. Using the most appropriate model, forecast the number of barrels, in billions, for 2010. Check how accurate your forecast is by locating the true value for 2010 on the Internet or in a library.
g. The actual physical capacity of the strategic oil reserve is 727 billion barrels of oil. If you knew that before making a forecast in (f), how would that change your forecast?

16.16 The data shown in the following table (and stored in **Solar Power**) represent the yearly amount of solar power installed (in megawatts) in the United States from 2000 through 2008:

Year	Amount of Solar Power Installed
2000	18
2001	27
2002	44
2003	68
2004	83
2005	100
2006	140
2007	210
2008	250

Source: Data extracted from P. Davidson, "Glut of Rooftop Solar Systems Sinks Price," *USA Today*, January 13, 2009, p. 1B.

a. Plot the data.
b. Compute a linear trend forecasting equation and plot the trend line.
c. Compute a quadratic trend forecasting equation and plot the results.
d. Compute an exponential trend forecasting equation and plot the results.
e. Using the models in (b) through (d), what are your annual trend forecasts of the yearly amount of solar power installed (in megawatts) in the United States in 2009 and 2010?

16.17 Electronics are being recycled more and more due to increased requirements of states and the availability of more companies doing the recycling. The data in the following table (and stored in **E-Cycling**) represent the tons of electronic items recycled from 1999 to 2007 (the last year for which data was available):

Year	Recycled Amount
1999	157
2000	190
2001	210
2002	250
2003	290
2004	320
2005	345
2006	377
2007	414

Source: Environmental Protection Agency, 2010.

a. Plot the data.
b. Compute a linear trend forecasting equation and plot the trend line.
c. Compute a quadratic trend forecasting equation and plot the results.
d. Compute an exponential trend forecasting equation and plot the results.
e. Which model is the most appropriate?
f. Using the most appropriate model, forecast the tons of electronic items recycled in 2008.

16.18 The data in the following table (and stored in **BBSalaries**) represent the average salary of Major League Baseball players on opening day from 2000 to 2010:

Year	Salary ($millions)
2000	1.99
2001	2.29
2002	2.38
2003	2.58
2004	2.49
2005	2.63
2006	2.83
2007	2.92
2008	3.13
2009	3.26
2010	3.27

Source: Data extracted from "Baseball Salaries," *USA Today*, April 6, 2009, p. 6C; and **mlb.com.**

a. Plot the data.
b. Compute a linear trend forecasting equation and plot the trend line.
c. Compute a quadratic trend forecasting equation and plot the results.
d. Compute an exponential trend forecasting equation and plot the results.

e. Which model is the most appropriate?

f. Using the most appropriate model, forecast the average salary for 2011.

16.19 The following data (stored in **Silver**) represent the price in London for an ounce of silver (in U.S. $) on the last day of the year from 1999 to 2009:

Year	Price ($)
1999	5.330
2000	4.570
2001	4.520
2002	4.670
2003	5.965
2004	6.815
2005	8.830
2006	12.900
2007	14.760
2008	10.790
2009	16.990

Source: Data extracted from **http://www.kitco.com/gold.londonfix.html.**

a. Plot the data.

b. Compute a linear trend forecasting equation and plot the trend line.

c. Compute a quadratic trend forecasting equation and plot the results.

d. Compute an exponential trend forecasting equation and plot the results.

e. Which model is the most appropriate?

f. Using the most appropriate model, forecast the price of silver at the end of 2010.

16.20 The data in **CPI-U** reflect the annual values of the consumer price index (CPI) in the United States over the 45-year period 1965 through 2009, using 1982 through 1984 as the base period. This index measures the average change in prices over time in a fixed "market basket" of goods and services purchased by all urban consumers, including urban wage earners (i.e., clerical, professional, managerial, and technical workers; self-employed individuals; and short-term workers), unemployed individuals, and retirees.

Source: Data extracted from Bureau of Labor Statistics, U.S. Department of Labor, **www.bls.gov.**

a. Plot the data.

b. Describe the movement in this time series over the 45-year period.

c. Compute a linear trend forecasting equation and plot the trend line.

d. Compute a quadratic trend forecasting equation and plot the results.

e. Compute an exponential trend forecasting equation and plot the results.

f. Which model is the most appropriate?

g. Using the most appropriate model, forecast the CPI for 2010 and 2011.

16.21 Although you should not expect a perfectly fitting model for any time-series data, you can consider the first differences, second differences, and percentage differences for a given series as guides in choosing an appropriate model. For this problem, use each of the time series presented in the following table and stored in **Tsmodel1**:

	Year				
	2000	**2001**	**2002**	**2003**	**2004**
Time series I	10.0	15.1	24.0	36.7	53.8
Time series II	30.0	33.1	36.4	39.9	43.9
Time series III	60.0	67.9	76.1	84.0	92.2
	2005	**2006**	**2007**	**2008**	**2009**
Time series I	74.8	100.0	129.2	162.4	199.0
Time series II	48.2	53.2	58.2	64.5	70.7
Time series III	100.0	108.0	115.8	124.1	132.0

a. Determine the most appropriate model.

b. Compute the forecasting equation.

c. Forecast the value for 2010.

16.22 A time-series plot often helps you determine the appropriate model to use. For this problem, use each of the time series presented in the following table and stored in **TsModel2**.

	Year				
	2000	**2001**	**2002**	**2003**	**2004**
Time series I	100.0	115.2	130.1	144.9	160.0
Time series II	100.0	115.2	131.7	150.8	174.1
	2005	**2006**	**2007**	**2008**	**2009**
Time series I	175.0	189.8	204.9	219.8	235.0
Time series II	200.0	230.8	266.1	305.5	351.8

a. Plot the observed data (Y) over time (X) and plot the logarithm of the observed data (log Y) over time (X) to determine whether a linear trend model or an exponential trend model is more appropriate. (Hint: If the plot of log Y vs. X appears to be linear, an exponential trend model provides an appropriate fit.)

b. Compute the appropriate forecasting equation.

c. Forecast the value for 2010.

16.5 Autoregressive Modeling for Trend Fitting and Forecasting

Frequently, the values of a time series are highly correlated with the values that precede and succeed them. This type of correlation is called *autocorrelation*. **Autoregressive modeling**[2] is a technique used to forecast time series with autocorrelation. A **first-order autocorrelation** refers to the association between consecutive values in a time series. A **second-order autocorrelation** refers to the relationship between values that are two periods apart. A ***p*th-order autocorrelation** refers to the correlation between values in a time series that are p periods apart. You can take into account the autocorrelation in data by using autoregressive modeling methods.

[2]The exponential smoothing model described in Section 16.3 and the autoregressive models described in this section are special cases of autoregressive integrated moving average (ARIMA) models developed by Box and Jenkins (see reference 2).

Equations (16.8), (16.9), and (16.10) define three autoregressive models. Equation (16.8) defines the **first-order autoregressive model** and is similar in form to the simple linear regression model [Equation (13.1) on page 522]. Equation (16.9) defines the **second-order autoregressive model** and is similar to the multiple regression model with two independent variables [Equation (14.2) on page 579]. Equation (16.10) defines the **pth-order autoregressive model** and is similar to the multiple regression model [Equation (14.1) on page 579]. In the equations for the autoregressive models, $A_0, A_1, \ldots, A_p$, represent the parameters and $a_0, a_1, \ldots, a_p$ represent the corresponding estimates. In contrast, in the equations for the regression models, $\beta_0, \beta_1, \ldots, \beta_k$, represent the regression parameters and $b_0, b_1, \ldots, b_k$ represent the corresponding estimates.

FIRST-ORDER AUTOREGRESSIVE MODEL

$$Y_i = A_0 + A_1 Y_{i-1} + \delta_i \tag{16.8}$$

SECOND-ORDER AUTOREGRESSIVE MODEL

$$Y_i = A_0 + A_1 Y_{i-1} + A_2 Y_{i-2} + \delta_i \tag{16.9}$$

*p*TH-ORDER AUTOREGRESSIVE MODELS

$$Y_i = A_0 + A_1 Y_{i-1} + A_2 Y_{i-2} + \cdots + A_p Y_{i-p} + \delta_i \tag{16.10}$$

where

Y_i = observed value of the series at time i

Y_{i-1} = observed value of the series at time $i - 1$

Y_{i-2} = observed value of the series at time $i - 2$

Y_{i-p} = observed value of the series at time $i - p$

$A_0, A_1, A_2, \ldots, A_p$ = autoregression parameters to be estimated from least-squares regression analysis

δ_i = a nonautocorrelated random error component (with mean = 0 and constant variance)

Selecting an appropriate autoregressive model can be complicated. You must weigh the advantages that are due to simplicity against the concern of not taking into account important autocorrelation in the data. You also must be concerned with selecting a higher-order model that requires estimates of numerous unnecessary parameters—especially if n, the number of values in the series, is small. The reason for this concern is that when computing an estimate of A_p, you lose p out of the n data values when comparing each data value with the data value p periods earlier. Examples 16.5 and 16.6 illustrate this loss of data values.

EXAMPLE 16.5

Comparison Schema for a First-Order Autoregressive Model

Consider the following series of $n = 7$ consecutive annual values:

	Year						
	1	**2**	**3**	**4**	**5**	**6**	**7**
Series	31	34	37	35	36	43	40

Show the comparisons needed for a first-order autoregressive model.

Year i	**First-Order Autoregressive Model** $(Y_i \text{ vs. } Y_{i-1})$
1	$31 \leftrightarrow \ldots$
2	$34 \leftrightarrow 31$
3	$37 \leftrightarrow 34$
4	$35 \leftrightarrow 37$
5	$36 \leftrightarrow 35$
6	$43 \leftrightarrow 36$
7	$40 \leftrightarrow 43$

SOLUTION Because there is no value recorded prior to Y_1, this value is not used for regression analysis. Therefore, the first-order autoregressive model is based on six pairs of values.

EXAMPLE 16.6

Comparison Schema for a Second-Order Autoregressive Model

Consider the following series of $n = 7$ consecutive annual values:

	Year						
	1	**2**	**3**	**4**	**5**	**6**	**7**
Series	31	34	37	35	36	43	40

Show the comparisons needed for a second-order autoregressive model.

Year i	**Second-Order Autoregressive Model** $(Y_i \text{ vs. } Y_{i-1} \text{ and } Y_i \text{ vs. } Y_{i-2})$
1	$31 \leftrightarrow \ldots$ and $31 \leftrightarrow \ldots$
2	$34 \leftrightarrow 31$ and $34 \leftrightarrow \ldots$
3	$37 \leftrightarrow 34$ and $37 \leftrightarrow 31$
4	$35 \leftrightarrow 37$ and $35 \leftrightarrow 34$
5	$36 \leftrightarrow 35$ and $36 \leftrightarrow 37$
6	$43 \leftrightarrow 36$ and $43 \leftrightarrow 35$
7	$40 \leftrightarrow 43$ and $40 \leftrightarrow 36$

SOLUTION Because no value is recorded prior to Y_1, two values are not used when performing regression analysis. Therefore, the second-order autoregressive model is based on five pairs of values.

After selecting a model and using the least-squares method to compute estimates of the parameters, you need to determine the appropriateness of the model. Either you can select a particular pth-order autoregressive model based on previous experiences with similar data or start with a model that contains several autoregressive parameters and then eliminate the higher-order parameters that do not significantly contribute to the model. In this latter approach, you use a t test for the significance of A_p, the highest-order autoregressive parameter in the current model under consideration. The null and alternative hypotheses are

$$H_0: A_p = 0$$
$$H_1: A_p \neq 0$$

Equation (16.11) defines the test statistic.

t TEST FOR SIGNIFICANCE OF THE HIGHEST-ORDER AUTOREGRESSIVE PARAMETER, A_p

$$t_{STAT} = \frac{a_p - A_p}{S_{a_p}} \tag{16.11}$$

where

A_p = hypothesized value of the highest-order parameter, A_p, in the autoregressive model

a_p = estimate of the highest-order parameter, A_p, in the autoregressive model

S_{a_p} = standard deviation of a_p

The t_{STAT} test statistic follows a t distribution with $n - 2p - 1$ degrees of freedom.[3]

[3]In addition to the degrees of freedom lost for each of the p population parameters you are estimating, p additional degrees of freedom are lost because there are p fewer comparisons to be made from the original n values in the time series.

For a given level of significance, α, you reject the null hypothesis if the t_{STAT} test statistic is greater than the upper-tail critical value from the t distribution or if the t_{STAT} test statistic is less than the lower-tail critical value from the t distribution. Thus, the decision rule is

$$\text{Reject } H_0 \text{ if } t_{STAT} < -t_{\alpha/2} \text{ or if } t_{STAT} > t_{\alpha/2};$$

$$\text{otherwise, do not reject } H_0.$$

Figure 16.11 illustrates the decision rule and regions of rejection and nonrejection.

FIGURE 16.11
Rejection regions for a two-tail test for the significance of the highest-order autoregressive parameter, A_p

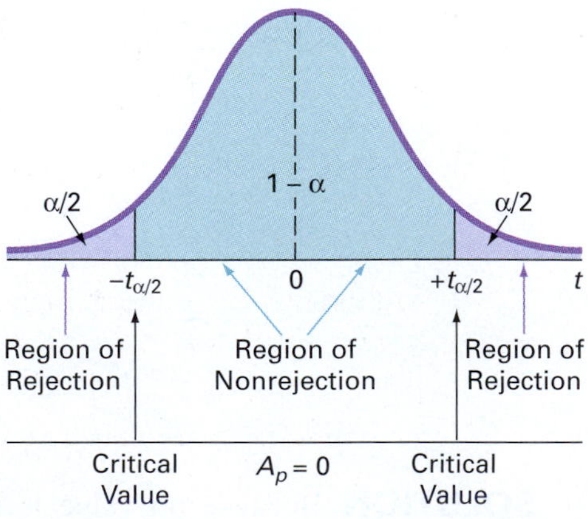

If you do not reject the null hypothesis that $A_p = 0$, you conclude that the selected model contains too many estimated autoregressive parameters. You then discard the highest-order term and estimate an autoregressive model of order $p - 1$, using the least-squares method. You then repeat the test of the hypothesis that the new highest-order parameter is 0. This testing and modeling continues until you reject H_0. When this occurs, you can conclude that the remaining highest-order parameter is significant, and you can use that model for forecasting purposes.

Equation (16.12) defines the fitted *p*th-order autoregressive equation.

FITTED *p*TH-ORDER AUTOREGRESSIVE EQUATION

$$\hat{Y}_i = a_0 + a_1Y_{i-1} + a_2Y_{i-2} + \cdots + a_pY_{i-p} \quad \textbf{(16.12)}$$

where

$\hat{Y}_i$ = fitted values of the series at time i

Y_{i-1} = observed value of the series at time $i - 1$

Y_{i-2} = observed value of the series at time $i - 2$

Y_{i-p} = observed value of the series at time $i - p$

$a_0, a_1, a_2, \ldots, a_p$ = regression estimates of the parameters $A_0, A_1, A_2, \ldots, A_p$

You use Equation (16.13) to forecast j years into the future from the current nth time period.

*p*TH-ORDER AUTOREGRESSIVE FORECASTING EQUATION

$$\hat{Y}_{n+j} = a_0 + a_1\hat{Y}_{n+j-1} + a_2\hat{Y}_{n+j-2} + \cdots + a_p\hat{Y}_{n+j-p} \quad \textbf{(16.13)}$$

where

$a_0, a_1, a_2, \ldots, a_p$ = regression estimates of the parameters $A_0, A_1, A_2, \ldots, A_p$

j = number of years into the future

$\hat{Y}_{n+j-p}$ = forecast of Y_{n+j-p} from the current time period for $j - p > 0$

$\hat{Y}_{n+j-p}$ = observed value for Y_{n+j-p} for $j - p \leq 0$

Thus, to make forecasts j years into the future, using a third-order autoregressive model, you need only the most recent $p = 3$ values (Y_n, Y_{n-1}, and Y_{n-2}) and the regression estimates a_0, a_1, a_2, and a_3.

To forecast one year ahead, Equation (16.13) becomes

$$\hat{Y}_{n+1} = a_0 + a_1Y_n + a_2Y_{n-1} + a_3Y_{n-2}$$

To forecast two years ahead, Equation (16.13) becomes

$$\hat{Y}_{n+2} = a_0 + a_1\hat{Y}_{n+1} + a_2Y_n + a_3Y_{n-1}$$

To forecast three years ahead, Equation (16.13) becomes

$$\hat{Y}_{n+3} = a_0 + a_1\hat{Y}_{n+2} + a_2\hat{Y}_{n+1} + a_3Y_n$$

and so on.

Autoregressive modeling is a powerful forecasting technique for time series that have autocorrelation. Exhibit 16.1 summarizes the steps to follow when constructing autoregressive models.

Sections EG16.5 and MG16.5 discuss an automated way of creating lagged predictor variables that are mentioned in step 2 of Exhibit 16.1.

EXHIBIT 16.1

Guide to Autoregressive Modeling

1. Choose a value for p, the highest-order parameter in the autoregressive model to be evaluated, realizing that the t test for significance is based on $n - 2p - 1$ degrees of freedom.
2. Create a set of p lagged predictor variables such that the first lagged predictor variable lags by one time period, the second variable lags by two time periods, and so on and the last predictor variable lags by p time periods (see Figure 16.12).
3. Perform a least-squares analysis of the multiple regression model containing all p lagged predictor variables (using Excel or Minitab).
4. Test for the significance of A_p, the highest-order autoregressive parameter in the model.
   a. If you do not reject the null hypothesis, discard the pth variable and repeat steps 3 and 4. The test for the significance of the new highest-order parameter is based on a t distribution whose degrees of freedom are revised to correspond with the revised number of predictors.
   b. If you reject the null hypothesis, select the autoregressive model with all p predictors for fitting [see Equation (16.12)] and forecasting [see Equation (16.13)].

To demonstrate the autoregressive modeling approach, return to the time series concerning the revenues for The Coca-Cola Company over the 15-year period 1995 through 2009. Figure 16.12 displays a worksheet that organizes the data for the first-order, second-order, and third-order autoregressive models. The worksheet contains the lagged predictor variables Lag1, Lag2, and Lag3 in columns C, D, and E. Use all three lagged predictors to fit the third-order autoregressive model. Use only Lag1 and Lag2 to fit the second-order autoregressive model, and use only Lag1 to fit the first-order autoregressive models. Thus, out of $n = 15$ values, $p = 1, 2$, or 3 values out of $n = 15$ are lost in the comparisons needed for developing the first-order, second-order, and third-order autoregressive models.

FIGURE 16.12

Worksheet data for developing first-order, second-order, and third-order autoregressive models on revenues for The Coca-Cola Company (1995–2009)

	A	B	C	D	E
1	Year	Revenues	Lag1	Lag2	Lag3
2	1995	18.0	#N/A	#N/A	#N/A
3	1996	18.5	18.0	#N/A	#N/A
4	1997	18.9	18.5	18.0	#N/A
5	1998	18.8	18.9	18.5	18.0
6	1999	19.8	18.8	18.9	18.5
7	2000	20.5	19.8	18.8	18.9
8	2001	20.1	20.5	19.8	18.8
9	2002	19.6	20.1	20.5	19.8
10	2003	21.0	19.6	20.1	20.5
11	2004	21.9	21.0	19.6	20.1
12	2005	23.1	21.9	21.0	19.6
13	2006	24.1	23.1	21.9	21.0
14	2007	28.9	24.1	23.1	21.9
15	2008	31.9	28.9	24.1	23.1
16	2009	31.0	31.9	28.9	24.1

Selecting an autoregressive model that best fits the annual time series begins with the third-order autoregressive model shown in Figure 16.13 on page 689.

From Figure 16.13, the fitted third-order autoregressive equation is

$$\hat{Y}_i = -11.6000 + 1.0259Y_{i-1} - 0.8876Y_{i-2} + 1.5180Y_{i-3}$$

where the first year in the series is 1998.

FIGURE 16.13

Excel and Minitab regression results for the third-order autoregressive model for The Coca-Cola Company revenues

	A	B	C	D	E	F	G
1	Third-Order Autoregressive Model						
2							
3	*Regression Statistics*						
4	Multiple R	0.9652					
5	R Square	0.9315					
6	Adjusted R Square	0.9059					
7	Standard Error	1.4232					
8	Observations	12					
9							
10	ANOVA						
11		*df*	*SS*	*MS*	*F*	*Significance F*	
12	Regression	3	220.5043	73.5014	36.2860	0.0001	
13	Residual	8	16.2049	2.0256			
14	Total	11	236.7092				
15							
16		*Coefficients*	*Standard Error*	*t Stat*	*P-value*	*Lower 95%*	*Upper 95%*
17	Intercept	-11.6000	7.4457	-1.5579	0.1579	-28.7698	5.5699
18	X Variable 1	1.0259	0.4229	2.4259	0.0415	0.0507	2.0011
19	X Variable 2	-0.8876	0.5874	-1.5111	0.1692	-2.2421	0.4669
20	X Variable 3	1.5180	0.6955	2.1827	0.0606	-0.0857	3.1218

Regression Analysis: Revenues versus Lag1, Lag2, Lag3

```
The regression equation is
Revenues = - 11.6 + 1.03 Lag1 - 0.888 Lag2 + 1.52 Lag3

12 cases used, 3 cases contain missing values

Predictor      Coef  SE Coef      T      P
Constant    -11.600    7.446  -1.56  0.158
Lag1         1.0259   0.4229   2.43  0.041
Lag2        -0.8876   0.5874  -1.51  0.169
Lag3         1.5180   0.6955   2.18  0.061

S = 1.42324   R-Sq = 93.2%   R-Sq(adj) = 90.6%

Analysis of Variance
Source          DF       SS      MS      F      P
Regression       3  220.504  73.501  36.29  0.000
Residual Error   8   16.205   2.026
Total           11  236.709
```

Next, you test for the significance of A_3, the highest-order parameter. The highest-order parameter estimate, a_3, for the fitted third-order autoregressive model is 1.518, with a standard error of 0.6955.

To test the null hypothesis:

$$H_0: A_3 = 0$$

against the alternative hypothesis:

$$H_1: A_3 \neq 0$$

using Equation (16.11) on page 686 and the worksheet results given in Figure 16.13,

$$t_{STAT} = \frac{a_3 - A_3}{S_{a_3}} = \frac{1.518 - 0}{0.6955} = 2.1827$$

Using a 0.05 level of significance, the two-tail t test with 8 degrees of freedom has critical values of ± 2.306. Because $-2.306 < t_{STAT} = 2.1827 < +2.306$ or because the p-value $= 0.0606 > 0.05$, you do not reject H_0. You conclude that the third-order parameter of the autoregressive model is not significant and can be deleted.

Next, you fit a second-order autoregressive model (see Figure 16.14).

FIGURE 16.14

Excel and Minitab regression results for the second-order autoregressive model for the Coca-Cola Company revenue data

	A	B	C	D	E	F	G
1	Second-Order Autoregressive Model						
2							
3	*Regression Statistics*						
4	Multiple R	0.9473					
5	R Square	0.8975					
6	Adjusted R Square	0.8770					
7	Standard Error	1.6180					
8	Observations	13					
9							
10	ANOVA						
11		*df*	*SS*	*MS*	*F*	*Significance F*	
12	Regression	2	229.1520	114.5760	43.7643	0.0000	
13	Residual	10	26.1803	2.6180			
14	Total	12	255.3323				
15							
16		*Coefficients*	*Standard Error*	*t Stat*	*P-value*	*Lower 95%*	*Upper 95%*
17	Intercept	1.6349	4.2228	0.3872	0.7067	-7.7741	11.0440
18	X Variable 1	1.3390	0.4448	3.0105	0.0131	0.3480	2.3300
19	X Variable 2	-0.3883	0.6115	-0.6350	0.5397	-1.7507	0.9742

Regression Analysis: Revenues versus Lag1, Lag2

```
The regression equation is
Revenues = 1.63 + 1.34 Lag1 - 0.388 Lag2

13 cases used, 2 cases contain missing values

Predictor     Coef  SE Coef      T      P
Constant     1.635    4.223   0.39  0.707
Lag1        1.3390   0.4448   3.01  0.013
Lag2       -0.3883   0.6115  -0.63  0.540

S = 1.61803   R-Sq = 89.7%   R-Sq(adj) = 87.7%

Analysis of Variance
Source          DF      SS      MS      F      P
Regression       2  229.15  114.58  43.76  0.000
Residual Error  10   26.18    2.62
Total           12  255.33
```

The fitted second-order autoregressive equation is

$$\hat{Y}_i = 1.6349 + 1.339Y_{i-1} - 0.3883\,Y_{i-2}$$

where the first year of the series is 1997.

From Figure 16.14, the highest-order parameter estimate is $a_2 = -0.3883$, with a standard error of 0.6115.

To test the null hypothesis:

$$H_0: A_2 = 0$$

against the alternative hypothesis:

$$H_1: A_2 \neq 0$$

using Equation (16.11) on page 686,

$$t_{STAT} = \frac{a_2 - A_2}{S_{a_2}} = \frac{-0.3883 - 0}{0.6115} = -0.635$$

Using the 0.05 level of significance, the two-tail t test with 10 degrees of freedom has critical values of ± 2.2281. Because $-2.2281 < t_{STAT} = -0.635 < 2.2281$ or because the p-value $= 0.5397 > 0.05$, you do not reject H_0. You conclude that the second-order parameter of the autoregressive model is not significant and should be deleted from the model. You then fit a first-order autoregressive model (see Figure 16.15).

FIGURE 16.15

Excel and Minitab regression results for the first-order autoregressive model for the Coca-Cola Company revenue data

	A	B	C	D	E	F	G
1	**First-Order Autoregressive Model**						
2							
3	*Regression Statistics*						
4	Multiple R	0.9490					
5	R Square	0.9007					
6	Adjusted R Square	0.8924					
7	Standard Error	1.5074					
8	Observations	14					
9							
10	**ANOVA**						
11		*df*	*SS*	*MS*	*F*	*Significance F*	
12	Regression	1	247.2561	247.2561	108.8135	0.0000	
13	Residual	12	27.2675	2.2723			
14	Total	13	274.5236				
15							
16		*Coefficients*	*Standard Error*	*t Stat*	*P-value*	*Lower 95%*	*Upper 95%*
17	Intercept	-0.5836	2.2702	-0.2571	0.8015	-5.5299	4.3626
18	X Variable 1	1.0694	0.1025	10.4314	0.0000	0.8460	1.2928

Regression Analysis: Revenues versus Lag1

```
The regression equation is
Revenues = - 0.58 + 1.07 Lag1

14 cases used, 1 cases contain missing values

Predictor      Coef   SE Coef      T      P
Constant     -0.584     2.270  -0.26  0.801
Lag1         1.0694    0.1025  10.43  0.000

S = 1.50741   R-Sq = 90.1%   R-Sq(adj) = 89.2%

Analysis of Variance
Source          DF      SS      MS       F      P
Regression       1  247.26  247.26  108.81  0.000
Residual Error  12   27.27    2.27
Total           13  274.52
```

From Figure 16.15, the fitted first-order autoregressive equation is

$$\hat{Y}_i = -0.5836 + 1.0694Y_{i-1}$$

where the first year of the series is 1996.

From Figure 16.15, the highest-order parameter estimate is $a_1 = 1.0694$, with a standard error of 0.1025.

To test the null hypothesis:

$$H_0: A_1 = 0$$

against the alternative hypothesis:

$$H_1: A_1 \neq 0$$

using Equation (16.11) on page 686,

$$t_{STAT} = \frac{a_1 - A_1}{S_{a_1}} = \frac{1.0694 - 0}{0.1025} = 10.4314$$

Using the 0.05 level of significance, the two-tail t test with 12 degrees of freedom has critical values of ± 2.1788. Because $t_{STAT} = 10.4314 > 2.1788$ or because the p-value $= 0.0000 < 0.05$, you reject H_0. You conclude that the first-order parameter of the autoregressive model is significant and should remain in the model.

The model-building approach has led to the selection of the first-order autoregressive model as the most appropriate for the given data. Using the estimates $a_0 = -0.5836$ and $a_1 = 1.0694$, as well as the most recent data value $Y_{14} = 31.0$, the forecasts of revenues from Equation (16.13) on page 687 at The Coca-Cola Company for 2010 and 2011 are

$$\hat{Y}_{n+j} = -0.5836 + 1.0694\,\hat{Y}_{n+j-1}$$

Therefore,

$$\text{2010: 1 year ahead, } \hat{Y}_{15} = -0.5836 + 1.0694(31.0) = 32.5678 \text{ billions of dollars}$$

$$\text{2011: 2 years ahead, } \hat{Y}_{16} = -0.5836 + 1.0694(32.5678) = 34.2444 \text{ billions of dollars}$$

Figure 16.16 displays the actual and predicted Y values from the first-order autoregressive model.

FIGURE 16.16

Plot of actual and predicted revenues from a first-order autoregressive model at The Coca-Cola Company

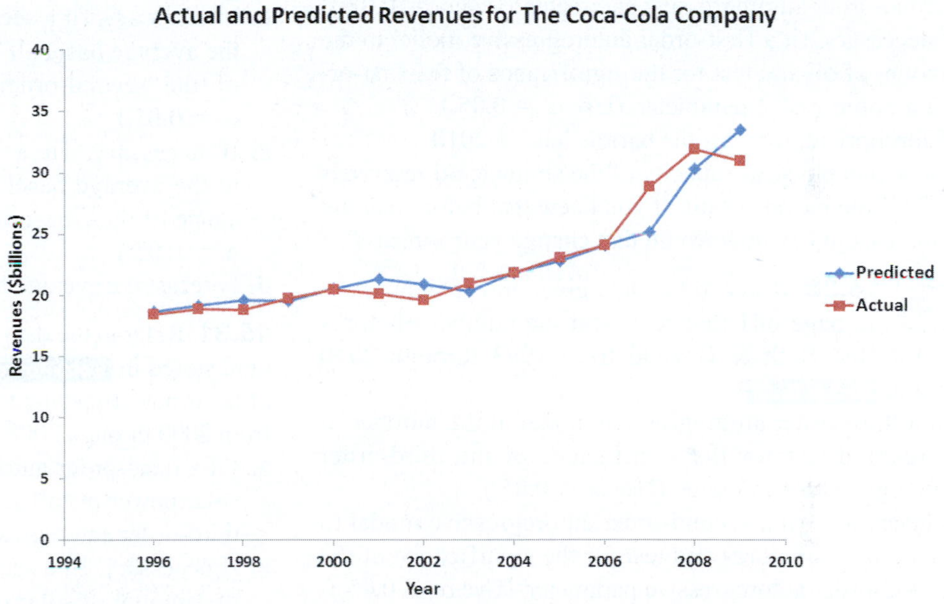

Problems for Section 16.5

LEARNING THE BASICS

16.23 You are given an annual time series with 40 consecutive values and asked to fit a fifth-order autoregressive model.

a. How many comparisons are lost in developing the autoregressive model?

b. How many parameters do you need to estimate?

c. Which of the original 40 values do you need for forecasting?

d. State the fifth-order autoregressive model.

e. Write an equation to indicate how you would forecast j years into the future.

16.24 A third-order autoregressive model is fitted to an annual time series with 17 values and has the following estimated parameters and standard errors:

$$a_0 = 4.50 \quad a_1 = 1.80 \quad a_2 = 0.80 \quad a_3 = 0.24$$

$$S_{a_1} = 0.50 \quad S_{a_2} = 0.30 \quad S_{a_3} = 0.10$$

At the 0.05 level of significance, test the appropriateness of the fitted model.

16.25 Refer to Problem 16.24. The three most recent values are

$$Y_{15} = 23 \quad Y_{16} = 28 \quad Y_{17} = 34$$

Forecast the values for the next year and the following year.

16.26 Refer to Problem 16.24. Suppose, when testing for the appropriateness of the fitted model, the standard errors are

$$S_{a_1} = 0.45 \quad S_{a_2} = 0.35 \quad S_{a_3} = 0.15$$

a. What conclusions can you reach?
b. Discuss how to proceed if forecasting is still your main objective.

APPLYING THE CONCEPTS

16.27 Refer to the data given in Problem 16.15 on page 682 that represent the amount of oil (in billions of barrels) held in the U.S. strategic reserve from 1981 through 2009 (stored in **Strategic**).
a. Fit a third-order autoregressive model to the amount of oil and test for the significance of the third-order autoregressive parameter. (Use $\alpha = 0.05$.)
b. If necessary, fit a second-order autoregressive model to the amount of oil and test for the significance of the second-order autoregressive parameter. (Use $\alpha = 0.05$.)
c. If necessary, fit a first-order autoregressive model to the amount of oil and test for the significance of the first-order autoregressive parameter. (Use $\alpha = 0.05$.)
d. If appropriate, forecast the barrels held in 2010.
e. The actual physical capacity of the strategic oil reserve is 727 billion barrels of oil. If you knew that before making a forecast in (d), how would that change your forecast?

SELF Test **16.28** Refer to the data given in Problem 16.12 on page 681 that represent the number of stores open for Bed Bath & Beyond from 1993 through 2010 (stored in **Bed & Bath**).
a. Fit a third-order autoregressive model to the number of stores and test for the significance of the third-order autoregressive parameter. (Use $\alpha = 0.05$.)
b. If necessary, fit a second-order autoregressive model to the number of stores and test for the significance of the second-order autoregressive parameter. (Use $\alpha = 0.05$.)
c. If necessary, fit a first-order autoregressive model to the number of stores and test for the significance of the first-order autoregressive parameter. (Use $\alpha = 0.05$.)
d. If appropriate, forecast the number of stores open in 2011 and 2012.

16.29 Refer to the data given in Problem 16.17 on page 682 that represent the tons of electronic items recycled from 1999 to 2007 (stored in **E-Cycling**).
a. Fit a third-order autoregressive model to the tons of electronic items recycled and test for the significance of the third-order autoregressive parameter. (Use $\alpha = 0.05$.)
b. If necessary, fit a second-order autoregressive model to the tons of electronic items recycled and test for the significance of the second-order autoregressive parameter. (Use $\alpha = 0.05$.)
c. If necessary, fit a first-order autoregressive model to the tons of electronic items recycled and test for the significance of the first-order autoregressive parameter. (Use $\alpha = 0.05$.)
d. Forecast the tons of electronic items recycled for 2008.

16.30 Refer to the data given in Problem 16.18 on page 682 (stored in **BBSalaries**) that represent the average baseball salary from 2000 through 2010.
a. Fit a third-order autoregressive model to the average baseball salary and test for the significance of the third-order autoregressive parameter. (Use $\alpha = 0.05$.)
b. If necessary, fit a second-order autoregressive model to the average baseball salary and test for the significance of the second-order autoregressive parameter. (Use $\alpha = 0.05$.)
c. If necessary, fit a first-order autoregressive model to the average baseball salary and test for the significance of the first-order autoregressive parameter. (Use $\alpha = 0.05$.)
d. Forecast the average baseball salary for 2011.

16.31 Refer to the data given in Problem 16.16 on page 682 (and stored in **SolarPower**) that represent the yearly amount of solar power installed (in megawatts) in the United States from 2000 through 2008.
a. Fit a third-order autoregressive model to the amount of solar power installed and test for the significance of the third-order autoregressive parameter. (Use $\alpha = 0.05$.)
b. If necessary, fit a second-order autoregressive model to the amount of solar power installed and test for the significance of the second-order autoregressive parameter. (Use $\alpha = 0.05$.)
c. If necessary, fit a first-order autoregressive model to the amount of solar power installed and test for the significance of the first-order autoregressive parameter. (Use $\alpha = 0.05$.)
d. Forecast the yearly amount of solar power installed (in megawatts) in the United States in 2009 and 2010.

16.6 Choosing an Appropriate Forecasting Model

In Sections 16.4 and 16.5, you studied six time-series methods for forecasting: the linear trend model, the quadratic trend model, and the exponential trend model in Section 16.4; and the first-order, second-order, and *p*th-order autoregressive models in Section 16.5. Is there a *best* model? Among these models, which one should you select for forecasting? The following guidelines are provided for determining the adequacy of a particular forecasting model. These guidelines are based on a judgment of how well the model fits the data and assume that you can use past data to predict future values of the time series:

- Perform a residual analysis.
- Measure the magnitude of the residuals through squared differences.
- Measure the magnitude of the residuals through absolute differences.
- Use the principle of parsimony.

A discussion of these guidelines follows.

Performing a Residual Analysis

Recall from Sections 13.5 and 14.3 that residuals are the differences between observed and predicted values. After fitting a particular model to a time series, you plot the residuals over the n time periods. As shown in Figure 16.17 Panel A, if the particular model fits adequately, the residuals represent the irregular component of the time series. Therefore, they should be randomly distributed throughout the series. However, as illustrated in the three remaining panels of Figure 16.17, if the particular model does not fit adequately, the residuals may show a systematic pattern, such as a failure to account for trend (Panel B), a failure to account for cyclical variation (Panel C), or, with monthly or quarterly data, a failure to account for seasonal variation (Panel D).

FIGURE 16.17

Residual analysis for studying error patterns

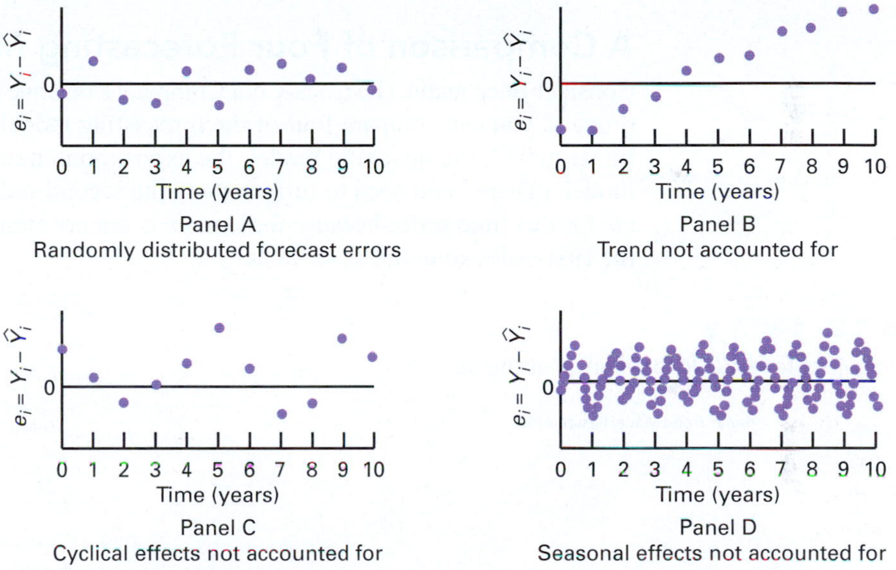

Measuring the Magnitude of the Residuals Through Squared or Absolute Differences

If, after performing a residual analysis, you still believe that two or more models appear to fit the data adequately, you can use additional methods for model selection. Numerous measures based on the residuals are available (see references 1 and 4).

In regression analysis (see Section 13.3), you have already used the standard error of the estimate (S_{YX}). For a particular model, this measure is based on the sum of squared differences between the actual and predicted values in a time series. If a model fits the time-series data perfectly, then the standard error of the estimate is zero. If a model fits the time-series data poorly, then S_{YX} is large. Thus, when comparing the adequacy of two or more forecasting models, you can select the model with the minimum S_{YX} as most appropriate.

However, a major drawback to using S_{YX} when comparing forecasting models is that whenever there is a large difference between even a single Y_i and $\hat{Y}_i$, the value of S_{YX} becomes overly inflated because the differences between Y_i and $\hat{Y}_i$ are squared. For this reason, many statisticians prefer the **mean absolute deviation (*MAD*)**. Equation (16.14) defines the *MAD* as the mean of the absolute differences between the actual and predicted values in a time series.

MEAN ABSOLUTE DEVIATION

$$MAD = \frac{\sum_{i=1}^{n} |Y_i - \hat{Y}_i|}{n} \quad \textbf{(16.14)}$$

If a model fits the time-series data perfectly, the *MAD* is zero. If a model fits the time-series data poorly, the *MAD* is large. When comparing two or more forecasting models, you can select the one with the minimum *MAD* as the most appropriate model.

Using the Principle of Parsimony

If, after performing a residual analysis and comparing the S_{YX} and *MAD* measures, you still believe that two or more models appear to adequately fit the data, you can use the principle of parsimony for model selection. As first explained in Section 15.4, **parsimony** guides you to select the regression model with the fewest independent variables that can predict the dependent variable adequately. In general, the principle of parsimony guides you to select the least complex regression model. Among the six forecasting models studied in this chapter, most statisticians consider the least-squares linear and quadratic models and the first-order autoregressive model as simpler than the second- and *p*th-order autoregressive models and the least-squares exponential model.

A Comparison of Four Forecasting Methods

Consider once again The Coca-Cola Company's revenue data. To illustrate the model selection process, you can compare four of the forecasting models used in Sections 16.4 and 16.5: the linear model, the quadratic model, the exponential model, and the first-order autoregressive model. (There is no need to further study the second-order or third-order autoregressive models for this time series because these models did not significantly improve the fit compared to the first-order autoregressive model.)

FIGURE 16.18

Residual plots for four forecasting methods

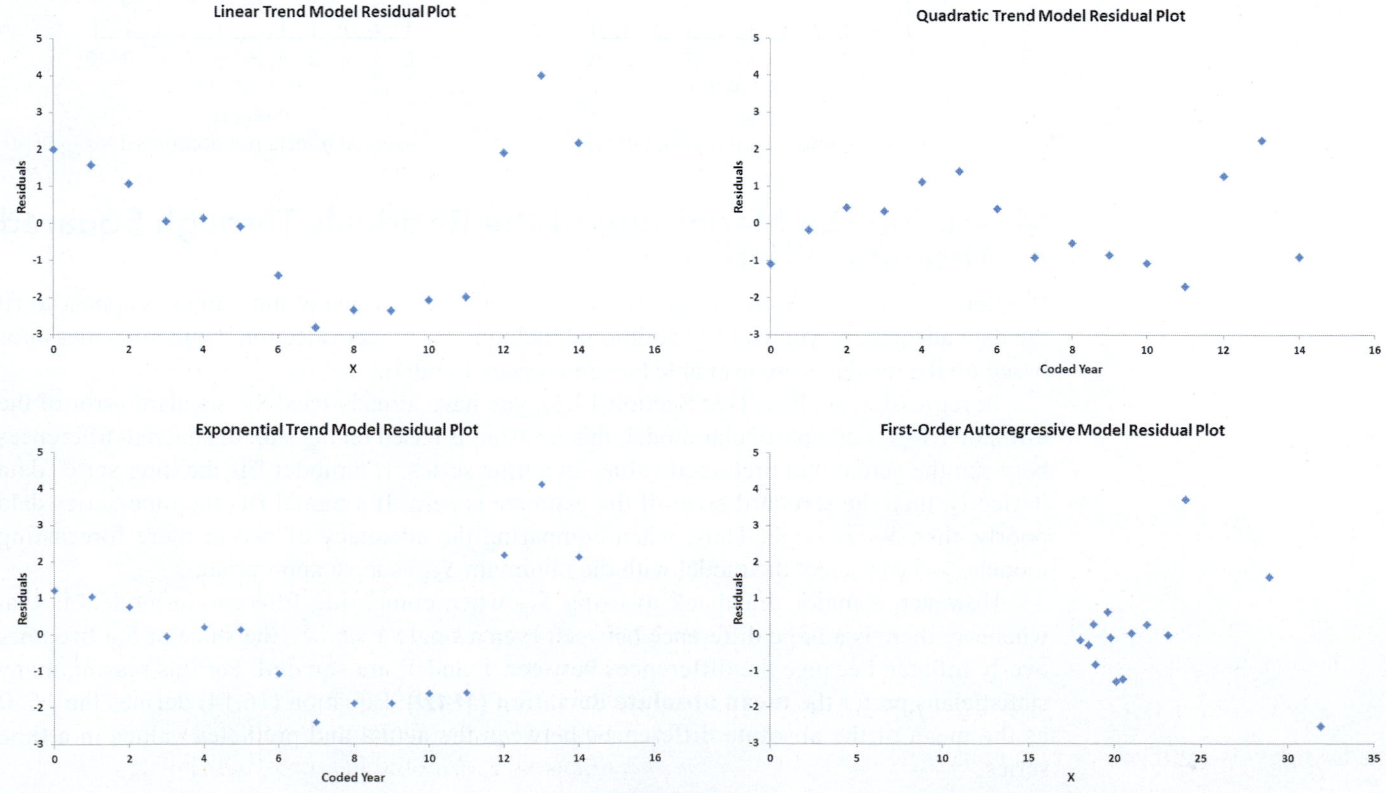

Figure 16.18 displays the residual plots for the four models. In reaching conclusions from these residual plots, you must use caution because there are only 15 values for the linear model, the quadratic model, and the exponential model and only 14 values for the first-order autoregressive model.

In Figure 16.18, observe that the residuals in the linear model, quadratic model, and exponential model are positive for the early years, negative for the intermediate years, and positive again for the latest years. For the autoregressive model, the residuals do not exhibit any systematic pattern.

To summarize, on the basis of the residual analysis of all four forecasting models, it appears that the first-order autoregressive model is the most appropriate, and the linear, quadratic, and exponential models are less appropriate. For further verification, you can compare the magnitude of the residuals in the four models. Figure 16.19 shows the actual values (Y_i) along with the predicted values $\hat{Y}_i$ the residuals (e_i), the error sum of squares (SSE), the standard error of the estimate (S_{YX}), and the mean absolute deviation (MAD) for each of the four models.

For this time series, S_{YX} and MAD provide fairly similar results. A comparison of the S_{YX} and MAD clearly indicates that the linear model provides the poorest fit followed by the exponential model. The first-order autoregressive model and the quadratic model provide the best fit. Although the quadratic model has a lower SSE and S_{YX}, the MAD for the first-order autoregressive model was slightly lower. Since the residual analysis showed a pattern in the residuals for the quadratic model, but not for the first-order autoregressive model, you should choose the first-order autoregressive model as the best model.

After you select a particular forecasting model, you need to continually monitor your forecasts. If large errors between forecasted and actual values occur, the underlying structure of the time series may have changed. Remember that the forecasting methods presented in this chapter assume that the patterns inherent in the past will continue into the future. Large forecasting errors are an indication that this assumption may no longer be true.

FIGURE 16.19
Table that summarizes and compares four forecasting methods, using SSE, S_{YX}, and MAD

		Linear		Quadratic		Exponential		First-order Autoregressive	
Year	Revenues	Predicted	Residual	Predicted	Residual	Predicted	Residual	Predicted	Residual
1995	18.0	16.0017	1.9983	19.0879	-1.0879	16.7947	1.2053	#N/A	#N/A
1996	18.5	16.9167	1.5833	18.6803	-0.1803	17.4570	1.0430	18.6654	-0.1654
1997	18.9	17.8317	1.0683	18.4761	0.4239	18.1454	0.7546	19.2001	-0.3001
1998	18.8	18.7467	0.0533	18.4753	0.3247	18.8609	-0.0609	19.6278	-0.8278
1999	19.8	19.6617	0.1383	18.6781	1.1219	19.6047	0.1953	19.5209	0.2791
2000	20.5	20.5767	-0.0767	19.0844	1.4156	20.3778	0.1222	20.5903	-0.0903
2001	20.1	21.4917	-1.3917	19.6942	0.4058	21.1814	-1.0814	21.3389	-1.2389
2002	19.6	22.4067	-2.8067	20.5074	-0.9074	22.0167	-2.4167	20.9111	-1.3111
2003	21.0	23.3217	-2.3217	21.5242	-0.5242	22.8849	-1.8849	20.3764	0.6236
2004	21.9	24.2367	-2.3367	22.7444	-0.8444	23.7874	-1.8874	21.8736	0.0264
2005	23.1	25.1517	-2.0517	24.1681	-1.0681	24.7254	-1.6254	22.8360	0.2640
2006	24.1	26.0667	-1.9667	25.7953	-1.6953	25.7004	-1.6004	24.1193	-0.0193
2007	28.9	26.9817	1.9183	27.6261	1.2739	26.7139	2.1861	25.1887	3.7113
2008	31.9	27.8967	4.0033	29.6603	2.2397	27.7674	4.1326	30.3217	1.5783
2009	31.0	28.8117	2.1883	31.8979	-0.8979	28.8624	2.1376	33.5299	-2.5299
		SSE	60.9063	SSE	18.2004	SSE	48.9221	SSE	27.2675
		S_{YX}	2.1645	S_{YX}	1.2315	S_{YX}	1.9399	S_{YX}	1.5074
		MAD	1.7269	MAD	0.9607	MAD	1.4889	MAD	0.9261

Problems for Section 16.6

LEARNING THE BASICS

16.32 The following residuals are from a linear trend model used to forecast sales:

2.0 −0.5 1.5 1.0 0.0 1.0 −3.0 1.5 −4.5 2.0 0.0 −1.0

a. Compute S_{YX} and interpret your findings.

b. Compute the MAD and interpret your findings.

16.33 Refer to Problem 16.32. Suppose the first residual is 12.0 (instead of 2.0) and the last residual is −11.0 (instead of −1.0).

a. Compute S_{YX} and interpret your findings

b. Compute the MAD and interpret your findings.

APPLYING THE CONCEPTS

16.34 Refer to the results in Problem 16.13 on page 681 (see GDP).

a. Perform a residual analysis.

b. Compute the standard error of the estimate (S_{YX}).

c. Compute the *MAD*.

d. On the basis of (a) through (c), are you satisfied with your linear trend forecasts in Problem 16.13? Discuss.

16.35 Refer to the results in Problem 16.15 on page 682 and Problem 16.27 on page 692 concerning the number of barrels of oil in the U.S. strategic oil reserve (stored in Strategic).

a. Perform a residual analysis for each model.

b. Compute the standard error of the estimate (S_{YX}) for each model.

c. Compute the *MAD* for each model.

d. On the basis of (a) through (c) and the principle of parsimony, which forecasting model would you select? Discuss.

SELF Test **16.36** Refer to the results in Problem 16.12 on page 681 and Problem 16.28 on page 692 concerning the number of Bed Bath & Beyond stores open (stored in Bed & Bath).

a. Perform a residual analysis for each model.

b. Compute the standard error of the estimate (S_{YX}) for each model.

c. Compute the *MAD* for each model.

d. On the basis of (a) through (c) and the principle of parsimony, which forecasting model would you select? Discuss.

16.37 Refer to the results in Problem 16.17 on page 682 and Problem 16.29 on page 692 concerning the amount of electronic items recycled (stored in E-Cycling).

a. Perform a residual analysis for each model.

b. Compute the standard error of the estimate (S_{YX}) for each model.

c. Compute the *MAD* for each model.

d. On the basis of (a) through (c) and the principle of parsimony, which forecasting model would you select? Discuss.

16.38 Refer to the results in Problem 16.18 on page 682 and Problem 16.30 on page 692 concerning the average baseball salary (stored in BBSalaries).

a. Perform a residual analysis for each model.

b. Compute the standard error of the estimate (S_{YX}) for each model.

c. Compute the *MAD* for each model.

d. On the basis of (a) through (c) and the principle of parsimony, which forecasting model would you select? Discuss.

16.39 Refer to the results in Problem 16.16 on page 682 and Problem 16.31 on page 692 concerning the yearly amount of solar power installed (in megawatts) in the United States from 2000 through 2008 (stored in SolarPower).

a. Perform a residual analysis for each model.

b. Compute the standard error of the estimate (S_{YX}) for each model.

c. Compute the *MAD* for each model.

d. On the basis of (a) through (c) and the principle of parsimony, which forecasting model would you select? Discuss.

16.7 Time-Series Forecasting of Seasonal Data

So far, this chapter has focused on forecasting annual data. However, many time series are collected quarterly or monthly, and others are collected weekly, daily, and even hourly. When a time series is collected quarterly or monthly, you must consider the impact of seasonal effects. In this section, regression model building is used to forecast monthly or quarterly data.

One of the companies of interest in the Using Statistics scenario is Wal-Mart Stores, Inc. In 2010, Wal-Mart Stores, Inc., operated more than 8,000 retail units in 15 countries and had revenues that exceeded $400 billion (Wal-Mart Stores, Inc., **investor.walmartstores.com**). Wal-Mart revenues are highly seasonal, and therefore you need to analyze quarterly revenues. The fiscal year for the company ends January 31. Thus, the fourth quarter of 2010 includes November and December 2009 as well as January 2010. Table 16.3 lists the

TABLE 16.3

Quarterly Revenues for Wal-Mart Stores, Inc., in Billions of Dollars (2005–2010)

	Year					
Quarter	**2005**	**2006**	**2007**	**2008**	**2009**	**2010**
1	64.8	71.6	79.6	86.4	95.3	93.5
2	69.7	76.8	84.5	93.0	102.7	100.9
3	68.5	75.4	83.5	91.9	98.6	99.4
4	82.2	88.6	98.1	107.3	107.9	113.7

Source: Data extracted from Wal-Mart Stores, Inc., **investor.walmartstores.com**.

quarterly revenues, in billions of dollars, from 2005 to 2010 (stored in WalMart). Figure 16.20 displays the time series.

FIGURE 16.20

Plot of quarterly revenues for Wal-Mart Stores, Inc., in billions of dollars (2005–2010)

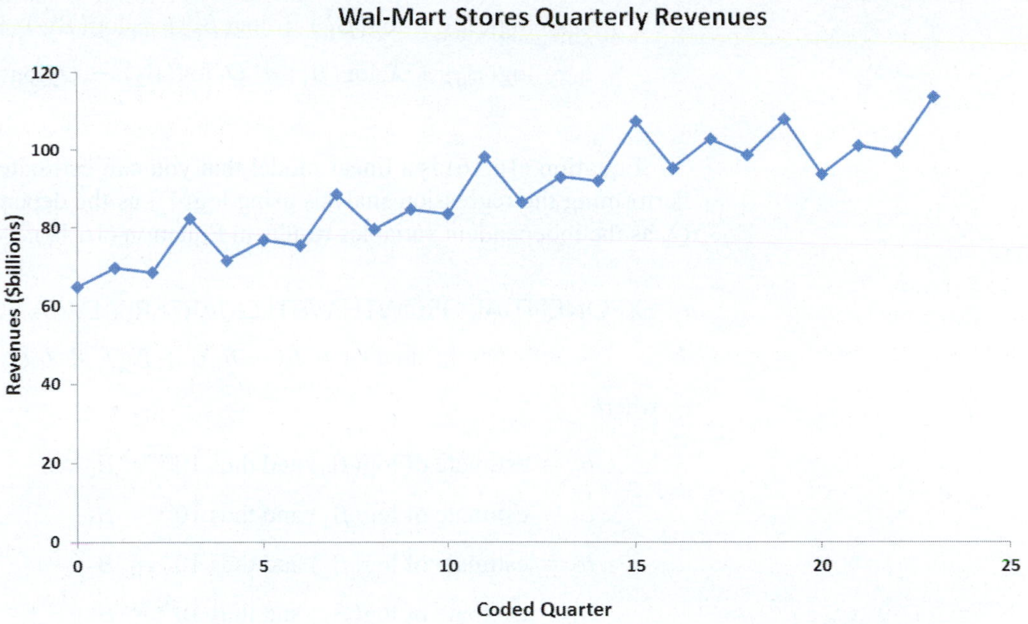

Least-Squares Forecasting with Monthly or Quarterly Data

To develop a least-squares regression model that includes a seasonal component, the least-squares exponential trend fitting method used in Section 16.4 is combined with dummy variables (see Section 14.6) to model the seasonal component.

Equation (16.15) defines the exponential trend model for quarterly data.

EXPONENTIAL MODEL WITH QUARTERLY DATA

$$Y_i = \beta_0 \beta_1^{X_i} \beta_2^{Q_1} \beta_3^{Q_2} \beta_4^{Q_3} \varepsilon_i \quad \textbf{(16.15)}$$

where

X_i = coded quarterly value, $i = 0, 1, 2, \ldots$

Q_1 = 1 if first quarter, 0 if not first quarter

Q_2 = 1 if second quarter, 0 if not second quarter

Q_3 = 1 if third quarter, 0 if not third quarter

β_0 = Y intercept

$(\beta_1 - 1) \times 100\%$ = quarterly compound growth rate (in %)

β_2 = multiplier for first quarter relative to fourth quarter

β_3 = multiplier for second quarter relative to fourth quarter

β_4 = multiplier for third quarter relative to fourth quarter

ε_i = value of the irregular component for time period i

The model in Equation (16.15) is not in the form of a linear regression model. To transform this nonlinear model to a linear model, you use a base 10 logarithmic transformation.[4] Taking the logarithm of each side of Equation (16.15) results in Equation (16.16).

[4]Alternatively, you can use base e logarithms. For more information on logarithms, see Section A.3 in Appendix A.

TRANSFORMED EXPONENTIAL MODEL WITH QUARTERLY DATA

$$\begin{aligned}\log(Y_i) &= \log(\beta_0\beta_1^{X_i}\beta_2^{Q_1}\beta_3^{Q_2}\beta_4^{Q_3}\varepsilon_i) \qquad \textbf{(16.16)}\\ &= \log(\beta_0) + \log(\beta_1^{X_i}) + \log(\beta_2^{Q_1}) + \log(\beta_3^{Q_2}) + \log(\beta_4^{Q_3}) + \log(\varepsilon_i)\\ &= \log(\beta_0) + X_i\log(\beta_1) + Q_1\log(\beta_2) + Q_2\log(\beta_3) + Q_3\log(\beta_4) + \log(\varepsilon_i)\end{aligned}$$

Equation (16.16) is a linear model that you can estimate using least-squares regression. Performing the regression analysis using $\log(Y_i)$ as the dependent variable and X_i, Q_1, Q_2, and Q_3 as the independent variables results in Equation (16.17).

EXPONENTIAL GROWTH WITH QUARTERLY DATA FORECASTING EQUATION

$$\log(\hat{Y}_i) = b_0 + b_1X_i + b_2Q_1 + b_3Q_2 + b_4Q_3 \qquad \textbf{(16.17)}$$

where

b_0 = estimate of $\log(\beta_0)$ and thus $10^{b_0} = \hat{\beta}_0$

b_1 = estimate of $\log(\beta_1)$ and thus $10^{b_1} = \hat{\beta}_1$

b_2 = estimate of $\log(\beta_2)$ and thus $10^{b_2} = \hat{\beta}_2$

b_3 = estimate of $\log(\beta_3)$ and thus $10^{b_3} = \hat{\beta}_3$

b_4 = estimate of $\log(\beta_4)$ and thus $10^{b_4} = \hat{\beta}_4$

Equation (16.18) is used for monthly data.

EXPONENTIAL MODEL WITH MONTHLY DATA

$$Y_i = \beta_0\beta_1^{X_i}\beta_2^{M_1}\beta_3^{M_2}\beta_4^{M_3}\beta_5^{M_4}\beta_6^{M_5}\beta_7^{M_6}\beta_8^{M_7}\beta_9^{M_8}\beta_{10}^{M_9}\beta_{11}^{M_{10}}\beta_{12}^{M_{11}}\varepsilon_i \qquad \textbf{(16.18)}$$

where

X_i = coded monthly value, $i = 0, 1, 2, \ldots$

M_1 = 1 if January, 0 if not January

M_2 = 1 if February, 0 if not February

M_3 = 1 if March, 0 if not March

.
.
.

M_{11} = 1 if November, 0 if not November

β_0 = Y intercept

$(\beta_1 - 1) \times 100\%$ = monthly compound growth rate (in %)

β_2 = multiplier for January relative to December

β_3 = multiplier for February relative to December

β_4 = multiplier for March relative to December

.
.
.

β_{12} = multiplier for November relative to December

ε_i = value of the irregular component for time period i

The model in Equation (16.18) is not in the form of a linear regression model. To transform this nonlinear model into a linear model, you can use a base 10 logarithm transformation. Taking the logarithm of each side of Equation (16.18) results in Equation (16.19).

TRANSFORMED EXPONENTIAL MODEL WITH MONTHLY DATA

$$\begin{aligned}\log(Y_i) &= \log(\beta_0\beta_1^{X_i}\beta_2^{M_1}\beta_3^{M_2}\beta_4^{M_3}\beta_5^{M_4}\beta_6^{M_5}\beta_7^{M_6}\beta_8^{M_7}\beta_9^{M_8}\beta_{10}^{M_9}\beta_{11}^{M_{10}}\beta_{12}^{M_{11}}\varepsilon_i) \qquad \textbf{(16.19)}\\ &= \log(\beta_0) + X_i\log(\beta_1) + M_1\log(\beta_2) + M_2\log(\beta_3)\\ &\quad + M_3\log(\beta_4) + M_4\log(\beta_5) + M_5\log(\beta_6) + M_6\log(\beta_7)\\ &\quad + M_7\log(\beta_8) + M_8\log(\beta_9) + M_9\log(\beta_{10}) + M_{10}\log(\beta_{11})\\ &\quad + M_{11}\log(\beta_{12}) + \log(\varepsilon_i)\end{aligned}$$

Equation (16.19) is a linear model that you can estimate using the least-squares method. Performing the regression analysis using $\log(Y_i)$ as the dependent variable and $X_i, M_1, M_2, \ldots,$ and M_{11} as the independent variables results in Equation (16.20).

EXPONENTIAL GROWTH WITH MONTHLY DATA FORECASTING EQUATION

$$\begin{aligned}\log(\hat{Y}_i) &= b_0 + b_1X_i + b_2M_1 + b_3M_2 + b_4M_3 + b_5M_4 + b_6M_5 + b_7M_6\\ &\quad + b_8M_7 + b_9M_8 + b_{10}M_9 + b_{11}M_{10} + b_{12}M_{11} \qquad \textbf{(16.20)}\end{aligned}$$

where

$$\begin{aligned}b_0 &= \text{estimate of } \log(\beta_0) \text{ and thus } 10^{b_0} = \hat{\beta}_0\\ b_1 &= \text{estimate of } \log(\beta_1) \text{ and thus } 10^{b_1} = \hat{\beta}_1\\ b_2 &= \text{estimate of } \log(\beta_2) \text{ and thus } 10^{b_2} = \hat{\beta}_2\\ b_3 &= \text{estimate of } \log(\beta_3) \text{ and thus } 10^{b_3} = \hat{\beta}_3\\ &\vdots\\ b_{12} &= \text{estimate of } \log(\beta_{12}) \text{ and thus } 10^{b_{12}} = \hat{\beta}_{12}\end{aligned}$$

Q_1, Q_2, and Q_3 are the three dummy variables needed to represent the four quarter periods in a quarterly time series. $M_1, M_2, M_3, \ldots, M_{11}$ are the 11 dummy variables needed to represent the 12 months in a monthly time series. In building the model, you use $\log(Y_i)$ instead of Y_i values and then find the regression coefficients by taking the antilog of the regression coefficients developed from Equations (16.17) and (16.20).

Although at first glance these regression models look imposing, when fitting or forecasting in any one time period, the values of all or all but one of the dummy variables in the model are equal to zero, and the equations simplify dramatically. In establishing the dummy variables for quarterly time-series data, the fourth quarter is the base period and has a coded value of zero for each dummy variable. With a quarterly time series, Equation (16.17) reduces as follows:

For any first quarter: $\log(\hat{Y}_i) = b_0 + b_1X_i + b_2$

For any second quarter: $\log(\hat{Y}_i) = b_0 + b_1X_i + b_3$

For any third quarter: $\log(\hat{Y}_i) = b_0 + b_1X_i + b_4$

For any fourth quarter: $\log(\hat{Y}_i) = b_0 + b_1X_i$

When establishing the dummy variables for each month, December serves as the base period and has a coded value of 0 for each dummy variable. For example, with a monthly time series, Equation (16.20) reduces as follows:

$$\text{For any January: } \log(\hat{Y}_i) = b_0 + b_1X_i + b_2$$
$$\text{For any February: } \log(\hat{Y}_i) = b_0 + b_1X_i + b_3$$
$$\vdots$$
$$\text{For any November: } \log(\hat{Y}_i) = b_0 + b_1X_i + b_{12}$$
$$\text{For any December: } \log(\hat{Y}_i) = b_0 + b_1X_i$$

To demonstrate the process of model building and least-squares forecasting with a quarterly time series, return to the Wal-Mart Stores, Inc., revenue data (in billions of dollars) originally displayed in Table 16.3 on page 696. The data are from the first quarter of 2005 through the last quarter of 2010. Figure 16.21 shows the regression results for the quarterly exponential trend model.

FIGURE 16.21

Excel and Minitab regression results for the quarterly revenue data for Wal-Mart Stores, Inc.

	A	B	C	D	E	F	G
1	Quarterly Revenues Model for Wal-Mart Stores						
2							
3	*Regression Statistics*						
4	Multiple R	0.9781					
5	R Square	0.9566					
6	Adjusted R Square	0.9474					
7	Standard Error	0.0155					
8	Observations	24					
9							
10	ANOVA						
11		*df*	*SS*	*MS*	*F*	*Significance F*	
12	Regression	4	0.1008	0.0252	104.6677	0.0000	
13	Residual	19	0.0046	0.0002			
14	Total	23	0.1054				
15							
16		*Coefficients*	*Standard Error*	*t Stat*	*P-value*	*Lower 95%*	*Upper 95%*
17	Intercept	1.8881	0.0087	215.9096	0.0000	1.8698	1.9064
18	Coded Quarter	0.0083	0.0005	17.8210	0.0000	0.0073	0.0092
19	Q1	-0.0618	0.0091	-6.8158	0.0000	-0.0808	-0.0428
20	Q2	-0.0391	0.0090	-4.3445	0.0003	-0.0580	-0.0203
21	Q3	-0.0557	0.0090	-6.2131	0.0000	-0.0745	-0.0370

Regression Analysis: Log(Revenues) versus Coded Quarter, Q1, Q2, Q3

```
The regression equation is
Log(Revenues) = 1.89 + 0.00826 Coded Quarter - 0.0618 Q1 - 0.0391 Q2 - 0.0557 Q3

Predictor            Coef    SE Coef       T      P
Constant          1.88813    0.00875  215.91  0.000
Coded Quarter   0.0082636  0.0004637   17.82  0.000
Q1              -0.061799   0.009067   -6.82  0.000
Q2              -0.039133   0.009007   -4.34  0.000
Q3              -0.055741   0.008972   -6.21  0.000

S = 0.0155184   R-Sq = 95.7%   R-Sq(adj) = 94.7%

Analysis of Variance
Source          DF        SS        MS       F      P
Regression       4  0.100825  0.025206  104.67  0.000
Residual Error  19  0.004576  0.000241
Total           23  0.105401
```

From Figure 16.21, the model fits the data extremely well. The coefficient of determination $r^2 = 0.9566$, the adjusted $r^2 = 0.9474$, and the overall F test results in an F_{STAT} test statistic of 104.6677 (p-value $= 0.000$). At the 0.05 level of significance, each regression coefficient is highly statistically significant and contributes to the model. The following summary includes the antilogs of all the regression coefficients:

Regression Coefficient	$b_i = \log \hat{\beta}_i$	$\hat{\beta}_i = \text{antilog}(b_i) = 10^{b_i}$
b_0: Y intercept	1.8881	77.2859
b_1: coded quarter	0.0083	1.0193
b_2: first quarter	−0.0618	0.8674
b_3: second quarter	−0.0391	0.9139
b_4: third quarter	−0.0557	0.8796

The interpretations for $\hat{\beta}_0$, $\hat{\beta}_1$, $\hat{\beta}_2$, $\hat{\beta}_3$, and $\hat{\beta}_4$ are as follows:

- The Y intercept, $\hat{\beta}_0 = 77.2859$ (in billions of dollars), is the *unadjusted* forecast for quarterly revenues in the first quarter of 2005, the initial quarter in the time series. *Unadjusted* means that the seasonal component is not incorporated in the forecast.

- The value $(\hat{\beta}_1 - 1) \times 100\% = 0.0193$, or 1.93%, is the estimated *quarterly compound growth rate* in revenues, after adjusting for the seasonal component.
- $\hat{\beta}_2 = 0.8674$ is the seasonal multiplier for the first quarter relative to the fourth quarter; it indicates that there is 13.26% less revenue for the first quarter than for the fourth quarter.
- $\hat{\beta}_3 = 0.9139$ is the seasonal multiplier for the second quarter relative to the fourth quarter; it indicates that there is 8.61% less revenue for the second quarter than for the fourth quarter.
- $\hat{\beta}_4 = 0.8796$ is the seasonal multiplier for the third quarter relative to the fourth quarter; it indicates that there is 12.04% less revenue for the third quarter than for the fourth quarter. Thus, the fourth quarter, which includes the holiday shopping season, has the strongest sales.

Using the regression coefficients b_0, b_1, b_2, b_3, b_4, and Equation (16.17) on page 698, you can make forecasts for selected quarters. As an example, to predict revenues for the fourth quarter of 2010 ($X_i = 23$),

$$\begin{aligned}\log(\hat{Y}_i) &= b_0 + b_1X_i \\ &= 1.8881 + (0.0083)(23) \\ &= 2.079\end{aligned}$$

Thus,

$$\log(\hat{Y}_i) = 10^{2.079} = 119.9499$$

The predicted revenue for the fourth quarter of fiscal 2010 is \$119.9499 billion. To make a forecast for a future time period, such as the first quarter of fiscal 2011 ($X_i = 24, Q_1 = 1$),

$$\begin{aligned}\log(\hat{Y}_i) &= b_0 + b_1X_i + b_2Q_1 \\ &= 1.8881 + (0.0083)(24) + (-0.0618)(1) \\ &= 2.0255\end{aligned}$$

Thus,

$$\hat{Y}_i = 10^{2.0255} = 106.0474$$

The predicted revenue for the first quarter of fiscal 2011 is \$106.0474 billion.

Problems for Section 16.7

LEARNING THE BASICS

16.40 In forecasting a monthly time series over a five-year period from January 2006 to December 2010, the exponential trend forecasting equation for January is

$$\log \hat{Y}_i = 2.0 + 0.01X_i + 0.10 \text{ (January)}$$

Take the antilog of the appropriate coefficient from this equation and interpret the

a. Y intercept, $\hat{b}_0$.
b. monthly compound growth rate.
c. January multiplier.

16.41 In forecasting daily time-series data, how many dummy variables are needed to account for the seasonal component day of the week?

16.42 In forecasting a quarterly time series over the five-year period from the first quarter of 2006 through the fourth quarter of 2010, the exponential trend forecasting equation is given by

$$\log \hat{Y}_i = 3.0 + 0.10X_i - 0.25Q_1 + 0.20Q_2 + 0.15Q_3$$

where quarter zero is the first quarter of 2006. Take the antilog of the appropriate coefficient from this equation and interpret the

a. Y intercept, $\hat{b}_0$.
b. quarterly compound growth rate.
c. second-quarter multiplier.

16.43 Refer to the exponential model given in Problem 16.42.

a. What is the fitted value of the series in the fourth quarter of 2008?

b. What is the fitted value of the series in the first quarter of 2008?

c. What is the forecast in the fourth quarter of 2010?

d. What is the forecast in the first quarter of 2011?

APPLYING THE CONCEPTS

SELF Test **16.44** The data in Toys R Us are quarterly revenues (in millions of dollars) for Toys R Us from 1996 through 2008.

Source: Data extracted from *Standard & Poor's Stock Reports*, November 1995, November 1998, and April 2002, New York: McGraw-Hill, Inc.; and Toys R Us, Inc., **www.toysrus.com**.

a. Do you think that the revenues for Toys R Us are subject to seasonal variation? Explain.

b. Plot the data. Does this chart support your answer in (a)?

c. Develop an exponential trend forecasting equation with quarterly components.

d. Interpret the quarterly compound growth rate.

e. Interpret the quarterly multipliers.

f. What are the forecasts for all four quarters of 2009?

16.45 Are gasoline prices higher during the height of the summer vacation season than at other times? The data in GasPrices give the mean monthly prices (in dollars per gallon) for unleaded gasoline in the United States from January 2006 to April 2010.

Source: Data extracted from Energy Information Administration, U.S. Department of Energy, **www.eia.doe.gov**.

a. Construct a time-series plot.

b. Develop an exponential trend forecasting equation with monthly components.

c. Interpret the monthly compound growth rate.

d. Interpret the monthly multipliers.

e. Write a short summary of your findings.

16.46 The data in Travel show the average traffic on Google recorded at the beginning of each month from January 2004 to August 2010 for searches from the United States concerning travel (scaled to the average traffic for the entire time period based on a fixed point at the beginning of the time period).

Source: Data downloaded from Google Trends, **www.google.com/trends**, August 13, 2010.

a. Plot the time-series data.

b. Develop an exponential trend forecasting equation with monthly components.

c. What is the fitted value in August 2010?

d. What are the forecasts for the last four months of 2010?

e. Interpret the monthly compound growth rate.

f. Interpret the July multiplier.

16.47 The following data (stored in Credit) are monthly credit card charges (in millions of dollars) for a popular credit card issued by a large bank (the name of which is not disclosed, at its request):

	Year		
Month	**2008**	**2009**	**2010**
January	31.9	39.4	45.0
February	27.0	36.2	39.6
March	31.3	40.5	
April	31.0	44.6	
May	39.4	46.8	
June	40.7	44.7	
July	42.3	52.2	
August	49.5	54.0	
September	45.0	48.8	
October	50.0	55.8	
November	50.9	58.7	
December	58.5	63.4	

a. Construct the time-series plot.

b. Describe the monthly pattern that is evident in the data.

c. In general, would you say that the overall dollar amounts charged on the bank's credit cards are increasing or decreasing? Explain.

d. Note that the December 2009 charges were more than $63 million, but those for February 2010 were less than $40 million. Was February's total close to what you would have expected?

e. Develop an exponential trend forecasting equation with monthly components.

f. Interpret the monthly compound growth rate.

g. Interpret the January multiplier.

h. What is the predicted value for March 2010?

i. What is the predicted value for April 2010?

j. How can this type of time-series forecasting benefit the bank?

16.48 The data in Silver-Q represent the price in London for an ounce of silver (in U.S. $) at the end of each quarter from 2004 through 2009.

Source: Data extracted from **http://www.kitco.com/gold.londonfix.html**.

a. Plot the data.

b. Develop an exponential trend forecasting equation with quarterly components.

c. Interpret the quarterly compound growth rate.

d. Interpret the first quarter multiplier.

e. What is the fitted value for the last quarter of 2009?

f. What are the forecasts for all four quarters of 2010?

g. Were the forecasts in (f) accurate? Explain.

16.49 The data in Gold represent the price in London for an ounce of gold (in U.S. $) at the end of each quarter from 2004 through 2009.

Source: Data extracted from **http://www.kitco.com/gold.londonfix.html**.

a. Plot the data.
b. Develop an exponential trend forecasting equation with quarterly components.
c. Interpret the quarterly compound growth rate.
d. Interpret the first quarter multiplier.
e. What is the fitted value for the last quarter of 2009?
f. What are the forecasts for all four quarters of 2010?
g. Were the forecasts in (f) accurate? Explain.

16.8 *Online Topic:* Index Numbers

Index numbers measure the value of an item (or group of items) at a particular point in time as a percentage of the value of an item (or group of items) at another point in time. To study this topic, read the **Section 16.8** online topic file that is available on this book's companion website. (See Appendix Section C to learn how to access the online topic files.)

THINK ABOUT THIS Let the Model User Beware

When you use a model, you must always review the assumptions built into the model and must always reflect how novel or changing circumstances may render the model less useful. No model can completely remove the risk involved in making a decision.

Implicit in the time-series models developed in this chapter is that past data can be used to help predict the future. While using past data in this way is a legitimate application of time-series models, every so often, a crisis in financial markets illustrates that using models that rely on the past to predict the future is not without risk.

For example, during August 2007, many hedge funds suffered unprecedented losses. Apparently, many hedge fund managers used models that based their investment strategy on trading patterns over long time periods. These models did not—and could not—reflect trading patterns contrary to historical patterns (G. Morgenson, "A Week When Risk Came Home to Roost," *The New York Times*, August 12, 2007, pp. B1, B7). When fund managers in early August 2007 needed to sell stocks due to losses in their fixed income portfolios, stocks that were previously stronger became weaker, and weaker ones became stronger—the reverse of what the models expected. Making matters worse was the fact that many fund managers were using similar models and rigidly made investment decisions solely based on what those models said. These similar actions multiplied the effect of the selling pressure, an effect that the models had not considered and that therefore could not be seen in the models' results.

This example illustrates that using models does not absolve you of the responsibility of being a thoughtful decision maker. Do go ahead and use models—when appropriately used, they will enhance your decision making—but don't use them mindlessly, for, in the words of a famous public service announcement, "a mind is a terrible thing to waste."

USING STATISTICS @ The Principled Revisited

In the Using Statistics scenario, you were the financial analyst for The Principled, a large financial services company. You needed to forecast the interest rate for three-month Treasury bills and revenues for Coca-Cola and Wal-Mart to better evaluate investment opportunities for your clients.

For three-month Treasury bills, you used moving averages and exponential smoothing methods to develop forecasts. You predicted that the interest rate for three-month Treasury bills at the end of 2010 would be 2.3%.

For The Coca-Cola Company, you used least-squares linear, quadratic, and exponential models and autoregressive models to develop forecasts. You evaluated these alternative models and determined that the first-order autoregressive model gave the best forecast, according to several criteria. You predicted that the revenue of The Coca-Cola Company would be \$32.5678 billion in 2010 and \$34.2444 billion in 2011.

For Wal-Mart Stores, Inc., you used a least-squares regression model with seasonal components to develop forecasts. You predicted that Wal-Mart Stores would have revenues of \$106.0474 billion in the first quarter of fiscal 2011.

Given these forecasts, you now need to determine whether your clients should invest, and if so, how much they should invest in Treasury bills and in these companies.

SUMMARY

In this chapter, you studied smoothing techniques, least-squares trend fitting, autoregressive models, and forecasting of seasonal data. Figure 16.22 provides a summary chart for the time-series methods discussed in this chapter.

When using time-series forecasting, you need to plot the time series and answer the following question: Is there a trend in the data? If there is a trend, then you can use the autoregressive model or the linear, quadratic, or exponential trend models. If there is no obvious trend in the time-series plot, then you should use moving averages or exponential smoothing to smooth out the effect of random effects and possible cyclical effects. After smoothing the data, if a trend is still not present, then you can use exponential smoothing to forecast short-term future values. If smoothing the data reveals a trend, then you can use the autoregressive model, or the linear, quadratic, or exponential trend models.

FIGURE 16.22
Summary chart of time-series forecasting methods

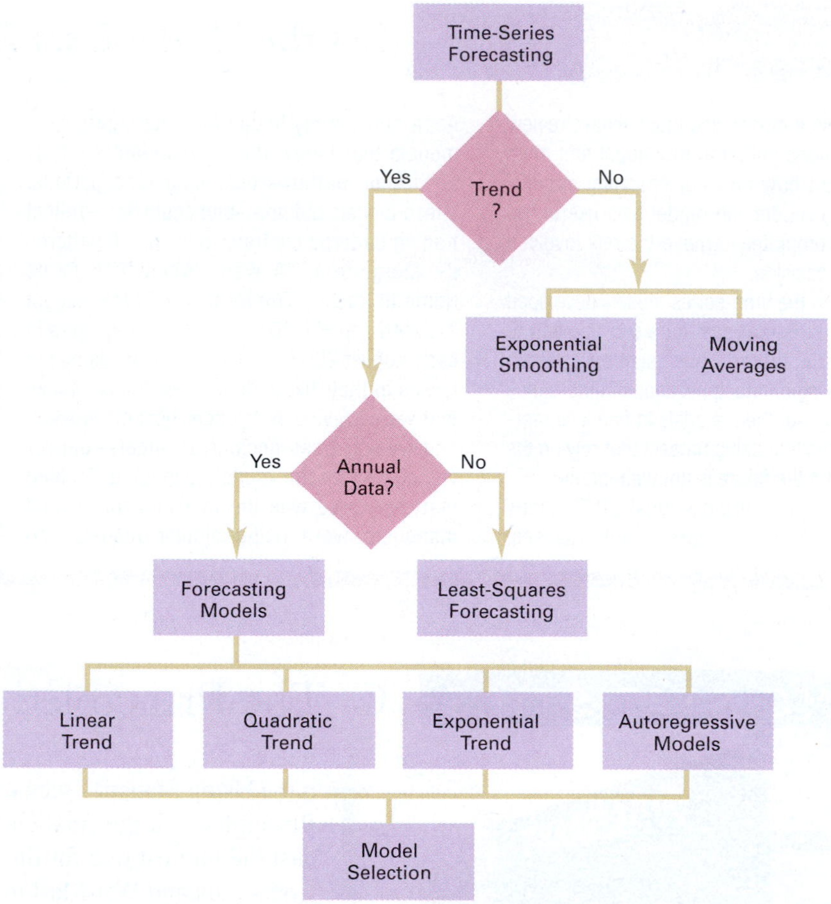

KEY EQUATIONS

Computing an Exponentially Smoothed Value in Time Period *i*

$$E_1 = Y_1 \quad \text{(16.1)}$$
$$E_i = WY_i + (1 - W)E_{i-1} \quad i = 2, 3, 4, \ldots$$

Forecasting Time Period *i* + 1

$$\hat{Y}_{i+1} = E_i \quad \text{(16.2)}$$

Linear Trend Forecasting Equation

$$\hat{Y}_i = b_0 + b_1X_i \quad \text{(16.3)}$$

Quadratic Trend Forecasting Equation

$$\hat{Y}_i = b_0 + b_1X_i + b_2X_i^2 \quad \text{(16.4)}$$

Exponential Trend Model

$$Y_i = \beta_0\beta_1^{X_i}\varepsilon_i \quad \text{(16.5)}$$

Transformed Exponential Trend Model

$$\log(Y_i) = \log(\beta_0\beta_1^{X_i}\varepsilon_i)$$
$$= \log(\beta_0) + \log(\beta_1^{X_i}) + \log(\varepsilon_i)$$
$$= \log(\beta_0) + X_i\log(\beta_1) + \log(\varepsilon_i) \quad \textbf{(16.6)}$$

Exponential Trend Forecasting Equation

$$\log(\hat{Y}_i) = b_0 + b_1X_i \quad \textbf{(16.7a)}$$
$$\hat{Y}_i = \hat{\beta}_0\,\hat{\beta}_1^{X_i} \quad \textbf{(16.7b)}$$

First-Order Autoregressive Model

$$Y_i = A_0 + A_1Y_{i-1} + \delta_i \quad \textbf{(16.8)}$$

Second-Order Autoregressive Model

$$Y_i = A_0 + A_1Y_{i-1} + A_2Y_{i-2} + \delta_i \quad \textbf{(16.9)}$$

***p*th-Order Autoregressive Models**

$$Y_i = A_0 + A_1Y_{i-1} + A_2Y_{i-2} + \cdots + A_pY_{i-p} + \delta_i \quad \textbf{(16.10)}$$

***t* Test for Significance of the Highest-Order Autoregressive Parameter, A_p**

$$t_{STAT} = \frac{a_p - A_p}{S_{a_p}} \quad \textbf{(16.11)}$$

Fitted *p*th-Order Autoregressive Equation

$$\hat{Y}_i = a_0 + a_1Y_{i-1} + a_2Y_{i-2} + \cdots + a_pY_{i-p} \quad \textbf{(16.12)}$$

***p*th-Order Autoregressive Forecasting Equation**

$$\hat{Y}_{n+j} = a_0 + a_1\hat{Y}_{n+j-1} + a_2\hat{Y}_{n+j-2} + \cdots + a_p\hat{Y}_{n+j-p} \quad \textbf{(16.13)}$$

Mean Absolute Deviation

$$MAD = \frac{\sum_{i=1}^{n}|Y_i - \hat{Y}_i|}{n} \quad \textbf{(16.14)}$$

Exponential Model with Quarterly Data

$$Y_i = \beta_0\beta_1^{X_i}\beta_2^{Q_1}\beta_3^{Q_2}\beta_4^{Q_3}\varepsilon_i \quad \textbf{(16.15)}$$

Transformed Exponential Model with Quarterly Data

$$\log(Y_i) = \log(\beta_0\beta_1^{X_i}\beta_2^{Q_1}\beta_3^{Q_2}\beta_4^{Q_3}\varepsilon_i) \quad \textbf{(16.16)}$$
$$= \log(\beta_0) + \log(\beta_1^{X_i}) + \log(\beta_2^{Q_1}) + \log(\beta_3^{Q_2})$$
$$+ \log(\beta_4^{Q_3}) + \log(\varepsilon_i)$$
$$= \log(\beta_0) + X_i\log(\beta_1) + Q_1\log(\beta_2)$$
$$+ Q_2\log(\beta_3) + Q_3\log(\beta_4) + \log(\varepsilon_i)$$

Exponential Growth with Quarterly Data Forecasting Equation

$$\log(\hat{Y}_i) = b_0 + b_1X_i + b_2Q_1 + b_3Q_2 + b_4Q_3 \quad \textbf{(16.17)}$$

Exponential Model with Monthly Data

$$Y_i = \beta_0\beta_1^{X_i}\beta_2^{M_1}\beta_3^{M_2}\beta_4^{M_3}\beta_5^{M_4}\beta_6^{M_5}\beta_7^{M_6}\beta_8^{M_7}\beta_9^{M_8}\beta_{10}^{M_9}\beta_{11}^{M_{10}}\beta_{12}^{M_{11}}\varepsilon_i \quad \textbf{(16.18)}$$

Transformed Exponential Model with Monthly Data

$$\log(Y_i) = \log(\beta_0\beta_1^{X_i}\beta_2^{M_1}\beta_3^{M_2}\beta_4^{M_3}\beta_5^{M_4}\beta_6^{M_5}\beta_7^{M_6}\beta_8^{M_7}\beta_9^{M_8}\beta_{10}^{M_9}\beta_{11}^{M_{10}}\beta_{12}^{M_{11}}\varepsilon_i)$$
$$= \log(\beta_0) + X_i\log(\beta_1) + M_1\log(\beta_2) + M_2\log(\beta_3)$$
$$+ M_3\log(\beta_4) + M_4\log(\beta_5) + M_5\log(\beta_6) + M_6\log(\beta_7)$$
$$+ M_7\log(\beta_8) + M_8\log(\beta_9) + M_9\log(\beta_{10})$$
$$+ M_{10}\log(\beta_{11}) + M_{11}\log(\beta_{12}) + \log(\varepsilon_i) \quad \textbf{(16.19)}$$

Exponential Growth with Monthly Data Forecasting Equation

$$\log(\hat{Y}_i) = b_0 + b_1X_i + b_2M_1 + b_3M_2 + b_4M_3 + b_5M_4 + b_6M_5$$
$$+ b_7M_6 + b_8M_7 + b_9M_8 + b_{10}M_9 + b_{11}M_{10} + b_{12}M_{11} \quad \textbf{(16.20)}$$

KEY TERMS

autoregressive modeling 684
causal forecasting method 666
cyclical effect 666
exponential smoothing 670
exponential trend model 676
first-order autocorrelation 684
first-order autoregressive model 684
forecasting 666
irregular effect 667
linear trend model 673
mean absolute deviation (*MAD*) 693
moving averages 668
parsimony 694
*p*th-order autocorrelation 684
*p*th-order autoregressive model 684
quadratic trend model 675
qualitative forecasting method 666
quantitative forecasting method 666
random effect 667
seasonal effect 667
second-order autocorrelation 684
second-order autoregressive model 684
time series 666
time-series forecasting method 666
trend 666

CHAPTER REVIEW PROBLEMS

CHECKING YOUR UNDERSTANDING

16.50 What is a time series?

16.51 What are the different components of a time-series model?

16.52 What is the difference between moving averages and exponential smoothing?

16.53 Under what circumstances is the exponential trend model most appropriate?

16.54 How does the least-squares linear trend forecasting model developed in this chapter differ from the least-squares linear regression model considered in Chapter 13?

16.55 How does autoregressive modeling differ from the other approaches to forecasting?

16.56 What are the different approaches to choosing an appropriate forecasting model?

16.57 What is the major difference between using S_{YX} and *MAD* for evaluating how well a particular model fits the data?

16.58 How does forecasting for monthly or quarterly data differ from forecasting for annual data?

APPLYING THE CONCEPTS

16.59 The following table (stored in **Polio**) represents the annual incidence rates (per 100,000 persons) of reported acute poliomyelitis recorded over five-year periods from 1915 to 1955:

Year	1915	1920	1925	1930	1935	1940	1945	1950	1955
Rate	3.1	2.2	5.3	7.5	8.5	7.4	10.3	22.1	17.6

Source: Data extracted from B. Wattenberg, ed., *The Statistical History of the United States: From Colonial Times to the Present,* ser. B303 (New York: Basic Books, 1976).

a. Plot the data.
b. Compute the linear trend forecasting equation and plot the trend line.
c. What are your forecasts for 1960, 1965, and 1970?
d. Using a library or the Internet, find the actually reported incidence rates of acute poliomyelitis for 1960, 1965, and 1970. Record your results.
e. Why are the forecasts you made in (c) not useful? Discuss.

16.60 The U.S. Department of Labor gathers and publishes statistics concerning the labor market. The file **Workforce** contains data on the size of the U.S. civilian noninstitutional population of people 16 years and over (in thousands) and the U.S. civilian noninstitutional workforce of people 16 years and over (in thousands) for 1984–2008. The workforce variable reports the number of people in the population who have a job or are actively looking for a job.

Source: Data extracted from Bureau of Labor Statistics, U.S. Department of Labor, **www.bls.gov**.

a. Plot the time series for the U.S. civilian noninstitutional population of people 16 years and older.
b. Compute the linear trend forecasting equation.
c. Forecast the U.S. civilian noninstitutional population of people 16 years and older for 2009 and 2010.
d. Repeat (a) through (c) for the U.S. civilian noninstitutional workforce of people 16 years and older.

16.61 The monthly wellhead and residential prices for natural gas (dollars per thousand cubic feet) in the United States from 2008 through 2009 are stored in **Natural Gas**.

Source: Data extracted from Energy Information Administration, U.S. Department of Energy, **www.eia.gov**, Natural Gas Monthly, July 2010.

For the wellhead price and the residential, price:
a. Do you think the price for natural gas has a seasonal component?
b. Plot the time series. Does this chart support your answer in (a)?
c. Compute an exponential trend forecasting equation for monthly data.
d. Interpret the monthly compound growth rate.
e. Interpret the month multipliers. Do the multipliers support your answers in (a) and (b)?
f. Compare the results for the wellhead prices and the residential prices.

16.62 The data in the following table (stored in **McDonalds**) represent the gross revenues (in billions of current dollars) of McDonald's Corporation from 1975 through 2009:

Year	Revenues	Year	Revenues	Year	Revenues
1975	1.0	1987	4.9	1999	13.3
1976	1.2	1988	5.6	2000	14.2
1977	1.4	1989	6.1	2001	14.8
1978	1.7	1990	6.8	2002	15.2
1979	1.9	1991	6.7	2003	16.8
1980	2.2	1992	7.1	2004	18.6
1981	2.5	1993	7.4	2005	19.8
1982	2.8	1994	8.3	2006	20.9
1983	3.1	1995	9.8	2007	22.8
1984	3.4	1996	10.7	2008	23.5
1985	3.8	1997	11.4	2009	22.7
1986	4.2	1998	12.4		

Source: Data extracted from *Moody's Handbook of Common Stocks,* 1980, 1989, and 1999; *Mergent's Handbook of Common Stocks,* Spring 2002; and **www.mcdonalds.com**.

a. Plot the data.
b. Compute the linear trend forecasting equation.
c. Compute the quadratic trend forecasting equation.
d. Compute the exponential trend forecasting equation.
e. Determine the best-fitting autoregressive model, using $\alpha = 0.05$.
f. Perform a residual analysis for each of the models in (b) through (e).
g. Compute the standard error of the estimate (S_{YX}) and the *MAD* for each corresponding model in (f).
h. On the basis of your results in (f) and (g), along with a consideration of the principle of parsimony, which model would you select for purposes of forecasting? Discuss.
i. Using the selected model in (h), forecast gross revenues for 2010.

16.63 Teachers' Retirement System of the City of New York offers several types of investments for its members. Among the choices are investments with fixed and variable rates of return. There are several categories of variable-return investments. The Diversified Equity Fund consists of investments that are primarily made in stocks, and the Stable-Value Fund consists of investments in corporate bonds and other types of lower-risk instruments. The data stored in **TRSNYC** represent the value of a unit of each type of variable-return investment at the beginning of each year from 1984 to 2010.

Source: Data extracted from Teachers' Retirement System of the City of New York, **www.trs.nyc.ny.us**.

For each of the two time series,
a. plot the data.
b. compute the linear trend forecasting equation.
c. compute the quadratic trend forecasting equation.
d. compute the exponential trend forecasting equation.
e. determine the best-fitting autoregressive model, using $\alpha = 0.05$.
f. Perform a residual analysis for each of the models in (b) through (e).
g. Compute the standard error of the estimate (S_{YX}) and the *MAD* for each corresponding model in (f).
h. On the basis of your results in (f) and (g), along with a consideration of the principle of parsimony, which model would you select for purposes of forecasting? Discuss.
i. Using the selected model in (h), forecast the unit values for 2011.
j. Based on the results of (a) through (i), what investment strategy would you recommend for a member of the Teachers' Retirement System of the City of New York? Explain.

REPORT WRITING EXERCISE

16.64 As a consultant to an investment company trading in various currencies, you have been assigned the task of studying long-term trends in the exchange rates of the Canadian dollar, the Japanese yen, and the English pound. Data from 1980 to 2009 are stored in **Currency**, where the Canadian dollar, the Japanese yen, and the English pound are expressed in units per U.S. dollar.

Develop a forecasting model for the exchange rate of each of these three currencies and provide forecasts for 2010 and 2011 for each currency. Write an executive summary for a presentation to be given to the investment company. Append to this executive summary a discussion regarding possible limitations that may exist in these models.

MANAGING ASHLAND MULTICOMM SERVICES

As part of the continuing strategic initiative to increase subscribers to the *3-For-All* cable/phone/Internet services, the marketing department is closely monitoring the number of subscribers. To help do so, forecasts are to be developed for the number of subscribers in the future. To accomplish this task, the number of subscribers for the most recent 24-month period has been determined and is stored in **AMS16**.

EXERCISES

1. Analyze these data and develop a model to forecast the number of subscribers. Present your findings in a report that includes the assumptions of the model and its limitations. Forecast the number of subscribers for the next four months.
2. Would you be willing to use the model developed to forecast the number of subscribers one year into the future? Explain.
3. Compare the trend in the number of subscribers to the number of new subscribers per month stored in **AMS13**. What explanation can you provide for any differences?

DIGITAL CASE

Apply your knowledge about time-series forecasting in this Digital Case.

The *Ashland Herald* competes for readers in the Tri-Cities area with the newer *Oxford Glen Journal* (*OGJ*). Recently, the circulation staff at the *OGJ* claimed that their newspaper's circulation and subscription base is growing faster than that of the *Herald* and that local advertisers would do better if they transferred their advertisements from the *Herald* to the *OGJ*. The circulation department of the *Herald* has complained to the Ashland Chamber of Commerce about *OGJ*'s claims and has asked the chamber to investigate, a request that was welcomed by *OGJ*'s circulation staff.

Open **ACC_Mediation216.pdf** to review the circulation dispute information collected by the Ashland Chamber of Commerce. Then answer the following:

1. Which newspaper would you say has the right to claim the fastest-growing circulation and subscription base? Support your answer by performing and summarizing an appropriate statistical analysis.

2. What is the single most positive fact about the *Herald*'s circulation and subscription base? What is the single most positive fact about the *OGJ*'s circulation and subscription base? Explain your answers.

3. What additional data would be helpful in investigating the circulation claims made by the staffs of each newspaper?

REFERENCES

1. Bowerman, B. L., R. T. O'Connell, and A. Koehler, *Forecasting, Time Series, and Regression*, 4th ed. (Belmont, CA: Duxbury Press, 2005).
2. Box, G. E. P., G. M. Jenkins, and G. C. Reinsel, *Time Series Analysis: Forecasting and Control*, 3rd ed. (Upper Saddle River, NJ: Prentice Hall, 1994).
3. Frees, E. W., *Data Analysis Using Regression Models: The Business Perspective* (Upper Saddle River, NJ: Prentice Hall, 1996).
4. Hanke, J. E., D. W. Wichern, and A. G. Reitsch, *Business Forecasting*, 7th ed. (Upper Saddle River, NJ: Prentice Hall, 2001).
5. *Microsoft Excel 2010* (Redmond, WA: Microsoft Corp., 2010).
6. *Minitab Release 16* (State College, PA: Minitab, Inc., 2010).

CHAPTER 16 EXCEL GUIDE

EG16.1 The IMPORTANCE of BUSINESS FORECASTING

There are no Excel Guide instructions for this section.

EG16.2 COMPONENT FACTORS of TIME-SERIES MODELS

There are no Excel Guide instructions for this section.

EG16.3 SMOOTHING an ANNUAL TIME SERIES

Moving Averages

In-Depth Excel Use the **COMPUTE worksheet** of the **Moving Averages workbook**, shown in Figure 16.2 on page 669, as a template for creating moving averages. The worksheet uses a series of **AVERAGE*(cell range that contains a sequence of L observed values)*** functions to compute moving averages for time-series data. For time periods in which no moving average can be computed, the worksheet uses the special worksheet value **#N/A** (not available).

For other problems, paste the time-series data into columns A and B and adjust the moving average entries in columns C and D. The COMPUTE worksheet also contains a superimposed chart, an exception to the general rule in this book that places each chart on its own chart sheet. To use this chart for other problems, double-click the chart titles and labels to change them to appropriate values. (The plot of points changes automatically when you change the data.)

To create the chart from scratch on its own chart sheet, open to the COMPUTE worksheet and:

1. Select the cell range **A1:D20**, the cell range of the time-series data and the moving averages.
2. Select **Insert ➔ Scatter** and select the second **Scatter** gallery choice in the second row of choices (**Scatter with Straight Lines and Markers**).
3. Relocate the chart to a chart sheet and adjust the chart formatting by using the instructions in Appendix Section F.4 on page 815, ignoring the instruction to select **None** from the **Legend** gallery.

Exponential Smoothing

In-Depth Excel Use the **COMPUTE worksheet** of the **Exponential Smoothing workbook**, shown in Figure 16.3 on page 670, as a template for creating exponentially smoothed values. In this worksheet, cells C2 and D2 contain the formula **=B2**, cell **C3** contains the formula **=0.5 * B3 + 0.5 * C2**, and cell **D3** contains the formula **=0.25 * B3 + 0.75 * D2**. The other formulas in columns C and D are the result of copying the C3 and D3 formulas down the columns. (Note that in the C3 and D3 formulas, the expression $1 - W$ has been simplified to the values 0.5 and 0.75, respectively.)

For other problems with fewer than 20 time periods, delete the excess rows. For problems with more than 20 time periods, select row 20, right-click, and click **Insert** in the shortcut menu. Repeat as many times as there are new rows. Then select cell range **C19:D19** and copy the contents of this range down through the new table rows.

The COMPUTE worksheet also contains a superimposed chart, an exception to the general rule in this book that places each chart on its own chart sheet. To use this chart for other problems, double-click the chart titles and labels to change them to appropriate values. (The plot of points changes automatically when you change the data.) To create the chart from scratch on its own chart sheet, open to the COMPUTE worksheet and select the cell range **A1:D20**, the cell range of the time-series data and the moving averages. Select **Insert ➔ Scatter** and select the second **Scatter** gallery choice in the second row of choices (**Scatter with Straight Lines and Markers**). Relocate the chart to a chart sheet and adjust the chart formatting by using the instructions in Appendix Section F.4 on page 815, ignoring the instruction to select **None** from the **Legend** gallery.

Analysis ToolPak Use **Exponential Smoothing** to create exponentially smoothed values. For example, to create the column C exponentially smoothed Three-Month U.S. Treasury bill rates (smoothing coefficient $W = 0.50$), shown in Figure 16.3 on page 670, open to the **DATA worksheet** of the **Treasury workbook** and:

1. Select **Data ➔ Data Analysis.**
2. In the Data Analysis dialog box, select **Exponential Smoothing** from the **Analysis Tools** list and then click **OK**.

In the Exponential Smoothing dialog box (shown below):

3. Enter **B1:B20** as the **Input Range**.
4. Enter **0.5** as the **Damping factor**. (The damping factor is equal to 1 − *W*.)
5. Check **Labels**, enter **C1** as the **Output Range**, and click **OK**.

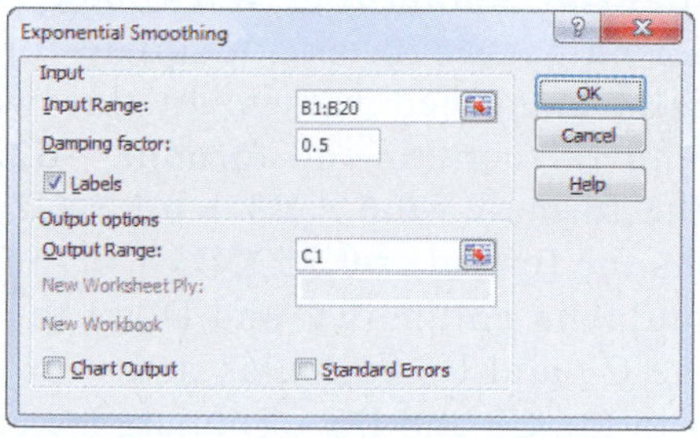

In the new column C:

6. Copy the last formula in cell **C19** to cell **C20**.
7. Enter the column heading **ES(W =.50)** in cell **C1**, replacing the #N/A value.

For other problems, to create exponentially smoothed values using a smoothing coefficient of $W = 0.25$, enter **0.75** as the damping factor in step 4. (The damping factor is equal to 1 − *W*.)

EG16.4 LEAST-SQUARES TREND FITTING and FORECASTING

The Linear Trend Model

Modify the Section EG13.2 instructions (see page 571) to create a linear trend model. Use the cell range of the coded variable as the *X* variable cell range (called the **X Variable Cell Range** in the *PHStat2* instructions, called the **cell range of X variable** in the *In-Depth Excel* instructions, and called the **Input X Range** in the *Analysis ToolPak* instructions). If you need to create coded values, enter them manually in a column. (If you have many coded values, you can use **Home ➔ Fill** (in the Editing group) **➔ Series** and in the Series dialog box, click **Columns** and **Linear**, and select appropriate values for **Step value** and **Stop value**.

The Quadratic Trend Model

Modify the Section EG15.1 instructions (see page 660) to create a quadratic trend model. Use the cell range of the coded variable and the squared coded variable as the *X* variables cell range (called the **X Variables Cell Range** in the *PHStat2* instructions, called the **cell range of X variables** in the *In-Depth Excel* instructions, and called the **Input X Range** in the *Analysis ToolPak* instructions). Use the Section EG15.1 instructions to create the squared coded variable.

To plot the quadratic trend, modify the Section EG13.2 *In-Depth Excel* instructions on page 571. Choose the polynomial type (not linear) by clicking **Polynomial** instead of **Linear** in step 2.

The Exponential Trend Model

Due to the limitations of Excel, creating an exponential trend model requires more work than creating the other trend models. First, modify the Section EG13.5 and EG13.2 instructions (see pages 572 and 571) to use the cell range of the log *Y* values as the *Y* variable cell range and the cell range of the coded variable as the *X* variable cell range. (The *Y* variable cell range and the *X* variable cell range are called the **Y Variable Cell Range** and **X Variable Cell Range** in the *PHStat2* instructions, called the **cell range of Y variable** and **cell range of X variable** in the *In-Depth Excel* instructions, and called the **Input Y Range** and **Input X Range** in the *Analysis ToolPak* instructions.) Use the Section EG15.2 instructions on page 660 to create the log *Y* values.

Using the modified instructions will create a regression results worksheet for a simple linear regression model and create additional columns for the logs of the residuals and the logs of the predicted *Y* values in a residual worksheet if using the *PHStat2* or *In-Depth Excel* instructions, or in the RESIDUAL OUTPUT area in the regression results worksheet, if using the *Analysis ToolPak* instructions. (If using the *Analysis ToolPak* instructions, note that the additional column for the logs of the residuals has the misleading label **Residuals**, and not the label **LOG(Residuals)**, as one might expect.)

To these results, add a column that contains the original (untransformed) *Y* values and a column of formulas that use the **POWER** function to transform the logs of the predicted *Y* values to the predicted *Y* values. To do so, first copy the original *Y* values to the empty column in the residuals worksheet (if using *PHStat2* or *In-Depth Excel*) or a column to the right of RESIDUALS OUTPUT area (if using the *Analysis ToolPak* instructions). Then create a new column that contains formulas in the form **=POWER(10, *log of predicted value*)** to compute the predicted *Y* values.

Use columns F and G of the **RESIDUALS worksheet** of the **Exponential Trend workbook** as a model for creating the two additional columns. This worksheet contains the values needed to create the Figure 16.9 plot that fits an exponential trend forecasting equation for The Coca-Cola Company revenues (see page 678). (In this worksheet, the formula **=POWER(10, C2)** was entered in cell G2 and copied down through row 16.)

Using the original X (time) variable column, the original Y variable column, and the predicted Y variable column, in that order, in the RESIDUALS worksheet, create and modify a scatter plot using the instructions given below. (Use these instructions even if you originally used PHStat2 or Analysis ToolPak to create the data for this plot.) For example, to create an exponential trend plot for The Coca-Cola Company revenue, open to the **RESIDUALS worksheet** of the **Exponential Trend workbook**. Select cell range **B1:B16** and while holding down the **Ctrl** key, select the cell range **F1:G16** and:

1. Select **Insert → Scatter** and select the **first Scatter gallery** choice (**Scatter with only Markers**).
2. Right-click one of the predicted revenues data points (typically a reddish square) and select **Format Data Series** from the shortcut menu.
3. Click **Marker Options** in the left pane and in the **Marker Options** right pane click **None**.
4. Back in the left pane, click **Line Style** and in the **Line Style** right pane enter **2** as the **Width**. Click **OK**.
5. Relocate the chart to a chart sheet and adjust the chart formatting by using the instructions in Appendix Section F.4 on page 815.

Model Selection Using First, Second, and Percentage Differences

Use arithmetic formulas to compute the first, second, and percentage differences. Use division formulas to compute the percentage differences and use subtraction formulas to compute the first and second differences. Use the **COMPUTE worksheet** of the **Differences workbook**, shown in Figure 16.10 on page 680 as a model for developing a differences worksheet. (Open to the **COMPUTE_FORMULAS worksheet** to see all formulas used.)

EG16.5 AUTOREGRESSIVE MODELING for TREND FITTING and FORECASTING

Creating Lagged Predictor Variables

Create lagged predictor variables by creating a column of formulas that refer to a previous row's (previous time period's) Y value. Enter the special worksheet value **#N/A** (not available) for the cells in the column to which lagged values do not apply.

Use the **COMPUTE worksheet** of the **Lagged Predictors workbook**, shown in Figure 16.12 on page 688 as a model for developing lagged predictor variables for the first-order, second-order, and third-order autoregressive models. When using lagged predictor variables, you select or refer to only those rows that contain lagged values. Unlike the general case in this book, you do not include rows that contain **#N/A**, nor do you include the row 1 column heading.

Autoregressive Modeling

Modify the Section EG14.1 instructions (see page 622) to create a third-order or second-order autoregressive model. Use the cell range of the first-order, second-order, and third-order lagged predictor variables as the X variables cell range for the third-order model. Use the cell range of the first-order and second-order lagged predictor variables as the X variables cell range for the second-order model (The X variables cell range is the **X Variables Cell Range** in the *PHStat2* instructions, called the **cell range of X variables** in the *In-Depth Excel* instructions, and called the **Input X Range** in the *Analysis ToolPak* instructions.) If using the *PHStat2* instructions, omit step 3 (clear, do *not* check, **First cells in both ranges contain label**). If using the *Analysis ToolPak* instructions, do not check **Labels** in step 4.

Modify the Section EG13.2 instructions (see page 571) to create a first-order autoregressive model. Use the cell range of the first-order lagged predictor variable as the X variable cell range (called the **X Variable Cell Range** in the *PHStat2* instructions, called the **cell range of X variable** in the *In-Depth Excel* instructions, and called the **Input X Range** in the *Analysis ToolPak* instructions). If using the *PHStat2* instructions, omit step 3 (clear, do *not* check, **First cells in both ranges contain label**). If using the *Analysis ToolPak* instructions, do not check **Labels** in step 4.

EG16.6 CHOOSING an APPROPRIATE FORECASTING MODEL

Measuring the Magnitude of the Residuals Through Squared or Absolute Differences

Use a two-part process to compute the mean absolute deviation (*MAD*). First, perform the appropriate residual analysis using either the Section EG13.5 or Section EG14.3 instructions (see pages 572 and 623). Then, add a column (or columns) of formulas to compute the mean absolute deviation (*MAD*) to the table that includes the residuals (in a residuals worksheet if using the *PHStat2* or *In-Depth Excel* instructions or as part of a regression results worksheet if using the *Analysis ToolPak* instructions).

For a linear, quadratic, or autoregressive model, add a column of formulas in the form **=ABS(*residual cell*)** to compute the absolute value of the residuals and then add the single formula in the form =AVERAGE(*cell range of the absolute values of the residuals*) to compute the *MAD*.

For an exponential model, you must first create the additional columns for the logs of the residuals and the logs of the "predicted *Y*" values using the "The Exponential Trend Model" instructions in Section EG16.4 on page 710. (As explained in that section, use columns F and G of the **RESIDUALS worksheet** of the **Exponential Trend workbook** as a model for creating the two additional columns.) To these two columns, add a third column of formulas in the form **=ABS(*original Y value cell* – *predicted Y value cell*)** to calculate the absolute value of the residuals. At the end of this column, add a single formula in the form **=AVERAGE(*cell range of residual absolute values*)** to compute the *MAD*. Use column H of the **RESIDUALS worksheet** of the **Exponential Trend workbook** as a model for creating this third column. In this worksheet, the formula **=ABS(F2 − G2)** was entered in cell **H2** and copied down through row 15, and the single formula **=AVERAGE(H2:H15)** was entered in cell **H16**.

A Comparison of Four Forecasting Methods

When you compare the four forecasting models, you use residual analysis to examine the models. Use the instructions in Section EG13.5 on page 572 to create residual plots for the linear trend model or first-order autoregressive models. Use the instructions in Section EG14.3 on page 623 to create residual plots for the quadratic trend model.

As is the case in other instructions in this Excel Guide, creating residual plots for the exponential trend model requires additional work. First create the additional columns for the logs of the residuals and the logs of the predicted *Y* values using the "The Exponential Trend Model" instructions of Section EG16.4 on page 710. (As explained in that section, use columns F and G of the **RESIDUALS worksheet** of the **Exponential Trend workbook** as a model for creating the two additional columns.)

To these two columns, add a third column of formulas in the form ***=original Y value cell - predicted Y value cell*** to calculate the residuals. Use column I of the **RESIDUALS worksheet** of the **Exponential Trend workbook** as a model for creating this third column. Then select the original *X* (time) variable column and the new column of computed residuals, in that order, and use the Section EG2.6 instructions for creating a scatter plot to create the exponential trend residual plot.

EG16.7 TIME-SERIES FORECASTING of SEASONAL DATA

Least-Squares Forecasting with Monthly or Quarterly Data

To develop a least-squares regression model for monthly or quarterly data, add columns of formulas that use the **IF** function to create dummy variables for the quarterly or monthly data. Enter all formulas in the form **=IF(*comparison*, 1, 0)**.

Figure EG16.1 shows the first four rows of columns F through K of a data worksheet that contains dummy variables. Columns F, G, and H contain the quarterly dummy variables Q1, Q2, and Q3 that are based on column B coded quarter values (not shown). Columns J and K contain the two monthly variables M1 and M6 that are based on column C month values (also not shown).

FIGURE EG16.1 Dummy variable formulas for quarterly and monthly data

	F	G	H	I	J	K
1	Q1	Q2	Q3		M1	M6
2	=IF(B2 = 1, 1, 0)	=IF(B2 = 2, 1, 0)	=IF(B2 = 3, 1, 0)		=IF(C2 ="January", 1, 0)	=IF(C2 = "June", 1, 0)
3	=IF(B3 = 1, 1, 0)	=IF(B3 = 2, 1, 0)	=IF(B3 = 3, 1, 0)		=IF(C3 ="January", 1, 0)	=IF(C3 = "June", 1, 0)
4	=IF(B4 = 1, 1, 0)	=IF(B4 = 2, 1, 0)	=IF(B4 = 3, 1, 0)		=IF(C4 ="January", 1, 0)	=IF(C4 = "June", 1, 0)
5	=IF(B5 = 1, 1, 0)	=IF(B5 = 2, 1, 0)	=IF(B5 = 3, 1, 0)		=IF(C5 ="January", 1, 0)	=IF(C5 = "June", 1, 0)

CHAPTER 16 MINITAB GUIDE

MG16.1 The IMPORTANCE of BUSINESS FORECASTING

There are no Minitab Guide instructions for this section.

MG16.2 COMPONENT FACTORS of TIME-SERIES MODELS

There are no Minitab Guide instructions for this section.

MG16.3 SMOOTHING AN ANNUAL TIME SERIES

Moving Averages

Use **Moving Average** to compute moving averages. For example, to compute the moving averages shown in column C of Figure 16.2 on page 669, open to the **Treasury worksheet**. Select **Stat ➔ Time Series ➔ Moving Average**. In the Moving Average dialog box (shown below):

1. Double-click **C2 Rate** in the variables list to add **Rate** to the **Variable** box.
2. Enter **3** in the **MA length** box.
3. Check **Center the moving averages**.
4. Click **Results**.

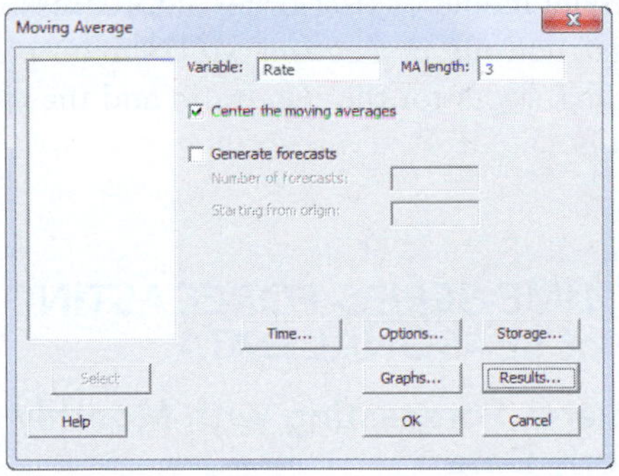

5. In the Moving Average - Results dialog box (not shown), click **Summary table and results table** and then click **OK**.
6. Back in the Moving Average dialog box, click **OK**.

For a seven-year moving average, enter **7** in the **MA length** box in step 2.

Exponential Smoothing

Use **Single Exp Smoothing** to compute exponential smoothed values. For example, to compute the exponential smoothed values shown in column C of Figure 16.3 on page 670, open to the **Treasury worksheet**. Select **Stat ➔ Time Series ➔ Single Exp Smoothing**. In the Single Exponential Smoothing dialog box (shown below):

1. Double-click **C2 Rate** in the variables list to add **Rate** to the **Variable** box.
2. Click **Use** and enter **0.50** in its box (for a *W* value of 0.50).
3. Click **Options**.

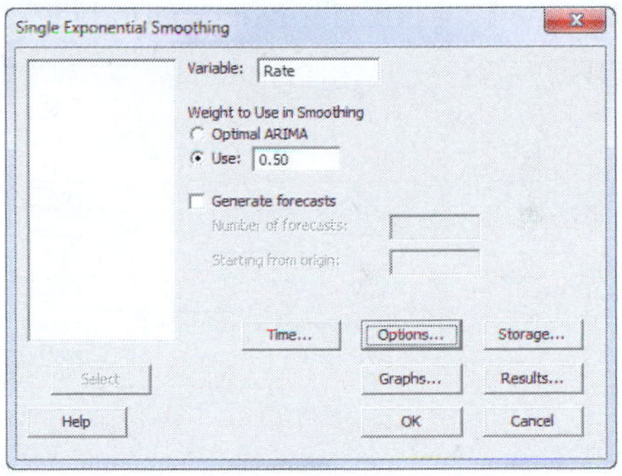

4. In the Single Exponential Smoothing - Options dialog box, enter **1** in the **Use average of first K observations** box and then click **OK.**
5. Back in the Single Exponential Smoothing dialog box, click **Results**.
6. In the Single Exponential Smoothing - Results dialog box, click **Summary table and results table** and then click **OK**.
7. Back in the Single Exponential Smoothing dialog box, click **OK**.

For a *W* value of 0.25, enter **0.25** in step 2.

MG16.4 LEAST-SQUARES TREND FITTING and FORECASTING

In Chapters 13 through 15, you used Minitab for the simple linear regression model and for a variety of multiple regression models. In this chapter, time-series models were developed assuming either a linear, quadratic, or exponential trend. For the linear trend model, see Section MG13.2 on page 573. For the quadratic and the exponential trend models, see Sections MG15.1 and MG15.2 on pages 661–662.

MG16.5 AUTOREGRESSIVE MODELING for TREND FITTING and FORECASTING

Creating Lagged Predictor Variables

Use **Lag** to create lagged predictor variables for autoregressive models. For example, to create the lagged variables shown in Figure 16.12 on page 688, open to the **Coca-Cola worksheet**. Select **Stat → Time Series → Lag**. In the Lag dialog box (shown below):

1. Double-click **C3 Revenues** in the variables list to add **Revenues** to the **Series** box.
2. Enter **C4** in the **Store lags in** box and press **Tab**.
3. Enter **1** in the **Lag** box (for a one-period lag).
4. Click **OK**.

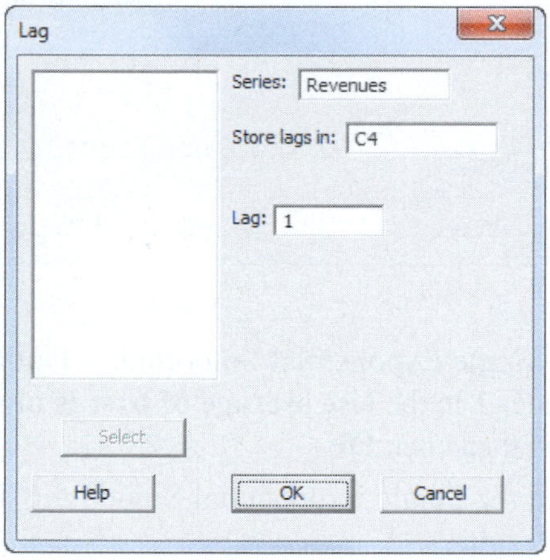

5. In the worksheet, enter **Lag1** as the name for column **C4**.
6. Again select **Stat → Time Series → Lag**. In the Lag dialog box, enter **C5** in the **Store lags in** box, press **Tab**, and enter **2** in the **Lag** box (for a 2-period lag). Click **OK**.
7. In the worksheet, enter **Lag2** as the name for column **C5**.
8. Reselect **Stat → Time Series → Lag**. In the Lag dialog box, enter **C6** in the **Store lags in** box, press **Tab**, and enter **3** in the **Lag** box (for a 3-period lag). Click **OK**.
9. In the worksheet, enter **Lag3** as the name for column **C6**.

Autoregressive Modeling

Modify the Section MG14.1 "Interpreting the Regression Coefficients" instructions (see page 625) to create a third-order or second-order autoregressive model. Add the names of the columns containing the first-order, second-order, and third-order lagged predictor variables to the **Predictors** box for the third-order model. Add the names of the columns containing the first-order, and second-order lagged predictor variables to the **Predictors** box for the second-order model.

Modify the Section MG13.2 instructions (see page 573) to create a first-order autoregressive model. In step 2, add the name of the column containing the first-order lagged predictor variable to the **Predictors** box.

MG16.6 CHOOSING an APPROPRIATE FORECASTING MODEL

A Comparison of Four Forecasting Methods

When you compare the four forecasting models, you use residual analysis to examine the models. Use the instructions in Section MG13.5 on page 574 to create residual plots for the linear trend model or first-order autoregressive models. Use the instructions in Section MG14.1 on page 625 to create residual plots for the quadratic and the exponential trend models.

MG16.7 TIME-SERIES FORECASTING of SEASONAL DATA

Least-Squares Forecasting with Monthly or Quarterly Data

Use **Calculator** to create dummy variables for the quarterly or monthly data. For example, to create the dummy quarterly variable Q1 for the Wal-Mart Stores quarterly revenues shown in Table 16.3 on page 696, open to the **WalMart**

worksheet. Select **Calc → Calculator**. In the Calculator dialog box:

1. Enter **C5** in the **Store result in variable** box.
2. Enter **IF(Quarter=1,1,0)** in the **Expression** box.
3. Click **OK**.
4. Enter **Q1** as the name for column **C5**.

In step 2, use the expression **IF(Quarter=2,1,0)** to create the dummy quarterly variable Q2 or use **IF(Quarter=3,1,0)** to create the quarterly variable Q3.

For monthly variables, first convert the values to text, if necessary, using **Change Data Type** (see Section MG1.2 on page 22). Then select **Calc → Calculator** and enter expressions such as **IF(Month="January",1,0)** in the **Expression** box.

17 Statistical Applications in Quality Management

Learning Objectives

In this chapter, you learn:

- How to construct a variety of control charts
- Which control chart to use for a particular type of data
- The basic themes of total quality management and Deming's 14 points
- The basic aspects of Six Sigma

USING STATISTICS

@ Beachcomber Hotel

You find yourself managing the Beachcomber Hotel, one of the resorts owned by T.C. Resort Properties (see Chapter 12). Your business objective is to continually improve the quality of service that your guests receive so that overall guest satisfaction increases. To help you achieve this improvement, T.C. Resort Properties has provided its managers with training in Six Sigma. In order to meet the business objective of increasing the return rate of guests at your hotel, you have decided to focus on the critical first impressions of the service that your hotel provides. Is the assigned hotel room ready when a guest checks in? Are all expected amenities, such as extra towels and a complimentary guest basket, in the room when the guest first walks in? Are the video-entertainment center and high-speed Internet access working properly? And do guests receive their luggage in a reasonable amount of time?

To study these guest satisfaction issues, you have embarked on an improvement project that focuses on the readiness of the room and the time it takes to deliver luggage. You would like to learn the following:

- Are the proportion of rooms ready and the time required to deliver luggage to the rooms acceptable?
- Are the proportion of rooms ready and the luggage delivery time consistent from day to day, or are they increasing or decreasing?
- On the days when the proportion of rooms that are not ready or the time to deliver luggage is greater than normal, are these fluctuations due to a chance occurrence, or are there fundamental flaws in the processes used to make rooms ready and to deliver luggage?

All companies, whether they manufacture products or provide services, as T.C. Resort Properties does in the Beachcomber Hotel scenario, understand that quality is essential for survival in the global economy. Quality has an impact on our everyday work and personal lives in many ways: in the design, production, and reliability of our automobiles; in the services provided by hotels, banks, schools, retailers, and telecommunications companies; in the continuous improvement in integrated circuits that makes for more capable consumer electronics and computers; and in the availability of new technology and equipment that has led to improved diagnosis of illnesses and improved delivery of health care services.

In this chapter you will learn how to develop and analyze control charts, a statistical tool that is widely used for quality improvement. You will then learn how businesses and organizations around the world are using control charts as part of two important quality improvement approaches: total quality management (TQM) and Six Sigma.

17.1 The Theory of Control Charts

A **process** is the value-added transformation of inputs to outputs. The inputs and outputs of a process can involve machines, materials, methods, measurement, people, and the environment. Each of the inputs is a source of variability. Variability in the output can result in poor service and poor product quality, both of which often decrease customer satisfaction.

Control charts, developed by Walter Shewhart in the 1920s (see reference 17), are commonly used statistical tools for monitoring and improving processes. A **control chart** analyzes a process in which data are collected sequentially over time. You use a control chart to study past performance, to evaluate present conditions, or to predict future outcomes. You use control charts at the beginning of quality improvement efforts to study an existing process (such charts are called *Phase 1 control charts*). Information gained from analyzing Phase 1 control charts forms the basis for process improvement. After improvements to the process are implemented, you then use control charts to monitor the processes to ensure that the improvements continue (these charts are called *Phase 2 control charts*).

Different types of control charts allow you to analyze different types of critical-to-quality (*CTQ* in Six Sigma lingo—see Section 17.8) variables—for categorical variables, such as the proportion of hotel rooms that are nonconforming in terms of the availability of amenities and the working order of all appliances in the room; for discrete variables such as the number of hotel guests registering complaints in a week; and for continuous variables, such as the length of time required for delivering luggage to the room.

In addition to providing a visual display of data representing a process, a principal focus of a control chart is the attempt to separate special causes of variation from common causes of variation.

THE TWO TYPES OF CAUSES OF VARIATION

Special causes of variation represent large fluctuations or patterns in data that are not part of a process. These fluctuations are often caused by unusual events and represent either problems to correct or opportunities to exploit. Some organizations refer to special causes of variation as **assignable causes of variation**.

Common causes of variation represent the inherent variability that exists in a process. These fluctuations consist of the numerous small causes of variability that operate randomly or by chance. Some organizations refer to common causes of variation as **chance causes of variation**.

Walter Shewhart (see reference 17) developed an experiment that illustrates the distinction between common and special causes of variation. The experiment asks you to repeatedly write the letter A in a horizontal line across a piece of paper:

AAAAAAAAAAAAAAAAA

When you do this, you immediately notice that the A's are all similar but not exactly the same. In addition, you may notice some difference in the size of the A's from letter to letter. This difference is due to common cause variation. Nothing special happened that caused the differences in the size of the A. You probably would have a hard time trying to explain why the largest A is bigger than the smallest A. These types of differences almost certainly represent common cause variation.

However, if you did the experiment over again but wrote half of the A's with your right hand and the other half of the A's with your left hand, you would almost certainly see a very big difference in the A's written with each hand. In this case, the hand that you used to write the A's is the source of the special cause variation.

Common and special cause variation have a crucial difference. Common causes of variation can be reduced only by changing the process. (Such systemic changes are the responsibility of management.) In contrast, because special causes of variation are not part of a process, special causes are correctable or exploitable without changing that process. (In the example, changing the hand to write the A's corrects the special cause variation but does nothing to change the underlying process of handwriting.)

Control charts allow you to monitor a process and identify the presence or absence of special causes. By doing so, control charts help prevent two types of errors. The first type of error involves the belief that an observed value represents special cause variation when it is due to the common cause variation of the process. Treating common cause variation as special cause variation often results in overadjusting a process. This overadjustment, known as **tampering**, increases the variation in the process. The second type of error involves treating special cause variation as common cause variation. This error results in not taking immediate corrective action when necessary. Although both of these types of errors can occur even when using a control chart, they are far less likely.

To construct a control chart, you collect samples from the output of a process over time. The samples used for constructing control charts are known as **subgroups**. For each subgroup (i.e., sample), you calculate a sample statistic. Commonly used statistics include the sample proportion for a categorical variable (see Section 17.2), the number of nonconformities (see Section 17.4), and the mean and range of a numerical variable (see Section 17.5). You then plot the values over time and add control limits around the center line of the chart. The most typical form of a control chart sets control limits that are within ±3 standard deviations[1] of the statistical measure of interest. Equation (17.1) defines, in general, the upper and lower control limits for control charts.

[1]Recall from Section 6.2 that in the normal distribution, $\mu \pm 3\sigma$ includes almost all (99.73%) of the values in the population.

CONSTRUCTING CONTROL LIMITS

$$\text{Process mean } \pm 3 \text{ standard deviations} \qquad \textbf{(17.1)}$$

so that

Upper control limit (UCL) = Process mean +3 standard deviations

Lower control limit (LCL) = Process mean −3 standard deviations

When these control limits are set, you evaluate the control chart by trying to find whether any pattern exists in the values over time and by determining whether any points fall outside the control limits. Figure 17.1 illustrates three different patterns.

FIGURE 17.1

Three control chart patterns

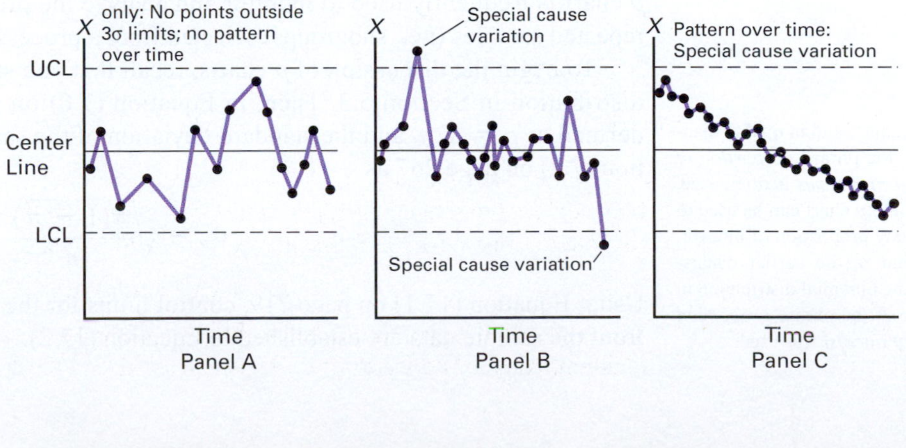

In Panel A of Figure 17.1, there is no apparent pattern in the values over time and there are no points that fall outside the 3 standard deviation control limits. The process appears stable and contains only common cause variation. Panel B, on the contrary, contains two points that fall outside the 3 standard deviation control limits. You should investigate these points to try to determine the special causes that led to their occurrence. Although Panel C does not have any points outside the control limits, it has a series of consecutive points above the mean value (the center line) as well as a series of consecutive points below the mean value. In addition, a long-term overall downward trend is clearly visible. You should investigate the situation to try to determine what may have caused this pattern.

Detecting a pattern is not always so easy. The following simple rule (see references 9, 13, and 19) can help you to detect a trend or a shift in the mean level of a process:

Eight or more *consecutive* points that lie above the center line or eight or more *consecutive* points that lie below the center line.[2]

[2]This rule is often referred to as the *runs rule*. A similar rule that some companies use is called the *trend rule*: eight or more consecutive points that increase in value or eight or more consecutive points that decrease in value. Some statisticians (see reference 5) have criticized the trend rule. It should be used only with extreme caution.

A process whose control chart indicates an out-of-control condition (i.e., a point outside the control limits or a series of points that exhibits a pattern) is said to be out of control. An **out-of-control process** contains both common causes of variation and special causes of variation. Because special causes of variation are not part of the process design, an out-of-control process is unpredictable. When you determine that a process is out of control, you must identify the special causes of variation that are producing the out-of-control conditions. If the special causes are detrimental to the quality of the product or service, you need to implement plans to eliminate this source of variation. When a special cause increases quality, you should change the process so that the special cause is incorporated into the process design. Thus, this beneficial special cause now becomes a common cause source of variation, and the process is improved.

A process whose control chart does not indicate any out-of-control conditions is said to be in control. An **in-control process** contains only common causes of variation. Because these sources of variation are inherent to the process itself, an in-control process is predictable. In-control processes are sometimes said to be in a **state of statistical control**. When a process is in control, you must determine whether the amount of common cause variation in the process is small enough to satisfy the customers of the products or services. If the common cause variation is small enough to consistently satisfy the customers, you then use control charts to monitor the process on a continuing basis to make sure the process remains in control. If the common cause variation is too large, you need to alter the process itself.

17.2 Control Chart for the Proportion: The *p* Chart

Various types of control charts are used to monitor processes and determine whether special cause variation is present in a process. **Attribute control charts** are used for categorical or discrete variables. This section introduces the ***p* chart**, which is used for categorical variables. The p chart gets its name from the fact that you plot the *proportion* of items in a sample that are in a category of interest. For example, sampled items are often classified according to whether they conform or do not conform to operationally defined requirements. Thus, the p chart is frequently used to monitor and analyze the proportion of nonconforming items in repeated samples (i.e., subgroups) selected from a process.

To begin the discussion of p charts, recall that you studied proportions and the binomial distribution in Section 5.3. Then, in Equation (7.6) on page 267, the sample proportion is defined as $p = X/n$, and the standard deviation of the sample proportion is defined in Equation (7.7) on page 267 as

[3]In this chapter, and in quality management, the phrase *proportion of nonconforming items* is often used, although the p chart can be used to monitor any proportion of interest. Recall that in the earlier discussions of the binomial distribution in Section 5.3, the phrase *proportion of items of interest* was used.

$$\sigma_p = \sqrt{\frac{\pi(1 - \pi)}{n}}$$

Using Equation (17.1) on page 719, control limits for the proportion of nonconforming[3] items from the sample data are established in Equation (17.2).

CONTROL LIMITS FOR THE *p* CHART

$$\bar{p} \pm 3\sqrt{\frac{\bar{p}(1-\bar{p})}{\bar{n}}}$$

$$\text{UCL} = \bar{p} + 3\sqrt{\frac{\bar{p}(1-\bar{p})}{\bar{n}}}$$

$$\text{LCL} = \bar{p} - 3\sqrt{\frac{\bar{p}(1-\bar{p})}{\bar{n}}} \qquad \textbf{(17.2)}$$

For equal n_i,

$$\bar{n} = n_i \text{ and } \bar{p} = \frac{\sum_{i=1}^{k} p_i}{k}$$

or, in general,

$$\bar{n} = \frac{\sum_{i=1}^{k} n_i}{k} \text{ and } \bar{p} = \frac{\sum_{i=1}^{k} X_i}{\sum_{i=1}^{k} n_i}$$

where

X_i = number of nonconforming items in subgroup i

n_i = sample (or subgroup) size for subgroup i

$p_i = \frac{X_i}{n_i}$ = proportion of nonconforming items in subgroup i

k = number of subgroups selected

$\bar{n}$ = mean subgroup size

$\bar{p}$ = proportion of nonconforming items in the k subgroups combined

Any negative value for the LCL means that the LCL does not exist.

To show the application of the *p* chart, return to the Beachcomber Hotel scenario on page 717. During the process improvement effort in the *Measure* phase of Six Sigma (see Section 17.8), a nonconforming room was operationally defined as the absence of an amenity or an appliance not in working order upon check-in. During the *Analyze* phase of Six Sigma, data on the nonconformances were collected daily from a sample of 200 rooms (stored in **Hotel1**). Table 17.1 on page 722 lists the number and proportion of nonconforming rooms for each day in the four-week period.

For these data, $k = 28$, $\sum_{i=1}^{k} p_i = 2.315$ and, because the n_i are equal, $n_i = \bar{n} = 200$. Thus,

$$\bar{p} = \frac{\sum_{i=1}^{k} p_i}{k} = \frac{2.315}{28} = 0.0827$$

TABLE 17.1
Nonconforming Hotel Rooms at Check-in over 28-Day Period

Day (i)	Rooms Studied (n_i)	Rooms Not Ready (X_i)	Proportion (p_i)	Day (i)	Rooms Studied (n_i)	Rooms Not Ready (X_i)	Proportion (p_i)
1	200	16	0.080	15	200	18	0.090
2	200	7	0.035	16	200	13	0.065
3	200	21	0.105	17	200	15	0.075
4	200	17	0.085	18	200	10	0.050
5	200	25	0.125	19	200	14	0.070
6	200	19	0.095	20	200	25	0.125
7	200	16	0.080	21	200	19	0.095
8	200	15	0.075	22	200	12	0.060
9	200	11	0.055	23	200	6	0.030
10	200	12	0.060	24	200	12	0.060
11	200	22	0.110	25	200	18	0.090
12	200	20	0.100	26	200	15	0.075
13	200	17	0.085	27	200	20	0.100
14	200	26	0.130	28	200	22	0.110

Using Equation (17.2),

$$0.0827 \pm 3\sqrt{\frac{(0.0827)(0.9173)}{200}}$$

so that

$$\text{UCL} = 0.0827 + 0.0584 = 0.1411$$

and

$$\text{LCL} = 0.0827 - 0.0584 = 0.0243$$

Figure 17.2 displays a p chart for the data of Table 17.1.

FIGURE 17.2
Excel and Minitab p charts for the nonconforming hotel rooms

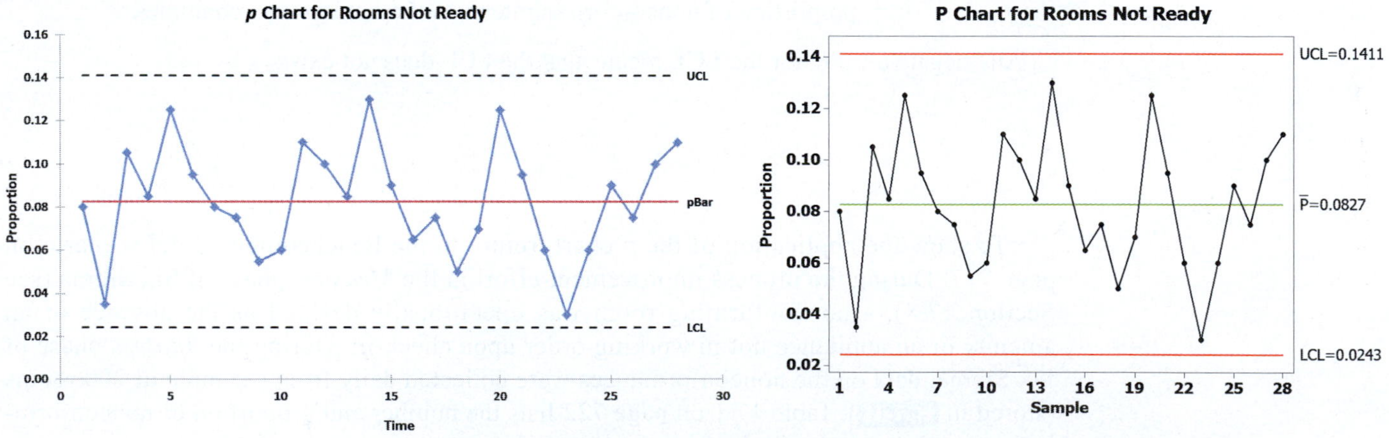

Figure 17.2 shows a process in a state of statistical control, with the individual points distributed around $\bar{p}$ without any pattern and all the points within the control limits. Thus, any improvement in the process of making rooms ready for guests must come from the reduction of common cause variation. Such reductions require changes in the process. These changes are the responsibility of management. Remember that improvements in quality cannot occur until changes to the process itself are successfully implemented.

This example illustrates a situation in which the subgroup size does not vary. As a general rule, as long as none of the subgroup sizes, n_i, differ from the mean subgroup size, $\bar{n}$, by more than

$\pm 25\%$ of $\bar{n}$ (see reference 9), you can use Equation (17.2) on page 721 to compute the control limits for the p chart. If any subgroup size differs by more than $\pm 25\%$ of $\bar{n}$, you use alternative formulas for calculating the control limits (see references 9 and 13). To illustrate the use of the p chart when the subgroup sizes are unequal, Example 17.1 studies the production of medical sponges.

EXAMPLE 17.1

Using the p Chart for Unequal Subgroup Sizes

Table 17.2 indicates the number of medical sponges produced daily for a period of 32 days and the number that are nonconforming (stored in **Sponge**). Construct a control chart for these data.

TABLE 17.2

Medical Sponges Produced and Number Nonconforming over a 32-Day Period

Day (i)	Sponges Produced (n_i)	Nonconforming Sponges (X_i)	Proportion (p_i)	Day (i)	Sponges Produced (n_i)	Nonconforming Sponges (X_i)	Proportion (p_i)
1	690	21	0.030	17	575	20	0.035
2	580	22	0.038	18	610	16	0.026
3	685	20	0.029	19	596	15	0.025
4	595	21	0.035	20	630	24	0.038
5	665	23	0.035	21	625	25	0.040
6	596	19	0.032	22	615	21	0.034
7	600	18	0.030	23	575	23	0.040
8	620	24	0.039	24	572	20	0.035
9	610	20	0.033	25	645	24	0.037
10	595	22	0.037	26	651	39	0.060
11	645	19	0.029	27	660	21	0.032
12	675	23	0.034	28	685	19	0.028
13	670	22	0.033	29	671	17	0.025
14	590	26	0.044	30	660	22	0.033
15	585	17	0.029	31	595	24	0.040
16	560	16	0.029	32	600	16	0.027

SOLUTION For these data,

$$k = 32, \sum_{i=1}^{k} n_i = 19{,}926$$

$$\sum_{i=1}^{k} X_i = 679$$

Thus, using Equation (17.2) on page 721,

$$\bar{n} = \frac{19{,}926}{32} = 622.69$$

$$\bar{p} = \frac{679}{19{,}926} = 0.034$$

so that

$$0.034 \pm 3\sqrt{\frac{(0.034)(1 - 0.034)}{622.69}}$$

$$= 0.034 \pm 0.022$$

Thus,

$$\text{UCL} = 0.034 + 0.022 = 0.056$$

$$\text{LCL} = 0.034 - 0.022 = 0.012$$

Figure 17.3 displays the Excel and Minitab control charts for the sponge data. Because Minitab calculates new control limits when the subgroup size changes from one time period (day) to another, the UCL and LCL appear as jagged lines in the Minitab chart.

FIGURE 17.3

Excel and Minitab *p* charts for the proportion of nonconforming medical sponges

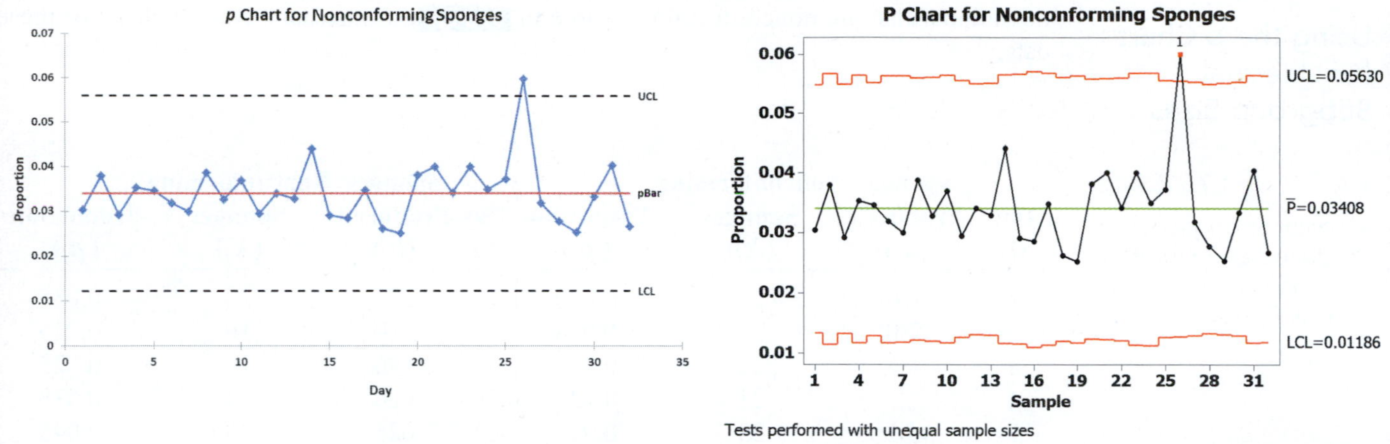

From Figure 17.3, you can see that day 26, on which there were 39 nonconforming sponges produced out of 651 sampled, is above the UCL. Management needs to determine the reason (i.e., root cause) for this special cause variation and take corrective action. Once actions are taken, you can remove the data from day 26 and then construct and analyze a new control chart.

Problems for Section 17.2

LEARNING THE BASICS

17.1 The following data were collected on nonconformances for a period of 10 days:

Day	Sample Size	Nonconformances
1	100	12
2	100	14
3	100	10
4	100	18
5	100	22
6	100	14
7	100	15
8	100	13
9	100	14
10	100	16

a. On what day is the proportion of nonconformances largest? Smallest?
b. What are the LCL and UCL?
c. Are there any special causes of variation?

17.2 The following data were collected on nonconformances for a period of 10 days:

Day	Sample Size	Nonconformances
1	111	12
2	93	14
3	105	10
4	92	18
5	117	22
6	88	14
7	117	15
8	87	13
9	119	14
10	107	16

a. On what day is the proportion of nonconformances largest? Smallest?
b. What are the LCL and UCL?
c. Are there any special causes of variation?

APPLYING THE CONCEPTS

17.3 A medical transcription service enters medical data on patient files for hospitals. The service has the business objective of improving the turnaround time (defined as the time between sending data and the time the client receives completed files). After studying the process, it was determined that turnaround time was increased by transmission errors. A transmission error was defined as data transmitted that did not go through as planned and needed to be retransmitted. For a period of 31 days, a sample of 125 transmissions were randomly selected and evaluated for errors and stored in **Transmit**. The following table presents the number and proportion of transmissions with errors:

Day (i)	Number of Errors (X_i)	Proportion of Errors (p_i)	Day (i)	Number of Errors (X_i)	Proportion of Errors (p_i)
1	6	0.048	17	4	0.032
2	3	0.024	18	6	0.048
3	4	0.032	19	3	0.024
4	4	0.032	20	5	0.040
5	9	0.072	21	1	0.008
6	0	0.000	22	3	0.024
7	0	0.000	23	14	0.112
8	8	0.064	24	6	0.048
9	4	0.032	25	7	0.056
10	3	0.024	26	3	0.024
11	4	0.032	27	10	0.080
12	1	0.008	28	7	0.056
13	10	0.080	29	5	0.040
14	9	0.072	30	0	0.000
15	3	0.024	31	3	0.024
16	1	0.008			

a. Construct a p chart.
b. Is the process in a state of statistical control? Why?

SELF Test **17.4** The following data (stored in **Canister**) represent the findings from a study conducted at a factory that manufactures film canisters. For 32 days, 500 film canisters were sampled and inspected. The following table lists the number of defective film canisters (the nonconforming items) for each day (the subgroup):

Day	Number Nonconforming	Day	Number Nonconforming
1	26	17	23
2	25	18	19
3	23	19	18
4	24	20	27
5	26	21	28
6	20	22	24
7	21	23	26
8	27	24	23
9	23	25	27
10	25	26	28
11	22	27	24
12	26	28	22
13	25	29	20
14	29	30	25
15	20	31	27
16	19	32	19

a. Construct a p chart.
b. Is the process in a state of statistical control? Why?

17.5 A hospital administrator has the business objective of reducing the time to process patients' medical records after discharge. She determined that all records should be processed within 5 days of discharge. Thus, any record not processed within 5 days of a patient's discharge is nonconforming. The administrator recorded the number of patients discharged and the number of records not processed within the 5-day standard for a 30-day period and stored in **MedRec**.

a. Construct a p chart for these data.
b. Does the process give an out-of-control signal? Explain.
c. If the process is out of control, assume that special causes were subsequently identified and corrective action was taken to keep them from happening again. Then eliminate the data causing the out-of-control signals and recalculate the control limits.

17.6 The bottling division of Sweet Suzy's Sugarless Cola maintains daily records of the occurrences of unacceptable cans flowing from the filling and sealing machine. The data in **Colaspc** lists the number of cans filled and the number of nonconforming cans for one month (based on a five-day workweek).

a. Construct a p chart for the proportion of unacceptable cans for the month. Does the process give an out-of-control signal?
b. If you want to develop a process for reducing the proportion of unacceptable cans, how should you proceed?

17.7 The manager of the accounting office of a large hospital has the business objective of reducing the number of incorrect account numbers entered into the computer system. A subgroup of 200 account numbers is selected from each day's output, and each account number is inspected to determine whether it is a nonconforming item. The results for a period of 39 days are stored in **Errorspc**.

a. Construct a p chart for the proportion of nonconforming items. Does the process give an out-of-control signal?
b. Based on your answer in (a), if you were the manager of the accounting office, what would you do to improve the process of account number entry?

17.8 A regional manager of a telephone company is responsible for processing requests concerning additions, changes, and deletions of telephone service. She forms a service improvement team to look at the corrections to the orders in terms of central office equipment and facilities required to process the orders that are issued to service requests. Data collected over a period of 30 days are stored in **Telespc**.

a. Construct a p chart for the proportion of corrections. Does the process give an out-of-control signal?
b. What should the regional manager do to improve the processing of requests for changes in telephone service?

17.3 The Red Bead Experiment: Understanding Process Variability

This chapter began with a discussion of common cause variation and special cause variation. Now that you have studied the p chart, this section presents a famous parable, the **red bead experiment**, to enhance your understanding of common cause and special cause variation. The red bead experiment involves the selection of beads from a bowl that contains 4,000 beads.[4] Unknown to the participants in the experiment, 3,200 (80%) of the beads are white and 800 (20%) are red. You can use several different scenarios for conducting the experiment. The one used here begins with a facilitator (who will play the role of company supervisor) asking members of the audience to volunteer for the jobs of workers (at least four are needed), inspectors (two are needed), chief inspector (one is needed), and recorder (one is needed). A worker's job consists of using a paddle that has five rows of 10 bead-size holes to select 50 beads from the bowl of beads.

[4]For information on how to purchase such a bowl, visit the Lightning Calculator website, **www.qualitytng.com**.

When the participants have been selected, the supervisor explains the jobs to them. The job of the workers is to produce white beads because red beads are unacceptable to the customers. Strict procedures are to be followed. Work standards call for the daily production of exactly 50 beads by each worker (a strict quota system). Management has established a standard that no more than 2 red beads (4%) per worker are to be produced on any given day.

Each worker dips the paddle into the box of beads so that when it is removed, each of the 50 holes contains a bead. The worker carries the paddle to the two inspectors, who independently record the count of red beads. The chief inspector compares their counts and announces the results to the audience. The recorder writes down the number and percentage of red beads next to the name of the worker.

When all the people know their jobs, "production" can begin. Suppose that on the first "day," the number of red beads "produced" by the four workers (call them Alyson, David, Peter, and Sharyn) was 9, 12, 13, and 7, respectively. How should management react to the day's production when the standard says that no more than 2 red beads per worker should be produced? Should all the workers be reprimanded, or should only David and Peter be warned that they will be fired if they don't improve?

Suppose that production continues for an additional two days. Table 17.3 summarizes the results for all three days.

TABLE 17.3

Red Bead Experiment Results for Four Workers over Three Days

	DAY			
WORKER	**1**	**2**	**3**	**All Three Days**
Alyson	9 (18%)	11 (22%)	6 (12%)	26 (17.33%)
David	12 (24%)	12 (24%)	8 (16%)	32 (21.33%)
Peter	13 (26%)	6 (12%)	12 (24%)	31 (20.67%)
Sharyn	7 (14%)	9 (18%)	8 (16%)	24 (16.0%)
All four workers	41	38	34	113
Mean	10.25	9.5	8.5	9.42
Percentage	20.5%	19%	17%	18.83%

From Table 17.3, on each day, some of the workers were above the mean and some below the mean. On Day 1, Sharyn did best, but on Day 2, Peter (who had the worst record on Day 1) was best, and on Day 3, Alyson was best. How can you explain all this variation? Using Equation (17.2) on page 721 to develop a p chart for these data,

$$k = 4 \text{ workers} \times 3 \text{ days} = 12, n = 50, \sum_{i=1}^{k} X_i = 113, \text{ and } \sum_{i=1}^{k} n_i = 600$$

Thus,

$$\bar{p} = \frac{113}{600} = 0.1883$$

so that

$$\bar{p} \pm 3\sqrt{\frac{\bar{p}(1-\bar{p})}{\bar{n}}}$$

$$= 0.1883 \pm 3\sqrt{\frac{0.1883(1-0.1883)}{50}}$$

$$= 0.1883 \pm 0.1659$$

Thus,

$$UCL = 0.1883 + 0.1659 = 0.3542$$

$$LCL = 0.1883 - 0.1659 = 0.0224$$

Figure 17.4 represents the *p* chart for the data of Table 17.3. In Figure 17.4, all the points are within the control limits, and there are no patterns in the results. The differences between the workers merely represent common cause variation inherent in an in-control process.

FIGURE 17.4
p chart for the red bead experiment

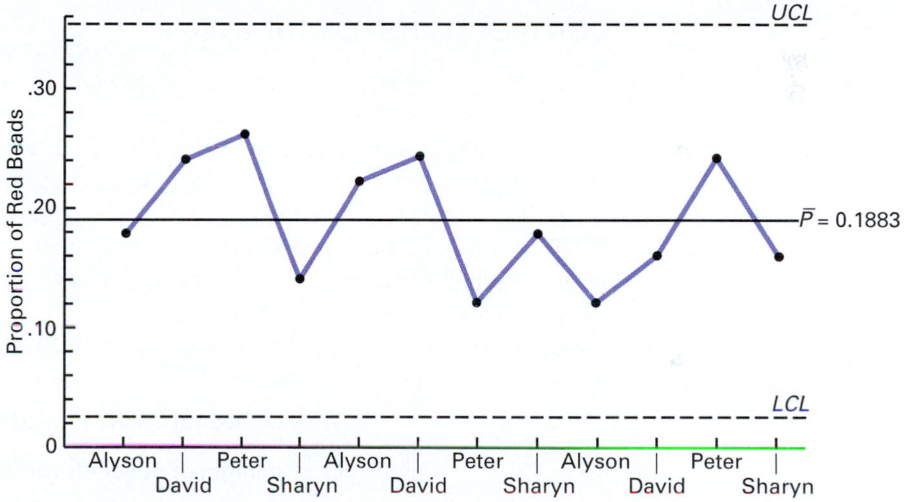

The parable of the red beads has four morals:

- Variation is an inherent part of any process.
- Workers work within a process over which they have little control. It is the process that primarily determines their performance.
- Only management can change the process.
- There will always be some workers above the mean and some workers below the mean.

Problems for Section 17.3

APPLYING THE CONCEPTS

17.9 In the red bead experiment, how do you think many managers would have reacted after Day 1? Day 2? Day 3?

17.10 (Class Project) Obtain a version of the red bead experiment for your class.

a. Conduct the experiment in the same way as described in this section.

b. Remove 400 red beads from the bead bowl before beginning the experiment. How do your results differ from those in (a)? What does this tell you about the effect of the process on the results?

17.4 Control Chart for an Area of Opportunity: The *c* Chart

Recall that you use a *p* chart for monitoring and analyzing the proportion of nonconforming items. Nonconformities are defects or flaws in a product or service. To monitor and analyze the number of nonconformities in an area of opportunity, you use a ***c* chart**. An **area of opportunity** is an individual unit of a product or service, or a unit of time, space, or area. Examples of "the number of nonconformities in an area of opportunity" would be the number of flaws in a square foot of carpet, the number of typographical errors on a printed page, and the number of hotel customers filing complaints in a given week.

Counting the number of nonconformities in an area of opportunity is unlike the process used to prepare a *p* chart in which you *classify* each unit as conforming or nonconforming. The *c* chart process fits the assumptions of a Poisson distribution (see Section 5.4). For the Poisson distribution, the standard deviation of the number of nonconformities is the square root of the mean number of nonconformities (λ). Assuming that the size of each area of opportunity remains constant,[5] you can compute the control limits for the number of nonconformities per area of opportunity using the observed mean number of nonconformities as an estimate of λ. Equation (17.3) defines the control limits for the *c* chart, which you use to monitor and analyze the number of nonconformities per area of opportunity.

[5]If the size of the unit varies, you should use a *u* chart instead of a *c* chart (see references 9, 13, and 19).

CONTROL LIMITS FOR THE *c* CHART

$$\bar{c} \pm 3\sqrt{\bar{c}}$$

$$UCL = \bar{c} + 3\sqrt{\bar{c}}$$

$$LCL = \bar{c} - 3\sqrt{\bar{c}} \quad \textbf{(17.3)}$$

where

$$\bar{c} = \frac{\sum_{i=1}^{k} c_i}{k}$$

k = number of units sampled

c_i = number of nonconformities in unit i

To help study the hotel service quality in the Beachcomber Hotel scenario on page 717, you can use a *c* chart to monitor the number of customer complaints filed with the hotel. If guests of the hotel are dissatisfied with any part of their stay, they are asked to file a customer complaint form. At the end of each week, the number of complaints filed is recorded. In this example, a complaint is a nonconformity, and the area of opportunity is one week. Table 17.4 lists the number of complaints from the past 50 weeks (stored in **Complaints**).

For these data,

$$k = 50 \text{ and } \sum_{i=1}^{k} c_i = 312$$

Thus,

$$\bar{c} = \frac{312}{50} = 6.24$$

TABLE 17.4

Number of Complaints in the Past 50 Weeks

Week	Number of Complaints	Week	Number of Complaints	Week	Number of Complaints
1	8	18	7	35	3
2	10	19	10	36	5
3	6	20	11	37	2
4	7	21	8	38	4
5	5	22	7	39	3
6	7	23	8	40	3
7	9	24	6	41	4
8	8	25	7	42	2
9	7	26	7	43	4
10	9	27	5	44	5
11	10	28	8	45	5
12	7	29	6	46	3
13	8	30	7	47	2
14	11	31	5	48	5
15	10	32	5	49	4
16	9	33	4	50	4
17	8	34	4		

so that using Equation (17.3) on page 728,

$$\bar{c} \pm 3\sqrt{\bar{c}}$$
$$= 6.24 \pm 3\sqrt{6.24}$$
$$= 6.24 \pm 7.494$$

Thus,

$$UCL = 6.24 + 7.494 = 13.734$$
$$LCL = 6.24 - 7.494 < 0$$

Therefore, the LCL does not exist.

Figure 17.5 displays the control chart for the complaint data of Table 17.4.

FIGURE 17.5

Excel and Minitab *c* charts for hotel complaints

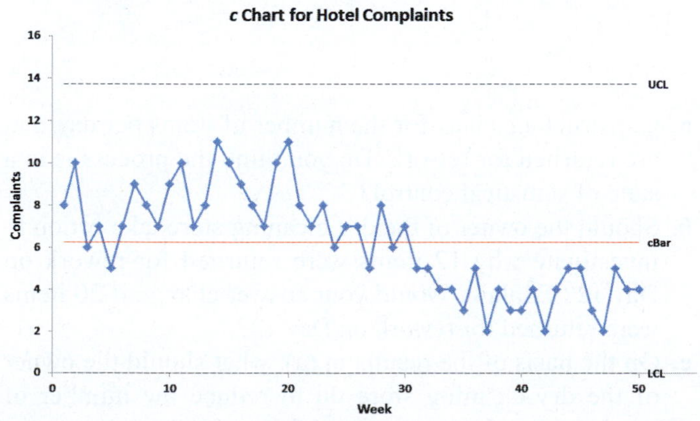

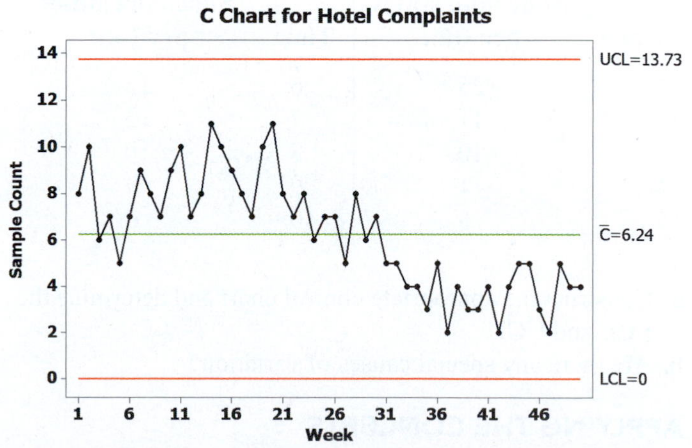

The c chart does not indicate any points outside the control limits. However, because there are eight or more consecutive points that lie above the center line and there are also eight or more consecutive points that lie below the center line, the process is out of control. There is a clear pattern to the number of customer complaints over time. During the first half of the sequence, the number of complaints for almost all the weeks is greater than the mean number of complaints, and the number of complaints for almost all the weeks in the second half are less than the mean number of complaints. This change, which is an improvement, is due to a special cause of variation. The next step is to investigate the process and determine the special cause that produced this pattern. When identified, you then need to ensure that this becomes a permanent improvement, not a temporary phenomenon. In other words, the source of the special cause of variation must become part of the permanent ongoing process in order for the number of customer complaints not to slip back to the high levels experienced in the first 25 weeks.

Problems for Section 17.4

LEARNING THE BASICS

17.11 The following data were collected on the number of nonconformities per unit for 10 time periods:

Time	Nonconformities per Unit	Time	Nonconformities per Unit
1	7	6	5
2	3	7	3
3	6	8	5
4	3	9	2
5	4	10	0

a. Construct the appropriate control chart and determine the LCL and UCL.
b. Are there any special causes of variation?

17.12 The following data were collected on the number of nonconformities per unit for 10 time periods:

Time	Nonconformities per Unit	Time	Nonconformities per Unit
1	25	6	15
2	11	7	12
3	10	8	10
4	11	9	9
5	6	10	6

a. Construct the appropriate control chart and determine the LCL and UCL.
b. Are there any special causes of variation?

APPLYING THE CONCEPTS

17.13 To improve service quality, the owner of a dry-cleaning business has the business objective of reducing the number of dry-cleaned items that are returned for rework per day. Records were kept for a four-week period (the store is open Monday through Saturday), with the results given in the following table and in the file **Dryclean**.

Day	Items Returned for Rework	Day	Items Returned for Rework
1	4	13	5
2	6	14	8
3	3	15	3
4	7	16	4
5	6	17	10
6	8	18	9
7	6	19	6
8	4	20	5
9	8	21	8
10	6	22	6
11	5	23	7
12	12	24	9

a. Construct a c chart for the number of items per day that are returned for rework. Do you think the process is in a state of statistical control?
b. Should the owner of the dry-cleaning store take action to investigate why 12 items were returned for rework on Day 12? Explain. Would your answer change if 20 items were returned for rework on Day 12?
c. On the basis of the results in (a), what should the owner of the dry-cleaning store do to reduce the number of items per day that are returned for rework?

SELF Test **17.14** The branch manager of a savings bank has recorded the number of errors of a particular type that each of 12 tellers has made during the past year. The results (stored in **Teller**) are as follows:

Teller	Number of Errors	Teller	Number of Errors
Alice	4	Mitchell	6
Carl	7	Nora	3
Gina	12	Paul	5
Jane	6	Salvador	4
Livia	2	Tripp	7
Marla	5	Vera	5

a. Do you think the bank manager will single out Gina for any disciplinary action regarding her performance in the past year?
b. Construct a *c* chart for the number of errors committed by the 12 tellers. Is the number of errors in a state of statistical control?
c. Based on the *c* chart developed in (b), do you now think that Gina should be singled out for disciplinary action regarding her performance? Does your conclusion now agree with what you expected the manager to do?
d. On the basis of the results in (b), what should the branch manager do to reduce the number of errors?

17.15 Falls are one source of preventable hospital injury. Although most patients who fall are not hurt, a risk of serious injury is involved. The data in **PtFalls** represent the number of patient falls per month over a 28-month period in a 19-bed AIDS unit at a major metropolitan hospital.
a. Construct a *c* chart for the number of patient falls per month. Is the process of patient falls per month in a state of statistical control?
b. What effect would it have on your conclusions if you knew that the AIDS unit was started only one month prior to the beginning of data collection?
c. Compile a list of factors that might produce special cause variation in this problem?

17.16 A member of the volunteer fire department for Trenton, Ohio, decided to apply the control chart methodology he learned in his business statistics class to data collected by the fire department. He was interested in determining whether weeks containing more than the mean number of fire runs were due to inherent, chance causes of variation, or if there were special causes of variation such as increased arson, severe drought, or holiday-related activities. The file **FireRuns** contains the number of fire runs made per week (Sunday through Saturday) during a single year.

Source: Data extracted from *The City of Trenton 2001 Annual Report*, Trenton, Ohio, February 21, 2002.

a. What is the mean number of fire runs made per week?
b. Construct a *c* chart for the number of fire runs per week.
c. Is the process in a state of statistical control?
d. Weeks 15 and 41 experienced seven fire runs each. Are these large values explainable by common causes, or does it appear that special causes of variation occurred in these weeks?
e. Explain how the fire department can use these data to chart and monitor future weeks in real-time (i.e., on a week-to-week basis)?

17.17 Rochester-Electro-Medical Inc. is a manufacturing company based in Tampa, Florida, that produces medical products. Management had the business objective of improving the safety of the workplace and began a safety sampling study. The following data (stored in **Safety**) represent the number of unsafe acts observed by the company safety director over an initial time period in which he made 20 tours of the plant.

Tour	Number of Unsafe Acts	Tour	Number of Unsafe Acts
1	10	11	2
2	6	12	8
3	6	13	7
4	10	14	6
5	8	15	6
6	12	16	11
7	2	17	13
8	1	18	9
9	23	19	6
10	3	20	9

Source: Data extracted from H. Gitlow, A. R. Berkins, and M. He, "Safety Sampling: A Case Study," *Quality Engineering,* 14 (2002), 405–419.

a. Construct a *c* chart for the number of unsafe acts.
b. Based on the results of (a), is the process in a state of statistical control?
c. What should management do next to improve the process?

17.5 Control Charts for the Range and the Mean

You use **variables control charts** to monitor and analyze a process when you have numerically measured data. Common numerical variables include time, money, and weight. Because numerical variables provide more information than categorical data, such as the proportion of nonconforming items, variables control charts are more sensitive than the p chart in detecting special cause variation. Variables charts are typically used in pairs, with one chart monitoring the variability in a process and the other monitoring the process mean. You must examine the chart that monitors variability first because if it indicates the presence of out-of-control conditions, the interpretation of the chart for the mean will be misleading. Although businesses currently use several alternative pairs of charts (see references 9, 13, and 19), this book considers only the control charts for the range and the mean.

The *R* Chart

You can use several different types of control charts to monitor the variability in a numerically measured characteristic of interest. The simplest and most common is the control chart for the range, the ***R* chart**. You use the range chart only when the sample size or subgroup is 10 or less. If the sample size is greater than 10, a standard deviation chart is preferable (see references 9, 13, and 19). Because sample sizes of 5 or less are typically used in many applications, the standard deviation chart is not illustrated in this book. An R chart enables you to determine whether the variability in a process is in control or whether changes in the amount of variability are occurring over time. If the process range is in control, then the amount of variation in the process is consistent over time, and you can use the results of the R chart to develop the control limits for the mean.

To develop control limits for the range, you need an estimate of the mean range and the standard deviation of the range. As shown in Equation (17.4), these control limits depend on two constants, the d_2 **factor**, which represents the relationship between the standard deviation and the range for varying sample sizes, and the d_3 **factor**, which represents the relationship between the standard deviation and the standard error of the range for varying sample sizes. Table E.9 contains values for these factors. Equation (17.4) defines the control limits for the R chart.

CONTROL LIMITS FOR THE RANGE

$$\bar{R} \pm 3\bar{R}\frac{d_3}{d_2}$$

$$\text{UCL} = \bar{R} + 3\bar{R}\frac{d_3}{d_2}$$

$$\text{LCL} = \bar{R} - 3\bar{R}\frac{d_3}{d_2} \qquad \textbf{(17.4)}$$

where

$$\bar{R} = \frac{\sum_{i=1}^{k} R_i}{k}$$

k = number of subgroups selected

You can simplify the computations in Equation (17.4) by using the D_3 **factor**, equal to $1 - 3(d_3/d_2)$, and the D_4 **factor**, equal to $1 + 3(d_3/d_2)$, to express the control limits (see Table E.9), as shown in Equations (17.5a) and (17.5b).

COMPUTING CONTROL LIMITS FOR THE RANGE

$$UCL = D_4\bar{R} \quad \textbf{(17.5a)}$$

$$LCL = D_3\bar{R} \quad \textbf{(17.5b)}$$

To illustrate the *R* chart, return to the Beachcomber Hotel scenario on page 717. As part of the *Measure* phase of a Six Sigma project (see Section 17.8), the amount of time to deliver luggage was operationally defined as the time from when the guest completes check-in procedures to the time the luggage arrives in the guest's room. During the *Analyze* phase of the Six Sigma project, data were recorded over a four-week period (see the file **Hotel2**). Subgroups of five deliveries were selected from the evening shift on each day. Table 17.5 summarizes the results for all 28 days.

TABLE 17.5

Luggage Delivery Times and Subgroup Mean and Range for 28 Days

Day	Luggage Delivery Times (in minutes)					Mean	Range
1	6.7	11.7	9.7	7.5	7.8	8.68	5.0
2	7.6	11.4	9.0	8.4	9.2	9.12	3.8
3	9.5	8.9	9.9	8.7	10.7	9.54	2.0
4	9.8	13.2	6.9	9.3	9.4	9.72	6.3
5	11.0	9.9	11.3	11.6	8.5	10.46	3.1
6	8.3	8.4	9.7	9.8	7.1	8.66	2.7
7	9.4	9.3	8.2	7.1	6.1	8.02	3.3
8	11.2	9.8	10.5	9.0	9.7	10.04	2.2
9	10.0	10.7	9.0	8.2	11.0	9.78	2.8
10	8.6	5.8	8.7	9.5	11.4	8.80	5.6
11	10.7	8.6	9.1	10.9	8.6	9.58	2.3
12	10.8	8.3	10.6	10.3	10.0	10.00	2.5
13	9.5	10.5	7.0	8.6	10.1	9.14	3.5
14	12.9	8.9	8.1	9.0	7.6	9.30	5.3
15	7.8	9.0	12.2	9.1	11.7	9.96	4.4
16	11.1	9.9	8.8	5.5	9.5	8.96	5.6
17	9.2	9.7	12.3	8.1	8.5	9.56	4.2
18	9.0	8.1	10.2	9.7	8.4	9.08	2.1
19	9.9	10.1	8.9	9.6	7.1	9.12	3.0
20	10.7	9.8	10.2	8.0	10.2	9.78	2.7
21	9.0	10.0	9.6	10.6	9.0	9.64	1.6
22	10.7	9.8	9.4	7.0	8.9	9.16	3.7
23	10.2	10.5	9.5	12.2	9.1	10.30	3.1
24	10.0	11.1	9.5	8.8	9.9	9.86	2.3
25	9.6	8.8	11.4	12.2	9.3	10.26	3.4
26	8.2	7.9	8.4	9.5	9.2	8.64	1.6
27	7.1	11.1	10.8	11.0	10.2	10.04	4.0
28	11.1	6.6	12.0	11.5	9.7	10.18	5.4
						Sums: 265.38	97.5

For the data in Table 17.5,

$$k = 28, \sum_{i=1}^{k} R_i = 97.5, \bar{R} = \frac{\sum_{i=1}^{k} R_i}{k} = \frac{97.5}{28} = 3.482$$

For $n = 5$, from Table E.9, $D_3 = 0$ and $D_4 = 2.114$. Then, using Equation (17.5),

$$UCL = D_4\bar{R} = (2.114)(3.482) = 7.36$$

and the LCL does not exist.

Figure 17.6 displays the R chart for the luggage delivery times. Figure 17.6 does not indicate any individual ranges outside the control limits or any obvious patterns. Therefore, you conclude that the R chart is in control.

FIGURE 17.6

Excel and Minitab R charts for the luggage delivery times (Minitab includes a companion $\overline{X}$ chart, discussed in the next subsection, with every R chart it creates.)

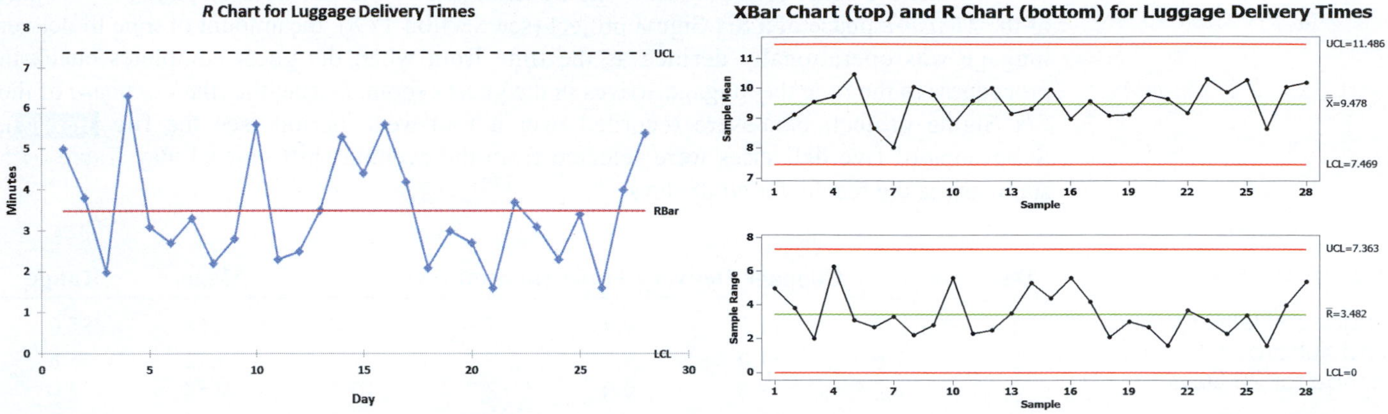

The $\overline{X}$ Chart

When you have determined from the R chart that the range is in control, you examine the control chart for the process mean, the **$\overline{X}$ chart**.

The control chart for $\overline{X}$ uses k subgroups collected in k consecutive periods of time. Each subgroup contains n items. You calculate $\overline{X}$ for each subgroup and plot these $\overline{X}$ values on the control chart. To compute control limits for the mean, you need to compute the mean of the subgroup means (called X double bar and denoted $\overline{\overline{X}}$ and the estimate of the standard error of the mean (denoted $\overline{R}/(d_2\sqrt{n})$). The estimate of the standard error of the mean is a function of the d_2 factor, which represents the relationship between the standard deviation and the range for varying sample sizes.[6] Equations (17.6) and (17.7) define the control limits for the $\overline{X}$ chart.

[6] $\overline{R}/d_2$ is used to estimate the standard deviation of the individual items in the population, and $\overline{R}/d_2\sqrt{n}$ is used to estimate the standard error of the mean.

CONTROL LIMITS FOR THE $\overline{X}$ CHART

$$\overline{\overline{X}} \pm 3\frac{\overline{R}}{d_2\sqrt{n}}$$

$$\text{UCL} = \overline{\overline{X}} + 3\frac{\overline{R}}{d_2\sqrt{n}}$$

$$\text{LCL} = \overline{\overline{X}} - 3\frac{\overline{R}}{d_2\sqrt{n}} \qquad \textbf{(17.6)}$$

where

$$\overline{\overline{X}} = \frac{\sum_{i=1}^{k}\overline{X}_i}{k}, \quad \overline{R} = \frac{\sum_{i=1}^{k}R_i}{k}$$

$\overline{X}_i$ = sample mean of n observations at time i

R_i = range of n observations at time i

k = number of subgroups

You can simplify the computations in Equation (17.6) by utilizing the A_2 **factor** given in Table E.9, equal to $3/d_2\sqrt{n}$. Equations (17.7a) and (17.7b) show the simplified control limits.

COMPUTING CONTROL LIMITS FOR THE MEAN, USING THE A_2 FACTOR

$$\text{UCL} = \bar{\bar{X}} + A_2\bar{R} \quad \textbf{(17.7a)}$$

$$\text{LCL} = \bar{\bar{X}} - A_2\bar{R} \quad \textbf{(17.7b)}$$

From Table 17.5 on page 733,

$$k = 28, \ \sum_{i=1}^{k}\bar{X}_i = 265.38, \ \sum_{i=1}^{k}R_i = 97.5$$

so that

$$\bar{\bar{X}} = \frac{\sum_{i=1}^{k}\bar{X}_i}{k} = \frac{265.38}{28} = 9.478$$

$$\bar{R} = \frac{\sum_{i=1}^{k}R_i}{k} = \frac{97.5}{28} = 3.482$$

Using Equations (17.7a) and (17.7b), since $n = 5$, from Table E.9, $A_2 = 0.577$, so that

$$\text{UCL} = 9.478 + (0.577)(3.482) = 9.478 + 2.009 = 11.487$$

$$\text{LCL} = 9.478 - (0.577)(3.482) = 9.478 - 2.009 = 7.469$$

Figure 17.7 displays the Excel $\bar{X}$ chart for the luggage delivery time data. (The Minitab $\bar{X}$ chart can be seen in Figure 17.6 on page 734.)

FIGURE 17.7

Excel $\bar{X}$ chart for the luggage delivery times

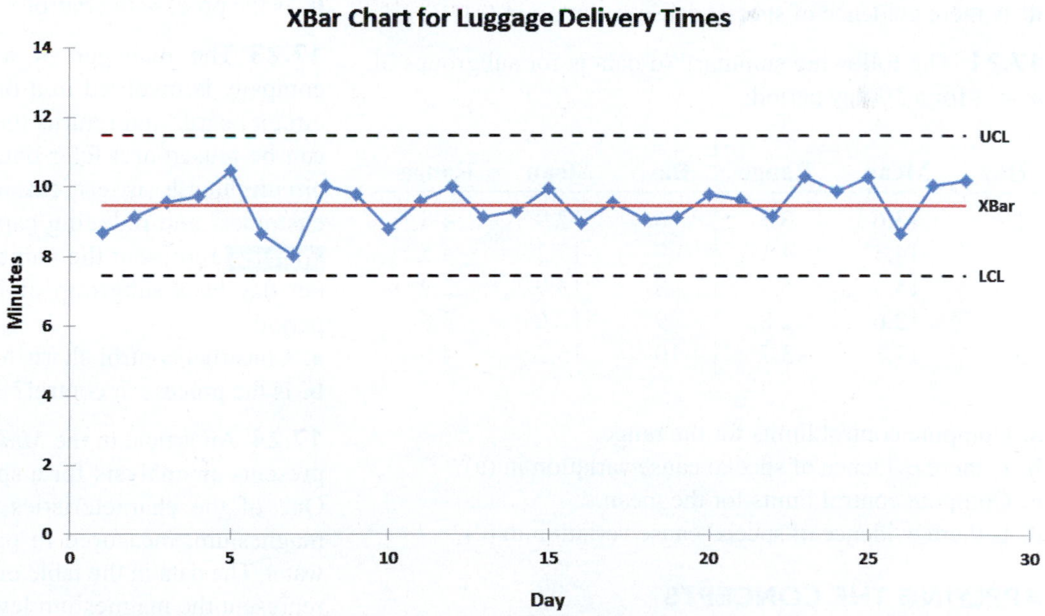

Figure 17.7 (or the Minitab results shown in Figure 17.6) does not reveal any points outside the control limits, and there are no obvious patterns. Although there is a considerable amount of variability among the 28 subgroup means, because both the R chart and the $\bar{X}$ chart are in control, you know that the luggage delivery process is in a state of statistical control. If you want to reduce the variation or lower the mean delivery time, you need to change the process.

Problems for Section 17.5

LEARNING THE BASICS

17.18 For subgroups of $n = 4$, what is the value of
a. the d_2 factor?
b. the d_3 factor?
c. the D_3 factor?
d. the D_4 factor?
e. the A_2 factor?

17.19 For subgroups of $n = 3$, what is the value of
a. the d_2 factor?
b. the d_3 factor?
c. the D_3 factor?
d. the D_4 factor?
e. the A_2 factor?

17.20 The following summary of data is for subgroups of $n = 3$ for a 10-day period:

Day	Mean	Range	Day	Mean	Range
1	48.03	0.29	6	48.07	0.22
2	48.08	0.43	7	47.99	0.16
3	47.90	0.16	8	48.04	0.15
4	48.03	0.13	9	47.99	0.46
5	47.81	0.32	10	48.04	0.15

a. Compute control limits for the range.
b. Is there evidence of special cause variation in (a)?
c. Compute control limits for the mean.
d. Is there evidence of special cause variation in (c)?

17.21 The following summary of data is for subgroups of $n = 4$ for a 10-day period:

Day	Mean	Range	Day	Mean	Range
1	13.6	3.5	6	12.9	4.8
2	14.3	4.1	7	17.3	4.5
3	15.3	5.0	8	13.9	2.9
4	12.6	2.8	9	12.6	3.8
5	11.8	3.7	10	15.2	4.6

a. Compute control limits for the range.
b. Is there evidence of special cause variation in (a)?
c. Compute control limits for the mean.
d. Is there evidence of special cause variation in (c)?

APPLYING THE CONCEPTS

SELF Test **17.22** The manager of a branch of a local bank has the business objective of reducing the waiting times of customers for teller service during the 12:00 noon-to-1:00 P.M. lunch hour. A subgroup of four customers is selected (one at each 15-minute interval during the hour), and the time, in minutes, is measured from when each customer enters the line to when he or she reaches the teller window. The results over a four-week period, stored in BankTime, are as follows:

Day	Time (Minutes)			
1	7.2	8.4	7.9	4.9
2	5.6	8.7	3.3	4.2
3	5.5	7.3	3.2	6.0
4	4.4	8.0	5.4	7.4
5	9.7	4.6	4.8	5.8
6	8.3	8.9	9.1	6.2
7	4.7	6.6	5.3	5.8
8	8.8	5.5	8.4	6.9
9	5.7	4.7	4.1	4.6
10	3.7	4.0	3.0	5.2
11	2.6	3.9	5.2	4.8
12	4.6	2.7	6.3	3.4
13	4.9	6.2	7.8	8.7
15	7.1	5.8	6.9	7.0
16	6.7	6.9	7.0	9.4
17	5.5	6.3	3.2	4.9
18	4.9	5.1	3.2	7.6
19	7.2	8.0	4.1	5.9
20	6.1	3.4	7.2	5.9

a. Construct control charts for the range and the mean.
b. Is the process in control?

17.23 The manager of a warehouse for a telephone company is involved in a process that receives expensive circuit boards and returns them to central stock so that they can be reused at a later date. Speedy processing of these circuit boards is critical in providing good service to customers and reducing capital expenditures. The data in Warehse represent the number of circuit boards processed per day by a subgroup of five employees over a 30-day period.
a. Construct control charts for the range and the mean.
b. Is the process in control?

17.24 An article in the *Mid-American Journal of Business* presents an analysis for a spring water bottling operation. One of the characteristics of interest is the amount of magnesium, measured in parts per million (ppm), in the water. The data in the table on page 737 (stored in SpWater) represent the magnesium levels from 30 subgroups of four bottles collected over a 30-hour period:
a. Construct a control chart for the range.
b. Construct a control chart for the mean.
c. Is the process in control?

Hour	Bottles 1	2	3	4
1	19.91	19.62	19.15	19.85
2	20.46	20.44	20.34	19.61
3	20.25	19.73	19.98	20.32
4	20.39	19.43	20.36	19.85
5	20.02	20.02	20.13	20.34
6	19.89	19.77	20.92	20.09
7	19.89	20.45	19.44	19.95
8	20.08	20.13	20.11	19.32
9	20.30	20.42	20.68	19.60
10	20.19	20.00	20.23	20.59
11	19.66	21.24	20.35	20.34
12	20.30	20.11	19.64	20.29
13	19.83	19.75	20.62	20.60
14	20.27	20.88	20.62	20.40
15	19.98	19.02	20.34	20.34
16	20.46	19.97	20.32	20.83
17	19.74	21.02	19.62	19.90
18	19.85	19.26	19.88	20.20
19	20.77	20.58	19.73	19.48
20	20.21	20.82	20.01	19.93
21	20.30	20.09	20.03	20.13
22	20.48	21.06	20.13	20.42
23	20.60	19.74	20.52	19.42
24	20.20	20.08	20.32	19.51
25	19.66	19.67	20.26	20.41
26	20.72	20.58	20.71	19.99
27	19.77	19.40	20.49	19.83
28	19.99	19.65	19.41	19.58
29	19.44	20.15	20.17	20.76
30	20.03	19.96	19.86	19.91

Source: Data extracted from Susan K. Humphrey and Timothy C. Krehbiel, "Managing Process Capability," *The Mid-American Journal of Business*, 14 (Fall 1999), 7–12.

17.25 The data in **Tensile** represent the tensile strengths of bolts of cloth. The data were collected in subgroups of three bolts of cloth over a 25-hour period.

a. Construct a control chart for the range.
b. Construct a control chart for the mean.
c. Is the process in control?

17.26 The director of radiology at a large metropolitan hospital has the business objective of improving the scheduling in the radiology facilities. On a typical day, 250 patients are transported to the radiology department for treatment or diagnostic procedures. If patients do not reach the radiology unit at their scheduled times, backups occur, and other patients experience delays. The time it takes to transport patients to the radiology unit is operationally defined as the time between when the transporter is assigned to the patient and when the patient arrives at the radiology unit. A sample of $n = 4$ patients was selected each day for 20 days, and the time to transport each patient (in minutes) was determined, with the results stored in **Transport**.

a. Construct control charts for the range and the mean.
b. Is the process in control?

17.27 A filling machine for a tea bag manufacturer produces approximately 170 tea bags per minute. The process manager monitors the weight of the tea placed in individual bags. A subgroup of $n = 4$ tea bags is taken every 15 minutes for 25 consecutive time periods. The results are stored in **Tea3**.

a. What are some of the sources of common cause variation that might be present in this process?
b. What problems might occur that would result in special causes of variation?
c. Construct control charts for the range and the mean.
d. Is the process in control?

17.28 A manufacturing company makes brackets for bookshelves. The brackets provide critical structural support and must have a 90-degree bend ± 1 degree. Measurements of the bend of the brackets were taken at 18 different times. Five brackets were sampled at each time. The data are stored in **Angle**.

a. Construct control charts for the range and the mean.
b. Is the process in control?

17.6 Process Capability

Often, it is necessary to analyze the amount of common cause variation present in an in-control process. Is the common cause variation small enough to satisfy customers with the product or service? Or is the common cause variation so large that there are too many dissatisfied customers, and a process change is needed?

Analyzing the capability of a process is a way to answer these questions. **Process capability** is the ability of a process to consistently meet specified customer-driven requirements. There are many methods available for analyzing and reporting process capability (see reference 3). This section begins with a method for estimating the percentage of products or services that will satisfy the customer. Later in the section, capability indices are introduced.

Customer Satisfaction and Specification Limits

Quality is defined by the customer. A customer who believes that a product or service has met or exceeded his or her expectations will be satisfied. The management of a company must listen to the customer and translate the customer's needs and expectations into easily measured **critical-to-quality (CTQ)** variables. Management then sets specification limits for these CTQ variables.

Specification limits are technical requirements set by management in response to customers' needs and expectations. The **upper specification limit (USL)** is the largest value a CTQ variable can have and still conform to customer expectations. Likewise, the **lower specification limit (LSL)** is the smallest value a CTQ variable can have and still conform to customer expectations.

For example, a soap manufacturer understands that customers expect their soap to produce a certain amount of lather. The customer can become dissatisfied if the soap produces too much or too little lather. Product engineers know that the level of free fatty acids in the soap controls the amount of lather. Thus, the process manager, with input from the product engineers, sets both a USL and a LSL for the amount of free fatty acids in the soap.

As an example of a case in which only a single specification limit is involved, consider the Beachcomber Hotel scenario on page 717. Because customers want their bags delivered as quickly as possible, hotel management sets a USL for the time required for delivery. In this case, there is no LSL. In both the luggage delivery time and soap examples, specification limits are customer-driven requirements placed on a product or a service. If a process consistently meets these requirements, the process is capable of satisfying the customer.

One way to analyze the capability of a process is to estimate the percentage of products or services that are within specifications. To do this, you must have an in-control process because an out-of-control process does not allow you to predict its capability. If you are dealing with an out-of-control process, you must first identify and eliminate the special causes of variation before performing a capability analysis. Out-of-control processes are unpredictable, and, therefore, you cannot conclude that such processes are capable of meeting specifications or satisfying customer expectations in the future. In order to estimate the percentage of product or service within specifications, first you must estimate the mean and standard deviation of the population of all X values, the CTQ variable of interest for the product or service. The estimate for the mean of the population is $\bar{\bar{X}}$, the mean of all the sample means [see Equation (17.6) on page 734]. The estimate of the standard deviation of the population is $\bar{R}$ divided by d_2. You can use the $\bar{\bar{X}}$ and $\bar{R}$ from in-control $\bar{X}$ and R charts, respectively. You need to find the appropriate d_2 value in Table E.9.

Assuming that the process is in control and X is approximately normally distributed, you can use Equation (17.8) to estimate the probability that a process outcome is within specifications. (If your data are not approximately normally distributed, see reference 3 for an alternative approach.)

ESTIMATING THE CAPABILITY OF A PROCESS

For a CTQ variable with an LSL and a USL:

$$P(\text{An outcome will be within specifications}) = P(\text{LSL} < X < \text{USL}) \quad \textbf{(17.8a)}$$

$$= P\left(\frac{\text{LSL} - \bar{\bar{X}}}{\bar{R}/d_2} < Z < \frac{\text{USL} - \bar{\bar{X}}}{\bar{R}/d_2}\right)$$

For a CTQ variable with only a USL:

$$P(\text{An outcome will be within specifications}) = P(X < \text{USL}) \quad \textbf{(17.8b)}$$

$$= P\left(Z < \frac{\text{USL} - \bar{\bar{X}}}{\bar{R}/d_2}\right)$$

For a CTQ variable with only an LSL:

$$P(\text{An outcome will be within specifications}) = P(\text{LSL} < X) \quad \textbf{(17.8c)}$$

$$= P\left(\frac{\text{LSL} - \bar{\bar{X}}}{\bar{R}/d_2} < Z\right)$$

where Z is a standardized normal random variable

In Section 17.5, you determined that the luggage delivery process was in control. Suppose that the hotel management has instituted a policy that 99% of all luggage deliveries must be completed in 14 minutes or less. From the summary computations on page 735:

$$n = 5 \quad \bar{\bar{X}} = 9.478 \quad \bar{R} = 3.482$$

and from Table E.9,

$$d_2 = 2.326$$

Using Equation (17.8b),

$$\begin{aligned} P(\text{Delivery is made within specifications}) &= P(X < 14) \\ &= P\left(Z < \frac{14 - 9.478}{3.482/2.326}\right) \\ &= P(Z < 3.02) \end{aligned}$$

Using Table E.2,

$$P(Z < 3.02) = 0.99874$$

Thus, you estimate that 99.874% of the luggage deliveries will be made within the specified time. The process is capable of meeting the 99% goal set by the hotel management.

Capability Indices

A common approach in business is to use capability indices to report the capability of a process. A **capability index** is an aggregate measure of a process's ability to meet specification limits. The larger the value of a capability index, the more capable the process is of meeting customer requirements. Equation (17.9) defines C_p, the most commonly used index.

C_p

$$C_p = \frac{\text{USL} - \text{LSL}}{6(\bar{R}/d_2)} = \frac{\text{Specification spread}}{\text{Process spread}} \quad \textbf{(17.9)}$$

The numerator in Equation (17.9) represents the distance between the upper and lower specification limits, referred to as the *specification spread*. The denominator, $6(\bar{R}/d_2)$, represents a 6 standard deviation spread in the data (the mean ± 3 standard deviations), referred to as the *process spread*. (Recall from Chapter 6 that approximately 99.73% of the values from a normal distribution fall in the interval from the mean ± 3 standard deviations.) You want the process spread to be small in comparison to the specification spread so that the vast majority of the process output falls within the specification limits. Therefore, the larger the value of C_p, the better the capability of the process.

C_p is a measure of process potential, not of actual performance, because it does not consider the current process mean. A C_p value of 1 indicates that if the process mean could be centered (i.e., equal to the halfway point between the USL and LSL), approximately 99.73% of the values would be inside the specification limits. A C_p value greater than 1 indicates that a process has the potential of having more than 99.73% of its outcomes within specifications. A C_p value less than 1 indicates that the process is not very capable of meeting customer requirements, for even if the process is perfectly centered, fewer than 99.73% of the process outcomes will be within specifications. Historically, many companies required a C_p greater than or equal to 1. Now that the global economy has become more quality conscious, many companies are requiring a C_p as large as 1.33, 1.5, or, for companies adopting Six Sigma management, 2.0.

To illustrate the calculation and interpretation of the C_p index, suppose a soft-drink producer bottles its beverage into 12-ounce bottles. The LSL is 11.82 ounces, and the USL is

12.18 ounces. Each hour, four bottles are selected, and the range and the mean are plotted on control charts. At the end of 24 hours, the capability of the process is studied. Suppose that the control charts indicate that the process is in control and the following summary calculations were recorded on the control charts:

$$n = 4 \qquad \bar{\bar{X}} = 12.02 \qquad \bar{R} = 0.10$$

To calculate the C_p index, assuming that the data are normally distributed, from Table E.9, $d_2 = 2.059$ for $n = 4$. Using Equation (17.9),

$$C_p = \frac{\text{USL} - \text{LSL}}{6(\bar{R}/d_2)}$$

$$= \frac{12.18 - 11.82}{6(0.10/2.059)} = 1.24$$

Because the C_p index is greater than 1, the bottling process has the potential to fill more than 99.73% of the bottles within the specification limits.

In summary, the C_p index is an aggregate measure of process potential. The larger the value of C_p, the more potential the process has of satisfying the customer. In other words, a large C_p indicates that the current amount of common cause variation is small enough to consistently produce items within specifications. For a process to reach its full potential, the process mean needs to be at or near the center of the specification limits. Capability indices that measure actual process performance are considered next.

CPL, CPU, and C_{pk}

To measure the capability of a process in terms of actual process performance, the most common indices are *CPL*, *CPU*, and C_{pk}. Equation (17.10) defines *CPL* and *CPU*.

CPL AND CPU

$$CPL = \frac{\bar{\bar{X}} - \text{LSL}}{3(\bar{R}/d_2)} \qquad \textbf{(17.10a)}$$

$$CPU = \frac{USL - \bar{\bar{X}}}{3(\bar{R}/d_2)} \qquad \textbf{(17.10b)}$$

Because the process mean is used in the calculation of *CPL* and *CPU*, these indices measure process performance—unlike C_p, which measures only potential. A value of *CPL* (or *CPU*) equal to 1.0 indicates that the process mean is 3 standard deviations away from the LSL (or USL). For CTQ variables with only an LSL, the *CPL* measures the process performance. For CTQ variables with only a USL, the *CPU* measures the process performance. In either case, the larger the value of the index, the greater the capability of the process.

In the Beachcomber Hotel scenario, the hotel management has a policy that luggage deliveries are to be made in 14 minutes or less. Thus, the CTQ variable delivery time has a USL of 14, and there is no LSL. Because you previously determined that the luggage delivery process was in control, you can now compute the *CPU*. From the summary computations on page 735,

$$\bar{\bar{X}} = 9.478 \qquad \bar{R} = 3.482$$

And, from Table E.9, $d_2 = 2.326$. Then, using Equation (17.10b),

$$CPU = \frac{\text{USL} - \bar{\bar{X}}}{3(\bar{R}/d_2)} = \frac{14 - 9.478}{3(3.482/2.326)} = 1.01$$

The capability index for the luggage delivery CTQ variable is 1.01. Because this value is slightly more than 1, the USL is slightly more than 3 standard deviations above the mean. To increase *CPU* even farther above 1.00 and therefore increase customer satisfaction, you need to investigate changes in the luggage delivery process. To study a process that has a *CPL* and a *CPU*, see the bottling process discussed in Example 17.2.

EXAMPLE 17.2

Computing CPL and CPU for the Bottling Process

In the soft-drink bottle-filling process described on pages 739–740, the following information was provided:

$$n = 4 \quad \bar{\bar{X}} = 12.02 \quad \bar{R} = 0.10 \quad \text{LSL} = 11.82 \quad \text{USL} = 12.18 \quad d_2 = 2.059$$

Compute the *CPL* and *CPU* for these data.

SOLUTION You compute the capability indices *CPL* and *CPU* by using Equations (17.10a) and (17.10b):

$$CPL = \frac{\bar{\bar{X}} - \text{LSL}}{3(\bar{R}/d_2)}$$

$$= \frac{12.02 - 11.82}{3(0.10/2.059)} = 1.37$$

$$CPU = \frac{\text{USL} - \bar{\bar{X}}}{3(\bar{R}/d_2)}$$

$$= \frac{12.18 - 12.02}{3(0.10/2.059)} = 1.10$$

Both the *CPL* and *CPU* are greater than 1, indicating that the process mean is more than 3 standard deviations away from both the LSL and USL. Because the *CPU* is less than the *CPL*, you know that the mean is closer to the USL than to the LSL.

The capability index, C_{pk} [shown in Equation (17.11)], measures actual process performance for quality characteristics with two-sided specification limits. C_{pk} is equal to the value of either the *CPL* or *CPU*, whichever is smaller.

C_{pk}

$$C_{pk} = \text{MIN}[CPL, CPU] \qquad \textbf{(17.11)}$$

A value of 1 for C_{pk} indicates that the process mean is 3 standard deviations away from the closest specification limit. If the characteristic is normally distributed, then a value of 1 indicates that at least 99.73% of the current output is within specifications. As with all other capability indices, the larger the value of C_{pk}, the better. Example 17.3 illustrates the use of C_{pk}.

EXAMPLE 17.3

Computing C_{pk} for the Bottling Process

The soft-drink producer in Example 17.2 requires the bottle filling process to have a C_{pk} greater than or equal to 1. Calculate the C_{pk} index.

SOLUTION In Example 17.2, $CPL = 1.37$ and $CPU = 1.10$. Using Equation (17.11):

$$C_{pk} = \text{MIN}[CPL, CPU]$$

$$= \text{MIN}[1.37, 1.10] = 1.10$$

The C_{pk} index is greater than 1, indicating that the actual process performance exceeds the company's requirement. More than 99.73% of the bottles contain between 11.82 and 12.18 ounces.

Problems for Section 17.6

LEARNING THE BASICS

17.29 For an in-control process with subgroup data $n = 4$, $\bar{\bar{X}} = 20$, and $\bar{R} = 2$, find the estimate of

a. the population mean of all X values.

b. the population standard deviation of all X values.

17.30 For an in-control process with subgroup data $n = 3$, $\bar{\bar{X}} = 100$, and $\bar{R} = 3.386$, compute the percentage of outcomes within specifications if

a. LSL = 98 and USL = 102.

b. LSL = 93 and USL = 107.5.

c. LSL = 93.8 and there is no USL.

d. USL = 110 and there is no LSL.

17.31 For an in-control process with subgroup data $n = 3$, $\bar{\bar{X}} = 100$, and $\bar{R} = 3.386$, compute the C_p, CPL, CPU, and C_{pk} if

a. LSL = 98 and USL = 102.

b. LSL = 93 and USL = 107.5.

APPLYING THE CONCEPTS

SELF Test **17.32** Referring to the data of Problem 17.24 on page 736, stored in SpWater, the researchers stated, "Some of the benefits of a capable process are increased customer satisfaction, increased operating efficiencies, and reduced costs." To illustrate this point, the authors presented a capability analysis for a spring water bottling operation. One of the CTQ variables is the amount of magnesium, measured in parts per million (ppm), in the water. The LSL and USL for the level of magnesium in a bottle are 18 ppm and 22 ppm, respectively.

a. Estimate the percentage of bottles that are within specifications.

b. Compute the C_p, CPL, CPU, and C_{pk}.

17.33 Refer to the data in Problem 17.25 on page 737 concerning the tensile strengths of bolts of cloth (stored in Tensile). There is no USL for tensile strength, and the LSL is 13.

a. Estimate the percentage of bolts that are within specifications.

b. Calculate the C_p and CPL.

17.34 Refer to Problem 17.27 on page 737 concerning a filling machine for a tea bag manufacturer (data stored in Tea3). In that problem, you should have concluded that the process is in control. The label weight for this product is 5.5 grams, the LSL is 5.2 grams, and the USL is 5.8 grams. Company policy states that at least 99% of the tea bags produced must be inside the specifications in order for the process to be considered capable.

a. Estimate the percentage of the tea bags that are inside the specification limits. Is the process capable of meeting the company policy?

b. If management implemented a new policy stating that 99.7% of all tea bags are required to be within the specifications, is this process capable of reaching that goal? Explain.

17.35 Refer to Problem 17.22 on page 736 concerning waiting time for customers at a bank (data stored in Banktime). Suppose management has set a USL of five minutes on waiting time and specified that at least 99% of the waiting times must be less than five minutes in order for the process to be considered capable.

a. Estimate the percentage of the waiting times that are inside the specification limits. Is the process capable of meeting the company policy?

b. If management implemented a new policy, stating that 99.7% of all waiting times are required to be within specifications, is this process capable of reaching that goal? Explain.

17.7 Total Quality Management

An increased interest in improving the quality of products and services in the United States occurred as a reaction to improvements of Japanese industry that began as early as 1950. Individuals such as W. Edwards Deming, Joseph Juran, and Kaoru Ishikawa developed an approach that focuses on continuous improvement of products and services through an increased emphasis on statistics, process improvement, and optimization of the total system. This approach, widely known as **total quality management (TQM)**, is characterized by these themes:

- The primary focus is on process improvement.
- Most of the variation in a process is due to the system and not the individual.
- Teamwork is an integral part of a quality management organization.
- Customer satisfaction is a primary organizational goal.
- Organizational transformation must occur in order to implement quality management.
- Fear must be removed from organizations.
- Higher quality costs less, not more, but requires an investment in training.

In the 1980s, the federal government of the United States increased its efforts to encourage the improvement of quality in American business. Congress passed the Malcolm Baldrige National Improvement Act of 1987 and began awarding the Malcolm Baldrige Award to companies making the greatest strides in improving quality and customer satisfaction. Deming became a prominent consultant to many Fortune 500 companies, including Ford and Procter & Gamble. Many companies adopted some or all the basic themes of TQM.

Today, quality improvement systems have been implemented in many organizations worldwide. Although most organizations no longer use the name TQM, the underlying philosophy and statistical methods used in today's quality improvement systems are consistent with TQM, as reflected by **Deming's 14 points for management**:

1. Create constancy of purpose for improvement of product and service.
2. Adopt the new philosophy.
3. Cease dependence on inspection to achieve quality.
4. End the practice of awarding business on the basis of price tag alone. Instead, minimize total cost by working with a single supplier.
5. Improve constantly and forever every process for planning, production, and service.
6. Institute training on the job.
7. Adopt and institute leadership.
8. Drive out fear.
9. Break down barriers between staff areas.
10. Eliminate slogans, exhortations, and targets for the workforce.
11. Eliminate numerical quotas for the workforce and numerical goals for management.
12. Remove barriers that rob people of pride of workmanship. Eliminate the annual rating or merit system.
13. Institute a vigorous program of education and self-improvement for everyone.
14. Put everyone in the company to work to accomplish the transformation.

Points 1, 2, 5, 7, and 14 focus on the need for organizational transformation and the responsibility of top management to assert leadership in committing to the transformation. Without this commitment, any improvements obtained will be limited.

One aspect of the improvement process is illustrated by the **Shewhart–Deming cycle**, shown in Figure 17.8. The Shewhart–Deming cycle represents a continuous cycle of "plan, do, study, and act." The first step, planning, represents the initial design phase for planning a change in a manufacturing or service process. This step involves teamwork among individuals from different areas within an organization. The second step, doing, involves implementing the change, preferably on a small scale. The third step, studying, involves analyzing the results, using statistical methods to determine what was learned. The fourth step, acting, involves the acceptance of the change, its abandonment, or further study of the change under different conditions.

FIGURE 17.8
Shewhart–Deming cycle

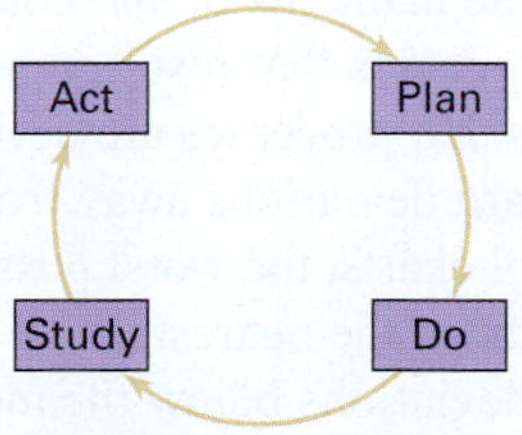

Point 3, cease dependence on inspection to achieve quality, implies that any inspection whose purpose is to improve quality is too late because the quality is already built into the product. It is better to focus on making it right the first time. Among the difficulties involved in inspection (besides high costs) are the failure of inspectors to agree on the operational definitions for nonconforming items and the problem of separating good and bad items. The following example illustrates the difficulties inspectors face.

Suppose your job involves proofreading the sentence in Figure 17.9, with the objective of counting the number of occurrences of the letter F. Perform this task and record the number of occurrences of the letter F that you discover.

FIGURE 17.9
An example of a proofreading process

Source: Adapted from W. W. Scherkenbach, *The Deming Route to Quality and Productivity: Road Maps and Roadblocks* (Washington, DC: CEEP Press, 1987).

FINISHED FILES ARE THE RESULT OF YEARS OF SCIENTIFIC STUDY COMBINED WITH THE EXPERIENCE OF MANY YEARS

People usually see either three *F*s or six *F*s. The correct number is six *F*s. The number you see depends on the method you use to examine the sentence. You are likely to find three *F*s if you read the sentence phonetically and six *F*s if you count the number of *F*s carefully. If such a simple process as counting *F*s leads to inconsistency of inspectors' results, what will happen when a much more complicated process fails to provide clear operational definitions?

Point 4, end the practice of awarding business on the basis of price tag alone, focuses on the idea that there is no real long-term meaning to price without knowledge of the quality of the product. In addition, minimizing the number of entities in the supply chain will reduce the variation involved.

Points 6 and 13 refer to training and reflect the needs of all employees. Continuous learning is critical for quality improvement within an organization. In particular, management needs to understand the differences between special causes and common causes of variation so that proper action is taken in each circumstance.

Points 8 through 12 relate to the evaluation of employee performance. Deming believed that an emphasis on targets and exhortations places an improper burden on the workforce. Workers cannot produce beyond what the system allows (as illustrated in the red bead experiment in Section 17.3). It is management's job to *improve* the system, not to raise the expectations on workers beyond the system's capability.

Although Deming's points are thought provoking, some have criticized his approach for lacking a formal, objective accountability (see reference 12). Many managers of large organizations, used to seeing financial analyses of policy changes, need a more prescriptive approach.

17.8 Six Sigma

Six Sigma is a quality improvement system originally developed by Motorola in the mid-1980s. After seeing the huge financial successes at Motorola, GE, and other early adopters of Six Sigma, many companies worldwide have now instituted Six Sigma to improve efficiency, cut costs, eliminate defects, and reduce product variation (see references 1, 4, 11, and 18). Six Sigma offers a more prescriptive and systematic approach to process improvement than TQM. It is also distinguished from other quality improvement systems by its clear focus on achieving bottom-line results in a relatively short three- to six-month period of time.

The name *Six Sigma* comes from the fact that it is a managerial approach designed to create processes that result in no more than 3.4 defects per million. The Six Sigma approach assumes that processes are designed so that the upper and lower specification limits are each six standard deviations away from the mean. Then, if the processes are monitored correctly with control charts, the worst possible scenario is for the mean to shift to within 4.5 standard deviations from the nearest specification limit. The area under the normal curve less than 4.5 standard deviations below the mean is approximately 3.4 out of 1 million. (Table E.2 reports this probability as 0.000003398.)

The DMAIC Model

To guide managers in their task of improving short-term and long-term results, Six Sigma uses a five-step process known as the **DMAIC model**—named for the five steps in the process:

- **Define** The problem is defined, along with the costs, the benefits, and the impact on the customer.
- **Measure** Important characteristics related to the quality of the service or product are identified and discussed. Variables measuring these characteristics are defined and

called *critical-to-quality (CTQ)* variables. Operational definitions for all the CTQ variables are then developed. In addition, the measurement procedure is verified so that it is consistent over repeated measurements.

- **Analyze** The root causes of *why* defects occur are determined, and variables in the process causing the defects are identified. Data are collected to determine benchmark values for each process variable. This analysis often uses control charts (discussed in Sections 17.2–17.5).
- **Improve** The importance of each process variable on the CTQ variable is studied using designed experiments (see Chapter 11 and references 9, 10, and 13). The objective is to determine the best level for each variable.
- **Control** The objective is to maintain the benefits for the long term by avoiding potential problems that can occur when a process is changed.

The *Define* phase of a Six Sigma project consists of the development of a project charter, performing a SIPOC analysis, and identifying the customers for the output of the process. The development of a project charter involves forming a table of business objectives and indicators for all potential Six Sigma projects. Importance ratings are assigned by top management, projects are prioritized, and the most important project is selected. A **SIPOC analysis** is used to identify the **S**uppliers to the process, list the **I**nputs provided by the suppliers, flowchart the **P**rocess, list the process **O**utputs, and identify the **C**ustomers of the process. This is followed by a Voice of the Customer analysis that involves market segmentation in which different types of users of the process are identified and the circumstances of their use of the process are identified. Statistical methods used in the *Define* phase include tables and charts, descriptive statistics, and control charts.

In the *Measure* phase of a Six Sigma project, members of a team identify the CTQ variables that measure important quality characteristics. Next, operational definitions (see Section 1.3) of each CTQ variable are developed so that everyone will have a firm understanding of the CTQ. Then studies are undertaken to ensure that there is a valid measurement system for the CTQ that is consistent across measurements. Finally, baseline data are collected to determine the capability and stability of the current process. Statistical methods used in the *Measure* phase include tables and charts, descriptive statistics, the normal distribution, the Analysis of Variance, and control charts.

The *Analyze* phase of a Six Sigma project focuses on the factors that affect the central tendency, variation, and shape of each CTQ variable. Factors are identified, and the relationships between the factors and the CTQs are analyzed. Statistical methods used in the *Analyze* phase include tables and charts, descriptive statistics, the Analysis of Variance, regression analysis, and control charts.

In the *Improve* phase of a Six Sigma project, team members carry out designed experiments to actively intervene in a process. The objective of the experiments is to determine the settings of the factors that will optimize the central tendency, variation, and shape of each CTQ variable. Statistical methods used in the *Improve* phase include tables and charts, descriptive statistics, regression analysis, hypothesis testing, the Analysis of Variance, and designed experiments.

The *Control* phase of a Six Sigma project focuses on the maintenance of improvements that have been made in the *Improve* phase. A risk abatement plan is developed to identify elements that can cause damage to a process. Statistical methods used in the *Control* phase include tables and charts, descriptive statistics, and control charts.

Roles in a Six Sigma Organization

Six Sigma requires that the employees of an organization have well-defined roles. The roles senior executive (CEO or president), executive committee, champion, process owner, master black belt, black belt, and green belt are critical to Six Sigma. More importantly, everyone must be properly trained in order to successfully fulfill their roles' tasks and responsibilities.

The role of the **senior executive** is critical for Six Sigma's ultimate success. The most successful, highly publicized Six Sigma efforts have all had unwavering, clear, and committed leadership from top management. Although Six Sigma concepts and processes can be initiated at lower levels, high-level success cannot be achieved without the leadership of the senior executive.

The members of the **executive committee** consist of the top management of an organization. They need to operate at the same level of commitment to Six Sigma as the senior executive.

Champions take a strong sponsorship and leadership role in conducting and implementing Six Sigma projects. They work closely with the executive committee, the black belt assigned to their project, and the master black belt overseeing their project. A champion should be a member of the executive committee, or at least someone who reports directly to a member of the executive committee. He or she should have enough influence to remove obstacles or provide resources without having to go higher in the organization.

A **process owner** is the manager of a process. He or she has responsibility for the process and has the authority to change the process on her or his signature. The process owner should be identified and involved immediately in all Six Sigma projects related to his or her own area.

A **master black belt** takes on a leadership role in the implementation of the Six Sigma process and as an advisor to senior executives. The master black belt must use his or her skills while working on projects that are led by black belts and green belts. A master black belt has successfully led many teams through complex Six Sigma projects. He or she is a proven change agent, leader, facilitator, and technical expert in Six Sigma.

A **black belt** works full time on Six Sigma projects. A black belt is mentored by a master black belt but may report to a manager for his or her tour of duty as a black belt. Ideally, a black belt works well in a team format, can manage meetings, is familiar with statistics and systems theory, and has a focus on the customer.

A **green belt** is an individual who works on Six Sigma projects part time (approximately 25%), either as a team member for complex projects or as a project leader for simpler projects. Most managers in a mature Six Sigma organization are green belts. Green belt certification is a critical prerequisite for advancement into upper management in a Six Sigma organization.

Recent research (see reference 4) indicates that more than 80% of the top 100 publicly traded companies in the United States use Six Sigma. So, you do need to be aware of the distinction between master black belt, black belt, and green belt if you are to function effectively in a Six Sigma organization.

In a Six Sigma organization, 25% to 50% of the organization will be green belts, only 6% to 12% of the organization will be black belts, and only 1% of the organization will be master black belts (reference 9). Individual companies, professional organizations such as the American Society for Quality, and universities such as the University of Miami offer certification programs for green belt, black belt, and master black belt. For more information on certification and other aspects of Six Sigma, see references 9, 10, and 13.

USING STATISTICS @ Beachcomber Hotel Revisited

In the Using Statistics scenario, you were the manager of the Beachcomber Hotel. After being trained in Six Sigma, you decided to focus on two critical first impressions: Is the room ready when a guest checks in? And, do guests receive their luggage in a reasonable amount of time?

You constructed a p chart of the proportion of rooms not ready at check-in. The p chart indicated that the check-in process was in control and that, on average, the proportion of rooms not ready was approximately 0.08 (i.e., 8%). You then constructed $\bar{X}$ and R charts for the amount of time required to deliver luggage. Although there was a considerable amount of variability around the overall mean of approximately 9.5 minutes, you determined that the luggage delivery process was also in control.

You have learned that an in-control process contains common causes of variation but no special causes of variation. Improvements in the outcomes of in-control processes must come from changes in the actual processes. Thus, if you want to reduce the proportion of rooms not ready at check-in and/or lower the mean luggage delivery time, you will need to change the check-in process and/or the luggage delivery process. From your knowledge of Six Sigma and statistics, you know that during the *Improve* phase of the DMAIC model, you will be able to perform and analyze experiments using different process designs. Hopefully you will discover better process designs that will lead to a higher percentage of rooms being ready on time and/or quicker luggage delivery times. These improvements should ultimately lead to greater guest satisfaction.

SUMMARY

In this chapter you have learned how to use control charts to distinguish between common causes and special causes of variation. For categorical variables, you learned how to construct and analyze p charts. For discrete variables involving a count of nonconformances, you learned how to construct and analyze c charts. For numerically measured variables, you learned how to construct and analyze $\bar{X}$ and R charts. The chapter also discussed managerial approaches such as TQM and Six Sigma that improve the quality of products and services.

KEY EQUATIONS

Constructing Control Limits

Process mean ±3 standard deviations

Upper control limit (UCL) = process mean +3 standard deviations

Lower control limit (LCL) = process mean −3 standard deviations **(17.1)**

Control Limits for the *p* Chart

$$\bar{p} \pm 3\sqrt{\frac{\bar{p}(1-\bar{p})}{\bar{n}}}$$

$$\text{UCL} = \bar{p} + 3\sqrt{\frac{\bar{p}(1-\bar{p})}{\bar{n}}}$$

$$\text{LCL} = \bar{p} - 3\sqrt{\frac{\bar{p}(1-\bar{p})}{\bar{n}}} \quad \textbf{(17.2)}$$

Control Limits for the *c* Chart

$$\bar{c} \pm 3\sqrt{\bar{c}}$$

$$\text{UCL} = \bar{c} + 3\sqrt{\bar{c}}$$

$$\text{LCL} = \bar{c} - 3\sqrt{\bar{c}} \quad \textbf{(17.3)}$$

Control Limits for the Range

$$\bar{R} \pm 3\bar{R}\frac{d_3}{d_2}$$

$$\text{UCL} = \bar{R} + 3\bar{R}\frac{d_3}{d_2}$$

$$\text{LCL} = \bar{R} - 3\bar{R}\frac{d_3}{d_2} \quad \textbf{(17.4)}$$

Computing Control Limits for the Range

$$\text{UCL} = D_4\bar{R} \quad \textbf{(17.5a)}$$

$$\text{LCL} = D_3\bar{R} \quad \textbf{(17.5b)}$$

Control Limits for the $\bar{X}$ Chart

$$\bar{\bar{X}} \pm 3\frac{\bar{R}}{d_2\sqrt{n}}$$

$$\text{UCL} = \bar{\bar{X}} + 3\frac{\bar{R}}{d_2\sqrt{n}}$$

$$\text{LCL} = \bar{\bar{X}} - 3\frac{\bar{R}}{d_2\sqrt{n}} \quad \textbf{(17.6)}$$

Computing Control Limits for the Mean, Using the A_2 Factor

$$\text{UCL} = \bar{\bar{X}} + A_2\bar{R} \quad \textbf{(17.7a)}$$

$$\text{LCL} = \bar{\bar{X}} - A_2\bar{R} \quad \textbf{(17.7b)}$$

Estimating the Capability of a Process

For a CTQ variable with an LSL and a USL:

$$P(\text{An outcome will be within specification}) = P(\text{LSL} < X < \text{USL})$$

$$= P\left(\frac{\text{LSL} - \bar{\bar{X}}}{\bar{R}/d_2} < Z < \frac{\text{USL} - \bar{\bar{X}}}{\bar{R}/d_2}\right) \quad \textbf{(17.8a)}$$

For a CTQ variable with only a USL:

$$P(\text{An outcome will be within specification}) = P(X < \text{USL})$$

$$= P\left(Z < \frac{\text{USL} - \bar{\bar{X}}}{\bar{R}/d_2}\right) \quad \textbf{(17.8b)}$$

For a CTQ variable with only an LSL:

$$P(\text{An outcome will be within specification}) = P(\text{LSL} < X)$$

$$= P\left(\frac{\text{LSL} - \bar{\bar{X}}}{\bar{R}/d_2} < Z\right) \quad \textbf{(17.8c)}$$

The C_p Index

$$C_p = \frac{\text{USL} - \text{LSL}}{6(\bar{R}/d_2)} = \frac{\text{Specification spread}}{\text{Process spread}} \quad \textbf{(17.9)}$$

CPL* and *CPU

$$CPL = \frac{\bar{\bar{X}} - \text{LSL}}{3(\bar{R}/d_2)} \quad \textbf{(17.10a)}$$

$$CPU = \frac{\text{USL} - \bar{\bar{X}}}{3(\bar{R}/d_2)} \quad \textbf{(17.10b)}$$

C_{pk}

$$C_{pk} = MIN[CPL, CPU] \quad \textbf{(17.11)}$$

KEY TERMS

A_2 factor 735
area of opportunity 728
assignable cause of variation 718
attribute control chart 720
black belt 746
c chart 728
capability index 739
champion 746
chance cause of variation 718
common cause of variation 718
control chart 718
critical-to-quality (CTQ) 738
d_2 factor 732
d_3 factor 732
D_3 factor 732
D_4 factor 732
Deming's 14 points for management 743
DMAIC model 744
executive committee 746
green belt 746
in-control process 720
lower control limit (LCL) 719
lower specification limit (LSL) 738
master black belt 746
out-of-control process 720
p chart 720
process 718
process capability 737
process owner 746
R chart 732
red bead experiment 726
senior executive 745
Shewhart–Deming cycle 743
SIPOC analysis 745
Six Sigma 744
special cause of variation 718
specification limit 738
state of statistical control 720
subgroup 719
tampering 719
total quality management (TQM) 742
upper control limit (UCL) 719
upper specification limit (USL) 738
variables control chart 732
$\bar{X}$ chart 734

CHAPTER REVIEW PROBLEMS

CHECKING YOUR UNDERSTANDING

17.36 What is the difference between common cause variation and special cause variation?

17.37 What should you do to improve a process when special causes of variation are present?

17.38 What should you do to improve a process when only common causes of variation are present?

17.39 Under what circumstances do you use a *p* chart?

17.40 What is the difference between attribute control charts and variables control charts?

17.41 Why are $\bar{X}$ and *R* charts used together?

17.42 What principles did you learn from the red bead experiment?

17.43 What is the difference between process potential and process performance?

17.44 A company requires a C_{pk} value of 1 or larger. If a process has $C_p = 1.5$ and $C_{pk} = 0.8$, what changes should you make to the process?

17.45 Why is a capability analysis *not* performed on out-of-control processes?

APPLYING THE CONCEPTS

17.46 According to the American Society for Quality, customers in the United States consistently rate service quality lower than product quality (American Society for Quality, *The Quarterly Quality Report*, **www.asq.org**, May 16, 2006). For example, products in the beverage, personal care, and cleaning industries, as well as the major appliance sector all received very high customer satisfaction ratings. At the other extreme, services provided by airlines, banks, and insurance companies all received low customer satisfaction ratings.

a. Why do you think service quality consistently rates lower than product quality?
b. What are the similarities and differences between measuring service quality and product quality?
c. Do Deming's 14 points apply to both products and services?
d. Can Six Sigma be used for both products and services?

17.47 Suppose that you have been hired as a summer intern at a large amusement park. Every day, your task is to conduct 200 exit interviews in the parking lot when customers leave. You need to construct questions to address the cleanliness of the park and the customers' intent to return. When you begin to construct a short questionnaire, you remember the control charts you learned in a statistics course, and you decide to write questions that will provide you with data to graph on control charts. After collecting data for 30 days, you plan to construct the control charts.

a. Write a question that will allow you to develop a control chart of customers' perceptions of cleanliness of the park.
b. Give examples of common cause variation and special cause variation for the control chart.
c. If the control chart is in control, what does that indicate and what do you do next?
d. If the control chart is out of control, what does this indicate and what do you do next?
e. Repeat (a) through (d), this time addressing the customers' intent to return to the park.
f. After the initial 30 days, assuming that the charts indicate in-control processes or that the root sources of special cause variation have been corrected, explain how the charts can be used on a daily basis to monitor and improve the quality in the park.

17.48 Researchers at Miami University in Oxford, Ohio, investigated the use of p charts to monitor the market share of a product and to document the effectiveness of marketing promotions. Market share is defined as the company's proportion of the total number of products sold in a category. If a p chart based on a company's market share indicates an in-control process, then the company's share in the marketplace is deemed to be stable and consistent over time. In the example given in the article, the RudyBird Disk Company collected daily sales data from a nationwide retail audit service. The first 30 days of data in the accompanying table (stored in **RudyBird**) indicate the total number of cases of computer disks sold and the number of RudyBird disks sold. The final 7 days of data were taken after RudyBird launched a major in-store promotion. A control chart was used to see if the in-store promotion would result in special cause variation in the marketplace.

Cases Sold Before the Promotion

Day	Total	RudyBird	Day	Total	RudyBird
1	154	35	16	177	56
2	153	43	17	143	43
3	200	44	18	200	69
4	197	56	19	134	38
5	194	54	20	192	47
6	172	38	21	155	45
7	190	43	22	135	36
8	209	62	23	189	55
9	173	53	24	184	44
10	171	39	25	170	47
11	173	44	26	178	48
12	168	37	27	167	42
13	184	45	28	204	71
14	211	58	29	183	64
15	179	35	30	169	43

Cases Sold After the Promotion

Day	Total	RudyBird
31	201	92
32	177	76
33	205	85
34	199	90
35	187	77
36	168	79
37	198	97

Source: Data extracted from C. T. Crespy, T. C. Krehbiel, and J. M. Stearns, "Integrating Analytic Methods into Marketing Research Education: Statistical Control Charts as an Example," *Marketing Education Review*, 5 (Spring 1995), 11–23.

a. Construct a p chart, using data from the first 30 days (prior to the promotion) to monitor the market share for RudyBird disks.
b. Is the market share for RudyBird in control before the start of the in-store promotion?
c. On your control chart, extend the control limits generated in (b) and plot the proportions for days 31 through 37. What effect, if any, did the in-store promotion have on RudyBird's market share?

17.49 The manufacturer of Boston and Vermont asphalt shingles constructed control charts and analyzed several quality characteristics. One characteristic of interest is the strength of the sealant on the shingle. During each day of production, three shingles are tested for their sealant strength. (Thus, a subgroup is operationally defined as one day of production, and the sample size for each subgroup is 3.) Separate pieces are cut from the upper and lower portions of a shingle and then reassembled to simulate shingles on a roof. A timed heating process is used to simulate the sealing process. The sealed shingle pieces are pulled apart, and the amount of force (in pounds) required to break the sealant bond is measured and recorded. This variable is called the *sealant strength*. The file **Sealant** contains sealant strength measurements on 25 days of production for Boston shingles and 19 days for Vermont shingles.

For the 25 days of production for Boston shingles,

a. construct a control chart for the range.
b. construct a control chart for the mean.
c. is the process in control?
d. Repeat (a) through (c), using the 19 production days for Vermont shingles.

17.50 A professional basketball player has embarked on a program to study his ability to shoot foul shots. On each day in which a game is not scheduled, he intends to shoot 100 foul shots. He maintains records over a period of 40 days of practice, with the results stored in **Foulspc**:

a. Construct a p chart for the proportion of successful foul shots. Do you think that the player's foul-shooting process is in statistical control? If not, why not?
b. What if you were told that the player used a different method of shooting foul shots for the last 20 days? How might this information change your conclusions in (a)?
c. If you knew the information in (b) prior to doing (a), how might you do the analysis differently?

17.51 The funds-transfer department of a bank is concerned with turnaround time for investigations of funds-transfer payments. A payment may involve the bank as a remitter of funds, a beneficiary of funds, or an intermediary in the payment. An investigation is initiated by a payment inquiry or a query by a party involved in the payment or any department affected by the flow of funds. When a query is received, an investigator reconstructs the transaction trail of the payment and verifies that the information is correct and that the proper payment is transmitted. The investigator then reports the results of the investigation, and the transaction is considered closed. It is important that investigations be closed rapidly, preferably within the same day. The number of new investigations and the number and proportion closed on the same day that the inquiry was made are stored in **FundTran**.

a. Construct a control chart for these data.
b. Is the process in a state of statistical control? Explain.
c. Based on the results of (a) and (b), what should management do next to improve the process?

17.52 A branch manager of a brokerage company is concerned with the number of undesirable trades made by her sales staff. A trade is considered undesirable if there is an error on the trade ticket. Trades with errors are canceled and resubmitted. The cost of correcting errors is billed to the brokerage company. The branch manager wants to know whether the proportion of undesirable trades is in a state of statistical control so she can plan the next step in a quality improvement process. Data were collected for a 30-day period and stored in **Trade**.

a. Construct a control chart for these data.
b. Is the process in control? Explain.
c. Based on the results of (a) and (b), what should the manager do next to improve the process?

17.53 As chief operating officer of a local community hospital, you have just returned from a three-day seminar on quality and productivity. It is your intention to implement many of the ideas that you learned at the seminar. You have decided to construct control charts for the upcoming month for the proportion of rework in the laboratory (based on 1,000 daily samples), the number of daily admissions, and time (in hours) between receipt of a specimen at the laboratory and completion of the work (based on a subgroup of 10 specimens per day). The data collected are summarized and stored in **HospAdm**. You are to make a presentation to the chief executive officer of the hospital and the board of directors. Prepare a report that summarizes the conclusions drawn from analyzing control charts for these variables. In addition, recommend additional variables to measure and monitor by using control charts.

17.54 A team working at a cat food company had the business objective of reducing nonconformance in the cat food canning process. As the team members began to investigate the current process, they found that, in some instances, production needed expensive overtime costs to meet the requirements requested by the market forecasting team. They also realized that data were not available concerning the stability and magnitude of the rate of nonconformance and the production volume throughout the day. Their previous study of the process indicated that output could be nonconforming for a variety of reasons. The reasons broke down into two categories: quality characteristics due to the can and characteristics concerning the fill weight of the container. Because these nonconformities stemmed from different sets of underlying causes, they decided to study them separately. The group assigned to study and reduce the nonconformities due to the can decided that at 15-minute intervals during each shift the number of nonconforming cans would be determined along with the total number of cans produced during the time period. The results for a single day's production of kidney cat food and a single day's production of shrimp cat food for each shift are stored in **CatFood3**. You want to study the process of producing cans of cat food for the two shifts and the two types of food. Completely analyze the data.

17.55 Refer to Problem 17.54. The production team at the cat food company investigating nonconformities due to the fill weight of the cans determined that at 15-minute intervals during each shift, a subgroup of five cans would be selected, and the contents of the selected cans would be weighed. The results for a single day's production of kidney cat food and a single day's production of shrimp cat food are stored in CatFood4. You want to study the process of producing cans of cat food for the two shifts and the two types of food. Completely analyze the data.

17.56 For a period of four weeks, record your pulse rate (in beats per minute) just after you get out of bed in the morning and then again before you go to sleep at night. Construct $\bar{X}$ and R charts and determine whether your pulse rate is in a state of statistical control. Discuss.

17.57 (Class Project) Use the table of random numbers (Table E.1) to simulate the selection of different-colored balls from an urn, as follows:

1. Start in the row corresponding to the day of the month in which you were born plus the last two digits of the year in which you were born. For example, if you were born October 3, 1990, you would start in row 93 (3 + 90). If your total exceeds 100, subtract 100 from the total.
2. Select two-digit random numbers.
3. If you select a random number from 00 to 94, consider the ball to be white; if the random number is from 95 to 99, consider the ball to be red.

Each student is to select 100 two-digit random numbers and report the number of "red balls" in the sample. Construct a control chart for the proportion of red balls. What conclusions can you draw about the system of selecting red balls? Are all the students part of the system? Is anyone outside the system? If so, what explanation can you give for someone who has too many red balls? If a bonus were paid to the top 10% of the students (the 10% with the fewest red balls), what effect would that have on the rest of the students? Discuss.

THE HARNSWELL SEWING MACHINE COMPANY CASE

Phase 1

For more than 40 years, the Harnswell Sewing Machine Company has manufactured industrial sewing machines. The company specializes in automated machines called pattern tackers that sew repetitive patterns on such mass-produced products as shoes, garments, and seat belts. Aside from the sales of machines, the company sells machine parts. Because the company's products have a reputation for being superior, Harnswell is able to command a price premium for its product line.

Recently, the operations manager, Natalie York, purchased several books related to quality. After reading them, she considered the feasibility of beginning a quality program at the company. At the current time, the company has no formal quality program. Parts are 100% inspected at the time of shipping to a customer or installation in a machine, yet Natalie has always wondered why inventory of certain parts (in particular, the half-inch cam rollers) invariably falls short before a full year lapses, even though 7,000 pieces have been produced for a demand of 5,000 pieces per year.

After a great deal of reflection and with some apprehension, Natalie has decided that she will approach John Harnswell, the owner of the company, about the possibility of beginning a program to improve quality in the company, starting with a trial project in the machine parts area. As she is walking to Mr. Harnswell's office for the meeting, she has second thoughts about whether this is such a good idea. After all, just last month, Mr. Harnswell told her, "Why do you need to go to graduate school for your master's degree in business? That is a waste of your time and will not be of any value to the Harnswell Company. All those professors are just up in their ivory towers and don't know a thing about running a business, like I do."

As she enters his office, Mr. Harnswell invites Natalie to sit down across from him. "Well, what do you have on your mind this morning?" Mr. Harnswell asks her in an inquisitive tone. She begins by starting to talk about the books that she has just completed reading and about how she has some interesting ideas for making production even better than it is now and improving profits. Before she can finish, Mr. Harnswell has started to answer: "Look, everything has been fine since I started this company in 1968. I have built this company up from nothing to one that employs more than 100 people. Why do you want to make waves? Remember, if it ain't broke, don't fix it." With that, he ushers her from his office with the admonishment of, "What am I going to do with you if you keep coming up with these ridiculous ideas?"

EXERCISES

1. Based on what you have read, which of Deming's 14 points of management are most lacking at the Harnswell Sewing Machine Company? Explain.
2. What changes, if any, do you think that Natalie York might be able to institute in the company? Explain.

Phase 2

Natalie slowly walks down the hall after leaving Mr. Harnswell's office, feeling rather downcast. He just won't listen to anyone, she thinks. As she walks, Jim Murante, the shop foreman, comes up beside her. "So," he says, "did you really think that he would listen to you? I've been here more than 25 years. The only way he listens is if he is shown something that worked after it has already been done. Let's see what we can plan together."

Natalie and Jim decide to begin by investigating the production of the cam rollers, which are precision-ground parts. The last part of the production process involves the grinding of the outer diameter. After grinding, the part mates with the cam groove of the particular sewing pattern. The half-inch rollers technically have an engineering specification for the outer diameter of the roller of 0.5075 inch (the specifications are actually metric, but in factory floor jargon, they are referred to as half-inch), plus a tolerable error of 0.0003 inch on the lower side. Thus, the outer diameter is allowed to be between 0.5072 and 0.5075 inch. Anything larger is reclassified into a different and less costly category, and anything smaller is unusable for anything other than scrap.

TABLE HS17.1

Diameter of Cam Rollers (in Inches)

	Cam Roller				
Batch	**1**	**2**	**3**	**4**	**5**
1	.5076	.5076	.5075	.5077	.5075
2	.5075	.5077	.5076	.5076	.5075
3	.5075	.5075	.5075	.5075	.5076
4	.5075	.5076	.5074	.5076	.5073
5	.5075	.5074	.5076	.5073	.5076
6	.5076	.5075	.5076	.5075	.5075
7	.5076	.5076	.5076	.5075	.5075
8	.5075	.5076	.5076	.5075	.5074
9	.5074	.5076	.5075	.5075	.5076
10	.5076	.5077	.5075	.5075	.5075
11	.5075	.5075	.5075	.5076	.5075
12	.5075	.5076	.5075	.5077	.5075
13	.5076	.5076	.5073	.5076	.5074
14	.5075	.5076	.5074	.5076	.5075
15	.5075	.5075	.5076	.5074	.5073
16	.5075	.5074	.5076	.5075	.5075
17	.5075	.5074	.5075	.5074	.5072
18	.5075	.5075	.5076	.5075	.5076
19	.5076	.5076	.5075	.5075	.5076
20	.5075	.5074	.5077	.5076	.5074
21	.5075	.5074	.5075	.5075	.5075
22	.5076	.5076	.5075	.5076	.5074
23	.5076	.5076	.5075	.5075	.5076
24	.5075	.5076	.5075	.5076	.5075
25	.5075	.5075	.5075	.5075	.5074
26	.5077	.5076	.5076	.5074	.5075
27	.5075	.5075	.5074	.5076	.5075
28	.5077	.5076	.5075	.5075	.5076
29	.5075	.5075	.5074	.5075	.5075
30	.5076	.5075	.5075	.5076	.5075

The grinding of the cam roller is done on a single machine with a single tool setup and no change in the grinding wheel after initial setup. The operation is done by Dave Martin, the head machinist, who has 30 years of experience in the trade and specific experience producing the cam roller part. Because production occurs in batches, Natalie and Jim sample five parts produced from each batch. Table HS17.1 presents data collected over 30 batches (stored in **Harnswell**).

EXERCISE

3. a. Is the process in control? Why?

b. What recommendations do you have for improving the process?

Phase 3

Natalie examines the $\overline{X}$ and R charts developed from the data presented in Table HS17.1. The R chart indicates that the process is in control, but the $\overline{X}$ chart reveals that the mean for batch 17 is outside the LCL. This immediately gives her cause for concern because low values for the roller diameter could mean that parts have to be scrapped. Natalie goes to see Jim Murante, the shop foreman, to try to find out what had happened to batch 17. Jim looks up the production records to determine when this batch was produced. "Aha!" he exclaims. "I think I've got the answer! This batch was produced on that really cold morning we had last month. I've been after Mr. Harnswell for a long time to let us install an automatic thermostat here in the shop so that the place doesn't feel so cold when we get here in the morning. All he ever tells me is that people aren't as tough as they used to be."

Natalie is almost in shock. She realizes that what happened is that, rather than standing idle until the environment and the equipment warmed to acceptable temperatures, the machinist opted to manufacture parts that might have to be scrapped. In fact, Natalie recalls that a major problem occurred on that same day, when several other expensive parts had to be scrapped. Natalie says to Jim, "We just have to do something. We can't let this go on now that we know what problems it is potentially causing." Natalie and Jim decide to take enough money out of petty cash to get the thermostat without having to fill out a requisition requiring Mr. Harnswell's signature. They install the thermostat and set the heating control so that the heat turns on a half hour before the shop opens each morning.

EXERCISES

4. What should Natalie do now concerning the cam roller data? Explain.

5. Explain how the actions of Natalie and Jim to avoid this particular problem in the future have resulted in quality improvement.

PHASE 4

Because corrective action was taken to eliminate the special cause of variation, Natalie removes the data for batch 17 from the analysis. The control charts for the remaining days indicate a stable system, with only common causes of variation operating on the system. Then, Natalie and Jim sit down with Dave Martin and several other machinists to try to determine all the possible causes for the existence of oversized and scrapped rollers. Natalie is still troubled by the data. After all, she wants to find out whether the process is giving oversizes (which are downgraded) and undersizes (which are scrapped). She thinks about which tables and charts might be most helpful.

EXERCISE

6. **a.** Construct a frequency distribution and a stem-and-leaf display of the cam roller diameters. Which do you prefer in this situation?
   b. Based on your results in (a), construct all appropriate charts of the cam roller diameters.
   c. Write a report, expressing your conclusions concerning the cam roller diameters. Be sure to discuss the diameters as they relate to the specifications.

PHASE 5

Natalie notices immediately that the overall mean diameter with batch 17 eliminated is 0.507527, which is higher than the specification value. Thus, the mean diameter of the rollers produced is so high that many will be downgraded in value. In fact, 55 of the 150 rollers sampled (36.67%) are above the specification value. If this percentage is extrapolated to the full year's production, 36.67% of the 7,000 pieces manufactured, or 2,567, could not be sold as half-inch rollers, leaving only 4,433 available for sale. "No wonder we often have shortages that require costly emergency runs," she thinks. She also notes that not one diameter is below the lower specification of 0.5072, so not one of the rollers had to be scrapped.

Natalie realizes that there has to be a reason for all this. Along with Jim Murante, she decides to show the results to Dave Martin, the head machinist. Dave says that the results don't surprise him that much. "You know," he says, "there is only 0.0003 inch variation in diameter that I'm allowed. If I aim for exactly halfway between 0.5072 and 0.5075, I'm afraid that I'll make a lot of short pieces that will have to be scrapped. I know from way back when I first started here that Mr. Harnswell and everybody else will come down on my head if they start seeing too many of those scraps. I figure that if I aim at 0.5075, the worst thing that will happen will be a bunch of downgrades, but I won't make any pieces that have to be scrapped."

EXERCISES

7. What approach do you think the machinist should take in terms of the diameter he should aim for? Explain.
8. What do you think that Natalie should do next? Explain.

MANAGING ASHLAND MULTICOMM SERVICES

The AMS technical services team has embarked on a quality improvement effort. Its first project relates to maintaining the target upload speed for its Internet service subscribers. Upload speeds are measured on a device that records the results on a standard scale in which the target value is 1.0. Each day five uploads are randomly selected, and the speed of each upload is measured. Table AMS17.1 on page 754 presents the results for 25 days (stored in AMS17).

EXERCISE

1. **a.** Construct the appropriate control charts for these data.
   b. Is the process in a state of statistical control? Explain.
   c. What should the team recommend as the next step to improve the process?

TABLE AMS17.1

Upload Speeds for 25 Consecutive Days

	Upload				
Day	**1**	**2**	**3**	**4**	**5**
1	0.96	1.01	1.12	1.07	0.97
2	1.06	1.00	1.02	1.16	0.96
3	1.00	0.90	0.98	1.18	0.96
4	0.92	0.89	1.01	1.16	0.90
5	1.02	1.16	1.03	0.89	1.00
6	0.88	0.92	1.03	1.16	0.91
7	1.05	1.13	1.01	0.93	1.03
8	0.95	0.86	1.14	0.90	0.95
9	0.99	0.89	1.00	1.15	0.92
10	0.89	1.18	1.03	0.96	1.04
11	0.97	1.13	0.95	0.86	1.06
12	1.00	0.87	1.02	0.98	1.13
13	0.96	0.79	1.17	0.97	0.95
14	1.03	0.89	1.03	1.12	1.03
15	0.96	1.12	0.95	0.88	0.99
16	1.01	0.87	0.99	1.04	1.16
17	0.98	0.85	0.99	1.04	1.16
18	1.03	0.82	1.21	0.98	1.08
19	1.02	0.84	1.15	0.94	1.08
20	0.90	1.02	1.10	1.04	1.08
21	0.96	1.05	1.01	0.93	1.01
22	0.89	1.04	0.97	0.99	0.95
23	0.96	1.00	0.97	1.04	0.95
24	1.01	0.98	1.04	1.01	0.92
25	1.01	1.00	0.92	0.90	1.11

REFERENCES

1. Arndt, M., "Quality Isn't Just for Widgets," *BusinessWeek*, July 22, 2002, pp. 72–73.
2. Automotive Industry Action Group (AIAG), *Statistical Process Control Reference Manual* (Chrysler, Ford, and General Motors Quality and Supplier Assessment Staff, 1995).
3. Bothe, D. R., *Measuring Process Capability* (New York: McGraw-Hill, 1997).
4. Cyger, M., "The Last Word—Riding the Bandwagon," *iSixSigma Magazine*, November/December 2006.
5. Davis, R. B., and T. C. Krehbiel, "Shewhart and Zone Control Charts Under Linear Trend," *Communications in Statistics: Simulation and Computation*, 31 (2002), 91–96.
6. Deming, W. E., *The New Economics for Business, Industry, and Government* (Cambridge, MA: MIT Center for Advanced Engineering Study, 1993).
7. Deming, W. E., *Out of the Crisis* (Cambridge, MA: MIT Center for Advanced Engineering Study, 1986).
8. Gabor, A., *The Man Who Discovered Quality* (New York: Time Books, 1990).
9. Gitlow, H., and D. Levine, *Six Sigma for Green Belts and Champions* (Upper Saddle River, NJ: Financial Times/Prentice Hall, 2005).
10. Gitlow, H., D. Levine, and E. Popovich, *Design for Six Sigma for Green Belts and Champions* (Upper Saddle River, NJ: Financial Times/Prentice Hall, 2006).
11. Hahn, G. J., N. Doganaksoy, and R. Hoerl, "The Evolution of Six Sigma," *Quality Engineering*, 12 (2000), 317–326.
12. Lemak, D. L., N. P. Mero, and R. Reed, "When Quality Works: A Premature Post-Mortem on TQM," *Journal of Business and Management*, 8 (2002), 391–407.
13. Levine, D. M., *Statistics for Six Sigma for Green Belts with Minitab and JMP* (Upper Saddle River, NJ: Financial Times/Prentice Hall, 2006).
14. *Microsoft Excel 2010* (Redmond, WA: Microsoft Corp., 2010).
15. *Minitab Release 16* (State College, PA: Minitab Inc., 2010).
16. Scherkenbach, W. W., *The Deming Route to Quality and Productivity: Road Maps and Roadblocks* (Washington, DC: CEEP Press, 1987).
17. Shewhart, W. A., *Economic Control of the Quality of Manufactured Product* (New York: Van Nostrand-Reinhard, 1931, reprinted by the American Society for Quality Control, Milwaukee, 1980).
18. Snee, R. D., "Impact of Six Sigma on Quality," *Quality Engineering*, 12 (2000), ix–xiv.
19. Vardeman, S. B., and J. M. Jobe, *Statistical Methods for Quality Assurance: Basics, Measurement, Control, Capability and Improvement* (New York: Springer-Verlag, 2009).
20. Walton, M., *The Deming Management Method* (New York: Perigee Books, 1986).

CHAPTER 17 EXCEL GUIDE

EG17.1 The THEORY of CONTROL CHARTS

There are no Excel Guide instructions for this section.

EG17.2 CONTROL CHART for the PROPORTION: The *p* CHART

PHStat2 Use **p Chart** to create a *p* chart and supporting worksheets that compute the control limits and plot points. For example, to create the Figure 17.2 *p* chart for the Table 17.1 nonconforming hotel room data on page 722, open to the **DATA worksheet** of the **Hotel1 workbook**. Select **PHStat → Control Charts → p Chart** and in the procedure's dialog box (shown below):

1. Enter **C1:C29** as the **Nonconformances Cell Range.**
2. Check **First cell contains label.**
3. Click **Size does not vary** and enter **200** as the **Sample/Subgroup Size.**
4. Enter a **Title** and click **OK.**

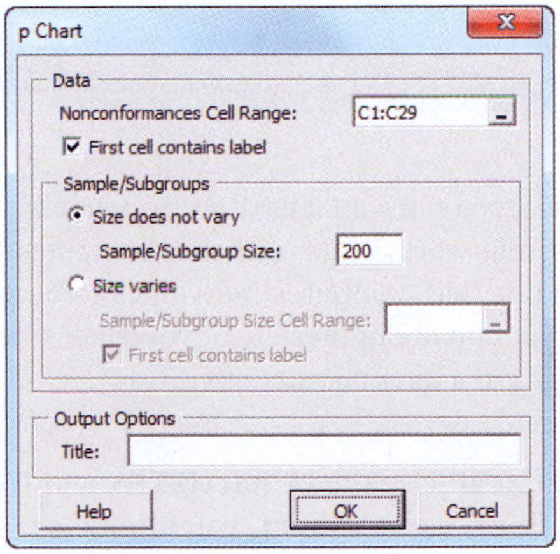

The procedure creates a *p* chart on its own chart sheet and two supporting worksheets: one that computes the control limits and one that computes the values to be plotted. For more information about these two worksheets, read the following *In-Depth Excel* instructions.

For problems in which the sample/subgroup sizes vary, replace step 3 with this step: Click **Size varies**, enter the cell range that contains the sample/subgroup sizes as the **Sample/Subgroup Cell Range**, and click **First cell contain label**.

In-Depth Excel Use the **pChartDATA** and **COMPUTE worksheets** of the **p Chart workbook** as a template for computing control limits and plot points. The pChartDATA worksheet uses formulas in column D that divide the column C number of nonconformances value by the column B subgroup/sample size value to compute the proportion (p_i) and uses formulas in columns E through G to display the values for the LCL, $\bar{p}$, and UCL that are computed in cells B12 through B14 of the COMPUTE worksheet. In turn, the COMPUTE worksheet (shown below) uses the subgroup sizes and the proportion values found in the pChartDATA worksheet to compute the control limits.

	A	B	
1	**p Chart Summary**		
2			
3	Intermediate Calculations		
4	Sum of Subgroup Sizes	5600	=SUM(pChartDATA!B:B)
5	Number of Subgroups Taken	28	=COUNT(pChartDATA!B:B)
6	Average Sample/Subgroup Size	200	=B4/B5
7	Average Proportion of Nonconforming Items	0.0827	=SUM(pChartDATA!C:C)/B4
8	Three Standard Deviations	0.0584	=3 * SQRT(B7 * (1 - B7)/B6)
9	Preliminary Lower Control Limit	0.0243	=B7 - B8
10			
11	p Chart Control Limits		
12	Lower Control Limit	0.0243	=IF(B9 > 0, B9, 0)
13	Center	0.0827	=B7
14	Upper Control Limit	0.1411	=B7 + B8

Computing control limits and plotting points for other problems requires changes to the **pChartDATA worksheet** of the **p Chart workbook**. First, paste the time period, subgroup/sample size, and number of nonconformances data into columns A through C of the pChartDATA worksheet. If there are more than 28 time periods, select cell range **D29:G29** and copy the range down through all the rows. If there are fewer than 28 time periods, delete the extra rows from the bottom up, starting with row 29.

Use the pChartDATA worksheet as the basis for creating a *p* chart. For example, to create the Figure 17.2 *p* chart for the nonconforming hotel room data on page 722, open to the pChartDATA worksheet which contains the Table 17.1 nonconforming hotel room data on page 722. Select the cell range **A1:A29** and while holding down the **Ctrl** key, select the cell range **D1:G29**. (This operation selects the cell range **A1:A29, D1:G29**.) Then:

1. Select **Insert → Scatter** and select the fourth choice from the **Scatter** gallery **(Scatter with Straight Lines and Markers)**.
2. Relocate the chart to a chart sheet and adjust chart formatting by using the instructions in Appendix Section F.4 on page 815.

At this point, a recognizable chart begins to take shape, but the control limit and center lines are improperly formatted and are not properly labeled. Use the following three sets of instructions to correct these formatting errors:

To reformat each control limit line:

1. Right-click the control limit line and select **Format Data Series** from the shortcut menu.
2. In the Format Data Series dialog box left pane, click **Marker Options** and in the **Marker Options** right panel, click **None**.
3. In the left pane, click **Line Style** and in the **Line Style** right panel, select the sixth choice (a dashed line) from the **Dash type** drop-down gallery list.
4. In the left pane, click **Line Color** and in the **Line Color** right panel, select the black color from the **Color** drop-down gallery list.
5. Click **Close**.

To reformat the center line:

1. Right-click the center line and select **Format Data Series** from the shortcut menu.
2. In the Format Data Series dialog box left pane, click **Marker Options** and in the **Marker Options** right panel, click **None**.
3. In the left pane, click **Line Color** and in the **Line Color** right panel, click **Solid line** and then select a red color from the **Color** drop-down gallery.
4. Click **Close**.

To label a control limit line or the center line:

1. Select **Layout → Text Box** (in Insert group) and starting slightly above and to the right of the line, drag the special cursor diagonally to form a new text box.
2. Enter the line label in the text box and then click on the chart background.

EG17.3 The RED BEAD EXPERIMENT: UNDERSTANDING PROCESS VARIABILITY

There are no Excel Guide instructions for this section.

EG17.4 CONTROL CHART for an AREA of OPPORTUNITY: The *c* CHART

PHStat2 Use **c Chart** to create a *c* chart and supporting worksheets that compute the control limits and plot points. For example, to create the Figure 17.5 *c* chart for the hotel complaint data on page 729, open to the **DATA worksheet** of the **Complaints workbook**. Select **PHStat → Control Charts → c Chart** and in the procedure's dialog box (shown below):

1. Enter **B1:B51** as the **Nonconformances Cell Range**.
2. Check **First cell contains label**.
3. Enter a **Title** and click **OK**.

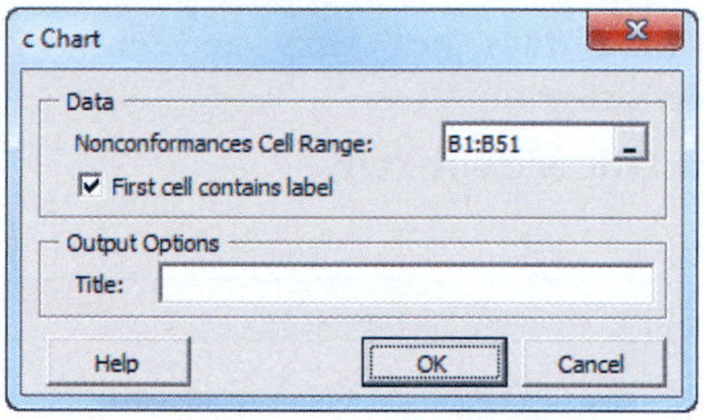

The procedure creates a *c* chart on its own chart sheet and two supporting worksheets: one that computes the control limits and one that computes the values to be plotted. For more information about these two worksheets, read the following *In-Depth Excel* instructions.

In-Depth Excel Use the **cChartDATA** and **COMPUTE worksheets** of the **c Chart workbook** as a template for computing control limits and plot points. The cChartDATA worksheet uses formulas in columns C through E to display the values for the LCL, cBar, and UCL that are computed in cells B10 through B12 of the COMPUTE worksheet. In turn, the COMPUTE worksheet (shown on page 757) computes sums and counts of the number of nonconformities found in the cChartDATA worksheet to help compute the control limits.

	A	B	
1	c Chart Summary		
2			
3	Intermediate Calculations		
4	Sum of NonConformities	312	=SUM(cChartDATA!B:B)
5	Number of Units Sampled	50	=COUNT(cChartDATA!B:B)
6	CBar	6.24	=B4/B5
7	Preliminary Lower Control Limit	-1.2540	=B6 - 3 * SQRT(B6)
8			
9	c Chart Control Limits		
10	Lower Control Limit	0.0000	=IF(B7 > 0, B7, 0)
11	Center	6.2400	=B6
12	Upper Control Limit	13.7340	=B6 + 3 * SQRT(B6)

Computing control limits and plotting points for other problems requires changes to the **cChartDATA worksheet** of the **c Chart workbook**. First, paste the time period and number of nonconformances data into columns A and B of the cChartDATA worksheet. If there are more than 50 time periods, select cell range **C51:E51** and copy the range down through all the rows. If there are fewer than 50 time periods, delete the extra rows from the bottom up, starting with row 51.

Use the cChartDATA worksheet as the basis for creating a *c* chart. For example, to create the Figure 17.5 *c* chart for the hotel complaint data on page 729, open to the cChartDATA worksheet which contains the Table 17.4 hotel complaint data on page 729. Select the cell range **B1:E51** and:

1. Select **Insert →Scatter** and select the fourth choice from the **Scatter** gallery **(Scatter with Straight Lines and Markers)**.
2. Relocate the chart to a chart sheet and adjust the chart formatting by using the instructions in Appendix Section F.4 on page 815.

At this point, a recognizable chart begins to take shape, but the control limit and center lines are improperly formatted and are not properly labeled. To correct these formatting errors, use the three sets of instructions given in the Section EG17.2 *In-Depth Excel* instructions.

EG17.5 CONTROL CHARTS for the RANGE and the MEAN

The *R* Chart and the $\bar{X}$ Chart

PHStat2 Use **R and XBar Charts** to create *R* and $\bar{X}$ charts and supporting worksheets that compute the control limits and plot points. For example, to create the Figure 17.6 *R* chart and the Figure 17.7 $\bar{X}$ chart for the Table 17.5 luggage delivery times (see pages 734 and 735), open to the **DATA worksheet** of the **Hotel2 workbook**. Because the PHStat2 procedure requires column cell ranges that contain either means or ranges, first add two columns that compute the mean and ranges on this worksheet. Enter the column heading **Mean** in cell **G1** and the heading **Range** in cell **H1**. Enter the formula **=AVERAGE(B2:F2)** in cell **G2** and the formula **=MAX(B2:F2) - MIN(B2:F2)** in cell **H2**. Select the cell range **G2:H2** and copy the range down through row 29.

With the two columns created, select **PHStat → Control Charts → R and XBar Charts**. In the procedure's dialog box (shown below):

1. Enter **5** as the **Subgroup/Sample Size**.
2. Enter **H1:H29** as the **Subgroup Ranges Cell Range**.
3. Check **First cell contains label**.
4. Click **R and XBar Charts**. Enter **G1:G29** as the **Subgroup Means Cell Range** and check **First cell contains label**.
5. Enter a **Title** and click **OK**.

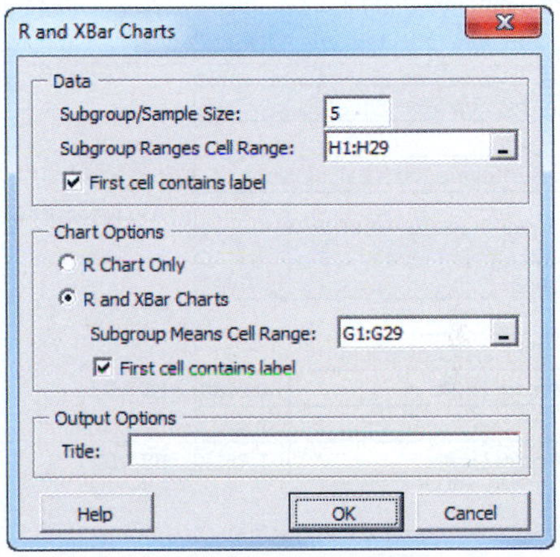

The procedure creates the two charts on separate chart sheets and two supporting worksheets: one that computes the control limits and one that computes the values to be plotted. For more information about these two worksheets, read the following *In-Depth Excel* section.

In-Depth Excel Use the **DATA**, **RXChartDATA**, and **COMPUTE worksheets** of the **R and XBar Chart workbook** as a template for computing control limits and plotting points. The RXChartDATA worksheet uses formulas in columns B and C to compute the mean and range values for the Table 17.5 luggage delivery times (see page 733 stored in the DATA worksheet. The worksheet uses formulas in columns D through I to display the values for the control limit and center lines, using values that are computed in the COMPUTE worksheet. Formulas in columns D and G use IF functions that will omit the lower control limit if the LCL value computed is less than 0. (To examine the formulas used in the worksheet, open to the **RXChartDATA_FORMULAS worksheet**.)

The COMPUTE worksheet (shown below) uses the computed means and ranges to compute $\overline{R}$ and $\overline{\overline{X}}$, the mean of the subgroup means. Unlike the COMPUTE worksheets for other control charts, you must manually enter the **Sample/Subgroup Size** in cell **B4** (**5**, as shown below) in addition to the D_3, D_4, and A_2 factors in cells **B8**, **B9**, and **B18** (**0**, **2.114**, and **0.577**, as shown). Use Table E.9 on page 812 to look up the values for the D_3, D_4, and A_2 factors.

	A	B	
1	**R and XBar Chart Summary**		
2			
3	Data		
4	Sample/Subgroup Size	5	
5			
6	R Chart Intermediate Calculations		
7	RBar	3.4821	=AVERAGE(RXChartDATA!C:C)
8	D_3 Factor	0	
9	D_4 Factor	2.114	
10			
11	R Chart Control Limits		
12	Lower Control Limit	0.0000	=B8 * B7
13	Center	3.4821	=B7
14	Upper Control Limit	7.3613	=B9 * B7
15			
16	XBar Chart Intermediate Calculations		
17	Average of Subgroup Averages	9.4779	=AVERAGE(RXChartDATA!B:B)
18	A_2 Factor	0.577	
19	A_2 Factor * RBar	2.0092	=B18 * B7
20			
21	XBar Chart Control Limits		
22	Lower Control Limit	7.4687	=B17- B19
23	Center	9.4779	=B17
24	Upper Control Limit	11.4871	=B17 + B19

Computing control limits and plotting points for other problems requires changes to the RXChartDATA or the DATA worksheet, depending on whether means and ranges have been previously computed. If the means and ranges have been previously computed, paste these values into column B and C of the RXChartDATA worksheet. If there are more than 28 time periods, select cell range **D29:I29** and copy the range down through all the rows. If there are fewer than 28 time periods, delete the extra rows from the bottom up, starting with row 29.

If the means and ranges have not been previously computed, changes must be made to the DATA worksheet. First, determine the subgroup size. If the subgroup size is less than 5, delete the extra columns, right-to-left, starting with column F. If the subgroup size is greater than 5, select column F, right-click, and click **Insert** from the short-cut menu. (Repeat as many times as necessary.) With the DATA worksheet so adjusted, paste the time and subgroup data into the worksheet, starting with cell A1. Then open to the RXChartDATA worksheet, and if the number of time periods is not equal to 28, adjust the number of rows using the instructions of the previous paragraph.

Use the RXChartDATA worksheet as the basis for creating R and $\overline{X}$ charts. For example, open to the **RXChartDATA worksheet** of the **R and XBar Chart workbook** which contains Table 17.5 luggage delivery times data on page 733. To create the Figure 17.6 R chart on page 734, select the cell range **C1:F29**. To create the Figure 17.7 $\overline{X}$ chart on page 735, select the cell range **B1:B29, G1:I29**, (while holding down the **Ctrl key**, select the cell range **B1:B29** and then the cell range **G1:I29**). In either case:

1. Select **Insert → Scatter** and select the fourth choice from the **Scatter** gallery **(Scatter with Straight Lines and Markers)**.
2. Relocate the chart to a chart sheet and adjust the chart formatting by using the instructions in Appendix Section F.4 on page 815.

At this point, a recognizable chart begins to take shape, but the control limit and center lines are improperly formatted and are not properly labeled. To correct these formatting errors, use the three sets of instructions given in the Section EG17.2 *In-Depth Excel* instructions.

EG17.6 PROCESS CAPABILITY

Use the **COMPUTE worksheet** of the **CAPABILITY workbook** as a template for computing the process capability indices discussed in Section 17.6.

EG17.7 TOTAL QUALITY MANAGEMENT

There are no Excel Guide instructions for this section.

EG17.8 SIX SIGMA

There are no Excel Guide instructions for this section.

CHAPTER 17 MINITAB GUIDE

MG17.1 The THEORY of CONTROL CHARTS

There are no Minitab Guide instructions for this section.

MG17.2 CONTROL CHART for the PROPORTION: The *p* CHART

Use **P** to create a *p* chart. For example, to create the Figure 17.2 *p* chart for the Table 17.1 nonconforming hotel room data on page 722, open to the **Hotel1 worksheet.** Select **Stat ➔ Control Charts ➔ Attribute Charts ➔ P**. In the P Chart dialog box (shown below):

1. Double-click **C3 Not ready** in the variables list to add **'Not ready'** to the **Variables** box.
2. Enter **200** in the **Subgroup sizes** box.
3. Click **P Chart Options**.

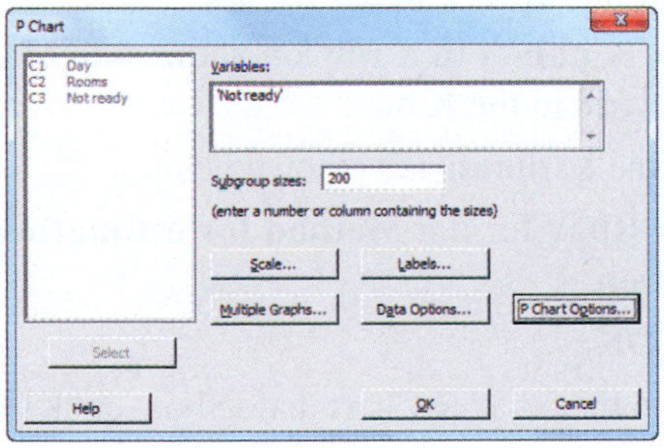

In the P Chart - Options box shown in the next column:

4. Click the **Tests** tab.
5. Select **Perform selected tests for special causes** from the drop-down list.
6. Check **1 point > K standard deviations from the center line** and enter **3** in the **K** box.
7. Check **K points in a row on same side of center line** and enter **8** in the **K** box.
8. Click **OK**.

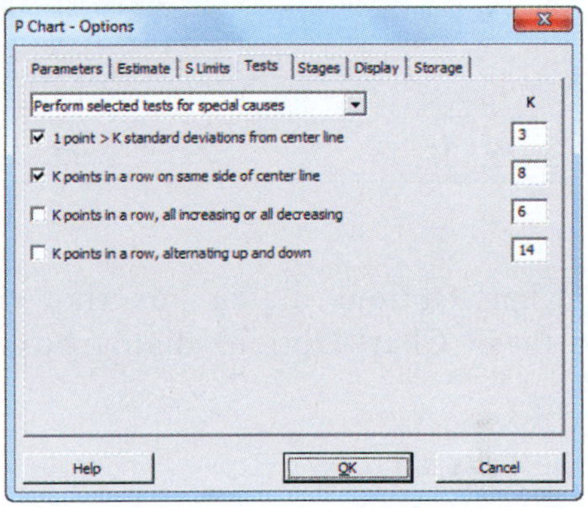

9. Back in the P Chart dialog box, click **OK**.

To omit points when estimating the center line and control limits, click the **Estimate** tab in the P Chart - Options dialog box and select **Omit the following subgroups when estimating parameters (eg, 3 12:15)** from the drop-down list and enter the points to omit in the box. If you create more than one control chart during the same session, Minitab remembers the list of points to omit and you must delete any points in the box that you want to be included in a subsequent control chart.

MG17.3 The RED BEAD EXPERIMENT: UNDERSTANDING PROCESS VARIABILITY

There are no Minitab Guide instructions for this section.

MG17.4 CONTROL CHART for an AREA of OPPORTUNITY: The *c* CHART

Use **C** to create a *c* chart. For example, to create the Figure 17.5 *c* chart for the hotel complaint data on page 729, open to the **Complaints worksheet**. Select **Stat ➔ Control Charts ➔ Attribute Charts ➔ C**. In the C Chart dialog box (shown below):

1. Double-click **C2 Complaints** in the variables list to add **Complaints** to the **Variables** box.
2. Click **C Chart Options**.

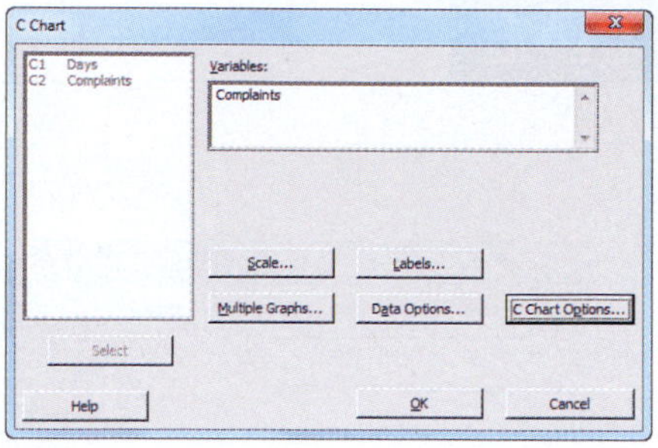

In the C Chart-Options dialog box (not shown, but similar to the P Chart-Options dialog box shown on page 759):

3. Click the **Tests** tab
4. Select **Perform selected tests for special causes** from the drop-down list.
5. Check **1 point > K standard deviations from the center line** and enter **3** in the **K** box.
6. Check **K points in a row on same side of center line** and enter **8** in the **K** box.
7. Click **OK.**
8. Back in the C Chart dialog box, click **OK**.

To omit points when estimating the center line and control limits, click the **Estimate** tab in the C Chart - Options dialog box and select **Omit the following subgroups when estimating parameters (eg, 3 12:15)** from the drop-down list and enter the points to omit in the box. If you create more than one control chart during the same session, Minitab remembers the list of points to omit and you must delete any points in the box that you want to be included in a subsequent control chart.

MG17.5 CONTROL CHARTS for the RANGE and the MEAN

The *R* Chart and the $\overline{X}$ Chart

Use **Xbar-R** to create *R* and $\overline{X}$ charts. For example, to create the Figure 17.6 *R* chart and the $\overline{X}$ chart for the Table 17.5 luggage delivery times (see pages 733–735), open to the **Hotel2 worksheet**. Select **Stat ➔ Control Charts ➔ Variable Charts for Subgroups ➔ Xbar-R**. In the Xbar-R Chart dialog box (shown below):

1. Select **Observations for a subgroup are in one row of columns** from the drop-down list and press **Tab**.
2. Enter **Time1-Time5** in the box below the drop-down list (as the shortcut way of entering the columns C2 through C6, Time1 through Time5).
3. Click **Xbar-R Options.**

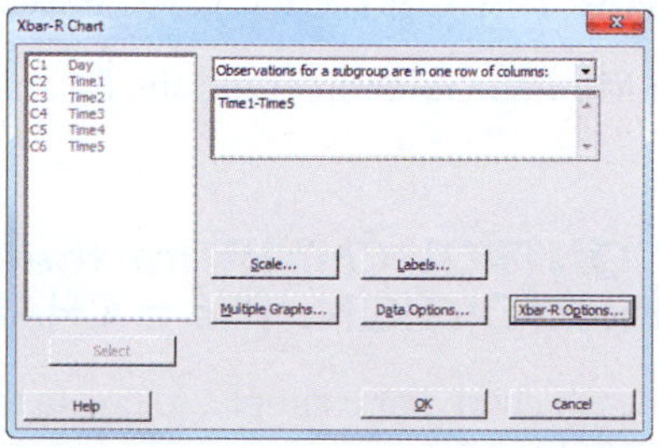

In the Xbar-R Chart-Options dialog box:

4. Click the **Tests** tab.
5. Select **Perform selected tests for special causes** from the drop-down list.
6. Check **1 point > K standard deviations from the center line** and enter **3** in the **K** box.
7. Check **K points in a row on same side of center line** and enter **8** in the **K** box.
8. Click the **Estimate** tab (shown below).
9. Select **Rbar** for the **Method for estimating standard deviation**.
10. Click **OK.**
11. Back in the Xbar-R Chart dialog box, click **OK**.

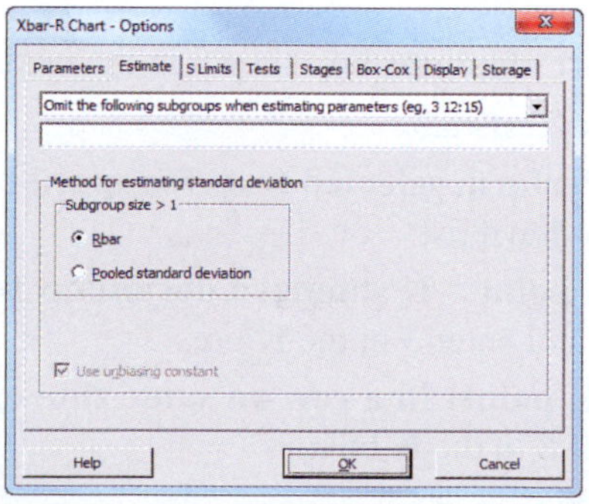

The Hotel2 worksheet contains data in unstacked order. When using worksheets with stacked data for other problems, select **All observations for a chart are in one column** from the drop-down list in step 1 and enter the name of the column that contains the stacked data in the box. You will also need to enter the subgroup size in a **Subgroup sizes** box that appears with this option.

To omit points when estimating the center line and control limits, select **Omit the following subgroups when estimating parameters (eg, 3 12:15)** from the drop-down list and enter the points to omit in the box in the Estimate tab of the Xbar-R Chart-Options dialog box shown above. If you create more than one control chart during the same session, Minitab remembers the list of points to omit and you must delete any points in the box that you want to be included in a subsequent control chart.

MG17.6 PROCESS CAPABILITY

There are no Minitab Guide instructions for this section.

MG17.7 TOTAL QUALITY MANAGEMENT

There are no Minitab Guide instructions for this section.

MG17.8 SIX SIGMA

There are no Minitab Guide instructions for this section.

18 A Roadmap for Analyzing Data

Learning Objectives

In this chapter, you learn:

- The steps involved in choosing which statistical methods to use to conduct a data analysis

USING STATISTICS

@ *YourBusiness*

As a student who is completing an introductory business statistics course, you find yourself needing to analyze data in other courses and in new business situations. Analyzing data is the last part of the **D**efine, **C**ollect, **O**rganize, **V**isualize, **A**nalyze (DCOVA) approach to which you were introduced in Chapter 2.

Determining what methods to use to analyze data may have seemed straightforward when doing homework problems from the chapters of this book, but in real-life situations it is much more difficult; after all, when doing a problem in the multiple regression chapter, you "knew" that methods of multiple regression would be used somewhere in your analysis. In your new situation, you might wonder if you should use multiple regression—or whether using simple linear regression would be better—or whether *any* type of regression would be appropriate. You also might wonder if you should use methods from more than one chapter to do your analysis. The question for you becomes: How can you apply the statistics you have learned to future situations that require you to analyze data?

Reviewing Table 18.1, a review and summary of the contents of this book, arranged by data analysis task, would be a good starting point.

TABLE 18.1
Commonly Used Data Analysis Tasks Discussed in This Book

DESCRIBING A GROUP OR SEVERAL GROUPS

For Numerical Variables:
Ordered array, stem-and-leaf display, frequency distribution, relative frequency distribution, percentage distribution, cumulative percentage distribution, histogram, polygon, cumulative percentage polygon **(Sections 2.3 and 2.5)**
Boxplot **(Section 3.3)**
Normal probability plot **(Section 6.3)**
Mean, median, mode, quartiles, geometric mean, range, interquartile range, standard deviation, variance, coefficient of variation **(Sections 3.1, 3.2, and 3.3)**
Index numbers **(*Online Topic* Section 16.8)**
For Categorical Variables:
Summary table, bar chart, pie chart, Pareto chart **(Sections 2.2 and 2.4)**
Contingency tables and Multidimensional tables **(Sections 2.2 and 2.7)**

MAKING INFERENCES ABOUT ONE GROUP

For Numerical Variables:
Confidence interval estimate of the mean **(Sections 8.1 and 8.2)**
t test for the mean **(Section 9.2)**
Chi-square test for a variance or standard deviation **(Section 12.5)**
For Categorical Variables:
Confidence interval estimate of the proportion **(Section 8.3)**
Z test for the proportion **(Section 9.4)**

COMPARING TWO GROUPS

For Numerical Variables:
Tests for the difference in the means of two independent populations **(Section 10.1)**
Wilcoxon rank sum test **(Section 12.6)**
Paired *t* test **(Section 10.2)**
Wilcoxon signed ranks test **(*Online Topic* Section 12.8)**
F test for the difference between two variances **(Section 10.4)**
For Categorical Variables:
Z test for the difference between two proportions **(Section 10.3)**
Chi-square test for the difference between two proportions **(Section 12.1)**
McNemar test for two related samples **(Section 12.4)**

COMPARING MORE THAN TWO GROUPS

For Numerical Variables:
One-way analysis of variance **(Section 11.1)**
Kruskal-Wallis rank test **(Section 12.7)**
Randomized block design **(Section 11.2)**
Friedman rank test for the randomized block design **(*Online Topic* Section 12.9)**
Two-way analysis of variance **(Section 11.3)**
For Categorical Variables:
Chi-square test for differences among more than two proportions **(Section 12.2)**

ANALYZING THE RELATIONSHIP BETWEEN TWO VARIABLES

For Numerical Variables:
Scatter plot, time-series plot **(Section 2.6)**
Covariance, coefficient of correlation, *t* test of correlation **(Sections 3.5 and 13.7)**
Simple linear regression **(Chapter 13)**
Time-series forecasting **(Chapter 16)**

TABLE 18.1 (Continued)

For Categorical Variables:
Contingency table, side-by-side bar chart **(Sections 2.2 and 2.4)**
Chi-square test of independence **(Section 12.3)**
ANALYZING THE RELATIONSHIP BETWEEN TWO OR MORE VARIABLES
For Numerical Dependent Variables:
Multiple regression **(Chapters 14 and 15)**
For Categorical Dependent Variables:
Logistic regression **(Section 14.7)**
Analytics and Data Mining **(*Online Topic* Section 15.7)**
ANALYZING PROCESS DATA
For Numerical Variables:
$\bar{X}$ and R control charts **(Section 17.5)**
For Categorical Variables:
p chart **(Section 17.2)**
For Counts of Nonconformities:
c chart **(Section 17.4)**

In the DCOVA approach, the first thing you do is to *define* the variables that you want to study in order to solve a business problem or meet a business objective. To do this, you must identify the type of business problem and then determine the type of variable—numerical or categorical—you are analyzing. (Recall that *numerical variables* have values that represent quantities, while *categorical variables* have values that can only be placed into categories, such as yes and no.)

In Table 18.1, the all-uppercase first-level headings identify types of business problems (e.g., whether you are describing a group or making inferences about a group, among other choices), and the second-level headings always include the two types of variables. The third-level (lowest) entries in Table 18.1 identify the specific statistical methods appropriate for a particular type of business problem and type of variable.

Choosing appropriate statistical methods for your data is the single most important task you face and is at the heart of "doing statistics." But this choosing process is also the single most difficult thing you do when applying statistics! How, then, can you ensure that you have made an appropriate choice? By asking a series of questions, you can guide yourself to the appropriate choice of methods.

The rest of this chapter presents questions that will help guide you in making this choice. Two lists of questions, one for numerical variables and the other for categorical variables, are presented in the next two sections. Having two lists makes the decision you face more manageable while also reinforcing the importance of identifying the type of variable that you seek to analyze.

18.1 Analyzing Numerical Variables

Exhibit 18.1 presents the list of questions to ask if you plan to analyze a numerical variable. Each question is independent of the others, and you can ask as many or as few questions as is appropriate for your analysis. How to go about answering these questions follows Exhibit 18.1.

EXHIBIT 18.1 QUESTIONS TO ASK WHEN ANALYZING NUMERICAL VARIABLES

When analyzing numerical variables, ask yourself, do you want to:

- Describe the characteristics of the variable (possibly broken down into several groups)?
- Reach conclusions about the mean and standard deviation of the variable in a population?

- Determine whether the mean and standard deviation of the variable differs depending on the group?
- Determine which factors affect the value of a variable?
- Predict the value of the variable based on the value of other variables?
- Determine whether the values of the variable are stable over time?

How to Describe the Characteristics of a Numerical Variable

You develop tables and charts and compute descriptive statistics to describe characteristics. Specifically, you can create a stem-and-leaf display, percentage distribution, histogram, polygon, boxplot, and normal probability plot (see Sections 2.3, 2.5, 3.3, and 6.3), and you can compute statistics such as the mean, median, mode, quartiles, range, interquartile range, standard deviation, variance, and coefficient of variation (see Sections 3.1, 3.2, and 3.3).

How to Reach Conclusions About the Population Mean or Standard Deviation

You have several different choices, and you can use any combination of these choices. To estimate the mean value of the variable in a population, you construct a confidence interval estimate of the mean (see Section 8.2). To determine whether the population mean is equal to a specific value, you conduct a *t* test of hypothesis for the mean (see Section 9.2). To determine whether the population standard deviation or variance is equal to a specific value, you conduct a χ^2 test of hypothesis for the standard deviation or variance (see Section 12.5).

How to Determine Whether the Mean or Standard Deviation Differs Depending on the Group

When examining differences between groups, you first need to establish which categorical variable divides your data into groups. You then need to know whether this grouping variable divides your data in two groups, as a gender variable would divide your data into male and female groups, or whether the variable divides your data into more than two groups (such as the four parachute suppliers discussed in Section 11.1). Finally, you must ask whether your data set contains independent groups or whether your data set contains matched or repeated measurements.

If the Grouping Variable Defines Two Independent Groups and You Are Interested in Central Tendency Which hypothesis tests you use depends on the assumptions you make about your data.

If you assume that your numerical variable is normally distributed and that the variances are equal, you conduct a pooled *t* test for the difference between the means (see Section 10.1). To evaluate the assumption of normality that this test includes, you can construct boxplots and normal probability plots for each group.

If you cannot assume that the variances are equal, you conduct a separate-variance *t* test for the difference between the means (see Section 10.1). To test whether the variances are equal, assuming that the populations are normally distributed, you can conduct an *F* test for the differences between the variances.

In either case, if you believe that your numerical variables are not normally distributed, you can perform a Wilcoxon rank sum test (see Section 12.6) and compare its results to those of the *t* test.

If the Grouping Variable Defines Two Groups of Matched Samples or Repeated Measurements If you can assume that the paired differences are normally distributed, you conduct a paired *t* test (see Section 10.2). If you cannot assume that the paired differences are normally distributed, you conduct a Wilcoxon signed ranks test (see *Online Topic* Section 12.8).

If the Grouping Variable Defines Two Independent Groups and You Are Interested in Variability If you can assume that your numerical variable is normally distributed, you conduct an F test for the difference between two variances (see Section 10.4).

If the Grouping Variable Defines More Than Two Independent Groups If you can assume that the values of the numerical variable are normally distributed, you conduct a one-way analysis of variance (see Section 11.1); otherwise, you conduct a Kruskal-Wallis rank test (see Section 12.7).

If the Grouping Variable Defines More Than Two Groups of Matched Samples or Repeated Measurements You have a design where the rows represent the blocks and the columns represent the levels of a factor. If you can assume that the values of the numerical variable are normally distributed, you conduct a randomized block design F test (see Section 11.2). If you cannot assume that the values of the numerical variable are normally distributed, you perform a Friedman rank test (see *Online Topic* Section 12.9).

How to Determine Which Factors Affect the Value of a Variable

If there are two factors to be examined to determine their effect on the values of a variable, you develop a two-factor factorial design (see Section 11.3).

How to Predict the Value of a Variable Based on the Value of Other Variables

You conduct least-squares regression analysis. If you have values over a period of time and you want to forecast the variable for future time periods, you can use moving averages, exponential smoothing, least-squares forecasting, and autoregressive modeling (see Chapter 16).

When predicting the values of a numerical dependent variable, which least-squares regression model you develop depends on the number of independent variables in your model. If there is only one independent variable being used to predict the numerical dependent variable of interest, you develop a simple linear regression model (see Chapter 13); otherwise, you develop a multiple regression model (see Chapters 14 and 15).

How to Determine Whether the Values of a Variable Are Stable over Time

If you are studying a process and have collected data on the values of a numerical variable over a time period, you construct R and $\bar{X}$ charts (see Section 17.5). If you have collected data in which the values are counts of the number of nonconformities, you construct a c chart (see Section 17.4).

18.2 Analyzing Categorical Variables

Exhibit 18.2 presents the list of questions to ask if you plan to analyze a categorical variable. Each question is independent of the others, and you can ask as many or as few questions as is appropriate for your analysis. How to go about answering these questions follows Exhibit 18.2.

EXHIBIT 18.2 QUESTIONS TO ASK WHEN ANALYZING CATEGORICAL VARIABLES

When analyzing categorical variables, ask yourself, do you want to:

- Describe the proportion of items of interest in each category (possibly broken down into several groups)?
- Reach conclusions about the proportion of items of interest in a population?
- Determine whether the proportion of items of interest differs depending on the group?
- Predict the proportion of items of interest based on the value of other variables?
- Determine whether the proportion of items of interest is stable over time?

How to Describe the Proportion of Items of Interest in Each Category

You create summary tables and use these charts: bar chart, pie chart, Pareto chart, or side-by-side bar chart (see Sections 2.2 and 2.4).

How to Reach Conclusions About the Proportion of Items of Interest

You have two different choices. You can estimate the proportion of items of interest in a population by constructing a confidence interval estimate of the proportion (see Section 8.3). Or, you can determine whether the population proportion is equal to a specific value by conducting a Z test of hypothesis for the proportion (see Section 9.4).

How to Determine Whether the Proportion of Items of Interest Differs Depending on the Group

When examining this difference, you first need to establish the number of categories associated with your categorical variable and the number of groups in your analysis. If your data contain two groups, you must also ask if your data contain independent groups or if your data contain matched samples or repeated measurements.

For Two Categories and Two Independent Groups You conduct either the Z test for the difference between two proportions (see Section 10.3) or the χ^2 test for the difference between two proportions (see Section 12.1).

For Two Categories and Two Groups of Matched or Repeated Measurements You conduct the McNemar test (see Section 12.4).

For Two Categories and More Than Two Independent Groups You conduct a χ^2 test for the difference among several proportions (see Section 12.2).

For More Than Two Categories and More Than Two Groups You develop contingency tables and use multidimensional contingency tables to drill down to examine relationships among two or more categorical variables (Sections 2.2 and 2.7). When you have two categorical variables, you conduct a χ^2 test of independence (see Section 12.3).

How to Predict the Proportion of Items of Interest Based on the Value of Other Variables

You develop a logistic regression model (see Section 14.7).

How to Determine Whether the Proportion of Items of Interest Is Stable over Time

If you are studying a process and have collected data over a time period, you can create the appropriate control chart. If you have collected the proportion of items of interest over a time period, you develop a *p* chart (see Section 17.2).

USING STATISTICS @ *YourBusiness* Revisited

This chapter summarizes all the methods discussed in the first 17 chapters of this book. The data analysis methods discussed in the book are organized in Table 18.1 according to whether each method is used for describing a group or several groups, for making inferences about one group or comparing two or more groups, or for analyzing relationships between two or more variables. Then, sets of questions are listed in Exhibits 18.1 and 18.2 to assist you in determining what method to use to analyze your data.

DIGITAL CASE

Whereas other Digital Cases asked you to apply your knowledge about the proper use of statistics, this case helps you remember how to properly apply that knowledge.

Guadalupe Cooper and Gilbert Chandler had worked very hard all semester long in their business statistics course. They now faced a final project in which they had to establish a plan to analyze a set of data that had been assigned to them by their instructor. As they looked through the online materials at the companion website for their statistics textbook, they found **DataAnalysisGuide.pdf** in the Digital Case materials. "Gee, this is like the material in Chapter 18, but in interactive form!" one of them noted. They both then knew what questions they needed to ask in order to get started on their final semester task.

CHAPTER REVIEW PROBLEMS

18.1 In many manufacturing processes, the term *work-in-process* (often abbreviated WIP) is used. At the BLK Publishing book manufacturing plants, WIP represents the time it takes for sheets from a press to be folded, gathered, sewn, tipped on end sheets, and bound together to form a book, and the book placed in a packing carton. The operational definition of the variable of interest, processing time, is the number of days (measured in hundredths) from when the sheets come off the press to when the book is placed in a packing carton. The company has the business objective of determining whether there are differences in the WIP between plants. Data have been collected from samples of 20 books at each of two production plants. The data, stored in WIP, are as follows:

Plant A

5.62	5.29	16.25	10.92	11.46	21.62	8.45	8.58	5.41	11.42
11.62	7.29	7.50	7.96	4.42	10.50	7.58	9.29	7.54	8.92

Plant B

9.54	11.46	16.62	12.62	25.75	15.41	14.29	13.13	13.71	10.04
5.75	12.46	9.17	13.21	6.00	2.33	14.25	5.37	6.25	9.71

Completely analyze the data.

18.2 Many factors determine the attendance at Major League Baseball games. These factors can include when the game is played, the weather, the opponent, whether the team is having a good season, and whether a marketing promotion is held. Popular promotions during a recent season included the traditional hat days and poster days and the newer craze, bobble-heads of star players. (Data extracted from T. C. Boyd and T. C. Krehbiel, "An Analysis of the Effects of Specific Promotion Types on Attendance at Major League Baseball Games," *Mid-American Journal of Business*, 2006, 21, pp. 21–32.) The file Baseball includes the following variables for a recent Major League Baseball season:

TEAM—Kansas City Royals, Philadelphia Phillies, Chicago Cubs, or Cincinnati Reds
ATTENDANCE—Paid attendance for the game
TEMP—High temperature for the day
WIN%—Team's winning percentage at the time of the game
OPWIN%—Opponent team's winning percentage at the time of the game
WEEKEND—1 if game played on Friday, Saturday, or Sunday; 0 otherwise
PROMOTION—1 if a promotion was held; 0 if no promotion was held

You want to predict attendance and determine the factors that influence attendance. Completely analyze the data for the Kansas City Royals.

18.3 Repeat Problem 18.2 for the Philadelphia Phillies.

18.4 Repeat Problem 18.2 for the Chicago Cubs.

18.5 Repeat Problem 18.2 for the Cincinnati Reds.

18.6 The file **RealEstate** contains data for a sample of 362 single-family homes located in five different communities in a suburban county outside a large city in the northeastern United States. The following variables are included:

1. Appraised value ($000)
2. Lot size (000 square feet)
3. Number of bedrooms
4. Number of bathrooms
5. Number of rooms
6. Age in years
7. Annual real estate taxes ($)
8. Type of Indoor parking facility—None One-car garage Two-car garage
9. Location—A B C D E
10. Architectural style—Cape Expanded ranch Colonial Ranch Split level
11. Type of heating fuel used—Gas Oil
12. Type of heating system—Hot air Hot water Other
13. Type of swimming pool—None Above ground In-ground
14. Eat-in kitchen—Absent Present
15. Central air-conditioning—Absent Present
16. Fireplace—Absent Present
17. Connection to local sewer system—Absent Present
18. Basement—Absent Present
19. Modern kitchen—Absent Present
20. Modern bathrooms—Absent Present

Prepare a report in which your objective is to compare the characteristics of single-family homes in the five communities. In addition, develop models to predict the assessed value of the house and the annual real estate taxes.

18.7 The file **Homes** contains information on all the single-family houses sold in a small city in the midwestern United States for one year. The following variables are included:

Price—Selling price of home, in dollars
Location—Rating of the location from 1 to 5, with 1 the worst and 5 the best
Condition—Rating of the condition of the home from 1 to 5, with 1 the worst and 5 the best
Bedrooms—Number of bedrooms in the home
Bathrooms—Number of bathrooms in the home
Other Rooms—Number of rooms in the home other than bedrooms and bathrooms

You want to be able to predict the selling price of the homes. Completely analyze the data.

18.8 Zagat's publishes restaurant ratings for various locations in the United States. The file **Restaurants2** contains the Zagat rating for food, decor, service, and price per person for a sample of 50 restaurants located in New York City and 50 restaurants located in suburban areas outside New York City.

You want to study differences in the cost of a meal between restaurants in New York City and suburban areas and also want to be able to predict the cost of a meal. Completely analyze the data.

Source: Data extracted from *Zagat Survey 2010, New York City Restaurants* and *Zagat Survey 2010–2011, Long Island Restaurants.*

18.9 The data in **Auto2008** represent different characteristics of 171 late-model automobiles. The variables included are make/model, length (in.), width (in.), height (in.), wheelbase (in.), weight (lbs.), maximum cargo load (lb.), cargo volume (cu. ft.), front shoulder room (in.), front leg room (in.), front head room (in.), horsepower, miles per gallon, acceleration (sec.) from 0 to 60 miles per hour, braking distance in feet from 60 miles per hour (dry), braking distance in feet from 60 miles per hour (wet), turning circle (ft.), country of origin (Asia, Europe, United States), vehicle type (4 door SUV, sedan, 4 door hatchback, coupe, minivan, wagon) transmission type (auto 4, auto 5, auto 6, auto 7, CVT, manual 5, manual 6).

You want to describe each of these variables in this sample of automobiles. In addition, you would like to predict the miles per gallon and dry braking distance and determine which variables are important in predicting these variables. Analyze the data.

Source: Data extracted from "Vehicle Ratings," *Consumer Reports*, April 2008, pp. 31–75.

18.10 The data in **UsedAutos** represent different characteristics of used automobiles advertised for sale in a recent year. The variables included are car, model, year of model (2000 = 0), asking price (in $000), miles driven by the car (in 000s), age in years, and type (coupe, minivan, pickup truck, sedan, sedan wagon, sports car, SUV, van, wagon).

You want to describe each of these variables, and you would like to predict the asking price of used autos. Analyze the data.

Source: Data extracted from The Newark Star Ledger, January 3, 2009, pp. 35–38.

18.11 The data in **Credit Unions** consist of different characteristics of 7,903 credit unions in the United States. The variables included are name, city, state, zip code, region, total assets ($), total investments ($), net income ($), total net worth ($), total amount of delinquent loans and leases ($), number of credit union members, number of potential members, number of full-time credit union employees, and number of credit union employees.

Your job is to present a report that summarizes descriptive characteristics of credit unions and highlight factors that differ among the credit unions. Analyze the data.

Source: **www.ncua.gov**, January 29, 2009.

18.12 The data in **Loans and Leases** consist of the different characteristics of 382 banks in the Tri-State New York City area as of June 30, 2008. The variables included are name, state, zip code, number of domestic and foreign offices, ownership type, regulator, Federal Reserve district, total deposits ($000), gross loans and leases ($000), real estate loans ($000), construction and development loans ($000), all real estate loans ($000), commercial real estate loans ($000), multifamily real estate loans ($000), 1–4 family real estate loans ($000), farmland loans ($000), commercial and industrial loans ($000), credit card loans ($000), related plans ($000), other loans to individuals ($000), and all other loans and leases ($000).

Your job is to present a report that summarizes descriptive characteristics of banks in the Tri-State New York City area and highlight factors that differ among the banks. Analyze the data.

Source: **www.fdic.gov.**

18.13 A mining company operates a large heap-leach gold mine in the western United States. The gold mined at this location consists of ore that is very low grade, having about 0.0032 ounce of gold in 1 ton of ore. The process of heap-leaching involves the mining, crushing, stacking, and leaching millions of tons of gold ore per year. In the process, ore is placed in a large heap on an impermeable pad. A weak chemical solution is sprinkled over the heap and is collected at the bottom after percolating through the ore. As the solution percolates through the ore, the gold is dissolved and is later recovered from the solution. This technology, which has been used for more than 30 years, has made the operation profitable. Due to the large amount of ore that is handled, the company is continually exploring ways to improve the process. As part of an expansion several years ago, the stacking process was automated with the construction of a computer controlled stacker. This stacker was designed to load 35,000 tons of ore per day at a cost that was less than the previous process that used manually operated trucks and bulldozers. However, since its installation, the stacker has not been able to achieve these results consistently. Data for a recent 35-day period that indicate the amount stacked (tons) and the downtime (minutes) are stored in the file **Mining**. Other data that indicate the causes for the downtime are stored in **Mining2**.

Analyze the data, making sure to present conclusions about the daily amount stacked and the causes of the downtime. In addition, be sure to develop a model to predict the amount stacked based on downtime.

Appendices

APPENDIX A Basic Math Concepts and Symbols

A.1 Rules for Arithmetic Operations

RULE	EXAMPLE
1. $a + b = c$ and $b + a = c$	$2 + 1 = 3$ and $1 + 2 = 3$
2. $a + (b + c) = (a + b) + c$	$5 + (7 + 4) = (5 + 7) + 4 = 16$
3. $a - b = c$ but $b - a \neq c$	$9 - 7 = 2$ but $7 - 9 \neq 2$
4. $(a)(b) = (b)(a)$	$(7)(6) = (6)(7) = 42$
5. $(a)(b + c) = ab + ac$	$(2)(3 + 5) = (2)(3) + (2)(5) = 16$
6. $a \div b \neq b \div a$	$12 \div 3 \neq 3 \div 12$
7. $\frac{a + b}{c} = \frac{a}{c} + \frac{b}{c}$	$\frac{7 + 3}{2} = \frac{7}{2} + \frac{3}{2} = 5$
8. $\frac{a}{b + c} \neq \frac{a}{b} + \frac{a}{c}$	$\frac{3}{4 + 5} \neq \frac{3}{4} + \frac{3}{5}$
9. $\frac{1}{a} + \frac{1}{b} = \frac{b + a}{ab}$	$\frac{1}{3} + \frac{1}{5} = \frac{5 + 3}{(3)(5)} = \frac{8}{15}$
10. $\left(\frac{a}{b}\right)\left(\frac{c}{d}\right) = \left(\frac{ac}{bd}\right)$	$\left(\frac{2}{3}\right)\left(\frac{6}{7}\right) = \left(\frac{(2)(6)}{(3)(7)}\right) = \frac{12}{21}$
11. $\frac{a}{b} \div \frac{c}{d} = \frac{ad}{bc}$	$\frac{5}{8} \div \frac{3}{7} = \left(\frac{(5)(7)}{(8)(3)}\right) = \frac{35}{24}$

A.2 Rules for Algebra: Exponents and Square Roots

RULE	EXAMPLE
1. $(X^a)(X^b) = X^{a+b}$	$(4^2)(4^3) = 4^5$
2. $(X^a)^b = X^{ab}$	$(2^2)^3 = 2^6$
3. $(X^a/X^b) = X^{a-b}$	$\frac{3^5}{3^3} = 3^2$
4. $\frac{X^a}{X^a} = X^0 = 1$	$\frac{3^4}{3^4} = 3^0 = 1$
5. $\sqrt{XY} = \sqrt{X}\sqrt{Y}$	$\sqrt{(25)(4)} = \sqrt{25}\sqrt{4} = 10$
6. $\sqrt{\frac{X}{Y}} = \frac{\sqrt{X}}{\sqrt{Y}}$	$\sqrt{\frac{16}{100}} = \frac{\sqrt{16}}{\sqrt{100}} = 0.40$

A.3 Rules for Logarithms

Base 10

Log is the symbol used for base-10 logarithms:

RULE	EXAMPLE
1. $\log(10^a) = a$	$\log(100) = \log(10^2) = 2$
2. If $\log(a) = b$, then $a = 10^b$	If $\log(a) = 2$, then $a = 10^2 = 100$
3. $\log(ab) = \log(a) + \log(b)$	$\log(100) = \log[(10)(10)] = \log(10) + \log(10) = 1 + 1 = 2$
4. $\log(a^b) = (b)\log(a)$	$\log(1{,}000) = \log(10^3) = (3)\log(10) = (3)(1) = 3$
5. $\log(a/b) = \log(a) - \log(b)$	$\log(100) = \log(1{,}000/10) = \log(1{,}000) - \log(10) = 3 - 1 = 2$

EXAMPLE

Take the base-10 logarithm of each side of the following equation:

$$Y = \beta_0 \beta_1^X \varepsilon$$

SOLUTION: Apply rules 3 and 4:

$$\begin{aligned}\log(Y) &= \log(\beta_0 \beta_1^X \varepsilon) \\ &= \log(\beta_0) + \log(\beta_1^X) + \log(\varepsilon) \\ &= \log(\beta_0) + X\log(\beta_1) + \log(\varepsilon)\end{aligned}$$

Base *e*

ln is the symbol used for base *e* logarithms, commonly referred to as natural logarithms. *e* is Euler's number, and $e \cong 2.718282$:

RULE	EXAMPLE
1. $\ln(e^a) = a$	$\ln(7.389056) = \ln(e^2) = 2$
2. If $\ln(a) = b$, then $a = e^b$	If $\ln(a) = 2$, then $a = e^2 = 7.389056$
3. $\ln(ab) = \ln(a) + \ln(b)$	$\ln(100) = \ln[(10)(10)] = \ln(10) + \ln(10) = 2.302585 + 2.302585 = 4.605170$
4. $\ln(a^b) = (b)\ln(a)$	$\ln(1{,}000) = \ln(10^3) = 3\ln(10) = 3(2.302585) = 6.907755$
5. $\ln(a/b) = \ln(a) - \ln(b)$	$\ln(100) = \ln(1{,}000/10) = \ln(1{,}000) - \ln(10) = 6.907755 - 2.302585 = 4.605170$

EXAMPLE

Take the base *e* logarithm of each side of the following equation:

$$Y = \beta_0 \beta_1^X \varepsilon$$

SOLUTION: Apply rules 3 and 4:

$$\begin{aligned}\ln(Y) &= \ln(\beta_0 \beta_1^X \varepsilon) \\ &= \ln(\beta_0) + \ln(\beta_1^X) + \ln(\varepsilon) \\ &= \ln(\beta_0) + X\ln(\beta_1) + \ln(\varepsilon)\end{aligned}$$

A.4 Summation Notation

The symbol Σ, the Greek capital letter sigma, represents "taking the sum of." Consider a set of n values for variable X. The expression $\sum_{i=1}^{n} X_i$ means to take the sum of the n values for variable X. Thus:

$$\sum_{i=1}^{n} X_i = X_1 + X_2 + X_3 + \cdots + X_n$$

The following problem illustrates the use of the symbol Σ. Consider five values of a variable X: $X_1 = 2, X_2 = 0, X_3 = -1, X_4 = 5$, and $X_5 = 7$. Thus:

$$\sum_{i=1}^{5} X_i = X_1 + X_2 + X_3 + X_4 + X_5 = 2 + 0 + (-1) + 5 + 7 = 13$$

In statistics, the squared values of a variable are often summed. Thus:

$$\sum_{i=1}^{n} X_i^2 = X_1^2 + X_2^2 + X_3^2 + \cdots + X_n^2$$

and, in the example above:

$$\begin{aligned}\sum_{i=1}^{5} X_i^2 &= X_1^2 + X_2^2 + X_3^2 + X_4^2 + X_5^2 \\ &= 2^2 + 0^2 + (-1)^2 + 5^2 + 7^2 \\ &= 4 + 0 + 1 + 25 + 49 \\ &= 79\end{aligned}$$

$\sum_{i=1}^{n} X_i^2$, the summation of the squares, is *not* the same as $\left(\sum_{i=1}^{n} X_i\right)^2$, the square of the sum:

$$\sum_{i=1}^{n} X_i^2 \neq \left(\sum_{i=1}^{n} X_i\right)^2$$

In the example given earlier, the summation of squares is equal to 79. This is not equal to the square of the sum, which is $13^2 = 169$.

Another frequently used operation involves the summation of the product. Consider two variables, X and Y, each having n values. Then:

$$\sum_{i=1}^{n} X_i Y_i = X_1Y_1 + X_2Y_2 + X_3Y_3 + \cdots + X_nY_n$$

Continuing with the previous example, suppose there is a second variable, Y, whose five values are $Y_1 = 1, Y_2 = 3, Y_3 = -2, Y_4 = 4$, and $Y_5 = 3$. Then,

$$\begin{aligned}\sum_{i=1}^{n} X_i Y_i &= X_1Y_1 + X_2Y_2 + X_3Y_3 + X_4Y_4 + X_5Y_5 \\ &= (2)(1) + (0)(3) + (-1)(-2) + (5)(4) + (7)(3) \\ &= 2 + 0 + 2 + 20 + 21 \\ &= 45\end{aligned}$$

In computing $\sum_{i=1}^{n} X_i Y_i$, you need to realize that the first value of X is multiplied by the first value of Y, the second value of X is multiplied by the second value of Y, and so on. These products are then summed in order to compute the desired result. However, the summation of products is *not* equal to the product of the individual sums:

$$\sum_{i=1}^{n} X_i Y_i \neq \left(\sum_{i=1}^{n} X_i\right)\left(\sum_{i=1}^{n} Y_i\right)$$

In this example,

$$\sum_{i=1}^{5} X_i = 13$$

and

$$\sum_{i=1}^{5} Y_i = 1 + 3 + (-2) + 4 + 3 = 9$$

so that

$$\left(\sum_{i=1}^{5} X_i\right)\left(\sum_{i=1}^{5} Y_i\right) = (13)(9) = 117$$

However,

$$\sum_{i=1}^{5} X_i Y_i = 45$$

The following table summarizes these results:

VALUE	X_i	Y_i	X_iY_i
1	2	1	2
2	0	3	0
3	−1	−2	2
4	5	4	20
5	7	3	21
	$\sum_{i=1}^{5} X_i = 13$	$\sum_{i=1}^{5} Y_i = 9$	$\sum_{i=1}^{5} X_i Y_i = 45$

Rule 1 The summation of the values of two variables is equal to the sum of the values of each summed variable:

$$\sum_{i=1}^{n} (X_i + Y_i) = \sum_{i=1}^{n} X_i + \sum_{i=1}^{n} Y_i$$

Thus,

$$\begin{aligned}\sum_{i=1}^{5} (X_i + Y_i) &= (2 + 1) + (0 + 3) + (-1 + (-2)) + (5 + 4) + (7 + 3) \\ &= 3 + 3 + (-3) + 9 + 10 \\ &= 22\end{aligned}$$

$$\sum_{i=1}^{5} X_i + \sum_{i=1}^{5} Y_i = 13 + 9 = 22$$

Rule 2 The summation of a difference between the values of two variables is equal to the difference between the summed values of the variables:

$$\sum_{i=1}^{n}(X_i - Y_i) = \sum_{i=1}^{n} X_i - \sum_{i=1}^{n} Y_i$$

Thus,

$$\sum_{i=1}^{5}(X_i - Y_i) = (2 - 1) + (0 - 3) + (-1 - (-2)) + (5 - 4) + (7 - 3)$$

$$= 1 + (-3) + 1 + 1 + 4$$

$$= 4$$

$$\sum_{i=1}^{5} X_i - \sum_{i=1}^{5} Y_i = 13 - 9 = 4$$

Rule 3 The sum of a constant times a variable is equal to that constant times the sum of the values of the variable:

$$\sum_{i=1}^{n} cX_i = c\sum_{i=1}^{n} X_i$$

where c is a constant. Thus, if $c = 2$,

$$\sum_{i=1}^{5} cX_i = \sum_{i=1}^{5} 2X_i = (2)(2) + (2)(0) + (2)(-1) + (2)(5) + (2)(7)$$

$$= 4 + 0 + (-2) + 10 + 14$$

$$= 26$$

$$c\sum_{i=1}^{5} X_i = 2\sum_{i=1}^{5} X_i = (2)(13) = 26$$

Rule 4 A constant summed n times will be equal to n times the value of the constant.

$$\sum_{i=1}^{n} c = nc$$

where c is a constant. Thus, if the constant $c = 2$ is summed 5 times,

$$\sum_{i=1}^{5} c = 2 + 2 + 2 + 2 + 2 = 10$$

$$nc = (5)(2) = 10$$

EXAMPLE

Suppose there are six values for the variables X and Y, such that $X_1 = 2, X_2 = 1, X_3 = 5, X_4 = -3, X_5 = 1, X_6 = -2$ and $Y_1 = 4, Y_2 = 0, Y_3 = -1, Y_4 = 2, Y_5 = 7$, and $Y_6 = -3$. Compute each of the following:

(a) $\sum_{i=1}^{6} X_i$

(b) $\sum_{i=1}^{6} Y_i$

(c) $\sum_{i=1}^{6} X_i^2$

(d) $\sum_{i=1}^{6} Y_i^2$

(e) $\sum_{i=1}^{6} X_iY_i$

(f) $\sum_{i=1}^{6} (X_i + Y_i)$

(g) $\sum_{i=1}^{6}(X_i - Y_i)$

(h) $\sum_{i=1}^{6}(X_i - 3Y_i + 2X_i^2)$

(i) $\sum_{i=1}^{6}(cX_i)$, where $c = -1$

(j) $\sum_{i=1}^{6}(X_i - 3Y_i + c)$, where $c = +3$

Answers

(a) 4 (b) 9 (c) 44 (d) 79 (e) 10 (f) 13 (g) −5 (h) 65 (i) −4 (j) −5

References

1. Bashaw, W. L., *Mathematics for Statistics* (New York: Wiley, 1969).
2. Lanzer, P., *Basic Math: Fractions, Decimals, Percents* (Hicksville, NY: Video Aided Instruction, 2006).
3. Levine, D., *The MBA Primer: Business Statistics* (Cincinnati, OH: South-Western Publishing, 2000).
4. Levine, D., *Statistics* (Hicksville, NY: Video Aided Instruction, 2006).
5. Shane, H., *Algebra 1* (Hicksville, NY: Video Aided Instruction, 2006).

A.5 Statistical Symbols

$+$ add

$-$ subtract

$=$ equal to

$\cong$ approximately equal to

$>$ greater than

$\geq$ greater than or equal to

$\times$ multiply

$\div$ divide

$\neq$ not equal to

$<$ less than

$\leq$ less than or equal to

A.6 Greek Alphabet

GREEK LETTER		LETTER NAME	ENGLISH EQUIVALENT	GREEK LETTER		LETTER NAME	ENGLISH EQUIVALENT
Α	α	Alpha	a	Ν	ν	Nu	n
Β	β	Beta	b	Ξ	ξ	Xi	x
Γ	γ	Gamma	g	Ο	ο	Omicron	ŏ
Δ	δ	Delta	d	Π	π	Pi	p
Ε	ε	Epsilon	ĕ	Ρ	ρ	Rho	r
Ζ	ζ	Zeta	z	Σ	σ	Sigma	s
Η	η	Eta	ē	Τ	τ	Tau	t
Θ	θ	Theta	th	Υ	υ	Upsilon	u
Ι	ι	Iota	i	Φ	ϕ	Phi	ph
Κ	κ	Kappa	k	Χ	χ	Chi	ch
Λ	λ	Lambda	l	Ψ	ψ	Psi	ps
Μ	μ	Mu	m	Ω	ω	Omega	ō

APPENDIX B Basic Computing Skills

B.1 Objects in a Window

When you open Excel or Minitab, you see a window that contains the objects listed in Table B.1 and shown in Figure B.1 on page 781. To effectively use Excel or Minitab, you must be familiar with these objects and their names.

TABLE B.1
Common Window Elements

Number	Element	Function
❶	Title bar	Displays the name of the program and contains the Minimize, Resize, and Close buttons for the program window. You drag and drop the title bar to reposition a program window onscreen.
❷	Minimize, Resize, and Close buttons	Changes the display of the program window. **Minimize** hides the window without closing the program, **Resize** permits you to change the size of the window, and **Close** removes the window from the screen and closes the program. A second set of these buttons that appear below the first set perform the three actions for the currently active workbook.
❸	Menu Bar and Toolbars	The menu bar is a horizontal list of words, where each word represents either a command operation or leads to another list of choices. Toolbars are sets of graphical icons that represent commands. The toolbar icons serve as shortcuts to menu bar choices. (Minitab and Excel 2003)
❹	Ribbon	A selectable area that combines the functions of a menu bar and toolbars. In the Ribbon, commands are arranged in a series of **tabs**, and the tabs are further divided into **groups.** Some groups contain **launcher buttons** that display additional choices presented in a dialog box or as a **gallery**, a set of pictorial choices. (Excel 2007 and Excel 2010)
❺	Workbook area	Displays the currently open worksheets. In Excel, this area usually displays the currently active worksheet in the workbook and shows the other worksheets as **sheet tabs** near the bottom of the workbook area.
❻	Scroll bar	Allows you to move through a worksheet vertically or horizontally to reveal rows and columns that cannot otherwise be seen.

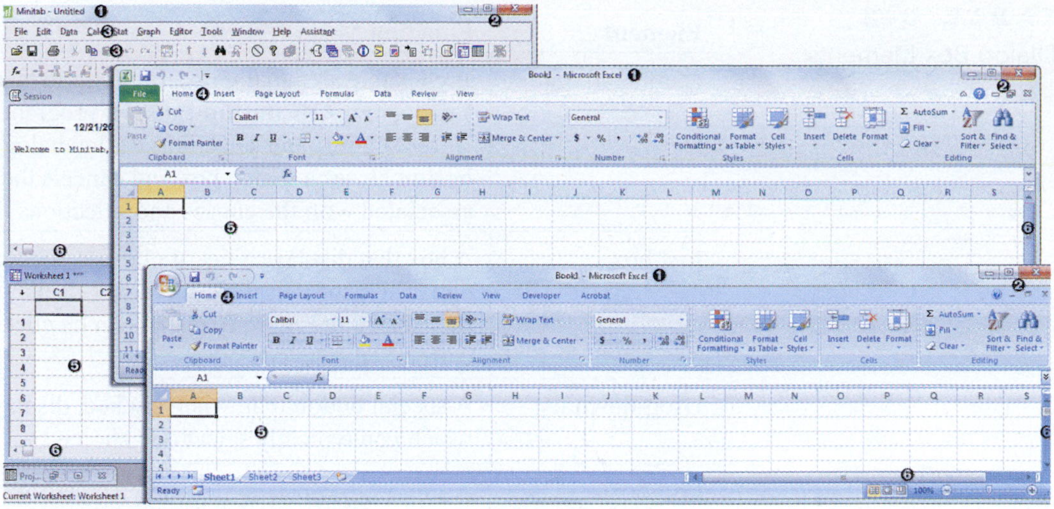

FIGURE B.1

Minitab, Excel 2010, and Excel 2007 windows (with number labels keyed to Table B.1)

B.2 Basic Mouse Operations

To interact with the objects in a window, you frequently use a mouse (or some other pointing device). Mouse operations can be divided into four types and assume a mouse with two buttons, one designated as the primary button (typically the left button) and the other button designated as the secondary button (typically the right button).

Click, **select**, **check**, and **clear** are operations in which you move the mouse pointer over an object and press the primary button. **Click** is used when pressing the primary button completes an action, as in "click (the) **OK** (button)." **Select** is used when pressing the primary button to choose or highlight one choice from a list of choices. **Check** is used when pressing the primary button places a checkmark in the dialog box's check box. (**Clear** reverses this action, removing the checkmark.)

Double-click is an operation in which two clicks are made in rapid succession. Most double-click operations enable an object for following use, such as double-clicking a chart in order to make changes to the chart. **Right-click** is an operation in which you move the mouse pointer over an object and press the *secondary* button. In the Excel Guide instructions, you will often right-click an object in order to display a pop-up **shortcut menu** of context-sensitive command operations.

Drag is an operation in which you hold down the primary button over an object and then move the mouse. (The drag operation ends when you release the mouse button.) Dragging is done to select multiple objects, such as selecting all the cells in a cell range, as well as to physically move an object to another part of the screen. The related **drag-and-drop** operation permits you to move one object over another to trigger an action. You drag the first object across the screen, and when the first object is over the second object, you release the primary mouse button. (In most cases, releasing the primary button causes the first object to reappear in its original position onscreen.)

Without a working knowledge of these mousing operations, you will find it difficult to understand and follow the instructions presented in the end-of-chapter Excel and Minitab Guides.

B.3 Dialog Box Interactions

When you interact with either Excel or Minitab, you will see **dialog boxes**, pop-up windows that contain messages or ask you to make entries or selections. Table B.2 identifies and defines the common objects found in dialog boxes which are shown in Figure B.2 on page 782.

TABLE B.2
Dialog Box Elements

Element	Function
Command button	A clickable area that tells a program to take some action. For example, a dialog box **OK button** causes a program to take an action using the current entries and selections of the dialog box. A dialog box **Cancel button** closes a dialog box and cancels the pending operation associated with the entries and selections in the dialog box.
List box	A box that displays a list of clickable choices. If a list exceeds the dimensions of a list box, list boxes display **scroll buttons** or **sliders** (not shown in Figure B.2) that can be clicked to reveal choices not currently displayed.
Drop-down list	A special button that, when clicked, displays a list of choices from which you typically select one choice.
Edit box	An area into which entries can be typed. Some edit boxes also contain drop-down lists or **spinner buttons** that can be used to make entries. A cell range edit box typically contains a clickable button that allows you to drag the mouse over a cell range as an alternative to typing the cell range.
Set of option buttons	A set of buttons that represent a set of mutually exclusive choices. Clicking one option button clears all the other option buttons in the set.
Check box	A clickable area that represents an optional action. A check box displays either a checkmark or nothing, depending on whether the optional action has been selected. Unlike with option buttons, clicking a check box does not affect the status of other check boxes, and more than one check box can be checked at a time. Clicking a check box that already contains a checkmark *clears* the check box. (To distinguish between the two states, instructions in this book use the verbs *check* and *clear*.)

FIGURE B.2
Excel 2010 Open (partially obscured) and Minitab Print dialog boxes

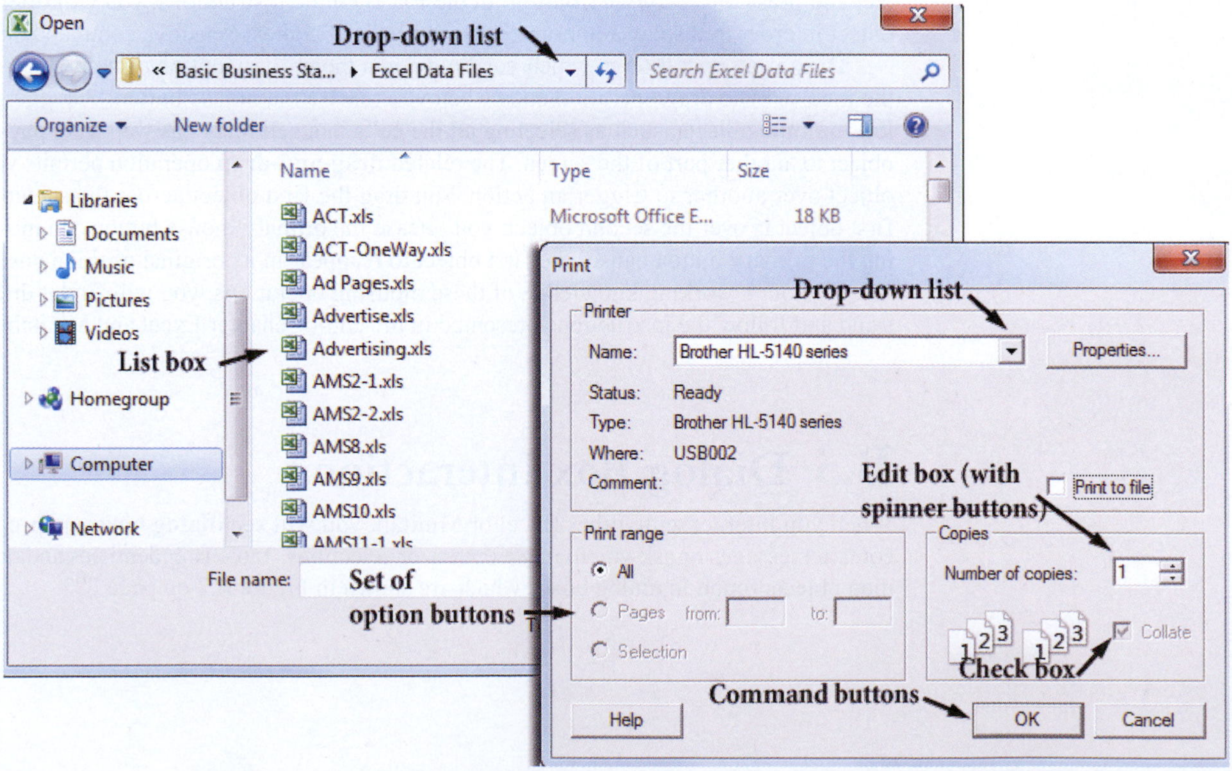

B.4 Unique Features

Excel 2007 This version of Excel uniquely features the **Office Button**, the circular logo in the upper left of the window that displays a menu of basic computing commands when clicked (see Figure B.1). The Office Button functions much like the File menu in Excel 2003 and Minitab and the File tab in Excel 2010.

Minitab Minitab (all versions) displays a session manager (shown in Figure MG1.1 on page 22), a window in which results are added as a continuous log. (All Minitab results, other than charts, shown throughout this book are copied from this session manager log.)

Minitab 16 Minitab 16 includes an Assistant feature that helps guide you through the choice of the statistical method to use. The Assistant appears as an additional choice on the Minitab menu bar and also provides direct clickable shortcuts to menu choices that might otherwise require several different mouse clicks to select. The Assistant is not explicitly used in this book due to its uniqueness to Minitab 16.

APPENDIX C Companion Website Resources

C.1 Visiting the Companion Website for This Book

The companion website for this book contains study resources, Excel workbook files, the free PHStat2 add-in, and the optional online topics. To visit this site, open a web browser and go to **www.pearsonhighered.com/levine**. On that web page, click the **Companion Website** link for this book. (Be careful; the web page lists several books, each with its own **Companion Website** link.) The link takes you to the home page of the companion website. On the home page, there are links for downloading the files for this book (see Section C.2), any updates or corrections to this book, and a horizontal menu of chapter numbers that you can use to display the companion materials for an individual chapter.

C.2 Downloading the Files for This Book

The companion website described in Section C.1 contains the links that will allow you to download the six sets of files listed below that support this book. (Section C.4 provides additional details about each set and contains a complete list of the files that comprise the first three sets.)

- **Data Files** Files that contain the data used in chapter examples or named in problems. These files are available in both **.xls** (Excel) and **.mtw** (Minitab) format.
- **Online Topics** A set of files in Adobe PDF format that contain the optional online topics for this book.
- **Excel Guide Workbooks** Workbooks that contain model solutions that can also be reused as templates for solving other problems.
- **Case Files** A mix of data and document files that support the "Managing Ashland MultiComm Services" running case and the end-of-chapter Digital Cases.
- **Visual Explorations Files** The files needed to use the Visual Explorations add-in workbook, the interactive Excel add-in that illustrates selected statistical concepts. (Not compatible with Mac Excel 2008.)
- **PHStat2 Readme File and PHStat2 Setup Program** Files that allow you to set up and install the free PHStat2 add-in. See Sections D.2, D.3, and G.1 for more information. (Requires Microsoft Windows–based Excel.)

To download a set of files, right-click its download link and click the "save as" choice from the shortcut menu (**Save Target As** in Internet Explorer, **Save Link As** in Mozilla Firefox). Other than PHStat2, each set is downloaded as a self-extracting archive of compressed files, which you extract and store in the folder of your choice.

C.3 Accessing the Online Topics Files

While you can download the set of online topic files for your own use while not connected to the Internet, you can also access these files individually while online. To do so, visit this book's companion website (see Section C.1). In the horizontal menu of chapter numbers, click the chapter number that corresponds to the chapter you want. Then, in that chapter's own web page, click the left menu link for the material you want to use online.

C.4 Details of Downloadable Files

Data Files

Data files are available as either Excel workbook files stored in **.xls** format, compatible with all Excel versions, or Minitab worksheet files, stored in the **.mtw** format, compatible with Minitab Release 14 or later. Data files organize the data for each variable by column, using the rules discussed in Sections EG1.2 and MG1.2. Throughout this book, the names of data files appear in a special typeface—for example, Bond Funds.

In the following alphabetical list, the variables included are presented in the order of their appearance in the file. Except where noted in the text, the Excel workbook files store data in a **DATA worksheet**.

ACT Method, ACT scores for condensed course, ACT scores for regular course (Chapter 11)

ACT-ONEWAY Group 1 ACT scores, group 2 ACT scores, group 3 ACT scores, group 4 ACT scores (Chapter 11)

AD PAGES Magazine name, magazine ad pages in 2008, and magazine ad pages in 2009 (Chapter 10)

ADVERTISE Sales ($thousands), radio ads ($thousands), and newspaper ads ($thousands) for 22 cities (Chapters 14 and 15)

ADVERTISING Sales ($millions) and newspaper ads ($thousands) (Chapter 15)

AMS2-1 Types of errors and frequency; types of errors and cost; types of wrong billing errors and cost (Chapter 2)

AMS2-2 Days and number of calls (Chapter 2)

AMS8 Rate willing to pay in $ (Chapter 8)

AMS9 Upload speed (Chapter 9)

AMS10 Update times for email interface 1 and email interface 2 (Chapter 10)

AMS11-1 Update time for system 1, system 2, and system 3 (Chapter 11)

AMS11-2 Media (cable or fiber) and interface (system 1, system 2, or system 3) (Chapter 11)

AMS13 Number of hours spent telemarketing and number of new subscriptions (Chapter 13)

AMS14 Week, number of new subscriptions, hours spent telemarketing, and type of presentation (formal or informal) (Chapter 14)

AMS16 Month and number of home delivery subscriptions (Chapter 16)

AMS17 Day and upload speed (Chapter 17)

ANGLE Subgroup number and angle (Chapter 17)

ANSCOMBE Data sets A, B, C, and D—each with 11 pairs of *X* and *Y* values (Chapter 13)

ATM TRANSACTIONS Cause, frequency, and percentage (Chapter 2)

AUDITS Year and number of audits (Chapters 2 and 16)

AUTO2008 Make/model, length (in.), width (in.), height (in.), wheelbase (in.), weight (lb.), maximum cargo load (lb.), cargo volume (cu. ft.), front shoulder room (in.), front leg room (in.), front head room (in.), horsepower, miles per gallon, acceleration from 0 to 60 mph (in sec.), braking from 60 mph dry (in sec.), braking from 60 mph wet (in sec.), turning circle (ft.), region of origin, vehicle type, and transmission type (Chapter 18)

AUTO2010 Car, miles per gallon, horsepower, and weight (in lb.) (Chapters 14 and 15)

BANK1 Waiting time (in minutes) of 15 customers at a bank located in a commercial district (Chapters 3, 9, 10, and 12)

BANK2 Waiting time (in minutes) of 15 customers at a bank located in a residential area (Chapters 3, 10, and 12)

BANKTIME Day, waiting times of four bank customers (A, B, C, and D) (Chapter 17)

BASEBALL Team; attendance; high temperature on game day; winning percentage of home team; opponent's winning percentage; game played on Friday, Saturday, or Sunday (0 = no, 1 = yes); and promotion held (0 = no, 1 = yes) (Chapter 18)

BB2009 Team, league (0 = American, 1 = National), wins, earned run average, runs scored, hits allowed, walks allowed, saves, and errors (Chapters 13 and 15)

BBCOST Team and fan cost index (Chapters 2 and 6)

BBREVENUE Team, revenue ($millions), and value ($millions) (Chapter 13)

BBSALARIES Year and average major league baseball salary ($millions) (Chapter 16)

BED & BATH Year, coded year, and number of stores open (Chapter 16)

BESTFUNDS Fund type (large cap value, large cap growth), 3-year return, 5-year return, 10-year return, expense ratio (Chapter 10)

BESTFUNDS2 Fund type (foreign large cap blend, small cap blend, midcap blend, large cap blend, diversified emerging markets), 3-year return, 5-year return, 10-year return, expense ratio (Chapter 11)

BESTFUNDS3 Fund type (intermediate municipal bond, short-term bond, intermediate term bond), 3-year return, 5-year return, 10-year return, expense ratio (Chapter 11)

BILL PAYMENT Form of payment and percentage (Chapter 2)

BOND FUNDS Fund number, type, assets, fees, expense ratio, 2009 return, 3-year return, 5-year return, risk, bins, and midpoints (Chapters 2, 3, 4, 6, 8, 10, 11, 12, and 15)

BOND FUNDS2008 Fund number, type, assets, fees, expense ratio, 2008 return, 3-year return, 5-year return, risk, bins, and midpoints (Chapters 2 and 3)

BOOKPRICES Author, title, bookstore price, and online price (Chapter 10)

BRAKES Part, gauge 1, and gauge 2 (Chapter 11)

BREAKFAST Menu choice, delivery time difference for early time period, and delivery time difference for late time period (Chapter 11)

BREAKFAST2 Menu choice, delivery time difference for early time period, and delivery time difference for late time period (Chapter 11)

BREAKSTW Operator and breaking strength for machines I, II, and III (Chapter 11)

BULBS Manufacturer (1 = A, 2 = B) and length of life in hours (Chapters 2, 10, and 12)

CABERNET California and Washington ratings and California and Washington rankings (Chapter 12)

CANISTER Day and number of nonconformances (Chapter 17)

CATFOOD Ounces eaten of kidney, shrimp, chicken liver, salmon, and beef cat food (Chapters 11 and 12)

CATFOOD2 Piece size (F = fine, C = chunky), coded weight for low fill height, and coded weight for current fill height (Chapter 11)

CATFOOD3 Type (1 = kidney, 2 = shrimp), shift, time interval, nonconformances, and volume (Chapter 17)

CATFOOD4 Type (1 = kidney, 2 = shrimp), shift, time interval, and weight (Chapter 17)

CD-FIVEYEAR Five-year CD rates 3/29/2010 and 8/23/2010 (Chapter 10)

CELLRATING City and ratings for Verizon, AT&T, T-Mobile, and Sprint (Chapter 11)

CEO-COMPENSATION Company, compensation of CEO in $millions, and return in 2009 (Chapters 2, 3, and 13)

CEREALS Cereal, calories, carbohydrates, and sugar (Chapters 3 and 13)

CHOCOLATECHIP Cost (cents) of chocolate chip cookies (Chapter 3)

CIGARETTETAX State and cigarette tax ($) (Chapters 2 and 3)

CIRCUITS Batch and thickness of semiconductor wafers by position (Chapter 11)

COCA-COLA Year, coded year, and operating revenues ($billions) at The Coca-Cola Company (Chapter 16)

COFFEE Expert, Rating of coffees, by brand A, B, C, and D (Chapters 10 and 11)

COFFEE PRICES Year and price per pound of coffee in the United States (Chapter 16)

COFFEESALES Coffee sales at $0.59, $0.69, $0.79, and $0.89 (Chapters 11 and 12)

COFFEESALES2 Coffee sales and price in $ (Chapter 15)

COLA Sales for normal and end-aisle locations (Chapters 10 and 12)

COLASPC Day, total number of cans filled, and number of unacceptable cans (Chapter 17)

COLLEGE BASKETBALL School, coach's total salary in $thousands, expenses, and revenues ($thousands) (Chapters 2, 3, and 13)

COMPLAINTS Day and number of complaints (Chapter 17)

CONCRETE1 Sample number and compressive strength after two days and seven days (Chapter 10)

CONCRETE2 Sample number and compressive strength after 2 days, 7 days, and 28 days (Chapter 11)

CPI-U Year, coded year, and value of CPI-U (the consumer price index) (Chapter 16)

CRACK Type of crack (0 = unflawed, 1 = flawed) and crack size (Chapters 10 and 12)

CREDIT Month, coded month, and credit charges (Chapter 16)

CREDIT UNIONS Name, city, state, zip code, region, total assets ($), total investments ($), net income ($), total net worth ($), total amount of delinquent loans and leases ($), number of current members, number of potential members, number of full-time credit union employees, and number of branches (Chapter 18)

CURRENCY Year, coded year, and exchange rates (against the U.S. dollar) for the Canadian dollar, Japanese yen, and English pound (Chapter 16)

CUSTSALE Week number, number of customers, and sales ($thousands) over a period of 15 consecutive weeks (Chapter 13)

DARKCHOCOLATE Cost ($) per ounce of dark chocolate bars (Chapters 2, 3, and 8)

DELIVERY Customer number, number of cases, and delivery time (Chapter 13)

DENTAL Annual family dental expenses (Chapter 8)

DIFFTEST Differences in the sales invoices and actual amounts (Chapter 8)

DIGITALCAMERAS Battery life (in shots) for subcompact cameras and compact cameras (Chapters 10 and 12)

DINNER Time to prepare and cook dinner (in minutes) (Chapter 9)

DISCOUNT Amount of discount not taken in $ (Chapter 8)

DJIA Year and Dow Jones Industrial Average at the end of the year (Chapter 16)

DOMESTICBEER Brand, alcohol percentage, calories, and carbohydrates in U.S. domestic beers (Chapters 2, 3, 6, and 15)

DOWMARKETCAP Company and market capitalization ($billions), (Chapters 3 and 6)

DRILL Depth, time to drill additional 5 feet, and type of hole (Chapter 14)

DRINK Amount of soft drink filled in 2-liter bottles (Chapters 2 and 9)

DRYCLEAN Days and number of items returned (Chapter 17)

E-CYCLING Year and recycled amount (Chapter 16)

ENERGY State and per capita kilowatt hour use (Chapter 3)

ENERGY PRICES Year, price of electricity, natural gas, and fuel oil (Chapter 16)

ERRORSPC Number of nonconforming items and number of accounts processed (Chapter 17)

ERWAITING Emergency room waiting time (in minutes) at the main facility and at satellite 1, satellite 2, and satellite 3 (Chapters 11 and 12)

ESPRESSO Tamp (the distance in inches between the espresso grounds and the top of the portafilter) and time (the number of seconds the heart, body, and crema are separated) (Chapter 13)

EURODOLLAR Year and six month Eurodollar deposit rate (Chapter 16)

FASTFOOD Amount spent on fast food in dollars (Chapters 3, 8, and 9)

FEDRECEIPT Year, coded year, and federal receipts ($billions) (Chapter 16)

FFCHAIN Rater and ratings for restaurants A, B, C, and D (Chapter 11)

FIFO Historical cost ($) and audited value ($) for inventory items (Chapter 8)

FIRERUNS Week and number of fire runs (Chapter 17)

FLYASH Fly ash percentage and strength in psi (Chapter 15)

FORCE Force required to break an insulator (Chapters 2, 3, 8, and 9)

FOULSPC Number of foul shots made and number taken (Chapter 17)

FREEPORT Address, appraised value ($thousands), property size (acres), house size (square feet), age, number of rooms, number of bathrooms, and number of cars that can be parked in the garage located in Freeport, New York (Chapter 15)

FRUIT Fruit and year, price ($), and quantity (Chapter 16)

FUNDTRAN Day, number of new investigations, and number of investigations closed (Chapter 17)

FURNITURE Days between receipt and resolution of complaints regarding purchased furniture (Chapters 2, 3, 8, and 9)

GASOLINE Year, gasoline price, 1980 price index, and 1995 price index (Chapter 16)

GAS PRICES Month and price per gallon ($) (Chapters 2 and 16)

GCFREEROSLYN Address, appraised value ($thousands), location, property size (acres), house size (square feet), age, number of rooms, number of bathrooms, and number of cars that can be parked in the garage (Chapter 15)

GCROSLYN Address, appraised value ($thousands), location, property size (acres), house size (square feet), age, number of rooms, number of bathrooms, and number of cars that can be parked in the garage (Chapters 14 and 15)

GDP Year and real gross domestic product (Chapter 16)

GLENCOVE Address, appraised value ($thousands), property size (acres), house size (square feet), age, number of rooms, number of bathrooms, and number of cars that can be parked in the garage in Glen Cove, New York (Chapters 14 and 15)

GOLD Quarter, coded quarter, price ($) (Chapter 16)

GOLFBALL Distance for designs 1, 2, 3, and 4 (Chapters 11 and 12)

GPIGMAT GMAT scores and GPA (Chapter 13)

GRADSURVEY ID number, gender, age (as of last birthday), graduate major (accounting, economics and finance, management, marketing/retailing, other, undecided), current graduate cumulative grade point average, undergraduate major (biological sciences, business, computers, engineering, other), undergraduate cumulative grade point average, current employment status (full-time, part-time, unemployed), number of different full-time jobs held in the past 10 years, expected salary upon completion of MBA ($thousands), amount spent for books and supplies this semester, satisfaction with student advising services on campus, type of computer owned, text messages per week, and wealth accumulated to feel rich (Chapters 2, 3, 4, 6, 8, 10, 11, and 12)

GRANULE Granule loss in Boston and Vermont shingles (Chapters 3, 8, 9, and 10)

HARNSWELL Day and diameter of cam rollers (in inches) (Chapter 17)

HEATINGOIL Monthly consumption of heating oil (gallons), temperature (degrees Fahrenheit), attic insulation (inches), and style (0 = not ranch, 1 = ranch) (Chapters 14 and 15)

HEMLOCKFARMS Asking price ($thousands), hot tub (0 = no, 1 = yes), rooms, lake view (0 = no, 1 = yes), bathrooms, bedrooms, loft/den, finished basement, and number of acres (Chapter 15)

HOMES Price ($thousands), location, condition, bedrooms, bathrooms, and other rooms (Chapter 18)

HOSPADM Day, number of admissions, mean processing time (in hours), range of processing times, and proportion of laboratory rework (over a 30-day period) (Chapter 17)

HOTEL1 Day, number of rooms studied, number of nonconforming rooms per day over a 28-day period, and proportion of nonconforming items (Chapter 17)

HOTEL2 Day and delivery time for subgroups of five luggage deliveries per day over a 28-day period (Chapter 17)

HOTELPRICES City and cost (in English pounds) of two-star, three-star, and four-star hotels (Chapters 2 and 3)

HOTELUK City and cost of a hotel room ($) (Chapter 3)

HOUSE1 Selling price ($thousands), assessed value ($thousands), type (new = 0, old = 1), and time period of sale for 30 houses (Chapters 13, 14, and 15)

HOUSE2 Assessed value ($thousands), size of heating area (in thousands of square feet), and age (in years) for 15 houses (Chapters 13 and 14)

HOUSE3 Assessed value ($thousands), size (in thousands of square feet), and presence of a fireplace for 15 houses (Chapter 14)

ICECREAM Daily temperature (in degrees Fahrenheit) and sales ($thousands) for 21 days (Chapter 13)

INDICES Year and yearly rate of return (in percentage) for the Dow Jones Industrial Average (DJIA), the Standards & Poor's 500 (S&P 500), and the technology-heavy NASDAQ Composite (NASDAQ) (Chapter 3)

INSURANCE Processing time in days for insurance policies (Chapters 3, 8, and 9)

INTAGLIO Surface hardness of untreated and treated steel plates (Chapter 10)

INVOICE Number of invoices processed and amount of time (in hours) for 30 days (Chapter 13)

INVOICES Amount recorded (in dollars) from sales invoices (Chapter 9)

ITEMERR Amount of error (in dollars) from 200 items (Chapter 8)

LARGEST BONDS Bond fund and one-year return of bond funds (Chapter 3)

LAUNDRY Detergent brand and dirt (in pounds) removed for cycle times of 18, 20, 22, and 24 (Chapter 11)

LOANS AND LEASES Name of bank, state, zip code, number of domestic and foreign offices, ownership type, regulator, Federal Reserve district, total deposits ($thousands), gross loans and leases ($thousands), all real estate loans ($thousands), construction and development loans ($thousands), commercial real estate ($thousands), multifamily residential real estate ($thousands), 1–4 family residential loans, ($thousands), farmland loans ($thousands), commercial and industrial loans ($thousands), credit card loans ($thousands), related plans ($thousands), other loans to individuals ($thousands), and all other loans and leases ($thousands) (Chapter 18)

LOGPURCH Upgraded (0 = no, 1 = yes), purchases ($thousands), and extra cards (Chapter 14)

LUGGAGE Delivery time (in minutes) for luggage in Wing A and Wing B of a hotel (Chapters 10 and 12)

MANAGERS Sales (ratio of yearly sales divided by the target sales value for that region), score from the Wonderlic Personnel Test, score on the Strong-Campbell Interest Inventory Test, number of years of selling experience prior to becoming a sales manager, and whether the sales manager has a degree in electrical engineering (Chapter 15)

MBA Success (0 = did not complete, 1 = completed), GPA, and GMAT (Chapter 14)

MCDONALDS Year, coded year, and annual total revenues ($billions) at McDonald's Corporation (Chapter 16)

MEASUREMENT Sample, in-line measurement, and analytical lab measurement (Chapter 10)

MEDICARE Difference in amount reimbursed and amount that should have been reimbursed for office visits (Chapter 8)

MEDREC Day, number of discharged patients, and number of records not processed for a 30-day period (Chapter 17)

METALS Year and the yearly rate of return (in percentage) for platinum, gold, and silver (Chapter 3)

MINING Day, amount stacked, and downtime in minutes (Chapter 18)

MINING2 Day, minutes of downtime due to mechanical, electrical, tonnage restriction, operator, and no feed (Chapter 18)

MMCDRATE Bank, money market rate, one-year CD rate, two-year CD rate, and five-year CD rate (Chapter 11)

MOISTURE Moisture content of Boston shingles and Vermont shingles (Chapter 9)

MOVIE Title, box office gross ($millions), and DVD revenue ($millions) (Chapter 13)

MOVIE ATTENDANCE Year and movie attendance (billions) (Chapter 16)

MOVIE SHARE Type of movie, number of movies, gross ($millions), and number of tickets (millions) (Chapter 2)

MOVIEGROSS Year and combined gross of movies ($millions) (Chapter 2)

MOVING Labor hours, cubic feet, number of large pieces of furniture, and availability of an elevator (Chapters 13 and 14)

MUTUAL FUNDS Category, objective, assets ($millions), fees, expense ratio, 2006 return, three-year return, five-year return, and risk (Chapter 2)

MYELOMA Patient, measurement before transplant, and measurement after transplant (Chapter 10)

NASCAR Year and number of accidents (Chapter 16)

NATURAL GAS Month, wellhead, price, and residential price (Chapter 16)

NBA2010 Team, number of wins, points per game (for team, opponent, and the difference between team and opponent), field goal (shots made) percentage (for team, opponent, and the difference between team and opponent), steals per game (for team, opponent, and the difference between team and opponent), and rebound percentage (for team, opponent, and the difference between team and opponent) (Chapters 14 and 15)

NBAVALUES Team, annual revenue ($millions), and value ($millions) for NBA franchises (Chapters 2, 3, and 13)

NEIGHBOR Selling price ($thousands), number of rooms, and neighborhood location (0 = east, 1 = west) (Chapter 14)

NEW HOME PRICES Year and mean price ($thousands) (Chapter 2)

OIL&GAS Week, price of oil per barrel, and price of a gallon of gasoline ($) (Chapter 13)

OMNIPOWER Bars sold, price (cents), and promotion expenses ($) (Chapter 14)

ORDER Time in minutes to fill orders for a population of 200 (Chapter 8)

O-RING Flight number, temperature, and O-ring damage index (Chapter 13)

PAINRELIEF Temperature and dissolve times (seconds) for Equate, Kroger, and Alka-Seltzer tablets (Chapter 11)

PALLET Weight of Boston shingles and weight of Vermont shingles (Chapters 2, 8, 9, and 10)

PARACHUTE Tensile strength of parachutes from suppliers 1, 2, 3, and 4; the sample means and the sample standard deviations for the four suppliers in rows 8 and 9 (Chapters 11 and 12)

PARACHUTE2 Loom and tensile strength of parachutes from suppliers 1, 2, 3, and 4 (Chapter 11)

PASTA Type of pasta (A = American, I = Italian), weight for 4-minute cooking time, and weight for 8-minute cooking time (Chapter 11)

PEN Gender, ad, and product rating (Chapters 11 and 12)

PERFORM Performance rating before and after motivational training (Chapter 10)

PETFOOD Shelf space (in feet), weekly sales ($), and aisle location (0 = back, 1 = front) (Chapters 13 and 14)

PHONE Time (in minutes) to clear telephone line problems and location (1 = I and 2 = II) (Chapters 10 and 12)

PHOTO Developer strength, density at 10 minutes, and density at 14 minutes (Chapters 11)

PIZZAHUT Gender (0 = female , 1 = male), price ($), and purchase (0 = the student selected another pizzeria, 1 = student selected Pizza Hut) (Chapter 14)

PIZZATIME Time period, delivery time for local restaurant, and delivery time for national chain (Chapter 10)

PLUMBINV Difference ($) between actual amounts recorded on sales invoices and amounts entered into the accounting system (Chapter 8)

POLIO Year and incidence rates per 100,000 persons of reported poliomyelitis (Chapter 16)

POTATO Percentage of solids content in filter cake, acidity (in pH), lower pressure, upper pressure, cake thickness, varidrive speed, and drum speed setting (Chapter 15)

POTTERMOVIES Title, first weekend gross ($millions), U.S. gross ($millions), and worldwide gross ($millions) (Chapters 2, 3, and 13)

PROPERTYTAXES State and property taxes per capita ($) (Chapters 2, 3, and 6)

PROTEIN Type of food, calories (in grams), protein, percentage of calories from fat, percentage of calories from saturated fat, and cholesterol (mg) (Chapters 2 and 3)

PTFALLS Month and patient falls (Chapter 17)

PUMPKIN Circumference and weight of pumpkins (Chapter 13)

REALESTATE Value ($thousands), lot size (thousands of sq. ft.), number of bedrooms, number of rooms, number of bathrooms, age in years, annual taxes ($), type of parking facility (none, one-car garage, two-car garage), location (A, B, C, D, E), style of house (cape, expanded ranch, colonial, ranch, split level), type of heating fuel (gas, oil), type of heating system (hot air, hot water, other), type of swimming pool (none, above ground, in ground), eat-in kitchen (absent, present), central air-conditioning (absent, present), fireplace (absent, present), connection to local sewer system (absent, present), basement (absent, present), modern kitchen (absent, present), and modern bathrooms (absent, present) (Chapter 18)

REDWOOD Height (ft.), breast height diameter (in.), and bark thickness (in.) (Chapters 13 and 14)

RENT Monthly rental cost (in dollars) and apartment size (in square footage) (Chapter 13)

RESTAURANTS Location, food rating, decor rating, service rating, summated rating, coded location (0 = city, 1 = suburban), and cost of a meal (Chapters 2, 3, 10, 13, and 14)

RESTAURANTS2 Location, food rating, decor rating, service rating, summated rating, coded location (0 = city, 1 = suburban), and cost of a meal (Chapter 18)

RETURN 2009 UNSTACKED Intermediate government return in 2009 and short-term corporate return in 2009 (Chapter 2)

ROSLYN Address, appraised value, property size (acres), house size (square feet), age, number of rooms, number of bathrooms, and number of cars that can be parked in the garage (Chapter 15)

RUDYBIRD Day, total cases sold, and cases of Rudybird sold (Chapter 17)

SAFETY Tour and number of unsafe acts (Chapter 17)

SATISFACTION Satisfaction (0 = unsatisfied, 1 = satisfied), delivery time difference in minutes (0 = no, 1 = yes), and whether the person had been a previous customer of the hotel (0 = no, 1 = yes) (Chapter 14)

SAVINGSRATE-MMCD Bank, location, rate for a money market account, and five-year CD (Chapters 2, 3, 6, and 8)

SCRUBBER Airflow, water flow, recirculating water flow, orifice diameter, and NTU (Chapter 15)

SEALANT Sample number, sealant strength for Boston shingles, and sealant strength for Vermont shingles (Chapter 17)

SEDANS Miles per gallon for 2010 family sedans (Chapters 3 and 8)

SHOPPING1 Product, Costco price ($), and store brand price ($) (Chapter 10)

SHOPPING2 Product, impulsive shopper price ($), savvy shopper price ($), Costco price ($), and store brand price ($) (Chapter 11)

SILVER Year and price of silver ($) (Chapter 16)

SILVER-Q Quarter, coded quarter, and price of silver ($) (Chapter 16)

SITE Store number, square footage (in thousands of square feet), and sales ($millions) (Chapter 13)

SOCCERVALUES Team, country, revenue ($millions), and value ($millions) (Chapter 13)

SOLAR POWER Year and amount of solar power installed (in megawatts) (Chapters 2 and 16)

SPONGE Day, number of sponges produced, number of nonconforming sponges, and proportion of nonconforming sponges (Chapter 17)

SPORTING Sales ($), age, annual population growth, income ($), percentage with high school diploma, and percentage with college diploma (Chapters 13 and 15)

SPWATER Sample number and amount of magnesium (Chapter 17)

STANDBY Standby hours, total staff present, remote hours, Dubner hours, and labor hours (Chapters 14 and 15)

STEEL Error in actual length and specified length (Chapters 2, 6, 8, and 9)

STOCK PERFORMANCE Decade and stock performance (%) (Chapters 2 and 16)

STOCKPRICES Week, and closing weekly stock price for GE, Discovery, and Apple (Chapters 2 and 13)

STRATEGIC Year and number of barrels (billions) in U.S. strategic oil reserve (Chapter 16)

STUDYTIME Gender and study time (Chapter 10)

SUPERMARKET Day, number of customers, and checkout time (minutes) (Chapter 13)

SUV Miles per gallon for 2010 small SUVs (Chapters 3, 6, and 8)

TAX Quarterly sales tax receipts ($thousands) (Chapter 3)

TAXES County taxes ($) and age of house (years) (Chapter 15)

TEA3 Sample number and weight of tea bags in ounces (Chapter 17)

TEABAGS Weight of tea bags in ounces (Chapters 3, 8, and 9)

TEABAGS2 Weight of tea bags in ounces (Chapter 12)

TELESPC Number of orders and number of corrections over 30 days (Chapter 17)

TELLER Number of errors by tellers (Chapter 17)

TENSILE Sample number and strength (Chapter 17)

TESTRANK Rank scores and training method used (0 = traditional, 1 = experimental) (Chapter 12)

THICKNESS Thickness, catalyst, pH, pressure, temperature, and voltage (Chapters 14 and 15)

TIMES Times to get ready (Chapter 3)

TOMATO Fertilizer and yield (Chapter 15)

TOMATO PRICE Year and price per pound ($) in the United States (Chapter 16)

TOYS R US Quarter, coded quarter, revenue ($millions), and three dummy variables for quarters (Chapter 16)

TRADE Days, number of undesirable trades, and total number of trades made over a 30-day period (Chapter 17)

TRANSMIT Day and number of errors in transmission (Chapter 17)

TRANSPORT Days and patient transport times (in minutes) (Chapter 17)

TRASHBAGS Weight required to break four brands of trash bags (Kroger, Glad, Hefty, Tuff Stuff) (Chapters 11 and 12)

TRAVEL Week and average traffic on Google for searches from the U. S. on travel scaled to the average traffic for the entire time period based on a fixed point at the beginning of the time period (Chapter 16)

TREASURY Year and interest rate (Chapter 16)

TROUGH Width of trough (Chapters 2, 3, 8, and 9)

TROUGH2 Width of trough (Chapter 12)

TRSNYC Year, unit value of the Diversified Equity Fund, and unit value of the Stable Value Fund (Chapter 16)

TSMODEL1 Year, coded year, and three time series (I, II, and III) (Chapter 16)

TSMODEL2 Year, coded year, and two time series (I and II) (Chapter 16)

UNDERGRADSURVEY ID number, gender, age (as of last birthday), class designation, major (accounting, computer information systems, economics and finance, international business, management, marketing, other, undecided) graduate school intention (yes, no, undecided), cumulative grade point average, current employment status, expected starting salary ($thousands), number of social networking sites registered for, satisfaction with student advisement services on campus, amount spent on books and supplies this semester, type of computer preferred (desktop, laptop, tablet/notebook/netbook), text messages per week, and wealth accumulated to feel rich (Chapters 2, 3, 4, 6, 8, 10, 11, and 12)

UNDERWRITING Score on end-of-training exam, score on proficiency exam, and training method (Chapter 14)

USEDAUTOS Car, model, year (2000 = 0), asking price in ($thousands), mileage (in thousands), age (in years), vehicle type, and region of origin (Chapter 18)

UTILITY Utilities charges ($) for 50 one-bedroom apartments (Chapters 2 and 6)

VB Time (in minutes) for nine students to write and run a Visual Basic program (Chapter 10)

VEGGIEBURGER Calories and fat in veggie burgers (Chapters 2 and 3)

WAIT Waiting times and seating times (in minutes) in a restaurant (Chapter 6)

WALMART Quarter and quarterly revenues ($billions) (Chapter 16)

WARECOST Distribution cost ($thousands), sales ($thousands), and number of orders (Chapters 13, 14, and 15)

WAREHSE Day, units handled, and employee number (Chapter 17)

WINE Expert, wine, and rating (Chapter 11)

WIP Processing times in days and plant number (Chapter 18)

WONDERLIC School, average Wonderlic score of football players trying out for the NFL, and graduation rate (Chapters 2, 3, and 13)

WORKFORCE Year, population, and size of the workforce in thousands (Chapter 16)

YARN Side-by-side aspect and breaking strength scores for 30 psi, 40 psi, and 50 psi (Chapter 11)

YIELD Cleansing step, new etching step yield, and standard etching step yield (Chapter 11)

YIELD-ONEWAY Yield for new method 1, new method 2, and standard (Chapter 11)

Downloadable Online Topics

The downloadable online topics contain the optional topics for this book. These files are stored in the Portable Document Format (PDF) format that can be viewed in many web browsers and utility programs, including Adobe Reader, the free program available for download at **get.adobe.com/reader/**.

The downloadable online topics for this book are:

Binomial	**Section 8.7**	**Section 15.7**
Poisson	**Section 9.6**	**Section 16.8**
Section 5.6	**Section 12.8**	**Chapter 19**
Section 6.6	**Section 12.9**	**ANOM**
Section 7.6	**Section 15.6**	**ANOP**

Excel Guide Workbooks

Excel Guide workbooks contain model solutions that can be reused as templates for solving other problems. The workbooks are featured in the *In-Depth Excel* instructions of the Excel Guides and also serve to document the worksheets created by many PHStat2 procedures and provide many of the illustrations of Excel results throughout this book.

All of these workbooks are stored in the **.xls** format, compatible with all Excel versions. Most contain a **COMPUTE worksheet** (often shown in this book) that presents results as well as a **COMPUTE_FORMULAS worksheet** that presents the COMPUTE worksheet in formulas view, which allows for the easy inspection of all worksheet formulas used in the worksheet.

The Excel Guide workbooks for this book are:

Bayes	**McNemar**
Binomial	**Moving Averages**
Boxplot	**Multiple Regression**
***c* Chart**	**Normal**
Capability	**NPP**
Chapter 2	**One-Way ANOVA**
Chi-Square	**Opportunity Loss**
Chi-Square Variance	***p* Chart**
Chi-Square Worksheets	**Paired T**
CIE Proportion	**Poisson**
CIE sigma known	**Pooled-Variance T**
CIE sigma unknown	**Portfolio**
CIE Total Difference	**Probabilities**
CIE Total	**Quartiles**
Correlation	**R and XBar Chart**
Covariance	**Random**
Descriptive	**Randomized Block**
Differences	**Sample Size Mean**
Discrete Random Variable	**Sample Size Proportion**
Expected Monetary Value	**SDS**
Exponential	**Separate-Variance T**
Exponential Smoothing	**Simple Linear Regression**
Exponential Trend	**StackedAndUnstacked**
F Two Variances	**T Mean**
Friedman Rank Test	**Two-Way ANOVA**
Hypergeometric	**Variability**
Index Numbers	**Wilcoxon**
Kruskal-Wallis Worksheets	**Z Mean**
Lagged Predictors	**Z Proportion**
Levene	**Z Two Proportions**

Other Downloadable Files

Case Files These files support the Managing Ashland MultiComm Services running case and the end-of-chapter Digital Cases; they come packaged as a self-extracting archive file. When this archive is expanded and extracted to the folder you choose, you will notice that some supporting files have been placed in one of three subfolders that the self-extraction process creates. The Digital Cases require Adobe Reader version 10 or later and some features of the selected Digital Case files may require the Adobe Flash or Adobe Air plug-ins.

Visual Explorations This Excel add-in is also packaged as a self-extracting archive file that expands to three files. The three files can be extracted to any folder you choose, and all three must be present together in the same folder for the add-in workbook to function properly.

PHStat2 readme file and PHStat2 setup file The files for the add-in, designed to be used with Windows-based Excel versions. The PHStat2 setup file is a self-extracting program that will install PHStat2 on a Windows-based system. If you plan to install PHStat2, first read Appendix Section D.2 and then download and read the PHStat2 readme file for the latest and most detailed instructions for installing PHStat2. You can also review the PHStat2 FAQs in Appendix G for additional information.

APPENDIX D Software Configuration Details

D.1 Checking for and Applying Updates

Excel

To check for and apply Excel updates, your system must be connected to the Internet. You can check and apply updates using one of two methods. If Internet Explorer is the default web browser on your system, use the Excel "check for updates" feature. In Excel 2010, select **File → Help → Check for Updates** and follow the instructions that appear on the web page that is displayed. In Excel 2007, click the **Office Button** and then **Excel Options** (at the bottom of the Office Button menu window). In the Excel options dialog box, click **Resources** in the left pane and then in the right pane click **Check for Updates** and follow the instructions that appear on the web page that is displayed.

If the first method fails for any reason, you can manually download Excel and Microsoft Office updates by opening a web browser and going to office.microsoft.com/officeupdate. On the web page that is displayed, you can find download links arranged by popularity as well as by product version. If you use this second method, you need to know the exact version and status of your copy of Excel. In Excel 2010, select **File → Help** and note the information under the heading "About Microsoft Excel." In Excel 2007, click the **Office Button** and then **Excel Options**. In the Excel options dialog box, click **Resources** in the left pane and then in the right pane note the detail line under the heading "about Microsoft Office Excel 2007." The numbers and codes that follow the words "Microsoft Office Excel" indicate the version number and updates already applied.

If you use Mac Excel, select **Help → Check for Updates** to begin Microsoft AutoUpdate for Mac, similar to Microsoft Update, described above, for checking and applying updates.

Special Notes About the Windows Update Service If you use a Microsoft Windows–based system and have previously turned on the Windows Update service, your system has not necessarily downloaded and applied all Excel updates. If you use Windows Update, you can upgrade for free to the Microsoft Update service that searches for and downloads updates for all Microsoft products, including Excel and Office. (You can learn more about the Microsoft Update service by visiting **www.microsoft.com/security/updates/mu.aspx**.)

Minitab

To check for and apply Minitab updates, your system must be connected to the Internet. Select **Help → Check for Updates**. Follow directions, if any, that appear in the Minitab Software Update Manager dialog box. If there are no new updates, you will see a dialog box that states "There are no updates available." Click **OK** in that dialog box and then click **Cancel** in the Update Manager dialog box to continue with your Minitab session.

D.2 Concise Instructions for Installing PHStat2

If your system can run the Microsoft Windows–based Excel 2003, Excel 2007, or Excel 2010, and has 15 MB of storage space free, you will be able to install and use PHStat2. If using PHStat2:

- Check for and apply all Excel updates by using the instructions in Section D.1.
- Download and read the PHStat2 readme file for the latest information about PHStat2 (see Appendix Section C.2).

- Download the PHStat2 setup program (see Appendix Section C.2).
- Install PHStat2 using the instructions in that section.
- Configure Excel to use PHStat2 (see Appendix Section D.3).

The PHStat2 setup program copies the PHStat2 files to your system and adds entries in the Windows registry file on your system. Run the setup program only after first logging on to Windows using a user account that has administrator privileges. (Running the setup program with a Windows user account that does not include these privileges will prevent the setup program from properly installing PHStat2.)

If your system runs Windows Vista, Windows 7, or certain third-party security programs, you may see messages asking you to "permit" or "allow" specific system operations as the setup program executes. If you do not give the setup program the necessary permissions, PHStat2 will *not* be properly installed on your computer.

After the setup completes, check the installation by opening PHStat2. If the installation ran properly, Excel will display a PHStat menu in the Add-Ins tab of the Office Ribbon (Excel 2007 or Excel 2010) or the Excel menu bar (Excel 2003). If you have skipped checking for and applying necessary Excel updates, or if some of the updates were unable to be applied, when you first attempt to use PHStat2, you may see a "Compile Error" message that talks about a "hidden module." If this occurs, repeat the process of checking for and applying updates to Excel. (If the bandwidth of the Internet connection is limited, you may need to use another connection.)

As you use PHStat2, check the PHStat2 website, **www.pearsonhighered.com/phstat**, on a regular basis to see if any free updates are available for your version. For more information about PHStat2 without going online, read Appendix Section G.1 on page 818.

D.3 Configuring Excel for PHStat2 Usage

To configure Excel security settings for PHStat2 usage:

1. In Excel 2010, select **File → Options**. In Excel 2007, click the Office Button and then click **Excel Options** (at the bottom of the Office Button menu window).

In the Excel Options dialog box:

2. Click **Trust Center** in the left pane and then click **Trust Center Settings** in the right pane (see the top of Figure D.1).

In the Trust Center dialog box:

3. Click **Add-ins** in the next left pane, and in the Add-ins right pane clear all of the checkboxes (see the bottom left of Figure D.1).
4. Click **Macro Settings** in the left pane, and in the Macro Settings right pane click **Disable all macros with notification** and check **Trust access to the VBA object model** (see the bottom right of Figure D.1).
5. Click **OK** to close the Trust Center dialog box.

Back in the Excel Options dialog box:

6. Click **OK** to finish.

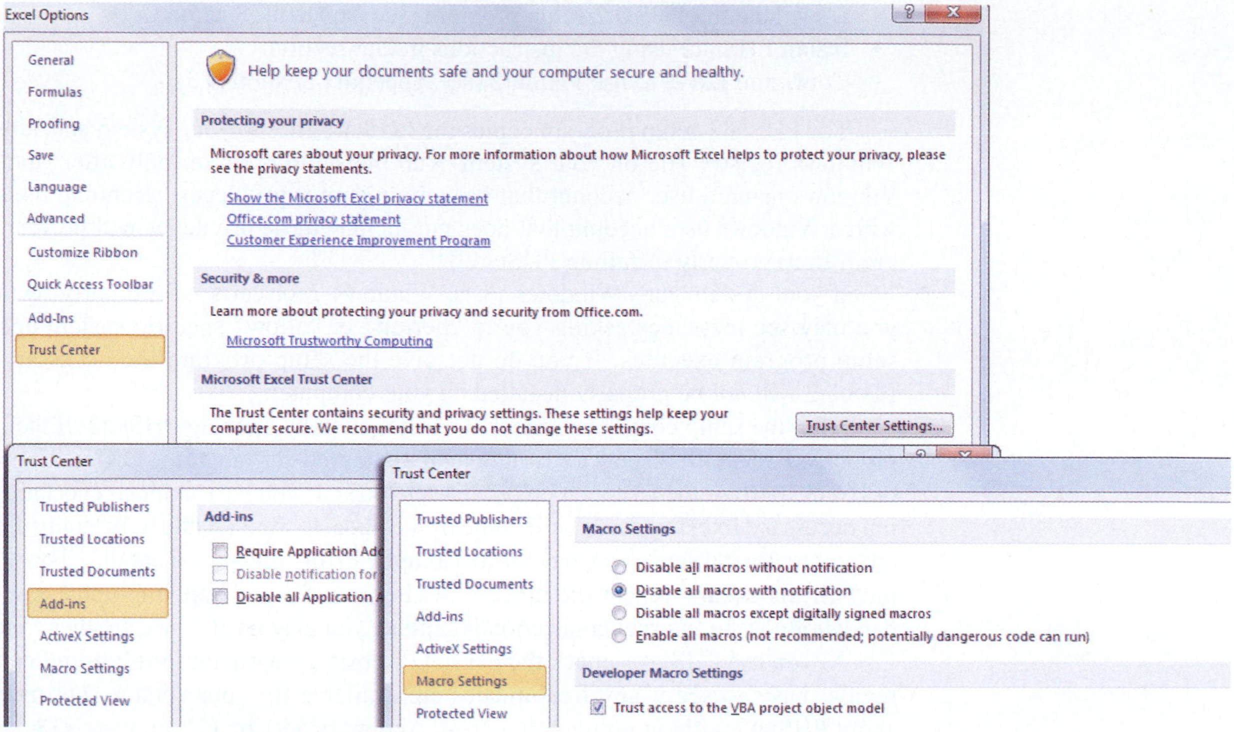

FIGURE D.1

Configuring Excel security settings

On some systems that have stringent security settings, you might need to modify step 5. For such systems, in step 5, click **Trusted Locations** in the left pane and then, in the Trusted Locations right pane, click **Add new location** to add the folder path to the PHStat2 add-in (typically C:\Program Files\PHStat2) and then click **OK**.

When you open PHStat2, Excel will display a Microsoft Excel Security Notice dialog box (shown below). Click **Enable Macros** to enable PHStat2 to open and function.

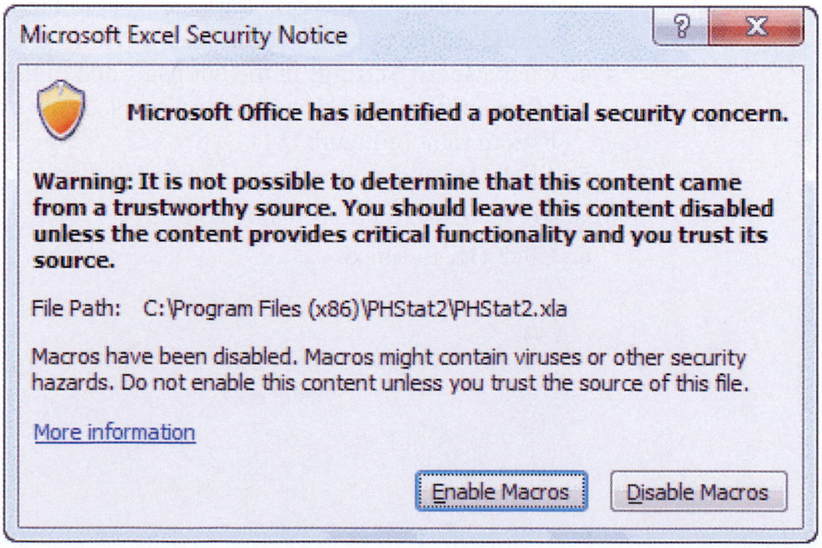

D.4 Using the Visual Explorations Add-in Workbook

To use the Visual Explorations add-in workbook, first download the set of three files that comprise Visual Explorations from this book's companion website (see Appendix C). Place the three files together in a folder of your choosing. Next, use the Section D.3 instructions for configuring Excel for PHStat2 usage. Then open the **Visual Explorations.xla** file in Excel and use the VisualExplorations menu in the **Add-Ins** tab to select individual procedures.

D.5 Checking for the Presence of the Analysis ToolPak

To check for the presence of the Analysis ToolPak add-in (needed only if you will be using the *Analysis ToolPak* Excel Guide instructions):

1. In Excel 2010, select **File ➔ Options**. In Excel 2007, click the **Office Button** and then click **Excel Options** (at the bottom of the Office Button menu window).

In the Excel Options dialog box:

2. Click **Add-Ins** in the left pane and look for the entry **Analysis ToolPak** in the right pane, under **Active Application Add-ins**.
3. If the entry appears, click **OK**.

If the entry does not appear in the **Active Application Add-ins** list, click **Go**. In the Add-Ins dialog box, check **Analysis ToolPak** in the **Add-Ins available** list and click **OK**. If Analysis ToolPak does not appear in the list, rerun the Microsoft Office setup program to install this component.

The Analysis ToolPak add-in is not included and is not available for Mac Excel 2008 but is included in older versions of Mac Excel.

APPENDIX E Tables

TABLE E.1
Table of Random Numbers

	Column							
Row	**00000 12345**	**00001 67890**	**11111 12345**	**11112 67890**	**22222 12345**	**22223 67890**	**33333 12345**	**33334 67890**
01	49280	88924	35779	00283	81163	07275	89863	02348
02	61870	41657	07468	08612	98083	97349	20775	45091
03	43898	65923	25078	86129	78496	97653	91550	08078
04	62993	93912	30454	84598	56095	20664	12872	64647
05	33850	58555	51438	85507	71865	79488	76783	31708
06	97340	03364	88472	04334	63919	36394	11095	92470
07	70543	29776	10087	10072	55980	64688	68239	20461
08	89382	93809	00796	95945	34101	81277	66090	88872
09	37818	72142	67140	50785	22380	16703	53362	44940
10	60430	22834	14130	96593	23298	56203	92671	15925
11	82975	66158	84731	19436	55790	69229	28661	13675
12	30987	71938	40355	54324	08401	26299	49420	59208
13	55700	24586	93247	32596	11865	63397	44251	43189
14	14756	23997	78643	75912	83832	32768	18928	57070
15	32166	53251	70654	92827	63491	04233	33825	69662
16	23236	73751	31888	81718	06546	83246	47651	04877
17	45794	26926	15130	82455	78305	55058	52551	47182
18	09893	20505	14225	68514	47427	56788	96297	78822
19	54382	74598	91499	14523	68479	27686	46162	83554
20	94750	89923	37089	20048	80336	94598	26940	36858
21	70297	34135	53140	33340	42050	82341	44104	82949
22	85157	47954	32979	26575	57600	40881	12250	73742
23	11100	02340	12860	74697	96644	89439	28707	25815
24	36871	50775	30592	57143	17381	68856	25853	35041
25	23913	48357	63308	16090	51690	54607	72407	55538
26	79348	36085	27973	65157	07456	22255	25626	57054
27	92074	54641	53673	54421	18130	60103	69593	49464
28	06873	21440	75593	41373	49502	17972	82578	16364
29	12478	37622	99659	31065	83613	69889	58869	29571
30	57175	55564	65411	42547	70457	03426	72937	83792
31	91616	11075	80103	07831	59309	13276	26710	73000
32	78025	73539	14621	39044	47450	03197	12787	47709
33	27587	67228	80145	10175	12822	86687	65530	49325
34	16690	20427	04251	64477	73709	73945	92396	68263
35	70183	58065	65489	31833	82093	16747	10386	59293
36	90730	35385	15679	99742	50866	78028	75573	67257
37	10934	93242	13431	24590	02770	48582	00906	58595
38	82462	30166	79613	47416	13389	80268	05085	96666
39	27463	10433	07606	16285	93699	60912	94532	95632
40	02979	52997	09079	92709	90110	47506	53693	49892
41	46888	69929	75233	52507	32097	37594	10067	67327
42	53638	83161	08289	12639	08141	12640	28437	09268
43	82433	61427	17239	89160	19666	08814	37841	12847
44	35766	31672	50082	22795	66948	65581	84393	15890
45	10853	42581	08792	13257	61973	24450	52351	16602
46	20341	27398	72906	63955	17276	10646	74692	48438
47	54458	90542	77563	51839	52901	53355	83281	19177
48	26337	66530	16687	35179	46560	00123	44546	79896
49	34314	23729	85264	05575	96855	23820	11091	79821
50	28603	10708	68933	34189	92166	15181	66628	58599
51	66194	28926	99547	16625	45515	67953	12108	57846
52	78240	43195	24837	32511	70880	22070	52622	61881
53	00833	88000	67299	68215	11274	55624	32991	17436
54	12111	86683	61270	58036	64192	90611	15145	01748
55	47189	99951	05755	03834	43782	90599	40282	51417
56	76396	72486	62423	27618	84184	78922	73561	52818
57	46409	17469	32483	09083	76175	19985	26309	91536

TABLE E.1
Table of Random Numbers (*continued*)

	Column							
Row	00000 12345	00001 67890	11111 12345	11112 67890	22222 12345	22223 67890	33333 12345	33334 67890
58	74626	22111	87286	46772	42243	68046	44250	42439
59	34450	81974	93723	49023	58432	67083	36876	93391
60	36327	72135	33005	28701	34710	49359	50693	89311
61	74185	77536	84825	09934	99103	09325	67389	45869
62	12296	41623	62873	37943	25584	09609	63360	47270
63	90822	60280	88925	99610	42772	60561	76873	04117
64	72121	79152	96591	90305	10189	79778	68016	13747
65	95268	41377	25684	08151	61816	58555	54305	86189
66	92603	09091	75884	93424	72586	88903	30061	14457
67	18813	90291	05275	01223	79607	95426	34900	09778
68	38840	26903	28624	67157	51986	42865	14508	49315
69	05959	33836	53758	16562	41081	38012	41230	20528
70	85141	21155	99212	32685	51403	31926	69813	58781
71	75047	59643	31074	38172	03718	32119	69506	67143
72	30752	95260	68032	62871	58781	34143	68790	69766
73	22986	82575	42187	62295	84295	30634	66562	31442
74	99439	86692	90348	66036	48399	73451	26698	39437
75	20389	93029	11881	71685	65452	89047	63669	02656
76	39249	05173	68256	36359	20250	68686	05947	09335
77	96777	33605	29481	20063	09398	01843	35139	61344
78	04860	32918	10798	50492	52655	33359	94713	28393
79	41613	42375	00403	03656	77580	87772	86877	57085
80	17930	00794	53836	53692	67135	98102	61912	11246
81	24649	31845	25736	75231	83808	98917	93829	99430
82	79899	34061	54308	59358	56462	58166	97302	86828
83	76801	49594	81002	30397	52728	15101	72070	33706
84	36239	63636	38140	65731	39788	06872	38971	53363
85	07392	64449	17886	63632	53995	17574	22247	62607
86	67133	04181	33874	98835	67453	59734	76381	63455
87	77759	31504	32832	70861	15152	29733	75371	39174
88	85992	72268	42920	20810	29361	51423	90306	73574
89	79553	75952	54116	65553	47139	60579	09165	85490
90	41101	17336	48951	53674	17880	45260	08575	49321
91	36191	17095	32123	91576	84221	78902	82010	30847
92	62329	63898	23268	74283	26091	68409	69704	82267
93	14751	13151	93115	01437	56945	89661	67680	79790
94	48462	59278	44185	29616	76537	19589	83139	28454
95	29435	88105	59651	44391	74588	55114	80834	85686
96	28340	29285	12965	14821	80425	16602	44653	70467
97	02167	58940	27149	80242	10587	79786	34959	75339
98	17864	00991	39557	54981	23588	81914	37609	13128
99	79675	80605	60059	35862	00254	36546	21545	78179
100	72335	82037	92003	34100	29879	46613	89720	13274

Source: Partially extracted from the Rand Corporation, *A Million Random Digits with 100,000 Normal Deviates* (Glencoe, IL, The Free Press, 1955).

TABLE E.2

The Cumulative Standardized Normal Distribution

Entry represents area under the cumulative standardized normal distribution from $-\infty$ to Z

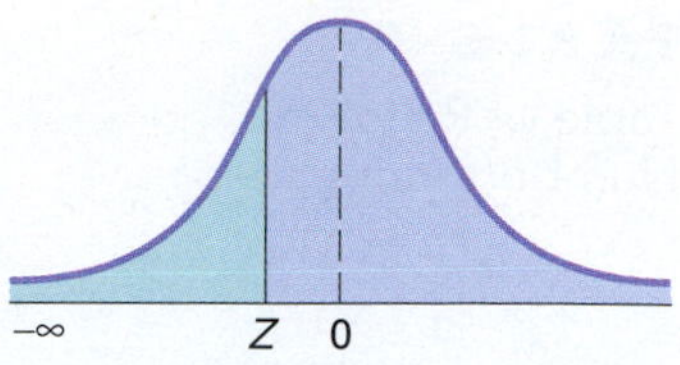

	Cumulative Probabilities									
Z	0.00	0.01	0.02	0.03	0.04	0.05	0.06	0.07	0.08	0.09
−6.0	0.000000001									
−5.5	0.000000019									
−5.0	0.000000287									
−4.5	0.000003398									
−4.0	0.000031671									
−3.9	0.00005	0.00005	0.00004	0.00004	0.00004	0.00004	0.00004	0.00004	0.00003	0.00003
−3.8	0.00007	0.00007	0.00007	0.00006	0.00006	0.00006	0.00006	0.00005	0.00005	0.00005
−3.7	0.00011	0.00010	0.00010	0.00010	0.00009	0.00009	0.00008	0.00008	0.00008	0.00008
−3.6	0.00016	0.00015	0.00015	0.00014	0.00014	0.00013	0.00013	0.00012	0.00012	0.00011
−3.5	0.00023	0.00022	0.00022	0.00021	0.00020	0.00019	0.00019	0.00018	0.00017	0.00017
−3.4	0.00034	0.00032	0.00031	0.00030	0.00029	0.00028	0.00027	0.00026	0.00025	0.00024
−3.3	0.00048	0.00047	0.00045	0.00043	0.00042	0.00040	0.00039	0.00038	0.00036	0.00035
−3.2	0.00069	0.00066	0.00064	0.00062	0.00060	0.00058	0.00056	0.00054	0.00052	0.00050
−3.1	0.00097	0.00094	0.00090	0.00087	0.00084	0.00082	0.00079	0.00076	0.00074	0.00071
−3.0	0.00135	0.00131	0.00126	0.00122	0.00118	0.00114	0.00111	0.00107	0.00103	0.00100
−2.9	0.0019	0.0018	0.0018	0.0017	0.0016	0.0016	0.0015	0.0015	0.0014	0.0014
−2.8	0.0026	0.0025	0.0024	0.0023	0.0023	0.0022	0.0021	0.0021	0.0020	0.0019
−2.7	0.0035	0.0034	0.0033	0.0032	0.0031	0.0030	0.0029	0.0028	0.0027	0.0026
−2.6	0.0047	0.0045	0.0044	0.0043	0.0041	0.0040	0.0039	0.0038	0.0037	0.0036
−2.5	0.0062	0.0060	0.0059	0.0057	0.0055	0.0054	0.0052	0.0051	0.0049	0.0048
−2.4	0.0082	0.0080	0.0078	0.0075	0.0073	0.0071	0.0069	0.0068	0.0066	0.0064
−2.3	0.0107	0.0104	0.0102	0.0099	0.0096	0.0094	0.0091	0.0089	0.0087	0.0084
−2.2	0.0139	0.0136	0.0132	0.0129	0.0125	0.0122	0.0119	0.0116	0.0113	0.0110
−2.1	0.0179	0.0174	0.0170	0.0166	0.0162	0.0158	0.0154	0.0150	0.0146	0.0143
−2.0	0.0228	0.0222	0.0217	0.0212	0.0207	0.0202	0.0197	0.0192	0.0188	0.0183
−1.9	0.0287	0.0281	0.0274	0.0268	0.0262	0.0256	0.0250	0.0244	0.0239	0.0233
−1.8	0.0359	0.0351	0.0344	0.0336	0.0329	0.0322	0.0314	0.0307	0.0301	0.0294
−1.7	0.0446	0.0436	0.0427	0.0418	0.0409	0.0401	0.0392	0.0384	0.0375	0.0367
−1.6	0.0548	0.0537	0.0526	0.0516	0.0505	0.0495	0.0485	0.0475	0.0465	0.0455
−1.5	0.0668	0.0655	0.0643	0.0630	0.0618	0.0606	0.0594	0.0582	0.0571	0.0559
−1.4	0.0808	0.0793	0.0778	0.0764	0.0749	0.0735	0.0721	0.0708	0.0694	0.0681
−1.3	0.0968	0.0951	0.0934	0.0918	0.0901	0.0885	0.0869	0.0853	0.0838	0.0823
−1.2	0.1151	0.1131	0.1112	0.1093	0.1075	0.1056	0.1038	0.1020	0.1003	0.0985
−1.1	0.1357	0.1335	0.1314	0.1292	0.1271	0.1251	0.1230	0.1210	0.1190	0.1170
−1.0	0.1587	0.1562	0.1539	0.1515	0.1492	0.1469	0.1446	0.1423	0.1401	0.1379
−0.9	0.1841	0.1814	0.1788	0.1762	0.1736	0.1711	0.1685	0.1660	0.1635	0.1611
−0.8	0.2119	0.2090	0.2061	0.2033	0.2005	0.1977	0.1949	0.1922	0.1894	0.1867
−0.7	0.2420	0.2388	0.2358	0.2327	0.2296	0.2266	0.2236	0.2206	0.2177	0.2148
−0.6	0.2743	0.2709	0.2676	0.2643	0.2611	0.2578	0.2546	0.2514	0.2482	0.2451
−0.5	0.3085	0.3050	0.3015	0.2981	0.2946	0.2912	0.2877	0.2843	0.2810	0.2776
−0.4	0.3446	0.3409	0.3372	0.3336	0.3300	0.3264	0.3228	0.3192	0.3156	0.3121
−0.3	0.3821	0.3783	0.3745	0.3707	0.3669	0.3632	0.3594	0.3557	0.3520	0.3483
−0.2	0.4207	0.4168	0.4129	0.4090	0.4052	0.4013	0.3974	0.3936	0.3897	0.3859
−0.1	0.4602	0.4562	0.4522	0.4483	0.4443	0.4404	0.4364	0.4325	0.4286	0.4247
−0.0	0.5000	0.4960	0.4920	0.4880	0.4840	0.4801	0.4761	0.4721	0.4681	0.4641

TABLE E.2

The Cumulative Standardized Normal Distribution (*continued*)

Entry represents area under the cumulative standardized normal distribution from $-\infty$ to Z

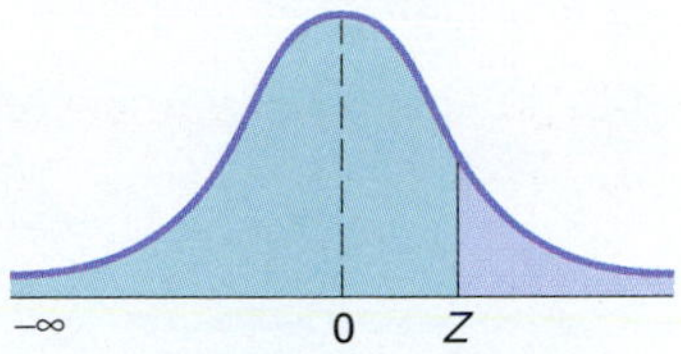

Cumulative Probabilities

Z	0.00	0.01	0.02	0.03	0.04	0.05	0.06	0.07	0.08	0.09
0.0	0.5000	0.5040	0.5080	0.5120	0.5160	0.5199	0.5239	0.5279	0.5319	0.5359
0.1	0.5398	0.5438	0.5478	0.5517	0.5557	0.5596	0.5636	0.5675	0.5714	0.5753
0.2	0.5793	0.5832	0.5871	0.5910	0.5948	0.5987	0.6026	0.6064	0.6103	0.6141
0.3	0.6179	0.6217	0.6255	0.6293	0.6331	0.6368	0.6406	0.6443	0.6480	0.6517
0.4	0.6554	0.6591	0.6628	0.6664	0.6700	0.6736	0.6772	0.6808	0.6844	0.6879
0.5	0.6915	0.6950	0.6985	0.7019	0.7054	0.7088	0.7123	0.7157	0.7190	0.7224
0.6	0.7257	0.7291	0.7324	0.7357	0.7389	0.7422	0.7454	0.7486	0.7518	0.7549
0.7	0.7580	0.7612	0.7642	0.7673	0.7704	0.7734	0.7764	0.7794	0.7823	0.7852
0.8	0.7881	0.7910	0.7939	0.7967	0.7995	0.8023	0.8051	0.8078	0.8106	0.8133
0.9	0.8159	0.8186	0.8212	0.8238	0.8264	0.8289	0.8315	0.8340	0.8365	0.8389
1.0	0.8413	0.8438	0.8461	0.8485	0.8508	0.8531	0.8554	0.8577	0.8599	0.8621
1.1	0.8643	0.8665	0.8686	0.8708	0.8729	0.8749	0.8770	0.8790	0.8810	0.8830
1.2	0.8849	0.8869	0.8888	0.8907	0.8925	0.8944	0.8962	0.8980	0.8997	0.9015
1.3	0.9032	0.9049	0.9066	0.9082	0.9099	0.9115	0.9131	0.9147	0.9162	0.9177
1.4	0.9192	0.9207	0.9222	0.9236	0.9251	0.9265	0.9279	0.9292	0.9306	0.9319
1.5	0.9332	0.9345	0.9357	0.9370	0.9382	0.9394	0.9406	0.9418	0.9429	0.9441
1.6	0.9452	0.9463	0.9474	0.9484	0.9495	0.9505	0.9515	0.9525	0.9535	0.9545
1.7	0.9554	0.9564	0.9573	0.9582	0.9591	0.9599	0.9608	0.9616	0.9625	0.9633
1.8	0.9641	0.9649	0.9656	0.9664	0.9671	0.9678	0.9686	0.9693	0.9699	0.9706
1.9	0.9713	0.9719	0.9726	0.9732	0.9738	0.9744	0.9750	0.9756	0.9761	0.9767
2.0	0.9772	0.9778	0.9783	0.9788	0.9793	0.9798	0.9803	0.9808	0.9812	0.9817
2.1	0.9821	0.9826	0.9830	0.9834	0.9838	0.9842	0.9846	0.9850	0.9854	0.9857
2.2	0.9861	0.9864	0.9868	0.9871	0.9875	0.9878	0.9881	0.9884	0.9887	0.9890
2.3	0.9893	0.9896	0.9898	0.9901	0.9904	0.9906	0.9909	0.9911	0.9913	0.9916
2.4	0.9918	0.9920	0.9922	0.9925	0.9927	0.9929	0.9931	0.9932	0.9934	0.9936
2.5	0.9938	0.9940	0.9941	0.9943	0.9945	0.9946	0.9948	0.9949	0.9951	0.9952
2.6	0.9953	0.9955	0.9956	0.9957	0.9959	0.9960	0.9961	0.9962	0.9963	0.9964
2.7	0.9965	0.9966	0.9967	0.9968	0.9969	0.9970	0.9971	0.9972	0.9973	0.9974
2.8	0.9974	0.9975	0.9976	0.9977	0.9977	0.9978	0.9979	0.9979	0.9980	0.9981
2.9	0.9981	0.9982	0.9982	0.9983	0.9984	0.9984	0.9985	0.9985	0.9986	0.9986
3.0	0.99865	0.99869	0.99874	0.99878	0.99882	0.99886	0.99889	0.99893	0.99897	0.99900
3.1	0.99903	0.99906	0.99910	0.99913	0.99916	0.99918	0.99921	0.99924	0.99926	0.99929
3.2	0.99931	0.99934	0.99936	0.99938	0.99940	0.99942	0.99944	0.99946	0.99948	0.99950
3.3	0.99952	0.99953	0.99955	0.99957	0.99958	0.99960	0.99961	0.99962	0.99964	0.99965
3.4	0.99966	0.99968	0.99969	0.99970	0.99971	0.99972	0.99973	0.99974	0.99975	0.99976
3.5	0.99977	0.99978	0.99978	0.99979	0.99980	0.99981	0.99981	0.99982	0.99983	0.99983
3.6	0.99984	0.99985	0.99985	0.99986	0.99986	0.99987	0.99987	0.99988	0.99988	0.99989
3.7	0.99989	0.99990	0.99990	0.99990	0.99991	0.99991	0.99992	0.99992	0.99992	0.99992
3.8	0.99993	0.99993	0.99993	0.99994	0.99994	0.99994	0.99994	0.99995	0.99995	0.99995
3.9	0.99995	0.99995	0.99996	0.99996	0.99996	0.99996	0.99996	0.99996	0.99997	0.99997
4.0	0.999968329									
4.5	0.999996602									
5.0	0.999999713									
5.5	0.999999981									
6.0	0.999999999									

TABLE E.3

Critical Values of t

For a particular number of degrees of freedom, entry represents the critical value of t corresponding to the cumulative probability $(1 - \alpha)$ *and a specified upper-tail area* (α).

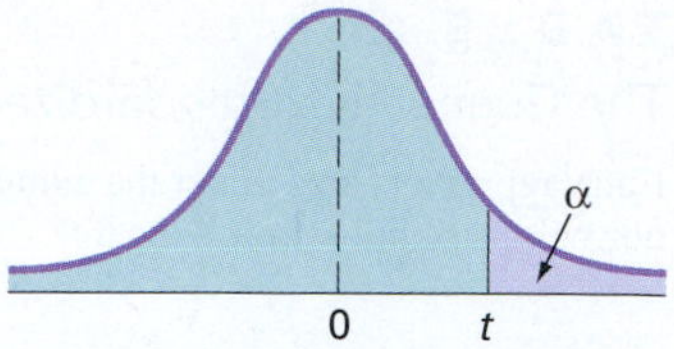

	Cumulative Probabilities					
	0.75	0.90	0.95	0.975	0.99	0.995
	Upper-Tail Areas					
Degrees of Freedom	0.25	0.10	0.05	0.025	0.01	0.005
1	1.0000	3.0777	6.3138	12.7062	31.8207	63.6574
2	0.8165	1.8856	2.9200	4.3027	6.9646	9.9248
3	0.7649	1.6377	2.3534	3.1824	4.5407	5.8409
4	0.7407	1.5332	2.1318	2.7764	3.7469	4.6041
5	0.7267	1.4759	2.0150	2.5706	3.3649	4.0322
6	0.7176	1.4398	1.9432	2.4469	3.1427	3.7074
7	0.7111	1.4149	1.8946	2.3646	2.9980	3.4995
8	0.7064	1.3968	1.8595	2.3060	2.8965	3.3554
9	0.7027	1.3830	1.8331	2.2622	2.8214	3.2498
10	0.6998	1.3722	1.8125	2.2281	2.7638	3.1693
11	0.6974	1.3634	1.7959	2.2010	2.7181	3.1058
12	0.6955	1.3562	1.7823	2.1788	2.6810	3.0545
13	0.6938	1.3502	1.7709	2.1604	2.6503	3.0123
14	0.6924	1.3450	1.7613	2.1448	2.6245	2.9768
15	0.6912	1.3406	1.7531	2.1315	2.6025	2.9467
16	0.6901	1.3368	1.7459	2.1199	2.5835	2.9208
17	0.6892	1.3334	1.7396	2.1098	2.5669	2.8982
18	0.6884	1.3304	1.7341	2.1009	2.5524	2.8784
19	0.6876	1.3277	1.7291	2.0930	2.5395	2.8609
20	0.6870	1.3253	1.7247	2.0860	2.5280	2.8453
21	0.6864	1.3232	1.7207	2.0796	2.5177	2.8314
22	0.6858	1.3212	1.7171	2.0739	2.5083	2.8188
23	0.6853	1.3195	1.7139	2.0687	2.4999	2.8073
24	0.6848	1.3178	1.7109	2.0639	2.4922	2.7969
25	0.6844	1.3163	1.7081	2.0595	2.4851	2.7874
26	0.6840	1.3150	1.7056	2.0555	2.4786	2.7787
27	0.6837	1.3137	1.7033	2.0518	2.4727	2.7707
28	0.6834	1.3125	1.7011	2.0484	2.4671	2.7633
29	0.6830	1.3114	1.6991	2.0452	2.4620	2.7564
30	0.6828	1.3104	1.6973	2.0423	2.4573	2.7500
31	0.6825	1.3095	1.6955	2.0395	2.4528	2.7440
32	0.6822	1.3086	1.6939	2.0369	2.4487	2.7385
33	0.6820	1.3077	1.6924	2.0345	2.4448	2.7333
34	0.6818	1.3070	1.6909	2.0322	2.4411	2.7284
35	0.6816	1.3062	1.6896	2.0301	2.4377	2.7238
36	0.6814	1.3055	1.6883	2.0281	2.4345	2.7195
37	0.6812	1.3049	1.6871	2.0262	2.4314	2.7154
38	0.6810	1.3042	1.6860	2.0244	2.4286	2.7116
39	0.6808	1.3036	1.6849	2.0227	2.4258	2.7079
40	0.6807	1.3031	1.6839	2.0211	2.4233	2.7045
41	0.6805	1.3025	1.6829	2.0195	2.4208	2.7012
42	0.6804	1.3020	1.6820	2.0181	2.4185	2.6981
43	0.6802	1.3016	1.6811	2.0167	2.4163	2.6951
44	0.6801	1.3011	1.6802	2.0154	2.4141	2.6923
45	0.6800	1.3006	1.6794	2.0141	2.4121	2.6896
46	0.6799	1.3002	1.6787	2.0129	2.4102	2.6870
47	0.6797	1.2998	1.6779	2.0117	2.4083	2.6846
48	0.6796	1.2994	1.6772	2.0106	2.4066	2.6822

TABLE E.3
Critical Values of t *(continued)*

	Cumulative Probabilities					
	0.75	0.90	0.95	0.975	0.99	0.995
	Upper-Tail Areas					
Degrees of Freedom	0.25	0.10	0.05	0.025	0.01	0.005
49	0.6795	1.2991	1.6766	2.0096	2.4049	2.6800
50	0.6794	1.2987	1.6759	2.0086	2.4033	2.6778
51	0.6793	1.2984	1.6753	2.0076	2.4017	2.6757
52	0.6792	1.2980	1.6747	2.0066	2.4002	2.6737
53	0.6791	1.2977	1.6741	2.0057	2.3988	2.6718
54	0.6791	1.2974	1.6736	2.0049	2.3974	2.6700
55	0.6790	1.2971	1.6730	2.0040	2.3961	2.6682
56	0.6789	1.2969	1.6725	2.0032	2.3948	2.6665
57	0.6788	1.2966	1.6720	2.0025	2.3936	2.6649
58	0.6787	1.2963	1.6716	2.0017	2.3924	2.6633
59	0.6787	1.2961	1.6711	2.0010	2.3912	2.6618
60	0.6786	1.2958	1.6706	2.0003	2.3901	2.6603
61	0.6785	1.2956	1.6702	1.9996	2.3890	2.6589
62	0.6785	1.2954	1.6698	1.9990	2.3880	2.6575
63	0.6784	1.2951	1.6694	1.9983	2.3870	2.6561
64	0.6783	1.2949	1.6690	1.9977	2.3860	2.6549
65	0.6783	1.2947	1.6686	1.9971	2.3851	2.6536
66	0.6782	1.2945	1.6683	1.9966	2.3842	2.6524
67	0.6782	1.2943	1.6679	1.9960	2.3833	2.6512
68	0.6781	1.2941	1.6676	1.9955	2.3824	2.6501
69	0.6781	1.2939	1.6672	1.9949	2.3816	2.6490
70	0.6780	1.2938	1.6669	1.9944	2.3808	2.6479
71	0.6780	1.2936	1.6666	1.9939	2.3800	2.6469
72	0.6779	1.2934	1.6663	1.9935	2.3793	2.6459
73	0.6779	1.2933	1.6660	1.9930	2.3785	2.6449
74	0.6778	1.2931	1.6657	1.9925	2.3778	2.6439
75	0.6778	1.2929	1.6654	1.9921	2.3771	2.6430
76	0.6777	1.2928	1.6652	1.9917	2.3764	2.6421
77	0.6777	1.2926	1.6649	1.9913	2.3758	2.6412
78	0.6776	1.2925	1.6646	1.9908	2.3751	2.6403
79	0.6776	1.2924	1.6644	1.9905	2.3745	2.6395
80	0.6776	1.2922	1.6641	1.9901	2.3739	2.6387
81	0.6775	1.2921	1.6639	1.9897	2.3733	2.6379
82	0.6775	1.2920	1.6636	1.9893	2.3727	2.6371
83	0.6775	1.2918	1.6634	1.9890	2.3721	2.6364
84	0.6774	1.2917	1.6632	1.9886	2.3716	2.6356
85	0.6774	1.2916	1.6630	1.9883	2.3710	2.6349
86	0.6774	1.2915	1.6628	1.9879	2.3705	2.6342
87	0.6773	1.2914	1.6626	1.9876	2.3700	2.6335
88	0.6773	1.2912	1.6624	1.9873	2.3695	2.6329
89	0.6773	1.2911	1.6622	1.9870	2.3690	2.6322
90	0.6772	1.2910	1.6620	1.9867	2.3685	2.6316
91	0.6772	1.2909	1.6618	1.9864	2.3680	2.6309
92	0.6772	1.2908	1.6616	1.9861	2.3676	2.6303
93	0.6771	1.2907	1.6614	1.9858	2.3671	2.6297
94	0.6771	1.2906	1.6612	1.9855	2.3667	2.6291
95	0.6771	1.2905	1.6611	1.9853	2.3662	2.6286
96	0.6771	1.2904	1.6609	1.9850	2.3658	2.6280
97	0.6770	1.2903	1.6607	1.9847	2.3654	2.6275
98	0.6770	1.2902	1.6606	1.9845	2.3650	2.6269
99	0.6770	1.2902	1.6604	1.9842	2.3646	2.6264
100	0.6770	1.2901	1.6602	1.9840	2.3642	2.6259
110	0.6767	1.2893	1.6588	1.9818	2.3607	2.6213
120	0.6765	1.2886	1.6577	1.9799	2.3578	2.6174
∞	0.6745	1.2816	1.6449	1.9600	2.3263	2.5758

TABLE E.4

Critical Values of χ^2

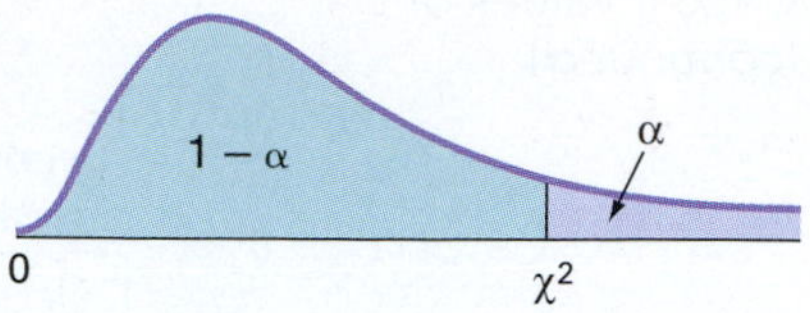

For a particular number of degrees of freedom, entry represents the critical value of χ^2 corresponding to the cumulative probability $(1 - \alpha)$ and a specified upper-tail area (α).

	Cumulative Probabilities											
	0.005	0.01	0.025	0.05	0.10	0.25	0.75	0.90	0.95	0.975	0.99	0.995
	Upper-Tail Areas (α)											
Degrees of Freedom	0.995	0.99	0.975	0.95	0.90	0.75	0.25	0.10	0.05	0.025	0.01	0.005
1			0.001	0.004	0.016	0.102	1.323	2.706	3.841	5.024	6.635	7.879
2	0.010	0.020	0.051	0.103	0.211	0.575	2.773	4.605	5.991	7.378	9.210	10.597
3	0.072	0.115	0.216	0.352	0.584	1.213	4.108	6.251	7.815	9.348	11.345	12.838
4	0.207	0.297	0.484	0.711	1.064	1.923	5.385	7.779	9.488	11.143	13.277	14.860
5	0.412	0.554	0.831	1.145	1.610	2.675	6.626	9.236	11.071	12.833	15.086	16.750
6	0.676	0.872	1.237	1.635	2.204	3.455	7.841	10.645	12.592	14.449	16.812	18.548
7	0.989	1.239	1.690	2.167	2.833	4.255	9.037	12.017	14.067	16.013	18.475	20.278
8	1.344	1.646	2.180	2.733	3.490	5.071	10.219	13.362	15.507	17.535	20.090	21.955
9	1.735	2.088	2.700	3.325	4.168	5.899	11.389	14.684	16.919	19.023	21.666	23.589
10	2.156	2.558	3.247	3.940	4.865	6.737	12.549	15.987	18.307	20.483	23.209	25.188
11	2.603	3.053	3.816	4.575	5.578	7.584	13.701	17.275	19.675	21.920	24.725	26.757
12	3.074	3.571	4.404	5.226	6.304	8.438	14.845	18.549	21.026	23.337	26.217	28.299
13	3.565	4.107	5.009	5.892	7.042	9.299	15.984	19.812	22.362	24.736	27.688	29.819
14	4.075	4.660	5.629	6.571	7.790	10.165	17.117	21.064	23.685	26.119	29.141	31.319
15	4.601	5.229	6.262	7.261	8.547	11.037	18.245	22.307	24.996	27.488	30.578	32.801
16	5.142	5.812	6.908	7.962	9.312	11.912	19.369	23.542	26.296	28.845	32.000	34.267
17	5.697	6.408	7.564	8.672	10.085	12.792	20.489	24.769	27.587	30.191	33.409	35.718
18	6.265	7.015	8.231	9.390	10.865	13.675	21.605	25.989	28.869	31.526	34.805	37.156
19	6.844	7.633	8.907	10.117	11.651	14.562	22.718	27.204	30.144	32.852	36.191	38.582
20	7.434	8.260	9.591	10.851	12.443	15.452	23.828	28.412	31.410	34.170	37.566	39.997
21	8.034	8.897	10.283	11.591	13.240	16.344	24.935	29.615	32.671	35.479	38.932	41.401
22	8.643	9.542	10.982	12.338	14.042	17.240	26.039	30.813	33.924	36.781	40.289	42.796
23	9.260	10.196	11.689	13.091	14.848	18.137	27.141	32.007	35.172	38.076	41.638	44.181
24	9.886	10.856	12.401	13.848	15.659	19.037	28.241	33.196	36.415	39.364	42.980	45.559
25	10.520	11.524	13.120	14.611	16.473	19.939	29.339	34.382	37.652	40.646	44.314	46.928
26	11.160	12.198	13.844	15.379	17.292	20.843	30.435	35.563	38.885	41.923	45.642	48.290
27	11.808	12.879	14.573	16.151	18.114	21.749	31.528	36.741	40.113	43.194	46.963	49.645
28	12.461	13.565	15.308	16.928	18.939	22.657	32.620	37.916	41.337	44.461	48.278	50.993
29	13.121	14.257	16.047	17.708	19.768	23.567	33.711	39.087	42.557	45.722	49.588	52.336
30	13.787	14.954	16.791	18.493	20.599	24.478	34.800	40.256	43.773	46.979	50.892	53.672

For larger values of degrees of freedom (df) the expression $Z = \sqrt{2\chi^2} - \sqrt{2(df) - 1}$ may be used and the resulting upper-tail area can be found from the cumulative standardized normal distribution (Table E.2).

TABLE E.5

Critical Values of F

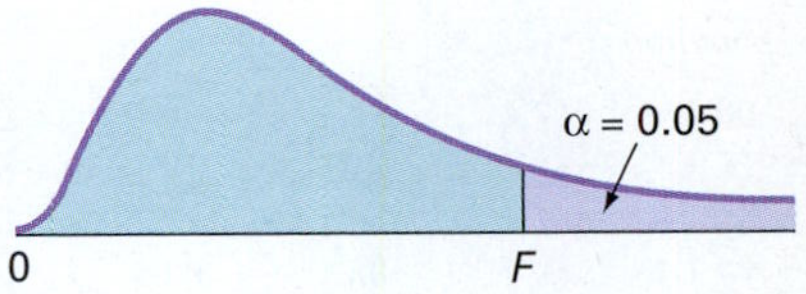

For a particular combination of numerator and denominator degrees of freedom, entry represents the critical values of F corresponding to the cumulative probability $(1 - \alpha)$ and a specified upper-tail area (α).

	Cumulative Probabilities = 0.95																		
	Upper-Tail Areas = 0.05																		
	Numerator, df_1																		
Denominator, df_2	1	2	3	4	5	6	7	8	9	10	12	15	20	24	30	40	60	120	∞
1	161.40	199.50	215.70	224.60	230.20	234.00	236.80	238.90	240.50	241.90	243.90	245.90	248.00	249.10	250.10	251.10	252.20	253.30	254.30
2	18.51	19.00	19.16	19.25	19.30	19.33	19.35	19.37	19.38	19.40	19.41	19.43	19.45	19.45	19.46	19.47	19.48	19.49	19.50
3	10.13	9.55	9.28	9.12	9.01	8.94	8.89	8.85	8.81	8.79	8.74	8.70	8.66	8.64	8.62	8.59	8.57	8.55	8.53
4	7.71	6.94	6.59	6.39	6.26	6.16	6.09	6.04	6.00	5.96	5.91	5.86	5.80	5.77	5.75	5.72	5.69	5.66	5.63
5	6.61	5.79	5.41	5.19	5.05	4.95	4.88	4.82	4.77	4.74	4.68	4.62	4.56	4.53	4.50	4.46	4.43	4.40	4.36
6	5.99	5.14	4.76	4.53	4.39	4.28	4.21	4.15	4.10	4.06	4.00	3.94	3.87	3.84	3.81	3.77	3.74	3.70	3.67
7	5.59	4.74	4.35	4.12	3.97	3.87	3.79	3.73	3.68	3.64	3.57	3.51	3.44	3.41	3.38	3.34	3.30	3.27	3.23
8	5.32	4.46	4.07	3.84	3.69	3.58	3.50	3.44	3.39	3.35	3.28	3.22	3.15	3.12	3.08	3.04	3.01	2.97	2.93
9	5.12	4.26	3.86	3.63	3.48	3.37	3.29	3.23	3.18	3.14	3.07	3.01	2.94	2.90	2.86	2.83	2.79	2.75	2.71
10	4.96	4.10	3.71	3.48	3.33	3.22	3.14	3.07	3.02	2.98	2.91	2.85	2.77	2.74	2.70	2.66	2.62	2.58	2.54
11	4.84	3.98	3.59	3.36	3.20	3.09	3.01	2.95	2.90	2.85	2.79	2.72	2.65	2.61	2.57	2.53	2.49	2.45	2.40
12	4.75	3.89	3.49	3.26	3.11	3.00	2.91	2.85	2.80	2.75	2.69	2.62	2.54	2.51	2.47	2.43	2.38	2.34	2.30
13	4.67	3.81	3.41	3.18	3.03	2.92	2.83	2.77	2.71	2.67	2.60	2.53	2.46	2.42	2.38	2.34	2.30	2.25	2.21
14	4.60	3.74	3.34	3.11	2.96	2.85	2.76	2.70	2.65	2.60	2.53	2.46	2.39	2.35	2.31	2.27	2.22	2.18	2.13
15	4.54	3.68	3.29	3.06	2.90	2.79	2.71	2.64	2.59	2.54	2.48	2.40	2.33	2.29	2.25	2.20	2.16	2.11	2.07
16	4.49	3.63	3.24	3.01	2.85	2.74	2.66	2.59	2.54	2.49	2.42	2.35	2.28	2.24	2.19	2.15	2.11	2.06	2.01
17	4.45	3.59	3.20	2.96	2.81	2.70	2.61	2.55	2.49	2.45	2.38	2.31	2.23	2.19	2.15	2.10	2.06	2.01	1.96
18	4.41	3.55	3.16	2.93	2.77	2.66	2.58	2.51	2.46	2.41	2.34	2.27	2.19	2.15	2.11	2.06	2.02	1.97	1.92
19	4.38	3.52	3.13	2.90	2.74	2.63	2.54	2.48	2.42	2.38	2.31	2.23	2.16	2.11	2.07	2.03	1.98	1.93	1.88
20	4.35	3.49	3.10	2.87	2.71	2.60	2.51	2.45	2.39	2.35	2.28	2.20	2.12	2.08	2.04	1.99	1.95	1.90	1.84
21	4.32	3.47	3.07	2.84	2.68	2.57	2.49	2.42	2.37	2.32	2.25	2.18	2.10	2.05	2.01	1.96	1.92	1.87	1.81
22	4.30	3.44	3.05	2.82	2.66	2.55	2.46	2.40	2.34	2.30	2.23	2.15	2.07	2.03	1.98	1.91	1.89	1.84	1.78
23	4.28	3.42	3.03	2.80	2.64	2.53	2.44	2.37	2.32	2.27	2.20	2.13	2.05	2.01	1.96	1.91	1.86	1.81	1.76
24	4.26	3.40	3.01	2.78	2.62	2.51	2.42	2.36	2.30	2.25	2.18	2.11	2.03	1.98	1.94	1.89	1.84	1.79	1.73
25	4.24	3.39	2.99	2.76	2.60	2.49	2.40	2.34	2.28	2.24	2.16	2.09	2.01	1.96	1.92	1.87	1.82	1.77	1.71
26	4.23	3.37	2.98	2.74	2.59	2.47	2.39	2.32	2.27	2.22	2.15	2.07	1.99	1.95	1.90	1.85	1.80	1.75	1.69
27	4.21	3.35	2.96	2.73	2.57	2.46	2.37	2.31	2.25	2.20	2.13	2.06	1.97	1.93	1.88	1.84	1.79	1.73	1.67
28	4.20	3.34	2.95	2.71	2.56	2.45	2.36	2.29	2.24	2.19	2.12	2.04	1.96	1.91	1.87	1.82	1.77	1.71	1.65
29	4.18	3.33	2.93	2.70	2.55	2.43	2.35	2.28	2.22	2.18	2.10	2.03	1.94	1.90	1.85	1.81	1.75	1.70	1.64
30	4.17	3.32	2.92	2.69	2.53	2.42	2.33	2.27	2.21	2.16	2.09	2.01	1.93	1.89	1.84	1.79	1.74	1.68	1.62
40	4.08	3.23	2.84	2.61	2.45	2.34	2.25	2.18	2.12	2.08	2.00	1.92	1.84	1.79	1.74	1.69	1.64	1.58	1.51
60	4.00	3.15	2.76	2.53	2.37	2.25	2.17	2.10	2.04	1.99	1.92	1.84	1.75	1.70	1.65	1.59	1.53	1.47	1.39
120	3.92	3.07	2.68	2.45	2.29	2.17	2.09	2.02	1.96	1.91	1.83	1.75	1.66	1.61	1.55	1.50	1.43	1.35	1.25
∞	3.84	3.00	2.60	2.37	2.21	2.10	2.01	1.94	1.88	1.83	1.75	1.67	1.57	1.52	1.46	1.39	1.32	1.22	1.00

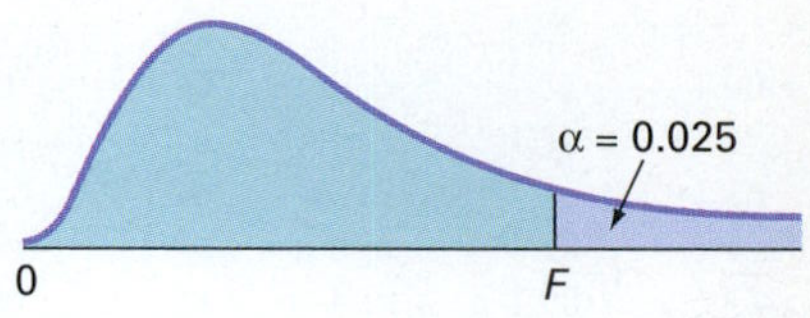

Cumulative Probabilities = 0.975																			
Upper-Tail Areas = 0.025																			
	Numerator, df_1																		
Denominator, df_2	**1**	**2**	**3**	**4**	**5**	**6**	**7**	**8**	**9**	**10**	**12**	**15**	**20**	**24**	**30**	**40**	**60**	**120**	**∞**
1	647.80	799.50	864.20	899.60	921.80	937.10	948.20	956.70	963.30	968.60	976.70	984.90	993.10	997.20	1,001.00	1,006.00	1,010.00	1,014.00	1,018.00
2	38.51	39.00	39.17	39.25	39.30	39.33	39.36	39.39	39.39	39.40	39.41	39.43	39.45	39.46	39.46	39.47	39.48	39.49	39.50
3	17.44	16.04	15.44	15.10	14.88	14.73	14.62	14.54	14.47	14.42	14.34	14.25	14.17	14.12	14.08	14.04	13.99	13.95	13.90
4	12.22	10.65	9.98	9.60	9.36	9.20	9.07	8.98	8.90	8.84	8.75	8.66	8.56	8.51	8.46	8.41	8.36	8.31	8.26
5	10.01	8.43	7.76	7.39	7.15	6.98	6.85	6.76	6.68	6.62	6.52	6.43	6.33	6.28	6.23	6.18	6.12	6.07	6.02
6	8.81	7.26	6.60	6.23	5.99	5.82	5.70	5.60	5.52	5.46	5.37	5.27	5.17	5.12	5.07	5.01	4.96	4.90	4.85
7	8.07	6.54	5.89	5.52	5.29	5.12	4.99	4.90	4.82	4.76	4.67	4.57	4.47	4.42	4.36	4.31	4.25	4.20	4.14
8	7.57	6.06	5.42	5.05	4.82	4.65	4.53	4.43	4.36	4.30	4.20	4.10	4.00	3.95	3.89	3.84	3.78	3.73	3.67
9	7.21	5.71	5.08	4.72	4.48	4.32	4.20	4.10	4.03	3.96	3.87	3.77	3.67	3.61	3.56	3.51	3.45	3.39	3.33
10	6.94	5.46	4.83	4.47	4.24	4.07	3.95	3.85	3.78	3.72	3.62	3.52	3.42	3.37	3.31	3.26	3.20	3.14	3.08
11	6.72	5.26	4.63	4.28	4.04	3.88	3.76	3.66	3.59	3.53	3.43	3.33	3.23	3.17	3.12	3.06	3.00	2.94	2.88
12	6.55	5.10	4.47	4.12	3.89	3.73	3.61	3.51	3.44	3.37	3.28	3.18	3.07	3.02	2.96	2.91	2.85	2.79	2.72
13	6.41	4.97	4.35	4.00	3.77	3.60	3.48	3.39	3.31	3.25	3.15	3.05	2.95	2.89	2.84	2.78	2.72	2.66	2.60
14	6.30	4.86	4.24	3.89	3.66	3.50	3.38	3.29	3.21	3.15	3.05	2.95	2.84	2.79	2.73	2.67	2.61	2.55	2.49
15	6.20	4.77	4.15	3.80	3.58	3.41	3.29	3.20	3.12	3.06	2.96	2.86	2.76	2.70	2.64	2.59	2.52	2.46	2.40
16	6.12	4.69	4.08	3.73	3.50	3.34	3.22	3.12	3.05	2.99	2.89	2.79	2.68	2.63	2.57	2.51	2.45	2.38	2.32
17	6.04	4.62	4.01	3.66	3.44	3.28	3.16	3.06	2.98	2.92	2.82	2.72	2.62	2.56	2.50	2.44	2.38	2.32	2.25
18	5.98	4.56	3.95	3.61	3.38	3.22	3.10	3.01	2.93	2.87	2.77	2.67	2.56	2.50	2.44	2.38	2.32	2.26	2.19
19	5.92	4.51	3.90	3.56	3.33	3.17	3.05	2.96	2.88	2.82	2.72	2.62	2.51	2.45	2.39	2.33	2.27	2.20	2.13
20	5.87	4.46	3.86	3.51	3.29	3.13	3.01	2.91	2.84	2.77	2.68	2.57	2.46	2.41	2.35	2.29	2.22	2.16	2.09
21	5.83	4.42	3.82	3.48	3.25	3.09	2.97	2.87	2.80	2.73	2.64	2.53	2.42	2.37	2.31	2.25	2.18	2.11	2.04
22	5.79	4.38	3.78	3.44	3.22	3.05	2.93	2.84	2.76	2.70	2.60	2.50	2.39	2.33	2.27	2.21	2.14	2.08	2.00
23	5.75	4.35	3.75	3.41	3.18	3.02	2.90	2.81	2.73	2.67	2.57	2.47	2.36	2.30	2.24	2.18	2.11	2.04	1.97
24	5.72	4.32	3.72	3.38	3.15	2.99	2.87	2.78	2.70	2.64	2.54	2.44	2.33	2.27	2.21	2.15	2.08	2.01	1.94
25	5.69	4.29	3.69	3.35	3.13	2.97	2.85	2.75	2.68	2.61	2.51	2.41	2.30	2.24	2.18	2.12	2.05	1.98	1.91
26	5.66	4.27	3.67	3.33	3.10	2.94	2.82	2.73	2.65	2.59	2.49	2.39	2.28	2.22	2.16	2.09	2.03	1.95	1.88
27	5.63	4.24	3.65	3.31	3.08	2.92	2.80	2.71	2.63	2.57	2.47	2.36	2.25	2.19	2.13	2.07	2.00	1.93	1.85
28	5.61	4.22	3.63	3.29	3.06	2.90	2.78	2.69	2.61	2.55	2.45	2.34	2.23	2.17	2.11	2.05	1.98	1.91	1.83
29	5.59	4.20	3.61	3.27	3.04	2.88	2.76	2.67	2.59	2.53	2.43	2.32	2.21	2.15	2.09	2.03	1.96	1.89	1.81
30	5.57	4.18	3.59	3.25	3.03	2.87	2.75	2.65	2.57	2.51	2.41	2.31	2.20	2.14	2.07	2.01	1.94	1.87	1.79
40	5.42	4.05	3.46	3.13	2.90	2.74	2.62	2.53	2.45	2.39	2.29	2.18	2.07	2.01	1.94	1.88	1.80	1.72	1.64
60	5.29	3.93	3.34	3.01	2.79	2.63	2.51	2.41	2.33	2.27	2.17	2.06	1.94	1.88	1.82	1.74	1.67	1.58	1.48
120	5.15	3.80	3.23	2.89	2.67	2.52	2.39	2.30	2.22	2.16	2.05	1.94	1.82	1.76	1.69	1.61	1.53	1.43	1.31
∞	5.02	3.69	3.12	2.79	2.57	2.41	2.29	2.19	2.11	2.05	1.94	1.83	1.71	1.64	1.57	1.48	1.39	1.27	1.00

continued

TABLE E.5
Critical Values of F (*continued*)

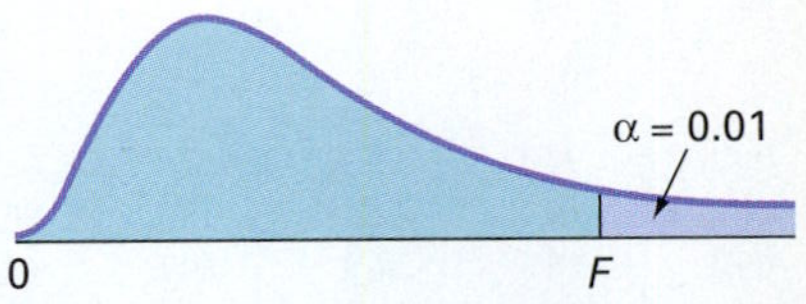

Denominator, df_2	Cumulative Probabilities = 0.99 / Upper-Tail Areas = 0.01 / Numerator, df_1: 1	2	3	4	5	6	7	8	9	10	12	15	20	24	30	40	60	120	∞
1	4,052.00	4,999.50	5,403.00	5,625.00	5,764.00	5,859.00	5,928.00	5,982.00	6,022.00	6,056.00	6,106.00	6,157.00	6,209.00	6,235.00	6,261.00	6,287.00	6,313.00	6,339.00	6,366.00
2	98.50	99.00	99.17	99.25	99.30	99.33	99.36	99.37	99.39	99.40	99.42	99.43	44.45	99.46	99.47	99.47	99.48	99.49	99.50
3	34.12	30.82	29.46	28.71	28.24	27.91	27.67	27.49	27.35	27.23	27.05	26.87	26.69	26.60	26.50	26.41	26.32	26.22	26.13
4	21.20	18.00	16.69	15.98	15.52	15.21	14.98	14.80	14.66	14.55	14.37	14.20	14.02	13.93	13.84	13.75	13.65	13.56	13.46
5	16.26	13.27	12.06	11.39	10.97	10.67	10.46	10.29	10.16	10.05	9.89	9.72	9.55	9.47	9.38	9.29	9.20	9.11	9.02
6	13.75	10.92	9.78	9.15	8.75	8.47	8.26	8.10	7.98	7.87	7.72	7.56	7.40	7.31	7.23	7.14	7.06	6.97	6.88
7	12.25	9.55	8.45	7.85	7.46	7.19	6.99	6.84	6.72	6.62	6.47	6.31	6.16	6.07	5.99	5.91	5.82	5.74	5.65
8	11.26	8.65	7.59	7.01	6.63	6.37	6.18	6.03	5.91	5.81	5.67	5.52	5.36	5.28	5.20	5.12	5.03	4.95	4.86
9	10.56	8.02	6.99	6.42	6.06	5.80	5.61	5.47	5.35	5.26	5.11	4.96	4.81	4.73	4.65	4.57	4.48	4.40	4.31
10	10.04	7.56	6.55	5.99	5.64	5.39	5.20	5.06	4.94	4.85	4.71	4.56	4.41	4.33	4.25	4.17	4.08	4.00	3.91
11	9.65	7.21	6.22	5.67	5.32	5.07	4.89	4.74	4.63	4.54	4.40	4.25	4.10	4.02	3.94	3.86	3.78	3.69	3.60
12	9.33	6.93	5.95	5.41	5.06	4.82	4.64	4.50	4.39	4.30	4.16	4.01	3.86	3.78	3.70	3.62	3.54	3.45	3.36
13	9.07	6.70	5.74	5.21	4.86	4.62	4.44	4.30	4.19	4.10	3.96	3.82	3.66	3.59	3.51	3.43	3.34	3.25	3.17
14	8.86	6.51	5.56	5.04	4.69	4.46	4.28	4.14	4.03	3.94	3.80	3.66	3.51	3.43	3.35	3.27	3.18	3.09	3.00
15	8.68	6.36	5.42	4.89	4.56	4.32	4.14	4.00	3.89	3.80	3.67	3.52	3.37	3.29	3.21	3.13	3.05	2.96	2.87
16	8.53	6.23	5.29	4.77	4.44	4.20	4.03	3.89	3.78	3.69	3.55	3.41	3.26	3.18	3.10	3.02	2.93	2.81	2.75
17	8.40	6.11	5.18	4.67	4.34	4.10	3.93	3.79	3.68	3.59	3.46	3.31	3.16	3.08	3.00	2.92	2.83	2.75	2.65
18	8.29	6.01	5.09	4.58	4.25	4.01	3.84	3.71	3.60	3.51	3.37	3.23	3.08	3.00	2.92	2.84	2.75	2.66	2.57
19	8.18	5.93	5.01	4.50	4.17	3.94	3.77	3.63	3.52	3.43	3.30	3.15	3.00	2.92	2.84	2.76	2.67	2.58	2.49
20	8.10	5.85	4.94	4.43	4.10	3.87	3.70	3.56	3.46	3.37	3.23	3.09	2.94	2.86	2.78	2.69	2.61	2.52	2.42
21	8.02	5.78	4.87	4.37	4.04	3.81	3.64	3.51	3.40	3.31	3.17	3.03	2.88	2.80	2.72	2.64	2.55	2.46	2.36
22	7.95	5.72	4.82	4.31	3.99	3.76	3.59	3.45	3.35	3.26	3.12	2.98	2.83	2.75	2.67	2.58	2.50	2.40	2.31
23	7.88	5.66	4.76	4.26	3.94	3.71	3.54	3.41	3.30	3.21	3.07	2.93	2.78	2.70	2.62	2.54	2.45	2.35	2.26
24	7.82	5.61	4.72	4.22	3.90	3.67	3.50	3.36	3.26	3.17	3.03	2.89	2.74	2.66	2.58	2.49	2.40	2.31	2.21
25	7.77	5.57	4.68	4.18	3.85	3.63	3.46	3.32	3.22	3.13	2.99	2.85	2.70	2.62	2.54	2.45	2.36	2.27	2.17
26	7.72	5.53	4.64	4.14	3.82	3.59	3.42	3.29	3.18	3.09	2.96	2.81	2.66	2.58	2.50	2.42	2.33	2.23	2.13
27	7.68	5.49	4.60	4.11	3.78	3.56	3.39	3.26	3.15	3.06	2.93	2.78	2.63	2.55	2.47	2.38	2.29	2.20	2.10
28	7.64	5.45	4.57	4.07	3.75	3.53	3.36	3.23	3.12	3.03	2.90	2.75	2.60	2.52	2.44	2.35	2.26	2.17	2.06
29	7.60	5.42	4.54	4.04	3.73	3.50	3.33	3.20	3.09	3.00	2.87	2.73	2.57	2.49	2.41	2.33	2.23	2.14	2.03
30	7.56	5.39	4.51	4.02	3.70	3.47	3.30	3.17	3.07	2.98	2.84	2.70	2.55	2.47	2.39	2.30	2.21	2.11	2.01
40	7.31	5.18	4.31	3.83	3.51	3.29	3.12	2.99	2.89	2.80	2.66	2.52	2.37	2.29	2.20	2.11	2.02	1.92	1.80
60	7.08	4.98	4.13	3.65	3.34	3.12	2.95	2.82	2.72	2.63	2.50	2.35	2.20	2.12	2.03	1.94	1.84	1.73	1.60
120	6.85	4.79	3.95	3.48	3.17	2.96	2.79	2.66	2.56	2.47	2.34	2.19	2.03	1.95	1.86	1.76	1.66	1.53	1.38
∞	6.63	4.61	3.78	3.32	3.02	2.80	2.64	2.51	2.41	2.32	2.18	2.04	1.88	1.79	1.70	1.59	1.47	1.32	1.00

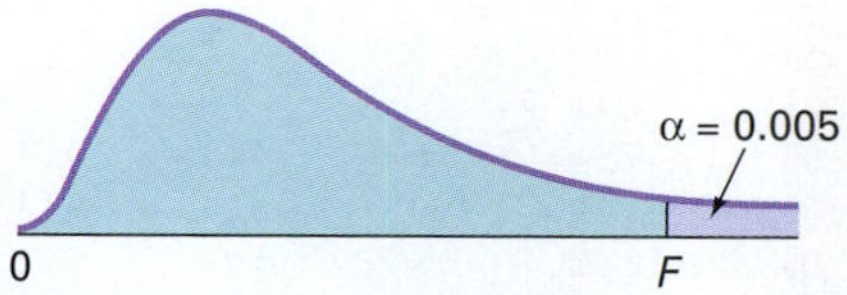

Cumulative Probabilities = 0.995																			
Upper-Tail Areas = 0.005																			
	Numerator, df_1																		
Denominator, df_2	1	2	3	4	5	6	7	8	9	10	12	15	20	24	30	40	60	120	∞
1	16,211.00	20,000.00	21,615.00	22,500.00	23,056.00	23,437.00	23,715.00	23,925.00	24,091.00	24,224.00	24,426.00	24,630.00	24,836.00	24,910.00	25,044.00	25,148.00	25,253.00	25,359.00	25,465.00
2	198.50	199.00	199.20	199.20	199.30	199.30	199.40	199.40	199.40	199.40	199.40	199.40	199.40	199.50	199.50	199.50	199.50	199.50	199.50
3	55.55	49.80	47.47	46.19	45.39	44.84	44.43	44.13	43.88	43.69	43.39	43.08	42.78	42.62	42.47	42.31	42.15	41.99	41.83
4	31.33	26.28	24.26	23.15	22.46	21.97	21.62	21.35	21.14	20.97	20.70	20.44	20.17	20.03	19.89	19.75	19.61	19.47	19.32
5	22.78	18.31	16.53	15.56	14.94	14.51	14.20	13.96	13.77	13.62	13.38	13.15	12.90	12.78	12.66	12.53	12.40	12.27	12.11
6	18.63	14.54	12.92	12.03	11.46	11.07	10.79	10.57	10.39	10.25	10.03	9.81	9.59	9.47	9.36	9.24	9.12	9.00	8.88
7	16.24	12.40	10.88	10.05	9.52	9.16	8.89	8.68	8.51	8.38	8.18	7.97	7.75	7.65	7.53	7.42	7.31	7.19	7.08
8	14.69	11.04	9.60	8.81	8.30	7.95	7.69	7.50	7.34	7.21	7.01	6.81	6.61	6.50	6.40	6.29	6.18	6.06	5.95
9	13.61	10.11	8.72	7.96	7.47	7.13	6.88	6.69	6.54	6.42	6.23	6.03	5.83	5.73	5.62	5.52	5.41	5.30	5.19
10	12.83	9.43	8.08	7.34	6.87	6.54	6.30	6.12	5.97	5.85	5.66	5.47	5.27	5.17	5.07	4.97	4.86	4.75	4.61
11	12.23	8.91	7.60	6.88	6.42	6.10	5.86	5.68	5.54	5.42	5.24	5.05	4.86	4.75	4.65	4.55	4.44	4.34	4.23
12	11.75	8.51	7.23	6.52	6.07	5.76	5.52	5.35	5.20	5.09	4.91	4.72	4.53	4.43	4.33	4.23	4.12	4.01	3.90
13	11.37	8.19	6.93	6.23	5.79	5.48	5.25	5.08	4.94	4.82	4.64	4.46	4.27	4.17	4.07	3.97	3.87	3.76	3.65
14	11.06	7.92	6.68	6.00	5.56	5.26	5.03	4.86	4.72	4.60	4.43	4.25	4.06	3.96	3.86	3.76	3.66	3.55	3.41
15	10.80	7.70	6.48	5.80	5.37	5.07	4.85	4.67	4.54	4.42	4.25	4.07	3.88	3.79	3.69	3.58	3.48	3.37	3.26
16	10.58	7.51	6.30	5.64	5.21	4.91	4.69	4.52	4.38	4.27	4.10	3.92	3.73	3.64	3.54	3.44	3.33	3.22	3.11
17	10.38	7.35	6.16	5.50	5.07	4.78	4.56	4.39	4.25	4.14	3.97	3.79	3.61	3.51	3.41	3.31	3.21	3.10	2.98
18	10.22	7.21	6.03	5.37	4.96	4.66	4.44	4.28	4.14	4.03	3.86	3.68	3.50	3.40	3.30	3.20	3.10	2.99	2.87
19	10.07	7.09	5.92	5.27	4.85	4.56	4.34	4.18	4.04	3.93	3.76	3.59	3.40	3.31	3.21	3.11	3.00	2.89	2.78
20	9.94	6.99	5.82	5.17	4.76	4.47	4.26	4.09	3.96	3.85	3.68	3.50	3.32	3.22	3.12	3.02	2.92	2.81	2.69
21	9.83	6.89	5.73	5.09	4.68	4.39	4.18	4.02	3.88	3.77	3.60	3.43	3.24	3.15	3.05	2.95	2.84	2.73	2.61
22	9.73	6.81	5.65	5.02	4.61	4.32	4.11	3.94	3.81	3.70	3.54	3.36	3.18	3.08	2.98	2.88	2.77	2.66	2.55
23	9.63	6.73	5.58	4.95	4.54	4.26	4.05	3.88	3.75	3.64	3.47	3.30	3.12	3.02	2.92	2.82	2.71	2.60	2.48
24	9.55	6.66	5.52	4.89	4.49	4.20	3.99	3.83	3.69	3.59	3.42	3.25	3.06	2.97	2.87	2.77	2.66	2.55	2.43
25	9.48	6.60	5.46	4.84	4.43	4.15	3.94	3.78	3.64	3.54	3.37	3.20	3.01	2.92	2.82	2.72	2.61	2.50	2.38
26	9.41	6.54	5.41	4.79	4.38	4.10	3.89	3.73	3.60	3.49	3.33	3.15	2.97	2.87	2.77	2.67	2.56	2.45	2.33
27	9.34	6.49	5.36	4.74	4.34	4.06	3.85	3.69	3.56	3.45	3.28	3.11	2.93	2.83	2.73	2.63	2.52	2.41	2.29
28	9.28	6.44	5.32	4.70	4.30	4.02	3.81	3.65	3.52	3.41	3.25	3.07	2.89	2.79	2.69	2.59	2.48	2.37	2.25
29	9.23	6.40	5.28	4.66	4.26	3.98	3.77	3.61	3.48	3.38	3.21	3.04	2.86	2.76	2.66	2.56	2.45	2.33	2.21
30	9.18	6.35	5.24	4.62	4.23	3.95	3.74	3.58	3.45	3.34	3.18	3.01	2.82	2.73	2.63	2.52	2.42	2.30	2.18
40	8.83	6.07	4.98	4.37	3.99	3.71	3.51	3.35	3.22	3.12	2.95	2.78	2.60	2.50	2.40	2.30	2.18	2.06	1.93
60	8.49	5.79	4.73	4.14	3.76	3.49	3.29	3.13	3.01	2.90	2.74	2.57	2.39	2.29	2.19	2.08	1.96	1.83	1.69
120	8.18	5.54	4.50	3.92	3.55	3.28	3.09	2.93	2.81	2.71	2.54	2.37	2.19	2.09	1.98	1.87	1.75	1.61	1.43
∞	7.88	5.30	4.28	3.72	3.35	3.09	2.90	2.74	2.62	2.52	2.36	2.19	2.00	1.90	1.79	1.67	1.53	1.36	1.00

Source: Reprinted from E. S. Pearson and H. O. Hartley, eds., *Biometrika Tables for Statisticians,* 3rd ed., 1966, by permission of the *Biometrika* Trustees.

TABLE E.6
Lower and Upper Critical Values, T_1, of the Wilcoxon Rank Sum Test

	α		n_1						
n_2	One-tail	Two-tail	4	5	6	7	8	9	10
4	0.05	0.10	11,25						
	0.025	0.05	10,26						
	0.01	0.02	—,—						
	0.005	0.01	—,—						
5	0.05	0.10	12,28	19,36					
	0.025	0.05	11,29	17,38					
	0.01	0.02	10,30	16,39					
	0.005	0.01	—,—	15,40					
6	0.05	0.10	13,31	20,40	28,50				
	0.025	0.05	12,32	18,42	26,52				
	0.01	0.02	11,33	17,43	24,54				
	0.005	0.01	10,34	16,44	23,55				
7	0.05	0.10	14,34	21,44	29,55	39,66			
	0.025	0.05	13,35	20,45	27,57	36,69			
	0.01	0.02	11,37	18,47	25,59	34,71			
	0.005	0.01	10,38	16,49	24,60	32,73			
8	0.05	0.10	15,37	23,47	31,59	41,71	51,85		
	0.025	0.05	14,38	21,49	29,61	38,74	49,87		
	0.01	0.02	12,40	19,51	27,63	35,77	45,91		
	0.005	0.01	11,41	17,53	25,65	34,78	43,93		
9	0.05	0.10	16,40	24,51	33,63	43,76	54,90	66,105	
	0.025	0.05	14,42	22,53	31,65	40,79	51,93	62,109	
	0.01	0.02	13,43	20,55	28,68	37,82	47,97	59,112	
	0.005	0.01	11,45	18,57	26,70	35,84	45,99	56,115	
10	0.05	0.10	17,43	26,54	35,67	45,81	56,96	69,111	82,128
	0.025	0.05	15,45	23,57	32,70	42,84	53,99	65,115	78,132
	0.01	0.02	13,47	21,59	29,73	39,87	49,103	61,119	74,136
	0.005	0.01	12,48	19,61	27,75	37,89	47,105	58,122	71,139

Source: Adapted from Table 1 of F. Wilcoxon and R. A. Wilcox, *Some Rapid Approximate Statistical Procedures* (Pearl River, NY: Lederle Laboratories, 1964), with permission of the American Cyanamid Company.

TABLE E.7

Critical Values of the Studentized Range, Q

Denominator, *df*	Upper 5% Points ($\alpha = 0.05$) Numerator, *df* 2	3	4	5	6	7	8	9	10	11	12	13	14	15	16	17	18	19	20
1	18.00	27.00	32.80	37.10	40.40	43.10	45.40	47.40	49.10	50.60	52.00	53.20	54.30	55.40	56.30	57.20	58.00	58.80	59.60
2	6.09	8.30	9.80	10.90	11.70	12.40	13.00	13.50	14.00	14.40	14.70	15.10	15.40	15.70	15.90	16.10	16.40	16.60	16.80
3	4.50	5.91	6.82	7.50	8.04	8.48	8.85	9.18	9.46	9.72	9.95	10.15	10.35	10.52	10.69	10.84	10.98	11.11	11.24
4	3.93	5.04	5.76	6.29	6.71	7.05	7.35	7.60	7.83	8.03	8.21	8.37	8.52	8.66	8.79	8.91	9.03	9.13	9.23
5	3.64	4.60	5.22	5.67	6.03	6.33	6.58	6.80	6.99	7.17	7.32	7.47	7.60	7.72	7.83	7.93	8.03	8.12	8.21
6	3.46	4.34	4.90	5.31	5.63	5.89	6.12	6.32	6.49	6.65	6.79	6.92	7.03	7.14	7.24	7.34	7.43	7.51	7.59
7	3.34	4.16	4.68	5.06	5.36	5.61	5.82	6.00	6.16	6.30	6.43	6.55	6.66	6.76	6.85	6.94	7.02	7.09	7.17
8	3.26	4.04	4.53	4.89	5.17	5.40	5.60	5.77	5.92	6.05	6.18	6.29	6.39	6.48	6.57	6.65	6.73	6.80	6.87
9	3.20	3.95	4.42	4.76	5.02	5.24	5.43	5.60	5.74	5.87	5.98	6.09	6.19	6.28	6.36	6.44	6.51	6.58	6.64
10	3.15	3.88	4.33	4.65	4.91	5.12	5.30	5.46	5.60	5.72	5.83	5.93	6.03	6.11	6.20	6.27	6.34	6.40	6.47
11	3.11	3.82	4.26	4.57	4.82	5.03	5.20	5.35	5.49	5.61	5.71	5.81	5.90	5.99	6.06	6.14	6.20	6.26	6.33
12	3.08	3.77	4.20	4.51	4.75	4.95	5.12	5.27	5.40	5.51	5.62	5.71	5.80	5.88	5.95	6.03	6.09	6.15	6.21
13	3.06	3.73	4.15	4.45	4.69	4.88	5.05	5.19	5.32	5.43	5.53	5.63	5.71	5.79	5.86	5.93	6.00	6.05	6.11
14	3.03	3.70	4.11	4.41	4.64	4.83	4.99	5.13	5.25	5.36	5.46	5.55	5.64	5.72	5.79	5.85	5.92	5.97	6.03
15	3.01	3.67	4.08	4.37	4.60	4.78	4.94	5.08	5.20	5.31	5.40	5.49	5.58	5.65	5.72	5.79	5.85	5.90	5.96
16	3.00	3.65	4.05	4.33	4.56	4.74	4.90	5.03	5.15	5.26	5.35	5.44	5.52	5.59	5.66	5.72	5.79	5.84	5.90
17	2.98	3.63	4.02	4.30	4.52	4.71	4.86	4.99	5.11	5.21	5.31	5.39	5.47	5.55	5.61	5.68	5.74	5.79	5.84
18	2.97	3.61	4.00	4.28	4.49	4.67	4.82	4.96	5.07	5.17	5.27	5.35	5.43	5.50	5.57	5.63	5.69	5.74	5.79
19	2.96	3.59	3.98	4.25	4.47	4.65	4.79	4.92	5.04	5.14	5.23	5.32	5.39	5.46	5.53	5.59	5.65	5.70	5.75
20	2.95	3.58	3.96	4.23	4.45	4.62	4.77	4.90	5.01	5.11	5.20	5.28	5.36	5.43	5.49	5.55	5.61	5.66	5.71
24	2.92	3.53	3.90	4.17	4.37	4.54	4.68	4.81	4.92	5.01	5.10	5.18	5.25	5.32	5.38	5.44	5.50	5.54	5.59
30	2.89	3.49	3.84	4.10	4.30	4.46	4.60	4.72	4.83	4.92	5.00	5.08	5.15	5.21	5.27	5.33	5.38	5.43	5.48
40	2.86	3.44	3.79	4.04	4.23	4.39	4.52	4.63	4.74	4.82	4.91	4.98	5.05	5.11	5.16	5.22	5.27	5.31	5.36
60	2.83	3.40	3.74	3.98	4.16	4.31	4.44	4.55	4.65	4.73	4.81	4.88	4.94	5.00	5.06	5.11	5.16	5.20	5.24
120	2.80	3.36	3.69	3.92	4.10	4.24	4.36	4.48	4.56	4.64	4.72	4.78	4.84	4.90	4.95	5.00	5.05	5.09	5.13
∞	2.77	3.31	3.63	3.86	4.03	4.17	4.29	4.39	4.47	4.55	4.62	4.68	4.74	4.80	4.85	4.89	4.93	4.97	5.01

continued

TABLE E.7

Critical Values of the Studentized Range, Q

Upper 1% Points ($\alpha = 0.01$)

Denominator, *df*	Numerator, *df* 2	3	4	5	6	7	8	9	10	11	12	13	14	15	16	17	18	19	20
1	90.00	135.00	164.00	186.00	202.00	216.00	227.00	237.00	246.00	253.00	260.00	266.00	272.00	277.00	282.00	286.00	290.00	294.00	298.00
2	14.00	19.00	22.30	24.70	26.60	28.20	29.50	30.70	31.70	32.60	33.40	34.10	34.80	35.40	36.00	36.50	37.00	37.50	37.90
3	8.26	10.60	12.20	13.30	14.20	15.00	15.60	16.20	16.70	17.10	17.50	17.90	18.20	18.50	18.80	19.10	19.30	19.50	19.80
4	6.51	8.12	9.17	9.96	10.60	11.10	11.50	11.90	12.30	12.60	12.80	13.10	13.30	13.50	13.70	13.90	14.10	14.20	14.40
5	5.70	6.97	7.80	8.42	8.91	9.32	9.67	9.97	10.24	10.48	10.70	10.89	11.08	11.24	11.40	11.55	11.68	11.81	11.93
6	5.24	6.33	7.03	7.56	7.97	8.32	8.61	8.87	9.10	9.30	9.49	9.65	9.81	9.95	10.08	10.21	10.32	10.43	10.54
7	4.95	5.92	6.54	7.01	7.37	7.68	7.94	8.17	8.37	8.55	8.71	8.86	9.00	9.12	9.24	9.35	9.46	9.55	9.65
8	4.74	5.63	6.20	6.63	6.96	7.24	7.47	7.68	7.87	8.03	8.18	8.31	8.44	8.55	8.66	8.76	8.85	8.94	9.03
9	4.60	5.43	5.96	6.35	6.66	6.91	7.13	7.32	7.49	7.65	7.78	7.91	8.03	8.13	8.23	8.32	8.41	8.49	8.57
10	4.48	5.27	5.77	6.14	6.43	6.67	6.87	7.05	7.21	7.36	7.48	7.60	7.71	7.81	7.91	7.99	8.07	8.15	8.22
11	4.39	5.14	5.62	5.97	6.26	6.48	6.67	6.84	6.99	7.13	7.25	7.36	7.46	7.56	7.65	7.73	7.81	7.88	7.95
12	4.32	5.04	5.50	5.84	6.10	6.32	6.51	6.67	6.81	6.94	7.06	7.17	7.26	7.36	7.44	7.52	7.59	7.66	7.73
13	4.26	4.96	5.40	5.73	5.98	6.19	6.37	6.53	6.67	6.79	6.90	7.01	7.10	7.19	7.27	7.34	7.42	7.48	7.55
14	4.21	4.89	5.32	5.63	5.88	6.08	6.26	6.41	6.54	6.66	6.77	6.87	6.96	7.05	7.12	7.20	7.27	7.33	7.39
15	4.17	4.83	5.25	5.56	5.80	5.99	6.16	6.31	6.44	6.55	6.66	6.76	6.84	6.93	7.00	7.07	7.14	7.20	7.26
16	4.13	4.78	5.19	5.49	5.72	5.92	6.08	6.22	6.35	6.46	6.56	6.66	6.74	6.82	6.90	6.97	7.03	7.09	7.15
17	4.10	4.74	5.14	5.43	5.66	5.85	6.01	6.15	6.27	6.38	6.48	6.57	6.66	6.73	6.80	6.87	6.94	7.00	7.05
18	4.07	4.70	5.09	5.38	5.60	5.79	5.94	6.08	6.20	6.31	6.41	6.50	6.58	6.65	6.72	6.79	6.85	6.91	6.96
19	4.05	4.67	5.05	5.33	5.55	5.73	5.89	6.02	6.14	6.25	6.34	6.43	6.51	6.58	6.65	6.72	6.78	6.84	6.89
20	4.02	4.64	5.02	5.29	5.51	5.69	5.84	5.97	6.09	6.19	6.29	6.37	6.45	6.52	6.59	6.65	6.71	6.76	6.82
24	3.96	4.54	4.91	5.17	5.37	5.54	5.69	5.81	5.92	6.02	6.11	6.19	6.26	6.33	6.39	6.45	6.51	5.56	6.61
30	3.89	4.45	4.80	5.05	5.24	5.40	5.54	5.65	5.76	5.85	5.93	6.01	6.08	6.14	6.20	6.26	6.31	6.36	6.41
40	3.82	4.37	4.70	4.93	5.11	5.27	5.39	5.50	5.60	5.69	5.77	5.84	5.90	5.96	6.02	6.07	6.12	6.17	6.21
60	3.76	4.28	4.60	4.82	4.99	5.13	5.25	5.36	5.45	5.53	5.60	5.67	5.73	5.79	5.84	5.89	5.93	5.98	6.02
120	3.70	4.20	4.50	4.71	4.87	5.01	5.12	5.21	5.30	5.38	5.44	5.51	5.56	5.61	5.66	5.71	5.75	5.79	5.83
∞	3.64	4.12	4.40	4.60	4.76	4.88	4.99	5.08	5.16	5.23	5.29	5.35	5.40	5.45	5.49	5.54	5.57	5.61	5.65

Source: Reprinted from E. S. Pearson and H. O. Hartley, eds., Table 29 of *Biometrika Tables for Statisticians,* Vol. 1, 3rd ed., 1966, by permission of the *Biometrika* Trustees, London.

TABLE E.8

Critical Values, d_L and d_U, of the Durbin-Watson Statistic, D (Critical Values Are One-Sided)[a]

	$\alpha = 0.05$										$\alpha = 0.01$									
	$k = 1$		$k = 2$		$k = 3$		$k = 4$		$k = 5$		$k = 1$		$k = 2$		$k = 3$		$k = 4$		$k = 5$	
n	d_L	d_U	d_L	d_U	d_L	d_U	d_L	d_U	d_L	d_U	d_L	d_U	d_L	d_U	d_L	d_U	d_L	d_U	d_L	d_U
15	1.08	1.36	.95	1.54	.82	1.75	.69	1.97	.56	2.21	.81	1.07	.70	1.25	.59	1.46	.49	1.70	.39	1.96
16	1.10	1.37	.98	1.54	.86	1.73	.74	1.93	.62	2.15	.84	1.09	.74	1.25	.63	1.44	.53	1.66	.44	1.90
17	1.13	1.38	1.02	1.54	.90	1.71	.78	1.90	.67	2.10	.87	1.10	.77	1.25	.67	1.43	.57	1.63	.48	1.85
18	1.16	1.39	1.05	1.53	.93	1.69	.82	1.87	.71	2.06	.90	1.12	.80	1.26	.71	1.42	.61	1.60	.52	1.80
19	1.18	1.40	1.08	1.53	.97	1.68	.86	1.85	.75	2.02	.93	1.13	.83	1.26	.74	1.41	.65	1.58	.56	1.77
20	1.20	1.41	1.10	1.54	1.00	1.68	.90	1.83	.79	1.99	.95	1.15	.86	1.27	.77	1.41	.68	1.57	.60	1.74
21	1.22	1.42	1.13	1.54	1.03	1.67	.93	1.81	.83	1.96	.97	1.16	.89	1.27	.80	1.41	.72	1.55	.63	1.71
22	1.24	1.43	1.15	1.54	1.05	1.66	.96	1.80	.86	1.94	1.00	1.17	.91	1.28	.83	1.40	.75	1.54	.66	1.69
23	1.26	1.44	1.17	1.54	1.08	1.66	.99	1.79	.90	1.92	1.02	1.19	.94	1.29	.86	1.40	.77	1.53	.70	1.67
24	1.27	1.45	1.19	1.55	1.10	1.66	1.01	1.78	.93	1.90	1.04	1.20	.96	1.30	.88	1.41	.80	1.53	.72	1.66
25	1.29	1.45	1.21	1.55	1.12	1.66	1.04	1.77	.95	1.89	1.05	1.21	.98	1.30	.90	1.41	.83	1.52	.75	1.65
26	1.30	1.46	1.22	1.55	1.14	1.65	1.06	1.76	.98	1.88	1.07	1.22	1.00	1.31	.93	1.41	.85	1.52	.78	1.64
27	1.32	1.47	1.24	1.56	1.16	1.65	1.08	1.76	1.01	1.86	1.09	1.23	1.02	1.32	.95	1.41	.88	1.51	.81	1.63
28	.33	1.48	1.26	1.56	1.18	1.65	1.10	1.75	1.03	1.85	1.10	1.24	1.04	1.32	.97	1.41	.90	1.51	.83	1.62
29	1.34	1.48	1.27	1.56	1.20	1.65	1.12	1.74	1.05	1.84	1.12	1.25	1.05	1.33	.99	1.42	.92	1.51	.85	1.61
30	1.35	1.49	1.28	1.57	1.21	1.65	1.14	1.74	1.07	1.83	1.13	1.26	1.07	1.34	1.01	1.42	.94	1.51	.88	1.61
31	1.36	1.50	1.30	1.57	1.23	1.65	1.16	1.74	1.09	1.83	1.15	1.27	1.08	1.34	1.02	1.42	.96	1.51	.90	1.60
32	1.37	1.50	1.31	1.57	1.24	1.65	1.18	1.73	1.11	1.82	1.16	1.28	1.10	1.35	1.04	1.43	.98	1.51	.92	1.60
33	1.38	1.51	1.32	1.58	1.26	1.65	1.19	1.73	1.13	1.81	1.17	1.29	1.11	1.36	1.05	1.43	1.00	1.51	.94	1.59
34	1.39	1.51	1.33	1.58	1.27	1.65	1.21	1.73	1.15	1.81	1.18	1.30	1.13	1.36	1.07	1.43	1.01	1.51	.95	1.59
35	1.40	1.52	1.34	1.58	1.28	1.65	1.22	1.73	1.16	1.80	1.19	1.31	1.14	1.37	1.08	1.44	1.03	1.51	.97	1.59
36	1.41	1.52	1.35	1.59	1.29	1.65	1.24	1.73	1.18	1.80	1.21	1.32	1.15	1.38	1.10	1.44	1.04	1.51	.99	1.59
37	1.42	1.53	1.36	1.59	1.31	1.66	1.25	1.72	1.19	1.80	1.22	1.32	1.16	1.38	1.11	1.45	1.06	1.51	1.00	1.59
38	1.43	1.54	1.37	1.59	1.32	1.66	1.26	1.72	1.21	1.79	1.23	1.33	1.18	1.39	1.12	1.45	1.07	1.52	1.02	1.58
39	1.43	1.54	1.38	1.60	1.33	1.66	1.27	1.72	1.22	1.79	1.24	1.34	1.19	1.39	1.14	1.45	1.09	1.52	1.03	1.58
40	1.44	1.54	1.39	1.60	1.34	1.66	1.29	1.72	1.23	1.79	1.25	1.34	1.20	1.40	1.15	1.46	1.10	1.52	1.05	1.58
45	1.48	1.57	1.43	1.62	1.38	1.67	1.34	1.72	1.29	1.78	1.29	1.38	1.24	1.42	1.20	1.48	1.16	1.53	1.11	1.58
50	1.50	1.59	1.46	1.63	1.42	1.67	1.38	1.72	1.34	1.77	1.32	1.40	1.28	1.45	1.24	1.49	1.20	1.54	1.16	1.59
55	1.53	1.60	1.49	1.64	1.45	1.68	1.41	1.72	1.38	1.77	1.36	1.43	1.32	1.47	1.28	1.51	1.25	1.55	1.21	1.59
60	1.55	1.62	1.51	1.65	1.48	1.69	1.44	1.73	1.41	1.77	1.38	1.45	1.35	1.48	1.32	1.52	1.28	1.56	1.25	1.60
65	1.57	1.63	1.54	1.66	1.50	1.70	1.47	1.73	1.44	1.77	1.41	1.47	1.38	1.50	1.35	1.53	1.31	1.57	1.28	1.61
70	1.58	1.64	1.55	1.67	1.52	1.70	1.49	1.74	1.46	1.77	1.43	1.49	1.40	1.52	1.37	1.55	1.34	1.58	1.31	1.61
75	1.60	1.65	1.57	1.68	1.54	1.71	1.51	1.74	1.49	1.77	1.45	1.50	1.42	1.53	1.39	1.56	1.37	1.59	1.34	1.62
80	1.61	1.66	1.59	1.69	1.56	1.72	1.53	1.74	1.51	1.77	1.47	1.52	1.44	1.54	1.42	1.57	1.39	1.60	1.36	1.62
85	1.62	1.67	1.60	1.70	1.57	1.72	1.55	1.75	1.52	1.77	1.48	1.53	1.46	1.55	1.43	1.58	1.41	1.60	1.39	1.63
90	1.63	1.68	1.61	1.70	1.59	1.73	1.57	1.75	1.54	1.78	1.50	1.54	1.47	1.56	1.45	1.59	1.43	1.61	1.41	1.64
95	1.64	1.69	1.62	1.71	1.60	1.73	1.58	1.75	1.56	1.78	1.51	1.55	1.49	1.57	1.47	1.60	1.45	1.62	1.42	1.64
100	1.65	1.69	1.63	1.72	1.61	1.74	1.59	1.76	1.57	1.78	1.52	1.56	1.50	1.58	1.48	1.60	1.46	1.63	1.44	1.65

[a] n = number of observations; k = number of independent variables.

Source: This table is reproduced from *Biometrika,* 41 (1951): pp. 173 and 175, with the permission of the *Biometrika* Trustees.

TABLE E.9
Control Chart Factors

Number of Observations in Sample/Subgroup (n)	d_2	d_3	D_3	D_4	A_2
2	1.128	0.853	0	3.267	1.880
3	1.693	0.888	0	2.575	1.023
4	2.059	0.880	0	2.282	0.729
5	2.326	0.864	0	2.114	0.577
6	2.534	0.848	0	2.004	0.483
7	2.704	0.833	0.076	1.924	0.419
8	2.847	0.820	0.136	1.864	0.373
9	2.970	0.808	0.184	1.816	0.337
10	3.078	0.797	0.223	1.777	0.308
11	3.173	0.787	0.256	1.744	0.285
12	3.258	0.778	0.283	1.717	0.266
13	3.336	0.770	0.307	1.693	0.249
14	3.407	0.763	0.328	1.672	0.235
15	3.472	0.756	0.347	1.653	0.223
16	3.532	0.750	0.363	1.637	0.212
17	3.588	0.744	0.378	1.622	0.203
18	3.640	0.739	0.391	1.609	0.194
19	3.689	0.733	0.404	1.596	0.187
20	3.735	0.729	0.415	1.585	0.180
21	3.778	0.724	0.425	1.575	0.173
22	3.819	0.720	0.435	1.565	0.167
23	3.858	0.716	0.443	1.557	0.162
24	3.895	0.712	0.452	1.548	0.157
25	3.931	0.708	0.459	1.541	0.153

Source: Reprinted from *ASTM-STP 15D* by kind permission of the American Society for Testing and Materials.

TABLE E.10
The Standardized Normal Distribution

Entry represents area under the standardized normal distribution from the mean to Z

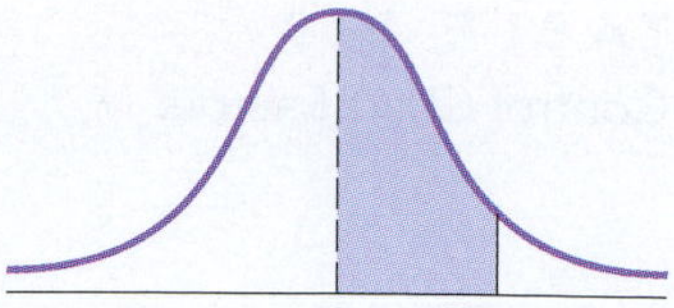

Z	.00	.01	.02	.03	.04	.05	.06	.07	.08	.09
0.0	.0000	.0040	.0080	.0120	.0160	.0199	.0239	.0279	.0319	.0359
0.1	.0398	.0438	.0478	.0517	.0557	.0596	.0636	.0675	.0714	.0753
0.2	.0793	.0832	.0871	.0910	.0948	.0987	.1026	.1064	.1103	.1141
0.3	.1179	.1217	.1255	.1293	.1331	.1368	.1406	.1443	.1480	.1517
0.4	.1554	.1591	.1628	.1664	.1700	.1736	.1772	.1808	.1844	.1879
0.5	.1915	.1950	.1985	.2019	.2054	.2088	.2123	.2157	.2190	.2224
0.6	.2257	.2291	.2324	.2357	.2389	.2422	.2454	.2486	.2518	.2549
0.7	.2580	.2612	.2642	.2673	.2704	.2734	.2764	.2794	.2823	.2852
0.8	.2881	.2910	.2939	.2967	.2995	.3023	.3051	.3078	.3106	.3133
0.9	.3159	.3186	.3212	.3238	.3264	.3289	.3315	.3340	.3365	.3389
1.0	.3413	.3438	.3461	.3485	.3508	.3531	.3554	.3577	.3599	.3621
1.1	.3643	.3665	.3686	.3708	.3729	.3749	.3770	.3790	.3810	.3830
1.2	.3849	.3869	.3888	.3907	.3925	.3944	.3962	.3980	.3997	.4015
1.3	.4032	.4049	.4066	.4082	.4099	.4115	.4131	.4147	.4162	.4177
1.4	.4192	.4207	.4222	.4236	.4251	.4265	.4279	.4292	.4306	.4319
1.5	.4332	.4345	.4357	.4370	.4382	.4394	.4406	.4418	.4429	.4441
1.6	.4452	.4463	.4474	.4484	.4495	.4505	.4515	.4525	.4535	.4545
1.7	.4554	.4564	.4573	.4582	.4591	.4599	.4608	.4616	.4625	.4633
1.8	.4641	.4649	.4656	.4664	.4671	.4678	.4686	.4693	.4699	.4706
1.9	.4713	.4719	.4726	.4732	.4738	.4744	.4750	.4756	.4761	.4767
2.0	.4772	.4778	.4783	.4788	.4793	.4798	.4803	.4808	.4812	.4817
2.1	.4821	.4826	.4830	.4834	.4838	.4842	.4846	.4850	.4854	.4857
2.2	.4861	.4864	.4868	.4871	.4875	.4878	.4881	.4884	.4887	.4890
2.3	.4893	.4896	.4898	.4901	.4904	.4906	.4909	.4911	.4913	.4916
2.4	.4918	.4920	.4922	.4925	.4927	.4929	.4931	.4932	.4934	.4936
2.5	.4938	.4940	.4941	.4943	.4945	.4946	.4948	.4949	.4951	.4952
2.6	.4953	.4955	.4956	.4957	.4959	.4960	.4961	.4962	.4963	.4964
2.7	.4965	.4966	.4967	.4968	.4969	.4970	.4971	.4972	.4973	.4974
2.8	.4974	.4975	.4976	.4977	.4977	.4978	.4979	.4979	.4980	.4981
2.9	.4981	.4982	.4982	.4983	.4984	.4984	.4985	.4985	.4986	.4986
3.0	.49865	.49869	.49874	.49878	.49882	.49886	.49889	.49893	.49897	.49900
3.1	.49903	.49906	.49910	.49913	.49916	.49918	.49921	.49924	.49926	.49929
3.2	.49931	.49934	.49936	.49938	.49940	.49942	.49944	.49946	.49948	.49950
3.3	.49952	.49953	.49955	.49957	.49958	.49960	.49961	.49962	.49964	.49965
3.4	.49966	.49968	.49969	.49970	.49971	.49972	.49973	.49974	.49975	.49976
3.5	.49977	.49978	.49978	.49979	.49980	.49981	.49981	.49982	.49983	.49983
3.6	.49984	.49985	.49985	.49986	.49986	.49987	.49987	.49988	.49988	.49989
3.7	.49989	.49990	.49990	.49990	.49991	.49991	.49992	.49992	.49992	.49992
3.8	.49993	.49993	.49993	.49994	.49994	.49994	.49994	.49995	.49995	.49995
3.9	.49995	.49995	.49996	.49996	.49996	.49996	.49996	.49996	.49997	.49997

APPENDIX F Additional Excel Procedures

F.1 Enhancing Workbook Presentation

You can enhance workbook presentation by using common formatting commands and rearranging the order of the worksheets and chart sheets in a workbook.

Table F.1 presents the shortcuts for worksheet formatting operations used to create the Excel Guide workbooks and the results shown throughout this book. These shortcuts can be found in the Home tab of the Excel Office Ribbon (see Figure F.1 on page 816).

TABLE F.1
Shortcuts to Common Formatting Operations

Number	Operation Name	Use
❶	Font Face and Font Size	Changes the text font face and size for cell entries and chart labels. Worksheets shown in this book have been formatted as **Calibri 11**. Many DATA worksheets have been formatted as **Arial 10**.
❷	Boldface	Toggles on (or off) boldface text style for the currently selected object.
❸	Italic	Toggles on (or off) italic text style for the currently selected object.
❹	Borders	Displays a gallery of choices that permit drawing lines (borders) around a cell or cell range.
❺	Fill Color	Displays a gallery of choices for the background color of a cell. Immediately to the right of **Fill Color** is the related **Font Color** (not used in any example in this book).
❻	Align Text	Aligns the display of the contents of a worksheet cell. Three buttons are available: **Align Text Left**, **Center**, and **Align Text Right**.
❼	Merge & Center	Merges (combines) adjacent cells into one cell and centers the display of the contents of that cell. In Excel 2007, this button is also a drop-down list that offers additional **Merge** and **Unmerge** choices.
❽	Percent	Formats the display of a number value in a cell as a percentage. The value 1 displays as 100%, the value 0.01 displays as 1%. To the immediate left of **Percent** is **Currency**, which formats values as dollars and cents. Do not confuse **Currency** formatting with the symbol used to identify absolute cell references (discussed in Section EG1.7 on page 21).
❾	Increase Decimal and Decrease Decimal	Adjusts the number of decimal places to display a number value in a cell.
❿	Format	Displays a gallery of choices that affect the row height and column width of a cell. The most common usage is to select a column and then select **Format ➔ AutoFit Column Width**.

FIGURE F.1
Home tab of the Excel Office Ribbon (with number labels keyed to Table F.1)

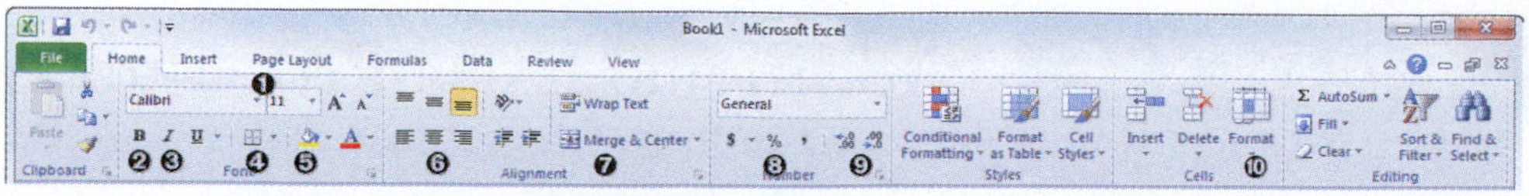

Use the **Move or Copy** command to rearrange the order of the worksheets and chart sheets in a workbook. To move or copy a worksheet, right-click the worksheet sheet tab and click **Move or Copy** in the shortcut menu that appears. In the Move or Copy dialog box, select the destination workbook from the **To book** drop-down list—select **(new book)** to place the worksheet in a new workbook—and select a position for the worksheet in the **Before sheet** list. If making a copy, also check **Create a copy**. Click **OK** to complete the move or copy operation.

Worksheet cell formatting can also be done through the **Format Cells** command. When editing a worksheet, right-click a cell and then click **Format Cells** from the shortcut menu. In the Format Cells dialog box that appears, you can perform all the formatting operations discussed in Table F.1 and more.

F.2 Useful Keyboard Shortcuts

In Excel, certain keys or keystroke combinations (one or more keys held down as you press another key) are keyboard shortcuts that act as alternate means of executing common operations. Table F.2 presents some common shortcuts that represent some of the common Excel operations described in this book. (Keystroke combinations are shown using a plus sign, as in **Ctrl+C**, which means "while holding down the **Ctrl** key, press the **C** key.")

TABLE F.2
Useful Keyboard Shortcuts

Key	Operation
Backspace	Erases typed characters to the left of the current position, one character at a time.
Delete	Erases characters to the right of the cursor, one character at a time.
Enter or Tab	Finalizes an entry typed into a worksheet cell. Implied by the use of the verb *enter* in the Excel Guides.
Esc	Cancels an action or a dialog box. Equivalent to the dialog box **Cancel** button.
F1	Displays the Excel help system.
Ctrl+C	Copies the currently selected worksheet entry or chart label.
Ctrl+V	Pastes the currently copied object into the currently selected worksheet cell or chart label.
Ctrl+X	Cuts the currently selected worksheet entry or chart label. You cut, and not delete, something in order to paste it somewhere else.
Ctrl+B	Toggles on (or off) boldface text style for the currently selected object.
Ctrl+I	Toggles on (or off) italic text style for the currently selected object.
Ctrl+F	Finds a **Find what** value.
Ctrl+H	Replaces a **Find what** value with the **Replace with** value.
Ctrl+Z	Undoes the last operation.
Ctrl+Y	Redoes the last operation.
Ctrl+`	Toggles on (or off) formulas view of worksheet.
Ctrl+Shift+Enter	Enters an array formula.

Note: Using the copy-and-paste keyboard shortcut, Ctrl+C and Ctrl+V, to copy formulas from one worksheet cell to another is subject to the same type of adjustment as discussed in Section EG1.7.

F.3 Verifying Formulas and Worksheets

If you use formulas in your worksheets, you should review and verify formulas before you use their results. To view the formulas in a worksheet, press Ctrl+` (grave accent key). To restore the original view, the results of the formulas, press Ctrl+` a second time.

As you create and use more complicated worksheets, you might want to visually examine the relationships among a formula and the cells it uses (called the *precedents*) and the cells that use the results of the formula (the *dependents*). Select **Formulas ➔ Trace Precedents** (or **Trace Dependents**). When you are finished, clear all trace arrows by selecting **Formulas ➔ Remove Arrows**.

F.4 Chart Formatting

Excel incorrectly formats the charts created by the *In-Depth Excel* instructions. Use the formatting adjustments in Table F.3 to properly format charts you create. Before applying these adjustments, relocate a chart to its own chart sheet. To do so, right-click the chart background and click **Move Chart** from the shortcut menu. In the Move Chart dialog box, click **New Sheet**, enter a name for the new chart sheet, and click **OK**.

TABLE F.3
Excel Chart Formatting Adjustments

Layout Tab Selection	Notes
Chart Title ➔ Above Chart	In the box that is added to the chart, double-click **Chart Title** and enter an appropriate title.
Axes Titles ➔ Primary Horizontal Axis Title ➔ Title Below Axis	In the box that is added to the chart, double-click **Axis Title** and enter an appropriate title.
Axes Titles ➔ Primary Vertical Axis Title ➔ Rotated Title	In the box that is added to the chart, double-click **Axis Title** and enter an appropriate title.
Axes Titles ➔ Secondary Horizontal ➔ Axis Title ➔ None and **Axes Titles ➔ Secondary Vertical Axis Title ➔ Rotated Title**	Only for charts that contain secondary axes.
Legend ➔ None	Turns off the chart legend.
Data Labels ➔ None	Turns off the display of values at plotted points or bars in the charts.
Data Table ➔ None	Turns off the display of a summary table on the chart sheet.
Axes ➔ Primary Horizontal Axis ➔ Show Left to Right Axis (or **Show Default Axis**, if listed)	Turns on the display of the *X* axis.
Axes ➔ Primary Vertical Axis ➔ Show Default Axis	Turns on the display of the *Y* axis.
Gridlines ➔ Primary Horizontal Gridlines ➔ None	Turns off the improper horizontal gridlines.
Gridlines ➔ Primary Vertical Gridlines ➔ None	Turns off the improper vertical gridlines.

Use all of the adjustments in Table F.3, unless a particular set of charting instructions tells you otherwise. To apply the adjustments, you must be open to the chart sheet that contains the chart to be adjusted. All adjustments are made by first selecting the **Layout** tab (under the Chart Tools heading). If a Layout tab selection cannot be made, the adjustment does not apply to the type of chart being adjusted. (Excel hides or disables chart formatting choices that do not apply to a particular chart type.)

Occasionally, when you open to a chart sheet, the chart is either too large to be fully seen or too small, surrounded by a chart frame mat that is too large. Click the **Zoom Out** or **Zoom In** buttons, located in the lower-right portion of the Excel window frame, to adjust the display.

F.5 Creating Histograms for Discrete Probability Distributions

You can create a histogram for a discrete probability distribution based on a discrete probabilities table. For example, to create a histogram based on the Figure 5.2 binomial probabilities worksheet on page 194, open to the **COMPUTE worksheet** of the **Binomial workbook**. Select the cell range **B14:B18**, the probabilities in the Binomial Probabilities Table, and:

1. Select **Insert → Column** and select the first **2-D Column** gallery choice **(Clustered Column)**.
2. Right-click the chart background and click **Select Data**.

In the Select Data Source dialog box:

3. Click **Edit** under the **Horizontal (Categories) Axis Labels** heading.
4. In the Axis Labels dialog box, enter =**COMPUTE!A14:A18** the cell range of the *X* axis values. (This cell range must be entered as a formula in the form =***SheetName!CellRange***.) Then, click **OK** to return to the Select Data Source dialog box.
5. Click **OK**.

In the chart:

6. Right-click inside a bar and click **Format Data Series** in the shortcut menu.

In the Format Data Series dialog box:

7. Click **Series Options** in the left pane. In the Series Options right pane, change the **Gap Width** slider to **Large Gap**. Click **Close**.

Relocate the chart to a chart sheet and adjust the chart formatting by using the instructions in Section F.4.

F.6 Pasting with Paste Special

Pasting data from one worksheet to another can sometimes cause unexpected side effects. When the two worksheets are in different workbooks, a simple paste creates an external link to the original workbook. This can lead to errors later if the first workbook is unavailable when the second one is being used. Even pasting between worksheets in the same workbook can lead to problems if what is being pasted is a cell range of formulas.

To avoid such side effects, use **Paste Special** in these special situations. To use this operation, copy the original cell range as you would do normally and select the cell or cell range to be the target of the paste. Right-click the target and click **Paste Special** from the shortcut menu. In the Paste Special dialog box (shown on page 819), click **Values** and then click **OK**. For the first case, Paste Special Values pastes the current values of the cells in the first workbook and not formulas that use cell references to the first workbook. For the second case, Paste Special Values pastes the current evaluation of the formulas copied and not the formulas themselves.

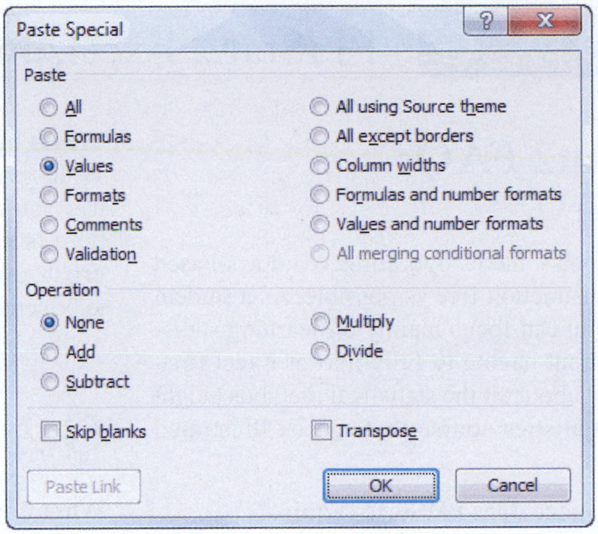

If you use PHStat2 and have data for a procedure in the form of formulas, use Paste Special Values to create columns of equivalent values before using the procedure. (PHStat2 will not work properly if data for a procedure are in the form of formulas.) Paste Special can paste other types of information, including cell formatting information. For a full discussion of Paste Special, see the Excel help system.

APPENDIX G PHStat2, Excel, and Minitab FAQs

G.1 PHStat2 FAQs

What is PHStat2?
PHStat2 is software that makes operating Windows-based Microsoft Excel as distraction free as possible. As a student studying statistics, you can focus mainly on learning statistics and not worry about having to fully master Excel first. PHStat2 contains just about all the statistical methods taught in an introductory statistics course that can be illustrated using Excel.

How much storage space does PHStat2 require?
PHStat2 requires about 3MB of storage space, although the PHStat2 setup program that you run to install PHStat2 (see Appendix Section D.2) requires about 15MB of storage space.

Are updates to PHStat2 available?
Yes, free minor updates to resolve issues or enhance functionality may be available for download from the PHStat2 website (**www.pearsonhighered.com/phstat**).

Where can I find the latest and most complete technical information for setting up PHStat2?
Download and read the PHStat2 readme file (see Appendix Section C.2) for the latest and most complete technical information for setting up PHStat2. The readme file expands on the concise installation and configuration instructions presented in Appendix Section D.2. Also check the PHStat2 website (**www.pearsonhighered.com/phstat**) for any technical issues created by Microsoft-supplied Excel updates distributed after the publication of this book.

Where can I get help setting up PHStat2?
If you need help setting up PHStat2, first review the "Troubleshooting PHStat2" section of the downloadable PHStat2 readme file. If your problem is still unresolved, visit the PHStat2 frequently asked questions web page and the web page for your version at the PHStat2 website (**www.pearsonhighered.com/phstat**) to see if your problem is addressed. If you need further assistance, click the **Contact Pearson Technical Support** on either web page for free technical support. (Pearson Technical Support cannot answer questions about the statistical applications of PHStat2 or questions about specific PHStat2 procedures.)

How can I identify which PHStat2 version I have?
Open Microsoft Excel with PHStat2 and select **PHStat → Help for PHStat**. In the dialog box that appears, note the XLA and DLL version numbers. If you downloaded and installed the PHStat2 version designed for this book, both of these numbers will not be lower than 3.0.

Where can I find tips for using PHStat2?
While your classmates and instructor can be the best sources of tips, you can check for any tips that may be posted on the new third-party PHStat2 community website **phstatcommunity.org** that, at the time of publication of this book, was scheduled to be activated by Fall 2011.

G.2 Excel FAQs

What does "Compatibility Mode" in the title bar mean?
Excel displays "Compatibility Mode" when the workbook you are currently using has been previously stored using the **.xls** file format that is compatible with all Excel versions. Compatibility Mode does not affect Excel functionality but will cause Excel to review your workbook for exclusive-to-Excel-2007-or-2010 formatting properties and objects the next time you save the workbook. (To preserve exclusive features in Excel 2010, select **File → Save As** and select **Excel Workbook (*.xlsx)** from the **Save as type** drop-down list. To preserve exclusive features in Excel 2007, click the **Office Button**, move the mouse pointer over **Save As**, and in the Save As gallery, click **Excel Workbook** to save the workbook in the **.xlsx** file format.)

If you open any of the Excel data or Excel Guide workbooks for this book, you will see "Compatibility Mode," as all workbooks for this book have been stored using the **.xls** format. Generally, it makes little difference whether you use compatibility mode or not. The one exception is when working with PivotTables, as explained in Section EG2.7 on page 86.

In Excel 2010, how can I specify the custom settings that you recommend?
Select **File → Options**. In the Excel Options dialog box, click **Formulas** in the left pane, and in the **Formulas** right pane, click **Automatic** under Workbook Calculation and verify that all check boxes are checked except **Enable iterative calculation**, **R1C1 reference style**, and **Formulas referring to empty cells**.

In Excel 2007, how can I specify the custom settings that you recommend?
Click the **Office Button** and then click **Excel Options**. In the Excel Options dialog box, click **Formulas** in the left pane, and in the **Formulas** right pane, click **Automatic** under Workbook Calculation and verify that all check boxes are checked except **Enable iterative calculation**, **R1C1 reference style**, and **Formulas referring to empty cells**.

What Excel security settings will allow the PHStat2 or Visual Explorations add-in to function properly?
Use the instructions in Appendix Section D.3 on page 793 for configuring Excel for PHStat2 for both add-ins.

I do not see the menu for the Visual Explorations (or PHStat2) add-in that I opened. Where is it?
Unlike earlier versions of Excel that allowed add-ins to add menus to the menu bar, Excel 2007 and 2010 places all add-in menus under the Add-ins tab. In order to see the menu, click **Add-ins** and then click the name of the add-in menu.

How can I install the Analysis ToolPak?
Close Excel and rerun the Microsoft Office or Microsoft Excel setup program. When the setup program runs, choose the option that allows you to add components which will be labeled either as **Change** or **Add or Remove Features**. (If you use Windows 7, open the **Programs and Features** Control Panel applet, select the entry for your version or Office or Excel, and then click **Change** at the top of the list of programs.)

In the Installation Options screen, double-click **Microsoft Office Excel** and then double-click **Add-ins.** Click the **Analysis ToolPak** drop-down list button and select **Run from My Computer**. (You may need access to the original Microsoft Office/Excel setup CD-ROMs or DVD to complete this task.) Upon successful installation, you will see **Data Analysis** as a choice in the **Analysis** group of the **Data** tab when you next open Excel.

G.3 FAQs for Minitab

Can I use Minitab Release 14 or 15 with this book?
Yes, you can use the Minitab Guide instructions, written for Minitab 16, with Release 14 or 15. For certain methods, there may be minor differences in labeling of dialog box elements. Any difference that is not minor is noted in the instructions.

Can I save my Minitab worksheets or projects for use with Release 14 or 15?
Yes. Select either **Minitab14** or **Minitab 15** (for a worksheet) or **Minitab 14 Project (*.MPJ)** or **Minitab 15 Project (*.MPJ)** (for a project) from the **Save as type** drop-down list in the save as dialog box. See Section MG1.3 on page 23 for more information about using the Save Worksheet As and Save Project As dialog boxes.

Self-Test Solutions and Answers to Selected Even-Numbered Problems

The following represent worked-out solutions to Self-Test Problems and brief answers to most of the even-numbered problems in the text. For more detailed solutions, including explanations, interpretations, and Excel and Minitab results, see the *Student Solutions Manual*.

CHAPTER 1

1.2 Small, medium, and large sizes imply order but do not specify how much more soft drink is added at increasing levels.

1.4 (a) The number of telephones is a numerical variable that is discrete because the outcome is a count. It is ratio scaled because it has a true zero point. **(b)** The length of the longest telephone call is a numerical variable that is continuous because any value within a range of values can occur. It is ratio scaled because it has a true zero point. **(c)** Whether someone in the household owns a Wi-Fi–capable cell phone is a categorical variable because the answer can be only yes or no. This also makes it a nominal-scaled variable. **(d)** Same answer as in (c).

1.6 (a) Categorical, nominal scale. **(b)** Numerical, continuous, ratio scale. **(c)** Numerical, discrete, ratio scale. **(d)** Numerical, discrete, ratio scale.

1.8 (a) Numerical, continuous, ratio scale. **(b)** Numerical, discrete, ratio scale. **(c)** Numerical, continuous, ratio scale. **(d)** Categorical, nominal scale.

1.10 The underlying variable, ability of the students, may be continuous, but the measuring device, the test, does not have enough precision to distinguish between the two students.

1.20 (a) All 3,727 full-time first-year students at the university. **(b)** The 2,821 students who responded to the survey. **(c)** The proportion of all 3,727 students who studied with other students. **(d)** The proportion of the sample of 2,821 responding students who studied with other students.

1.22 (a) Adults living in the United States, aged 18 and older. **(b)** The 1,006 adults living in the United States, aged 18 and older, who were selected in the sample. **(c)** Because the 20% is based on the sample, it is a statistic. (d) Because the 58% is based on the sample, it is a statistic.

1.26 (a) Categorical, categorical, numerical discrete, categorical.

1.28 Gender, graduate major, undergraduate major, employment status, satisfaction with MBA advisory services, and preferred type of computer are categorical variables. Age, graduate grade point average, undergraduate grade point average, number of full-time jobs, expected starting salary, spending for textbooks and supplies, advisory rating number of text messages sent in a typical week, and the amount of wealth needed to feel rich are numerical variables.

CHAPTER 2

2.6 (a) Table of frequencies for all student responses:

	STUDENT MAJOR CATEGORIES			
GENDER	A	C	M	Totals
Male	14	9	2	25
Female	6	6	3	15
Totals	20	15	5	40

(b) Table based on total percentages:

	STUDENT MAJOR CATEGORIES			
GENDER	A	C	M	Totals
Male	35.0%	22.5%	5.0%	62.5%
Female	15.0	15.0	7.5	37.5
Totals	50.0	37.5	12.5	100.0

Table based on row percentages:

	STUDENT MAJOR CATEGORIES			
GENDER	A	C	M	Totals
Male	56.0%	36.0%	8.0%	100.0%
Female	40.0	40.0	20.0	100.0
Totals	50.0	37.5	12.5	100.0

Table based on column percentages;

	STUDENT MAJOR CATEGORIES			
GENDER	A	C	M	Totals
Male	70.0%	60.0%	40.0%	62.5%
Female	30.0	40.0	60.0	37.5
Totals	100.0	100.0	100.0	100.0

2.8 (a) The percentages are 48.52, 6.04, 21.33, 19.61, and 4.49. **(b)** Almost half the electricity is generated from coal. About 20% of the electricity is generated from natural gas, and about 20% is generated from nuclear power.

2.10 (a) Table of row percentages:

	GENDER		
ENJOY SHOPPING FOR CLOTHING	Male	Female	Total
Yes	38%	62%	100%
No	74	26	100
Total	48	52	100

Table of column percentages:

	GENDER		
ENJOY SHOPPING FOR CLOTHING	Male	Female	Total
Yes	57%	86%	72%
No	43	14	28
Total	100	100	100

Table of total percentages:

ENJOY SHOPPING FOR CLOTHING	GENDER: Male	Female	Total
Yes	27%	45%	72%
No	21	7	28
Total	48	52	100

(b) A higher percentage of females enjoy shopping for clothing.

2.12 The percentage of online retailers who require three or more clicks to be removed from an e-mail list has increased drastically from 2008 to 2009.

2.14 73 78 78 78 85 88 91.

2.16 (a) 10 but less than 20, 20 but less than 30, 30 but less than 40, 40 but less than 50, 50 but less than 60, 60 but less than 70, 70 but less than 80, 80 but less than 90, 90 but less than 100. **(b)** 10. **(c)** 15, 25, 35, 45, 55, 65, 75, 85, 95.

2.18 (a)

Electricity Costs	Frequency	Percentage
\$80 up to \$99	4	8%
\$100 up to \$119	7	14
\$120 up to \$139	9	18
\$140 up to \$159	13	26
\$160 up to \$179	9	18
\$180 up to \$199	5	10
\$200 up to \$219	3	6

(b)

Electricity Costs	Frequency	Percentage	Cumulative %
\$ 99	4	8.00%	8.00%
\$119	7	14.00	22.00
\$139	9	18.00	40.00
\$159	13	26.00	66.00
\$179	9	18.00	84.00
\$199	5	10.00	94.00
\$219	3	6.00	100.00

(c) The majority of utility charges are clustered between \$120 and \$180.

2.20 (a)

Width	Frequency	Percentage
8.310–8.329	3	6.12%
8.330–8.349	2	4.08
8.350–8.369	1	2.04
8.370–8.389	4	8.16
8.390–8.409	5	10.20
8.410–8.429	16	32.65
8.430–8.449	5	10.20
8.450–8.469	5	10.20
8.470–8.489	6	12.24
8.490–8.509	2	4.08

(b)

Width	Percentage Less Than
8.310	0
8.330	6.12
8.350	10.20
8.370	12.24
8.390	20.40
8.410	30.60
8.430	63.25
8.450	73.45
8.470	83.65
8.490	95.89
8.51	100.00

(c) All the troughs will meet the company's requirements of between 8.31 and 8.61 inches wide.

2.22 (a)

Bulb Life (hrs)	Percentage, Mfgr A	Percentage, Mfgr B
650–749	7.5%	0.0%
750–849	12.5	5.0
850–949	50.0	20.0
950–1,049	22.5	40.0
1,050–1,149	7.5	22.5
1,150–1,249	0.0	12.5

(b)

% Less Than	Percentage Less Than, Mfgr A	Percentage Less Than, Mfgr B
750	7.5%	0.0%
850	20.0	5.0
950	70.0	25.0
1,050	92.5	65.0
1,150	100.0	87.5
1,250	100.0	100.0

(c) Manufacturer B produces bulbs with longer lives than Manufacturer A. The cumulative percentage for Manufacturer B shows that 65% of its bulbs lasted less than 1,050 hours, contrasted with 92.5% of Manufacturer A's bulbs, which lasted less than 950 hours. None of Manufacturer A's bulbs lasted more than 1,149 hours, but 12.5% of Manufacturer B's bulbs lasted between 1,150 and 1,249 hours. At the same time, 7.5% of Manufacturer A's bulbs lasted less than 750 hours, whereas all of Manufacturer B's bulbs lasted at least 750 hours.

2.24 (b) The Pareto chart is best for portraying these data because it not only sorts the frequencies in descending order but also provides the cumulative line on the same chart. **(c)** You can conclude that friends/family account for the largest percentage, 45%. When other, news media, and online user reviews are added to friends/family, this accounts for 83%.

2.26 (b) 88%. **(d)** The Pareto chart allows you to see which sources account for most of the electricity.

2.28 (b) Since electricity consumption is spread over many types of appliances, a bar chart may be best in showing which types of appliances used the most electricity. **(c)** Air conditioning, lighting, and clothes washers/other accounted for 58% of the residential electricity use in the United States.

2.30 (b) A higher percentage of females enjoy shopping for clothing.

2.32 The percentage of online retailers who require three or more clicks to be removed from an e-mail list has increased drastically from 2008 to 2009.

2.34 50 74 74 76 81 89 92.

2.36 (a)

Stem unit:	10	Stem unit:	10	Stem unit:	10
11	4	22	0 2 3 4	33	[illegible]
12		23		[illegible]	
13	5	24			
14	1 5 6	25			
15	1 8	[illegible]			
16	1 2 4 [illegible]				
17	[illegible] 6				

30		37	
31	5	38	
32	6	39	
		40	
		41	1

[illegible]esults are concentrated between \$160 and \$225.

2.38 (c) The majority of utility charges are clustered between \$120 and \$180.

2.40 The property taxes per capita appear to be right-skewed, with approximately 90% falling between \$399 and \$1,700 and the remaining 10% falling between \$1,700 and \$2,100. The center is at about \$1,000.

2.42 (d) All the troughs will meet the company's requirements of between 8.31 and 8.61 inches wide.

2.44 (c) Manufacturer B produces bulbs with longer lives than Manufacturer A.

2.46 (b) Yes, there is a strong positive relationship between X and Y. As X increases, so does Y.

2.48 (c) There appears to be very little relationship between the first weekend gross and either the U.S. gross or the worldwide gross of Harry Potter movies.

2.50 (c) There appears to be a positive relationship between the coaches' salary and revenue. Yes, this is borne out by the data.

2.52 (b) There is a great deal of variation in the returns from decade to decade. Most of the returns are between 5% and 15%. The 1950s, 1980s, and 1990s had exceptionally high returns, and only the 1930s and 2000s had negative returns.

2.54 (b) There has been a steady increase in the amount of solar power installed in the United States between 2000 and 2008. During that time, the yearly amount of solar power installed has increased from 44 megawatts to 250 megawatts. The yearly rate of increase appears to have accelerated since 2006.

2.56 (a)

	A	B	C	D	E
1	PivotTable of Type, Risk, and Fees				
2					
3	Count of Type		Fees		
4	Type	Risk	No	Yes	Grand Total
5	Intermediate Government	Above Average	9.44%	8.89%	18.33%
6		Average	10.56%	5.56%	16.11%
7		Below Average	10.56%	5.00%	15.56%
8	Intermediate Government Total		30.56%	19.44%	50.00%
9	Short Term Corporate	Above Average	11.11%	2.78%	13.89%
10		Average	12.78%	4.44%	17.22%
11		Below Average	16.67%	2.22%	18.89%
12	Short Term Corporate Total		40.56%	9.44%	50.00%
13	Grand Total		71.11%	28.89%	100.00%

(b) Although the ratio of fee-yes to fee-no bond funds for intermediate government category seems to be about 2-to-3 (19% to 31%), the ratio for above-average-risk intermediate government bond funds is closer to 1-to-1 (8.9% to 9.4%). While the group "intermediate government funds that do not charge a fee" has nearly equal numbers of above average risk, average risk, and below risk funds, the group "short term corporate bond funds that do not charge a fee" contains about 50% more below-average-risk funds than above-average-risk ones. The pattern of risk percentages differs between the fee-yes and fee-no funds in each of bond fund categories. **(c)** The results for type, fee, and risk, in the two years are similar.

[illegible] (a)

Count of [illegible]	Fees								
	No			No	Yes			Yes	Grand
Category	[illegible]	[illegible]	Low	Total	Average	High	Low	Total	Total
Large cap	33	[illegible]	201	251	79	51	69	199	450
Mid-cap	52	[illegible]	[illegible]	[illegible]	22	45	10	77	174
Small cap	[illegible]	[illegible]	[illegible]	[illegible]	30	58	4	92	244
Grand Total	180	[illegible]	[illegible]	[illegible]	[illegible]	154	83	368	868

(b) Large-cap funds without fees are fa[illegible] large-cap funds with fees are more likely to [illegible] Mid-cap and small-cap funds, regardless of fees, [illegible] while average or high risk.

2.78 (c) The publisher gets the largest portion (64.8%) of the revenue. About half (32.3%) of the revenue received by the publisher covers manufacturing costs. The publisher's marketing and promotion account for the next largest share of the revenue, at 15.4%. Author, bookstore employee salaries and benefits, and publisher administrative costs and taxes each account for around 10% of the revenue, whereas the publisher after-tax profit, bookstore operations, bookstore pretax profit, and freight constitute the "trivial few" allocations of the revenue. Yes, the bookstore gets twice the revenue of the authors.

2.80 (b) The pie chart may be best since with only three categories it enables you to see the portion of the whole in each category. **(d)** The pie chart may be best since with only four categories since it enables you to see the portion of the whole in each category. **(e)** The online content is not copy-edited or fact-checked as carefully as print content. Only 41% of the online content is copy-edited as carefully as print content and only 57% of the online content is fact-checked as carefully as the print content.

2.82 (a)

DESSERT ORDERED	GENDER: Male	Female	Total
Yes	71%	29%	100%
No	48	52	100
Total	53	47	100

DESSERT ORDERED	GENDER: Male	Female	Total
Yes	30%	14%	23%
No	70	86	77
Total	100	100	100

DESSERT ORDERED	GENDER: Male	Female	Total
Yes	16%	7%	23%
No	37	40	77
Total	53	47	100

DESSERT ORDERED	BEEF ENTRÉE: Yes	No	Total
Yes	52%	48%	100%
No	25	75	100
Total	31	69	100

DESSERT ORDERED	BEEF ENTRÉE: Yes	No	Total
Yes	38%	16%	23%
No	62	84	77
Total	100	100	100

DESSERT ORDERED	BEEF ENTRÉE: Yes	No	Total
Yes	12%	11%	23%
No	19	58	77
Total	31	69	100

(b) If the owner is interested in finding out the percentage of males and females who order dessert or the percentage of those who order a beef entrée and a dessert among all patrons, the table of total percentages is most informative. If the owner is interested in the effect of gender on ordering of dessert or the effect of ordering a beef entrée on the ordering of dessert, the table of column percentages will be most informative. Because dessert is usually ordered after the main entrée, and the owner has no direct control over the gender of patrons, the table of row percentages is not very useful here. **(c)** 30% of the men ordered desserts, compared to 14% of the women; men are more than twice as likely to order dessert as women. Almost 38% of the patrons ordering a beef entrée ordered dessert, compared to 16% of patrons ordering all other entrées. Patrons ordering beef are more than 2.3 times as likely to order dessert as patrons ordering any other entrée.

2.84 (a) 23575R15 accounts for over 80% of the warranty claims. **(b)** 91.82% of the warranty claims are from the ATX model. **(c)** Tread separation accounts for 73.23% of the warranty claims among the ATX model. **(d)** The number of claims is evenly distributed among the three incidents; other/unknown incidents account for almost 40% of the claims, tread separation accounts for about 35% of the claims, and blowout accounts for about 25% of the claims.

2.86 (c) The alcohol percentage is concentrated between 4% and 6%, with the largest concentration between 4% and 5%. The calories are concentrated between 140 and 160. The carbohydrates are concentrated between 12 and 15. There are outliers in the percentage of alcohol in both tails. The outlier in the lower tail is due to the non-alcoholic beer O'Doul's with only a 0.4% alcohol content. There are a few beers with alcohol content as high as around 10.5%. There are a few beers with calorie content as high as around 302.5 and carbohydrates as high as 31.5. There is a strong positive relationship between percentage alcohol and calories, and calories and carbohydrates and a moderately positive relationship between percentage alcohol and carbohydrates.

2.88 (c) The money market yield is concentrated between 0.95 and 1.35. The five-year CD is concentrated between 2.8 and 3.1. In general, the five-year CD has the higher yield. There appears to be a positive relationship between the yield of the money market and the five-year CD.

2.90 (a)

Frequency (Boston)

Weight (Boston)	Frequency	Percentage
3,015 but less than 3,050	2	0.54%
3,050 but less than 3,085	44	11.96
3,085 but less than 3,120	122	33.15
3,120 but less than 3,155	131	35.60
3,155 but less than 3,190	58	15.76
3,190 but less than 3,225	7	1.90
3,225 but less than 3,260	3	0.82
3,260 but less than 3,295	1	0.27

(b)

Frequency (Vermont)

Weight (Vermont)	Frequency	Percentage
3,550 but less than 3,600	4	1.21%
3,600 but less than 3,650	31	9.39
3,650 but less than 3,700	115	34.85
3,700 but less than 3,750	131	39.70
3,750 but less than 3,800	36	10.91
3,800 but less than 3,850	12	3.64
3,850 but less than 3,900	1	0.30

(d) 0.54% of the Boston shingles pallets are underweight, and 0.27% are overweight. 1.21% of the Vermont shingles pallets are underweight, and 3.94% are overweight.

2.92 (c)

Calories	Frequency	Percentage	Limit	Percentage Less Than
50 but less than 100	3	12%	100	12%
100 but less than 150	3	12	150	24
150 but less than 200	9	36	200	60
200 but less than 250	6	24	250	84
250 but less than 300	3	12	300	96
300 but less than 350	0	0	350	96
350 but less than 400	1	4	400	100

Cholesterol	Frequency	Percentage	Limit	Percentage Less Than
0 but less than 50	2	8%	50	8%
50 but less than 100	17	68	100	76
100 but less than 150	4	16	150	92
150 but less than 200	1	4	200	96
200 but less than 250	0	0	250	96
250 but less than 300	0	0	300	96
300 but less than 350	0	0	350	96
350 but less than 400	0	0	400	96
400 but less than 450	0	0	450	96
450 but less than 500	1	4	500	100

The sampled fresh red meats, poultry, and fish vary from 98 to 397 calories per serving, with the highest concentration between 150 to 200 calories. One protein source, spareribs, with 397 calories, is more than 100 calories above the next-highest-caloric food. The protein content of the sampled foods varies from 16 to 33 grams, with 68% of the values falling between 24 and 32 grams. Spareribs and fried liver are both very different from other foods sampled—the former on calories and the latter on cholesterol content.

2.94 (b) There is a downward trend in the amount filled. **(c)** The amount filled in the next bottle will most likely be below 1.894 liter. **(d)** The scatter plot of the amount of soft drink filled against time reveals the trend of the data, whereas a histogram only provides information on the distribution of the data.

CHAPTER 3

3.2 (a) Mean = 7, median = 7, mode = 7. **(b)** Range = 9, $S^2 = 10.8$, $S = 3.286$, $CV = 46.948\%$. **(c)** Z scores: 0, −0.913, 0.609, 0, −1.217, 1.522. None of the Z scores are larger than 3.0 or smaller than −3.0. There is no outlier. **(d)** Symmetric because mean = median.

3.4 (a) Mean = 2, median = 7, mode = 7. **(b)** Range = 17, $S^2 = 62$ $S = 7.874$, $CV = 393.7\%$. **(c)** 0.635, −0.889, −1.270, 0.635, 0.889. **(d)** Left-skewed because mean $<$ median.

3.6 −0.085.

3.8 (a)

	Grade X	Grade Y
Mean	575	575.4
Median	575	575
Standard deviation	6.40	2.07

(b) If quality is measured by central tendency, Grade X tires provide slightly better quality because X's mean and median are both equal to the expected value, 575 mm. If, however, quality is measured by consistency, Grade Y provides better quality because, even though Y's mean is only slightly larger than the mean for Grade X, Y's standard deviation is much smaller. The range in values for Grade Y is 5 mm compared to the range in values for Grade X, which is 16 mm.

(c)

	Grade *X*	Grade *Y*, Altered
Mean	575	577.4
Median	575	575
Standard deviation	6.40	6.11

When the fifth *Y* tire measures 588 mm rather than 578 mm, *Y*'s mean inner diameter becomes 577.4 mm, which is larger than *X*'s mean inner diameter, and *Y*'s standard deviation increases from 2.07 mm to 6.11 mm. In this case, *X*'s tires are providing better quality in terms of the mean inner diameter, with only slightly more variation among the tires than *Y*'s.

3.10 (a) Mean $= \dfrac{63.26}{9} = 7.0289$,

Median $=$ 5*th* ranked value $= 7.38$

$$\text{Variance} = (4.20 - 7.0289)^2 + (5.03 - 7.0289)^2 + (5.86 - 7.0289)^2$$
$$+(6.45 - 7.0289)^2 + (7.38 - 7.0289)^2 + (7.54 - 7.0289)^2$$
$$+(8.46 - 7.0289)^2 + (8.47 - 7.0289)^2 + (9.87 - 7.0289)^2$$
$$= \frac{26.2809}{9 - 1} = 3.2851,$$

Standard deviation $= \sqrt{3.2851} = 1.8125$, range $= 9.87 - 4.20 = 5.67$,

Coefficient of variation $= \dfrac{1.8125}{7.0289} \times 100\% = 25.79\%$

(c) The mean is only slightly smaller than the median, so the data are only slightly right-skewed. **(d)** The mean cost is \$7.03, and the median cost is \$7.38. The average scatter of cost around the mean is \$1.81. The difference between the highest cost and the lowest cost is \$5.67.

3.12 (a) Mean $= 20.9231$, median $= 21$, mode $= 21$ **(b)** $S^2 = 7.4338$, $S = 2.7265$, range $= 10$, coefficient of variation $= 13.03\%$, and Z scores are 1.13, 0.76, 0.39, 0.03, 0.39, 0.39, −1.07, −1.07, 1.86, 1.86, 1.86, −0.71, −0.71, −0.71, 0.03, 0.03, 0.03, 0.03, 0.03, −1.07, −0.71, 0.03, 0.39, 0.39, −1.81, −1.81. **(c)** Because the mean is very close to the median, the data are approximately symmetric. **(d)** The distributions of MPG of the sedans is right-skewed, while the MPG of the SUVs is symmetric. The mean MPG of sedans is 3.93 higher than that of SUVs. The average scatter and the range of the MPG of sedans is much higher than that for SUVs.

3.14 (a) Mean $= 0.9257$, median $= 0.88$ **(b)** Variance $= 0.1071$, standard deviation $= 0.3273$, range $= 0.96$, $CV = 35.36\%$. There is no outlier because none of the Z scores has an absolute value that is greater than 3.0. **(c)** The data appear to be right-skewed because the mean is greater than the median.

3.16 (a) Mean $=$ \$134.0, median $=$ \$121.0. **(b)** Range $=$ \$80, variance $= 998.00$, standard deviation $=$ \$31.59. **(c)** The price paid by U.S. travelers is right-skewed because the mean is greater than the median. **(d) (a)** Mean $=$ \$117.33, median $=$ \$114.00. **(b)** Range $=$ \$75, variance $= 624.67$, standard deviation $=$ \$24.99. **(c)** The price paid by U.S. travelers is now almost symmetric because the mean is only slightly greater than the median due to the much lower price in the first city (\$85).

3.18 (a) Mean $= 7.11$, median $= 6.68$. **(b)** Variance $= 4.336$, standard deviation $= 2.082$, range $= 6.67$, $CV = 29.27\%$.
(c) Because the mean is greater than the median, the distribution is right-skewed. **(d)** The mean and median are both greater than 5 minutes. The distribution is right-skewed, meaning that there are some unusually high values. Further, 13 of the 15 bank customers sampled (or 86.7%) had waiting times greater than 5 minutes. So the customer is likely to experience a waiting time in excess of 5 minutes. The manager overstated the bank's service record in responding that the customer would "almost certainly" not wait longer than 5 minutes for service.

3.20 (a) $[(1 - 0.6331) \times (1 - 0.1705)]^{1/2} - 1 = 0.5517 - 1 = -44.83\%$ per year. **(b)** $= (\$1{,}000) \times (1 - 0.4483) \times (1 - 0.4483) = \$304.37$. **(c)** The result for Taser was worse than the result for GE, which was worth \$461.18.

3.22 (a) Platinum $= 10.95\%$, gold $= 20.65\%$, silver $= 17.65\%$ per year. **(b)** Gold had a higher return than silver and a much higher return than platinum. **(c)** All the metals had positive returns, whereas the three stock indices all had returns that were close to 0.

3.24 (a) 4, 9, 5. **(b)** 3, 4, 7, 9, 12. **(c)** The distances between the median and the extremes are close, 4 and 5, but the differences in the tails are different (1 on the left and 3 on the right), so this distribution is slightly right-skewed. **(d)** In Problem 3.2 (d), because mean $=$ median, the distribution is symmetric. The box part of the graph is symmetric, but the tails show right-skewness.

3.26 (a) −6.5, 8, 14.5. **(b)** −8, −6.5, 7, 8, 9. **(c)** The shape is left-skewed. **(d)** This is consistent with the answer in Problem 3.4 (d).

3.28 (a) $Q_1 = \dfrac{14 + 1}{4} = 3.75$ ranked value = 4th ranked value = \$0.68,

$Q_3 = \dfrac{3(14 + 1)}{4} = \dfrac{45}{4} = 11.25$ ranked value = 11th ranked value = \$1.14,

Interquartile range $= 1.14 - 0.68 =$ \$0.46. **(b)** Five-number summary: 0.55 0.68 0.88 1.14 1.51. **(c)** The distribution is right-skewed.

3.30 (a) $Q_1 = 19$, $Q_3 = 22$, interquartile range $= 3$. **(b)** Five-number summary: 16 19 21 22 26. **(c)** The MPG of SUVs is approximately symmetric since the distance from the smallest value to the median is the same as the distance from the median to the largest value although the other comparisons are inconsistent.

3.32 (a) Commercial district five-number summary: 0.38 3.2 4.5 5.55 6.46. Residential area five-number summary: 3.82 5.64 6.68 8.73 10.49. **(b)** Commercial district: The distribution is left-skewed. Residential area: The distribution is slightly right-skewed. **(c)** The central tendency of the waiting times for the bank branch located in the commercial district of a city is lower than that of the branch located in the residential area. There are a few long waiting times for the branch located in the residential area, whereas there are a few exceptionally short waiting times for the branch located in the commercial area.

3.34 (a)

Average of 3-Year Return	Risk			
Type	Above Average	Average	Below Average	Grand Total
Intermediate government	5.6515	5.7862	4.8214	5.4367
Short-term corporate	−0.0440	2.6355	3.2294	2.1156
Grand total	3.1966	4.1583	3.9484	3.7761

(b)

StdDev of 3-Year Return	Risk			
Type	Above Average	Average	Below Average	Grand Total
Intermediate government	2.4617	1.1457	1.2784	1.8066
Short-term corporate	3.6058	1.7034	1.4886	2.6803
Grand total	4.1197	2.1493	1.6001	2.8227

(c) Across the three different risk levels, intermediate government funds have the highest average three-year returns but the lowest standard deviation. **(d)** Similarly to the 2006–2008 three-year returns, intermediate government funds have the highest average three-year returns but the lowest standard deviation across the three different risk levels.

3.36 (a)

Average of Return 2008		Risk			
Type	**Fees**	**Above Average**	**Average**	**Below Average**	**Grand Total**
Intermediate government	No	9.0294	6.9053	4.0368	6.5709
	Yes	3.8863	7.1700	4.5444	4.9937
Intermediate government total		6.5358	6.99656	4.200	5.9576
Short-term corporate	No	10.7315	−1.6174	0.4600	−3.2607
	Yes	−10.2000	−1.6250	0.7250	−3.5941
Short-term corporate total		−10.6252	−1.6140	0.492	−3.3237
Grand total		−0.8612	2.5450	2.1661	1.316

(b)

StdDev of Return 2008		Risk			
Type	**Fees**	**Above Average**	**Average**	**Below Average**	**Grand Total**
Intermediate government	No	5.6635	3.6998	3.5178	4.7322
	Yes	6.5778	2.8744	3.2055	5.0712
Intermediate government total		6.5675	3.3870	3.3694	4.8999
Short-term corporate	No	8.6070	4.0613	3.3503	7.1587
	Yes	7.2928	5.4013	3.5790	6.9786
Short-term corporate total		8.2199	4.3480	3.3220	7.0874
Grand total		11.2319	5.8231	3.8020	7.6530

(c) The intermediate government funds have the highest average 2008 returns but the lowest standard deviation among all different combinations of risk level and whether there is a fee charged with the exception that they have the highest average 2008 returns and the highest standard deviation among the below average risk funds that do not charge a fee. **(d)** In contrast to the 2008 returns, the intermediate government funds have the lowest average 2009 returns for all combinations of risk level and whether the funds charged a fee with the except of the below average risk funds that do not charge a fee where the intermediate government funds have the highest average 2008 returns. Unlike the 2008 returns, the intermediate government funds have the lowest standard deviations only among the above average risk funds that do not charge a fee, the average risk funds that either charge a fee or do not charge a fee, and the below average risk funds that charge a fee.

3.38 (a) Population mean, $\mu = 6$. **(b)** Population standard deviation, $\sigma = 1.673$, population variance, $\sigma^2 = 2.8$.

3.40 (a) 68%. **(b)** 95%. **(c)** Not calculable, 75%, 88.89%. **(d)** $\mu - 4\sigma$ to $\mu + 4\sigma$ or −2.8 to 19.2.

3.42 (a) Mean $= \dfrac{662{,}960}{51} = 12{,}999.22$, variance $= \dfrac{762{,}944{,}726.6}{51} = 14{,}959{,}700.52$, standard deviation $= \sqrt{14{,}959{,}700.52} = 3{,}867.78$. **(b)** 64.71%, 98.04%, and 100% of these states have mean per capita energy consumption within 1, 2, and 3 standard deviations of the mean, respectively. **(c)** This is consistent with 68%, 95%, and 99.7%, according to the empirical rule. **(d) (a)** Mean $= \dfrac{642{,}887}{50} = 12{,}857.74$, variance $= \dfrac{711{,}905{,}533.6}{50} = 14{,}238{,}110.67$, standard deviation $= \sqrt{14{,}238{,}110.67} = 3{,}773.34$. **(b)** 66%, 98%, and 100% of these states have a mean per capita energy consumption within 1, 2, and 3 standard deviations of the mean, respectively. **(c)** This is consistent with 68%, 95%, and 99.7%, according to the empirical rule.

3.44 Covariance = 65.2909, $r = +1.0$.

3.46 (a) $\text{cov}(X, Y) = \dfrac{\sum_{i=1}^{n}(X_i - \bar{X})(Y_i - \bar{Y})}{n-1} = \dfrac{800}{6} = 133.3333$.

(b) $r = \dfrac{\text{cov}(X, Y)}{S_X S_Y} = \dfrac{133.3333}{(46.9042)(3.3877)} = 0.8391$.

(c) The correlation coefficient is more valuable for expressing the relationship between calories and sugar because it does not depend on the units used to measure calories and sugar. **(d)** There is a strong positive linear relationship between calories and sugar.

3.48 (a) $cov(X, Y) = 4{,}473{,}270.3$ **(b)** $r = 0.7903$ **(c)** There is a positive linear relationship between the coaches' salary and revenue.

3.62 (a) Mean = 43.89, median = 45, 1st quartile = 18, 3rd quartile = 63. **(b)** Range = 76, interquartile range = 45, variance = 639.2564, standard deviation = 25.28, $CV = 57.61\%$. **(c)** The distribution is right-skewed because there are a few policies that require an exceptionally long period to be approved. **(d)** The mean approval process takes 43.89 days, with 50% of the policies being approved in less than 45 days. 50% of the applications are approved between 18 and 63 days. About 67% of the applications are approved between 18.6 and 69.2 days.

3.64 (a) Mean = 8.421, median = 8.42, range = 0.186, $S = 0.0461$. The mean and median width are both 8.42 inches. The range of the widths is 0.186 inch, and the average scatter around the mean is 0.0461 inch. **(b)** 8.312, 8.404, 8.42, 8.459, 8.498. **(c)** Even though mean = median the left tail is slightly longer, so the distribution is slightly left-skewed. **(d)** All the troughs in this sample meet the specifications.

3.66 (a), (b)

	Calories	Fat
Mean	108.3333	3.375
Median	110	3.25
Standard deviation	19.4625	1.7597
Sample variance	378.7879	3.0966
Range	70	5.5
First quartile	90	1.5
Third quartile	120	5
Interquartile range	30	3.5
Coefficient of variation	17.97%	52.14%

(c) The distribution of calories and total fat are symmetrical.

(d) $r = \dfrac{\text{cov}(X, Y)}{S_X S_Y} = 0.6969$.

(e) The number of calories of the veggie burgers centers around 110, and its distribution is symmetrical. The amount of fat centers around 3.3 grams per serving, and its distribution is symmetrical. There is a positive linear relationship between calories and fat.

3.68 (a) Boston: 0.04, 0.17, 0.23, 0.32, 0.98; Vermont: 0.02, 0.13, 0.20, 0.28, 0.83. **(b)** Both distributions are right-skewed. **(c)** Both sets of shingles did quite well in achieving a granule loss of 0.8 gram or less.

Only two Boston shingles had a granule loss greater than 0.8 gram. The next highest to these was 0.6 gram. These two values can be considered outliers. Only 1.176% of the shingles failed the specification. Only one of the Vermont shingles, had a granule loss greater than 0.8 gram. The next highest was 0.58 gram. Thus, only 0.714% of the shingles failed to meet the specification.

3.70 (a) The correlation between calories and protein is 0.4644. **(b)** The correlation between calories and cholesterol is 0.1777. **(c)** The correlation between protein and cholesterol is 0.1417. **(d)** There is a weak positive linear relationship between calories and protein, with a correlation coefficient of 0.46. The positive linear relationships between calories and cholesterol and between protein and cholesterol are very weak.

3.72 (a), (b)

Property Taxes per Capita ($)	
Mean	1,040.863
Median	981
Standard deviation	428.5385
Sample variance	183,645.2
Range	1,732
First quartile	713
Third quartile	1,306
Interquartile range	593
Coefficient of variation	41.17%

(c), (d) The distribution of the property taxes per capita is right-skewed, with a mean value of $1,040.83, a median of $981, and an average spread around the mean of $428.54. There is an outlier in the right tail at $2,099, while the standard deviation is about 41.17% of the mean. 25% of the states have property tax that falls below $713 per capita, and 25% have property taxes that are higher than $1,306 per capita.

CHAPTER 4

4.2 (a) Simple events include selecting a red ball. **(b)** Selecting a white ball.

4.4 (a) $60/100 = 3/5 = 0.6$. **(b)** $10/100 = 1/10 = 0.1$. **(c)** $35/100 = 7/20 = 0.35$. **(d)** $9/10 = 0.9$.

4.6 (a) Mutually exclusive, not collectively exhaustive. **(b)** Not mutually exclusive, not collectively exhaustive. **(c)** Mutually exclusive, not collectively exhaustive. **(d)** Mutually exclusive, collectively exhaustive.

4.8 (a) Needs three or more clicks to be removed from an email list. **(b)** Needs three or more clicks to be removed from an email list in 2009. **(c)** Does not need three or more clicks to be removed from an email list. **(d)** "Needs three or more clicks to be removed from an email list in 2009" is a joint event because it consists of two characteristics.

4.10 (a) A respondent who answers quickly. **(b)** A respondent who answers quickly who is over 70 years old. **(c)** A respondent who does not answer quickly. **(d)** A respondent who answers quickly and is over 70 years old is a joint event because it consists of two characteristics, answering quickly and being over 70 years old.

4.12 (a) $796/3{,}790 = 0.21$. **(b)** $1{,}895/3{,}790 = 0.50$. **(c)** $796/3{,}790 + 1{,}895/3{,}790 - 550/3{,}790 = 2{,}141/3790 = 0.5649$. **(d)** The probability of "is engaged with their workplace *or* is a U.S. worker" includes the probability of "is engaged with their workplace" plus the probability of "is a U.S. worker" minus the joint probability of "is engaged with their workplace *and* is a U.S. worker."

4.14 (a) $360/500 = 18/25 = 0.72$. **(b)** $224/500 = 56/125 = 0.448$. **(c)** $396/500 = 99/125 = 0.792$. **(d)** $500/500 = 1.00$.

4.16 (a) $10/30 = 1/3 = 0.33$. **(b)** $20/60 = 1/3 = 0.33$. **(c)** $40/60 = 2/3 = 0.67$. **(d)** Because $P(A/B) = P(A) = 1/3$, events A and B are independent.

4.18 $\frac{1}{2} = 0.5$.

4.20 Because $P(A \text{ and } B) = 0.20$ and $P(A)P(B) = 0.12$, events A and B are not independent.

4.22 (a) $536/1{,}000 = 0.536$. **(b)** $707/1{,}000 = 0.707$. **(c)** $P(\text{Answers quickly}) = 1{,}243/2{,}000 = 0.6215$ which is not equal to $P(\text{Answers quickly} \mid \text{between 12 and 50}) = 0.536$. Therefore, answers quickly and age are not independent.

4.24 (a) $550/1{,}895 = 0.2902$. **(b)** $1{,}345/1{,}895 = 0.7098$. **(c)** $246/1{,}895 = 0.1298$. **(d)** $1{,}649/1{,}895 = 0.8702$.

4.26 (a) $0.025/0.6 = 0.0417$. **(b)** $0.015/0.4 = 0.0375$. **(c)** Because $P(\text{Needs warranty repair} \mid \text{Manufacturer based in U.S.}) = 0.0417$ and $P(\text{Needs warranty repair}) = 0.04$, the two events are not independent.

4.28 (a) 0.0045. **(b)** 0.012. **(c)** 0.0059. **(d)** 0.0483.

4.30 0.095.

4.32 (a) 0.736. **(b)** 0.997.

4.34 (a) $P(B' \mid O) = \dfrac{(0.5)(0.3)}{(0.5)(0.3) + (0.25)(0.7)} = 0.4615.$

(b) $P(O) = 0.175 + 0.15 = 0.325$.

4.36 (a) $P(\text{Huge success} \mid \text{Favorable review}) = 0.099/0.459 = 0.2157$; $P(\text{Moderate success} \mid \text{Favorable review}) = 0.14/0.459 = 0.3050$; $P(\text{Break even} \mid \text{Favorable review}) = 0.16/0.459 = 0.3486$; $P(\text{Loser} \mid \text{Favorable review}) = 0.06/0.459 = 0.1307$. **(b)** $P(\text{Favorable review}) = 0.459$.

4.38 $3^{10} = 59{,}049$.

4.40 (a) $2^7 = 128$. **(b)** $6^7 = 279{,}936$. **(c)** There are two mutually exclusive and collectively exhaustive outcomes in (a) and six in (b).

4.42 (8)(4)(3)(3) = 288.

4.44 $5! = (5)(4)(3)(2)(1) = 120$. Not all the orders are equally likely because the teams have a different probability of finishing first through fifth.

4.46 $n! = 6! = 720$.

4.48 $\dfrac{10!}{4!6!} = 210$.

4.50 4,950.

4.60 (a)

	Age		
Goals	**18–25**	**26–40**	**Total**
Getting Rich	405	310	715
Other	95	190	285
Total	500	500	1,000

(b) Simple event: "Has a goal of getting rich." Joint event: "Has a goal of getting rich and is between 18–25 years old." **(c)** $P(\text{Has a goal of getting rich})$. **(d)** $P(\text{Has a goal of getting rich and is in the 26–40-year-old group}) = 310/1000 = 0.31$. **(e)** Not independent.

4.62 (a) 99/200. **(b)** 127/200. **(c)** 129/200. **(d)** 29/200. **(f)** 10/100.

4.64 (a) 0.4712. **(b)** Because the probability that a fatality involved a rollover, given that the fatality involved an SUV, a van, or a pickup is 0.4712, which is almost twice the probability that a fatality involved a rollover with any vehicle type, at 0.24, SUVs, vans, and pickups are generally more prone to rollover accidents.

CHAPTER 5

5.2 (a) $\mu = 0(0.10) + 1(0.20) + 2(0.45) + 3(0.15) + 4(0.05) + 5(0.05) = 2.0.$

(b) $\sigma = \sqrt{\begin{array}{l}(0-2)^2(0.10) + (1-2)^2(0.20) + (2-2)^2(0.45) + \\ (3-2)^2(0.15) + (4-2)^2(0.05) + (5-2)^2(0.05)\end{array}}$
$= 1.183.$

5.4 (a)

X	P(X)
\$ − 1	21/36
\$ + 1	15/36

(b)

X	P(X)
\$ − 1	21/36
\$ + 1	15/36

(c)

X	P(X)
\$ − 1	30/36
\$ + 4	6/36

(d) \$−0.167 for each method of play.

5.6 (a) 2.1058. **(b)** 1.4671.

5.8 (a) 90; 30. **(b)** 126.10, 10.95. **(c)** −1,300. **(d)** 120.

5.10 (a) 9.5 minutes. **(b)** 1.9209 minutes.

5.12

$X{*}P(X)$	$Y{*}P(Y)$	$(X-\mu_X)^2{*}P(X)$	$(Y-\mu_Y)^2{*}P(Y)$	$(X-\mu_X)(Y-\mu_Y){*}P(XY)$
−10	5	2,528.1	129.6	−572.4
0	45	1,044.3	5,548.8	−2,407.2
24	−6	132.3	346.8	−214.2
45	−30	2,484.3	3,898.8	−3,112.2

(a) $E(X) = \mu_X = \sum_{i-1}^{N} X_i P(X_i) = 59, E(Y) = \mu_Y = \sum_{i-1}^{N} Y_i P(Y_i) = 14.$

(b) $\sigma_X = \sqrt{\sum_{i-1}^{N}[X_i - E(X)]^2 P(X_i)} = 78.6702.$

$\sigma_Y = \sqrt{\sum_{i=1}^{N}[Y_i - E(Y)]^2 P(Y_i)} = 99.62.$

(c) $\sigma_{XY} = \sum_{i=1}^{N}[X_i - E(X)][Y_i - E(Y)]P(X_iY_i) = -6{,}306.$

(d) Stock *X* gives the investor a lower standard deviation while yielding a higher expected return, so the investor should select stock *X*.

5.14 (a) \$71; \$97. **(b)** 61.88; 84.27. **(c)** 5,113. **(d)** Risk-averse investors would invest in stock *X*, whereas risk takers would invest in stock *Y*.

5.16 (a) $E(X) = \$66.20$; $E(Y) = \$63.01$. **(b)** $\sigma_X = \$57.22$; $\sigma_Y = \$195.22$. **(c)** $\sigma_{XY} = \$10{,}766.44$. **(d)** Based on the expected value criteria, you would choose the common stock fund. However, the common stock fund also has a standard deviation more than three times higher than that for the corporate bond fund. An investor should carefully weigh the increased risk. **(e)** If you chose the common stock fund, you would need to assess your reaction to the small possibility that you could lose virtually all of your entire investment.

5.18 (a) 0.0768. **(b)** 0.9130. **(c)** 0.3370. **(d)** 0.6630.

5.20 (a) 0.40, 0.60. **(b)** 1.60, 0.98. **(c)** 4.0, 0.894. **(d)** 1.50, 0.866.

5.22 (a) 0.2128. **(b)** 0.3153. **(c)** 0.9294. **(d)** $\mu = 4.95$ $\sigma = 0.9307$.

5.24 (a) 0.0834. **(b)** 0.2351. **(c)** 0.6169. **(d)** 0.3831.

5.26 Given $\pi = 0.848$ and $n = 3$,

(a) $P(X=3) = \frac{n!}{x!(n-x)!}\pi^x(1-\pi)^{n-x} = \frac{3!}{3!0!}(0.848)^3(0.152)^0 = 0.6098.$

(b) $P(X=0) = \frac{n!}{x!(n-x)!}\pi^x(1-\pi)^{n-x} = \frac{3!}{0!3!}(0.848)^0(0.152)^3 = 0.0035.$

(c) $P(X \geq 2) = P(X=2) + P(X=3)$
$= \frac{3!}{2!1!}(0.848)^2(0.152)^1 + \frac{3!}{3!0!}(0.848)^3(0.152)^0 = 0.9377.$

(d) $E(X) = n\pi = 3(0.848) = 2.544$ $\sigma_X = \sqrt{n\pi(1-\pi)}$
$= \sqrt{3(0.848)(0.152)} = 0.6218.$

5.28 (a) 0.2565. **(b)** 0.1396. **(c)** 0.3033. **(d)** 0.0247.

5.30 (a) 0.0337. **(b)** 0.0067. **(c)** 0.9596. **(d)** 0.0404.

5.32 (a) $P(X < 5) = P(X=0) + P(X=1) + P(x=2) + P(X=3) + P(X=4)$

$= \frac{e^{-6}(6)^0}{0!} + \frac{e^{-6}(6)^1}{1!} + \frac{e^{-6}(6)^2}{2!} + \frac{e^{-6}(6)^3}{3!} + \frac{e^{-6}(6)^4}{4!}$

$= 0.002479 + 0.014873 + 0.044618 + 0.089235 + 0.133853$

$= 0.2851.$

(b) $P(X=5) = \frac{e^{-6}(6)^5}{5!} = 0.1606.$

(c) $P(X \geq 5) = 1 - P(X < 5) = 1 - 0.2851 = 0.7149.$

(d) $P(X = 4 \text{ or } X = 5) = P(X=4) + P(X=5) = \frac{e^{-6}(6)^4}{4!} + \frac{e^{-6}(6)^5}{5!}$

$= 0.2945.$

5.34 (a) $P(X=0) = 0.0204$. **(b)** $P(X \geq 1) = 0.9796$.
(c) $P(X \geq 2) = 0.9000$.

5.36 (a) 0.0176. **(b)** 0.9093. **(c)** 0.9220.

5.38 (a) 0.2618. **(b)** 0.8478. **(c)** Because Ford had a lower mean rate of problems per car in 2009 compared to Dodge, the probability of a randomly selected Ford having zero problems and the probability of no more than two problems are both higher than their values for Dodge.

5.40 (a) 0.2441. **(b)** 0.8311. **(c)** Because Dodge had a lower mean rate of problems per car in 2009 compared to 2008, the probability of a randomly selected Dodge having zero problems and the probability of no more than two problems are both lower in 2009 than their values in 2008.

5.42 (a) 0.238. **(b)** 0.2. **(c)** 0.1591. **(d)** 0.0083.

5.44 (a) If $n = 6, A = 25$, and $N = 100$,

$P(X \geq 2) = 1 - [P(X=0) + P(X=1)]$

$$= 1 - \left[\frac{\binom{25}{0}\binom{100-25}{6-0}}{\binom{100}{6}} + \frac{\binom{25}{1}\binom{100-25}{6-1}}{\binom{100}{6}}\right].$$

$= 1 - [0.1689 + 0.3620] = 0.4691.$

(b) If $n = 6, A = 30$, and $N = 100$,

$P(X \geq 2) = 1 - [P(X=0) + P(X=1)]$

$$= 1 - \left[\frac{\binom{30}{0}\binom{100-30}{6-0}}{\binom{100}{6}} + \frac{\binom{30}{1}\binom{100-30}{6-1}}{\binom{100}{6}}\right].$$

$= 1 - [0.1100 + 0.3046] = 0.5854.$

(c) If $n = 6, A = 5$, and $N = 100$,

$$P(X \geq 2) = 1 - [P(X = 0) + P(X = 1)]$$

$$= 1 - \left[\frac{\binom{5}{0}\binom{100-5}{6-0}}{\binom{100}{6}} + \frac{\binom{5}{1}\binom{100-5}{6-1}}{\binom{100}{6}}\right].$$

$$= 1 - [0.7291 + 0.2430] = 0.0279$$

(d) If $n = 6, A = 10$, and $N = 100$,

$$P(X \geq 2) = 1 - [P(X = 0) + P(X = 1)]$$

$$= 1 - \left[\frac{\binom{10}{0}\binom{100-10}{6-0}}{\binom{100}{6}} + \frac{\binom{10}{1}\binom{100-10}{6-1}}{\binom{100}{6}}\right].$$

$$= 1 - [0.5223 + 0.3687] = 0.1090$$

(e) The probability that the entire group will be audited is very sensitive to the true number of improper returns in the population. If the true number is very low ($A = 5$), the probability is very low (0.0279). When the true number is increased by a factor of 6 ($A = 30$), the probability the group will be audited increases by a factor of more than 20 (0.5854).

5.46 (a) $P(X = 4) = 0.00003649$. **(b)** $P(X = 0) = 0.5455$. **(c)** $P(X \geq 1) = 0.4545$. **(d)** $X = 6$. **(a)** $P(X = 4) = 0.0005$. **(b)** $P(X = 0) = 0.3877$. **(c)** $P(X \geq 1) = 0.6123$.

5.48 (a) $P(X = 1) = 0.2424$. **(b)** $P(X \geq 1) = 0.9697$. **(c)** $P(X = 3) = 0.2424$. **(d)** Because there were now 12 funds to consider, the probability that 3 would be short-term corporate funds decreased from 0.3810 to 0.2424.

5.54 (a) 0.64. **(b)** 0.64. **(c)** 0.3020. **(d)** 0.0060. **(e)** The assumption of independence may not be true.

5.56 (a) If $\pi = 0.50$ and $n = 12$, $P(X \geq 9) = 0.0730$. **(b)** If $\pi = 0.75$ and $n = 12$, $P(X \geq 9) = 0.6488$.

5.58 (a) 0.1074. **(b)** 0.2684. **(c)** 0.6242. **(d)** Mean $= 2.0$, standard deviation $= 1.2649$.

5.60 (a) $\mu = n\pi = 13.6$ **(b)** $\sigma = \sqrt{n\pi(1 - p)} = 2.0861$. **(c)** $P(X = 15) = 0.1599$. **(d)** $P(X \leq 10) = 0.0719$. **(e)** $P(X \geq 10) = 0.9721$.

5.62 (a) If $\pi = 0.50$ and $n = 38$, $P(X \geq 33) = 0.00000213$. **(b)** If $\pi = 0.70$ and $n = 38$, $P(X \geq 33) = 0.0137$. **(c)** If $\pi = 0.90$ and $n = 38$, $P(X \geq 33) = 0.8252$. **(d)** Based on the results in (a)–(c), the probability that the Standard & Poor's 500 Index will increase if there is an early gain in the first five trading days of the year is very likely to be close to 0.90 because that yields a probability of 82.52% that at least 33 of the 38 years the Standard & Poor's 500 Index will increase the entire year.

5.64 (a) The assumptions needed are (i) the probability that a golfer loses a golf ball in a given interval is constant, (ii) the probability that a golfer loses more than one golf ball approaches 0 as the interval gets smaller, and (iii) the probability that a golfer loses a golf ball is independent from interval to interval. **(b)** 0.0067. **(c)** 0.6160. **(d)** 0.3840.

5.66 (a) Virtually 0. **(b)** 0.00000037737. **(c)** 0.00000173886. **(d)** 0.000168669. **(e)** 0.0011998. **(f)** 0.00407937. **(g)** 0.006598978. **(h)** 0.0113502. **(i)** 0.976601.

CHAPTER 6

6.2 (a) 0.9089. **(b)** 0.0911. **(c)** +1.96. **(d)** −1.00 and +1.00.

6.4 (a) 0.1401. **(b)** 0.4168. **(c)** 0.3918. **(d)** +1.00.

6.6 (a) 0.9599. **(b)** 0.0228. **(c)** 43.42. **(d)** 46.64 and 53.36.

6.8 (a) $P(34 < X < 50) = P(-1.33 < Z < 0) = 0.4082$. **(b)** $P(X < 30) + P(X > 60) = P(Z < -1.67) + P(Z > 0.83) = 0.0475 + (1.0 - 0.7967) = 0.2508$. **(c)** $P(Z < -0.84) \cong 0.20$, $Z = -0.84 = \frac{X - 50}{12}$, $X = 50 - 0.84(12) = 39.92$ thousand miles, or 39,920 miles. **(d)** The smaller standard deviation makes the Z values larger. **(a)** $P(34 < X < 50) = P(-1.60 < Z < 0) = 0.4452$. **(b)** $P(X < 30) + P(X > 60) = P(Z < -2.00) + P(Z > 1.00) = 0.0228 + (1.0 - 0.8413) = 0.1815$. **(c)** $X = 50 - 0.84(10) = 41.6$ thousand miles, or 41,600 miles.

6.10 (a) 0.9878. **(b)** 0.8185. **(c)** 86.16%. **(d)** Option 1: Because your score of 81% on this exam represents a Z score of 1.00, which is below the minimum Z score of 1.28, you will not earn an A grade on the exam under this grading option. Option 2: Because your score of 68% on this exam represents a Z score of 2.00, which is well above the minimum Z score of 1.28, you will earn an A grade on the exam under this grading option. You should prefer Option 2.

6.12 (a) 0.9461. **(b)** 0.0032. **(c)** 0.0045. **(d)** 29.6714.

6.14 With 39 values, the smallest of the standard normal quantile values covers an area under the normal curve of 0.025. The corresponding Z value is −1.96. The middle (20th) value has a cumulative area of 0.50 and a corresponding Z value of 0.0. The largest of the standard normal quantile values covers an area under the normal curve of 0.975, and its corresponding Z value is +1.96.

6.16 (a) Mean $= 20.9231$, median $= 21$, $S = 2.7265$, range $= 10$, $6S = 6(2.7265) = 16.359$, interquartile range $= 3$, $1.33(2.7265) = 3.6262$. The mean is slightly less than the median. The range is much less than $6S$, and the interquartile range is less than $1.33S$. **(b)** The normal probability plot does not appear to be highly skewed. The data may be symmetrical but not normally distributed.

6.18 (a) Mean $= 1{,}040.863$, median $= 981$, range $= 1{,}732$, $6(S) = 2{,}571.2310$, interquartile range $= 593$, $1.33(S) = 569.9562$. There are 62.75%, 78.43%, and 94.12% of the observations that fall within 1, 1.28, and 2 standard deviations of the mean, respectively, as compared to the approximate theoretical 66.67%, 80%, and 95%. Because the mean is slightly larger than the median, the interquartile range is slightly larger than 1.33 times the standard deviation, and the range is much smaller than 6 times the standard deviation, the data appear to deviate slightly from the normal distribution. **(b)** The normal probability plot suggests that the data appear to be slightly right-skewed.

6.20 (a) Interquartile range $= 0.0025$, $S = 0.0017$, range $= 0.008$, $1.33(S) = 0.0023$, $6(S) = 0.0102$. Because the interquartile range is close to $1.33S$ and the range is also close to $6S$, the data appear to be approximately normally distributed. **(b)** The normal probability plot suggests that the data appear to be approximately normally distributed.

6.22 (a) Five-number summary: 82 127 148.5 168 213; mean $= 147.06$, mode $= 130$, range $= 131$, interquartile range $= 41$, standard deviation $= 31.69$. The mean is very close to the median. The five-number summary suggests that the distribution is approximately symmetrical around the median. The interquartile range is very close to $1.33S$. The range is about $50 below $6S$. In general, the distribution of the data appears to closely resemble a normal distribution. **(b)** The normal probability plot confirms that the data appear to be approximately normally distributed.

6.24 (a) $(20 - 0)/120 = 0.1667$. **(b)** $(30 - 10)/120 = 0.1667$. **(c)** $(120 - 35)/120 = 0.7083$. **(d)** Mean $= 60$, standard deviation $= 34.641$.

6.26 (a) 0.1. **(b)** 0.3333. **(c)** 0.3333. **(d)** Mean = 4.5, standard deviation = 0.8660.

6.28 (a) 0.6321. **(b)** 0.3679. **(c)** 0.2326. **(d)** 0.7674.

6.30 (a) 0.7769. **(b)** 0.2231. **(c)** 0.1410. **(d)** 0.8590.

6.32 (a) For $\lambda = 2, P(X \leq 1) = 0.8647$. **(b)** For $\lambda = 2, P(X \leq 5) = 0.99996$. **(c)** For $\lambda = 1, P(X \leq 1) = 0.6321$, for $\lambda = 1, P(X \leq 5) = 0.9933$.

6.34 (a) 0.6321. **(b)** 0.3935. **(c)** 0.0952.

6.36 (a) 0.8647. **(b)** 0.3297. **(c)(a)** 0.9765. **(b)** 0.5276.

6.46 (a) 0.4772. **(b)** 0.9544. **(c)** 0.0456. **(d)** 1.8835. **(e)** 1.8710 and 2.1290.

6.48 (a) 0.2734. **(b)** 0.2038. **(c)** 4.404 ounces. **(d)** 4.188 ounces and 5.212 ounces.

6.50 (a) Waiting time will more closely resemble an exponential distribution. **(b)** Seating time will more closely resemble a normal distribution. **(c)** Both the histogram and normal probability plot suggest that waiting time more closely resembles an exponential distribution. **(d)** Both the histogram and normal probability plot suggest that seating time more closely resembles a normal distribution.

6.52 (a) 0.999968 **(b)** 0.0668 **(c)** 0.0013 **(d)** 1.6653 **(e)** 0.8080 to 1.592 **(f)** 1.0, 0.30, 0.10, 1.935, 0.4875 to 1.91255.

CHAPTER 7

7.2 Sample without replacement: Read from left to right in three-digit sequences and continue unfinished sequences from the end of the row to the beginning of the next row:
Row 05: 338 505 855 551 438 855 077 186 579 488 767 833 170
Rows 05–06: 897
Row 06: 340 033 648 847 204 334 639 193 639 411 095 924
Rows 06–07: 707
Row 07: 054 329 776 100 871 007 255 980 646 886 823 920 461
Row 08: 893 829 380 900 796 959 453 410 181 277 660 908 887
Rows 08–09: 237
Row 09: 818 721 426 714 050 785 223 801 670 353 362 449
Rows 09–10: 406
Note: All sequences above 902 and duplicates are discarded.

7.4 A simple random sample would be less practical for personal interviews because of travel costs (unless interviewees are paid to go to a central interviewing location).

7.6 Here all members of the population are equally likely to be selected, and the sample selection mechanism is based on chance. But selection of two elements is not independent; for example, if *A* is in the sample, we know that *B* is also and that *C* and *D* are not.

7.8 (a)

Row 16: 2323 6737 5131 8888 1718 0654 6832 4647 6510 4877
Row 17: 4579 4269 2615 1308 2455 7830 5550 5852 5514 7182
Row 18: 0989 3205 0514 2256 8514 4642 7567 8896 2977 8822
Row 19: 5438 2745 9891 4991 4523 6847 9276 8646 1628 3554
Row 20: 9475 0899 2337 0892 0048 8033 6945 9826 9403 6858
Row 21: 7029 7341 3553 1403 3340 4205 0823 4144 1048 2949
Row 22: 8515 7479 5432 9792 6575 5760 0408 8112 2507 3742
Row 23: 1110 0023 4012 8607 4697 9664 4894 3928 7072 5815
Row 24: 3687 1507 7530 5925 7143 1738 1688 5625 8533 5041
Row 25: 2391 3483 5763 3081 6090 5169 0546
Note: All sequences above 5,000 are discarded. There were no repeating sequences.

(b) 089 189 289 389 489 589 689 789 889 989
1089 1189 1289 1389 1489 1589 1689 1789 1889 1989
2089 2189 2289 2389 2489 2589 2689 2789 2889 2989
3089 3189 3289 3389 3489 3589 3689 3789 3889 3989
4089 4189 4289 4389 4489 4589 4689 4789 4889 4989

(c) With the single exception of invoice 0989, the invoices selected in the simple random sample are not the same as those selected in the systematic sample. It would be highly unlikely that a simple random sample would select the same units as a systematic sample.

7.10 Before accepting the results of a survey of college students, you might want to know, for example: Who funded the survey? Why was it conducted? What was the population from which the sample was selected? What sampling design was used? What mode of response was used: a personal interview, a telephone interview, or a mail survey? Were interviewers trained? Were survey questions field-tested? What questions were asked? Were the questions clear, accurate, unbiased, and valid? What operational definition of "vast majority" was used? What was the response rate? What was the sample size?

7.12 (a) The four types of survey errors are coverage error, nonresponse error, sampling error, and measurement error. **(b)** When people who answer the survey tell you what they think you want to hear, rather than what they really believe, this is the halo effect, which is a source of measurement error. Also, every survey will have sampling error that reflects the chance differences from sample to sample, based on the probability of particular individuals being selected in the particular sample.

7.14 Before accepting the results of the survey, you might want to know, for example: Who funded the study? Why was it conducted? What was the population from which the sample was selected? What sampling design was used? What mode of response was used: a personal interview, a telephone interview, or a mail survey? Were interviewers trained? Were survey questions field-tested? What other questions were asked? Were the questions clear, accurate, unbiased, and valid? What was the response rate? What was the margin of error? What was the sample size? What frame was used?

7.16 (a) Virtually 0. **(b)** 0.1587. **(c)** 0.0139. **(d)** 50.195.

7.18 (a) Both means are equal to 6. This property is called unbiasedness. **(c)** The distribution for $n = 3$ has less variability. The larger sample size has resulted in sample means being closer to μ.

7.20 (a) When $n = 2$, because the mean is larger than the median, the distribution of the sales price of new houses is skewed to the right, and so is the sampling distribution of $\bar{X}$ although it will be less skewed than the population. **(b)** If you select samples of $n = 100$, the shape of the sampling distribution of the sample mean will be very close to a normal distribution, with a mean of \$274,300 and a standard deviation of \$9,000. **(c)** 0.9996. **(d)** 0.2796

7.22 (a) $P(\bar{X} > 3) = P(Z > -1.00) = 1.0 - 0.1587 = 0.8413$. **(b)** $P(Z < 1.04) = 0.85; \bar{X} = 3.10 + 1.04(0.1) = 3.204$. **(c)** To be able to use the standardized normal distribution as an approximation for the area under the curve, you must assume that the population is approximately symmetrical. **(d)** $P(Z < 1.04) = 0.85; \bar{X} = 3.10 + 1.04(0.05) = 3.152$.

7.24 (a) 0.40. **(b)** 0.0704.

7.26 (a) $\pi = 0.501, \sigma_p = \sqrt{\dfrac{\pi(1-\pi)}{n}} = \sqrt{\dfrac{0.501(1-0.501)}{100}} = 0.05$

$P(p > 0.55) = P(Z > 0.98) = 1.0 - 0.8365 = 0.1635$.

(b) $\pi = 0.60, \sigma_p = \sqrt{\dfrac{\pi(1-\pi)}{n}} = \sqrt{\dfrac{0.6(1-0.6)}{100}} = 0.04899$.

$P(p > 0.55) = P(Z > -1.021) = 1.0 - 0.1539 = 0.8461.$

(c) $\pi = 0.49, \sigma_P = \sqrt{\dfrac{\pi(1-\pi)}{n}} = \sqrt{\dfrac{0.49(1-0.49)}{100}} = 0.05$

$P(p > 0.55) = P(Z > 1.20) = 1.0 - 0.8849 = 0.1151.$

(d) Increasing the sample size by a factor of 4 decreases the standard error by a factor of 2.

(a) $P(p > 0.55) = P(Z > 1.96) = 1.0 - 0.9750 = 0.0250.$
(b) $P(p > 0.55) = P(Z > -2.04) = 1.0 - 0.0207 = 0.9793.$
(c) $P(p > 0.55) = P(Z > 2.40) = 1.0 - 0.9918 = 0.0082.$

7.28 (a) 0.7889. **(b)** 0.6746. **(c)** 0.8857. **(d) (a)** 0.9458. **(b)** 0.9377. **(c)** 0.9920.

7.30 (a) 0.8422 **(b)** The probability is 90% that the sample percentage will be contained within 5.58% (0.3042 to 0.4158) symmetrically around the population percentage. **(c)** The probability is 95% that the sample percentage will be contained within 6.65% (0.2935 to 0.4265) symmetrically around the population percentage.

7.32 (a) 0.0336. **(b)** 0.0000. **(c)** Increasing the sample size by a factor of 5 decreases the standard error by a factor of $\sqrt{5}$. The sampling distribution of the proportion becomes more concentrated around the true proportion of 0.59 and, hence, the probability in (b) becomes smaller than that in (a).

7.44 (a) 0.4999. **(b)** 0.00009. **(c)** 0. **(d)** 0. **(e)** 0.7518.

7.46 (a) 0.8944. **(b)** 4.617; 4.783. **(c)** 4.641.

7.48 (a) 0.0668. **(b)** 0.6912. **(c)** 0.9998.

CHAPTER 8

8.2 $114.68 \le \mu \le 135.32$.

8.4 Yes, it is true because 5% of intervals will not include the population mean.

8.6 (a) You would compute the mean first because you need the mean to compute the standard deviation. If you had a sample, you would compute the sample mean. If you had the population mean, you would compute the population standard deviation. **(b)** If you have a sample, you are computing the sample standard deviation, not the population standard deviation needed in Equation (8.1). If you have a population and have computed the population mean and population standard deviation, you don't need a confidence interval estimate of the population mean because you already know the mean.

8.8 Equation (8.1) assumes that you know the population standard deviation. Because you are selecting a sample of 100 from the population, you are computing a sample standard deviation, not the population standard deviation.

8.10 (a) $\bar{X} \pm Z \cdot \dfrac{\sigma}{\sqrt{n}} = 350 \pm 1.96 \cdot \dfrac{100}{\sqrt{64}}$; $325.50 \le \mu \le 374.50$.
(b) No, the manufacturer cannot support a claim that the bulbs have a mean of 400 hours. Based on the data from the sample, a mean of 400 hours would represent a distance of 4 standard deviations above the sample mean of 350 hours. **(c)** No. Because σ is known and $n = 64$, from the Central Limit Theorem, you know that the sampling distribution of $\bar{X}$ is approximately normal. **(d)** The confidence interval is narrower, based on a population standard deviation of 80 hours rather than the original standard deviation of 100 hours. $\bar{X} \pm Z \cdot \dfrac{\sigma}{\sqrt{n}} = 350 \pm 1.96 \cdot \dfrac{80}{\sqrt{64}}$, $330.4 \le \mu \le 369.6$. Based on the smaller standard deviation, a mean of 400 hours would represent a distance of 5 standard deviations above the sample mean of 350 hours. No, the manufacturer cannot support a claim that the bulbs have a mean life of 400 hours.

8.12 (a) 2.2622. **(b)** 3.2498. **(c)** 2.0395. **(d)** 1.9977. **(e)** 1.7531.

8.14 $-0.12 \le \mu \le 11.84$, $2.00 \le \mu \le 6.00$. The presence of the outlier increases the sample mean and greatly inflates the sample standard deviation.

8.16 (a) $32 \pm (2.0096)(9)/\sqrt{50}$; $29.44 \le \mu \le 34.56$ **(b)** The quality improvement team can be 95% confident that the population mean turnaround time is between 29.44 hours and 34.56 hours. **(c)** The project was a success because the initial turnaround time of 68 hours does not fall within the interval.

8.18 (a) $5.64 \le \mu \le 8.42$. **(b)** You can be 95% confident that the population mean amount spent for lunch at a fast-food restaurant is between \$5.64 and \$8.42.

8.20 (a) $19.82 \le \mu \le 22.02$. **(b)** You can be 95% confident that the population mean miles per gallon of 2010 small SUVs is between 19.82 and 22.02. **(c)** Because the 95% confidence interval for population mean miles per gallon of 2010 small SUVs overlaps with that for the population mean miles per gallon of 2010 family sedans, you are unable to conclude that the population mean miles per gallon of 2010 small SUVs is lower than that of 2010 family sedans.

8.22 (a) $31.12 \le \mu \le 54.96$. **(b)** The number of days is approximately normally distributed. **(c)** No, the outliers skew the data. **(d)** Because the sample size is fairly large, at $n = 50$, the use of the t distribution is appropriate.

8.24 (a) $\$0.7367 \le \$1.1147$. **(b)** The population distribution needs to be normally distributed. **(c)** Both the normal probability plot and the boxplot show that the distribution of the cost of dark chocolate bars is right-skewed.

8.26 $0.19 \le \pi \le 0.31$.

8.28 (a) $p = \dfrac{X}{n} = \dfrac{135}{500} = 0.27$, $p \pm Z\sqrt{\dfrac{p(1-p)}{n}} = 0.27 \pm 2.58\sqrt{\dfrac{0.27(0.73)}{500}}$; $0.2189 \le \pi \le 0.3211$. **(b)** The manager in charge of promotional programs concerning residential customers can infer that the proportion of households that would purchase an additional telephone line if it were made available at a substantially reduced installation cost is somewhere between 0.22 and 0.32, with 99% confidence.

8.30 (a) $0.4762 \le \pi \le 0.5638$. **(b)** No, you cannot, because the interval estimate includes 0.50 (50%). **(c)** $0.5062 \le \pi \le 0.5338$. Yes, you can, because the interval is above 0.50 (50%). **(d)** The larger the sample size, the narrower the confidence interval, holding everything else constant.

8.32 (a) $0.784 \le \pi \le 0.816$. **(b)** $0.5099 \le \pi \le 0.5498$. **(c)** Many more people think that e-mail messages are easier to misinterpret.

8.34 $n = 35$.

8.36 $n = 1{,}041$.

8.38 (a) $n = \dfrac{Z^2\sigma^2}{e^2} = \dfrac{(1.96)^2(400)^2}{50^2} = 245.86$. Use $n = 246$.

(b) $n = \dfrac{Z^2\sigma^2}{e^2} = \dfrac{(1.96)^2(400)^2}{25^2} = 983.41$. Use $n = 984$.

8.40 $n = 97$.

8.42 (a) $n = 167$. **(b)** $n = 97$.

8.44 (a) $n = 246$. **(b)** $n = 385$. **(c)** $n = 554$. **(d)** When there is more variability in the population, a larger sample is needed to accurately estimate the mean.

8.46 (a) $p = 0.28; 0.2522 \le \pi \le 0.3078$. **(b)** $p = 0.19; 0.1657 \le \pi \le 0.2143$. **(c)** $p = 0.07; 0.0542 \le \pi \le 0.0858$. **(d) (a)** $n = 1{,}937$. **(b)** $n = 1{,}479$. **(c)** $n = 626$.

8.48 (a) If you conducted a follow-up study to estimate the population proportion of individuals who view oil companies favorably, you would use $\pi = 0.84$ in the sample size formula because it is based on past information on the proportion. **(b)** $n = 574$.

8.50 $\$10{,}721.53 \le \text{Total} \le \$14{,}978.47$.

8.52 (a) 0.054. **(b)** 0.0586. **(c)** 0.066.

8.54 $(3{,}000)(\$261.40) \pm (3{,}000)(1.8331)\dfrac{(138.8046)}{\sqrt{10}}\sqrt{\dfrac{3{,}000 - 10}{3{,}000 - 1}}$.

$\$543{,}176.96 \le \text{Total} \le \$1{,}025{,}224.04$.

8.56 $\$5{,}443 \le \text{Total difference} \le \$54{,}229$.

8.58 (a) 0.0542. **(b)** Because the upper bound is higher than the tolerable exception rate of 0.04, the auditor should request a larger sample.

8.66 $940.50 \le \mu \le 1007.50$. Based on the evidence gathered from the sample of 34 stores, the 95% confidence interval for the mean per-store count in all of the franchise's stores is from 940.50 to 1,007.50. With a 95% level of confidence, the franchise can conclude that the mean per-store count in all its stores is somewhere between 940.50 and 1,007.50, which is larger than the original average of 900 mean per-store count before the price reduction. Hence, reducing coffee prices is a good strategy to increase the mean customer count.

8.68 (a) $14.085 \le \mu \le 16.515$. **(b)** $0.530 \le \pi \le 0.820$. **(c)** $n = 25$. **(d)** $n = 784$. **(e)** If a single sample were to be selected for both purposes, the larger of the two sample sizes ($n = 784$) should be used.

8.70 (a) $8.049 \le \mu \le 11.351$. **(b)** $0.284 \le \pi \le 0.676$. **(c)** $n = 35$. **(d)** $n = 121$. **(e)** If a single sample were to be selected for both purposes, the larger of the two sample sizes ($n = 121$) should be used.

8.72 (a) $\$25.80 \le \mu \le \$31.24$. **(b)** $0.3037 \le \pi \le 0.4963$. **(c)** $n = 97$. **(d)** $n = 423$. **(e)** If a single sample were to be selected for both purposes, the larger of the two sample sizes ($n = 423$) should be used.

8.74 (a) $\$36.66 \le \mu \le \$40.42$. **(b)** $0.2027 \le \pi \le 0.3973$. **(c)** $n = 110$. **(d)** $n = 423$. **(e)** If a single sample were to be selected for both purposes, the larger of the two sample sizes ($n = 423$) should be used.

8.76 (a) $\pi \le 0.2013$. **(b)** Because the upper bound is higher than the tolerable exception rate of 0.15, the auditor should request a larger sample.

8.78 (a) $n = 27$. **(b)** $\$402{,}652.53 \le \text{Population total} \le \$450{,}950.79$.

8.80 (a) $8.41 \le \mu \le 8.43$. **(b)** With 95% confidence, the population mean width of troughs is somewhere between 8.41 and 8.43 inches. **(c)** The assumption is valid as the width of the troughs is approximately normally distributed.

8.82 (a) $0.2425 \le \mu \le 0.2856$. **(b)** $0.1975 \le \mu \le 0.2385$. **(c)** The amounts of granule loss for both brands are skewed to the right, but the sample sizes are large enough. **(d)** Because the two confidence intervals do not overlap, you can conclude that the mean granule loss of Boston shingles is higher than that of Vermont shingles.

CHAPTER 9

9.2 Because $Z_{STAT} = +2.21 > 1.96$, reject H_0.

9.4 Reject H_0 if $Z_{STAT} < -2.58$ or if $Z_{STAT} > 2.58$.

9.6 p-value $= 0.0456$.

9.8 p-value $= 0.1676$.

9.10 H_0: Defendant is guilty; H_1: Defendant is innocent. A Type I error would be not convicting a guilty person. A Type II error would be convicting an innocent person.

9.12 H_0: $\mu = 20$ minutes. 20 minutes is adequate travel time between classes. H_1: $\mu \ne 20$ minutes. 20 minutes is not adequate travel time between classes.

9.14 (a) $Z_{Stat} = \dfrac{350 - 375}{\dfrac{100}{\sqrt{64}}} = -2.0$. Because $Z_{Stat} = -2.00 < -1.96$, reject H_0. **(b)** p-value $= 0.0456$. **(c)** $325.5 \le \mu \le 374.5$. **(d)** The conclusions are the same.

9.16 (a) Because $-2.58 < Z_{Stat} = -1.7678 < 2.58$, do not reject H_0. **(b)** p-value $= 0.0771$. **(c)** $0.9877 \le \mu \le 1.0023$. **(d)** The conclusions are the same.

9.18 $t_{STAT} = 2.00$.

9.20 ± 2.1315.

9.22 No, you should not use a t test because the original population is left-skewed, and the sample size is not large enough for the t test to be valid.

9.24 (a) $t_{STAT} = (3.57 - 3.70)/0.8/\sqrt{64} = -1.30$. Because $-1.9983 < t_{STAT} = -1.30 < 1.9983$ and p-value $= 0.1984 > 0.05$, there is no evidence that the population mean waiting time is different from 3.7 minutes. **(b)** Because $n = 64$, the central limit theorem should ensure that the sampling distribution of the mean is approximately normal. In general, the t test is appropriate for this sample size except for the case where the population is extremely skewed or bimodal.

9.26 (a) $-1.9842 < t_{STAT} = 1.1364 < 1.9842$. There is no evidence that the population mean retail value of the greeting cards is different from \$2.50. **(b)** p-value $= 0.2585 > 0.05$. The probability of getting a t_{STAT} statistic greater than $+1.1364$ or less than -1.1364, given that the null hypothesis is true, is 0.2585.

9.28 (a) Because $-2.306 < t_{STAT} = 0.8754 < 2.306$, do not reject H_0. There is not enough evidence to conclude that the mean amount spent for lunch at a fast food restaurant, is different from \$6.50. **(b)** The p-value is 0.4069. If the population mean is \$6.50, the probability of observing a sample of nine customers that will result in a sample mean farther away from the hypothesized value than this sample is 0.4069. **(c)** The distribution of the amount spent is normally distributed. **(d)** With a small sample size, it is difficult to evaluate the assumption of normality. However, the distribution may be symmetric because the mean and the median are close in value.

9.30 (a) Because $-2.0096 < t_{STAT} = 0.114 < 2.0096$, do not reject H_0. There is no evidence that the mean amount is different from 2 liters. **(b)** p-value $= 0.9095$. **(d)** Yes, the data appear to have met the normality assumption. **(e)** The amount of fill is decreasing over time. Therefore, the t test is invalid.

9.32 (a) Because $t_{STAT} = -5.9355 < -2.0106$, reject H_0. There is enough evidence to conclude that mean widths of the troughs is different from 8.46 inches. **(b)** The population distribution is normal. **(c)** Although the distribution of the widths is left-skewed, the large sample size means that the validity of the t test is not seriously affected.

9.34 (a) Because $-2.68 < t_{STAT} = 0.094 < 2.68$, do not reject H_0. There is no evidence that the mean amount is different from 5.5 grams. **(b)** $5.462 \le \mu \le 5.542$. **(c)** The conclusions are the same.

9.36 p-value $= 0.0228$.

9.38 p-value $= 0.0838$.

9.40 p-value $= 0.9162$.

9.42 $t_{STAT} = 2.7638$.

9.44 $t_{STAT} = -2.5280$.

9.46 (a) $t_{STAT} = -1.7094 < -1.6604$. There is evidence that the population mean waiting time is less than 36.5 hours. **(b)** p-value $= 0.0453 < 0.05$. The probability of getting a t_{STAT} statistic less than -1.7094, given that the null hypothesis is true, is 0.0453. **(c)** The results are different because in this problem you have conducted a one-tail test with the entire rejection region in the lower tail.

9.48 (a) $t_{STAT} = (32 - 68)/9/\sqrt{50} = -28.2843$. Because $t_{STAT} = -28.2843 < -2.4049$, reject H_0. p-value $= 0.0000 < 0.01$, reject H_0. **(b)** The probability of getting a sample mean of 32 minutes or less if the population mean is 68 minutes is 0.0000.

9.50 (a) H_0: $\mu \leq 900$; H_1: $\mu > 900$. **(b)** A Type I error occurs when you conclude that the mean number of customers increased above 900 when in fact the mean number of customers is not greater than 900. A Type II error occurs when you conclude that the mean number of customers is not greater than 900 when in fact the mean number of customers has increased above 900. **(c)** Because $t_{STAT} = 4.4947 > 2.4448$ or p-value $= 0.0000 < 0.01$, reject H_0. There is enough evidence to conclude the population mean number of customers is greater than 900. **(d)** The probability that the sample mean is 900 customers or more when the null hypothesis is true is 0.0000.

9.52 $p = 0.22$.

9.54 Do not reject H_0.

9.56 (a) $Z_{STAT} = 9.61$, p-value $= 0.0000$. Because $Z_{STAT} = 9.61 > 1.645$ or $0.0000 < 0.05$, reject H_0. There is evidence to show that more than half the readers of online magazines have linked to an advertiser's website. **(b)** $Z_{STAT} = 1.20$, p-value $= 0.115$. Because $Z_{STAT} = 1.20 < 1.645$, do not reject H_0. There is insufficient evidence to show that more than half of the readers of online magazines have linked to an advertiser's website. **(c)** The sample size had a major effect on being able to reject the null hypothesis. **(d)** You would be very unlikely to reject the null hypothesis with a sample of 20.

9.58 H_1: $\pi = 0.6$; H_1: $\pi \neq 0.6$. Decision rule: If $Z_{STAT} > 1.96$ or $Z_{STAT} < -1.96$, reject H_0.

$$p = \frac{650}{1{,}000} = 0.65$$

Test statistic:

$$Z_{STAT} = \frac{p - \pi}{\sqrt{\dfrac{\pi(1 - \pi)}{n}}} = \frac{0.65 - 0.60}{\sqrt{\dfrac{0.6(1 - 0.6)}{1{,}000}}} = 3.2275$$

Because $Z_{STAT} = 3.2275 > 1.96$ or p-value $= 0.0012 < 0.05$, reject H_0 and conclude that there is evidence that the percentage of young job seekers who prefer to look for a job in a place they want to reside is different from 60%.

9.60 (a) H_0: $\pi \leq 0.08$. No more than 8% of students at your school are omnivores. H_1: $\pi > 0.08$. More than 8% of students at your school are omnivores. **(b)** $Z_{STAT} = 3.6490 > 1.645$; p-value $= 0.0001316$. Because $Z_{STAT} = 3.6490 > 1.645$ or p-value $= 0.0001316 < 0.05$, reject H_0. There is enough evidence to show that the percentage of omnivores at your school is greater than 8%.

9.70 (a) Buying a site that is not profitable. **(b)** Not buying a profitable site. **(c)** Type I. **(d)** If the executives adopt a less stringent rejection criterion by buying sites for which the computer model predicts moderate or large profit, the probability of committing a Type I error will increase. Many more of the sites the computer model predicts that will generate moderate profit may end up not being profitable at all. On the other hand, the less stringent rejection criterion will lower the probability of committing a Type II error because more potentially profitable sites will be purchased.

9.72 (a) Because $t_{STAT} = 3.248 > 2.0010$, reject H_0. **(b)** p-value $= 0.0019$. **(c)** Because $Z_{STAT} = -0.32 > -1.645$, do not reject H_0. **(d)** Because $-2.0010 < t_{STAT} = 0.75 < 2.0010$, do not reject H_0. **(e)** Because $Z_{STAT} = -1.61 > -1.645$, do not reject H_0.

9.74 (a) Because $t_{STAT} = -1.69 > -1.7613$, do not reject H_0. **(b)** The data are from a population that is normally distributed. **(d)** With the exception of one extreme value, the data are approximately normally distributed. **(e)** There is insufficient evidence to state that the waiting time is less than five minutes.

9.76 (a) Because $t_{STAT} = -1.47 > -1.6896$, do not reject H_0. **(b)** p-value $= 0.0748$. If the null hypothesis is true, the probability of obtaining a t_{STAT} of -1.47 or more extreme is 0.0748. **(c)** Because $t_{STAT} = -3.10 < -1.6973$, reject H_0. **(d)** p-value $= 0.0021$. If the null hypothesis is true, the probability of obtaining a t_{STAT} of -3.10 or more extreme is 0.0021. **(e)** The data in the population are assumed to be normally distributed. **(f)** Both boxplots suggest that the data are skewed slightly to the right, more so for the Boston shingles. However, the very large sample sizes mean that the results of the t test are relatively insensitive to the departure from normality.

9.78 (a) $t_{STAT} = -21.61$, reject H_0. **(b)** p-value $= 0.0000$. **(c)** $t_{STAT} = -27.19$, reject H_0. **(d)** p-value $= 0.0000$. **(e)** Because of the large sample sizes, you do not need to be concerned with the normality assumption.

CHAPTER 10

10.2 (a) $t = 3.8959$. **(b)** $df = 21$. **(c)** 2.5177. **(d)** Because $t_{STAT} = 3.8959 > 2.5177$, reject H_0.

10.4 $3.73 \leq \mu_1 - \mu_2 \leq 12.27$.

10.6 Because $t_{STAT} = 2.6762 < 2.9979$ or p-value $= 0.0158 > 0.01$, do not reject H_0. There is no evidence of a difference in the means of the two populations.

10.8 (a) Because $t_{STAT} = 5.7883 > 1.6581$ or p-value $= 0.0000 < 0.05$, reject H_0. There is evidence that the mean amount of Goldfish crackers eaten by children is higher for those who watched food ads than for those who did not watch food ads. **(b)** $5.79 \leq \mu_1 - \mu_2 \leq 11.81$. **(c)** The results cannot be compared because (a) is a one-tail test and (b) is a confidence interval that is comparable only to the results of a two-tail test.

10.10 (a) H_0: $\mu_1 = \mu_2$, where Populations: 1 = Males, 2 = Females. H_1: $\mu_1 \neq \mu_2$. Decision rule: $df = 170$. If $t_{STAT} < -1.974$ or $t_{STAT} > 1.974$, reject H_0.

Test statistic:

$$S_p^2 = \frac{(n_1 - 1)(S_1^2) + (n_2 - 1)(S_2^2)}{(n_1 - 1) + (n_2 - 1)}$$

$$= \frac{(99)(13.35^2) + (71)(9.42^2)}{99 + 71} = 140.8489$$

$$t_{STAT} = \frac{(\bar{X}_1 - \bar{X}_2) - (\mu_1 - \mu_2)}{\sqrt{S_p^2\left(\dfrac{1}{n_1} + \dfrac{1}{n_2}\right)}}$$

$$= \frac{(40.26 - 36.85) - 0}{\sqrt{140.8489\left(\dfrac{1}{100} + \dfrac{1}{72}\right)}} = 1.859.$$

Decision: Because $-1.974 < t_{STAT} = 1.859 < 1.974$, do not reject H_0. There is not enough evidence to conclude that the mean computer anxiety experienced by males and females is different. **(b)** p-value $= 0.0648$. **(c)** In order to use the pooled-variance t test, you need to assume that the populations are normally distributed with equal variances.

10.12 (a) Because $t_{STAT} = -4.1343 < -2.0484$, reject H_0. **(b)** p-value $= 0.0003$. **(c)** The original populations of waiting times are approximately normally distributed. **(d)** $-4.2292 \le \mu_1 - \mu_2 \le -1.4268$.

10.14 (a) Because $t_{STAT} = 4.10 > 2.024$, reject H_0. There is evidence of a difference in the mean surface hardness between untreated and treated steel plates. **(b)** p-value $= 0.0002$. The probability that two samples have a mean difference of 9.3634 or more is 0.0002 if there is no difference in the mean surface hardness between untreated and treated steel plates. **(c)** You need to assume that the population distribution of hardness of both untreated and treated steel plates is normally distributed. **(d)** $4.7447 \le \mu_1 - \mu_2 \le 13.9821$.

10.16 (a) Because $t_{STAT} = -7.8124 < -1.9845$ or p-value $= 0.0000 < 0.05$, reject H_0. There is evidence of a difference in the mean number of calls for cell phone users under age 12 and cell phone users who are between 13 and 17 years of age. **(b)** You must assume that each of the two independent populations is normally distributed.

10.18 $df = 19$.

10.20 (a) $t_{STAT} = (-1.5566)/(1.424)/\sqrt{9} = -3.2772$. Because $t_{STAT} = -3.2772 < -2.306$ or p-value $= 0.0112 < 0.05$, reject H_0. There is enough evidence of a difference in the mean summated ratings between the two brands. **(b)** You must assume that the distribution of the differences between the two ratings is approximately normal. **(c)** p-value $= 0.0112$. The probability of obtaining a mean difference in ratings that results in a test statistic that deviates from 0 by 3.2772 or more in either direction is 0.0112 if there is no difference in the mean summated ratings between the two brands. **(d)** $-2.6501 \le \mu_D \le -0.4610$. You are 95% confident that the mean difference in summated ratings between brand A and brand B is somewhere between -2.6501 and -0.4610.

10.22 (a) Because $-2.2622 < t_{STAT} = 0.0332 < 2.2622$ or p-value $= 0.9743 > 0.05$, do not reject H_0. There is not enough evidence to conclude that there is a difference between the mean prices between Costco and store brands. **(b)** You must assume that the distribution of the differences between the prices is approximately normal. **(c)** $-\$1.612 \le \mu_D \le \$1.66$. You are 95% confident that the mean difference between the prices is between $-\$1.612$ and \$1.66. **(d)** The results in (a) and (c) are the same. The hypothesized value of 0 for the difference in the price of shopping items between Costco and store brands is within the 95% confidence interval.

10.24 (a) Because $t_{STAT} = 1.8425 < 1.943$, do not reject H_0. There is not enough evidence to conclude that the mean bone marrow microvessel density is higher before the stem cell transplant than after the stem cell transplant. **(b)** p-value $= 0.0575$. The probability that the t statistic for the mean difference in microvessel density is 1.8425 or more is 5.75% if the mean density is not higher before the stem cell transplant than after the stem cell transplant. **(c)** $-28.26 \le \mu_D \le 200.55$. You are 95% confident that the mean difference in bone marrow microvessel density before and after the stem cell transplant is somewhere between -28.26 and 200.55.

10.26 (a) Because $t_{STAT} = -9.3721 < -2.4258$, reject H_0. There is evidence that the mean strength is lower at two days than at seven days. **(b)** The population of differences in strength is approximately normally distributed. **(c)** $p = 0.000$.

10.28 (a) Because $-2.58 \le Z_{STAT} = -0.58 \le 2.58$, do not reject H_0. **(b)** $-0.273 \le \pi_1 - \pi_2 \le 0.173$.

10.30 (a) $H_0: \pi_1 \le \pi_2$. $H_1: \pi_1 > \pi_2$. Populations: $1 = 2009$, $2 = 2008$. **(b)** Because $Z_{STAT} = 5.3768 > 1.6449$ or p-value $= 0.0000 < 0.05$, reject H_0. There is sufficient evidence to conclude that the population proportion of large online retailers who require three or more clicks to be removed from an e-mail list is greater in 2009 than in 2008. **(c)** Yes, the result in (b) makes it appropriate to claim that the population proportion of large online retailers who require three or more clicks to be removed from an e-mail list is greater in 2009 than in 2008.

10.32 (a) $H_0: \pi_1 = \pi_2$. $H_1: \pi_1 \ne \pi_2$. Decision rule: If $|Z_{STAT}| > 2.58$, reject H_0.

Test statistic: $\bar{p} = \dfrac{X_1 + X_2}{n_1 + n_2} = \dfrac{707 + 536}{1{,}000 + 1{,}000} = 0.6215$

$$Z_{STAT} = \frac{(p_1 - p_2) - (\pi_2 - \pi_2)}{\sqrt{\bar{p}(1-\bar{p})\left(\dfrac{1}{n_1} + \dfrac{1}{n_2}\right)}} = \frac{(0.707 - 0.536) - 0}{\sqrt{0.6215(1 - 0.6215)\left(\dfrac{1}{1{,}000} + \dfrac{1}{1{,}000}\right)}}.$$

$Z_{STAT} = 7.8837 > 2.58$, reject H_0. There is evidence of a difference in the proportion who believe that e-mail messages should be answered quickly between the two age groups. **(b)** p-value $= 0.0000$. The probability of obtaining a difference in proportions that gives rise to a test statistic below -7.8837 or above $+7.8837$ is 0.0000 if there is no difference in the proportion of people in the two age groups who believe that e-mail messages should be answered quickly.

10.34 (a) Because $Z_{STAT} = 7.2742 > 1.96$, reject H_0. There is evidence of a difference in the proportion of adults and users ages 12–17 who oppose ads. **(b)** p-value $= 0.0000$. The probability of obtaining a difference in proportions that is 0.16 or more in either direction is 0.0000 if there is no difference between the proportion of adults and users ages 12–17 who oppose ads.

10.36 (a) 2.20. **(b)** 2.57. **(c)** 3.50.

10.38 (a) Population B: $S^2 = 25$. **(b)** 1.5625.

10.40 $df_{\text{numerator}} = 24$, $df_{\text{denominator}} = 24$.

10.42 Because $F_{STAT} = 1.2109 < 2.27$, do not reject H_0.

10.44 (a) Because $F_{STAT} = 1.2995 < 3.18$, do not reject H_0. **(b)** Because $F_{STAT} = 1.2995 < 2.62$, do not reject H_0.

10.46 (a) $H_0: \sigma_1^2 = \sigma_2^2$. $H_1: \sigma_1^2 \ne \sigma_2^2$.

Decision rule: If $F_{STAT} > 1.556$, reject H_0.

Test statistic: $F_{STAT} = \dfrac{S_1^2}{S_2^2} = \dfrac{(13.35)^2}{(9.42)^2} = 2.008$.

Decision: Because $F_{STAT} = 2.008 > 1.556$, reject H_0. There is evidence to conclude that the two population variances are different. **(b)** p-value $= 0.0022$. **(c)** The test assumes that each of the two populations is normally distributed. **(d)** Based on (a) and (b), a separate-variance t test should be used.

10.48 (a) Because $F_{STAT} = 5.1802 > 2.34$ or p-value $= 0.0002 < 0.05$, reject H_0. There is evidence of a difference in the variability of the battery life between the two types of digital cameras. **(b)** p-value $= 0.0002$. The probability of obtaining a sample that yields a test statistic more extreme than 5.1802 is 0.0002 if there is no difference in the two population variances. **(c)** The test assumes that the two populations are both normally distributed. **(d)** Based on (a) and (b), a separate-variance t test should be used.

10.50 Because $F_{STAT} = 2.7684 > 2.2693$, or p-value $= 0.0156 < 0.05$, reject H_0. There is evidence of a difference in the variance of the yield at the two time periods.

10.58 (a) \$0.59 coffee: $t_{STAT} = 2.8167 > 1.7613$ (or p-value $= 0.0069 < 0.05$), so reject H_0. There is evidence that reducing the price to

\$0.59 has increased mean daily customer count. \$0.79 coffee: $t_{STAT} = 2.0894 > 1.7613$ (or p-value $= 0.0277 < 0.05$), so reject H_0. There is evidence that reducing the price to \$0.79 has increased mean daily customer count. **(b)** Because $F_{STAT} = 1.3407 < 2.9786$, or p-value $= 0.5906 > 0.05$, do not reject H_0. There is not enough evidence of a difference in the variance of the daily customer count for \$0.59 and \$0.79 coffee. Because $-2.0484 < t_{STAT} = 0.7661 < 2.0484$ or p-value $= 0.4500 > 0.05$, do not reject H_0. There is insufficient evidence of a difference in the mean daily customer count for \$0.59 and \$0.79 coffee. **(c)** Since both \$0.59 and \$0.79 coffee increased daily customer count, you should recommend that the price of coffee should be reduced. However, since there is no significant difference in the mean daily customer count between the two prices, you should price the coffee at \$0.79 per 12-ounce cup.

10.60 (a) Because $F_{STAT} = 1.3349 < 1.7787$, or p-value $= 0.3236 > 0.05$, do not reject H_0. There is not enough evidence of a difference in the variance of the salary of Black Belts and Green Belts. **(b)** The pooled-variance t test. **(c)** Because $t_{STAT} = 5.7032 > 1.96$ or p-value $= 0.0000 < 0.05$, reject H_0. There is evidence of a difference in the mean salary of Black Belts and Green Belts.

10.62 (a) Because $F_{STAT} = 22.7067 > F_\alpha = 1.6275$, reject H_0. There is enough evidence to conclude that there is a difference between the variances in age of students at the Western school and at the Eastern school. **(b)** Because there is a difference between the variances in the age of students at the Western school and at the Eastern school, schools should take that into account when designing their curriculum to accommodate the larger variance in age of students in the state university in the Western United States. **(c)** It is more appropriate to use a separate-variance t test. **(d)** Because $F_{STAT} = 1.3061 < 1.6275$, do not reject H_0. There is not enough evidence to conclude that there is a difference between the variances in years of spreadsheet usage of students at the Western school and at the Eastern school. **(e)** Using the pooled-variance t test, because $t_{STAT} = -4.6650 < -2.5978$, reject H_0. There is enough evidence of a difference in the mean years of spreadsheet usage of students at the Western school and at the Eastern school.

10.64 (a) Because $t_{STAT} = 3.3282 > 1.8595$, reject H_0. There is enough evidence to conclude that the introductory computer students required more than a mean of 10 minutes to write and run a program in Visual Basic. **(b)** Because $t_{STAT} = 1.3636 < 1.8595$, do not reject H_0. There is not enough evidence to conclude that the introductory computer students required more than a mean of 10 minutes to write and run a program in Visual Basic. **(c)** Although the mean time necessary to complete the assignment increased from 12 to 16 minutes as a result of the increase in one data value, the standard deviation went from 1.8 to 13.2, which reduced the value of t statistic. **(d)** Because $F_{STAT} = 1.2308 < 3.8549$, do not reject H_0. There is not enough evidence to conclude that the population variances are different for the Introduction to Computers students and computer majors. Hence, the pooled-variance t test is a valid test to determine whether computer majors can write a Visual Basic program in less time than introductory students, assuming that the distributions of the time needed to write a Visual Basic program for both the Introduction to Computers students and the computer majors are approximately normally distributed. Because $t_{STAT} = 4.0666 > 1.7341$, reject H_0. There is enough evidence that the mean time is higher for Introduction to Computers students than for computer majors. **(e)** p-value $= 0.000362$. If the true population mean amount of time needed for Introduction to Computer students to write a Visual Basic program is no more than 10 minutes, the probability of observing a sample mean greater than the 12 minutes in the current sample is 0.0362%. Hence, at a 5% level of significance, you can conclude that the population mean amount of time needed for Introduction to Computer students to write a Visual Basic program is more than 10 minutes. As illustrated in part **(d)**, in which there is not enough evidence to conclude that the population variances are different for the Introduction to Computers students and computer majors, the pooled-variance t test performed is a valid test to determine whether computer majors can write a Visual Basic program in less time than introductory students, assuming that the distribution of the time needed to write a Visual Basic program for both the Introduction to Computers students and the computer majors are approximately normally distributed.

10.66 From the boxplot and the summary statistics, both distributions are approximately normally distributed. $F_{STAT} = 1.056 < 1.89$. There is insufficient evidence to conclude that the two population variances are significantly different at the 5% level of significance. $t_{STAT} = -5.084 < -1.99$. At the 5% level of significance, there is sufficient evidence to reject the null hypothesis of no difference in the mean life of the bulbs between the two manufacturers. You can conclude that there is a significant difference in the mean life of the bulbs between the two manufacturers.

10.68 Playing a game on a video game system: Because $Z_{STAT} = 15.74 > 1.96$ and p-value $= 0.0000 < 0.05$, reject H_0. There is evidence that there is a difference between boys and girls in the proportion who played a game on a video game system. Reading a book for fun: Because $Z_{STAT} = -2.1005 < -1.96$ and p-value $= 0.0357 < 0.05$, reject H_0. There is evidence that there is a difference between boys and girls in the proportion who have read a book for fun. Gave product advice to parents: Because $-1.96 < Z_{STAT} = 0.7427 < 1.96$ and p-value $= 0.4576 > 0.05$, do not reject H_0. There is insufficient evidence that there is a difference between boys and girls in the proportion who gave product advice to parents. Shopped at a mall: Because $Z_{STAT} = -6.7026 < -1.96$ and p-value $= 0.0000 < 0.05$, reject H_0. There is evidence that there is a difference between boys and girls in the proportion who shopped at a mall.

10.70 The normal probability plots suggest that the two populations are not normally distributed. An F test is inappropriate for testing the difference in two variances. The sample variances for Boston and Vermont shingles are 0.0203 and 0.015, respectively. Because $t_{STAT} = 3.015 > 1.967$ or p-value $= 0.0028 < \alpha = 0.05$, reject H_0. There is sufficient evidence to conclude that there is a difference in the mean granule loss of Boston and Vermont shingles.

CHAPTER 11

11.2 (a) $SSW = 150$. **(b)** $MSA = 15$. **(c)** $MSW = 5$. **(d)** $F_{STAT} = 3$.

11.4 (a) 2. **(b)** 18. **(c)** 20.

11.6 (a) Reject H_0 if $F_{STAT} > 2.95$; otherwise, do not reject H_0. **(b)** Because $F_{STAT} = 4 > 2.95$, reject H_0. **(c)** The table does not have 28 degrees of freedom in the denominator, so use the next larger critical value, $Q_\alpha = 3.90$. **(d)** Critical range $= 6.166$.

11.8 (a) $H_0\colon \mu_A = \mu_B = \mu_C = \mu_D$ and H_1: At least one mean is different.

$$MSA = \frac{SSA}{c-1} = \frac{1{,}986.475}{3} = 662.1583.$$

$$MSW = \frac{SSW}{n-c} = \frac{495.5}{36} = 13.76389.$$

$$F_{STAT} = \frac{MSA}{MSW} = \frac{662.1583}{13.76389} = 48.1084.$$

$$F_{0.05,3,36} = 2.8663.$$

Because the p-value is approximately 0 and $F_{STAT} = 48.1084 > 2.8663$, reject H_0. There is sufficient evidence of a difference in the mean strength of the four brands of trash bags.

(b) Critical range $= Q_\alpha\sqrt{\frac{MSW}{2}\left(\frac{1}{n_j} + \frac{1}{n_{j'}}\right)} = 3.79\sqrt{\frac{13.7639}{2}\left(\frac{1}{10} + \frac{1}{10}\right)}$

$= 4.446.$

From the Tukey-Kramer procedure, there is a difference in mean strength between Kroger and Tuffstuff, Glad and Tuffstuff, and Hefty and Tuffstuff. **(c)** ANOVA output for Levene's test for homogeneity of variance:

$$MSA = \frac{SSA}{c-1} = \frac{24.075}{3} = 8.025.$$

$$MSW = \frac{SSW}{n-c} = \frac{198.2}{36} = 5.5056.$$

$$F_{STAT} = \frac{MSA}{MSW} = \frac{8.025}{5.5056} = 1.4576.$$

$$F_{0.05,3,36} = 2.8663.$$

Because p-value $= 0.2423 > 0.05$ and $F_{STAT} = 1.458 < 2.866$, do not reject H_0. There is insufficient evidence to conclude that the variances in strength among the four brands of trash bags are different. **(d)** From the results in (a) and (b), Tuffstuff has the lowest mean strength and should be avoided.

11.10 (a) Because $F_{STAT} = 12.56 > 2.76$, reject H_0. **(b)** Critical range $=$ 4.67. Advertisements A and B are different from Advertisements C and D. Advertisement E is only different from Advertisement D. **(c)** Because $F_{STAT} = 1.927 < 2.76$, do not reject H_0. There is no evidence of a significant difference in the variation in the ratings among the five advertisements. **(d)** The advertisements underselling the pen's characteristics had the highest mean ratings, and the advertisements overselling the pen's characteristics had the lowest mean ratings. Therefore, use an advertisement that undersells the pen's characteristics and avoid advertisements that oversell the pen's characteristics.

11.12 (a) Because the p-value for this test, 0.922, is greater than the level of significance, $\alpha = 0.05$ (or the computed F test statistic, 0.0817, is less than the critical value $F = 3.6823$), you cannot reject the null hypothesis. You conclude that there is insufficient evidence of a difference in the mean yield between the three methods used in the cleansing step. **(b)** Because there is no evidence of a difference between the methods, you should not develop any multiple comparisons. **(c)** Because the p-value for this test, 0.8429, is greater than the level of significance, $\alpha = 0.05$ (or the computed F test statistic, 0.1728, is less than the critical value, $F = 3.6823$), you cannot reject the null hypothesis. You conclude that there is insufficient evidence of a difference in the variation in the yield between the three methods used in the cleansing step. **(d)** Because there is no evidence of a difference in the variation between the methods, the validity of the conclusion reached in (a) is not affected.

11.14 (a) Because $F_{STAT} = 53.03 > 2.92$, reject H_0. **(b)** Critical range $= 5.27$ (using 30 degrees of freedom). Designs 3 and 4 are different from Designs 1 and 2. Designs 1 and 2 are different from each other. **(c)** The assumptions are that the samples are randomly and independently selected (or randomly assigned), the original populations of distances are approximately normally distributed, and the variances are equal. **(d)** Because $F_{STAT} = 2.093 < 2.92$, do not reject H_0. There is no evidence of a significant difference in the variation in the distance among the four designs. **(e)** The manager should choose Design 3 or 4.

11.16 (a) $SSE = 75$. **(b)** $MSA = 15$, $MSBL = 12.5$, $MSE = 3.125$. **(c)** $F_{STAT} = 4.8$. **(d)** $F_{STAT} = 4$.

11.18 (a) df numerator $= 5$, df denominator $= 24$. **(b)** $Q = 4.17$. **(c)** Critical range $= 2.786$.

11.20 (a) $MSE = 3$, $SSE = 36$. **(b)** $SSBL = 72$. **(c)** $SST = 144$. **(d)** Because $F_{STAT} = 6 < 6.9266$, do not reject H_0. There is insufficient evidence of a treatment effect. Because $F_{STAT} = 4 < 4.82$, do not reject H_0. There is insufficient evidence of a block effect.

11.22 (a) Because $F_{STAT} = 5.185 > 3.07$, reject H_0. **(b)** Because $F_{STAT} = 5 > 2.49$, reject H_0.

11.24 (a) H_0: $\mu_{.1} = \mu_{.2} = \mu_{.3} = \mu_{.4}$ where *1* = Verizon, *2* = AT&T, *3* = T-Mobile, *4* = Sprint H_1: Not all $\mu_{.j}$ are equal where $j = 1, 2, 3, 4$
Excel output:

ANOVA

Source of Variation	SS	df	MS	F	P-value	F crit
Rows	109.6579	18	6.0921	1.2356	0.2679	1.79823
Columns	1,431.2630	3	477.0877	96.7662	1.04E-21	2.7758
Error	266.2368	54	4.93031			
Total	1807.158	75				

$F_{STAT} = 96.7662$. Since the p-value is virtually $0 < 0.05$, reject H_0. There is evidence of a difference in the mean cell rating for the four cell phone services.
(b)

Tukey Multiple Comparisons

Group	Sample Mean	Sample Size	Comparison	Absolute Difference	Std. Error of Difference	Critical Range	Results
Verizon-1	78.3158	19	**Group 1 to Group 2**	7.5263	0.5094	1.9052	**Means are different**
AT&T - 2	70.7895	19	**Group 1 to Group 3**	5.26316	0.509	1.9052	**Means are different**
T-Mobile - 3	73.0526	19	**Group 1 to Group 4**	12.052	0.509	1.9052	**Means are different**
Sprint - 4	66.2631	19	**Group 2 to Group 3**	2.2632	0.50940	1.9052	**Means are different**
			Group 2 to Group 4	4.5263	0.5094	1.9052	**Means are different**
Other Data			**Group 3 to Group 4**	6.7895	0.5094	1.9052	**Means are different**

Level of significance 0.05
Numerator d.f. 4
Denominator d.f. 54
MSW 4.930
Q Statistic 3.74

The mean cell rating for the four cell phone services are significantly different from each other with Verizon highest followed by T-Mobile, AT&T, and then Sprint.

11.26 (a) $F_{STAT} = 18.2879$. Since the p-value is virtually $0 < 0.05$, reject H_0. There is evidence of a difference between the mean price of an impulsive shopper, a savvy shopper, if you shop at a warehouse club such as Costco, or if you purchase store-brands. **(b)** The assumptions needed are: (i) Samples are randomly and independently drawn, (ii) populations are normally distributed, (iii) populations have equal variances, and (iv) no interaction effect between treatments and blocks. **(c)** Critical range $= 3.2674$ The absolute differences are group 1 to group $2 = 6.292$, group 1 to group $3 = 7.598$, group 1 to group $4 = 7.622$, group 2 to group $3 = 1.306$, group 2 to group $4 = 1.33$, group 3 to group $4 = 0.024$. The mean of impulsive shoppers differs from the other three while being a savvy shopper, shopping at Costco or purchasing at store-brands do not differ from each other at 5% level of significance. **(d)** $F_{STAT} = 23.8081$ and p-value $= 0.0000 < 0.05$, Reject H_0. There is evidence of a significant block effect in this experiment. The blocking has been advantageous in reducing the experimental error.

11.28 (a) Because $F_{STAT} = 268.26 > 3.114$, reject H_0. There is enough evidence to conclude that there is a difference in the mean compressive strength after 2, 7, and 28 days. **(b)** Critical range $= 0.1651$. At the 0.05 level of significance, all of the comparisons are significant. **(c)** $RE = 2.558$. **(e)** The compressive strength of the concrete increases over the three time periods.

11.30 (a) 40. **(b)** 60 and 55. **(c)** 10. **(d)** 10.

11.32 (a) Because $F_{STAT} = 6.00 > 3.35$, reject H_0. **(b)** Because $F_{STAT} = 5.50 > 3.35$, reject H_0. **(c)** Because $F_{STAT} = 1.00 < F = 2.73$, do not reject H_0.

11.34 $df_B = 4$, $df_{\text{TOTAL}} = 44$, $SSA = 160$, $SSAB = 80$, $SSE = 150$, $SST = 610$, $MSB = 55$, $MSE = 5$. For A: $F_{STAT} = 16$. For B: $F_{STAT} = 11$ For AB: $F_{STAT} = 2$.

11.36 (a) Because $F_{STAT} = 1.37 < 4.75$, do not reject H_0. **(b)** Because $F_{STAT} = 23.58 > 4.75$, reject H_0. **(c)** Because $F_{STAT} = 0.70 < 4.75$, do not reject H_0. **(e)** Developer strength has a significant effect on density, but development time does not.

11.38 (a) H_0: There is no interaction between brand and water temperature. H_1: There is an interaction between brand and water temperature. Because $F_{STAT} = \frac{253.1552}{12.2199} = 20.7167 > 3.555$ or the p-value $= 0.0000214 < 0.05$, reject H_0. There is evidence of interaction between brand of pain reliever and temperature of the water. **(b)** Because there is an interaction between brand and the temperature of the water, it is inappropriate to analyze the main effect due to brand. **(c)** Because there is an interaction between brand and the temperature of the water, it is inappropriate to analyze the main effect due to water temperature. **(e)** The difference in the mean time a tablet took to dissolve in cold and hot water depends on the brand, with Alka-Seltzer having the largest difference and Equate with the smallest difference.

11.40 (a) $F_{STAT} = 0.1523$, p-value $= 0.9614 > 0.05$, do not reject H_0. There is not enough evidence to conclude that there is an interaction between the brake discs and the gauges. **(b)** $F_{STAT} = 7.7701$, p-value is virtually $0 < 0.05$, reject H_0. There is sufficient evidence to conclude that there is an effect due to brake discs. **(c)** $F_{STAT} = 0.1465$, p-value $= 0.7031 > 0.05$, do not reject H_0. There is inadequate evidence to conclude that there is an effect due to the gauges. **(d)** From the plot, there is no obvious interaction between brake discs and gauges. **(e)** There is no obvious difference in mean temperature across the gauges. It appears that Part 1 has the lowest, Part 3 the second lowest, and Part 2 has the highest average temperature.

11.52 (a) Because $F_{STAT} = 1.485 < 2.54$, do not reject H_0. **(b)** Because $F_{STAT} = 0.79 < 3.24$, do not reject H_0. **(c)** Because $F_{STAT} = 52.07 > 3.24$, reject H_0. **(e)** Critical range $= 0.0189$. Washing cycles for 22 and 24 minutes are not different with respect to dirt removal, but they are both different from 18- and 20-minute cycles. **(f)** 22 minutes. (24 minutes was not different, but 22 does just as well and would use less energy.) **(g)** The results are the same.

11.54 (a) Because $F_{STAT} = 0.075 < 3.68$, do not reject H_0. **(b)** Because $F_{STAT} = 4.09 > 3.68$, reject H_0. **(c)** Critical range $= 1.489$. Breaking strength is significantly different between 30 and 50 psi.

11.56 (a) Because $F_{STAT} = 1.97 < 3.89$, do not reject H_0. **(b)** Because $F_{STAT} = 4.87 > 4.75$, reject H_0. **(c)** Because $F_{STAT} = 5.67 > 3.89$, reject H_0. **(e)** Critical range $= 1.30$. Mean breaking strength under 30 psi is significantly different from 40 psi and 50 psi. **(f)** The mean breaking strength is highest under 30 psi. **(g)** The two-factor experiment gave a more complete set of results than the one-factor experiment. Not only was the side-to-side aspect factor significant, the application of the Tukey procedure on the air-jet pressure factor determined that breaking strength scores are highest under 30 psi.

11.58 (a) Because $F_{STAT} = 0.1899 < 4.1132$, do not reject H_0. There is insufficient evidence to conclude that there is any interaction between type of breakfast and desired time. **(b)** Because $F_{STAT} = 30.4434 > 4.1132$, reject H_0. There is sufficient evidence to conclude that there is an effect that is due to type of breakfast. **(c)** Because $F_{STAT} = 12.4441 > 4.1132$, reject H_0. There is sufficient evidence to conclude that there is an effect that is due to desired time. **(e)** At the 5% level of significance, both the type of breakfast ordered and the desired time have an effect on delivery time difference. There is no interaction between the type of breakfast ordered and the desired time.

11.60 Population 1 = foreign large-cap blend, 2 = small-cap blend, 3 = mid-cap blend, 4 = Large-cap blend, 5 = diversified emerging markets; Three-year return: Levene test: $F_{STAT} = 0.4148$. Since the p-value $= 0.7971 > 0.05$, do not reject H_0. There is insufficient evidence to show a difference in the variance of return among the 5 different types of mutual funds at a 5% level of significance. $F_{STAT} = 14.3127$. Since the p-value is virtually zero, reject H_0. There is sufficient evidence to show a difference in the mean three-year returns among the five different types of mutual funds at a 5% level of significance. Critical range = 2.83. Groups 3 and 4. (Mid-cap blend and large-cap blend) are lower than diversified emerging markets. All other comparisons are not significant. Five-year return: Levene test: $F_{STAT} = 0.9671$. Since the p-value $= 0.4349 > 0.05$, do not reject H_0. There is insufficient evidence to show a difference in the variance of return among the 5 different types of mutual funds at a 5% level of significance. $F_{STAT} = 62.4531$ Since the p-value is virtually zero, reject H_0. There is sufficient evidence to show a difference in the mean five-year returns among the five different types of mutual funds at a 5% level of significance. Critical range $= 2.3171$. At the 5% level of significance, there is sufficient evidence that the mean five-year returns of the diversified emerging market funds is significantly higher than the others. Also, the mean five-year returns of the large-cap blend funds are significantly lower than that of the foreign large-cap funds. Ten-year return: Levene test: $F_{STAT} = 0.7854$. Since the p-value $= 0.5407 > 0.05$, do not reject H_0. There is insufficient evidence to show a difference in the variance of return among the five different types of mutual funds at a 5% level of significance. $F_{STAT} = 11.9951$. Since the p-value is virtually zero, reject H_0. There is sufficient evidence to show a difference in the mean 10-year returns among the five different types of mutual funds at a 5% level of significance. Critical range $= 3.3372$. At the 5% level of significance, there is sufficient evidence that the mean 10-year returns of the diversified emerging market funds is significantly higher than the others. Expense ratio: Levene test: $F_{STAT} = 0.59$. Since the p-value $= 0.6716 > 0.05$, do not reject H_0. There is insufficient evidence to show a difference in the variance in expense ratios among the 5 different types of mutual funds at a 5% level of significance. $F_{STAT} = 4.1069$. Since the p-value $= 0.0064 < 0.05$, reject H_0. There is sufficient evidence to show a difference in the mean among the five different types of mutual funds at a 5% level of significance. Critical range $= 0.479$. At the 5% level of significance, there is sufficient evidence that the mean expense ratio of the diversified emerging market funds is significantly higher than the foreign large-cap funds.

11.62 (a) $F_{STAT} = 7.6863$. Since the p-value is virtually $0 < 0.05$, reject H_0. There is evidence of a difference in the mean rating scores among the wines. **(b)** The assumptions needed are: (i) samples are randomly and independently drawn, (ii) populations are normally distributed, (iii) populations have equal variances and (iv) no interaction effect between treatments and blocks. **(c)** Critical range $= 3.5593$. The mean ratings of the eight different type of wines in ascending order are California Beaujolais (red) \$10.50, French burgundy (red) \$10.69, California white \$13.59, French white \$10.59, Italian red \$8.50, French white \$9.75, French burgundy (red) \$11.75, and Italian white \$8.50. At the 5% level of significance, the mean rating of French burgundy (red) \$11.75 is significantly higher than French white \$10.59 and the other types that have lower mean rating, and the mean rating of Italian white \$8.50 is also significantly higher than French white \$10.59 and the other types that have lower mean rating. There is no significant differences in mean rating among the other pairs. **(d)** Based upon the results in (c), none of the country of origin, the type of wine, or the price has had an effect on the ratings. **(e)** RE = 1.555.

CHAPTER 12

12.2 (a) For $df = 1$ and $\alpha = 0.05$, $\chi^2_\alpha = 3.841$. **(b)** For $df = 1$ and $\alpha = 0.025$, $\chi^2 = 5.024$. **(c)** For $df = 1$ and $\alpha = 0.01$, $\chi^2_\alpha = 6.635$.

12.4 (a) All $f_e = 25$. **(b)** Because $\chi^2_{STAT} = 4.00 > 3.841$, reject H_0.

12.6 (a) Because $\chi^2_{STAT} = 28.9102 > 3.841$, reject H_0. There is enough evidence to conclude that there is a significant difference between the proportion of retail websites that require three or more clicks to be removed from an email list in 2009 as compared to 2008. **(b)** p-value = 0.0000. The probability of obtaining a test statistic of 28.9102 or larger when the null hypothesis is true is 0.0000. **(c)** You should not compare the results in (a) to those of Problem 10.30 (b) because that was a one-tail test.

12.8 (a) H_0: $\pi_1 = \pi_2$. H_1: $\pi_1 \neq \pi_2$. Because $\chi^2_{STAT} = (536 - 621.5)^2/621.5 + (464 - 378.5)^2/378.5 + (707 - 621.5)^2/621.5 + (293 - 378.5)^2/378.5 = 62.152 > 6.635$, reject H_0. There is evidence of a difference in the proportion who believe that e-mail messages should be answered quickly between the two age groups. **(b)** p-value = 0.0000. The probability of obtaining a difference in proportions that gives rise to a test statistic greater than 62.152 is 0.0000 if there is no difference in the proportion of people in the two age groups who believe that e-mail messages should be answered quickly. **(c)** The results of (a) and (b) are exactly the same as those of Problem 10.32. The χ^2 in (a) and the Z in Problem 10.32 (a) satisfy the relationship that $\chi^2 = 62.152 = Z^2 = (7.8837)^2$, and the p-value in (b) is exactly the same as the p-value computed in Problem 10.32 (b).

12.10 (a) Since $\chi^2_{STAT} = 52.9144 > 3.841$, reject H_0. There is evidence that there is a significant difference between the proportion of adults and users ages 12–17 who oppose ads on websites. **(b)** p-value 0.0000. The probability of obtaining a test statistic of 52.9144 or larger when the null hypothesis is true is 0.0000.

12.12 (a) The expected frequencies for the first row are 20, 30, and 40. The expected frequencies for the second row are 30, 45, and 60. **(b)** Because $\chi^2_{STAT} = 12.5 > 5.991$, reject H_0.

12.14 (a) Because the calculated test statistic $\chi^2_{STAT} = 48.6268 > 9.4877$, reject H_0 and conclude that there is a difference in the proportion who oppose ads on websites between the age groups. **(b)** The p-value is virtually 0. The probability of a test statistic greater than 48.6268 or more is approximately 0 if there is no difference between the age groups in the proportion who oppose ads on websites. **(c)** The 18–24 and 25–34 age groups are each different from the 50–64 and 65–89 age groups. The 35–49 age group is different from the 65–89 group.

12.16 (a) H_0: $\pi_1 = \pi_2 = \pi_3$. H_1: At least one proportion differs.

f_0	f_e	$(f_0 - f_e)$	$(f_0 - f_e)^2/f_e$
48	42.667	5.333	0.667
152	157.333	−5.333	0.181
56	42.667	13.333	4.166
144	157.333	−13.333	1.130
24	42.667	−18.667	8.167
176	157.333	18.667	2.215
			16.526

Decision rule: $df = (c - 1) = (3 - 1) = 2$. If $\chi^2_{STAT} > 5.9915$, reject H_0.

Test statistic: $\chi^2_{STAT} = \sum_{\text{all cells}} \frac{(f_0 - f_e)}{f_e} = 16.526$.

Decision: Because $\chi^2_{STAT} = 16.526 > 5.9915$, reject H_0. There is a significant difference in the age groups with respect to major grocery shopping day. **(b)** p-value = 0.0003. The probability that the test statistic is greater than or equal to 16.526 is 0.0003, if the null hypothesis is true.

(c)

Pairwise Comparisons	Critical Range	$\lvert p_j - p_{j'} \rvert$
1 to 2	0.1073	0.04
2 to 3	0.0959	0.16*
1 to 3	0.0929	0.12*

There is a significant difference between the 35–54 and over-54 groups and between the under-35 and over-54 groups. **(d)** The stores can use this information to target their marketing to the specific groups of shoppers on Saturday and the days other than Saturday.

12.18 (a) Because $\chi^2_{STAT} = 6.50 > 5.9915$, reject H_0. There is evidence of a difference in the percentage who often listen to rock music among the age groups. **(b)** p-value = 0.0388. **(c)** The 16–29 group is different from the 50–64 age group.

12.20 $df = (r - 1)(c - 1) = (3 - 1)(4 - 1) = 6$.

12.22 $\chi^2_{STAT} = 92.1028 > 16.919$, reject H_0 and conclude that there is evidence of a relationship between the type of dessert ordered and the type of entrée ordered.

12.24 (a) H_0: There is no relationship between the commuting time of company employees and the level of stress-related problems observed on the job. H_1: There is a relationship between the commuting time of company employees and the level of stress-related problems observed on the job.

f_0	f_e	$(f_0 - f_e)$	$(f_0 - f_e)^2/f_e$
9	12.1379	−3.1379	0.8112
17	20.1034	−3.1034	0.4791
18	11.7586	6.2414	3.3129
5	5.2414	−0.2414	0.0111
8	8.6810	−0.6810	0.0534
6	5.0776	0.9224	0.1676
18	14.6207	3.3793	0.7811
28	24.2155	3.7845	0.5915
7	14.1638	−7.1638	3.6233
			9.8311

Decision rule: If $\chi^2_{STAT} > 13.277$, reject H_0.

Test statistic: $\chi^2_{STAT} = \sum_{\text{all cells}} \frac{(f_0 - f_e)^2}{f_e} = 9.8311$.

Decision: Because $\chi^2_{STAT} = 9.8311 < 13.277$, do not reject H_0. There is insufficient evidence to conclude that there is a relationship between the commuting time of company employees and the level of stress-related problems observed on the job. **(b)** Because $\chi^2_{STAT} = 9.831 > 9.488$, reject H_0. There is enough evidence at the 0.05 level to conclude that there is a relationship.

12.26 Because $\chi^2_{STAT} = 129.520 > 21.026$, reject H_0. There is a relationship between when the decision is made of what to have for dinner and the type of household.

12.28 (a) H_0: $\pi_1 \geq \pi_2$ and H_1: $\pi_1 < \pi_2$, where 1 = beginning, 2 = end. Decision rule: If $Z < -1.645$, reject H_0.

Test statistic: $Z_{STAT} = \frac{B - C}{\sqrt{B + C}} = \frac{9 - 22}{\sqrt{9 + 22}} = -2.3349$.

Decision: Because $Z_{STAT} = -2.3349 < -1.645$, reject H_0. There is evidence that the proportion of coffee drinkers who prefer Brand A is lower at the beginning of the advertising campaign than at the end of the advertising campaign. **(b)** p-value $= 0.0098$. The probability of a test statistic less than -2.3349 is 0.0098 if the proportion of coffee drinkers who prefer Brand A is not lower at the beginning of the advertising campaign than at the end of the advertising campaign.

12.30 (a) Because $Z_{STAT} = -2.2361 < -1.645$, reject H_0. There is evidence that the proportion who prefer Brand A is lower before the advertising than after the advertising. **(b)** p-value $= 0.0127$. The probability of a test statistic less than -2.2361 is 0.00127 if the proportion who prefer Brand A is not lower before the advertising than after the advertising.

12.32 (a) Because $Z_{STAT} = -3.8996 < -1.645$, reject H_0. There is evidence that the proportion of employees absent fewer than five days was lower in Year 1 than in Year 2. **(b)** The p-value is virtually 0. The probability of a test statistic smaller than -3.8996 is virtually 0 if the proportion of employees absent fewer than five days was not lower in Year 1 than in Year 2.

12.34 (a) 9.2604 and 44.1814. **(b)** 8.9065 and 32.8523. **(c)** 7.2609 and 24.9958.

12.36 10.417.

12.38 (a) 6.262 and 27.488. **(b)** 7.261.

12.40 You must assume that the data in the population are normally distributed to be able to use the chi-square test of a population variance or standard deviation. If the data selected do not come from an approximately normally distributed population, the accuracy of the test can be seriously affected.

12.42 (a) H_0: $\sigma = \$200$. H_1: $\sigma \neq \$200$.
Decision rule: $df = 24$. If $\chi^2_{STAT} < 12.401$ or $\chi^2_{STAT} > 39.364$, reject H_0.

$$\text{Test statistic: } \frac{(n-1)S^2}{\sigma^2} = \frac{(24)237.52^2}{200^2} = 33.849$$

Decision: Because $12.401 < \chi^2_{STAT} = 33.849 < 39.364$, do not reject H_0. There is insufficient evidence to conclude that the standard deviation of the amount of auto repairs is not equal to \$200. **(b)** You must assume that the data in the population are normally distributed to be able to use the chi-square test of a population variance or standard deviation. **(c)** p-value $=$ 0.1748. The p-value of 0.1748 is the probability of obtaining a result greater from the sample value of \$237.52 when the null hypothesis is true.

12.44 (a) Because $\chi^2_{STAT} = 1.2245 < 13.848$, reject H_0. There is sufficient evidence to conclude that the standard deviation of the diameter of doorknobs is less than 0.035 inch in the redesigned production process. **(b)** You must assume that the data in the population are normally distributed to be able to use the chi-square test of a population variance or standard deviation. **(c)** p-value $= 0.0230$. The probability of a test statistic equal to or more extreme than the result from this sample data is 0.0230 if the population standard deviation is no less than 0.035 inch.

12.46 (a) Because $\chi^2_{STAT} = 1.5315 < 30.135$, do not reject H_0. There is insufficient evidence to conclude that the standard deviation of the weight of the teabags is greater than 0.5 gram. **(b)** You must assume that the data in the population are normally distributed to be able to use the chi-square test of a population variance or standard deviation.

12.48 (a) 31. **(b)** 29. **(c)** 27. **(d)** 25.

12.50 40 and 79.

12.52 (a) The ranks for Sample 1 are 1, 2, 4, 5, and 10. The ranks for Sample 2 are 3, 6.5, 6.5, 8, 9, and 11. **(b)** 22. **(c)** 44.

12.54 Because $T_1 = 22 > 20$, do not reject H_0.

12.56 (a) The data are ordinal. **(b)** The two-sample t test is inappropriate because the data can only be placed in ranked order. **(c)** Because $Z_{STAT} = -2.2054 < -1.96$, reject H_0. There is evidence of a significance difference in the median rating of California Cabernets and Washington Cabernets.

12.58 (a) H_0: $M_1 = M_2$, where Populations: 1 = Wing A, 2 = Wing B. H_1: $M_1 \neq M_2$.

Population 1 sample: Sample size 20 Sum of ranks 561

Population 2 sample: Sample size 20 Sum of ranks 259

$$\mu_{T_1} = \frac{n_1(n+1)}{2} = \frac{20(40+1)}{2} = 410$$

$$\sigma_{T_1} = \sqrt{\frac{n_1 n_2(n+1)}{12}} = \sqrt{\frac{20(20)(40+1)}{12}} = 36.9685$$

$$Z_{STAT} = \frac{T_1 - \mu_{T_1}}{S_{T_1}} = \frac{561 - 410}{36.9685} = 4.0846$$

Decision: Because $Z_{STAT} = 4.0846 > 1.96$ (or p-value $= 0.0000 < 0.05$), reject H_0. There is sufficient evidence of a difference in the median delivery time in the two wings of the hotel. **(b)** The results of (a) are consistent with the results of Problem 10.67.

12.60 (a) Because $Z_{STAT} = -4.118 < -1.645$, reject H_0. There is enough evidence to conclude that the median crack size is less for the unflawed sample than for the flawed sample. **(b)** You must assume approximately equal variability in the two populations. **(c)** Using both the pooled-variance t test and the separate-variance t test allowed you to reject the null hypothesis and conclude in Problem 10.17 that the mean crack size is less for the unflawed sample than for the flawed sample. In this test, using the Wilcoxon rank sum test with large-sample Z approximation also allowed you to reject the null hypothesis and conclude that the median crack size is less for the unflawed sample than for the flawed sample.

12.62 (a) Because $-1.96 < Z_{STAT} = 1.956 < 1.96$ (or the p-value $= 0.0504 > 0.05$), do not reject H_0. There is not enough evidence to conclude that there is a difference in the median battery life between subcompact cameras and compact cameras. **(b)**You must assume approximately equal variability in the two populations. **(c)** Using the pooled-variance t-test, you reject the null hypothesis ($t = 2.8498 > 2.0167$; p-value $= 0.0067 < 0.05$) and conclude that there is evidence of a difference in the mean battery life between the two types of digital cameras in Problem 10.11 (a). However, in Problem 10.48, the F test for the ratio of two variances shows a significant difference between the variances in the battery life. Therefore, the pooled-variance t test is not valid for these data. The separate-variance t test, however, also shows evidence of a difference in the mean battery life between the two types of digital cameras ($t = 2.3248 > 2.1009$; p-value $= 0.0320 < 0.05$). The difference in results can be explained by the fact that the Wilcoxon rank sum test assumes equal variances not normality and the separate-variance test assumes normality but not equal variances.

12.64 (a) Decision rule: If $H > \chi^2_U = 15.086$, reject H_0. **(b)** Because $H = 13.77 < 15.086$, do not reject H_0.

12.66 (a) $H = 13.517 > 7.815$, p-value $= 0.0036 < 0.05$, reject H_0. There is sufficient evidence of a difference in the median waiting time in the four locations. **(b)** The results are consistent with those of Problem 11.9.

12.68 (a) $H = 19.3269 > 9.488$, reject H_0. There is evidence of a difference in the median ratings of the ads. **(b)** The results are consistent with those of Problem 11.10. **(c)** Because the combined scores are not true continuous variables, the nonparametric Kruskal-Wallis rank test is more appropriate because it does not require that the scores be normally distributed.

12.70 (a) Because $H = 22.26 > 7.815$ or the p-value is approximately 0, reject H_0. There is sufficient evidence of a difference in the median strength of the four brands of trash bags. **(b)** The results are the same.

12.78 (a) Because $\chi^2_{STAT} = 0.412 < 3.841$, do not reject H_0. There is insufficient evidence to conclude that there is a relationship between a student's gender and pizzeria selection. **(b)** Because $\chi^2_{STAT} = 2.624 < 3.841$, do not reject H_0. There is insufficient evidence to conclude that there is a relationship between a student's gender and pizzeria selection. **(c)** Because $\chi^2_{STAT} = 4.956 < 5.991$, do not reject H_0. There is insufficient evidence to conclude that there is a relationship between price and pizzeria selection. **(d)** p-value $= 0.0839$. The probability of a sample that gives a test statistic equal to or greater than 4.956 is 8.39% if the null hypothesis of no relationship between price and pizzeria selection is true.

12.80 (a) Because $\chi^2_{STAT} = 11.895 < 12.592$, do not reject H_0. There is not enough evidence to conclude that there is a relationship between the attitudes of employees toward the use of self-managed work teams and employee job classification. **(b)** Because $\chi^2_{STAT} = 3.294 < 12.592$, do not reject H_0. There is insufficient evidence to conclude that there is a relationship between the attitudes of employees toward vacation time without pay and employee job classification.

12.82 (a) Because $Z_{STAT} = -1.7889 < -1.645$, reject H_0. There is enough evidence of a difference in the proportion of respondents who prefer Coca-Cola before and after viewing the ads. **(b)** p-value $= 0.0736$. The probability of a test statistic that differs from 0 by 1.7889 or more in either direction is 0.0736 if there is no difference in the proportion of respondents who prefer Coca-Cola before and after viewing the ads. **(c)** The frequencies in the second table are computed from the row and column totals of the first table. **(d)** Because the calculated test statistic $\chi^2_{STAT} = 0.6528 < 3.8415$, do not reject H_0 and conclude that there is no evidence of a significant difference in preference for Coca-Cola before and after viewing the ads. **(e)** p-value $= 0.4191$. The probability of a test statistic larger than 0.6528 is 41.91% if there is not a significant difference in preference for Coca-Cola before and after viewing the ads. **(f)** The McNemar test performed using the information in the first table takes into consideration the fact that the same set of respondents is surveyed before and after viewing the ads while the chi-square test performed using the information in the second table ignores this fact. The McNemar test should be used because of the related samples (before–after comparison).

CHAPTER 13

13.2 (a) Yes. **(b)** No. **(c)** No. **(d)** Yes.

13.4 (a) The scatter plot shows a positive linear relationship. **(b)** For each increase in shelf space of an additional foot, predicted weekly sales are estimated to increase by \$7.40. **(c)** $\hat{Y} = 145 + 7.4X = 145 + 7.4(8) = 204.2$, or \$204.20.

13.6 (b) $b_0 = -2.37$, $b_1 = 0.0501$ **(c)** For every cubic foot increase in the amount moved, predicted labor hours are estimated to increase by 0.0501. **(d)** 22.67 labor hours.

13.8 (b) $b_0 = -384.7934$, $b_1 = 4.4564$. **(c)** For each additional million-dollar increase in revenue, the value is predicted to increase by an estimated \$4.4564 million. Literal interpretation of b_0 is not meaningful because an operating franchise cannot have zero revenue. **(d)** 283.6654 million.

13.10 (b) $b_0 = 10.473$, $b_1 = 0.3839$. $\hat{Y} = b_0 + b_1X$. $\hat{Y} = 10.473 + 0.3839$. **(c)** For each increase of one additional increase of million dollars of box office gross, the predicted DVD revenue is estimated to increase by \$0.3839 million. **(d)** $\hat{Y} = b_0 + b_1X$. $\hat{Y} = 10.473 + 0.3839(75) =$ \$39.2658 million.

13.12 $r^2 = 0.90$. 90% of the variation in the dependent variable can be explained by the variation in the independent variable.

13.14 $r^2 = 0.75$. 75% of the variation in the dependent variable can be explained by the variation in the independent variable.

13.16 (a) $r^2 = \dfrac{SSR}{SST} = \dfrac{20{,}535}{30{,}025} = 0.684$. 68.4% of the variation in sales can be explained by the variation in shelf space.

(b) $S_{YX} = \sqrt{\dfrac{SSE}{n-2}} = \sqrt{\dfrac{\sum_{i=1}^{n}(Y_i - \hat{Y}_i)^2}{n-2}} = \sqrt{\dfrac{9{,}490}{10}} = 30.8058.$

(c) Based on (a) and (b), the model should be useful for predicting sales.

13.18 (a) $r^2 = 08892$. 88.92% of the variation in labor hours can be explained by the variation in cubic feet moved. **(b)** $S_{YX} = 5.0314$ **(c)** Based on (a) and (b), the model should be very useful for predicting the labor hours.

13.20 (a) $r^2 = 0.9695$. 96.95% of the variation in the value of a baseball franchise can be explained by the variation in its annual revenue. **(b)** $S_{YX} = 46.1275$. **(c)** Based on (a) and (b), the model should be very useful for predicting the value of a baseball franchise.

13.22 (a) $r^2 = 0.5452$. 54.52% of the variation in DVD revenue can be explained by the variation in box office gross. **(b)** $S_{YX} = 15.3782$. The variation of DVD revenue around the prediction line is \$15.3782 million. The typical difference between actual DVD revenue and the predicted DVD revenue using the regression equation is approximately \$15.3782 million. **(c)** Based on (a) and (b), the model is useful for predicting DVD revenue. **(d)** Other variables that might explain the variation in DVD revenue could be the amount spent on advertising, the timing of the release of the DVDs, and the type of movie.

13.24 A residual analysis of the data indicates a pattern, with sizable clusters of consecutive residuals that are either all positive or all negative. This pattern indicates a violation of the assumption of linearity. A curvilinear model should be investigated.

13.26 There does not appear to be a pattern in the residual plot. The assumptions of regression do not appear to be seriously violated.

13.28 Based on the residual plot, there does not appear to be a curvilinear pattern in the residuals. The assumptions of normality and equal variance do not appear to be seriously violated.

13.30 Based on the residual plot, there appears to be a nonlinear pattern in the residuals. A curvilinear model should be investigated. There is some right-skewness in the residuals, and there is some violation of the equal-variance assumption.

13.32 (a) An increasing linear relationship exists. **(b)** There is evidence of a strong positive autocorrelation among the residuals.

13.34 (a) No, because the data were not collected over time. **(b)** If a single store had been selected and studied over a period of time, you would compute the Durbin-Watson statistic.

13.36 (a)

$$b_1 = \frac{SSXY}{SSX} = \frac{201399.05}{12495626} = 0.0161$$

$$b_0 = \overline{Y} - b_1\overline{X} = 71.2621 - 0.0161\,(4{,}393) = 0.458$$

(b) $\hat{Y} = 0.458 + 0.0161X = 0.458 + 0.0161(4{,}500) = 72.908$, or \$72,908. **(c)** There is no evidence of a pattern in the residuals over time.

(d) $D = \frac{\sum_{i=2}^{n}(e_i - e_{i-1})^2}{\sum_{i=1}^{n} e_i^2} = \frac{1{,}243.2244}{599.0683} = 2.08 > 1.45$. There is no evidence of positive autocorrelation among the residuals. **(e)** Based on a residual analysis, the model appears to be adequate.

13.38 (a) $b_0 = -2.535, b_1 = .06073$. **(b)** \$2,505.40. **(d)** $D = 1.64 > d_U = 1.42$, so there is no evidence of positive autocorrelation among the residuals. **(e)** The plot shows some nonlinear pattern, suggesting that a nonlinear model might be better. Otherwise, the model appears to be adequate.

13.40 (a) 3.00. **(b)** ± 2.1199. **(c)** Reject H_0. There is evidence that the fitted linear regression model is useful. **(d)** $1.32 \le \beta_1 \le 7.68$.

13.42 (a) $t_{STAT} = \frac{b_1 - \beta_1}{S_{b_1}} = \frac{7.4}{1.59} = 4.65 > 2.2281$. Reject H_0. There is evidence of a linear relationship between shelf space and sales. **(b)** $b_1 \pm t_{\alpha/2}S_{b_1} = 7.4 \pm 2.2281(1.59)$ $3.86 \le \beta_1 \le 10.94$.

13.44 (a) $t_{STAT} = 16.52 > 2.0322$; reject H_0. There is evidence of a linear relationship between the number of cubic feet moved and labor hours. **(b)** $0.0439 \le \beta_1 \le 0.0562$.

13.46 (a) $t_{STAT} = 29.8157 > 2.0484$ or because the p-value is approximately 0, reject H_0 at the 5% level of significance. There is evidence of a linear relationship between annual revenue and franchise value. **(b)** $4.1502 \le \beta_1 \le 4.7626$.

13.48 (a) $t_{STAT} = 4.8964 > 2.086$ or because the p-value is virtually $0 < 0.05$; reject H_0. There is evidence of a linear relationship between box office gross and sales of DVDs. **(b)** $3.3072 \le \beta_1 \le 5.3590$.

13.50 (a) (% daily change in BGU) $= b_0 + 3.0$ (% daily change in Russell 1000 index). **(b)** If the Russell 1000 gains 10% in a year, BGU is expected to gain an estimated 30%. **(c)** If the Russell 1000 loses 20% in a year, BGU is expected to lose an estimated 60%. **(d)** Risk takers will be attracted to leveraged funds, and risk-averse investors will stay away.

13.52 (a), (b) First weekend and U.S. gross: $r = 0.2526$, $t_{STAT} = -0.5221 < 2.7764$, p-value $= 0.6292 > 0.05$. Do not reject H_0. At the 0.05 level of significance, there is a insufficient evidence of a linear relationship between First weekend sales and U.S. gross. First weekend and worldwide gross: $r = 0.4149$, $t_{STAT} = -0.912 < 2.7764$, p-value $= 0.4134 > 0.05$. Do not reject H_0. At the 0.05 level of significance, there is a insufficient evidence of a linear relationship between first weekend sales and worldwide gross. U.S. gross and worldwide gross: $r = 0.9414$, $t_{STAT} = 5.5807 > 2.7764$, p-value $= 0.0051 < 0.05$. Reject H_0. At the 0.05 level of significance, there is evidence of a linear relationship between U.S. gross and worldwide gross.

13.54 (a) $r = 0.5497$. There appears to be a moderate positive linear relationship between the average Wonderlic score of football players trying out for the NFL and the graduation rate for football players at selected schools. **(b)** $t_{STAT} = 3.9485$, p-value $= 0.0004 < 0.05$. Reject H_0. At the 0.05 level of significance, there is a significant linear relationship between the average Wonderlic score of football players trying out for the NFL and the graduation rate for football players at selected schools. **(c)** There is a significant linear relationship between the average Wonderlic score of football players trying out for the NFL and the graduation rate for football players at selected schools, but the positive linear relationship is only moderate.

13.56 (a) $15.95 \le \mu_{Y|X=4} \le 18.05$. **(b)** $14.651 \le Y_{X=4} \le 19.349$.

13.58 (a) $\hat{Y} = 145 + 7.4(8) = 204.2$ $\hat{Y} \pm t_{\alpha/2}S_{YX}\sqrt{h_i}$

$$= 204.2 \pm 2.2281(30.81)\sqrt{0.1373}$$
$$178.76 \le \mu_{Y|X=8} \le 229.64.$$

(b) $\hat{Y} \pm t_{\alpha/2}S_{YX}\sqrt{1 + h_i}$

$$= 204.2 \pm 2.2281(30.81)\sqrt{1 + 0.1373}$$
$$131.00 \le Y_{X=8} \le 277.40.$$

(c) Part (b) provides a prediction interval for the individual response given a specific value of the independent variable, and part (a) provides an interval estimate for the mean value, given a specific value of the independent variable. Because there is much more variation in predicting an individual value than in estimating a mean value, a prediction interval is wider than a confidence interval estimate.

13.60 (a) $20.799 \le \mu_{Y|X=500} \le 24.542$. **(b)** $12.276 \le Y_{X=500} \le 33.065$. **(c)** You can estimate a mean more precisely than you can predict a single observation.

13.62 (a) $261.279 \le \mu_{Y|X=150} \le 306.0519$. **(b)** $186.5618 \le Y_{X=150} \le 350.769$. **(c)** Part (b) provides a prediction interval for an individual response given a specific value of X, and part (a) provides a confidence interval estimate for the mean value, given a specific value of X. Because there is much more variation in predicting an individual value than in estimating a mean, the prediction interval is wider than the confidence interval.

13.74 (a) $b_0 = 24.84, b_1 = 0.14$. **(b)** For each additional case, the predicted delivery time is estimated to increase by 0.14 minutes. **(c)** 45.84. **(d)** No, 500 is outside the relevant range of the data used to fit the regression equation. **(e)** $r^2 = 0.972$. **(f)** There is no obvious pattern in the residuals, so the assumptions of regression are met. The model appears to be adequate. **(g)** $t_{STAT} = 24.88 > 2.1009$; reject H_0. **(h)** $44.88 \le \mu_{Y|X=150} \le 46.80$. $41.56 \le Y_{X=150} \le 50.12$.

13.76 (a) $b_0 = -122.3439, b_1 = 1.7817$. **(b)** For each additional thousand dollars in assessed value, the estimated selling price of a house increases by \$1.7817 thousand. The estimated selling price of a house with a 0 assessed value is \$ − 122.3439 thousand. However, this interpretation is not meaningful because the assessed value cannot be below 0. **(c)** $\hat{Y} = -122.3439 + 1.78171X = -122.3439 + 1.78171(170) = 180.5475$ thousand dollars. **(d)** $r^2 = 0.9256$. So 92.56% of the variation in selling price can be explained by the variation in assessed value. **(e)** Neither the residual plot nor the normal probability plot reveals any potential violation of the linearity, equal variance, and normality assumptions. **(f)** $t_{STAT} = 18.6648 > 2.0484$, p-value is virtually 0. Because p-value < 0.05, reject H_0. There is evidence of a linear relationship between selling price and assessed value. **(g)** $1.5862 \le \beta_1 \le 1.9773$.

13.78 (a) $b_0 = 0.30, b_1 = 0.00487$. **(b)** For each additional point on the GMAT score, the predicted GPA is estimated to increase by 0.00487. Because a GMAT score of 0 is not possible, the Y intercept does not have a practical interpretation. **(c)** 3.222. **(d)** $r^2 = 0.798$. **(e)** There is no obvious pattern in the residuals, so the assumptions of regression are met. The model appears to be adequate. **(f)** $t_{STAT} = 8.43 > 2.1009$; reject H_0. **(g)** $3.144 \le \mu_{Y|X=600} \le 3.301$, $2.866 \le Y_{X=600} \le 3.559$. **(h)** $.00366 \le \beta_1 \le .00608$.

13.80 (a) There is no clear relationship shown on the scatter plot. **(c)** Looking at all 23 flights, when the temperature is lower, there is likely to be some O-ring damage, particularly if the temperature is below 60 degrees. **(d)** 31 degrees is outside the relevant range, so a prediction should not be made. **(e)** Predicted $Y = 18.036 - 0.240X$, where X = temperature and Y = O-ring damage **(g)** A nonlinear model would be more appropriate. **(h)** The appearance on the residual plot of a nonlinear pattern indicates that a nonlinear model would be better. It also appears that the normality assumption is invalid.

13.82 (a) $b_0 = -6.2448, b_1 = 2.9576$. **(b)** For each additional million-dollar increase in revenue, the franchise value will increase by an estimated \$2.9576 million. Literal interpretation of b_0 is not meaningful because an operating franchise cannot have zero revenue. **(c)** \$437.3901 million. **(d)** $r^2 = 0.981$. 98.1% of the variation in the value of an NBA franchise can be explained by the variation in its annual revenue. **(e)** There does not appear to be a pattern in the residual plot. The assumptions of regression do not appear to be seriously violated. **(f)** $t_{STAT} = 38.0207 > 2.0484$ or because the p-value is approximately 0, reject H_0 at the 5% level of significance. There is evidence of a linear relationship between annual revenue and franchise value. **(g)** $431.0467 \leq \mu_{Y|X=150} \leq 443.7334$. **(h)** $408.8257 \leq Y_{X=150} \leq 465.9544$. **(i)** The strength of the relationship between revenue and value is stronger for baseball and NBA franchises than for European soccer teams.

13.84 (a) $b_0 = -2{,}629.222$, $b_1 = 82.472$. **(b)** For each additional centimeter in circumference, the weight is estimated to increase by 82.472 grams. **(c)** 2,319.08 grams. **(d)** Yes, since circumference is a very strong predictor of weight. **(e)** $r^2 = 0.937$. **(f)** There appears to be a nonlinear relationship between circumference and weight. **(g)** p-value is virtually $0 < 0.05$; reject H_0. **(h)** $72.7875 \leq \beta_1 \leq 92.156$.

13.86 (b) $\hat{Y} = 931{,}626.16 + 21{,}782.76X$. **(c)** $b_1 = 21{,}782.76$ For each increase of the median age of the customer base by one year, the latest one-month sales total is estimated to increase by \$21,782.76. $b_0 = 931{,}626.16$ Since age cannot be 0, there is no direct interpretation for b_0. **(d)** $r^2 = 0.0017$. Only 0.17% of the total variation in the franchise's latest one-month sales total can be explained by using the median age of the customer base. **(e)** The residuals are very evenly spread out across different ranges of median age. **(f)** Because $-2.0281 < t_{STAT} = 0.2482 < 2.0281$, do not reject H_0. There is insufficient evidence to conclude that there is a linear relationship between the one-month sales total and the median age of the customer base. **(g)** $-156{,}181.50 \leq \beta_1 \leq 199{,}747.02$.

13.88 (a) There is a positive linear relationship between total sales and the percentage of the customer base with a college diploma. **(b)** $\hat{Y} = 789{,}847.38 + 35{,}854.15X$. **(c)** $b_1 = 35{,}854.15$ For each increase of 1% of the customer base having received a college diploma, the latest one-month mean sales total is estimated to increase by \$35,854.15. $b_0 = 789{,}847.38$ Although this is outside the range of the data, it would mean that the estimated sales when the percentage of the customer base with a college diploma was 0 would be \$789,847.38 **(d)** $r^2 = 0.1036$. 10.36% of the total variation in the franchise's latest one-month sales total can be explained by the percentage of the customer base with a college diploma. **(e)** The residuals are evenly spread out around zero. **(f)** Because $t_{STAT} = 2.0392 > 2.0281$, reject H_0. There is enough evidence to conclude that there is a linear relationship between one-month sales total and percentage of customer base with a college diploma. **(g)** $b_1 \pm t_{\alpha/2} S_{b_1} = 35{,}854.15 \pm 2.0281(17{,}582.269)$, $195.75 \leq \beta_1 \leq 71{,}512.60$.

13.90 (a) The correlation between compensation and stock performance is -0.0281. **(b)** $t_{STAT} = -0.3924 > -1.96$. The correlation between compensation and stock performance is not significant. **(c)** The lack of correlation between compensation and stock performance was surprising (or maybe it shouldn't have been!).

CHAPTER 14

14.2 (a) For each one-unit increase in X_1, you estimate that Y will decrease 2 units, holding X_2 constant. For each one-unit increase in X_2, you estimate that Y will increase 7 units, holding X_1 constant. **(b)** The Y intercept, equal to 50, estimates the value of Y when both X_1 and X_2 are 0.

14.4 (a) $\hat{Y} = -2.72825 + 0.047114X_1 + 0.011947X_2$. **(b)** For a given number of orders, for each increase of \$1,000 in sales, the distribution cost is estimated to increase by \$47.114. For a given amount of sales, for each increase of one order, the distribution cost is estimated to increase by \$11.95. **(c)** The interpretation of b_0 has no practical meaning here because it would represent the estimated distribution cost when there were no sales and no orders. **(d)** $\hat{Y} = -2.72825 + 0.047114(400) + 0.011947(4500) = 69.878$, or \$69,878. **(e)** $\$66{,}419.93 \leq \mu_{Y|X} \leq \$73{,}337.01$. **(f)** $\$59{,}380.61 \leq Y_X \leq \$80{,}376.33$. **(g)** The interval in (e) is narrower because it is estimating the mean value, not an individual value.

14.6 (a) $\hat{Y} = 156.4 + 13.081X_1 + 16.795X_2$. **(b)** For a given amount of newspaper advertising, each increase by \$1,000 in radio advertising is estimated to result in an increase in sales of \$13,081. For a given amount of radio advertising, each increase by \$1,000 in newspaper advertising is estimated to result in an increase in sales of \$16,795. **(c)** When there is no money spent on radio advertising and newspaper advertising, the estimated mean sales is \$156,430.44. **(d)** Holding the other independent variable constant, newspaper advertising seems to be more effective because its slope is greater.

14.8 (a) $\hat{Y} = 400.8057 + 456.4485X_1 - 2.4708X_2$ where X_1 = land area, X_2 = age. **(b)** For a given age, each increase by one acre in land area is estimated to result in an increase in appraised value by \$456.45 thousands. For a given land area, each increase of one year in age is estimated to result in a decrease in appraised value by \$2.47 thousands. **(c)** The interpretation of b_0 has no practical meaning here because it would represent the estimated appraised value of a new house that has no land area. **(d)** $\hat{Y} = 400.8057 + 456.4485(0.25) - 2.4708(45) =$ \$403.73 thousands. **(e)** $372.7370 \leq \mu_{Y|X} \leq 434.7243$. **(f)** $235.1964 \leq Y_X \leq 572.2649$.

14.10 (a) $MSR = 15$, $MSE = 12$. **(b)** 1.25. **(c)** $F_{STAT} = 1.25 < 4.10$; do not reject H_0. **(d)** 0.20. **(e)** 0.04.

14.12 (a) $F_{STAT} = 97.69 > 3.89$. Reject H_0. There is evidence of a significant linear relationship with at least one of the independent variables. **(b)** p-value $= 0.0001$. **(c)** $r^2 = 0.9421$. 94.21% of the variation in the long-term ability to absorb shock can be explained by variation in forefoot absorbing capability and variation in midsole impact. **(d)** $r^2_{adj} = 0.935$.

14.14 (a) $F_{STAT} = 74.13 > 3.467$; reject H_0. **(b)** p-value $= 0$. **(c)** $r^2 = 0.8759$. 87.59% of the variation in distribution cost can be explained by variation in sales and variation in number of orders. **(d)** $r^2_{adj} = 0.8641$.

14.16 (a) $F_{STAT} = 40.16 > 3.522$. Reject H_0. There is evidence of a significant linear relationship. **(b)** p-value < 0.001. **(c)** $r^2 = 0.8087$. 80.87% of the variation in sales can be explained by variation in radio advertising and variation in newspaper advertising. **(d)** $r^2_{adj} = 0.7886$.

14.18 (a)–(e) Based on a residual analysis, there is no evidence of a violation of the assumptions of regression.

14.20 (a) There appears to be a quadratic relationship in the plot of the residuals against both radio and newspaper advertising. (b) Since the data are not collected over time, the Durbin-Watson test is not appropriate. **(c)** Curvilinear terms for both of these explanatory variables should be considered for inclusion in the model.

14.22 (a) The residual analysis reveals no patterns. (b) Since the data are not collected over time, the Durbin-Watson test is not appropriate. **(c)** There are no apparent violations in the assumptions.

14.24 (a) Variable X_2 has a larger slope in terms of the t statistic of 3.75 than variable X_1, which has a smaller slope in terms of the t statistic of 3.33. **(b)** $1.46824 \leq \beta_1 \leq 6.53176$. **(c)** For X_1: $t_{STAT} = 4/1.2 = 3.33 > 2.1098$, with 17 degrees of freedom for $\alpha = 0.05$. Reject H_0. There is evidence that X_1 contributes to a model already containing X_2. For X_2: $t_{STAT} = 3/0.8 = 3.75 > 2.1098$, with 17 degrees of freedom for

$\alpha = 0.05$. Reject H_0. There is evidence that X_2 contributes to a model already containing X_1. Both X_1 and X_2 should be included in the model.

14.26 (a) 95% confidence interval on β_1: $b_1 \pm tS_{b_1}$, 0.0471 ± 2.0796 (0.0203), $0.0049 \le \beta_1 \le 0.0893$. **(b)** For X_1: $t_{STAT} = b_1/S_{b_1} = 0.0471/0.0203 = 2.32 > 2.0796$. Reject H_0. There is evidence that X_1 contributes to a model already containing X_2. For X_2: $t_{STAT} = b_1/S_{b_1} = 0.0112/0.0023 = 5.31 > 2.0796$. Reject H_0. There is evidence that X_2 contributes to a model already containing X_1. Both X_1 (sales) and X_2 (orders) should be included in the model.

14.28 (a) $9.398 \le \beta_1 \le 16.763$. **(b)** For X_1: $t_{STAT} = 7.43 > 2.093$. Reject H_0. There is evidence that X_1 contributes to a model already containing X_2. For X_2: $t_{STAT} = 5.67 > 2.093$. Reject H_0. There is evidence that X_2 contributes to a model already containing X_1. Both X_1 (radio advertising) and X_2 (newspaper advertising) should be included in the model.

14.30 (a) $227.5865 \le \beta_1 \le 685.3104$. **(b)** For X_1: $t_{STAT} = 4.0922$ and p-value $= 0.0003$. Because p-value < 0.05, reject H_0. There is evidence that X_1 contributes to a model already containing X_2. For X_2: $t_{STAT} = -3.6295$ and p-value $= 0.0012$. Because p-value < 0.05 reject H_0. There is evidence that X_2 contributes to a model already containing X_1. Both X_1 (land area) and X_2 (age) should be included in the model.

14.32 (a) For X_1: $F_{STAT} = 1.25 < 4.96$; do not reject H_0. For X_2: $F_{STAT} = 0.833 < 4.96$; do not reject H_0. **(b)** 0.1111, 0.0769.

14.34 (a) For X_1: $SSR(X_1 | X_2) = SSR(X_1 \text{ and } X_2) - SSR(X_2) =$

$$3{,}368.087 - 3{,}246.062 = 122.025,\ F_{STAT} = \frac{SSR(X_1|X_2)}{MSE} = \frac{122.025}{477.043/21} = 5.37 > 4.325.$$

Reject H_0. There is evidence that X_1 contributes to a model already containing X_2. For X_2: $SSR(X_2 | X_1) = SSR(X_1 \text{ and } X_2) - SSR(X_1) = 3{,}368.087 - 2{,}726.822 = 641.265$,

$$F_{STAT} = \frac{SSR(X_2|X_1)}{MSE} = \frac{641.265}{477.043/21} = 28.23 > 4.325.$$ Reject H_0.

There is evidence that X_2 contributes to a model already containing X_1. Because both X_1 and X_2 make a significant contribution to the model in the presence of the other variable, both variables should be included in the model.

$$\textbf{(b)}\ r^2_{Y1.2} = \frac{SSR(X_1|X_2)}{SST - SSR(X_1 \text{ and } X_2) + SSR(X_1|X_2)}$$

$$= \frac{122.025}{3{,}845.13 - 3{,}368.087 + 122.025} = 0.2037.$$

Holding constant the effect of the number of orders, 20.37% of the variation in distribution cost can be explained by the variation in sales.

$$r^2_{Y2.1} = \frac{SSR(X_2|X_1)}{SST - SSR(X_1 \text{ and } X_2) + SSR(X_2|X_1)}$$

$$= \frac{641.265}{3{,}845.13 - 3{,}368.087 + 641.265} = 0.5734$$

Holding constant the effect of sales, 57.34% of the variation in distribution cost can be explained by the variation in the number of orders.

14.36 (a) For X_1: $F_{STAT} = 55.28 > 4.381$. Reject H_0. There is evidence that X_1 contributes to a model containing X_2. For X_2: $F_{STAT} = 32.12 > 4.381$. Reject H_0. There is evidence that X_2 contributes to a model already containing X_1. Because both X_1 and X_2 make a significant contribution to the model in the presence of the other variable, both variables should be included in the model. **(b)** $r^2_{Y1.2} = 0.7442$. Holding constant the effect of newspaper advertising, 74.42% of the variation in sales can be explained by the variation in radio advertising. $r^2_{Y2.1} = 0.6283$. Holding constant the effect of radio advertising, 62.83% of the variation in sales can be explained by the variation in newspaper advertising.

14.38 (a) Holding constant the effect of X_2, for each increase of one unit of X_1, Y increases by 4 units. **(b)** Holding constant the effect of X_1, for each increase of one unit of X_2, Y increases by 2 units. **(c)** Because $t_{STAT} = 3.27 > 2.1098$, reject H_0. Variable X_2 makes a significant contribution to the model.

14.40 (a) $\hat{Y} = 243.7371 + 9.2189X_1 + 12.6967X_2$, where X_1 = number of rooms and X_2 = neighborhood (east = 0) **(b)** Holding constant the effect of neighborhood, for each additional room, the selling price is estimated to increase by 9.2189 thousands of dollars, or \$9,218.9. For a given number of rooms, a west neighborhood is estimated to increase the selling price over an east neighborhood by 12.6967 thousands of dollars, or \$12,696.7. **(c)** $\hat{Y} = 243.7371 + 9.2189(9) + 12.6967(0) = 326.7076$, or \$326, 707.6. $\$309{,}560.04 \le Y_X \le \$343{,}855.1$. $\$321{,}471.44 \le \mu_{Y|X} \le \$331{,}943.71$. **(d)** Based on a residual analysis, the model appears to be adequate. **(e)** $F_{STAT} = 55.39$, the p-value is virtually 0. Because p-value < 0.05, reject H_0. There is evidence of a significant relationship between selling price and the two independent variables (rooms and neighborhood). **(f)** For X_1:$t_{STAT} = 8.9537$, the p-value is virtually 0. Reject H_0. Number of rooms makes a significant contribution and should be included in the model. For X_2:$t_{STAT} = 3.5913$, p-value $= 0.0023 < 0.05$, Reject H_0. Neighborhood makes a significant contribution and should be included in the model. Based on these results, the regression model with the two independent variables should be used. **(g)** $7.0466 \le \beta_1 \le 11.3913$. **(h)** $5.2378 \le \beta_2 \le 20.1557$. **(i)** $r^2_{adj} = 0.851$. **(j)** $r^2_{Y1.2} = 0.825$. Holding constant the effect of neighborhood, 82.5% of the variation in selling price can be explained by variation in number of rooms. $r^2_{Y2.1} = 0.431$. Holding constant the effect of number of rooms, 43.1% of the variation in selling price can be explained by variation in neighborhood. **(k)** The slope of selling price with number of rooms is the same, regardless of whether the house is located in an east or west neighborhood. **(l)** $\hat{Y} = 253.95 + 8.032X_1 - 5.90X_2 + 2.089X_1X_2$. For X_1X_2, p-value $= 0.330$. Do not reject H_0. There is no evidence that the interaction term makes a contribution to the model. **(m)** The model in (b) should be used.

14.42 (a) Predicted time = 8.01 + 0.00523 Depth − 2.105 Dry. **(b)** Holding constant the effect of type of drilling, for each foot increase in depth of the hole, the drilling time is estimated to increase by 0.00523 minutes. For a given depth, a dry drilling hole is estimated to reduce the drilling time over wet drilling by 2.1052 minutes. **(c)** 6.428 minutes, $6.210 \le \mu_{Y|X} \le 6.646$, $4.923 \le Y_X \le 7.932$. **(d)** The model appears to be adequate. **(e)** $F_{STAT} = 111.11 > 3.09$; reject H_0. **(f)** $t_{STAT} = 5.03 > 1.9847$; reject H_0. $t_{STAT} = -14.03 < -1.9847$; reject H_0. Include both variables. **(g)** $0.0032 \le \beta_1 \le 0.0073$. **(h)** $-2.403 \le \beta_2 \le -1.808$. **(i)** 69.0%. **(j)** 0.207, 0.670. **(k)** The slope of the additional drilling time with the depth of the hole is the same, regardless of the type of drilling method used. **(l)** The p-value of the interaction term $= 0.462 > 0.05$, so the term is not significant and should not be included in the model. **(m)** The model in part (b) should be used.

14.44 (a) $\hat{Y} = 31.5594 + 0.0296X_1 + 0.0041X_2 + 0.000017159X_1X_2$, where X_1 = sales, X_2 = orders, p-value $= 0.3249 > 0.05$. Do not reject H_0. There is not enough evidence that the interaction term makes a contribution to the model. **(b)** Because there is insufficient evidence of any interaction effect between sales and orders, the model in Problem 14.4 should be used.

14.46 (a) The p-value of the interaction term $= 0.002 < 0.05$, so the term is significant and should be included in the model. **(b)** Use the model developed in this problem.

14.48 (a) For $X_1 X_2$, p-value $= 0.2353 > 0.05$. Do not reject H_0. There is insufficient evidence that the interaction term makes a contribution to the model. **(b)** Because there is not enough evidence of an interaction effect between total staff present and remote hours, the model in Problem 14.7 should be used.

14.50 Holding constant the effect of other variables, the natural logarithm of the estimated odds ratio for the dependent categorical response will increase by 2.2 for each unit increase in the particular independent variable.

14.52 0.4286.

14.54 (a) ln(estimated odds ratio) $= -6.94 + 0.13947X_1 + 2.774X_2 = -6.94 + 0.13947(36) + 2.774(0) = -1.91908$.

$$\text{Estimated odds ratio} = e^{-1.91908} = 0.1467.$$

Estimated Probability of Success = Odds Ratio/(1 + Odds Ratio) = 0.1467/(1 + 0.1467) = 0.1280. **(b)** From the text discussion of the example, 70.16% of the individuals who charge \$36,000 per annum and possess additional cards can be expected to purchase the premium card. Only 12.80% of the individuals who charge \$36,000 per annum and do not possess additional cards can be expected to purchase the premium card. For a given amount of money charged per annum, the likelihood of purchasing a premium card is substantially higher among individuals who already possess additional cards than for those who do not possess additional cards. **(c)** ln(estimated odds ratio) $= -6.94 + 0.13947X_1 + 2.774X_2 = -6.94 + 0.13947(18) + 2.774(0) = -4.42954$.

$$\text{Estimated odds ratio} = e^{-4.42954} = 0.0119.$$

Estimated Probability of Success = Odds Ratio/(1 + Odds Ratio) = 0.0119/(1 + 0.0119) = 0.01178. **(d)** Among individuals who do not purchase additional cards, the likelihood of purchasing a premium card diminishes dramatically with a substantial decrease in the amount charged per annum.

14.56 (a) ln(estimated odds) $= -121.95 + 8.053$ GPA $+ 0.1573$ GMAT. **(b)** Holding constant the effect of GMAT score, for each increase of one point in GPA, ln(estimated odds) increases by an estimate of 8.053. Holding constant the effect of GPA, for each increase of one point in GMAT score, ln(estimated odds) increases by an estimate of 0.1573. **(c)** 0.197. **(d)** Deviance statistic $= 8.122 < 40.133$, do not reject H_0, so model is adequate. **(e)** For GPA: $Z_{STAT} = 1.60 < 1.96$, do not reject H_0. For GMAT: $Z_{STAT} = 2.07 > 1.96$, reject H_0. **(f)** ln(estimated odds) $= 2.765 + 1.02$ GPA. **(g)** ln(estimated odds) $= -60.15 + 0.099$ GMAT. **(h)** Use model in (g).

14.68 (a) $\hat{Y} = -3.9152 + 0.0319X_1 + 4.2228X_2$, where X_1 = number cubic feet moved and X_2 = number of pieces of large furniture. **(b)** Holding constant the number of pieces of large furniture, for each additional cubic foot moved, the labor hours are estimated to increase by 0.0319. Holding constant the amount of cubic feet moved, for each additional piece of large furniture, the labor hours are estimated to increase by 4.2228. **(c)** $\hat{Y} = -3.9152 + 0.0319(500) + 4.2228(2) = 20.4926$. **(d)** Based on a residual analysis, the errors appear to be normally distributed. The equal-variance assumption might be violated because the variances appear to be larger around the center region of both independent variables. There might also be violation of the linearity assumption. A model with quadratic terms for both independent variables might be fitted. **(e)** $F_{STAT} = 228.80$, p-value is virtually 0. Because p-value < 0.05, reject H_0. There is evidence of a significant relationship between labor hours and the two independent variables (the amount of cubic feet moved and the number of pieces of large furniture). **(f)** The p-value is virtually 0. The probability of obtaining a test statistic of 228.80 or greater is virtually 0 if there is no significant relationship between labor hours and the two independent variables (the amount of cubic feet moved and the number of pieces of large furniture). **(g)** $r^2 = 0.9327.93.27\%$ of the variation in labor hours can be explained by variation in the number of cubic feet moved and the number of pieces of large furniture. **(h)** $r^2_{adj} = 0.9287$. **(i)** For X_1: $t_{STAT} = 6.9339$, the p-value is virtually 0. Reject H_0. The number of cubic feet moved makes a significant contribution and should be included in the model. For X_2: $t_{STAT} = 4.6192$, the p-value is virtually 0. Reject H_0. The number of pieces of large furniture makes a significant contribution and should be included in the model. Based on these results, the regression model with the two independent variables should be used. **(j)** For X_1: $t_{STAT} = 6.9339$, the p-value is virtually 0. The probability of obtaining a sample that will yield a test statistic farther away than 6.9339 is virtually 0 if the number of cubic feet moved does not make a significant contribution, holding the effect of the number of pieces of large furniture constant. For X_2: $t_{STAT} = 4.6192$, the p-value is virtually 0. The probability of obtaining a sample that will yield a test statistic farther away than 4.6192 is virtually 0 if the number of pieces of large furniture does not make a significant contribution, holding the effect of the amount of cubic feet moved constant. **(k)** $0.0226 \le \beta_1 \le 0.0413$. You are 95% confident that the mean labor hours will increase by between 0.0226 and 0.0413 for each additional cubic foot moved, holding constant the number of pieces of large furniture. In Problem 13.44, you are 95% confident that the labor hours will increase by between 0.0439 and 0.0562 for each additional cubic foot moved, regardless of the number of pieces of large furniture. **(l)** $r^2_{Y1.2} = 0.5930$. Holding constant the effect of the number of pieces of large furniture, 59.3% of the variation in labor hours can be explained by variation in the amount of cubic feet moved. $r^2_{Y2.1} = 0.3927$. Holding constant the effect of the number of cubic feet moved, 39.27% of the variation in labor hours can be explained by variation in the number of pieces of large furniture.

14.70 (a) $\hat{Y} = -120.0483 + 1.7506X_1 + 0.3680X_2$, where X_1 = assessed value and X_2 = time since assessment. **(b)** Holding constant the time period, for each additional thousand dollars of assessed value, the selling price is estimated to increase by 1.7506 thousand dollars. Holding constant the assessed value, for each additional month since assessment, the selling price is estimated to increase by 0.3680 thousand dollars. **(c)** $\hat{Y} = -120.0483 + 1.7506(170) + 0.3680(12) = 181.9692$ thousand dollars. **(d)** Based on a residual analysis, the model appears to be adequate. **(e)** $F_{STAT} = 223.46$, the p-value is virtually 0. Because p-value < 0.05, reject H_0. There is evidence of a significant relationship between selling price and the two independent variables (assessed value and time since assessment). **(f)** The p-value is virtually 0. The probability of obtaining a test statistic of 223.46 or greater is virtually 0 if there is no significant relationship between selling price and the two independent variables (assessed value and time since assessment). **(g)** $r^2 = 0.9430$. 94.30% of the variation in selling price can be explained by variation in assessed value and time since assessment. **(h)** $r^2_{adj} = 0.9388$. **(i)** For X_1: $t_{STAT} = 20.4137$, the p-value is virtually 0. Reject H_0. The assessed value makes a significant contribution and should be included in the model. For X_2: $t_{STAT} = 2.8734$, p-value $= 0.0078 < 0.05$. Reject H_0. The time since assessment makes a significant contribution and should be included in the model. Based on these results, the regression model with the two independent variables should be used. **(j)** For X_1: $t_{STAT} = 20.4137$, the p-value is virtually 0. The probability of obtaining a sample that will yield a test statistic farther away than 20.4137 is virtually 0 if the assessed value does not make a significant contribution, holding time since assessment constant. For X_2: $t_{STAT} = 2.8734$, the p-value is virtually 0. The probability of obtaining a sample that will yield a test statistic farther away than 2.8734 is virtually 0 if the time since assessment does not make a significant contribution holding the effect of the assessed value constant. **(k)** $1.5746 \le \beta_1 \le 1.9266$. You are 95% confident that the selling price will increase by an amount somewhere between \$1.5746 thousand and \$1.9266 thousand for each additional thousand-dollar increase in assessed value, holding constant the time since assessment. In Problem 13.76, you are 95% confident that the selling price will increase by an amount somewhere between \$1.5862 thousand and \$1.9773 thousand for each additional thousand-dollar increase in assessed value, regardless of the time since assessment. **(l)** $r^2_{Y1.2} = 0.9392$. Holding constant the effect of the time since assessment, 93.92% of the variation in selling price can be explained by variation in the assessed value. $r^2_{Y2.1} = 0.2342$. Holding constant the effect of the assessed value, 23.42% of the variation in selling price can be explained by variation in the time since assessment.

14.72 (a) $\hat{Y} = 163.7751 + 10.7252X_1 - 0.2843X_2$, where X_1 = size and X_2 = age. **(b)** Holding age constant, for each additional thousand square feet, the assessed value is estimated to increase by \$10.7252 thousand. Holding size constant, for each additional year, the assessed value is estimated to decrease by \$0.2843 thousand. **(c)** $\hat{Y} = 163.7751 + 10.7252(1.75) - 0.2843(10) = 179.7017$ thousand dollars. **(d)** Based on a residual analysis, the errors appear to be normally distributed. The equal-variance assumption appears to be valid. There might be a violation of the linearity assumption for age. You might want to include a quadratic term in the model for age. **(e)** $F_{STAT} = 28.58$, p-value $= 0.0000272776$. Because p-value $= 0.0000 < 0.05$, reject H_0. There is evidence of a significant relationship between assessed value and the two independent variables (size and age). **(f)** p-value $= 0.0000272776$. The probability of obtaining an F_{STAT} test statistic of 28.58 or greater is virtually 0 if there is no significant relationship between assessed value and the two independent variables (size and age). **(g)** $r^2 = 0.8265$. 82.65% of the variation in assessed value can be explained by variation in size and age. **(h)** $r^2_{adj} = 0.7976$. **(i)** For X_1: $t_{STAT} = 3.5581$, p-value $= 0.0039 < 0.05$. Reject H_0. The size of a house makes a significant contribution and should be included in the model. For X_2: $t_{STAT} = -3.4002$, p-value $= 0.0053 < 0.05$. Reject H_0. The age of a house makes a significant contribution and should be included in the model. Based on these results, the regression model with the two independent variables should be used. **(j)** For X_1: p-value $= 0.0039$. The probability of obtaining a sample that will yield a test statistic farther away than 3.5581 is 0.0039 if the size of a house does not make a significant contribution, holding age constant. For X_2: p-value $= 0.0053$. The probability of obtaining a sample that will yield a test statistic farther away than -3.4002 is 0.0053 if the age of a house does not make a significant contribution, holding the effect of the size constant. **(k)** $4.1572 \le \beta_1 \le 17.2928$. You are 95% confident that the mean assessed value will increase by an amount somewhere between \$4.1575 thousand and \$17.2928 thousand for each additional thousand-square-foot increase in the size of a house, holding constant the age. In Problem 13.77, you are 95% confident that the mean assessed value will increase by an amount somewhere between \$9.4695 thousand and \$23.7972 thousand for each additional thousand-square-foot increase in heating area, regardless of the age. **(l)** $r^2_{Y1.2} = 0.5134$. Holding constant the effect of age, 51.34% of the variation in assessed value can be explained by variation in the size. $r^2_{Y2.1} = 0.4907$. Holding constant the effect of the size, 49.07% of the variation in assessed value can be explained by variation in the age. **(m)** Based on your answers to (b) through (l), the age of a house does have an effect on its assessed value.

14.74 (a) $\hat{Y} = 167.6892 - 19.2757X_1 - 6.6882X_2$, where X_1 = ERA and X_2 = league (American = 0 National = 1) **(b)** Holding constant the effect of the league, for each additional ERA, the number of wins is estimated to decrease by 19.2757. For a given ERA, a team in the National League is estimated to have 6.6882 fewer wins than a team in the American League. **(c)** 80.9484 wins. **(d)** Based on a residual analysis, the errors appear to be somewhat right skewed. There is no apparent violation of other assumptions. **(e)** $F_{STAT} = 12.7547 > 3.35$, p-value $= 0.0001$. Because p-value < 0.05, reject H_0. There is evidence of a significant relationship between wins and the two independent variables (ERA and league). **(f)** For X_1: $t_{STAT} = -5.0220 < -2.0518$, the p-value is virtually 0. Reject H_0. ERA makes a significant contribution and should be included in the model. For X_2: $t_{STAT} = -2.0502 > -2.0518$, p-value $= 0.0502 > 0.05$. Do not reject H_0. The league does not make a significant contribution and should not be included in the model. Based on these results, the regression model with only the ERA as the independent variable should be used. **(g)** $-27.1512 \le \beta_1 \le -11.4002$. **(h)** $-13.3818 \le \beta_2 \le 0.0054$. **(i)** $r^2_{adj} = 0.4477$. 44.77% of the variation in wins can be explained by the variation in ERA and league after adjusting for number of independent variables and sample size. **(j)** $r^2_{Y1.2} = 0.4830$. Holding constant the effect of league, 48.30% of the variation in number of wins can be explained by the variation in ERA. $r^2_{Y2.1} = 0.1347$. Holding constant the effect of ERA, 13.47% of the variation in number of wins can be explained by the variation in league. **(k)** The slope of the number of wins with ERA is the same, regardless of whether the team belongs to the American League or the National League. **(l)** For X_1X_2: $t_{STAT} = 0.5777 < 2.0555$ the p-value is $0.5685 > 0.05$. Do not reject H_0. There is no evidence that the interaction term makes a contribution to the model. **(m)** The model with one independent variable (ERA) should be used.

14.76 The r^2 of the multiple regression is very low, at 0.0645. Only 6.45% of the variation in thickness can be explained by the variation of pressure and temperature. The F test statistic for the combined significant of pressure and temperature is 1.621, with p-value $= 0.2085$. Hence, at a 5% level of significance, there is not enough evidence to conclude that both pressure and temperature affect thickness. The p-value of the t test for the significance of pressure is $0.8307 > 0.05$. Hence, there is insufficient evidence to conclude that pressure affects thickness, holding constant the effect of temperature. The p-value of the t test for the significance of temperature is 0.0820, which is also > 0.05. There is insufficient evidence to conclude that temperature affects thickness at the 5% level of significance, holding constant the effect of pressure. Hence, neither pressure nor temperature affects thickness individually.

The normal probability plot does not suggest any potential violation of the normality assumption. The residual plots do not indicate potential violation of the equal variance assumption. The temperature residual plot, however, suggests that there might be a nonlinear relationship between temperature and thickness.

The r^2 of the multiple regression model is very low, at 0.0734. Only 7.34% of the variation in thickness can be explained by the variation of pressure, temperature, and the interaction of the two. The F test statistic for the model that includes pressure and temperature is 1.214, with a p-value of 0.3153. Hence, at a 5% level of significance, there is insufficient evidence to conclude that pressure, temperature, and the interaction of the two affect thickness. The p-value of the t test for the significance of pressure, temperature, and the interaction term are 0.5074, 0.4053, and 0.5111, respectively, which are all greater than 5%. Hence, there is insufficient evidence to conclude that pressure, temperature, or the interaction individually affects thickness, holding constant the effect of the other variables.

The pattern in the normal probability plot and residual plots is similar to that in the regression without the interaction term. Hence the article's suggestion that there is a significant interaction between the pressure and the temperature in the tank cannot be validated.

CHAPTER 15

15.2 (a) Predicted HOCS is 2.8600, 3.0342, 3.1948, 3.3418, 3.4752, 3.5950, 3.7012, 3.7938, 3.8728, 3.9382, 3.99, 4.0282, 4.0528, 4.0638,

4.0612, 4.045, 4.0152, 3.9718, 3.9148, 3.8442, and 3.76. **(c)** The curvilinear relationship suggests that HOCS increases at a decreasing rate. It reaches its maximum value of 4.0638 at GPA = 3.3 and declines after that as GPA continues to increase. **(d)** An r^2 of 0.07 and an adjusted r^2 of 0.06 tell you that GPA has very low explanatory power in identifying the variation in HOCS. You can tell that the individual HOCS scores are scattered widely around the curvilinear relationship.

15.4 (a) $\hat{Y} = -4.5056 + 20.9262X_1 + 4.1052X_2$ where X_1 = alcohol % and X_2 = carbohydrates. **(b)** $\hat{Y} = 13.0505 + 13.4035X_1 + 4.7205X_2 + 0.6237X_1^2 - 0.0229X_2^2$, where X_1 = alcohol % and X_2 = carbohydrates. **(c)** $F_{STAT} = 7.7018$ p-value $= 0.0007 < 0.05$, so reject H_0. At the 5% level of significance, the quadratic terms are significant together. Hence, the model in (b) is better. $t_{STAT} = 3.8904$, and the p-value is virtually 0. Reject H_0. There is enough evidence that the quadratic term for alcohol % is significant at the 5% level of significance. $t_{STAT} = -1.5659$, p-value = 0.1197. Do not reject H_0. There is insufficient evidence that the quadratic term for carbohydrates is significant at the 5% level of significance. The normal probability plot suggests some left-skewness in the errors. However, because of the large sample size, the validity of the results is not seriously impacted. The residual plots of the alcohol percentage and carbohydrates in the quadratic model do not reveal any remaining nonlinearity. **(d)** The number of calories in a beer depends quadratically on the alcohol percentage but linearly on the number of carbohydrates. The alcohol percentage and number of carbohydrates explain about 97.68% of the variation in the number of calories in a beer.

15.6 (b) Predicted yield = 6.643 + 0.895 AmtFert − 0.00411 AmtFert^2. **(c)** Predicted yield = 6.643 + 0.895(70) − 0.00411(70)^2 = 49.168 pounds. **(d)** The model appears to be adequate. **(e)** $F_{STAT} = 157.32 > 4.26$; reject H_0. **(f)** p-value $= 0.0000 < 0.05$, so the model is significant. **(g)** $t_{STAT} = -4.27 < -2.2622$; reject H_0. There is a significant quadratic effect. **(h)** p-value $= 0.002 < 0.05$, so the quadratic term is significant. **(i)** 97.2% of the variation in yield can be explained by the quadratic model. **(j)** 96.6%.

15.8 (a) 215.37. **(b)** For each additional unit of the logarithm of X_1, the logarithm of Y is estimated to increase by 0.9 units, holding all other variables constant. For each additional unit of the logarithm of X_2, the logarithm of Y is estimated to increase by 1.41 units, holding all other variables constant.

15.10 (a) $\hat{Y} = -146.4770 + 90.1592\sqrt{X_1} + 28.3833\sqrt{X_2}$, where X_1 = alcohol % and X_2 = carbohydrates. **(b)** The normal probability plot suggests that the errors are normally distributed. The residual plots of the square-root transformation of alcohol percentage and carbohydrates do not reveal any remaining nonlinearity. **(c)** $F_{STAT} = 988.7901$. Because the p-value is virtually 0, reject H_0 at the 5% level of significance. There is evidence of a significant linear relationship between calories and the square root of the percentage of alcohol and the square root of the number of carbohydrates. **(d)** $r^2 = 0.9357$. So 93.47% of the variation in calories can be explained by the variation in the square root of the percentage of alcohol and the square root of the number of carbohydrates. **(e)** Adjusted $r^2 = 0.9347$. **(f)** The model in Problem 15.4 is slightly better because it has a higher r^2.

15.12 (a) Predicted ln(Yield) = 2.475 + 0.0185 AmtFert. **(b)** 32.95 pounds. **(c)** A quadratic pattern exists, so the model is not adequate. **(d)** $t_{STAT} = 6.11 > 2.2281$; reject H_0. **(e)** 78.9%. **(f)** 76.8%. **(g)** Choose the model from Problem 15.6. That model has a much higher adjusted r^2 of 96.6%.

15.14 1.25.

15.16 $R_1^2 = 0.64$, $VIF_1 = \dfrac{1}{1 - 0.64} = 2.778$, $R_2^2 = 0.64$,

$VIF_2 = \dfrac{1}{1 - 0.64} = 2.778$. There is no evidence of collinearity.

15.18 $VIF = 1.0 < 5$. There is no evidence of collinearity.

15.20 $VIF = 1.0428$. There is no evidence of collinearity.

15.22 (a) 35.04. **(b)** $C_p > 3$. This does not meet the criterion for consideration of a good model.

15.24 Let Y = selling price, X_1 = assessed value, X_2 = time since assessment, and X_3 = whether house was new (0 = no, 1 = yes). Based on a full regression model involving all of the variables, all the VIF values (1.32, 1.04, and 1.31, respectively) are less than 5. There is no reason to suspect the existence of collinearity. Based on a best-subsets regression and examination of the resulting C_p values, the best models appear to be a model with variables X_1 and X_2, which has $C_p = 2.84$, and the full regression model, which has $C_p = 4.0$. Based on a regression analysis with all the original variables, variable X_3 fails to make a significant contribution to the model at the 0.05 level. Thus, the best model is the model using the assessed value (X_1) and time since assessment (X_2) as the independent variables. A residual analysis shows no strong patterns. The final model is $\hat{Y} = -120.0483 + 1.7506X_1 + 0.3680X_2$, $r^2 = 0.9430$, $r^2_{adj} = 0.9388$. Overall significance of the model: $F_{STAT} = 223.4575$, $p < 0.001$. Each independent variable is significant at the 0.05 level.

15.30 (a) An analysis of the linear regression model with all of the six possible independent variables does not reveals any variables with $VIF > 5.0$. A best-subsets regression produces numerous models that have C_p values less than or equal to $k + 1$. The model that includes points scored and points allowed can be selected since it is simpler and has adjusted r^2 similar to the other models. The best linear model is determined to be

$$\hat{Y} = 46.6301 + 2.7402X_1 + -2.7969\,X_2$$

The overall model has $F = 268.0845$ (2 and 27 degrees of freedom) with a p-value that is virtually 0. $r^2 = 0.9521$, $r^2_{adj} = 0.9485$. A residual analysis does not reveal any strong patterns. The errors appears to be normally distributed. **(b)** An analysis of the linear regression model with all of the possible independent variables reveals that point difference has a VIF value in excess of 5.0. A best-subsets regression reveals that only the regression model with field goal % difference, steal % difference, and rebound % difference has a C_p value less than or equal to $k + 1$. Analysis of the p-value of the slope coefficients for the rebound difference reveals that it is not significant ($0.0609 > .05$). Dropping rebound % difference, the best linear model is determined to be

$$\hat{Y} = 40.9108 + 4.408X_1 + 3.0381X_2.$$

$r^2 = 0.7442$, $r^2_{adj} = 0.7253$. The normal probability plot reveals some left-skewness in the residuals. The residual plot does not reveal any strong patterns. **(c)** The model in (a) with a higher adjusted r^2 of 0.9485 is better than that in (b) in predicting the number of wins.

15.32 (a) Best model: predicted appraised value = 136.794 + 276.0876 land + 0.1288 house size (sq ft) − 1.3989 age. **(b)** The adjusted r^2 for the best model in 15.32(a), 15.33(a), and 15.34(a) are, respectively, 0.81, 0.8117 and 0.8383. The model in 15.34(a) has the highest explanatory power after adjusting for the number of independent variables and sample size.

15.34 (a) Predicted appraised value = 110.27 + 0.0821 house size (sq ft). **(b)** The adjusted r^2 for the best model in 15.32(a), 15.33(a), and 15.34(a) are, respectively, 0.81, 0.8117 and 0.8383. The model in 15.34(a) has the highest explanatory power after adjusting for the number of independent variables and sample size.

15.36 Let Y = appraised value, X_1 = land area, X_2 = interior, X_3 = age, X_4 = number of rooms, X_5 = number of bathrooms, X_6 = garage size, X_7 = 1 if Glen Cove and 0 otherwise, and X_8 = 1 if Roslyn and 0 otherwise. **(a)** All *VIF*s are less than 5 in a full regression model involving all the variables: There is no reason to suspect collinearity between any pair of variables. The following is the multiple regression model that has the smallest C_p (9.0) and the highest adjusted r^2 (0.891):

$$\text{Appraised Value} = 49.4 + 343\text{ Land} + 0.115\text{ House Size} - 0.585\text{ Age} - 8.24\text{ Rooms} + 26.9\text{ Baths} + 5.0\text{ Garage} + 56.4\text{ Glen Cove} + 210\text{ Roslyn}$$

The individual t test for the significance of each independent variable at the 5% level of significance concludes that only X_1, X_2, X_5, X_7, and X_8 are significant individually. This subset, however, is not chosen when the C_p criterion is used. The following is the multiple regression result for the model chosen by stepwise regression:

$$\text{Appraised Value} = 23.4 + 347\text{ Land} + 0.106\text{ House Size} - 0.792\text{ Age} + 26.4\text{ Baths} + 57.7\text{ Glen Cove} + 213\text{ Roslyn}$$

This model has a C_p value of 7.7 and an adjusted r^2 of 89.0. All the variables are significant individually at the 5% level of significance. Combining the stepwise regression and the best-subsets regression results along with the individual t-test results, the most appropriate multiple regression model for predicting the appraised value is

$$\hat{Y} = 23.40 + 347.02X_1 + 0.10614X_2 - 0.7921X_3 + 26.38X_5 + 57.74X_7 + 213.46X_8$$

(b) The estimated appraised value in Glen Cove is 57.74 thousand dollars above Freeport for two otherwise identical properties. The estimated appraised value in Roslyn is 213.46 thousand dollars above Freeport for two otherwise identical properties.

15.38 In the multiple regression model with catalyst, pH, pressure, temperature, and voltage as independent variables, none of the variables has a *VIF* value of 5 or larger. The best-subsets approach showed that only the model containing X_1, X_2, X_3, X_4, and X_5 should be considered, where X_1 = catalyst, X_2 = pH, X_3 = pressure, X_4 = temp, and X_5 = voltage. Looking at the p-values of the t statistics for each slope coefficient of the model that includes X_1 through X_5 reveals that pH level is not significant at the 5% level of significance (p-value = 0.2862). The multiple regression model with pH level deleted shows that all coefficients are significant individually at the 5% level of significance. The best linear model is determined to be $\hat{Y} = 3.6833 + 0.1548X_1 - 0.04197X_3 - 0.4036X_4 + 0.4288X_5$. The overall model has $F = 77.0793$ (4 and 45 degrees of freedom), with a p-value that is virtually 0. $r^2 = 0.8726$, $r^2_{adj} = 0.8613$. The normal probability plot does not suggest possible violation of the normality assumption. A residual analysis reveals a potential nonlinear relationship in temperature. The p-value of the squared term for temperature (0.1273) in the following quadratic transformation of temperature does not support the need for a quadratic transformation at the 5% level of significance. The p-value of the interaction term between pressure and temperature (0.0780) indicates that there is not enough evidence of an interaction at the 5% level of significance. The best model is the one that includes catalyst, pressure, temperature, and voltage which explains 87.26% of the variation in thickness.

CHAPTER 16

16.2 (a) 1959. **(b)** The first four years and the last four years.

16.4 (b)–(d)

Year	Attendance	*MA*(3)	*ES*(*W* = 0.5)	*ES*(*W* = 0.25)
2001	1.44		1.4400	1.4400
2002	1.60	1.5200	1.5200	1.4800
2003	1.52	1.5333	1.5200	1.4900
2004	1.48	1.4600	1.5000	1.4875
2005	1.38	1.4200	1.4400	1.4606
2006	1.40	1.3933	1.4200	1.4455
2007	1.40	1.3867	1.4100	1.4341
2008	1.36	1.3933	1.3850	1.4156
2009	1.42		1.4025	1.4167

(e) A smoothing coefficient of $W = 0.25$ smoothes out the attendance more than $W = 0.50$. The exponential smoothing with $W = 0.50$ assigns more weight to the more recent values and is better for forecasting, while the exponential smoothing with $W = 0.25$, which assigns more weight to more distant values, is better suited for eliminating unwanted cyclical and irregular variations.

16.6 (b), (c), (e)

Decade	Performance(%)	*MA*(3)	*ES*(*W* = 0.5)	*ES*(*W* = 0.25)
1830s	2.8		2.8000	2.8000
1840s	12.8	7.4000	7.8000	5.3000
1850s	6.6	10.6333	7.2000	5.6250
1860s	12.5	8.8667	9.8500	7.3438
1870s	7.5	8.6667	8.6750	7.3828
1880s	6.0	6.3333	7.3375	7.0371
1890s	5.5	7.4667	6.4188	6.6528
1900s	10.9	6.2000	8.6594	7.7146
1910s	2.2	8.8000	5.4297	6.3360
1920s	13.3	4.4333	9.3648	8.0770
1930s	−2.2	6.9000	3.5824	5.5077
1940s	9.6	8.5333	6.5912	6.5308
1950s	18.2	12.0333	12.3956	9.4481
1960s	8.3	11.0333	10.3478	9.1611
1970s	6.6	10.5000	8.4739	8.5208
1980s	16.6	13.6000	12.5370	10.5406
1990s	17.6	11.2333	15.0685	12.3055
2000s	−0.5		7.2842	9.1041

(d) $\hat{Y}_{2010} = E_{2000} = 7.2842$ **(e)** $\hat{Y}_{2010} = E_{2000} = 9.1041$. **(f)** The exponentially smoothed forecast for 2010 with $W = 0.5$ is lower than that with $W = 0.25$. The exponential smoothing with $W = 0.5$ assigns more weight to the more recent values and is better for forecasting, while the exponential smoothing with $W = 0.25$ which assigns more weight to more distanct values is better suited for eliminating unwanted cyclical and irregular variations. **(g)** According to the exponential smoothing with $W = 0.25$, there appears to be a general upward trend in the performance of the stocks in the past.

16.8 (b),(c),(e)

Year	Audits	MA(3)	*ES*(*W* = 0.5)	*ES*(*W* = 0.25)
2001	3,305		3,305.0000	3,305.0000
2002	3,749	3,461.3333	3,527.0000	3,416.0000
2003	3,330	3,821.6667	3,428.5000	3,394.5000
2004	4,386	4,191.6667	3,907.2500	3,642.3750
2005	4,859	4,507.0000	4,383.1250	3,946.5313
2006	4,276	4,186.3333	4,329.5625	4,028.8984
2007	3,424	3,784.6667	3,876.7813	3,877.6738
2008	3,654	3,616.3333	3,765.3906	3,821.7554
2009	3,771		3,768.1953	3,809.0665

(d) $\hat{Y}_{2010} = E_{2009} = 3{,}768.1953$ **(e)** $\hat{Y}_{2010} = E_{2009} = 3{,}809.0665$ **(f)** The exponentially smoothed forecast for 2010 with $W = 0.5$ is lower than that with $W = 0.25$. The exponential smoothing with $W = 0.5$ assigns more weight to the more recent values and is better for forecasting, while the exponential smoothing with $W = 0.25$ which assigns more weight to more distance values is better suited for eliminating unwanted cyclical and irregular variations.

16.10 (a) The Y intercept $b_0 = 4.0$ is the fitted trend value reflecting the real total revenues (in millions of dollars) during the origin, or base year, 1989. **(b)** The slope $b_1 = 1.5$ indicates that the real total revenues are increasing at an estimated rate of \$1.5 million per year. **(c)** Year is 1993, $X = 1992 - 1988 = 4$, $\hat{Y}_5 = 4.0 + 1.5(4) = 10.0$ million dollars. **(d)** Year is 2010, $X = 2009 - 1988 = 21$, $\hat{Y}_{20} = 4.0 + 1.5(21) = 35.5$ million dollars. **(e)** Year is 2013, $X = 2012 - 1988 = 24$, $\hat{Y}_{23} = 4.0 + 1.5(24) = 40$ million dollars.

16.12 (b) Linear trend: $\hat{Y} = -129.0234 + 69.3034\,X$, where X is relative to 1993. **(c)** Quadratic trend: $\hat{Y} = -1.0439 + 21.3111X + 2.8231X^2$, where X is relative to 1993. **(d)** Exponential trend: $\log_{10}\hat{Y} = 1.6704 + 0.0918X$, where X is relative to 1993. **(e)** Linear trend: $\hat{Y}_{2011} = -129.0234 + 69.3034(18) = 1{,}118.4379 = 1{,}118$, $\hat{Y}_{2012} = -129.0234 + 69.3034(19) = 1{,}187.7413 = 1{,}188$. Quadratic trend: $\hat{Y}_{2011} = -1.0439 + 21.3111\,(18) + 2.8231(18)^2 = 1{,}297.2328 = 1{,}297$, $\hat{Y}_{2012} = -1.0439 + 21.3111\,(19) + 2.8231(19)^2 = 1{,}422.9978 = 1{,}423$. Exponential trend: $\hat{Y}_{2011} = 10^{1.6704+0.0918(18)} = 2{,}106.1491 = 2{,}106$, $\hat{Y}_{2012} = 10^{1.6704+0.0918(19)} = 2{,}602.1172 = 2{,}602$ **(f)** The quadratic trend model fits the data better and, hence, of the models fit, its forecast should be used.

16.14 (b) $\hat{Y} = 257.1858 + 70.9110X$, where X = years relative to 1978. **(c)** $X = 2010 - 1978 = 32$, $\hat{Y} = 257.1858 + 70.9110\,(32) = \$2{,}526.3377$ billion, $X = 2011 - 1978 = 33$, $\hat{Y} = 257.1858 + 70.9110\,(33) = \$2{,}597.2487$ billion. **(d)** There is an upward trend in federal receipts between 1978 and 2009. The trend appears to be nonlinear. A quadratic trend or an exponential trend model could be explored.

16.16 (b) Linear trend: $\hat{Y} = -8.9556 + 28.35X$, where X is relative to 2000. **(c)** Quadratic trend: $\hat{Y} = 23.1152 + 0.8608X + 3.4361X^2$, where X is relative to 2000. **(d)** Exponential trend: $\log_{10}\hat{Y} = 1.3220 + 0.1403X$, where X is relative to 2000. **(e)** Linear trend: $\hat{Y}_{2009} = -8.9556 + 28.35(9) = 246.1944$ megawatts, $\hat{Y}_{2010} = -8.9556 + 28.35(10) = 274.5444$ megawatts. Quadratic trend: $\hat{Y}_{2009} = 23.1152 + 0.8608(9) + 3.4361(9)^2 = 309.1905$ megawatts, $\hat{Y}_{2010} = 23.1152 + 0.8608(10) + 3.4361(10)^2 = 375.3381$ megawatts. Exponential trend: $\hat{Y}_{2009} = 10^{1.3220+0.1403(9)} = 384.1023$ megawatts, $\hat{Y}_{2010} = 10^{1.3220+0.1403(10)} = 530.5360$ megawatts.

16.18 (b) Linear trend: $\hat{Y} = -2.0905 + 0.1232X$, where X is relative to 2000. **(c)** Quadratic trend: $\hat{Y} = 2.0819 + 0.1289X - 0.00057X^2$, where X is relative to 2000. **(d)** Exponential trend: $\log_{10}\hat{Y} = 0.3270 + 0.0201X$, where X is relative to 2000. **(e)** Investigating the first, second, and percentage differences suggests that the linear and quadratic trend models have the best fit. **(f)** Using the linear trend model, $\hat{Y}_{2011} = 2.0905 + 0.1232(11) = \$3.4455$ millions. Using the quadratic trend model, $\hat{Y}_{2011} = 2.0819 + 0.1289(11) - 0.00057(11)^2 = \$3{,}4306$ millions. Using the exponential trend model, $\hat{Y}_{2011} = 10^{0.3270+0.0201(11)} = \$3.5339$ millions

16.20 (b) There has been an upward trend in the CPI in the United States over the 45-year period. The rate of increase became faster in the late 1970s but tapered off in the early 1980s. **(c)** Linear trend: $\hat{Y} = 16.4483 + 4.4791X$. **(d)** Quadratic trend: $\hat{Y} = 20.1201 + 3.9668X + 0.0116X^2$. **(e)** Exponential trend: $\log_{10}\hat{Y} = 1.5480 + 0.0200X$. **(f)** The quadratic trend appears to be a better model, according to the narrow spread of the second differences. **(g)** Quadratic trend: For 2010: $\hat{Y}_{2010} = 20.1201 + 3.9668(458) + 0.0116(45)^2 = 222.2044$. For 2011: $\hat{Y}_{2011} = 20.1201 + 3.9668(46) + 0.0116(46)^2 = 227.2308$.

16.22 (a) For Time Series I, the graph of Y vs. X appears to be more linear than the graph of log Y vs. X, so a linear model appears to be more appropriate. For Time Series II, the graph of log Y vs. X appears to be more linear than the graph of Y vs. X, so an exponential model appears to be more appropriate. **(b)** Time Series I: $\hat{Y} = 100.082 + 14.9752X$, where X = years relative to 1999. Time Series II: $\hat{Y} = 99.704(1.1501)^X$, where X = years relative to 1999. **(c)** Forecasts for 2009: Time Series I: 249.834; Time Series II: 403.709.

16.24 $t_{STAT} = 2.40 > 2.2281$; reject H_0.

16.26 (a) $t_{STAT} = 1.60 < 2.2281$; do not reject H_0.

16.28 (a) Because p-value $= 0.8566 > 0.05$ level of significance, the third-order term can be dropped **(b)** Because the p-value is virtually 0 and is less than the 0.05 level of significance, the second-order term cannot be dropped. **(c)** It is not necessary to fit a first-order regression. **(d)** The most appropriate model for forecasting is the second-order autoregressive model: $\hat{Y}_{2011} = 14.2403 + 1.9498Y_{2010} - 0.9696Y_{2009} = 1{,}153.5399 = 1{,}154$ stores. $\hat{Y}_{2012} = 14.2403 + 1.9498Y_{2011} - 0.9696\hat{Y}_{2010} = 1{,}196.8472 = 1{,}197$ stores.

16.30 (a) Because p-value $= 0.8237 > 0.05$ level of significance, the third-order term can be dropped. **(b)** Because p-value $= 0.3971 > 0.05$ level of significance, the second-order term can be dropped. **(c)** Because the p-value is virtually 0, the first-order term cannot be dropped. **(d)** The most appropriate model for forecasting is the first-order autoregressive model: $\hat{Y}_{2011} = 0.4419 + 0.8815Y_{2010} = \$3.3246$ millions.

16.32 (a) 2.121. **(b)** 1.50.

16.34 (c) $MAD = 439.8557$. **(d)** The residuals in the linear trend model show strings of consecutive positive and negative values. The linear trend model is inadequate in capturing the nonlinear trend.

16.36 (b), (c)

	Linear	Quadratic	Exponential	AR2
SSE	110,671.8438	28,296.3123	578,885.304	2,142.5328
S_{YX}	83.1684	43.4329	190.2113	12.8378
MAD	66.1130	35.3306	102.0806	8.4826

(d) The residuals in the three trend models show strings of consecutive positive and negative values. The autoregressive model performs well for the historical data and has a fairly random pattern of residuals. The autoregressive model also has the smallest values in MAD and S_{YX}. Based on the principle of parsimony, the autoregressive model would be the best model for forecasting.

16.38 (b), (c)

	Linear	Quadratic	Exponential	AR1
SSE	0.0571	6.4530	0.0670	0.0918
S_{YX}	0.0797	0.8981	0.0863	0.1071
MAD	0.0645	0.6611	0.0675	0.07526

(d) The residuals in the linear, quadratic and exponential trend models show strings of consecutive positive and negative values. The autoregressive model perform well for the historical data and have a fairly random pattern of residuals. The linear trend model, however, has the smallest values in *MAD* and S_{YX}. The autoregressive model would be the best model for forecasting due to its fairly random pattern of residuals even though it has slightly larger *MAD* and S_{YX} than the linear model.

16.40 (a) $\log\hat{\beta}_0 = 2$, $\hat{\beta}_0 = 10^2 = 100$. This is the fitted value for January 2005 prior to adjustment with the January multiplier. **(b)** $\log\hat{\beta}_1 = 0.01$, $\hat{\beta}_1 = 10^{0.01} = 1.0233$. The estimated monthly compound growth rate is 2.33%. **(c)** $\log \hat{\beta}_2 = 0.1, \hat{\beta}_2 = 10^{0.1} = 1.2589$. The January values in the time series are estimated to have a mean 25.89% higher than the December values.

16.42 (a) $\log \hat{\beta}_0 = 3.0, \hat{\beta}_0 = 10^{3.0} = 1{,}000$. This is the fitted value for the first quarter of 2005 prior to adjustment by the quarterly multiplier. **(b)** $\log \hat{\beta}_1 = 0.1, \hat{\beta}_1 = 10^{0.1} = 1.2589$. The estimated quarterly compound growth rate is $(\hat{\beta}_1 - 1)100\% = 25.89\%$. **(c)** $\log\hat{\beta}_3 = 0.2$, $\hat{\beta}_3 = 10^{0.2} = 1.5849$.

16.44 (a) The retail industry is heavily subject to seasonal variation due to the holiday season, and so are the revenues for Toys R Us. **(b)** There is an obvious seasonal effect in the time series. **(c)** $\log_{10}\hat{Y} = 3.6210 + 0.0030X - 0.3669Q_1 - 0.3715Q_2 - 0.3445Q_3$. **(d)** $\log_{10}\hat{\beta}_1 = 0.0030$. $\hat{\beta}_1 = 10^{0.0030} = 1.0069$. The estimated quarterly compound growth rate is $(\hat{\beta}_1 - 1)100\% = 0.69\%$. **(e)** $\log_{10}\hat{\beta}_2 = -0.3669$. $\hat{\beta}_2 = 10^{-0.3669} = 0.4296$. $(\hat{\beta}_2 - 1)\ 100\% = -57.0391\%$. The first-quarter values in the time series are estimated to be 57.04% below the fourth-quarter values. $\log_{10}\hat{\beta}_3 = -0.3715$. $\hat{\beta}_3 = 10^{-0.3715} = 0.4251$. $(\hat{\beta}_3 - 1)\ 100\% = 57.49\%$. The second-quarter values in the time series are estimated to be 57.49% below the fourth-quarter values. $\log_{10}\hat{\beta}_4 = -0.3445$. $\hat{\beta} = 10^{-0.3445} = 0.4523$. $(\hat{\beta}_4 - 1)\ 100\% = 54.77\%$. The third-quarter values in the time series are estimated to be 54.77% below the fourth-quarter values. **(f)** Forecasts for 2009: $\hat{Y}_{53} = \$2{,}560.7240$ millions; $\hat{Y}_{54} = \$2{,}551.4693$ millions; $\hat{Y}_{55} = \$2{,}733.2744$ millions; $\hat{Y}_{56} = \$6{,}084.0383$ millions.

16.46 (b) $\log \hat{Y} = 0.0801 - 0.0038$ coded month $- 0.1067$ M1 $+ 0.0794$ M2 $+ 0.1008$ M3 $+ 0.0761$ M4 $+ 0.0795$ M5 $+ 0.1084$ M6 $- 0.1101$ M7 $+ 0.0874$ M8 $+ 0.0204$ M9 $+ 0.0106$ M10 $+ 0.0051$ M11. **(c)** $\hat{Y}_{79} = 0.5069$. **(d)** Forecasts for the last four months of 2009 are September: 0.4306, October: 0.4173, November: 0.4084, December: 0.4001. **(e)** $\log_{10}\hat{\beta}_1 = -0.0038$; $\hat{\beta}_1 = 10^{-0.0038} = 0.9912$. The estimated monthly compound growth rate is $(\hat{\beta}_1 - 1)\ 100\% = -0.8775\%$. **(f)** $\log_{10}\hat{\beta}_8 = 0.1101$; $\hat{\beta}_8 = 10^{0.1101} = 1.2885$. $(\hat{\beta}_8 - 1)\ 100\% = 28.8457\%$. The July values in the time series are estimated to be 28.8457% above the December values.

16.48 (b) $\log \hat{Y} = 0.8087 + 0.0188$ coded quarter $- 0.0559$ Q1 $+ 0.0076$ Q2 $- 0.0064$ Q3. **(c)** $\log_{10}\hat{\beta}_1 = 0.8087\ \hat{\beta}_1 = 10^{0.8087} = 1.0444$; $(\hat{\beta}_1 - 1)100\% = 4.4359\%$. The estimated *quarterly* compound growth rate in the price of silver is 4.4359%, after adjusting for the seasonal component. **(d)** $\log_{10}\hat{\beta}_2 = 0.0559$; $\hat{\beta}_2 = 10^{0.0559} = 1.1373$; $(\hat{\beta}_2 - 1)\ 100\% = 13.7344\%$. The first-quarter values in the time series are estimated to have a mean 13.7344% above the fourth-quarter values. **(e)** Last quarter, 2009: $\hat{Y}_{23} = 17.4670$. **(f)** 2010: First quarter: 20.7473 second quarter: 19.3860, third quarter: 20.1937, fourth quarter: 20.7787. **(g)** The forecasts in (f) were not accurate because the price of silver experienced a drastic decline in 2010, and the exponential trend model was not very good at picking up this drastic decline.

16.60 (b) Linear trend: $\hat{Y} = 174{,}246.8308 + 2{,}408.3608X$, where X is relative to 1984. **(c) 2009:** $\hat{Y}_{2009} = 174{,}246.8308 + 2{,}408.3608(25) = 234{,}455.85$ thousands, **2010:** $\hat{Y}_{2010} = 174{,}246.8308 + 2{,}408.3608(26) = 236{,}864.2108$ thousands

(d) Linear trend: $\hat{Y} = 114{,}542.0985 + 1673.7185X$, where X is relative to 1984.**(c) 2009:** $\hat{Y}_{2009} = 114{,}542.0985 + 1{,}673.7185(25) = 156{,}385.06$ thousands, **2010:** $\hat{Y}_{2010} = 114{,}542.0985 + 1{,}673.7185(26) = 158{,}058.7785$ thousands

16.62 (b) Linear trend: $\hat{Y} = -2.0352 + 0.6727X$, where X is relative to 1975. **(c)** Quadratic trend: $\hat{Y} = 1.3011 + 0.0661X + 0.0178X^2$, where X is relative to 1975. **(d)** Exponential trend: $\log_{10}\hat{Y} = 0.1549 + 0.0391X$, where X is relative to 1975. **(e)** AR(3): $\hat{Y}_i = 0.3441 + 1.5575Y_{i-1} - 1.0741Y_{i-2} + 0.5517Y_{i-3}$. Test of A_3: p-value $= 0.0641 > 0.05$. Do not reject H_0 that $A_3 = 0$. Third-order term can be deleted. AR(2): $\hat{Y}_i = 0.2610 + 1.5418Y_{i-1} - 0.5393Y_{i-2}$. Test of A_2: p-value $= 0.05001 > 0.05$. Do not reject H_0 that $A_2 = 0$. Second-order term can be deleted. AR(1): $\hat{Y}_i = 0.3455 + 1.0325Y_{i-1}$. Test of A_1: p-value is virtually 0. Reject H_0 that $A_1 = 0$. A first-order autoregressive model is appropriate. **(f)** The residuals in the first three models show strings of consecutive positive and negative values. The autoregressive model has a fairly random pattern of residuals.
(g)

	Linear	Quadratic	Exponential	First-Order Aotoregressive
SSE	100.2117	7.7125	107.3081	8.1811
S_{YX}	1.7426	0.4909	1.8033	0.5056
MAD	1.4587	0.3309	1.0215	0.3221

(h) The residuals in the first three models show strings of consecutive positive and negative values. The autoregressive model performs well for the historical data and has a fairly random pattern of residuals. It also has the smallest values in the standard error of the estimate, *MAD*, and *SSE*. Based on the principle of parsimony, the autoregressive model would probably be the best model for forecasting. **(i)** $\hat{Y}_{2010} = 0.3455 + 1.0325Y_{2009} = \$23.7831$ billions.

CHAPTER 17

17.2 (a) Day 4, Day 3. **(b)** LCL = 0.0397, UCL = 0.2460. **(c)** No, proportions are within control limits.

17.4 (a) $n = 500, \bar{p} = 761/16{,}000 = 0.0476$.

$$\text{UCL} = \bar{p} + 3\sqrt{\frac{\bar{p}(1-\bar{p})}{n}}$$

$$= 0.0476 + 3\sqrt{\frac{0.0476(1-0.0476)}{500}} = 0.0761$$

$$\text{LCL} = \bar{p} - 3\sqrt{\frac{\bar{p}(1-\bar{p})}{n}}$$

$$= 0.0476 - 3\sqrt{\frac{0.0476(1-0.0476)}{500}} = 0.0190$$

(b) Because the individual points are distributed around $\bar{p}$ without any pattern and all the points are within the control limits, the process is in a state of statistical control.

17.6 (a) UCL = 0.0176, LCL = 0.0082. The proportion of unacceptable cans is below the LCL on Day 4. There is evidence of a pattern over time because the last eight points are all above the mean, and most of the earlier points are below the mean. Therefore, this process is out of control.

17.8 (a) UCL = 0.1431, LCL = 0.0752. Days 9, 26, and 30 are above the UCL. Therefore, this process is out of control.

17.12 (a) UCL = 21.6735, LCL = 1.3265. **(b)** Yes, time 1 is above the UCL.

17.14 (a) The 12 errors committed by Gina appear to be much higher than all others, and Gina would need to explain her performance.

(b) $\bar{c} = 66/12 = 5.5$, UCL = 12.5356, LCL does not exist. The number of errors is in a state of statistical control because none of the tellers is outside the UCL. **(c)** Because Gina is within the control limits, she is operating within the system and should not be singled out for further scrutiny. **(d)** The process needs to be studied and potentially changed, using principles of Six Sigma and/or total quality management.

17.16 (a) $\bar{c} = 3.0566$. **(b)** LCL does not exist, UCL = 8.3015. **(c)** There are no weeks outside the control limits. Therefore, this process is in control. Note, however that the first eight weeks are below the mean. **(d)** Because these weeks are within the control limits, the results are explainable by common cause variation.

17.18 (a) $d_2 = 2.059$. **(b)** $d_3 = 0.880$. **(c)** $D_3 = 0$. **(d)** $D_4 = 2.282$. **(e)** $A_2 = 0.729$.

17.20 (a) $\bar{R} = 0.247$, R chart: UCL = 0.636; LCL does not exist. **(b)** According to the R chart, the process appears to be in control, with all points lying inside the control limits, without any pattern and no evidence of special cause variation. **(c)** $\bar{\bar{X}} = 47.998$, $\bar{X}$ chart: UCL = 48.2507; LCL = 47.7453. **(d)** According to the $\bar{X}$ chart, the process appears to be in control, with all points lying inside the control limits, without any pattern and no evidence of special cause variation.

17.22 (a) $\bar{R} = \dfrac{\sum_{i=1}^{k} R_i}{k} = 3.275$, $\bar{\bar{X}} = \dfrac{\sum_{i=1}^{k} \bar{X}_i}{k} = 5.941$. R chart: $UCL = D_4\bar{R} = 2.282(3.275) = 7.4736$. LCL does not exist. $\bar{X}$ chart: $UCL = \bar{\bar{X}} + A_2\bar{R} = 5.9413 + 0.729(3.275) = 8.3287$. $LCL = \bar{\bar{X}} - A_2\bar{R} = 5.9413 - 0.729(3.275) = 3.5538$. **(b)** The process appears to be in control because there are no points outside the control limits, there is no evidence of a pattern in the range chart, there are no points outside the control limits, and there is no evidence of a pattern in the $\bar{X}$ chart.

17.24 (a) $\bar{R} = 0.8794$, LCL does not exist, UCL = 2.0068. **(b)** $\bar{\bar{X}} = 20.1065$, LCL = 19.4654, UCL = 20.7475. **(c)** The process is in control.

17.26 (a) $\bar{R} = 8.145$, LCL does not exist, UCL = 18.5869; $\bar{\bar{X}} = 18.12$, UCL = 24.0577, LCL = 12.1823. **(b)** There are no sample ranges outside the control limits, and there does not appear to be a pattern in the range chart. The mean is above the UCL on Day 15 and below the LCL on Day 16. Therefore, the process is not in control.

17.28 (a) $\bar{R} = 0.3022$, LCL does not exist, UCL = 0.6389; $\bar{\bar{X}} = 90.1312$, UCL = 90.3060, LCL = 89.9573. **(b)** On Days 5 and 6, the sample ranges were above the UCL. The mean chart may be erroneous because the range is out of control. The process is out of control.

17.30 (a) $P(98 < X < 102) = P(-1 < Z < 1) = 0.6826$. **(b)** $P(93 < X < 107.5) = P(-3.5 < Z < 3.75) = 0.99968$. **(c)** $P(X > 93.8) = P(Z > -3.1) = 0.99903$. **(d)** $P(X < 110) = P(Z < 5) = 0.999999713$.

17.32 (a) $P(18 < X < 22)$

$$= P\left(\frac{18 - 20.1065}{0.8794/2.059} < Z < \frac{22 - 20.1065}{0.8794/2.059}\right)$$

$$= P(-4.932 < Z < 4.4335) = 0.9999$$

(b)

$$C_p = \frac{(USL - LSL)}{6(\bar{R}/d_2)} = \frac{(22 - 18)}{6(0.8794/2.059)} = 1.56$$

$$CPL = \frac{(\bar{\bar{X}} - LSL)}{3(\bar{R}/d_2)} = \frac{(20.1065 - 18)}{3(0.8794/2.059)} = 1.644$$

$$CPU = \frac{(USL - \bar{\bar{X}})}{3(\bar{R}/d_2)} = \frac{22 - 20.1065)}{3(0.8794/2.059)} = 1.477$$

$$C_{pk} = \min(CPL, CPU) = 1.477$$

17.34 $\bar{R} = 0.2248$, $\bar{\bar{X}} = 5.509$, $n = 4$, $d_2 = 2.059$. **(a)** $P(5.2 < X < 5.8) = P(-2.83 < Z < 2.67) = 0.9962 - 0.0023 = 0.9939$. **(b)** Because only 99.39% of the tea bags are within the specification limits, this process is not capable of meeting the goal of 99.7%.

17.46 (a) The main reason that service quality is lower than product quality is because the former involves human interaction, which is prone to variation. Also, the most critical aspects of a service are often timeliness and professionalism, and customers can always perceive that the service could be done more quickly and with greater professionalism. For products, customers often cannot perceive a better or more ideal product than the one they are getting. For example, a new laptop is better and contains more interesting features than any laptop the owner has ever imagined. **(b)** Both services and products are the results of processes. However, measuring services is often harder because of the dynamic variation due to the human interaction between the service provider and the customer. Product quality is often a straightforward measurement of a static physical characteristic such as the amount of sugar in a can of soda. Categorical data are also more common in service quality. **(c)** Yes. **(d)** Yes.

17.48 (a) $\bar{p} = 0.2702$, LCL = 0.1700, UCL = 0.3703. **(b)** Yes, RudyBird's market share is in control before the in-store promotion. **(c)** All seven days of the in-store promotion are above the UCL. The promotion increased market share.

17.50 (a) $\bar{p} = 0.75175$, LCL = 0.62215, UCL = 0.88135. Although none of the points are outside the control limits, there is a clear pattern over time, with the last 13 points above the center line. Therefore, this process is not in control. **(b)** Because the increasing trend begins around Day 20, this change in method would be the assignable cause. **(c)** The control chart would have been developed using the first 20 days, and then a different control chart would be used for the final 20 points because they represent a different process.

17.52 (a) $\bar{p} = 0.1198$, LCL = 0.0205, UCL = 0.2191. **(b)** Day 24 is below the LCL; therefore, the process is out of control. **(c)** Special causes of variation should be investigated to improve the process. Next, the process should be improved to decrease the proportion of undesirable trades.

17.54 Separate p charts should be developed for each food for each shift:

Kidney—Shift 1: $\bar{p} = 0.01395$, UCL = 0.02678, LCL = 0.00112. Although there are no points outside the control limits, there is a strong increasing trend in nonconformances over time.

Kidney—Shift 2: $\bar{p} = 0.01829$, UCL = 0.03329, LCL = 0.00329. Although there are no points outside the control limits, there is a strong increasing trend in nonconformances over time.

Shrimp—Shift 1: $\bar{p} = 0.006995$, UCL = 0.01569, LCL = 0. There are no points outside the control limits, and there is no pattern over time.

Shrimp—Shift 2: $\bar{p} = 0.01023$, UCL = 0.021, LCL = 0. There are no points outside the control limits, and there is no pattern over time.

The team needs to determine the reasons for the increase in nonconformances for the kidney product. The production volume for kidney is clearly decreasing for both shifts. This can be observed from a plot of the production volume over time. The team needs to investigate the reasons for this.

Index

D

Q

R

The Cumulative Standardized Normal Distribution

Entry represents area under the cumulative standardized normal distribution from $-\infty$ to Z

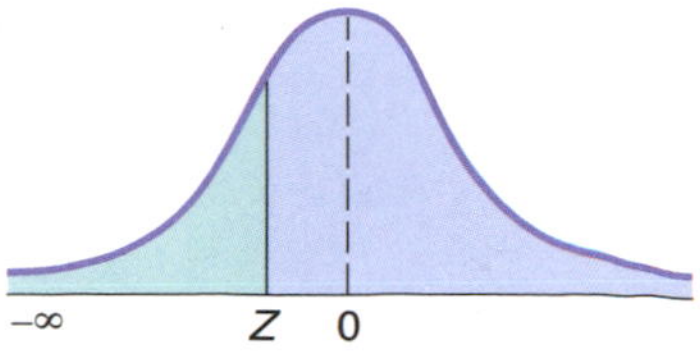

	Cumulative Probabilities									
Z	**0.00**	**0.01**	**0.02**	**0.03**	**0.04**	**0.05**	**0.06**	**0.07**	**0.08**	**0.09**
−6.0	0.000000001									
−5.5	0.000000019									
−5.0	0.000000287									
−4.5	0.000003398									
−4.0	0.000031671									
−3.9	0.00005	0.00005	0.00004	0.00004	0.00004	0.00004	0.00004	0.00004	0.00003	0.00003
−3.8	0.00007	0.00007	0.00007	0.00006	0.00006	0.00006	0.00006	0.00005	0.00005	0.00005
−3.7	0.00011	0.00010	0.00010	0.00010	0.00009	0.00009	0.00008	0.00008	0.00008	0.00008
−3.6	0.00016	0.00015	0.00015	0.00014	0.00014	0.00013	0.00013	0.00012	0.00012	0.00011
−3.5	0.00023	0.00022	0.00022	0.00021	0.00020	0.00019	0.00019	0.00018	0.00017	0.00017
−3.4	0.00034	0.00032	0.00031	0.00030	0.00029	0.00028	0.00027	0.00026	0.00025	0.00024
−3.3	0.00048	0.00047	0.00045	0.00043	0.00042	0.00040	0.00039	0.00038	0.00036	0.00035
−3.2	0.00069	0.00066	0.00064	0.00062	0.00060	0.00058	0.00056	0.00054	0.00052	0.00050
−3.1	0.00097	0.00094	0.00090	0.00087	0.00084	0.00082	0.00079	0.00076	0.00074	0.00071
−3.0	0.00135	0.00131	0.00126	0.00122	0.00118	0.00114	0.00111	0.00107	0.00103	0.00100
−2.9	0.0019	0.0018	0.0018	0.0017	0.0016	0.0016	0.0015	0.0015	0.0014	0.0014
−2.8	0.0026	0.0025	0.0024	0.0023	0.0023	0.0022	0.0021	0.0021	0.0020	0.0019
−2.7	0.0035	0.0034	0.0033	0.0032	0.0031	0.0030	0.0029	0.0028	0.0027	0.0026
−2.6	0.0047	0.0045	0.0044	0.0043	0.0041	0.0040	0.0039	0.0038	0.0037	0.0036
−2.5	0.0062	0.0060	0.0059	0.0057	0.0055	0.0054	0.0052	0.0051	0.0049	0.0048
−2.4	0.0082	0.0080	0.0078	0.0075	0.0073	0.0071	0.0069	0.0068	0.0066	0.0064
−2.3	0.0107	0.0104	0.0102	0.0099	0.0096	0.0094	0.0091	0.0089	0.0087	0.0084
−2.2	0.0139	0.0136	0.0132	0.0129	0.0125	0.0122	0.0119	0.0116	0.0113	0.0110
−2.1	0.0179	0.0174	0.0170	0.0166	0.0162	0.0158	0.0154	0.0150	0.0146	0.0143
−2.0	0.0228	0.0222	0.0217	0.0212	0.0207	0.0202	0.0197	0.0192	0.0188	0.0183
−1.9	0.0287	0.0281	0.0274	0.0268	0.0262	0.0256	0.0250	0.0244	0.0239	0.0233
−1.8	0.0359	0.0351	0.0344	0.0336	0.0329	0.0322	0.0314	0.0307	0.0301	0.0294
−1.7	0.0446	0.0436	0.0427	0.0418	0.0409	0.0401	0.0392	0.0384	0.0375	0.0367
−1.6	0.0548	0.0537	0.0526	0.0516	0.0505	0.0495	0.0485	0.0475	0.0465	0.0455
−1.5	0.0668	0.0655	0.0643	0.0630	0.0618	0.0606	0.0594	0.0582	0.0571	0.0559
−1.4	0.0808	0.0793	0.0778	0.0764	0.0749	0.0735	0.0721	0.0708	0.0694	0.0681
−1.3	0.0968	0.0951	0.0934	0.0918	0.0901	0.0885	0.0869	0.0853	0.0838	0.0823
−1.2	0.1151	0.1131	0.1112	0.1093	0.1075	0.1056	0.1038	0.1020	0.1003	0.0985
−1.1	0.1357	0.1335	0.1314	0.1292	0.1271	0.1251	0.1230	0.1210	0.1190	0.1170
−1.0	0.1587	0.1562	0.1539	0.1515	0.1492	0.1469	0.1446	0.1423	0.1401	0.1379
−0.9	0.1841	0.1814	0.1788	0.1762	0.1736	0.1711	0.1685	0.1660	0.1635	0.1611
−0.8	0.2119	0.2090	0.2061	0.2033	0.2005	0.1977	0.1949	0.1922	0.1894	0.1867
−0.7	0.2420	0.2388	0.2358	0.2327	0.2296	0.2266	0.2236	0.2206	0.2177	0.2148
−0.6	0.2743	0.2709	0.2676	0.2643	0.2611	0.2578	0.2546	0.2514	0.2482	0.2451
−0.5	0.3085	0.3050	0.3015	0.2981	0.2946	0.2912	0.2877	0.2843	0.2810	0.2776
−0.4	0.3446	0.3409	0.3372	0.3336	0.3300	0.3264	0.3228	0.3192	0.3156	0.3121
−0.3	0.3821	0.3783	0.3745	0.3707	0.3669	0.3632	0.3594	0.3557	0.3520	0.3483
−0.2	0.4207	0.4168	0.4129	0.4090	0.4052	0.4013	0.3974	0.3936	0.3897	0.3859
−0.1	0.4602	0.4562	0.4522	0.4483	0.4443	0.4404	0.4364	0.4325	0.4286	0.4247
−0.0	0.5000	0.4960	0.4920	0.4880	0.4840	0.4801	0.4761	0.4721	0.4681	0.4641